ROUTLEDGE HANDBOOK
OF CHINESE ARCHITECTURE

This handbook, representing the collaboration of 40 scholars, provides a multi-faceted exploration of roughly 6,000 years of Chinese architecture, from ancient times to the present.

This volume combines a broad-spectrum approach with a thematic framework for investigating Chinese architecture, integrating previously fragmented topics and combining the scholarship of all major periods of Chinese history. By organizing its approach into five parts, this handbook:

- Traces the practices and traditions of ancient China from imperial authority to folk culture.
- Unveils a rich picture of early modern and republican China, revealing that modernization was already beginning to emerge.
- Describes the social, intellectual, ideological, and formal enterprises of socialist architecture.
- Frames a window on a complex and changing contemporary China by focusing on autonomy, state practices, and geopolitics of design, ultimately identifying its still evolving position on the world stage.
- Examines the existing cultural and political theories to highlight potential avenues for future transformations in Chinese architecture that also retain Chinese identity.

Providing a pioneering combination of ancient and modern Chinese architecture in one coherent study, this book is a must-read for scholars, students, and educators of Chinese architecture, architectural history and theory, and the architecture of Asia.

Jianfei Zhu is Professor of East Asian Architecture at Newcastle University UK, author of *Chinese Spatial Strategies* (2004) and *Architecture of Modern China* (2009) with Routledge, as well as *Forms and Politics* (2018) and works on space, power, visuality, and geopolitics with a Chinese focus.

Chen Wei is Professor, Director, History and Theory Research Institute, Southeast University China, eminent historian and architect on literati gardens and author of *Private Gardens* (1999), *Collected Works of Chen Wei* (2015), *Ornament of Jiangnan* (2016), *Walking Along the Grand Canal* (2 vols, 2013) in Chinese.

Li Hua, PhD (AA), Professor, Deputy Director, History and Theory Research Institute, Southeast University, is author of '"Composition" and Regularisation of Architectural Production in Contemporary China' (2010) and other papers in China's top journal *Jianzhu Xuebao*, and editor-in-chief of bilingual AS series on architectural theory.

ROUTLEDGE HANDBOOK OF CHINESE ARCHITECTURE

Social Production of Buildings and Spaces in History

Edited by
Jianfei Zhu, Chen Wei, and Li Hua

LONDON AND NEW YORK

Cover image: China Academy of Art, Phase II of Xiangshan Campus, Hangzhou, completed in 2007. Architect: Wang Shu (with Lu Wenyu). Photo taken in 2018. © Jianfei Zhu.

First published 2023
by Routledge
4 Park Square, Milton Park, Abingdon, Oxon OX14 4RN

and by Routledge
605 Third Avenue, New York, NY 10158

Routledge is an imprint of the Taylor & Francis Group, an informa business

© 2023 selection and editorial matter, Jianfei Zhu, Chen Wei and Li Hua; individual chapters, the contributors

British Library Cataloguing-in-Publication Data
A catalogue record for this book is available from the British Library

Library of Congress Cataloging-in-Publication Data
Names: Zhu, Jianfei, 1962– editor.
Title: Routledge handbook of Chinese architecture : social production of buildings and spaces in history / edited by Jianfei Zhu, Li Hua and Chen Wei.
Description: Abingdon, Oxon : Routledge, 2023. | Includes bibliographical references and index.
Identifiers: LCCN 2022021927 (print) | LCCN 2022021928 (ebook) | ISBN 9780415729222 (hardback) | ISBN 9781032363363 (paperback) | ISBN 9781315851112 (ebook)
Subjects: LCSH: Architecture—China. | Architecture and society—China.
Classification: LCC NA1540 .R68 2023 (print) | LCC NA1540 (ebook) | DDC 720.951—dc23/eng/20220603
LC record available at https://lccn.loc.gov/2022021927
LC ebook record available at https://lccn.loc.gov/2022021928

ISBN: 978-0-415-72922-2 (hbk)
ISBN: 978-1-032-36336-3 (pbk)
ISBN: 978-1-315-85111-2 (ebk)

DOI: 10.4324/9781315851112

Typeset in Bembo
by Apex CoVantage, LLC

CONTENTS

ACKNOWLEDGEMENTS

On 30 March 2012, one of us, Jianfei Zhu, then serving at Melbourne University, received an email from Leanne Hinves, Editor in Asian Studies at Routledge of Taylor and Francis, with an invitation to publish a reader entitled *Routledge Handbook of Chinese Architecture*. From then on, the project has been always with us, for nearly a decade, until 2020 (with Jianfei now at Newcastle in the UK), when completion finally arrived on the horizon as something real and reachable.

In the process, a team of us – Jianfei with Chen Wei and Li Hua of Southeast University China – as editors of different expertise, was formed in 2012. The project with a guiding idea and a framework was established among us and was approved with Routledge in April 2013. Invitations to contributors were sent in September 2013. By May 2016, all chapters but two had arrived and by May 2017 all except one had been submitted to us – but many were in Chinese or incomplete English. While all papers need rechecking, most in fact need careful translation, sometimes full and careful retranslation. This alone took several years to complete. With the final chapter arriving in early 2021, the morning glory of completion finally emerged on the horizon. Today, we are pleased to present you this volume of some undertaking.

We would like to thank Routledge (Taylor and Francis), Melbourne University of Australia, Southeast University of China, and Newcastle University of the UK, for their sustained support and timely funding, without which the current volume would not be possible. We are grateful to many editors at Routledge, especially Leanne Hinves for her initial contact and guidance (in and since 2012) and her assistants, Helena Hurd and Lucy McClune, for continuing support from 2012 on. We are thankful to Stephanie Rogers and her assistants, Georgina Bishop (since 2016) and Emily Pickthall (since 2020), for their support, patience, and faith in the project. Most importantly, we are thankful to the 40 contributing authors worldwide who together have produced 44 chapters on some 17 topic clusters on a vast and fascinating subject matter – whose names are presented in the following pages. Your contributions are critical and substantial, without which the volume could not exist. We would also like to thank the unsung heroes, those translators whose work is instrumental and indispensable – especially Zou Chunshen, a renowned English language scholar in China; Alexandra Harrer, an accomplished scholar in ancient Chinese architecture at Tsinghua University Beijing; Ling Jie and Zhao Yue, top graduate students at Southeast University Nanjing; Helen Chen and Maggie Ma, committed postgraduates at Melbourne University; Wang Lu, helpful PhD candidate at Newcastle University;

and David Gregory and Yang Liyan, long-standing supportive collaborators of author Jiang Feng (South China University of Science and Technology, Guangzhou).

Research is a social and collective endeavour. While one may not get fully acknowledged, fragments of one's ideas and work live on anonymously in a wider intellectual universe. Many names are not listed here; but you are there and we are together. This book comes from a boundless community of the 40 scholars and many more behind them, and now it returns to a wider world of flying signs and travelling messages for all. We are grateful to all who have helped one way or another. We look forward to further collaborations for years and decades to come.

Jianfei Zhu, Chen Wei, Li Hua
5 July 2021

TRANSLATORS

Part IV

Part V

CONTRIBUTORS

Chang Yu-yu PhD (Southeast), Associate Professor, Institute of Architectural Design and Theory, College of Civil Engineering and Architecture, Zhejiang University, Hangzhou, China

Chau, Hing-Wah PhD (Melbourne), Course Chair in Building Design, Researcher at Institute for Sustainable Industries & Liveable Cities, Victoria University, Melbourne, Australia

Chen Wei Professor, School of Architecture; Director of Architectural History and Theory Research Institute, Southeast University, Nanjing, China

Cheng Jianjun Professor, School of Architecture, South China University of Technology, Guangzhou; Advisor in Heritage Studies at National Administration of Cultural Heritage, Beijing, China

Ding, Guanghui PhD (Nottingham), Associate Professor in Architecture, Beijing University of Civil Engineering and Architecture, Beijing, China

Dong Wei Professor and UNESCO Chair in Cultural Resource Management, School of Architecture, Southeast University; Chair, Urban Planning History and Theory Academic Committee, Urban Planning Society of China

Feng, Jiang Professor in Architecture, Director of Architectural History and Culture Research Center, School of Architecture, South China University of Technology, Guangzhou, China

Fu, Chao-ching PhD (Edinburgh), Professor Emeritus in Architecture, College of Planning and Design, National Cheng Kung University, Tainan, Taiwan

Fu Xinian Academician at Chinese Academy of Engineering; Senior Architect, Architectural History Research Institute, CADG (China Architecture Design and Research Group), Beijing, China

Gu Kai Associate Professor, Department of Landscape Architecture, School of Architecture, Southeast University, Nanjing, China

Heng Chye Kiang PhD (UC Berkeley), Provost's Chair Professor and immediate past Dean, School of Design and Environment, National University of Singapore

Ho Puay Peng PhD (SOAS, London), UNESCO Chair on Architectural Heritage Conservation and Management in Asia; Head and Professor, Department of Architecture, National University of Singapore

Ji Qiu PhD (Southeast); Lecturer in early modern architecture at Pantianshou School of Architecture and Design, Ningbo University, Ningbo, China

Kan, Har Ye DDes (Harvard GSD), AICP; Community Planner, Michigan, USA

Kögel, Eduard Lecturer, Bauhaus-Universität Weimar, Germany; Research Advisor and Programme Curator at ANCB (Aedes Network Campus Berlin); Managing Director of Chinese-architects.com

Li Baihao Professor, Urban Planning, School of Architecture, Southeast University, Nanjing; Vice Chairman and Secretary General, Planning History and Theory Academic Committee, Urban Planning Society of China

Li Haiqing Associate Professor, School of Architecture, Southeast University, Nanjing, China

Li Hua PhD (AA), Professor, Architectural History and Theory Research Institute, School of Architecture, Southeast University, Nanjing, China

Li, Shiqiao Weedon Professor in Asian Architecture, Director of the PhD in the Constructed Environment Programme, School of Architecture, University of Virginia, Charlottesville, Virginia, USA

Li Xiangning Dean, Professor of Architectural History, Theory and Criticism, College of Architecture and Urban Planning, Tongji University, Shanghai, China

Lu, Duanfang Professor of Architecture and Urbanism, Associate Dean (Research Education), School of Architecture Design and Planning, University of Sydney, Australia

Lu Yongyi Professor, Department of Architecture, College of Architecture and Urban Planning, Tongji University, Shanghai, China

Pan Guxi Emeritus Professor of Architectural History, former deputy Head, School of Architecture, Southeast University, Nanjing, China

Qian Feng Associate Professor, College of Architecture and Urban Planning, Tongji University, Shanghai, China

Rowe, Peter G. Raymond Garbe Professor of Architecture and Urban Design, Harvard University Distinguished Service Professor, Cambridge, Massachusetts, USA; Honorary Professor, Tsinghua University, Beijing, China

Shen Yang Associate Professor, Architectural History and Theory Research Institute, School of Architecture, Southeast University, Nanjing, China

Song, Ke PhD (Melbourne), Academic Tutor at Melbourne University Australia for many years, currently Assistant Professor at School of Architecture, Harbin Institute of Technology, Shenzhen, China.

Steinhardt, Nancy S. Professor of East Asian Art and Curator of Chinese Art, University of Pennsylvania, Philadelphia, Pennsylvania, USA

Wang, David PhD (Michigan), Professor of Architecture Emeritus at Washington State University, Pullman, Washington, USA

Wang Guixiang Professor Emeritus and former Director, Institute of Architectural History and Heritage Conservation, Tsinghua University, Beijing, China; Editor of *Jianzhushi Xuekan* (journal of architectural history)

Wang Jianguo PhD (Southeast), Professor and former Dean, School of Architecture, Southeast University, Nanjing, China; Academician at Chinese Academy of Engineering

Wang Xiaoqian PhD (Southeast), Associate Professor, School of Architecture, Southeast University, Nanjing, China

Wu, Ming PhD (Melbourne), Academic Tutor in Architecture at Melbourne University; Co-Founder and Design Director, Studio W Architects, Melbourne, Australia

Xu, Jia PhD (Melbourne), Registered Architect Class 1 (China); Studio Principal at Hangzhou Design Institute (1990s–2000s); Lecturer at Zhejiang University of Science & Technology (Hangzhou China) in the 2010s

Xu Subin PhD (Tokyo), Professor, School of Architecture, Tianjin University; Visiting Professor at Chinese University of Hong Kong, China

Xue, Charlie Qiuli Associate Professor, Department of Architecture and Civil Engineering, City University of Hong Kong, China

Zhang Tianjie PhD (NUS), Professor and Deputy Director, Institute of Urban Heritage Preservation & Regeneration, School of Architecture, Tianjin University, Tianjin, China

Zhou Qi PhD (Illinois Inst of Tech), Professor in History and Heritage of Early Modern Architecture, School of Architecture, Southeast University, Nanjing, China

Zhu, Jianfei PhD (UCL), Professor of East Asian Architecture, Newcastle University, United Kingdom; Visiting Professor at Southeast University (Nanjing) and China Academy of Art (Hangzhou), China

Zhuge Jing Associate Professor, Architectural History and Theory Research Institute, School of Architecture, Southeast University, Nanjing, China

FIGURES

TABLES

Introduction

1

REASSEMBLING FOR A CHINESE ARCHITECTURE

Notes for a New Departure

Jianfei Zhu, Chen Wei, and Li Hua

This collection of papers on the topic of "Chinese architecture," as prepared in recent years, reflects inevitably the conditions, problems, and anxieties of our time in the field of architecture and urban design (and planning) of China. In many ways, this collection, especially its conception and framework, is a conscious response to the issues we face in the field of our time. To explain this, we need to briefly review the development of the scholarship on "Chinese architecture," as a process of constructing *and* deconstructing, that is, a development of building up a body of historical knowledge of this architecture, followed by a quickening and explosive proliferation of research production in multiple directions, to the point where a deconstruction of the constructed body occurred. Our question, then, is how to depart from here, on a new platform with a new critical self-awareness.[1]

Constructing: 1940s, 1965–80, and 2002–3

There were studies on historical architecture of China by German architect Ernst Boerschmann (1873–1949) and Japanese architectural historians Tadashi Sekino (1868–1935) and Ito Chuta (1867–1954) in the early twentieth century.[2] While the former worked on religious structures based on field trips of 1906–14, the latter two, as Japanese working on East Asian and Japanese architecture amid imperial expansion, had extensive access to the sites and texts over these decades (1900s–30s). While Sekino had focused on Buddhist architecture, Chuta developed a brief history of Chinese architecture, which included a historical narrative ending in Sui and North–South dynasties (600). Systematic and comprehensive research on ancient Chinese architecture started with a team of Chinese architectural scholars, in the Society of Research in Chinese Architecture (*Zhongguo Yingzao Xueshe*), which was in operation from 1930 to 1945. Established and headed by a senior state official, Zhu Qiqian (1871–1964), work was carried out in two areas, structural research and textual study. While Liang Sicheng (1901–72), graduating from University of Pennsylvania in 1927, was leading on structural research, Liu Dunzhen (1897–1968), graduating from Tokyo Higher College of Engineering (later Tokyo Institute of Technology) in 1922, was supervising research on historical literature. The society conducted extensive field work and documentation across China while reading historical literature; its many breakthroughs included the discovery in 1937 of Foguangsi Temple (857) of the Tang dynasty (618–907), one of the few earliest surviving timber architectures from the past in

DOI: 10.4324/9781315851112-2

modern China. These pioneering investigations were published in the *Journal of the Society of Research in Chinese Architecture* (*zhongguo yingzao xueshe huikan*) from 1930 to 1945, in 7 volumes or 23 issues, with more than 100 papers over 5600 pages.[3]

In the last years of World War II, in the "anti-Japanese war" in China, hiding in the inland province of Sichuan, and in poverty and ill health, Liang Sicheng, with his wife Lin Hui-yin (1904–55) and their assistants, completed two monumental manuscripts summarizing the work of the society into a system. These were *Zhongguo Jianzhu Shi* (a history of Chinese architecture), completed in 1944 in Chinese, and *A Pictorial History of Chinese Architecture*, completed in 1946 in English. While the first was printed for limited circulation in 1954 (after the founding of the People's Republic of China in 1949) and was not fully published until 1998, the second was not published until after the Cultural Revolution (1966–76), in the United States by MIT Press in 1984.[4] The manuscripts of 1944 and 1946, coming from Liang, who studied in Pennsylvania, marked the first moment when scholarship on "Chinese architecture" (*zhongguo jianzhu*), as a modern construction inspired by western perspectives and standards, came into being. In many ways, the basic framework of knowledge on the ancient building tradition – including its methodological assumption with a western gaze on architecture as objects, and its nationalist ideology of a strong tradition responding to a time of crisis in war with superior powers, as established in the 1944–46 manuscripts – had a long impact in the development of modern Chinese scholarship on China's ancient building tradition in the following decades.

If the 1944–6 manuscripts marked the first moment in a systematic modern construction of a body of knowledge on "Chinese architecture," then the second such moment was 1980. When mainland China was unified as the People's Republic in 1949, nation-wide effort was made to study further and to write up a new and more comprehensive history of Chinese architecture in the light of a Marxist materialism (which was considered to be superior to the earlier approach). A team of architectural historians, under Liu Dunzhen's editorship, completed the manuscript in 1965, where social and material conditions were emphasized. But the outbreak of the Great Proletarian Cultural Revolution in 1966 suspended the project altogether. When the movement or turmoil (1966–76) was out of the way, and after many revisions, the book was finally published in 1980, titled as *Zhongguo Gudai Jianzhushi* (a history of ancient Chinese architecture).[5] With a more social emphasis, it was also consciously titled as *gudai* (ancient) to differentiate that there was by now a modern and socialist architecture of China proudly developing. Adopting a chronological structure like Liang's 1944 manuscript, but with an added emphasis on social and material conditions, this 1980s book covered all major dynasties from pre-history to the Qing (ending in 1911), with 643,000 words over 418 pages. It manifested the achievement of the effort of the People's Republic in the field from 1949 to the late 1970s. Its methods and ideological assumption must be examined in relation to Liang's attempt of the 1940s, a point to which we will soon return.

The reform era of China since 1978, i.e. the 1980s and 1990s, witnessed another wave of discoveries and productions, in great quantity and at a faster pace. The collective approach to produce a chronological and coherent architecture of China had resulted in another, hitherto the largest, compilation. Using the same title as the 1980 publication, it is nevertheless much bigger; the five-volume *Zhongguo Gudai Jianzhushi* (a history of ancient Chinese architecture) was published from 2001 to 2003. Under five chief editors (Liu Xujie, Fu Xin-ian, Guo Daiheng, Pan Guxi, and Sun Dazhang), five teams of authors worked for the five volumes respectively. From the first to the fifth, the volumes cover Chinese dynasties in a grand continuous historical lineage. They are, from the first to the last, "primitive society and Xia, Shang, Zhou, Qin and Han dynasties";[6] "Jin, North-South, Sui-Tang and Five Period dynasties";[7] "Song, Liao, Jin and Xixia dynasties";[8] "Yuan and Ming dynasties";[9] and, finally, "Qing dynasty."[10] In quantity, the five-volume book printed some 6,762,000 words over 3342 pages. It is a hundred-fold increase of the 1980 book in quantity, indicating a massive profusion at a fast pace.

Publications in English in the field were an associated process. Among the systematic and comprehensive works after the war, one of the earliest was Andrew Body's *Chinese Architecture and Town Planning: 1500 BC–AD 1911* (1962), as assisted by Cambridge-based Joseph Needham and his massive history on China's science and technology.[11] But the major breakthrough came in the 1980s and after. Apart from Liang's *A Pictorial History of Chinese Architecture* (1984), a work of the 1940s (and in fact the 1930s), other major publications absorbed new scholarships from China after the war as accumulated up to the 1980s – a decade of blossoming of publications in China with its opening up after a decade of the Cultural Revolution (1966–76). Some of the best of these new publications included Laurence G. Liu's *Chinese Architecture* (1989)[12] and Nancy S. Steinhardt's *Chinese Imperial City Planning* (1990).[13]

But if we aim to examine the underlying assumptions, especially its nationalist outlook and sentiment of these attempts in and through the wars in China, as it was resisting imperialist aggressions, we need to look closer at these publications in China.

In Liang Sicheng's war-time manuscript of 1944 (that is, in a "war of resistance" against a powerful Japan attacking and occupying much of China from the northeast down and from the east coast in), in a Preface titled "Why Should We Study Chinese Architecture?" Liang says:

> Chinese architecture is a technology lasting continuously over two thousand years and has evolved into an artistic system; . . . if we are determined to contribute to a revival of this country and this nation, we must then study and protect the historical artefacts of our country; we therefore cannot ignore the research on Chinese architecture. . . . Besides the need to protect the ancient buildings in China today, a more important issue is design and creation in the future for a revival in architecture. . . . For a revival of the Chinese spirit (*zhongguo jingshen*), the architects will endeavour for a synthesis of aesthetics and rationality. This creative torch of fire had already been ignited before the war of resistance – the so-called "Palace Style" is a case in point. . . . The effort testifies the rise of the Chinese spirit, and it has infinite significance.[14]

Liang further says, in Chapter 1, "Characteristics of Chinese Architecture":

> Chinese architecture is an independent structural system, developing and lasting over a long history, and is found across a vast territory. . . . Over thousands of years, with a variety of forms, the timber structural system – pure and unique – persisted consistently. Wherever our nation reached, the system established a cultural manifestation – from metropolises to borderlands, and from cities to villages.[15]

This is one of the earliest formal statements made by the Chinese architectural community, as backed up by the society's research and the manuscript, declaring that "Chinese architecture" was a unique structural and artistic system lasting over millenniums and developing over a vast territory, a system that was also in need of research and revival in new ways, for a nation it had always embodied, in its rebirth and new ascendance.

If that statement sounded combatant as written in war-time, then the post-war statement from the People's Republic was more balanced, clarifying the relations between Han (Chinese) and other ethnic groups in China, with a certain ideological tone, while maintaining the same message of uniqueness, long continuity, and vast geography. In the 1965–80 book edited by Liu Dunzhen, the Introduction says that

> China is a country with large land, rich resource and a populous demography; it is composed of many nationalities; it is a great country with a long historical culture and is rich in a revolutionary tradition. The different nationalities of China have jointly developed because of long-standing communication and convergence in economy and cultural development. In architecture, the buildings of Han people were most extensive in geographic expanse and most prolific in quantity, but at the same time, architecture of different nationalities have added their unique characters, contributing to a rich spectrum of varieties.[16]

In the 2001–3 statement, there appears to be a stronger global confidence, and the same message remains – a unique architectural system with long continuity over a vast land. The Preface of the five-volume *Zhongguo Jianzhu Shi* (a history of Chinese architecture) says,

> The Chinese nation (*zhonghua minzu*) is one of the oldest in the world in history and civilizational development . . . , it has developed a complete architectural system with unique Chinese characteristics. No nation can quite match in its architecture for historical length, geographic expanse, quantity and scale, and the rich variety in typology, structure, form, and construction, as we find in Chinese architecture. . . . The great achievements of traditional Chinese architecture have been acknowledged worldwide, and these should be celebrated and remembered by the following generations of the Chinese people forever.[17]

On the purpose of the project, it says,

> The purpose of writing the history of ancient Chinese architecture is firstly to discover and compile its glorious achievements over several thousand years . . . and to present to all peoples of the world . . . a permanent . . . heritage of all mankind. Secondly, it is to treat the tradition as a priceless treasure and a great monument. . . . Thirdly, it is to assemble and summarize the basic rules, guiding principles and practical measures of the building practices of the ancient masters . . . for us to study in our architectural practice in the future . . . for the creation of new architectural forms with Chinese national and historical characteristics. Fourthly, since architecture is an important part of the great Chinese civilization, we must also develop a book of complete record . . . and to use it as a textbook and guidebook for our work, research and study in the future.[18]

On the effort of compiling the book of 67 million words, it says

> This is a task that is extremely large and complex, an effort that is tough and long-term. It requires persistent hard work and a relentless struggle of many generations, and a cooperation of scholars across many disciplines – a project more comprehensive and more in-depth than normally expected anywhere.[19]

The production of the manuscripts, expanding in scale over these three moments, has produced a body of knowledge on "Chinese architecture" or "ancient Chinese architecture," whose content, scope and depth had been growing gradually. These three efforts should be considered as a continuous effort of constructing this body of knowledge. Growing over time, polishing and enriching on the way, reflecting the time each was produced (war-time of the 1940s, socialist modernity of the 1980s, and globalization of the 2000s), they have maintained a core message, as reflected in the statements of the three productions, of 1945–55, 1965–80, and 2001–3, as cited earlier. They were all saying that there had been in China a unique system of architecture developed continuously over a long history and upon a vast land, a system that was internally consistent and externally rich with variations; that though there were local variations and ethnic differences, a pervasive Chinese or Han architectural tradition remained as a major system; that this architectural system represented the culture and spirit of China; and that we need to study it in order to create new forms of architecture for the nation in the future in a sustaining continuity of China.

Our reading of the project of constructing the body of knowledge known as "Chinese architecture" is that, though it indeed contained a wealth of empirical work and rational understanding, it had been historically entangled with a nationalist project of survival and resistance in the 1930s and 1940s, a collective socialist modernization of the 1950s–80s, and a "great renaissance of Chinese nation" in a more global setting since the 1990s. A certain nationalism runs thorough all these. As a nationalist ideology embedded in the production of historical knowledge, a certain subjective construction was at work, which had privileged unity over difference, the main over the minor, continuity over breaks or departures, consistency over complexity, and homogeneity over heterogeneity.[20] A recursive interconnection was made between objective research and ideological projection in a constructed scholarship.

Within the production of knowledge, such construction of a unifying knowledge of "Chinese architecture" – more strictly speaking "ancient (pre-modern) Chinese architecture" – implies four strategic priorities in research and outlook that have been at work. 1) In terms of historical time, the focus is on a Chinese history or a history where Han culture had been predominant for a substantial period of time. 2) In terms of geographical place, the focus is on territories where Chinese or Han had been predominant or defining for characterization, or places where Chinese or Han culture was significant in some mutual interactions. 3) In terms of typology, the focus is on those as typically found in the main culture or its territories, chiefly capital cities, palaces, temples and pagodas, schools and academies, urban and rural houses, and the gardens of late imperial time. 4) In terms of methodology, the preferred approach is a chronological history of dynasties where a linear time of the nation, unifying with an epistemological power in research, overrides and frames local histories – where local varieties are not rejected but contained and harmonized into a grand narrative of the nation and its national architecture. While we acknowledge the empirical and rational content of the histories constructed from the 1930s to the 2000s, we must nevertheless raise questions on underlying positions and ideological perspectives.

Deconstructing: A Profusion of Studies Since the 1990s

The third moment in constructing "ancient Chinese architecture" (2001–3), with its massive effort of "many generations," with nearly 70 million words over thousands of pages, had already revealed a tension – to a breaking point in terms of the effort – between the internal content expanding to a large quantity, and the external framework of the "book" (and its linear history) insisting on unity and a continuous narrative. In reality, since the late twentieth century and especially since 2000, there has been a great profusion of studies and publications on all aspects of architecture of China developing in all directions. In effect, the old scholarly category of a "history of (ancient) Chinese architecture" has been challenged and has been increasingly replaced by "studies on architecture of China," in all time periods and on all possible cases, with diverse methods and perspectives.[21] The situation amounts to a deconstruction of the established discourse by the massive new studies "exploding" in all directions. In this condition, new or other or alien elements have entered the terrain, delivering a critical force deconstructing the old framework, in four dimensions.

On the *temporal* dimension, there have emerged new or other "times." While China's modern and contemporary architecture has been studied increasingly by many publications, the major "new time" coming into the picture is the so-called early modern, covering a time from late Qing (up to 1911) and colonial (since 1840) to the republican (since 1911) and up to 1949 (the founding of the People's Republic). Here the main breakthroughs included Wang Tan and Fujimori Terunobu's publications on *zhongguo jindai jianzhu* (early modern architecture of China) in the 1990s,[22] Wu Jiang's *Shanghai Bainian Jianzhushi (1840–1949)* (a century of architecture in Shanghai) (1997),[23] and Jeffrey Cody's *Building in China: Henry K. Murphy's Adaptive Architecture 1914–1935* (2001).[24] More specialized studies are also important, including those on technology (Li Haiqing), education (Xu Subin), and the profession (Wang Haoyu, Lai Delin). Above all, the most significant publication so far in this area is a five-volume compendium published in 2016, *Zhongguo Jindai Jianzhushi* (a history of early modern Chinese architecture), edited by Lai Delin, Wu Jiang, and Xu Subin – a massive production with teams of authors that rivals (but also adopts some methods of) the five-volume *History of Chinese Architecture* of 2001–3.[25]

On the *geographic* dimension, there are also new or different "spaces" emerging – those that had not been "Chinese" in a classical sense. The northern regions, which is one group of these spaces, was dominated at times by non-Han cultures; they were actually covered in the previous "constructive" discourse, but now they have emerged as a category or "subject" of its own. Nancy S. Steinhardt's *Liao Architecture* (1997) on the Liao dynasty and its Khitan people, and her *China's Early Mosques* (2015), covering a variety of sites and territories of this Muslim tradition in many regions including Xinjiang, are some of the main productions here.[26] Another new space or terrain not typically "Chinese" that has been heavily studied recently are the colonial-modern cities, such as Shanghai, which was insignificant as a site or place until the colonial time after 1840.

On the *typological* dimension, there are new or different types and type-related cases emerging as a new focus of research. The first are those historical cases receiving new and special treatment as a case of its own, such as mosques, *literati* gardens, and rural houses and settlements. The second are new modern typologies (such as libraries, universities, stadiums, parks, train stations), which have been chiefly studied in "early modern Chinese architecture," as discussed previously. The third are modern public and state architecture designs with a special nationalist intention, in and beyond the "early modern" period. And the fourth are the socialist typologies and their associated aspects (planning, design, use, structure, process). On nationalism or the national-style in architecture, Fu Chao-ching's *Zhongguo Gudian Shiyang Xin Jianzhu* (a new architecture of classical styles in China) (1993) is prominent.[27] On socialist typologies, or more accurately socialist production of space and form, there are those on design (Jianfei Zhu 2009, Shuishan Yu 2012),[28] on space and organization – such as *danwei* or the work-unit (David Bray 2005, Duanfang Lu 2006),[29] on third-world aid projects (Duanfang Lu 2010, Cole Roskam 2015, Ke Song 2021),[30] and on the design institute and its mode of design production (Charlie Q. L. Xue and Guanghui Ding 2018).[31]

On the *methodological* dimension, we are witnessing a more serious challenge and a broader profusion of perspectives, leading architectural scholarship on China into a wider open space with more potential. Here, the new methods or perspectives included: the study of Chinese gardens for design thinking rather than a chronological history (Peng Yigang 1986, and Tong Ming, Dong Yugan, and Ge Ming in 2009);[32] criticism of the architectural design of contemporary

China (Jianfei Zhu 1997, Li Xiangning 2011, Guanghui Ding 2016);[33] critique of historical writing on Chinese architecture (Hsia Chu-joe 1989/1993, Zhuge Jing 2014);[34] spatial politics in imperial or modern China (Jianfei Zhu 1994 and 2004, Duanfang Lu 2006);[35] history of ideas in architecture of modern China (Shiqiao Li 2009);[36] phenomenology in relation to architecture of China (Peng Nu, Zhi Wenjun, and Dai Chun 2009);[37] and political and cultural critique on architecture and China (Hsia Chu-joe 1993, Jianfei Zhu 2018).[38] With this profusion of new methods and perspectives on spaces and buildings of China, there is a clear tendency toward reflexivity and criticality, and the use of social theories, critical thinking, and cultural studies, for methodological aspirations to move beyond chronological history. Two recent publication series in China, both periodical collections of essays, are good evidence: *Jianzhu Wenhua Yanjiu* (cultural studies in architecture), edited by Ding Wowo and Hu Heng since 2009,[39] and *Jianzhu Yanjiu* (architectural studies), edited by Mark Cousins, Chen Wei, Li Hua, and Ge Ming since 2011.[40]

This Book: A New and Reflexive Departure

If we have correctly depicted the transformation of intellectual landscape into the architecture of China, then the main character defining this scholarship is now shifting, in recent decades, from a "history of ancient Chinese architecture" to studies on buildings, spaces, and cultures of China ancient, modern, and contemporary. In this major transformation, the homogenizing unity of (ancient) Chinese architecture, and its associated unifying national identity, is being challenged. What is being called for and what has emerged are a development in three aspects: 1) a rising *multiplicity* (in time, space, typology, method, and perspective), including multiple histories, multiple identities (subjects and subjectivities), and multiple epistemologies; 2) a rising use of *social and cultural theories* with more methodological reflexivity and innovation; and 3) an increasing importance of *modern* conditions, typologies and perspectives.

The key issue we are facing now, in preparing for the current collection, may be descried as follows: how to deal with unity, chronological history, and ancient history, in the study on architecture of China? In this book, as an attempt to frame a new departure, we aim for not an either–or solution but an assemblage of systems that may not be in harmony or consistent with each other. Between unity and multiplicity, we aim to trace possible shapes of some identity (of China and architecture of China) while allowing multiple diversities and differences. Between ancient and modern histories, we aim to adopt a contemporary perspective in which current, modern, early modern, and pre-modern can be collected, without forcing any homogeneity or consistency, although underlying threads and currents are to be explored. Between chronological history and sociological methodology, again we aim to contain both and to adopt a social and sociological framework in which local histories and broader historical transformations are attached below and above.[41] In such an approach, the narrative is no longer a unifying progression, but a dynamic assemblage of diverse systems working with their own logic and life-force.

Following these ideas, assuming that the current collection is exploring possible shapes of an identity of China and architecture of China while allowing diversities in all dimensions – as an assemblage of differing systems, we propose that this book adopt the following seven principles in organizing the content.

1) Ancient, early modern, modern, and contemporary times and narratives are accommodated *together* and side by side, so that the body of knowledge is no longer exclusively about the ancient or classical tradition.
2) *Social production* is used as a central idea, so that architecture is considered as a social product and a social space, as well as a social process in which spaces and building are produced.

3) *Agent* – as individuals, groups, and institutions who deliver the production,– and their social forms, such as "masters," "architects," "offices," and "design institutes" – is emphasized as a focus of inquiry.

4) *State* or state government, as a primary agent, is emphasized; against this or in relation to the state as a main agent, other agents can be identified as working with or against (logically at least) the state, such as the gentry or the scholar-official class, vernacular masters and builders, modern "free" architects, state design institutes, and the so-called autonomous voices emerging more recently.

5) *Categories* are used together as *clusters*, for a social study on architecture of China as situated in a historical context. Since issues covered by certain categories are related, clusters work as a motor for dynamic research. Here clusters include agents and institutions; space and form; city and country; production and transfer of knowledge in research, teaching, and professional practice; institutional control of these practices; historical discontinuities and historical situations that sustain or resist a chronological continuity.

6) *Special conditions* of a certain period are respected without forcing the cases into a homogenizing totality. For example, both "republican" and "socialist" (Parts II and II) are historically special and discontinuous with times before and after; yet, they are assembled and studied side by side.

7) A *contemporary perspective* is used to organize different times and periods as if we are seeing them from today's vantage point, privileging the current and the modern, while respecting the ancient and the distant, so that an either–or selection of the modern and the ancient is avoided, and an assemblage of times and conditions – without homogenizing and without a methodological privilege of the classical – is attempted.

8) To resist nationalism for an open collection of systems, but also to reconstruct a certain identity, research here is assumed as studies of a culture of China or a cultural China at a level above the political constructs of states and nations, as well as the historical time of the modern and the historical when the attempts were made, even though these conditions and constructs are important locally. As an assemblage of local orders, culture here *transcends nationhood, modernity, and antiquity.*

The Book: Assembling Multiple Systems

With these rules in mind, the content of the book is organized into five parts and 17 sections. With each section containing two to four pieces, the book together presents 45 essays by 40 contributing authors from all around the world. These five parts are: 1) ancient or dynastic, that is, imperial and pre-modern times up to the end of the Qing (1911), as a long tradition of established practices; 2) early modern and republican time (from late Qing to 1949) concerning modernization; 3) modern or socialist, that is, Mao time of the People's Republic (from 1949 to the late 1970s), on aspects of socialist modernization; 4) contemporary practices from post-Mao reform and opening up to a more globalized time after 2000, covering various issues of this new condition; and finally 5) theorization, where reflective, critical, and theoretical studies are made and methodological issues discussed.

A Long History of Timber Architecture and Political Planning

In Part I, "Ancient and Dynastic Tradition," the three sections trace the practices of ancient China in three spheres, namely, imperial authority, the gentry class with its cultural practice, and folk culture and vernacular practice. In the first, Nancy S. Steinhardt addresses the practice of capital city planning that serviced the purpose of state authority; Fu Xinian examines one of the most renowned product of this planning – Beijing, the capital city with its palaces and altars of Ming China (1368–1644); Heng Chye Kiang studies further a crucial transformation of planning and use of the capital city from Sui-Tang (581–906) to Song (960–1276) dynasties when liberalization and commercialization occurred; whereas Pan Guxi provides an examination of a 1103 state guidebook on building construction, *Yingzao Fashi* (building standard) from the late Northern Song dynasty (960–1127). The four pieces together provide a glimpse of the rule of the state over city planning and building construction at some of the key moments in imperial China.

The second section, on the gentry (scholar-official) class, contains chapters from Gu Kai, Chen Wei, Jia Xu, and Shen Yang. While Shen examines the education regime of the imperial state at its highest level in Beijing of the Ming and Qing (1368–1644–1911), the other three deal with a more relaxed culture of garden and landscape design: Gu and Chen on the scholar or literati gardens of the Jiangnan region, with Xu on landscape urbanism in the same region – in the city of Hangzhou.

In the third part on folk or vernacular China, Dong Wei and Cheng Jianjun work on the northern and southern schools of fengshui practice respectively, whereas Chang Yu-yu reveals to us how building practice, centering on timber buildings, was actually carried out by vernacular masters and builders in southern China. Ho Puay Peng, on the other hand, provides a broader picture of house forms in vernacular China. The three sections – on the practice of the state, literati, and commoners – may begin to demonstrate some of the richness and complexity of Chinese society in pre-modern times for the production and use of spaces and buildings, in relation to state ideology, elite culture, and a rich life-world of the population.

Modernization in Early Modern China

In Part II, "Republican and Early Modern Transformation," the three sections address respectively the arrival of "architecture" in the modern western sense; the adoption of modern architectural technology and the rise of a modern "Chinese" style; and the issue of modern city building and planning as imported from the west. In the first, Xu Subin outlines the earliest national education programs on "architecture" as inspired from the west and adopted from Japan in the 1900s, while Wang Xiaoqian examines how the first modern Chinese state (Republic of China) – based in Nanjing – was developing and institutionalizing the profession of the architect as a new practice in the 1930s. In the second section on styles and technologies, Li Haiqing details the adoption of modern building technologies, including steel-and-concrete, steel frame, and large-span structural types as well as limitations and comparative backwardness in the 1930s, whereas Zhou Qi and Ji Qiu's chapter examines the rise of a Native or Palace Style for state and public architecture in capital city Nanjing of the same period. In the third section concerning modern city construction, Li Baihao describes how modern industrial cities in China came into being with a mixture of western influence and the Chinese state's effort for modernization, in the case of Wuhan in central China, whereas Zhang Tianjie studies the rise of urban parks across China since the 1910s, as promoted by the new Chinese state for building a new social space for the public with cultural, athletic, leisure, and ideological functions. These six chapters reveal to us a rich picture of early modern China where, from urban construction to building technology, and from architectural education to the institution of the profession, a wholesale modernization was on the way.

Socialist China: Achievements Despite the Turbulence

In Part III, "Socialist–Maoist Modernization," the three sections are: urban planning and spatial construction under socialist ideology; frames for design practice, university education, and knowledge production (for design and historical research); and design positions including nationalism and modernism in Mao China from 1949 to the early 1980s. Within the first section, Li Baihao outlines socialist urban planning of the time over a few phases where collectivist ideology, industrialization drive, political campaigns, and pragmatic planning for war preparation dominated as priorities from time to time; whereas Duanfang Lu examines a renowned socialist formation of work-unit called *danwei*, addressing its spatial social organization and its underlying political economy, concluding with eight aspects of Maoist urbanism as found in these territories.

In the second section on the framing for design, education, and knowledge, Ke Song examines the design institute as a system for design production; Qian Feng studies the formation of a teaching system with Soviet and American influence (both with a French Beaux-Art background) as well as a shifting emphasis between disruption and affirmation over these decades; Li Hua examines the formation of ideas of "spatial composition" in design research as a modernist attempt with a Beaux-Arts tradition in Mao China – a line of inquiry that finally surfaced in the 1980s; Zhuge Jing further studies the issue of historical writing in Mao China by observing Liang Sicheng and Liu Dunzhen's approaches, detecting a stronger impact by Liu on the 1980s publications – emphasizing typology and social use, gardens and houses, and a Marxist-materialist perspective.

In the third section on design positions, Jianfei Zhu examines the formation of the national-style or the "big-roof" approach in the first decade of the People's Republic, where diverse formal and ideological strands intersected at this moment in the northern (imperial) capital Beijing; while Eduard Kögel, Lu Yongyi, and Jiang Feng investigate several lines of modernist and functionalist development in southern China with vernacular connections. While Eduard Kögel outlines a broader history of regional modernism, Lu Yongyi examines specifically Shanghai's Tongji University architectural education with a modernist tradition; and Jiang Feng profiles another case based in Guangzhou centering on the Canton Fair and its various buildings (such as hotels) that displayed modernist and sub-tropical features. With these three sections (city and space, knowledge and design framing, and design positions) and the ten essays, some key characteristics of the architecture of socialist China as a social, intellectual, ideological, and formal enterprise are described, for a primary outline and basic features.

China in the World: Problems and Possibilities

In Part IV, "Contemporary Histories: China in the World," there are five sections. These are: ascendance of (semi-)autonomous architects; state design institutes going through market reform; the building of CBDs and their landmarks to engage with global economy; urban–rural reintegration with mega-cities; and Hong Kong and Taiwan's architecture as important alternatives to the mainland in a geopolitical observation.

In the first section, Li Xiangning and Hing-Wah Chau examine the rise of free and (semi-) independent architects and their designs, which have been attracting international attention since 2000; while Li outlines an overall landscape of the situation, Chau provides a case study on a few selected architects – Yung Ho Chang, Liu Jiakun, and Wang Shu.

In the second section, on the design institute in market reform, Charlie Q. L. Xue and Guanghui Ding outline the reform for the institutes to make themselves a market force while maintaining a collectivist and statist base; Jianfei Zhu argues that the practice of these institutions amounts to a critique of "critical thinking" – as found in the west with an oppositional logic rather than a relational ethics.

In the next section, on CBDs and landmarks in China's major cities as "global objects," Peter G. Rowe and Har Ye Kan's chapter examines Chang'an Avenue of Beijing and Century Boulevard in Pudong of Shanghai, as territories in which these global objects were constructed with a territorial rationale; whereas Ming Wu's essay argues for a local reading based on China's modern history rather than an international critique that sees the objects as a matter of branding and commercial gain in a Marxist formula.

In the section on urban–rural reintegration, Wang Jianguo examines the urbanization of China in the reform era (1978–2008,) using Nanjing as an example, to detect problems and to offer advice; identifying the causes of the problem as including developmentalism and excessive exploitation, Wang suggests that the solution for a "new urbanization" should include measures such as urban–rural holism, compact design, reuse of local wisdom, and heritage protection, among others.

In the section on geopolitical differentiations, Chao-ching Fu and Ke Song examine nationalist and modernist design practices outside mainland China, with Fu focusing on Taiwan and Song on both Hong Kong and Taiwan. Fu studies a "Chinese Cultural Renaissance" as reflected in state and public architecture in Taiwan from the 1960s to 1980s, as part of a broader neo-classical or national-style architecture of modern China since Nanjing of the 1930s, a modern tradition now resurfaced in Taiwan in these decades due to several political agendas, including a critique of mainland's Cultural Revolution. Song, on the other hand, examines a critical and autonomous design practice in Taiwan and Hong Kong, focusing on a few key figures, including Wang Da-hong, Chen Chi-kwan, and Rocco Yim. Relations and interactions can be traced between Hong Kong, Taiwan, and mainland China in a geopolitical map of the territories with ongoing interactions. On the whole, the five sections of this art on contemporary China – autonomy, state practice, the CBDs as global objects, urban–rural social morphology, and geopolitics of design – together frame a possible window on a complex and changing China still evolving on the world stage.

Theorizing: Architecture Beyond Architecture

In Part V, "Theorization," there are three sections – culture, politics, and methodology. In the first, on traditional theories concerning building and culture, or contemporary theories on the ancient architecture of China, there are chapters by Wang Guixiang and David Wang that fall into the first case on ancient theories and categories, as well as studies by Shiqiao Li and Jianfei Zhu on the second approach, using new categories to examine the culture and architecture of ancient China. Wang Guixiang provides a broad reading of ancient Chinese categories from which "ten lamps of architecture" are discovered – ten ideas as grouped in five clusters – perfection, ritual, appreciation, style, and layout. David Wang examines a functionalist use of Confucian ritualism in Xun Zi (310s–230s BCE) and a rationalist idea from Zhu Xi (1130–1200), as well as a generic concept of the gentry (scholar-official) to develop a theory of architecture that is more internally Chinese – for a tectonic ethics and the role of the architect–scholar–teacher. Shiqiao Li, on the other hand, tests new concepts for explaining that cultures of China include its spaces and cities – Chinese writing and its plastic force as "figuration" to ensure a dominance of writing over speech, and texts over buildings, and a formation of "colonies of beauty and violence" such as the body, the desk, the garden, and the city. Jianfei Zhu examines the rationale of the Chinese script, its proximity to matter and world, and its instant vastness as an empire of signs; the chapter aims to establish a connection between an "empire of signs" and "signs of an empire," between signifying culture and state politics, in three realms – sign systems, expressive surfaces, and tectonic construction.

In the second section, on political ethics, Shiqiao Li outlines a theory of politics and architecture of China as different from the European tradition – while the latter approximated abstraction with purifying ideas of equality and universal values, the former resided in an immanent world of concrete things in a vast empire of entities organized through structures of hierarchy; the chapter enlists various cases in ancient, modern, and contemporary China in which profusion and hierarchy remain central in society and architecture. Jianfei Zhu, on the other hand, uses the setting of imperial Beijing as a case to reveal a comparability of the theory of power of Han Fei (280–233 BCE) and a panoptic model of state control of Jeremy Bentham (1748–1832); it also reveals a bifurcation of the two cultures, where the west moved to a disciplinary yet open system while China an internalized state ethics with cosmology, high rituals, and disciplinary control all interconnected; the chapter delivers a dialogue between cultures and poses difficult questions on directions of political ethics of the future.

The third section – on research methods and possible future directions as reflected in this collection – is best placed at the end of the book. On the whole, the 45 chapters presented in this book, we hope, manifest an attempt to reassemble an architecture of China or an assemblage of bodies of knowledge on this subject matter, as one that retains its identity while allowing difference, adopts a social approach while accommodating historical narratives, and privileges the current perspective while acknowledging the weight and importance of ancient traditions that were both imperial and vernacular, centralized and pluralistic, established yet open to new transformations.

Notes

1 A draft of the current chapter was presented at "A World of Architectural History" conference, University College London, 3 November 2018.
2 Ernst Boerschmann, *Picturesque China: Architecture and Landscape, a Journey Through Twelve Provinces*, trans. Louis Hamilton (New York: Brentano's, 1923); Ito Chuta's 1931 book in a Chinese translation in 1937 and a Chinese scholar Le Jiazao's work in 1934 were all reprinted recently: Yidong Zhongtai (Ito Chuta), *Zhongguo Jianzhushi* (A History of Chinese Architecture), trans. Chen Qingquan (Changsha: Hunan Daxue Chubanshe, 2016); Le Jiazao, *Zhongguo Jianzhushi* (A History of Chinese Architecture) (Shanghai: Shanghai Shudian, 1996).
3 The initial journal issues published from July 1930 to October 1945 were republished in one book as follows: Zhongguo Yingzao Xueshe, *Zhongguo Yingzao Xueshe Juibian, Gong 23 Ce* (*Journal of the Society of Research in Chinese Architecture*, in 23 issues) (Beijing: Zhishi Chanquan Chubanshe, 2006).
4 Liang Ssu-ch'eng, *A Pictorial History of Chinese Architecture: A Study of the Development of Its Structural System and the Evolution of Its Types*, ed. Wilma Fairbank (Cambridge, MA: MIT Press, 1984). Liang Sicheng, *Zhongguo Jianzhu Shi* (A History of Chinese Architecture) (Tianjin: Baihua Wenyi Chubanshe, 1998).
5 Liu Dunzhen, ed., *Zhongguo Gudai Jianzhushi* (A History of Ancient Chinese Architecture), (Beijing: Zhongguo Jianzhu Gongye Chubanshe, 1980).
6 Liu Xujie, ed., *Zhongguo Gudai Jianzhushi, diyijuan* (A History of Ancient Chinese Architecture), vol. 1 (Beijing: Zhongguo Jianzhu Gongye Chubanshe, 2003).
7 Fu Xinian, ed., *Zhongguo Gudai Jianzhushi, dierjuan* (A History of Ancient Chinese Architecture), vol. 2 (Beijing: Zhongguo Jianzhu Gongye Chubanshe, 2001).
8 Guo Daiheng, ed., *Zhongguo Gudai Jianzhushi, disanjuan* (A History of Ancient Chinese Architecture), vol. 3 (Beijing: Zhongguo Jianzhu Gongye Chubanshe, 2003).
9 Pan Guxi, ed., *Zhongguo Gudai Jianzhushi, disijuan* (A History of Ancient Chinese Architecture), vol. 4 (Beijing: Zhongguo Jianzhu Gongye Chubanshe, 2001).

10 Sun Dazhang, ed., *Zhongguo Gudai Jianzhushi, diwujuan* (A History of Ancient Chinese Architecture), vol. 5 (Beijing: Zhongguo Jianzhu Gongye Chubanshe, 2002).
11 Andrew Body, *Chinese Architecture and Town Planning: 1500 BC – AD 1911* (London: Tiranti, 1962).
12 Laurence G. Liu, *Chinese Architecture* (London: Academy Editions, 1989).
13 Nancy S. Steinhardt, *Chinese Imperial City Planning* (Honolulu: Hawaii University Press, 1990).
14 Liang, *Zhongguo*, 2–5.
15 Liang, *Zhongguo*, 11.
16 Liu, *Zhongguo*, 1.
17 Liu, *Zhongguo*, 4.
18 Liu, *Zhongguo*, 6.
19 Liu, *Zhongguo*, 6.
20 Prasenjit Duara, *Rescuing History from the Nation: Questioning Narratives of Modern China* (Chicago: Chicago University Press, 1995), 17–50.
21 The situation has attracted methodological studies on the condition of the field. Some of the most prominent ones include: Chen Wei, "Yuedu Liangbu Zhongguo Jianzhu Tongshi: Tiwei Yige Shiji Shixue Mingmai (Reading Two Survey Histories of Chinese Architecture: To Appreciate the Lifeline of Historical Research Over a Century)," *Jianzhushi* 4 (2008): 85–90; Zhuge Jing, "Xunzhao Zhongguo de Jianzhu Chuantong: 1953–2003 nian Zhongguo Jianzhu Shixueshi Gangyao (In Search of Architectural Traditions of China: Outline of a History of Chinese Architecture History from 1953 to 2003)," *Shidai Jianzhu: Time + Architecture* 1 (2014): 166–169; Lai Delin, "Jingxue, Jingshizixue, Xinshixue yu Yingzaoxue he Jianzhu Shixue: Xiandai Zhongguo Jianzhu Shixue de Xingcheng Zhaisi (Old in New: Reflections on the Influence of Classics, Pragmatism and New History of Late Imperial China on the Modern Historiography of Chinese Architecture)," *Jianzhu Xuebao* 9–10 (2014): 108–116; Chen Wei, "Zhou Xiang 'He': 2004–2014 nian Zhongguo Jianzhu Lishi Yanjiu Dongxiang (Moving Towards 'Combination': Research Trends in Chinese Architectural History, 2004–2014)," *Jianzhu Xuebao* 9–10 (2014): 100–107; Wang Guixiang, "Jianzhu Shixue de Weiji yu Zhengbian (Crises and Arguments in Methodology for Architectural History)," *Jianzhushi* 4 (2017): 6–15. Outside China, parallel self-reflection of the discipline can be found in: Nancy S. Steinhardt, "Chinese Architectural History in the Twenty-First Century," *Journal of the Society of Architectural Historians* 73, no. 1 (March 2014): 38–60.
22 Wang Tan and Fujimori Terunobu, eds., *Zhongguo Jindai Jianzhu Zonglan – Tianjin Pian: The Architectural Heritage of Modern China – Tianjin* (Beijing: Zhongguo Jianzhu Gongye Chubanshe, 1989). Under Wang and Fujimori, and others including Zhang Fuhe and Muramatsu Shin, some 15 Chinese cities are covered, one by a book (of surveys), after the first on Tianjin in 1989; these are six cities, including Wuhan, Nanjing, and Guangzhou in 1992; five, including Beijing in 1993; and four, including Dalian in 1995.
23 Wu Jiang, *Shanghai Bainian Jianzhushi (1840–1949)* (A Century of Architecture in Shanghai) (Shanghai: Tongji Daxue Chubanshe, 1997).
24 Jeffrey W. Cody, *Building in China: Henry K. Murphy's 'Adaptive Architecture' 1914–1935* (Hong Kong: The Chinese University of Hong Kong Press, 2001).
25 Lai Delin, Wu Jiang and Xu Subin, eds., *Zhongguo Jindai Jianzhushi* (A History of Early Modern Chinese Architecture), vol. 1–5 (Beijing: Zhongguo Jianzhu Gongye Chubanshe, 2016).
26 See Nancy S. Steinhardt's two books in this regard: *Liao Architecture* (Honolulu: Hawaii University Press, 1997) and *China's Early Mosques* (Edinburgh: Edinburgh University Press, 2015). There are more books recently on non-Han architecture, such as: Wang Xiaodong et al., *Keshi Gaotai Minju* (Terraced Vernacular Houses in Kashgar) (Nanjing: Dongnan Daxue Chubanshe, 2014).
27 Fu Chao-ching, *Zhongguo Gudian Shiyang Xin Jianzhu* (A New Architecture of Classical Styles in China) (Taipei: Nantian Shuju, 1993).
28 Jianfei Zhu, *Architecture of Modern China: A Historical Critique* (London: Routledge 2009); Shuishan Yu, *Chang'an Avenue and the Modernization of Chinese Architecture* (Seattle: University of Washington Press, 2012).
29 David Bray, *Social Space and Governance in Urban China: The Danwei System from Origins to Reform* (Stanford: Stanford University Press, 2005); Duanfang Lu, *Remaking Chinese Urban Form: Modernity, Scarcity and Space, 1949–2005* (London: Routledge, 2006).
30 Duanfang Lu, ed., *Third World Modernism: Architecture, Development and Identity* (London: Routledge, 2010); Cole Roskam, "Non-Aligned Architecture: China's Designs on and in Ghana and Guinea, 1955–1992," *Architectural History* 58 (2015): 161–191; Ke Song, "China's Foreign Aid Architecture in

a Transitional Period, 1964–1976," *Journal of Asian Architecture and Building Engineering* (January 2021), online, https://doi.org/10.1080/13467581.2020.1869012.

31 Charlie Q.L. Xue and Guanghui Ding, *A History of Design Institutes in China: From Mao to Market* (London: Routledge, 2018).

32 Peng Yigang, *Zhongguo Gudian Yuanlin Fenxi* (Analysis of Classical Chinese Gardens) (Beijing: Zhongguo Jianzhu Gongye Chubanshe, 1986); Tong Ming, Dong Yugan and Ge Ming, eds., *Yuanlin yu Jianzhu* (Gardens and Architecture) (Beijing: Zhongguo Shuilishuidian Chubanshe, 2009).

33 Jianfei Zhu, "Beyond Revolution: Notes on Contemporary Chinese Architecture," *AA Files* 35 (1998): 3–14; Li Xiangning, "Key Concepts of Chinese Architecture Today," *AV Monographs* 150 (2011): 6–15; Guanghui Ding, *Constructing a Place of Critical Architecture in China: Intermediate Criticality in the Journal Time + Architecture* (London: Routledge, 2012).

34 Hsia Chu-joe, "Yingzao Xueshe: Liang Sicheng Jianzhushi Lunshu Gouzhao zhi Lilun Fenxi (Society of Research in Chinese Architecture: A Theoretical Analysis of the Narrative Structure of Liang Sicheng's Architectural History)," in *Kongjian, Lishi yu Sheji: Lunwen Xuan 1987–1992* (Space, History and Design: A Collection of Essays 1987–1992), ed. Hsia Chu-joe (Taipei: Taiwan Shehui Yanjiu, 1993), 1–40. See also Zhuge, "Xunzhao (In Search of)," 166–169.

35 Jianfei Zhu, "A Celestial Battlefield," *AA Files* 28 (Autumn 1994): 48–60; Jianfei Zhu, *Chinese Spatial Strategies: Imperial Beijing, 1420–1911* (London: Routledge Curzon, 2004); Duanfang Lu, *Remaking Chinese Urban Form: Modernity, Scarcity and Space, 1949–2005* (London: Routledge, 2006).

36 Li Shiqiao, *Xiandai Sixiang zhongde Jianzhu* (Architecture in Modern Thought) (Beijing: Zhongguo Shuilishuidian Chubanshe, 2009).

37 Peng Nu, Zhi Wenjun and Dai Chun, eds., *Xianxiangxue yu Jianzhu de Duihua* (Conversations Between Phenomenology and Architecture) (Shanghai: Tongji Daxue Chubanshe, 2009).

38 Hsia Chu-joe, *Kongjian* (Space); Zhu Jianfei, *Xingshi yu Zhengzhi: Jianzhu Yanjiu de Yizhong Fangfa, Ershinian Gongzuo Huigu 1994–2014* (Forms and Politics: An Approach to Thinking in Architecture, Collection of Essays 1994–2014) (Shanghai: Tongji Daxue Chubanshe, 2018).

39 Ding Wowo and Hu Heng, eds. *Jianzhu Wenhua Yanjiu: Studies of Architecture and Culture*, vol. 1 (Beijing: Zhongyang Bianyi Chubanshe, 2009).

40 Mark Cousins, Chen Wei, Li Hua and Ge Ming, eds., *Architecture Studies: Jianzhu Yanjiu, vol. 1: Words, Buildings & Drawings* (Beijing: Zhongguo Jianzhu Gongye Chubanshe, 2011).

41 We are aware of a parallel debate in the English-speaking world concerning methodology in architectural history. From Porphyrios' 1985 essay to Nancy Stieber-led group debate in December 2005, the argument seems to suggest that a reflective scholar is expected to be critical of history writing itself, to be critical of any methods, and to be open to multiple approaches in social science and humanities. We are contributing to this argument with a specific case from China. For the initial discussions in English, see Demetri Porphyrios, "On Critical History," in *Architecture Criticism Ideology*, ed. Joan Ockman (Princeton: Princeton University Press, 1985), 16–21; Nancy Stieber, "Learning from Interdisciplinarity: Introduction," *Journal of the Society of Architectural Historians* 64, no. 4 (December 2005): 417–18; and the whole section: 417–40.

Bibliography

Boerschmann, Ernst. *Picturesque China: Architecture and Landscape, a Journey Through Twelve Provinces*. Translated by Louis Hamilton. New York: Brentano's, 1923.

Boyd, Andrew. *Chinese Architecture and Town Planning: 1500 BC – AD 1911*. London: Tiranti, 1962.

Bray, David. *Social Space and Governance in Urban China: The 'Danwei' System from Origins to Reform*. Stanford: Stanford University Press, 2005.

Chen Wei. "Yuedu Liangbu Zhongguo Jianzhu Tongshi: Tiwei Yige Shiji Shixue Mingmai (Reading Two Survey Histories of Chinese Architecture: To Appreciate the Lifeline of Historical Research Over a Century)." *Jianzhushi* 4 (2008): 85–90.

———. "Zhou Xiang 'He': 2004–2014 nian Zhongguo Jianzhu Lishi Yanjiu Dongxiang (Moving Towards 'Combination': Research Trends in Chinese Architectural History, 2004–2014)." *Jianzhu Xuebao* 9–10 (2014): 100–107.

Cody, Jeffrey W. *Building in China: Henry K. Murphy's 'Adaptive Architecture' 1914–1935*. Hong Kong: The Chinese University of Hong Kong Press, 2001.

Cousins, Mark, Chen Wei, Li Hua and Ge Ming, eds. *Architecture Studies: Jianzhu Yanjiu, vol. 1: Words, Buildings & Drawings*. Beijing: Zhongguo Jianzhu Gongye Chubanshe, 2011.

Ding, Guanghui. *Constructing a Place of Critical Architecture in China: Intermediate Criticality in the Journal Time + Architecture*. London: Routledge, 2012.

Ding, Wowo and Hu Heng, eds. *Jianzhu Wenhua Yanjiu: Studies of Architecture and Culture*, vol. 1. Beijing: Zhongyang Bianyi Chubanshe, 2009.

Duara, Prasenjit. *Rescuing History from the Nation: Questioning Narratives of Modern China*. Chicago: Chicago University Press, 1995.

Fu Chao-ching. *Zhongguo Gudian Shiyang Xin Jianzhu* (A New Architecture of Classical Styles in China). Taipei: Nantian Shuju, 1993.

Fu Xinian, ed. *Zhongguo Gudai Jianzhushi, dierjuan* (A History of Ancient Chinese Architecture), vol. 2. Beijing: Zhongguo Jianzhu Gongye Chubanshe, 2001.

Guo Daiheng, ed. *Zhongguo Gudai Jianzhushi, disanjuan* (A History of Ancient Chinese Architecture), vol. 3. Beijing: Zhongguo Jianzhu Gongye Chubanshe, 2003.

Hsia Chu-joe. *Kongjian, Lishi yu Sheji: Lunwen Xuan 1987–1992* (Space, History and Design: A Collection of Essays 1987–1992). Taipei: Taiwan Shehui Yanjiu, 1993.

———. "Yingzao Xueshe: Liang Sicheng Jianzhushi Lunshu Gouzhao zhi Lilun Fenxi (Society of Research in Chinese Architecture: A Theoretical Analysis of the Narrative Structure of Liang Sicheng's Architectural History)." In *Kongjian, Lishi yu Sheji: Lunwen Xuan 1987–1992* (Space, History and Design: A Collection of Essays 1987–1992), edited by Hsia Chu-joe, 1–40. Taipei: Taiwan Shehui Yanjiu, 1993.

Lai Delin. "Jingxue, Jingshizixue, Xinshixue yu Yingzaoxue he Jianzhu Shixue: Xiandai Zhongguo Jianzhu Shixue de Xingcheng Zhaisi (Old in New: Reflections on the Influence of Classics, Pragmatism and New History of Late Imperial China on the Modern Historiography of Chinese Architecture)." *Jianzhu Xuebao* 9–10 (2014): 108–116.

Lai Delin, Wu Jiang and Xu Subin, eds. *Zhongguo Jindai Jianzhushi* (A History of Early Modern Chinese Architecture), vol. 1–5. Beijing: Zhongguo Jianzhu Gongye Chubanshe, 2016.

Le Jiazao. *Zhongguo Jianzhushi* (A History of Chinese Architecture). Shanghai: Shanghai Shudian, 1996.

Li Shiqiao. *Xiandai Sixiang zhongde Jianzhu* (Architecture in Modern Thought). Beijing: Zhongguo Shuilishuidian Chubanshe, 2009.

Li Xiangning. "Key Concepts of Chinese Architecture Today." *AV Monographs* 150 (2011): 6–15.

Liang Sicheng. *Zhongguo Jianzhu Shi* (A History of Chinese Architecture). Tianjin: Baihua Wenyi Chubanshe, 1998.

Liang Ssu-ch'eng. *A Pictorial History of Chinese Architecture: A Study of the Development of Its Structural System and the Evolution of Its Types*. Edited by Wilma Fairbank. Cambridge, MA: MIT Press, 1984.

Liu Dunzhen, ed. *Zhongguo Gudai Jianzhushi* (A History of Ancient Chinese Architecture). Beijing: Zhongguo Jianzhu Gongye Chubanshe, 1980.

Liu, Laurence G. *Chinese Architecture*. London: Academy Editions, 1989.

Liu Xujie, ed. *Zhongguo Gudai Jianzhushi, diyijuan* (A History of Ancient Chinese Architecture), vol. 1. Beijing: Zhongguo Jianzhu Gongye Chubanshe, 2003.

Lu, Duanfang. *Remaking Chinese Urban Form: Modernity, Scarcity and Space, 1949–2005*. London: Routledge, 2006.

———, ed. *Third World Modernism: Architecture, Development and Identity*. London: Routledge, 2010.

Ockman, Joan, ed. *Architecture Criticism Ideology*. Princeton: Princeton University Press, 1985.

Pan Guxi, ed. *Zhongguo Gudai Jianzhushi, disijuan* (A History of Ancient Chinese Architecture), vol. 4. Beijing: Zhongguo Jianzhu Gongye Chubanshe, 2001.

Peng Nu, Zhi Wenjun and Dai Chun, eds. *Xianxiangxue yu Jianzhu de Duihua* (Conversations Between Phenomenology and Architecture). Shanghai: Tongji Daxue Chubanshe, 2009.

Peng Yigang. *Zhongguo Gudian Yuanlin Fenxi* (Analysis of Classical Chinese Gardens). Beijing: Zhongguo Jianzhu Gongye Chubanshe, 1986.

Porphyrios, Demetri. "On Critical History." In *Architecture Criticism Ideology*, ed. Joan Ockman, 16–21. Princeton: Princeton University Press, 1985.

Roskam, Cole. "Non-Aligned Architecture: China's Designs on and in Ghana and Guinea, 1955–1992." *Architectural History* 58 (2015): 161–91.

Song, Ke. "China's Foreign Aid Architecture in a Transitional Period, 1964–1976." *Journal of Asian Architecture and Building Engineering* (January 2021), online, https://doi.org/10.1080/13467581.2020.1869012.

Steinhardt, Nancy S. *Chinese Imperial City Planning*. Honolulu: Hawaii University Press, 1990.

———. *Liao Architecture*. Honolulu: Hawaii University Press, 1997.

———. "Chinese Architectural History in the Twenty-First Century." *Journal of the Society of Architectural Historians* 73, no. 1 (March 2014): 38–60.

———. *China's Early Mosques*. Edinburgh: Edinburgh University Press, 2015.

Stieber, Nancy. "Learning from Interdisciplinarity: Introduction." *Journal of the Society of Architectural Historians* 64, no. 4 (December 2005): 417–418 (and the whole section: 417–440).

Sun Dazhang, ed. *Zhongguo Gudai Jianzhushi, diwujuan* (A History of Ancient Chinese Architecture), vol. 5. Beijing: Zhongguo Jianzhu Gongye Chubanshe, 2002.

Tong Ming, Dong Yugan and Ge Ming, eds. *Yuanlin yu Jianzhu* (Gardens and Architecture). Beijing: Zhongguo Shulishudian Chubanshe, 2009.

Wang Guixiang. "Jianzhu Shixue de Weiji yu Zhengbian (Crises and Arguments in Methodology for Architectural History)." *Jianzhushi* 4 (2017): 6–15.

Wang Tan and Fujimori Terunobu, eds. *Zhongguo Jindai Jianzhu Zonglan – Tianjin Pian: The Architectural Heritage of Modern China – Tianjin*. Beijing: Zhongguo Jianzhu Gongye Chubanshe, 1989.

Wang Xiaodong et al. *Keshi Gaotai Minju* (Terraced Vernacular Houses in Kashgar). Nanjing: Dongnan Daxue Chubanshe, 2014.

Wu Jiang. *Shanghai Bainian Jianzhushi (1840–1949)* (A Century of Architecture in Shanghai). Shanghai: Tongji Daxue Chubanshe, 1997.

Xue, Charlie Q.L. and Guanghui Ding. *A History of Design Institutes in China: From Mao to Market*. London: Routledge, 2018.

Yidong Zhongtai (Ito Chuta). *Zhongguo Jianzhushi* (A History of Chinese Architecture). Translated by Chen Qingquan. Changsha: Hunan Daxue Chubanshe, 2016.

Yu, Shuishan. *Chang'an Avenue and the Modernization of Chinese Architecture*. Seattle: University of Washington Press, 2012.

Zhongguo Yingzao Xueshe. *Zhongguo Yingzao Xueshe Juibian, Gong 23 Ce* (Journal of the Society of Research in Chinese Architecture, in 23 issues). Beijing: Zhishi Chanquan Chubanshe, 2006.

Zhu, Jianfei. "A Celestial Battlefield." *AA Files* 28 (Autumn 1994): 48–60.

———. "Beyond Revolution: Notes on Contemporary Chinese Architecture." *AA Files* 35 (1998): 3–14.

———. *Architecture of Modern China: A Historical Critique*. London: Routledge 2009.

———. *Chinese Spatial Strategies: Imperial Beijing, 1420–1911*. London: Routledge Curzon, 2004.

———. *Xingshi yu Zhengzhi: Jianzhu Yanjiu de Yizhong Fangfa, Ershinian Gongzuo Huigu 1994–2014* (Forms and Politics: An Approach to Thinking in Architecture, Collection of Essays 1994–2014). Shanghai: Tongji Daxue Chubanshe, 2018.

Zhuge Jing. "Xunzhao Zhongguo de Jianzhu Chuantong: 1953–2003 nian Zhongguo Jianzhu Shixueshi Gangyao (In Search of Architectural Traditions of China: Outline of a History of Chinese Architecture History from 1953 to 2003)." *Shidai Jianzhu: Time + Architecture* 1 (2014): 166–169.

Glossary

Chang Yu-yu	张玉瑜
Chang'an Avenue	长安（街）
Charlie Q. L. Xue	薛求理
Chen Chi-kwan	陈其宽
Chen Wei	陈薇
Cheng Jianjun	程建军
Dai Chun	戴春
danwei	单位
David Wang	王元生
Ding Wowo	丁沃沃
Dong Wei	董卫
Dong Yugan	董豫赣
Duanfang Lu	卢端芳
fengshui	风水
Foguangsi (Temple)	佛光寺
Fu Chao-ching	傅朝卿
Fu Xinian	傅熹年

Ge Ming	葛明
Gu Kai	顾凯
Guanghui Ding	丁光辉
Guangzhou	广州
gudai	古代
Guo Daiheng	郭戴妲
Han	汉（朝）
Han (people, culture)	汉（人、文化）
Han Fei	韩非
Har Ye Kan	简夏仪
Heng Chye Kiang	王才强
Hing-Wah Chau	周庆华
Hsia Chu-joe	夏铸九
Hu Heng	胡恒
Ji Qiu	季秋
Jia Xu	徐佳
Jianfei Zhu	朱剑飞
Jiang Feng	冯江
Jianzhu Wenhua Yanjiu	建筑文化研究
Jin	晋（朝）
Jin	金（朝）
Ke Song	宋科
Lai Delin	赖德霖
Li Baihao	李百浩
Li Haiqing	李海清
Li Hua	李华
Li Xiangning	李翔宁
Liang Sicheng	梁思成
Liao	辽（代）
Lin Huiyin	林徽因
Liu Dunzhen	刘敦桢
Liu Jiakun	刘家琨
Liu Xujie	刘叙杰
Lu Yongyi	卢永毅
Mao (era of)	毛泽东（时期）
Ming	明（朝）
Ming Wu	吴名
Nanjing	南京
Pan Guxi	潘谷西
Peng Nu	彭怒
Peng Yigang	彭一刚
Ho Puay Peng	何培斌
Pudong	浦东
Qian Feng	钱锋
Qin	秦（朝）
Qing	清（朝）
Rocco (S. Y.) Yim	严迅奇

Shang	商（朝）
Shanghai	上海
Shanghai Bainian Jianzhushi	上海百年建筑史
Shen Yang	沈暘
Shiqiao Li	李世桥
Shuishan Yu	于水山
Song	宋（朝）
Sui-Tang	隋唐（朝）
Sun Dazhang	孙大章
Taiwan	台湾
Tang	唐（朝）
Tong Ming	童明
Tongji	同济（大学）
Wang Da-hong	王大闳
Wang Guixiang	王贵祥
Wang Haoyu	王浩娱
Wang Jianguo	王建国
Wang Shu	王澍
Wang Tan	汪坦
Wang Xiaoqian	汪晓茜
Wu Jiang	伍江
Wuhan	武汉
Xia	夏（朝）
Xinjiang	新疆
Xixia	西夏（王朝）
Xu Subin	徐苏斌
Xun Zi	荀子
Yingzao Fashi	营造法式
Yuan	元（朝）
Yung Ho Chang	张永和
Zhang Tianjie	张天洁
Zhi Wenjun	支文军
Zhongguo Gudai Jianzhushi	中国古代建筑史
Zhongguo Gudian Shiyang Xin Jianzhu	中国古典式样新建筑
zhongguo jianzhu	中国建筑
Zhongguo Jianzhu Shi	中国建筑史
zhongguo jindai jianzhu	中国近代建筑
Zhongguo Jindai Jianzhushi	中国近代建筑史
zhongguo jingshen	中国精神
Zhongguo Yingzao Xueshe	中国营造学社
zhongguo yingzao xueshe huikan	中国营造学社汇刊
zhonghua minzu	中华民族
Zhou	周（朝）
Zhou Qi	周琦
Zhu Qiqian	朱启钤
Zhu Xi	朱熹
Zhuge Jing	诸葛净

PART I

ANCIENT AND DYNASTIC TRADITION

State Governance Over Building and City Planning

2

THE CHINESE CITY IN THE SERVICE OF THE STATE

Nancy S. Steinhardt

States could not exist in China without cities. Nor could rulers endure in China without states. Thus were rulers, cities, and states integral to one another, and eventually to the concept of empire. Cities of rulers were not necessarily the largest or wealthiest in China, but through three millennia of premodern history, rulers' cities were distinct from other urban environments. Cities in the service of the state, and of course its ruler, emerged in China in the second millennium BCE, several millennia after the rise of urbanism on the Chinese landscape.

China's Earliest Cities

The beginning of urbanism in China is determined by one's definition of a city. Historically and linguistically, the clearest defining feature of the premodern Chinese city is a wall, and in fact, the Chinese character *cheng* translates as either wall or city, depending on context. Walled, pottery-producing settlements whose inhabitants used stone implements and buried their dead in cemeteries trace to the sixth millennium BCE. An example is a village in Li county, Hunan province, enclosed by an earthen wall, six meters wide at the base, narrowing to about 1.5 meters at the top, and roughly rectangular in shape.[1] The wall was surrounded by a ditch, perhaps anticipating the moats that would become standard in Chinese cities for the rest of the premodern period. In Aohanqi, Inner Mongolia, a ditch, but without wall remains, encompassed another settlement of similar size, dated 6200–5400 BCE.[2] Remains of what might have been more complex settlements, also without walls, have been found in Wuyang county of Henan province where pottery kilns, sacrificial dog burials, urn burials, 45 building foundations, 349 tombs, 370 ash pits, and thousands of other objects at a site dated 7000–5800 BCE suggest that workshops and tombs, as well as residences, were components of the Chinese city.[3] In the fifth millennium BCE, the world-renowned Yangshao culture settlement in Banpo, Shaanxi, just east of Xi'an, came into existence. A millennium later, the 500-hectare site included houses of at least three sizes, three cemeteries, a pottery workshop, and animal pens.[4] Banpo may be the earliest example of the relation between a ruler and his city: a large structure known as the Great House (*dafangzi*) dominates the site. That centralized building may have been the residence of a ruler whose population and service buildings were around him. A nearly circular wall, surrounded by a moat, enclosed a Yangshao settlement in Zhengzhou, Henan, dated 3300–2800

DOI: 10.4324/9781315851112-5

BCE. The wall was framed by wooden planks between which earth was pounded into layers.[5] Like the moat, walls of pounded layers (*hangtu*) trace back 7000 years.

Major changes occurred in the third millennium BCE. The first was size. Cities served populations that spread as many as 90 kilometers. Taosi in Xiangfen, southern Shanxi, is an example. A city with multiple walls, Taosi is a precursor to or very early example of a state with an urban center. Without texts or definitive information from archaeology, one cannot deem Taosi a state served by a city, but it likely was. The second important feature of Taosi is its Great House. As at Banpo, one assumes a ruler or priestly class used it.

Urbanism also flourished in the third millennium BCE in the Longshan culture. More than 50 Longshan settlements with walls and building foundations of the rammed-earth technique have been uncovered along the Yellow and Yangzi Rivers. Since its discovery in the 1920s, China's most famous Longshan city has been at Chengziya in Shandong.[6] Dated ca. 2600 BCE, the wall was an irregular rectangle, roughly 445 by 540 meters. The contemporary city Pingliangtai, in Huaiyang, Henan, is the earliest evidence of a squarish city, an idealized shape that would be specified for a ruler's city 2500 years later. Two other features of Pingliangtai would be part of many future Chinese state and imperial capitals: a prominent entry at the center of the south wall and the long avenue from it that divided the city into east and west sectors (Figure 2.1).[7]

Urban centers that flourished in ca. 3000 BCE also provide evidence of ritual architecture. Niuheliang, in Liaoning, is an example from ca. 4700–2900 BCE.[8] In south China at Yuhang, near Shanghai, ritual altars and jade objects attest to ceremonies of ca. 3300–2000 BCE.[9] Whether ancestors, gods, or kings were the focus of ritual, the presence of walls of *terre pisé* construction and altars from Mongolia to Zhejiang to the Yellow River confirms shared practices across the regions that would unite when large capital cities were built to serve dynasties and empires.

Shang (ca. 1600–1046) cities were huge by comparison with earlier times, and some were certainly built by kings for the purpose of serving states. K.C. Chang has argued that early Bronze Age Chinese cities were almost exclusively administrative centers constructed by and for the ruling elite.[10] Archaeological evidence supports his ideas. Texts of the Zhou dynasty (1046–221 BCE) inform us that the movement of the capital was a standard practice of Shang royalty. Written records also relate that orientation of a city was considered prior to construction, and that it was determined by the position of stars and rays of the sun and verified by tools such as a plumb-line.[11]

Erlitou, near Luoyang, stretches 400 hectares. So far, no outer wall has been defined. Dated ca. 1900–ca. 1500 BCE, to date seven palatial complexes, bronze vessels, bronze plaques inlaid with turquoise, and jade, lacquer, bone, and pottery document the complexity of Erlitou urban life. Erlitou was probably the first of seven capitals used by the Shang kings.[12] There is little doubt the Shang city at Erligang near Zhengzhou also was one of the capitals. The most important urban center in the first half of the Shang dynasty, the Erligang outer wall measured just a few meters short of seven kilometers with parts as wide as 30 meters at the base. Another five meters of wall have been uncovered south and west of this main wall, suggesting either that the city was significantly larger or that it had multiple sections. The wall was constructed of pounded earthen layers lined by wooden planks. The largest palace foundation so far is 2000 square meters.[13] At Yanshi, adjacent to Luoyang and dated ca. 1600 BCE, an outer wall enclosed an area of 100 hectares and an inner wall shared the southern and part of the western boundaries. A palace foundation was roughly centered in the inner city, so that the spatial configuration of this mid-second millennium BCE site can be viewed as three concentric entities. The outermost wall was more than twice as thick as the inner city-enclosure and was surrounded by a moat. Seven gates provided access to the outer city and wide boulevards ran through it. Ritual

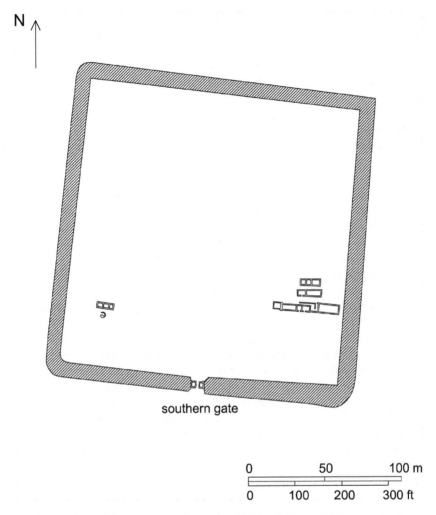

N ↑

southern gate

```
0              50            100 m
0      100     200     300 ft
```

Figure 2.1   Plan of Pingliangtai, Huaiyang, Henan, mid-third millennium BCE.

Source: Drawn by Sijie Ren.

sectors for animal offerings, pottery workshops, and a drainage system were among the urban features.[14] Shang cities that do not have clear ties to rulers include one at Panlongcheng near Wuhan, Hubei, and one in Gucheng in Yuanqu county, Shanxi.[15] They may have been military outposts for states that were centered in Henan.

Shang China's most important capital was also in Henan, at Yinxu (ruins of Yin), northwest of Anyang. It spanned about 36 hectares on either side of the Huan River. Among the remains are a royal cemetery known as Xibeigang, more than 3000 other tombs, 2200 sacrificial burials, about 200 residential foundations, thousands of artifacts in bronze, bone, ivory, jade, stone, pottery, and horn, and a few fragments of painting. A rectangular, Shang-period wall has been found.[16] Every Shang capital served its state.[17]

From Yinxu on, the name of every capital and the state it served, when it flourished, and who ruled there is documented. Western Zhou (1046–770 BCE) had primary capitals at Feng and Hao, both in near Chang'an (Xi'an), and Eastern Zhou (770–221 BCE) had its capital in Luoyang. Extensive knowledge about Zhou cities comes from written records contemporary to the cities themselves, including inscriptions on bronze vessels and philosophical treatises of China's classical age (the age of Confucius [ca. 551–479 BCE] through the Han dynasty), and from later official histories, local records, and scholarly discourse.

One passage about the city in service of the state is preeminent. It is a prescription for a ruler's city (Wangcheng) in the "Kaogong ji" (Record of [the investigation of] crafts) section of the *Zhou li* (Rituals of Zhou). A ruler's city is to be a square whose wall positions are determined by measuring out from a midpoint according to the sun's shadows. Each side of the wall is nine *li*, the number nine associated with Chinese royalty. Major thoroughfares cross the entire city from wall to opposite wall. The central thoroughfares, however, are blocked by the ruler's palace, positioned in its own walled enclosure. It faces south with markets behind it, a temple to the ruler's ancestors on the east and altars to soil and the five grains on the west.[18] Qufu in Shandong, where Confucius was born in 551 BCE, and Anyi in Shanxi were of this plan. Both were constructed in the Eastern Zhou, a time of unprecedented city building in China when every ruler of a state had a capital, and every ruler had his own army and aspired to extend his control. At times, as many as 100 cities co-existed. Each had an enclosed palace area distinct from the outer wall.[19] Two patterns of urbanism co-existed with the plan prescribed in "Kaogong ji": palaces in the north center of a greater walled area and multiple walls that were not concentric.

The importance of markets as a component of the city of a Zhou state is emphasized in texts of the period. Bamboo slips excavated in a tomb in Linyi, Shandong, contain sections of a document known as *Shifa* (Rules about markets).[20] One reads that markets were administered by officials, specific products were sold in prescribed locations, and misconduct in the marketplace was punished. *Zuo zhuan* informs us that market officials were on duty in the first half of Eastern Zhou. The writings of third-century-BCE official Xunzi record that in the earlier part of Eastern Zhou, market officers were largely responsible for maintenance, cleaning, traffic flow, security, and price control, and in later Eastern Zhou their job expanded to merchandise inspection, settlement of disputes, loans, and tax collection for sales, property, and imported goods. One also learns that each state market had its own name. Excavation at Zhou capitals usually yields seals that name officials in charge of state-controlled minting of coins and bronze foundries in the vicinity of palaces, suggesting that these industries were controlled by the state, whereas workshops for goods such as farming tools and pottery most often were farther from palaces. More than 30,000 coins excavated at the capital of the Yan state in Hebei suggest the sizable wealth of a ruler's city. An early fourth-century massacre in Yan has led to the theory that too large an urban population posed a challenge to royal control of a city's production, so that reduction of the urban population was an assertion of power by the ruler to regain control of his state.[21] The seven states that survived at the end of the Zhou dynasty were united in 221 BCE by China's First Emperor, Shi Huangdi (259–210 BCE) of the Qin dynasty (221–206 BCE). Shi Huangdi's vision of empire and the role of the city in it would be carried forward for the next four hundred years by rulers of the Western (206 BCE–CE 9) and Eastern (25–220) Han dynasties (and an interregnum dynasty Xin [9–23]).

China's First Imperial Cities

Shi Huangdi of Qin built his capital, Xianyang, northeast of the early Zhou capitals Hao and Feng. Remains of palaces and countless other foundations have been uncovered there along with the infamous pits that contained thousands of life-size warriors to guard the First Emperor in the afterlife. The outer boundary of Xianyang has not been determined. Probably no capital was intended to serve a ruler more than this short-lived one.

The two capitals of Han China, like their Zhou predecessors, were located in Chang'an and Luoyang. Each is copiously documented. Two features of the Western Han capital are noteworthy. First, Chang'an's outer wall was more irregular than any other capital's, with only the eastern boundary a straight line. The outer wall of the 25.7 km–perimeter city has been accurately drawn since the eleventh century. Scholars have tried to explain the unusual shape as a representation of the two constellations Ursa Major and Ursa Minor, thus linking the city that served the empire with forces of the cosmos. A more practical explanation is that the northern wall was determined by the position of the Wei River. The second unique feature was the amount of space occupied by palaces. Five palaces were inside the walls and an additional palace was beyond the western boundary. Eight major streets emanated from gates of the outer wall, but palaces made it impossible for any one of them to extend the total length or width of the city. The palaces inside the wall occupied fully two-thirds of Chang'an, more than in any previous capital. The ratio of palace: city space at Eastern Han Luoyang would be 1:10. When other imperial architecture such as dynastic altars and the Mingtang (Numinous Hall) for monthly ceremonies, Biyong (Jade Ring Moat) whose functions included imperial education, and Lingtai (Spirit Altar) for observing the heavens, all that trace to Eastern Zhou, are included, even more of the first Han capital was a city almost exclusively for concerns of the state (Figure 2.2). In addition, 11 emperor and empress mausoleums and funerary cities beyond each of them spread north and southeast of Chang'an. Palaces, mausoleums, ritual architecture, and markets, all institutions of a Chinese capital since Zhou times, can be archaeologically confirmed at Western Han Chang'an. Kilns, bronze foundries, and a mint also were part of the ruler's city.[22]

Eastern Han Luoyang had a population twice Chang'an's, but it was less than half the size. From inception, the emperor intended that his capital be austere and his reign frugal, including imperial burial, compared to the earlier Han or Qin. This point is emphasized in a *fu* (prose-poem) about Han Luoyang that states that when constructing his capital, the first Eastern Han emperor looked to the architecture of Chang'an, decided that it exceeded the norm, and "reduced it again and again." When "those who saw it deemed it narrow and vulgar, the emperor . . . ridiculed it as too opulent and uncomfortable."[23] Eastern Han Luoyang had twelve gates, ten major street segments, the same ceremonial and sacrificial structures as Chang'an, and two palaces, although they were never used simultaneously. The two palaces show Luoyang to be transitional in the course of Chinese imperial planning: whereas Chang'an was largely a city of palaces, after Eastern Han Luoyang, all Chinese capitals would have only one palace area. Beginning with Luoyang, palace sectors also would always be positioned along a central north–south axial line through the city.

Chinese Cities in the Age of Disunion (Third Through Sixth Centuries)

More than 30 dynasties, kingdoms, and states were built for rulers in the four centuries following Han and before reunification of China in 589 under the Sui (581–618). Immediately upon the fall of Han, Cao Cao (155–220) established a power base for the Wei kingdom at Ye in southern Hebei. In China's southeast, the Sun family set up a capital for the Wu kingdom in Jianye, today Nanjing. In May of 221, Liu Bei (161–223) declared himself emperor of Shu-Han, ruling from Chengdu in Sichuan. Thus there were Three Kingdoms, each with a city for its ruler, each with a different plan, and each plan resonating a scheme of the first millennium BCE: Ye had its palace area in the north center, Jianye's palatial halls were near the center of the

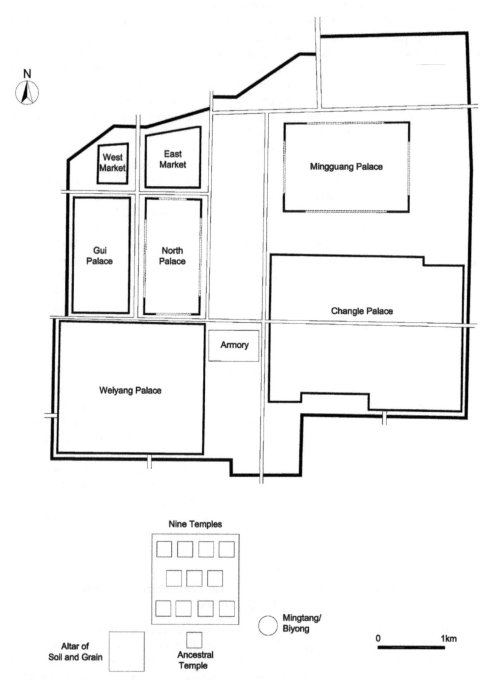

Figure 2.2 Plan of Western Han Chang'an, Xi'an, Shaanxi, ca. 206 BCE–9 CE.

Source: Drawn by Sijie Ren.

city, and Chengdu had multiple adjacent walled areas.[24] Imperial ritual architecture of Han was maintained in all three.

A dozen cities housed China's important imperial and ritual architecture of the century from ca. 280 to 386. Luoyang remained important, becoming the capital of Jin in 265. It was burned in 313.[25] Jianye became Jiankang under the dynasty Jin in 313. Jiankang was an economically prosperous and beautiful city, bounded by mountains and encircled by waterways. Its main north–south thoroughfare, Vermilion Oriole Road, was lined with exotic plantings and flowering trees. This long axis through a capital would remain a feature of Chinese imperial planning through the nineteenth century. Jiankang had a national academy and ritual halls and altars; its palace contained 3500 bays of rooms.[26]

While Eastern Jin ruled from Jiankang, Sixteen Kingdoms (304–439) rose and fell in the north. Their founders and shapers were primarily of non-Chinese origin, yet most sought to adopt or adapt Chinese ways to enhance their imperial ambitions. Walled cities and Chinese-style buildings and ritual structures in them were essential for the rulers because they were important symbols of imperial China. Cities of the Sixteen Kingdoms thus had: at least two walled enclosures, outer and inner; outer walls often fortified, sometimes with battlements that extended beyond the walls; towers above walls for lookout and an advantage from which to shoot arrows; ancestral temples and imperial altars; water in, around, or directed to them. All were features of earlier Chinese capitals. Noteworthy cities of the Sixteen Kingdoms were Pingyang in southern Shanxi, Xiangguo in southern Hebei, Tongwan in northern Shaanxi, and Ye, Cao Cao's city, ruled by the strongmen Shi Hu and Shi Le from the years 331–384.[27] The walls of fourth-century Ye were heavily fortified and brick-faced. The inner walled city had five parallel building axes along which palaces, government offices, and parkland were arranged. Wolongcheng (Reclining Dragon City), today Guzang, in Wuwei county of Gansu, was one of the most interesting of the Sixteen Kingdoms capitals. An intriguing passage in the eleventh-century chronicle *Zizhi tongjian* (Comprehensive Mirror for Aid in Government) says the city had five "clusters" (*cuanju*) of buildings, each with a palace.[28] The passage is clarified in *Jinshu* (History of the Jin Dynasty), in which one reads of a hall painted in five colors, with another hall on each of its four sides. The four halls were used in different seasons.[29] The relation of architecture to time and space and the emperor's progression through architecture as a metaphor for passage of time is a Chinese notion. The principle of centrality in a four-sided configuration traces to Wangcheng. In China's northeast and extending to North Korea, more than 150 walled towns of the Goguryeo kingdom have been identified.[30] The most important urban remains are in Huanren, Liaoning, Ji'an, Jilin, and P'yŏngyang in North Korea. Located on high ground and enclosed by stone walls, the fortified cities are known as *shancheng* (mountain castles.)

Luoyang of the Northern Wei flourished only from 493 to 534, but together with Jiankang, which had a continuous history (first as Jianye) until 589, it is one of the two most important cities of the period. Northern Wei Luoyang represents the transformation from a city focused on imperial architecture to one that would spread to include dozens of residential wards for a large urban population (Figure 2.3). Northern Wei Luoyang also represents the urban transformation of China into a Buddhist nation. Some 1367 temples and monasteries are recorded by Luoyang resident Yang Xuanzhi (d. 555?) in *Luoyang qielan ji* (Record of Buddhist monasteries of Luoyang).[31] The city is an excellent case study in the sinification process of a non-native dynasty, in this case the Tuoba, whose Emperor Xiaowen (r. 471–99) promulgated sweeping social and cultural reforms, as well as an urban building program aimed at making his kingdom more Chinese. By the sixth century, religious architecture became a component of a Chinese city in service of the state.

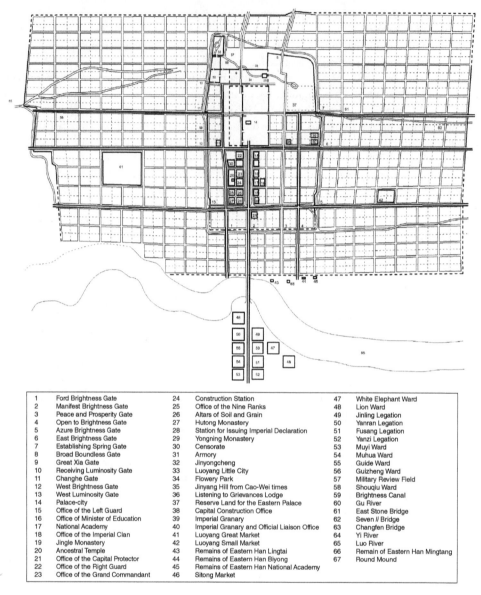

1	Ford Brightness Gate	24	Construction Station	47	White Elephant Ward
2	Manifest Brightness Gate	25	Office of the Nine Ranks	48	Lion Ward
3	Peace and Prosperity Gate	26	Altars of Soil and Grain	49	Jinling Legation
4	Open to Brightness Gate	27	Hutong Monastery	50	Yanran Legation
5	Azure Brightness Gate	28	Station for Issuing Imperial Declaration	51	Fusang Legation
6	East Brightness Gate	29	Yongning Monastery	52	Yanzi Legation
7	Establishing Spring Gate	30	Censorate	53	Muyi Ward
8	Broad Boundless Gate	31	Armory	54	Muhua Ward
9	Great Xia Gate	32	Jinyongcheng	55	Guide Ward
10	Receiving Luminosity Gate	33	Luoyang Little City	56	Guizheng Ward
11	Changhe Gate	34	Flowery Park	57	Military Review Field
12	West Brightness Gate	35	Jinyang Hill from Cao-Wei times	58	Shouqiu Ward
13	West Luminosity Gate	36	Listening to Grievances Lodge	59	Brightness Canal
14	Palace-city	37	Reserve Land for the Eastern Palace	60	Gu River
15	Office of the Left Guard	38	Capital Construction Office	61	East Stone Bridge
16	Office of Minister of Education	39	Imperial Granary	62	Seven li Bridge
17	National Academy	40	Imperial Granary and Official Liaison Office	63	Changfen Bridge
18	Office of the Imperial Clan	41	Luoyang Great Market	64	Yi River
19	Jingle Monastery	42	Luoyang Small Market	65	Luo River
20	Ancestral Temple	43	Remains of Eastern Han Lingtai	66	Remain of Eastern Han Mingtang
21	Office of the Capital Protector	44	Remains of Eastern Han Biyong	67	Round Mound
22	Office of the Right Guard	45	Remains of Eastern Han National Academy		
23	Office of the Grand Commandant	46	Sitong Market		

Figure 2.3 Plan of Northern Wei Luoyang, Henan, 493–534.

Source: Drawn by Sijie Ren.

Luoyang's Northern Wei predecessor, Pingcheng (Datong) in Shanxi, established in 398, marked the end of Northern Wei as a grasslands empire. Like Luoyang and Jiankang, it was a city of walls, palaces, ritual altars, gardens, major avenues, arsenals, granaries, government offices, and noble and aristocratic residences. Pingcheng contained nearly 100 Buddhist establishments with a total of 2000 monks or nuns.[32] In the 460s, five Buddhist caves were opened just outside Pingcheng at Yungang. From the fifth century through the Tang dynasty, cave-temples would be an important focus of state-sponsored patronage.

In 534, Northern Wei split into Eastern Wei (534–50) with a capital at Ye and Western Wei (535–57), whose capital was in Chang'an. In 535, 76,000 laborers worked on construction of the new city at Ye.[33] During the ninth and tenth moons of 539, 100,000 people worked on the imperial residences.[34] In the first moon of 540, the court moved in.[35] Ten years later, Eastern Wei fell to Northern Qi (550–77), who also used Ye as the primary capital. In 577, Northern Qi fell to Northern Zhou (550–581).

Luoyang and Ye were rulers' cities that would have profound influences on Chinese imperial urbanism for the next 300 years. In terms of architecture, a major north–south axis ran from the south central gate of the outer wall to the central entrance of the palace-city and onward to the north outer wall gate, dozens of government bureaus were in the city, there was an arsenal, and the population resided in the many wards. Mansions of the wealthy consisted of multiple court-yards of buildings, those in the front for entertainment and the back ones where the owners resided, and often with gardens.[36] If records can be trusted, Northern Qi Ye had 4000 religious establishments and 80,000 male and female members of the clergy.[37]

In Northern Zhou Chang'an, by contrast, Emperor Wudi executed his guards and destroyed many of the buildings constructed before the formal establishment of his dynasty in 572.[38] Promulgating an anti-elaboration policy, Wudi urged a return to past architecture and encour-aged construction in earth and wood. His successor Xuandi, who reigned for only about a year between 578 and 580, also encouraged earth and wood construction.[39] In 581, rule was in the hands of Yang Jian (541–604), who took power and established the capital of his dynasty Sui at Daxing (Chang'an). Excavation has not conclusively determined how much of Han Chang'an was used by the Northern Zhou or even what remained when Northern Zhou took control. It is believed three Han gates were in use.[40] When the founder of the Tang (618–907) entered Chang'an in 617, he stayed in Changlegong,[41] perhaps remaining from Qin–Han times.

Cities in Service of Great Empires, ca. 600–ca. 1400

The 800 years from the reunification of China under the Sui dynasty in 581 until Zhu Di's ascension (1360–1424) to Yongle emperor in Beijing in 1402 saw the construction and flourish-ing of capitals with populations of more than a million and urbanism that supported and pro-tected state ambitions across China. Chang'an was the first Chinese capital to reach a population of one million. It was also a city that served the state according to patterns established during the previous millennium. Chang'an was not only the largest city in the world in the eighth century, its population was also probably the most international. The internationalism is confirmed by goods sold in the seven markets.[42] The wine business, including wine shops where female com-panionship from West and Central Asia was available, jewelry sales, and moneylending were all pursuits of non-Chinese residents. The large foreign presence did not alter a city whose plan and buildings were configured to serve the ruler and his state.

Chang'an was a city of 108 wards in addition to two wards that contained the east and west markets (Figure 2.4). All 110 were opened at dawn and closed at dusk so that the govern-ment could control the movement of its population in and out of them. In addition to control through the ward system, the city was designed to enhance the ultimate position of the emperor who resided in a palace-city in the north center, looking down on this people and sequestered from them. Earlier rulers' cities had designated areas for the palaces separate from enclosed spaces for government offices. By Sui-Tang times, the three distinct areas, palace-city, administra-tive (imperial)-city, and outer city, were institutionalized. Linking itself with past capitals, the approach to the palace area was via the wide Vermillion Bird Road, divided into three sections for imperial passage in the center and unidirectional passage on either side. The road ended in

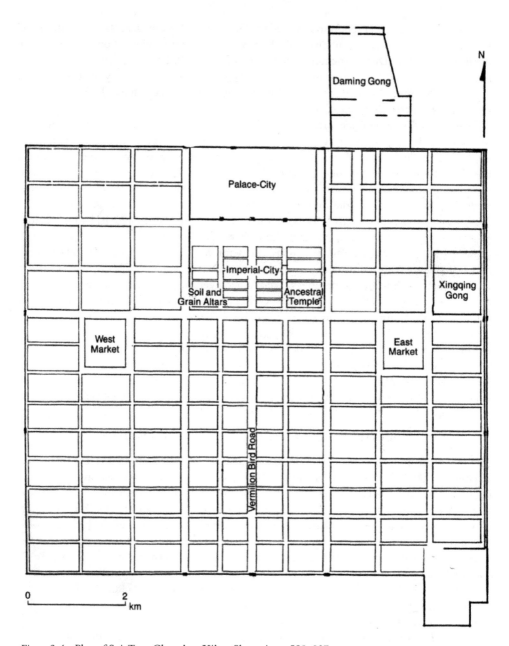

Figure 2.4 Plan of Sui-Tang Chang'an, Xi'an, Shaanxi, ca. 589–907.

Source: From Steinhardt, *Chinese Imperial City Planning*, 11; Published with permission and courtesy of University of Hawai'i Press.

a T-shape in front of the emperor's own spaces, with imperial bureaus on either side. Although the major north–south and east–west streets formed a grid, the broken and unbroken lines of the east–west streets (due to the locations of markets and imperial architecture) have been likened to the trigrams of the *Yijing* (Book of Changes).[43] The association of a ruler's city with a classical text is another aspect of the relation between ruler and state in China.

The second Sui-Tang capital, Luoyang, had exceptionally strong ties to one ruler, usurper Empress Wu Zetian. First used as a Sui capital in 605 when Emperor Yangdi moved population there, as early as 655 Empress Wu had begun to spend most of her time in this eastern capital. Beginning in 684, a year after the death of her husband, third Tang emperor Gaozong, Wu Zetian made Luoyang the primary capital. Luoyang had followed the form of Sui-Tang Chang'an from the beginning, although topography and tomb remains resulted in an urban scheme whose wards were primarily south and west of the palace-city and imperial-city (administrative districts). Imperial architecture that served the state was erected or enhanced under Empress Wu. It included a Mingtang and Tiantan (Altar to Heaven), the second to become increasingly important in later Chinese rulers' cities.[44] Empress Wu also built an enormous cave-temple named Fengxiansi at the Longmen caves outside Luoyang. Here, too, she continued a pattern of imperial patronage of religious architecture: cave-temples Yungang, Longmen, and Gongxian of Northern Wei and Xiangtangshan and Tianlongshan of Eastern Wei and Northern Qi; and vast Buddhist and Daoist urban monasteries. Every Tang ruler also had a splendid tomb, most joint burials with their wives, another longstanding component of state architecture.[45]

An international population was never a necessary component of rulers' cities in China, but probably it was crucial to national success. In the Song dynasty (960–1279), the largest foreign populations were in the international trade entrepôts along China's southeastern coast, particularly Guangzhou and Quanzhou in Fujian, Hangzhou in Zhejiang, Yangzhou in Jiangsu, the last the city on the Yangzi River that joined the Yellow River via the Grand Canal. Records suggest international trading activity in Quanzhou in the Tang dynasty, possibly as early as 741.[46] Guangzhou, however, was closer to the Indian Ocean and the likely first point of entry to China for ships sailing from the West. In 748, Persian, Indian, and Malayan ships were docked in Guangzhou. In 758, Arab and Persian merchants set fire to the port.[47] The Guangzhou port closed to foreign merchants until 792. In 916, 120,000 people, including Muslims, Jews, and Hindus, died in international riots as the result of trade. Still, Guangzhou was the most important international seaport in China into the tenth century when the trade superintendency, the office responsible for taxing imported goods, was located there.[48] Before the Song dynasty, Guangzhou was the only legal port of entry into China for foreign merchants as well as the only port where direct trade between the Chinese and foreigners was permitted. Reform policies of Wang Anshi (1021–1086) led to the opening of Quanzhou in 1087 and the establishment of a trade superintendency in that port.[49] Quanzhou from 1000 to 1400 has been called "the emporium of the world,"[50] comparable to Hong Kong in the late twentieth century.[51] Government restrictions on spices, medicines, and valuables from abroad prohibited their sale in private markets without first going through the official storehouse.[52] It appears that both Guangzhou and Quanzhou received approximately two million strings of cash from abroad in the year 1159.[53] Fuzhou, in Fujian, also had an office that supervised the government monopoly on imported goods.[54] Thus, China's greatest trade cities also served the state.

Biangjing (also known as Bianliang and Bianzhou), Kaifeng today, was the capital of Song China from 960 to 1227. With a population of more than 1.7 million, the outer wall was not a perfect rectangle; nor was the palace-city in the center or north center. The city did have all the necessary institutions of Chinese imperial kingship. The second Song capital, built when the Song dynasty had regrouped in the south after the loss of north China to peoples from the north, was even more irregular. Located at Hangzhou on West Lake, the Song wall, like earlier walls of Hangzhou, was irregularly shaped. The Song palaces were in the south, approached by a long north–south thoroughfare. Like Tang Chang'an and Biangjing, Hangzhou had a population of between one and two million.[55]

Capitals contemporary to Song established by non-Chinese dynasties in the north help understand the relation between ruler and his city. Between 918 and 1044, the Liao dynasty (907–1125) built five capitals: Shangjing, the upper capital, at Linhuang (Balinzuoqi) in Inner Mongolia in 918; the eastern capital in Liaoyang, Liaoning, in 919; the southern capital, also known as Yanjing, in today's Beijing in 947; the central capital in Ningcheng, Inner Mongolia, in 1007; and the western capital at Datong in 1044. The first two cities were "double cities," a name for a capital with adjacent walls and the palace area in one of them. The eastern capital had its palaces in the north center of the northern city, approached by a long avenue from a central gate in the south city wall, like the plans of Sui-Tang capitals. This would be the con-figuration of the Liao central capital. The Jin (1115–1234) conquered Liao and the northern part of the Song dynasty. Jin ruled from six capitals, no more than five at a time; four had been Liao imperial cities. The Jin capital with the greatest impact on later Chinese urbanism was the central capital (Zhongdu), which encompassed the Liao southern capital, and part of which would be incorporated into the Mongol capital Dadu and later versions of Beijing. The Jin ruler moved building pieces from the Song capital at Kaifeng to the central capital, thereby linking himself and his city with the Song dynasty. The palaces of this central capital, established in 1153 by Hailingwang, were located in the approximate center of Jin Zhongdu and were approached by a long, T-shaped avenue that became a plaza directly in front of the palaces. If records can be trusted, 800,000 men and 4000 troops aided in the construction. The Jin central capital had three concentric walls: palace-city, administrative-city, and outer city. There was a main palace, a hall where imperial gifts were received, an eastern palace where the crown prince lived, and a palace for the empress dowager. There was also a ritual pleasure island to which magical stone known as *genyue* was moved from the Song dynasty capital Bianjing after the Jin conquered it. And there were an Ancestral Temple and Altars of Soil and Grain.[56] Imperial tombs, today in Fangshan, were another part of the Jin imperial vision shared with earlier Chinese capitals.[57]

Beijing and Its Predecessor

Khubilai's Khan's capital Dadu was constructed to serve the state more closely than any city that had come before it. Already in 1256, Khubilai had built a capital called Shangdu, upper capital, in Inner Mongolia, for the purpose of displaying Mongol power in the manner of a Chinese ruler. The large outer area was primarily a hunting ground for Mongol royalty, who would spend about four months a year here after they moved south into China. The second and third city walls, around the palace and administrative areas, were concentric. The positions of eight Buddhist or Daoist monasteries in them were inspired by the Eight Trigrams in the *Yijing*. Khu-bilai's minister Liu Bingzhong presented the idea for the design.[58] Liu also selected the design for Dadu. It was based on the passage on Wangcheng in the *Rituals of Zhou*.

Different from every city that had come before it, a point was marked for the midpoint of Dadu before the outer wall was constructed. It was designed "center marker." A "central pavilion" was built above it. The east and west walls and the north and south walls of Dadu were equidistant from the marker. In the end, Khubilai's palace was not positioned on top of the marker. It was located along the main north–south axis of the city, but to the south so that water that had been channeled into the city by the Jin for their island with *genyue* ran right through the Mongol capital. Nevertheless, the capital of the Mongol Khan more closely fol-lowed the idealized plan of a classical Chinese than any previous capital for any ruler of any Chinese state.[59] Further, publications during the period of Mongolian rule rewrote the history of Chinese imperial planning to show that the capital of the Mongols fit into a lineage that started with Wangcheng. The plan of Biangjing published in *Shilin guangji* (Record of a Forest of Affairs) in the 1330s and the plan of Hangzhou published in *Lin'anxian zhi* (Record of Lin'an [Hangzhou]), issued in the period 1265–1274, both had clear city centers (Figure 2.5). The books ensured that after the Song cities no longer endured, history would record them as the ancestors of the Mongol city.[60] It is because of the Mongol city that Beijing today has the plan it does.

Beijing was not constructed immediately upon the fall of the Mongols in 1368. With Mongol supporters still in the north, the first emperor of the Ming dynasty (1368–1644) established his capital in Nanjing. In 1402, the Yongle emperor (r. 1402–1424) attained succession and in 1406 began construction of his capital, in the north, that would become Beijing. Yongle's capital was smaller than Khubilai's. The north wall was 2.9 kms farther south, but the central building line of the palaces was the same and all palaces were east of the body of water that had been channeled into the city by the Jin dynasty. Between 1419 and 1421, the southern boundary was extended about a kilometer southward, but the city was still smaller than the Mongol capital.

Beijing is the culmination of two thousand years of Chinese imperial planning, the ideal space toward which all Chinese architecture in service of the state had been headed. The emperor was at the center, served by all the buildings around him and the people who built and occupied them. The core of imperial Beijing is the Three Great Halls of the innermost enclosure, the Forbidden City, also known as the Inner City, equivalent of palace-cities of earlier times. The Hall of Supreme Harmony where the emperor held audience, celebrated the New

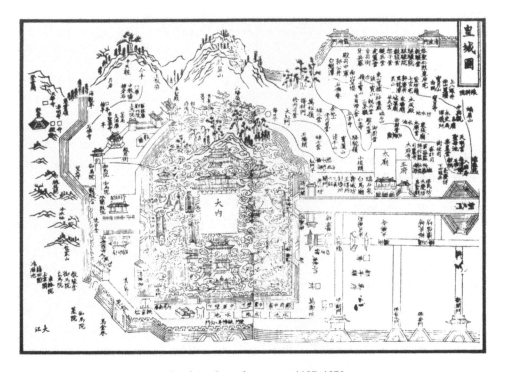

Figure 2.5 Plan of Hangzhou in Southern Song dynasty, ca. 1127–1279.

Source: From *Xianshun Lin'an zhi* (Record of Lin'an [Hangzhou] during the Xianshun period), 1867 edition.

Year, the winter solstice, and his birthday, and announced the names of successful candidates for officialdom, is the most important building in the city and one of the most important in China. The square-shaped Hall of Central Harmony, where the emperor examined seeds for the harvest and made final preparation before entering the Hall of Supreme Harmony, is behind it. Third is Preservation of Harmony Hall, where the emperor honored successful scholars of the highest rank, made high official appointments, and held banquets for foreign dignitaries.

The central hall is equidistant from the other two and elevated with them on a triple-layer, I-shaped, marble platform, a spatial configuration reserved for China's most eminent architecture. Directly behind the Three Great Halls are the Back Halls, of the same plan, equidistant from one another and raised on a single I-shaped platform. The back halls were private imperial chambers, the emperor's bedroom, empress' throne room, and the empress' bedroom. Following a dictum of the *Rituals of Zhou*, the text that had guided the plan of Khubilai's city, the hall of audience was in front, and the private chambers behind.

Like emperors in earlier times, Yongle used his palace-city to inspire his tomb. The tomb is the focus of a cemetery of 13 Ming emperors. As at the Western Han cemetery, the dynastic founder's is the central tomb. The configuration carries the central role of the emperor in space and history beyond his city to link him with earlier emperors of China for whom imperial architecture displayed their power.

Changes made in Ming and Qing (1644–1911) Beijing further enhanced the display of royal power in the City of the Chinese State. The Jiajing (r. 1522–1566) emperor added a southern walled area that extended Beijing to include the Altar of Heaven and Altar of Agriculture. The total area of Beijing was thereupon 62 sq kms. The Altar of Heaven complex was enclosed by a horseshoe-shaped wall whose form combines the perfect shape circle, representing heaven, and square, representing earth. The plans of the three buildings of the Altar of Heaven complex employ the same shapes; together the three halls take the I-shaped plan. The emperor performed the most sacred annual ceremonies of the Chinese calendar here. Details of the symbolic architecture include three round, marble terraces representing the worlds of heaven, earth, and man at the Circular Mound, whose flagstones are arranged in multiples of nine, a numerical symbol of the Chinese emperor; and four large and 24 smaller interior pillars, the ones symbolizing the seasons and the others representing the 12 moons of the Chinese lunar calendar and the 12 hours into which the Chinese day that divide the Hall for Prayer for a Prosperous Year. In addition, Altars of Agriculture (or First Crops), Soil and Grain, Earth, Sun, Moon, Silkworms, and Jupiter were enclosed within Beijing's walls. Not as much of Beijing as Western Han Chang'an was occupied by imperial architecture, but architecture for the emperor or his ceremonies, or that served imperial ambitions, was positioned in every part of the city beyond the Forbidden City or governmental offices.[61]

Chinese rulers constructed cities and architecture to serve and enhance their roles in the state from earliest times. Whether city-states, large imperial capitals, or commercial centers, any city with a palace, imperial altar, or temple, or that paid taxes on some level, served imperial ambitions of the Chinese government. Not every ruler's city in China has the same plan, nor is each plan derived from Wangcheng, but the first emperor through the last had the mandate to reign from the most powerful center in the Chinese universe. The image and power of a ruler's city was so strong that when foreign kingdoms overtook China, a conqueror built a Chinese-style capital. The Chinese city was also a center of production, services, and manufacturing, but its most important role was to serve its state or empire. Most of China greatest monumental architecture was in or around cities. The focus on city, ruler, and service of the state, and the resulting urban uniformity, are defining and distinguishing features of China.

Notes

1 Hunan Institute of Archaeology, "Hunan Lixian, Mengxi Bashidang Xin Shiqi shidai zaoqi yizhi faxian jianbao (Brief Excavation Report on Remains of the Early Neolithic Period at Bashidang, Mengxi, Lixian, Hunan)," *Wenwu*, no. 12 (1996): 26–39.

2 Inner Mongolia Archaeology Unit, Institute of Archaeology, Chinese Academy of Social Science, "Nei Menggu Aohanqi Xinglongwa Juluo Yizhi 1992-nian Fajue Jianbao (Brief Report on the Remains from the 1992 Excavation at Xinglongwa Aohanqi, Inner Mongolia)," *Kaogu*, no. 1 (1997): 1–26.

3 Henan Cultural Relics Research Institute, *Wuyang Jiahu* (Jiahu in Wuyang), 2 vols (Beijing: Kexue Chubanshe, 1999).

4 Xi'an Banpo Museum, *Xi'an Banpo* (Banpo in Xi'an) (Beijing: Cultural Relics Press, 1982).

5 Training Program for Archaeology Team Directors, State Cultural Relics Bureau, "Zhengzhou Xishan Yangshao Shidai Chengzhi de Fajue (Excavation of City Remains from the Yangshao Period Xishan Area of Zhengzhou)," *Wenwu*, no. 7 (1999): 4–15.

6 Li Ji, *Ch'eng-tzu-yai; the Black Pottery Cultures at Lung-shan-chên in Li-ch'êng-hsien, Shantung* (New Haven: Yale University Press, 1956).

7 Henan Archaeology Research Institute et al., "Henan Huaiyang Pingliangtai Longshan Wenhua Chengzhi Shijue Jianbao (Brief Report on Excavation of City Remains of the Longshan Culture Site Pingliangtai in Huaiyang, Henan)," *Wenwu*, no. 3 (1983): 21–36.

8 Cultural Bureau of Chaoyang City and Liaoning Provincial Institute of Archaeology, *Niuheliang Site* (Beijing: Academy Press, 2004).

9 Fanshan Archaeology Unit, Zhejiang Archaeology Research Institute, "Zhejiang, Yuhang, Fanshan, Liangzhu Mudi Fajue Jianbao (Brief Excavation Report of Liangzhu Tombs in Fangshan, Yuhang, Zhejiang), *Wenwu*, no. 1 (1988): 1–31; Zhejiang Cultural Relics and Archaeology Research Institute, *Yaoshan* (Yaoshan) (Beijing: Wenwu Chubanshe, 2003).

10 For Kwang-chih Chang (1931–2001)'s key ideas about Chinese archaeology, see *The Archaeology of Ancient China* (New Haven: Yale University Press, 4 editions from 1963 to 1986).

11 Nancy Steinhardt, *Chinese Imperial City Planning* (Honolulu: University of Hawaii Press, 1990), 30–32.

12 Chinese Academy of Social Sciences Archaeology Institute, *Yanshi Erlitou: 1959 nian – 1978 nian Kaogu Baojue Baogao* (Archaeology Report on Excavations of the Years 1959–1978 at Erlitou, Yanshi) (Beijing: Zhongguo Dabaike quanzhu chubanshe, 1999); K.C. Chang, *Shang Archaeology* (New Haven and London: Yale University Press, 1980), 342–346.

13 Henan Cultural Relics and Archaeology Research Institute, *Zhengzhou Shangcheng: 1952–1985-nian Kaogu Fajue Jianbao* (Excavation Report on 1952–1985 at the Shang City at Zhengzhou) (Beijing: Cultural Relics Press, 2001); Henan Cultural Relics and Archaeology Research Institute, *Zhengzhou Shangcheng Kaogu Xinfaxian yu Yanjiu, 1985–1992* (New Discoveries and Research in Archaeology of the Shang City at Zhengzhou, 1985–1992) (Zhengzhou: Zhongzhou guji chubanshe, 1993); Robert Bagley et al., *Art and Archaeology of the Erligang Civilization* (Princeton: P.Y. and Kinmay W. Tang Center, 2014).

14 Second Henan Archaeology Unit, Institute of Archaeology, Chinese Academy of Social Science, "Henan Yanshi Shangcheng Gongcheng Beibu 'Dahuogou' Fajue Jianbao (Brief Excavation Report on the 'Large Ash Trench' Excavated in the Northern Part of the Palace-City of the Shang City at Yanshi, Henan)," *Kaogu*, no. 7 (2000): 1–2; *Kaogu*, no. 2 (1999): 1–40 (four articles); *Kaogu*, no. 6: 1–19 (three articles); and Han-Wei Luoyang Archaeology Unit, Archaeology Research Institute, Chinese Academy of Social Science, "Yanshi Shangcheng de Chubu Kantan he Fajue" (Early Stages of Survey and Excavation of the Shang City at Yanshi), *Kaogu*, no. 6 (1984): 488–506.

15 Hubei Cultural Relics and Archaeology Research Institute, *Panlongcheng: 1963–1994-nian Kaogu Fajue Baogao* (Report on Excavations at Panlongcheng from 1963–1994), 2 vols (Beijing: Cultural Relics Press, 2001).

16 Anyang, Henan Province Local History Committee, *Anyangshi Zhi* (Record of Anyang), 4 vols (Zhengzhou: Zhongzhou guji chubanshe, 1998).

17 Robin Yates argues this point in "The City State in Ancient China," *The Archaeology of City-States: Cross-Cultural Approaches*, ed. Deborah Nichols and Thomas Charlton (Washington, DC: Smithsonian, 1997), 71–90. Liu Li views China's earliest cities, including those of Shang, primarily as ritual centers; see Liu Li, "Ancestor Worship: An Archaeological Investigation of Ritual Activities in Neolithic North China," *Journal of East Asian Archaeology* 2, no. 1–2 (2000): 129–164.

18 Guanzhong Collected Writings, *Guanzhong Congshu* (Collected Writings of Guanzhong) (Taipei: Yiwen Publishing Company, 1970), *juan* 2/11a–12b.

19 For background on Eastern Zhou cities and states, see Li Xueqin, *Eastern Zhou and Qin Civilizations* (New Haven and London: Yale University Press, 1985), 1–262.

20 Shandong Provincial Museum and Linyi Archaeology Unit, "Linyi Yinqueshan Sizuo Xi Han Muzang (Four Western Han Tombs from Yinqueshan, Linyi)," *Kaogu*, no. 6 (1975): 363–379.

21 Texts referred to in this paragraph are summarized in Chen Shen, "Compromise and Conflicts: Production and Commerce in the Royal Cities of Eastern Zhou, China," *The Social Construction of Ancient Cities*, ed. Monica L. Smith (Washington, DC: Smithsonian Books, 2003), 290–310.

22 Liu Qingzhu and Li Shufang, *Han Chang'ancheng* (Han Chang'an) (Beijing: Wenwu Chubanshe, 2003), among many other writings by these authors on this city.

23 Xiao Tong, "Eastern Metropolis Rhapsody," *Wen Xuan* (Selection of Refined Literature), in *Rhapsodies on Metropolises and Capitals*, trans. David R. Knechtges, vol. 3 (Princeton: Princeton University Press, 1982), 247.

24 Steinhardt, *Chinese Imperial City Planning*, 72–78.

25 Arthur Waley, "Lo-yang and Its Fall," in *The Secret History of the Mongols and Other Pieces* (London: George Allen and Unwin Ltd., 1963), 47–55.

26 The major source of information on Jiankang is Xu Song (eighth century), *Jiankang Shilu* (Veritable record of Jiankang); information on Eastern Jin Jiankang is found in *juan* 5 and 7.

27 Fu Xinian, *Zhongguo Gudai Jianzhu Shi* (History of Chinese Ancient Architecture), vol. 2 (Beijing: China Architecture and Building Press, 2001), 42–59; Edward Schafer, "The Yeh chung chi," *T'oung Pao* 76, no. 4–5 (1990): 147–207.

28 Sima Guang (1019–1086), *Baihua Zizhi Tongjian* (Comprehensive Mirror for Aid in Government, with Modern Chinese Translations) (Beijing: Zhonghua shuju, 1993), *juan* 95, 2237.

29 Fang Xuanling (579–648), *Jinshu* (Standard History of Jin) (Beijing: Zhongguo shuju, 1974), *juan* 86, 2237–2238.

30 Wang Mianhou, *Gaogouli Gucheng Yanjiu* (Research on Goguryeo Cities) (Beijing: Cultural Relics Press, 2002).

31 Yang Hsüan-chih, *A Record of Buddhist Monasteries of Lo-yang*, trans. Wang Yi-t'ung (Princeton: Princeton University Press, 1984); W.J.F. Jenner, *Memories of Loyang* (Oxford: Clarendon Press, 1981.

32 Wei Shou (506–572), *Weishu* (Standard History of Wei) (Beijing: Zhonghua shuju, 1974), *juan* 114, 3030–3039.

33 Sima Guang, *Zizhi Tongjian, juan* 157, 4867.

34 Sima Guan, *Zizhi Tongjian, juan* 158, 4877.

35 Wei Shou, *Weishu, juan* 12, 303–304.

36 Fu Xinian, *Zhongguo Gudai Jianzhu Shi*, 92.

37 Daoxuan, *Xu Gaoseng Zhuan* (Biographies of Eminent Monks, Continued), *Xuxiu Siku Quanshu* (Siku Quanshu Restored), vol. 128 (Shanghai: Shanghai Guji Chubanshe, 1995), *juan* 10, 4908.

38 Linghu Defen, *Zhoushu* (Standard History of Zhou) (Beijing: Zhonghua Shuju, 1974), *juan* 6, 107.

39 Linghu Defen, *Zhoushu, juan* 7, 124.

40 Chinese Academy of Sciences Archaeology Institute, *Xin Zhongguo de Kaogu Faxian he Yanjiu* (Archaeological Discoveries and Research in New China) (Beijing: Cultural Relics Press, 1984), 395.

41 Sima Guang, *Zizhi Tongjian, juan* 184, 5761.

42 Victor (Cunrui) Xiong, *Sui-Tang Chang'an: A Study in the Urban History of Medieval China* (Ann Arbor: University of Michigan Center for Chinese Studies, 2000), 166–168.

43 Victor (Cunrui) Xiong, "Re-evaluation of the Naba-Chen Theory on the Exoticism of Daxingcheng, the First Sui Capital," *Papers on Far Eastern History* 35 (March 1987): 149.

44 Luoyang Cultural Relics Official Bureau, *Gudu Luoyang* (Ancient City of Luoyang) (Beijing: Chaohua Chubanshe, 1999), 150–153.

45 On the Tang tombs, see Zheng Cheng and Hui Li, *Tang Shibaling Shike* (Tang: Eighteen Tombs of Sculpture) (Xi'an: Shaanxi Renmin Meishu Chubanshe, 1988); Nara Prefectural Archaeology Research Institute and Kashihara National Archaeology Museum, *Daitō Kōtei Ryō* (Imperial Tombs of the Great Tang) (Nara: Nara Kenritsu Kashihara Kōkogaku Kenkyūjo Fuzoku Hakubutsukan, 2010).

46 Hugh Clark, *Community, Trade, and Networks: Southern Fujian Province from the Third to the Thirteenth Century* (Cambridge and New York: Cambridge University Press, 1991), 32–33.

47 Fadlo George Hourani and John Carswell, *Arab Seafaring in the Indian Ocean in Ancient and Early Medieval Times* (Princeton: Princeton University Press, 1995), 62–63.

48 Clark, *Community, Trade, and Networks*, 49.
49 Hugh Clark, "Muslims and Hindus in the Culture and Morphology of Quanzhou from the Tenth to the Thirteenth Century," *Journal of World History* 6, no. 1 (Spring 1995): 58–59.
50 Angela Schottenhammer, *Emporium of the World: Maritime Quanzhou 1000–1400* (Leiden: Brill, 2001).
51 Billy Kee-long So, *Prosperity, Region, and Institutions in Maritime China: The South Fukien Pattern, 946–1368* (Cambridge, MA: Harvard University Asia Center, 2000), 2.
52 Clark, "Muslims and Hindus," 52–54.
53 Clark, *Community, Trade, and Networks*, 134–135.
54 Clark, *Community, Trade, and Neworks*, 48–49.
55 On Song cities, see Steinhardt, *Chinese Imperial City Planning*, 137–147. On Hangzhou, see Arthur C. Moule, "Hang-chou to Shang-tu A.D. 1276," *T'oung Pao* 16 (1915): 393–419; Moule, "Marco Polo's Description of Quinsai," *T'oung Pao* 33 (1937): 105–128; and Moule, *Quinsai with Other Notes on Marco Polo* (Cambridge: Cambridge University Press, 1957).
56 On Liao and Jin capitals see Steinhardt, *Chinese Imperial Planning*, 122–133.
57 Beijing Cultural Relics Research Institute, *Beijing Jindai huangling* (Jin Imperial Tombs in Beijing) (Beijing: Wenwu chubanshe, 2006).
58 Nancy Steinhardt, "Imperial Architecture Along the Mongolian Road to Dadu," *Ars Orientalis* 19 (1989): 62–65.
59 Nancy Steinhardt, "The Plan of Khubilai Khan's Imperial City," *Artibus Asiae* 44, no. 2–3 (1983): 137–158.
60 Steinhardt, *Chinese Imperial City Planning*, 146–147.
61 Basic information of the kind here on the city of Beijing is found in numerous books. See, for example, Juliet Bredon, *Peking*, 2nd ed. (Shanghai: Kelly and Walsh, 1922); L.C. Arlington and William Lewisohn, *In Search of Old Peking* (Peking: Henri Vetch, 1935); Yu Zhuoyun, *Palaces of the Forbidden City* (New York and London: Viking Press and Allen Lane, 1984).

Bibliography

An Jinhuai et al. "Yanshi Shangcheng Ruogan Wenti de Zai Tantao (Further Discussion of Questions Regarding the Shang City at Yanshi)." *Kaogu*, no. 6 (1998): 14–19.
Anyang, Henan Province Local History Committee, *Anyangshi Zhi* (Record of Anyang), 4 vols. (Zhengzhou: Zhongzhou guji chubanshe, 1998).
Bagley, Robert et al. *Art and Archaeology of the Erligang Civilization*. Princeton: P.Y. and Kinmay W. Tang Center, 2014.
Beijingshi Wenwu Yanjiusuo. *Beijing Jindai Huangling* (Jin Imperial Tombs in Beijing). Beijing: Wenwu chubanshe, 2006.
Bredon, Juliet. *Peking*, 2nd ed. Shanghai: Kelly and Walsh, 1922.
Chang, Kwang-chih. *Shang Archaeology*. New Haven and London: Yale University Press, 1980.
———. *The Archaeology of Ancient China*, 4th ed. New Haven: Yale University Press, 1986.
Chen Shen. "Compromise and Conflicts: Production and Commerce in the Royal Cities of Eastern Zhou, China." In *The Social Construction of Ancient Cities*, edited by Monica L. Smith, 290–310. Washington, DC: Smithsonian Books, 2003.
Chinese Academy of Social Sciences, Archaeology Institute. *Xin Zhongguo de Kaogu Faxian he Yanjiu* (Archaeological Discoveries and Research in New China). Beijing: Cultural Relics Press, 1984.
———. *Yanshi Erlitou: 1959-nian – 1978-nian Kaogu Baojue Baogao* (Archaeology Report on Excavations of the Years 1959–1978 at Erlitou, Yanshi). Beijing: Zhongguo Dabaike quanzhu chubanshe, 1999.
Clark, Hugh. *Community, Trade, and Networks: Southern Fujian Province from the Third to the Thirteenth Century*. Cambridge and New York: Cambridge University Press, 1991.
———. "Muslims and Hindus in the Culture and Morphology of Quanzhou from the Tenth to the Thirteenth Century." *Journal of World History* 6, no. 1 (Spring 1995): 49–74.
Cultural Bureau of Chaoyang City and Liaoning Provincial Institute of Archaeology. *Niuheliang Site*. Beijing: Academy Press, 2004.
Daoxuan. *Xu Gaoseng Zhuan* (Biographies of Eminent Monks, Continued). *Xuxiu Siku Quanshu* (*Siku Quanshu* Restored), vol. 128. Shanghai: Shanghai guji chubanshe, 1995.
Du Jinpeng et al. "Shilun Yanshi Shangcheng Dongbeiyu Kaogu Xinshouhuo (New Achievements in Archaeology in the Northeast Corner of the Shang City at Yanshi)." *Kaogu*, no. 6 (1998): 9–13, 38.

———. "Shilun Yanshi Shangcheng Xiaocheng de Jige Wenti (Some Questions About the Small Shang City at Yanshi)." *Kaogu*, no. 2 (1999): 35–40.

Fang Xuanling (579–648). *Jinshu* (Standard History of Jin). Beijing: Zhongguo Shuju, 1974.

Fanshan Archaeology Unit, Zhejiang Archaeology Research Institute. "Zhejiang Yuhang, Fanshan Liangzhu Mudi Fajue Jianbao (Brief Excavation Report of Liangzhu Tombs in Fangshan, Yuhang, Zhejiang)." *Wenwu*, no. 1 (1988): 1–31.

Fu Xinian. *Zhongguo Gudai Jianzhu Shi* (History of Chinese Ancient Architecture), vol. 2: *Liang Jin, Nanbeichao, Sui-Tang, Wudai Jianzhu* (Architecture of the Two Jins, Northern and Southern Dynasties, Sui-Tang, and Five Dynasties). Beijing: China Architecture and Building Press, 2001.

Guanzhong Congshu. *Guanzhong Congshu* (Collected Writings of Guanzhong). Taipei: Yiwen Publishing Company, 1970.

Han-Wei Luoyang Archaeology Unit, Archaeology Research Institute, Chinese Academy of Social Science. "Yanshi Shangcheng de Chubu Kantan he Fajue (Early Stages of Survey and Excavation of the Shang City at Yanshi)." *Kaogu*, no. 6 (1984): 488–506.

Henan Archaeology Research Institute et al. "Henan Huaiyang Pingliangtai Longshan Wenhua Chengzhi Shijue Jianbao (Brief Report on Excavation of City Remains of the Longshan Culture Site Pingliangtai in Huaiyang, Henan)." *Wenwu*, no. 3 (1983): 21–36.

Henan Cultural Relics and Archaeology Research Institute. *Zhengzhou Shangcheng Kaogu Xinfaxian yu Yanjiu, 1985–1992* (New Discoveries and Research in Archaeology of the Shang City at Zhengzhou, 1985–1992). Zhengzhou: Zhongzhou guji chubanshe, 1993.

———. *Wuyang Jiahu* (Jiahu in Wuyang), 2 vols. Beijing: Kexue Chubanshe, 1999.

———. *Zhengzhou Shangcheng: 1952–1985-nian Kaogu Fajue Jianbao* (Excavation Report on 1952–1985 at the Shang City at Zhengzhou). Beijing: Cultural Relics Press, 2001.

Hourani, Fadlo George and John Carswell. *Arab Seafaring in the Indian Ocean in Ancient and Early Medieval Times*. Princeton: Princeton University Press, 1995.

Hubei Cultural Relics and Archaeology Research Institute. *Panlongcheng: 1963–1994-nian Kaogu Fajue Baogao* (Report on Excavations at Panlongcheng from 1963–1994), 2 vols. Beijing: Cultural Relics Press, 2001.

Hunan Institute of Archaeology. "Hunan Lixian, Mengxi Bashidang Xin Shiqi Shidai Zaoqi Yizhi Faxian Jianbao (Brief Excavation Report on Remains of the Early Neolithic Period at Bashidang, Mengxi, Lixian, Hunan)." *Wenwu*, no. 12 (1996): 26–39.

Inner Mongolia Archaeology Unit, Institute of Archaeology, Chinese Academy of Social Science. "Nei Menggu Aohanqi Xinglongwa Juluo Yizhi 1992-nian Fajue Jianbao (Brief Report on the Remains from the 1992 Excavation at Xinglongwa Aohanqi, Inner Mongolia)." *Kaogu*, no. 1 (1997): 1–26.

Jenner, W.J.F. *Memories of Loyang*. Oxford: Clarendon Press, 1981.

Knechtges, David R., trans. *Wen Xuan*, vol. 3. Princeton: Princeton University Press, 1982.

Li Ji. *Ch'eng-tzu-yai; the Black Pottery Cultures at Lung-shan-chên in Li-ch'êng-hsien, Shantung*. New Haven: Yale University Press, 1956.

Li Xueqin. *Eastern Zhou and Qin Civilizations*. New Haven and London: Yale University Press, 1985.

Linghu Defen. *Zhoushu* (Standard History of Zhou). Beijing: Zhonghiua Shuju, 1974.

Liu Li. "Ancestor Worship: An Archaeological Investigation of Ritual Activities in Neolithic North China." *Journal of East Asian Archaeology* 2, no. 1–2 (2000): 129–164.

Liu Qingzhu and Li Shufang. *Han Chang'ancheng* (Han Chang'an). Beijing: Wenwu Chubanshe, 2003.

Luoyang Cultural Relics Official Bureau. *Gudu Luoyang* (Ancient City of Luoyang). Beijing: Chaohua Chubanshe, 1999.

Moule, Arthur C. "Hang-chou to Shang-tu A.D. 1276." *T'oung Pao* 16 (1915): 393–419.

———. "Marco Polo's Description of Quinsai." *T'oung Pao* 33 (1937): 105–128.

———. *Quinsai with Other Notes on Marco Polo*. Cambridge: Cambridge University Press, 1957.

Nara Prefectural Archaeology Research Institute and Kashihara National Archaeology Museum. *Daitō Kōtei Ryō* (Imperial Tombs of the Great Tang). Nara: Nara Kenritsu Kashihara Kōkogaku Kenkyūjo Fuzoku Hakubutsukan, 2010.

Schafer, Edward. "The Yeh chung chi." *T'oung Pao* 76, no. 4–5 (1990): 147–207.

Schottenhammer, Angela. *Emporium of the World: Maritime Quanzhou 1000–1400*. Leiden: Brill, 2001.

Second Henan Archaeology Unit, Institute of Archaeology, Chinese Academy of Social Science. "Henan Yanshi Shangcheng Dongbeiyu Fajue Jianbao (Brief Excavation Report of the Northeast Corner of the Shang City at Yanshi, Henan)." *Kaogu*, no. 6 (1998): 1–8.

————. "Henan Yanshi Shangcheng Gongcheng Beibu 'Dahuogou' Fajue Jianbao (Brief Excavation Report on the 'Large Ash Trench' Excavated in the Northern Part of the Palace-City of the Shang City at Yanshi, Henan)." *Kaogu*, no. 7 (2000): 1–12.

————. "Henan Yanshi Shangcheng IV chu 1996-nian Fajue Jianbao (Brief Report on the 1996 Excavations of Section IV of the Shang City at Yanshi, Henan)." *Kaogu*, no. 7 (2000): 13–23.

————. "Henan Yanshi Shangcheng Xiaocheng Fajue Jianbao (Brief Excavation Report of the Small Shang City at Yanshi, Henan)." *Kaogu*, no. 2 (1999): 2–11.

Shandong Provincial Museum and Linyi Archaeology Unit. "Linyi Yinqueshan Sizuo Xi Han Muzang (Four Western Han Tombs from Yinqueshan, Linyi)." *Kaogu*, no. 6 (1975): 363–379.

Sima Guang (1019–1086). *Baihua Zizhi Tongjian* (Comprehensive Mirror for Aid in Government, with Modern Chinese Translations). Beijing: Zhonghua Shuju, 1993.

So, Billy Kee-long. *Prosperity, Region, and Institutions in Maritime China: The South Fukien Pattern, 946–1368*. Cambridge, MA: Harvard University Asia Center, 2000.

Steinhardt, Nancy. "The Plan of Khubilai Khan's Imperial City." *Artibus Asiae* 44, no. 2–3 (1983): 137–158.

————. "Imperial Architecture along the Mongolian Road to Dadu." *Ars Orientalis* 19 (1989): 59–93.

————. *Chinese Imperial City Planning*. Honolulu: University of Hawaii Press, 1990.

Training Program for Archaeology Team Directors, State Cultural Relics Bureau. "Zhengzhou Xishan Yangshao Shidai Chengzhi de Fajue (Excavation of City Remains from the Yangshao Period Xishan Area of Zhengzhou)." *Wenwu*, no. 7 (1999): 4–15.

Waley, Arthur. "Lo-yang and Its Fall." In *The Secret History of the Mongols and Other Pieces*, edited by Arthur Waley, 47–55. London: George Allen and Unwin Ltd., 1963.

Wang Mianhou. *Gaogouli Gucheng Yanjiu* (Research on Goguryeo Cities). Beijing: Cultural Relics Press, 2002.

Wang Xuerong. "Yanshi Shangcheng Buju de Tansuo he Sikao (Exploration and Pondering the Layout of the Shangcity of Yanshi)." *Kaogu*, no. 2 (1999): 24–34.

Wei Shou (506–572). *Weishu* (Standard History of Wei). Beijing: Zhonghua Shuju, 1974.

Xi'an Banpo Museum. *Xi'an Banpo* (Banpo in Xi'an). Beijing: Cultural Relics Press, 1982.

Xiong, Victor (Cunrui). "Re-evaluation of the Naba-Chen Theory on the Exoticism of Daxingcheng, the First Sui Capital." *Papers on Far Eastern History* 35 (1987): 136–166.

————. *Sui-Tang Chang'an: A Study in the Urban History of Medieval China*. Ann Arbor: University of Michigan Center for Chinese Studies, 2000.

Xu Hong. *Xian Qin Chengshi Kaoguxue* (Archaeology of Pre-Qing Cities). Beijing: Beijing Yanshan Chubanshe, 2000.

Xu Song (8th century). *Jiankang Shilu* (Veritable Record of Jiankang), 8 vols. Beijing: Zhonghua Shuju, 1984.

Yang Hsüan-chih. *A Record of Buddhist Monasteries of Lo-yang*. Translated by Wang Yi-t'ung. Princeton: Princeton University Press, 1984.

Yates, Robin. "The City State in Ancient China." In *The Archaeology of City-States: Cross-cultural Approaches*, edited by Deborah Nichols and Thomas Charlton, 71–90. Washington, DC: Smithsonian Books, 1997.

Yu Zhuoyun. *Palaces of the Forbidden City*. New York and London: Viking Press and Allen Lane, 1984.

Zhejiang Cultural Relics and Archaeology Research Institute. *Yaoshan* (Yaoshan). Beijing: Wenwu Chubanshe, 2003.

Zheng Cheng and Hui Li. *Tang Shibaling Shike* (Tang: Sculpture at Eighteen Tombs). Xi'an: Shaanxi Renmin Meishu Chubanshe, 1988.

Glossary

Anyang	安阳
Anyi	安邑
Aohanqi	敖汉旗
Balinzuoqi	巴林左旗
Banpo	半坡
Beijing	北京
Biangjing	汴京

Bianliang	汴梁
Bianzhou	汴州
biyong	辟雍
Cao Cao	曹操
Chang'an	长安
Changlegong	长乐宫
cheng	城
Chengdu	成都
Chengziya	城子崖
cuanju	攒聚
Dadu	大都
dafangzi	大房子
Datong	大同
Daxing	大兴
Erligang	二里岗
Erlitou	二里头
Fangshan (county)	方山（县）
Feng	沣
Fengxiansi	奉先寺
fu	赋
Fujian	福建
Fuzhou	福州
Gansu	甘肃
Gaozong	高宗
genyue	艮岳
Goguryeo (Gaogouli)	高句丽
Gongxian	巩县
Guangzhou	广州
Gucheng	故城
Guzang (city)	姑臧（城）
Hailingwang	海陵王
Han (dynasty)	汉（朝）
hangtu	夯土
Hangzhou	杭州
Hao	镐
Hebei	河北
Henan	河南
Huaiyang	淮阳
Huan River	洹河
Huanren (county)	桓仁（县）
Hubei	湖北
Hunan	湖南
Ji'an (city)	吉安（城）
Jiajing (emperor)	嘉靖（皇帝）
Jiankang	建康
Jiangsu	江苏
Jianye	建邺

Jilin	吉林
Jin (state/dynasty)	金（国/朝）
Jinshu	晋书
K.C. Chang (Zhang Guangzhi)	张光直
Kaifeng	开封
Kaogong ji	考工记
li	里
Liao (dynasty)	辽（代）
Liaoning	辽宁
Liaoyang	辽阳
Lin'anxian zhi	临安县志
Linhuang (prefecture)	臨（临）潢（府）
Linyi	临沂
lingtai	灵台
Liu Bei	刘备
Liu Bingzhong	刘秉忠
Longmen	龙门
Longshan	龙山
Luoyang Qielan Ji	洛阳伽蓝记
Luoyang	洛阳
Mingtang	明堂
Nanjing	南京
Ningcheng	宁城
Niuheliang	牛河梁
P'yŏngyang (Pingrang)	平壤
Panlongcheng	盘龙城
Pingcheng	平城
Pingyang (city)	平阳（城）
Qi (state)	齐（国/朝）
Qin (dynasty)	秦（朝）
Quanzhou	泉州
Qufu	曲阜
Shaanxi	陕西
shancheng	山城
Shandong	山东
Shang (dynasty)	商（朝）
Shangdu	上都
Shanghai	上海
Shangjing	上京
Shanxi	山西
Shi Le	石勒（人名）
Shi Hu	石虎（人名）
Shi Huangdi	始皇帝
Shifa	市法
Shilin guangji	事林广记
Shu-Han	蜀汉
Song (dynasty)	宋（朝）

Sui (dynasty)	隋（朝）
Sun (Quan)	孙（权）
Tang (dynasty)	唐（朝）
Taosi	陶寺
Tianlongshan	天龙山
Tiantan	天坛
Tongwan (city)	统万（城）
Tuoba (state)	拓拔（国）
Wang Anshi	王安石
wangcheng	王城
Wei (river)	渭（河）
Wei (state/dynasty)	魏（国/朝）
Wolongcheng	卧龙城
Wu (state)	吴（国）
Wu Zetian	武则天
Wudi	武帝
Wuhan	武汉
Wuwei (city)	武威（城）
Wuyang (county)	舞阳（县）
Xi'an	西安
Xiangfen	襄汾
Xiangguo (city)	襄国（城）
Xiangtangshan	响堂山
Xianyang	咸阳
Xiaowen (emperor)	萧文（皇帝）
Xibeigang	西北岗
Xin (dynasty)	新（朝）
Xuandi	宣帝
Yan (state)	燕（国）
Yang Jian	杨坚
Yang Xuanzhi	杨炫之
Yangdi	炀帝
Yangshao	仰韶
Yangzhou	扬州
Yanjing	燕京
Yanshi	偃师
Ye (city)	邺（城）
Yijing	易经
Yin (dynasty)	殷（朝）
Yinxu	殷墟
Yongle (emperor)	永乐（皇帝）
Yuanqu	垣曲
Yuhang	余杭
Yungang	云冈
Zhejiang	浙江
Zhengzhou	郑州
Zhongdu	中都

Zhou (state/dynasty)	周（国／朝）
Zhou li	周礼
Zhu Di	朱棣
Zizhi Tongjian	资治通鉴
Zuo Zhuan	左传

3

TYPICAL DESIGN FEATURES OF MING PALACES AND ALTARS IN BEIJING

Fu Xinian

One of the most important characteristics of Chinese traditional architecture is the arrangement of buildings around courtyards.[1] The courtyard as a fundamental feature of Chinese space goes hand-in-hand with the basic tenet of spatial growth: architecture, and thus courtyards, unfold on the horizontal plane; with the exception of Buddhist pagodas, vertical projection is rare in Chinese architecture.[2] Palaces, monasteries, and vernacular construction consist of individual buildings that enclose one or more courtyards of varying dimensions in response to function. Even if a seemingly endless number of courtyards with a variety of buildings and spatial designs unfolds, hierarchy of buildings and space can still be distinguished. One has to assume that major architectural projects were planned from inception, for if not, the kind of spatial organization inherent in the Chinese building system could not have been achieved.

Three major treatises or technical manuals that survive about Chinese traditional architecture, *Yingzao fashi* (Building standards), *Lu Ban jing* (Classic of Lu Ban), and *Gongbu Gongcheng zuofa* (Engineering methods), focus on individual building construction. No premodern records or documents specifically address urban planning or the general plan and layout of large architectural complexes. We can explore this topic only through surviving examples.

Historical texts wax eloquent about palaces, imperial temples, and shrines of China's early dynasties, but little survives, even when the archaeological record is factored in, to really understand Chinese imperial construction before the Ming dynasty. From Ming and Qing China, palaces, hunting parks, dynastic altars, royal mansions, and great imperial Buddhist and Daoist monasteries survive. The palaces of the Forbidden City, the Ancestral Temple (Taimiao), the Altar of Soil and Grain (Shejitan), and the Altar of Heaven (Tiantan) preserve layouts close to their original arrangements. Ming inherited the imperial building tradition of Song and Yuan and transmitted it to Qing. Here we focus on the Forbidden City, Ancestral Temple, and Altar of Heaven, all in Beijing. Each one is discussed in numerous other publications. Here we concentrate on the most important features that relate to the planning of imperial building complexes.

Palaces of the Forbidden City in Beijing

The Forbidden City, also known as Danei (Great Within) and Gugong (Old Palace) in Chinese, was begun in 1417 and completed in 1420 during the Yongle reign (1402–1424). The main architectural complex of the Forbidden City is the three buildings in the southern section

DOI: 10.4324/9781315851112-6

known as the Three Front Halls (Qiansandian). From front to back they are the Hall of Supreme Harmony (Taihedian), Hall of Central Harmony (Zhonghedian), and Hall of Preservation of Harmony (Baohedian). Directly behind are the Hall of Heavenly Purity (Qianqinggong) and Hall of Earthly Repose (Kunninggong), the two larger of the Three Back Halls (Housangong), named *gong*, or palaces, in Chinese even though they are halls. Only these two stood in the early fifteenth century and thus are referred to as the Two Back Halls when this period is discussed. On the left and right sides of the Back Halls are the Six Eastern and Six Western Palaces (Dongxi liugong). All these building compounds have their main halls positioned centrally within a courtyard that is surrounded by corridors, some with attached buildings, and side halls.

Relation Between the Forbidden City Halls and the Ming City of Beijing

Following the victory of General Xu Da (1332–1385) and fall of the Yuan capital Dadu in 1368, the Ming emperor changed the name of the administrative district to Beipingfu (Northern Peace prefecture). There was concern that the area enclosed by the Yuan city wall was too large to defend, so the northern wall was disbanded in the same year and a new wall was built 3,000 m to the south. The other three sides of the wall remained unchanged. In the eleventh moon of 1416, the Yongle emperor renamed the city Beijing (northern capital). In 1420, in addition to construction of palaces, state temples, and royal mansions, the south city wall was moved farther south. Between 1416 and 1449, gate-towers and watchtowers of the outer wall were built, as were government buildings in front of the palace, but outside the main approach to it. Additionally, storehouses and other necessary structures of the imperial government were erected at various places within the city. The speed and logic of construction order and placement seem to indicate that when the decision was made to establish Beijing as the capital, the Yongle emperor already had a plan. No known document confirms this. The assessment is based on the dates and locations of buildings. We use Figure 3.1 for reference.

The outer wall of the Forbidden City measured 753 m east-to-west by 961 m north-to-south. The distance between the outer edges of its northern wall and the northern wall of the outer city of Beijing was 2,904 m; the distance between the outer edges of its southern wall and the southern wall of the outer city was 1,448.9 m. The ratio of the north–south length from the north sides of the outer wall to the Forbidden City north wall was 2,904 m: 961 m = 3.02.:1; and of the counterpart southern walls, 1,448.9 m: 961 m = 1.51:1.

Over the course of history, Chinese linear measurement was imprecise. Usually based on *bu* (pace) or *zhangsheng* (rope length, equal to 1 *zhang*), measurement becomes less precise with varying topography. We assume a 1 to 2 percent deviation. Using the numbers given earlier, the distance between the northern wall of the Forbidden City and the northern city wall is three times the north–south length of the palace complex, and the distance between its southern wall and the southern city wall is 1.5 times the north–south length. It appears that when Beijing was built, the north–south length of the city was set to the value of 5.5 times the north–south length of the Forbidden City, and the Forbidden City, in turn, was positioned in such a way that the distance to the southern city wall measured one-half its distance to the northern outer wall. The east–west width of the Ming city of Beijing measured 6,637 m, and compared to the east–west width of the Forbidden City, their proportional relationship was 6,637 m: 753 m = 8.81:1, which rounds up to 9:1, with a deviation of 2 percent.

The dimensions of the city are more problematic to measure in the east–west direction because of physical barriers like the Three Lakes and Jishui Pond. The central axes of neither the palace complex nor the outer city are aligned with the midpoint of the city's east–west dividing

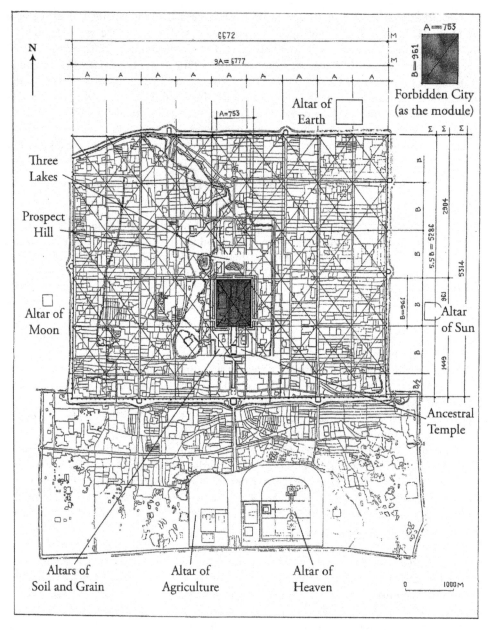

Figure 3.1 Plan of Beijing in Qianlong period (1736–1796).

Source: Permission and courtesy of Princeton University Press, with Nancy S. Steinhardt and Alexandra Harrer.

line. Probably because of the Three Lakes, the Forbidden City was moved 129 m east of the north–south central axis. However, we cannot completely rule out the influence of geomancy or of an unknown numerical reason for the discrepancy. Indeed, certain numbers are puzzling. Why is the width of the Forbidden City 236.2 *zhang* or its length 302.95 *zhang*? One would expect easily divisible whole numbers.

Still, when Beijing was planned under Yongle, the width of the Forbidden City was designed on the basis of one-ninth the city's width plus a certain fraction. One-ninth, and even 1/5.5, the proportional relations of the Forbidden City and outer walls, appear to be proportions that lend themselves to further easy division, as did, perhaps, the area of the outer city, which was 49.5 times the area of the Forbidden City, which rounds up to 50 times.

The eastern and western walls of Ming Beijing and its Forbidden City follow their coun-terparts at the Yuan capital Dadu. Thus, we can say that the proportional relation based on the number nine was inherited from the Yuan dynasty. The Yuan capital has been surveyed and measured. Introducing the variable *a* as the width of the Yuan palace-city and the variable *b* as the north–south length between the North Imperial Garden and palace-city, we can confirm that the east–west width of Dadu measured $9a$, and its north–south length measured $5b$. The dimensions of Yuan Dadu were thus based on modular units. The city area was 45 times the area of the palace-city (Figure 3.2).

The numbers nine and five are noteworthy. The classical Chinese text of the first millennium BCE, the *Book of Changes* (Yijing), often refers to these two numbers as *guiwei* (honored posi-tions), which are explained in commentary and sub-commentary as numbers that symbolize the superior man. Later they became associated with sovereignty and the position of an emperor. Commoners were not allowed to use them. The use of multiples of nine and five at Dadu sug-gests their potency was understood in the Yuan dynasty.

In the replacement of one dynasty with another one, *wangqi*, or imperial energy of the former dynasty, must also be replaced. Xu Da's movement of the northern city wall of Dadu southward may be explained by the need for protective measures against the *wangqi* of the Yuan dynasty, and if so, when the Ming chose Beijing as their capital, there must have been changes. They should have torn down and replaced or altered the Yuan wall and palaces simply because they could not have carried on with the same architectural *wangqi*. However, because of the Three Lakes and other natural obstacles such as ponds in the eastern part of the city, the eastern and western walls of both Dadu and the palace-city were not moved. Since the east–west dimension already had a fixed ratio of 9:1 (outer wall: palace-city), it was possible to change the proportional relationship only in the north–south direction. In doing this, by shifting southward, the ratio was altered to 5.5: 1. This decision increased the area of the pal-ace complex to 1/50 of the city's area, a proportion probably inspired by a line in the *Book of Changes* that suggests that since the palace measured 1/50 of the city's area, the city and the palace matched "forty-nine parts and the one part" specified in the text. Builders stressed the idea of "harmony with nature and balance of opposite forces" for the outer city and palace-city to ensure the continuation of the dynasty. When the Ming transformed Dadu into their capital, even though the eastern and western walls were determined by topography, they searched for other means of accomplishing the analogy of nine and five and the number 50. The southward movement of the wall was required, but the neighborhood system of 50 wards was continued. Still, because the Yuan palace contained the dynasty's imperial energy, the Ming had no choice but to destroy it. The palace architecture most representative for Yuan sovereignty, Yanchunge (Pavilion of Prolonged Spring), the residence of the emperor and his wives, came to be located outside the Ming Forbidden City. The Ming piled up the soil and debris from the dismantled buildings at their former location to symbolize repression so that the Yuan never would regain authority. The Ming also planted trees on top of the mound to form Jingshan (Prospect Hill), located north of the new Forbidden City. In Ming times, this artificial hill was often referred to as Zhenshan (Repression Hill). The new Beijing thus built on Yuan Dadu in the most lit-eral sense, retaining the modular units (length and width of the imperial buildings) but with modification.

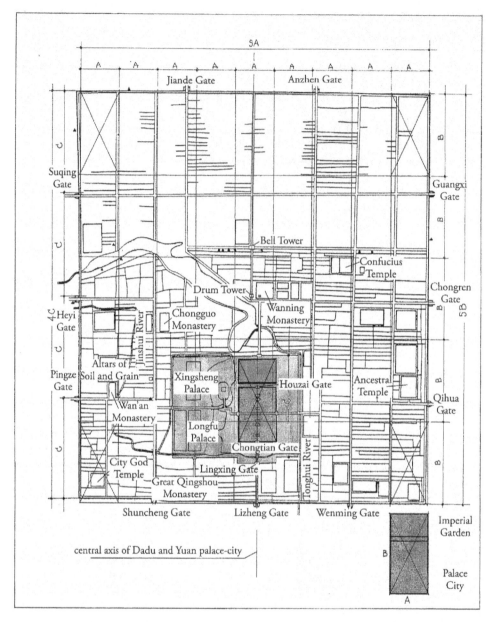

Figure 3.2 Plan of Dadu, capital of Yuan dynasty, with emphasis on centrality of palaces along central axis of city and measurements that are multiples of nine and five.

Source: Permission and courtesy of Princeton University Press, with Nancy S. Steinhardt and Alexandra Harrer.

The Modular Relationship Between the Palaces of the Forbidden City and Each Compound

The Forbidden City is a large palace complex that consists of several dozen compounds of different sizes. The most important building groups are along the central axis, and the secondary ones are symmetrically arranged on both of its sides. The principal architecture along the central axis, the Three Front Halls and Back Halls, are in their original Ming positions but have been repeatedly damaged and rebuilt. The Ming reconstructed the Three Front Halls in 1440, 1562, 1615, and 1625. The Qing widened the Hall of Supreme Harmony from a nine-bay into an eleven-bay building and altered the inclined corridors on both sides that connected to the east and west side buildings. They also added fire partition walls to the east and west side buildings. The Two Back Halls were repaired in 1440, 1521, 1598, and 1604 in the Ming period. Additionally, the small Jiaotaidian (Hall of Mutual Ease) was built between Qianqing (Heavenly Purity) Hall and Kunning (Earthly Repose) Hall, from about the 1520s to the 1540s. In many ways, the Three Front Halls and Two Back Halls did not change significantly: the total area covered by each palace compound, the podiums on which the gates, halls, corridors, and side buildings stand, and the location and size of the white marble *gong*-shaped platforms that support each group remain as they were in the Yongle reign. Thus, we can still conjecture about design regulations that might have been imposed.

The back cluster is 218 m long and 118 m wide, giving way to a rectangular palace courtyard based on a length: width ratio of 11:6. The Three Front Halls can be conceived as 348 m north–south and 234 m east–west, resulting in a length: width ratio as seen in Figure 3.3. Through further analysis, we discover that the east–west width of the Three Front Halls (234 m) is twice the width of the Back Palaces (118 m). This relationship cannot be accidental. Further examination shows that the distance between the central axes of the front eaves columns of the Gate of Supreme Harmony (Taihemen) and Gate of Heavenly Purity (Qianqingmen), the entrance to the Back Palaces, measures 437 m, which is twice the north–south length of the Back Palaces (218 m). In other words, when designing the Three Front Halls, the builders used the distance between the front eaves of the Gates of Supreme Harmony and Heavenly Purity as the north–south length of the new building cluster and at the same time made this measurement twice the length of the back building cluster. By doing so, the area of the Three Front Halls was exactly four times the area of the Back Halls.

The Six Eastern and Six Western Palaces are further confirmation of the modular basis for the plan of imperial architecture in Ming Beijing. Situated east and west of the Back Halls, buildings are aligned in two north–south rows of three palaces on each side. Further north are the Five Eastern and Western Lodges (Qian donxi wusuo), where originally five double-courtyard complexes, each courtyard a *siheyuan* (enclosed by buildings on four sides) formation, were aligned on either side of the main axis. (Today only three survive on the west.) The distance between the outer edge of the southern wall of the Six Eastern and Six Western Palaces southernmost palaces and the outer edge of the northern wall of the Five Eastern and Western Lodges measures 216 m, so close to the north–south length of the Back Halls (218 m) that we can work with the assumption that the same dimensions were intended (Figure 3.4).

Modular Relationship Between the Back Palaces and Architecture of the Imperial-City

The distance between Meridian Gate (Wumen) and Great Ming Gate (Da Mingmen; later known as Great Qing Gate [Da Qingmen]), the present-day China Gate (Zhonghuamen), also uses the length of the Back Halls as the module (Figure 3.5). The distance from Meridian Gate through Duanmen (Primordial Gate) to Tian'anmen (Heavenly Peace Gate), measured from the northernmost and southernmost side walls of their east and west waiting rooms for officials, is 438.6 m, just 2.6 m longer than twice the length of the Back Halls. The distance from the south face of the gate piers of Tian'anmen to the southern end of Thousand-pace Corridor (Qian-bulang), north of Great Ming Gate, is three times the length of the Back Halls. The distance

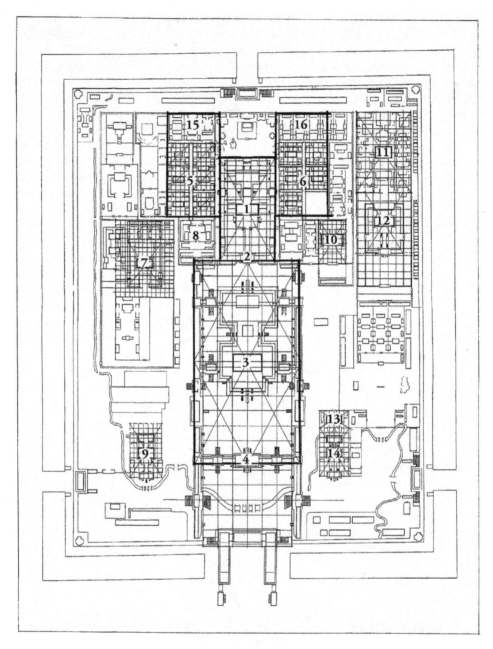

Figure 3.3 Front and Back Halls of the Forbidden City, Beijing.

Source: Permission and courtesy of Princeton University Press, with Nancy S. Steinhardt and Alexandra Harrer.

between the Eastern and Western Three Gates in front of the Gate of Heavenly Peace is 356 m, which is three times the width of the Back Halls. The front of the Beijing imperial-city of Ming times, the part between Tian'an and Great Ming Gates, is three times the length and width of the Back Halls. Finally, the distance between the north wall of Prospect Hill and the east–west

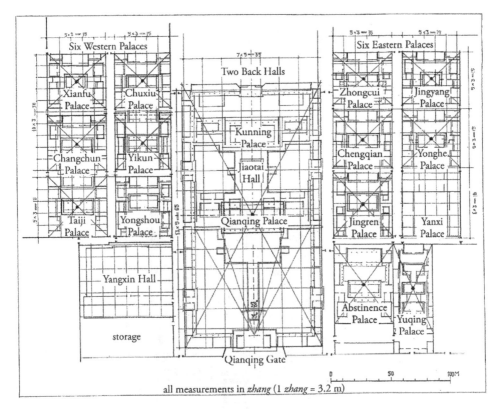

Figure 3.4 Modular relationships between Back Halls, Six Eastern and Six Western Palaces, and Five Eastern and Five Western Lodges of Forbidden City, Beijing.

Source: Permission and courtesy of Princeton University Press, with Nancy S. Steinhardt and Alexandra Harrer.

wall next to Great Ming Gate is 2,828 m, 13 times the length of the Back Halls. All this confirms the use of the length and width of the Back Halls as the modules for design throughout the imperial sectors of the capital (see Figure 3.5).

Modular Layout Programs Inside Palace Compounds

Three features dominate planning inside the palatial compounds of the Forbidden City. The first is the centrality of the main hall. The focal buildings of the Three Front Halls, Back Halls, Six Eastern and Western Palaces, and Palace of Repose and Longevity are in the geometrical center. If we draw diagonal lines between opposite corners of the compounds, the points of intersection are in the center of the main hall (Figures 3.3 and 3.4).[3]

Second, a square grid network (*fanggewang*) with cell edges of 10 *zhang*, 5 *zhang*, or 3 *zhang* that was applied to sections of the Forbidden City was also employed in individual palaces. The 10-*zhang*-square grid is applied to the Three Front Halls, which divides the area into 7 cells (*ge*) in the east–west direction and 11 cells in the north–south direction. The grid is independent of the module of the Back Halls that defines the outer contour of the Three Front Halls. The depth of the front courtyard corresponds to 6 squares if we set the boundary lines in the north along the walls east and west of the Hall of Supreme Harmony and in the south along the

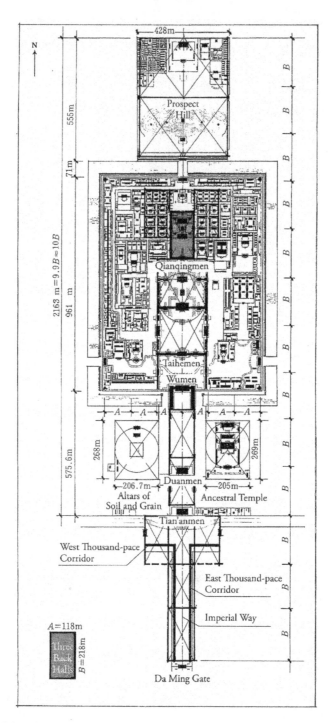

Figure 3.5 Modular relationships between gates along the main axis of Beijing form Great Ming-Qing
Gate to Prospect Hill, Forbidden City, Beijing.

Source: Permission and courtesy of Princeton University Press, with Nancy S. Steinhardt and Alexandra Harrer.

northern podium edges of the east and west side gates of the Gate of Supreme Harmony. The width, also 6 squares in distance, is measured between the front edges of the podium of the two side pavilions, Embodying Benevolence (Tiren) and Spreading Propriety (Hongyi). The front courtyard thus measures as a 60-*zhang* square. If we calculate the north–south length only to the beginning of the front platform (*yuetai*) in front of the Hall of Supreme Harmony, then the front courtyard measures 4 squares long and is equal to 40 *zhang*. The platform beneath the Hall of Supreme Harmony also is 4 squares wide and equal to 40 *zhang*. More remarkable, the central axes of the left- and right-side gates of the Hall of Supreme Harmony are aligned at a distance of 2 squares, equal to 20 *zhang* from the central axis of the hall. The width of the podium of the hall is also 2 squares and equal to 20 *zhang* (Figure 3.5). Furthermore, the areas between the Gate of Heavenly Peace and Meridian Gate and between Meridian Gate and Jinshui Bridge (in front of Tian'anmen) also are laid out according to the 10-*zhang*-square grid.

The Back Halls and the Six Eastern and Six Western Palaces use a 5-*zhang*-square grid because they are smaller than the Three Front Halls. The Back Halls correspond to 7 squares in the east–west direction and 13 in the north–south direction. The whole compound measures 35 by 65 *zhang*. The front courtyard is 6 squares wide, equal to 30 *zhang*. The individual compounds of the Six Eastern and Six Western Palaces are 3 squares in depth and width.

The best examples of the use of the 5-*zhang*-square grid are the Imperial Ultimate (Huangji) Hall and Joyful Longevity (Leshou) Hall complexes, both built in 1771–1776.[4] Looking from south to north, the elongated palatial layout consists of a 2-square horizontal lane, a 4-square open space in front of the principal gate of the palace, an 8-square outer palace court, and a 10-square inner palace court, which adds up to 24 squares in length, equal to 120 *zhang*. The total width of the compound measures 7 squares, and, more precisely, the open spaces in front of Repose and Longevity Gate, the principal gate, and the outer palace courtyard are both 5 squares wide, equal to 25 *zhang*; the podiums of Imperial Ultimate Hall, the main hall of the outer courtyard, and Joyful Longevity Hall, the main hall of the inner courtyard, are both 3 squares wide and equal to 15 *zhang*. Even smaller palatial buildings, such as the Martial Valor (Wuying) Hall, Compassionate Repose (Cining) Palace, and Ancestor Worship (Fengxian) Hall, use the smaller, 3-*zhang*-square grid as the basis for layout.

Last, the numerical relationships with the numbers nine and five between Yuan Dadu and the Inner Court of the Forbidden City were continued in the Ming. Most explicit is the ratio between the widths of compounds and platforms at the Three Front Halls, 234:130 m, or 9:5. Since the north–south length of the *gong*-shaped platform is almost 228 m, roughly the same as 234 m, the length: width ratio of the *gong*-shaped platform is also 9:5. The *gong*-shaped platform of the Back Halls, 97 by 56 m, also corresponds to this ratio. Thus, the Outer Court and Inner Court of the Forbidden City are the most numerically correct and symbolic.

Meaning and Function of the Proportions

Three characteristics repeatedly recur in the planning and design of the Forbidden City: the length and width measurements of the Back Halls as basic modules; positioning of the main building of a compound in the geometric center; and the use of a square grid. Sometimes the solutions to these planning and design agendas are ingenious; other times they also convey symbolic meanings.

The use of an architectural module allows craftsmen to manipulate the difference in size between building sites, to attach importance to them, and to attach symbolic meaning. The most important buildings inside the Forbidden City are the Three Front Halls and the Back Halls. The former is the place where the most important state ceremonies were held, and the latter included the living quarters of the emperor and empress. Together these were the sacred spaces of the Chinese dynasties. Quadrupling the area of the Back Halls that represent the ruling family increased the power of the family. The design relationships based on the measurements of the Back Palaces – for example, its length for the distance from Prospect Hill to Great Ming Gate or its area for the combined surface of the Six Eastern and Six Western Palaces and the Five Eastern and Western Lodges – were aimed at demonstrating that imperial power commands everything, encompasses everything, and can change everything.

The concept of geometric centrality has a long history in China. One finds it at the predynastic Zhou site in Fengchu, Qishan, Shaanxi province. *Lüshi chunqiu* (Springs and Autumns of Master Lü) states that the palace and temple are at the center of the capital. Palaces, state temples, and great Buddhist and Daoist monasteries were designed like this throughout Chinese history, but centrality is even more pronounced in Ming-Qing Beijing, where the center is synonymous with the power of the emperor.

The square grid has a history almost as long. Daming Palace and Luoyang Palace in the Tang capitals Chang'an and Luoyang, respectively, used a 50-*zhang*-square grid that was further developed at Yuan Dadu. The 5-*zhang*-square grid was employed at the Confucian Temple in Qufu, and the 3-*zhang*-square grid was the basis of the Confucian Temple and Temple of the Eastern Peak in Beijing. Later, in the Ming period, in the Forbidden City, craftsmen used three different grid systems simultaneously: as a symbol of the state, a 10-*zhang* system for the Outer Court (the Three Front Halls) and reaching south to the Gate of Heavenly Peace; the 5-*zhang* system for the Inner Court, including the Back Halls and Imperial Ultimate Hall; and a 3-*zhang*-square grid for auxiliary architecture, for example at Martial Valor (Wuying) and Literary Gems (Wenhua) Halls and Compassionate Repose (Cining) Palace, where the empress dowager resided. The choice of a square grid system depended on the importance and size of the architectural cluster.

The use of large or small grid cells can be compared to the use of different scales for different building sizes, a design method discussed in previous essays on Tang and Song modules. As for the use of modular proportions in building complexes, they are also employed in the late imperial Ancestral Temple (Taimiao) and Temple of Heaven (Tiantan) complexes in imperial Beijing.

The Ancestral Temple in Beijing

The Ancestral Temple in Beijing, which at the end of the twentieth century was the People's Cultural Palace, was southeast of the Forbidden City on the east side of the Imperial Way between Meridian Gate and the Gate of Heavenly Peace. The Altar of Soil and Grain was situated almost precisely opposite the Ancestral Temple on the western side of the Imperial Way. Construction at the Ancestral Temple began in 1420. The extant architecture dates to 1545 with extensive repair between 1736 and 1739. The building complex is surrounded by a double wall consisting of an inner and outer layer. The southern outer wall has a gate with three doorways that is centrally positioned and flanked by left- and right-side gates. The northern wall has only a central gate, known as North Gate, with three doorways. The southern inner wall has a centrally positioned five-bay gate named Halberd Gate (Jimen), with solid doors at the three central bays and a one-bay gate on either side. The northern wall and the north wall of the back hall are parallel to each other, with gates on either side of the back hall. Inside the inner wall, along the central axis, three halls are aligned: a sacrificial hall (*jidian*) is in front; the resting hall (*qindian*) for imperial tablets, that is, for the souls of the emperor and his wives, is next, the two halls standing on a *gong*-shaped platform; and in the back is the storage place for ancestral tablets of preceding generations, the back hall, positioned on top of a low platform and separated from the hall in front of it by an east–west partition wall. The sacrificial hall is 11 bays wide and its eastern and western side halls are 15 bays each. The resting hall and back hall are nine bays wide, and their side halls are five bays on each side.[5]

Today, the outer wall of the Ancestral Temple measures 271.60 m north–south by 206.87 m east–west. The dimensions are close to the length: width ratio of 4:3. The measurements are close to those of the Altar of Soil and Grain, whose dimensions are 267.9 m north–south and 206.7 m east–west. These numbers suggest there was a grand plan when construction started in the early Ming dynasty. Converted into Ming *chi*, the Ancestral Temple was 650 by 850 *chi*. The inner wall of the Taimiao measures 207.45 m north–south by 114.56 m east–west, which is equivalent to a ratio of 9:5. These are the numbers used in the Three Great Halls. The width of the outer wall, 206.87 m, is essentially the length of the inner wall, 207.45 m. Again, between the widths of the outer and inner walls, we observe a 9:5 ratio.

If we draw diagonal lines between opposite corners of the inner wall, then their point of intersection lies in the middle of the front hall. If we inscribe a circle with this point of intersection as its center, and the distance from there to the southern (or northern) inner wall is its radius, then the outermost corners of the southern sides of both the east and west side buildings of the front hall and the outermost corners of the northern sides of both east and west side buildings of the back hall are on the arc of the circle. This must all have been planned from the beginning.

The layout of the Taimiao applies the 5-*zhang*-square grid. Converted into Ming *chi*, the outer wall is 65 *zhang* wide and 85.2 *zhang* long, and the inner wall is 36 *zhang* wide and 65 *zhang* long. Accordingly, the area enclosed by the outer wall corresponds to 13 cells east-to-west and 17 cells north-to-south. The area inside the inner wall measures 7 squares east–west by 13 squares north–south. The reason the inner wall width is 36 rather than 35 *zhang* is to maintain the length: width ratio of 9:5 ($65 \times 5/9 = 36.1$).

Observing the layout top-down, we see on a 5-*zhang* grid that the important buildings are aligned with the lateral grid lines: the northern bank of Jinshui, the northern and southern edges of the podium beneath Halberd Gate, the edges of the front hall's northern and southern platform sides, and the partition wall to the south of the back hall. The central axes of side staircases and gates are aligned with the longitudinal grid lines, for example in the case of the outer wall of South Gate and of the front and back halls. Several structures have the size of a single grid cell, which is to say that they are restricted to a depth of about 5 *zhang*. They include Halberd Gate, the upper level of the approach platform of the front hall, and the platform connecting the front and middle halls. The distance between the front of Halberd Gate's northern staircases and the front hall's southern staircases measures 5 grid cells, equal to 25 *zhang*. The upper level of the front hall's approach platform is 3 squares wide, equal to 15 *zhang*. In summary, the figures clearly demonstrate that the square grid was used as the basis for laying out the Ancestral Temple. The two characteristics that we saw in the palaces of the Forbidden City, the main hall positioned in the geometric center and the importance of the numbers nine and five, also exist in the design of the Ancestral Temple. They were the most important measurements in the planning and design of large-scale Ming imperial architecture.

Altar of Heaven

The Altar of Heaven complex is situated south of Beijing's inner city on the eastern side of the north–south avenue that runs from the front gate of the inner city (Zhengyangmen) to the front gate of the outer city (Yongdingmen). Just on the other side of the avenue was the Altar to Mountains and Rivers. Construction began in 1420. It was originally built slightly to the east, but in 1553, when Beijing was expanded southward, the Temple of Heaven came to be located within the outer city west of Zhengyang Gate and the main axial line of Beijing.

Originally known as the Altar of Heaven and Earth (Tianditan), it was the site for imperial sacrifices to heaven and earth. The altar complex was built according to rules and regulations implemented at the Great Sacrifice Hall (Dasidian) in Nanjing, built in 1378. In 1530, the sacrificial complex was divided into two sites: a place for sacrifices to heaven centered around a structure known as the Circular Mound (Yuanqiu), which was situated south of the Great Sacrifice Hall and corresponds to the present site of the same name; and another place in the northern suburbs for sacrifices to earth called Ditan (Altar of Earth). In line with traditions regarding the Mingtang (Numinous Hall), a circular structure was built at the foundation of Great Sacrifice Hall in 1545. Known then as Great Ceremonial Banquet Hall (Daxiangdian; hereafter Great Banquet Hall) and today as Hall for Prayer for a Prosperous Year (Qiniandian), it was the place to perform the ritual known as qigu (praying for grain) each spring. From then on, the Altar of Heaven complex consisted of two parts – the Hall for Prayer for a Prosperous Year in the north and the Circular Mound in the south. They were separated by a partition wall but connected by a gate known as Chengzhenmen (Achieving Purity Gate), north of which was a north–south thoroughfare directly leading to Gate of Prayer for a Prosperous Year (Qinianmen) and strongly emphasizing the north–south axis between the ritual precincts.

Among the late imperial sacrificial architecture still extant, the Altar of Heaven has the most distinctive features. The circle and square distinguish it, but there are more spatial relationships. Chinese traditional altars and state temples (tanmiao) always have a clear axis and symmetry, as we have seen at the Forbidden City and the Ancestral Temple. The north–south axis of the Altar of Heaven, however, is positioned off center, which seems highly unusual for a place where sacrifices to heaven were offered. There are explanations.

A description and illustration of the Altar of Heaven and Earth during the Yongle reign period is recorded in Da Ming huidian (Statues of the Great Ming); we refer to it hereafter as the Yongle Plan. The Circular Mound and Hall for Prayer for a Prosperous Year, built in 1530 and 1543, respectively, are also shown on a drawing in the same text; we refer to it as the Jiajing Plan. The illustrations offer information about the construction process and characteristics of the current Altar of Heaven complex. There were four stages in its development.

Plan and Features of the Altar of Heaven and Earth of 1419

According to the Yongle Plan and Da Ming huidian, the Yongle Altar of Heaven and Earth was built according to the rules and regulations, formulated in the former capital Nanjing, that had been established by the Hongwu emperor, the founder of the Ming dynasty, in 1368. The complex was surrounded by a single (rather than a double) wall that was half a square on the south side and a semicircle on the north. A gate was installed on each side. The main gate was located in the south, and a passageway ran from there toward the north, directly to Great Sacrifice Hall, the center of the altar complex and the central position on the north–south axis. The building cluster around this hall was rectangular and surrounded by an earthen double wall with a gate on each side of the outer single wall, which was lower. To the north of its northern gate was the Heavenly Storage (Tianku). After passing through South Gate, one reached Great Sacrifice Gate, behind which, in the center of the courtyard, was the 11-bay Great Sacrifice Hall on top of a tall podium that, in fact, was an altar. This is why the early Ming text records, "The structure is on an altar." East- and west-side buildings stood in the foreground of the hall on both sides. The inner wall ran from Great Sacrifice Gate directly to the left and right sides of Great Sacrifice Hall and encompassed a courtyard shaped like half a square in the south and a semicircle in the north, which echoed the plan of the sacrificial complex's outer enclosure. Finally, in the southwest corner of the Altar of Heaven and Earth was Abstinence Palace (Zhai-gong); its front gate was oriented to the east, facing the passageway from Great Sacrifice Hall to South Gate.[6]

If we compare this plan of the Yongle period with the current lay of the land, we can still see that the terrain was elevated in the north and sunken in the south. Today the land close to Chengzhen Gate at the southern end of the north–south thoroughfare, an elevated pathway known as Danbi Bridge, still rises several dozen centimeters above ground, and at the northern end next to the Hall for Prayer for a Prosperous Year, it reaches a height of 3.35 m. This is an almost 3-m gap in height. Therefore, before building the altar, it probably was necessary to erect a high platform to a height slightly taller than that of South Gate. Through comparison of the present-day Hall for Prayer for a Prosperous Year complex with the former Great Sacrifice Hall complex depicted on the Yongle Plan, we see that the main hall switched from a rectangular to a circular ground plan and was placed on top of a newly built three-tier circular altar. However, neither the auxiliary buildings nor the basic layout has changed much. The large, rectangular platform of the Hall for Prayer for a Prosperous Year and the north–south thoroughfare probably existed already in the Yongle period. Today the location of Abstinence Hall southwest of Hall for Prayer for a Prosperous Year and its proximity to the western and southern walls of the inner enclosure also are consistent with the data on the Yongle Plan. Thus, we assume that the wall now situated to the west of Abstinence Palace corresponds to the western wall of the Altar of Heaven and Earth during the Yongle period.

The Yongle Plan depicts the axial and symmetrical temple layout along a straight line that links the present Hall for Prayer for a Prosperous Year to Danbi Bridge and Chengzhen Gate. This line corresponds to the historical central axis. Thus, we place the eastern and western walls on either side of the axis. Today the area east of Danbi Bridge is enclosed by a double wall. But, since the distance from the outer eastern wall to the central axis is close to the distance from the western wall to the central axis (635.7 m), we identify the outer eastern wall, rather than the inner eastern wall, as the eastern wall of the Yongle period. Next, the southern front gate of the sacrificial complex (Chengzhenmen) corresponds to the south gate depicted on the Yongle Plan. The original southern wall must have been located along an imaginary line extending from this gate sideways. In its current condition, the southward bend of the southern wall dates to the late Ming period when the enlargement of Abstinence Palace made it necessary to move the wall south. The distance from the center of the Hall for Prayer for a Prosperous Year to Chengzhen Gate measures 493.5 m, and northward, to the northern outer wall, it measures 498.2 m. The two figures basically match. Thus, we believe that the outer northern wall corresponded to the wall of the Yongle period. The Yongle Plan depicts a gate in the eastern and western walls of the Altar of Heaven and Earth, with the west gate positioned north of Abstinence Palace. Thus, we may conclude that the current west gate of the Altar of Heaven complex's inner district is the western gate of the Yongle period. Then, to determine the historical location of the opposite gate, we may place the eastern gate in the corresponding position of the eastern outer wall. The two gates are connected by a thoroughfare whose central axis is placed at a distance of 247.5 m from Qiniandian's center (to the north); the south distance from Chengzhen Gate measures 245.8 m – in other words, almost equidistant.

We can now reconstruct the plan of the Yongle-period Altar of Heaven and Earth in 1420. The altar was 1289.2 m wide and 991.7 m long. The high platform beneath Great Sacrifice Hall measured 162 m (east–west) by 187.5 m (north–south), and the hall on top of it was shifted slightly northward away from the platform center. The center of the hall was the center of the entire temple compound. The plan was very similar to the plan today.[7] A passageway joined the south of the hall to Chengzhen Gate.

The reconstruction drawing of the Yongle-period Altar of Heaven and Earth is based on actual measurements, which makes it possible to identify design patterns. Similar to the palaces in the Forbidden City that use the Back Halls as the basic design module, the architecture here builds on the width of the platform beneath the Hall for Prayer for a Prosperous Year. The east–west width of the entire complex is eight times this module and the north–south length is six times this module. The dimensions of Abstinence Palace are the width and length of the Hall for Prayer for a Prosperous Year platform.

When the Altar of Heaven and Earth was planned in 1419, the craftsmen first set the dimensions of the Great Sacrifice Hall cluster according to ritual requirements. Then they laid out the site, for which they used the platform width as a module, and determined the total length and width as six and eight times that width, respectively. They arranged architecture, particularly Chengzhenmen and the passageway (Danbiqiao), in a south–north sequence, to form the main central axis of the Altar of Heaven and Earth in order to achieve an axial and symmetrical layout. They placed the main hall of the Great Sacrifice Hall complex in the geometrical center. They enhanced this relationship by placing the connecting line of east and west gates at the midpoint of the distance between Great Sacrifice Hall's center and Chengzhenmen. The point of intersection corresponded to one-fourth the length of the total complex if measured from the southern wall. This design is grounded in a simple and solemn modular relationship that clearly emphasized axial planning and the idea of a geometric center.

The Circular Mound Altar of 1530

In 1530, once the decision was made to divide the Altar of Heaven and Earth into two sacrificial sites, the Circular Mound for sacrifices to heaven was built south of the Altar of Heaven and Earth. Its main architectural features included the altar proper and a low earthen double wall, a circular low wall inside and a square low wall outside. The Circular Mound that stands today on a three-tier podium due south of the central axis of the Altar of Heaven and Earth is in the same location as the altar that stood in the sixteenth century. The dimensions of the Ming altar and of the circular and square low earthen walls of the complex are recorded in the statutes of the Ming dynasty. This is important because the current Circular Mound dates to the Qing period and is slightly larger than the Ming version. Beyond the square low wall is the wall of the southern part, or inner district, of the present Altar of Heaven, which is enclosed by a rectangle with a gate on each side. The northern gate follows the former south gate (Chengzhenmen); the enclosed area is 504.9 m north–south. Calculated from the central axis of the Circular Mound, its width is 407.5 m east to the eastern wall of the current inner district and 635.7 m west to the western wall of the current inner district. The total east–west width is the sum of these two figures and equals 1043.2 m. The precinct of the Circular Mound is on the eastern side of its courtyard; this off-axis positioning is puzzling. In historical records, the situation appears differently. The *Ming shilu* (Veritable records of the Ming) describes the newly established "Yuanqiu sidian" (Sacrificial rites of the Circular Mound) of 1530, and the *Qinsi yuanqiu li* (Imperial ceremonies of the Circular Mound) of 1575 describes the route the emperor followed, leaving through its south gate (Zhaohengmen) before entering Abstinence Palace. In other words, the emperor had to leave the Circular Mound through Zhaoheng Gate, turn west, go straight, and pass through the Zhaigong (Abstinence Palace) Gate of the north wall, which would have been possible only if he were standing outside the western wall of the Circular Mound complex. Therefore, when construction began, the western wall must have been located east of its current position. The eastern wall should thus be mirrored at the Circular Mound's central axis on the western side to give us the position of the western wall. We may further conclude that when construction began, the east–west width of the Circular Mound complex was 407.5 m by 2, or 815 m. Converted into the mid-Ming length of a *chi*, which was 0.3184 m, we calculate the actual dimensions of the altar precinct as follows:

north–south length: 504.9 / 0.3184 (m/*zhang*) = 158.6 *zhang*
east–west width: 815 / 0.3184 (m/*zhang*) = 256 *zhang*

The *Da Ming huidian, juan* 187, records the following measurements: the diameter of the lowest tier of the Ming-period Circular Mound complex is 12 *zhang*; the circumference of the circular low wall is 97.75 *zhang* with a diameter of 31.1 *zhang*; and the circumference of the square low wall is 204.85 *zhang* with the length of each side measuring 51.2 *zhang*. If we compare these figures with the width and depth of the Circular Mound complex, we discover that only the side length of the square wall could possibly have a proportional relationship with the altar precinct's dimensions. Based on the side length of the square low wall, 51.2 *zhang*, we calculate the dimensions again, as follows:

length: 158.6 *zhang* / 51.2 = 3.1
width: 256 *zhang* / 51.2 = 5

Taking into account the possible inaccuracy of historical records and survey measurements, the Circular Mound complex was most likely designed on the basis of a module equal to the square low wall's side length of 51.2 *zhang*, and its length: width ratio was set at 3:5.

If we compare these measurements with those of the Altar of Heaven and Earth, we see that the Circular Mound corresponds to Great Sacrifice Hall. The area surrounded by the circular low wall corresponds to the courtyard compound enclosed by Great Sacrifice Gate and its inner low wall. The square low wall corresponds to the outer wall and the high platform of the Great Sacrifice Hall compound. The former Altar of Heaven and Earth took the width of the outer low wall (the width of the high platform) as the basic modular unit, as did the new altar precinct of the Circular Mound. The means of determining their modules was the same.

Outside the Circular Mound precinct, the eastern and western walls of the Altar of Heaven and Earth (also known as Great Altar walls [Datanqiang]) were extended southward so that their southern ends connected to the newly erected wall in the east–west direction. By doing so, a second wall layer was formed with the aim of protecting the emperor from the view of onlookers when he made sacrifices to heaven.

At closer inspection, we find the distance from the central axis of the east–west thoroughfare of the Altar of Heaven and Earth northward to the north wall is 745.9 m, and the distance southward to the south wall of the Circular Mound precinct is 750.7 m. The difference is only 4.38 m, or a 6 percent divergence, so they can be regarded as the same. This shows that a plan to unify the new and old altar districts must have existed when the Circular Mound was designed. It further demonstrates that the east–west thoroughfare of the Altar of Heaven and Earth became the line that divided the unified temple complex into northern and southern sections, and that the location of the southern wall of the Circular Mound complex was determined accordingly. Finally, following the Altar of Heaven and Earth's old planning technique of taking the outer wall's width as the basic module, the builders of the Circular Mound calculated the square wall's width as one-third of the district's north–south depth and established it as the new module for the whole altar district.[8]

Altar of Heaven Complex After the Modification of 1545

After the construction of the Circular Mound, a plan was developed to remove Great Sacrifice Hall and replace it with the Altar for Prayer for Grain (Qigutan). This was accomplished in 1545. The lower part of the structure, a three-tier podium with a base diameter of 91 m, is the altar proper, above which is built Great Banquet Hall, a circular structure with a diameter of 24.5 m and crowned with triple eaves and a conical roof (*yuanzhuiding*). It was renamed Hall for Prayer for a Prosperous Year (Qinian) in 1751. The gates and side buildings positioned all around it follow the old rules and regulations from the Yongle period.

The high platform below the Hall for Prayer for a Prosperous Year is 162 m east–west and 187.5 m north–south. A double gate is in front. A wall is positioned on the left and right sides of the second gate at a distance of 160 m from the northern low wall. In other words, the platform appears as a square of 160 m on each side. The center of the Hall for Prayer for a Prosperous Year is 24.7 m north of the center of this square, and the distance by which the building shifted back is equivalent to its diameter.

Similar to the Forbidden City and the Ancestral Temple, the Hall for Prayer for a Prosperous Year cluster also uses a square grid as the basis for its layout. The side of the platform, 160 m, converts to 50 *zhang*. Using a 5-*zhang*-square grid, its length and width correspond to 10 squares each. The diameter of the bottom podium step of the Hall for Prayer for a Prosperous Year matches the width of the Prayer for a Prosperous Year Gate, both 2 squares, or 10 *zhang*. The diameter of the middle tier of the three-tier platform of Hall for Prayer for a Prosperous Year measures 5 squares, equal to 25 *zhang*. The north–south length of the east and west side buildings corresponds to 3 squares, or 15 *zhang*, and the distance from the northern edge of the podium of Prosperous Year Gate to the bottom step of the three-tier altar is the same. The layouts of the remaining buildings also build on the square grid, with which they have fixed proportional relationships.[9]

Further, even though the complex is longer in the north–south direction, the large platform beneath the Hall for Prayer for a Prosperous Year can be considered a square if one starts measuring from the second Prayer for a Prosperous Year Gate (the inner rather than the outer one). The remaining space, in the form of the short southward projection, was there to provide the space for another gate (the outer Prayer for a Prosperous Year Gate). The platform width was the module for the altar complex.

After the Hall for Prayer for a Prosperous Year was built, the Altar of Heaven complex was expanded to include the Hall for Prayer for a Prosperous Year complex in the north and the Circular Mound complex in the south. The boundaries were set to the western wall of the present inner district and to the northern, eastern, and southern walls of the present outer district. The area was 1,289.2 m east–west and 1,650 m north–south. The main entrance was moved from the south gate (Chengzhenmen) to the west gate (Xitianmen [West Heavenly Gate]).[10]

Temple of Heaven After Construction of the Outer City of Beijing

The Temple of Heaven was incorporated into Beijing when the outer city was built in 1553. The avenue between the main south gate of the inner city (Zhengyang Gate) and the main south gate of the outer city (Yongding Gate) extended Beijing's central axis. At that time, the west gate of the Altar of Heaven's inner district had already become the front gate of the whole sacrificial complex. It was thus necessary to build another outer gate and wall facing the avenue to counterbalance the Altar of Agriculture (First Crops [Xiannongtan]) situated at the same position on the opposite (west) side of the avenue. By then, the south wall of the Altar of Heaven complex had already been built to the south of the Circular Mound, and through its westward extension and connection to the newly built western wall facing the avenue, the temple complex was fully enclosed. A double wall was thus formed at the southern and western sides of the temple complex. Corresponding walls should have been built at the northern and eastern sides to close the encircling double ring of inner and outer walls. However, the area of the former Altar of Heaven and Earth had already become very large. North of the temple was a pond, and the eastern side already reached the outer avenue of Chongwen Gate. It was impossible to expand the temple compound toward these directions. The only possibility was to use the existing northern and eastern walls as the new outer walls and to build other walls parallel to them further inside. These new walls connected to the southern and western inner walls, thereby closing the inner wall ring. As a result, the center of the double wall and the main temple axis shifted eastward, where it is today.[11]

The east–west wall that divided the northern section from the Circular Mound in the south was still straight. Upon the extension of Abstinence Palace in 1588, this wall had to move south, although only part of it was moved. Since Chengzhen Gate could not move farther south, only the short wall sections on both its sides were altered, changed into curved shapes to connect to the eastern and western ends of the wall that had been successfully moved south, parallel to their original positions. This is the present situation.[12]

Not surprisingly, then, an important building complex like that of the Altar of Heaven followed proportional relationships during renovations. The distance from the new eastern inner wall of the Altar of Heaven to the eastern platform edge of the Hall for Prayer for a Prosperous Year located to its west is twice the width of this platform. The distance from the new northern inner wall to Chengzhen Gate measures 723.1 m, which is twice the length of Danbi Bridge (361.3 m). By intentionally using this figure – twice 361.3 m – for the positioning of the northern inner wall, the outer south gate is placed at the division between the northern and southern sectors. We further find sufficient evidence for the use of a module when setting the locations of the northern and eastern walls. After erection of the double wall, the Altar of Heaven complex underwent change, mainly because the original strict layout focusing on axial symmetry turned into a layout where the main axis was shifted eastward. Afterward, neither the inner district nor outer district of the Altar of Heaven was aligned with the actual center of the whole sacrificial complex.[13]

When construction began in 1420, the craftsmen used the high platform beneath Great Sacrifice Hall as a module. They applied a strict symmetrical layout in line with the cardinal axes, and they put the main hall in the geometrical center of the then much smaller sacrificial complex. Afterward, when the Circular Mound was built to the south, the center of the temple complex shifted southward to the thoroughfare between the east and west gates. The new position determined the north–south length of the Circular Mound complex, and one-third of that distance became the side length of its square (outer) low wall. The whole complex still was axially aligned and symmetrical, and it also possessed a clear geometrical center. To adjust to the new urban layout of the city of Beijing, after the establishment of the outer city to the south, the craftsmen could do nothing but expand westward, and only then was the axial design abandoned. The area in the east and north was reduced, but even this solution relied as much as possible on modules and proportional relationships. Here we can see that at each stage the architectural planning and design, whether as new construction or as alteration, take advantage of the accumulated knowledge of previous generations, and the craftsmen strive for consistency in the choice of planning methods while maintaining the same high level of quality.

Conclusions

Through analysis of the Ming system of palace and state temple architecture, we can now confirm that site layouts had a certain amount of regularity. When a large building complex with multiple courtyard compounds was planned, the width or length of a particular compound was used as the module. Accordingly, the dimensions of large building clusters within that complex were a multiple of this figure (for example, the Three Front Halls were four times the Back Halls of the Forbidden City) and the measurements of small clusters were a fraction (for example, the Back Halls were equal to the combined area of the Six Eastern and Western Palaces plus the Five Eastern and Western Lodges). The aim was to regulate the relationship between building clusters of different sizes and to control the dimensions of the outer contours of the entire building complex. In the case of multilayer buildings, the outer courtyard's width becomes the inner courtyard's length. Finally, the main building of a particular compound was positioned at the geometric center of the entire building complex.

Using a square grid for the architectural layout inside a compound was another effective method of regulating the relationship between building dimensions and the site, one that was common in site planning. Taking this a step further and putting it into the context of modular design, the Song module *cai* and Qing module *doukou* that regulate the scale and grade of the individual building, everything from city to large and small compounds to palace complex is based on modularity and systematic planning. The words harmony and integrated coherence are appropriate to describe it.

Notes

1   This is a reprint of the essay first published in English in Fu Xinian, *Traditional Chinese Architecture: Twelve Essays*, ed. Nancy S. Steinhardt and trans. Alexandra Harrer (Princeton: Princeton University Press, 2017), 315–347, chapter 12. It is published here with permission and courtesy of Princeton University Press, with Nancy S. Steinhardt and Alexandra Harrer. Minor editorial corrections are made; the first five illustrations are included here. The paper itself, in Chinese, was first published in 1992 and republished a few times in the 1990s and 2000s. See: Editorial Group, *Jianzhu Lishi Yanjiu* (Research in Architectural History), vol. 3 (Beijing: China Architecture & Building Press, 1992), 25–48; Editorial Group, *Zhongguo Kexue Jishu Qianyan: Zhongguo Gongcheng Yuan Ban* (Frontiers of Research in Science and Technology in China: The Chinese Academy of Engineering Edition), (Shanghai: Shanghai Jiaoyu Chubanshe, 1997), 633–668; Zheng Xinmiao and Zhu Chengru, eds., *Zhongguo Zijincheng Xuehui Lunwenji* (Collection of Essays: From the Imperial Palace Research Society), vol. 5 (Beijing: Zijincheng Chubanshe, 2007), 141–166; Fu Xinian, *Fu Xinian Jianzhu Lunwen Ji* (Architectural Essays by Fu Xinian) (Tianjin: Baihua Wenyi Chubanshe, 2009), 380–405. [Editors' Note].
2   In this chapter, Fu Xinian divides Chinese building complexes into three types: the individual building; a group of buildings arranged around one or more courtyards to form clusters, referred to here as compounds, and as precincts if they are enclosed by walls; and a large building complex, here referred to as an architectural ensemble, that comprises several building clusters, courtyard compounds, or themed districts. Fu then measures the modular basis for each type and proposes parallel or shared understandings of spatial planning and overriding proportional relationships in China over the centuries. The chapter thus explains the implications of a modular building system far beyond individual structures. The use of the word "typical" in this chapter is to emphasize typical designs over centuries, not typical features of the Ming dynasty. Yet another major contribution of this chapter is the final section, a detailed study of the changes in the most important spaces for imperial ritual in Beijing in the Ming and Qing periods. Names of the many buildings of imperial Beijing are given in English for structures widely known by those names (such as Hall of Supreme Harmony), always with the Chinese name provided at the first use and thereafter occasionally as a reminder to the reader; in cases such as Tian'anmen (Heavenly Peace Gate), for which the Chinese name is widely known, the structure's Chinese name is sometimes used, and in these cases, the English name is provided as a reminder. [Translators' Note]

3 We are publishing five illustrations from the paper. For a further illustration here, see Fu, *Traditional Chinese*, 328 [Editors' Note].
4 See Fu, *Traditional Chinese*, 328 [Editors' Note].
5 See Fu, *Traditional Chinese*, 332 [Editors' Note].
6 See Fu, *Traditional Chinese*, 335 [Editors' Note].
7 See Fu, *Traditional Chinese*, 337 [Editors' Note].
8 See Fu, *Traditional Chinese*, 339 [Editors' Note].
9 See Fu, *Traditional Chinese*, 341 [Editors' Note].
10 See Fu, *Traditional Chinese*, 342 [Editors' Note].
11 See Fu, *Traditional Chinese*, 344 [Editors' Note].
12 See Fu, *Traditional Chinese*, 345 [Editors' Note].
13 See Fu, *Traditional Chinese*, 345 [Editors' Note].

Bibliography

Editorial Group. *Jianzhu Lishi Yanjiu* (Research in Architectural History), vol. 3. Beijing: China Architecture & Building Press, 1992.

———. *Zhongguo Kexue Jishu Qianyan: Zhongguo Gongcheng Yuan Ban* (Frontiers of Research in Science and Technology in China: The Chinese Academy of Engineering Edition). Shanghai: Shanghai Jiaoyu Chubanshe, 1997.

Fu Xinian. *Fu Xinian Jianzhu Lunwen Ji* (Architectural Essays by Fu Xinian). Tianjin: Baihua Wenyi Chubanshe, 2009.

———. *Traditional Chinese Architecture: Twelve Essays*. Edited by Nancy S. Steinhardt and Translated by Alexandra Harrer. Princeton and Oxford: Princeton University Press, 2017.

Liu Chang. *The Forbidden City*. Beijing: Qinghua Daxue Chubanshe, 2012.

Wang Guixiang. *Temple of Heaven*. Beijing: Qinghua Daxue Chubanshe, 2012.

Zheng Xinmiao and Zhu Chengru, eds. Zhongguo Zijincheng Xuehui Lunwenji (Collection of Essays: From the Imperial Palace Research Society), vol. 5. Beijing: Zijincheng Chubanshe, 2007.

Zheng Zhihai and Qu Zhijing. *The Forbidden City in Beijing*. Beijing: Jizhou Publishing House, 2000.

Glossary

Baohedian	保和殿
Beijing	北京
Beipingfu	北平府
bu	步
cai	材
Chang'an	长安
Chengzhenmen	成贞门
Chengzhen (Gate)	成贞（门）
chi	尺
Chongwen (Gate)	崇文（门）
Cining (Palace)	慈宁宫
Danei	大内
Daming Palace	大明宫
Da Mingmen	大明门
Da Ming huidian	大明会典
Danbiqiao	丹陛桥
Danbi (Bridge)	丹陛（桥）
Da Qingmen	大清门
Dasidian	大祀殿
Datanqiang	大坛墙

Daxiangdian	大享殿
Ditan	地坛
Dongxi	liugong 东西六宫
doukou	斗口
Duanmen	端门
fanggewang	方格网
Fengchu (village)	凤雏（村）
Fengxian (Hall)	奉先殿
ge	格
gong	宫
Gongbu Gongcheng zuofa	工部工程做法
Gugong	故宫
guiwei	贵位
Hongwu (emperor)	洪武（皇帝）
Hongyi	弘义
Housangong	后三宫
Huangji (Hall)	皇极殿
Jiajing (Plan)	嘉靖（图）
Jiaotaidian	交泰殿
jidian	祭殿
Jimen	戟门
Jingshan	景山
Jinshui (Bridge)	金水（桥）
Jishui (Pond)	积水潭
Kunninggong	坤宁宫
Kunning (Hall)	坤宁宫
Leshou (Hall)	乐寿堂
Lu Ban jing	鲁班经
Luoyang Palace	洛阳宫
Luoyang	洛阳
Lüshi Chunqiu	吕氏春秋
Ming (dynasty)	明（朝）
Ming shilu	明书录
Mingtang	明堂
Nanjing	南京
Qishan (county)	岐山（县）
Qianbulang	千步廊
Qian donxi	wusuo 乾东西五所
Qianqinggong	乾清宫
Qianqing (Hall)	乾清宫
Qianqingmen	乾清门
Qiansandian	前三殿
qigu	祈谷
Qigutan	祈谷坛
qindian	寝殿
Qing (dynasty)	清（朝）

Qiniandian	祈年殿
Qinianmen	祈年门
Qinsi yuanqiu li	秦祀圜丘礼
Qufu (county/city)	曲阜（县/市）
Shaanxi (province)	陕西（省）
Shejitan	社稷坛
siheyuan	四合院
Song (dynasty)	宋（朝）
Taimiao	太庙
Taihedian	太和殿
Taihemen	太和门
tanmiao	坛庙
Tang (dynasty)	唐（朝）
Tian'anmen	天安门
Tianditan	天地坛
Tianku	天库
Tiantan	天坛
Tiren	体仁
wangqi	王气
Wenhua (Hall)	文华(殿)
Wumen	午门
Wuying (Hall)	武英殿
Xiannongtan	先农坛
Xitianmen	西天门
Xu Da	徐达
Yanchunge	延春阁
Yijing	易经
Yingzao fashi	营造法式
Yongdingmen	永定门
Yongle (Plan)	永乐（图）
Yongle (Reign)	永乐年间
Yuan Dadu	元大都
Yuan (dynasty)	元（朝）
Yuanqiu	圜丘
Yuanqiu sidian	圜丘祀典
yuanzhuiding	圆锥顶
yuetai	月台
Zhaigong	斋宫
zhang	丈
zhangsheng	丈绳
Zhaohengmen	照衡门
Zhengyangmen	正阳门
Zhenshan	镇山
Zhonghedian	中和殿
Zhonghuamen	中华门
Zhou (dynasty/era)	周（朝/代）

4

IMPERIAL CITIES

Critical Changes in Urban Paradigm
from Sui-Tang to Song

Heng Chye Kiang

The Sui-Tang and Song imperial cities were fundamentally different; the former were closed, hierarchical, and, to a large extent, functionally zoned, while the latter were open, complex, and heterogeneous in urban fabric. The attitude of the ruling regime towards the management and control of the cities was also very different. Two imperial encounters of the same city – Kaifeng – 360 years apart illustrate well the different attitudes that gave rise to two very dissimilar urban paradigms.[1]

In 595, Emperor Wen of the Sui dynasty (henceforth Sui Wendi) stopped at Bianzhou (modern Kaifeng) on his way back from the *feng* sacrifice at Taishan after the reunification of China and was offended by the sight of opulence, the proliferation of "unscrupulous" characters, and the disconcerting condition of the city. He saw a city in which non-authorized commercial activities flourished; ward walls had been torn down or punctured to provide direct access to the streets for houses and shops alike. Sui Wendi curbed these itinerant commercial and artisanal activities, blocked street-access gates that had been illegally opened, relocated boat dwellers who had settled outside the city walls, ordered refugees from the north to return to their land, and prohibited, among other things, people from living off non-agricultural occupations.[2]

The autocratic control of the city by Sui Wendi was typical of the prevailing official attitude towards merchant activities and illustrates the strict control that the government had on the population. City folks lived in walled residential compounds and were permitted to leave the wards only during certain hours of the day. This dual system of enclosed residential wards together with designated curfew hours had been in practice in China as early as the Qin period (221–207 BC).[3] The *li* system, which was already in place during the tyranny of Qin Shi Huang 秦始皇, was even more oppressive than the later *fang* system practiced during the Sui and Tang periods. Only one gate was allowed in each walled ward.[4] The population, hence confined to the residential quarters, was easy to conscript for the army. Although such an extreme walled residential ward *li* system, which had its origin in the ultra-Legalist Qin dynasty, was gradually relaxed, subsequent dynasties continued to employ the essentials of the system as a population control tool. Emperor Wen, upon seeing that the uncontrolled flourish of commercial activities had compromised the walled wards, duly restored the integrity of the system and the agricultural livelihood of its populace.

In contrast, the attitude espoused by Chai Rong – also known as Emperor Shizong, who inherited Kaifeng (the same city at which Sui Wendi had stopped over 360 years earlier) from

DOI: 10.4324/9781315851112-7

his adopted father in 954 during the Later Zhou dynasty – was very different. He, too, found a prosperous city that had grown beyond its walls and was teeming with commercial activities. Instead of the demolition of physical structures and relocation of inhabitants, his approach was much more measured. His first task was to order the building of a new circuit wall out of considerations for its defense. The court was responsible for determining the location of critical infrastructures within the city and the distance of pollutive industries and installations from the urban limits. The rest of the city fabric – of houses, shops, entertainment precincts, temples, and shrines, etc. – were left very much to the initiative of the people after certain broad rules and guidelines were laid out. Where urban management is concerned, two decrees that he issued in 954 and 956 amply demonstrate the different approach adopted. The 954 decree reads:

> Chinese and foreigners converge on the Eastern Capital, well served by land and water routes. Thanks to prolonged peace, the city's prosperity increases daily. However, as the city is old and the system still incomplete, all the guards' barracks are mostly narrow, and there is no site to locate the various government bureaus. Furthermore, there are limited inns and shops within the wards and markets, and an endless influx of artisans and merchants. The increase in rental property being unstable, it is extremely difficult to supply and manage the poor households [with housing]. Additionally, houses adjoin one another; roads and streets are damp and narrow; and people suffer from the heat and humidity in summer and worry about frequent fires.
>
> For the convenience of the State and the people, the city must be expanded. The office [in charge of the city walls] should be ordered to build an outer wall around the four sides of the capital. Markers must first be erected; wait for the end of winter and the beginning of spring when spared from agricultural chores to order appropriate numbers of men from the nearby suburbs to construct [the walls]. Once spring chores begin, they should be dismissed. If the earth works are still unfinished, construction will resume the following year.
>
> Henceforth, cemeteries, kilns and *caoshi* (rural markets) must be located seven *li* beyond the markers. Within the markers, await planning decisions from the court to determine the [locations of] army barracks, roads and lanes, granaries and various public offices and government bureaus. Once this is done, order the common people to build them.[5]

In addition to the city expansion works, and despite protests, roadways where encroachment by add-on structures encumbered traffic flow were also widened, some to as much as 30 paces.[6] A decree issued in 956 states:

> The capital city is big and prosperous. Horses from ten thousand countries gallop here; great numbers from the four directions gather here. . . . The recently built capital is congested with people and activities. Alleyways are narrow. When it rains and snows, there is the problem of mud. When it is windy and dry, there is the worry of fire. Whenever it is humid and sweltering hot, it is easy to produce miasma.
>
> Recently the capital is expanded, and the streets and wards enlarged. Although it is laborious for the moment, eventually we will secure the big benefits. . . . Of the thousands and tens of thousands of households, all want an easy and comfortable life, and to reduce the discomfort of heat and chill during the peak of summer and winter.
>
> Hence, within the capital, for streets fifty paces wide, households on both sides are permitted to use up to five paces for planting trees, digging wells, and building sheds. For streets with widths between 25 and 30 paces, each may use up to three paces.[7]

Interestingly, both the Sui (581–618) and Later Zhou (951–960) were short lived dynasties that set the stage for the better known and longer dynasties – Tang (618–906) and Song (N Song: 960–1127; S Song: 1127–1279) – that succeeded them, respectively. The Tang and Song dynasties continued the use of the capitals of their predecessors as well as their urban management philosophy and practice, the latter due largely to the prevailing socio-economic and political context of that time.

Chang'an in the Sui and Tang periods and Kaifeng in the Later Zhou and Northern Song periods represent two stages in the development of the Chinese medieval city. These capital cities reflected the respective periods that produced them: one rooted in a strong aristocratic power with a highly hierarchical social structure, and the other shaped by a diverse, mercantile society managed by pragmatic professional bureaucrats. While the medieval capital of Chang'an was a highly controlled and disciplined city with restricted commercial activity, Song Kaifeng established a new urban structure that boasted a complex urban fabric with vibrant pluralistic streets.

The emergence of this new urban paradigm is one of the most dramatic and important changes in Chinese urban history and parallels an equally significant change in the social makeup of the Chinese society. This new paradigm remained dominant and mostly intact until contact with the West, and the advent of modern technologies, industries, and government during the last 170 years has transformed the urban landscape. Interestingly, recent developments during the Maoist period and today's contemporary Chinese cities once again recall the historical experiences of cities during the Sui and Tang eras when powerful centralized control and the ability to muster vast resources dictated the physical form, internal structure, organization, and management of these medieval urban centers.

Sui-Tang Chang'an

Sui-Tang Chang'an began its 300-plus years of glorious history during the Sui dynasty, when Sui Wendi decided that he needed a new capital in preparation for his unification of China. The previous year, he had usurped the throne after the untimely demise of a very capable Northern Zhou ruler who had in 577 united northern China and set the stage for China's unification. Instead of refurbishing the 800-year-old Han capital of Chang'an that he inherited from his Northern Zhou predecessors, Sui Wendi chose to build a new monumental city.

The young Vice Inspector General, Yuwen Kai, was entrusted in 582, when he was only 27 years of age, with the building of a new capital, Daxingcheng – a grand city, larger than any ever built prior to the modern world, from which the united China would be ruled (Figure 4.1).

General Description

Like many other Chinese cities, Daxingcheng – later known as Chang'an – was a walled city organized around a gridiron plan, 9.72 kilometers by 8.65 kilometers or about 84 square kilometers in size. The checkerboard layout of Chang'an was formed by 14 latitudinal (E–W) and 11 longitudinal avenues (N–S) dividing the city into an axially symmetrical plan of, theoretically, 130 large and small wards. The tree-lined avenues of Chang'an were of considerable proportions: the main N–S avenue, Zhuque dajie (also known as Tianjie or Heavenly Street), measured 155 meters wide. Even the other principal avenues were sizable at widths of between 120 meters and 134 meters. The Palace City and the Imperial City, in the north center, together occupied an area of some 16 blocks. The two markets each took up an area of two wards. At the southeastern corner, Qujiang Lake and its adjacent park took up an area of at least two other blocks, leaving the city with 108 blocks or wards for residential purposes.

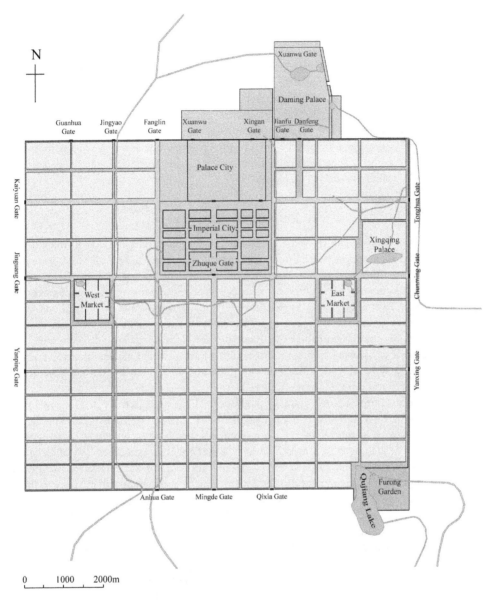

N

Xuanwu Gate

Daming Palace

Guanhua Gate   Jingyao Gate   Fanglin Gate   Xuanwu Gate   Xingan Gate   Jianfu Gate   Danfeng Gate

Palace City

Kaiyuan Gate

Jinguang Gate

Yanping Gate

Imperial City

Zhuque Gate

Xingqing Palace

Tonghua Gate

Chunming Gate

Yanxing Gate

West Market

East Market

Qujiang Lake

Furong Garden

Anhua Gate   Mingde Gate   Qixia Gate

0   1000   2000m

Figure 4.1   Plan of Tang period Chang'an (by author).

Source: © Heng Chye Kiang.

The fortified Palace City, 2.82 kilometers by 1.49 kilometers, contained the many halls in which the emperor conducted his affairs and the imperial household lived. To its south, an immense imperial square, 2.82 kilometers by 220 meters, separated the Palace and the Imperial Cities. Here, at this imperial square before the palace, the emperor conducted the rituals of First Prime (first day of the lunar year) and Winter Solstice; announced amnesties; and received foreign dignitaries. To the south was the Imperial City – the 5.2 square kilometer administrative heart of the empire, which contained government offices with civil and military functions, headquarters of the imperial guards, and residence and offices of the crown prince. It was also here that the emperor came to conduct ritual sacrifices at the imperial ancestral temple (*tai miao*) and imperial heavenly altar (*tai she*).[8]

In short, there was a clear and defined separation of official functions as well as state machinery from other functions of the city, although a few of the less critical official departments were in the wards close to the major N–S thoroughfare. No individual without good reasons was allowed into the Imperial City, much less the Palace Cities,[9] and no individual could ascend a tall structure or high ground with a vantage point looking into the Imperial or Palace Cities. If caught trespassing, the offender would be meted out with a sentence of one-year imprisonment; similarly, three years for scaling the walls of the Imperial City, and banishment of more than 3,000 *li* away for scaling the Palace City walls.

Residential Wards

The 108 residential wards, which housed residential compounds, religious establishments, and occasional government offices, were also tightly controlled (Figure 4.2). All the wards were surrounded by thick earthen walls about 3 meters high.[10] In essence, Chang'an resembled a collection of semi-autonomous walled cities or urban "villages" separated by wide avenues within a fortified precinct. Even if not always successful, the Tang government was adamant about maintaining the integrity of these walls, judging by the repeated edicts during the Late Tang period that forbade not only the destruction of walls but also the illegal piercing of doors in them.[11]

The residential wards were of different sizes and can be classified generally into five major categories. The smallest ones were found on both sides of the Heavenly Street, while the largest wards were located to both sides of the Imperial City.[12]

The smaller wards immediately south of the Imperial City were each divided into two parts by a street running E–W and further subdivided into 12 sectors; all other wards were subdivided and organized into 16 sectors by a set of main crossroads (about 20 meters wide) and intersecting secondary roads (about 5 to 6 meters wide).[13] A tertiary orthogonal network of *xiang* and even narrower *qu*, streets and alleys, mostly E–W in direction, served the quarters within the wards. Although much narrower at just over 2 meters, horse trains could still circulate in them, serving the interior of the wards (Figures 4.2 and 4.3).[14]

The people of Chang'an who lived in these walled wards were subject to stringent supervision and forbidden to leave the wards during curfew hours. The gates were closed off at night by the ward headman (*fangzheng*), and unless an official permit was issued, as in the case of an emergency, no one was allowed out in the avenues at night.[15] Within the wards, however, people could move around freely. Few activities went on within the wards in the evening, as shown by a poem written by Quan Deyu (759–818) that says: "A thousand doors were quiet when the ward gates were opened and closed."[16]

Only temples or monastic establishments and houses of officials above the third rank were allowed to have a gate that directly opened on to the avenues (an exception to this rule was the *sanjue*, or house located against the ward wall, which had the other three sides of its compound blocked by adjacent properties). Thanks to this privilege, many aristocrats, high officials, and temples chose to locate their premises near the gates, at the corner of or along the periphery of the wards, to have direct access to the main avenues. In contrast, most houses, religious buildings and, in some cases, government bureaus fronted the smaller interior streets and alleys.

Beginning in the winter of 636, drums were set up in the six major avenues to announce the opening and closing of the ward gates. According to the treatise on officials in the New History of Tang, the drums were beaten 3,000 times at 5 a.m. before the opening of the gates and once

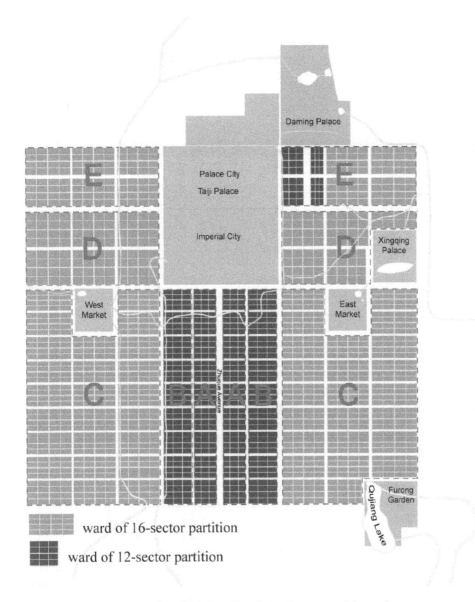

Figure 4.2 Five categories of wards in Tang Chang'an and structure of the wards.

Source: Drawings by author. © Heng Chye Kiang.

again at sunset for 800 times to announce the closing of the gates. These drums were important in the daily rhythm of the city and were often mentioned in stories and poems of the Tang period.[17] Coupled with the stringent temporal control were harsh penalties imposed on those who flouted the rules: ordinary civilians, for example, caught climbing the ramparts, market, or ward walls were liable to a punishment of 70 blows of the rod. The walls of these wards were as much for the protection of the inhabitants of the wards as for the control of the inhabitants within the wards, guarding against popular unrest.[18] These walls made it easy for the police to

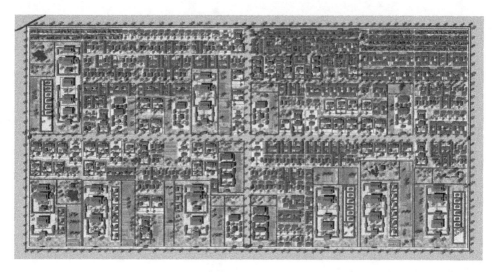

Figure 4.3   Digital reconstruction of Pingkang ward.

Source: Digital reconstruction by author. © Heng Chye Kiang.

ensure the security of the city. The walls also facilitated the arrest of criminals by confining them within the ward, where the crime was committed, or providing them with no nooks and corners in which to hide if they were outside.[19] At the external corners of the wards, that is, the junctions of the avenues, were guard posts manned by detachments of the Jinwu Guard.

Not only were spatial and temporal constraints imposed in the wards, sumptuary laws also strictly regulated the designation, size, *jian* (number of bays of construction), design, and decorations of the houses of nobles, officials, and commoners.[20] Officials of the third rank and above, for example, could not have halls of more than five bays of construction in a row and a front gate of more than three bays, while officials of the sixth rank and below could not have halls of more than three bays and a gate of more than one bay.[21] The houses and gates of common folks were simple with little or no decoration; only officials could decorate house beams, rafters, and dougong (corbel and bracket sets) with paintings or use roof tiles with animal designs.[22] Officials above the fifth rank could use the prominent "*wutou*" gate for their residence.[23]

However, when the central authority was weak – as was the case during the aftermath of the An Lushan rebellion – or when the state was in the hands of indulgent rulers, officials and magnates defied sumptuary laws and built ostentatious residences with multiple halls and exclusive gardens.[24] The residence of the famous General Guo Ziyi, which took up a quarter of Qinren Ward or about 12 hectares, for example, was so vast that "within the residence, one travels from one courtyard to another on horseback or in carriages; servants entering and leaving the main gate do not even know each other."[25] Two wards farther south in Yongchong Ward, the property of Imperial Grand Secretary Li Sheng (during the 780s) was large enough for horse polo games to be played within his compound.[26] Such was the extent of luxurious living enjoyed by nobles and officials within the wards.

Market Wards

Situated at the eastern end of the Silk Route, Chang'an was an international bazaar with brisk trading activities that took place in two specially designated wards – the East and West

Markets – symmetrically disposed along the main axis south of the palace (Figure 4.4). These wards were probably the busiest centers of commerce in the world at the time, packed with one- and two-story structures and stocked with goods from all parts of China, Central Asia, and the South Seas. Found here were also numerous restaurants, wine shops, and brothels.[27]

Besides housing foreign merchants and distant traders in inns large and small, local families also lived and worked in the markets. Although many kinds of merchandise were imported, many were produced in workshops within the markets and bore trademarks of their makers, suggesting a rather developed economy in which products were easily differentiable.[28] There were also "proto-banks" and safe deposit firms in which merchants could deposit their money before major transactions to avoid physically moving large sums of money about. A certificate was issued confirming the availability of funds and the new owner of the certificate could then redeem it if he so wished.[29]

Measuring 600 by 600 paces or about the size of two residential wards, the markets were the veritable "downtowns" of the city.[30] A perimeter wall, some 4 meters thick, pierced with two gates on each side, kept all trading within the ward.[31] A 120 meter-wide road encircled the outer perimeter of the market, spatially segregating the markets from the rest of the city.[32] Within the market walls ran another narrower perimeter road.[33] Four roads linked the gates, subdividing the market into approximately 9 square quarters.[34] The quarters were further served within by a network of alleyways.

Figure 4.4 Digital reconstruction of the East Market.

Source: Digital reconstruction by author. © Heng Chye Kiang.

Given the immense sizes of these markets, such "downtowns" were far from being homogeneous. Rather, socio-economic differences were clearly expressed in the layout of shops and subsequent occupation of empty plots of land. Larger shops owned by wealthy merchants fronted the major roadways, while retail shops and stalls, one after another, neatly lined the small alleyways.[35] At the entrance of each street was a sign naming the street in accordance to the types of businesses that plied their trades such as Garment Street (*yihang*) or Butcher Street (*rouhang*).[36] Every shop, too, had its sign. There were an enormous number of shops in the market; Japanese pilgrim Ennin noted in his diary that a fire in 843 destroyed some 4,000 shops on 12 (of the 220) streets (*hang*) in the East Market.[37]

At the center of the market were the Price Regulating Office (*Changping shu*) and the Price Equalizing Office (*Pingzhun shu*), which were responsible for maintaining the price of grain and other commodities at a fair level.[38] Beside them was the Market Office (*Shishu*), which supervised and regulated all aspects of commercial activities: maintaining public order; enforcing strict trading hours; supervising weights, measures, the quality of money in circulation, and the quality of goods on sale; issuing certificates of sale for slaves and livestock; and preventing unscrupulous trading practices.[39] Owners were forbidden to erect lean-to extensions in front of their shops or to encroach on the public ways.[40] The movement of vehicles and horses were also strictly controlled; any mishaps were liable to severe punishment.[41] Public executions were also conducted at specific locations known as *duliu*, or "Lone Willow," in these markets, and the heads of criminals were paraded and displayed there as a public warning.[42]

Trading time and even access were also strictly regulated. No officials above the fifth rank were allowed to enter the markets, which were opened for business only for a few hours a day.[43] At noon, the opening was signaled by 300 drum beats. One and three-quarter hours before sundown, 300 gong beats sounded the end of transactions of the market.[44]

Although Chang'an's unique cityscape may have been the consequence of it being the capital of the Tang dynasty, its spatial and urban management characteristics were found in other cities, such as Luoyang, Yangzhou, Yizhou, and many other administrative seats. The spatial and temporal control began to break down in these cities only during the second half of the Tang period, when the An Lushan rebellion and internal political upheavals after a long period of economic development weakened the government's control of the ward and market systems. Ward walls were breached, and shops and workshops began appearing outside the designated market wards. Initially, commercial activities took place on a very discreet scale within the residential wards, but they soon increased. Wards located close to markets and palaces were especially successful in attracting businesses. Night life thrived in these wards. The loosening of urban management and attendant urban transformation that began in the latter half of the Tang dynasty subsequently gave rise to a different kind of city during the Later Zhou and Song periods.

Later Zhou and Song Kaifeng

Emperor Chai Rong's approach to planning the thriving capital city Kaifeng laid the foundation for a very different kind of city in the Song period. The two decrees that he promulgated in 954 and 956 are important in revealing his attitude on urban management and control. Unlike the Sui and Tang emperors' autocratic control over the city, Chai Rong's approach indicates a significant loosening of central control over the process of city-making. First, agricultural production was the main priority and therefore dictated the pace of city development. In other words, building works were only conducted during lulls in the agrarian cycle.

Second, where detailed planning of the city was concerned, the central authorities seemed content to be involved only in the general zoning of road networks and sites that would facilitate critical government functions. Installations that were pollutive, such as cemeteries and kilns, were relegated to areas distant from the city. *Caoshi* or rural markets, which began to proliferate in numbers, thus causing the growth of extramural suburbs and burdening the administrative system, were also forbidden within proximity of the city. The rest of city building – houses, shops, non-hazardous industries, and open spaces – seems to have been left to the initiative of the common people.

Third, the shoulders of major thoroughfares (that is, avenues measuring 50 paces or about 75 meters in width) could be used by adjacent households for planting trees, digging wells, and building sheds. The use of these street edges indicates significant erosion or even the disappearance of ward walls, which in turn implies the decreased significance, if not the disappearance, of monofunctional residential wards. By now, most shops and houses probably had entrances fronting the streets and avenues. The phenomenon of *qinjie*, or street encroachment, must have been widespread. No longer was it a battle to maintain the integrity of the ward walls but, rather, a matter of preventing the encroachment of roadways by ad hoc structures. Instead of clearing the encroaching structures, the streets were widened when necessary to 30 paces across. Inhabitants were then permitted to use up to 20 percent of the street width, along its edges, for their own intents and purposes. In this way, the imperial edict limited the extent of street encroachment instead of eradicating it.

The cityscape of Song Kaifeng that was built upon Chai Rong's legacy was significantly different from that of Sui-Tang Chang'an. Song Kaifeng was less regular in shape and more modest in size, about three-fifths the size of Tang Chang'an. The city had three concentric circuit walls; the innermost protected the Imperial City, which held some governmental apparatus and the palace complex. The remaining official bureaus are located elsewhere across the city among houses, shops, temples, and entertainment precincts. Together with the demolition of the ward walls, the Song city's mixed-use urban fabric became continuous, rendering the visual and physical distinction of the different district less obvious (Figure 4.5).

Instead of a grid of wide avenues as was the case in Chang'an, three major commercial streets together with four imperial avenues constituted Kaifeng's primary structure, to which secondary and tertiary streets and alleys attached to form a closely knit road network. While spatially, Chang'an's wide thoroughfares were dividers that separated walled wards, those of Kaifeng remained narrow enough to serve as busy channels of activity and spatial connectors. The presence of street-encroaching structures also reduced the physical width of the roadways, making them even more congested. The roads in Kaifeng were also far less regulated. Although there were still frequent guard posts set up in the streets, the narrower width of the roadways, the presence of street-front shops, sheds, and stands, and the urban congestion all served to minimize the visual and physical impact of these installations.

As the ward walls fell, and stalls, shops, taverns, restaurants, brothels, and the like left the confines of the enclosed market to line main streets and side alleys, the urban fabric became more complex. The proliferation of these pluralistic streets throughout the city not only had a great impact on the structure of the city but also altered the urban tissue. The rigid zoning and segregation of activities in the city gave way to diverse neighborhoods where market forces determined to a large extent the allocation of activities. The distinction and location of the different urban tissues typical of residential, commercial, and administrative functions so definite in Tang Chang'an was no longer as clear in Song Kaifeng. Public and private spaces became accessible to large cross-sections of the populace.

The abolition of curfews also made the streets active with market and entertainment activities throughout the day and, in some places, throughout the night. Socially, the Song capital was also more complex. While senior officials were not allowed into Tang Chang'an's walled

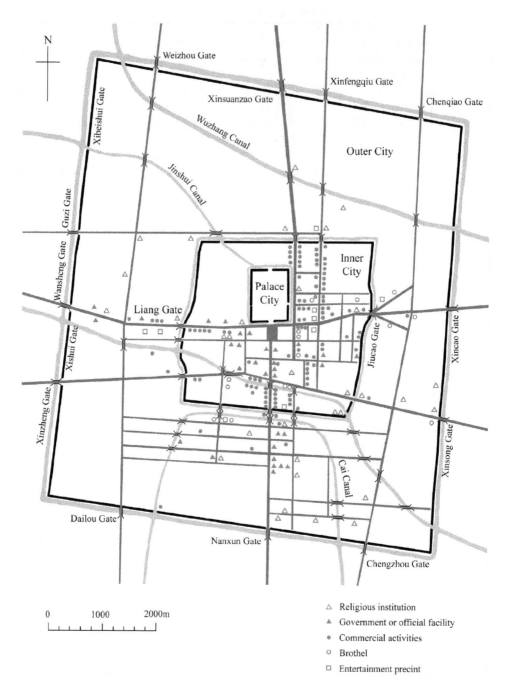

Figure 4.5 Reconstruction of the plan of Song Kaifeng.

Source: © Heng Chye Kiang.

markets, many of the prime commercial properties that contributed to the hustle and bustle of Kaifeng's busy thoroughfares were owned by Song officials. Womenfolk of noble families jostled with the common people in the streets of Kaifeng to watch gambling and celebrations during popular festivals. A rich mix of activities, functions, and social classes were seen in the major commercial arteries of the city.

Forces Behind Chinese City-Making

As described, Chang'an's scale was unprecedented – a consequence of Emperor Sui Wendi's ambition and perhaps also of Yuwen Kai's youth and inexperience.[45] As I have argued in another article, the unique layout of the city was a quest by Yuwen Kai to invent an urban paradigm for the impending unification of China that would reconcile two great traditions of imperial city planning from the north and south – a city plan that is, in itself, symbolic of the unification of the physical realm.[46] When a more mature Yuwen Kai proceeded to plan Luoyang at the age of 49 in 604, he standardized the ward size and configuration, thus reducing the eastern capital to approximately half the size of Chang'an.

The ability to dictate the layout and size of Chang'an was possible only because of the power of a regime that had absolute control of land and authority. This control and authority extended from the layout of the city to the strict zoning of land use and from the spatial segregation of activities to the enforcement of temporal and social regiments during much of the Tang period.

The control of land was equally matched by the ability of the Sui-Tang dynasties to: muster the vast capital, labor, and expertise needed to erect the city and ward walls; build the imposing avenues; construct the drainage infrastructure; and establish and sustain an administration capable of enforcing the stringent physical, social, economic, and temporal sanctions. The very wide major avenues, the walled wards, and the stringent system of urban management and harsh punishment for deviant behavior were as much for the protection of the populace as they were for an emperor anxious of popular unrest and personal safety.

Defense, security, population control, and ethnic distinction have been the constant preoccupations of the imperial court, and the walled enclosures prevalent in Tang cities were not relegated entirely to the pages of history. Even during the Song dynasty, there were hints and shades of the ward system appearing within the Chinese city. In the northern frontier towns, for instance, where incursions by nomadic tribes were frequent, the walled ward system survived till the late imperial period. Late in the Northern Song period between 1068 and 1077, Shen Kuo revived the ward system with its gates and household registers in border towns that the Khitans often invaded.[47]

Preserving ethnic identity later led the Manchu rulers to establish distinct walled districts in many cities for the exclusive residential use of its people when they conquered China in the seventeenth century. About 34 cities in the north and northwest China became twin cities in which totally separate walled enclosures were erected for Manchus and Chinese to enforce ethnic segregation.[48] Curfew was also practiced with the help of gates at the entrances of alleyways. Beijing's inner city had 1199 such gates, while its outer city had 449, which were closed in the evening to maintain security and urban order.[49] In some cities, this practice of neighborhood gates persisted well until a couple of decades ago and is still a recent memory.

Closer in time, the urbanism of walled wards found its renaissance in the Maoist urban system established after the communist liberation of China, especially since the 1960s. This system centered around the work unit or *danwei* saw the erection of walls around multifunctional compounds – work space, housing, schools, clinics, and even entertainment – large and small for reasons of security and, particularly, boundary definition, turning the city once again into a collection of walled enclosures.

The economic reform that followed only exacerbated the city of the work units. To begin with, the rapid economic development, urbanization, and the absolute ownership of land by the Chinese State gave rise to the numerous masterplans of new townships, urban districts, and townships throughout China. Bolstered by the capacity to realize them, the ambitions of many such plans could easily rival that of Sui Wendi.

Many contemporary Chinese cities are built up of a kit of parts of large government precincts, walled work units, industrial parks, logistic parks, university parks, central business districts, commercial enclaves, gated residential precincts, et cetera. Some of these are the heritage of the Maoist city; others are a habitual continuation of the practice from that era, and for yet others, the product of contemporary economic and social conditions. Today, the scale of the modern gated residential communities often dwarfs the walled wards of Sui-Tang Chang'an. In certain urban areas, the return to a cityscape of gated monofunctional residential enclave walls is rather prominent. A curious parallel to the forces that gave rise to the Sui-Tang cityscape appears to be at play. The ability of the Chinese developer today to raise colossal capital and harness expertise at a global scale make possible the acquisition and development of vast tracts of land released by a government that has almost absolute ownership and control of land. Coupled with the trend of building gated communities and concern for safety and exclusivity, we are seeing a return to the monofunctional residential precincts that typified the Tang residential wards. We have come full circle.

Social, economic, and political changes during the second half of the Tang period and especially the Song dynasty had led, first, to relaxation in the spatial and temporal control of the capital and, subsequently, to a revolutionary change in the urban fabric and management of the Chinese city during the Song period. Hopefully, similar forces in contemporary China as well as international urban trends and practices can help speed up a necessary urban transformation to make its cities and urban fabric less segregated and monofunctional and rather, like the Song cities, more inclusive, with more mix, both in scale and use, and better served by public transportation.

Notes

1 During the Song period, Kaifeng was known as Dongjing or Eastern Capital. It was also commonly known as Bianjing or Daliang. It came to be known also as Bianliang only after the Yuan Period.
2 Zhonghua shuju ed., *Sui Shu* (Official History of Sui), vol. 56 (1973), 1386.
3 See Miyazaki Ichisada, "Kandai no risei to Todai no josei (The Han *li* System and the Tang *fang* System), *Toyoshi Kenkyu* (The Journal of Oriental Researches), 21, no. 3. 271–294.
4 Miyazaki Ichisada, "Les villes en Chine à l'époque des Han," *T'oung Pao*, XLVIII, 4–5 (1960): 376–392.
5 Wang Pu (922–982) ed., *Wudai huiyao* (Important Documents of the Five Dynasties) (Shanghai: Commercial Press, 1936), c. 26, 320.
6 See Sima Guang (1019–1086), *Zizhi tongjian* (Comprehensive Mirror for Aiding Government) (Taipei: Yuanda chuban gongsi, 1983), c. 292, 2030.
7 Wang, *Wudai*, c. 26, 317.
8 There are two other palace compounds in Tang Chang'an. In 634, Daming Palace was built just northeast of the Palace City by Emperor Taizong. In 714, Xingqing Palace was founded when Emperor Xuanzong converted the ward in which he resided before his enthronement into a palace complex.
9 Zhang Yonglu, "Tangdai Chang'an cheng fangli guanli zhidu (Management System of *fang* and *li* in Tang Chang'an), *Renwen zazhi* (Journal of the Humanities), no. 3 (1981): 85–88.
10 Ward walls were made of rammed earth and had a thickness of about 2.5 to 3 meters at the base. See Ma Dezhi, "Tangdai Chang'an cheng kaogu jilüe (Brief Archaeological Report on Tang Chang'an)," *Kaogu* (Archaeology), no. 11 (1963): 595–611.

11 Wang Pu (922–982), ed., *Tang Huiyao* (Important Documents of the Tang Period) (Shanghai: Shanghai guji chubanshe, 1991), c. 86, 1867–1868.

12 See Heng Chye Kiang, *Journal of the Society of Architectural Historian* 73, no. 1 (March 2014): 91–117 for categorization of the wards.

13 Ma Dezhi, "Tang Chang'an and Luoyang," *Kaogu*, no. 6 (1982): 642. See also Ma Dezhi, "Tangdai Chang'an cheng Anding fang fajue ji (Record of the Excavation of Anding Ward of Tang Period Chang'an)," *Kaogu*, no. 4(1989): 319–324.

14 Ma, "Tang Chang'an," 642.

15 Congshu jicheng ed., *Tang lu shuyi* (Tang Legal Code) (Beijing: Commercial Book Press, 1939), c. 8, 179.

16 Quan Deyu's poem "Song Li chengmen baguan gui Songyang 送李城门罢官归嵩阳," in *Quan Tangshi* (Complete Tang Poems) (Beijing: Zhonghua shuju, 1960), c. 324–329, 3638.

17 Bai Juyi described in a poem written in 805 that "Early in the morning I ride in my carriage to send off the Elevated Persons; the East was still not lightened. 'I have gotten up too early,' I say to myself, but already there are horses and carriages about. The torches of cavalrymen cast shadows high and low; street drums (announcing the dawn) can be heard far and near . . ." See Howard S. Levy, Translations from *Po Chü-I's Collected Works*, vol. 1 (New York: Paragon Book Reprint Cor, 1971), 35. Other poems and stories include the poem "The Watchman's Drum in the Streets of Officials" by Li He (791–817); "Renshi zhuan" by Shen Jiji's (c. 750–800); "Guanjie gu" by Li He; "Liwa Zhuan" by Bai Xingjian (775–826), etc.

18 For etymology of *fang*, see Etienne Balazs, *Chinese Civilization and Bureaucracy* (New Haven, CT: Yale University Press, 1964), 69.

19 See also the rescript of 831 in Wang, *Tang Huiyao*, c. 86, 1837, which specifically relates the connection between ward walls and crime. These rules were suspended only three days a year, on and around the night of the First Prime – the 14th, 15th, and 16th days of the 1st lunar month – permitting city folks to stroll the streets at night in order to enjoy the New Year Lantern Festival. This was the culmination of festivities following the New Year when households erected bamboo poles and hung banners from them. See Edwin O. Reischauer, trans., *Ennin's Diary: The Record of a Pilgrimage to China in Search of the Law* (New York: The Ronald Press Company, 1955), 311.

20 Sumptuary laws were instituted to minimize or limit the exercise of economic power such that wealth alone did not guarantee the right to consume and to ensure that the official class was guaranteed the exclusive enjoyment of it (a lifestyle), unthreatened by any propertied class. See T'ung-Tsu Ch'ü, "Chinese Class Structure and Its Ideology," *Chinese Thought and Institutions*, ed. J. Fairbank (Chicago: University of Chicago, 1957), 235–250.

21 Wang, *Tang Huiyao*, c. 31, 14b–15a; Zhonghua shuju, *Xin Tang shu* (New History of the Tang Dynasty) (Shanghai: Zhonghua shuju, 1975), c. 24, 12b.

22 Wang, *Tang Huiyao*, c. 31, 15a.

23 Wang, *Tang Huiyao*, c. 31, 14b.

24 E.H. Schafer, "The Last Days of Ch'ang-an," *Oriens Extremus* 10 (1963): 139. In the poem "Shangzhai," Bai Juyi described an ostentatious official residence surrounded by high walls with a vermillion gate facing the main avenue that had six or seven main halls built at great cost.

25 Song Minqiu (1019–1079), *Chang'an zhi* (Record of Chang'an) in *Song-Yuan fangzhi congkan* (Collection of Song and Yuan Period Gazetteers), vol. 8 (Beijing: Zhonghua shuju, 1990), c. 8, 6a.

26 See Xu Song (1781–1848), *Tang liangjing chengfang kao* (Study of the Walls and Wards of the Two Tang Capitals) (first published in 1848, reissued in 1985 by Beijing: Zhonghua shuju, 1st ed.), 65–66. For the playing of polo in China, see James Liu, "Nansong zhongye maqiu shuailuo he wenhua de bianqian (Cultural Shifts and the Decline of Polo Playing in Mid-Southern Song)," *Lishi yanjiu* (Historical Research), no. 2 (1980), 99–104; also "Polo and Cultural Change from T'ang to Sung China," *Harvard Journal of Asiatic Studies* 45 (1985): 203–224.

27 See Song, *Chang'an*, c. 8, 11a–11b, for description of East Market, and c. 10, 7a for West Market; Denis Twitchett, "Merchant, Trade and Government in Late T'ang," *Asia Major*, vol. XIV Part 1 (September 1968), 63–95, 70. Twitchett, "The T'ang Market System," *Asia Major*, no. 12, Part 2 (1966): 211, 217.

28 Su Bai, "Sui Tang Chang'an cheng he Luoyang cheng (Sui-Tang Chang'an and Luoyang)," *Kaogu*, no. 6 (1978): 418.

29 See Kato Shigeshi, "Guifang kao (Study of Early "Banks")," in *Zhongguo jingjishi kaozheng* (Research on Chinese Economic History), trans. Wu Jie (Beijing: Shangwu yinshu guan, 1959), 395–412.

30 Actual archaeological excavations reveal dimensions of 1000 × 924 meters for the East Market and 1031 x 927 meters for the West Market. See Ma, "Tangdai Chang'an cheng kaogu jiliie," 600. See also Heng Chye Kiang, "A Contest of Wills in the Tang Market" *Journal of Southeast Asian Architecture* 1 (September 1996): 92–104.

31 The perimeter wall for the East Market is thicker, between 6 and 8 meters; see Ma, "Tangdai Chang'an cheng kaogu jiliie," 607.

32 Archaeological excavations within the West Market showed wheel ruts of a width of 1.35 meters within its confines. See Ma, "Brief Archaeological Report on Tang Chang'an," 606.

33 This road was 14 meters wide in the West Market; see Ma, "Brief Archaeological Report on Tang Chang'an," 605.

34 In the less congested East Market, the roads were about 30 meters wide, while those in the West Market were 16 meters across. Ma, "Brief Archaeological Report on Tang Chang'an," 607.

35 See Twitchett, "The T'ang Market System," 209. See also Duan Chengshi, *Jianxia zhuan*, c. 1, "Chezhong nüzi," where he mentions the neat little alleys.

36 See Kato, "On the Hang or the Associations of Merchants in China," 53.

37 Reischauer, trans., *Ennin's Diary*, 333. See also Kato, "On the Hang or the Associations of Merchants in China," 50; see also Wang, *Tang Huiyao*, c. 44, 923.

38 Twitchett, "The T'ang Market System," 218.

39 Twitchett, "Merchant, Trade and Government in Late T'ang," 68–70; *Tang liu dian* (Tang Six Code), c. 20, 5b; Adachi Kiroku's *Choan shiseki no kenkyu* (Study of Tang Chang'an), 2 vols., Tokyo: Toyo bunko ronshu, 1933 or Adachi, *Chang'an shiji kao* (Research on the Remains of Chang'an), trans. Yang Lian (Shanghai: Shangwu yinshu guan, 1935), 122.

40 Wang, *Tang Huiyao*, c. 86, 1867 and 1874.

41 See Twitchett, "The T'ang Market System," 210.

42 Twitchett, "The T'ang Market System," 217; Song, *Chang'an zhi*, c. 10, 7a. See also Xu, *Tang liangjing*, 75, 118.

43 The contempt held against commercial activities was so pronounced that any contact with merchant activities was deemed unrespectable. Wang, *Tang Huiyao*, c. 86, 1873.

44 See *Tang liu dian*, vol. 20, but Wang, *Tang Huiyao*, records 200 drum beats instead, c. 86, 1874.

45 Luoyang, also planned by Yuwen Kai some 22 years later, was only about half the size of Chang'an.

46 For a detailed elaboration of this theory, see Heng Chye Kiang, *A Digital Reconstruction of Tang Chang'an* (Beijing: China Architecture and Building Press, 2006), c. 5.

47 *CB*, c. 267, p. 4a; Umehara Kaoru, in "Song Period Kaifeng and Its City Structure," thinks that this was only a border defense strategy and not the general condition of Song cities.

48 Chang Sen Dou, "The Morphology of Walled Capitals," in *The City in Late Imperial China*, ed. G.W. Skinner (Stanford, CA: Stanford University Press, 1975), 92.

49 *Da Qing Huidian Shili* (Collected Statutes of the Qing Dynasty, with Substatutes Based on Precedent), c. 934.

Bibliography

Chang, Sen-dou. "The Historical Trend of Chinese Urbanization." *Annals, Association of American Geographers* LIII, no. 2 (June 1963): 109–143.

———. "Some Observations on the Morphology of Chinese Walled Cities." *Annals, Association of American Geographers* LX, no. 1 (March 1970): 63–91.

Cunrui Xiong. *Sui-Tang Chang'an: A Study in Urban History of Medieval China*. Ann Arbor: The University of Michigan, 2000.

Elvin, Mark. "Chinese Cities Since the Sung Dynasty." In *Towns in Societies*, edited by Philip Abrams and E.A. Wrigley, 79–89. Cambridge: Cambridge University Press, 1978.

Elvin, Mark and William Skinner, eds. *The Chinese City Between Two World*. Stanford: Stanford University Press, 1974.

Gernet, Jacques. *Daily Life in China on the Eve of the Mongol Invasion, 1250–1276*. Stanford: Stanford University Press, 1962.

Heng Chye Kiang. "Kaifeng and Yangzhou: The Birth of the Commercial Street." In *Streets: Critical Perspectives on Public Space*, edited by Z. Çelik et al., 45–56. Berkeley: University of California Press, 1994.

———. *A Digital Reconstruction of Tang Chang'an*. Beijing: China Architecture and Building Press, 2006.

———. "Visualizing Everyday Life in the City: A Categorization System for Residential Wards in Tang Chang'an." *Journal of the Society of Architectural Historian* 73, no. 1 (March 2014).

Kracke Jr, E.A. "Sung K'ai-feng: Pragmatic Metropolis and Formalistic Capital." In *Crisis and Prosperity in Sung China,* edited by John W. Haeger, 49–77. Tucson: The University of Arizona Press, 1975.

Li Shiqiao. *Understanding the Chinese City.* London: Sage Publications Ltd., 2014.

Mote, Frederick. "A Millennium of Chinese Urban History: Form, Time, and Space Concepts in Soochow." *Rice University Studies* 59, no. 4 (1974): 35–65.

Skinner, G. William, ed. *The City in Late Imperial China.* Stanford: Stanford University Press, 1977.

Steinhardt, Nancy S. *Chinese Imperial City Planning.* Honolulu: University of Hawaii Press, 1990.

Tatsuhiko Seo. "The Urban Systems of Chang'an in the Sui and Tang Dynasties A.D. 583–907." In *Historic Cities of Asia: An Introduction to Asian Cities from Antiquity to Pre – Modern Times,* edited by M.A.J. Beg, 129–186. Kuala Lumpur: Percetakan Ban Huat Seng, 1986.

Wheatley, Paul. "The Ancient Chinese City as a Cosmological Symbol." *Ekistics,* no. 39 (March 1975): 147–158.

Wright, Arthur. "Symbolism and Function: Reflections on Chang'an and Other Great Cities." *The Journal of Asian Studies* XXIV, no. 4 (August 1965): 667–679.

Wu Liangyong. "A Brief History of Ancient Chinese City Planning." In *Urbs et Regio,* vol. 38. Kassel: Gesamthochschulbibliothek, 1986.

Zhou Baozhu. *Songdai Dongjing yanjiu* (A Study of Dongjing of the Song Dynasty). Kaifeng: Henan University Press, 1998.

Glossary

An Lushan	安禄山
Bianjing	汴京
Bianliang	汴梁
Bianzhou	汴州
caoshi	草市
Chai Rong	柴荣
Chang'an	长安
Changping shu	常平署
danwei	单位
Daliang	大梁
Daxingcheng	大兴城
Dongjing	东京
dougong	斗拱
duliu	独柳
fangzheng	坊正
feng	封
Guo Ziyi	郭子仪
Han (dynasty)	汉朝
hang	行
jian	间
Jinwu	金吾
Kaifeng	开封
Later Zhou	后周
li	里
Li Sheng	李晟
Luoyang	洛阳
Manchu	满族

Northern Song	北宋
Northern Zhou	北周
Pingzhun shu	平准署
rouhang	肉行
sanjue	三绝
Shen Kuo	沈括
Shishu	市署
Shizong	世宗（后周）
Song (dynasty)	宋朝
Sui (dynasty)	隋朝
Sui Wendi	隋文帝
tai miao	太庙
tai she	太社
Taishan	泰山
Tang (dynasty)	唐朝
Tianjie	天街
Qin (dynasty)	秦朝
Qinren Ward	亲仁坊
qinjie	侵街
qu	曲
Quan Deyu	权德舆
Qujiang Lake	曲江池
wutou	乌头
xiang	巷
Yangzhou	扬州
yihang	衣行
Yizhou	益州
Yongchong Ward	永崇坊
Yuan (dynasty)	元朝
Yuwen Kai	宇文恺
Zhuque dajie	朱雀大街

5

YINGZAO FASHI

The Book and Methodical Issues
for Studying It

Pan Guxi

The book *of Yingzao Fashi* is a budget control document for building construction released by the Chinese government in the eleventh century.[1] This chapter discusses a range of issues concerning the document, including background, writing genre, content, and implications. Some arguments regarding the study of the book are also discussed.

Yingzao Fashi: For Budget Control

Fashi is a term extensively used in the official documents of the Song dynasty. It connotes by-laws, regulations, or fixed formulas. In this context, anything that was a regulation or a by-law in nature could be termed as a *Fashi*. For example, in his fifth year (1072) as a ruler of the Song dynasty, Emperor Shenzong issued an imperial edict regarding the functionalities of government agencies, which stated: "The one who submits a memo to the imperial court shall: send the memo to Men Xia Sheng (the administrative office of state council) if it is about a *Fashi*, or otherwise to the Premier or Vice-Premier meeting."[2] It is apparent that *Fashi* has a broad range of meaning when referring to government acts, by-laws, or regulations. In this context, the book of *Yingzao Fashi* is a government by-law that has to be observed by officials and workforces in building construction, rather than a non-binding professional manual. According to the preface and annotations written by Li Jie for the book, the Song government made the book a budget control tool to regulate the expenditures of building projects. In his annotations to the book of *Yingzao Fashi*, Professor Liang Sicheng observed that "the book is a monograph prepared by the Song officials for architectural design and construction. It acts a bit like today's design handbook and building standards."[3] The definition carries some truth. However, fundamentally speaking, the two are different in nature. To make the point, let's look at the historical background that prompted the birth of the book.

In the Northern Song dynasty, especially in its late days, building industry was dominated by malpractice and corruption. Some officials who took care of building renovation and maintenance would, before the start of the project, submit to the authorities concerned an application with an overestimated material budget, or a fake building construction proposal. They would also cheat on the working hours and materials that would be consumed through inside jobs. Upon the completion of the project, they would produce a false balance sheet to ask for credit. The quality of the project was most affected, as this compromised the durability of the building

DOI: 10.4324/9781315851112-8

structures. To counter malpractice and corruption, the State Treasury proposed in 1023 an accountability system in an attempt to hold accountable the officials in charge of the project, the heads responsible for design and implementation, and the foremen taking care of the construction activities. The system had a range of strict requirements for establishing a project and for reviewing the material budget. It asked the parties concerned to "develop a fixed formula for calculating the working loads and materials needed for building or renovating structures of three to five bays each, with defined manpower and fixated formula."[4] Here, the expression "defined functionalities and fixated formula" speaks of the budget control that heralded the eventual release of *Yingzao Fashi*. Unfortunately, the proposed system failed to achieve forceful implementation, let alone the eradication of malpractice and corruption in the industry.

In 1054, Emperor Renzong issued an imperial decree, stating:

> I was told when building or renovating in the capital city, the responsible officials would overestimate the functionalities and materials needed, in an attempt to win the reward for the false saving. As a result, building construction and renovation is not done in a proper manner. From today on, one must send a solid functionality and material application to the authorities concerned. All the officials, foremen and craftsmen involved in the project shall be held accountable in case the building breaks down in seven years.[5]

The decree may sound rigorous, but the reality is something else. Officials, superior or inferior, would collaborate to submit a false assessment report. Corruption remained rampant. For example, in 1069, when a Ganying Pagoda was built, the officials in charge made a false estimate for 340,000 labors. However, a re-assessment made by an official dispatched by the imperial court proved that the project only needed one-fifth of the original estimate. Upon the completion of the project, this official was promoted.

Emperor Shenzong was an ambitious man with a commitment to reform. He appointed a number of the reformists, including Wang Anshi, and pursued the "new deals." The reformists thought the corruption of the building industry intolerable. Consequentially, an imperial decree during the years of Emperor Shenzong (1068–1077) asked for a by-law to enhance control of building projects. Unfortunately, the preparation of the by-law did not proceed forcefully. The book of *Yingzao Fashi* was not completed until 1091 – the sixth year of the Yuanyou period under Emperor Zhezong, and it was put into effect a year after.[6] The first edition of *Yingzao Fashi* encountered many hurdles and proved impractical for actual use. In 1097, Emperor Zhezong ordered the book to be rewritten. The official put in charge of the rewrite was a superintendent of Jiang Zuo Jian (office for construction) named Li Jie. It took some three years for Li and his team to complete the masterpiece, and this is the book of *Yingzao Fashi* that people see today (Figures 5.1, 5.2, 5.3, and 5.4).

One can see from this account that *Yingzao Fashi*, whatever the edition, is designed to provide counter-strategies for fencing off malpractice in the building industry, including overestimation, cheating on working hours and materials to be consumed, and embezzlement of national wealth. It is a well-focused by-law for project budget control. Li made it clear in his annotations that the first edition of *Yingzao Fashi* was abolished due to not having effective control of the materials. His edition of *Yingzao Fashi* focuses on "a strict control of the materials to be used. It is applicable internally and externally." He was fully confident about this. He believed that the by-law was feasible and practicable and should be enforced both within and outside of the capital city. Readers can feel the weight of the by-law, especially in those volumes concerning "Manpower" (*gongxian*, standards of manpower) and "Materials" (*liaoli*, cases for

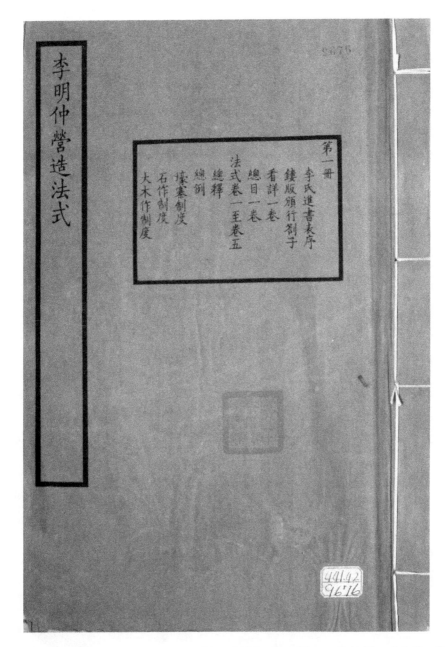

Figure 5.1 Cover of the book in its 1920s edition: *Li Mingzhong Yingzao Fashi* (Shanghai: The Commercial Press, 1929).

Source: Collection of Architecture Library, Southeast University (National Central University).

the use of materials). Li established a low–medium–high grade system for the craftsmen in line with their ranking. He also set up standards for calculating the length of laboring, including short, medium, and long working-days based on the seasons. He developed a range of methods to estimate the amount of labor to be used, based on the unit weight of materials, the distance

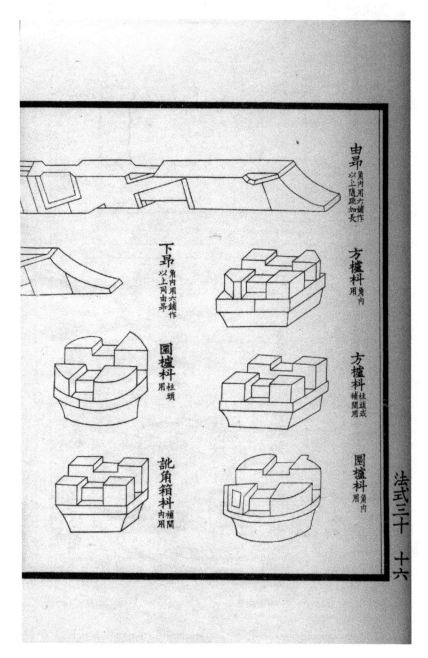

Figure 5.2　A variety of bracket sets (figure 16 of volume 30) in *Yingzao Fashi*. Collection of Architecture Library, Southeast University (National Central University).

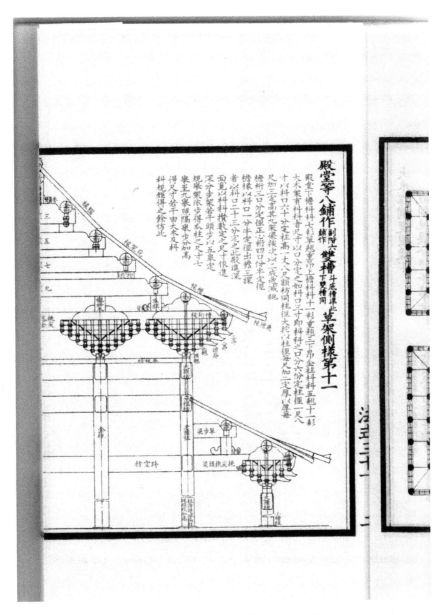

Figure 5.3 Section of a structure (figure 2 of volume 31) in *Yingzao Fashi*. Collection of Architecture Library, Southeast University (National Central University).

of delivery, and the use of materials. The clearly and distinctly defined sections and entries can even make today's reader gasp in admiration.

Highlights of *Yingzao Fashi*

The preceding discussion discusses the nature of *Yingzao Fashi*. Referring to it as a by-law concerning the budget control of building projects is not by any means intended to belittle it, as

八架椽屋前後三椽栿用四柱

法式三十一　十五

Figure 5.4　Section of a structure (figure 15 of volume 31) in *Yingzao Fashi*.

Source: Collection of Architecture Library, Southeast University (National Central University).

it was so both historically and objectively. In a society where Confucianism was the orthodox norm, and intelligentsia and bureaucrats disdained craftsmanship, an official needed courage to write a masterpiece that mirrored the reality of building activities at the time. Li's qualifications as a man with abundant building and project experience and his hard-working personality enabled *Yingzao Fashi* to reach a higher level. It deserves recognition as the most complete and immortal masterpiece on ancient Chinese architecture. It provides the key to open the door to the science and art of architecture of the Song dynasty.

The edition of *Yingzao Fashi* prior to Li's was described by Li as

> A document that only speaks of manpower and materials, without a system that allows a range of differentiation. The prescribed limit for the functionalities and materials are too widely set to fence off the corruption. It is only a by-law for certain purposes. It does not work for different techniques and settings. It is an empty document, hardly feasible and applicable.[7]

Unfortunately, one is not able to compare the notes, as the first edition of *Yingzao Fashi* has been lost. Based on Li's criticism, the first edition had an inappropriate layout of contents, only a pile of material specifications, and was without applicable generic methods. As a result, the applications described in the edition could not cope with changing designs and demands. The methods mentioned in the first edition are possibly those proposed by the authorities concerned under Emperor Renzong: firstly, to use the amount of labor time and building material for certain kinds of buildings as a standard to assess the cost of other buildings (similar to the Qing practice, as in the cases enlisted in *Gongcheng Zuofa*) and, secondly, to acknowledge that the estimated allowance has too wide a margin. The first edition became a useless budget control by-law that was quickly abandoned.

Li worked hard not to repeat the same mistakes in his edition of *Yingzao Fashi*. He took two measures. Firstly, he made the budget control specific to individual parts or components, arranged in a classified differentiation of work types, allowing any project to have a budget control plan. To facilitate practical use, he also established dimensions of the parts under "Regulating System" (*zhidu*, system to regulate dimensions), placed it before the budgeting sections, supplied drawings, and established methods for shifting the budget according to the changing dimensions of a certain part. Li Jie established a three-step layout of the book for dimension regulating, budget identification, and size shifting; it was also the process for using the book when proposing a budget. Secondly, the compilation of the book was based on the actual contemporary practice of building to secure the reliability and applicability of *Yingzao Fashi*.

Layout for Three Steps

Li's three steps may be described as follows:

Step One: Specifying the dimensions. Here the book enlists typical or representational dimensions of various parts, for assessing the cost of manpower and materials. This is volumes 3 to 15 of the book, which includes 13 work types under "Regulating System." For the ease of use, the dimensions cited for a part are representational; sometimes only one dimension is cited. For example, for the stone tablet, those with a height of 1 *zhang* 8 *chi* are quoted, whereas in reality there were a variety of scales for stone tablets for officials of different levels in the Song dynasty.[8]

Step Two: Determining the budget for a part. Based on a sample selected from the "Regulating System," one can then calculate the amount of labor and material based on the information provided in volumes 16–28 under "Manpower" and "Materials." As there is a variety of sizes and scales in reality, and the book cannot exhaust all calculation for parts of all sizes, calculation is still based on that of a typical sample provided. For example, for a bracket set in the basic timber structure of a building, the sample provided is that of grade six (for a section called *cai*), and the calculation for a bracket of different grade (and the corresponding grade of *cai*) will have to be determined with an increase or decrease, and the actual amounts of expenditure will be not listed.

Step Three: Increasing or decreasing in a comparative scale. Based on calculations from "Manpower" and "Materials" for a certain sample of a part, compared with the actual form and dimensions of the part needed in a real project, and checked on the scale of complexity, size, and difficulty, one can arrive at a budget for manpower and material required by the project in reality. Concerning increase and decrease in a comparative scale, the book has general rules:

1   If "Manpower" has already provided methods of measuring increase and decrease (for example, that a column base uses a standard base in bare form in a square shape of 2.5 × 2.5 *chi*, and further manpower assessment is based on the sides of the square being 3, 3.5, 4, 5 and 6 *chi*, plus an assessment on that used for carving and decoration), then follow it in a real project; if this is not the case, then calculate the sum based on a sample part before adding up or reducing based on reasonable deduction for a real project.

2   When calculating the use of materials, follow a grade provided in the book. If the style or the scale is different from what is provided, or when there are no specifications at all in the book, then adopt a type whose form and scale are the nearest to the real one, obtain the assessment for the "near" model, and then make a reasonable deduction.

These two general rules allow Li's *Yingzao Fashi* to have a unified standard while allowing flexibility for diverse design requirements. The labor and material budget controls defined by the book are applicable to all projects. "Increasing and decreasing in a comparative scale," however, left some corruption loopholes for actual implementation. Yet, undoubtedly, *Yingzao Fashi* had made great progress compared to when there were no such rules; the building of Ganying Pagoda, for instance, incurred a 400% overestimation of the actual cost. Li's *Yingzao Fashi* would have achieved great savings for government expenditures, if it had been forcefully implemented at all levels across the nation.

The Nature of the Book Determines Its Content

The three-step system developed by Li is a chain and a coherent whole aimed at the same objective – the integrity of the use of labor and material, cost-saving, and quality. The part on "Regulating Systems" serves the same purpose. It is worth discussing how we should estimate this "regulating" of the sizes and forms. In the past, people tended to have high expectations for what the book could offer. Some people thought that this section should have included the specifications of all components and even the architectural designs for building official structures in the Song dynasty. As a matter of fact, expectation has gone beyond the historical missions of *Yingzao Fashi*. As previously mentioned, the "Regulating System" is organized only to show the style, form, and size of typical components, to allow for an assessment of labor and material. It is not meant to include all the styles or sizes available at the time. Though they are important, it is unnecessary for *Yingzao Fashi* to address architectural issues of function and form.

With that in mind, one can understand why Li chose not to list all the popular architectural practices available at the time in the capital city and why no provisions were made to tell the width of a bay, the height of a column, the depth of a room, etc., as well as why nothing was mentioned about master planning, group organization, and spatial design, even though Song-dynasty architecture performed very well in all of these aspects. Today, when studying Song dynasty architecture, one is in dire need of this information. Unfortunately, *Yingzao Fashi* is unable to provide these details. Perhaps we should not blame Li for the unaccomplished missions. In any case, it is a work completed 890 years ago.

If we compare another architecture and construction manuscript popular in the Northern Song dynasty, Yu Hao's *Mu Jing* (Book on timber construction), the nature and characteristics of *Yingzao Fashi* would become clearer. However, *Mu Jing* has been lost. Only a few quotes survived in *Mengxi Bitan* (*Dream Pool Essays*) by Shen Kuo. Here, let's compare the two on building a path of steps.

Mengxi Bitan (volume 18) quotes the *Mu Ji* like this:

> The steps can be steep, flat or slow, depending on the grade. Take a men-drawn carriage in the royal palace as an example. When climbing the steps from the bottom level with the carriage, steep steps would facilitate the bearers' gestures of dropping arms in the front and extended arms in the rear. Slow steps are designed to accommodate the gestures of flat elbows in the front and the flat shoulders in the rear. The flat steps are desirable for the dropping arms in the front and the flat shoulders in the rear.[9]

It is apparent that the slope of steps is determined by the requirement of the use for the palace, that is, the function of architecture. This differs significantly from the focus of *Yingzao Fashi*, where there are also some lines on a step path:

> Regulating for Step Path: The width goes with that of a bay. Each step shall be 1 chi tall with two footstep stone pieces. Each of piece is 5 *cun* tall and 1 *chi* deep. The flanking pieces on the two sides shall be 1 *chi* 8 *cun* wide, and the height shall be the same as the triangle stones at the end on the ground. The triangle stones are at the two ends, when the overall height is 4.5–5 *chi*, there shall be three layers above, and when it is 6–8 *chi* high, five to six layers above; the periphery defines the ground layer, and retreating inside by 2 *cun* there is the second layer; the ground surface shall be filled with soil and pieces of stone, each with a depth the same as that for the step.[10]

Here the specification is for the dimensions of the footsteps (1 *chi* deep and 5 *cun* tall), so as to determine the use of manpower and material and form a sample unit for cost calculation; it does not care about the steep, slow, and gentle slope of the step path and its associated functions. In the same book, we find specification for the use of "Manpower" for a stone step path:

> Regarding a stone piece for a foot step, each is 3 *chi* wide, 2 *chi* deep and 6 *cun* high; and to arrange manpower, installing one such a piece counts as one unit of manpower.[11]

This is for measuring labor, and it uses a piece of stone of $0.6 \times 2 \times 3$ *chi* in dimension for calculating; it is different from the "Regulating" of part and component sizes, where it uses 0.5×1 *chi* as the standard dimensions for a piece. To summarize, for the same category of step path, different dimensions are used to illustrate different problems.

Closely Connected to Building Practice

Let's now look at how *Yingzao Fashi* was written in close connection with contemporary building practice. Li was not born to a scholarly family. He became an imperial official because of his father, also an imperial official. Li was promoted, from a mid-level position to a senior one in the then-Office of Construction, due to his solid performance in handling major projects. He was a man of action with practical knowledge as well as an expert in building construction management. When he received the emperor's decree to revise *Yingzao Fashi*, he had been working at the Office for six years, where he had presided over a range of major building projects, including the Wuwangfu Palaces, and gathered rich experience. That explains why Li dared in his edition of *Yingzao Fashi* to criticize the officials in charge of building projects, calling them laymen. He stated that those who presided over the management of the projects had no knowledge of building construction: "Those in charge don't have practical knowledge, not knowing that *cai* is the unit for measuring, and instead using *dou* for that purpose; corruption is inevitable and lawful inspection is in disorder."[12] That is, he laughed at those who mistakenly used *dou* for *cai* as a unit of measurement – basic knowledge needed for construction and management. Li Jie, for sure, was very confident, saying that "without a refined knowledge on construction, how could I revise and renew the whole set of practice from the past?"[13] His rich knowledge and experience provided favorable conditions for him to set up new rules for building construction.

In the course of rewrite, he learnt from carpenter builders in the field. Li's *Yingzao Fashi* included 3,555 entries, or 92% of the total of the book, "as practical working methods collected from practice as proven and tested, and adopted from place to place, time to time."[14] If we exclude the inessential provisions in the first two volumes that are copied from the old classics, the book is a 100% collection of proven practical knowledge accumulated from craftsmen's practice. Li also gathered craftsmen together to discuss the entries one by one.

> The participants are the experienced craftsmen of various ranks. They are particular about the rules. They are able to compare the strength and weakness of various methods, and review the procedures for scaling up and down for the parts, material and labor force.[15]

Li not only learnt from the grassroots experience but also approached the rewrite with a serious and fastidious attitude. The book of *Yingzao Fashi*, which stemmed from such efforts, eventually found its mark in implementation. It isn't an exaggeration to say that Li's great book reflects the accomplishments in building construction achieved in the Northern Song dynasty as well as the wisdom and experience of the craftsmen at the time.

The rational layout of the book and its close connection with practice quickly won the approval of imperial authority, and it was adopted in the capital area for testing. Three years later, Li proposed to disseminate the practice, through formal release of the book in small prints as an imperial document, for people to follow in other places. This was approved by Emperor Huizong, and Li's *Yingzao Fashi* was printed and released in 1103. After that, the book had several reprints. Even when the Song moved its capital to the south, and the old capital city was no longer a political center, Wang Huan, a magistrate of Pingjiang Prefecture, ordered reprints in Suzhou to accommodate the need for it in construction practice, which shows the broad applicability of the book.

Research Methods: Discussion

Today when studying *Yingzao Fashi*, one cannot just look at the information on its own, focusing on a clarification of the regulation, manpower, and material systems described in the book. One must read more about the many aspects of Song dynasty architecture provided by the book. However, the study should be based on objective and historical reality and not on subjective projections. In this regard, Professor Liang Sicheng has established a good example; he started with an investigation into a large number of real buildings, then compared several editions of *Yingzao Fashi*, checked the texts closely, adopted rigorous scientific attitude, and offered hitherto the most precise and visually concrete explanation of the volumes based on the logic of the timber structure of the time.

Unfortunately, people now tend to overstate the architectural capability of the Song dynasty, though with good intentions. For example, some researchers believe that the "eight grades of *cai*" for the timber structure is a sequence of figures of "geometric progression" calculated from the strength of the beams involved, so that China was ahead of Europe by six centuries; that is, China had already reached what Galileo discovered much later – a preliminary method of calculating a beam's flexural strength through experiments with the performance of cantilever beams.[16]

This conclusion is debatable. If we leave aside the problem of mathematical calculation adopted by the authors first, and just focus on the information provided in *Yingzao Fashi*, we can ascertain that the "eight grades of *cai*" are the result of empirical measuring rather than scientific research and experiments. Firstly, these eight grades do not really follow a geometric sequence and cannot be moved around to suit any numerical order; instead, these grades are based on reality and can be shifted for real building structures. *Yingzao Fashi* made this clear as a general rule in its *zongli* section (general guide to the use) and has provided another grade between Grade Seven and Eight, a grade of *cai* of 5 *cun*, to be used specifically for army's military barracks.[17] Secondly, Li Jie clearly said that his rules and provisions were collected from real practice – a result of experience accumulated in a tradition and a crystallization of the wisdom of the craftsmen. We can therefore conclude that, unless there is solid evidence proving that there was a method of calculation similar to Galileo's, the researchers' claim is not persuasive.

In the course of studying *Yingzao Fashi*, I personally think that we might have achieved a more precise understanding of the book if we had studied it from an engineering and practical perspective. For example, on the issue of raising the corner columns and of tilting the peripheral columns, people have long accepted the explanation that it is meant to adjust people's vision and to increase the feel of stability of the external appearance of an architectural structure. But this leads to many problems: when the corner columns are enclosed by an enclosure wall, the tilting of the wall replaces the needs for the tilting of the columns and makes the special treatment of the corner posts unnecessary. Secondly, the upward projection of the eaves because of the raising of the corner posts is the opposite of the treatment of the cornice in Greek architecture, so how can you explain the opposing practice by saying that they aim for the same visual effect? Further, in the Qing dynasty, the raising and the tilting of corner posts were no longer in use; does this suggest a decline in the aesthetic design of the architecture of the Qing? These questions make us skeptical of those purely aesthetic explanations and prompt us to seek alternative ways – for example a structure and construction viewpoint – to explain the raising and the tilting of the corner posts.

In terms of physical mechanics, the raising and tilting of corner posts add an inward force to enhance a structural integrity to the timber building structure. This is very important in the process of constructing the building. In the Tang and Song dynasties, a palace of the highest rank adopts timber structures that place one on top of another – the whole structure has a level of the frame of columns, a second level of the frame of brackets, and a third layer of the roof frame; only lintels are used to link between the columns; and the physical integrity of the column frame is weak. When the raising and tilting are adopted for the corner columns, the horizontal force of the static weight of the roof would press the column heads to bend inwards, and the lintels are also pressed inward, so that an outward disintegration of the structure because of the outward move of the column heads can be avoided during the process of construction (especially when the lintel is connected to the column via a direct mortise-and-tenon joint). When the building is completed, the enclosing walls consolidate the stability of the corner columns and stability to the overall structure; meanwhile, the tilting of the posts also helps resist strong winds and other horizontal forces.

The raising of the corner posts ensures that the column heads are not on a level plane but are instead a concave plane with the four corners flying upward, and the second-level bracket frame therefore sits one this curve plane. This ensures the bracket and the roof frames are bent inward slightly, adding thus a cohesive force and stability to the whole timber structure.

However, the raising and the tilting bring about troubles in the building process. Firstly, the dimensions on the plan of column heads are different from that of the plan of column bases, and the staking of key lines during construction requires a careful outward shift of the position for these columns; the sections of the column at the top and base are also not perpendicular to the central axis of the column. Secondly, for installing bracket sets on top of the columns, the whole frame of the brackets must be put together on the ground first, a process called *ankan jiaoge zhanzhuai* (placing, correcting, cutting, stretching, and pulling), before they are taken apart, raised atop of the columns, and assembled into one frame again. Because of the raising of the corner posts, the frame of brackets sits on a curved and concave plane, so the first assembling of the bracket sets on the ground requires the sets to be placed on a gradually raised height; measured timber cushions are needed for this, as otherwise when the bracket sets are re-assembled atop the columns, the joining of the parts will not work properly. As we can see, raising and tilting are a subtle change in the dimensions of the parts, yet this has great impact on the plans and the structure as a whole, bringing about a lot of trouble in the building process.

Because of this, in the Ming and Qing dynasties, improvements were made to enhance the overall integration of the parts of the structure: two types of tie-beams are used in between the columns; brackets or bracket sets are no long used, and columns, beams, and purlins come to joint directly; a "dark floor" on top of the columns is removed and the layering of the three frames is replaced with an overall frame of full-height columns. These measures greatly improved the overall stability of the timber structures and made the raising and tilting of corner columns unnecessary. The new techniques eventually made craftsmen abandon the old practice, which was time- and labor-consuming.

Notes

1 The chapter was first published in Chinese as "Guanyu *Yingzao Fashi* de Xingzhi, Tedian, Yanjiu-fangfa," *Dongnan Daxue Xuebao (Ziran Kexue Ban)*, vol. 20, no. 5 (20 September 1990): 1–7. Translated and published here with permission and courtesy of the Editorial Office of *Journal of Southeast University* (Natural Science Edition).
2 Xu Songji, comp., *Song Huiyao Jigao* (Collection of Official Documents of the Song dynasty), Beijing: Zhonghua Shuju, 1957; vol. 58, "Officials, Section 1," 2339.
3 Liang Sicheng, *Yingzao Fashi Zhushi* (Notes for Li Jie's *Yingzao Fashi*) (Beijing: China Architecture and Building Press, 1983), 5.
4 Xu, *Song*, vol. 58, "Officials, Section 1," 2997.
5 Xu, *Song*, vol. 75, "Officials, Section 30," 2999.
6 Yuan Tuotuo, comp., *Song Shi* (History of the Song Dynasty), vol. 165, "Officials, Office of Construction" (Beijing: Zhonghua Shuju, 1975), 3918–3919, where it says "In the seventh year of Yuanyou, the book of *Yingzao Fashi* complied by Jiang Zuo Jian was completed and declared."
7 Li Jie, *Yingzao Fashi* (Rules and Regulations on Building Construction) (Shanghai: The Commercial Press, 1929), Book 1, "Zhazi, Kan Xiang" (Annotations, details), p. 1.
8 In the Song dynasty, 1 *zhang* = 10 *chi* = 100 *cun* = 3.07 meters.
9 Hu Daojing, *Xin Jiaozheng Mengxi Bitan* (Shen Kuo's Classic *Mengxi Bitan* as Newly Edited and Corrected) (Beijing: Zhonghua Shuju, 1957), 570.

10 Li, *Yingzao*, Book 1, "Shizuo Zhidu" (Rules for Stonework), 7.

11 Li, *Yingzao*, Book 3, "Shizuo Gongxian" (Labour for Stonework), 9.

12 Li, *Yingzao*, Book 1, "Jingxinxiu Yingzao Fashi xu" (Preface to the Newly Edited *Yingzao Fashi*), 1.

13 Li, *Yingzao*, Book 1, "Jingxinxiu Yingzao Fashi xu" (Preface to the Newly Edited *Yingzao Fashi*), 1.

14 Li, *Yingzao*, Book 1, "Yingzao Fashi Kan Xiang, Zong Zhuzuo Kan Xiang" (On Using the Book, on General Cases and Rules), 12.

15 Li, *Yingzao*, Book 1, "Yingzao Fashi Kan Xiang, Zong Zhuzuo Kan Xiang" (On Using the Book, on General Cases and Rules), 12.

16 Du Gongchang, Chen Mingda, "Cong Yingzao Fashi Kan Beijing de Lixue Chengjiu (Beijing's Achievement in the Science of Mechanics Based on a Study of the Book *Yingzao Fashi*)," *Jianzhu Xuebao* (Architectural Journal), no. 1 (1977): 36–52.

17 Li, *Yingzao*, Book 1, "Da Mu Zuo Zhidu Yi: Cai" (Major Timber Structure, Regulation One: *Cai*), 1–2.

Bibliography

Du Gongchang and Chen Mingda. "Cong Yingzao Fashi Kan Beijing de Lixue Chengjiu (Beijing's Achievement in the Science of Mechanics Based on a Study of the Book *Yingzao Fashi*)." *Jianzhu Xuebao* (Architectural Journal), no. 1 (1977): 36–52.

Hu Daojing. *Xin Jiaozheng Mengxi Bitan* (Shen Kuo's Classic *Mengxi Bitan* as Newly Edited and Corrected), 570. Beijing: Zhonghua Shuju, 1957.

Li Jie. *Yingzao Fashi* (Rules and Regulations on Building Construction). Shanghai: The Commercial Press, 1929.

Liang Sicheng. *Yingzao Fashi Zhushi* (Notes for Li Jie's *Yingzao Fashi*). Beijing: China Architecture and Building Press, 1983.

Xu Songji, comp. *Song Huiyao Jigao* (Collection of Official Documents of the Song Dynasty). Beijing: Zhonghua Shuju, 1957.

Yuan Tuotuo, comp., *Song Shi* (History of the Song Dynasty). Beijing: Zhonghua Shuju, 1975.

Glossary

ankan jiaoge zhanzhuai	安勘绞割展拽
cai	材
chi	尺
cun	寸
dou	斗
Ganying Pagoda	感应塔
Gongcheng Zuofa	工程做法
gongxian	功限
Jiang Zuo Jian	将作监
Li Jie	李诫
Liang Sicheng	梁思成
liaoli	料例
Men Xia Sheng	门下省
Mengxi Bitan	梦溪笔谈
Ming dynasty	明朝
Mu Jing	木经
Pingjiang Prefecture	平江府
Qing dynasty	清朝
Renzong (Emperor)	仁宗（皇帝）
Shen Kuo	沈括
Shenzong (Emperor)	神宗（皇帝）

Song dynasty	宋朝
Tang dynasty	唐朝
Wang Anshi	王安石
Wang Huan	王唤
Wuwangfu Palaces	五王府
Yingzao Fashi	营造法式
Yu Hao	喻皓
Yuanyou	元祐
zhang	丈
Zhezong (Emperor)	哲宗（皇帝）
zhidu	制度
zongli	总例

Literati Culture and Social Production

6

LITERATI GARDENS OF THE JIANGNAN REGION

Characters and Mutations

Gu Kai

The *literati* gardens of the Jiangnan region of China have garnered great fame both at home and abroad, as representative of the greatest achievements of Chinese garden art – most noticeably, these gardens conspicuously display not only the features of traditional gardens but also the ideals of a living environment in Chinese culture.

"Jiangnan," literally "south of the river," refers to a region of China that includes the southern parts of Jiangsu Province, the city of Shanghai, and the northern parts of Zhejiang Province, distributed around the great Taihu Lake. This region boasts several conditions superior for garden making. Geographically, there are plains with well-developed river and canal systems that provide abundant water indispensable for gardens as well as for transporting stones, an important element in garden making. Climatically, four distinctive seasons and abundant rainfall make plants thrive in rich varieties. Economically, this is the richest region in China since the Tang and Song dynasties (618–907, 960–1279), a condition crucial for the art of garden making to develop. Culturally, this has been the most developed region of China since the Southern Song dynasty (1127–1279) and has produced a significant percentage of the population's educated and wealthy families as well as a shared culture of appreciation, which have allowed the gardens to develop and thrive. In addition, this region produces Taihu stones or rocks, providing specially formed rockeries and stone pieces highly appreciated in and much needed for garden making. Because of these factors, Jiangnan has been the center of garden culture and has led the trend of garden making in China since the time of the Southern Song.

Most gardens in Jiangnan are private, owned by the *literati* or wealthy scholars and officials. In the history of garden making in China, the two principal categories are private and royal gardens, which influenced other garden types such as temple gardens, government office gardens, and shrine gardens, among others. The development of royal gardens led early on, while after the Six Dynasties (222–589), private gardens arose suddenly, developing independent methods and styles and becoming the source of inspiration for royal gardens. In Jiangnan, there were royal gardens during the periods of the Six Dynasties, Southern Tang dynasty (937–976), and Southern Song dynasty. In Jiangnan, while all royal gardens had vanished, private gardens continued to develop and prosper, among which the *literati* gardens were considered as of the highest quality, taking the lead in China after the Southern Song.

Academic research on the gardens of this region first appeared in the 1930s. *Jiangnan Yuanlin Zhi* (record of Jiangnan gardens), completed in 1937 by Professor Tong Jun (1900–1983),

DOI: 10.4324/9781315851112-10

initiated the study of Chinese gardens in a modern scholarly manner. In this book, a great number of gardens in Jiangnan were surveyed and mapped, while related historical literature was also studied.[1] In the 1950s, a team of scholars led by Professor Liu Dunzhen (1897–1968) delivered by then the most systematic and rigorous study of the Jiangnan gardens as found in Suzhou; the study was resulted in *Suzhou Gudian Yuanlin* (Chinese classical gardens of Suzhou); this had triggered a nation-wide wave of studies on Chinese gardens.[2] These two master scholars, both with a disciplinary background in architecture, laid down a foundation for modern scholarship in China on Jiangnan gardens, and their influence can still be felt today. Since the 1980s, there have emerged more studies of Jiangnan gardens, especially with cultural history perspectives or explanations. The studies listed here have all focused on the existing gardens; while they have provided rich and thorough considerations of these gardens, they also suffer from a lack of understanding when it comes to a variety of cases and types in history that have disappeared in modern times.

Departing from existing scholarship, this chapter expands the scope of perspective by covering not only the existing cases but also a broader history, including early periods, for a more comprehensive understanding of Jiangnan gardens. We examine both persistent characters and historical mutations of these gardens; the study concludes with three concrete examples that detail the features and historical evolution.

Persistent Characters

Since the Six Dynasties, from about the third to sixth centuries, when *literati* gardens in Jiangnan first appeared, some conspicuous and stable features have developed that are also basic traits of gardens in China.

Pursuit and Theme: Nature

With owners who cultivated cultural knowledge and aspiration, the gardens in Jiangnan manifested distinctive ideas, one of which was acquiring nature, or a world of nature. A belief in "Heaven and humans as one" runs through all intellectual schools in China, whether Confucianism or Taoism; and all cultivated Chinese see seeking and maintaining harmony between humans and nature, following the ways of nature, and seeing naturalness as ultimate beauty as a supreme goal. This culture requires one to follow the ways of Heaven and Earth and to be inspired by ancient priests and hermits living amid nature – living with freedom by becoming one with nature and with cosmological spirit. The reference to "*youruo ziran*" (like nature or nature-like) in the literature of Six Dynasties indicates that this is an ideal in garden making, as does the phrase "*suiyou renzuo, wanzi tiankai*" (though manmade, it feels naturally created) found in *Yuanye* (The graft of gardens), the classic on garden making in Jiangnan of the late Ming dynasty (1600–1644).[3] Based on this, the design focuses on the use of *shan* (hills, rocks), *shui* (water, streams, ponds), and *huamu* (flowers-and-woods, or plants) as entities that refer to or signify scenes of nature.

Of all the themes and images of nature followed and expressed in garden making, *shanshui* ("mountain-and-water," that is, hills and rocks with ponds and streams) is the most prominent, as it best fits and strongly expresses a love of nature in Chinese culture. From the Six Dynasties on, *shanshui* has become a great feature in Chinese artistic culture, as found in poems, essays, paintings, and, most importantly, in garden design. While other garden cultures have often focused on the theme of plants, Chinese gardens regard the construction of a realm of "mountain-and-water" as the highest ideal; and most of the *literati* gardens of Jiangnan centered on the building of scenes and images of *shanshui* as a core design idea.

In building a scene of *shunshui* or "mountain-and-water," the use of artificial rocks is central. There is a long tradition of doing this, as found either in the making of small hills and ponds in the miniature scholar gardens of the Tang dynasty, or in the creation of larger hills with more realistic features in the late Ming, as represented by the works of Zhang Nanyuan (1587–1671), a renowned painter and garden designer. Since the late Ming period, ideas and images of painterly representations of "mountain-and-water" became gradually adopted as a standard for garden making and appreciation, and the building of "mountain-and-water" scenes became more important; any garden owners, if they had any resources, would create artificial hills with rocks; today, most surviving gardens of that time contain these carefully constructed rock hills.

Artificial hills must be accompanied by scenes of water, to form a garden in which "water flows with hills and hills come to life because of water." Such a combination in a *shanshui* garden creates the best effect for association with a pure nature and manifests a certain painterly landscape of well; we can find this in the design of a stream gully inside and a pond outside the rocky hills in the Huanxiu Shanzhuang Garden, and the placing of a ravine in between islands in the Zhuozheng Yuan Garden, both located in Suzhou.

Aside from "mountain" and "water" elements, plants (*huamu* or "flowers-and-woods") are another key element for the careful arrangement and creation of naturalness in the garden; sometimes scenes of water and plants are designed together, to create a theme of water-and-plant (*shuimu*) in the garden. In the *literati* gardens of Jiangnan, the changes of the four seasons and the corresponding sceneries of the plants, especially the blossoming of flowers in spring, are highly appreciated.

Method and Profile: Flexibility with Interdependence

Regarding how to represent or construct a natural world in the garden, the basic principle followed in the *literati* gardens of Jiangnan is *yindi zhiyi*, that is, depending on the site and following the condition. With no universal models for all conditions, the specific site and its special situations are fully utilized; and the gardens are designed with great flexibility. In Chinese philosophy, the idea of *guiyin* (respecting the contingent) mirrors the *yindi zhiyi* idea in garden marking. Zheng Yuanxun (1598–1645), a renowned figure in the late Ming dynasty, once claimed "*yuanyou yiyi, wu chengfa*" (each garden is unique, there is no fixed method) in his preface to the classic *Yuanye* (the craft of gardens). With such guidance, while structural layout may be similar, the actual arrangement of scenes and entities is flexible and different, with no simple model to copy from; though gardens are abundant, each is very different from others.

The late Ming garden-making master of the Jiangnan region, Ji Cheng (1582–1642), in his classic *Yuanye*, has elaborated the principles of *yin* – interdependence on contingent situations – and enlisted six types of site situation that one needs to follow and adapt with flexibility: hilly land with woods, urban land, village land, rural and wilderness land, land next to a house, and land by a river or a lake.

Sui Yuan (garden of ease or casual following), owned and created by Yuan Mei (1716–97), a famed man of letters in Nanjing during the Qing dynasty (1644–1911), is a conspicuous example of garden making through the ideas of following and interdependence, with a clear, articulated theory and skillful pragmatic application. In his *Sui Yuan Ji* (record of the Sui Yuan garden), he says,

> following the high site I place a towering building for a grand view over the river;
> following the low land I place a pavilion to view the stream; following the narrow gap

> I place a bridge to cross a gully; and following the running water I place a boat; and, further, following the humping and slanting of the land I place stone peaks, whereas following the lush scene with open visions I place a building to face it . . .[4]

This garden, adopting the word *sui* (following with ease) for its name, builds along and upon the land profile as it rises and falls, constructing views by the hillside and bridging pathways across waters and streams; it fully demonstrates the method of *jiushi qujing* (creating scenes by using the immediate local topography and its dynamic profile) and the overall ideas of *yin* and *sui*, depending on and following with ease.

The principle of flexibility manifests not only in the adaptation of local site conditions, but also in projecting a uniqueness for each garden as developed out of its special situation. For example, in Suzhou, many gardens have special characters. Zhuozheng Yuan (garden of a humble administrator) has a large pond and simple and austere buildings, with a character of purity and simplicity; Liu Yuan (garden for lingering) maintains a dual focus on buildings and mountain-and-water scenery, with its petite courtyards deep, mysterious, and serene, and its buildings richly decorated without looking vulgar; Wangshi Yuan (garden of a master of nets) is known for its compact design, with delicate and deep spaces, and a maze of journeys within; whereas Canglang Ting (garden of surging waves) is known for its long history, a favor of antiquity, and an aura of tranquility. Like poetry and painting, garden making in Jiangnan prefers not to follow any model or type, but rather to develop its own special character in a specific case, making the collection of the *literati* gardens of the region richly variegated.

Pause, Move and View: Architecture for Living and Experiencing

What is pursued in a *literati* garden in Jiangnan is not just a collection of scenes of nature without humans. People's activities – including residing, visiting and meandering with moments of pause, walking and viewing – are taken into full account in garden making. In ancient Chinese thinking, heaven and human are considered as one, without the separation of nature and artificiality made in western culture.[5] In China, an ideal world is one in which nature and humans live in harmony, and garden making is a manifestation of this ideal, especially in the scholar gardens of Jiangnan.

In ancient Chinese theories on art and representation, a key perspective for judging a landscape painting is to see if the world depicted is "walkable," "visible," "enjoyable," and "habitable"; this also applies to judgments of garden making. Scenery is indeed important, but the most important consideration is the presence of humans, who form the soul of garden design. You may ignore one of the key elements –s "mountain," "water," "flowers," and "woods" – but without a trace of humans, a garden design is never complete.

In the Chinese tradition, the idea of "another world" beyond or above the current reality is not much explored or contemplated upon; gardens as an ideal realm of everyday life contain various pragmatic functions. Apart from viewing and enjoying oneself while lingering around and moving through a garden, other functions are also included. A scholar or *literati* garden is a place for contemplating, learning, and cultivating of oneself, a place in which one can begin to follow the Confucian idea of "having a sincere intent, regulating one's mind, disciplining one's body, managing one's family, governing the state, and bringing peace and justice to the world." In such a serene place, one can read and collect books. A garden is also an ideal place for social gathering among the cultivated, while the garden itself is often what the scholars make poems about in such gatherings. Some famous cultural gatherings are followed in later generations. There are also other garden activities, such as acting as a school for kids, a temple for religious worship, a landscape for family tours and banqueting, and a guesthouse for temporary residence, among other programs and functions.

Consideration of the presence of humans in garden design mainly manifests in the arrangement of functional sites and touring pathways, and these are closely related to the arrangement of buildings or built structures. Architecture is important in this sense. A variety of types cater to a variety of programs of activities: *ting* (pavilions without walls) for pause and rest during a meandering tour in order to enjoy the garden; *tang* (meeting halls) for gathering and receiving friends; *tai* (platforms or terraces) for open-air gathering to enjoy a play or theatrical performance; *ge* (pavilions with windows) for broad viewing over the garden; *zhai* (study) for quiet reading alone; and *lang* (covered walkways or galleries) for connecting places.

Overall, in terms of formal effect, the *literati* gardens of Jiangnan present not a human-free wilderness or a rural rusticity, as in other garden cultures, but instead a harmonious oneness between nature and artificiality.

Texts and Imagination: Cultural Meaning

The gardens provide not only the pleasure of viewing scenes of nature, but also a place for exploring *shiyi* or poetic ideas and sentiments. Based on educated scholars' historical knowledge and cultural learning, the views, scenes, and entities of the garden generate abundant associations that go much beyond the spatial-temporal limits of the physical garden, creating a spiritual reading derived from a cosmological imagination and a historical dialogue with ancient sages or authors. Because of this, the scholar gardens of Jiangnan are endowed with rich cultural meaning, with a deep deposit of ideas and imagination for the cultivated.

The creation of this kind of *yijing* or a realm of ideas and imagination is done at the most direct level with the use of words. In a scholar garden, texts are used profusely: the name of the garden, the title for a view, the poetic words on the tablets and couplets, and those on stone carvings: these bring in a world of art and literature found in poems, calligraphy, and seal carvings, but also express the intentions and associations behind the making of a specific garden and the character of the owner of the place, adding layers of *shiqing huayi* (poetic emotions and painterly ideas) to the *yijing* (realm of ideas and imagination) of the sceneries of the garden.

The use of texts reveals the culture and longing of the owner of the garden. Firstly, giving a name to a garden reveals the desire, sentiment, or self-understanding of the master of the project; for example, garden names of Zhuozheng (a humble administrator), Wangshi (a master of nets or a fisherman), and Canglang (surging waves) expressed clearly a desire to retire and retreat into a pure natural world, revealing a self-understanding of detachment, dignity, and purity. Secondly, the use of texts also aids in highlighting and deepening an appreciation of certain scenery; for example, in Zhuozheng Yuan, the naming of a pavilion "Liu Ting Ge" (pavilion for the remaining and the sound) derives from a poetic phrase, *"liu de ku he ting yu sheng"* (with the remaining withered lotus leaves, I hear the rain drops hitting upon them), from the poet Li Shangyin (813–858) of Tang dynasty. Some of these words also refer to a mode of experiencing; for example, in Yi Yuan (garden of pleasant harmony), the phrase *"jing zuo can zhong miao"* – sitting in repose and feeling the miscellaneous wonderfulness – is inscribed, expressing a mode of aesthetic appreciation, that is, to see, to listen, and to observe with sensitivity and a focused mind.

Since these textual inscriptions play an important role in constructing cultural meaning and elevating the realm of ideas, they are considered indispensable in garden making. In Tong Jun's *Jiangnan Yuanlin Zhi* (record of Jiangnan gardens), there is an account of the history of Yan Yuan (garden of swallows) of the city of Changshu. When the Gui family sold the garden, they removed all the tablets and couplets, which delivered to the garden "a great harm no less than from a war destruction."[6] We can glean the importance of textual inscriptions for the gardens from this.

Besides texts, there are also sceneries and entities that contain specific cultural meanings, allowing them to act as allusions, because of certain historical myths or narratives. This especially applies to the use of plants; with cultural meanings attached, the plants act beyond merely a visual and formal feature, instead adding layers of cultural suggestions. For example, pine trees, bamboo, and plum flowers are considered "three friends in severe winter" and represent strength and nobility; the moral metaphor is widely used, such as through the plants used around the Sui Han Ting (pavilion of yearly winter) in the Zhan Yuan (garden for viewing and admiring) of Nanjing. Further, certain compositions for a scenery also contain a specific meaning as established over history. For example, the caves in an artificial hill of rocks refer to the legendary dwellings of ancient spirits; a hut on top of a hill suggests a detached dwelling of a sage or priest; and a pastoral openness reveals an admiration for the historical figure of Tao Yuanming (365–427), known for his love of nature and life of retreat into wilderness.

Historical Mutations

Although *literati* gardens in Jiangnan have stable features, as previously described, they have not always remained the same over history. In the late Ming period (from the late sixteenth to mid-seventh centuries), obvious changes can be found in how gardens were appreciated and how they were constructed.

Shifts in Aesthetic Appreciation

In the late Ming dynasty, as garden making became increasingly popular, and as it reached a peak in quality of design and quantity of production, an important change in the ways gardens were appreciated occurred, marking a shift from a focus on *shiyi* (appropriate ideas) to *huayi* (painterly ideas).

Since the very beginning in Chinese cultural and art history, people's appreciation of gardens for their natural sceneries was always about a communication between natural scenes and a human's inner world, a correspondence summarized in the phrase *shiyi*, appropriate or adequate to the ideas of the mind – that is to say, the purpose of garden marking is for scenes of nature to make the mind settle adequately, appropriately, and comfortably.[7] This idea emerged in the time of the Six Dynasties (222–589) and was fully established by the middle years of the Tang dynasty (618–907), with impact on the following times and dynasties. Before the time of late Ming, gardens had been always regarded as a medium of dialogue between nature and the inner world; the design of meandering pathways in the garden always aimed to obtain pleasure and communication in the mind with the landscape of nature; to meet the mind adequately or *shiyi* was the main purpose, while the arrangement of things and sceneries as formal design remained secondary.

Closely associated with the *shiyi* approach was a persistent and basic purpose in garden marking: the union between individuals and nature. On the one hand, it was concerned about the pursuit of the individual, especially his retreat; it was about how to collaborate with the ruler to manage the politics and economy of the state, while retaining a certain autonomy and independence of one's self.[8] On the other hand, it cared about how a natural landscape was appreciated in an individual's mind, how the building of views and sceneries helped to construct one's inner world. The problem here was how an appreciation of the landscape related to the building of one's inner mind, while how the entities and scenes were organized, though important, was not regarded as primary.

While the idea of *shiyi* had been predominant in garden making, the new idea of *huayi* (painterly ideas) emerged abruptly in the late Ming and came into dominance thereafter. Indeed, both garden making and landscape painting followed the ideas and poetics of "mountain-and-water," but using painting as guidance for garden making was not found before the Ming dynasty (1368–1644); and only when we reach late Ming do we find a self-conscious use of such ideas. A cultural leader of late Ming, Dong Qichang (1555–1636), stated that "a garden can be depicted in a painting" (*yuan ke hua*) and "a painting can be constructed in a garden" (*hua ke yuan*), and placed the two ideas side by side, on equal footing; this marked the moment in China's cultural history when painting and gardening were interconnected, and garden making could now be compared to and considered as landscape painting (*yi hua wei yuan*).[9] After that, more scholars began to talk about garden making as painting, which was well manifested in Ji Cheng *Yuanye, The Graft of Gardens*, where painterly ideas for garden design were repeatedly described. From here onwards, garden making based on painterly ideas (*huayi*) was widely accepted as the norm in the *literati* gardens of the Jiangnan region, and the painterly ideas of "mountain-and-water" became the objective and the principle of garden making. This self-conscious transition in the conception and appreciation of gardens was clearly materialized in the active practice of garden making in the time of the late Ming.

Behind this transformation were two shifts concerning the two aspects of the idea of *shiyi*. Firstly, for the status of the individual, late Ming witnessed a transition from a personalized perspective to a shared appreciation in garden making and garden culture; as it became more of a shared and social pursuit of art, it increasingly needed an established and externalized frame of reference for discussion and criticism. The Chinese landscape painting, which already had a system of theory long-since developed, can now be borrowed for the discussion on garden art and garden making. Secondly, there was also a shift in the making of natural scenery; in the increasingly social pursuit of garden making, how to observe nature and how to appreciate and arrange the form of a natural landscape became increasingly important. "Painterly ideas," widely understood and appreciated, could now lend a convenient frame of reference for discussion; to see a natural scene was now increasingly likened to the viewing of a painting or a "painterly surface" with its formal and compositional issues; a formal composition in garden making could even become its primary purpose. The sophisticated theory and practice in landscape painting for "mountain" and "water" could also lend practical suggestions on how to deal with complex arrangements of entities and sceneries in garden design. At the same time, economic prosperity and the profusion of gardens also led to the expansion of professional masters in garden design and making, providing a social basis for building complex sceneries with painterly ideas and images.

As garden making acquired increasingly a social and shared nature, and as the painting image was being increasingly adopted for the design of natural sceneries, "painterly ideas" replaced the "appropriate ideas." This had a great impact on the methods and techniques of garden making in the late Ming and after.

Changes in Method and Technique

Generally, before the late Ming, garden making was regarded as a private interest rather than a specialized art; and there were few discussions on garden-making methods, let alone theories or artistic standards. In such a situation, *literati* gardens in Jiangnan were normally built small in size and with a simple appearance. However, in late Ming, garden-making methods changed greatly with the establishment of "painterly ideas" as an aesthetic principle. Correspondingly, new methods came into being for arranging garden elements, such as "mountain," "water," "flowers," and "woods," and for architectural structures, as well as for arranging the overall garden.

1   *Compiling hills and rocks.* In the early gardens, when "appropriate ideas" (*shiyi*) were predominant, the profile of the hills did not need to follow actual forms; symbolic reference, associational imagination, and a simple collection of small-scale rocks were enough for projecting an "idea of mountains." Strange-looking rocks (especially rocks from the Taihu Lake) were employed for appreciation; the peculiar look of the stones was viewed as a reference to mountain peaks, and thus they acquired the name of "stone peaks." When these rocks were erected together, the various "peaks" formed an overall profile that was much appreciated. Into the late Ming dynasty, the compilation of artificial hills with rocks as a focus in garden making received the influence of the "painterly ideas" (*huayi*) most directly, and the focus on the forms of peaks of the rocks then shifted to the pursuit of a painterly image of the rocky hills as a whole. Following a certain landscape (or "mountain-and-water") painting style of a renowned painter, and a certain style of brush strokes using ink and water as applied on the painting, the compilation of rocks for making artificial hills acquired an entirely new look.

2   *Organizing water bodies.* Before the late Ming, garden ponds were often straight or rectangular in shape. The paradigm of "appropriate ideas" in the early times emphasized the inner world as triggered by viewing a certain scenery; in the case of using water bodies, what was important were the reflections mirroring the sky and the moving clouds, along with the floating lotus leaves and the swimming fish, whereas the shape of the bank was not important. Since straight banks were easy to make and maintain, the approach was widely adopted; historical records also reveal that many early masters constructed water bodies with straight lines. However, when we reach the late Ming, people were increasingly interested in the "painterly ideas"; the natural and irregular profile of the water bodies were increasingly appreciated, and ponds with straight lines were out of favor. Historical texts also recorded criticism of square ponds. Today, as existing gardens are mostly from late Ming or after, there are hardly any ponds with straight lines in the Jiangnan region.

3   *Laying out plants.* In early gardens with "appropriate ideas" dominating, plants and trees were organized in groups to create a natural atmosphere until the middle of the Ming dynasty. In the late Ming, the arrangement of shrubs and trees acquired new inspiration because of the "painterly ideas" being adopted; the early practice of planting trees (especially orchards) to form a grove was gradually replaced, and more focus was placed on appreciating the form of flowers and shrubs on their own or in an arranged formation. The appreciation focused not only on the color, fragrance, and posture of single plants, but also on the various contrasts in arranged formations, such as the straight and the curvy, the strong and the soft, the dense and the sparse, and the bright and the dim, in the lines, postures, textures, and colors of the plants placed together; the combination between trees and shrubs and between evergreen and deciduous plants was also carefully arranged. The matching of the plants with buildings, rocks, and water bodies was also carefully designed; for example, high trees with pavilions and covered walkways, branches with cliffs, and shrubs with shores of ponds, to form contrasting or harmonious views and scenes.

4   *Arranging built structures.* In early gardens with "appropriate ideas," scholarly gardens were small, and there were only a few buildings scattered around, with simpler forms. In the late Ming, because of the "painterly ideas," garden making shifted from an emphasis on the inner mind to a focus on external forms and a sensual experience of these formal dispositions.

For this purpose, buildings or built structures were more actively used; there were more of them, in higher density, and with more formal elaborations. Covered walkways were much more used, creating zigzag pathways and complex spatial forms. Combined with screening walls, doorways and widow openings, the twisting, covered passageways created spatial effects of separating, connecting, flowing around, filtering through, layering, and contrasting; these structures make a garden infinitely rich for someone to meander in and through.

Because of these specific techniques undergoing change, the overall profile of the gardens of Jiangnan in the late Ming was dramatically different from those of the past. Whether it was for "mountain-and-water" or for "flowers-and-woods," the building of views and scenes acquired a strong sense of formal arrangement inspired by landscape paintings. The abundant use of built structures in skillful manners had also made the gardens richer and more complex in spatial construction, with a greater spatial and visual effect. The ancient and natural "sparseness" was now replaced by an artistic "intricacy." The main features of the surviving gardens of Jiangnan that we see today are the result of the impact of these profound transformations.

Case Studies in the *Literati* Gardens of Jiangnan

There has been fairly good conservation of the scholar gardens of Jiangnan, as we can see today. Below, we analyze a few typical examples to show case-persistent characters and historical evolutions of the scholar gardens of the Jiangnan region.

Jichang Yuan Garden of Wuxi

Jichang Yuan is located to the east of Hui Mountain and northwest of Xi Mountain in the western suburb of Wuxi. In 1527, Qin Jin returned to his hometown after his retirement from office and made a garden here, where there was a convent for monks. He reshaped the earth mound, dredged the spring canal, and erected a few pavilions based on site topography; the garden scenery as a result was simple and serene. Later on, younger generations of the Qin made three major expansions and transformations.

The first attempt was made in 1560, when Qin Han and Qin Liang, father and son, rebuilt the garden according to renowned garden poem *Chi Shang Pian* (on the pond) by the poet Bai Juyi (772–846). They made a new pond, compiled rockeries, and built pavilions and bridges; the garden now had more views and scenes, and its water landscape was most impressive.

In 1592, Qin Yao made the second attempt to transform the garden. It took him seven years to complete. He adopted a poetic phrase from renowned writer-official Wang Xizhi (303–361) for a new name of the garden – Ji Chang Yuan, garden for fresh openness; Qin's friend Wang Zhideng (1535–1612) wrote a prose or "record" for the garden, and another friend, Song Maojin (?–1620), made an album of paintings depicting the scenes of the garden. The garden had 20 scenes, each with a title; though there were built structures (halls, pavilions, walkways, platforms), the views and scenes look natural, as stones, water bodies, and plants still dominated the landscape.

The last important change occurred in 1667–1668 when Qin Dezao and Qin Songling, father and son, invited professional garden master-builder Zhang Shi – nephew of Zhang Nanyuan (1587–1671), the best garden master of the time – to rebuild the garden. This work established the appearance of the garden as we see today. Later, the garden was visited by multiple famous people, and a large quantity of garden records, poems, and paintings were made and left for the following times, making the garden highly renowned throughout China. Kangxi

Emperor (1654–1722) visited the garden seven times in six tours to the Jiangnan region of China; this made the garden even more famous. Qinglong Emperor (1711–1799), following his grandfather Kangxi, not only visited the garden multiple times but also made a garden in Beijing, the Huishan Yuan (garden with Hui hills), later renamed Xiequ Yuan (garden of harmonious features), in the Summer Palace (Qingyi Yuan, later known later as Yihe Yuan), based on Jichang Yuan.

Today's Jichang Yuan is about one hectare in size, and its strongest feature is the main scene with hills and water bodies. Here in the garden, you find a linear pond called *jin hui yi* (a lake of brocade ripples) as the center of the landscape; to the southwest there are dense woods and groves, while to the east and the north there are built structures (Figure 6.1). This design of "mountain" and "water" departs greatly from normal residential gardens; its special effect is achieved by utilizing the topographic conditions fully, by organizing scenes and views of hills, and by matching elements carefully together.

When he started to create the garden, Qin Jin utilized existing topography to make artificial hills with a winding creek inside, running into a rectilinear pond; such an arrangement has been kept ever since. To improve the sceneries of the hills, Qin Han piled rocks to form artificial hills, whereas Qin Yao add more rocks to form caves. In Qin Songling's time, Zhang Shi made a big change by building a hillside slope with scattered rocks and earth mounds, as well as lush groves, as if they were all natural. The fluctuating hill ridge points to Xi Mountain and is parallel to Hu Mountain nearby. Seen from the pavilions and walkway galleries in the east, the artificial hill slope looks like it is part of Hui Mountain, extending into the garden. With small sceneries of hills and slopes inside connecting to large hills and mountains at a distance outside, the

Figure 6.1 Jichang Yuan Garden, Wuxi: "Mountain-and-water," a main view.
Source: © Gu Kai.

111

experience of the garden is much expanded. This is an excellent example of following natural conditions of the site for garden making.

For creating water scenery, again local natural conditions were fully utilized, as found in introducing an Erquan spring outside into the garden, to create an excellent water landscape. In Qin Jin's time, a creek with running water was made to create a view and sound effect; in Qin Han's time, a pond with winding shores was made; and in Qin Yao's time, water scenery became the most conspicuous feature of the garden, and the pond was greatly enlarged. With Zhang Shi's transformation, the vast water surface becomes the center of the entire garden for organizing various scenes; at the same time, layering of space is also much enriched and elaborate.

This is achieved with several arrangements: 1) the foot of the hills as shores stretch into the water here and there; 2) the Crane Step shores with leaning Chinese ash trees on this side of the bank are responding to a boathouse-like Pavilion of Understanding Fish on the other (east) side of the water, suddenly forming a narrow opening of the pond and creating a spatial drama between the wide and the narrow, the near and the far; 3) two spaces of the water surface are thus created, with the southern side small and the northern one wide and open, with a long Seven Star Bridge cutting across aslant; and 4) a covered bridge is also added across the northeast corner of the pond, blocking sights into that corner and creating a sense of water flowing endlessly into unknown distance. In this manner, space is made to block and to connect, to wind and to twist, creating a rich layering of multiple views and distances near and far.

The combining of "mountain" and "water" is also manifested in the Gully of Eight Sounds. This is an artificially created winding ravine made of yellow stones within the artificial hills of rocks, over some 30 meters long, being narrow and wide, winding and twisting, into and through the rocky hills, creating a sense of depth as if one is in deep and serene woods with the sound of flowing water. The musical effect of the sound of spring water running and flowing is much appreciated.

The presentation or revelation of the sceneries is closely associated with the placing of viewing points and associated built structures. The scenes of hills, apart from a Mei Ting (pavilion of plum flowers) hiding aside, are mainly on the western side, corresponding to the pavilions and walking galleries on the eastern side; these pavilions are placed near and far from the water, providing static views, whereas the walking galleries, as they shift and move around, provide dynamic observations. An open terrace in front the main hall, Jia Shu Tang (hall of fine trees), forms the major place for viewing; there, you can observe "mountain" and "water" together, as well as the layered views across the water surface. Several main paths converge at this point; here on the terrace, one can also view Xi Mountain and its Long Guan Pagoda (dragon light tower) on top at distance; this is an excellent example for the technique of borrowing views – distant views of hills and mountains outside the garden can suddenly be brought into the garden, expanding the spatial scope of the place immensely (Figure 6.2).

The building of "mountain" and "water" in Jichang Yuan has expressed the basic features of scholar gardens of Jiangnan. The core idea is the construction of hills and water bodies as sceneries of a natural landscape. Another key idea is to follow and take full advantage of the contingent site conditions, using their unique features as the basis for garden making. The introduction of Erquan Spring into the site to form ponds and streams and to borrow views of Xi and Hui Mountains from afar have made the garden a rich place in its endless extension or immensity. Master Zhang Shi's transformation has made the artificial hills, valleys, and streams feel as they would in a real mountain. Built structures are also important. The use of texts in tablets and couplets provides culture, elegance, and imagination. With these, this garden stands out as the leading example of all in the Jiangnan region.

Figure 6.2   Jichang Yuan Garden: Long Guan Pagoda and Xi Mountain at distance viewed from the front of the main hall.

Source: © Gu Kai.

The historical evolution of garden making in the region is also reflected in the shift in design for this garden. As in Jichang Yuan, the owner of the property did what he could in the careful design for new ideas of the time. If the first development, in the Jiajing era (1522–1566), was a progression from the simple to the complex, then the second change, in the Wanli era (1573–1620), manifested many new interests and inspirations (such as the covered walkway across the pond). When we reach the third major transformation, in the reign of Emperor Kangxi (1662–1722, the early Qing dynasty), the change was more radical; old ideas, even if they were about wonderful scenes, were discarded for new ones. This third transformation typically manifested a dramatic leap occurring in the late Ming dynasty, or from the Ming (1368–1644) to Qing dynasty (1644–1911), in the overall evolution of garden making in China and especially in the Jiangnan region.

Zhuozheng Yuan Garden of Suzhou

Suzhou turns out to be the core place for the development of the garden culture of the Jiangnan region in the Ming (1368–1644) and Qing (1644–1911) dynasties; it is here that we find the maximum concentration of these gardens. Of all of Suzhou's existing gardens today, Zhuozheng Yuan (garden of a humble administrator), located in the northeast of the city, is the largest in size, most renowned in popularity, and most complex in historical evolution.

In 1513, Wang Xianchen created Zhuozheng Yuan at the deserted site of an old Buddhist temple. The garden scenery was mainly made of water and plants, with buildings sparsely dotted about, and the overall landscape remained natural; Wen Zhengming (1470–1559), a leading figure in the *literati* culture of the region, wrote essays, made paintings, and composed poems about this garden. In the early years of Kangxi Emperor's reign (1662–1722), Wang Yongning, son-in-law of late Ming military general Wu Sangui (1612–78), acquired this garden; he added many structures and built artificial hills, making great changes and laying down the basic structure for the garden that we see today. After this, the garden changed hands and the site plot was reduced and expanded a few times; the buildings were also reconstructed and transformed throughout history. The garden that we see today was shaped in the late Qing dynasty.

Today, the middle section of the garden is where all the best scenes are located; here you can discern the features of the garden in its early days. This section is three acres in size, with a pond in the middle; built structures are found around the lake, many of which are alongside water, giving the garden the atmosphere of a water village.

In this section, the Hall of Distant Fragrance as the main building forms a central focus, from which scenes on all sides can be viewed and appreciated (Figure 6.3). To its immediate north, there is a terrace facing the pond and hills of rocks on the other shore of the pond, to be appreciated as a scenery in the hall or on the terrace; such a "hall–terrace–pond–hill" arrangement can be found in other gardens as well. The pond is quite open and wide and extends in an east–west direction; the scene of the hills, facing the pond, is arranged in the same direction. To the south, there is a smaller pond with rocks (Figure 6.4). To the southeast, the use of rocks, walls, buildings, and walking galleries forms an increasingly compact and serene series of small spaces (as one walks down to the southeast), creating rich spatial experiences with these minute "gardens-within-gardens." To the west is another series of small spaces forming a symmetry to those to the east; here water is the theme, and a series of quiet and deep water-courts and water scenes are arranged, forming a characteristic water garden well known in the region. Looking north from the pavilion of Xiao Cang Lang (small surging waves), one sees a covered Small Flying Rainbow Bridge and its reflection in the water; through the bridge and the reflection one sees further the Fragrant Island Building, the Pavilion with Lotus and Breezes on Four Sides, and a Hill View House, with their shrubs, step by step, as they stretch further into distance. The layered views and spaces create a sense of infinity.

Besides the central section outlined previously, there are other parts attached. For example, the Hall of Magnolia at the southwest corner forms a courtyard of flowers and rocks, with interesting views; the Pavilion of Green Ripples at the northeast corner provides side views

Figure 6.3   Zhuozheng Yuan Garden, Suzhou: Main hall with its northern terrace facing other shores over the pond.

Source: © Gu Kai.

Figure 6.4   Zhuozheng Yuan Garden: Small hills and a pond to the south of the main hall.

Source: © Gu Kai.

of the main pond with rocks; the Hill View House (storied) at the northwest provides broad views beyond and down to the garden and is connected to the Pavilion of Lotus and Breezes on Four Sides at a central point through a covered walking gallery (Winding Path with Willow Shades). On the east–west line, a "half-pavilion" on the eastern and western ends (Lean Against a Rainbow Pavilion and Opening to Another World, respectively) allows penetrating views into distant ends through layers of open structures; few other gardens in Jiangnan can match the composition of these deep views.

Since its inception, Zhuozheng Yuan has attracted attention near and far, because of its magnitude, its high quality, and the high regarded accorded to it. It is considered not only the very best of gardens of Suzhou, but also a classic for private gardens of Jiangnan and even of China. The central section, as the main body of the work, maintains a fine balance between density and sparsity, openness and seclusion, with built structures abundant but not overcrowding, and with the water bodies broadly open but also enriched with layered scenes of "mountain-and-water." These are unmatched by other gardens.

Wangshi Yuan Garden in Suzhou

This garden is located in the southeast of Suzhou and is built on the site of a ruined Garden of Hermit Fishermen from the Southern Song dynasty (1127–1279). The garden that we see today is a product from the middle of the Qing dynasty (1644–1911). In the reign of Qianlong Emperor (1735–96), Song Zongyuan built a villa here and named it "Wangshi Yuan" (garden of a master of nets, or garden of a fisherman). About 1794, Qu Yuancun bought this garden house and reorganized it thoroughly, turning it into a renowned garden in Suzhou. This garden now had eight themed and titled scenes; besides the main hall, Hillside House with Plum Blossoms and Iron Stones, the other seven scenes have all survived today. In 1876, Li Hongyi acquired the property and made changes to it – the water body and the buildings in the eastern section were demolished and replaced by new courtyard buildings, leaving the pond much reduced. The garden changed hands a few times after, whereas the landscape garden remained largely the same. Today, the garden maintains a pattern of residence in the east and garden in the west; it is 1.5 acres in total, of which 0.8 acres are for the garden; it is one of the smallest but most finely designed gardens of Suzhou (Figure 6.4).

Wangshi Yuan has a "main garden" and an "inner garden." The main garden is centered on the pond, to express ideas of water, fishing, fishermen in retreat; here buildings are placed around the pond. On the northern side, there are studies or book-rooms (for reading and storing books and artworks), namely Pavilion for Viewing Pine Trees and Fine Paintings, Study for Humbling One's Mind, and Study with Five Peaks; in the south, a group of buildings form a zigzagging courtyard for living and dining, which are named Pavilion with Small Hills and Osmanthus Trees, House of Harmony, and Chamber for Playing Zither; on the eastern edge, at the foot of tall walls for courtyard houses of the east, shrubs and rocks are placed with a "half pavilion," the Duck Hunting Gallery; and on the western side, a pavilion called Breeze Blowing with Moon Arriving is built upon rocks and into the pond, providing a place to view the moon (Figure 6.5). Beyond the western wall of the pond, there is another zone called "inner garden"; it has been renowned for its peonies in the past; a tiny pond with rocks and plants creates a serene inner space in this inner garden.

The main pond is about 0.1 acre in size, in roughly a square shape; the water body is kept as a unified whole, with small extensions only at the southeast and northwest corners. Without lotus planted in the water, the clear surface reflects sky and clouds as well as buildings and plants, making the garden fresh and open. The water bank is made up of yellow sands and stone pieces,

Figure 6.5 Wangshi Yuan Garden, Suzhou: Pavilions and covered walkways to the west of the pond.
Source: © Gu Kai.

with shores projecting in and out of the pond. The buildings, the covered walkways, and the plants, zigzagging here and there, all run around the pond in the middle. The whole garden is small, yet there are plenty of open pavilions; views are allowed across the open pond in various directions, for a rather free space in which rich, multiple, and shifting perspectives – like a Chinese painting – are accommodated.

This garden has a compact plan, delicate structures, balanced spatial scales, and layered views, creating a certain immensity and infinite reading within a small plot size. It is an excellent example of a small-scale Jiangnan garden from the late Qing dynasty with fine buildings and water scenery.

Conclusion

The scholar gardens of Jiangnan region embody the high achievement of the art of garden making of China. Its primary theme of a great natural world, its flexible method with local site conditions, its ingenious matching and mixing of nature and artificiality, and its rich cultural meaning for the educated *literati* or scholars have formed persistent characters of a special art of garden making, while over time historical evolutions also occurred, creating important features of new times in aesthetic reading and pragmatic construction – which must be appreciated in our current study of the gardens remaining today.

Notes

1 Tong Jun, *Jiangnan Yuanlin Zhi* (Record of Jiangnan Gardens), 2nd edition (Beijing: Zhongguo Jianzhu Gongye Chubanshe, 1987).
2 Liu Dunzhen, *Suzhou Gudian Yuanlin* (Chinese Classical Gardens of Suzhou) (Beijing: Zhongguo Jianzhu Gongye Chubanshe, 1979).

3 Ji Cheng, *Yuanye Zhushi* (Annotation on *Craft of Gardens*), ed. Chen Zhi, 2nd ed. (Beijing: Zhongguo Jianzhu Gongye Chubanshe, 1988).
4 Chen Zhi and Zhang Gongchi, eds., *Zhongguo Lidai Mingyuanji Xuanzhu* (Selected Annotation of Chinese Records of Famous Gardens) (Hefei: Anhui Kexue Jishu Chubanshe, 1983), 361.
5 David L. Hall and Roger T. Ames, "The Cosmological Setting of Chinese Gardens," *Studies in the History of Gardens & Designed Landscapes* 18, no. 3 (Autumn 1998): 178.
6 Tong, *Jiangnan*, 33.
7 Gu Kai, *Mingdai Jiangnan Yuanlin Yanjiu* (Gardens of the Jiangnan Region in the Late Ming Period) (Nanjing: Dongnan Daxue Chubanshe, 2010), 232.
8 Wang Yi, *Yuanlin yu Zhongguo Wenhua* (Garden Making and Chinese Culture) (Shanghai: Shanghai Renmin Chubanshe, 1990), 195.
9 Gu Kai, *Mingdai*, 212.

Bibliography

Chen Zhi and Zhang Gongchi, eds. *Zhongguo Lidai Mingyuanji Xuanzhu* (Selected Annotation of Chinese Records of Famous Gardens). Hefei: Anhui Kexue Jishu Chubanshe, 1983.

Gu Kai. *Mingdai Jiangnan Yuanlin Yanjiu* (Gardens of the Jiangnan Region in the Late Ming Period). Nanjing: Dongnan Daxue Chubanshe, 2010.

Hall, David L., and Roger T. Ames. "The Cosmological Setting of Chinese Gardens." *Studies in the History of Gardens & Designed Landscapes* 18, no. 3 (Autumn 1998): 178.

Ji Cheng. *Yuanye Zhushi* (Annotation on *Craft of Gardens*). Edited by Chen Zhi, 2nd ed. Beijing: Zhongguo Jianzhu Gongye Chubanshe, 1988.

Liu Dunzhen. *Suzhou Gudian Yuanlin* (Chinese Classical Gardens of Suzhou). Beijing: Zhongguo Jianzhu Gongye Chubanshe, 1979.

Pan Guxi, ed. *Jiangnan Lijing Yishu* (Landscape Architecture in the Jiangnan Region). Nanjing: Dongnan Daxue Chubanshe, 2001.

Tong Jun. *Jiangnan Yuanlin Zhi* (Record of Jiangnan Gardens), 2nd ed. Beijing: Zhongguo Jianzhu Gongye Chubanshe, 1987.

Wang Yi. *Yuanlin yu Zhongguo Wenhua* (Garden Making and Chinese Culture). Shanghai: Shanghai Renmin Chubanshe, 1990.

Glossary

Bai Juyi	白居易
Canglang (Ting)	沧浪（亭）
Changshu	常熟
Chi Shang Pian	池上篇
Dong Qichang	董其昌
Erquan Spring	二泉
ge	阁
Gui (family)	桂氏（家族）
guiyin	贵因
hua ke yuan	画可园
huamu	花木
Huanxiu Shanzhuang	环秀山庄
huayi	画意
Hui (mountain)	惠山
Huishan Yuan	惠山园
Ji Cheng	计成
Jia Shu Tang	嘉树堂
Jiajing	嘉靖

Jiangnan	江南
Jiangnan Yuanlin Zhi	江南园林志
Jiangsu (province)	江苏（省）
Jichang Yuan	寄畅园
jin hui yi	锦汇漪
jing zuo can zhong miao	静坐参众妙
jiushi qujing	就势取景
Kangxi	康熙
lang	廊
Li Hongyi	李鸿裔
Li Shangyin	李商隐
liu de ku he ting yu sheng	留得枯荷听雨声
Liu Dunzhen	刘敦桢
Liu Ting Ge	留听阁
Liu Yuan	留园
Mei Ting	梅亭
Ming (dynasty)	明（朝）
Nanjing	南京
Qianlong	乾隆
Qin (family)	秦氏（家族）
Qin Dezao	秦德藻
Qin Han	秦瀚
Qin Jin	秦金
Qin Liang	秦梁
Qin Songling	秦松龄
Qin Yao	秦燿
Qing (dynasty)	清（朝）
Qingyi Yuan	清漪园
Qu Yuancun	瞿远村
shan	山
Shanghai	上海
shanshui	山水
shiqing huayi	诗情画意
shiyi	适意
shui	水
shuimu	水木
Song (dynasty)	宋（朝）
Song Maojin	宋懋晋
Song Zongyuan	宋宗元
sui	随
Sui Han Ting	岁寒亭
Sui Yuan	随园
Sui Yuan Ji	随园记
suiyou renzuo	虽有人作
Suzhou	苏州
Suzhou Gudian Yuanlin	苏州古典园林
tai	台
Taihu (lake or rock)	太湖（太湖石）

tang	堂
Tang (dynasty)	唐（朝）
Tao Yuanming	陶渊明
ting	亭
Tong Jun	童寯
Wang Xianchen	王献臣
Wang Xizhi	王曦之
Wang Yongning	王永宁
Wang Zhideng	王穉（稚）登
Wangshi (Yuan)	网师（园）
Wanli	万历
wanzi tiankai	宛自天开
Wen Zhengming	文征明
wu chengfa	无成法
Wu Sangui	吴三桂
Wuxi	无锡
Xi (mountain)	锡山
Xiao Cang Lang	小沧浪
Xiequ Yuan	谐趣园
Yan Yuan	燕园
yi hua wei yuan	以画为园
Yi Yuan	怡园
Yihe Yuan	颐和园
yijing	意境
yin	因
yindi zhiyi	因地制宜
youruo ziran	有若自然
yuan ke hua	园可画
Yuan Mei	袁枚
Yuanye	园冶
yuanyou yiyi	园有异易
zhai	斋
Zhan Yuan	瞻园
Zhang Nanyuan	张南垣
Zhang Shi	张鉽
Zhejiang (province)	浙江（省）
Zheng Yuanxun	郑元勋
Zhuozheng (Yuan)	拙政（园）

7

CANG LANG PAVILION OF SUZHOU

Sentiment, Scenery, Aura, and Meaning

Chen Wei

In the treasures of classical Chinese literature, a popular poem goes: "The Cang Lang Water is clear enough to wash my hat tassels, though it could be turbid as well to wash my feet." This poem has passed on for generations, not just because of the beautiful lines, but also due to a spiritual purity and high taste revealed – a precious sense of noble detachment and resoluteness upheld by the Chinese literati comes into our mind immediately, purifying our mind and soul at the same time.

The story of the Chinese garden I am sharing with you is about a Cang Lang Pavilion whose ideas and meaning originated from this poem.

The birth of the Cang Lang Pavilion was about one thousand years after this poem, which was titled *Cang Lang Water*; the pavilion was built in Suzhou of the Song dynasty – a city praised in words like "there is heaven high above and there are Suzhou and Hangzhou on earth." Society in Suzhou then was peaceful and wealthy, and the environment was poetic and picturesque, while culturally it was a city of rich traditions; a disillusioned high official named Su Shunqin casually arrived here and settled down; a ruined old house and wild water winding around appeared to him to be a scene clear and beautiful; he purchased the place and built a garden there, and named it "Cang Lang Pavilion."

From then on, the garden went through transformations for a thousand years, but its charm remained. Today, Cang Lang Pavilion is a World Heritage site and the oldest of all heritage classical gardens of Suzhou. Space and time interact, and poetic thoughts are in our minds, when we observe the history of the pavilion. This garden has existed for one thousand years physically, yet, spiritually, it has carried a history of two millennia. To share a story about it may reveal a lot on the essence of classical Chinese gardens.

Episode One: The Water of Cang Lang

Cang Lang Water in Geography

In *Shu Yu Gong* (the book of Yu Gong), it says: a river has its source in Mount Bozhong in Shaanxi Province; its eastern stream was called Han River, and further east, the branch is called Cong Lang Water.

DOI: 10.4324/9781315851112-11

In *Yuan Liaofan Yugong Tushuo* (illustrated book of Yu Gong by Yuan Liaofan), it says that Cang Lang is Han River; it originates from a place called Nancang in the Changde county of Hunan Province; named as Cang River, it flows northeast to the west of Hanshou county; there it joins a river called Lang, and the joint stream, called Cang Lang Water, flows further north to Canggangkou before merging into the Long River.

Contained in *Shi Ji* (Records of the Grand Historian), there are three narratives of the Cang Lang Water:

1) It is a branch of the Han River, located in Jingzhou according to *Shu Kong Zhuan*; and is known as Cang Lang Water, also as Xia Water, which is effectively a branch of the Han according to *Zheng Xuan Shu Zhu*; also, Xia Water is an ancient name of Cang Lang Water as recorded in *Liu Chengzhi Yongchu Shanshui Ji*.

2) Cang Lang is the name of a place, located in the north of Jun county of Hubei Province; in *Shui Jing Zhu* (Commentary on the water classic), it says that there is an island in the Han River in the northwest of Wudang county that is called Cang Lang Zhou, and scholar Cai Shen agreed on this in his writings after. *Hu Wei Yu Gong Zhuizhi* said that Cang Lang is a name for place, not river. In yet another book, *Yan Ruoqu Sishu Shidi*, it is said the Cang Lang is not a river name, but a place name, and it refers to an island in the Han River some forty *li* northwest of Wudang county; this island is called Chan Lang, and therefore waters flowing from there on is called Cang Lang Water.

3) It is simply a section of the Han River. According to *Zhang Heng Nandu Fu*, Cang Lang is the moat that circulates the walls of a city; and scholar Li Shan further says that in the State of Chu, a square-shaped wall forms a city while the Han water around it forms a moat. From these we know that Cang Lang Water is part of the Han River.

Cang Lang Water in Classical Legends

The formation and course of the Cang Lang river through the physical geography of rivers and mountains across the ancient Chinese land is in itself perhaps not so important, but the poem and the song for the Cang Lang Water have bestowed upon this water course a special message and meaning.

Mengzi Li Lou Shang introduces a children's folk song that sings, "The Cang Lang Water is clear enough to wash my hat tassels, though it could be turbid as well to wash my feet."

Chu Ci: Yu Fu depicts that a smiling fisherman says nothing but sings the lines while pedaling the boat: "The Cang Lang Water is clear enough to wash my hat tassels, though it could be turbid as well to wash my feet."

Huan Yu Ji says that the fisherman washes his hat tassels where the Cang and the Lang waters join their currents; and here we have a narrative that integrates geographic and legendary information together.

In the reign of Qingxiang King of the Chu State, famous poet Qu Yuan found his second exile in the Yangtze River delta, that is, the Jiangnan region. When told of the Qin army having conquered the capital of the Chu state, the lamentation and indignation of losing one's homeland drove Qu sad and crazy; he wandered along the river; and his utterly miserable and gaunt look bewildered the fisherman who asked him why he looked this way. Qu replied, "I am clear alone in a world of turbid chaos, I am awake alone in a world where everyone is drunk." The fisherman advised Qu to take it easy and to follow the majority, and not to be alone in alertness with high mind. Yet Qu refused and wrote a poem, *Huaisha Fu* (Embracing the sand), before leaping into the river, drowning himself, to offer himself to fish rather than to be alive in a world of dirt and dust. At this, the fisherman paddled the boat, singing, "the Cang Lang Water is clear enough to wash my hat tassels, though it could be turbid as well to wash my feet."

This is not a mean legend, for it reveals a high mind and noble outlook, to be "*huaizhi bao-qing, duwu piexi*" – to cherish ideals and concerns, to the point of absolute loneliness, as written in Qu's poem. The meaning of Cang Lang Water is now gaining quality and richness.

Cang Lang Water in Literature

The Cang Lang Water to the east of the Han River is, from this moment on, forever a river clean and clear in the minds of the cultured. The disillusioned officials and scholars employed it for watering the field of their heart and cherished it as their spiritual home. In this sense, the high palace and the distant country had no meaning to them, and in "Cang Lang" alone did they find a world of rest, peace, and detachment. In classical Chinese literature, the poetries composed in the Tang and Song dynasties reveal this most clearly.[1]

The following nine excerpts are from the Tang dynasty (618–907):

> Nostalgia for wild mountains
> Associates with the pure cleanness of
> Cang Lang Water.
> Silent wildness betrays a
> Noble man's wisdom.
> (Wang Bo, *Shan Ting Xing Xu*)

> Seeing the decay of
> Whirling old trees,
> Adoring the remained
> Clean purity of
> Cang Lang Water.
> (Liu Changqing, *Ji Cui Xianggong Wen*)

> Born at the riverside
> But envy the Cang Lang Water.
> Yearning for a secluded life,
> But cannot resign from the
> Wealth of being an official.
> (Bai Juyi, *Chushou Hangzhou*)

> While offering sacrifice,
> Secluded weeds became afresh.
> Cang Lang Water
> Secures the presence of
> Hermits.
> (Luo Binwang, *Linquan Sishou*)

Words wrote out
Traces of birds,
Poems sang out the
Cry of monkeys.
Outside, Cang Lang Water
Reminding me of the cleanness
Like washing one's hat tassels with
Cang Lang Water.
    (Xu Hun, *Zeng Pei Chushi*)

Flat tides rest the boat,
Bright moon suggests a view
From the tall building.
Fishermen who sang the Song of
Cang Lang Water in old days
Now became grey haired.
    (Xu Hun, *Song Kehuan Jingzhu*)

Autumn water washes
Paddy rice reddish,
Cooking smoke betrays the
Smell of fish.
A heavy dinner
Lasts out the night,
A sound sleep
Awakes at dawn.
No court visit in the morning,
No garrison over the night.
Two of us,
Though passengers,
Feel like a boatman.
Being a prefecture official
Worrying about folks'
Livelihood and well-being.
Years' work expects
Accomplishments, before the
Retirement in three years.
Eventually, I would enjoy
Cang Lang Water,
Washing my hat tassels.
    (Bai Juyi, *Chuxia Jianghan*)

Writing festival scrolls in snow
For a riverside house.
Watching seasonal plough
From a deserted temple.
Outside, Cang Lang Water,

Came the mixed sound of
Wind and rain.
    (Qi Ji, *Jida Wuling*)

Further, the following are from the Song dynasty (960–1276):

Long hatred upon long lament,
Cutting hurt feeling into
A short poem.
Who dances for me?
Who listens to my cry?
I grow fragrant orchids over
Extended areas for years,
Eating simple and elegant.
Outside, Cang Lang Water
Washes clean my hat tassels.
A cup of wine at hand
Exceeds the fame after death,
Myriads of things in the world
Tells you a light hair may
Heavier than a huge mountain.
A permanent truth be:
Departure, most miserable,
When from a live soul,
Things, the happiest,
When making a new friend.
I no longer indulge in
Becoming wealthy, but would rather
Make friends with gulls.
    (Xin Qiji, *Shuidiao Getou*)

Legend fisherman named Ren,
Catches loads of fish with a hook
Feeding millions of folks.
Effort, how hard it be,
Hardly solve the entanglement of
Fishing lines.
Escaping fish, giant they are,
Growing fatter,
Fighting soldiers, hungry they were,
On the brink of death.
Helpless tiny fish
Swarm in the Cang Lang Water.
    (Wang Anshi, *Zayong Bashou*)

One became contaminated
Even in an environment

Meant to be clean.
Cang Lang Water,
Saint it be, saves no
Contaminated souls,
No matter how long
It washes.
> (Shi Huikai, *Jisong Bashiqi Shou*)

Folks wash their hat tassels
Using Cang Lang Water,
I love Cang Lang Water
Because of its cleanness.
Prosperous, a state is,
But plain living forges
Hard working spirit.
> (Liu Zai, *Song Fushou Gui*)

Fully contaminated, I am,
Found no Cang Lang Water
To clean my dirt.
Inviting friends to wine
At a shady retreat on a green hill,
Listening to the gurgling spring water,
Adoring the cleanness of stone plates.
> (Wang Yan, *Yong Yuanyun Da Xiushu*)

Sing a new song amid
Plum trees, attempting to
Melt the frozen buds.
I did this, in line with the
God of Spring.
No better, the latter generation,
Than the former.
Two of us, speechless.
Facing Cang Lang Water,
Drunken for helplessness.
> (Wu Wenying, *Jin Lvge: He Xinlang*)

Imperial learning builds
My fame,
Content with the integrity of
My senior years.
Elapses of time left
Luling Temple untouched.
Celebrating Cang Lang Water,
Plain regime regulates

Fine communities.
Criminal codes, available now
Bring virtue and fame to the village.
    (Wang Mai, *Wan Chongqing Chen Shilang*)

Heard old story about
Cang Lang Pavilion,
Never washed using
Cang Lang Water.
Sage's relics, though a
Spectacular scene.
A bridge flies across the
Wooden ends, and the immense
Water circles the rampart. The
Water course runs along the
Fortified posts and city walls for
Several miles,
Things, prosperous or decaying,
Though destined by Heaven,
Observation tells the future.
A world, protected by Heaven,
Heads for a course smooth.
Minister or gentleman,
Kind or noble,
Escapes no fate of
Literary inquisition.
Truth gave way to slander,
Weak bred lament.
Lines from a drunken genteel
Shining for a long time.
Keep in mind the
Harm done by smearing,
Respect the good
Bestowed by the virtue.
Folks in my vicinity
Sighed for an unfair world.
Toasting for victims,
Forgetting slander and praise.
Awakened drunkard
Fancy meeting an acquaintance
Departed for two decades.
Old, though he is,
Smart and wise remains.
Chatting came with
Indignation and lament.
Desiring to tear down the

Red curtain, opening up to the
Brightness, wind
Please send my words to lord.
　　　(Hu Cheng, *Cang Lang Yong*)

Qiu Yuan, a Song-dynasty poet, also shared his respect of the integrity of Cang Lang Water with a friend he was seeing off, saying that they shall always remember to purify themselves using Cang Lang Water, in a prose titled *Song Zhang Juchuan Gui Chongde*.

Li Hong, another poet of the Song, stated in a poem (*Bie Wuxing Congyou*) that he enjoyed washing his feet on his riverside trip using Cang Lang Water.

Fan Zhongyan, a reformist in the Northern Song dynasty, took the position of state councilor in 1043. He gathered other reformists, including Su Shunqin, a then-government official, to launch a reform campaign. Su then became a major target of conservatives and was removed from office. In the spring of 1045, Su brought his family to Suzhou, where he built the Cang Lang Pavilion. For this, Mei Yaochen, a realistic poet in the Northern Song dynasty, dedicated a poem (*Jiti Su Zimei Cang Lang Ting*) to the pavilion as follows:

Buying Cang Lang Water,
Living on Cang Lang Water,
Becoming
A Cang Lang guest,
An intimating Cang Lang partner,
An old Cang Lang man, then
A Cang Lang soul, forever.
Where is the Cang Lang Water?
The neighbour of Dongting Lake.

All the lines – praising, lamenting, hating, loving, crying – are built on sentiments of the high integrity symbolized in and by Cang Lang Water. A geographical water system generated numerous anecdotes and poetic lines about it, and the glorification reached its peak in the Song dynasty.

Episode Two: The Scenery of Cang Lang

Original Wilderness

After a southern boat tour, Su Shunqin one day set out to visit the prefecture school in Suzhou, where he saw lush grasses and trees in the east, with tall piers erected above the waters, which were unlikely scenes in a city area. He followed a waterside trail that led him to an open wasteland amid bamboo and miscellaneous flowers. The spacious wild land is bordered by water in three directions.[2] This is the Cang Lang Water that connects to the southern water system of the city of Suzhou (Figure 7.1).

The water comes from a wetland. According to *Wu Jun Zhi*, Annuals of Wu County, "The wetland has accumulated water over a dozen *mu*, and folks heaped up hills to retain water."[3] Another source, *Shilin Shihua*, says that "the wetland has an accumulated water surface over a dozen *mu*, and was flanked with small hills, where land and water meander and embraced each other."[4] All of these suggest a primary wilderness at an early stage of the Cang Lang Water.

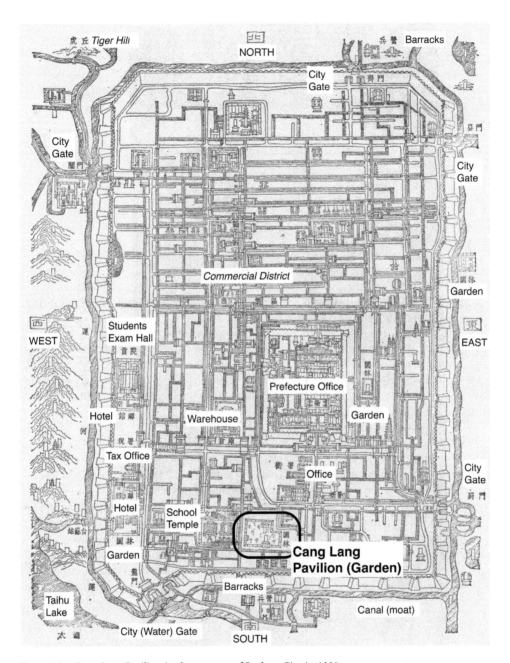

Figure 7.1   Cang Lang Pavilion in the context of Suzhou City in 1229.

Source: adapted from Liu Dunzhen, *Zhongguo Gudai Jianzhushi* (A history of ancient Chinese architecture), (Beijing: China Architecture & Building Press, 1980), 110, Figure 111–1; illustration now in public domain.

Overwhelming Terrains

As Su Shunqin said,

> the small bridge connects to an open space in the south, without the traces of civic residences. The space is surrounded and shaded by lush green trees. I asked an old man about the site. He replied: "This is a deserted garden of Sun Chengyou, a royal relative of the King of Wuyue State." A glimpse of the jagged terrains shows the ruin traces of an abandoned garden. I adored the site. After a survey back-and-forth, I bought the site for forty thousand bucks.[5]

The site apparently makes a desirable place for a garden, thanks to the timbered hills and circling waters.

Pavilion Riding the Cang Lang Water

Then,

> I erected a pavilion in the north, with a name of Cang Lang. The pavilion enjoys the view of bamboo in the south and water in the north. From the water, one saw endless bamboo forests further north. The clear stream and green bamboos, blended with the alternating presence of sunshine and shadow, would be particularly charming and entertaining in a day having breezes and moon.[6]

The presence of the pavilion secures a finishing touch to the garden, making it a beautiful Cang Lang landscape amid hills and waters that have survived hundreds of years.

It marks a laudable process from enlightened site selection to carving a limited geographic river system into an elegant, manmade garden. Upon the completion of the garden, the owner started to trace the meaning of Cang Lang Water:

> Wearing casual clothes, I often went to the pavilion by boat. There, I would play to my heart, forgetting to go back, or composing poems over a cup of wine, or making a loud shout towards the sky. Even a hermit would not come here. I only play with fish and birds for fun. My body got rest, and so did my mind, free from anxieties. What I heard and smelled are original, which led me to the truth of life. Looking back to the fame and interests I pursued in the past – balancing every detail of interests; what a shame comparing with the fun I enjoyed here! I'm removed from office. Fortunately, I got this nice place, resting my body and soul in the wildness. I'm saved from competing with others for personal gains. My mind and body finally found their roots, with an enriched heart and heartfelt laughs. I didn't forget why I'm dwelling here. I have freed myself from being vulgar.[7]

Episode Three: The Aura of Cang Lang

Cang Lang Pavilion or Big Cloud Temple

One hundred years later, the Cang Lang Pavilion built and named during the Song dynasty became a temple, where

> a Buddhist monk named Wen Ying lived at a Big Cloud hut surrounded by the water, or the Cang Lang Pavilion in Su's term . . . the Cang Lang Pavilion became a Big

Cloud Temple for the presence of monks. Having been Big Cloud Temple in name for two hundred years, monks managed to collect the details of the relics, and rebuilt the dreamland composed by Su, and eventually the Big Cloud was re-named Cang Lang Pavilion.[8]

Presumably, one hundred years after the Song dynasty and two hundred years before the Ming dynasty, the Cang Lang Pavilion was indeed the Big Cloud Temple for the monks in the Yuan dynasty.[9]

Monks' Adoration of Cang Lang Pavilion

As a monks' congregation place, the Cang Lang Pavilion survived the chaotic period of State of Wuyue, where

> warlords passed their wealth on to the following generations. Their descendants and relatives became rich and influential. They squandered money building luxurious residences and landscapes. Fortunately, the Cang Lang Pavilion built by Su was much respected and protected by monks. It explains why a long-famed scholar would not have been easily melted like ice. . . . The monks there were dubbed as Cang Lang Monks.[10]

Though a congregation place for monks, the Cang Lang Pavilion eventually won the dwellers' respect.

Lakes, Hills, and Mountains in Perspective

The garden witnessed ups and downs over hundreds of years. The city's height was growing. In the Ming dynasty,

> the change of dynasties brought up the changes to the royal court and streets. I used to climb up Mount Gusu, visiting a platform on the top, overlooking the vast expanse of five lakes and verdant green hills, and the residences and landscape gardens built in ancient time by Tai Bo and Yu Zhong, competed for by King He Lu of Wu and King Fu Chai of Wu, and operated by Zi Xu, Wen Zhong and Fan Li; unfortunately, there are all gone.[11]

The Cang Lang Pavilion, which initially sat by the water, may have possibly been moved to the top of the hill. This can be inferred from an essay on the rebuilding by Song Luo of the Qing dynasty, in *Chongxiu Cang Lang Ting Ji*:

> the pavilion resumed its old look, open and facing the mountain peaks southwest of the city. The pavilion's eaves were covered by verdant canopies, with old trees standing by. The pavilion looks as if it were built hundreds of years ago.[12]

What, then, is the aura in, of, and around Cang Lang and the pavilion? In a monk's mind, Cang Lang is not merely a pavilion, but an idea of water and of purity, as the name suggests. Scholars and the learned shared this thought as well. For example, in the Song dynasty, a monk named Shi Huikai offered the following words praising Cang Lang and the idea of integrity symbolized: "Cang Lang Water, saint it be, saves no contaminated souls, no matter how long it washes," demonstrating the literati and cultural mindset of a Buddhist priest.[13] The point is not the rise or fall of a temple or a pavilion; the point is that Cang Lang and its associated pavilion prevailed as a conceptual point of reference, though the pavilion itself may have eventually left the waterside and been relocated to the hilltop. There, it could "see" the five lakes and the mountain ranges and further afield; and the spiritual quality of the place was developed from an aura bestowed by nature.

Episode Four: The Meaning of Cang Lang

In the years that followed the reign of Emperor Kangxi,[14] the Cang Lang Pavilion was not only bestowed with the ancient-styled calligraphy of three Chinese characters – Cang Lang Ting – in an adorned name plate, but also expanded into a garden based on the sentiment, scenery, and aura developed around Cang Lang Water and the Pavilion. The process took a few steps.

In the Years of Emperor Kangxi (r. 1661–1722)

This period saw the building or rebuilding of the following five structures:

1) Cang Lang Ting (pavilion). It was "rebuilt and relocated to the hilltop, . . . with its initial look restored."[15] It should be a restoration of the pavilion of the Ming dynasty some one hundred years before.
2) Zi Sheng Xuan (veranda). "Along the northern foothills, facing slightly to the east, was built a small veranda titled *zi sheng* or self-restrain, a phrase adopted from Su's *Stories of Cang Lang Ting*."[1617]
3) Guan Yu Chu (waterside hall). This is a "three-bay structure, with earthen hills in the front, and clear streams in the rear. It is named after a fish-viewing place named by Su in his poem."[18]
4) Bu Qi Lang (covered walkway). This is located "in the south of the pavilion, with stone steps, winding railings, and is projected from a long wall like wings stretching, and is named after a path described as winding steps by Su Shunqin."[19]
5) Su Gong Ci (ancestral temple). "Walking out of the covered corridor, there stands a majestic hall; a wooden figure of Su Shunqin sits in the middle; and a name plate next to the door reads *Su Gong Ci* – temple dedicated to Master Su; this is actually an old building renovated into a new hall."[20]

These buildings and the surrounding scenery, as should be obvious by now, created a set of landscape architecture that is essentially about meaning and signification. There may be renovation, restoration, adopting ideas, transferring sentiment, shifting views, and worshiping ancestors; the garden and its structures may be newly built or renovated from the past. All these do not matter; what matters is that Cang Lang Pavilion embodies ideas.

In the Reign of Emperor Qianlong (r. 1735–1796)

During this time, two more structures were added:

1) Ming Huan Ci (ancestral temples for the famous). Officials, one after another, came here and renovated the garden, and they also built an ancestral hall for worshiping the masters.

2) Jian Xin Lou (new-building). To promote and celebrate the spirit of high officials out-posted to distant places, "a new building was completed by the side of the pavilion, for worshipping the lofty spirit of the officials."[21]

By now, Cang Lang Pavilion had been transformed into a state garden, with officials coming and going frequently. The meaning of "Cang Lang" had also shifted, from the idea of a noble detachment after disillusionment in the court to that of a celebrated honesty and dedication for officials serving at the court. Emperor Qianlong thus wrote a poem, *Ti Cang Lang Ting* (On the Cang Lang Pavilion), in which he said, "hereby I advise those who are visiting the garden, be diligent, hard-working, kind-hearted, to live up to your reputation." So, from this moment on, you are covered by "Cang Lang" anyway, whether you are in or out of the court, successful or failing, on the rise or in decline (Figure 7.2).

In the Years of Emperors Daoguang and Tongzhi (r. 1820–1850, 1861–1875)

Two more efforts were made in this period:

1) Ming Xian Ci (sage temple) with *keshi huaxiang* (inscription of drawings onto stone tablets). This is a temple that exhibits inscriptions of drawings of some five hundred famed historical figures of Suzhou, based on collections of rare drawings; named Sage Temple, it stands near the pavilion, offering a site for yearly worship."[22]

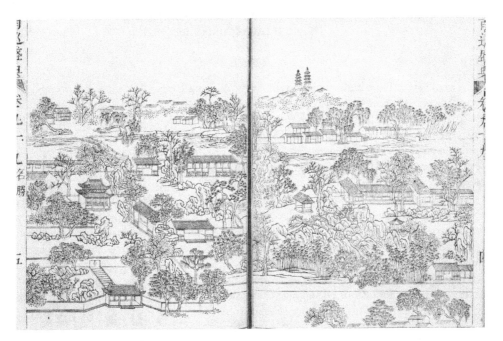

Figure 7.2 A drawing of Cang Lang Pavilion in *Nanxun Shengdian* (Festive scenes in the Emperor's southern inspection tour) made in the Qianlong reign (1735–96).

Source: From Gao Jin et al, comp. *Nanxun Shengdian* (Festival scenes in the Emperor's southern inspection tour) (Beijing: Imperial Court, 1771), vol. 99, p 4.

2) Ming Dao Tang (hall of knowing the truth). A court official Zhang Shusheng noted that "in 1863 when I visited the State of Wu, all properties public or private got looted. In August 1872, I was authorized to restore order there. I then ordered to have all the damaged premises repaired or reconstructed, including altars, temples, residences, palaces, students' examination halls, and government offices, the Pavilion was also included." Further, "A three-bay hall is also built on a dry highland in the rear of the Pavilion, and the hall is named Ming Dao Tang – hall of knowing the truth, following Su Shunqin's words – *guanting wuxie, zedao ziming*, or seeing and listening to all sides you will know the truth."[23]

By now, we can be assured of a few observations. First, Cang Lang Pavilion had become a state garden rebuilt and maintained through government efforts. Second, apart from maintaining the Pavilion, the rest of the constructions were quite free and flexible, and what was kept as essential was the spirit or the ideas and meaning of the creation made by Su Shunqin. "Of the constructions made today, only the Pavilion is at the hilltop and follows the initial practice of the Song dynasty; whereas the rest are made quite freely, without adhering to the old pattern of Su." Third, the fame of Cang Lang Pavilion has been passed on for generations, mainly to encourage people to remember and to learn from the good deeds of the sages and heroes.

> The beautiful Cang Lang Pavilion survived the passage of a thousand years, harvested the praise and adoration in numerous poetries and articles for the spiritual integrity it symbolized. The presence of Sage Temple inspires people to be clean, honest, and constructive.[24]

Sentiment, Scenery, Aura, and Meaning: Cang Lang Pavilion Through Interconnecting

Return

From a river stream to a built pavilion in the name of Cang Lang, what we have witnessed is a necessary progression from the geographical river and its associated legends into a sentiment that was gradually perfected and perfectly embodied in the Pavilion in the Tang and Song period; whereas development into the garden of Cang Lang has employed a specific urban-geographical condition and the aura it generates for the making of hills and rocks, temples and waters, for beautiful sceneries and a taste of wilderness and its poetic feeling, so that the meaning of purity in the water of Cang Lang could be alluded to and manifested.

In the process, subject and object have been interrelated and integrated and have settled deeply into the human mind, so that subjective ideas can be embodied in the rocks, hills, water, bamboo, or concrete activity. In a psychological and subjective sense, this is a "return", from a large realm to the small space and back into a large world. In a spatial-temporal perspective, we are witnessing a process from a distant Cang Lang river into a local Cang Lang stream that is now bestowed with meaning, and this meaning then refers back to a sentiment of Cang Lang developed over a thousand years; and here the garden of Cang Lang is employed to deliver this "return" across time and space, and in between sentiment and scenery.

Flexibility

The second thousand years after the Pavilion was built witnessed constant change in content, function, theme, scenery, and even viewing perspective – that this flexible change was allowed

Figure 7.3 Section: measured drawing of the garden of Cang Lang Pavilion in the 1950s.

Source: From Liu Dnzhen, *Suzhou Gudian Yuanlin* (Classical gardens in Suzhou), (Beijing: Zhongguo Jianzhu Gongye Chubanshe, 1979), p. 390; printed here with permission and courtesy of Liu Dunzhen's family.

or accommodated is the main reason why classical Chinese gardens have survived to today. This garden can be transferred to another owner, be purchased and sold,[25] tolerate the adding of new structures – as long as one retains the meaning and the theme of the Cang Lang Pavilion, all is fine (Figure 7.3).

When it was transitioned from a residential garden to a Buddhist temple, the aura and the meaning remained in the heart. Even the pavilion itself was relocated from waterside to hilltop, as the city was growing and views needed to be clear and open for a greater perspective; what was constant was the necessity of appreciating nature. As a record says, "when relaxing in a suburban place, the clear air and perspective purify my ears and eyes, and clean my heart and soul, so that I can manage worldly issues and material things well."[26]

Further, the function of a private garden can be changed to that of a state garden; whether favored and not in the imperial court, whether serving a disillusioned gentry or a governor in office, all is fine as long as all understand and appreciate the meaning of Cang Lang and the purity and integrity it symbolizes. As said in a poem,

> bright moon and fresh breeze can be purchased for four-thousand yuan today, yet the ancient poets and generals who resided the place, as inscribed in a pair of white marble walls, stood alone, with no one to match and compare.[27]

In the long process of transformation, what has remained unchanged is that crucial communication between scenery and aura (Figure 7.4).

Meaning

Sentiment, scenery, and aura – and a construct of meaning with aura, views, and feelings when nature and artifice are combined – are the highest state found in the Chinese classical gardens. This state, combined with human understanding and flexibility, creates *yiwei*, a touch and a flavor that has a message silently understood. The Cang Lang Pavilion of the Qing dynasty is a garden with such touch and message. By the Qing dynasty, the garden no longer had the clear theme and simple scenes of the Song time: it was complex and secular, and its content was also long, heavy, and multi-layered; as the French novelist Marcel Proust said, the recalled and reconstructed are forever richer and more meaningful then the original (*In Search of Lost Time*). The garden by this time had accumulated a lot and obtained a heaviness and multiplicity. For

Figure 7.4   Current condition of Cang Lang Pavilion on hilltop.
Source: © Chen Wei (2003).

example, the once aloof purity of the meaning of Cang Lang Water had now been blended with Ming Xian Ci and Ming Dao Tang – Sage Temple and Hall for Knowing the Truth, as well as stone tablets for the emperors and figures such as Liang Boluan. The secular content is evidenced in the couplets found in the garden: "Rains fill-up three springs making farmers happy, winds travel in four quarters making officials clean"; the atmosphere is also found in words like "bright light and brilliant color are gathering here," as inscribed in the garden.[28] Frankly, with scenery, function, and owner all changing over time, how can one retain a simple and pure theme on its own?

Locality

At a physical level, although Cang Lang Pavilion had undergone numerous changes within the garden boundary, the locality – constituted by relations with the water system of the city and the surrounding environment – remained not much changed. This is very important. This brings us back to the urban geography of Suzhou for Cang Lang Water and the context in which the garden was located. Comparing Suzhou city maps of the Qing and Song dynasties, together with certain descriptions, we will be able to understand the following points.

Firstly, a school temple was located nearby. The *Cang Lang Ting Ji* of the Song time says: "One day, passing by a county school, I looked east and found lush green woods, with rich water streams flowing around, quiet unlike a city place."[29] The *Ji Cang Lang Ting* of the Qing dynasty adds that "renting a boat, I went into the city through the Panmen Water City Gate, then docked and went into the county school to read, then immediately I arrived at the 'Cang Lang Pavilion' garden."[30]

Secondly, the site was quiet and spacious. The same essay of the Song also says, "the place was open and spacious, with no neighboring houses, and trees are everywhere, left or right, covering and folding."[31] The piece of the Qing cited then says:

> the landscape here is amazing, yet the buildings are dilapidated in a state of ruin; to the left and right is Jinshasi Temple and Jicaoan Temple . . . ; to the front it is Zhengyi Shuyuan College, and to the side there is Keyuan Garden, and these buildings are very fine and elegant.[32]

Thirdly, the site was surrounded with water. In the Song, it had "water on three sides";[33] in the Ming it was "surrounded by water";[34] and in the Qing it had "water around on four sides."[35]

We can therefore say that the water system – itself constant over a long time – around the garden is the primary condition that secures the birth of the meaning of Cang Lang Water and the historical inheritance of the Pavilion, whereas a cultural atmosphere around the place – rich and serene – adds further a special air and aura to the southern quarter of the water city Suzhou, delivering a purity to the meaning of the waters that has been flowing along and washing through ceaselessly (Figure 7.5).

In other words, the birth, transformation, protection, and carrying-forward of a garden is an interactive effort – with shared concern – between a humanist–spiritual intent and an

Figure 7.5   The outside of Cang Lang Pavilion as related to the water system of the city of Suzhou.
Source: © Chen Wei (2003).

urban landscape–architectural exercise, especially in the love and care of the mountain-water landscape.

The process of interactions between the sentiment, scenery, aura, and meaning of Cang Lang Pavilion should, perhaps, be clear by now: the longing for mountains and waters, the dialogue between sentiment and scenery, and the deep meaning expressed, as found in the essence of classical Chinese gardens, contain so much a love of will and spirit, a special understanding of the environment, and a humanist care of the bewitching entanglement between social reality and noble detachment.

The Cang Lang Pavilion has a history of one thousand years, but contains a story of two millennia. Herein we find a special charm so emblematic of the Chinese literati garden!

Notes

1 English translation of the poems used in this chapter has been made by the translator of this chapter, Zou Chunshen.
2 Su Shunqin, "Cang Lang Ting Ji (A story of Chan Lang Pavilion)," in *Wu Xian Zhi* (Annals of Wu County), vol. 39, *Minguo Wuxianzhi* (Annals of Wu County Edited in the Republican Era), comp. Cao Yunyuan and Li Genyuan (Nanjing: Jiangsu Guji Chubanshe, 1991), 617. The information is checked against another source: Gao Shixian and Wu Rulin, eds., *Suxue Shiji* (Collection of Su Shunqin's Writings), vol. 13 (Shanghai: Zhonghua Shuju, 1912), 3.
3 Fan Chengda, *Wu Jun Zhi* (Annals of Wu County) (Nanjing: Jiangsu Guji Chubanshe, 1986), 187. 1 mu = 0.6667 hectare.
4 Ye Mengde, *Shilin Shihua Jiaozhu* (Poems and Stories of a Stone Forest, Checked and Noted), checked and Noted by Lu Mingxin (Beijing: Remmin Wenxue Chubanshe, 2011), 10.
5 Su, "Cang Lang Ting Ji," 617; also checked with Gao and Wu, *Shuxue Shiji*, vol. 13, 3.
6 Su, "Cang Lang Ting Ji," 617; also checked with Gao and Wu, *Shuxue Shiji*, vol. 13, 3.
7 Su, "Cang Lang Ting Ji," 617; also checked with Gao and Wu, *Shuxue Shiji*, vol. 13, 3–4.
8 Gui Youguang, "Cang Lang Ting Ji (Stories of Cang Lang Pavilion)," in *Wu Xian Zhi* (Annals of Wu County), vol. 39, *Minguo Wuxianzhi* (Annals of Wu County Edited in the Republican Era), comp. Cao Yunyuan and Li Genyuan (Nanjing: Jiangsu Guji Chubanshe, 1991), 617.
9 Since the author Gui Youguan, who lived from 1506 to 1571, wrote this piece in his middle age, we can thus infer that the temple was built in the Yuan and lasted for two hundred years.
10 Gui, "Cang Lang Ting Ji," 617.
11 Gui, "Cang Lang Ting Ji," 617.
12 Song Luo, "Chongxiu Cang Lang Ting Ji (Rebuild of the Cang Lang Pavilion)," in *Wu Xian Zhi* (Annals of Wu County), vol. 39, *Minguo Wuxianzhi* (Annals of Wu County edited in the Republican era), comp. Cao Yunyuan and Li Genyuan (Nanjing: Jiangsu Guji Chubanshe, 1991), 617.
13 Gui, "Cang Lang Ting Ji," 617.
14 Zhang Shusheng, "Chongxiu Cang Lang Ting Ji (Rebuild of the Cang Lang Pavilion)," in *Wu Xian Zhi* (Annals of Wu County), vol. 39, *Minguo Wuxianzhi* (Annals of Wu County Edited in the Republican Era), comp. Cao Yunyuan and Li Genyuan (Nanjing: Jiangsu Guji Chubanshe, 1991), 618.
15 Song Luo says, "I'm earnestly planning the rebuilding, possibly on the top of the hill. I obtained ancient-styled characters of Cang Lang Pavilion for a name plate, making it look as old as it were before"; see Song, "Chongxiu Cang Lang Ting Ji," 617.
16 Su Shunqin's original statement was "shi weizhi suoyi zishen zhidao" (it was because I had not known the ways of self-restraint). See Song, "Chongxiu Cang Lang Ting Ji," 617.
17 Song, "Chongxiu Cang Lang Ting Ji," 617.
18 Song, "Chongxiu Cang Lang Ting Ji," 618.
19 Song, "Chongxiu Cang Lang Ting Ji," 618.
20 Song, "Chongxiu Cang Lang Ting Ji," 618.
21 Liang Zhangkui, "Chongxiu Cang Lang Ting Ji (Rebuild of the Cang Lang Pavilion)," in *Wu Xian Zhi* (Annals of Wu County), vol. 39, *Minguo Wuxianzhi* (Annals of Wu County Edited in the Republican Era), comp. Cao Yunyuan and Li Genyuan (Nanjing: Jiangsu Guji Chubanshe, 1991), 618.
22 Zhang, "Chongxiu Cang Lang Ting Ji," 618.
23 Zhang, "Chongxiu Cang Lang Ting Ji," 618.

24 Zhang, "Chongxiu Cang Lang Ting Ji," 618.
25 It is recorded that the site was a Qian family's garden; it was bought by Su Shunqin, who then built and named Cang Lang Pavilion; and, later on, it changed hands to Master Zhang and then to Han Shizhong. See Liang, "Chongxiu Cang Lang Ting Ji," 618.
26 Song, "Chongxiu Cang Lang Ting Ji," 618.
27 Chen Qiyuan, "Yongxianzhai Biji (Notes of a Lazy and Relaxing Residence)," in *Yongxianzhai Biji* (Notes of a Lazy and Relaxing Residence), vol. 5, by Chen Qiyuan (Beijing: Zhonghua Shuju, 1989), 112.
28 Guo, "Ji Cang Lang Ting (About Cang Lang Pavilion)," in *Guo Songtao Riji* (Diary of Guo Songtao), vol. 1, by Guo Songtao (Changsha: Hunan Renmin Chubanshe, 1981), 39.
29 Su, "Cang Lang Ting Ji," 617; also checked with Gao and Wu, *Shuxue Shiji*, vol. 13, 3.
30 Guo, "Ji Cang Lang Ting," 39.
31 Su, "Cang Lang Ting Ji," 617; also checked with Gao and Wu, *Shuxue Shiji*, vol. 13, 3.
32 Guo, "Ji Cang Lang Ting," 39–40.
33 The description is "there is a deserted land, about fifty and sixty xun on each side, with waters on three sides." See Su, "Cang Lang Ting Ji," 617; also checked with Gao and Wu, *Shuxue Shiji*, vol. 13, 3.
34 The text is as follows: "Monk Wen Ying resides in Big Cloud Temple, which is surrounded with waters; this actually was Su's Cang Lang Pavilion." See Gui, "Cang Lang Ting Ji," 617.
35 The description says, "the site has waters around on the four sides, and the landscape here is amazing." See Guo, "Ji Cang Lang Ting," 39.

Bibliography

Cao Yunyuan and Li Genyuan, comp. *Wu Xian Zhi* (Annals of Wu County), vol. 39, *Minguo Wuxianzhi* (Annals of Wu County Edited in the Republican Era). Nanjing: Jiangsu Guji Chubanshe, 1991.

Chen Congzhou, Jiang Qiting and Zhao Houjun, eds. *Yuan Zong* (Writings on Gardens). Shanghai: Tongji Daxue Chubanshe, 2004.

Chen Qiyuan. *Yongxianzhai Biji* (Notes of a Lazy and Relaxing Residence). Beijing: Zhonghua Shuju, 1989.

Fan Chengda. *Wu Jun Zhi* (Annals of Wu County). Nanjing: Jiangsu Guji Chubanshe, 1986.

Gao Shixian and Wu Rulin, eds. *Suxue Shiji* (Collection of Su Shunqin's writings). Shanghai: Zhonghua Shuju, 1912.

Gui Youguang. "Cang Lang Ting Ji (Stories of Cang Lang Pavilion)." In *Wu Xian Zhi* (Annals of Wu County), vol. 39, *Minguo Wuxianzhi* (Annals of Wu County Edited in the Republican Era), comp by Cao Yunyuan and Li Genyuan, 617. Nanjing: Jiangsu Guji Chubanshe, 1991.

Guo Songtao. *Guo Songtao Riji* (Diary of Guo Songtao). Changsha: Hunan Renmin Chubanshe, 1981.

Liang Zhangkui. "Chongxiu Cang Lang Ting Ji (Rebuild of the Cang Lang Pavilion)." In *Wu Xian Zhi* (Annals of Wu County), vol. 39, *Minguo Wuxianzhi* (Annals of Wu County Edited in the Republican Era), comp by Cao Yunyuan and Li Genyuan, 618. Nanjing: Jiangsu Guji Chubanshe, 1991.

Liu Dunzhen. *Suzhou Gudian Yuanlin* (Classical Gardens of Suzhou). Beijing: Zhongguo Jianzhu Gongye Chubanshe, 1979.

Song Luo. "Chongxiu Cang Lang Ting Ji (Rebuild of the Cang Lang Pavilion)." In *Wu Xian Zhi* (Annals of Wu County), vol. 39, *Minguo Wuxianzhi* (Annals of Wu County Edited in the Republican Era), comp by Cao Yunyuan and Li Genyuan, 617. Nanjing: Jiangsu Guji Chubanshe, 1991.

Su Shunqin. "Cang Lang Ting Ji (A story of Chan Lang Pavilion)." In *Wu Xian Zhi* (Annals of Wu County), vol. 39, *Minguo Wuxianzhi* (Annals of Wu County Edited in the Republican Era), comp by Cao Yunyuan and Li Genyuan, 617. Nanjing: Jiangsu Guji Chubanshe, 1991.

Tang Guizhang. *Tang Song Ci Jianshang Chidian* (Dictionary for Study and Appreciation of Poetries from the Tang and Song Dynasties). Nanjing: Jiangsu Guji Chubanshe, 1986.

Ye Mengde. *Shilin Shihua Jiaozhu* (Poems and Stories of a Stone Forest, Checked and Noted). Checked and noted by Lu Mingxin. Beijing: Renmin Wenxue Chubanshe, 2011.

Zhang Shusheng. "Chongxiu Cang Lang Ting Ji (Rebuild of the Cang Lang Pavilion)." In *Wu Xian Zhi* (Annals of Wu County), vol. 39, *Minguo Wuxianzhi* (Annals of Wu County Edited in the Republican Era), comp by Cao Yunyuan and Li Genyuan, 618. Nanjing: Jiangsu Guji Chubanshe, 1991.

Zhu Changwen. *Wujun Tujing Xuji* (Further Notes on the Illustrations and Writings of Wu County). Nanjing: Jiangsu Guji Chubanshe, 1986.

Glossary

Bai Juyi	白居易
Bie Wuxing Congyou	别吴兴从游
Bozhong (mountain)	嶓冢山
Bu Qi Lang	步碕廊
Cai Shen	蔡沈
Cang Lang	沧浪
Cang Lang Ting Ji	沧浪亭记
Cang Lang Ting	沧浪亭
Cang Lang Yong	沧浪咏
Cang Lang Zhou	沧浪洲
Canggangkou	沧港口
Changde (county)	常德县
Chongxiu Cang Lang Ting Ji	重修沧浪亭记
Chu (State of)	楚国
Chu Ci: Yu Fu	楚辞：渔夫
Chushou Hangzhou	出守杭州（长庆二年七月自中书舍人出守杭州，路次蓝溪）
Chuxia Jianghan	初下江汉（初下江汉，舟中作，寄两省给舍）
Dongting Lake	洞庭湖
Fan Li	范蠡
Fan Zhongyan	范仲淹
Fu Chai	夫差
Guan Yu Chu	观鱼处
guanting wuxie, zedao ziming	观听无邪，则道自明
Gusu	姑苏
Han (river)	汉水
Hangzhou	杭州
Hanshou county	汉寿县
He Lu	阖闾
Hu Cheng	胡珵
Hu Wei Yu Gong Zhuizhi	胡渭禹贡锥指
Huaisha Fu	怀沙赋
huaizhi baoqing, duwu piexi	怀质报情，独无匹兮
Huan Yu Ji	寰宇记
Hubei (province)	湖北省
Hunan (province)	湖南省
Ji Cang Lang Ting	记沧浪亭
Ji Cui Xianggong Wen	祭崔相公文
Jian Xin Lou	建新楼
Jicaoan Temple	结草庵
Jida Wuling	寄答武陵（寄答武陵幕中何支使二首）
Jin Lvge: He Xinlang	金缕歌：贺新郎（陪履斋先生沧浪看梅）
Jingzhou	荆州
Jinshasi Temple	金沙寺
Jisong Bashiqi Shou	偈颂八十七首
Jiti Su Zimei Cang Lang Ting	寄题苏子美沧浪亭

Jun county	均县
keshi huaxiang	刻石画像
Keyuan garden	可园
li	里
Li Hong	李洪
Li Shan	李善
Linquan Sishou	林泉四首（同辛簿简仰酬思玄上人林泉四首）
Liu Changqing	刘长卿
Liu Chengzhi Yongchu Shanshui Ji	刘澄之永初山水记
Liu Zai	刘宰
Luo Binwang	骆宾王
Mei Yaochen	梅尧臣
Mengzi Li Lou Shang	孟子离娄上
Ming Dao Tang	明道堂
Ming Huan Ci	名宦祠
Ming Xian Ci	名贤祠
Nancang	南沧
Panmen Water City Gate	盘门水城
Qi Ji	齐己
Qingxiang King	頃襄王
Qiu Yuan	仇远
Qu Yuan	屈原
Shaanxi	陕西省
Shan Ting Xing Xu	山亭兴序
Shi Huikai	释慧开
Shilin Shihua	石林诗话
Shu Kong Zhuan	书孔传
Shu Yu Gong	书禹贡
Shui Jing Zhu	水经注
Shuidiao Getou	水调歌头（水调歌头，壬子三山被召，陈端仁给事饮饯席）
Song (dynasty)	宋朝
Song Fushou Gui	送傅守归
Song Kehuan Jingzhu	送客还荆渚（将赴京师蒜山津送客还荆渚）
Song Luo	宋荦
Song Zhang Juchuan Gui Chongde	送张巨川归崇德
Su Gong Ci	苏公祠
Su Shunqin	苏舜钦
Sun Chengyou	孙承祐
Suzhou	苏州
Tai Bo	太伯
Ti Cang Lang Ting	题沧浪亭
Wan Chongqing Chen Shilang	挽崇清陈侍郎（五首其五）
Wang Anshi	王安石
Wang Bo	王勃
Wang Mai	王迈
Wang Yan	王炎
Wen Ying	文瑛

Wen Zhong	文种
Wu (state of)	吴（国）
Wu Jun Zhi	吴郡志
Wu Wenying	吴文英
Wudang county	武当县
Wuyue State	吴越国
Xia (waters)	夏水
Xin Qiji	辛弃疾
Xu Hun	许浑
Yan Ruoqu Sishu Shidi	阎若璩四书释地
yiwei	意味
Yong Yuanyun Da Xiushu	用元韵答秀叔
Yu Zhong	虞仲
Yuan Liaofan Yugong Tushuo	袁了凡禹贡图说
Zayong Bashou	杂咏八首
Zeng Pei Chushi	赠裴处士
Zhang Heng Nandu Fu	张衡南都赋
Zhang Shusheng	张树声
Zheng Xuan Shu Zhu	郑玄书注
Zhengyi Shuyuan College	正谊书院
Zi Sheng Xuan	自胜轩
Zi Xu	子胥

8

LANDSCAPE URBANISM

Urban–Rural Relations in Hangzhou of Southern Song China

Jia Xu

With considerable social, economic, political, and intellectual developments, the Song dynasty (960–1279) is one of the crucial formative periods of Chinese history. Yet, at the same time, this creative age was greatly impaired by tribal invasions from Inner Asia.[1] In 1126, the Jurchen army eventually obtained administrative control over the northern territory of the country, including its capital, Kaifeng; this drove the Song state into the south and, historically, divided the era into two halves, Northern Song (960–1127) and Southern Song (1127–1279). In 1138, Hangzhou, seat of a provincial capital in the Northern Song near the southeastern coast, was selected as the new capital. It was known as Xingzai (a temporary residence of the emperor) or Lin'an (a temporary abode) at that time.[2]

Most historical studies on Hangzhou as capital of the Southern Song fall into two groups, one on spatial, urban, and geographic characteristics, and the other to do with social and socio-economic development – the first revealed aspects of spatial construction, and the second development and urban social life.[3] Hangzhou's special situation contributes to the split in studying this city. On the one hand, as the south-most imperial capital city, it shared similarities with cities of the Lower Yangtze-River Region, where hilly topography contributed to irregular formal urban planning; on the other, as a successor of the Northern Song capital, Kaifeng, where society was increasingly open, Hangzhou of the south was also considered pragmatic, economy-oriented, and socially open (where state politics and military might were downplayed).[4] In this context, the spatial-morphological studies focused on Hangzhou as a hybrid city with a mixture of formal planning and informal natural conditions.[5] The social studies, on the other hand, concluded that it was an "open city" following the tradition of the Northern Song as a high period of commercialization and urbanization that put China ahead of other countries.[6]

Although there are some overlaps between these two camps, the approaches are basically either spatial or social, missing important areas in between. The interrelationship between natural landscape, urban space, and social life has not been investigated as a central focus. This is what this chapter aims to address. Focusing on certain sites in the scenic landscape that had fostered activities of urban life, this social-spatial analysis examines an urban–rural dynamic in Southern Song Hangzhou and explores how this relationship, if any, contributed to the lives of the population and the development of the city. Further, different from former studies, which are often based on archaeological discoveries and textual reading, this study is aided by a spatial reconstruction of the city using reconstructive mapping, through which sites and activities are

DOI: 10.4324/9781315851112-12

plotted and examined. By plotting sites, tracing trajectories of social life, and depicting abstract relationships and complex social phenomena in a more perceptible and tangible way, this study aims to be more rigorous and concrete.

Landscape and the City

The spatial configuration of Hangzhou as a dynastic capital was greatly restricted by its complex topography. Bordered by the Qiantang River to its east, the West Lake to its west, and the Phoenix Mountain to its south, Hangzhou was also encroached upon by the Wushan Hill in its southwestern corner and was characterized by the four major north–south arteries compressed to the east. As such, Hangzhou was an exceptionally unsatisfying capital city in terms of its formal layout. It had two sets of city walls, making two "cities," the Capital City and the Imperial City. The former was restricted to an irregular narrow plain, with mountain ridges acting as boundary to the southwest and with walls on other sides – these were pierced by a free-running road system with seven wall gates to the east, four to the west, and one each to the south and the north. The Imperial City was built at the southern end of the city and was partially hidden in the Phoenix Mountain. It drew most imperial institutions toward it, leaving the middle part of the Capital City mainly to noble residential compounds and major commercial facilities, and the northern part to residences and facilities for ordinary people (Figure 8.1).[7]

Yet, at the same time, the city fit well into its landscape. For institutions and compounds of royal authority, unsatisfying localities were explained by *fengshui* theory, with special relations with landscape. As the Dragon Mountain and the Phoenix Mountain both originated from one of the cradles of Daoism, the Tianmu Mountain, they were believed to be auspicious sites in Hangzhou. Thus, the Imperial City was partially constructed in the Phoenix Mountain, with the major southern wall gate facing its highest peak, as this was believed to be an arrangement reinforcing the authority of the imperial court. In the same token, the Altar of Heaven and Earth was built at the foot of the Dragon Mountain, the Imperial Ancestral Shrine was backed by the highest peak of the Wushan Hill, and most other important imperial institutions were situated at locations semi-surrounded and "protected" by the winding Wushan Hill (Figure 8.1).[8] Further, buildings in these compounds were either well integrated with natural surroundings or closely combined with manmade scenic landscapes. Inclusion of a garden was the most prominent feature in the Imperial City, and the Northern Imperial City, an extension outside. In the former, almost half of the area was designed as a rear garden, which was extravagant compared with the Outer Court composed of only two main palaces.[9] Similarly, the rare garden in the Northern Imperial City occupied more than two-thirds of the total area, which comprised a huge manmade lake and a lofty manmade hill imitating famous scenic spots in Hangzhou.[10] The official compound of Lin'anfu Prefecture was another significant example, comprising many halls, galleries, and pavilions used for recreation in a well-designed environment.[11]

Residential compounds and private gardens belonging to nobles and officials where daily activities and social gatherings unfolded were located in two types of places. The first were formal and urban and concentrated in the central areas inside the city where commercial activities were also found. The second were landscape-oriented, located in scarcely populated suburban or natural places with beautiful scenery; these include the various sides of the Phoenix and Wushan Hills within the city, the flat and hilly plains around the West Lake outside the city walls to the west, and the more hilly and mountainous sites further away to the south.[12]

Marketplaces and entertaining precincts accommodating commercial and leisure activities were concentrated along the Imperial Way in the city. Outside the city walls, they clustered near city gates and radiated out to suburban and rural areas with beautiful scenery

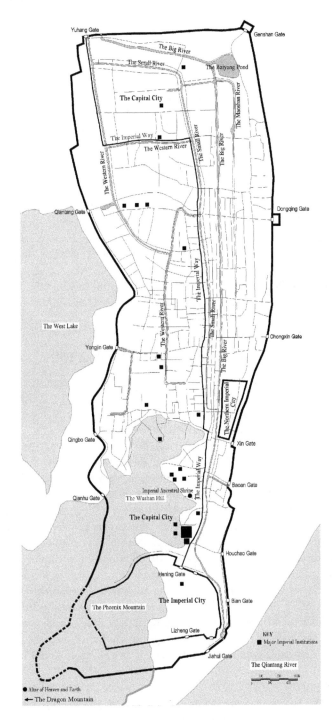

Figure 8.1   A general layout of Southern Song Hangzhou.

Source: © Jia Xu.

and convenient routes for travel. The West Lake was the biggest marketplace district, just outside the western city walls.[13] Further away, marketplaces were found in and around some 15 market towns along the main arteries, including the Qiantang River and the Grand Canal; some of these were highly urbanized and acted like satellite towns in a modern sense (Figure 8.2).[14]

For temples and religious grounds providing sites for social and religious activities, the majority (439 out of 550) were scattered among the scenic landscape in suburban and rural areas, which either dotted flat or hilly lands surrounding the West Lake, or congregated along the Qiantang River or on the Wulinshan Mountain further away from the city. This affinity to nature and landscape can be found in the distribution of the temples within the city as well. Almost one-fifth of these temples (21 out of 111) were situated in scenic landscape areas, and especially around the Wushan Hill (Figures 8.3 and 8.4).[15]

The above spatial observation shows that landscape, from designed gardens to natural land features such as hills, mountains, and the lake, was closely related to the urban fabric of the city and significantly overlapped with key civic centers for the social activities of the local population. It can be argued that although the irregular patterns of landscape restricted the use of a rigid and formalist planning of the city for an imperial capital, it was actively employed and played a great role in shaping the city and its life. The following two sections will concentrate on the urbanization of two "natural" sites, the Wushan Hill in the city and the West Lake outside the city, and will attempt to reveal the underlying forces of their transformations and the impact they asserted on the life of the local population.

Landscape in the City: The Wushan Hill

Transforming the Hill

The Wushan Hill was the only hill protruding into the Capital City. Following the tradition of constructing temples in serene mountains and hills, the local population had erected temples on it since antiquity (770–403 BC, known as Spring and Autumn period).[16] Before the Southern Song dynasty, there existed at least five temples on Wushan.[17] When the Southern Song court settled at the foot of the Phoenix Mountain to its south, with most of the imperial administrative institutions constructed along its eastern foot, the position of Wushan became pivotal and strategic to the Southern Song government. Although the hill became "imperial," it was only partially closed to the public. Several key positions were strictly guarded and forbidden, including the areas above the Imperial Ancestral Shrine and several important official temples.[18] Other sites, though guarded, were open to the public. In addition, some 12 temples – guarded but open to the population – were newly erected on the hill.[19]

Most of the temples were introduced onto the hill by the government (11 out of 17, or 9 out of 12 if we exclude the existing ones). The rest, which originated in local community, were lately recognized and promoted by the government, with an elevated social status or enlarged physical territory. It is clear that during the Southern Song, the transformation of Wushan as a major religious ground within the city walls was led and reinforced by the imperial authority.

This religious ground was closely related to imperial worship and official cult. At least two temples of the five existing ones and six of the twelve newly constructed ones were adopted by the government as official temples used for its own services, which were dedicated to major deities in Daoist or Buddhist traditions, enshrined guardian deities of the royal household, or employed as imperial bureaus for compiling calendar and promulgate decrees. Thus, the hill

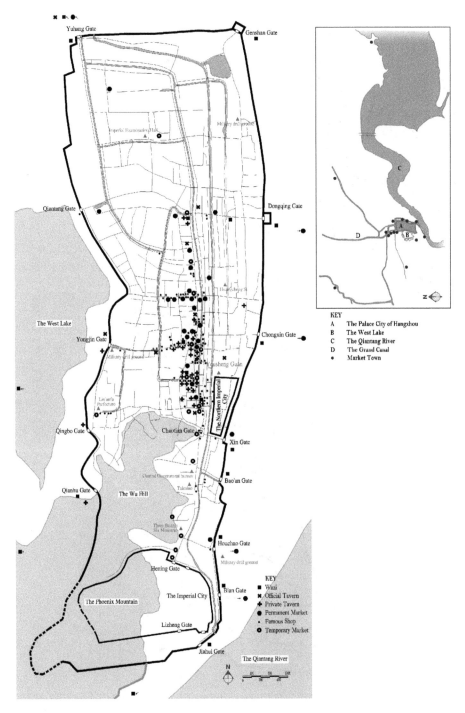

Figure 8.2 A layout of marketplaces and entertaining precincts in and around the city of Southern Song Hangzhou.

Source: © Jia Xu.

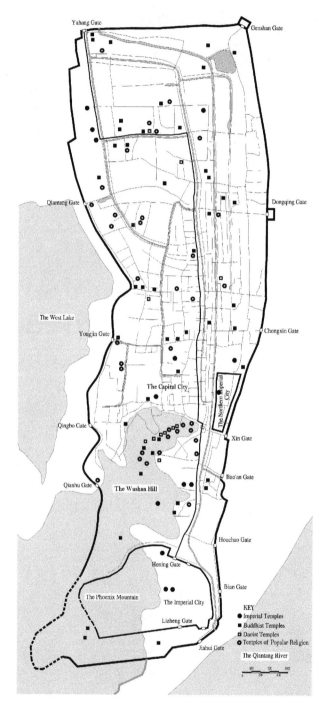

Figure 8.3 A layout of temples located in the city of Southern Song Hangzhou.
Source: © Jia Xu.

Figure 8.4 A layout of temples located around the city of Southern Song Hangzhou.
Source: © Jia Xu.

became a major site where the emperor and his officials prayed for the welfare of the court and dynasty on key dates of the year, such as summer and winter solstice, vernal equinox, and the birthdays of the royal family. By these efforts, the site on the hill was connected to the core of imperial worship centered on the Imperial Ancestral Shrine located at the eastern foot of the hill, and its status was greatly elevated.

However, the court did not monopolize this territory, instead sharing it with the public. Most temples were open to the local population for daily religious observances. At least two of the existing temples and three of the newly constructed ones were especially popular among the local residents, who held big public ceremonies around birthdays of the enshrined gods and deities. During these periods, the relevant temple compounds saw the participants involved in the most diverse activities. Daoist priests recited scriptures and played religious music. Local residents burned incenses and prayed for good fortune. Officials, eunuchs, and devoted wealthy families, organized in various associations, presented live horses and birds, and other treasures, while people of different occupational and professional associations offered their best products and performances as a gesture of gratitude.[20]

It should be noted that most of these five temples were already celebrated among the population before the Southern Song, and were now either extended on the former site or relocated to the hill. Two temples were enlarged with new buildings, for worshipping several supreme gods and deities.[21] Two were relocated to the hill from a celebrated temple of native religion outside the city walls, one a must-go place of burning incense around winter solstice and the other holding the largest congregation on the birthday of the temple god.[22] The rest was reconstructed at least six times after frequent conflagrations, instead of moving off the hill, to dispel inauspicious signs.[23] With these constructions, more customs and activities were introduced and more of the public was invited onto the hill by the royal authority. The Wushan Hill was thereby enlivened as a major site in the city for popular religion and secular life, besides being a key locality for imperial worship.

A Centripetal Civil Center Based on Temples and the Landscape

Although temples in imperial China had a tendency to be dispersed outside the city, the blooming of Wushan as a religious ground in the vicinity of the political core and urban center is not an exception. A similar social religious center based on Xiangguosi Temple was formed in the Northern Song capital, Kaifeng, in a similar locality where several commercial streets intersected not far from the Imperial City. As the most prominent temple in Kaifeng, Xiangguosi Temple served both the court as an imperial temple and the local population as a public urban space, with unremitting religious activities carried on in its main buildings and a big market opened daily in its central court.[24]

The popularity of both places among the local residents was inseparable from their closeness to the urban center of the city, which was convenient for attendants to congregate. Yet, compared to the religious ground in Kaifeng based on one temple, the consolidation in Hangzhou depended on various temples and was further propelled by the natural landscape of the site. Since hills and mountains were believed to be the most desirable environment for temple gods, temples set in such places were believed to please and assist spirits and immortals so that more miracles ensued. When the Southern Song imperial court moved to Hangzhou in crisis, the authority strategically utilized this relation between temples and locations to secure its governance[25] and constantly built temples of its own onto the Wushan Hill. Meanwhile, as it was also believed that the quantity of devotees gathered from society could bring about a supporting power of deities, the government actively constructed additional buildings to the existing compounds and initiated extra religious events to attract more local residents to the site.

Of course, none of the temples on Wushan on their own was comparable to Xiangguosi Temple of the Northern Song in scale, grandeur, and fame. Yet, as a whole, this religious ground in Hangzhou was more influential in the scope of impact, the diversity of the visiting population, the multiplicity of rites and ceremonies, and the excitement of the lively activities. By following the tradition of constructing temples among hills, and after the example of the Northern Song in treating temples as urban centers and in promoting public activities there, a thriving ground of religious and secular life more significant than its predecessor was formed on the Wushan Hill. It can be argued that it benefited from its special topography and location, and that Wushan continued its role as a focus of religious life and became a central civil center for the city in the Southern Song era.

Landscape Outside the City: The West Lake

Transforming the West Lake

As the only big water body outside Hangzhou, West Lake supplied fresh water to the city and was crucial to its sustenance and development. Since the Tang dynasty (618–907), local governors had continuously carried out various projects for maintaining the lake. In this process, efforts of beautifying the landscape emerged, initially as a by-product of the projects of dredging, and later as a major project on its own.

Following this tradition, the Southern Song government took a positive role in the construction and transformation of the lake. On the one hand, the court allocated funding every year for refurbishing buildings and planting flowers and bushes around the lake and on the Su Causeway.[26] On the other hand, the more privileged Southern Song governors, who were scholar-officials themselves, continuously added new buildings here and there in prominent locations around the lake. With their endeavors, the accessibility of the lake and its surrounding hills were improved by the introduction of a new causeway. The attractiveness and the amenity of the area was enhanced by the construction of new facilities such as lookouts and piers, teahouses and taverns, as well as shrines and resting pavilions.[27] As more scenic and historic spots came into being, a collection of "Ten Scenes of the West Lake" came into fame in the middle of the Southern Song.[28] Hence, the lake was "polished" into a delicate and cultivated landscape and won a great reputation across the whole country.

Meanwhile, under a culture highly appreciative of the beauty of landscape, the lake attracted more imperial and private gardens to it in the Southern Song period. Among gardens that had both their locations and names recorded in gazetteers and essays, 80 percent (59 out of 74) congregated in this area (Figure 8.5).[29] For example, private gardens owned by high-ranking officials were sited among the hills around the lake, gardens that belonged to eunuchs and palace attendants encircled the western part of the lake, while imperial gardens occupied the best place along the narrow eastern bank parallel to the western city wall.[30] With these compounds knitted into a vast landscape, this suburban area was no longer "forest-like without human habitation,"[31] but was instead populated with "endless high buildings and platforms stretching for miles."[32]

Along with the transformation of this area into a series of scenic spots and as an idyllic residential area, markets, taverns, teahouses, and restaurants were formed or opened by merchants who followed the outward flow of local residents seeking more opportunities. Around the lake, markets congregated along causeways and on bridges.[33] On the lake, some boats served as "mobile shops" carrying foods, wines, teas, fruits and other small items, while others as "mobile Wazi" (a pleasure ground or theatre) carrying actors, actresses, and prostitutes with, at times, gaming facilities.[34] On each of the two islands in the middle of the lake, there was a marvelous palace for weddings and social parties, according to Marco Polo.[35] As mentioned by Lu You (1125–1210) in a poem, the West Lake became a marketplace and an entertaining precinct during the Southern Song.[36]

With all the leisure, commercial, and entertaining facilities crowding onto and around the lake, more social activities took place in this constructed landscape. All year round, the lake offered enjoyment suitable for all members of society, such as an idyllic lifestyle imbued with the changing views of the four seasons for scholar-officials, commercial and entertaining activities carrying on endlessly for the general public, and the banquets and gatherings held by various social groups and societies in private gardens or natural surroundings. Because of a huge sum of money squandered in activities in this area, the lake was also nicknamed a "Gold Swallowing Pot" (*xiaojin guo*).[37]

Figure 8.5 A layout of imperial gardens and private gardens in and around the city of Southern Song Hangzhou.

Source: © Jia Xu.

The busy life on and around the lake reached its height around birthdays of certain deities and other public festivals such as the Lantern Festival, Cold-Food Day, Tomb-Sweeping Day, and Mid-autumn Festival. On these special occasions, the lake became a center for the hustle and bustle of the city. The Southern Song government also introduced new events and customs, such as dragon-boat racing and the rite of releasing captured animals, which further energized life around this area. On these special days, with night-curfew suspended and city gates open all day long, crowds of people flocked to view the spectacular scenes and enjoyed themselves on and around the lake.[38]

The active life of the population also attracted the involvement of the emperors, which in turn attracted more involvement of ordinary people. During the reign of Chunxi (1174–1189), when the country prospered during a period of peace, Emperor Gaozong and Xiaozong visited the lake several times in a dragon boat, followed by about a hundred boats of court officials, in a rare and spectacular scene. As normal life was permitted as usual, the whole area was covered with more crowds of people. The lake was covered with more boats, some of them rented by sightseers, some owned by traders selling things like fruits, wines, flowers, toys, lacquers, pearls, and hairpins, and other boats carrying performers such as musicians, singers, dancers, acrobats, and puppeteers.[39]

A Centrifugal "Urban" Center Based on Gardens and the Landscape

Hangzhou is not the only city with numerous private gardens constructed outside the city walls. The Northern Song capital, Kaifeng, is again another good example. It had five grand imperial gardens dominating areas outside of the four city gates in four directions. Also, other private gardens, more than a hundred in total, spread through the natural topography around the city, covering a vast area.[40]

Yet, in terms of spatial configuration, like most imperial capitals, gardens in Kaifeng were distributed around the city on a flat land without a specific center established. In Hangzhou, gardens instead took advantage of the special topography to the west of the city; there they congregated around the West Lake. With the engagement of the royal court and the management of the scholar-official, scenic spots, commercial shops, and entertaining facilities were constructed to connect isolated private gardens into a land of cultivated landscape. By adopting ideas, manners, and techniques usually used in traditional Chinese private garden design, the West Lake was transformed into a "public" garden for the enjoyment of the majority. In other words, the vast field surrounding Kaifeng remained as a suburban area while that around Hangzhou, especially places to its west, was constructed into a "park," in a sense comparable to the modern practice, though neither the concept nor the term existed then.

Moreover, in terms of social activity, the privileged owned the private gardens in Kaifeng, and these were open to the local population during the limited periods of time, mainly the key festivals. Although banquets and literary gatherings were held in these occasions, the major theme was limited to enjoying seasonal views of the landscape, and the main visitors were limited to the upper circle of society.[41] Yet, in Hangzhou, visitors were composed of people from all levels of society, including emperors and their household, high officials, scholar-officials, merchants, traders, and other ordinary people. They frequented the area to engage in all sorts of activities in their daily life, as well as special events linked to the area on a yearly cycle of dates and festivals. In this sense, with no social centers formed, the suburban area in Kaifeng was still subordinate to the city and its association with the city was comparatively weak. The area around the West Lake, however, formed a centrifugal "urban" center based on landscape, providing not only a busy urban life comparable to those inside the city, but also a tranquil and leisurely life in a natural surrounding hard to find in the city.

Conclusion: Urban–Rural Dynamic Emanating From the Landscape

The city of Southern Song Hangzhou was closely tied to its landscape. With its general layout greatly affected by the special natural textures of topography, Hangzhou deviated from the rules of formal urban planning for a typical Chinese imperial capital as prescribed in *Kaogongji*; these formal rules included square-ness, centrality of the Imperial City, an orthogonal structure in relation to the four cardinal points, and a chessboard-like road system – in other words, a strict geometric form with centrality, symmetry, and, implicitly or explicitly, a dominance of north over south.[42] Deviating from and even opposing these rules, the city of Hangzhou as imperial capital of the Southern Song nevertheless adapted itself well into the irregular and hilly topography and its natural surroundings, while maintaining some formality and symbolic features of a typical imperial capital, such as the Imperial Way, as a quasi-axis.

Within the city walls, patches of natural land were utilized and "created" in the form of gardens and courtyards, interlocking with governmental apparatus, residential compounds, and entertaining halls and pavilions on a small scale. On a larger scale, plots of aesthetically appealing places, such as the Wushan Hill, were well maintained and knitted into the texture of a crowded metropolitan environment. The embracing of these irregular natural features challenged an artificial and geometrical order that would normally be imposed in the tradition and introduced elements of rural areas into the built environment to enhance the attractiveness of the city. Beyond the city walls, numerous commercial and leisure facilities, and the gardens and temples as well, also animated the use of large zones of the country with landscape attractions, as we find around the West Lake. The construction of these buildings and compounds transformed the former desolate suburban area into a cultivated leisure zone associated closely with the life of the city. Hence, spatial combinations and juxtapositions of natural landscape and urban texture inside and outside the city walls had brought about not only an impact on the city and its life, but also a crucial connection and a blurring of the division between a populated city and a natural countryside.

Meanwhile, just as observed in the cases of the Wushan Hill and the West Lake, scenic sites offered rich opportunities for the flourishing of social activities and became a central locus of urban life. Based on the natural and hilly features in the city, constructions typically dispersed into the country, such as temples and gardens, were brought back into the heart of the city and enlivened it with rich and variegated social activities. Based on the leisure zones outside the city, the daily life of the population broke through the confinement of the city walls and propelled, as it were, the dispersion and extension of urban centers toward city edges and further afield. Hence, the exceptionally close ties found between the built fabric and the natural landscape, inside and outside of the city, contributed to not only the life and the economy of the city but also the social status of the suburban and country areas, turning them into an urban–rural hybrid infused with the rich and vital life of the city. During the Southern Song dynasty, the city of Hangzhou and its natural landscape inside and out developed into a reciprocal and mutually constructive relationship, through which a two-way influence and transformation was enacted.

We may argue that there is a "paradigm" in Southern Song Hangzhou, as it was endowed with the natural environment with scenic sites and the associated activities and vitalities. It is a new or different "paradigm" in the Chinese tradition; it is especially different from the dominant cases in the north represented by Chang'an of the Sui and Tang (581–907) and Beijing of the Ming and Qing dynasties (1420–1911). In this new model, there is a free combination of an artificial urban texture and a natural environment, as well as an extensive intermingling of the two at all scales both inside and outside of the city walls. The juxtaposition and coexistence of the two nourished an unprecedented and thriving metropolis and its social life. In other words, the embracing of the landscape and the rural condition in an urban layout – in a broad sense –

did not impair the development of urbanization and commercialization, but on the contrary strengthened these functions by providing a new space – either more suitable in the case of the religious hillsides or more accommodating in the case of the open and "participatory" lake – for urban life and social negotiation. Hence, as a model based on an urban–rural dynamic growing from the great potentials of the natural landscape, this new paradigm offers us new possibilities for acquiring an open and human-centric world that today's problematic modernization has promised, yet failed to provide.[43]

Notes

1 John King Fairbank, *China: A New History* (Cambridge, MA: The Belknap Press of Harvard University Press, 2006), 88.
2 Xu Jijun, *Nansong Ducheng Lin'an* (The Southern Song Capital Lin'an) (Hangzhou: Hangzhou Chubanshe, 2008), 1–3.
3 Major books on the spatial morphology of Southern Song Hangzhou include: Zhang Jing, *Liangsong Kaifeng Lin'an: Huangcheng Gongyuan Yanjiu* (Kaifeng and Lin'an in the Song Dynasty: A Research on the Palace City). Shandong: Qilu Shushe, 2008; Tang Junsheng, and Du Zhengxian. *Nansong Lin'ancheng Kaogu* (Archaeological Findings in the City of Southern Song Linan) (Hangzhou: Hangzhou Chubanshe, 2008); Fu Boxing and Hu Ansheng, *Nansong Huangcheng Tanmi* (The Secret of the Southern Song Imperial City) (Hangzhou: Hangzhou Chubanshe, 2002); Que Weimin, *Hangzhou Chengchi Ji Xihu Lishi Tushuo* (An Illustrated History of Hangzhou and the West Lake) (Hangzhou: Zhejiang Renmin Chubanshe, 2000). Major books on the social analysis of Southern Song life include: Xu Jijun, *Nansong Lin'an Shehui Shenghuo* (Social Life in Southern Song Lin'an) (Hangzhou: Hangzhou Chubanshe, 2011); Lin Zhengqiu, *Nansong Lin'an Wenhua* (Culture in Southern Song Lin'an) (Hangzhou: Hangzhou Chubanshe, 2010); Bao Chengzhi, *Nansong Lin'an Zongjiao* (Religion in Southern Song Lin'an) (Hangzhou: Hangzhou Chubanshe, 2010); Fang Jianxin, *Nansong Lin'an Dashiji* (Major Events in Southern Song Lin'an) (Hangzhou: Hangzhou Chubanshe, 2008); Jacques Gernet, *Daily Life in China: On the Eve of the Mongol Invasion 1250–1276* (Stanford, CA: Stanford University Press, 1962). Besides these books, many monographs on Southern Song Hangzhou that cover both realms have been published recently, including: Xin Wei, ed., *Nansongshi Ji Nansong Ducheng Lin'an Yanjiu Xu* (A Research on the History of the Southern Song Dynasty and Its Capital Lin'an, the Second Collection) (Beijing: Renmin Chubanshe, 2013); He Zhongli, ed., *Nansongshi Ji Nansong Ducheng Lin'an Yanjiu* (A Research on the History of the Southern Song Dynasty and Its Capital Lin'an) (Beijing: Renmin Chubanshe, 2009); Xu Jijun, *Nansong Ducheng Lin'an* (The Southern Song Capital Lin'an) (Hangzhou: Hangzhou Chubanshe, 2008); Lin Zhengqiu, *Nansong Ducheng Lin'an Yanjiu* (A Research on the Southern Song Capital Lin'an) (Beijing: Zhongguo Wenshi Chubanshe, 2006). The third group has touched on the spatial-physical and social-historical but remains at the level of factual description. The current research aims to move further to an analytical level. In addition, a recent piece has also combined historical study with conservation research: Jing Xie, "Disembodied Historicity: Southern Song Imperial Street in Hangzhou," in *Journal of the Society of Architectural Historians* 75, no. 2 (June 2016): 182–200.
4 K.A. Krache, Jr., "Sung K'ai-feng: Pragmatic Metropolis and Formalistic Capital," in *Crisis and Prosperity in Sung China*, ed. John Winthrop Haeger (Tucson: University of Arizona Press, 1975), 49.
5 F.W. Mote, "The Transformation of Nanjing, 1350–1400," in *The City in Late Imperial China*, ed. G. William Skinner (Stanford, CA: Stanford University Press, 1977), 107.
6 Valerie Hanson, *Changing Gods in Medieval China, 1127–1276* (Princeton, NJ: Princeton University Press, c.1990), 3; Hisayuki Miyakawa, "The Naito Hypothesis," in *Change in Sung China: Innovation or Revolution?*, ed. James T.C. Liu and Peter J. Golas (Lexington: Heath, 1969), 4–8; Chye Kiang Heng, *Cities of Aristocrats and Bureaucrats: The Development of Medieval Chinese* (Honolulu: University of Hawai'i Press, 1999), 205–209.
7 Guo Daiheng, *Zhongguo Gudai Jianzhushi* (The History of Chinese Imperial Architecture), vol. 3 (Beijing: Zhongguo Jiancai Gongye Chubanshe, 2003), 35–45.
8 They were constructed at three locales. The first locale was for the central governmental apparatus, the second was for the Imperial Ancestral Shrine, while the third was for the dormitory of high officials. Behind them, Chaotian Gate stood where the mountain ended. See Zhu Peng, "Nansong Guji Kao (A Record on the Relics of the Southern Song Dynasty)," in *Xihu Wenxian Jicheng* (A Collection of

Records on the West Lake), ed. Wang Guoping, vol. 2 (Hangzhou: Hangzhou Chubanshe, 2004), 441–442.

9 Zhang Jing, *Liangsong Kaifeng Lin'an: Huangcheng Gongyuan Yanjiu* (Kaifeng and Lin'an in the Song Dynasty: A Research on the Palace City) (Shandong: Qilu Shushe, 2008), fig S8 in Appendix.

10 Zhang, *Liangsong*, 175–183.

11 Qian Shuoyou, ed., *Xianchun Lin'an Zhi* (A Record of Lin'an in the Reign of Xianchun), vol. 15 (Hangzhou: Zhejiang Guji Chubanshe, 2012), 4354–4362; Ouyang Xiu, "Youmei Tang Ji (A Record on the Hall of Youmei Tang)," in *Xihu*, vol. 14, ed. Wang, 9–10.

12 Zhou Hui, *Qingbo Zazhi Jiaozhu* (An Annotated Records on Hangzhou,) ed. Liu Yongxiang (Beijing: Zhonghua Shuju, 1994), 117; Wu Zimu, "Mengliang Lu (A Record on a Dream)," in *Xihu*, ed. Wang, vol. 11, 150–152; vol. 12, 161; vol. 18, 232.

13 Zhu, "Nansong," 435.

14 Wu, "Mengliang," vol. 13, 172.

15 These maps are based on information mainly collected from Qian, *Xianchun*, vol. 13, 515–552; vol. 71–85, 2525–3150.

16 Ding Bing, *Wulin Fangxiang Zhi* (A Record of the Roads and Lanes in Wulin) (Hangzhou: Zhejiang Renmin Chubanshe, 2010), 415–417.

17 Information related to these temples is collected from Qian, *Xianchun*, vol. 71, 2528–2537; vol. 73, 2293–2294, 2581; vol. 75, 2655–2658, 2666 and Ding, *Wulin*, vol. 3, 352.

18 Ding, *Wulin*, vol. 2, 283, 557.

19 Information related to these temples is collected from Qian, *Xianchun*, vol. 13, 540–545; vol. 71, 2526–2527; vol. 73, 2584, 2594–2597, 2716–2720; vol. 75, 2667–2669; Ding, *Wulin*, vol. 2, 239–244, 568–575; vol. 3, 25–27, 80–81, 265, 271, 299; Wu, "Mengliang," vol. 1, 65; vol. 8, 128. Tian Rucheng, *Xihu Youlan Zhi* (A Tourist Record of the West Lake) (Shanghai: Shanghai Guji Chubanshe, 1998), vol. 12, 135, 139.

20 Wu, "Mengliang," vol. 1, 65–67; vol. 2, 73; vol. 19, 239; Zhou, "Wulin," vol. 3, 302.

21 Ding, *Wulin*, vol. 3, 271–272; Qian, *Xianchun*, vol. 75, 2667.

22 Ding, *Wulin*, vol. 3, 299; Qian, *Xianchun*, vol. 73, 2594–2595.

23 Ding, *Wulin*, vol. 2, 446–447.

24 Duan Yuming, *Xiangguosi Temple: Zai Tangsong Diguo de Shengshen yu Fansu Zhijian* (Xiangguosi Temple: Between the Sacred and the Secular of the Tang and Song Dynasties) (Chengdu: Bashu Shushe, 2004), 207, 243–245, 254–255.

25 This can be read from an inscription on a tablet in Ningshou Guan Temple, which has the following statement: "Ningshou Guan Temple is sited at the foot of the Qibao Hill (the hill of seven treasures, which is a peak of the Wushan Hill). Embraced by lake and river, the temple is well supported. With The Imperial Way in front and a lofty peak behind, its location is the best in the city. . . . This is the right place for a temple which is erected to assist and guard the country, suppress the surrounding countries and bring peace to the land. In this sense, the temple is incomparable by any other temples and altars." See Ding, *Wulin*, vol. 2, 575.

26 Wu, "Mengliang," vol. 1, 65.

27 Wu, "Mengliang," vol. 12, 160–164.

28 These scenes fell into five pairs, namely, "Twin Peaks Piercing the Cloud" and "Three Pools Mirroring the Moon," "Spring Dawn at the *Su* Causeway" and "Autumn Moon Over the Came Lake," "Orioles Singing in the Willows" and "Fish Viewing at Flower Harbor," "Lingering Snow on *Duan* Bridge" and "Evening Glow at *Leifeng* Pagoda," "Evening Bell Ringing at *Nanping* Hill" and "Breeze-Ruffled Lotus at *Quyuan* Garden." See Zhai Hao, *Hushan Bianlan* (An Overview of Scenic Spots), vol. 1 (Shanghai: Shanghai Guji Chubanshe, 1998), 27–29.

29 This map is based on information mainly collected from Zhou Mi, "Wulin Jiushi (Memories of Wulin)," in *Xihu*, ed. Wang, vol. 5, 326–349; Guanpu Naide Weng, "Ducheng Jisheng (A record on the prosperity of the capital)," in *Xihu*, ed. Wang, vol. 2, 41; and Qian, *Xianchun*, vol. 13, 553–560.

30 Wu, "Mengliang," vol. 12, 161–164.

31 Zhou, *Qingbo*, 117.

32 Lu Jiansan, *Xihu Bicong* (Essays on the West Lake) (Hangzhou: Zhejiang Renmin Chubanshe, 1981), 15.

33 Tian, *Xihu*, vol. 2, 17–18. Zhou, "Wulin," vol. 3, 299.

34 Wu, "Mengliang," vol. 12, 168–169.

35 Marco Polo, *The Travels of Marco Polo*, trans. Harmondsworth Ronald Latham (Middlesex: Penguin Books, 1958), 218.

36 Zhu, "Nansong," 435.
37 Zhou, "Wulin," vol. 3, 299–301.
38 Wu, "Mengliang," vol. 1, 66–67 and vol. 2, 71. Xihu Laoren, "Xihu Laoren Fansheng Lu (A Record on Prosperity by an Old Man of the West Lake)," in *Xihu*, ed. Wang, vol. 3, 11, 13; Zhou, "Wulin," vol. 3, 299–301.
39 Zhou, "Wulin," vol. 3, 299–300 and vol. 7, 379–380.
40 Zhou Baozhu, *Songdai Dongjing Yanjiu* (A Research on the Eastern Capital of the Southern Song Dynasty) (Kaifeng: Henan Daxue Chubanshe, 1992), 457.
41 Guo, *Zhongguo*, vol. 3, 31.
42 Jianfei Zhu, *Chinese Spatial Strategies: Imperial Beijing 1420–1911* (New York: Routledge, 2003), 33.
43 Jianfei Zhu, *Architecture of Modern China: A Historical Critique* (London: Routledge, 2009), 220–228.

Bibliography

Bao Chengzhi. *Nansong Lin'an Zongjiao* (Religion in Southern Song Lin'an). Hangzhou: Hangzhou Chubanshe, 2010.

Ding Bing. *Wulin Fangxiang Zhi* (A Record of the Roads and Lanes in Wulin). Hangzhou: Zhejiang Renmin Chubanshe, 1990.

Duan Yuming. *Xiangguosi Temple: Zai Tang Song Diguo de Shensheng yu Fansu Zhijian* (Xiangguosi Temple: Between the Sacred and the Secular of the Tang and Song Dynasties). Chengdu: Bashu Shushe, 2004.

Fang Jianxin. *Nansong Lin'an Dashiji* (Major Events in Southern Song Lin'an). Hangzhou: Hangzhou Chubanshe, 2008.

Guanpu Naide Weng. "Ducheng Jisheng (A Record on the Prosperity of the Capital)." In *Xihu Wenxian Jicheng* (A Collection of Records on the West Lake), edited by Wang Guoping, vol. 2, 25–45. Hangzhou: Hangzhou Chubanshe, 2004.

Guo Daiheng. *Zhongguo Gudai Jianzhushi* (The History of Chinese Imperial Architecture), vol. 3. Beijing: Zhongguo Jiancai Gongye Chubanshe, 2003.

Haeger, John Winthrop, ed. *Crisis and Prosperity in Sung China*. Tucson: University of Arizona Press, 1975.

Hanson, Valerie. *Changing Gods in Medieval China, 1127–1276*. Princeton, NJ: Princeton University Press, 1990.

He Zhongli, ed. *Nansongshi Ji Nansong Ducheng Lin'an Yanjiu* (A Research on the History of the Southern Song Dynasty and Its Capital Lin'an). Beijing: Renmin Chubanshe, 2009.

Heng, Chye Kiang. *Cities of Aristocrats and Bureaucrats: The Development of Medieval Chinese*. Honolulu: University of Hawai'i Press, 1999.

Krache, K.A., Jr. "Sung K'ai-feng: Pragmatic Metropolis and Formalistic Capital." In *Crisis and Prosperity in Sung China*, edited by John Winthrop Haeger, 49–78. Tucson: University of Arizona Press, 1975.

Lin Zhengqiu. *Nansong Ducheng Lin'an Yanjiu* (A Research on the Southern Song Capital Lin'an). Beijing: Zhongguo Wenshi Chubanshe, 2006.

———. *Nansong Lin'an Wenhua* (Culture in Southern Song Lin'an). Hangzhou: Hangzhou Chubanshe, 2010.

Liu, James T.C. and Peter J. Golas, eds. *Change in Sung China: Innovation or Revolution?*, Lexington: Heath, 1969.

Lu Jiansan. *Xihu Bicong* (Essays on the West Lake). Hangzhou: Zhejiang Renmin Chubanshe, 1981.

Miyakawa, Hisayuki. "The Naito Hypothesis." In *Change in Sung China: Innovation or Revolution?*, edited by James T.C. Liu and Peter J. Golas, 4–8. Lexington: Heath, 1969.

Mote, F.W. "The Transformation of Nanjing, 1350–1400." In *The City in Late Imperial China*, edited by Skinner, G. William, 101–154. Stanford, CA: Stanford University Press, 1977.

Ouyang Xiu. "Youmei Tang Ji (A Record on the Hall of Youmei Tang)." In *Xihu Wenxian Jicheng* (A Collection of Records on the West Lake), edited by Wang Guoping, vol. 14, 9–10. Hangzhou: Hangzhou Chubanshe, 2004.

Polo, Marco. *The Travels of Marco Polo*. Translated and with an introduction by Ronald Latham. Harmondsworth, Middlesex: Penguin Books, 1958.

Qian Shuoyou, ed. *Xianchun Lin'an Zhi* (A Record of Lin'an in the Reign of Xianchun). Hangzhou: Zhejiang Guji Chubanshe, 2012.

Skinner, G. William, ed. *The City in Late Imperial China*. Stanford, CA: Stanford University Press, 1977.

Tang Junsheng and Du Zhengxian. *Nansong Lin'ancheng Kaogu* (Archaeological Findings in the City of Southern Song Lin'an). Hangzhou: Hangzhou Chubanshe, 2008.

Tian Rucheng. *Xihu Youlan Zhi* (A Tourist Record of the West Lake). Shanghai: Shanghai Guji Chubanshe, 1998.

Wang Guoping, ed. *Xihu Wenxian Jicheng* (A Collection of Records on the West Lake). Hangzhou: Hangzhou Chubanshe, 2004.

Wushan Zimu. "Mengliang Lu (A Record on a Dream)." In *Xihu Wenxian Jicheng* (A Collection of Records on the West Lake), edited by Wang Guoping, vol. 2, 47–254. Hangzhou: Hangzhou Chubanshe, 2004.

Xie, Jing. "Disembodied Historicity: Southern Song Imperial Street in Hangzhou." *Journal of the Society of Architectural Historians* 75, no. 2 (June 2016): 182–200.

Xihu Laoren. "Xihu Laoren Fansheng Lu (A Record on Prosperity by an Old Man of the West Lake)." In *Xihu Wenxian Jicheng* (A Collection of Records on the West Lake), edited by Wang Guoping, vol. 2–3, 1–23. Hangzhou: Hangzhou Chubanshe, 2004.

Xin Wei, ed. *Nansongshi Ji Nansong Ducheng Lin'an Yanjiu Xu* (A Research on the History of the Southern Song Dynasty and Its Capital Lin'an, the Second Collection). Beijing: Renmin Chubanshe, 2013.

Xu Jijun. *Nansong Ducheng Lin'an* (The Southern Song Capital Lin'an). Hangzhou: Hangzhou Chubanshe, 2008.

———. *Nansong Lin'an Shehui Shenghuo* (Social Life in Southern Song Lin'an). Hangzhou: Hangzhou Chubanshe, 2011.

Zhai Hao. *Hushan Bianlan* (An Overview of Scenic Spots). Shanghai: Shanghai Guji Chubanshe, 1998.

Zhang Jing. *Liangsong Kaifeng Lin'an: Huangcheng Gongyuan Yanjiu* (Kaifeng and Lin'an in the Song Dynasty: A Research on the Palace City). Shandong: Qilu Shushe, 2008.

Zhou Baozhu. *Songdai Dongjing Yanjiu* (A Research on the Eastern Capital of the Northern Song Dynasty). Kaifeng: Henan Daxue Chubanshe, 1992.

Zhou Hui. *Qingbo Zazhi Jiaozhu* (An Annotated Records on Hangzhou). Edited by Liu Yongxiang. Beijing: Zhonghua Shuju, 1994.

Zhou Mi. "Wulin Jiushi (Memories of Wulin)." In *Xihu Wenxian Jicheng* (A Collection of Records on the West Lake), edited by Wang Guoping, vol. 2, 255–426. Hangzhou: Hangzhou Chubanshe, 2004.

Zhu, Jianfei. *Chinese Spatial Strategies: Imperial Beijing 1420–1911*. New York: Routledge, 2003.

———. *Architecture of Modern China: A Historical Critique*. London: Routledge, 2009.

Zhu Peng. "Nansong Guji Kao (A Record on the Relics of the Southern Song Dynasty)." In *Xihu Wenxian Jicheng* (A Collection of Records on the West Lake), edited by Wang Guoping, vol. 2, 427–502. Hangzhou: Hangzhou Chubanshe, 2004.

Glossary

Chunxi	淳熙
fengshui	风水
Gaozong	高宗
Hangzhou	杭州
Kaogongji	考工记
Lin'an	临安
Lin'an Fu (prefecture)	临安府
Lu You	陆游
Qiantang River	钱塘江
Su Causeway	苏堤
Tianmu (mountain)	天目山
Wazi	瓦子
Wulinshan (mountain)	武林山
Wushan (hill)	吴山
Xiangguosi (temple)	相国寺
xiaojin guo	销金锅
Xiaozong	孝宗
Xingzai	行在

9

CONFUCIAN AUTHORITY

Analysis of School-Temples at Imperial Academy of Beijing

Shen Yang

In ancient China, "Confucian orthodox tradition" (*daotong*) referred specifically to the passing down of correct Confucian teaching (*dao*) from one generation to the next. The practice can also be understood as endeavors to secure some autonomy of education and learning without political interference, yet in reality this was hardly ever achieved under the authoritarian rule of the emperor. In the practical teaching of Confucian classics, educational institutions were established, and the most material embodiment of the institutions were the "school-temples" (*miaoxue*). School-temples were official schools where Confucian classics were taught – schools to which Confucian temples were also attached, allowing ritual tributes to be paid to Confucius and other prominent scholars of Confucian learning. Students in school-temples were expected not only to study the classics but also to worship the ancient sages. Learning of knowledge and cultivating of personality were combined; rational study and spiritual worshipping were conjoined – a culture that was rather oriental in essence.

In ancient China, authoritarian political dynasties came and went, yet Confucian orthodoxy – as based on the thought of Confucius – remained supreme and highly respected. When Confucius was regarded as "the teacher of all emperors," a special combination of Confucian orthodoxy and imperial power was fully revealed. At this point, we may inquire as to the relations between them; did orthodoxy teaching survive because it relied on imperial power, or did the authority remain because it relied on Confucian teaching? It is an important historical question worthy of reflection.

To respond to this question with an architectural perspective, it is important to conduct an analysis on the spatial construction of school-temples. This chapter examines the Imperial Academy – known as Guozijian – of Beijing.[1] This case is important on two grounds. Firstly, Guozijian was the highest-ranking educational institution and scholarly academy of imperial China; it was the largest in scale, and most supreme in hierarchy, of all colleges or academies of the empire; it represented all school-temples in the country. Secondly, the practice of combining a school and a temple within one institution originated in the capital city, Jiankang (today's Nanjing) of Eastern Jin dynasty (266–420),[2] was established as a system in the Tang and Song dynasties (618–1279), and matured in the last three dynasties – Yuan, Ming, and Qing (dominated each by Mongolian, Han, and Manchurian ethnic groups respectively, 1279–1911) – whose capital and Imperial Academy were all located in Beijing. Here in Beijing over the last three dynasties, the school-temple evolved into a mature architectural system; yet, due to ethnic

DOI: 10.4324/9781315851112-13

and cultural difference between these three authorities, the relative importance of school and temple buildings shifted over time, creating a diachronic differentiation and a base for comparison across these periods.

Establishing in the Yuan: Temple Over School

In 1271, Yuan dynasty established its capital, Dadu, where the city of Zhongdu of Jin dynasty (1115–1234) was located (where Beijing is located today). There was already a Confucian temple in the southern part of the city built in the Jin dynasty, revealing an intention to revive the school-temple practice. But later on, the school building with the temple was not intended to use the temple much for Confucius worship or Confucian learning; rather, it relied on the Taoist priests of the Jin tradition. The school or the academy was simply a language and translation institution, but it formally adopted the Han Chinese practice of building schools with temples, so that the authority appeared more acceptable to the Chinese who were the majority in the empire – as a political gimmick.[3] After that, Confucians and Taoists entered a heated debate on the management and property rights of the school and the temple, until the Yuan emperor Kublai Kahn adjudicated a win for the Confucians, which considerably excited the Confucian society.

The Imperial Academy of the Yuan was very special; it changed the practice of one academy managing several departments into a new practice of three parallel academies – "Mongolian Academy," "Imperial Academy," and "Huihui (Chinese-Muslin) Academy," revealing an ethnic complexity. But the Imperial Academy itself, the center of Confucian learning, was not built until some ten years after the Mongolian Academy was built, with the mounting pressure of Confucian scholar-officials of various ethnic origins – Han (Chinese), Mongolian, and Chinese-Muslin (Huihui).[4] After decades of development, the city of Dadu witnessed a filling up and densification of its middle and southern parts – as occupied increasingly by commoners' houses; as the Imperial Academy required a lot of space and might later expand, it was placed in the northern part and was closer to the east, on a spacious location with a plot size of 90 *mu* (1 *mu* = 0.0667 hectares), subdivided into 50 *mu* for the temple and 40 *mu* for the school.[5] Although it was planned for the school to be built first, in reality the temple structures were completed first, and the funding for school buildings was much delayed; the school was finally completed five years after the temple, revealing a political culture of privileging worship over learning.

Both temple and school compounds faced the street. The Confucian Temple here adopted the layout of the Temple of Confucius in Qufu – hometown of Confucius, more specifically the section from Dachengmen Gate to Dachengdian Hall; the main hall in Beijing was similar in scale to that in Qufu. The school, to the west of the Temple, had spacious courtyards; teachers and teacher-officials' residences and their lecture halls were located in the middle, whereas to the east and west of the compound were the six departments for teaching and studying. The compound had many different kinds of trees and the green landscape was well organized with rich layers; the environment was elegant and serene, and facilities for staff and students – living, dining, and bathing – were fully provided.[6] Later on, within the compound, Chongwenge Building (a library) was added to house classics and rare books, in a scale and style similar to the Kuiwenge Building (library) built in the Ming dynasty in Qufu's Temple of Confucius (23.35 m high, 17.62 m north to south, and 30.10 m east to west). Grand and beautiful, the new library added glory to the Confucian School of Beijing.[7]

Regarding the ritual staff in the Confucian Temple, the joining of the towering figure of Confucian scholar Xu Heng (1209–1281) revealed the authority's strong promotion of neo-Confucianism.[8] Neo-Confucianism, or the Cheng-Zhu school of Confucian thought, grew into the dominant state ideology in the middle of the Yuan dynasty (1279–1368); the sages and masters before Zhu Xi, Cheng Yi and Cheng Hao (1130–1200, 1033–1107, 1032–1085), and even the followers of Zhu and Cheng brothers, were increasingly revered; and the trend continued uninterrupted to the end of the Yuan.[9]

Yuan rulers understood too well the underlying relationship between Confucian doctrines and the politics of imperial rule, so they respected Confucian learning greatly; they gave the title of Wenxuanwang – King of Culture, the highest ever bestowed – to Confucius. They also prescribed the use of the highest class of ritual format for worshipping Confucius – at the same level as for the emperor. The layout of Imperial Academy in Dadu followed the pattern of "temple to the east and school to the west" – the east being a superior position in the tradition – and although the two were next to each other, the temple compound was bigger and more independent. Indeed, the scale and spaciousness of the temple here surpassed all Confucius temples of capital cities of the past. The supreme numbers of 9 and 5 were used for the planning and building of the temple, matching the dimensions reserved for buildings for the supreme emperor. All of these revealed Yuan rulers' respect for Confucius and Confucian learning, rather than a real understanding and study of Confucian thought, as well expressed in the phrase "all towns and cities of the empire regardless of size must have a school-temple in which the temple is the most important."[10] The respect for Confucian scholars was limited to those already established; the building of schools and the promotion of teaching and learning were not so much emphasized. This was reflected in the privileging of temple over school and was probably to do with the relatively short history of Yuan, which lasted fewer than one hundred years.[11]

Transforming in the Ming: School Over Temple

In contrast to the Yuan rulers who privileged temple over school, the Ming emperors reversed their priority; this was most clearly manifested in the "Great Debate on the Rituals" under Jiajing Emperor (r. 1521–1567), which revealed a dominance of imperial authority over – and a manipulation of – Confucian orthodoxy; this was in total contrast to the Yuan time, when the rulers revered Confucian doctrines. The transformation left its marks in school and temple structures of the Imperial Academy at an architectural level.

In the first era of Ming dynasty, the capital was located in Nanjing. Due to a strong need for talents to build the country, large numbers of students were recruited, and a new Imperial Academy was built at the foot of Jimingshan Hill; the government considered school education critical to the survival and development of the state. The large scale of the academy and the speed of construction were beyond imagination; within two years, the project was completed. The school was completed before the temple; the layout remained in the form of "temple to the east and school to the west."

In location and height, the temple was formally superior to the school, in real spatial organization; however, the design centered on the school.[12] The axis of the whole complex started at the southern end in the Chengxianjie block; some three hundred trees properly lined up on the two sides of the axial street looking north. When you reached the northern end, it was the Guozijian block, beyond which stood the Confucian school. Although both temple and school compounds extended northwards into deeper spaces, and although the temple was to the east in a superior position, the eastern position was in fact off-center (from the viewpoint of the northbound approach on the axis). However, because of the axial approach on the Chengxianjie Street and the two blocks building up along the approach, the school attained a central and critical position as the core to the whole complex. The deep and reserved look of the temple front, and the fences outside the gate, certainly imparted a distant and dignified image. The temple might indeed have been the spiritual center of the academy, but it lacked the commanding and critical position the school had in the overall spatial layout and spatial use of the system. In the Imperial Academy of Nanjing, the status of the school was surely rising to rival that of the temple (Figure 9.1).

The east–west spatial spine, defined by the east–west street outside the school-temple and the east–west blocks (including Chengxianjie Fang), along with the north–south space of the Chengxianjie Street, formed a T-shaped intersection and defined an open space in the Imperial Academy; the T-shaped space, the Jiandong river, and the bridges together formed a group of carefully divided communal spaces for ritual, learning, and everyday life. Apart from funneling traffic and dividing spaces, the T-shaped intersection also displayed a revered dignity and the authority of the academy.[13] The Imperial Academy was basically a sealed-off complex. Students could not come in and out freely; within, life was much self-sustained. The T-shaped space was a basic ground, linking various buildings together, and was the only open space with a street-plaza quality, serving a certain urban function. When the emperor came here to inspect in early Ming, staff and students all gathered at the east end of the Chengxianjie Street to welcome and to see off the sage ruler, revealing a ritual and symbolic importance of the space.

Under Yongle Emperor (r. 1402–1424), the capital was relocated to Beijing, and the Imperial Academy there used the old site left by the Yuan dynasty. By now, Chongwenge Library of the Yuan academy was much destroyed; upon the site, a new Yiluntang Hall was built, and to the west of the school compound an archery exercise ground was created. The Yuan authority – ruled by Mongolians – was strict on the Han Chinese population and did not allow the exercise of archery; therefore, an exercise ground as such was not built in the academy of the Yuan and was part of the eradication of the ritual and practice in the Yuan time. Now, in the Ming, this ancient ritual was recovered; the imperial decree requested all schools in the empire to imitate

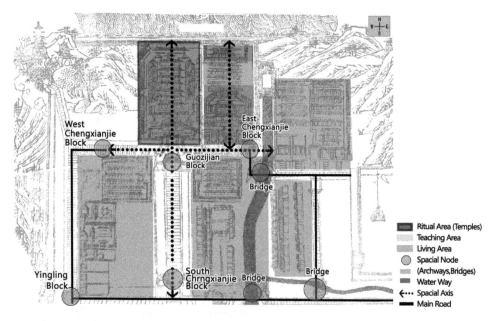

Figure 9.1 Spatial organization of the Imperial Academy in Nanjing of the Ming dynasty.
Source: © Shen Yang.

the practice of Northern Song dynasty (960–1127) and to build archery grounds, asking all students to practice the art; a pavilion for Observing the Virtue – Guandeting, or other similar names – was requested to be built at the center of these grounds.

In the Ming, imperial authority was much centralized and autocratic, reaching a height of power previously unmatched; it did not allow other authorities to counter imperial power, and the Confucian temple became a major problem. In early Ming, Emperor Zhu Yuanzhang (r. 1368–1398) decreed that the common use of Confucian temples should be terminated, which aroused intense reactions among Confucian scholars and scholar-officials. Under Emperor Jiajing (r. 1402–1424), changes were made to the practice of using Confucian temples – the titles for Confucius were demoted, the name of the main hall was changed from Dachengdian (hall of great achievement) to Kongzimiao (Temple for Confucius), and the various ritual practices were reduced. One dramatic measure then was the replacing of the statues of Confucius and his followers with wooden tablets. This iconoclastic destruction, however, prompted great anger only among the scholar-officials or gentry of the imperial court; commoners did not respond to it too much – unlike the iconoclastic movement in Europe that aroused intense conflicts among Christians. In China, with the statues replaced by the wooden tables, with the sages' names written on them, the image of Confucian teaching became increasingly distant to the population, especially to many illiterate commoners.[14] Further, by removing the statues, it reduced the space needed, which led to the shortening of the side galleries of the temples – places where statues of the lesser deities (followers of Confucius) were previously placed.

The addition of two side galleries to a temple hall was a common practice since the Song dynasty (960–1279), yet the scale (number of bays and the overall length) was not fixed. From Song to Qing (1644–1911), the dimensions were determined by the number of statues of these lesser deities to be included in the galleries. Since the Tang dynasty (618–907), the ritual practice for worshipping Confucius grew into a massive cultural system, allowing later generations to contribute to its growth, with a purpose of paying tribute to the sage Confucius and encouraging students to study and strive forth. Worshipping at a Temple of Confucius included a segment of paying tribute to the lesser deities, and these deities were placed and worshipped with a strict hierarchy. Since these deities could not be placed together in a crowded fashion in the main hall, it was sensible to place them in a linear order from the center down, in the galleries that stretched from the main hall in the middle down on the two sides; this also allowed rooms for further extensions. The side galleries were the ideal typology for this practice. If we liken the main hall Dachengdian to the emperor, then the two side galleries were like civilian and military ministers guarding on the flanks. With the main hall on the high platform, the horizontal extension of the two side galleries created a good spatial composition of order and hierarchy; architecture and space here became a concrete manifestation of social and religious structures.

Taking into account the doctrines of Confucian teaching and the need of imperial authority, it was only natural that Confucianism was regarded as a national-societal foundation and the core of moral teaching; and the hierarchical order it promoted was also naturally materialized into the architecture space of the complex.[15] The side galleries were there to create a "closed space"; because of the galleries, the courtyard gained a certain identity and autonomy against the outside, and the main hall became the focus of the enclosed realm. Rudolf Arnheim referred to this realm as a constructed space or extrinsic space, and its purpose was "to control relationships between objects and to provide a scale and a standard for the visual experience."[16] In the Ming and Qing dynasties, courtyards with side galleries withered; only Confucian temples maintained the practice of this thousand-year long tradition, without imitating the ancient typology rigidly – they followed the actual needs of the time for functional or spiritual purposes. The reduction of the length of side galleries limited the space in front of the main hall Dachengdian, making it inferior to the space in front of the main lecture hall of the school; this effectively reduced and lowered the standing of the Confucian temple, the symbol of Confucius orthodoxy.

Further, in the Ming dynasty, a Qishengsi was built at the end of the axis of the complex; it was dedicated to Confucius' father, which highlighted Confucius as a son and a minister of someone else, reducing the standing of the sage as teacher of all time. At the same time, to the north of the lecture hall, a group of pavilions (Jingyiting or Pavilion for Respecting One) was added, and all Confucian schools nationwide – following a decree – must follow this; these pavilions contained the essays written by Emperor Jiajing, "Advice on Respecting One" (Jingyizhen) and "Notes on Five Advices" (Wuzhenzhu). These were Jiajing's own reflective notes based on reading classics; it is interesting to observe that with these interpretative writings, an imperial power now became a symbol of Confucian orthodoxy. These pieces implied that the emperor had understood the secret of thinking from the ancient Emperor Yao and Emperor Shun, so that an emperor can be a teacher, yet a teacher cannot become an emperor. The confrontation of the Jingyiting pavilions with the main Confucian temple delivered a reconstruction of the symbolic system of orthodox tradition and dislocated – if not negated entirely – the importance of Confucianism as the main official doctrine.[17]

Expanding in the Qing: Temple and School as Equals

In Qing dynasty, the Imperial Academy of Beijing, as a major site to promote Confucian and ritualist doctrines of the empire and to celebrate greatness of imperial authority, enjoyed care and privileges from the government. In terms of its overall layout, apart from expanding the institution by transforming southern nearby buildings into Southern Academy, the major development was the building of Biyong – a circular-shaped place for rituals and lecturing – inside the school compound by Qianlong Emperor (r. 1735–1796). Qianlong's own selfish plan was to deliver lectures on the fiftieth anniversary of his reign, so that he could become the first imperial ruler to lecture at Biyong, which resulted in the ritual practice described as *linyong shixue*, "visiting Biyong to inspect school and learning."[18] The initially too-open and spacious compound was now enriched; with the newly added Drum Pavilion and Bell Pavilion to the east and west respectively, the overall space from the front gate to the Yiluntang (main library complex) was now more rhythmic, with layers of spaces building up one after another.[19]

The addition of Biyong surely revealed Qianlong's personal interest and political message. In terms of architecture, it added something in not just the physical layout, but also the use of spaces in the ritual practice of paying tribute to Confucius.

Within the Imperial Academy, this manifested in the different paths the emperor adopted from paying tribute to Confucius in the temple to inspecting learning in the school. Before Biyong was built, Emperors Shunzhi, Kangxi, and Yongzheng had all inspected Yiluntang Library and delivered lectures; Kangxi had also offered his calligraphic writing of "*yi lun tang*" for a front plaque of the library. In those days, when the emperor came to inspect the Imperial Academy, he went to Dachengdian – the main hall of the Confucian temple – first, then came out, entered into an eastern side chamber in the southern front court to change his attire, then came out southwards and ascended to a sedan chair to be carried; the trajectory moved first west, then northward, into the gate of the school, and then northward to the Yiluntang Library; there the emperor delivered his rites of lecturing. But, after Biyong was built, several gates to the west and northwest of Dachendian (the main hall of the temple) were opened; upon completing the rituals for the sage Confucius, the emperor then moved through the western and northwestern gates into Yiluntang Library and rested in its eastern Warm Chamber to change his attire and have a meal before coming out to lecture (Figure 9.2). When the emperor

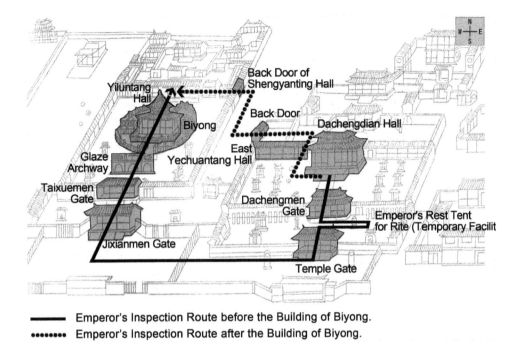

——— Emperor's Inspection Route before the Building of Biyong.

•••••••• Emperor's Inspection Route after the Building of Biyong.

Figure 9.2　Imperial Academy in Beijing of the Qing after the adding of Biyong and the new route adopted for the Emperor's inspection.

Source: © Shen Yang.

lectured in Biyong, ministers, officials, teachers, and students – four thousand in total in ten groups – all lined up outside the bridges to the east, west, and south. The formation of the crowd extended southward beyond the arches; the formation was very orderly, and the spectacle was very impressive.[20]

Outside the Imperial Academy, the ritual trajectory the emperor adopted – as he moved out of this palace city into the academy – was also very telling. As early as the ninth year of Jiajing era (1530) of Ming dynasty, the palace city itself already had collective shrines for 11 gods: Fuxi, Shennong, Huangdi, Rao, Shun, Yu, Tang, Wen, Wu, Zhougong, and Confucius – with Fuxi and Confucius the first and the last in the Confucian orthodox tradition.[21] Into the Qing, Shunzhi Emperor worshipped Confucius in Hongdedian Hall, whereas Kangxi Emperor built a Chuanxindian Hall on the eastern side of Wenhuadian compound, to worship the first nine gods at the center and the last two, Zhougong and Confucius, on the two sides. Yong-zheng Emperor followed this practice; Qianlong Emperor visited and worshipped here upon his ascendance to the throne; in the sixtieth year of his reign, he visited and paid tribute to the gods here as well (Figure 9.3). These worshipping rituals within the palace city were part of the emperor's life, whereas his trip out to inspect the Imperial Academy was a more elaborate political and cultural exercise, and the journey and the process certainly aimed for manifesting and promoting his image as a sage ruler.[22] In Ming dynasty, to reach the Imperial Academy to the northeast, the emperor would come southwards first, to go beyond the Golden River Bridges, then turn east and north; on his way back, he still needed to pass the bridges to return northwards. In early Qing, this practice was maintained; but in the Qianlong reign, the emperor now came out of the palace city via the eastern gate – Donghuamen; this was probably because

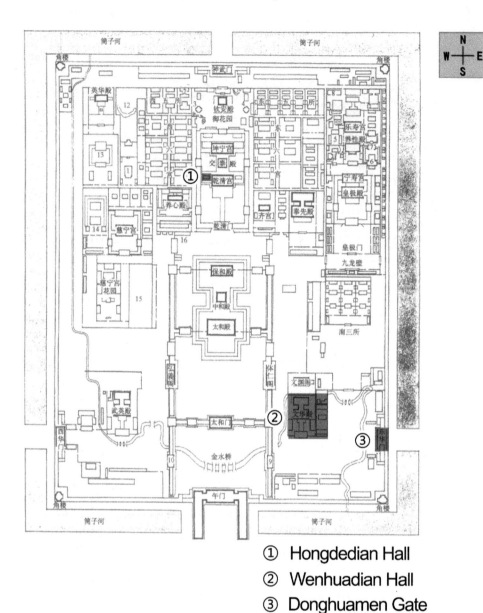

① **Hongdedian Hall**
② **Wenhuadian Hall**
③ **Donghuamen Gate**

Figure 9.3 Sites for worshipping Confucius with the Palace City in the Qing dynasty.
Source: © Shen Yang.

Emperor Qianlong cared a lot about Chuanxindian in the Wenhuadian Compound, which was located just inside the eastern gate, Donghuamen. This change to use Donghuamen was specified in the imperial decree *Linyongyi Zhu* (notes on the ritual of inspecting the academy) issued on the fiftieth year of his reign (1785), two years after Biyong was built in the imperial school (Figure 9.4).

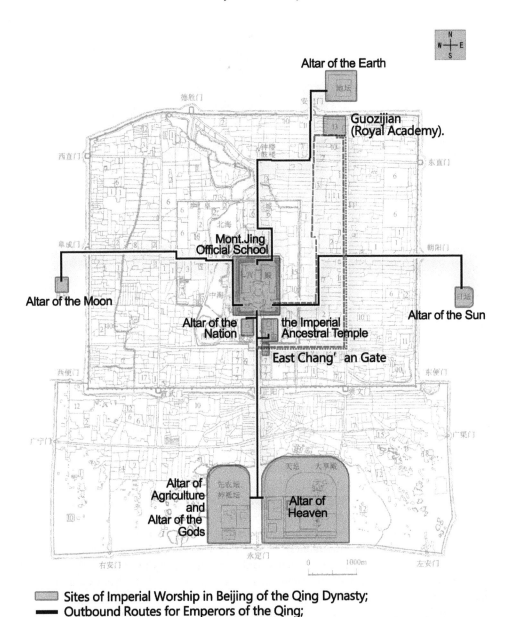

N
W—E
S

Altar of the Earth
地坛

Guozijian
(Royal Academy).

德胜门
安

西直门

东直门

北海

Mont.Jing
Official School

阜成门

朝阳门

Altar of the Moon
日坛

Altar of the Sun

Altar of the
Nation

the Imperial
Ancestral Temple

East Chang' an Gate

西便门

东便门

广宁门

广渠门

天坛   大享殿

Altar of
Agriculture
and
Altar of the
Gods

先农坛

Altar of
Heaven

右安门

永定门

0   1000m

左安门

▦ Sites of Imperial Worship in Beijing of the Qing Dynasty;
▬ Outbound Routes for Emperors of the Qing;
▬▬ Possible Routes for the Qianlong Emperor for Guozijian(Royal Academy);
▪▪▪▪ Route for Emperors of the Ming and Early Qing for Guozijian (Royal Acasdemy)

Figure 9.4   Routes Emperor Qianlong took for the Imperial Academy and other sites.

Source: © Shen Yang.

By now, the Imperial Academy of Beijing as we know it today was fully established (Figure 9.5). In the Imperial Academy, temple and school compounds were parallel and next to each other, each with their own axis and axial articulation, and had their own transitional spaces, to facilitate circulation and logistical service. In the northern area, despite some messy

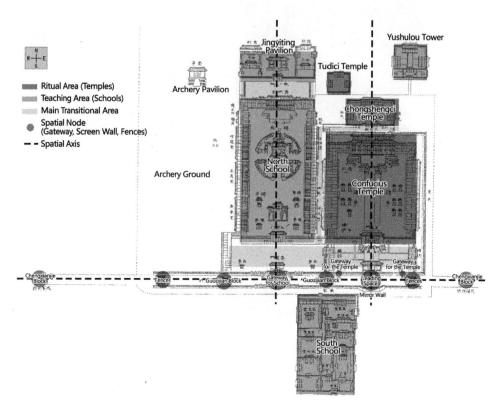

Figure 9.5 Spatial organization of the Imperial Academy in Beijing of the Qing dynasty.
Source: © Shen Yang.

arrangement, the placing of Yushulou Library and Tudici Temple to the east and west retained the basic symmetrical layout of the Confucian temple. In the south, outside the gates of the Imperial Academy ran an east–west street Chengxianjie; it was not as wide as the one in Nan-jing but maintained a clear thoroughness for east–west movement. Passing through two street arches, two fence lines, two academy arches, and two stone tablets (Xiamabei), the east–west street was carefully marked and articulated, forming an urban front and urban extension of the Imperial Academy. Whenever the emperor was coming here to inspect the academy, all officials, scholars, and students kneeled down on the street to welcome the sage ruler; this street therefore displayed multiple characteristics – ceremonial, urban-social, and traffic-utilitarian. For temple and school, each had a grand entry with the gate retreating back (northward) forming a fan-shaped open space in front; each also had a Mirror (or Shadow) Wall, *zhaobi*, on the opposite or southern side of the street facing the gate (the one facing the temple had a fan-shape opening northwards); these two carefully defined front spaces formed two climaxes on the east–west street. Yet, the deep spaces and the tall enclosing walls of the academy imparted an aloof look; the academy was not open for the public to visit, let alone for them to pay tribute.[23] It is not surprising that many commoners came and went through here without knowing nor noticing anything beyond the closed gates.[24]

Further, the class nature of the academy, as revealed in its operation, was also very differ-ent from, if not opposite to, a universal care of all people as striven for in the initial Confucian thought. When Kangxi Emperor paid a visit and tribute to the Confucian Temple in Qufu, he offered his calligraphic script, which said "Teaching and Moral Exemplification for Ten Thousand Generations" (*wanshi shi biao*). The use of these words implied that the believers and practitioners of official Confucianism or Confucian orthodoxy were in reality imperial rulers (known as *di wang shi* or imperial teacher) and scholar-officials. In effect, for all ritual practices in the academy, from annual celebrations to monthly rites, the use of the institution was monopolized by these two groups of people.[25] In other words, Confucius and the other deities were the guardians of gentries and scholar-officials. In the Ming and Qing, if scholar-officials were mistreated by imperial authority, they would go to a Confucian temple to complain, a practice known as "crying at temple" (*kumiao*), which verifies our observation here.[26]

Conclusion: Confucian Orthodoxy Controlled by Imperial Authority?

In reality, school-temple (*miaoxue*) initially had no temple; to build a Confucian temple in or with a school was entirely based on the condition of Confucianism being elevated to the position of an intellectual orthodoxy, and on the necessity of paying ritual tribute to Confucius on the school ground. Once educational schools and Confucian temples became interconnected and were generally accepted all over the country, the symbolic significance of the setup then surpassed its function as merely a school for teaching and learning.

The phrasing of *miaoxue*, temple-school (or school-temple), covers up the initial condition that there are schools without temples. Such a phrase has also elevated the importance of temples. Despite efforts such as Jiajing of Ming adding weight and putting buildings to the schools for a rebalance, there was never really a full equalization of the two. Without the campaign of "promoting Confucianism alone above one hundred schools of thought" by Han Dynasty's Emperor Wudi (r. 141–87 BC), and without the singular imperial promotion and sanctioning of Confucianism as the correct orthodoxy of all learning in the follow dynasties, the formation of the school-temple institution is unthinkable. The subsequent studies and interpretations of Confucian orthodoxy, especially by great scholars such as Han Yu (768–824) and Zhu Xi (1130–1200), determined the ways of thinking, respecting, and worshipping Confucianism in the times that followed.

As a tool to establish a correct culture and its symbolic system, the school-temple institution delivered an idealized cultural system in the real world upon the figure of Confucius as *suwang* (pure and primary king of all time) for the kings and emperors to rule over society. The system of Confucian thought was then institutionalized for state purposes; its moral orthodoxy was externalized into a state ideology. In our current study of the institution over the three dynasties Yuan, Ming, and Qing in Beijing, the relative importance of school and temple changed over time – temple over school, school over temple, and both as important – but what remained consistent was imperial authority's use of learning and culture, and a mixture of idealism and pragmatic considerations – a combination of idealism and instrumentalism.[27] Whether school or temple was emphasized was entirely dependent on the emperor's pragmatic considerations at that particular time.

We can therefore suggest that the school-temple institution was a constructed system that was both open and closed; it was open because of its flexibility as based on a fundamental Confucian care for humans, and it was closed because it manifested an absolute domination of state power and authority. This contradiction ensured that the institution was not a simple addition of a temple to a school, but rather a Confucian and symbolic orthodox system employed if not manipulated in every aspect by the imperial authority.

Notes

1 The system of Guozisi (imperial temple) was first established in the Northern Qi dynasty (550–577); later the Sui dynasty (581–619) followed the practice and changed the name to Guozijian (Imperial Academy).

2 See Xu Song (Tang Dynasty), *Jiankang Shilu* (A Memoir of Jiankang) (Beijing: Sikuguan 1781). See also Gao Mingshi, *Dongya Jiaoyu Quan Xingcheng Lun* (A History of the Formation of the Educational Sphere in East Asia) (Shanghai: Shanghai Guji Chubanshe, 2003), 52.

3 Wang Jianjun, *Yuandai Guozijian Yanjiun* (A Study of the Imperial Academy of the Yuan Dynasty) (Macao: Aoya Zhoukan Chuban Youxian Gongsi, 2003), 26.

4 Wang, *Yuandai*, 94–112.

5 Cheng Jufu (Yuan Dynasty), "Dayuan guoxue xiansheng miaobei (Temple Tablets for the Sages in the Academy of the Yuan Dynasty)," in *Xue Lou Ji* (Collection from the Pavilion in the Snow), vol. 6, Cheng Jufu (Beijing: Sikuguan, 1780), 1–3 (of vol. 6).

6 See Wang, *Yuandai*, 121; see also: Jiang Dongcheng, "Yuan Dadu kongmiao, guozixue de jianzhu moshi yu jizhi guimo tanxi (A Preliminary Inquiry into the Scale of Construction and the Scale Foundation for the Confucian Temple and Imperial Academy in the Yuan Capital Dadu)," *Gugong Bowuyuan Yuankan: Palace Museum Journal*, no. 2 (2007): 18.

7 See Wu Cheng (Yuan Dynasty), "Congwenge bei (Tablets at Congwen Pavilion)," in *Wu Wenzheng ji* (Collection of Wu Wenzheng's Writings), vol. 50 (Beijing: Sikuguan, 1789), 1–7 (of vol. 50).

8 Song Lian et al. (Ming Dynasty), eds., *Yuan Shi* (History of the Yuan Dynasty) (Beijing: Zhonghua Shuju, 2005), 557.

9 Jiang, "Yuan Dadu," 20.

10 Zhao Chengxi, "Yonghe xian chong xiu miaoxue Ji (Recording the Reconstruction of the School-Temple in the County of Yonghe)," in *Quan Yuan Wen* (Complete Works of the Yuan Dynasty), ed. Li Xiusheng (Nanjing: Jiangsu Guji Chubanshe, 1999), 234–235.

11 Qu Yingjie, *Kongmiao Shihua* (A History of the Confucian Temple) (Beijing: Zhongguo Dabaike Quanshu Chubanshe, 1998), 95.

12 See Xu Hong, "Ming Nanjing guozijian de xiaoyuan guihua (Campus Planning for the Imperial Academy of Nanjing in the Ming Dynasty)," in *Diqijie Mingshi Guoji Xueshu Taolunhui Lunwenji* (Proceedings of the Seventh International Symposium on Ming History), ed. Zhao Yi and Lin Fengping (Changchun: Dongbei Shifan Daxue Chubanshe, 1999), 569.

13 For example, in 1394 (the 27th year of the Hongwu Era), a student named Zhao Lin was decapitated and his head placed on top of a post in this open space, because he was found, as claimed, guilty of libel of teachers.

14 See Huang Jinxing, *Shengxian yu Shengtu* (Sages and Saints) (Beijing: Beijing Daxue Chubanshe, 2005), 144–187, 205–233.

15 On Confucian thought and its impact on the design of Confucian temples, please see: Pan Guxi, "Cong Qufu kan rujia sixiang dui jianzhu de yingxian (Confucian Thought and Its Influence on the Architecture in the City of Qufu)," *Kongzi Yanjiu* (Studies on Confucius), no. 2 (1986): 67–70. See also Li Bingnan, "Rujia xueshuo dui Zhongguo gudai jianzhu de yingxiang (The Influence of Confucianism on Ancient Chinese Architecture)," *Yunnan Shehui Kexue* (Social Sciences in Yunnan), no. 3 (1999): 88–94.

16 Quoted from: Wu Hong, *Liyi Zhong de Meishu: Wu Hong Zhongguo Gudai Meishu Shi Wenbian* (Fine Arts in Ritual Practice: Wu Hong's Essays in the Fine Arts of Classical China) (Beijing: Sanlian Shudian, 2005), 553.

17 Jiang, "Yuan Dadu," 23–27.

18 Wen Qing and Li Zhongfang (Qing Dynasty), eds., *Qinding Guozijian Zhi, Juan 24, Biyongzhi Liu: Linyong* (Verified History of the Imperial Academy, vol. 24: History of Biyong Two: Imperial Inspection of the School at Biyong), punctuated and checked by Guo Yanan (Beijing: Beijing Guji Chubanshe, 2000), 362.

19 The Imperial Academy used to have a Bell Room and Drum Room in front of Yiluntang Hall, with the first located to the west and the second east. At 7:00 am, the Bell rings and class starts; there is a rest at noon, and the afternoon class ends at 5:00 pm with the beating of the Drum. When the emperor comes to inspect, Bell ringing and Drum beating are used together. After some debates on ritual format, the Bell and Drum were moved further south, but the first was still to the west and the second east, for signaling morning and evening respectively. There were texts prescribing the Bell and Drum

to be placed to the east and west, but in reality, it was opposite. This is probably because the ringing of the Bell on the west in the morning receives sun light from the east as viewed from a central position very comfortably; and the same is true the other way around in the afternoon – for the beating of the Drum to the east at dust receiving the glow of sunset.

20 Wen Qing and Li Zhongfang (Qing Dynasty), eds., *Qinding Guozijian Zhi, Juan 19, Biyong Zhi* (Verified History of the Imperial Academy, vol. 19: History of Biyong) (Beijing: Beijing Guji Chubanshe, 2000), 313.

21 Zhang Tingyu et al. (Qing Dynasty), eds., *Ming Shi, Juan 50, Zhi Di 26 – Li 4 – Shengshi* (History of the Ming Dynasty, vol. 50, History 26 – Rituals 4 – Paying Tribute to Sage Teachers) (Beijing: Zhonghua Shuju, 1974), 1291.

22 Jianfei Zhu, "Tianchao shachang: Qing gugong ji Beijing de zhengzhi kongjian goucheng gangyao (A Celestial Battlefield: The Forbidden City and Beijing in the Late Imperial China)," trans. Xin Xifang. *Jianzhushi: The Architect*, no. 74 (1997): 107–108, 111, and its endnote 21.

23 Anonymous (Yuan Dynasty), *Miaoxue Dianli* (Rituals at School-Temples) (Beijing: Sikuguan, 1781), 4 (of vol. 1) and 19 (of vol. 2).

24 See Zhao Yingkui (Qing Dynasty), *Wenmiao Beikao* (Recording and Examining the Confucian Temple) (Beijing: Dejutang, 1847), 1.

25 Zhang, *Ming Shi*, 1297.

26 See Chen Guodong, "Kumiao yu fen rufu: Mingmo Qingchu shengyuanceng de shehuixing dongzuo (Crying at the Confucian Temple and Burning the Confucian Dress: Social Actions of the Scholar Class in the Late Ming and Early Qing Period)," *Xin Shixue* (New History), no. 31 (1992): 69–94; Zhou Zhibin, "Lun Qingchu Suzhou de 'kumiao an' (On the Case of "Crying at a Temple" in Suzhou in the Early Qing Dynasty)," *Xuehai* (Sea of Studies), no. 6 (2001): 124–127; Zhang Zhilu, "Laizhoufu zhi kumiao (Crying at the Confucian Temple in the Laizhou Prefecture)," *Chunqiu* (Spring and Autumn), no. 3 (1996): 32–33.

27 See Jianfei Zhu, "Bianxin, Fuke, Hanfei, Ming-Qing Beijing: Quanli kongjian de kua wenhua taolun (Bentham, Foucault, Hanfei and Ming-Qing Beijing: A Cross-Cultural Discussion on Power and Space in Beijing of the Ming and Qing Period)," *Shidai Jianzhu: Time + Architecture*, no. 2 (2003): 106.

Bibliography

Anonymous (Yuan Dynasty). *Miaoxue Dianli* (Rituals at School-Temples). Beijing: Sikuguan, 1781.

Chen Guodong. "Kumiao yu fen rufu: Mingmo Qingchu shengyuanceng de shehuixing dongzuo (Crying at the Confucian Temple and Burning the Confucian Dress: Social Actions of the Scholar Class in the Late Ming and Early Qing Period)." *Xin Shixue* (New History), no. 31 (1992): 69–94.

Cheng Jufu (Yuan dynasty). *Xue Lou Ji* (Collection from the Pavilion in the Snow). Beijing: Sikuguan, 1780.

Editorial Committee, ed. *Wenyuange Siku Quanshu* (The Wenyuange Collection of Complete Four Libraries), electronic ed. Shanghai: Shanghai Renmin Chubanshe, 1999.

———, ed. *Zhongri Wenhua Yanjiu Wenku* (A Library of Studies of Chinese and Japanese Cultures). Shanghai: Shanghai Guji Chubanshe, 2003.

Gao Mingshi. *Dongya Jiaoyu Quan Xingcheng Lun* (A History of the Formation of the Educational Sphere in East Asia). Shanghai: Shanghai Guji Chubanshe, 2003.

Huang Jinxing. *Shengxian yu Shengtu* (Sages and Saints). Beijing: Beijing Daxue Chubanshe, 2005.

Jiang Dongcheng. "Yuan Dadu kongmiao, guozixue de jianzhu moshi yu jizhi guimo tanxi (A Preliminary Inquiry into the Scale of Construction and the Scale Foundation for the Confucian Temple and Imperial Academy in the Yuan Capital Dadu)." *Gugong Bowuyuan Yuankan: Palace Museum Journal*, no. 2 (2007): 10–27.

Li Bingnan. "Rujia xueshuo dui Zhongguo gudai jianzhu de yingxiang (The Influence of Confucianism on Ancient Chinese Architecture)." *Yunnan Shehui Kexue* (Social Sciences in Yunnan), no. 3 (1999): 88–94.

Li Xiusheng, ed. *Quan Yuan Wen* (Complete Works of the Yuan Dynasty). Nanjing: Jiangsu Guji Chubanshe, 1999.

Pan Guxi. "Cong Qufu kan rujia sixiang dui jianzhu de yingxian (Confucian Thought and Its Influence on the Architecture in the City of Qufu)." *Kongzi Yanjiu* (Studies on Confucius), no. 2 (1986): 67–70.

Qu Yingjie. *Kongmiao Shihua* (A History of the Confucian Temple). Beijing: Zhongguo Dabaike Quanshu Chubanshe, 1998.

Song Lian et al. (Ming Dynasty), ed. *Yuan Shi* (History of the Yuan Dynasty). Beijing: Zhonghua Shuju, 2005.

Wang Jianjun. *Yuandai Guozijian Yanjiun* (A Study of the Imperial Academy of the Yuan Dynasty). Macao: Aoya Zhoukan Chuban Youxian Gongsi, 2003.

Wen Qing and Li Zhongfang (Qing dynasty), eds. *Qinding Guozijian Zhi* (Verified History of the Imperial Academy), punctuated and checked by Guo Yanan. Beijing: Beijing Guji Chubanshe, 2000.

Wu Cheng (Yuan dynasty). *Wu Wenzheng ji* (Collection of Wu Wenzheng's Writings). Beijing: Sikuguan, 1789.

Wu Hong. *Liyi Zhong de Meishu: Wu Hong Zhongguo Gudai Meishu Shi Wenbian* (Fine Arts in Ritual Practice: Wu Hong's Essays in the Fine Arts of Classical China). Beijing: Sanlian Shudian, 2005.

Xu Hong. "Ming Nanjing guozijian de xiaoyuan guihua (Campus Planning for the Imperial Academy of Nanjing in the Ming Dynasty)." In *Diqijie Mingshi Guoji Xueshu Taolunhui Lunwenji* (Proceedings of the Seventh International Symposium on Ming History), edited by Zhao Yi and Lin Fengping, 561–576. Changchun: Dongbei Shifan Daxue Chubanshe, 1999.

Xu Song (Tang Dynasty). *Jiankang Shilu* (A Memoir of Jiankang). Beijing: Sikuguan, 1781.

Zhang Tingyu et al. (Qing dynasty), eds. *Ming Shi* (History of the Ming Dynasty). Beijing: Zhonghua Shuju, 1974.

Zhang Zhilu. "Laizhoufu zhi kumiao (Crying at the Confucian Temple in the Laizhou Prefecture)." *Chunqiu* (Spring and Autumn), no. 3 (1996): 32–33.

Zhao Chengxi. "Yonghe xian chong xiu miaoxue Ji (Recording the Reconstruction of the School-Temple in the County of Yonghe)." In *Quan Yuan Wen* (Complete Works of the Yuan Dynasty), edited by Li Xiusheng, 234–235. Nanjing: Jiangsu Guji Chubanshe, 1999.

Zhao Yi and Lin Fengping, eds. *Diqijie Mingshi Guoji Xueshu Taolunhui Lunwenji* (Proceedings of the Seventh International Symposium on Ming History). Changchun: Dongbei Shifan Daxue Chubanshe, 1999.

Zhao Yingkui (Qing Dynasty). *Wenmiao Beikao* (Recording and Examining the Confucian Temple). Beijing: Dejutang, 1847.

Zhou Zhibin. "Lun Qingchu Suzhou de 'kumiao an' (On the Case of "Crying at a Temple" in Suzhou in the Early Qing Dynasty)." *Xuehai* (Sea of Studies), no. 6 (2001): 124–127.

Zhu, Jianfei. "Tianchao shachang: Qing gugong ji Beijing de zhengzhi kongjian goucheng gangyao (A Celestial Battlefield: The Forbidden City and Beijing in the Late Imperial China)." Translated by Xin Xifang. *Jianzhushi: The Architect*, no. 74 (1997): 101–112.

———. "Bianxin, Fuke, Hanfei, Ming-Qing Beijing: Quanli kongjian de kua wenhua taolun (Bentham, Foucault, Hanfei and Ming-Qing Beijing: A Cross-Cultural Discussion on Power and Space in Beijing of the Ming and Qing Period)." *Shidai Jianzhu: Time + Architecture*, no. 2 (2003): 104–109.

Glossary

Biyong	辟雍
Cheng Hao	程颢
Cheng Yi	程颐
Cheng-Zhu (school)	程朱理学
Chengxianjie (street)	成贤街
Chengxianjie Fang	成贤街坊
Chongwenge	崇文阁
Chuanxindian	传心殿
Dachengdian	大成殿
Dachengmen	大成门
Dadu (city)	大都（城）
dao	道
daotong	道统
di wang shi	帝王师
Donghuamen	东华门

Eastern Jin (dynasty)	东晋（朝）
Fuxi	伏羲
Guandeting	观德亭
Guozijian	国子监
Han Yu	韩愈
Hongdedian	弘德殿
Huangdi	皇帝
Huihui (ethnicity)	回回（族）
Jiajing (emperor)	嘉靖（皇帝）
Jiandong (river)	监东（河）
Jiankang (city)	建康（城）
Jimingshan (hill)	鸡鸣山
Jin (dynasty)	金（朝）
Jingyiting	敬一亭
Jingyizhen	敬一箴
Kangxi (emperor)	康熙（皇帝）
Kongzimiao	孔子庙
Kuiwenge	奎文阁
kumiao	哭庙
linyong shixue	临雍视学
Linyongyi Zhu	临雍仪注
miaoxue	庙学
Ming (dynasty)	明（朝）
mu	亩
Nanjing	南京
Qianlong (emperor)	乾隆（皇帝）
Qing (dynasty)	清（朝）
Qishengsi	启圣寺
Qufu (city)	曲阜
Rao	尧
Shennong	神农
Shun	舜
Shunzhi (emperor)	顺治（皇帝）
Song (dynasty)	宋（朝）
suwang	素王
Tang	汤
Tang (dynasty)	唐（朝）
Tudici	土地祠
wanshi shi biao	万世师表
Wen	文
Wenhuadian	文华殿
Wenxuanwang	文宣王
Wu	武
Wudi	武帝
Wuzhenzhu	五箴注
Xiamabei	下马碑
Xu Heng	许衡

Yao	尧
yi lun tang	彝伦堂
Yiluntang	彝伦堂
Yongle (emperor)	永乐（皇帝）
Yongzheng (emperor)	雍正（皇帝）
Yu	禹
Yuan (dynasty)	元（朝）
Yushulou	御书楼
zhaobi	照壁
Zhongdu (city)	中都（城）
Zhougong	周公
Zhu Xi	朱熹
Zhu Yuanzhang	朱元璋

Folk Culture and Vernacular Practice

10

FENGSHUI PRACTICE AND URBAN DEVELOPMENT IN ANCIENT CHINA

An Outline

Dong Wei

Fengshui, meaning "wind and water" in Chinese, as a system of practice and a tradition of discourse was a unique phenomenon in the history of designing cities and architecture in ancient China. Fengshui was meant to find relations between a built environment and the fate of families and countries residing there. Connecting space, time, and life together, it created a body of discourse and knowledge that, though seemingly complex, was in fact rather concise and clear; with this, it also generated a profession and a system of practice, forming a singular cultural tradition. This tradition has caught enormous attention and generated diverse and different studies, commentaries, and viewpoints. By providing a concise outline, this chapter aims to clarify the origins and development of fengshui with a historical perspective and academic methods.

First Stage or Early Exercises: Luoyi City for the Zhou Dynasty

The origin of fengshui was closely associated with the rituals people used of ancient times for avoiding bad fate and obtaining good fortune. With this, fengshui became a practice of finding a most favourable site and plan for cities, towns, and villages in a given natural setting, by observing and reading the natural world around them. In the ancient Shang and Zhou dynasties (1766–256 BC), divination was widely used in all affairs political or personal – it was a way of building connections with gods on high, for establishing a harmony with nature through forms of rituals, so that people may be protected with a positive future. Some of these ritual practices later developed into a culture called "wind and water" or fengshui.

Divination in the earliest stage was a state affair. It was carried out by state officials, with aims, procedures, and ritual forms. The building of Luoyi as the capital city of Zhou dynasty (1766–256 BC) was the earliest recorded case in China in which divination was used for selecting and building a city. Around 1118 BC, King Wu of Zhou (Zhou Wuwang, ?–1043 BC), upon conquering the previous Shang dynasty, brought Duke of Zhou (?–?) and others to observe the forms and distributions of the landscape between River Luo and Mountain Mang, and concluded that it was here that the capital should be built. Around 1116 BC, Zhou sent Duke of Shao (?–?) to observe the place for selecting a site; Zhou then went there himself to observe the territory, travelling up and down between the three rivers of Luo, Jian, and Chan, using various means of divination for ideal sites (Figure 10.1).[1] We can tell from this case – known

DOI: 10.4324/9781315851112-15

Figure 10.1   Officials inspecting sites for planning and building.

Source: From: Anonymous, Shang Shu (Book of documents) of 551 BC – 479 BC, reprinted in Sun Jiading and Zhang Baixi, comp. *Qinding Shujing Tushuo* (The book of classics with illustrations), (Beijing: Qing Palace, 1874), vol 32, p 2.

as "Building Capital Luo by Duke of Zhou" (*zhougong yingluo*) – that fengshui was a process for serving a political purpose; more precisely, it was a technical ritual for a political project of the state.

The story of Zhou and Shao observing the land for ideal sites for the capital city of Zhou dynasty is well known and is regarded as a typical case where fengshui was practiced. It is indeed a classical case and a milestone in history, although we must understand that the divining rituals then were different from the fengshui practice developed later. At this time, city planning was still in a formative stage; the ideas for arranging in a terrain and for communication with gods remained simple, direct, and intuitive. People believed that worshiping, sacrificing, and divining were rituals for predicting future; and since building palaces and cities was important for the state and society, the rituals were then essential and necessary for establishing a certain authority and imperial orthodoxy. If these ideas and rituals were considered as constituting the content of fengshui, then the subsequent development of the tradition was a thorough deviation from the simple and direct thought of urban planning of this classical age – a proximate imitation and a secular reconstruction of the rituals of the early time.

Middle Stage or Growth: City Planning From Han to Tang Dynasties

In the Han dynasty – including Western Han (202 BC–9 AD) and Eastern Han (25–220), scholarship was blossoming, and many books were published then. It is a time often attributed as the birth era for the many books of fengshui. Yet, in *Shi Ji* (Records of the Grand Historian, 91 BC), Sima Qian (145–86 BC) talked about *yin* and *yang* from *Yi Jing* or *I Ching* (the Book of Changes), but not *kanyu* ("heaven and earth") and *fengshui* ("wind and water") – two phrases for geomancy. In the Eastern Han period, more theories of Yin and Yang, and of Five Elements, came into being. Here, in *Han Shu* (Book of Han, 82 AD), Ban Gu (32–92 AD) discussed these and criticized the use of Five Elements for interpreting one's fortune and misfortune.[2] In the following periods (Wei, Jin, and Northern and Southern dynasties, 220–589), fengshui culture witnessed a turning point: the relatively simple ideas of geomancy as a ritual for siting and designing capital cities were in retreat, replaced by a specialized practice of artisans using numbers and techniques of Yin Yang and Five Element theories. The love for beautiful landscape, for abstract conversations, and for mysterious theories – so characterized by this time period of Chinese history – had also pushed the development of fengshui in this direction.

With rationalist Confucianism becoming increasingly a dominant imperial ideology, the practice of using divination for siting and designing capital cities was in decline, as found in the following time – Sui dynasty (581–618) – and its effort in building Daxing and Luoyang, its central and eastern capitals. Chang'an, the capital city of Han dynasty, was in ruin after many wars at the dawn of the Sui dynasty. In 581, the first emperor of Sui (Emperor Wen of Sui, Yang Jian, 541–604, r. 581–604), resided and ruled the empire in an old palace at a corner of Chang'an. The dilapidated buildings and the environment were not satisfying. So, in the following year, he ordered high officials, including Prime Minister Gao Jiong (541–607) and Minister of Construction Liu Long (?-?) and eminently Yuwen Kai (555–612), to look for new sites and to supervise the construction of a new capital for the Sui empire, in an open terrain to the southeast of Chang'an.[3] Similar to Luoyi city of the Zhou dynasty mentioned above, the new capital, known as Daxing, demonstrated a grand and geometric projection of imperial authority in spatial design, rather than a calculation in fengshui terms as practiced in later times (Figure 10.2).

The second emperor of Sui (Emperor Yang of Sui, Yang Guang, 569–618, r. 604–618) conquered a coup d'état and decided to move his power base eastward, to Luoyang (officially

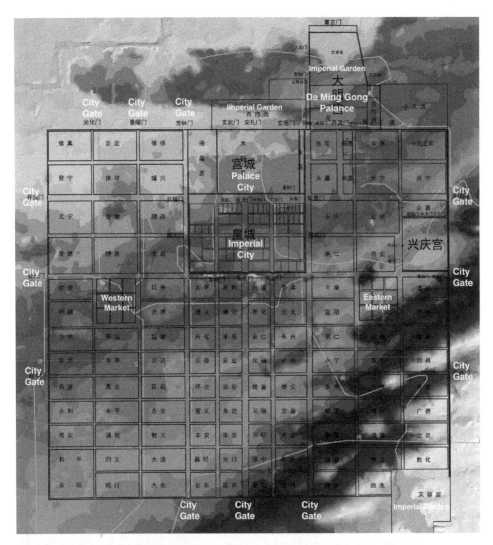

Figure 10.2 Capital City for the Sui (581–619) and Tang (618–907) dynasties (known as "Daxing" in the Sui and "Chang'an" in the Tang) based on GIS topographic analysis: higher in the south-east and lower in the north-west, with "imperial city" and "daminggong royal palace" on sites higher than the "palace city," a situation that opens to many fengshui interpretations.

Source: © Dong Wei, Chen Mengjiao and Huang Huiyan.

became the capital in 605), in order to control eastern regions better. He published a decree and described clearly his vision for the planning of the new capital (Figure 10.3).[4]

It is interesting to note that officials of Tang dynasty (618–907), Wei Zheng (580–643) and Yan Shigu (581–645), in their compilation of *Sui Shu* (Book of Sui, 636), had positively described the building of the two capitals, Daxing and Luoyang, but without mentioning the use of fengshui ideas or techniques. Yet, in a book published some 200 years later, *Yuanhe Junxian Tuzhi* (Yuanhe maps and records of prefectures and counties, 813), there was a depiction of the use of fengshui ideas for the making of the city of Luoyang, a narrative that was later on much quoted,

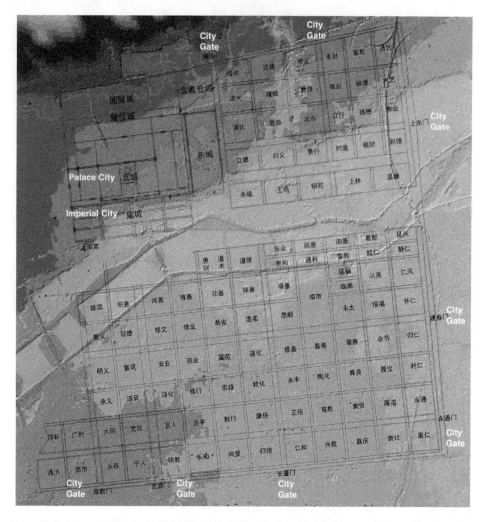

Figure 10.3 Luoyang City in the Sui-Tang time (581–907) based on GIS topographic analysis: "imperial city" and "palace city" on higher sites to the north-west, against the backdrop of Mountain Mang overlooking the city; the planning intention was to avoid floods, yet it was flooded from time to time in the Sui and Tang period.

Source: © Dong Wei, Liu Yuansha and Huang Huiyan.

for celebrating the city in positive fengshui terms.[5] In reality, Emperor Yang of Sui disliked the mystic fengshui and yin yang theories and ordered books of these types to be burnt, and decreed to execute anyone resisting the rule.[6] This reveals to us that, from Sui to mid- and late Tang, in a space of 200 years, there was a crucial shift in the development of fengshui: as we reach late Tang, fengshui ideas became popular, more accepted, and indispensable in the various projects of building and construction. This is why the author of the book, Li Jifu (758–814), though he held a high standing as a prime minister, still had to adopt fengshui terms to describe various developments in order to follow predominate social ideas and cultural practice of the time.

We can tell that, from Wei-Jin to Sui dynasty, in about 300 years, there was a gradual shift from ideas of imperial systems and rituals for city planning based on hierarchical culture and ancestral worship, towards a more secular practice where a mystic culture of fengshui, of Yin and Yang ideas, and of Five Elements was more adopted; whereas in the next 200 years, from Sui to mid Tang dynasty, a strong folk culture for fengshui ideas and practices was fully established and thriving. The two capital cities of Sui, Daxing (also known as Chang'an of Sui) and Luoyang, stood in the middle of this shift, as classical cases to witness the emergence of the culture of fengshui – as we know it later on, that is, as a popular or folk cultural tradition. Initially, fengshui ideas were not so important for Daxing and Luoyang, but as fengshui grew and became popular, new interpretative narratives for explaining the two cities came into being, as a favourable topic and case for the new fengshui masters. It is not surprising that in Li's *Maps and Records of Prefectures and Counties* (813), and in many historical accounts like this, a fengshui narrative was made upon Yu Wenkai's planning of Daxing and Luoyang.

Late Stage or Secularization: Visualization, Interpretation, and Intervention

Fengshui practice, as a spatial operation using some formal ideas, gradually developed into a system of graphic analysis with spatial concepts and cosmological interpretations – a rich iconology – through the Song and Ming dynasties (960–1279, 1368–1644). Song is a turning point in China in writing and publishing; one of the key breakthroughs then was a great proliferation of local records and folk literature published and printed with vivid writing and rich graphic illustrations. In this context, graphic or iconological narratives in fengshui practice became more popular, giving rise to an interpretative fengshui cultural practice that used visual diagrams and depictions to illustrate ideal forms and types. Interestingly, as urbanization blossomed, fengshui was used for interpreting and re-interpreting an existing settlement, and for offering visions for modifications to the existing built fabric. In the process, these graphic illustrations were crucial and instrumental. The work on Luoyang of the Jin and Yuan time (1115–1234, 1271–1368) serves as a good example.

The Luoyang city of Jin-Yuan time (1115–1368), built upon the old fabric of the once eastern capital of the great Sui and Tang dynasties, was now a reduced city – practically a normal prefecture in northern China. There was a Wenfengta – "pagoda of literature" – at its southeast corner, which was built in the Northern Song (960–1127). According to fengshui interpretations, the pagoda – rebuilt several times at the same spot in the following dynasties – was sited there for correcting or rebalancing a topographic situation of the city where the northwest was high and the southeast low. According to *Chongxiu Wenfengta Ji* (Notes on the rebuilding of Wenfengta, 1651), the pagoda was once destroyed by Li Zicheng (1606–1645) and his armies at the end of the Ming dynasty (1368–1644), and was then rebuilt later by local prefecture officials Yang Suo (?–?) and Wu Panlong (?–?) on the same spot.[7]

The actual history runs like this. After the An-Lushan Rebellion (755–763), Tang empire (618–907) was in decline and the city was much ruined. At the beginning of Northern Song, Emperor Taizu, Zhao Kuangyin (927–976, r. 960–976), intended to build his capital at Luoyang; but the idea was not implemented; the city became his western capital, and its overall layout, as left from the Tang, generally survived. So, if Wenfengta Pagoda was indeed built in the Northern Song, its position was in fact on a river bank called Xintan – a busy dock reserved for the royal palace for a long time, from Sui to Song (589–1127). Obviously, the pagoda acted as a lighthouse for guiding boats and ships (Figure 10.4). At the same time, the location was at a low spot in the topography of the city, so making a tower here was also befitting in fengshui terms. Late in the Jin dynasty (1115–1234), around 1223, the city walls of Luoyang were reconstructed, and the pagoda was now wrapped into the city by the new walls (Figure 10.5). Later on, when the city became prosperous and social life vibrant, people came forward to offer

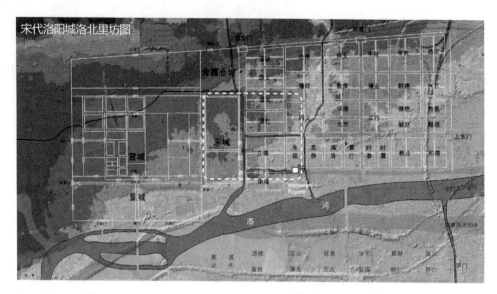

Figure 10.4 Wenfengta Pagoda (white dot) in Luoyang of the Northern Song dynasty (960–1127) is located next to Luo River and its branch streams, on the northern bank of a royal dock. Later city of Luoyang of the Ming-Qing is marked by a dashed outline.

Source: © Dong Wei, Liu Yuansha and Huang Huiyan.

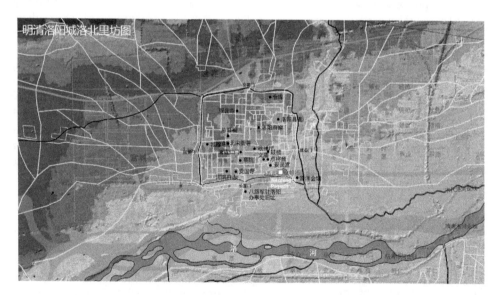

Figure 10.5 Luoyang of the Ming-Qing time (1368–1911) as descending from the Jin-Yuan period (1115–1368): smaller and occupying the eastern section and other three blocks of the old Luoyang of the Sui-Tang time (581–907). By now Wenfengta Pagoda is wrapped up into the city at its lower south-east corner.

Source: © Dong Wei, Liu Yuansha and Huang Huiyan.

interpretations on the great site and performance of the pagoda in formal and fengshui terms, producing charming stories on how fengshui can change a city's fortune and contribute to the culture of society – with a "Pagoda of Literature."

Conclusion

From a historical perspective, fengshui made important contributions to the planning and construction of cities in ancient China. In today's terms, fengshui had two major contributions. Firstly, it provided a spatial interpretation, in that it employed geomantic concepts and observations to deliver an explanatory narrative on an existing city and its space, bestowing a certain fengshui meaning "after" the fact. Secondly, it provided a projective design and planning, in that it used geomantic ideas, observations, and analyses for the building of a new city or settlement to come, envisioning a fengshui significance "before" the fact. In actual practice, these two processes were often interwoven and mutually productive. At a more practical level, since fengshui – as a body of ideas and techniques – had only a generic core of functional imperatives and a broad platform for interpretation, it left a huge room for individual fengshui masters to exercise their own views, skills, and capacities a lot. This is one of the reasons why fengshui reviews often have huge gaps and differences between each other.

In historical evolution, the early use of fengshui was clearly associated with imperial authorities, and from Qin and Han time on there was an increasing injection of visions of some officials and emperors in the hope of strengthening the prospect of the dynasty through a grand urban planning and construction. In the Tang and Song time, local aristocrats gained more power, and fengshui ideas and techniques were used to enhance their prospect and influence. And when we move on to the Ming and Qing time (1368–1911), we no longer see many cases of a grand city planning and construction using fengshui ideas; instead, fengshui was more used for interpretation and for minor or partial modification for improvement, for some existing urban or rural settlements. This in turn was also reflected in the scale a fengshui master was able to control in a particular exercise. As a result, many practical guides for fengshui talked about houses and domestic spaces only, and discussed broader settlements only in the theory section of the book. In relation to that, later use of fengshui was also increasingly interpretative, with its interventional function in decline.

In summary, over three thousand years, fengshui has shifted from a practical method for planning and designing a settlement to a conceptual method for reading and explaining a settlement; and, with this, it has produced several landmarks at some turning points. Because of this, we must not use one standard to judge the cultural tradition of fengshui, which had multiple meanings and values.

Notes

1 Zeng Yuanqian, *Shangshu Zhengdu* (Shangshu: A Guide to Correct Reading), vol. 4 (Beijing: Zhonghua Shuju, 1964), 147–199.
2 Ban Gu, *Han Shu Di Liu Ce: Yiwen Zhi* (Book of Han, vol. 6: Treaties on Literature), noted by Yan Shigu (Beijing: Zhonghua Shuju, 1962), 1774–1776.
3 Wei Zheng, *Sui Shu, Juanyi, Di Ji Diyi* (Book of Sui, vol. 1, Biography of the Emperors, Part One), as Collected in *Sibu Congkan* (All Books in Four Types), Edition of Dade Era of the Yuan Dynasty (1297–1307) and reprinted by Shanghai Hanfenlou (Shanghai: The Commercial Press, 1930), 16.
4 Wei, *Sui Shu, Juanyi, Di Ji Disan* (Book of Sui, vol. 1, Biography of the Emperors, Part Three), as collected in *Sibu Congkan*, 2–4.

5 Li Jipu, *Yuanhe Junxian Tuzhi* (Yuanhe Maps and Records of Prefectures and Counties), noted by He Cijun (Beijing: Zhonghua Shuju, 1983), 129–133.
6 Wei, *Sui Shu, Juanyi, Di Ji Disi* (Book of Sui, vol. 1, Biography of the Emperors, Part Four), as collected in *Sibu Congkan*, 9.
7 Next to the Wenfengta Pagoda, a tablet was erected on which, in 1651 (in the Shunzhi Reign of the Qing dynasty), a text – *Chongxiu Wenfengta Ji* (a Record for Rebuilding the Pagoda) – was inscribed. It says: "Wenfengta Pagoda of Luoyang City was initially built in Northern Song, and was then rebuilt several times in the Jin, Yuan and Ming dynasties; at the end of the Ming, the rebel forces of Li destroyed it. . . . We are now rebuilding it, in order to retain the great tradition of learning in Luoyang, and to revive its great fortune of culture and civilization, and to connect the cosmos above and human culture below."

Bibliography

Anonymous. *Chongxiu Wenfengta Ji* (A Record for Rebuilding the Pagoda). Inscription on a Stone Tablet Next to Wenfengta Pagoda of Luoyang, 1651.

Ban Gu. *Han Shu Di Liu Ce: Yiwen Zhi* (Book of Han, Volume Six: Treaties on Literature). Noted by Yan Shigu. Beijing: Zhonghua Shuju, 1962.

Dong Wei. *Suitang Chang'an cheng kongjian xingtai jiqi bianqian yanjiu* (Inquiry into spatial Forms and Their Historical Evolutions of the City of Chang'an of the Sui and Tang Dynasties). Unpublished paper. In collaborations with Xi'an Institute of Surveying and Mapping, Xian Jiaotong University and Tsinghua University. Funded by National Natural Science Foundation of China (scheme number: 51178096).

Dong Wei. *Suitang Luoyang cheng kongjian xingtai jiqi bianqian yanjiu* (Inquiry into Spatial Forms and Their Historical Evolutions of the City of Luoyang of the Sui and Tang Dynasties). Unpublished paper. Supported by Luoyang Municipal Bureau of Planning and Luoyang Bureau of Cultural Heritage. Funded by National Natural Science Foundation of China (scheme number: 51178096).

Li Jipu. *Yuanhe Junxian Tuzhi* (Yuanhe Maps and Records of Prefectures and Counties). Noted by He Cijun. Beijing: Zhonghua Shuju, 1983.

Li Ruentian. "Ziran tiaojian dui Luoyang chengshi lishi fazhan de yingxiang (The Impact of Natural Conditions Upon the Historical Development of the City of Luoyang)." In *Zhongguo Kudu Yanjiu, di san ji* (Research in Ancient Chinese Capitals) (Third Annual Symposium of the Society of Research in Ancient Chinese Capitals in 1985), vol. 3, 179–191. Hangzhou: Zhejiang Renmin Chubanshe, 1987.

Wang Duo. "Tangsong Luoyang sijia yuanlin de fengge (Styles of Private Gardens of the City of Luoyang in the Tang and Song Dynasties)." In *Zhongguo Kudu Yanjiu, di san ji* (Research in Ancient Chinese Capitals) (Third Annual Symposium of the Society of Research in Ancient Chinese Capitals in 1985), vol. 3, 234–253. Hangzhou: Zhejiang Renmin Chubanshe, 1987.

Wang Zhu, Bi Ludao and Zhang Qian, eds. *Dili Xinshu Jiaoli* (An Examination on the Book *Dili Xinshu* – New Book on Geography). Complied by Jin Shenjia. Xiangtan: Xiangtan Daxue Chubanshe, 2012.

Wei Zheng. *Sui Shu, Juanyi, Di Ji* (Book of Sui, Volume One, Biography of the Emperors). Collected in *Sibu Congkan* (All Books in Four Types), edition of Dade Era of the Yuan dynasty (1297–1307) and reprinted by Shanghai Hanfenlou. Shanghai: The Commercial Press, 1930.

Yang Zhigang. "*Sima Shi Shuyi* he *Zhu Zi Jiali* Yanjiu (A Study on *Sima Shi Shuyi* and *Zhuzhi Jiali*)." *Zhejiang Xuekan* 78, no. 1 (1993): 108–114.

Zeng Yuanqian. *Shangshu Zhengdu* (Shangshu: A Guide to Correct Reading), vol. 4. Beijing: Zhonghua Shuju, 1964.

Zhou Baozhu. "Beisong siqi de xijing Luoyang (Western Capital Luoyang in the Northern Song Dynasty)." *Shixue Yuekan* 4 (2001): 109–117.

Glossary

An-Lushan Rebellion	安史之乱
Ban Gu	班固
Chan (river)	瀍水
Chang'an	长安
Chongxiu Wenfengta Ji	重修文峰塔记

Daxing	大兴
Duke of Shao	召公
Duke of Zhou	周公
Emperor Wen of Sui	隋文帝
Emperor Yang of Sui	隋炀帝
fengshui	风水
fengshui	风水
Gao Jiong	高颎
Han (dynasty)	汉（朝）
Han Shu	汉书
Jian (river)	涧水
Jin (dynasty)	晋（朝）
Jin (dynasty)	金（朝）
kanyu	堪舆
King Wu of Zhou	周武王
Li Jifu	李吉甫
Li Zicheng	李自成
Liu Long	刘龙
Luo (river)	洛水
Luoyang	洛阳
Luoyi	洛邑
Mang (mountain)	邙山
Shang (dynasty)	商（朝）
Shi Ji	史记
Sima Qian	司马迁
Sui (dynasty)	隋（朝）
Sui Shu	隋书
Taizu (emperor)	宋太祖
Tang (dynasty)	唐（朝）
Wei (dynasty)	魏（朝）
Wei Zheng	魏征
Wenfengta	文峰塔
Wu Panlong	武攀龙
Xintan	新潭
Yan Shigu	颜师古
Yang Guang	杨广
Yang Jian	杨坚
Yang Suo	杨所
Yi Jing (I Ching)	易经
Yin Yang (yin yang)	阴阳
Yu Wenkai	宇文恺
Yuan (dynasty)	元（朝）
Yuanhe Junxian Tuzhi	元和郡县图志
Zhao Kuangyin	赵匡胤
Zhou (dynasty)	周（朝）
Zhou Wuwang	周武王
zhougong yingluo	周公营洛

11

YANG YUNSONG AND THE JIANGXI SCHOOL OF FENGSHUI PRACTICE IN SOUTHERN CHINA

Cheng Jianjun

There is a long history of fengshui practice in China, with many schools competing. But if we examine the situation more closely, it is clear that since the Han (202 BC–220 AD) and Tang (618–907) dynasties, the school of Jiangxi province – the Jiangxi School – dominated as most influential, so much so that the royal palaces of the Ming and Qing in the north employed fengshui masters from Jiangxi for their imperial projects (1420–1911). People therefore often say that "Chinese fengshui is located in Jiangxi". This is all because of Yang Yunsong (834–906), a royal fengshui master of the Tang empire – he left the center of power to avoid danger during the Huang Chao Rebellion (874–884) and returned to his home town, Ganzhou in the Jiangxi province. He brought with him a secret palace manuscript, *Zang Shu* (*Book of Burial*, by Guo Pu, 276–324) and taught the art and technique to his followers in the region (such as Yudu and Yangxianling). In Ganzhou, fengshui practice even became an occupation, a tradition that has extended from Tang to modern times.

Yang Yunsong and the Jiangxi School of Fengshui

For a long time, fengshui doctrines have often been divided into two – "formal" and "rational" schools, that is, a *xing-shi* (forms and tendencies) school and a *li-qi* (rationality and vitality) school. Zhao Yizhi, a scholar of the Qing dynasty (1644–1911), once said that Chinese fengshui practices could be divided into the Jiangxi method and Fujian method, and that the Jiangxi method originated in Yang Yunsong of Ganzhou, who emphasized forms and tendencies, the origins and endings of the formal tendencies (of the landscape) for determining sites and positions, to ensure the matching of "dragons" (mountains), "eyes" (caves), "hills", and "waters" (*long, xue, sha, shui* respectively). This description is broadly fine but not exactly accurate: Yang's books, *Yilong Jing* (Manual for questioning the dragons) and *Hanlong Jing* (Manual for moving the dragons), talked about formal methods, whereas Yang's *Qingnang Aoyu* (Secret talks on green bags) and *Yuchi Jing* (Manual of the jade ruler) and his student Zeng Wenchan's *Tianyu Jingxu* (Manual of the heavenly jade) talked about rational methods. In addition, the two pointers of the compass used in the rationalist method – *zhengzhen* and *fengzhen* – were also invented by Yang himself.

DOI: 10.4324/9781315851112-16

The so-called formal method was based on the idea of "following and riding on dynamic flows" (*cheng sheng qi*) from Guo Pu's *Zang Shu* or *Book of Burial* — which actually advocated both formal (observing formal currents and tendencies) and rational methods (rationalizing precise sites and directions). Guo Pu said in *Zang Shu*: "a dynamic propensity (*shi*) is hardest, a good formal (*xing*) condition is less so, and an actual positioning (*fang*) is even less (in one's fengshui exercise to discover a favorable terrain)".[1] *Shi* (propensity) and *xing* (form) are about the formal method, whereas *fang* (positioning) is about the rational method. Yang Yunsong and Zeng Wenchan, in their fengshui practice, used intuitive observations to search for "dragons", "eyes", "waters" (*long, xue, shui* or mountains, caves/sites, and river flows) — which were part of the formal method — and they used the compass to position the dragons, to follow and ride on the vitality, to shift to or away from the hills and to collect water flows. These were parts of the "rational" method; these theories and practices were based on the natural conditions of land and topography rather than scholastic divisions. Similarly, on the other side, a master of the rational school, Wang Ji (1007–1076), advocated the ideas and methods of the formal approach as well. So, the division between the formal and the rational is not very meaningful; any established fengshui practice would only have some subtle emphasis towards this or that school. Whatever the persuasion, they all agreed that a formal exercise was primary, whereas technical calculations concerned the more practical matters. We can say that Jiangxi School appreciated both methods and was initially centered on the idea of "following and riding on dynamic flows" (*cheng sheng qi*), but later on witnessed a proliferation into many branch schools and groups.

One of the groups in Ganzhou, Yuchi Tang (Hall of jade rulers), is often regarded as having inherited directly from the teaching of Yang, following closely the theory and practice of that specific lineage of Guo-Yang-Zeng (Guo Pu, Yang Yunsong, and Zeng Wenchan). Its classical theory emphasized on the relations between *xuan* (the deep and mysterious) and *qiao* (openings), that is, between a cave site (for building) and an entry for water to flow in. It suggested that if the two were well related, we could then follow and ride on the dynamic flows of energies or vitalities. Its later theory added another key word and dimension — *guan* (opening or closing towards), which is *xiang* (orientation), so the old set of two key points, cave site and water entry, now became a series of three key elements — site, orientation, and water entry (and indeed, *xuan-guan*, deep site and open operation, became a common phrase). These doctrines of master Yang, with vast practice, obtained a great number of theories and experiences and secured the position of a major fengshui school in China; it was widely accepted and practiced, especially among the Hakka people in Jiangxi, Fujian, and Guangdong provinces, and it obtained the name "Yang Jiupin" — master Yang who rescues people from poverty (by bringing good fortune using fengshui).

Basic Intentions of Fengshui: Storing Vitality and Obtaining Water

Generally speaking, fengshui practice is a comprehensive evaluation of climate, geology, geomorphology, ecology, the landscape, and other environmental systems and factors; it is also an overall assessment of adoption and avoidance of building layouts and practical techniques. Simply put, it is a process for selecting and organizing a suitable setting for the living and the dead. For selecting a good site, the key point is vitality or vital flows and currents, and the key advice is to retain and to gather "wind" and "air" (vitalities). For fengshui masters gathering vitalities, "wind" and "water" (vitality and river flow) are two of the several important key elements, hence the name of *feng-shui* (wind and water).

Wind and Water

In Yang Yunsong's framework, "wind" (*feng*) refers to "flow of vitality" (*sheng qi*); it describes an ecological condition of a building site and its surroundings, that is, the ecological and landscape situation of a realm of "cave or eye" (*xue*) in relation to its context in fengshui's terminology. Guo Pu says clearly in *Book of Burial* that

> to bury is to retain, and to retain is to follow and to ride on flows of vitality; the air of *yin* and *yang*, when released, becomes wind and vital flows; these vital flows travel in land and, when developing outward, give life to ten thousand things.[2]

The so-called flow of vitality can be understood as a traveling energy of many elements in land and can be described as elements of "earth", for the growth of ten thousand things; the lively flow is a flow within and from earth – when it grows out of earth, it becomes wind. The idea of "wind" here refers to a vital flow of earth, an earthly vitality and energy, which is also regarded as the vitality and energy of dragons – so it is not the wind we talk about today. The core and the aim of fengshui are to obtain and to utilize this "lively air" or flow of vitality. This lively air or flow of vitality is made of the *yin* elements of earth and *yang* aspects of water; as water flows out of earth, the *yin* and *yang* elements here retain a relationship of balance, unification, and interdependence. The purpose of Chinese fengshui is to follow and to ride on this lively air or flow of vitality – the air or flow here includes that from earth and that from water.

Storing Vitality and Obtaining Water

Guo Pu in *Book of Burial* says "for fengshui methods, obtaining water is most crucial, and retaining air (vital flow) is also important".[3] In ancient China, the siting of cities, towns, and villages were closely associated with assessment of land and water in fengshui terms. In Yang's fengshui practice, it is important to examine the relationship between the "arriving dragon" (*ru shou long*, the main mountain) and "mouth of water" (*shui kou*, where a river or a stream arrives into the scene), and to determine the trajectory of the "dragon vein" (*long mai*) from an ancestral mountain to the arriving mountain and its characteristics in terms of the Five Elements, in order to ascertain if the chosen site, the "cave" (*xue*), is a "true end of the dragon" (*zhen long xue di*). For the method to achieve this, one needs to use direct visual observation on the form and propensity of the terrain, as well as the compass, to determine various positioning and characterization.[4]

A good site as a "true end of the dragon" must be able to "protect air (vitality) and obtain water" (*cang feng de shui*). For that, it is necessary to "follow vitality internally" and "absorb vitality externally". To follow and ride on vitality internally (*nei cheng sheng qi*) means to employ some vital life force, also referred to as dragon's life energy – dynamic elements from within and upon the terrain of the "cave" (site), a kind of internal air and vitality, which should not dissipate by spreading and diminishing outward. To absorb vitality externally (*wai jie tang qi*) is to secure harmony between the site and the surrounding environment, including aspects of the landscape and of local climate – as "external air". One of the main advices is "facing mountains and waters" (*chao shan chao shui*) – so the practice is also called "obtaining water" (*de shui*). Explaining the advice through another theory (Twelve Palaces for Long Life), to store vitality is to bring it to *muku*, "graveyard", a constellation in Chinese astrology; to obtain water is also to bring dragon's air and vitality to *muku*, and an entry for water to flow, aligned to a direction of *muku*, is where the dragon rests and resides. My understanding is that this is the true meaning of "obtaining water", and is also the initial real meaning of the advice for a "correspondence between the deep site (*xuan*) and the entry of water flow (*qiao*)" – or *xuan qiao xiang ying* – in the fengshui school of master Yang.

Methods in Fengshui Practice

Methods of assessing a site in fengshui practice can be broadly described as three interrelated steps, namely formal, rational, and shifting-assuring. Their ideas and methods are briefly outlined as follows.

Formal Method

Here the main methods are direct visual observation. For collecting dragon's vitality *within* the terrain, there are two methods. The first is to observe the origins of air and flow and their lively force or vitality by examining the dynamic forms of mountains (the dragon) – it was called reviewing the dragon, or simply "dragon method" (*long fa*). The second is to observe the gathering of air and flow, that is, the more static situation centering upon the site – considered as the cave or the eye (*xue*) – is referred as "cave method" (*xue fa*). For collecting vitality from *outside* of the terrain, the methods here are about finding a good relationship with mountains and rivers in the surroundings outside the immediate terrain. Here, "mountain method" (*feng fa* or *sha fa*) refers to direct observations on the mountains and hills near and far, and "water method" (*shui fa*) refers to direct review and observation of the flow of water in various forms. These four methods constitute the so-called formal method (*xing fa*). *Book of Burial* says, a good site should have "dynamic forms (of mountains and hills as a backdrop) like ten thousand horses galloping from heaven down to earth, and should look like multiple roofs, with vibrant trees and lush greens growing around". It also says, "if the shape (of the mountains and hills) looks like the crown of a tree, the site is prosperous and happy, whereas if it looks like the scattered beads of an abacus, all things will be in chaos".[5] This is the advice based on a direct visual observation of the form and the propensity of the landscape.

Rational Method

Initially, rationality (*li*) here referred to managing *qi* (air and flow of vitality or life force), and in Chinese medicine it referred to managing the inner *qi* of the human body – for example, "reduce heat when *qi* is in discordance, and add nutritious intake if *qi* is weak and voided". In Yang's fengshui framework, reason or rationality here refers to rationally knowing and managing. In the phrase "managing the flow" (*li qi*), *qi* refers to air or flow of life force, which include water and ten thousand things animate or inanimate, and *li-qi* together refers to knowing the dynamic operations of *qi* and managing it for our human purpose. In the overall process of assessing a terrain, knowing and managing constitute the second step, allowing a deeper understanding of and engagement with of the vital forces of the place in its totality.

The actual operation involves the use of the compass (and other devices and diagrams) at a central point of the site to assess the positioning and characters – in astrological terms – of the Arrival Dragon (*ru shou long*, the mountain that arrives onto the terrain) and Water Mouth (*shui kou*, where rivers or streams arrive into the terrain). First, it needs to find out where Water Mouth belongs – gold, water, wood, and fire; then it needs to discover to which dragon the mountain belongs – in a distribution of 72 dragons. If it is found that the Water Mouth and Arriving Dragon belong to the same constellation in Chinese astrology, the next step is to see if the flow of vitality from the dragon comes directly onto the site and if propensities and forms (of the dragon mountain) are in correspondence. If the Water Mouth and Arriving Dragon in question are found not to be in the same constellation, then the site (where observation is made) has to be shifted left or right, until the two are in the same area in the Chinese celestial terms. One is advised never to choose a site where the two are not the same.

Removing Hills and Collecting Water Bodies for Assuring the Site

This is the third step in assessing the terrain; it involves "removing hills and collecting waters" (and other procedures such as "ascertaining the site with dragons"). It is a process of observing external flows of vitality and ways of managing them. Guo Pu in *Book of Burial* says, "external flows can support the storing of internal flows; while outside flows come laterally (in front of the site), inside flows (within and behind the site) settle and reside".[6] These expressions suggest a dialectic and mutually interdependent considerations of internal vitality and those from outside (front, left, and right from the perspective of the site).

More specifically, "removing hills" (*xiao sha*) refers to some shifting of the site so that hills and mountains to the left, right, and ahead, the array of peaks facing us, can be best positioned, for the most favorable prospect for the site – the actual process includes a "meeting of the dragons", and a correspondence of dragons and water flows, for the sites of the living (houses) and the dead (graves). "Collecting waters" (*na shui*) refers to an assessment of the entry points where rivers and streams arrive, their forms, bodies, directions, and qualities, and their overall liveliness and resourcefulness.

Principles and Techniques in Fengshui

Yang's fengshui practice, for example in its assessment and employment of a Water Mouth (where a water body arrives at the terrain), employs special terms, theories, and techniques – such as "double hills with five elements", "unity of three", "four water mouths", "twelve palaces of longevity", and "72 dragons".

Unity of Three

In assessing terrain, Yang's fengshui theory emphasizes relations between a building site ("cave", the deep, the mysterious) and water's entry point ("opening", "water mouth"), and says that "departing water goes to rest while arriving water comes in for prosperity". These ideas of rest and growth or prosperity come from a theory of "unity of three" (*sanhe lun*). It refers to the three stages of life of all things – "birth", "growth", "graveyard". The assessment of the site and the flow of water bodies in terms of the three is based on a series of diagrams with ancient Chinese symbolic systems, as documented in Yang's *Manuel of the Jade Ruler* (*Yuchi Jing*). More precisely, the three stages of the 12 Earthly Branches (used for 12 two-hours a day, 12 months in a lunar year, 12 animals of the zodiac and other systems, all parallel to each other) – Zi, Chou, Yin, Mao, Chen, Si, Wu, Wei, Shen, You, Xu, Hai – counting from noon or eleventh month on – are expressed in the characters of the four of the Five Elements (gold, wood, water, fire, earth). One of the earliest famous expressions of this is found in *Huainanzi* (Writings of the Huanan masters) by Liu An (179–122 BC) of West Han Dynasty (202 BC–9 AD): the three stages of birth, growth, and death of the four elements are, respectively, Hai, Mao, Wei for wood; Yin, Wu, Xu for fire; Si, You, Chou for gold; and Shen, Zi, Chen for water (Figure 11.1).

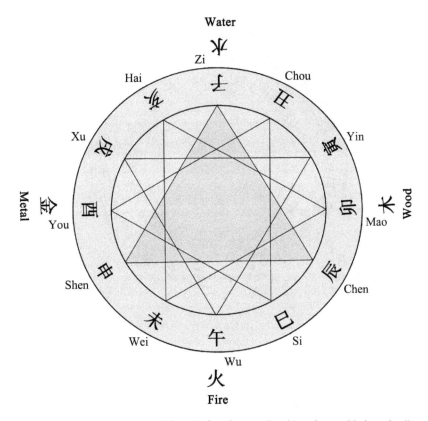

Figure 11.1 Diagram showing "unity of three," "five elements," and "twelve earthly branches."
Source: © Jianjun Cheng.

Twelve Palaces of Longevity

In fengshui theory, the three stages of life are regarded as not refined enough, and a more elaborate staging of the life process was therefore created – the twelve palaces. Following and corresponding to the twelve Earthly Branches, the palaces for the cycle are: Birth, Bath, Attire, Coming-of-Age, Prosperity Peak, Aging, Sickness, Death, Graveyard, Repose, Womb, and Cultivation. The Twelve Palace theory was widely used within and beyond fengshui practice.

Four Zones of Water Mouths

How do fengshui masters identify and analyze water bodies and flows? They employ the compass with a set of diagrams and symbolic references. In this framework, land is divided into four directions with corresponding natural elements and astrological constellations: east relates to wood and Zhen, west gold and Dui, north water and Kan, and south fire and Li. In Yang's theory of assessing a terrain, the compass, with the use of other diagrams and systems (double hills, Five Elements, twelve palaces), divides directions into four zones for water mouths, matching the cardinal points and their references; and each zone has three of the twelve palaces. In

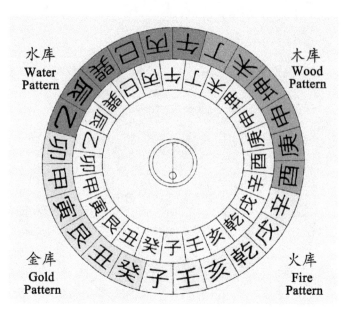

水库
Water
Pattern

木库
Wood
Pattern

金库
Gold
Pattern

火库
Fire
Pattern

Figure 11.2 Four zones of "water mouths" on the twelve and twenty-four points (branches, seasons, and orientations).

Source: © Jianjun Cheng.

assessing a real "water mouth", the compass pointers can detect the fortune and character of that entry of water in terms of its position in the cycle of life and longevity as framed in the symbolic and astrological system (Figure 11.2).

On the whole, Yang's theory inherited Guo Pu's essence of "storing and riding on dynamic flows" (*zang cheng sheng qi*). He uses formal methods to examine hills and water bodies, to search and assess dragons (mountains) and the cave (a suitable site), and to shift positions for "eliminating" hills and collecting water flows (*xiao sha na shui*). He then uses rational methods to ensure a unity of three aspects, including that of dragons, water bodies, and orientations, by using Earthly Branches and their associated systems and descriptions of time, space, and life. Yang emphasizes that dragons and water bodies must originate from a prosperous region, while rivers and streams must also flow away into sites of graveyard and storage.

Spiritual Tablets of Master Yang

Due to the popularity of Yang Yunsong in the Hakka regions of southern China, Yang's talisman was prevailing there, which usually included objects with characters such as "Yang", "Yang Yunsong", or "Yang Who Saves the Poor" written or inscribed, for expelling evil spirits. A typical form was a special cubic bamboo or wood artifact with characters written on four sides, which was used in an initiation ritual for building a house or a tomb. Referred to as Fortune Wood of Master Yang (*yang gong fu mu*), it was placed on the site facing the coming mountain. The process of preparing included: making the wood, writing on the wood, wrapping it with red cloth, worshipping the wood, placing the wood, and saying farewell to the wood.[7] The object was often made of fir, peach wood, or bamboo. Selection of the shape and dimensions of such a tablet must follow strict rules and the associated symbolic meaning. Solemn rites for worshipping master Yang were conducted before and during erecting such a spiritual tablet. In modern times, procedures have been much simplified. Sometimes, characters are written on paper – red paper for building a house suggesting celebration and happiness, and yellow paper for a graveyard or tomb for expelling evil spirits.

Case Studies

I have conducted case studies to test how fengshui theories are applied. As Yang's school or Jiangxi School was popular in the southern Hakka regions – southern Jiangxi, western Fujian, and northern Guangdong especially – and was also brought north by the imperial authorities, I will cite two cases: a Hakka round-shaped house tower in Fujian, and the Forbidden Palace of Beijing, to show their use of fengshui ideas in relation to water bodies and water flows.

Eryi Lou House Tower in Hua'an of Fujian

Eryi Lou House Tower is located in Dadi Village, Xiandu County, Hua'an Prefecture, in western Fujian Province. It was completed in 1770, after 30 years' construction, by Jiang Shixiong with his six sons and 17 grandsons. It is very large in scale, in the shape of a drum or cylinder, with a diameter of 71.2 meters; it has a four-story outer circular building and a single-story inner circular building. It accommodated some 400 people at one time. The 600-square meter courtyard in the center provides a public open space for daily life and communication for the residents of the large family. With stones at the lower parts and rammed earth further up, the outer wall is 2.5 meter thick and 0.8 meter at the top floor (fresco paintings are found on the walls; with high cultural values, it is now listed as a national heritage).

Eryi Building is perfectly situated in the environment. It sits in the southeast, is facing northwest, and is surrounded by hills and mountains. It rests against Centipede Mountain (*wugong shan*) to its back to the southeast, with the mountain's dragon vein winding and twisting down from Stone Cup Mountain (*beishi shan*) in the distance, with dynamic propensity; in fengshui terms, it has an arriving dragon "shifting lively with vitality" (*ququ ruhuo*) and an arriving range like "a bell covering the ground" (*xingru fuzhong*). Next to the arriving range, on a platform, stands the round building, like a pearl. In front of the building, a broad perspective opens up, with a spectacular view of farmlands. Two clear streams flow in from both sides, converging in front of the building, then running away to irrigate the fields. The axis of the main gate extends to Big Turtle Mountain (*dagui shan*) at the center of the vista, and further on to Mount Nine Dragons (*jiulong shan*) further away – the open view covers a "shrine" (*an*) and an "orientation" (*chao*), that is, a terminal landmark and a vast distant backdrop – using fengshui terms for the ideal prospect in the front of a building. A Lion Hill (*shizi shan*) runs to the left, and a Tiger Hill (*huxing shan*) comes in to protect to the right, creating a balance and a gradual opening of spaces extending into the distance. The selection of the site and the building of the house created a favorable ecological setting and a great landscape – with the qualities of "storing winds and gathering flows" (*cang feng ju qi*) and characters for nurturing one's mind, eye, body, and life.

In a closer study (using Earthly Branches), it is found that the stream from the left falls into the zone of "Prosperity Peak", and the stream from the right the zone of "Birth" – both are the best in the twelve palaces of longevity. Further, the location of their joining belongs to "Repose" and that of their exit – a Water Mouth – belongs to "Graveyard" in the Twelve Palace system. This fits well with the advice that an arriving water body be on the rise or growth and the departing flow goes to rest and to be stored. For the relations between the building site (*xuan*, the deep and mysterious) and the arrival points of water bodies (water mouths and

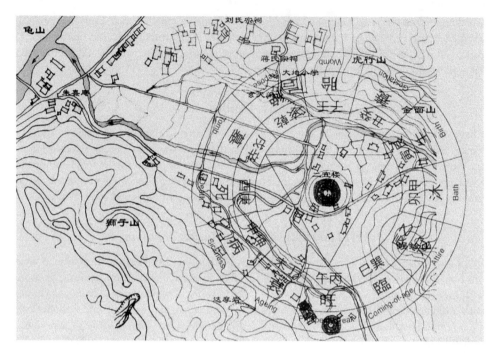

Figure 11.3 Distribution of water entries (water mouths) for Eryi Building of Fujian.

Source: © Jianjun Cheng.

openings, *shui kou* and *qiao*), both belong "Fire" of the Five Elements – which fits well the advice that the two should be consistent and connected. The arrangement reveals the teaching of Yang's school of fengshui closely (Figure 11.3).

Water Design in the Forbidden City of Imperial Beijing

Fengshui ideas were used for not only vernacular buildings but also religious temples, and even imperial palaces, such as the Forbidden City of Beijing, of the Ming and Qing dynasties (1420–1911). The planning of the palace city followed the rules of *Zhou Li Kaogong Ji* ("Notes on construction" in *Rites of Zhou*), for grand imperial ceremonies and for presenting an auspicious outlook: following the decree from heaven, the imperial authority is justified and is to last forever, with its mountains and waters living on in prosperity and perpetuity. The palace city sits in the north and faces down to the south; it has a Perspective Hill (Jingshan) to the north (built with earth dug up nearby, which also created Central and South Lakes or Zhongnanhai to the west) and a Golden River (*jinshui he*) surrounding the palace city as a moat, thus offering an ideal situation of the building as protected by hills and water flows, for "storing vitality" (*ju qi*). In between is the vast palatial complex – the palace city or the Forbidden City – which is well protected by walls and gates; such a design is ideal for storing wind and air, with static forms and dynamic propensities, and with openness in front and closure at back, with an aura that is both peaceful and celebrated, austere, and spectacular.

Inside the Forbidden City, there is an Inner Golden River (*nei jinshui he*), which enters from the northwest corner, then winds down to the south, passing by key front buildings including – from west to east – Hall of Martial Grace, Gate of Supreme Harmony, Hall of Civil Glory, and

Library of Deep Culture; it takes the shape of a bow, symbolizing protection in front of the Gate of Supreme Harmony; it then winds on eastward, out of the Forbidden City. The trajectory is slow and graceful, shifting between going and returning in posture. According to fengshui analysis, the arriving water is in the Coming-of-Age (or Becoming-an-Official, *lin guan*) position and the departing point is in the Repose position (in an alternative assessment using the center of Hall of Supreme Harmony, the arriving and departing points are Prosperity Peak and Repose respectively). In either case, it fits well the teaching of fengshui – "arriving water is to become prosperous and departing water is to rest and to be stored". Further, in an analysis of the arriving dragons in terms of the Five Elements (and other references such as "72 dragons"), the dragon belongs to "earth" and is judged as consistent with the astrological constellations of the site and the water flow.[8] These are not coincidences, but evidence of a careful design that closely followed teachings of Yang Yunsong – with or by some successors of Yang in fengshui design (Figure 11.4).

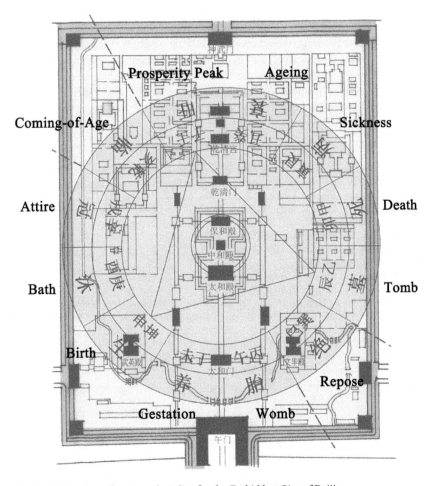

Figure 11.4 Distribution of water and vitality for the Forbidden City of Beijing.

Source: © Jianjun Cheng.

There were historical connections between the fengshui pattern of the Forbidden City and Yang's fengshui teaching. The Forbidden City in Beijing was constructed in 1406–20. Some of the designer-builders, including Lei Fada (1619–1693) and his family, were from Jiangxi Province. Because of Yang Yunsong's wide influence, Jiangxi fengshui masters were invited to assess the terrains and to site and design the imperial tombs of the Ming and Qing dynasties in Beijing and northern China. For example, in 1407, Liao Junqing (1350–1413), a fengshui master from Jiangxi, was invited to assess terrain for siting and design of Ming Tombs, including its main Changling Tomb, to the west of Beijing. His excellent service won him titles and abundant reward.[9] Liao was an offspring of Liao Yu (943–1018), and both Liao Yu and Zeng Wenchan (854–916) were the students of Yang Yunsong. Although Liao died before the completion of the Forbidden City, there was enough overlap in time and circles of contact. It is reasonable to assume an involvement of Liao and his Jiangxi contact – an impact of Yang in terms of fengshui teaching.

Conclusion

Fengshui teaching had a wide impact in ancient China on selecting sites and planning building design. It was widely used for not only vernacular structures but also temples, imperial tombs, and royal palaces and their government compounds. Regionally, it also asserted impact in other countries of East Asia, such as Japan and Korea, where Han culture was broadly adopted and absorbed. With more fieldwork and more analysis to come, fengshui, as part of the culture behind the production of buildings and built environment in China, will surely bring us a richer and deeper understanding of architecture and its intentions.

Notes

1 Guo Pu, *Zang Jing* (Book of Burial), in *Gujin Tushu Jicheng, Yishu Dian, Kanyu Bu, Huikao Shiwu* (Collection of Books Past and Present: Arts and Techniques; Geomancy, part 15), ed. Chen Menglei and Jiang Tingxi (Beijing: Imperial Palace, 1726), in *Siku Quanshu Kanyu Lei Dianji Yanjiu* (Inquiry into the Books on Fengshui as Collected in *Complete Books in Four Libraries*) (Shanghai: Shanghai Guji Chubanshe, 2007), 192.
2 Guo Pu, *Zang Jing,* in Li Dingxin, *Siku Quanshu*, 192.
3 Guo Pu, *Zang Jing,* in Li Dingxin, *Siku Quanshu*, 192.
4 Li Dingxin, *Siku Quanshu*, 647.
5 Guo Pu, *Zang Jing,* in Li Dingxin, *Siku Quanshu*, 194.
6 Guo Pu, *Zang Jing,* in Li Dingxin, *Siku Quanshu*, 192.
7 Chen Jinguo, *Fengshui de Lishi Renlei Xue Tansuo: Xinyang, Yishi yu Xiangtu Shehui, Shang* (A historical and Anthropological Study on Fengshui: Belief, Ritual and Folk Society, Part 1) (Beijing: Zhongguo Shehui Kexue Chubanshe, 2005), 372.
8 Chen Ran, "Zijincheng fengshui geju tanmi (Inquiry into the Use of Fengshui for the Design of the Forbidden City)", in *Fengshui Wenhua Luncong* (Essays in Fengshui Culture), ed. Wu Xiaoheng (Beijing: Dazhong Wenyi Chubanshe, 2008), 285–290.
9 Chen Ran, "Zijingcheng fengshui", 286.

Bibliography

Chen Jinguo. *Fengshui de Lishi Renlei Xue Tansuo: Xinyang, Yishi yu Xiangtu Shehui, Shang* (A Historical and Anthropological Study on fengshui: Belief, Ritual and Folk Society, Part 1). Beijing: Zhongguo Shehui Kexue Chubanshe, 2005.
Chen Menglei and Jiang Tingxi, eds. *Gujin Tushu Jicheng* (Collection of Books Past and Present). Beijing: Imperial Palace, 1726.

Chen Ran. "Zijincheng fengshui geju tanmi (Inquiry into the Use of Fengshui for the Design of the Forbidden City)". In *Fengshui Wenhua Luncong* (Essays in Fengshui Culture), edited by Wu Xiaoheng, 285–290. Beijing: Dazhong Wenyi Chubanshe, 2008.

Cheng Jianjun. *Jingtian Weidi: Zhongguo Luopan Xiangjie* (Measuring Heaven and Earth: A Detailed Explanation on the Chinese Compass). Beijing: Zhongguo Dianying Chubanshe, 2005.

———. "Fengshui 'shuikou' linian yu Zhongguo minju (Concepts of the "Water Mouth" and Vernacular Houses in China)". In *Fengshui Wenhua Luncong* (Essays on Fengshui Culture), edited by Wu Xiaoheng, 245–253. Beijing: Dazhong Wenyi Chubanshe, 2008.

Editorial Committee, ed. *Fujian Tulou* (Tulou Buildings of Fujian Province: Application for the World Heritage). Beijing: Zhongguo Dabaike Quanshu Chubanshe, 2007.

Gao Yunfei. *Lingnan chuantong cunluo renju rehuanjing yanjiu* (A Study on Thermal Environment of Lingnan Traditional Villages). PhD Thesis. South China University of Technology, Guangzhou, 2007.

Guo Pu. "Zang Jing (Book of Burial)". In *Gujin Tushu Jicheng, Yishu Dian, Kanyu Bu, Huikao Shiwu* (Collection of Books Past and Present: Arts and Techniques; Geomancy, part 15), edited by Chen Menglei and Jiang Tingxi (Beijing: Imperial Palace, 1726). In *Siku Quanshu Kanyu Lei Dianji Yanjiu* (Inquiry into the Books on Fengshui as Collected in *Complete Books in Four Libraries*), edited by Li Dingxin, 192. Shanghai: Shanghai Guji Chubanshe, 2007.

Hua'an Tulou World Heritage Application Team, ed. *Hua'an Tulou* (Tulou Building of Hua'an). Zhangzhou: Hua'an Tulou World Heritage, 2002.

Huang Hanmin. *Fujian Tulou* (Tulou Buildings of the Fujian Province). Taipei: Hansheng Zazhishe, 1994.

———. *Fujian Tulou: Zhongguo Chuantong Minju de Guibao* (Fujian Tulou: The Treasure of Chinese Vernacular Architecture). Beijing: SDX Joint Publishing, 2003.

Li Dingxin. *Siku Quanshu Kanyu Lei Dianji Yanjiu* (Inquiry into the Books on Fengshui as Collected in *Complete Books in Four Libraries*). Shanghai: Shanghai Guji Chubanshe, 2007.

Liu Bingzhong and Li Feng, eds. *Pingsha Yuchi Jing* (Book of the Jade Ruler of Pingsha). Haikou: Hainan Chubanshe, 2003.

Wu Weiguang. *Weilongwu jianzhu xingtai de tuxiangxue yanjiu* (An Iconographical Study on the Architectural Form of Weilongwu). PhD Thesis. South China University of Technology, Guangzhou, 2008.

Wu Xiaoheng, ed. *Fengshui Wenhua Luncong* (Essays in Fengshui Culture). Beijing: Dazhong Wenyi Chubanshe, 2008.

Glossary

an	案
Beijing	北京
beishi shan	杯石山
cang feng de shui	藏风得水
cang feng ju qi	藏风聚气
Changling	长陵
chao	朝
chao shan chao shui	朝山朝水
Chen	辰
cheng sheng qi	乘生气
Chou	丑
Dadi (village)	大地（村）
dagui shan	大龟山
de shui	得水
Dui	兑
Eryi Lou	二宜楼
fang	方
feng	风
feng fa	峰法

fengshui (feng-shui)	风水
fengzhen	缝针
Fujian	福建
Ganzhou	赣州
guan	关
Guo Pu	郭璞
Hai	亥
Han	汉
Hanlong Jing	撼龙经
Hua'an (prefecture)	华安（县）
Huainanzi	淮南子
Huang Chao	黄巢
huxing shan	虎行山
Jiang Shixiong	蒋士雄
Jiangxi	江西
Jingshan	景山
jinshui he	金水河
jiulong shan	九龙山
ju qi	聚气
Kan	坎
Kaogong Ji	考工记
Lei Fada	雷发达
li	理
Li	离
li qi (li-qi)	理气
Liao Junqing	廖均卿
Liao Yu	廖瑀
lin guan	临官
Liu An	刘安
long	龙
long fa	龙法
long mai	龙脉
Mao	卯
Ming (dynasty)	明（朝）
muku	墓库
na shui	纳水
nei cheng sheng qi	内乘生气
nei jinshui he	内金水河
qiao	窍
Qing (dynasty)	清（朝）
Qingnang Aoyu	青囊奥语
ququ ruhuo	屈曲如活
ru shou long	入首龙
sanhe lun	三合论
sha	砂
sha fa	砂法
Shen	申
sheng qi	生气

shi	势
shizi shan	狮子山
shui	水
shui fa	水法
shui kou	水口
Si	巳
Tang (dynasty)	唐（朝）
Tianyu Jingxu	天玉经序
wai jie tang qi	外接堂气
Wang Ji	王伋
Wei	未
Wu	午
wugong shan	蜈蚣山
Xiandu (county)	仙都（镇）
xiang	向
xiao sha	消砂
xiao sha na shui	消砂纳水
xing	形
xing fa	形法
xing-shi	形势
xingru fuzhong	形如覆钟
Xu	戌
xuan	玄
xuan qiao xiang ying	玄窍相应
xuan-guan	玄关
xue	穴
xue fa	穴法
yang gong fu mu	杨公符木
Yang Jiupin	杨救贫
Yang Yunsong	杨筠松
Yangxianling	杨仙岭
Yilong Jing	疑龙经
Yin	寅
You	酉
Yuchi Jing	玉尺经
Yuchi Tang	玉尺堂
Yudu	于都
zang cheng sheng qi	葬乘生气
Zang Shu	葬书
Zeng Wenchan	曾文辿
Zhao Yizhi	赵翼之
Zhen	震
zhen long xue di	真龙穴的
zhengzhen	正针
Zhongnanhai	中南海
Zhou Li	周礼
Zi	子

12

CARPENTRY IN VERNACULAR BUILDING PRACTICE

The Master's Way

Chang Yu-yu

In traditional Chinese architecture, a timber frame with wooden posts and beams typically provides the basic structure of the building, to which wood, brick, stone, and other materials are added, to complete the building. In this practice, "major carpentry" (*damuzuo*) or structural woodwork, as it provides the design and construction for the main structure, constitutes the leading and foundational work, above and along with other divisions of labor, such as tilework, stonework, earthwork, and paintwork. Besides imperial and governmental projects, an overwhelming number of vernacular houses and temples were constructed by local builders. Of these, the chief master of major carpentry (*damu jiangshi*) occupies the top position in a hierarchical organization of the builders and leads the whole team to complete projects with regional characteristics, using special skills handed down over generations, in a unique historical transfer of knowledge from masters to apprentices.

In a Chinese culture that privileges statecraft and systems of thought rather than vernacular techniques, there were few literary works recording these technical bodies of knowledge. That the masters were secret about their skills to protect their professional positions added another reason for the lack of written records. The *chuandou* timber system that was practiced in southern China, as it circulated mostly among local craftsmen, suffers from this problem more. Apart from a publication *Yingzao Fayuan* (Methods of building construction)[1] that covers a bit on the craftsmanship of Xuangshang Group[2], there is very little available to us in historical description or modern study on how constructions have been carried out in the local vernacular contexts – local knowledge hides in the dense layers of silent practice. The local building tradition of Fujian Province embodies one of the key versions of the *chuandou* building tradition of southern China. To expose a local building tradition and to examine *chuandou* structure, this chapter focuses on a folk system of practice in Fujian and examines its tradition of training and organization, its structural characteristics, and its ways of communication for design and construction.

Training and lineage: The Chief Master of Major Carpentry

In a team of builders in the folk practice, there are three levels of people in each section of the work as determined by skills and experience – apprentice, artisan, and master. However, in structural timberwork or "major carpentry," there is another level above these, a singular position occupied by one person in the term – *damu jiangshi* or chief master of major carpentry.

DOI: 10.4324/9781315851112-17

He is not only the head of the section of structural carpentry but also leads the entire team of builders at the top of the pyramid of workmanship. All sections are to follow the overall design and command of the chief master in a coordinated manner. But in terms of training, the starting point for an apprentice to reach this position, if ever, is actually the same as those in other sections. For a young apprentice in the folk tradition, he typically has two pathways to become a chief master – to join a master's team as an apprentice-student, or to learn in and inherit one's own family business.

After joining a master's team as an apprentice-student, it takes three years and four months to complete the program. Before starting, the student's kowtowing and paying tribute to the master constitute an important initiation and a rite of passage. He must first pay tribute to the Guardian God and Sage Teacher of the profession, to confirm his reverence to the profession, sincerity for the career, and determination to work hard in learning. He then needs to convey to the master that parental respect, life-long gratitude, and an entire willingness to study are to be dedicated to the master. For this, he needs to write these words down on and sign a formal letter, and then reverently present it to the master in a kneeling posture – a ritual called "seeking for admission." When the apprenticeship has been completed, the rule is that students shall never compete with the master for business and must return to help when called upon.

For the second pathway, where one learns in and inherits one's own family tradition, there are two types in terms of the business – those from a large clan[3] and those within a smaller family. Obviously, in these cases, one has already been destined to follow the profession since young, but in some cases, a student may also go through a formal apprenticeship with a fixed master.

For an apprentice, his study is combined with his practice. What he learns are the basic skills needed for all artisans in the trade. An apprentice is an artisan at the lowest level; when he completes the program after three years and four months, he becomes the second-stage artisan and begins to earn a salary. After years of practice with a lot of experience, a few most competent ones may become stage-three senior artisans or masters; among these masters, one may be further elevated – as a candidate successor for the existing head – to be a chief master of major carpentry.

Typically, within local communities, despite the presence of many artisans and masters, there are only a few highly respected chief masters – and only they are entrusted with prestigious commissions of state offices, renowned temples, and large mansions. However, when an apprentice is studying as a first-stage artisan, there is no plan for teaching and cultivating one to become the chief master, nor can any student-artisan just learn some skills to obtain an executive capability. A student can learn some technical knowledge from the program of studying and working, yet certain executive and overall competence can only be learned by examining existing ancient buildings. Chief masters – as we will find – have learned a lot by closely observing these ancient masterpieces.

Due to the pragmatic nature of the craftsmanship, teaching centers less on imparting abstract knowledge and more on empirical learning through hands-on work experience. The emphasis on direct personal learning with a master also reveals a reverence in the tradition for unspoken knowledge and intuitive experience gained through embodied practice. Such a pattern of learning and imparting knowledge also secures the historical durability of the culture of building. As explained by themselves, most chief masters' methods were initially learned during their apprenticeship – from large-scale work on structural frames, assemblage, dimensions of parts, styles, and sculpture work, to small-scale techniques such as the use of tools and of measuring rulers. With the inheriting of knowledge over generations in this manner, great wisdom is shaped, accumulated, and embodied into the styles of vernacular architecture. In this process, the practice of apprenticeship becomes a coordinate system for anchoring a specific regional architecture.

Characteristics and Design Principles of The *Chuandou* Structure

In a typical building in traditional Chinese architecture, the structural frame constitutes longitudinal timber frames jointed together by lateral beams and purlins. Between every two longitudinal frames, that is, when a bay is created, there is a so-called *kaijian* (lateral spacing and opening) in the lateral direction and a *bujia* (step distance between two rows of purlins) in the longitudinal direction; by creating a basic spatial unit, these mark two basic measures of spacing or distance respectively. In this three-dimensional structural unit, the careful placing of the altitude of the purlins (each resting on posts) determines the curving profile of the roof on top. The building of this basic unit reveals two major technical problems for constructing the whole building – maintaining stability for the vertical posts and securing stability for the beams, the purlins, and the roof frame above.

Ancient Chinese timber architecture had two basic structural types. In the north, a *tailiang* (raising-the-beam) structure was widely used: on the longitudinal direction, beams that rest on posts support purlins on top that in turn support roof elements, and, importantly, smaller posts are placed on the beams, supporting smaller beams further up, achieving three to five levels of beams. In the south, a *chuandou* (beams-going-through) structure was often used – beams go through posts, and posts go straight to the top to support purlins and the roof, in the longitudinal framework. The types here reveal important differences in stability consideration, structural design, and method of assemblage.

In the design of the *chuandou* structure, we can detect three important techniques used for raising the stability of the frame – spreading the load onto the posts, lateral pull and connection, and three-dimensional consolidation. The first secures the roof weight, passing down directly to the posts, which are horizontally interconnected by beams going through them for the whole structural plane; the second ensures a stable framework by using the beams and lintels laterally passing through the posts of different bays; and the third refers to all members compiling and coming together here onto the post via mortise-and-tenon joineries, so that the mortises on the post play a central role to secure stability in all directions of the whole structure. In this way, stability relies on the interrelations of the parts going into or through the post; the careful design of the mortises for the tenons is therefore central to the whole process. For the chief master of major carpentry, the post marks not only a spatial position but also the beginning of the whole construction (Figure 12.1).

The importance of the post comes from the contribution the mortise-and-tenon joineries – gathering onto the post – are making for the entire structure. The design of the mortises is therefore central to a reasonable distribution of forces. Based on accumulated experience, the chief masters often have a very clear idea on this: he needs to determine a distribution of forces based on the position and the shape of the parts, and then he needs to specify the types of the tenons on the two ends of a structural member and provide specific design if necessary.

The principal idea in designing the mortise-tenon joineries is to protect stability of those that receive pressure. This is manifested through several methods. When several members come to intersect with the post, the tenons of the parts not receiving pressures need to give way to those receiving force or bearing load, and "reduced tenons" (*jian sun*) will be used here to secure enough absorption of pressure into the post. In terms of placing, those receiving pressure use "upper tenons" (*shang sun*) and those being pulled use "lower tenons" (*xia sun*) to secure a good locking relationship. Those receiving weight or pressure can also use "through tenons" (*tou sun*) with hardwood keys inserted on the other side to secure; and members not receiving force – such as simple bracket sets (*cha gong*) – may just be slotted into the post. For mortise-tenon joineries that act as an ornament or as parts to be pulled, the carving for mortise holes requires

Figure 12.1 Example of the *chuandou* structure commonly used in Fujian Province.

Source: Photo taken inside Liujitang Temple, Hanjiang District, Putian City, 2004. © Chang Yu-yu.

a loose approach for ease and flexibility. Apart from the rules of "giving way," chief masters also use differentiated heights for the different members coming into the post in a way that enhances overall stability. For the section of the members, the masters can use round shape or a rectangular of 3:2 or 3:1 ratio, depending on the situation, with the same principle (Figure 12.2).

Most of these methods are well established and have been handed down over generations. A second-stage artisan can manage all these without special explanations. The drawings of the chief master thus often don't give special designs and notations on these. The third-stage artisan, as masters, act as a connecting point between the ideas of the chief master and the actual carving and chiseling of the artisans – by translating the chief's drawings into ink lines marked onto the parts and members for the artisans to work on.

When the members are assembled, one is unable to see the internal locking of the tenons and mortises, but the ink lines that survived on the posts usually indicate the quality of the work. It is usually said that good skills are evidenced in "fine workmanship and rich ink lines." This saying suggests that, when one examines the work, one checks if the board or part has been "roughly flattened," "finely planned," and "smoothly polished" – the three required steps. One then checks the ink lines on the post: the left and right sides of a mortise can be slightly eased, whereas the top and bottom sides are expected to be tighter – and if the holes are a bit too big, the ink lines will be faint or nearly invisible, which indicates a lesser craftsmanship. On the whole, masters loosely place members together first and then, when the frame is checked for positioning and adjusted, press the frame together with all its joineries into a tight whole.

Figure 12.2 The various mortise-tenon joineries used for the round-shaped beam frames in Fujian.

Source: Photo taken in Zhangzhou and Quanzhou regions, 2003. © Chang Yu-yu.

If the survival of the ink lines after assemblage indicates the competence of artisans and masters, then the accuracy of the mortise holes carved out on the posts attests to the capacity of the chief master supervising the whole project. All beams, regardless of whether their sectional shapes are round or rectangular, adopt tenon heads in the shape of a rectangle – of difference sizes and ratios. Here, at the point where beams are coming into the post, they may arrive in four or six directions; and where mortises are carved into the post, the depth cannot be longer than one-third of the diameter of the post, to ensure the integrity of the wooden column. Since the diameter imposes restrictions on the dimensions of the mortises and tenons, this dimension – along with the position – of the posts takes great priority and has to be decided first. Yet, in the chief master's drawings, we usually cannot find the diameters of the posts marked out clearly. Why is that?

In these traditional buildings, the posts are wooden columns in a round shape with the diameter at top being smaller than that at base. However, natural tree material comes in all shapes and sizes. When these timber pieces are collected into the building site, they are initially shaped into embryonic posts – and other parts – of different lengths and of varying diameter differentials for the two ends of each post. The chief master then makes flexible but careful decisions as to which one goes where for the posts. This requires a cautious planning in design, budgeting, material collection for the posts' diameters and the size of the building beforehand, and then a flexible redesign when the embryonic posts are actually distributed to the points for a finer specification on diameters and heights of the columns – using diameters at the top of the posts for planning the mortises. This perhaps echoes Laozi's renowned saying in *Tao Te Ching* (or *Laozi* or *Lao Tzu*), "solid material gives us utility, and void openness provides greater function" (*you zhi yiwei li, wu zhi yiwei yong*). The unspecified diameters of the post in the drawings and the void holes of the mortises reveal in fact complex and active thinking by the chief master in managing the structural frame of the building. Other masters and artisans, in their respective work, also exercise concrete skills and active flexibility.

In this process, where the diameters of the posts and the dimensions of the mortise-tenon joineries determine the sizes of other parts, the major beam (*da liang*), biggest in size and longest in span, plays a determining role. Taking priority in the design of its joineries over that of others, its size and the diameters of the columns it connects with become the starting point for determining dimensions of other parts and members. In this process, all other parts – no matter how rich and complex they may look – can be designed and determined one by one, in an orderly manner without confusion.

There are non-structural parts and members where ornamental considerations are important. For the overall structure and the building, ornamental and aesthetic preference are important, at times more than the economy of material use and the efficiency of the structure. Regional styles emerge at this point and are secured for their durability through collective sharing within and between teams, and generational inheritance over a long time. The masters take great pride in their work, not just its technical calculations, but also the overall grandeur and beauty of the completed building they have made.

Drawings and Communications of The Chief Master

If you visit a building site where structural woodwork is underway, you will find that it is not easy to find drawings of the plans, sections, elevations, and details we normally use. If you ask supervising masters for these, they may show you a cedar-wood stick – or a bamboo stick split open – of several meters long with signs and notations marked. And if you ask the chief master if there are more drawings, he may finally manage to find and show an untidy sheet – tucked in somewhere amid work cabinets – with a very simple plan of the building. So, how do they manage the whole process of design and construction? What system of visual communication do they use?

In southern China, such as in Fujian Province, vernacular builders, mainly chief masters, use these ways of visual communication from design to completion: floorplan drawing, sectional drawing, roof profile drawing ("water diagrams" or *shui gua tu*), drawing of notations and measurements, and special ruler sticks called *gao chi*. In practice, a specific team uses only some of these means of visual communication.

Floorplan Drawing

This drawing uses single axial lines to describe the column grid of the whole building, with each column or post marked by its center point; positions of doors, orientations of the building, and notations in fengshui terms (using Luban Chi measuring rulers) are also marked. This drawing is made only at the beginning of design; when confirmed, the interval distances between the posts are translated and drawn onto a long cedar-wood stick with several faces – known as wooden "stick of zhang" (*zhang gao*) – *zhang* being a Chinese unit of measuring (1 *zhang* = 320 cm); and the smaller distances and dimensions are marked onto a smaller "stick of chi" (*chi gao*) – chi being 1/10 of zhang. The long stick of zhang or "Zhang Gao," marking distances from center to center for the posts, is the most important reference for the whole process. The drawing, by comparison, is not as important. It may be left aside, or sometimes used for managing the construction by adding notes (names of the beams, dimensions of mortises, and the progression of construction).

Sectional Drawing

For builders working with the *chuandou* structure in the south, a sectional drawing describes a frame – as a structural plane or truss – on a longitudinal section of the building and is described as "a surface of frames assembled with tenons" by the builders. Depending on the actual situation, it can be simple or complex – a sketch, a visual drawing for communication with the client, or a working drawing for use in construction. Similar to the idea of the Zhang Gao, a cedar-wood board is used on which the section is marked with dimensions at the scale of 1:10 or 1:20. With this "standard board" (*yang ban tu*) on display, all in the team can go and check (Figure 12.3).

Figure 12.3   Standard drawing on a cedar-wood board at 1:10.

Source: Photo taken on construction site for Zhizhi'an Nunnery in Wuyishan region, 2003. © Chang Yu-yu.

Roof Profile Drawing

Also known as "water diagram" (*shui gua tu*), this depicts the design of the roof profile. Based on the overall longitudinal span, the height of the roof ridge, the height of the eaves, and the two sloping lines on the two sides, the relative heights of each purlin are determined after subtle adjustments in order to secure an elegant and concave curve of the roof profile, for the front and back of the roof. The critical issue here is the height of each purlin. The actual process here is a secret guarded by the chief masters, to protect their trade. Sometimes, when a building is going through restoration, a board may be found in the building on which methods for determining the curve profile are described. At times, a roof profile drawing, with details of beams and posts, may be drawn onto a cedar-wood board at the scale of 1:10 for the team to see and check.

Drawing of Dotations and Measurements

In this drawing, dimensions of tenons and mortises are designed and recorded. Eave-purlins and lintels going through several posts are usually made of several boards to make an overall height/width ratio at 5:1; and tenon heads are divided into upper, middle, and lower positions for them to interlock together. The chief master is responsible for determining the shapes and dimensions of the section of each member, and especially of the tenons and mortises, all to be marked on this drawing with an overall longitudinal frame drawn as well for basic reference. When confirmed, supervising masters translate these into timber parts and boards with ink lines, and artisans (second-stage carpenter builders) proceed further to cut and polish to shape the parts to the expected refinement (Figure 12.4).

Measuring Sticks

The main measuring stick is known as Gao Chi (bamboo or wood stick as a ruler); it is longer than one zhang in traditional Chinese measurement (1 zhang = 320 cm); in modern terms, it is more than 3 meters long and has a width and thickness of about 10–12 cm and 3–6 cm respectively (that is, 3–4 *cun* and 1–2 cun respectively; 1 cun = 3.2 cm). With marks and words on the faces of the stick, it is used as the master stick for transferring and checking almost all

Figure 12.4 Drawing with notes and numbers, for dimensions of parts and mortis-tenon joineries for rectangular-shaped beam frames.

Source: Photo taken inside the Lei Tingyi Construction Group, Fu'an City, 2004. © Chang Yu-yu.

dimensions by the supervising masters under the chief master, although lower-level apprentices and artisans may not always understand its meanings and messages. We will come back to this soon.

As we can see, in the folk building practice, "design" has a meaning different from ours which involves smaller scales and numerous drawings. In the folk practice here, designing, planning, construction, and managing are more interrelated, whereby visual and material communication has multiple functions. Design and construction being closely related, supervising masters play a central role for connecting the ideas of the chief master to the production work of artisans and builders at junior levels, to secure a certain totality and grandeur to be fully realized in the final product.

Today, the various secret or invisible techniques – with complex notations, regional differences of standard, and local religious values attached – of the chief masters are in danger of disappearing, because of the shrinking labor force in the trade and the onslaught of modern technologies and measuring methods. To survive with modern systems of design, construction, and management, this ancient practice is confronting crisis, which in turn reveals its values more.

Gao Chi: As Drawings for a Building

Adopting the *chuandou* structure in southern China, a single story temple with three bays would use hundreds of parts, interconnected via mortise-tenon joineries with all the posts; if we add all pieces in lateral and longitudinal directions, it could have more than 400 parts altogether for this building. These parts can be efficiently made with some standardization and the use of a modular system, but to supervise all this in an orderly manner, one needs to have a method to specify and check immediately all shapes and sizes of the parts. For this, the chief master uses the bamboo or cedar-wood stick – which constitutes the most special and most secret technique of the trade – which is called Gao Chi 篙尺 (literally, it means wooden or bamboo stick as a measuring ruler).

This stick should be longer than the tallest middle post, or as long as the length from the top to the lower edge of the lowest mortise hole on the post. Often, it is about 3 to 4 meters long, and with a width of some 12 to 13 cm for one face or side of the stick; for a single story building, only one side of the stick is used, whereas for a larger building with multiple roofs and elaborate corner eaves, all four sides are used for marking. In marking the various lengths for the various parts on the stick, the reading/marking sequence starts from the tallest point and moves down, that is, from the height of the roof ridge – following the declining roof – to that of the purlins, all the way down, until there is no member any more on the post. In this way, all heights of all parts, as well as the shapes and sizes of the joineries to be connected to the post, are marked onto the stick, in a single unifying summary as embodied on the stick.

How can all this rich information be marked on a linear surface only 12 cm wide? The practice uses two methods: marking with zones and the use of signs and phrases. The first refers to marking on the stick according to zones of the roof – front slope, front slope in the longitudinal direction, middle ridge, back slope in the longitudinal direction, and back slope. The second refers to the core function of the stick – the noting of lengths, signs, member names, and technical phrases on the surface or surfaces. On the stick, the chief master uses 1:1 scale to note all dimensions. Signs are marked as well to refer to various items such as purlins, bracket sets, major beams, diagonal pieces, and posts of different types. The words on the stick include member names and construction methods. There are also difference between teams and local traditions; some don't use words, and some just write the name of the parts, while some mark all types of members – about 40 of them – with names of parts and phrases of assembling methods (Figure 12.5).

With these lengths and signs marked based on the heights and relations of assemblage, we can visualize that when the stick moves around in a three-dimensional space, it can create literally at full scale a skeleton structure of the entire building. In this sense, the actual production is a physical materialization by the artisans and master builders, who all follow closely the chief master with the commanding Gao Chi. In this manner, this long stick of rich and detailed information works as the only material form of all design and working drawings we use today. Further, it also serves for managing, supervising, and checking the construction immediately and directly. As it contains so much information, when the building is completed, it is stored following the local tradition within the building so that it can assist with future repair or any further work.

The rather obscure and coded methods of notating, as core skills of the chief masters, have been kept as their most protected professional secret, to be passed on to the younger generations only through a special process of recruiting and teaching. From our perspective, these long sticks and their methods reflect subtle regional differences as well as the specific approaches of the place and the particular team. While serving as a unification of information within a team – for example, two masters can work on two parts of a building using the same stick to ensure

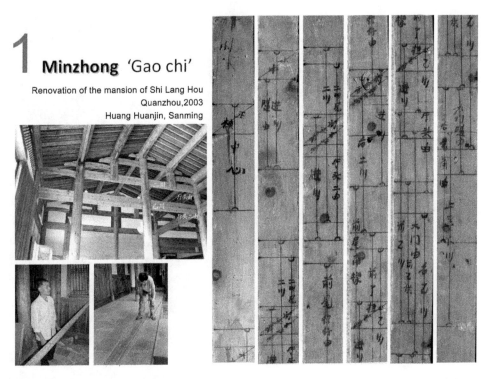

1 Minzhong 'Gao chi'

Renovation of the mansion of Shi Lang Hou
Quanzhou, 2003
Huang Huanjin, Sanming

Figure 12.5 The Gao Chi master sticks of different schools and traditions in Fujian, with their different methods of notation: Minzhong (central Fujian), Fu'an, Quanzhou and Putian for the first, second, third and fourth respectively.

Source: Photo taken in these places, 2003–04. © Chang Yu-yu.

2 Fu'an 'Gao chi'

Shunjigong Temple, Yangtou, 2004
Lei Tingyi, Fuan

3 Quanzhou 'Gao chi'

an octanglar pavilion, 2004
Liang Shizhi , Quanzhou

Figure 12.5 (Continued)

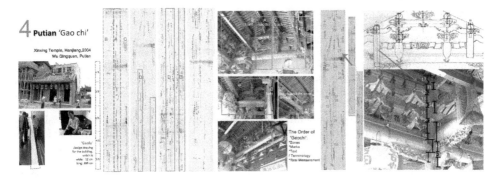

Figure 12.5 (Continued)

exact consistency – the sticks can also serve for us a means for appreciation across teams and regions. There are nevertheless issues here; if the building has more elaboration, the master stick can be too complex; and if you are skilled in one region or team, it can be very obscure to read if you join another team or teams elsewhere.

Acting as a means of visual communication, as "drawings" for design and construction at once, the master stick is particularly efficient for the *chuandou* structural construction, which uses the mortise-tenon joinery extensively. As a set of 1:1 or real scale working drawings all marked onto one stick for quick checking, it is especially useful for traditional Chinese building construction, including the *chuandou* structural approach, compared to the modern practice of many drawings at reduced scales where checking is not so immediate. Today, for working with modern procedures and standards, including the planning boards for approving all constructions, modern drawings must be produced. Nevertheless, the chief masters still use the Gao Chi stick onto which all dimensions are translated, and are readjusted and refined, before construction can start.

Conclusion

In this complete and mature building tradition in China, the most basic and technical craftsmanship and the design thinking of the chief master are well integrated into one operating practice. In the system, every artisan and builder at the various stages may fully participate in their specific role for reading and making. With their dedication, and with the operation of the system, the whole building is made with pride and happiness, as if it grows out of the hands and the minds of the workers. The method and the operation have surely contributed to the charm and beauty of the traditional architecture of China.

Notes

1 *Yingzao Fayuan* (Methods of building construction) was initially written by a renowned chief master of the Xiangshanbang school, Yao Chengzu (1866–1938), in 1929. Thirty years later, in 1959, it was published by China Architecture and Building Press (*Zhongguo jianzhu gongye chubanshe*), with Zhang Zhigang's editing and expansion, and Liu Dunzhen's checking and supervising, over the chaotic and war-torn times of 1930s and 1940s, with Liu's leadership and Zhang's work in the 1930s and 1950s. This book explains the construction methodology of the Xiangshanbang school; it covers groundwork,

woodwork, joinery work, stonework, wall construction, roofwork, as well as costs, labor management, garden work, and other miscellaneous issues.

2 Xiangshanbang, or groups from Xiangshan areas, refers to a collective of teams and groups of artisan builders working in or coming from the Xiangshan region by Taihu Lake in Suzhou prefecture. In the early Ming dynasty (1410s–20s), they were called to work in Beijing for the building of the imperial palace. Kuai Xiang (1398–1481), due to his supreme skills and knowledge, is regarded as the founding father of effectively a school of building in the folk architecture of China. This collective and its tradition represent the achievement of Suzhou-style architecture in the region around the Taihu Lake.

3 In southern China, villages were often made up of families of one or a few clans; and certain trades were developed as family business over generations. If there were enough artisans and masters and if their skills were strong enough in a village or a rural settlement, then this village or place may have become associated with that trade – as "artisan villages," such as the "carpenter villages" in Xiangyun county of Nan'an city or Xidi village of Huian county in the Quanzhu region, or "stonemason villages" in the Futian area, of Fujian Province.

Bibliography

Bin Huizhong. *Zhongguo Baizu Chuantong Minju Yingzao Jiyi* (Building Craftsmanship for the Vernacular Courtyard Houses of Bai Ethnicity in China). Shanghai: Tongji Daxue Chubanshe, 2011.

Chang Yu-yu. *Fujian Chuantong Damu Jiangshi Jiyi Yanjiu* (The Chief Master in Structural Carpentry in Traditional Chinese Building Practice of the Fujian Region: A Study of Its Craftsmanship). Nanjing: Dongnan Daxue Chubanshe, 2010.

———. "Chuantong yingzao tixi de damuzuo gongzuo tujian xitong: xingshi, tezheng yu gongneng (Working Drawing System of Structural Carpentry in Traditional Construction)." *Jianzhu Xuebao* 11 (2017): 104–109.

Chang Yu-yu and Shi Hongchao. "Yuyan, fangfa ji cailiao: chuantong yingzao tixi de damuzuo gongzuo tujian xitong xilie yanjiu (Language, Method and Material: Working Drawing System of Structural Carpentry in Traditional Construction – Part of a Series of Studies)." *Xin Jianzhu* 4 (2017): 140–145.

Guo, Qinghua and Yuyu Chang. *The Weiwu at Dafuzhen: Unseen Details of Chinese Vernacular.* Stuttgart: Edition Axel Menges, 2016.

Le Zhi. *Zhongguo Gudai Louge Shouli Jizhi Yanjiu* (Structural Analysis of Ancient Chinese Pavilions and Pavilion Towers). Nanjing: Dongnan Daxue Chubanshe, 2014.

Shi Hongchao. *Zhejiang Chuantong Jianzhu Damu Gongyi Yanjiu* (A Study on Craftsmanship of Structural Carpentry in Traditional Chinese Building Practice of the Zhejiang Region). PhD Thesis. Dongnan Daxue (Southeast University), Nanjing, 2016.

Yao Chengzu, Zhang Zhigang and Liu Dunzhen. *Yingzao Fayuan* (Methods of Building Construction). Beijing: Zhongguo Jianzhu Gongye Chubanshe, 1959.

Glossary

bujia	步架
cha gong	插栱
chi	尺
chi gao	尺篙
chuandou	穿斗
cun	寸
da liang	大梁
damu jiangshi	大木匠师
damuzuo	大木作
fengshui	风水
Fujian (province)	福建（省）
gao chi (**Gao Chi**)	篙尺

jian sun	减榫
kaijian	开间
Lao Tzu	老子
Laozi (**Laozi**)	老子
Luban Chi	鲁班尺
shang sun	上榫
shui gua tu	水卦图
tailiang	抬梁
Tao Te Ching	道德经
tou sun	透榫
wu zhi yiwei yong	无之以为用
xia sun	下榫
Xiangshanbang	象山帮
yang ban tu	样板图
Yingzao Fayuan	营造法源
you zhi yiwei li	有之以为利
zhang	丈
zhang gao (**Zhang Gao**)	丈篙

13

VERNACULAR ARCHITECTURE

Themes and Variations Over a Large Country

Ho Puay Peng

The vernacular environment in China is complex and multi-dimensional.[1] China's current territory covers a large geographical region with many climatic and topographical variations. These conditions exert different degrees of influence on the form of the village and build-ings, resulting in a number of distinctive vernacular forms seen in China. However, it is also discernible that the vernacular environment and built form in a wide geographical region pre-dominantly follow certain general characteristics. The reason for such congruence in form must have been the cultural milieu of the vernacular environment within the Han cultural circle. The cultural milieu would affect not just the way the village environment is used, but also the perception of the built form, spatial conception, and issues such as materials, construction tech-niques, and decorations. It is therefore necessary to consider holistically all aspects of culture, climate, topography, materials, construction technology, means of production, and economy in a reading of the vernacular environment in China. This chapter will narrate the vernacular form of China in the context of its geo-cultural generalities with specific examples to highlight idiosyncratic variations.

It is without doubt that cultural manifestation is complex, and it is not possible to over-generalize. However, Chinese society had generally been homogenous for the last two mil-lennia due to the adoption of Confucianism as the state ideology that became the overarching cultural framework for all levels of society.[2] The main focus of this Confucian framework in the vernacular environment was the clan system prevalent particularly in southern China since the 11th century. Here, most villages are inhabited by people with the same surname and with blood relations. The clan is in turn branched out into several lineages. This social relationship is expressed and community behaviour dictated physically through the distribution of buildings in the villages.[3] The other significant aspect of Chinese vernacular architecture is the reliance on agriculture predominantly in most parts of China. This means of production necessitates the economical use of available land for farming and the proximity to water sources. Thus, villages in China are often very compact, almost like a small town in Europe, and are closely related to rivers flowing through or near the village. In addition, it is essential to have open space for farming activities in the design of individual houses.

Vernacular architecture[4] in China is distinguished by the range of its form. The range of house or village form is a reflection of the geographical locations and cultural entities within the vast Chinese territories. However, despite the varieties of house form, most village houses are

DOI: 10.4324/9781315851112-18

shaped around a central courtyard or a series of courtyards. In addition, vernacular architecture in China expresses the immediacy of its relationship with social, environmental, constructional, and cultural influences. Finally, the difference in Chinese vernacular architecture when compared with other vernacular traditions is its improvisation from primarily official architecture or, at times, contesting the sumptuary codes.[5] Official architecture has a strong presence in the architectural history of China, be it the imperial palace, government offices, mansions of aristocrats, or officially sanctioned temples and monasteries. The main construction materials are timber and brick, and the main form is a compound with multiple courtyards. There are also sumptuary codes controlling the use of these forms and imperial construction manuals specifying the details of the form. Improvisation seen in vernacular architecture is essentially the degree of approximation to the official form. Other forms of improvisation include adaptation to the physical landscape and prevailing culture, and the idiosyncratic responses from the owners and occupiers of the buildings.

Village Layout

While there are buildings in cities that can be considered part of the vernacular tradition in China, such as the *hutong* houses in Beijing or shop houses, guild buildings, temples, and opera stages in towns and cities, most vernacular buildings, unlike official constructions, are present in tens of thousands of villages all over China. The layout and form of villages in China comprise several types, all of which are influenced by climate, terrain, availability of materials, and local culture. Predominantly, most Han ethnic villages are very compact. Houses, ancestral halls, study halls, and temples form a concentrated building group, usually located between hills and rivers. One can clearly see a hierarchy of importance among the hundreds of buildings in the village, and the entire ensemble is not unlike small towns in southern Europe. In some villages, particularly those located in flat terrain, houses are organized in a grid pattern. Other villages built over a longer period of time would show a more casual pattern. Some ethnic minorities who are heavily influenced by Han culture, such as the Bai or Naxi people of Yunnan province, would also have villages in the same form as the Han Chinese. On more hilly terrain, Han Chinese villages might adopt a more dispersed form with buildings located on terraces along the contours, connected by steps and paths. However, villages would still be built as compact as possible so that land for agriculture can be maximized, such as those seen in Nanxijiang, Yongjia county, Zhejiang province.[6] Villages of minorities, such as the Miao and Dong people of Guizhou province, or Dai people of Yunnan province, will also display a similar dispersed form on hilly terrain. Under certain circumstances, the village form would change to suit. For example, in areas where the need for defence was greatest, villages and houses would be heavily fortified with stone or brick walls, such as those walled villages seen in southern China.[7] There are villages in the loess region in Shanxi and Shaanxi provinces where houses are sunken into the ground, resulting in a dispersed layout. Similarly, in southern Fujian province, earthen houses in round or square shapes were placed in the hillside randomly, with no perceivable pattern. Needless to say, individual yurts in Inner Mongolia would also be randomly located in the extensive plain. In summary, the layout of buildings of a Chinese settlement follows primarily a grid pattern, except where terrain and culture placed some constraints on the regular layout.

It is essential to trace the development path of a village in order to fully understand the village form. Donglong of Ningdu county is a small village located deep in the mountains in the south-eastern corner of Jiangxi province (Figure 13.1).[8] Currently there are two lineages of the Li clan and a very small number of other surnames found in this predominantly farming village. Lineage registry of the late Qing dynasty records a story narrating an encounter the founding

Figure 13.1   Donglong village, Ningdu county, Jiangxi province, showing the extensive village among the hills. Pagoda to the right serves as the *fengshui* pagoda for safekeeping the village's wealth.

Source: © Ho Puay Peng.

ancestor of the village had with a disguised *fengshui* master in the late 10th century. When this ancestor, Li Yijun, came to reside at the locality, there were clans of other surnames living in the same valley. The disguised *fengshui* master was not well received by other clans except by the founding ancestor of the Li clan. Through the hospitality of Li Yijun, he was put up for three years. Before the master departed from the locale, he gave the son of Li Yijun guidance to the best *fengshui* sites around the valley. With this guidance, the Lis buried their ancestors in the best locations. Allegedly after a few generations, they prospered in terms of both the number of descendants and wealth. Slowly, the Li clan took over most of the land of the valley and elbowed out the original settlers. This pattern of development and the narrative of the *fengshui* master are common in the southern villages. The *fengshui* master's advice is a convenient means to provide legitimacy for occupying the site. The clan at Donglong later developed into two major branches, and thus there are two main ancestral halls; one can be traced all the way back to the focal ancestor who settled in at the site in the 10th century, while the other was traced back to the branch ancestor.

Site Selection and *Fengshui*

The selection of site for locating a village is based on the reading of the landscape using the traditional practice of geomancy.[9] Known as *fengshui*, literally, wind and water, the landscape is read according to its form to determine the prevalent direction of the village, house, or tomb in order to bring good fortune to the family and to avoid bad luck. In northern villages, south-facing is essential for having good sunlight and warmth, and thus best *fengshui* would have the

216

villages or houses facing south. In south China, such directive would not be necessary, and thus landform is of primarily concern. Hills are regarded as protection to the site and water is seen to bring in good spirit; thus, hills and rivers are essential components of *fengshui*. Different readings are associated with different hill form or direction of the water; thus, there are auspicious sites as well as those that will bring bad influences to the living. The placement of the tomb is also critical as its *fengshui* would cast effect on the descendants. For example, a good *fengshui* site would be one with a high hill protecting it in the back, secondary hills on the two sides, and a stream or river flowing from left to right of the site. Beyond the river there should also be distant hills to shelter the site from the front. The site is known as the dragon lair, in which the occupier will feel very much protected and good fortune will be brought in by the river. It is also desirable for the river to have a bend before and after the site so that the flow can be moderated and the benefit the water brought to the site would be sustained. In sites that cannot fulfil all the condition for a good *fengshui* site, there are remedial actions, such as the building of a pagoda in place of the river bend or creating a pond in place of the river.

The reliance on reading the physical landscape for auspicious site is most prevalent in south China with hilly terrain and lots of watercourses. This is usually known as the Form School of *fengshui*, which had begun in Jiangxi province. However, there is another school of *fengshui* known as the Compass School, which originated in the Fujian province and requires the examination of the movement of heavenly bodies and its relationship with the birthday of the main protagonist. Birthday is expressed in year, month, day, and hour, and how these four sets of figures[10] can be in tune with the cosmic figures of heavenly constellations and the earthly direction of the site. Synchronization of these figures as read in the multi-ring compass is said to bring best fit of the heavenly and earthly breath to the fortune of the protagonist, who might be house owner, village head for the villagers, or the descendants of the ancestor who lies in the tomb. In most cases, both the landform and compass will be read by the *fengshui* master for the placement of villages, houses, or the tombs. These readings will be recorded in the lineage registry of the village in text or in topographical drawing or representation.[11]

At the centre of these *fengshui* representations is always the focal ancestral hall, which is usually the largest and most decorative building in the village, with a large open space in front of it. The hall might or might not be in the physical centre of the village, depending on the development history of the village. In some cases, when there was no space at the centre of the existing village, the hall will be built at the fringe of the village. Thus, the focal ancestral hall could be built much later than the founding of the village, at a time when some descendants had achieved high official status or accumulated sufficient wealth. There might be a smaller ancestral hall built before a larger one is built when the circumstances are right.

Ancestral Hall and Ancestral Worship: South China Villages

The largest ancestral halls normally consist of an extensive compound with three or four buildings placed one behind another along a central axis, interspersed by courtyards, with the long side of the rectangular building facing the approach.[12] Each of these halls serves a specific purpose. The first building is the entrance, the second the main worship hall, which doubles up as community hall, and the last building houses the ancestral tablets. The entrance building faces the outer courtyard and thus the façade is decorated to impress; there might be two rooms inside the gate serving as offices. The second building along the axis is usually the grandest of the three. Between the entrance and the worship hall is a large courtyard for gatherings and different ceremonies. The scale of the courtyard also allows the large hall to be appreciated and awed. Depending on the political status of any one of the members of the clan, the hall can be as wide as having five inter-columnal bays for high-ranking official, but commonly the main hall is three bays wide. This large hall is empty to allow for different activities to take place. The last hall houses the spirit tablets of the ancestors, laid out in rows starting with the focal ancestor in the middle of the top row. It is believed that a part of the spirit of the deceased is present in the tablet. The building is low and the courtyard between the second and last halls is narrow, befitting the role of the last hall as memorial space.

The focal ancestral hall is both the symbol of clan solidarity as well as a communal space. It is the spiritual centre of clan life. The hall serves as the site for worshipping the ancestors during the spring and fall rituals that are opened to members of the clan as recorded in the lineage registry. These ceremonies establish the identity of the clan with its hierarchy and order. Following Confucian precepts, the clan aims to live harmoniously together, thus abiding by rules and practices dutifully such as those of filial piety, loyalty, and chastity. Marriage ceremonies are held at the ancestral hall, and so are funerals in some vernacular traditions. Good behaviours are rewarded and bad deeds are punished; judgements are delivered with the elder presiding at the ancestral hall. But the most important role the ancestral hall plays is for ritual worship of the ancestors, safeguarding lineage purity with the maintenance of the lineage registry, and managing clan properties and lands. In the trading village of Xiamei in Jianyang county, Fujian province, the Zou family, one of the few wealthy tea merchants of the village, built an ancestral hall in 1790 (Figure 13.2) Located at an awkward corner of the main artery of the village, the façade was designed to impress with flamboyant decoration in brick and plaster carvings. Thus, the aim of this extraordinary architecture is not just to remember the ancestors, but also to display the wealth of the clan for business purposes.[13]

Figure 13.2   Extensive façade of the Zou ancestral hall in Xiamei township, Jianyang county, Fujian province; projection of an image for the clan to visitors and business partners.

Source: © Ho Puay Peng.

For lineages other than the focal lineage within the clan that might have illustrious descendants, sub-lineage ancestral halls might be built to worship these ancestors who might not get worshipped at the focal ancestral hall. These halls are smaller in size than the focal ancestral hall, unless the lineage ancestor was of very high political or social status; it is then permissible for the hall to be larger and more lavish than the focal ancestral hall. There can also be more than just one lineage ancestral hall, such as Liukeng village of the Dong clan in Le'an county in the northern Jiangxi province. In this village, founded in the 10th century, there are around 500 buildings, among which are more than 60 ancestral halls.[14] There is a focal ancestor hall, several main lineage ancestral halls, and many more family or individual ancestral halls. The number of ancestral halls in this village is probably one of the largest in China; most villages in southern China that followed more closely the Confucian ideology might have 6–7 ancestral halls. An example is the village of Peitian; there is a major focal ancestral hall located at the fringe of the village due to the lack of land in the centre of the village, and around sub-lineage ancestral halls, and many family ancestral halls that are located in large houses.

While the architecture of the focal ancestral hall is usually the most impressive among village buildings, some lineage ancestral halls are considerably larger and more lavish than most. A case in point is the ancestral hall dedicated to Luo Dongshu in the village of Chengkan in She county, southern Anhui province.[15] Luo lived in the 13th century and was a famous Confucian scholar who refused to serve in the Mongolian Yuan dynasty government. The hall, however, was built in the 16th century first by members of the lineage and later completed by Luo Yinghe (1540–1630), a high official. The hall is located at the edge of the village, possibly because the compound that was envisaged is larger than any available vacant site at the centre of the village. The hall complex comprises four layers of buildings along the central axis, starting with a wooden gate with vertical timber members, an entrance hall with huge door drums and a high threshold showing the status of the lineage, a main hall, and terminating in a double-storied building housing ancestral tablets. The fact that Luo Yinghe was a high official explains why a wooden gate, used mainly in official buildings, and a double-storied building were built for an ancestor who had no official status. It is probably also the reason why the last building, built or enlarged by Luo Yinghe, is a building of nine bays grouped into three sections. A building of nine bays was definitely only reserved for the emperor, such as the throne hall. In this building, known also as the Baolunge [Pavilion for Precious Decrees], with the upper storey used to house the decrees of the emperor given to Luo and the lower storey for ancestral tablets, there are extensive paintings of brocaded patterns and floral motives on beams and ceilings (Figure 13.3). These decorations again are only found in imperial buildings. The idiosyncratic design of Baolunge can be said to respond to the usage of the building for storing imperial decrees, but it is probably more for showing off the status of the Luo lineage by exceeding the standard prescribed for an ancestral hall. It is also interesting to note that tourist literature refers the scale of the building to the fact that Luo Dongshu was a famous Confucian scholar, and thus the hall was built to imitate the temple of Confucius in Qufu, Shandong province, where the hometown of Confucius is. This idea of the high standing of Luo was constructed to conceal the fact that the building was built way above what was allowed in a strict authoritarian society.

Ancestral Hall: North China Villages

Villages in north China are usually smaller and more compact than southern villages. This is possibly due to the frequent warfare that took place in north China and the massive shift of the population to the south when north China was overtaken by the Jurchen, who established the Jin dynasty in 1115. In the next few centuries, population movements continued, particularly at

Figure 13.3 Double-storied Baolunge of the ancestral hall dedicated to Luo Dongshu in Chengkan
  village, She county, Anhui province. Notice the size of the building containing nine inter-
  columnal spaces and the highly decorative wooden structural members of the building.

Source: © Ho Puay Peng.

the time of Mongolian invasion. Unlike villages in the south, northern villages are not normally
occupied by a single-surname clan. The clan relationship within the village, even in a single-
surname village, is also not as strong as those in the south. Thus, not many villages contain
imposing ancestral halls compared to villages in south China. In addition, because north China
suffered more from warfare than south China, there are thus not many ancestral halls left in
the villages. The ancestral halls that have been preserved are usually small in scale.[16] The architecture of these buildings, such as those houses used at the same time for ancestral worship in
the village of Cuandixia in the mountains west of Beijing, is simple, looking much like a plain
house.[17] However, rituals and clan solidarity have begun to make a comeback in recent years
with invented traditions and aggrandized ancestral halls. This occurs in a more tolerant political
regime and a societal atmosphere that encourages harmony and cohesion. It is also likely that
cultural devices and invention are employed in service of the increasingly popular tourism need.

Houses in South China

When a clan gathered in a settlement, their houses were mostly very simple, limited by means.
Local materials were used and simple construction techniques employed to erect the houses.
Only at a later time, when the villages are more established, can certain formal planning be
detected in the villages, especially in regions where land is relatively flat. In order to maximise
land for agriculture, most houses were built to abut each other and leave a small footprint. The
most economical way of building would be to have a grid pattern of rows of houses separated

by small lanes. This is the village form adopted in south China, as seen in numerous villages in Pearl River Delta, for example, those in the New Territories, Hong Kong. The houses face a general direction, possibly chosen due to good *fengshui*. A house is around 5 metres across and 15 metres deep. The small frontage ensures that every house faces the access lane as well as having a share of the good *fengshui*. The organization of the interior of the house is very simple. Village houses in the New Territories, Hong Kong, can serve as an illustration. In the form of a rectangle, a house can be divided into two parts; the front portion usually has an open-air courtyard, with two side chambers housing a kitchen and a store on either side of the courtyard. The rear part of the house is usually a building with a pitch roof. The interior is not normally subdivided into rooms, but a screen demarcates the living space at the front and a sleeping space behind the screen. In some houses, the upper part of the sleeping space will be decked to provide more storage space. Facing the front entrance on the upper part of the interior is usually a niche housing ancestral tablets or images of deities or both.

Larger houses in south China are an embellishment over the simple layout just described. The basic spatial arrangement would remain as the simple house, except that the body of the house would likely be three times the size of a small common house, increased in the lateral direction. In larger houses, the entrance might be a separate building with a recessed entrance and two side chambers. The courtyard would be much larger than the simple house and could be used for many purposes, including festive ritual or dining. The main building would be likewise divided into three parts; the central part is for living, and again the niche for ancestor or deity would occupy the upper portion of the back wall. On either side of the central living space could be either enclosed to form two bedrooms or could be open with an upper floor used as sleeping space. On the side of the courtyard between the entrance and the main building, there can also be two side buildings used as bedrooms or additional space for living. While the basic construction between the small and big houses is not that different, the features that mark a house of means are the scale of decorative elements in the form of ridge decoration in plaster relief, wooden eaves board, paintings and plaster relief on the top of the wall, and many others. Houses in south China are usually constructed with a pitch roof using grey concave tiles on a wooden structure with large rounded purlins supporting closely packed rafters over which roof tiles are laid. The gable walls that support the purlins are usually of cavity wall construction with grey bricks sitting on granite courses. The granite courses can be one, three or five courses, rising up to 2 metres tall in some houses. The number of courses of granite used symbolises wealth and protection from burglary.

Large houses in south China are owned by rich landowners and usually occupied the best position in the village, such as those located along the front edge of the village in Peitian village in Liancheng county in western Fujian province. The village of Wu clan was first built at the foot of the protective *fengshui* hill. When rich traders and landowners of the village wanted to enlarge their houses or build new mansions, they could not find large pieces of land in the existing village, and thus large houses were built on land outside the village either to the front or the side of the existing village houses. Around 20 large houses were built in the 19th century and are monumental in scale, not because of the larger size of the main building but because of the addition of many buildings making up the compound. If the nucleus of a Chinese house consists of four buildings surrounding a courtyard, the large houses would consist of many courtyard units (Figure 13.4). This is due to the sumptuary law governing the size of the main building, usually three bays in width. However, the law did not stipulate the number of courtyard units a house can contain. Thus, the multiplication of courtyard units, lay out in a neat grid pattern, would indicate both the extent of the family and its wealth. The main building will be in the centre of the front of the compound, with a few courtyard units placed along the central axis at

Figure 13.4 Two courtyards of a large mansion of Jishu Hall, Peitian village, Liancheng county, Fujian province.

Source: © Ho Puay Peng.

the rear of the main building. To either side of the main building, more courtyard units would be added. Because of the size of the large houses, they are usually referred to as *minjian gugong*, the vernacular Forbidden City.

How does the house support the lifestyle of the villagers? The agricultural community of south China is usually rice growers, and thus the need of rice production is met with the use of space inside and in the front yard of the houses. In smaller villages, production will be grouped in the main open space located either in front of the main ancestral hall or to the side of the village. For larger houses, all agricultural activities will be held in the compound. The house is but a unit within the village community; thus, some family activities such as festive celebrations and ritual service for the immediate ancestors will be held within the household, usually in the main building of the house. However, there are also many activities held collectively, such as the spring and autumn ancestral worships and the Lunar New Year celebration. There would also be temple festivals and communal worships taking place at the hall. In some regions, a large house can also serve as an ancestral hall. A case in point is the Jishu Hall of Peitian village mentioned earlier.[18] The wealthiest merchant family of the village, Wu Changtong and Wu Yinzhai, built this hall in 1824–34 as a grand mansion with three large courtyards and corresponding buildings. At the same time, the family was also looking for a site to build the lineage ancestral hall, as their wealth had been accumulating. However, he was not successful in securing a site in the village large enough for the ancestral hall. Eventually, in 1847, the descendants had to add a building to the back of his house to serve as the ancestral hall, but such a move created huge controversy in the village. While some felt that the combination of the space for the living and the ancestors was unwise, others thought it would be easy for the descendants to worship the ancestors regularly in such spatial arrangement. But in land-tight villages, this approach of combining the ancestral hall and the house, though unorthodox, provides a workable solution. The method for adding an ancestral hall to the house was adapted by many households in Peitian village, as well as other villages in south China. It is also clear that some improvisations occurred in the vernacular environment to the extent of challenging the fundamental cultural precepts with justifications.

Houses in North China

The common form of houses in north China is usually composed of a series of courtyards with corresponding buildings unless in steep terrain, in which case the form would be less extensive. They are in general less elaborate and extensive than houses in south China. Each house would also consist of a main building surrounded by subsidiary buildings, forming a courtyard in the centre. The predominant material for construction is grey brick, with brick-carving as the main form of decoration. There are colourful elements in wood carving, such as the eaves board. As timber was in shorter supply in north China, timber members are of a smaller size than those in south China. Due to warfare and more frequent occurrence of famine in north China, most extant houses are from the 18th century or later. Thus, the size and decoration of houses is more impoverished than those in well-established villages in the south.

The 18th century also saw the rise of the merchant class in north China who had business extending to the entire empire. These merchants constructed extensive mansions in north China, such as the bankers and salt merchants of Shanxi province, or large landlords of Hebei and Henan provinces.[19] The extensive mansions in central Shanxi province can contain more than 200 buildings in the form of courtyard units.[20] They are usually fortified with a high defensive wall surrounding the compound and watch towers at strategic positions. The mansions of the Qiao family in Qi county and the Wang family in Lingshi county are excellent examples.[21] The fortified rectangular compound has a central "street" leading from the main gate to the shrine housing the protector deity. To either side of the street are five compounds, each with a gate opening to the street. Each compound is composed of three courtyards, with a gate building, main hall, and the double-storied residential block on axis. Side buildings next to the courtyards are usually very elongated with a lean-to roof. There are plenty of wood and brick carvings, particularly the gate canopies known as hanging-flower gates. While a large part of the building is in monotone, the colourful wooden decorations provide a strong contrast and exhibit the wealth of the family in no uncertain terms.

Other large merchant mansions might have even more courtyards and buildings, creating a sense of depth and mystery for visitors. The size of these large compounds is also an indication of the size of the extensive family, which may be in the hundreds; they often lived together as each member of the family could have a courtyard unit to himself. In most of these compounds, there would be buildings delegated to the worship of ancestors and protector deities. There are elaborate room and storage facilities for food and goods, or even wealth. In larger compounds, there might also be buildings dedicated to the enjoyment of opera, such as that of the manor estate of the Shi family at Yangliuqing, Tianjin.[22] The opera stage is housed in a separate building that includes a "stall" for the audience. In the case of Chinese opera, the performance is usually carried out on a small stage, and the audience is usually seated at separate tables with food and drinks served. Thus, a large building is necessary, and not all merchants can afford the luxury of an opera building in the compound.

Apart from these house forms, there are also subterranean houses in the loess region of Shanxi and Shannxi provinces on either side of the Yellow River. Taking advantage of the soft ground, these houses consist of a large sunken courtyard with rooms opened into the walls of the courtyard.[23] Entrance into the house is through a dog-leg tunnel descending into the courtyard from the surface of the flat ground. In the courtyard is usually a tree to distinguish the house from the ground. The rooms are barrel vaulted for better support and would have a large heated bed along the side wall. The bed, known as *kang*, would be where all activities in the room were held; resting, working, sleeping, and eating can all be done in the warmth of the bed. Other rooms will be reserved for livestock. Agriculture activities will be held on the surface of the ground. The house form, similar to the troglodyte underground houses of the northern Safari desert, is cool in the summer and warm in the winter. The villagers help each other in the excavation of the large courtyard while the family will dig the rooms themselves. While the climate is very dry, the wall of the courtyard would still have to be maintained once a year due to occasional rain. A similar form of earth housing is also found in Shanxi province with rooms dug into the cliff face and a courtyard formed by timber frame buildings placed at the foot of the cliff. There can be many levels of earthen rooms and many rooms on one level in more well-to-do houses. These rooms are not connected internally, and are only accessible from the terrace. The space between the door to the barrel-vaulted rooms is usually used to place a small altar dedicated to the earth god, or the god of heaven. One great example is in the town of Qikou, in Lin county, Shanxi province, by the bank of the Yellow River (Figure 13.5).[24]

Figure 13.5   View of Qikou town, Lin county, Shanxi province showing layers of buildings constructed from the hill to the Yellow River. Some buildings are simply a façade over the habitable caves dug into the loess hillside.

Source: © Ho Puay Peng.

Earthen Houses in Fujian Province

Large fortified houses in western Fujian province are another form of earthen architecture seen in China.[25] These are large houses dispersed in a village either along the contours or on the flat plain in Longyan and Yongjing counties. The exterior wall of these large round or square houses is constructed using pounded earth. The houses are usually four stories tall with only small windows on the upper two floors. The inside of the earthen wall is a wooden construction of four floors encircling a large courtyard in the middle. The diameter of a large round house can be around 80 metres and smaller ones around 20. It is the same for square houses in form and size. Rooms of equal size are open off the circumscribing veranda on each floor. Members of the family sharing a house are assigned a vertical segment for their use. So there could be 20 segments for a house on average. The ground floor room is usually for dining, with a kitchen built into the courtyard. The second floor is for grain storage and the last two floors for living. At the centre of the courtyard is usually an ancestral hall that also houses images of deities.[26] In other houses, the centre of the house might just be an open courtyard used for agricultural and communal activities. In these houses, tablets and images of ancestors or deities would be housed on the ground floor in the segment across from the entrance. Thus, a fortified house is a community on its own, self-sufficient in food and, with a well in the courtyard, water. This would sustain the residents if the fortified house ever came under siege. It is also known that many houses were built not by one family but as a cooperative, with many relations or friends buying a share in the house. Price can either be paid in cash, grain, or labour for the construction of the house. It will take many years to complete a house as the labour needed to construct the exterior wall using pounded earth, which is up to one metre at the bottom, is considerable. It is hard to speculate why there are both round and square houses. Obviously round houses are seen to be more egalitarian, and thus many were built during the 1950s after Communist rule, although the oldest round houses can be traced all the way back to the 15th century.[27] In the neighbouring Chaozhou region in eastern Guangdong province, a similar house form can be found; there are also square or octagonal fortified houses, usually two stories high.[28] This can be seen as the continuation of the tradition of building fortified houses in the mountainous border of the Chinese empire for defence and protection.

Ethnic Villages

There are many ethnic groups in China located in Jiangxi, Yunnan, and Guizhou provinces. Their villages are usually located in hilly terrain and houses are individually dispersed through the contour, such as those in Miao villages. The houses are usually of timber construction, on stilts, and not symmetrical. In Dong villages, the centre of the village is usually occupied by a drum tower as the centre for the communal life. Houses are rather compactly laid out.[29] There might also be altars dedicated to the mother goddess of the villagers. In Bai villages of Yunnan province, houses are in courtyard form, very much similar to houses seen in Han villages.[30] The only differences are the decorative motif and the form itself. The courtyard tends to be smaller than southern Han houses but with two stories, having a more complex spatial arrangement. The centre of the village is around a temple, an ancestral hall, or a stage for opera performance.

In the Tibetan plateau, houses are packed together due to the scarcity of flat land. So, a village can be like a small town in form. Houses are also organized around a courtyard, with two- to three-story buildings on two sides. In the courtyard is the external staircase going to the upper level. The principal room is on the first floor, which is also a Buddha hall for prayer and meditation. The external walls are of pounded earth or brick and the interior are of timber construction. A special technique in the preparation of the roof allows for waterproofing. The openings into the courtyard are large and in stark contrast to the blank exterior wall. Wood carvings are well executed, serving as a symbol for wealth. Obviously, the centre of communal life in a village is to be found in the monastery of Tibetan Buddhism. The monastery is usually much grander than the house, but using similar building techniques and form.

Summary

Unlike the official or religious building tradition, vernacular architecture in China should be regarded in a holistic environment encompassing different building types serving a full range of communal, production, and family needs. The structure of the village and its buildings cannot be fully appreciated outside the context of the environments in which they are located. These environments can be either the overarching social concern for propriety, order, and communal harmony or the physical environment of the climate, terrain, and available building materials, or the cultural dimensions of belief system, building tradition, and living pattern. In this intricate web of relationships, the vernacular environment of China presents a rich tapestry of form that is a reflection of both the broad cultural milieu of traditional China and the specificity of the individual building and village. However, there are many instances of improvisation seen in Chinese vernacular form that are responding to specific individual circumstances. It is this direct corresponding relationship between the influencing factors, idiosyncratic context, and built forms that makes the study into Chinese vernacular environment interesting and enduring.

Notes

1 China here refers to the current territory of the People's Republic of China. This territory was not a constant throughout the last 2,000 years.

2 There is considerable literature discussing the formation of a Confucian state in China since the Han dynasty. See in particular: Thomas A. Wilson, *Genealogy of the Way: The Construction and Uses of the Confucian Tradition in Late Imperial China* (Stanford: Stanford University Press, 1995); Derk Bodde, *Chinese Thought, Society, and Science: The Intellectual and Social Background of Science and Technology in Premodern China* (Honolulu: Univ. of Hawaii Press, 1991); and Lionel M Jensen, *Manufacturing Confucianism: Chinese Traditions & Universal Civilization* (Durham: Duke University Press, 1997).

3 See James L. Watson and Patricia Ebrey, eds., *Kinship Organization in Late Imperial China, 1000–1940* (Berkeley: University of California Press, 1986).

4 The term vernacular architecture is here used to refer to buildings built with little design input from architectural professionals. In the context of China, these buildings would be those built involving a master craftsman with the help of craftsmen from different building trades. This tradition is distinguished from the official tradition where form and construction method were dictated and regulated by official, sometimes encoded in a building manual, such as *Yingzao fashi*, promulgated in 1103. Thus, the term Chinese vernacular architecture would cover all building forms in cities, towns, or villages other than those governed by official regulations.

5 Throughout the imperial era, the State promulgated different laws and codes for differentiating the different social class in the society. These codes regulated the dress and behaviour as well as buildings in terms of size, structure, and decoration.

6 See detailed account of the villages in Nanxijiang region in Chen Zhihua ed., *Nanxijiang zhongyou xiangtu jianzhu* (Vernacular Architecture in the Middle Reaches of Nanxijiang) (Taipei: Hansheng Publishing House, 1992); Ruan Yisan, ed., *Nanxijiang zongzu cunluo* (Clan Villages in Nanxijiang) (Fuzhou: Fujian Art Press, 2003).

7 Defence might be one reason for wall villages in south China, from eastern Fujian province to central Guangdong province, with high perimeter walls built in stone, pounded earth, or bricks. However, the situation might be more complex; there are village clusters with only a small number of walled compounds in among common houses, or there might be villages next to each other having either

defensive or common forms. It could be that with more wealth, people in these turbulent regions would opt for erecting a defensive structure for protection of all villagers as a collective action.

8 Research on Donglong, Peitian, and Xiamei villages in Jiangxi, Fujian, and Zhejiang provinces were conducted with the grant given by Research Grant Committee General Research Fund: Tradition and Transformation: An Investigation into the Development of Vernacular Architecture Practices in Southeast China, 2006–2009.

9 For more information on the practice of *fengshui* in Chinese villages, see Ole Bruun, *Fengshui in China: Geometric Divination Between State Orthodoxy and Popular Religion* (Honolulu: University of Hawai'i Press, 2003), Fan Wei, "Village *Fengshui* Principles," in *Chinese Landscapes: The Village as Place*, ed. Ronald G. Knapp (Honolulu: University of Hawai'i Press, 1992), 35–45; Puay-peng Ho, "China's Vernacular Architecture," in *Asia's Old Dwellings*, ed. Ronald G. Knapp (Oxford: Oxford University Press, 2003), 322–324.

10 Each of the year, month, day, or hour is denoted by two characters, and thus the birthday is expressed in eight characters.

11 *Fengshui* is about the siting of tombs and buildings; these are all recorded in the lineage registry in the form of *fengshui* diagram, supplemented by text describing the nature of the sites. The lineage registry of a village is usually updated every two or three generations. Thus, the reading of the site's *fengshui* can be explained in terms of its effect.

12 See Puay-peng Ho, "Ancestral Halls: Family, Lineage, and Ritual," in *House Home Family: Living and Being Chinese*, ed. Ronald G. Knapp and Lo Kai-yin (Honolulu: University of Hawai'i Press, 2005), 295–323.

13 See a brief description of Xiamei and the ancestral hall of Zou clan in Xiao Chunrei, *Yangguang xia de giaohua menlou* (Carved Gate Towers Under the Sun) (Fuzhou: Haichao Photographic art Publisher, 2002), 92–99.

14 For a detailed account of the village of Liukeng, see Li Qiuxiang and Chen Zhihua, *Liukengcun* (Chongqing: Chongqing Publishing House, 2001) and Zhou Luanshu, ed., *The First Village Through the Ages- Liukeng* (Nanchang: Jiangxi Education Publishing House, 1999).

15 For a brief description of the village and the history of the clan, see Ma Yonghu, *Hexie youxu de xiang-cun shequ- Chengkan* (Hefei: Hefei Industrial University Press, 2005).

16 There are large ancestral halls in north China, similar to the size of small or medium size ancestral halls in south China. One good example is found in the village of Ding clan, Dingcun, in Xianfen county in Shanxi province, which is a three-layer building compound with three bays in the front façade. See Li Qiuxiang, *Dingcun* (Beijing: Tsinghua University Press, 2007), 79–80, 116–117.

17 See the web site of the village, https://en.wikipedia.org/wiki/Cuandixia. Accessed 27 December 2021.

18 See a broad introduction to the village of Peitian in Zheng Zhenman, *Peitian* (Beijing: Joint Publishing House, 2005).

19 For Henan architecture, see Zuo Manchang, ed., *Henan minju* (Vernacular Buildings of Henan) (Beijing: China Architecture and Building Press, 2007).

20 For a detailed survey of large houses in central Shanxi province, see Shanxi Provincial Construction Bureau, *Shanxi gucunzhen* (Ancient Villages and Towns of Shanxi Province) (Beijing: China Architecture and Building Press, 2007).

21 There are several books that give a good description of the many buildings in Qiao Mansion, such as Zhang Chengde and Fau Tuixiang eds., *Residential Courtyard of Shanxi Merchant- Wang Family* (Taiyuan: Shanxi Renmin Publishing House, 1997); Zhang Chengde ed., *Residential Courtyard of Shanxi Merchant- Qiao Family* (Taiyuan: Shanxi Renmin Publishing House, 1997); Zhang Xin and Chen Jie, *The Wang's Grand Courtyard in Illustration* (Taiyuan: Shanxi Jinji Publishing House, 2007).

22 Shi mansion was first constructed in 1875 and is now designated as the National Protected Monument.

23 There are many forms of subterranean houses in the loess regions, which are well captured in Hou Jiyao, ed., *Yaodong in China* (Zhengzhou: Henan Science and Technology Press, 1999). See also Ronald G. Knapp, *Chinese Houses: The Architectural Heritage of a Nation* (North Clarendon: Tuttle Publishing, 2005), 274–281.

24 See a detailed account of Xikou town and surrounding villages in Chen Zhihua, *Guzhen Xikou* (Ancient Town Xikou) (Taipei: Hansheng Publishing House, 2004).

25 There are many publications on this form of houses; see Huang Hanmin, *Fujian tulou* (Earthen Towers of Fujian Province) (Taipei: Hansheng Publishing House, 1994); Huang Hanmin and Chen Limu, *Fujian tulou jianzhu* (Architecture of Earthen Towers of Fujian Province) (Fuzhou: Fujian Science and Technology Press, 2012).

26 This is a common feature in vernacular architecture throughout China; ancestors are considered to be spirits that will bestow benefit to their descendants, and thus they are worshipped in the same manner as deities that will also bring tangible benefit to the household. Thus, most houses would have a niche for either ancestral spirits or deities who are considered to be efficacious, or both.

27 See a recent PhD dissertation with in-depth research on the building of earthen houses with significant findings not seen in other research on these structures in Zheng Jing, *Socio-Political System and Vernacular Architectural Forms: A Study on* Tulou *in China (1958–1983)* (Dissertation, The Chinese University of Hong Kong, Hong Kong, 2012); Zheng Jing, "Tulou and Population Mobility: Architectural Transformations in Southwestern Fujian Since the Qing Dynasty," *Global Hakka Studies* (May 2014): 123–164.

28 See Yang Yaolin and Huang Chongyue, eds., *Hakka Enclosed Houses in Guangdong and Hong Kong* (Beijing: Wenwu Press, 2001).

29 See Cao Weiqiong, ed., *The Folkloric Heritage of Guizhou Villages* (Guiyang: Guizhou Renmin Publishing House, 2001); Cai Ling, *Traditional Villages and Architecture of Dong Nationality's Habitation Region* (Beijing: China Architecture and Building Press, 2007).

30 See Zhang Zengtang, ed., *Yunnan Dali Baizu jianzhu* (Architecture of the Bai People in Yunnan Dali) (Kunming: Yunnan University Press, 1992).

Bibliography

Bodde, Derk. *Chinese Thought, Society, and Science: The Intellectual and Social Background of Science and Technology in Pre-Modern China.* Honolulu: University of Hawai'i Press, 1991.

Bruun, Ole. *Fengshui in China: Geometric Divination Between State Orthodoxy and Popular Religion.* Honolulu: University of Hawai'i Press, 2003.

Cai Ling. *Traditional Villages and Architecture of Dong Nationality's Habitation Region.* Beijing: China Architecture and Building Press, 2007.

Cao Weiqiong, ed. *The Folkloric Heritage of Guizhou Villages.* Guiyang: Guizhou Renmin Publishing House, 2001.

Chen Zhihua, ed. *Nanxijiang zhongyou xiangtu jianzhu* (Vernacular Architecture in the Middle Reaches of Nanxijiang). Taipei: Hansheng Publishing House, 1992.

———. *Guzhen Xikou* (Ancient Town Xikou). Taipei: Hansheng Publishing House, 2004.

Fan Wei. "Village *Fengshui* Principles." In *Chinese Landscapes: The Village as Place*, edited by Ronald G. Knapp, 35–45. Honolulu: University of Hawai'i Press, 1992.

Ho, Puay-peng. "China's Vernacular Architecture." In *Asia's Old Dwellings*, edited by Ronald G. Knapp, 322–324. Oxford: Oxford University Press, 2003.

———. "Ancestral Halls: Family, Lineage, and Ritual." In *House Home Family: Living and Being Chinese*, edited by Ronald G. Knapp and Lo Kai-yin, 295–323. Honolulu: University of Hawai'i Press, 2005.

Hou Jiyao ed. *Zhongguo yaodong* (Cave Dwellings of China). Zhengzhou: Henan Science and Technology Press, 1999.

Huang Hanmin. *Fujian tulou* (Earthen Towers of Fujian Province). Taipei: Hansheng Publishing House, 1994.

Huang Hanmin and Chen Limu. *Fujian tulou jianzhu* (Architecture of Earthen Towers of Fujian Province). Fuzhou: Fujian Science and Technology Press, 2012.

Jensen, Lionel M. *Manufacturing Confucianism: Chinese Traditions & Universal Civilization.* Durham: Duke University Press, 1997.

Knapp, Ronald G. *China's Vernacular Architecture: House Form and Culture.* Honolulu: University of Hawai'i Press, 1989.

———, ed. *Chinese Landscape: The Village as Place.* Honolulu: University of Hawai'i Press, 1992.

———. *China's Living Houses: Folk Beliefs, Symbols, and Household Ornamentation.* Honolulu: University of Hawai'i Press, 1999.

———. *China's Old Dwellings.* Honolulu: University of Hawai'i Press, 2000.

———, ed. *Asia's Old Dwellings.* Oxford: Oxford University Press, 2003.

———. *Chinese Houses: The Architectural Heritage of a Nation.* North Clarendon: Tuttle Publishing, 2005.

Knapp, Ronald G. and Lo Kai-yin, eds. *House Home Family: Living and Being Chinese.* Honolulu: University of Hawai'i Press, 2005.

Li Qiuxiang. *Dingcun* (Ding Village). Beijing: Tsinghua University Press, 2007.

Li Qiuxiang and Chen Zhihua. *Liukengcun* (Liukeng Village). Chongqing: Chongqing Publishing House, 2001.

Ma Yonghu. *Hexie youxu de xiangcun shequ- Chengkan* (Harmonious and Orderly Village Community: Chengkan Village). Hefei: Hefei Industrial University Press, 2005.

Ruan Yisan, ed. *Nanxijiang zongzu cunluo* (Clan Villages in Nanxijiang). Fuzhou: Fujian Art Press, 2003.

Shanxi Provincial Construction Bureau. *Shanxi gucunzhen* (Ancient Villages and Towns of Shanxi Province). Beijing: China Architecture and Building Press, 2007.

Watson, James L. and Patricia Ebrey, eds. *Kinship Organization in Late Imperial China, 1000–194*. Berkeley: University of California Press, 1986.

Wilson, Thomas A. *Genealogy of the Way: The Construction and Uses of the Confucian Tradition in Late Imperial China*. Stanford: Stanford University Press, 1995.

Xiao Chunrei. *Yangguang xia de giaohua menlou* (Carved Gate Towers Under the Sun) Fuzhou: Haichao Photographic art Publisher, 2002.

Yang Yaolin and Huang Chongyue, eds. *Hakka Enclosed Houses in Guangdong and Hong Kong*. Beijing: Wenwu Press, 2001.

Zhang Chengde, ed. *Residential Courtyard of Shanxi Merchant- Qiao Family*. Taiyuan: Shanxi People's Publishing House, 1997.

Zhang Chengde and Fau Tuixiang, eds. *Residential Courtyard of Shanxi Merchant- Wang Family*. Taiyuan: Shanxi Renmin Publishing House, 1997.

Zhang Xin and Chen Jie. *The Wang's Grand Courtyard in Illustration*. Taiyuan: Shanxi Economic Publishing House, 2007.

Zhang Zengtang, ed. *Yunnan Dali Baizu jianzhu* (Architecture of the Bai People in Yunnan Dali). Kunming: Yunnan University Press, 1992.

Zheng Jing. *Socio-Political System and Vernacular Architectural Forms: A Study on 'Tulou' in China (1958–1983)*. Dissertation. The Chinese University of Hong Kong, Hong Kong, 2012.

———. "Tulou and Population Mobility: Architectural Transformations in Southwestern Fujian Since the Qing Dynasty." *Global Hakka Studies* (May 2014): 123–164.

Zheng Zhenman. *Peitian* (Peitian Village). Beijing: Joint Publishing House, 2005.

Zhou Luanshu, ed. *The First Village Through the Ages- Liukeng*. Nanchang: Jiangxi Education Publishing House, 1999.

Zuo Manchang, ed. *Henan minju* (Vernacular Buildings of Henan) Beijing: China Architecture and Building Press, 2007.

Glossary

Bai (people)	白族
Baolunge	宝纶阁
Chaozhou (city)	潮州市
Chengkan (village)	呈坎村
Cuandixia (village)	爨底下（村）
Dai (people)	傣族
Dingcun	丁村
Dong (people)	侗族
Dong (clan)	董（家）
Donglong (village)	东龙村
fengshui	风水
Fujian (province)	福建省
Guangdong (province)	广东省
Guizhou (province)	贵州省
Han (people)	汉族
Hebei (province)	河北省
Jiangxi (province)	江西省
Jianyang (county)	建阳县

Jishu hall	继述堂
kang	炕
Le'an (county)	乐安县
Li Yijun	李翊俊
Li (clan)	李家
Liancheng (county)	连城县
Lin (county)	临县
Lingshi (county)	灵石县
Liukeng (village)	流坑（村）
Longyan (city, region)	龙岩（市或地区）
Luo Dongshu	罗东舒
Luo Yinghe	罗应鹤
Miao (people)	苗族
minjian gugong	民间故宫
Nanxijiang (river)	楠溪江
Naxi (people)	纳西族
Ningdu (county)	宁都县
Peitian (village)	培田（村）
Qi (county)	祁县
Qiao (clan)	乔家
Qikou (town)	碛口镇
Qufu (city)	曲阜（市）
Shaanxi (province)	陕西省
Shanxi (province)	山西省
She (county)	歙县
Shi (clan)	石家
Suichang (county)	遂昌县
Wang (clan)	王家
Wu Changtong	吴昌同
Wu Yinzhai	吴引斋
Xiamei (village)	下梅（村）
Xianfen (county)	襄汾县
Yangliuqing (town)	杨柳青（镇）
Yingzao fashi	营造法式
Yongjia (county)	永嘉县
Yongjing (county)	永靖县
Yunnan (province)	云南省
Zhejiang (province)	浙江省
Zou (clan)	邹家

PART II

REPUBLICAN AND EARLY MODERN TRANSFORMATION

The Arrival of "Architecture": Profession, Knowledge, and Education

14

EMERGENCE OF "ARCHITECTURE"

In the Reform Years of Late Qing Dynasty

Xu Subin

At what time can we witness the birth of architecture as a modern academic discipline and a modern educational system in early modern China?

Since the 1990s, studies on the architectural education of modern China have delivered substantial results, providing a foundation for answering this question. If we observe the development of architectural education of modern China, we find that there was an "active" process and a "passive" one – the first followed a nationalist trend, the second a colonialist trajectory. Studies on education and design production in the architecture of modern China went hand in hand, and they have all started with a focus on Suzhou College of Technology (Suzhou Gongye Zhuanmen Xuexiao) and National Central University of Nanjing.[1] Other studies have also started on new territory, such as an early time – the New Policy of the late Qing dynasty – or new topics – architectural education in the academies of fine art.[2] Entering the twenty-first century, scholarship is moving further forward, as reflected in new and deep studies on key individuals and specific schools.[3] At the same time, survey histories on architectural education of early modern China have also begun.[4] On the whole, we can say that those studies focusing on "active" architectural education have focused on Suzhou College of Technology, starting in the 1920s, whereas those engaging in the "passive" process have centered on Harbin China–Russia College of Technology (Haerbin Zhong'e Gongye Xuexiao) and Southern Manchurian College of Technology (Nanman Zhou Gongye Zhuanmen Xuexiao).[5]

This chapter examines the "active" process. It aims to push the birth date of Chinese modern architecture education to a time beyond the Suzhou College of the Republican era – to an early time of the so-called New Policy in the late Qing dynasty. I explored this in my PhD thesis (*Comparing, Exchanging and Illuminating: A Study on the History of Architecture in Early Modern China and Japan*, Tianjin University 1991) and have written more on this in my book *The Birth of Architecture in Early Modern China* (Tianjin University Press, 2010). Building upon these studies, the current chapter examines the early situation in the introduction of architecture discipline through a framework much accepted then – Chinese and Western knowledge conceived as essence and instrument, respectively. This chapter argues that the introduction of architecture as Western instrumental technology was merely a surface process, whereas an assertion of Chinese learning as core essence – amid promotion of Chinese studies during the New Policy time of the late Qing – acted as a central agenda in the process.

DOI: 10.4324/9781315851112-21

Education Reform of the Late Qing and Ideas of "Chinese" and "Western" Knowledge

Education programs adopted in the late Qing revealed a scheme of thinking on "Chinese" and "Western" knowledge, in which the first was regarded as foundational or essential and the second instrumental or useful. And for the first, classical learning in the Chinese tradition provided its core content.

The earliest discussion on architectural education in China is found in the 1902 *Imperial Guideline for Peking University* (Qinding jingshi daxuetang zhangcheng). Following the Boxer Uprising (1899–1901), the Chinese Qing government initiated a project of political reform with new ideas in many spheres, including education. A reformist, Zhang Baixi (1847–1907), was appointed as a minister to manage Peking University (as minister for education and president of the university). In 1902, Zhang drafted *Imperial Guideline*, and this effectively became the origin of a new education system in China. This guideline made a reference to Japan's new education system. On university disciplines, it says

> for the specific university disciplines, a student need to choose only after graduating a foundation course; following the examples in Japan, we now establish a guideline for the distribution of the disciplines: the first is politics, the second literature, the third science, the fourth agriculture, the fifth engineering, the sixth commerce, and the seventh medicine.[6]

The education system in modern Japan, in turn, was based on those in the countries of Europe; Japan for sure had also evolved to gradually establish its own approach. The Japanese government formulated a modern university system and established Tokyo Imperial University in 1886; by 1902, the discipline-based internal university division of Tokyo Imperial University included the University of Law, University of Medicine, University of Engineering, University of Literature, University of Science, and University of Agriculture.[7] As we can see, apart from the discipline of commerce, all of the disciplines in China's *Imperial Guideline* had almost entirely followed the pattern in Japan.

Why did Zhang follow Japan's examples? Firstly, this was to do with the Chinese reformists' determination to learn from Japan after the Sino-Japanese War (1894–95); the consequence of the war prompted the reformists in China not only to critically review its own political system but also to observe the achievement of Japan in adopting industrialization for nation building. Industrialization, in turn, was much based on a modern university education. China therefore began sending students to Japan in 1896 and started to observe Japan's university system. Secondly, the university system was already well established in Japan and was considered more appropriate for China, which shared a common oriental culture. By 1902, there were many travel books and diaries in China on visits to Japan, recording various aspects of this Asian neighbor. The most well-known author was Yao Xiguang,[8] who published *Riben Xuexiao Shulue* (An outline of schools and colleges in Japan) in 1898[9] and *Dongying Xuexiao Jugai* (Examples of schools and colleges of Japan) in 1899.[10] These clearly generated an impact in China on developing a modern education system.

In August 1902, Zhang submitted his *Imperial Guideline for Institutions of Learning* (Qinding xuetang zhangcheng) to the authority, but it was set aside due to the complex political situation of the time. But soon, Emperor Guangxu (r. 1889–1898) requested Zhang Zhidong (1837–1909)[11] to revise the submitted *Guideline* with Zhang Baixi and Rong Qing (1859–1917).[12] Different from Zhang Baixi in outlook, Rong adopted conservative views; in a historical record,

Qing History: Biographies (volume 226), it is said that "Baixi insisted on reform with new ideas, whereas Rong Qing added traditional studies to counterbalance from time to time." Zhang Zhidong, meanwhile, aimed for a third path between the traditionalists and the reformists.[13] But the reformists also appreciated the importance of native classical learning. Kang Youwei (1858–1927), a renowned reformist, wrote an essay as early as 1898 to promote the continuing importance of Confucianism.[14] Liang Qichao (1873–1929), another famous reformist, adopted in 1902 for the first time the term *guoxue* – national learning or Chinese learning – launching national and nationalist studies in modern China; Liang advised that we should critically inherit the tradition of Confucian learning – to retain its old essence and to absorb new ideas.[15]

These ideas were clearly reflected in the revised *Guideline*. On 27 June 1903, Zhang Zhidong, along with Zhang Baixi and Rong Qing, started to rework guidelines for Peking University and other universities of the provinces; after some four rounds of revision, they finalized and named it *Revised Guideline for Institutions of Learning* (which was later named *Confirmed Guideline for Institutions of Learning*) and submitted it to the emperor on 13 January 1904; it was approved and a decree was issued for implementation in the capital and the provinces on the same day. Since that year was called *guimao* in the Chinese calendar, the document was also known as the Guimao Education System. This is the first national decree for education issued by the Qing authority after the abolition of the ancient and long-standing civil service examination system (*keju zhi*). In this *Revised Guideline*, Zhang Zhidong explains the relations between Chinese classical learning and new Western knowledge as follows:

> All studies in any schools must prioritize the teaching of royalty and piety as their core, and regard the learning of Chinese classics as their foundation, so that the minds of the students can be guided to the pure and correct. With this, we can then adopt western knowledge and intelligence, and technologies and skills, to train students to be competent and useful in all specialized fields, to become experts for nation building, and they will not be misguided and distracted.

The new *Confirmed Guideline* (*Zouding xuetang zhangcheng*) had two clear characteristics: the "classical and historical studies" of Chinese tradition were considered as the core, whereas Western knowledge in "politics, technology, and history" was also included in the curriculum structure. According to this *Guideline*, there should be in China universities of classical learning, of law and politics, of literature, of medicine, of sciences, of agriculture, of engineering, and of commerce. Compared to its early draft (1902), this *Guideline* of 1904 added the university for classical learning, which clearly emphasized the importance of the classical knowledge of Chinese tradition. In the *Guideline*, classical learning had 11 specialized departments – Zhou Yi (studies of I Ching or Yi Jing), Shang Shu (the Book of Documents), Mao Shi (the Classic of Poems), Chunqiu Zuozhuan (Commentary on the Chronicle *Spring and Autumn Annals*), Chunqiu Sanzhuan (three classics from the Spring and Autumn era), Zhou Li (the Rites of Zhou), Yi Li (a classic on rites and rituals), Li Ji (the Book of Rites), Lun Yu (The Analects by Confucius), Meng Zi (The Book of Mencius), and Li Xue (Neo-Confucianism). These comprised the core knowledge for Confucian learning and Confucian culture.

As to the study of "Western knowledge," Zhang Zhidong's *Exhortation to Learning* (*Quanxue Pian*) of 1898 was clear about the approach:

> for going abroad to study, the west is not as good as the east; countries of the east are closer and the trip is economic so we can send more students; it is easier to visit and observe since it is closer; eastern languages are closer to Chinese and is easier to learn;

western knowledge can be very complex and those not adequate were already deleted and shortened; China and eastern countries share similar culture; so it is easier for us to learn, and we can learn more efficiently.[16]

This observation was made regarding the lessons and experiences of going abroad to study in Europe and North America. It is clear that learning from Japan was the focus in developing the new education system.

The Guimao Education System of 1903–4 in China was closer – in terms of timing – to the new system adopted in Japan in 1900 (Year 33 of the Meiji era).[17] In terms of institutional structure, it was also very close: from "Tongru Yuan" to "Mengyang Yuan" (Japanese terms for universities and kindergartens respectively), the Chinese framework was almost entirely based on Japan's.[18] *Confirmed Guideline for Institutions of Learning* included seven chapters and 72 sections, covering guidelines for schools of all levels. Those that covered the discipline of architecture included *Guideline for Universities (Daxeutang zhangcheng)*; *Guideline for Practical Colleges of Higher Learning in Medicine, Engineering, and Commerce (Gaodeng nonggongshang shiye xuetang zhangcheng)*; and *Guideline for Technical Colleges (Yitu xuetang zhangcheng)*.

The Discipline of "Architecture" in *Guideline for Universities*

With classical Chinese learning as its foundation, *Guideline for Universities* introduced the specialization of "architecture" (*jianzhu xuemen*). Departing from the time *The Compete Books in Four Collections (Siku quanshu)* was compiled, "architecture" now was no longer an index or a tool of classical knowledge but instead a specialized body of knowledge with values of its own. This process was much to do with Wu Rulun (1840–1903)[19] – provost at Peking University – and his observations on Japan.

Wu's study on Japan is clearly reflected in *Confirmed Guideline for Institutions of Learning* of 1904, especially its listing of specializations in engineering.[20] The Guideline says, "there are nine specializations in engineering,"[21] and in Wu's Japan travel diary, *Diaries of the Eastern Tour (Dongyou Conglu)*, it comments on the Engineering College of Tokyo Imperial University, saying, "this college has nine disciplines, each taking three years to complete." If we compare the two lists, they were almost the same aside from some small difference in wording (*jixie gongxue ke* in Japan was *jixie gongxue men* in China for mechanical engineering, and *zaobing xueke* in Japan was *zaobingqi xuemen* in China for ordnance engineering) (Table 14.1).

For the discipline of architecture, the situation was the same. If we compare *Confirmed Guideline for Institutions of Learning* and Wu's *Diaries of the Eastern Tour*, we can find that the two lists of teaching content remained very close (Table 14.2).

The twofold ideas of architecture – as fine art and as science – that came from England found their way into Japan through two stages of development. In the first stage, in early Meiji era (1868–1912), with an emphasize on industrialization, the science and engineering side of architecture was much privileged, and the architecture discipline was placed within the curriculum structure at Universities or Colleges of Engineering; in the second stage, however, ideas of architecture as an aesthetic issue and a nationalist topic were brought into the curriculum to enrich the teaching program.[22] Late in the Meiji era, the disciplinary curriculum content for architecture combined these two sides well. Yet, in China, when the discipline of architecture was introduced, the major precondition was the privileging of classical Chinese learning – which in a way prevented cultural issues from emerging in the first place, for a while.

China fully embraced the scientific and technological side of the teaching from Japan; the curriculum in China almost entirely followed that of architectural teaching at Tokyo Imperial

Table 14.1 College of Engineering disciplinary list at Tokyo Imperial University and in China's *Confirmed Guideline for Institutions of Learning*: comparison.

College of Engineering Disciplines at Tokyo Imperial University (1902)	Disciplines at Colleges of Engineering specified by Confirmed Guideline (1904)
第一 土木工学科 Civil Engineering	一 土木工学门 Civil Engineering
第二 机械工学科 Mechanical Engineering	二 机器工学门 Mechanical Engineering
第三 造船学科 Shipbuilding	三 造船学门 Shipbuilding
第四 造兵学科 Ordnance Engineering	四 造兵器学门 Ordnance Engineering
第五 电气工学科 Electrical Engineering	五 电气工学门 Electrical Engineering
第六 建筑学科 Architecture	六 建筑学门 Architecture
第七 应用化学科 Applied Chemistry	七 应用化学门 Applied Chemistry
第八 火药学科 Gunpowder Engineering	八 火药学门 Gunpowder Engineering
第九 采矿冶金学科 Mining & Metallurgy	九 采矿冶金学门 Mining & Metallurgy

Source: Left column: Wu Rulun, *Dongyou Conglu* (Diaries of the eastern tour) (Tokyo: Sanseido Books, 1902), 24–25; Right column: Taga Akigorou, *Kindai Chugoku Kyoiku-shi Shiryo – Shinmatsu Hen* (Sources for a history of education in early modern China: late Qing) (Tokyo: Nihon Gakujutsu Shinko-kai, 1972), 251.

Table 14.2 Teaching subjects in the architecture discipline for a College of Engineering at Tokyo Imperial University and in China's *Confirmed Guideline for Institutions of Learning*: comparison.

Year	Subjects for Architecture at Tokyo Imperial University (1902)	Subjects for Architecture in Confirmed Guideline (1904)
1	数学 Mathematics	算学 Mathematics
	热机关 Thermomechanics	热机关 Thermomechanics
	应用力学 Applied Dynamics	应用力学 Applied Dynamics
	测量 Surveying	测量 Surveying
	地质学 Geology	地质学 Geology
	应用规矩 Applied Geometry & Drafting	应用规矩 Applied Geometry & Drafting
	建筑材料 Building Material	建筑材料 Building Material
	家屋构造 House Construction	房屋构造 Building Construction
	建筑意匠 Architectural Design	建筑意匠 Architectural Design
	建筑历史 Architectural History	建筑历史 Architectural History
	日本建筑 Japanese Architecture	
	配景法 Landscape Design	配景法及装饰法 （选修） Landscape and Ornament (Elective)
	自在画 Freehand Drawing	自在画 Freehand Drawing
	应用力学制图和演习 Graphic Statics & Exercise	应用力学制图和演习 Graphic Statics & Exercise
	测量实习 Surveying Practice	测量实习 Surveying Practice
	制图及配景图 Drafting of Building & Landscape	制图及配景图 Drafting of Building & Landscape
	计画及制图 Design & Drafting	计画及制图 Design & Drafting

(Continued)

University; even subjects like seismology were adopted as electives; ornamentation and landscape design were combined as one subject; there was no thesis design, but "upon the end of year three for graduation, students must submit their graduation projects, with their own writings and drawings," revealing that there was in effect thesis design or thesis essay, exactly as in

Table 14.2 (Continued)

Year	Subjects for Architecture at Tokyo Imperial University (1902)	Subjects for Architecture in Confirmed Guideline (1904)
2	卫生工学 Hygiene	卫生工学 Hygiene
	装饰法 Ornamentation	配景法及装饰法 Landscape & Ornamentation
	日本建筑 Japanese Architecture	
	水力学 Hydraulics	水力学 Hydraulics
	建筑意匠 Architectural Design	建筑意匠 Architectural Design
	施工法 Methods of Building Construction	施工法 Methods of Building Construction
	建筑条例 Building Regulations	
	制造冶金学 Metallurgical Manufacturing	冶金制器学 Metallurgical Manufacturing
	美学 Aesthetics	美学 Aesthetics
	自在画 Freehand Drawing	自在画 （选修） Freehand Drawing (Elective)
	装饰画 Ornamental Fine Art	装饰画 （选修） Ornamental Fine Art (Elective)
	计画及制图 Design & Drafting	计画及制图 Design & Drafting
	实地演习 Site Practice	实地演习 （不定） Site Practice (To Be Confirmed)
3	地震学 Seismology	地震学（选修） Seismology (Elective)
	装饰画 Ornamental Fine Art	装饰画 （选修） Ornamental Fine Art (Elective)
	自在画 Freehand Drawing	自在画 （选修） Freehand Drawing (Elective)
	计画及制图 Design & Drafting	计画及制图 Design & Drafting
	实地演习 Site Practice	实地演习（不定） Site Practice (To Be Confirmed)
	卒业计画 Thesis Design	

Source: Left column: Wu Rulun, *Dongyou Conglu* (Diaries of the eastern tour) (Tokyo: Sanseido Books, 1902), 39–42; Right column: Taga Akigorou, *Kindai Chugoku Kyoiku-shi Shiryo – Shinmatsu Hen* (Sources for a history of education in early modern China: late Qing) (Tokyo: Nihon Gakujutsu Shinko-kai, 1972), 255–256.

Japan.[23] Building regulations, as a subject, was not taught as in Japan, since such rules for building industry had not been established in China yet.

However, beyond the technical side, the situation was more complex. When introducing technologies from the West in architecture, Japan also had full consideration of two aspects of architecture in terms of design ideas. The first concerned architecture as art, and the second architecture as a national expression. And in Japan's national architecture, both the artistic and the technological sides were studied, in parallel. The artistic side of considerations were reflected in subjects such as architectural ideas, architectural history, aesthetics, landscape design, ornamentation, freehand drawing, and decorative painting, among others. These were also adopted in China, and the most noted was aesthetics, an entirely new subject in late Qing dynasty. In a broader sphere of intellectual culture, the period from the early twentieth century to the New Culture Movement (1915–1923) witnessed the beginning of aesthetics in China, as best represented in Wang Guowei (1877–1927). Wang encountered and studied Western thoughts when he was in Shanghai in the late nineteenth century; from 1902, he studied in Western philosophy. He gradually introduced into China the philosophy, aesthetics, and art theory of Schopenhauer, Kant, Nietzsche, and Schiller.[24] The appearance of Aesthetics in the architectural teaching curriculum reflected an acceptance of Western cultural ideas and Wang's effort directly or indirectly in China.

In the 1880s, Japan turned to nationalism in its societal consciousness; in the 1890s, scholars in literature, anthropology, archaeology, and fine art all turned increasingly to an emphasis on Japan's own culture and tradition, for positioning Japan in the world. In this context, nationalist thinking on Japanese architecture came into being. The instituting of the subject of "Japanese architecture" in the teaching curriculum was a reflection of nationalism in the discipline of architecture in Japan, and an imprint in architecture of the reflexive thinking on national culture and history at the establishing of Japan as a modern nation-state. In China, however, national-ist thinking was reflected in the independent teaching program of Chinese classical learning, rather than a subject like "Chinese architecture" in architectural teaching. This means that, in China, nationalism and architecture had not come together; China had not yet entered a time for reflexive thinking on a national architecture or architectural tradition – this happened later in the Republican time (after 1911 and mainly in the 1930s).

Architectural Teaching for Colleges of Higher Learning and Technical Colleges

Parallel to *Guideline for Universities*, there were also *Guideline for Practical Colleges of Higher Learning in Agriculture, Engineering and Commerce* and *Guideline for Technical Colleges*, both established on 13 January 1904. Teaching subjects of architecture at "practical colleges of higher learning" formed part of the earliest practice of architectural education in China.

"Practical colleges" or education for practical professions in China was also based on a ref-erence to the practice in Japan. Wu Rulun's *Diaries of the Eastern Tour* of 1902 explained such education practice in Japan in great detail, which directly influenced China in that area.

Among all the practical colleges, those Practical Colleges of Higher Learning were equiva-lent to the Higher College of Engineering in Japan. When Wu was in Japan in 1902, the new decree for standardizing institutions of learning in Japan – Special College Degree (1903) – was not published yet; and in 1901, as a special case in Japan, Tokyo College of Engineering was upgraded to Tokyo Higher College of Engineering. So, what Wu had introduced into China as a model of the College of Higher Learning in Engineering was specifically Tokyo Higher College of Engineering. Colleges of Higher Learning in Engineering included the disciplines of building design (*jianzhu ke*) and drafting (*tugao huihua ke*) (which was called *gongye tuan ke* and *tuan ke* in Tokyo Higher College and Tokyo College of Art respectively) (Tables 14.3 and 14.4). The name *tuan fa* in Japan was renamed *tugao fa* in China – two different wordings for drafting.

For Colleges of Mid-Level Learning in Engineering in China, the disciplinary teaching framework followed Colleges of Engineering in Japan exactly (Table 14.5). Those related to

Table 14.3 Subjects in architecture at Tokyo Higher College of Engineering and in China's Colleges of Higher Learning in Engineering (as specified by *Guideline of Practical Colleges of Higher Learning in Agriculture, Engineering and Commerce*): comparison.

Architecture Subjects at Tokyo Higher College of Engineering (1906)	*Architecture Subjects at China's Colleges of Higher Learning in Engineering (1904)*
应用力学、建筑用材料、建筑沿革、 　家屋构造、 卫生工学、制图及意匠、工场实修 Applied Mechanics, Building Materials, 　History of Building, House Construction, 　Hygiene, Drafting and Design, Site Practice	应用力学、房屋构造法、工场用具及制造法、 　建筑沿革、施工法、配景法、制图及绘画法 Applied Mechanics, Building Construction, 　Instruments and Methods, History of Building, 　Construction Methods, Landscape Design, 　Drafting and Drawing

Source: Left column: Tokyo Koto Kogyo Gakko, ed. *Tokyo Koto Kogyo Gakko Ichiran* (Tokyo Higher Col-lege of Engineering: Survey) (Tokyo: Tokyo Koto Kogyo Gakko, 1907), 38; Right column: Taga Akig-orou, *Kindai Chugoku Kyoiku-shi Shiryo – Shinmatsu Hen* (Sources for a history of education in early modern China: late Qing) (Tokyo: Nihon Gakujutsu Shinko-kai, 1972), 345.

Table 14.4 Drafting program at Tokyo Higher College of Engineering and China's Colleges of Higher Learning in Engineering (as specified by *Guideline of Practical Colleges of Higher Learning in Agriculture, Engineering and Commerce*): comparison.

Drafting Subjects at Tokyo Higher College of Engineering (1902)	*Drafting Subjects at China's Colleges of Higher Learning in Engineering (1904)*
图案法（有职故实、建筑装饰）、工艺史、应用解剖、绘画、用器画、工场实修、图案实修	一图稿法、二配景法、三绘画、四工艺史、五应用解剖、六用器画、七工场实习及图稿实习
Graphics (Building & Ornamentation), History of Technology, Applied Anatomy, Drawing & Painting, Depiction of Objects, Site Practice, Drafting Practice	1 Graphics, 2 Landscape Design, 3 Drawing and Painting, 4 History Technology, 5 Applied Anatomy, 6 Depiction of Objects, 7 Site Practice and Drafting Practice

Source: Left column: Wu Rulun, *Dongyou Conglu* (Diaries of the eastern tour) (Tokyo: Sanseido Books, 1902), 165; Right column: Taga Akigorou, *Kindai Chugoku Kyoiku-shi Shiryo – Shinmatsu Hen* (Sources for a history of education in early modern China: late Qing) (Tokyo: Nihon Gakujutsu Shinko-kai, 1972), 346.

Table 14.5 Disciplines at Japan's Colleges of Engineering and China's Colleges of Mid-Level Learning in Engineering: comparison.

Disciplines at Japan's Colleges of Engineering (1902)	*Disciplines at China's Colleges of Mid-Level Learning in Engineering (1904)*
土木科 Civil Engineering	土木科 Civil Engineering
金工科 Metalwork Engineering	金工科 Metalwork Engineering
造船科 Shipbuilding	造船科 Shipbuilding
电气科 Electrical Engineering	电气科 Electrical Engineering
木工科 Timberwork Engineering	木工科 Timberwork Engineering
矿业科 Mining Engineering	矿业科 Mining Engineering
染织科 Textile Engineering	染织科 Textile Engineering
窑业科 Kiln Industry	窑业科 Kiln Industry
漆工科 Lacquer Work	漆工科 Lacquer Work
图案绘画科 Graphics & Drafting	图稿绘画科 Graphics & Drafting

Source: Left column: Wu Rulun, *Dongyou Conglu* (Diaries of the eastern tour) (Tokyo: Sanseido, 1902), 142–144; Right column: Taga Akigorou, *Kindai Chugoku Kyoiku-shi Shiryo – Shinmatsu Hen* (Sources for a history of education in early modern China: late Qing) (Tokyo: Nihon Gakujutsu Shinko-kai, 1972), 352–353.

building design included timber building engineering (*mugong ke*) and drafting (*tugao huihua ke*) (which was called *tuan huihua ke* in Japan) (Table, 14.6 and 14.7). Timber building engineering covered house construction and the history of building, whereas drafting covered the history of architecture, design ideas, and drawing. In addition, for colleges of engineering in Japan, there was no "junior-level" college of engineering, and in China among practical colleges of junior-level learning, there was no colleges of engineer, either; but in 1909, China established the system of Colleges of Junior-Level Education in Engineering. A college of engineering that was upgraded from a technical college (*yitu xuetang*) in China then was roughly the same as a professional college of mid-level learning of engineering.

Table 14.6 Timber Building Engineering at Japan's Colleges of Engineering and China's Colleges of Mid-Level Learning in Engineering: comparison.

Timber Building Engineering Subjects at Japan's Colleges of Engineering (1902)	*Timber Building Engineering at China's Colleges of Mid-Level Learning in Engineering (1904)*
应用力学、家屋构造、工场用（具）及制作法、建筑沿革、施工法、配景法、制图及绘画等	一房屋构造、二建筑沿革、三施工法、四配景法、五制图及绘画、六工场用具及制作法、七应用力学、八实习
Applied Mechanics, House Construction, Instruments and Methods, History of Building, Construction Methods, Landscape Design, Drafting & Drawing	1 Building Construction, 2 History of Building, 3 Construction Methods, 4 Landscape Design, 5 Drafting & Drawing, 6 Instruments and Methods, 7 Applied Mechanics, 8 Practice

Source: Left column: Wu Rulun, *Dongyou Conglu* (Diaries of the eastern tour) (Tokyo: Sanseido, 1902), 144; Right column: Taga Akigorou, *Kindai Chugoku Kyoiku-shi Shiryo – Shinmatsu Hen* (Sources for a history of education in early modern China: late Qing) (Tokyo: Nihon Gakujutsu Shinko-kai, 1972), 352.

Table 14.7 Drafting Subjects at Japan's Colleges of Engineering and China's Colleges of Mid-Level Learning in Engineering: comparison.

Drafting Subjects in Japan's Colleges of Engineering (1902)	*Drafting Subjects in China's Colleges of Mid-Level Learning in Engineering (1904)*
配景法、解剖大意、工艺史、建筑沿革大意、绘画、应用化学大意、各种工艺品图案等	一配景法、二解剖大意、三工艺史、四建筑沿革大意、五绘画、六应用化学大意、七各种工艺品图样、八实习
Landscape Design, Introduction to Anatomy, History of Technology, Outline History of Building, Fine Art, Introduction to Applied Chemistry, Industrial Design and Graphics	1 Landscape Design, 2 Introduction to Anatomy, 3 History of Technology, 4 Outline History of Building, 5 Fine Art, 6 Introduction to Applied Chemistry, 7 Industrial Design & Graphics, 8 Practice

Source: Left column: Wu Rulun, *Dongyou Conglu* (Diaries of the eastern tour) (Tokyo: Sanseido, 1902), 144; Right column: Taga Akigorou, *Kindai Chugoku Kyoiku-shi Shiryo – Shinmatsu Hen* (Sources for a history of education in early modern China: late Qing) (Tokyo: Nihon Gakujutsu Shinko-kai, 1972), 353.

As we can see, like universities, practical colleges also followed Japanese examples and were a simplified version of the university-level curriculum. As Japan was also improving its system, the learning process in China included shifts and changes as well. In addition, the Higher College of Engineering in Japan belonged to the Ministry of Education, whereas in China it belonged to Ministry of Agriculture, Industry, and Commerce. This reflected the importance of strengthening industry and commerce in China during its New Policy reform in late Qing dynasty.

Actual practice in architectural education began in China at the Practical Colleges of Higher Learning (*gaodeng shiye xuetang*) and Technical Colleges (*yitu xuetang*). In 1904, Tianjin Zhili Practical College of Higher Learning had a short course program in which design and drafting (*yijiang tuan ke*) were established, taught by a Japanese professor, Matsunaga Chyozaburo. In the same year, the Technical College at Ministry of Agriculture, Industry and Commerce in Beijing established building engineering and drafting courses; Japanese professors Harada Takeo, Kawabuchi Kunpei, and Akino Sotoya were invited to teach drafting, while Nakayama Kinjiro and Oguro Chujiro were invited to teach building engineering; in 1909, these courses were combined to form architecture as a disciplinary program, with Haraguchi Yoshitsugu of Japan as its leading professor. At this point, the practice of architectural education in modern China had started.[25]

Conclusion

The birth of architecture as a discipline in modern China was the result of education reform of the New Policy of late Qing government – when it was preparing for transferring toward a constitutional monarch. Architecture as an academic discipline arrived in 1904 when the new education system came into being. From this moment on, the art and culture of building, in other words architecture, departed from the classical sphere of *Books of Political Knowledge* (*zhengshu lei*) and was no longer a phenomenon of ritual systems or institutions; at this moment, it became a discipline with its own system of skills and knowledge. This is a revolutionary transformation made to the culture of building in modern China.

The system of architectural education then was characterized by the principle of Chinese and Western knowledge as considered foundational and pragmatic, respectively. With the background of promoting "national learning" in the New Policy of the Qing, Chinese classical learning was enshrined as basic or foundational, whereas the discipline of architecture was introduced as Western technology for pragmatic use – introduced by adopting comprehensively the teaching system of architecture in Japan. In the process, with adjustment and reorganization, the dual content of architecture as "art" and "science" were introduced into China – this should be confirmed and appreciated. However, unlike Japan during Meiji Restoration, which had already considered substantially its national tradition and its national architecture, China had not reached that point, and there were no reflections or studies on a native and national tradition in architecture in China. In this aspect, the introduction of architecture remained premature and incomplete, in a transition from tradition to modernity.

Notes

1 Qi Kang and Yan Longyu, "Jindai jiuanzhu jiaoyu shilue (Notes on a History of Architectural Education in Early Modern China)," in *Zhongguo Jianzhuye Nianjian 1986–1987* (Yearbook in the Building Industry of China 1986–1987), ed. Editorial Committee (Beijing: Zhongguo Jianzhu Gongye Chubanshe, 1988), 414–415; Xu Subin, "Dongjing gaodeng gongye xuexiao yu liushiying (Tokyo Higher College of Engineering and Liushiying)," *Nanfang jianzhu* 3 (1994): 10–14; Xu Subin, "Zhongguo jindai jianzhu jiaoyu de qishi he Suzhou gongzhuan jianzhuke (The Birth of China's Early Modern Architectural Education and the Architecture Discipline at Suzhou College of Technology)," *Zhongguo*, ed. Editorial, 15–18; Lai Delin, "Zhongguo jindai jiaoyu de xianxingzhe: Jiangsu shengli Suzhou gongye zhuanmen xuexiao jianzhuke (A Pioneer in China's Early Modern Architectural Education: The Architecture Discipline at Suzhou College of Technology of Jiangsu Province)," in *Jianzhu Lishi yu Lilun* (Architectural History and Theory), ed. Yang Hongxun and Liu Tuo (Beijing: Zhongguo Gongye Chubanshe, 1997), 71–77; Pan Guxi and Shan Yong, "Guanyu Suzhou gongzhuan yu zhongyang daxue jianzhuke (The Architecture Discipline at Suzhou College of Technology and National Central University)," *Jianzhu Shi* 90 (October 1999): 89–97; Zhang Liangben, "Jiangmen shuxue: Wei jinian zhongyang daxue jianzhuxi chengli 70 zhounian tan zhongguo jianzhu jiaoyu (On China's Architectural Education for Celebrating the 70th Anniversary of Central University Department of Architecture)," *Xin Jianzhu* 2 (1999): 58–65.

2 Whereas I studied the establishing of architectural education in late Qing dynasty, Lai Delin's study touched on the architectural department in the College of Art at Peking University. For these, see: Xu Subin, *Bijiao, Jiaowang, Qishi: Zhongri jinxiandai jianzhushi zhi yanjiu* (Comparing, Exchanging and Illuminating: A Study on the History of Architecture of Early Modern China and Japan) (PhD Thesis,

Tianjin University, Tianjin, 1991); Lai Delin, *Zhongguo Jindai Jianzhushi Yanjiu* (A Study for an Architectural History of Early Modern China) (PhD Thesis, Tsinghua University, Beijing, 1992).

3 Wen Yuqing, "Taoli buyan xiazi chengxi – Tianjin gongshang xueyuan jianzhuxi jiqi jiaoxue tixi pingshu (1937–1952) (Silent Achievement: Department of Architecture at Tianjin College of Commerce and Its System of Teaching, 1937–1952)," in *Zhongguo Jindai Jianzhu Xueshu Sixiang* (Leading Ideas in the Discipline of Architecture in Early Modern China), ed. Zhao Chen and Wu Jiang (Beijing: Zhongguo Jianzhu Gongye Chubanshe, 2003), 77–86; Wu Jiang and Qian Feng, "Huang Zuoshen he tade jianzhu jiaoyu sixiang (Huang Zuoshen and His Thoughts for Architectural Education)," in *Zhongguo*, ed. Zhao and Wu, 87–91; Wen Yuqing and Sun Lian, "Ji Tianjin gongshang xueyuan jianzhuxi (On the Department of Architecture at Tianjin College of Commerce)," in *Jianzhu Baijia Huiyilu Xubian* (Memoirs of One Hundred Architects: Part two), ed. Yang Yongsheng (Beijing: Zhishi Chanquan Chubanshe, 2003), 21–26; Peng Changxin and Yang Xiaochuan, "Xiangqin daxue jianzhu gongcheng xuexi yu lingnan zaoqi xiandai zhuyi de chuanbo he yanjiu (Department of Architecture and Civil Engineering at Xiangqin University and the Development of an Early Modern Architecture in the South)," *Xin Jianzhu* (New Architecture) 10 (2002): 54–56; Wei Qiufang, *Xu Zhong Xiansheng de Jianzhu Jiaoyu Sixiang yu Tianjin Daxue Jianzhuxi* (Xu Zhong's Thoughts for Architectural Education and the Development of Tianjin University Department of Architecture) (MA Thesis, Tianjin University, Tianjin, 2005); Liu Mi, *Zhijiang Daxue Jianzhu Jiaoyu Lishi Yanjiu* (Architectural Education at Zhijiang University: A Historical Inquiry) (MA Thesis, Tongji University, Shanghai, 2008); Yang Miaomiao, "Liu Dunzhen dui zhongguo jindai jianzhu jiaoyu de zhaoshi yu fazhan de yingxiang (Liu Dunzhen's Influence on the Birth and Development of Architectural Education in Early Modern China)," *Jianzhu Chuangzuo* 3 (2009): 137–145; Liu Zhao, *Zhongguo Jindai Jianzhu Jiaoyu de Xianqu Liu Futai Yanjiu* (Studies on Liu Futai – a Pioneer for Architectural Education in Early Modern China) (MA Thesis, Tianjin University, Tianjin, 2010); Li Baiyu, *Woguo Jindai Jianzhu Jiaoyu Xianqu – Hua Nangui Yanjiu* (Studies on Hua Nangui – a Pioneer for Architectural Education in Early Modern China) (MA Thesis, Tianjin University, Tianjin, 2010); Shen Zhensen, *Zhongguo Jindai Jianzhu de Xianquzhe – Jianzhushi Shen Liyuan Yanjiu* (Studies on Architect Shen Liyuan – a Pioneer for Architectural Education in Early Modern China) (MA Thesis, Tianjin University, Tianjin, 2002); Shen Zhensen, *Shen Liyuan* (Shen Liyuan: A Study) (Beijing: Zhongguo Jianzhu Gongye Chubanshe, 2012); Chen Ying and Liu Deming, *Haerbin Gongye Daxue Zaoqi Jianzhu Jiaoyu* (Architecture Education in Early Development at Harbin Institute of Technology) (Beijing: Zhongguo Jianzhu Gongye Chubanshe, 2010); Zhang Sheng, *Jingjinji Diqu Tumu Gongxue Beijingxia de Jindai Jianzhu Jiaoyu Yanjiu* (Inquiry into Early Modern Education of Architecture in the Context of Civil Engineering in the Beijing-Tianjin-Hebei Region of China) (PhD Thesis, Tianjin University, Tianjin, 2011).

4 Among the following, the first two are the primary studies; the third touches on a history of design education, whereas the fourth has also explored many issues concerning architectural education: Qian Feng, *Xiandai Jianzhu Jiaoyu zai Zhongguo 1920s-1980s* (Architecture Education in Modern China 1920s-1980s) (PhD Thesis, Tongji University, Shanghai, 2005); Qian Feng and Wu Jiang, *Zhongguo Jindai Jianzhu Jiaoyushi* (A History of architecture education in modern China) (Beijing: Zhongguo Jianzhu Gongye Chubanshe, 2008); Yuan Xiyang, *Zhongguo Yishu Sheji Jiaoyu Fazhan Lichen Yanjiu* (Inquiry into a History of Design Education in China) (Beijing: Beijing Ligong Daxue Chubanshe, 2003); Lai Delin, *Zhongguo Jindai Jianzhushi Yanjiu* (Studies in Architecture History of Modern China) (Beijing: Qinghua Daxue Chubanshe, 2007).

5 Chen and Liu, *Haerbin*. I have also touched on Southern Manchurian College of Technology; see: Xu, *Bijiao*.

6 Taga Akigorou, *Kindai Chugoku Kyoiku-shi Shiryo – Shinmatsu Hen* (Sources for a History of Education in Early Modern China: Late Qing) (Tokyo: Nihon Gakujutsu Shinko-kai, 1972), 129–130.

7 Tokyo Teikoku-Daigaku, ed., *Tokyo Teikoku-Daigaku Goju-nen-shi, Ge-satsu* (A Fifty-Year History of Tokyo Imperial University), vol. 2 (Tokyo: Tokyo Teikoku-Daigaku, 1932), 11.

8 Yao Xiguang (1857–?) was born in Dantu of Jiangsu province of China; he was posted to Japan in 1878 as a staffer for He Ruzhang, China's ambassador for Japan. In 1898, Yao was dispatched by Zhang Zhidong to Japan for a study of its education system.

9 Yao Xiguang, *Riben Xuexiao Shulue* (An Outline of Schools and Colleges in Japan) (Hangzhou: Zhejiang Shuju, 1898).

10 Yao Xiguang, *Dongying Xuexiao Jugai* (Examples of Schools and Colleges of Japan) (1899).

11 Zhang Zhidong (1837–1909) was a renowned statesman of the Qing government; in different periods, he was the provincial minister of education in Hubei and Sichuan, the governor of Shanxi, Guangxi, Guangdong, Hubei, and Hunan, and was once a Minister of Grand Council (or the military office).

12 Rong Qing (1859–1917) was then a newly arrived senior official at the ministry of education; he was a member of the Mongolian section of Plain Yellow Banner – part of a military–civilian organization of the Qing society; he obtained in 1886 the title of Jinshi – the highest-ranking degree in the national civil service examination system; he was once Minister for the Ministry of Punishment.

13 In his well-known *Exhortation to Learning* (*Quanxue Pian*) of 1898, Zhang Zhidong says "there are five principles for a learning institution; the first is balancing new and old knowledge; the studying of classics and ancient books, of Chinese history, of political theory, and of geography belongs to the old knowledge, whereas studies in western politics, technology and history belong to the new knowledge; we should regard the old as essence and the new as tools; and neither should be ignored." Upon Western technology, Zhang further says, "western technology includes mathematics, geometry, mining technology, medicine, acoustics, optics, chemistry, and electrics."

14 Tang Zhijun, ed., *Kang Youwei Zhenglunji* (Kang Youwei: Writings on Politics), vol. 1 (Beijing: Zhonghua Shuju, 1981), 279–284.

15 Lian Yantang, "Liang qichao duiyu guoxue yanjiu de kaichuangxing gongxian (Liang Qichao's Pioneering Contribution to the Study of National Learning)," *Wenxue Yichan* 6 (2009): 99–110.

16 Zhang Zhidong, *Exhortation to Learning* (Quanxue Pian), vol. 2, Section Two: Travelling and Studying, 1898.

17 Monbu Sho, ed., *Gakusei Kyuju-nen-shi* (A Ninety-Year History of the Education System) (Tokyo: Okura-syo Insatsu-kyoku, 1964), 586.

18 There were already studies on China's learning of Japan's education system. See for example, Wang Xiaoqiu, "Keishi-dagaku-do to nihon (Peking University and Japan)," in *Seiyo Kindai Bunmei to Chuka Seikai* (Early Modern Western Culture and the Chinese World), ed. Hazama Naoki (Kyoto: Kyoto Daigaku Gakujutsu Syupan-sha, 2001), 72–88.

19 Wu Rulun (1840–1903), from Tongcheng County of Anhui Province, obtained the titles of Juren and Jinshi – the second and the first highest-ranking degree in China's civil service examination system – at the age of 25 and 26. In 1902, amid a political change towards New Policy under Empress Dowager Cixi, Minister Zhang Baixi nominated Wu to be the Provost of Peking University. Wu reluctantly accepted it and visited Japan to observe its education system from June to October 1902; he died of a medical condition in February 1903.

20 On Wu Rulun's visit to Japan, see: Rong Yingyu, "Wu Rulun to 'toyu-soroku' – aru 'yomu-ha' no kyoiku kaikaku-an (Wu Rulun's *Diaries in the Eastern Tour*: Reformists and Education Reform)," in *Kindai Nihon to Ajia* (Modern Japan and Asia), ed. Hirano Ken'ichiro Hen (Tokyo: Tokyo Daigaku Shupan-kai, 2000), 45–71.

21 Taga, *Kindai*, 251.

22 Xu Subin, *Jindai Zhongguo Jianzhuxu de Dansheng* (The Birth of Architecture in Modern China) (Tianjin: Tianjin Daxue Chubanshe, 2010), 25–50 (Chapter Two).

23 Taga, *Kindai*, 256.

24 Nie Zhenbin, "Huiwang bainian: 20 shiji de zhongguo meixue (Review Over a Hundred Years: Chinese Aesthetics of the Twentieth Century)," in *Zhongguo Meixue Nianjian 2001* (Yearbook in Chinese Aesthetics 2001), ed. Ru Xin and Zeng Fanren (Zhengzhou: Henan Renmin Chubanshe, 2003), 2.

25 Xu Subin, "Qingmo tuan, mugong, jianzhu jiaoyu de shixing zhi yanjiu (A Study on the Early Practice of Teaching in Design Drafting, Building Engineering and Architecture in the Late Qing Dynasty)," in *Tianjin Shi Shehui Kexuejie Disanjie Xueshu Nianhui Youxiu Lunwenji, Kexue Fazhan: Yiren Weiben, Gongjian Hexie* (A Collection of Outstanding Papers of the Third Academic Conference in Social Sciences in Tianjin: Scientific Development – Building Harmony with Humanism), ed. Tianjin Shehui Kexuejie Lianghehui (Tianjin: Tianjin Renmin Chubanshe, 2007), 590–599.

Bibliography

Chen Ying and Liu Deming. *Haerbin Gongye Daxue Zaoqi Jianzhu Jiaoyu* (Architecture Education in Early Development at Harbin Institute of Technology). Beijing: Zhongguo Jianzhu Gongye Chubanshe, 2010.

Editorial Committee, ed. *Zhongguo Jianzhuye Nianjian 1986–1987* (Yearbook in the Building Industry of China 1986–1987). Beijing: Zhongguo Jianzhu Gongye Chubanshe, 1988.

Hazama Naoki, ed. *Seiyo Kindai Bunmei to Chuka Seikai* (Early Modern Western Culture and the Chinese World). Kyoto: Kyoto Daigaku Gakujutsu Syupan sha, 2001.

Hirano Ken'ichiro, ed. *Kindai Nihon to Ajia* (Modern Japan and Asia). Tokyo: Tokyo Daigaku Shupan-kai, 2000.

Lai Delin. *Zhongguo Jindai Jianzhushi Yanjiu* (A Study for an Architectural History of Early Modern China). PhD Thesis. Tsinghua University, Beijing, 1992.

———. "Zhongguo jindai jiaoyu de xianxingzhe: Jiangsu shengli Suzhou gongye zhuanmen xuexiao jianzhuke (A Pioneer in China's Early Modern Architectural Education: The Architecture Discipline at Suzhou College of Technology of Jiangsu Province)." In *Jianzhu Lishi yu Lilun* (Architectural History and Theory), edited by Yang Hongxun and Liu Tuo, 71–77. Beijing: Zhongguo Gongye Chubanshe, 1997.

———. *Zhongguo Jindai Jianzhushi Yanjiu* (Studies in Architecture History of Modern China). Beijing: Qinghua Daxue Chubanshe, 2007.

Li Baiyu. *Woguo Jindai Jianzhu Jiaoyu Xianqu – Hua Nangui Yanjiu* (Studies on Hua Nangui – a Pioneer for Architectural Education in Early Modern China). MA Thesis. Tianjin University, Tianjin, 2010.

Lian Yantang. "Liang qichao duiyu guoxue yanjiu de kaichuangxing gongxian (Liang Qichao's Pioneering Contribution to the Study of National Learning)." *Wenxue Yichan* 6 (2009): 99–110.

Liu Mi. *Zhijiang Daxue Jianzhu Jiaoyu Lishi Yanjiu* (Architectural education at Zhijiang University: a historical inquiry). MA Thesis. Tongji University, Shanghai, 2008.

Liu Zhao. *Zhongguo Jindai Jianzhu Jiaoyu de Xianqu Liu Futai Yanjiu* (Studies on Liu Futai – a Pioneer for Architectural Education in Early Modern China). MA Thesis. Tianjin University, Tianjin, 2010.

Monbu Sho, ed. *Gakusei Kyuju-nen-shi* (A Ninety-Year History of the Education System). Tokyo: Okura-syo Insatsu-kyoku, 1964.

Nie Zhenbin. "Huiwang bainian: 20 shiji de zhongguo meixue (Review Over a Hundred Years: Chinese Aesthetics of the Twentieth Century)." In *Zhongguo Meixue Nianjian 2001* (Yearbook in Chinese Aesthetics: 2001), edited by Ru Xin and Zeng Fanren, vol. 2. Zhengzhou: Henan Renmin Chubanshe, 2003.

Pan Guxi and Shan Yong. "Guanyu Suzhou gongzhuan yu zhongyang daxue jianzhuke (The Architecture Discipline at Suzhou College of Technology and National Central University)." *Jianzhu Shi* 90 (October 1999): 89–97.

Peng Changxin and Yang Xiaochuan. "Xiangqin daxue jianzhu gongcheng xuexi yu lingnan zaoqi xiandai zhuyi de chuanbo he yanjiu (Department of Architecture and Civil Engineering at Xiangqin University and the Development of an Early Modern Architecture in the South)." *Xin Jianzhu* 10 (2002): 54–56.

Qi Kang and Yan Longyu. "Jindai jiuanzhu jiaoyu shilue (Notes on a History of Architectural Education in Early Modern China)." In *Zhongguo Jianzhuye Nianjian 1986–1987* (Yearbook in the Building Industry of China 1986–1987), edited by Editorial Committee, 414–415. Beijing: Zhongguo Jianzhu Gongye Chubanshe, 1988.

Qian Feng. *Xiandai Jianzhu Jiaoyu zai Zhongguo 1920s-1980s* (Architecture Education in Modern China 1920s-1980s). PhD Thesis. Tongji University, Shanghai, 2005.

Qian Feng and Wu Jiang. *Zhongguo Jindai Jianzhu Jiaoyushi* (A History of Architecture Education in Modern China). Beijing: Zhongguo Jianzhu Gongye Chubanshe, 2008.

Rong Yingyu. "Wu Rulun to 'toyu-soroku' – aru 'yomu-ha' no kyoiku kaikaku-an (Wu Rulun's *Diaries the Eastern Tour*: Reformists and Education Reform)." In *Kindai Nihon to Ajia* (Modern Japan and Asia), edited by Hirano Ken'ichiro, 45–71. Tokyo: Tokyo Daigaku Shupan-kai, 2000.

Ru Xin and Zeng Fanren, eds. *Zhongguo Meixue Nianjian 2001* (Yearbook in Chinese Aesthetics: 2001). Zhengzhou: Henan Renmin Chubanshe, 2003.

Shen Zhensen. *Zhongguo Jindai Jianzhu de Xianquzhe – Jianzhushi Shen Liyuan Yanjiu* (Studies on Architect Shen Liyuan – a Pioneer for Architectural Education in Early Modern China). MA Thesis. Tianjin University, Tianjin, 2002.

———. *Shen Liyuan* (Shen Liyuan: A Study). Beijing: Zhongguo Jianzhu Gongye Chubanshe, 2012.

Taga Akigorou. *Kindai Chugoku Kyoiku-shi Shiryo – Shinmatsu Hen* (Sources for a History of Education in Early Modern China: Late Qing). Tokyo: Nihon Gakujutsu Shinko-kai, 1972.

Tang Zhijun, ed. *Kang Youwei Zhenglunji* (Kang Youwei: Writings on Politics), vol. 1. Beijing: Zhonghua Shuju, 1981.

Tianjin Shehui Kexuejie Lianghehui, ed. *Tianjin Shi Shehui Kexuejie Disanjie Xueshu Nianhui Youxiu Lunwenji, Kexue Fazhan: Yiren Weiben, Gongjian Hexie* (A Collection of Outstanding Papers of the Third Academic Conference in Social Sciences in Tianjin: Scientific Development – Building Harmony with Humanism). Tianjin: Tianjin Renmin Chubanshe, 2007.

Tokyo Koto Kogyo Gakko, ed. *Tokyo Koto Kogyo Gakko Ichiran* (Tokyo Higher College of Engineering: Survey). Tokyo: Tokyo Koto Kogyo Gakko, 1907.

Tokyo Teikoku-Daigaku, ed. *Tokyo Teikoku-Daigaku Goju-nen-shi, Ge-satsu* (A Fifty-Year History of Tokyo Imperial University), vol. 2. Tokyo: Tokyo Teikoku-Daigaku, 1932.

Wang Xiaoqiu. "Keishi-dagaku-do to nihon (Peking University and Japan)." In *Seiyo Kindai Bunmei to Chuka Seikai* (Early Modern Western Culture and the Chinese World), edited by Hazama Naoki, 72–88. Kyoto: Kyoto Daigaku Gakujutsu Syupan-sha, 2001.

Wei Qiufang. *Xu Zhong Xiansheng de Jianzhu Jiaoyu Sixiang yu Tianjin Daxue Jianzhuxi* (Xu Zhong's Thoughts for Architectural Education and the Development of Tianjin University Department of Architecture). MA Thesis. Tianjin University, Tianjin, 2005.

Wen Yuqing. "Taoli buyan xiazi chengxi – Tianjin gongshang xueyuan jianzhuxi jiqi jiaoxue tixi pingshu (1937–1952) (Silent Achievement: Department of Architecture at Tianjin College of Commerce and Its System of Teaching, 1937–1952)." In *Zhongguo Jindai Jianzhu Xueshu Sixiang* (Leading Ideas in the Discipline of Architecture in Early Modern China), edited by Zhao Chen and Wu Jiang, 77–86. Beijing: Zhongguo Jianzhu Gongye Chubanshe, 2003.

Wen Yuqing and Sun Lian. "Ji Tianjin gongshang xueyuan jianzhuxi (On the Department of Architecture at Tianjin College of Commerce)." In *Jianzhu Baijia Huiyilu Xubian* (Memoirs of One Hundred Architects: Part Two), edited by Yang Yongsheng, 21–26. Beijing: Zhishi Chanquan Chubanshe, 2003.

Wu Jiang and Qian Feng. "Huang Zuoshen he tade jianzhu jiaoyu sixiang (Huang Zuoshen and His Thoughts for Architectural Education)." In *Zhongguo Jindai Jianzhu Xueshu Sixiang* (Leading Ideas in the Discipline of Architecture in Early Modern China), edited by Zhao Chen and Wu Jiang, 87–91. Beijing: Zhongguo Jianzhu Gongye Chubanshe, 2003.

Wu Rulun. *Dongyou Conglu* (Diaries of the Eastern Tour). Tokyo: Sanseido Books, 1902.

Xu Subin. "Zhongguo jindai jianzhu jiaoyu de qishi he Suzhou gongzhuan jianzhuke (The Birth of China's Early Modern Architectural Education and the Architecture Discipline at Suzhou College of Technology)." In *Zhongguo Jianzhuye Nianjian 1986–1987* (Yearbook in the Building Industry of China 1986–1987), edited by Editorial Committee, 15–18. Beijing: Zhongguo Jianzhu Gongye Chubanshe, 1988.

———. *Bijiao, Jiaowang, Qishi: Zhongri Jinxiandai Jianzhushi zhi Yanjiu* (Comparing, Exchanging and Illuminating: A Study on the History of Architecture of Early Modern China and Japan). PhD Thesis. Tianjin University, Tianjin, 1991.

———. "Dongjing gaodeng gongye xuexiao yu liushiying (Tokyo Higher College of Engineering and Liushiying)." *Nanfang jianzhu* 3 (1994): 10–14.

———. "Qingmo tuan, mugong, jianzhu jiaoyu de shixing zhi yanjiu (A Study on the Early Practice of Teaching in Drafting, Building Engineering and Architecture in the Late Qing Dynasty)." In *Tianjin Shi Shehui Kexuejie Disanjie Xueshu Nianhui Youxiu Lunwenji, Kexue Fazhan: Yiren Weiben, Gongjian Hexie* (A Collection of Outstanding Papers of the Third Academic Conference in Social Sciences in Tianjin: Scientific Development – Building Harmony with Humanism), edited by Tianjin Shehui Kexuejie Lianghehui, 590–599. Tianjin: Tianjin Renmin Chubanshe, 2007.

———. *Jindai Zhongguo Jianzhuxu de Dansheng* (The Birth of Architecture in Modern China). Tianjin: Tianjin Daxue Chubanshe, 2010.

Yang Hongxun and Liu Tuo, eds. *Jianzhu Lishi yu Lilun* (Architectural History and Theory). Beijing: Zhongguo Gongye Chubanshe, 1997.

Yang Miaomiao. "Liu Dunzhen dui zhongguo jindai jianzhu jiaoyu de zhaoshi yu fazhan de yingxiang (Liu Dunzhen's Influence on the Birth and Development of Architectural Education in Early Modern China)." *Jianzhu Chuangzuo* 3 (2009): 137–145.

Yang Yongsheng, ed. *Jianzhu Baijia Huiyilu Xubian* (Memoirs of One Hundred Architects: Part Two). Beijing: Zhishi Chanquan Chubanshe, 2003.

Yao Xiguang. *Riben Xuexiao Shulue* (An Outline of Schools and Colleges in Japan). Hangzhou: Zhejiang Shuju, 1898.

———. *Dongying Xuexiao Jugai* (Examples of Schools and Colleges of Japan). 1899.

Yuan Xiyang. *Zhongguo Yishu Sheji Jiaoyu Fazhan Lichen Yanjiu* (Inquiry into a History of Design Education in China). Beijing: Beijing Ligong Daxue Chubanshe, 2003.

Zhang Liangben. "Jiangmen shuxue: wei jinian zhongyang daxue jianzhuxi chengli 70 zhounian tan zhongguo jianzhu jiaoyu (On China's Architectural Education for Celebrating the 70th Anniversary of Central University Department of Architecture)." *Xin Jianzhu* 2 (1999): 58–65.

Zhang Sheng. *Jingjinji Diqu Tumu Gongxue Beijingxia de Jindai Jianzhu Jiaoyu Yanjiu* (Inquiry into Early Modern Education of Architecture in the Context of Civil Engineering in the Beijing-Tianjin-Hebei Region of China). PhD Thesis. Tianjin University, Tianjin, 2011.

Zhang Zhidong. *Exhortation to Learning* (*Quanxue Pian*). 1898.

Zhao Chen and Wu Jiang, eds. *Zhongguo Jindai Jianzhu Xueshu Sixiang* (Leading Ideas in the Discipline of Architecture in Early Modern China). Beijing: Zhongguo Jianzhu Gongye Chubanshe, 2003.

Glossary

Akino Sotoya	秋野外也
Beijing	北京
Chunqiu Sanzhuan	春秋三转
Chunqiu Zuozhuan	春秋左传
Daxeutang zhangcheng	大学堂章程
Dongying Xuexiao Jugai	东瀛学校举概
Dongyou Conglu	东游丛录
Gaodeng nonggongshang shiye xuetang zhangcheng	高等农工商实业学堂章程
gaodeng shiye xuetang	高等实业学堂
gongye tuan ke	工业图案科
Guangxu	光绪
guimao	癸卯
guoxue	国学
Haerbin Zhong'e Gongye Xuexiao	哈尔滨中俄工业学校
Harada Takeo	原田武雄
Haraguchi Yoshitsugu	原口吉次
jianzhu ke	建筑科
jianzhu xuemen	建筑学门
jixie gongxue ke	机械工学科
jixie gongxue men	机械工学门
Kang Youwei	康有为
Kawabuchi Kunpei	川渊薰平
keju zhi	科举制
Li Ji	礼记
Li Xue	理学
Liang Qichao	梁启超
Lun Yu	论语
Mao Shi	毛诗
Matsunaga Chyozaburo	松长长三郎
Meiji	明治
Meng Zi	孟子
Mengyang Yuan	蒙养院
mugong ke	木工科
Nakayama Kinjiro	中山金次郎
Nanjing	南京
Nanman Zhou Gongye Zhuanmen Xuexiao	南满州工业专门学校
Oguro Chujiro	小黑忠次郎
Qinding jingshi daxuetang zhangcheng	钦定京师大学堂
Qinding xuetang zhangcheng	钦定学堂章程

Quanxue Pian	劝学篇
Riben Xuexiao Shulue	日本学校述略
Rong Qing	荣庆
Shang Shu	尚书
Shanghai	上海
Siku quanshu	四库全书
Suzhou	苏州
Suzhou Gongye Zhuanmen Xuexiao	苏州工业专门学校
Tianjin	天津
Tongru Yuan	通儒院
tuan fa	图案法
tuan huihua ke	图案绘画科
tuan ke	图案科
tugao fa	图稿法
tugao huihua ke	图稿绘画科
Wang Guowei	王国维
Wu Rulun	吴汝纶
Yao Xiguang	姚锡光
Yi Jing	易经
Yi Li	仪礼
yijiang tuan ke	意匠图案科
yitu xuetang	艺徒学堂
Yitu xuetang zhangcheng	艺徒学堂章程
zaobing xueke	造兵学科
zaobingqi xuemen	造兵器学门
Zhang Baixi	张百熙
Zhang Zhidong	张之洞
zhengshu lei	政书类
Zhili	直隶
Zhou Li	周礼
Zhou Yi	周易
Zouding xuetang zhangcheng	奏定学堂章程

15

THE ARCHITECT AS A PROFESSION IN REPUBLICAN CHINA

Rising Under the State

Wang Xiaoqian

The history of early modern China is often considered as composed of two periods – the late Qing dynasty (1840–1911) and the Republic of China (1912–49). The time is characterized as painful and chaotic in anticipation of the arrival of a new era. In architecture, early modern practice was a bridging phrase between a declining old system and a rising new one; it was also a time of synthesis between Chinese and western traditions. Further, it marked a transition from the old building practice to a new system of division between free architects and contracted builders. In short, it was a time when the content of the profession and the format of practice were totally altered, and it marked one of the key characteristics of modernization for the architecture of China.

> The emergence and development of the Chinese architect is a great change in the history of early modern Chinese architecture. It was a breakthrough on the practice of family inheritance, oral teaching, and craftsmanship of the feudal society. It changed the long-standing separation between the literati-intellectual and the artisan-builder; it established a system of the professionals equipped with scientific knowledge and design skills. . . . The process had greatly facilitated the development of architecture in modern and early modern China.[1]

Identity and Identification of the Architect

"Professional architect" refers to those who, while engaging in architectural design in a design institution, have an education, with a defined scope of work and responsibility, and have been specially recognized and qualified as such. In the early twentieth century, professional systems of architects – entirely originating in the west – were introduced to the foreign concession areas in China and showcased as advanced examples. Realizing the scientific and progressive merits of the practice, the Republican government of China began to promulgate a similar system for accreditation, which laid a legal foundation for the identity and private practice of professional architects, even though the process was difficult and the period of implementation was short.

In early Republican time, the government showed a strong tendency for institutionalization with an aim to promote national unity through administrative means. New systems regulated

DOI: 10.4324/9781315851112-22

by legislation were beneficial to the political and economic development of the country. However, the professional transformation of architects in the early modern era basically evolved on a bottom-up basis. Considering the particular social context of China at the time, laws and regulations for architectural practice were firstly enacted by local municipal governments, which were apparently keener for modernization than the central government. With political unrest, local governments could provide forward-looking systems to secure a local stability of the place they controlled.

In the *Building Regulations of Public Works Bureau in Guangzhou* (*guangzhoushi gongwuju qudi jianzhu zhangcheng*) (1920), the prototype of the professional institution of architects first appeared. According to Chapter 2, "Regulations for Licensing" (*lingzhao banfa*), the name and address of the draftsperson should be included in the drawings submitted by the contractor. Although the role of the "draftsperson" was not clearly defined, the initial recognition of the professional identity of the architect by the government was made clear.[2] The term "architect" first appeared in non-governmental and professional documents, such as the completion brief for the design of Sun Yat-sen Mausoleum in 1925. Later, various names and duty descriptions for the new profession were found in building regulations issued by local governments. For example, according to the *Regulations for Registration of Architects and Engineers in Special Municipality of Shanghai* (*Shanghai tebieshi jianzhushi gongchengshi dengji zhangcheng*) (1927), the name and business number of the designer should be included in the drawings submitted to the Public Works Bureau (*gongwuju*).[3] *Regulations for Qualification of Architectural Engineers in Special Municipality of Beiping* (*Beiping tebieshi jianzhu gongchengshi zhiye qudi guize*) (1929) was regarded as one of the earliest records of a professional architectural legislation system in early modern China established by a local government. The chaotic situation of the name of this new profession continued until the announcement of *Regulations for Management of Architects* (*Jianzhushi guanli guize*) by the Republican government in 1944. The term "architect" (*jianzhushi*) was subsequently revised as "architectural technician" (*jianzhuke gongye jishi*) under the *Regulations for the Registration of Technicians* (*Jishi dengjifa*) in 1947.

The building of a system of professional architects in Republican China was largely based on an idealized framework of a modernized state with full political organizations. There were, however, huge gaps between ideas and reality, between government expectations and actual situations – in identifying, regulating, and licensing for the architects. Western models were improperly copied and adopted. For instance, government enacted *Regulations for the Registration of Technicians* in June 1929, which was the first important legal document on licensing for technicians and classified technicians into three categories: agricultural, mineral, and industrial. Industrial technicians were further classified into civil engineering, chemistry, electrical, and other sub-categories, except architecture. Under such a system of qualification assessment for technicians, it was difficult for those with an architectural background to apply for a license. In addition, in order to become a registered technician, an applicant should have graduated from a local or overseas university or a higher educational institute after studying a specialized course for more than three years and should have relevant working experience of more than two years with a certificate. Alternatively, the applicant should pass a relevant examination, or have published works of specialized subjects, or have the achievement of improving or inventing relevant techniques.[4]

Although the intention was to maintain the professional standard of the technicians, it was controversial whether the drawings prepared by architects could be classified as "works of specialized subjects." Such demanding entry requirements caused some people who had previously engaged in building construction to lose their qualifications. In fact, the high academic requirements did not correspond with the general low educational level in China at that time,

Figure 15.1   Certificate of a national technician in the Republic of China (1936).
Source: © Wang Xiaoqian.

resulting in a substantial reduction of technicians available. As a result, it was difficult to implement such regulations – a situation that had crucial impacts on local building design industries. For instance, after implementation in Shanghai during the period from 1930 to 1935, there were only 173 qualified architects, most of whom had civil engineering backgrounds or were western architects. This substantially affected the localization of the profession and strengthened the hegemony of foreign architects in Shanghai.[5]

Due to the lack of applicants, the Executive Yuan (*xingzheng yuan*) – the executive branch of the government – requested to postpone the implementation of such regulations twice until the promulgation of a new rule in 1931 – *Regulations for Registration of Agricultural, Industrial, and Mining Technicians and Associates under the Ministry of Industry* (*Shiyebu nonggongkuang jifu dengji tiaoli*) (Figure 15.1).

Establishing Professional Societies of Chinese Architects

The first generation of Chinese architects studying overseas – represented by Zhuang Jun and Lu Yanzhi – returned to China in the 1920s and 1930s. They aimed to obtain the same social status enjoyed by their western counterparts by promoting a scientific and rational professional practice, on one hand, and to play the role of social advocacy by establishing professional societies, on the other. At that time, the majority of the general public did not understand the importance of architectural design and mistakenly regarded architects as contractors or engineers.

In 1927, the first architects' professional group in modern China, the Society of Chinese Architects (*zhongguo jianzhushi xuehui*), was established, launched by Fan Wenzhao, Zhuang

Jun, Lu Yanzhi, Zhang Guangqi, Wu Zhengying, and so on. The headquarters of the Society was in Shanghai, while branches were set up in Nanjing, Chongqing, and Kunming in succession. During preparation, American architect Henry Murphy provided detailed guidance. Since most of the organizers had western educational backgrounds, the Society followed the western approach of establishing rules, standards, and a self-restraint mechanism for the industry. As such, several committees were founded, such as the Code of Conduct Committee, Architectural Terminology Committee, Society Building Preparation Committee, and Publication Committee. In addition, relevant regulations and professional codes of conduct were compiled and published, including the *Charter for the Society of Chinese Architects* (*zhongguo jianzhushi xuehui zhangcheng*), *Regulations for Architects Practice* (*jianzhushi yewu guize*), and the *Rules for Chinese Architects* (*zhongguo jianzhushi gongshou jieyue*). These efforts contributed a great deal to the building of an autonomous governance of the profession in China.

The Society was proactive in enhancing its social influence and professional image by organizing a series of activities, such as academic forums and exhibitions. In addition, the most important and prestigious architectural periodical in the Republic of China, *Zhongguo Jianzhu: The Chinese Architect*, was published, playing a crucial role in raising the social status of architects and their competitive advantage; the publication also bridged a connection between profession and society, disseminated architectural knowledge, and pushed forward research in architecture.

In addition to the nationwide Society, professional groups of architects were established in various cities in China after the 1930s. After the promulgation of relevant regulations at the national level, such as the *Regulations for the Registration of Technicians* and the *Building Regulations* (*jianzhufa*), the duties, responsibilities, and qualifications of the architect were clearly defined, so the practitioners could began to organize themselves into societies and associations – such as the Association of Shanghai Builders (*Shanghai shi jianzhu xiehui*) and the Association of Architectural Technicians (*jianzhu jishi gonghui*) in Beiping, Guangzhou, and Nanjing – who often worked as professional guilds.

In 1947, the Nanjing Association of Architectural Technicians (*Nanjing shi jianzhu jishi gonghui*) was founded in Nanjing, capital of the Republic of China. The Association set the local practice template of the *Building Contract Agreement* (*gongcheng weituo qiyue*), which classified building types, defined architects' duties, and set the standard of fees, providing a comprehensive guidance for architects to carry out normative practice. Facing the market competition of lowering fees, the Association responded resolutely on behalf of all its members to protect the profession. In addition, the Association provided criticism and recommendations to the Nanjing Works Bureau (*Nanjing gongwuju*) on urban planning and city management. During the transformation and development of a modern architectural practice in China, these professional groups contributed tremendously to the institutionalization, standardization, and modernization of the entire industry.

Although the professional groups of Chinese architects were non-governmental in the Republic of China, the central government was willing to participate in their activities. The professional groups were also eager to interact and communicate with the government to gain state recognition. For example, government officials were often invited to the annual meetings of the Society of Chinese Architects. For the inaugural ceremony of the Nanjing Association of Architectural Technicians in September 1947, a letter was sent to the Ministry of Civil Service (*neizhengbu*) inviting "an official to attend and to deliver guidance (*paiyuan zhidao*)."[6] The director of the Construction Department (*yingjiansi*), Ha Xiongwen, himself previously an architect, attended the ceremony and delivered an inspiring speech, sharing his views as an official voice on the coordination and development of the industry – facilitating a dialogue between state authority and the profession.

Encouraged and guided by state regulations, the standard for entering professional societies became stringent. At that time, membership in the Society of Chinese Architects was classified into three levels: full member, associate member, and honorable member. The requirements for entering the Society included: being a graduate from a local or overseas university or a higher educational institute with a minimum of three years of working experience; holding a position as a full-time architectural professor for more than three years; holding the qualification of being an industrial technician; having a self-employed architectural business for several years with completed projects; or having made improvements, inventions, and publications in the field of architecture.

According to the statistics, after four years of the establishment of the Society of Chinese Architects, there were only 55 members in total in 1931, of whom 39 were full members and 16 associate members; 41 studied abroad, comprising 74.5% of all members (Figure 15.2).[7]

The entry requirements of the Society were consistent with those stipulated in the state-announced *Regulations for the Registration of Technicians*. Obviously, the professional society was following state practice in raising the bar for membership, so as to approximate the ideas and standards of the state; these would be important to gain official support, to win approval for a professional autonomy, and to raise social status and public recognition, as its counterparts in the UK and USA.

Figure 15.2 Group photo of some members of the Society of Chinese Architects.

Source: Photo taken in 1933. Source: *Zhongguo Jianzhu: The Chinese Architect* 1, no. 1 (1933): 37.

Architectural Expression as Political Discourse: Practice in the Capital

If there was state control over the institutionalization of the profession of the architect through regulations and a rational-scientific spirt, then there was also state influence on the profession's design work – through the ideology of the state, which was often embraced by the architects themselves. This can be verified in the design practice of the architects in Nanjing, then the capital of China. In the late 1920s, after the victory of the Northern Expedition (*beifa zhanzheng*),[8] the Republican government – not quite established as a national authority yet – wanted to strengthen and consolidate its will to control and lead quickly by building Nanjing as its new capital; so, the planning and building of the capital were given enormous symbolic weight and significance. For this purpose, "scientific rationalism" and "nationalism" were the key principal ideas in the planning document – *Shoudu Jihua* or *Capital Plan*. The first principle was about using scientific methods of "urban planning" (*dushi jihua*) to reform the existing city and to turn the city and the nation from chaotic backwardness to an orderly civilization; whereas the second principle was about using physical forms and images to express the correct and authorized ideas of the party-state ruled by Kuomintang – the Chinese Nationalist Party (Figure 15.3).

Drafting the *Capital Plan* involved many disputes within the government. There were three versions for a *Grand Plan of Nanjing* (*shoudu da jihua*), followed by the alternations of the site of capitol by the designers Lu Yanzhi and Henry Murphy as authorized by Chiang Kai-shek and Sun Ke – revealing constant political control over the design of material space. Apart from rational planning, *Capital Plan* dictated specifically the spatial layout and formal style of the key buildings of the capital, thus asserting a long-lasting impact on the image of the city of Nanjing. The art of architecture was considered of a paramount importance; in the chapter

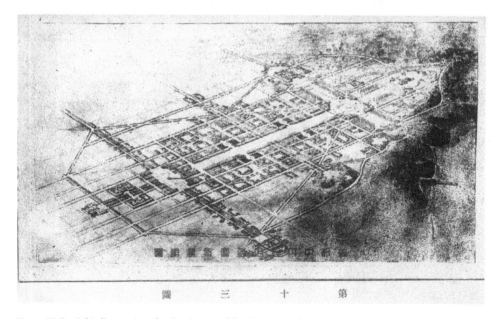

Figure 15.3 A bird's eye view for the design of the Capitol in *Capital Plan* (1929).

Source: Guodu Sheji Jishu Zhunyuan Banshichu (Technical office for Capital Plan), ed. *Shoudu Jihua* (Capital Plan) (Nanjing: Nanjing Chubanshe, 2006), 47, fig 13.

"Selection of the Style of Architecture," it specified that "the use of Chinese Native Forms are encouraged and, for government and public buildings, this is especially so."[9] For sure, this was based on political considerations by the government. A political statement can be constructed through spatial and formal design: that is, by adopting traditional space and form, a certain national culture is inherited and manifested and a national sentiment is communicated, so that the population can experience the greatness of the nation-state and come to identify themselves with state authority.

In *Capital Plan*, the architectural features of "Chinese Native Forms" (*zhongguo guyou zhi xingshi*) were precisely explained: ornamental details in the Chinese tradition; adopting features of palatial architecture; striking colors for the buildings. The government buildings designed by the first generation of Chinese architects in Nanjing in the 1927–37 period clearly manifested this guidance, whereas many other formal features and variations were subsequent developments. Large-scale government buildings, such as the Ministry of Roads and Railways, Lizhishe Society, the Examinational Yuan (*kaoshi yuan*), the Legislative Yuan (*lifa yuan*), the Academia Sinica (*zhongyang yanjiu yuan*), and the Archives and Exhibition Halls for the Chinese Nationalist Party (*guomindang zhongyang dangshi shiliao chenlieguan*) all adopted "Chinese Native Forms" and were all located within the city walls, along the main urban axis – the Zhongshan Avenue – to display honor and pride as architecture of the state (Figures 15.4 and 15.5). The cost for these buildings was often enormous, exceeding the budget easily; in the case of Sun Yat-sen Mausoleum, for example, the cost was eight times higher than the initial budget.

The government's request produced a wave of Chinese classical revival buildings, but also severely restricted the creative potential of the architects. Influential architects such as Tong Jun once critically said, "there were a few public buildings in the palatial manner, dictated by the clients with selected styles."[10] Due to this strong government request, the early modern architecture of Nanjing in the Republic era – though there as a strong western influence – retained a

Figure 15.4   Examination Yuan: government buildings with "Chinese Native styles" in the 1930s.

Source: Photo taken in 2014. © Wang Xiaoqian.

Figure 15.5 Auditorium, Lizhishe Society: government buildings with "Chinese Native styles" in the 1930s.

Source: Photo taken in 2014. © Wang Xiaoqian.

strong Chinese nationalist flavor, setting the city apart from others such as Shanghai and Guang-zhou in the image of the buildings.

Capital Plan and the urban construction and architectural design it produced can be con-sidered part of the governance of state authority, and a continuation of the political practice of China from its feudal and imperial past as an empire. Architecture here clearly represented authority symbolically. The situation also reflected a relationship between a guiding force of the state and a target scenario of modernization of the nation the force aimed at achieving.[11]

Conclusion

The first generation of professional Chinese architects emerged in the Republican era, in a process that was full of struggles. The new regime, having eradicated the old feudalist system, aimed to achieve modernization, yet cannot quite rid itself off a feudalist authoritarian tradi-tion – a dilemma that defined much of modern China in a larger picture. For the building of the profession of the architect in China, the final establishment of the position of the profession was a result of the efforts of many parties: the local governments' adoption of the various regu-lations; the efforts of the societies of architects; the guided orientation of design practice – all these must be unified under the central leadership of the Republican or nationalist government. In fact, judging from the regulations and policies released by the government, together with the feedbacks it is clear that these organizations delivered a positive force for the practicing subject to leave behind the artisan practice of the past and to move onto a specialist, rationalist, and scientific path; the pioneering and experimenting significance of the process must be fully acknowledged. However, governance of the state over the identity and practice of the profession also revealed an anxious rush to a leadership that was modern, quantified, and authoritative – which was unrealistic at the time and encountered problems and hindrances. As a whole, the process of building the profession remained more of form than content. The chaotic situation of China then, in both politics and economy, necessarily rendered institutional rules and regulations somewhat empty and yet to be fully realized.

Notes

1 Pan Guxi, ed., *Zhongguo Jianzhushi* (A History of Chinese Architecture) (Beijing: Zhongguo Jianzhu Gongye Chubanshe, 2009), 395.
2 Editorial Group, ed., "Guangzhoushi Gongwuju Qudi Jianzhu Zhangcheng (Building Regulations of Public Works Bureau in Guangzhou)," in *Guomin Zhemgfu Fagui Daquan: Jianshe* (Complete Regulations of the National Government: Construction) (Shanghai: Central Press, 1928), 570.
3 Shanghaishi Zhengfu (Shanghai Municipal Government), "Yingzao: Shanghai Tebieshi Jianzhushi Gongchengshi Dengji Zhangcheng (Construction: Regulations for Registration of Architects and Engineers in Special Municipality of Shanghai)," in *Shanghai Shi Zhengfu Fagui Huibian* (Shanghai Government Regulations: Complete Collection) (Shanghai: Central Press, 1945), 231.
4 Xu Baiqi, ed., "Jishi Dengjifa (Regulations for the Registration of Technicians)," in *Zhonghua Minguo Fagui Daquan* (Complete Regulations of Republican China) (Shanghai: Shangwu Yinshuguan, 1937), 3622–3625.
5 Lai Delin, *Zhongguo Jindai Jianzhushi Yanjiu* (Studies in Modern Chinese Architectural History) (Beijing: Qinghua Daxue Chubanshe, 2007).
6 Li Haiqing, *Zhongguo Jianzhu Xiandai Zhuanxing* (Transformation in Modern Chinese Architecture) (Nanjing: Dongnan Daxue Chubanshe, 2004), 294.
7 Society of Chinese Architects, "Zhongguo Jianzhushi Xuehui Huiyuanbiao (A Table of the Members of the Society of Chinese Architects)," *Zhongguo Jianzhu: The Chinese Architect* 1, no. 1 (1933): 39–40.
8 The Northern Expedition was a military campaign of 1926–1928 for a unification of the Republic of China. The troops led by Chiang Kai-shek, starting from the south, fought northward against local warlords and completed much of the plan. Upon a rough (i.e. not complete) unification of the nation, Nanjing was selected as the national capital in 1927.
9 Guodu Sheji Jishu Zhunyuan Banshichu (Technical Office for Capital Plan), ed., *Shoudu Jihua* (Capital Plan) (Nanjing: Nanjing Chubanshe, 2006), 60.
10 Tong Jun, "Woguo Gonggongjianzhu Waiguan de Jiantao (Review on the Appearance of Public Architecture in China)," in *Tongjun Wenji* (Collection of writings of Tong Jun), vol. 1 (Beijing: Zhongguo Jianzhu Gongye Chubanshe, 2000), 118.
11 Li, *Zhongguo*, 153–155.

Bibliography

Editorial Group, ed. *Guomin Zhemgfu Fagui Daquan: Jianshe* (Complete Regulations of the National Government: Construction). Shanghai: Central Press, 1928.

Guodu Sheji Jishu Zhunyuan Banshichu (Technical Office for Capital Plan), ed. *Shoudu Jihua* (Capital Plan). Nanjing: Nanjing Chubanshe, 2006.

Lai, Delin. *Zhongguo Jindai Jianzhushi Yanjiu* (Studies in Modern Chinese Architectural History). Beijing: Qinghua Daxue Chubanshe, 2007.

Li, Haiqing. *Zhongguo Jianzhu Xiandai Zhuanxin* (Transformation in Modern Chinese Architecture). Nanjing: Dongnan Daxue Chubanshe, 2004.

Pan, Guxi, ed. *Zhongguo Jianzhushi* (A History of Chinese Architecture). Beijing: Zhongguo Jianzhu Gongye Chubanshe, 2009.

Shanghaishi Zhengfu (Shanghai Municipal Government), comp. *Shanghai Shi Zhengfu Fagui Huibian* (Shanghai Government Regulations: Complete Collection). Shanghai: Central Press, 1945.

Society of Chinese Architects. "Zhongguo Jianzhushi Xuehui Huiyuanbiao (A Table of the Members of the Society of Chinese Architects)." *Zhongguo Jianzhu: The Chinese Architect* 1, no. 1 (1933): 39–40.

Wang, Xiaoqian. *Dajiang Zuji: Minguo Shidai de Nanjing Zhiye Jianzhushi* (Building in Nanjing: Professional Architects in Republican China). Nanjing: Dongnan Daxue Chubanshe, 2014.

Xu Baiqi, ed. *Zhonghua Minguo Fagui Daquan* (Complete Regulations of Republican China). Shanghai: Shangwu Yinshuguan, 1937.

Glossary

beifa zhanzheng	北伐战争
Beiping tebieshi	北平特别市
chenlieguan	陈列馆
Chiang Kai-shek	蒋介石
Chongqing	重庆
dangshi	党史
dengji tiaoli	登记条例
dengji zhangcheng	登记章程
dushi jihua	都市计划
Fan Wenzhao	范文照
gongcheng weituo qiyue	工程委托契约
gongchengshi	工程师
gongshou jieyue	公守诚约
gongwuju	工务局
Guangzhou	广州
guangzhoushi	广州市
guomindang	国民党
Ha Xiongwen	哈雄文
jianzhu jishi gonghui	建筑技师公会
jianzhufa	建筑法
jianzhuke gongye jishi	建筑科工业技师
jianzhushi	建筑师
Jianzhushi guanli guize	建筑师管理规则
Jishi dengjifa	技师登记法
kaoshi yuan	考试院
Kunming	昆明
Kuomintang	国民党
lifa yuan	立法院
lingzhao banfa	领照办法
Lizhishe Society	励志社
Lu Yanzhi	吕彦直
Nanjing	南京
Nanjing shi	南京市
neizhengbu	内政部
paiyuan zhidao	派员指导
Qing (dynasty)	清（朝）
qudi jianzhu zhangcheng	取缔建筑章程
Shanghai	上海
Shanghai shi jianzhu xiehui	上海市建筑协会

Shanghai tebieshi	上海特别市
shiliao	史料
Shiyebu nonggongkuang jifu	实业部农工矿技副
shoudu da jihua	首都大计划
Shoudu Jihua	首都计划
Sun Ke	孙科
Sun Yat-sen	孙中山
Tong Jun	童寯
Wu Zhengying	巫振英
xingzheng yuan	行政院
yewu guize	业务规则
yingjiansi	营建司
Zhang Guangqi	张光圻
zhangcheng	章程
zhiye qudi guize	职业取缔规则
zhongguo guyou zhi xingshi	中国固有之形式
zhongguo Jianzhu	中国建筑
zhongguo jianzhushi xuehui	中国建筑师学会
Zhongshan Avenue	中山大道
zhongyang	中央
zhongyang yanjiu yuan	中央研究院
Zhuang Jun	庄俊

Modern Building Practice: Style and Technology

16

BUILDING TECHNOLOGY IN REPUBLICAN CHINA AND ITS HISTORICAL LEGACIES

Li Haiqing

Building technology in the Republic of China had an inseparable and close association with subsequent development in new China. Its significant impact has even been extended to building activities in contemporary China. If successes and failures nowadays are reviewed without reflection on that particular period, this will unavoidably lead to a lack of a comprehensive understanding. Regrettably, for various reasons, this issue has been ignored deliberately or inadvertently for a long time.

In the academic context of mainland China, the "period of the Republic of China" is commonly referred to as a unique historical period lasting for 38 years, from the successful overthrow of the feudal monarchy at the Xinhai Revolution of 1911 to the retreat of the Chinese Nationalist Party to Taiwan in 1949. From the perspective of global patterns, two unprecedented world wars occurred, and colonies or semi-colonial regions declared independence one after another to become modern nations and countries during and after this period. The hegemony of Western powers established since the sixteenth century gradually declined and new systems began to establish under the influence of the Cold War. This global political pattern directly influenced the status of building technology in China – once the largest semi-colonial country in the world – and enabled building technology of the Republic of China to be completely inherited by the new China – the People's Republic. The inheritance can be divided into two aspects:

The first aspect was the inheritance of persons, which mainly depended on personal or inter-personal continuity across the divide between "old" and "new" China (that is, the Republic and the People's Republic). Whether in the Academia Sinica or in local construction companies, it remained the same. On 26 March 1948, 81 persons were selected as the first batch of members of the Academia. After 1949, 59 of them remained in mainland China, which was 73% of the total.[1] Among them were two experts in architecture and civil engineering – Liang Sicheng and Mao Yisheng. Both had significant impacts on the development of the new or People's Republic. Those who became academic members of the Academy of Sciences of the People's Republic – such as Yang Tingbao and Liu Dunzhen – were those who chose to stay on the mainland. Well-known architects, such as Zhuang Jun, Zhao Shen, Chen Zhi, Tong Jun, Lin Keming, Dong Dayou, Xi Fuquan, and Ha Xiongwen, also chose to stay. A few scholars and many owners of large building companies (such as Tao Guilin of the Fu Ji Construction Company) migrated overseas or moved to Hong Kong and Taiwan. Ordinary architects and

DOI: 10.4324/9781315851112-24

professionals, and especially technicians and engineers of the building industry, could not easily escape the war and chaos; they stayed, waited, and restarted their professional services when needed once again – the technical and professional forces who served in the early days of the new China all came from the Republican era.

The second aspect was the inheritance of objects in relation to material conditions and economic context. Apparently, it was impossible to promptly relocate materials, construction machinery, and equipment. At the end of the 1940s, the Republican government was in a precarious situation. The most urgent items to be moved to Taiwan, obviously, were those with strategic significances – large amounts of gold reserves, residual armed forces, military supplies, valuable ancient art treasures, etc., so there was no way for the government to take care of building machinery and equipment. In addition, because of the careful arrangement of the underground organization of the Communist Party, large amounts of materials, machinery, and equipment of many important industrial companies were unable to be relocated in a timely manner due to the effective "factory protection" campaigns by workers[2] – material conditions of building technology in the new China were also taken over from the Republican era.

Therefore, the foundation of building technology in the People's Republic was in fact the accumulation of nearly 30 years of development in the Republic of China. There was an inseparable, direct continuity between the two periods.

Although the past 30 years witnessed tremendous progress in research on early modern Chinese architecture, building technology and its history had little success. Due to political tensions and ideological opposition between the mainland and Taiwan, gaps cannot be covered and studies and exchanges in between cannot be made – for a long while; specialized research as a topic of its own upon building technology of the Republican era was never quite established, and great gaps remain today.

The research on early modern Chinese architecture on the mainland started with the book *Zhongguo Jianzhu Shi* (Architectural history of China) by Liang Sicheng in 1944,[3] yet not much was advanced further after that due to political conditions. In the mid-1980s, Wang Tan and other scholars broke the ice and led a vigorous development of systematic research in the field.[4] *Zhongguo Jindai Jianzhu Zonglan* (Early modern architecture in China: a comprehensive survey), a Sino-Japanese co-edited and multi-volume project, led by Zhang Fuhe and others, provided a comprehensive and systematic study of early modern buildings across the nation for the first time.[5] Concurrent representative studies included: research on early modern architecture from the perspective of cultural history by Yang Bingde,[6] specialized survey on the real estate market, architectural institutions, and architectural education by Lai Delin,[7] the establishment of Chinese architectural education and discipline based on Chinese-Japanese comparison by Xu Subin,[8] the panoramic review of Shanghai's modern architecture (1840s–1940s) by Wu Jiang,[9] specialized research on architecture of Christian universities by Dong Li,[10] and the review of "new architecture of Chinese classical style" as a stylistic history by Fu Chao-Ching.[11]

Based on the above work, the amount of research on the building technology of early modern China is gradually increasing and mainly includes: firstly, comprehensive research on early modern architectural history involving building technology, such as Sha Yongjie's comparative research on modern architecture in China and Japan following a "architecture–society–people" connection.[12] Secondly, research on early modern architectural history involving regional characteristics of building technology, such as Chen Li's research on Qingdao architecture during the German colonial period;[13] Peng Changxin's analysis of modern building structural technology in Lingnan;[14] and Wang Xin's review of modern building technology in Jiangsu from the aspects of structure, materials, and engineering.[15] Thirdly, specialized research on early modern architectural history involving building technology based on particular perspectives, such as

Qian Haiping's research on Chinese architectural modernization based on a reading of professional periodicals published in the Republic of China.[16]

Fourthly, specialized research on early modern architectural history involving regional background and building technology, such as Tang Fang's research on building codes in Shanghai's International Settlement;[17] Zeng Juan's discussion about the application of new types of materials in modern landscape architecture in Lingnan;[18] the study of construction technology of historical architecture of the Chinese Eastern Railway by Chen Haijiao and Liu Daping;[19] Zhang Haiao's research on the workmanship of fair-face brick walls in modern Shanghai;[20] Chen Zhihong's introduction of construction industry in modern Minnan and the workmanship of the "Jiageng architecture" in Xiamen;[21] as well as Qin Lin's dissection of the construction process of modern timber vernacular architecture of the Tujiazu ethnic minority group in the south-east of Chongqing.[22]

Fifthly, research on building technology involving heritage protection and utilization, such as Guo Xuan's exploration of integrating regionality and modernity of preservation technology, with a focus on preservation problems of war heritage in Chongqing.[23] Sixthly, case study research, such as Liu Yishi's investigation of the dome form and construction technology of the Auditorium at Tsinghua University.[24]

Despite the interest among overseas scholars in the building technology of early modern China, the research results so far are limited. Both Bao Muping and Shin Muramatsu claimed that the approach in Japan on early modern architecture was decisively different from that in China – the Japanese approach typically starts with technology before moving on to discuss on forms, styles, and ideas.[25] Natalie Delande has argued that the key player of building activities in early modern Shanghai was the engineer working in both building design and construction management.[26] Torsten Warner's research was on German architecture in Qingdao, which covered building practice and civil engineering.[27]

On the whole, there are various research methods adopted by the Chinese and overseas scholars. Although the outcomes are fruitful, the work so far on building technology and its development history is very limited. Research outcomes focusing on the overall development of building technology in the Republic of China are extremely rare – which is a serious defect. This is the key motivation for launching this research.

Phases of Building Technology Development in Republican China

The Republic of China lasted over 38 years amid political instability and two world wars. The scale of the building activity and the level of development in the use of building technology varied greatly, with ups and downs, as domestic and international political conditions evolved over these turbulent decades. As a whole, the history has three phases:

The first phase was the 16 years before the establishment of the Republican Government (under Kuomintang or the Chinese Nationalist Party) in Nanjing in 1927. In this early period of the Republic, the First World War broke out. Western powers were engaged in the war outside Eastern Asia, leaving a window of time for China's own capital and industry to develop at an unprecedented rate. The division of the country among warlords in the absence of a centralized state authority facilitated the development of various cities with a fresh air. Industrialization promoted urbanization, changing the profile of the city dramatically. New building technologies such as the use of reinforced concrete – totally different from the old Chinese building system – came into China and began to develop.

The second phase was from the establishment of the Republican Government in Nanjing in 1927 to the outbreak of war in 1937 – known as the "Golden Decade." The government formally unified the country. Industrialization and urbanization developed further in economically developed areas along the eastern coast with Shanghai as the centre. After the rapid development of building activities in China in the first 20 years of the twentieth century, a short climax was reached. Different types of reinforced concrete framed building structures, high-rise steel structures, and long-span structures were constructed.

The third phase was the 12-year war period from 1937 to 1949. During the eight-year war of resistance against Japan, cities and villages in economically developed areas along the eastern coast were seriously damaged. There was a downturn in building activities. At the strategic rear, the south-western and north-western regions had a relatively fast development in terms of industrialization and urbanization. After the victory of the war of resistance, a civil war (between nationalists and communists) broke out. Construction activities shrank rapidly within a short period of time under the condition of destitution. This situation continued until 1950. Large-scale construction work began again after the establishment of the People's Republic of China.

Major Trends in the Development of Building Technology in Republican China

In a pace nearly synchronic with the outside world, the importing of new building technologies included reinforced concrete, steel, high-rise and large-span structures, and their associated technologies. The development of building materials, building services installations, and building structural technology, and the renovation of construction technology and construction management, constituted the key aspects of the development of building technology in Republican China.

Structure

The introduction of reinforced concrete structural system to China was closely related to building activities in Shanghai, Tianjin, and Guangzhou along the eastern coast. Considering the poor geological conditions of both Shanghai and Tianjin, typical mixed structure by bricks (stones) and timber or bricks (stones) and reinforced concrete could not achieve significant building height, resulting in a pronounced demand for reinforced concrete framed structures. The first case of using reinforced concrete framed structures was the six-storey high Shanghai Telephone Company, completed in 1908. It was designed by Davies & Thomas Civil Engineers and Architects (Xin Ruihe Yanghang) and its structural calculation was done by Yha Tai Engineers and Architects (Xietai Yanghang).[28] Other examples included the Sun Company in Shanghai, completed in 1936, and the Bohai Commercial Building, completed in 1936. The former was designed by Kwan, Chu, and Yang Architects (Jitai Gongchengsi), with its main span reaching 7 m; whereas the latter was designed by the French company Brossand Mopin (Yonghe Gongchengsi), with an eight-storey high main tower.[29] In this period, a number of reinforced concrete framed buildings were completed in Nanjing, Beijing, Guangzhou, Wuhan, Yingkou, Dalian, Jinan, Wuxi, and Wuhu. These building structures were mainly designed by foreign design firms, but Chinese architects and engineers had entered into this design market.[30] The building industry in mainland China could even completely undertake the construction of reinforced concrete framed buildings with various heights.

Similarly, the introduction of steel structural technology to China was closely related to building activities in Shanghai and Guangzhou. Since high-rise buildings could effectively increase the plot ratio and unsalable materials were imported from Europe and the US to Shanghai, so developers could utilize cheap materials and labour force and shifted their investment focus to high-rise buildings in the late 1920s. During the ten-year period from 1929 to 1938, 31 high-rise buildings – each more than ten storeys high – were completed in Shanghai.[31] Since the building boom in the 1920s, there was unprecedented improvement in the design and construction level. This paved the path for applying the steel structural technology to high-rise buildings. Palmer & Turner Architects and Surveyors (Gonghe Yanghang) had an impressive design outcome in this aspect. Completed in 1917, the seven-storey building for Dodwell & Co. Ltd., also known as the Tianxiang Yanghang Building (renamed the Union Building or Youli Yinghang Dalou), was the first building to use a steel framed structure in Shanghai.[32] The Hong Kong & Shanghai Bank (Huifeng Yinhang) Building was completed in 1923, while the eight-storey Customs House Phase III was completed in 1927. Both buildings were precedent cases using precast reinforced concrete piles.[33] In 1934, the Broadway Mansions on the Bund and the Shanghai Joint Savings Society (Sihang Chuxuhui) Building – the International Hotel now – were completed, reaching 21 and 24 storeys high respectively (Figure 16.1). In 1937, the 15-storey Oi Kwan Building (renamed Aiqun Hotel) in Guangzhou designed by Chan Wing Gee (Chen Rongzhi) was completed. It was a steel framed structure and the highest building in Southern China at that time. Steel framed structures became the sole structural solution for high-rise buildings with 20 storeys or above. The heights of steel framed structures and structural spans gradually increased. The market of designing steel framed high-rise structures was nearly monopolized by foreign architectural design firms, but for constructing steel framed structures, the Chinese construction industry could completely undertake the work and had dominated the market.

In the Republican era, the application of long-span structural technology was extended from industrial buildings to civil buildings; and the technology used then was classified as truss, three-hinge steel frame, and reinforced concrete portal frame. Among them, steel trusses were mostly used. The National Assembly building in Beijing, completed in 1913, had a structural span of 24 metres, using steel-timber roof trusses. The Tsinghua University Stadium (now the front stadium of the Tsinghua University Stadium) was completed in 1919, having six steel trusses. The Auditorium at Tsinghua University, completed in 1921, was built by an in-situ reinforced concrete shell structure, reaching the international construction level at that time.[34] The Southeast University Stadium was completed in 1922, having a steel-timber assembled roof trusses and reaching 20 metres in span. The Shenyang Station of the Peking-Mukden Railway was completed in 1927, using semi-circular steel roof trusses and reaching 20 metres in span. Many long-span structures in China were completed in 1931, such as the Sun Yat-sen Memorial Hall in Guangzhou using fink steel trusses and reaching 30 metres in span (Figure 16.2); the assembly hall of the National Central University in Nanjing had a dome roof supported by steel arching trusses of about 30 metres in span, and the extension of the Tsinghua University Stadium used pointed arching steel trusses of about 27 metres in span.

In 1936, the True Light Theatre (now the Capital Cinema) was completed using steel trusses of 24 metres in span. In the same year, the Lunghwa (Longhua) aircraft depot of the Eurasia Aviation Corporation was built using ladder-shaped steel trusses, achieving 32 metres in span.[35] The application of three-hinge steel frames significantly promoted the advancement of long-span structural technology in early modern Chinese architecture. The Wuhan University Stadium was completed in the early 1930s using lightweight, three-hinge steel frames and achieving 21.5 metres in span; while the Shanghai Central Stadium was completed in 1936 with three-hinge steel frames of 42.7 metres in span. This was the longest single span

影攝架鋼築構廈大層二十二行四海上

Figure 16.1   The construction of steel framed structure of the Joint Savings Society Building, Shanghai, completed in 1934.

Source: Jianzhu Yuekan 1, no. 5 (May 1933): 5.

of building structures ever recorded in Republican China. Three-hinge steel frames were superior in terms of span, while trusses were more flexible in material selection and structural forms. Undoubtedly, industrial buildings, transport facilities, assembly halls, and stadiums were important architectural typologies promoting the development of long-span building technology.

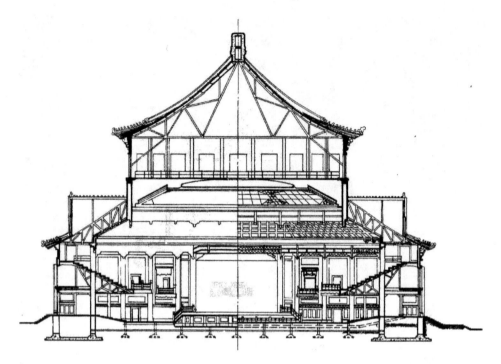

Figure 16.2   Section of the Sun Yat-sen Memorial Hall, Guangzhou, completed in 1931.

Source: *Zhongguo Jianzhu* 1, no. 1 (July 1933): 4.

Material and Equipment

Building materials and technology were under unprecedented development in the Republic of China. During the First World War, the Chinese cement industry had great development opportunities. Before the outbreak of the war of resistance (against Japan in 1937), large-scale cement companies increased to nine. The big four companies were Qixin, Zhongguo, Huashang, and Xicun. Most of them were limited companies. They introduced the whole set of mechanized production line for rolling stones, grinding, transportation, and packaging, but generally produced limestone-based Portland cement only. Later, they also produced low temperature burning soil cement, slag cement, and white cement. In the mid-1930s, the total cement consumption in China was about 5 million barrels, but only 4.68 million barrels could be produced, so the market demand could not be satisfied and cement was relatively expensive. Apart from major construction projects, most ordinary residential buildings were still constructed of bricks and timber.

The Chinese steel industry had some development from the Self-Strengthening Movement in the late Qing dynasty to the 1920s, but the production amount was still limited. Steel for construction purpose relied on import because only a minority of local steel factories could produce certain types of steel. In the mid-1930s, there were about ten large to medium size steel factories in China, but production capacity was generally low.[36] During the eight years from 1926 to 1933, the annual production amount did not exceed 20 thousand tons, and the total amount in eight years was merely 99.9 thousand tons. Due to rapid urban development in these eight years, the demand for steel significantly expanded, so the supply relied heavily on import.[37] The recession of European and American markets initiated by the global economic crisis from 1929 to 1933 led to the influx of a large amount of unsalable steel to China. For nearly all major construction projects, imported steel was used. In some cases, prefabricated members were directly manufactured overseas and delivered to China for installation. Having said that, there were many factories producing small rolled steel members and manufacturing reinforcement bars, steel doors, and windows.[38]

Regarding machine-made bricks and tiles, after the establishment of the Republican Government in Nanjing, the most developed centres for manufacturing bricks and tiles were located in Shanghai, Nanjing, and surrounding regions. Before the war of resistance (starting in 1937), there were more than ten types that were produced, such as solid clay bricks, hollow clay bricks, runner bricks, and lightweight cinder bricks. In addition, different types of flat tiles, grey tiles, Chinese cylindrical tiles, Spanish cylindrical tiles, English hip tiles, and relevant tile accessories were manufactured. Chinese brick and tile manufacturing industries experienced a transition from manual to mechanical production then. The level of industrialization and the variety of bricks and tiles produced could, basically, satisfy the demand of the local market.[39]

The building ceramics industry was initiated in the early twentieth century and substantially developed in the Republican era, especially in the 1920s. Until the outbreak of the war of resistance, there were sizeable building ceramics factories in Tianjin, Shanghai, Wuhan, Hunan, Sichuan, and Guangzhou. The Taishan Bricks and Tiles Factory and the Xingye Ceramics Company had the most variety of products to offer. For major public building projects, nearly all types of ceramics products were locally produced, despite the fact that some local products might not have a surface finish as good as imported products. Other building materials, such as natural stones, glass, prefabricated panels, and architectural ironmongery, were mostly mass produced mechanically after the 1920s.[40]

In the Republic of China, especially the 1920s, there was a significant increase in plumbing, electrical, heating, ventilation, and air-conditioning installations in buildings, promoting the degree of specialization in local manufacturing of equipment and installation. Only a few important construction projects used imported equipment. For heating equipment, the American-Chinese Company Federal Inc. (Yingfeng Yanghang) in Shanghai imported automatic coal burning machines from Canada in 1934, allowing automatic refilling and burning the coal in the production. China Gas Stoves Company in Beijing produced various types of coal burning boilers and heating radiators (steam), which were sold throughout the country. Air-conditioning and lift installations relied heavily on import. Lift suppliers such as Otis and Schindler opened branches in China. Most high-rise buildings were installed with imported lifts. Light fittings, electric bells, electric wires, and relevant building accessories were generally manufactured locally.[41]

In summary, the overall level of industries of building materials, equipment manufacturing, and installation had great improvements in Republican China. However, there was uneven development in various aspects. The steel industry and high-tech, large-scale manufacturing of electrical equipment were very weak. Poor material-economic conditions significantly affected the modern transformation of Chinese architecture.

Construction

The spread of new structural systems and the associated use of new materials initiated a chain reaction for the development of building technology and project management. Entering the twentieth century, Chinese building technology closely followed international development, and a new batch of professionals with technical education backgrounds emerged. This led to a significant leap, which could be expressed by three aspects: the development of new construction methods based on actual needs, the import of new types of construction machinery and equipment to increase productivity, and the enhancement of the construction process and technology management.

Firstly, regarding the use of new construction methods in terms of foundation construction, due to the poor geological conditions of eastern coastal regions and the sharp increase of the number of high-rise buildings, new types of foundation appeared, such as timber piles, reinforced concrete cast-in-place piles, precast reinforced concrete piles, sand-gravel cushions, and pressurized caisson foundation. For example, the Cathay Mansion (Huamao Gongyu) in Shanghai and the Oi Kwan Building in Guangzhou used reinforced concrete cast-in-place piles. The Russo-Chinese Bank Building (or Huasheng Building) in Shanghai used sand-gravel cushions. The piers of the Qiantang River Bridge in Hangzhou used pressurized caisson foundations. For retaining construction, due to the common provision of basements for high-rise buildings, braced excavation technology for deep trenches appeared. For example, the China Merchants Bank (Tongshang Yingyang) Building in Shanghai used U-shaped steel sheet piles and wooden sheet piles during construction (Figure 16.3). For the construction of the superstructure, there was some innovation in scaffolding technology, which was particularly prominent for high-rise buildings. It was common for scaffolding to have Chinese-fir as vertical members, bamboo as horizontal members, and hemp rope for joint lashing, which was subsequently replaced by galvanized wire. New methods increased the efficiency of building construction and resolved some engineering difficulties. Chinese construction professionals and artisans could promptly master the building construction technology imported from the West.[42]

Secondly, for the use of new construction machinery and equipment since 1900, there was a period of importing from the West followed by a gradual localization in manufacturing; as a result, the precision of building technology and efficiency of the labour force improved. For staking the lines, modern surveying instruments were widely used; the manufacturing of levels and theodolites was localized. For foundation construction, steam (electric) pile rigs were commonly used. Service drainage initially relied on hand pumps, which were subsequently replaced by steam (electric) centrifugal pumps. For the construction of bridges and piers, different types of excavating machinery were used. For reinforced concrete construction, imported concrete mixers and mortar mixers were initially used, but Chinese artisans could master such technology quickly. In 1919, locally made concrete mixers developed. After the 1930s, mechanized equipment, including machinery conveyor belt loaders, was gradually promoted (Figure 16.4). In the Hong Kong & Shanghai Bank Building, automatic reinforcement bar bending machines were used. To cope with the construction of high-rise buildings, different types of vertical lifting machinery, such as wooden head framed hoists (electrical driven) and steel framed hoists, were developed. For the Qiantang River Bridge, 720-ton gantry cranes with rails were used.[43]

Thirdly, for the management of building construction, the Chinese approach was becoming more scientific and systematic, due to the gradual rise of the level of training and education, as well as the impact of international influence. For example, construction progress charts were used to strengthen the arrangement of work sequences and monitor the construction periods in a tangible and visualized manner.

Ornamentation

In the Republic of China, especially after the establishment of the Republican Government in Nanjing, the division of labour in architectural decoration became more detailed and the craftsmanship became more refined. Various types of techniques for fair-face brick walls were developed.

Figure 16.3 The steel sheet piles for the foundation construction of the China Merchants Bank Building, Shanghai, completed in 1933.

Source: Jianzhu Yuekan 2, no. 5 (May 1934): 4.

It was common to use *xianxiangfeng* (a slender stick of incense) as the fine jointing for early brick walls, but more than ten different styles were used later. More specialized tools for brick and tile work were developed. For example, stirring plates for mortar mixing, mercury level bars for level calibration, *yangtiepi* (western iron plates), or *yuantao* (round covers) for controlling the width of brick-wall jointing. Handy trowels for tilework replaced heavy shovels. More accurate measuring rulers were used to determine the width of brick-wall jointing. For masonry work, more exquisite

Figure 16.4   The use of conveyor belt loaders in and after the 1930s.

Source: Jianzhu Yuekan 4, no. 12 (December 1936): 35.

craftsmanship was developed. After the 1920s, washed grano finish, rubbed grano finish, artificial stone finish, and other new craftsmanship were widely used by Chinese artisans. Various types of walls, floor tiles, and mosaic tiles were also commonly applied to external walls and internal floor finishes. Around the year 1933, Shanghai merchants introduced wall papers from Europe and the US. Large numbers of solid timber boards were used for indoor flooring. Flooring work was undertaken by professional companies in Shanghai and Guangzhou, which used new girdling machines. In addition, new types of decorative accessories, such as doors and windows, handles, staircase handrails, fireplaces, light fittings, and aluminium alloy and glass blocks were used. Although the internal and external finishes of some famous buildings, such as the Hong Kong & Shanghai Bank Building, the International Hotel, and the Sassoon House were completed by Chinese artisans, the overall effect was completely different from traditional treatment.[44]

Summary

In general, from the 1920s onwards, due to the fast development of reinforced concrete structures, steel structures, and large-span structures, and associated technologies, the market for various building materials expanded, which greatly facilitated the development of building material production and equipment manufacturing, as well as the growth of installing industry as well. The market displayed a few characteristics: firstly, there was an increase in the production of building materials such as cement and machine-made bricks and tiles; secondly, the division of labour between equipment manufacturing and installation industry was more refined; and thirdly, the variety of the materials for finishing had been much expanded. Despite the prosperity of the industry, however, there were many gaps, and productivity was still low; and this determined a weak and poor material-technological basis for the modern transformation of architecture of China.

Characters and Impacts: Reflecting on Building Technology of the Republican Era

Based on a spatial observation of the nation, it is clear that the development of the building technology of the Republic of China displays complexity and multiplicity, and that the huge regional disparity and urban–rural difference were the concrete manifestations of complexity and multiplicity. As historical legacies, this situation still asserts a profound impact on building activities in China today.

Regional Disparity

Firstly, regional disparity resulting from the early, uneven development of modern building technology is an avoidable yet often neglected core problem.

For the use of building materials, the divergence between regions was quite apparent due to different natural geographical conditions and level of building material industries. For example, both Dahua Cinema in Nanjing and YMCA Cinema in Chongqing were built in the 1930s and designed by Yang Tingbao; however, the former used reinforced concrete columns, brick walls, and steel roof frames, whereas the latter used brick columns, a mixed structural wall system of rammed earth, double bamboo fencing, and hollow bricks, as well as timber frames.[45] In the 1930s, the Shanghai Public Works Department had five building material factories for manufacturing various types of tubes, panels, and piles through mechanized mass production (Figure 16.5). By comparison, in the 1940s, adobe brick walls and straw roofs were still used for the US 14th Air Force barrack at the Chungking Paishiyiek Airfield (also the Chongqing Baishiyi Military Airport) in the great rear region of the war of resistance.

Figure 16.5 Mechanized manufacturing of prefabricated reinforced concrete parts, including tubes, panels, piles, and chimneys, in a factory on Damuqiao Road in southern Shanghai, established by Shanghai Public Works Department since 1934.

Source: Shanghaishi Gongwuju (Shanghai Public Works Department), *Shanghaishi Gongwuju zhi Shinian* (Ten years of Shanghai Public Works Department) (Shanghai: Shanghaishi Gongwuju, 1937), 139.

From the perspective of construction tools, differences across regions were very notable. For example, in the major renovation work of the Qingdao-Jinan Railway in 1925–1926, large-scale lifting mechanical equipment installed on platform trailers running along railway tracks had already been used. In the 1930s, road rollers empowered by internal combustion engines were used by the Shanghai government for repairing roadwork.[46] In sharp contrast, until the 1940s, in several military airports in south-western regions, the repair work was still labour intensive, using stone rollers, iron spades, earth shovels, shoulder poles, manure baskets, and even animal-drawn vehicles for transportation purpose.[47]

From this perspective, in the Republic of China, various types of new materials and machinery started to play an important role in building construction in Shanghai, Nanjing, cities along the Qingdao-Jinan Railway, and the economically developed areas along the eastern coast. On the contrary, in remote regions, traditional materials and tools were still used for building activities.

There was a parallel relationship between the regional divergence at the level of building technology and an overall disparity in the level of industrialization of the whole country at that time. Firstly, the industrialization in China was still in its infancy. Relevant research indicated that such industrialization lacked the support of heavy industry sectors and coordination with agricultural development. The overall level lagged substantially behind with serious disorder in the proportion of light and heavy industries, with an extreme imbalance in regional distribution. In the 1930s, Japan successfully achieved national industrialization, while the production amount of major industrial products – and the number of products per capita – in China were below that in Japan.[48] In addition, the extreme imbalance of regional distribution of industrialization showed an abnormal situation. During the Beiyang Government period (1912–28), with the division of the country among warlords, strong forces in various areas promoted industrial development within their areas of control, leading to a wide spread of industrialized regions in China and enabling original impoverished regions to have faster development.

However, on the whole, Chinese industries still mainly concentrated in coastal areas and trading ports. This situation changed after the establishment of the Republican Government in Nanjing. Under the threat of growing aggression by Japan in the 1930s, a state industrialization strategy of having a national defence industry as the focus and basic industry was implemented. Industrial development was initiated in strategic deep areas, such as the steel factory in Xiangtan (in Hunan), iron ores in Chaling (in Hunan) and Lingxiang (in Hubei), copper ore factories in Dazhi and Yangxin (in Hubei) and Pengxian (in Sichuan), coal ores in Gaokeng (in Jiangxi), Tianhe (in Jiangxi), Yuxian (in Henan), oil mines in Baxian and Daxian (in Sichuan), the aircraft engine plant Yongli Gas Plant, and Tianli Ammonia Manufacturing Company in Xiangtan (in Hunan), among others.[49] However, most factories were small in scale and low in productivity. On the whole, industrial development – though limited – still concentrated in several large to medium sized cities along the coast. Therefore, some scholars argued that industrialization in China did not happened in any real and serious sense until 1949.[50]

Urban–Rural Difference

Secondly, the urban–rural difference in a dualistic pattern of building technology development was a salient feature of Republican China – as a whole and at a basic level. This has been neglected for a long time due to the constraint of historical research in architecture. For example, in Nanjing, there were over 80 kiln operators in the city in the early Republican time, producing traditional grey bricks and small tiles. Due to manual or cow-driven soil compression, manual shaping, natural drying, having firewood or coal as the fuel, and using earth kilns for burning, productivity was very low. Subsequently, bricks and tiles were manufactured mechanically for a gradual increase of productivity. After 1927, massive construction work commenced in the capital, and the demand for bricks and tiles increased sharply. The brick-and tile-making industries were gradually transformed from manual operation of rural kilns to mechanical production of urban factories. Before the war of resistance, the annual production of clay bricks and tiles reached about 100 million blocks and 4 million pieces respectively. After the war of resistance (1937–45), the industries of manufacturing bricks and tiles developed further. In 1947, there were 54 brick and tile factories in urban areas employing 18,000 workers, which was two-thirds of the total number of workers working in more than 800 factories in Nanjing. Further, there were more than 50 side-lined kiln operators in the outskirts. The annual production of clay bricks and tiles was about 210 million blocks and 8.4 million pieces in Nanjing respectively, which doubled the amount before the war of resistance.[51] Analyses of old photos of buildings of Nanjing's Puzhen, Hangzhou's countryside,[52] and Shangdong's Laizhou City[53] reveal that large-scale public buildings in the city, residential buildings under the real estate development model, and large numbers of self-built houses were constructed of bricks, tiles, and even reinforced concrete, at a relatively high level of industrialization. Comparatively, in rural regions, large numbers of self-built houses by farmers were constructed with cheaper traditional materials and methods, such as *caofang* (grass house) using rammed earth walls and straw roofs.

Since in the same region and period, village houses were still built by traditional materials and methods, it was natural that manually operated traditional tools were often used in material manufacturing and building construction. A detailed analysis of the two-man framed saws for dividing large timber parts for building in Kunming of the 1940s[54] and the Jiacun in Zhejiang of the 1930s,[55] of the hand moulds for shaping the bricks by kiln operators in Tiantaishan in Zhe-jiang,[56] and of the timber framed moulds and timber hammers for erecting rammed earth houses in Lushan of Jiangxi,[57] and with a comparison with the large saws for cutting large timber parts in a sawmill in Beijing of 1900,[58] it is clear that traditional, manually operated tools for building construction were widely in use and played a critical role.

There was a close relationship between the great urban–rural difference in building tech-nology and the dualistic industrialization model of China at that particular time. The so-called dualistic model referred to the coexistence of two types of industrialization on a dualistic structure of city and countryside – an "urban low-level industrialization" and a "rural semi-industrialization." The two were competing and yet mutually influencing each other.[59] This characterization, developed by historian Peng Nansheng on the history of China's industrializa-tion, captured vividly the situation and was well reflected in building technology in China then. In rural China, the progression was from "traditional craftsmanship" to "primitive industriali-zation" – the native subject adopted a craft mode of production using very limited machinery (such as the hand-operated brick-making machinery). In urban China, on the other hand, development was at a faster rate, from "traditional craftsmanship" to "primitive industrializa-tion," and further onto "low-level industrialization" – the new labour subject, having left coun-tryside behind, adopted a more mechanized mode of production using a sizeable number of mechanical facilities (excavators, pile drivers, heavy cranes, tower cranes, fulling machines, and rollers) as well as many factory-produced building materials, equipment, and parts (machine-made clay bricks, steel bars, cement, even profile steel, air-conditioning, lifts, fire-alarm systems, kitchen facilities, and ceramic bathroom wares).[60]

Concluding Reflections

How were complexity and multiplicity in the use of building technology formed? What was behind the transformative mechanism? What were the main reasons facilitating the development of building technology in this period? It is unlikely these problems will be effectively explained unless more accurate models of political and economic theories are used. This would be the focus of future direction of this research. As of now, a more urgent and concerning question is as follows: what is the historical importance of the Republican era with its development of building technology, given that half a century has passed since the end of that era? What is the significance, if any, for us today? This perhaps can be answered with a reference to the issues we face at the present.

On 12–13 December 2013, a working meeting on urbanization was held in the central government in Beijing; it was suggested that in the cities "people should be able to see the mountains and the rivers, and sustain a nostalgic longing for country life." Clearly, state government and the leadership were very concerned with the destruction of nature and environment, the loss of ecological balance, the homogenization of cities, and the disappearance of local character and traditions – as the consequences of a rough and fast urbanization development of the past three decades. Admittedly, the loss of ecological balance and the erosion of the spiritual homeground are not unrelated to the chaotic and disordered practice of building construction. And this is also related to the fast closing of the gaps across regions and between city and countryside. The pace is so fast, so drastic, and so out of control. Regional and urban–rural disparities had been the result of natural (geographical and climatic) and socio-politico-economic conditions; while the big gaps have been a problem in many aspects, a fast reduction or even an erasure of them can also be a problem with unknown and unpredictable consequences.

On the one hand, for some regions with specific natural conditions and construction traditions, pursuing new materials and structures blindly for so-called technological advancement may cause adverse impact to the natural environment, often in the interest of securing irrational figures of economic indicators. For example, Motuo in Xizang (Tibet) was the last county in China to be accessible by roads and the traffic there is still very dangerous, relying on primitive transportation methods. Since it is located between the two main tectonic plates of the Pacific Ocean and Indian Ocean, various natural disasters, such as earthquakes, mudslides, and landslides, occur frequently, causing road blockage and expensive logistics cost. Ordinary 325# Portland cement is sold in mainland China at RMB 300–400/ton, but after delivery to Motuo, the selling price is increased sharply to about RMB 20,000/ ton, some 50 to 60 times of the ordinary price. It is also extremely difficult for construction machinery and equipment to arrive on site. Insistence on using new types of building materials and methods only incurs high construction cost. It is preferable to use locally available materials there, such as timber stilts and rubble masonry, which are effective in practice.

On the other hand,

> people like to visit other places with culture and tradition, and to obtain different aesthetic experience; the International Style is a product of multinational enterprises, and is utterly boring and homogenizing; modernism was not defeated by the new theorists of architecture, but by the public.[61]

If the development of technology brings about only a uniformity of the cities and homogenization of the villages, then this would be very wrong and disappointing, not just because it ruins our expectation to see and experience the other and the different or "to live elsewhere" as in tourism.

In the past 60 years, and especially in the most recent 30 years, urban and rural development in mainland China has witnessed many irrational behaviours, which may well be the result of not understanding properly the positive message of regional disparity and urban–rural differentiation as manifested in the building technology development of the Republican era. Artificial attempts based on political projections, as evidenced in early socialist China on the development of Beijing – involving a debate between various parties such as scholars, party leaders, and Russian advisors – could be a serious factor distorting the situation.[62] It is time to review regional disparity and urban–rural difference, as evidenced in the Republican period as studied in this chapter, in all angles and perspectives, for a rational assessment that goes beyond either a political or an instrumentalist projection.

Notes

1 Cheng Ji, "Zhongyangyanjiuyuan Diyijie Yuanshi de Quxiang (The Directions of the First Batch of Members of Academia Sinica)," *Ziran Bianzhengfa Tongxun* (Journal of Dialectics of Nature), no. 2 (2011): 36–40, 70.

2 Huang Jianzhi and Yuan Gang, "Shanghai Jianzhuye de Xinsheng (New Life of the Building Industry in Shanghai)," in *Dongfang "Bali": Jindai Shanghai Jianzhu Shihua* (Eastern "Paris": History of Architecture of Modern Shanghai), ed. Shanghai Jianzhu Shigongzhi Bianweihui Bianxie Bangongshi (Editorial Committee of the Office of the Shanghai Building Construction Chronicles) (Shanghai: Shanghai Wenhua Chubanshe, 1991), 208–215.

3 Liang Sicheng, *Zhongguo Jianzhushi* (History of Chinese Architecture) (Tianjin: Baihua Wenyi Chubanshe, 2005).

4 Wang Tan, "Diyici Zhongguo Jindai Jianzhushi Yanjiu Taolunhui Lunwen Zhuanji (Conference Proceeding of the First Symposium of the Research on the History of Architecture of Early Modern China)," *Huazhong Jianzhu* (Journal of Architecture of Central China), no. 2 (1987): 4–7.

5 Zhang Fuhe, "Zhongguo Jindai Jianzhushi Yanjiu Ershinian (Twenty Years of Research on Chinese Modern Architectural History) (1986–2006)," in *Zhongguo Jindai Jianzhu Yanjiu yu Baohu* (Research and Preservation of Early Modern Chinese Architecture), ed. Zhang Fuhe, vol. 5 (Beijing: Tsinghua University Press, 2012), 1–15.

6 Yang Bingde, *Zhongguo Jindai Zhongxi Jianzhu Wenhua Jiaorongshi* (History of Cultural Exchange of Modern Chinese and Western Architecture in China) (Wuhan: Hubei Jiaoyu Chubanshe, 2003).

7 Lai Delin, *Zhongguo Jindai Jianzhushi Yanjiu* (Research on Chinese Modern Architectural History) (PhD Thesis, Tsinghua University, Beijing, 1992).

8 Xu Subin, *Bijiao, Jiaowang, Qishi: Zhongri Jin Xiandai Jianzhushi zhi Yanjiu* (Comparison, Exchange, Revelation: Research on Chinese and Japanese Modern Architectural History) (PhD Thesis, Tianjin University, Tianjin, 1992).

9 Wu Jiang, *Shanghai Bainian Jianzhushi (1840–1949)* (One Hundred Years of Shanghai Architectural History, 1840–1949) (PhD Thesis, Tongji University, Tongji, 1993).

10 Dong Li, *Zhongguo Jiaohui Daxue Jianzhu Yanjiu* (Research on Architecture of Christian Universities in China) (PhD Thesis, Southeast University, Nanjing, 1995).

11 Fu Chao-ching, *Zhongguo Gudian Shiyang Xinjianzhu: Ershi Shiji Zhongguo Xinjianzhu Guanzhihua de Lishi Yanjiu* (Neo-Classical Chinese Architecture: Historical Research of the Institutionalization of a New Architecture of China in the Twentieth Century) (Taipei: Nantian Shuju Co. Ltd., 1993).

12 Sha Yongjie, *Zhongri Jindai Jianzhu Fazhan Guocheng Bijiao Yanjiu* (Comparative Research on the Development of Modern Architecture in China and Japan) (PhD Thesis, Tongji University, Tongji, 1999).

13 Chen Li, *Dezu Shiqi Qingdao Jianzhu Yanjiu* (Research on Architecture in Qingdao in the German Colonial Period) (PhD Thesis, Tianjin University, Tianjin, 2007).

14 Peng Changxin, *Xiandaixing, Difangxing: Lingnan Chengshi Jianzhu de Jindai Zhuanxing* (Modernity and Regionality: Modern Transformation of Urban Architecture in the Lingnan Region) (Shanghai: Tongji University Press, 2012).

15 Wang Xin, *Jiangsu Jindai Jianzhu Wenhua Yanjiu* (Research on Modern Architectural Culture of the Jiangsu Province) (PhD Thesis, Southeast University, Nanjing, 2006).

16 Qian Haiping, *Yi Zhongguo Jianzhu yu Jianzhu Yuekan wei Zilaoyuan de Zhongguo Jianzhu Xiandaihua Jincheng Yanjiu* (Research on the Process of Modernization of Chinese Architecture Based on the Resources of Both *Zhongguo Jianzhu* and *Jianzhu Yuekan*) (PhD Thesis, Zhejiang University, Hangzhou, 2011).

17 Tang Fang, *Dushi Jianzhu Kongzhi: Jindai Shanghai Gonggong Zujie Jianzhu Fagui Yanjiu* (Control of Urban Architecture: Research on the Building Codes of Modern Shanghai's International Settlement) (1845–1943) (PhD Thesis, Tongji University, Tongji, 2012).

18 Zeng Juan, "Lun Jindai Lingnan Sijia Yuanlin Zaoyuan Cailiao Gexin yu Jiyi Fazhan (On the Innovation of Materials and Development of Craftsmanship for Constructing the Modern Private Gardens in the Lingnan Region)," *Zhongguo Yuanlin* (Chinese Landscape), no. 10 (2009): 99–102.

19 Chen Haijiao and Liu Daping, "Anda, Zhaodong ji Jiangjia Huochezhan deng Zhongdong Tielu Zhanfang Jianzhu de Jianzao Jishu Chutan (Preliminary Investigation into the Building Construction of Railway Stations of the Chinese-Eastern Line Including Those at Anda, Zhaodong, and Jianjia)," *Jianzhu Lishi yu Lilun di Shiyi Ji* (Architectural History and Theory), vol. 11, published as *2001 nian Zhongguo Jianzhushixue Xueshu Nianhui Lunwenji – Lanzhou Ligong Daxue Xuebao Di 37 Juan* (Conference Proceeding of the 2011 Annual Meeting the Society of Architectural Historiography of China – Journal of Lanzhou University of Technology), vol. 37 (Lanzhou: Lanzhou University of Technology, (2011), 218–233.

20 Zhang Haiao, *Jindai Shanghai Qingshui Zhuanqiang Jianzhu Tezheng Yanjiu Chutan* (Preliminary Investigation into the Characteristics of Buildings with Fair-Faced Brick Walls in Modern Shanghai) (Master Thesis, Tongji University, Tongji, 2008).

21 Chen Zhihong, *Minnan Qiaoxiang Jindai Diyuxing Jianzhu Yanjiu* (Research on Modern Regional Architecture in the Hometowns of Overseas Chinese in the South of Fujian Province) (PhD Thesis, Tianjin University, Tianjin, 2005).

22 Qin Lin, "Jinxiandai Yudongnan Tujiazu Mugou Minju Jianzao Liucheng (Construction Process of Modern Timber Vernacular Architecture of the Tujiazu Ethnic Minority in the Southeast of Chongqing)," in *Zhongguo Jindai Jianzhu Yanjiu yu Baohu* (Research and Preservation on Early Modern Chinese Architecture), vol. 8, ed. Zhang Fuhe (Beijing: Tsinghua University Press, 2012), 626–634.

23 Guo Xuan, "Jiyu Diyu de Kangzhan Yichan Baohu yu Liyong: Yi Peidu Chongqing Weili (Region-Based Reservation and Utilization of War Heritage: The Case of the Secondary Capital Chongqing)," *Xibu Renju Huanjing Xuekan* (Journal of Human Settlements of West China), no. 4 (2013): 24–31.

24 Liu Yishi, "Qinghua Daxue Dalitang Qiongding Jiegou Xingshi ji Jianzao Jishu Kaoxi (Investigation into the Structural Form and Construction Technology for the Dome of the Auditorium at Tsinghua University)," *Jianzhu Xuebao* (Architectural Journal), no. 11 (2013): 32–37.

25 Bao Muping and Shin Muramatsu, "Zhongguo Jindai Jianzhu Jishushi Yanjiu de Jichu Wenti (Basic Problems for the Historical Research on Early Modern Architectural Technology of China)," in *Zhongguo Gongye Jianzhu Yichan Diaocha yu Yanjiu: 2008 Zhongguo Gongye Jianzhu Yichan Guoji Xueshu Yantaohui Lunwenji* (Survey and Research on the Industrial Architecture Heritage of China: Conference Proceedings of the 2008 International Academic Seminar on the Industrial Architecture Heritage of China), ed. Liu Boying (Beijing: Tsinghua University Press, 2009), 192–205.

26 Natalie Delande, "Gongchengshi Zhanzai Jianzhu Duiwu de Qianlie: Shanghai Jindai Jianzhu Lishi shang Jishu Wenhua de Zhongyao Diwei (Engineers at the Forefront: The Important Position of Technological Culture in the Architectural History of Early Modern Shanghai)," in *Diwuci Zhongguo Jindai Jianzhushi Yanjiu Taolunhui Lunwenji* (Conference Proceeding of the 5th Seminar of the Research on the Early Modern Chinese Architectural History), ed. Wang Tan and Zhang Fuhe (Beijing: Zhongguo Jianzhu Gongye Chubanshe, 1998), 96–106.

27 Hua Na (Torsten Warner), *Jindai Qingdao de Chengshi Guihua yu Jianshe* (Urban Planning and Development of Modern Qingdao), ed. and trans. Qingdao Municipal Archives (Nanjing: Southeast University Press, 2011).

28 Wu Jiang, *Shanghai Bainian Jianzhushi* (History of Architecture of Shanghai, 1840s-1940s) (Shanghai: Tongji University Press, 1997), 74.

29 Li Zhuo, "Tianjin Bohai Shangye Dalou (Tianjin Bohai Commercial Building)," in *20th Century Chinese Architecture* (20 Shiji Zhongguo Jianzhu), ed. Yang Yongsheng and Gu Mengchao, 162 (Tianjin: Tianjin Kexue Jishu Chubanshe, 1999).

30 Li Haiqing, *Zhongguo Jianzhu Xiandai Zhuanxing* (Modern Transformation of Chinese Architecture) (Nanjing: Southeast University Press, 2004), 158–159. Information is based on the statistics published by old periodicals, *Zhongguo Jianzhu* and *Jianzhu Yuekan* in the 1930s.

31 Li, *Zhongguo*, 166.

32 Zheng Shiling, *Shanghai Jindai Jianzhu Fengge* (Styles in the Architecture of Early Modern Shanghai) (Shanghai: Shanghai Jiaoyu Chubanshe, 1999), 205.

33 Delande, "Gongchengshi," 102.

34 Liu, "Qinghua," 32–37.

35 Li, *Zhongguo*, 179–193.

36 *Jianzhu Yuekan* 3, no. 1 (January 1935): 61–63.

37 *Jianzhu Yuekan* 3, no. 1 (January 1935): 61–63.

38 *Jianzhu Yuekan* 2, no. 3 (March 1934): advertisement.

39 Li, *Zhongguo*, 199–201.

40 Li, *Zhongguo*, 201–202.

41 Li, *Zhongguo*, 203–205.

42 Li, *Zhongguo*, 216–219.

43 Li, *Zhongguo*, 219–221.

44 Li, *Zhongguo*, 222–227.

45 Nanjing Gomngxueyuan Jianzhu Yanjiusuo (Institute of Research in Architecture at Nanjing Institute of Technology), ed., *Yang Tingbao Jianzhu Sheji Zuopinji* (Monograph of the Architectural Works of Yang Tingbao) (Nanjing: Nanjing Gongxueyuan Chubanshe, 1983), 94–98,131–132.

46 Shanghaishi Gongwuju (Shanghai Public Works Department), *Shanghaishi Gongwuju zhi Shinian* (Ten Years of Shanghai Public Works Department) (Shanghai: Shanghaishi Gongwuju, 1937).

47 Zhang Dongpan, *Guojia Jiyi* (Memory of the Country) (Taiyuan: Shanxi Renmin Chubanshe, 2010), 297.

48 Song Zheng, *Zhongguo Gongyehua Lishi Jingyan Yanjiu* (Research on the Historical Experience of Industrialization of China) (Dalian: Dongbei Caijing Daxue Chubanshe, 2013), 38–45.

49 Song, *Zhongguo*, 36.

50 Cao Haiying, "Zhongguo Gongyehua: Lishi Jincheng he Xianzhuang Fenxi (China's Industrialization: An Analysis of Historical Evolution and Current Status)," *Sheke Zongheng* (Social Sciences Review), no. 12 (2008): 41–42.

51 Nanjingshi Difangzhi Bianzuan Weiyuanhui (Editorial Committee of Nanjing Local Records), ed., *Jianzhu Cailiao Gongye Zhi* (Records of the Building Material Industries) (Nanjing: Nanjing Chubanshe, 1991), 90–93.

52 La Sen (H. Allen Larsen) and Di Bai (William L. Dibble), *Feihudui Duiyuan Yanzhong de Zhongguo 1944–1945* (China in the Eyes of Flying Tigers Members 1944–1945) (Shanghai: Wenyi Chubanshe Zongshe, 2010), 144–147.

53 Feng Keli, ed., *Lao Zhaopian* (Old Photos), vol. 76 (Jinan: Shandong Huabao Chubanshe, 2011), back cover.

54 La and Di, *Feihudui*, 30.

55 Lu Daofu (Rudolf P. Hommel), *Shouyi Zhongguo: Zhongguo Shougongye Diaocha Tulu* (Chinese Craftsmanship: A Pictorial Survey Catalogue of the Industry of Chinese Craftsmanship) (1921–1930) (Beijing: Beijing Ligong Daxue Chubanshe, 2012), 244.

56 Lu, *Shouyi*, 286.

57 Lu, *Shouyi*, 314.

58 Feng Keli, ed., *Lao Zhaopian* (Old Photos), vol. 75 (Jinan: Shandong Huabao Chubanshe, 2011), 124.

59 Peng Nansheng, "Bangongyehua: Jindai Xiangcun Shougongye Fazhan Jincheng de Yizhong Miaoshu (Semi-Industrialization: A Description of Development Process of the Industry of Craftsmanship in the Early Modern Villages)," *Shixue Yuekan* (Journal of Historical Science), no. 7 (2003): 97–108.

60 Li Haiqing, "Cong 'Zhongguo' + 'Xiandai' dao 'Xiandai' @ 'Zhongguo': Guanyu Wangshu Huo Pulizikejiang yu Zhongguo Bentuxing Xiandai Jianzhu de Taolun (From 'China' + 'Modern' to 'Modern' @ 'China': On Wang Shu's Winning of the Pritzker Prize and China's Regionalist Modern Architecture)," *Jianzhushi* (Architect), no. 1 (2013): 39–45.

61 Han Baode, "Dasheng de Jianzhuguan (A Philosophy of Architecture Based on Mahayana Buddhism)," *Shijie Jianzhu* (World Architecture), no. 5 (1990): 68–74.

62 Jianfei Zhu, *Architecture of Modern China: A Historical Critique* (London: Routledge, 2009), 75–104; see also Zhu Tao, *Liangsicheng yu Tade Shidai* (Liang Sicheng and His Era) (Nanning: Guangxi Shifan Daxue Chubanshe, 2014), 227–280.

Bibliography

Bao Muping and Shin Muramatsu. "Zhongguo Jindai Jianzhu Jishushi Yanjiu de Jichu Wenti (Basic Problems for the Historical Research on Early Modern Architectural Technology of China)." In *Zhongguo Gongye Jianzhu Yichan Diaocha yu Yanjiu: 2008 Zhongguo Gongye Jianzhu Yichan Guoji Xueshu Yantaohui Lunwenji* (Survey and Research on the Industrial Architecture Heritage of China: Conference

Proceedings of the 2008 International Academic Seminar on the Industrial Architecture Heritage of China), edited by Liu Boying, 192–205. Beijing: Tsinghua University Press, 2009.

Cao Haiying. "Zhongguo Gongyehua: Lishi Jincheng he Xianzhuang Fenxi (China's Industrialization: An Analysis of Historical Evolution and Current Status)." *Sheke Zongheng* (Social Sciences Review), no. 12 (2008): 41–42.

Chen Haijiao and Liu Daping. "Anda, Zhaodong ji Jiangjia Huochezhan deng Zhongdong Tielu Zhanfang Jianzhu de Jianzao Jishu Chutan (Preliminary Investigation into the Building Construction of Railway Stations of the Chinese-Eastern Line Including Those at Anda, Zhaodong, and Jianjia)." In *Jianzhu Lishi yu Lilun di Shiyi Ji* (Architectural History and Theory, vol. 11), published as *2001 nian Zhongguo Jianzhushixue Xueshu Nianhui Lunwenji – Lanzhou Ligong Daxue Xuebao Di 37 Juan* (Conference Proceeding of the 2011 Annual Meeting the Society of Architectural Historiography of China – Journal of Lanzhou University of Technology, vol. 37, 218–233, Lanzhou: Lanzhou University of Technology, 2011).

Chen Li. *Dezu Shiqi Qingdao Jianzhu Yanjiu* (Research on Architecture in Qingdao in the German Colonial Period). PhD Thesis. Tianjin University, Tianjin, 2007.

Chen Zhihong. *Minnan Qiaoxiang Jindai Diyuxing Jianzhu Yanjiu* (Research on Modern Regional Architecture in the Hometowns of Overseas Chinese in the South of Fujian Province). PhD Thesis. Tianjin University, Tianjin, 2005.

Cheng Ji. "Zhongyangyanjiuyuan Diyijie Yuanshi de Quxiang (The Directions of the First Batch of Members of Academia Sinica)." *Ziran Bianzhengfa Tongxun* (Journal of Dialectics of Nature), no. 2 (2011): 36–70.

Delande, Natalie. "Gongchengshi Zhanzai Jianzhu Duiwu de Qianlie: Shanghai Jindai Jianzhu Lishi shang Jishu Wenhua de Zhongyao Diwei (Engineers at the Forefront: The Important Position of Technological Culture in the Architectural History of Early Modern Shanghai)." In *Diwuci Zhongguo Jindai Jianzhushi Yanjiu Taolunhui Lunwenji* (Conference Proceeding of the 5th Seminar of the Research on the Early Modern Chinese Architectural History), edited by. Wang Tan and Zhang Fuhe, 96–106. Beijing: Zhongguo Jianzhu Gongye Chubanshe, 1998.

Dong Li. *Zhongguo Jiaohui Daxue Jianzhu Yanjiu* (Research on Architecture of Christian Universities in China). PhD Thesis. Southeast University, Nanjing, 1995.

Feng Keli, ed. *Lao Zhaopian* (Old Photos), vol. 75–76. Jinan: Shandong Huabao Chubanshe, 2011.

Fu Chao-ching. *Zhongguo Gudian Shiyang Xinjianzhu: Ershi Shiji Zhongguo Xinjianzhu Guanzhihua de Lishi Yanjiu* (Neo-Classical Chinese Architecture: Historical Research of the Institutionalization of a New Architecture of China in the Twentieth Century). Taipei: Nantian Shuju Co. Ltd., 1993.

Guo Xuan. "Jiyu Diyu de Kangzhan Yichan Baohu yu Liyong: Yi Peidu Chongqing Weili (Region-Based Reservation and Utilization of War Heritage: The Case of the Secondary Capital Chongqing)." *Xibu Renju Huanjing Xuekan* (Journal of Human Settlements of West China), no. 4 (2013): 24–31.

Han Baode. "Dasheng de Jianzhuguan (A Philosophy of Architecture Based on Mahayana Buddhism)." *Shijie Jianzhu* (World Architecture), no. 5 (1990): 68–74.

Hua Na (Torsten Warner). *Jindai Qingdao de Chengshi Guihua yu Jianshe* (Urban Planning and Development of Modern Qingdao). Edited and translated by Qingdao Municipal Archives. Nanjing: Southeast University Press, 2011.

Huang Jianzhi and Yuan Gang, "Shanghai Jianzhuye de Xinsheng (New Life of the Building Industry in Shanghai)." In *Dongfang "Bali": Jindai Shanghai Jianzhu Shihua* (Eastern "Paris": History of Architecture of Modern Shanghai), edited by Shanghai Jianzhu Shigongzhi Bianweihui Bianxie Bangongshi (Editorial Committee of the Office of the Shanghai Building Construction Chronicles), 208–215. Shanghai: Shanghai Wenhua Chubanshe, 1991.

Jianzhu Yuekan 2, no. 3 (March 1934).

Jianzhu Yuekan 3, no. 1 (January 1935).

La Sen (H. Allen Larsen) and Di Bai (William L. Dibble). *Feihudui Duiyuan Yanzhong de Zhongguo 1944–1945* (China in the Eyes of Flying Tigers Members 1944–1945). Shanghai: Wenyi Chubanshe Zongshe, 2010.

Lai Delin. *Zhongguo Jindai Jianzhushi Yanjiu* (Research on Chinese Modern Architectural History). PhD Thesis. Tsinghua University, Tsinghua, 1992.

Li Haiqing. *Zhongguo Jianzhu Xiandai Zhuanxing* (Modern Transformation of Chinese Architecture). Nanjing: Southeast University Press, 2004.

———. "Cong 'Zhongguo' + 'Xiandai' dao 'Xiandai' @ 'Zhongguo': Guanyu Wangshu Huo Pulizikejiang yu Zhongguo Bentuxing Xiandai Jianzhu de Taolun (From 'China' + 'Modern' to 'Modern' @ 'China':

On Wang Shu's Winning of the Pritzker Prize and China's Regionalist Modern Architecture)." *Jianzhushi* (Architect), no. 1 (2013): 39–45.

Li Zhuo. "Tianjin Bohai Shangye Dalou (Tianjin Bohai Commercial Building)." In *20th Century Chinese Architecture* (20 Shiji Zhongguo Jianzhu), edited by Yang Yongsheng and Gu Mengchao, 161–163. Tianjin: Tianjin Kexue Jishu Chubanshe, 1999.

Liang Sicheng. *Zhongguo Jianzhushi* (History of Chinese Architecture). Tianjin: Baihua Wenyi Chubanshe, 2005.

Liu Boying, ed. *Zhongguo Gongye Jianzhu Yichan Diaocha yu Yanjiu: 2008 Zhongguo Gongye Jianzhu Yichan Guoji Xueshu Yantaohui Lunwenji* (Survey and Research on the Industrial Architecture Heritage of China: Conference Proceedings of the 2008 International Academic Seminar on the Industrial Architecture Heritage of China). Beijing: Tsinghua University Press, 2009.

Liu Yishi. "Qinghua Daxue Dalitang Qiongding Jiegou Xingshi ji Jianzao Jishu Kaoxi (Investigation into the Structural Form and Construction Technology for the Dome of the Auditorium at Tsinghua University)." *Jianzhu Xuebao* (Architectural Journal), no. 11 (2013): 32–37.

Lu Daofu (Rudolf P. Hommel). *Shouyi Zhongguo: Zhongguo Shougongye Diaocha Tulu* (Chinese Craftsmanship: A Pictorial Survey Catalogue of the Industry of Chinese Craftsmanship) (1921–1930). Beijing: Beijing Ligong Daxue Chubanshe, 2012.

Nanjing Gomngxueyuan Jianzhu Yanjiusuo (Institute of Research in Architecture at Nanjing Institute of Technology), ed. *Yang Tingbao Jianzhu Sheji Zuopinji* (Monograph of the Architectural Works of Yang Tingbao). Nanjing: Nanjing Gongxueyuan Chubanshe, 1983.

Nanjingshi Difangzhi Bianzuan Weiyuanhui (Editorial Committee of Nanjing Local Records), ed. *Jianzhu Cailiao Gongye Zhi* (Records of the Building Material Industries). Nanjing: Nanjing Chubanshe, 1991.

Peng Changxin. *Xiandaixing, Difangxing: Lingnan Chengshi Jianzhu de Jindai Zhuanxing* (Modernity and Regionality: Modern Transformation of Urban Architecture in the Lingnan Region). Shanghai: Tongji University Press, 2012.

Peng Nansheng. "Bangongyehua: Jindai Xiangcun Shougongye Fazhan Jincheng de Yizhong Miaoshu (Semi-Industrialization: A Description of Development Process of the Industry of Craftsmanship in the Early Modern Villages)." *Shixue Yuekan* (Journal of Historical Science), no. 7 (2003): 97–108.

Qian Haiping. *Yi Zhongguo Jianzhu yu Jianzhu Yuekan wei Zilaoyuan de Zhongguo Jianzhu Xiandaihua Jincheng Yanjiu* (Research on the Process of Modernization of Chinese Architecture Based on the Resources of Both *Zhongguo Jianzhu* and *Jianzhu Yuekan*). PhD Thesis. Zhejiang University, Hangzhou, 2011.

Qin Lin. "Jinxiandai Yudongnan Tujiazu Mugou Minju Jianzao Liucheng (Construction Process of Modern Timber Vernacular Architecture of the Tujiazu Ethnic Minority in the Southeast of Chongqing)." In *Zhongguo Jindai Jianzhu Yanjiu yu Baohu* (Research and Preservation on Early Modern Chinese Architecture), edited by Zhang Fuhe, vol. 8, 626–634. Beijing: Tsinghua University Press, 2012.

Sha Yongjie. *Zhongri Jindai Jianzhu Fazhan Guocheng Bijiao Yanjiu* (Comparative Research on the Development of Modern Architecture in China and Japan). PhD Thesis. Tongji University, Tongji, 1999.

Shanghai Jianzhu Shigongzhi Bianweihui Bianxie Bangongshi (Editorial Committee of the Office of the Shanghai Building Construction Chronicles), ed. *Dongfang "Bali": Jindai Shanghai Jianzhu Shihua* (Eastern "Paris": History of Architecture of Modern Shanghai). Shanghai: Shanghai Wenhua Chubanshe, 1991.

Shanghaishi Gongwuju (Shanghai Public Works Department). *Shanghaishi Gongwuju zhi Shinian* (Ten Years of Shanghai Public Works Department). Shanghai: Shanghaishi Gongwuju, 1937.

Song Zheng. *Zhongguo Gongyehua Lishi Jingyan Yanjiu* (Research on the Historical Experience of Industrialization of China). Dalian: Dongbei Caijing Daxue Chubanshe, 2013.

Tang Fang. *Dushi Jianzhu Kongzhi: Jindai Shanghai Gonggong Zujie Jianzhu Fagui Yanjiu* (Control of Urban Architecture: Research on the Building Codes of Modern Shanghai's International Settlement) (1845–1943). PhD Thesis. Tongji University, Tongji, 2012.

Wang Tan. "Diyici Zhongguo Jindai Jianzhushi Yanjiu Taolunhui Lunwen Zhuanji (Conference Proceeding of the First Symposium of the Research on the History of Architecture of Early Modern China)." *Huazhong Jianzhu* (Journal of Architecture of Central China), no. 2 (1987): 4–7.

Wang Tan and Zhang Fuhe, eds. *Diwuci Zhongguo Jindai Jianzhushi Yanjiu Taolunhui Lunwenji* (Conference Proceeding of the 5th Seminar of the Research on the Early Modern Chinese Architectural History). Beijing: Zhongguo Jianzhu Gongye Chubanshe, 1998.

Wang Xin. *Jiangsu Jindai Jianzhu Wenhua Yanjiu* (Research on Modern Architectural Culture of the Jiangsu Province). PhD Thesis. Southeast University, Dhaka, 2006.

Wu Jiang. *Shanghai Bainian Jianzhushi (1840–1949)* (One Hundred Years of Shanghai Architectural History, 1840–1949). PhD Thesis. Tongji University, Tongji, 1993.

————. *Shanghai Bainian Jianzhushi* (History of Architecture of Shanghai, 1840s–1940s). Shanghai: Tongji University Press, 1997.

Xu Subin. *Bijiao, Jiaowang, Qishi: Zhongri Jin Xiandai Jianzhushi zhi Yanjiu* (Comparison, Exchange, Revelation: Research on Chinese and Japanese Modern Architectural History). PhD Thesis. Tianjin University, Tianjin, 1992.

Yang Bingde. *Zhongguo Jindai Zhongxi Jianzhu Wenhua Jiaorongshi* (History of Cultural Exchange of Modern Chinese and Western Architecture in China). Wuhan: Hubei Jiaoyu Chubanshe, 2003.

Yang Yongsheng and Gu Mengchao, eds. *20th Century Chinese Architecture* (20 Shiji Zhongguo Jianzhu). Tianjin: Tianjin Kexue Jishu Chubanshe, 1999.

Zeng Juan. "Lun Jindai Lingnan Sijia Yuanlin Zaoyuan Cailiao Gexin yu Jiyi Fazhan (On the Innovation of Materials and Development of Craftsmanship for Constructing the Modern Private Gardens in the Lingnan Region)." *Zhongguo Yuanlin* (Chinese Landscape), no. 10 (2009): 99–102.

Zhang Dongpan. *Guojia Jiyi* (Memory of the Country). Taiyuan: Shanxi Renmin Chubanshe, 2010.

Zhang Fuhe, ed. *Zhongguo Jindai Jianzhu Yanjiu yu Baohu* (Research and Preservation of Early Modern Chinese Architecture), vol. 5, 8. Beijing: Tsinghua University Press, 2012.

————. "Zhongguo Jindai Jianzhushi Yanjiu Ershinian (Twenty Years of Research on Chinese Modern Architectural History) (1986–2006)." In *Zhongguo Jindai Jianzhu Yanjiu yu Baohu* (Research and Preservation of Early Modern Chinese Architecture), edited by Zhang Fuhe, vol. 5, 1–15. Beijing: Tsinghua University Press, 2012.

Zhang Haiao. *Jindai Shanghai Qingshui Zhuanqiang Jianzhu Tezheng Yanjiu Chutan* (Preliminary Investigation into the Characteristics of Buildings with Fair-Faced Brick Walls in Modern Shanghai). Master Thesis. Tongji University, Tongji, 2008.

Zheng Shiling. *Shanghai Jindai Jianzhu Fengge* (Styles in the Architecture of Early Modern Shanghai). Shanghai: Shanghai Jiaoyu Chubanshe, 1999.

Zhu, Jianfei. *Architecture of Modern China: A Historical Critique*. London: Routledge, 2009.

Zhu Tao. *Liangsicheng yu Tade Shidai* (Liang Sicheng and His Era). Nanning: Guangxi Shifan Daxue Chubanshe, 2014.

Glossary

Aiqun Hotel (Oi Kwan Building)	爱群大厦
Baishiyi (Paishiyiek) Military Airfield	白市驿军用机场
Bao Muping	包慕萍
Baxian	巴县
Beijing	北京
Beiyang Government	北洋政府
Bohai	渤海
caofang	草房
Chaling	茶陵
Chen Haijiao	陈海娇
Chen Li	陈雳
Chen Rongzhi (Chan Wing Gee)	陈荣枝
Chen Zhihong	陈志宏
Chen Zhi	陈植
Chongqing (Chungking)	重庆
Dahua Cinema	大华大戏院
Dalian	大连
Daxian	达县
Dazhi	大治
Dong Dayou	董大酉
Dong Li	董黎

Fu Chao-ching	傅朝卿
Fu Ji Construction Company	馥记营造厂
Gaokeng	高坑
Gonghe Yanghang (Palmer & Turner Architects and Surveyors)	公和洋行
Guangzhou	广州
Guo Xuan	郭璇
Ha Xiongwen	哈雄文
Hangzhou	杭州
Henan	河南
Hong Kong	香港
Huamao Gongyu (Cathay Mansion)	华懋公寓
Huashang	华商
Huasheng Building	华胜大楼
Hubei	湖北
Huifeng Yinhang (Hong Kong & Shanghai Bank）	汇丰银行
Hunan	湖南
Jiacun	甲村
Jiageng architecture	嘉庚建筑
Jiangsu	江苏
Jiangxi	江西
Jinan	济南
Jitai Gongchengsi (Kwan, Chu, and Yang Architects）	基泰工程司
Kunming	昆明
Kuomintang (Guomindang)	国民党
Lai Delin	赖德霖
Laizhou City	莱州城
Liang Sicheng	梁思成
Lin Keming	林克明
Lingnan	岭南
Lingxiang	灵乡
Liu Daping	刘大平
Liu Dunzhen	刘敦桢
Liu Yishi	刘亦师
Lunghwa (Longhua) aircraft depot	龙华飞机库
Lushan	庐山
Mao Yisheng	茅以升
Minnan	闽南
Motuo	墨脱
Mukden (Fengtian)	奉天 / 沈阳
Nanjing	南京
Peking-Mukden Railway	京奉铁路
Peng Changxin	彭长歆
Peng Nansheng	彭南生
Pengxian	彭县
Puzhen	浦镇
Qian Haiping	钱海平
Qiantang River	钱塘江

Qin Lin	覃琳
Qingdao	青岛
Qixin	启新
Sha Yongjie	沙永杰
Shangdong	山东
Shanghai	上海
Shenyang	沈阳
Shin Muramatsu	村松伸
Sichuan	四川
Sihang Chuxuhui (Joint Savings Society）	四行储蓄会
Sun Yat-sen	孙逸仙／孙中山
Taishan	泰山
Taiwan	台湾
Tang Fang	唐方
Tao Guilin	陶桂林
Tianhe	天河
Tianli Company	天利公司
Tiantaishan	天台山
Tianxiang Yanghang (Dodwell & Co. Ltd.）	天祥洋行
Tong Jun	童寯
Tongshang Yingyang (China Merchants Bank)	通商银行
Tsinghua University	清华大学
Tujiazu	土家族
Wang Tan	汪坦
Wang Xin	王昕
Wu Jiang	伍江
Wuhan	武汉
Wuhu	芜湖
Wuxi	无锡
Xi Fuquan	奚福泉
Xiamen	厦门
Xiangtan	湘潭
xianxiangfeng	线香缝
Xicun	西村
Xietai Yanghang (Yha Tai Engineers and Architects)	协泰洋行
Xin Ruihe Yanghang	新瑞和洋行
Xingye	兴业
Xinhai Revolution	辛亥革命
Xizang	西藏
Xu Subin	徐苏斌
Yang Bingde	杨秉德
Yang Tingbao	杨廷宝
yangtiepi	洋铁皮
Yangxin	阳新
Yingfeng Yanghang (Federal Inc.)	英丰洋行
Yingkou	营口
Yonghe Gongchengsi (Brossand Mopin)	永和工程司
Yongli Gas Plant	永利煤气厂

Youli Yinghang Dalou (Union Building)	有利银行大楼
yuantao	圆套
Yuxian	禹县
Zeng Juan	曾娟
Zhang Fuhe	张复合
Zhang Haiao	张海翱
Zhao Shen	赵深
Zhejiang	浙江
Zhongguo Jianzhu Shi	中国建筑史
Zhongguo Jindai Jianzhu Zonglan	中国近代建筑总论
Zhongguo	中国
Zhuang Jun	庄俊

17

CHINESE CLASSICAL REVIVAL

Nanjing, Capital of Republican China (1910s–40s)

Zhou Qi and Ji Qiu

The debate on formal issues in Chinese modern architecture was mainly influenced by two factors: grand narratives of the nation-state and national style to represent the willpower of the government on the one hand, and micro-transformations, including the change of design positions of architects and the accumulation of architectural historical knowledge, on the other. Perhaps the latter is less attractive in scholarly analysis, but it is nevertheless very important and shows a clear and crucial clue for explaining the emergence of certain designs.

In early modern China, the estrangement between architects and Chinese traditional timber structures gradually disappeared with increasing knowledge and research development on the history of ancient Chinese architecture. Architects imitated and created traditional forms with the use of new materials, technology, and spatial design. This chapter aims to explain this line of formal design following the trajectory of the architects. The architects of Nanjing – the capital of the Republic of China – and the works they created are the primary case to study this "mutation of the big roof." Nanjing, a city with a history of 2,500 years, plays important political and economic roles in modern China. Since the Xinhai or Republican Revolution in China (1911), Nanjing as the capital of the Republic of China has established a crucial position in China's modernization. The architectural trend during this period of time was influenced by western modern architecture, on one hand, and Chinese classicism reflecting a nationalism, on the other. The earliest attempt to incorporate Chinese formal features into a modern building was found in the introduction of western Christianity – along with its building practice – into China. Subsequently, Chinese state authority explicitly required the use of traditional forms for important government buildings. With the change in the use of modern materials and technology, it was impossible to completely adopt a traditional timber structure and to create classical architecture. The changes of building functions also required compromise and coordination to a certain extent.

American architects Dwight H. Perkins (1867–1941) and Henry K. Murphy (1857–1954) initiated the new form of Chinese-style big-roof architecture in Nanjing in the early twentieth century. Major sources of their knowledge of Chinese architectural history were the Forbidden City in Beijing and relevant writing by German architect and historian Ernst Boerschmann (1873–1949). A Chinese architect, Lǚ Yanzhi (1894–1929), graduated from Connell University in the US and worked at Murphy's architectural office for several years. Leaving Murphy and practicing himself later on, he became more skilful in the use of Chinese forms; his design

DOI: 10.4324/9781315851112-25

for the Sun Yat-sen Mausoleum proved to be a great success. Among others in China after studying aboard, the key representatives were Liang Sicheng (Liang Ssu-ch'eng, 1901–72) and Liu Dunzhen (also as Liu Tun-chen or Liu Tun-Tseng, 1897–1968). Both of them had profound achievement in the historical research of Chinese architecture. Through these research outcomes, American- and European-trained Chinese architects could gain the knowledge of Chinese traditional wooden structures. Their subsequent divergence in design perspective originated from their education background, as to whether it was the Beaux-Arts or the modern model and their personal preference in a range of attitudes from the radical to the moderate.

Early Exploration: Nanking University (1910s) and Ginling College (1920s)

The first batch of western Catholic missionaries came to China for preaching at the turn of the sixteenth century, whereas the Protestant missionaries first arrived in China in 1807. Later, the missionary work was interrupted by the prohibition imposed by the Qing-dynasty authority and the upheavals caused by the Taiping Rebellion (1850–64). When the Taiping force was defeated in the late century, Christianity formally returned to Nanjing. To facilitate their preaching, missionaries started to attempt to combine Christian doctrines with Chinese Confucianism. As described, the majority of western missionaries now held the Bible in one hand and *The Four Books* in the other to facilitate the spread of Christianity in China. Early buildings built by the Christian churches in Nanjing included churches, hospitals, and schools – for example, the French Catholic Church in the fifth year of the reign of Emperor Tongzhi (1866), the Jesus Church and the American Hospital in the eleventh year of the reign of Emperor Guangxu (1885), the Macklin Hospital in 1892, the Mingde College for Girls in 1884, the Methodist Nanking University (Huiwen Shuyuan) in 1888, the Department of Foundation Studies of Aurora University in 1912, and the early buildings of Ginling College in 1913–15.

In 1910, the Union Christian College (Hongyu Shuyuan) was merged into the Methodist Nanking University to form the University of Nanking. Arthur J. Bowen had become the president of the Methodist Nanking University in 1907 and served as the first president of the newly formed University of Nanking. Over 2,000 *mu* of land on the southwestern side of Gulou (drum tower) was purchased for constructing the new campus of the university.[1] The founding president, John C. Ferguson (Fu Kaisen), and Arthur J. Bowen explicitly required the use of Chinese traditional architectural style for the new campus. Teaching buildings of the University of Nanking were mainly designed by Perkins, Fellows & Hamilton Office in Chicago in the US. The key partner of this architectural firm was Dwight H. Perkins, who was a member of the Prairie School. His representative work, the Carl Schurz High School, Chicago, was completed in 1910. It is regarded as one of the most important early twentieth-century architecture in the United States, expressing elements of both the Chicago and Prairie Schools.

The design of the University of Nanking reflects an imitation – in a somewhat simple way – of Chinese northern imperial architecture by Perkins (Figures 17.1 and 17.2). According to the early planning scheme, a central plaza rather than a courtyard was formed by the disposition of teaching buildings. The complete system of roof, *dougong* bracket, post, and beam of Chinese traditional architecture was substantially simplified in the design of the University of Nanking. The clock tower was located at the end of the main axis in the centre of the main facade of the North Teaching Building, destroying the overall hip-and-gable roof, which could never happen in a proper Chinese architecture. Western instead of Chinese timber frames were used inside the roof. The most delicate structural element – *dougong* (an elaborate bracket set) – was replaced by corbelling of bricks. There was no Chinese column on the facades; instead, vertical

Figure 17.1 Methodist Nanking University (now Nanjing University), the main quadrangle, Nanjing, 1910s; Architect: Perkins, Fellows & Hamilton.

Source: From and by permission of Special Collections, Yale Divinity School Library (RG 11, United Board for Christian Higher Education in Asia Records).

Figure 17.2 Assembly Hall, Methodist Nanking University (now Nanjing University), Nanjing, 1910s; Architect: Perkins, Fellows & Hamilton.

Source: © Author (2014).

windows similar to those used in the Carl Schurz High School were adopted. Teaching buildings at the University of Nanking were constructed by using old bricks of the Ming Dynasty city wall of Nanjing. Such city wall was over 37 km in length and building was started in the fourteenth century by the founding emperor of the dynasty, Zhu Yuanzhang. As a result of the declining power of the Qing dynasty after 1907, part of the city-wall bricks was dismantled and sold by local dignitaries as private properties. Foreigners took this opportunity to buy building materials in large quantities. Chinese northern cylindrical tiles were used for roofs of teaching buildings instead of the less curvy roof tiles typically in the south – the so-called small grey roof tile (*xiaoqingwa*) or butterfly tile (*hudiewa*).

For Chinese architects who came to practice later on, this early imitation of Chinese traditional architecture by western architects was superficial and "romantic." Chinese architecture was regarded as an exotic condiment and was helpful to serve the ultimate purpose of preaching. Adding Chinese traditional roofs on western architecture was not authentic and difficult to coordinate in terms of building form.

The Ginling College (also known as Jinling Women's College), designed by the American architect Henry K. Murphy, was a great achievement, surpassing the building forms of the University of Nanking. This is because Murphy had more knowledge of traditional architecture of China than other western architects. Although he had made many mistakes and lacked his own systematic approach, he was an active participant rather than a bystander in the development of architecture in China.

When Murphy first met the president of the Tsinghua School, Zhou Daichun, in 1914, William K. Fellows, one of the partners of the Chicago architectural firm of Perkins, Fellows & Hamilton, persuaded Zhou to appoint his firm for architectural design.[2] Zhou, however, selected Murphy instead. Similarly, the founding president of Ginling College, Matilda C. Thurston, was also more interested in Murphy and his practice in Changsha. Although the Perkins, Fellows & Hamilton Office pre-emptively positioned themselves in the market, they could not compete with Murphy later.

Although the school board of the Ginling College originally did not intend to build modern teaching buildings over two storeys high with Chinese roofs on top, Mrs. Thurston preferred the building style under the roof to be Chinese. In a letter written by Mrs. Thurston to Murphy, she stated:

> The roof is, of course, the most distinctive feature of the Chinese style; but the essence of the style runs all through, in the fenestration, the relation of voids and solids, the mass and the detail. We feel that it is not worth while to attempt to get the spirit of these wonderful Chinese buildings at all, in modern work, unless we can work with something more than the top.[3]

Murphy was good at implementing these ideas in the design of Ginling College (Figure 17.3). He was aware of the integrity of Chinese roofs, which could not be interrupted by building mass, such as the clock tower of the North Teaching Building at the University of Nanking. He also had a better understanding of Chinese courtyards and the architectural axis of building clusters, which were connected by covered walkways for strengthening courtyard enclosures. In addition, he could comprehend the structural authenticity of Chinese architecture, including the relationship between structure and decoration, as well as the form of the *dougong* bracket set – and how to imitate it properly in a modern design. Chinese traditional colour was also used in the design, ranging from grey bricks and black roof tiles to red columns and yellow walls, together with carved beams, painted rafters, and sculptured figures on roof ridges. Although

Figure 17.3 Ginling College (now Suiyuan campus of Nanjing Normal University), Nanjing, 1910s, Architect: Henry K. Murphy.

Source: © Author (2014).

the buildings were durable concrete structures, they could reflect Chinese architecture in a new and adaptive manner.

However, Murphy's design also showed some deficiencies in his knowledge of Chinese architectural history. He did not clearly comprehend the structural performance of *dougong*.

Dougong sets were almost completely misaligned with columns and densely arranged between roofs and walls. Double columns appeared on the facade, and the proportions between columns were not carefully arranged.

The completed buildings of the Ginling College fully expressed Murphy's design intentions. In fact, both Ginling in Nanjing and Yenching University of Beijing materialized Murphy's design ideas and were much approved by the Chinese government at the time. In 1928, the Nationalist government decided to apply similar "adaptive Chinese architecture" to government projects and invited Murphy to act as the architectural consultant for the urban planning of the capital Nanjing for one year.

A Representative Case of Classical Revival: Sun Yat-sen Mausoleum (1920s)

The Sun Yat-sen Mausoleum, one of the most important buildings in modern China, was designed by Lǚ Yanzhi, who was talented but unfortunately died young, before the completion of the mausoleum. It was built for the burial of Sun Yat-sen, the "father of modern China." After the Republican Revolution of 1911, Sun was appointed to serve as the Provisional President of the Republic of China, but later stepped down for Yuan Shikai to succeed. Sun's prominent historical contributions were to overthrow the Qing dynasty, to end the 2,000-year history of monarchy in China, and to establish the Chinese Republic. His will was to be buried at Purple Mountain of Nanjing after his death.

The Sun Yat-sen Mausoleum – and the Zhongshan Avenue (Sun Zhongshan being another name of Sun Yat-sen) for burial and receiving the coffin of Sun Yat-sen – had significant implications for the urban planning and design of modern Nanjing. The Zhongshan, by connecting the Yangtze River in the northwest and the Sun Yat-sen Mausoleum in the far east, redefined the urban core and its structure for the city of Nanjing. In 1928, shortly after the reunification of the whole country, the Nationalist government started to prepare the relocation of Sun Yat-sen's body from Beijing to Nanjing. Finally, upon the completion of the buildings of Sun Yat-sen Mausoleum, a state funeral was held on 1 June 1929 and Sun's body was buried after three days of public memorial service. In 1933, Zhongshan Avenue was the first bituminous road in Nanjing, having a total length of 13 kilometres with three segments: Zhongshan North Road, Zhongshan Road, and Zhongshan South Road, with the Gulou (drum tower) and Xinjiekou (new intersection) as key nodes.

Lǚ Yanzhi was a 1918 graduate from the Department of Architecture at Cornell University. His interest in Chinese architecture was aroused during his work at Murphy's office (Murphy and Dana Architects) in New York. He worked there for two years and learned about classical Chinese architecture. After that, he worked at Murphy's Shanghai office (Murphy, McGill, and Hamlin Architects) for one year. He left Murphy's office in March 1922 and won the international design competition of the Sun Yat-sen Mausoleum three years later. In his resignation letter to Murphy in 1922, Lǚ praised the design of Ginling College and expressed a strong desire "to extend the sphere of [my] usefulness" and "to combat the ever present 'comprador' architecture, which is disfiguring our bigger cities and countryside."[4]

The Sun Yat-sen Mausoleum as designed by Lǚ Yanzhi has a grand and open site. The spatial sequence along the lengthy central axis and the internal memorial spaces can fulfil the needs of various commemorative activities. Lǚ avoided the use of traditional ornaments reminiscent of feudal imperial power, eliminated some details in relation to superstition and hierarchical systems, such as stone sculptural figures, and replaced dragon motifs with non-hierarchical geometric decoration of clouds, curly grass, and mountains. Similarly, the use of blue glazed roof tiles – instead of the golden yellow glazed tiles of the Forbidden City – was another sign of a position against monarchy.[5]

The English annotations and British units on architectural drawings, and the proportional relationship of facade composition, might reveal Lü's limited understanding of Chinese building modulus. He was mainly inspired by the sinophilic atmosphere of Murphy's office and may not have had an in-depth knowledge about classical Chinese architecture itself. The composed masses at the four corners of the Sacrificial Hall of the Sun Yat-sen Mausoleum were similar to the elevation treatment of the Ginling College in terms of the proportion of bays and column spacing – a trace of Murphy for sure.

New Architecture with Traditional Chinese Forms (1930s)

The so-called Golden Decade of fast development, also known as the Nanjing Decade, began with the moment that Nanjing was confirmed as the capital of China on 18 April 1927 and lasted until capital was relocated to Chongqing on 20 November 1937 (on the eve of Japanese attack on and invasion of Nanjing). Much happened during the course of the decade. In 1930, Zhu Qiqian (1871–1964) established Zhongguo Yingzao Xueshe – Society for Research in Chinese Architecture – aiming to carry out systematic research on traditional Chinese architecture. Two well-known architects, Liang Sicheng (1901–72) and Liu Dunzhen (1897–1968), were invited to join and lead actual research work. Stable political and economic conditions, together with the progress of historical research, offered architects in Nanjing in the 1930s a good prospect for commissioning and adopting historical ideas. What emerged from this period in hindsight were two major design trends: a close reproduction of the historical forms, especially the big roofs (Figure 17.4), and a more innovative approach that abandoned the use of the big roofs (Figure 17.5).

In the Sun Yat-sen Memorial Park – including but much larger than the mausoleum – there are cases where traditional Chinese timber architectural forms were faithfully reproduced using

Figure 17.4 Scriptorium in Sun Yat-sen Memorial Park, Nanjing, 1936; Architect: Lu Shusen.

Source: Permission and courtesy of © Wang Wei (2014).

Figure 17.5 Ministry of Foreign Affairs, Nanjing, 1935: Architect: Allied Architects.

Source: *Zhongguo Jianzhu: The Chinese Architect* 3, no. 3 (1935): 21.

reinforced concrete. These include: Xiaohongshan Residence (Chiang Kai-shek Villa) by Chen Pinshan (1934), the Scriptorium by Lu Shusen (1937), and the Sacrificial Hall for Tan Yankai by Kwan, Chu, and Yang Architects (1932) (Figure 17.4). Apart from adding window openings for functional needs, decorative approaches, materials, and external forms basically complied with – if at times simplified – the northern official construction methods of traditional timber structures. *Dougong* brackets of the Scriptorium were complicated and detailed, but they were eliminated in both Xiaohongshan Residence and Tan Yankai Sacrificial Hall due to the idea that *dougong* sets had lost structural necessity in late imperial China. Other Chinese-style ornamentations, such as sculptured figures on roof ridges, internal and external coloured painting, railings, and column bases were comparatively authentic to the old tradition. In and since the 1930s, Chinese architects in both well-established organizations and private practices had the ability to complete these types of design commissions.

Designs of this approach along the major urban avenues included: the Central Museum, the Central Archives of the History of the Chinese Nationalist Party, the building clusters for the Central Party Supervision Commission, and the Lizhishe Society. Kwan, Chu, and Yang Architects designed two of these projects with similar heights along the Zhongshan East Road, on the two sides of the central axis of the Ming Palace (perpendicular to the Road).

The first was the building clusters for the Central Archives of the History of the Chinese Nationalist Party (1935) on the site of the old West Palace of the Ming; the ensemble included a main tower, police pavilions, and an entrance gateway – a complex nicknamed "West Palace." The second was the buildings for the Central Party Supervision Commission (1937) on the old site of Wenhua Hall of the Ming Palace – and the new complex was referred to as "East Palace." The two ensembles to the east and west, similar in style and scale, were two storeys high and constructed with reinforced concrete.

The buildings of the Lizhishe Society (1931) were designed by Fan Wenzhao and Zhao Shen. The large assembly hall was three storeys high and constructed mainly with reinforced concrete, but beams, rafters, and eaves were timber structures. Its floor area was 1,360 m² and could accommodate a total of 500 people. The other two buildings were three-storey brick–timber mixed structures. Building number one had a *wudian* roof (a roof with four slopes and five ridges), whereas its two wings had *xieshan* roofs (half-hipped, half-gabled). Building number three had some roof variations, having a *xieshan* roof in the middle and *wudian* roofs for both wings.

In the design competition for the National Central Museum in Nanjing in June 1935, high-quality entries submitted by architects were received and experienced jury members were involved. A total of 13 Chinese architects were invited to participate. Five of them received awards: Xu Jingzhi, Yang Tingbao, Tong Jun, Lu Qianshou, and Xi Fuquan. The winning entry was submitted by Xu Jingzhi. He proposed to locate large buildings with Chinese roofs at a prominent location for the visitors upon entering. The jury panels included the two architectural historians of the Society of Research in Chinese Architecture, Liang Sicheng and Liu Dunzhen. They emphasized the need to use Chinese traditional characteristics for the design. Finally, Xu Jingzhi's scheme was required to be modified to a Liao-dynasty style.

By this time, architects and historians had much better knowledge than before on traditional Chinese architecture: they now had more refined classifications of the tradition, could design with more accuracy for a certain style, were more knowledgeable about the characteristics of a certain historical period, and began to appreciate certain regional characteristics as well.

New National Style (1930s)

Despite increasing knowledge about the past, some architects in China adopted a radical position that opposed the use of Chinese roofs. Instead, they preferred to include some Chinese ornamentation on parts of the facade. By doing so, traditional Chinese architectural form was converted to decorative elements. Examples of this approach include the Ministry of Foreign Affairs Building in Nanjing, designed by Allied Architects, and the National Grand Assembly Hall and the National Art Gallery, designed by Xi Fuquan (Figure 17.5).

The two architectural firms – Kwan, Chu, and Yang Architects and Allied Architects – were in direct competition in the design for the Ministry of Foreign Affairs, which manifests well the opposition between the conservative and the radical in design at that time. In this case, the radical approach was finally adopted. The original scheme by Kwan, Chu, and Yang Architects was a building with a Chinese big roof. However, due to the lack of budget, it was subsequently simplified by Allied Architects using a flat roof solution. The design outcome was well received. It was praised as one of the most modernized buildings in Nanjing, expressing Chinese architectural aesthetics, on one hand, and fulfilling functional needs and operational requirements, on the other. It was simple and majestic without excessive ornamentation.[6]

Yang Tingbao (1901–82), one of the partners with Kwan, Chu, and Yang Architects, adopted a variety of design approaches and followed a memorialist and a functionalist principle. On one hand, both the Central Archives of the History of the Chinese Nationalist Party and the buildings for the Central Party Supervision Commission were strong in a memorialist sense. They were two groups of buildings following pure Chinese styles and delicate designs replicating with each other and imitating closely the northern official timber structures. On the other hand, the Central Hospital was strong in a functionalist sense and only partially decorated with Chinese ornamentation. The Dahua Cinema was an Art Deco work with simplified Chinese decorations and line patterns.

Comparatively, the three young partners of Allied Architects (Zhao Shen, Chen Zhi, and Tong Jun) aimed to eliminate ornamentation and emphasized structure and functions in many of their designs, such as the modern Metropolitan Hotel (*shoudu fandian*). Their clear understanding about traditional structure was reflected in a statement by Tong Jun (1900–83):

> The Chinese builder never sacrificed the structural for any decoration, however, attractive. On all the great epochs of Chinese architecture, the spirit remained distinctly Chinese, no matter how much foreign influence it had assimilated.[7]

The design strategy of the German-trained Xi Fuquan (1903–83) was distinctively different from the above two architectural firms. He never hesitated when it came to emphasizing functions and weakening Chinese ornamentation. In fact, he never designed any architecture with a Chinese big roof on top. During his study in Germany, he was heavily influenced by the Bauhaus. His architectural design often expressed an attempt for experimentation and for a radical departure, which differentiated his work from the majority of Chinese architects. After two months of the announcement of the competition result of the National Central Museum, the preparatory committee of the National Grand Assembly Hall and the National Art Gallery selected Xi's design proposal in August 1935, which was coherent with his competition entry for the National Central Museum design. Xi was more successful in Shanghai, as manifested in works such as the Lunghwa (Longhua) airport depot of the Eurasia Aviation Corporation in 1935, which had similar floor area as the Xiaohongshan Residence, which had Chinese architectural features. However, the construction cost of the former one was less than half of the latter (over $300,000 for Xiaohongshan) and the construction period was largely reduced (over two years for Xiaohongshan). Nevertheless, the merits of his work were substantially underestimated in the conservative atmosphere and the decorative-laden context of Nanjing.

Tong Jun – who thoroughly opposed the use of Chinese big roofs – was an exemplar of the radical architects of that time. He appreciated principles of modern architecture. He stated the following, which may serve to conclude this short, design-based historical review:

> Whether genius can blend it with Chinese architecture, or as the tendency goes, rather the reverse, the temple roof definitely has had its day. . . . Whether a building has a Chinese or modernistic exterior, its plan can only be one thing: a logical and scientific arrangement of rooms according to the most up-to-date knowledge available. Naturally the façade, a product of the plan, could be nothing but modernistic. Any attempt to give it local "colour" will require study, research, and originality, which constitute China's contribution to world architecture. Such contribution, it must be added, should have structural significance, which was once so ingeniously displayed in the design of the Chinese temple.[8]

Notes

1 *Mu*, a unit of area (1 *mu* = 0.0667 hectares).
2 Jeffrey William Cody, *Henry K. Murphy, an American architect in China, 1914–1935* (PhD Thesis, Cornell University, Ithaca, NY, 1989), 53–54.
3 Cody, "Henry," 161–164. Jeffrey William Cody, *Building in China: Henry K. Murphy's "Adaptive Architecture" 1914–1935* (Hong Kong: The Chinese University of Hong Kong, 2001), 109. Mrs. Thurston's 25 July 1918 letter to Murphy.
4 Cody, "Henry," 241; Cody, *Building in China,"* 148. Lü's 3 March 1922 resignation letter to Murphy.

5 See also the following on the design of the mausoleum: Delin Lai, "Searching for a modern Chinese monument: The design of the Sun Yat-sen Mausoleum in Nanjing," *Journal of the Society of Architectural Historians*, vol. 64, no. 1 (March 2005): 22–55.

6 *Zhongguo Jianzhu: The Chinese Architect,* no. 1 (July 1933): 11.

7 Tong Jun, *Tong Jun Wenji 1* (Collection of Tong Jun's Writing), vol. 1 (Beijing: Jianzhu Gongye Chubanshe, 2000), 103.

8 Tong, *Tong Jun*, 88.

Bibliography

Cody, Jeffrey William. *Henry K. Murphy, an American Architect in China, 1914–1935*. PhD Thesis. Cornell University, Ithaca, NY, 1989.

———. *Building in China: Henry K. Murphy's "Adaptive Architecture" 1914–1935*. Hong Kong: The Chinese University of Hong Kong, 2001.

Jianzhu Yuekan: The Builder (November 1932–April 1937, 54 issues).

Lai, Delin. "Searching for a Modern Chinese Monument: The Design of the Sun Yat-sen Mausoleum in Nanjing." *Journal of the Society of Architectural Historians* 64, no. 1 (March 2005): 22–55.

Nanjing Gongxueyuan Jianzhu Yanjiushi, ed. *Yang Tingbao Jianzhu Sheji Zuopinji* (Collection of Yang Tingbao's Architectural Design Works). (Beijing: Zhongguo Jianzhu Chubanshe, 1983).

Tong, Jun. *Tong Jun Wenji 1* (Collection of Tong Jun's Writing), vol. 1. Beijing: Jianzhu Gongye Chubanshe, 2000.

Wang Huanlu, ed. *Shouduzhi* (Record of the Capital). Shanghai: Zhongzheng Bookshop, 1937.

Zhongguo Jianzhu: The Chinese Architect (November 1932–April 1937, 30 issues).

Glossary

Chen Pinshan	陈品善
Chen Zhi	陈植
Chiang Kai-shek	蒋介石
Dahua Cinema	大华大戏院
dougong	斗拱
Fan Wenzhao	范文照
Fu Kaisen	福开森
Ginling College	金陵女子大学
Guangxu	光绪
Gulou	鼓楼
Hongyue Shuyuan	宏育书院
hudiewa	蝴蝶瓦
Huiwen Shuyuan	汇文书院
Jinling Women's College	金陵女子大学
Kwan, Chu, and Yang Architects	基泰工程司
Liang Sicheng (Ssu-ch'eng)	梁思成
Liao (style)	辽（式）
Liu Dunzhen (Tun-chen, Tun-Tseng)	刘敦桢
Lizhishe Society	励志社
Lu Qianshou	陆谦受
Lu Shusen	卢树森
Lü Yanzhi	吕彦直
Lunghwa (Longhua) airport depot	龙华飞机棚厂
Macklin Hospital	马林医院
Ming (Dynasty) Palace	明（朝）故宫

Mingde College for Girls	明德女子中学
mu	亩
Nanjing	南京
Nanking	南京
Shanghai	上海
shoudu fandian	首都饭店
Sun Yat-sen	孙中山
Taiping Rebellion	太平天国ff动
Tan Yankai	谭延恺
Tong Jun	童寯
Tongzhi	同治
Tsinghua School	清华学校
Wenhua Hall	文华殿
wudian **roof**	庑殿顶
Xi Fuquan	奚福泉
Xiaohongshan Residence	小红山官邸
xiaoqingwa	小青瓦
xieshan **roof**	歇山顶
Xinhai Revolution	辛亥革命
Xinjiekou	新街口
Xu Jingzhi	徐敬直
Yang Tingbao	杨廷宝
Yangtze River	长江
Yenching University	燕京大学
Yuan Shikai	袁世凯
Zhao Shen	赵深
Zhongguo Yingzao Xueshe	中国营造学社
Zhongshan Avenue	中山大道
Zhongshan Road	中山路
Zhou Daichun	周诒春
Zhu Qiqian	朱启钤
Zhu Yuanzhang	朱元璋

Modern City Construction
and Spatial Formation

18

FROM HANKOU TOWN TO GREATER WUHAN

Urban Spatial Organizations in Early Modern China

Li Baihao

China has been a unified state since the Qin dynasty (221–206 BC); it had a centralized government and an inclusive system for managing and building cities across the nation. There were administrative cities for the state, the provinces, the prefectures, and the counties (*ducheng*, *shengcheng*, *fucheng* or *zhoucheng*, and *xiancheng*, respectively). These cities, facilitating and manifesting state governance, military defense, and social organization, revealed clearly the Chinese cultural ideas of statehood, of "all-under-heaven," of "nine-quarters" of the empire, and of the cosmic order (expressed as *guojia*, *tianxia*, *jiuzhou*, and *yuzhou* respectively).

Many cities in Chinese history were large in scale and formal in layout; the enclosed city walls, the high towers and gates on the walls, the solemn palaces and the offices, and the strictly planned state officials' residential quarters all manifested a great symbolic image. It revealed a concept of urban building very different from that in Europe, where cities grew around churches and plazas, and where urban public spaces were shaped gradually for the civic and daily life of the population.

Between City and Country: Hankou

From the Song dynasty (960–1279) onwards, however, despite the continuation of the practice described earlier, there emerged "modern" cities in the western sense. The trend was clearer in the Ming and Qing dynasties (1368–1911). At intersections of busy roads or sites of vibrant local economy, market towns developed gradually, with a habitable condition and a convenient layout, without city walls or palace compounds, where natural landscape such as hills and rivers were often integrated with urban habitation. In old China, these market towns were neither "cities" (*cheng*) nor "countryside" (*xiang*) but somewhere in between, yet they were sizable towns or market towns (*shi*).

Old Hankou was an ideal case for towns of this kind. Today, Hankou is a district of the large city of Wuhan on the middle reaches of Yangtze River; in fact, Hankou, along with Hanyang on the south of Han River and Wuchang on the southeast of Yangtze River, have been referred to as the Three Towns of Wuhan.[1] An ideal example of an assembled city, Wuhan is made up of Hankou Town, Hanyang County, and Wuchang City, which, though different in political

DOI: 10.4324/9781315851112-27

hierarchy and socioeconomic function, came together because of the rivers joining stream at this point.

Located to the northwest of the Yangtze River and north of the Han River, Hankou Town was administrated under Hanyang County. In the Ming dynasty (1368–1644), due to the changed course of Han River and the increasing importance of water transportation, Hankou Town emerged as a prosperous center of commercial exchange between north and south and was regarded as one of the "Four Famous Towns" and "Four Settlements under Heaven" of China. Because of this, scholar Liu Xianting (1648–1695) in his *Notes* (*Guangyang Zaji*) famously said that "there was Beijing in the north, Foshan in the south, Suzhou in the east and Hankou in the west."[2]

Towns (*zhen*) were not formally included in the state-led urban administrative system, nor were villages based on agriculture as a productive base. These towns didn't need to follow a strict ritualistic layout with symmetry and geometrical outlines; instead, they grew naturally according to the topography of the site for habitation and commerce, thus creating a friendly city that may express an ideal image for the local population.

Commerce based on water transport was essential in this case. Many docks were built from west to east along the bank of Han River. The docks were the starting point for connecting to the world outside and were also the birthplace of urban residential spaces. Streets (*jie*) parallel to the river and laneways (*xiang*) perpendicular to the riverbank thus emerged, forming a pattern of east–west roads and north–south lanes – a "fishbone" spatial morphology, as often described.[3]

Concentration of active businesses led to the emergence of autonomous associations and a general tolerance in society. Morphologically, row houses, with a shop in front and residential quarter at back, emerged and concentrated in an orderly manner along the road, forming commercial streets for various products and services, often with well-known specialties attached to the streets. Some 38 guilds were founded, testifying to the prosperity of an inland city of the time; there were schools, academies, and temples as well as civic organizations such as fire brigades, facilitating the rich and vibrant lifeworld of the population in Hankou.[4]

Of the three towns of Wuhan, Hanyang had a long history, Wuchang less so, and Hankou had the shortest history, having emerged only in the Ming and Qing. Yet, it is in this small inland town, which hardly had any commercial connection with the outside world, that we witness sudden development, almost overnight, into an international trading port.

The Birth of a Modern City

In the traditional Chinese sense, Hankou, which had no city walls, government offices, drum and bell towers, or a city temple, was not a "city" in a strict sense, let alone a city to be modernized. Yet, since opening in 1861, Hankou was like a motor, transforming very quickly a small town into a modern and international city, at a rate faster, it seems, than any other open ports in China.

The British established the first foreigners' settlement in Hankou, the British Concession, to the east of the old city, on the north bank of the Yangtze River, next to the Chinese settlement (Figure 18.1). Soon, Russia, France, Germany, and Japan all established their Concessions along the river, creating a co-presence of Chinese and international settlements. Hankou, with Shanghai and Tianjin, was one of the three cities that had the largest number of Concessions in a city across China. Though the British Concession was on lowland, it was seamlessly connected to the old city. This marked Hankou apart from other opening ports such as Shanghai, where Concessions were invariably distant from the old city. Breaking the idea that "Chinese

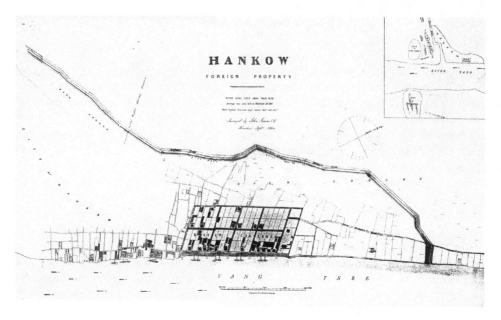

Figure 18.1   Planning of the British Concession in Hankou (1864).

Source: John Gavin (Hankou, 1864).

and foreigners should reside apart," this adjacency perhaps revealed an open and accommodating mindset on the part of the local Hankou population.

Despite this, and although Chinese and international settlements had a common interest in livelihood and development, approaches to urban building were indeed very different and, in fact, in sharp contrast. The ideas and practice of urban administration, civic design and construction, and ways of life from the western world, as manifested in the Concessions, delivered strong impressions to the Chinese, setting up advanced examples to learn, pushing forward urban construction of Hankou step by step.

Morphologically, the opening changed the spatial organization of the city. A closed locality based on inland and small waterways was shifting towards openness and the sea, building up a foundation for an international metropolis to come; the city center was shifting from facing the small Han River to engaging the large Yangtze River, from the Chinese to the international settlement; the streets were extending further from those parallel to the Han to those along the Yangtze; the overall urban space was growing in this direction as a linear city; *malu* (roads built with modern technology) were replacing *jie* and *xiang* (streets and lanes of the old); urban blocks and continuous façades were introduced, and a homogenous urban space emerged.

The opening-up also changed the economy of the city, reorganized its social structure, and changed the concept and method of urban construction. Hankou, like many Chinese cities then, learned western methods of development by imitating how things were done in the Concessions. But the process was led by the Chinese authority. If the opening was a starting point towards an urban modernity, then the 18 years since 1889 – when Zhang Zhidong (1837–1909) was the Governor General (*huguang zongdu*) and pushed for a "New Policy of Hubei" – was the critical period when Hankou was fully transformed into a modern international city.[5]

Under Zhang, large enterprises such as steel plants, arsenals, and textile and linen mills were built, laying down a solid foundation from which a modern industry could arise. He also transformed old academies, instituted modern schools, and organized students to be sent abroad to study – efforts at developing a modern education system. In the meantime, domestic and international banks were opening their branches here, making Hankou a financial hub. In transportation, the Beijing–Hankou Railway Line was completed and in operation, and shipping routes along the Yangtze also opened, establishing Hankou as a key node in a modern network of production across the country.[6]

By now, Hankou was very different from its past: docks, plants, railway lines, commercial firms, banks, schools, colleges, modern roads, and large buildings had arrived and, as elements and symbols, altered the old town into a modern city.

Establishing the Municipality of Hankou

In the early twentieth century, open-minded and well-informed intellectuals and officials, especially those well versed and those who traveled east and west, gradually realized that China's development should be neither a reproduction of the Concession's model nor a continuation of the tradition of a "large and unified empire" (*dayitong jianguo*), but instead an unprecedented establishment of municipalities, with urban administration and local autonomy, so as "to develop the nation by developing the cities" (*xingshi yi da xingguo*).[7]

In 1897, Liang Qichao (1873–1929) proposed the idea of "local autonomy" (*difang zizhi*); in 1909, the Qing government announced a Decree for Establishing Local Autonomy of Cities, Towns, and Townships (*cheng zhen xiang difang zizhi*), initiating the first step in Chinese history for establishing separate administration over these settlement entities. In 1911, the Parliament of Jiangsu Province announced a System of Cities and Townships of Jiangsu Province, or *Jiangsu Sheng Shi Xiang Zhi*, which used the word *shi* (meaning city, market, market-town, and municipality) for the first time. In 1921, Guangdong Province authority issued Temporary Regulations for Establishing Guangzhou Municipality, which established in Guangzhou the first municipality in China in the modern sense. In the same year, the Northern Government (*beiyang zhengfu*) announced the Autonomous Municipality System and the Guide to Establishing Autonomous Municipality (which also used the word *shi*), initiating a government-led transformation towards the "municipality system" known as *shizhi*. The Republican Government (*guomin zhengfu*), in 1928, issued Organization of Municipalities and Organization of Special Municipalities, and announced a new Organization of Municipalities in 1930; in 1943, a revision was supplied. By now, after some 50 years, legislation for establishing municipality in China had been established. This was exactly a century after Shanghai, in 1843, opened as a treaty port.[8]

In the protracted process of establishing the system, Chinese political culture from the past was incorporated, making a model that, though it originated in the west, was very different from that origin. It was more about governance than for autonomy, more authoritarian than democratic, and more determined by the mayor than the urban population – a municipality with strong centralized control.

In this nation-wide attempt at establishing a municipal system, Hankou was unique in its early start and swift development. Firstly, because of the influence of the Concessions, a Road and Civil Engineering Bureau was established in 1905. Secondly, in 1926, when the Northern Expedition from Guangzhou was pushing north successfully, the Republican Government in Guangzhou endorsed a Political Affairs Committee of Hubei (a province that included Hankou), which established Temporary Regulations for Establishing Hankou Municipality, based on the regulation for Guangzhou Municipality; and, with this, Hankou Municipality was established, with Liu Wendao (1893–1967) as its first mayor – this was the second city in China with a modern municipality system after Guangzhou. Thirdly, Hankou was the largest inland port in China, and the second largest of any port in the nation after Shanghai; with this national importance, in 1929, three years after the municipality's establishment, Hankou was elevated to the status of Special Municipality, one of a few in China, which were directly under the supervision of the Executive Yuan (*xingzheng yuan*) of the Republican Government.[9]

In this process, Guangzhou and Hankou, with their process and experience in establishing a modern municipality, became a model to learn from in Shanghai, Nanjing, Hangzhou, and Chongqing.

If the British Concession had initiated the modernizing process of Hankou, then it was the establishing of the municipality system that was the real driving force that brought modern planning and construction practice to Hankou.

The Unfolding of Modern Urban Construction

The main function of the Road and Civil Engineering Bureau of both Hankou and Shanghai, established in 1905 and 1895 respectively, was to plan and build *malu* or modern roads of the Macadam system, the western-style urban roads in the Concessions – straight, broad, orderly, covered on the road surface with single-sized crushed stone layers, with raised pedestrian walkways on the two sides, and rows of trees and street lamps at regular intervals.[10]

For sure, all Chinese cities had their own streets (*jie*) and laneways (*xiang*), forming a road system. However, *jie* and *xiang* cannot be compared with *malu* in quality, orderliness, and convenience. So, changing Chinese *jie* and *xiang* into western *malu* was then the beginning of transforming Chinese cities to reduce the gap with the western model and to change the face of the city. This was the starting point for modern urban planning and building in China. The opening of the cities and ports for development was actually a process of widening and extending the old streets into modern *malu*, and further into a network of these modern roads. From a line to a net of lines, and further into a system of nets of lines, consciously or unconsciously, the Chinese gradually developed their own practice of modern urban planning and construction.[11]

Due to the destruction of wars and a fire in 1911, one-fifth of the buildings of Hankou were burned down. To rebuild the city was urgently needed; this was a good opportunity for a new and well-ordered city similar to the Concessions to be planned and constructed. In 1912, based on street plans of Paris and London, Hankou Construction Corporation proposed a Hankou Town Plan (excluding the Concessions), which included as many as 306 streets and avenues in a radial and grid plan, displaying a spatial vision that was excessive and idealistic (Figure 18.2).[12]

Due to existing conditions, private land ownership, and protests from the local population, however, the 1912 plan remained a dream on paper. The authorities had to make an alternative plan, this time based more closely on the roads and patterns of the existing city. In this plan, the city was divided into several districts; major roads were widened, some streets and laneways were made straight, and new ones were opened for connection, creating a new pattern of modern roads with horizontal ones parallel to the river and vertical ones perpendicular to the riverbank (Figure 18.3). In dividing the urban blocks, western formal blocks and Chinese streets and lanes were combined, creating a hybrid spatial morphology of "avenues/blocks outside and streets/lanes inside" (*wai jiekuo nei jiexiang*). As this plan took serious consideration of the existing condition and organized traffic routes well, it was quickly realized, and shaped the old areas of Hankou that we see today.[13]

Because of the opening of Beijing–Hankou Railway Line in 1905, the destruction of city walls (of 1864) in 1907, and the building of a ring road on the foundation of the walls, a new urban area between the old city and the railway line became active and prosperous. The population increased, land prices soared, and new plans were made to develop further along the rail

Figure 18.2   Map for building streets for the complete town of Hankou (1912).

Source: Hankou Construction Corporation, 1912.

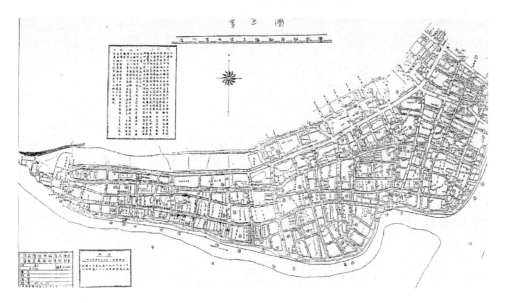

Figure 18.3 Planning for major modern roads in the old town of Hankou (1930).

Source: Hankou Municipal Government, Attached map, in *Hankou Shi Jianshe Gaikuang* (1930), no pagination.

line. According to the 1916 New Hankou Plan, to the north of the railway line and in the northwest of the city, there should be 5 roads parallel and 15 perpendicular to the rail line, to form a new city district (Figure 18.4). Unfortunately, due to a shortage of funding and division by the rail line, this plan was still not realized by 1938 (when war broke out and Japanese forces sacked the city).[14]

In fact, from 1911 when the fire broke out to the early 1930s, Hankou developed quickly and experienced an economic boom; the property market was very active, and a special urban residential typology, the *lifen* house, emerged and spread quickly.[15]

As is well known, after the Opium War (1840–50s), western ideas and practices entered China at full scale, and, as western culture spread widely, China entered a process of transformation from agricultural to industrial civilization. A new architectural system, different from the local tradition, arrived in China and settled in Shanghai first, the earliest port in opening up; the traditional system of building and living was challenged, and threatened, accordingly. Because of population density, urban land scarcity, and the needs of modern urban living, a property market emerged and houses became a commodity. With this, a new type of urban residential architecture, one that extended the old tradition and its living patterns and spaces but also incorporated modern city living and its residential forms – that is, the well-known *lilong* house – emerged in Shanghai.

This new urban housing typology had absorbed traditional Chinese layout and inside–outside integration, including a genre of traditional residential culture, and had also adopted western collectivity in construction and an emphasis on the look of the outside. It facilitated a transformation from rural to urban and from traditional to modern in the making of a new residential form. The process embodied ideas and practices of "east–west synthesis" and of "Chinese learning for essence and western learning for utility," as proposed then in early modern China.

Figure 18.4   City map of Hankou (1916).

Source: Hankou Municipal Government, 1916.

If the formation of modernity in the west was a process of differentiation, then the process in China was that of transforming and absorbing under the influence of western culture. Modern housing culture in China was also formed in this manner. The *lilong* housing of Shanghai, the *lifen* housing in Hankou, and the *liyuan* houses in Qingdao, among others, all manifested – in general layout, formal image, planning, and spatial organization – a strong foreign influence as well as a continuation of the local tradition; the names also reflected even different local traditions in China.

Compared with the *lilong* housing of Shanghai, the *lifen* housing in Hankou revealed a stronger local character. In the overall layout, modern roads defined an urban block in the western sense; within the block, streets and laneways of the local Hankou tradition dominated where, regardless of orientation and ceremonial prescription, front gates of the houses faced each other on the two sides of a main laneway, while rear gates also faced each other on the two sides of a small laneway, maintaining a special urban pattern of large and small laneways in alternation. In the hot summer, the main laneways were used for traffic in daytime and for chatting, relaxing, and enjoying the breeze in the evening. Within each house, there was a symmetrical plan, three bays across and several layers of space in depth, with a courtyard in the middle. The seamless integration of urban and architectural, external and internal, and natural and artificial spaces adapted well to the local climate, characterized with hot summer and cold winter; the integration also expressed a Chinese spatiality where space flows between "dark, grey and white" areas. On the outside, especially for the main gate, western styles and decorations were applied, emphasizing visual effects and a look of the new (Figure 18.5).[16]

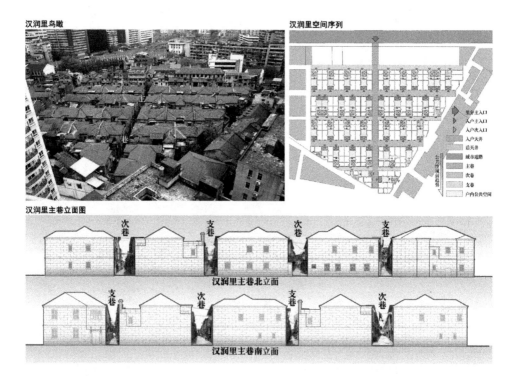

Figure 18.5 The *Lifen* housing in Hankou: the case of Hanrenli (1917–19).

Source: © Li Baihao.

Building Greater Wuhan

Wuhan was never a city; it was instead a composition of Hanyang County, Wuchang Prefecture City, and Hankou Town, at the point where the small Han River joined the mighty Yangtze River. Here, Hanyang had the longest history; Wuchang was the seat of government of two provinces, that is, for the Governor General of Hubei and Hunan (*huguang zongdu*); both Hanyang and Wuchang had political and military importance. Hankou, by contrast, was young and a market town. However, due to swift development at the turn of the twentieth century, it quickly transformed itself into an international metropolis and was referred to as "Greater Hankou," providing a basis for Greater Wuhan to arrive.

Before the war (of resistance against Japan, part of the Pacific War) ended in 1945, there were already several plans for the three cities to be considered together, and most of them were based around Hankou as the center. Earlier, in 1929, there was also a Wuhan Special Municipality Urban Construction Outline that proposed to connect the three towns together, although it was suspended due the short life of Wuhan as a Special Municipality. In any case, the attempt to plan Hanyang, Wuchang, and Hankou together never stopped over these years.

Late in the war (1938–45), when victory was clearly in sight, the Chinese Republican Government began to prepare post-war recovery actively. As a political, economic, and cultural hub of the nation, Wuhan was a major focus. In this period, the planning documents for the Wuhan Region (led by Wu Shilin, Zhu Jieping, and Bao Ding) presented not only a spatial organization of Greater Wuhan but also a "regional planning" exercise, the first in modern China's urban planning history.

In July 1945, before the three towns were officially joined, Hubei Provincial Government established an urban and civil construction team, to work on the construction plan of Greater Wuhan; they issued a document titled "Outline of the Plan for Greater Wuhan" and proposed a planning at three scales: urban core areas (composed of the three towns), Greater Wuhan City (60 km in north–south and east–west dimensions), and Wuhan Region (about 12,000 km²). In spatial terms, it included not only Wuchang, Hanyang, and Hankou but also neighboring towns such as Huangpi, Echeng, and Huanggang.[17]

The document included these key words: greater Wuhan, region for construction, regional planning, railway line across the Yangtze River, tunnels under the river, redistribution of land, decentralization plan, green belt, multi-focal plan, and concerted managing over flooding and water course. They revealed a set of focuses and an array of targets for spatial reorganization. It is well known that the Republican Government had already issued urban planning law and had asked every city government to establish an urban planning committee to propose city planning schemes. Yet, Wuhan's effort was not limited by the phrase "urban planning"; instead, based on the situation of the three towns still separated and the development tendencies of the place, the authority introduced the idea of "regional planning" – which was innovative and pioneering indeed in China's planning history.[18]

In December 1945, Wuhan Regional Planning Committee issued "Outline for the Execution of Wuhan Regional Planning." In April 1946, the committee produced a preliminary study for Wuhan regional planning. In August 1947, "Outline for Land Use and Transportation for the Three Towns of Wuhan" was issued by the committee. These three documents as crucial studies together shaped the Greater Wuhan plan. This plan defined Wuhan's future as one of the "modern industrialized metropolises"; it emphasized constructing harbors, to allow ships to dock at Wuhan, and to put Wuhan and Shanghai together as "Two Cities of the Sea" (*haishang shuangcheng*). It stipulated that a "satellite city of heavy industry" be built in the Qingshan area downstream; it prescribed that, based on history, the cities of Wuhan be developed with "individuality," making Wuchang, Hankou, and Hanyang respectively a "political–cultural city," an "industrial–commercial city," and a "garden–residential city." The plan also asked that green belts be built around urban centers, to limit the continuation of urban building.[19]

At the end of 1947, civil war (between Republican and Communist forces) escalated; the authority could no longer afford to work on the planning, and so the Wuhan regional planning exercise came to an end.

On 24 May 1949, Wuhan Municipality Government of the People's Republic of China was established. By then, a Greater Wuhan had already arrived in reality.

Notes

1 Pi Mingxiu, *Jindai Wuhan Chengshi Shi* (An Urban History of Early Modern Wuhan) (Beijing: Zhongguo Shehui Kexue Chubanshe, 1993), 6–9.
2 Liu Xianting, *Guangyang Zaji* (Notes by Guangyang), commented and checked by Wang Beiping and Xia Zhihe (Beijing: Zhonghua Shuju Chubanshe, 1957), 193.
3 Wang Gang, "Jiedao de xingcheng: 1861 nian yiqian Hankou jiedao lishi xing kaocha (Formation of Streets: A Historical Study on Street Patterns of pre-1861 Hankou)," *Xin Jianzhu* (New Architecture), no. 4 (2010): 122–128.
4 Luo Weilian (William T. Rowe), *Hankou: Yige Zhongguo Chengshi de Chongtu he Shequ (1796–1895)* (Hankou: Conflict and Community in a Chinese City, 1796–1895), trans. Lu Xiqi and Luo Dufang, proofed by Ma Zhao and Xiao Zhizhi (Beijing: Zhongguo Renmin Daxue Chubanshe, 2008), 94–106.
5 Tu Wenxue, *Wenhua Hankou* (The Culture of Hankou) (Wuhan: Wuhan Chubanshe, 2006), 79–90.
6 Tu Wenxue, "'Hubei Xin Zheng' yu jindai Wuhan de jueqi (the New Policy of Hubei and the Rise of Early Modern Wuhan)," *Jianghan Daxue Xeubao (shehuikexue ban)* (Journal of Jianghan University, Social Science Edition) 27, no. 1 (2010): 71–77.
7 Qiu Zhizhong, "Jianguo bi xian jianshi lun (On Developing the Nation by Developing the Cities)," *Shizheng pinglun* (Municipality Review), no. 8 (1948): 13–40.
8 Weng Youwei and Zhang Xuewu, *Jindai Xifang Shizhi de Yinru yu Jindai Zhongguo Chengshi Zhidu de Zhuanxing, Jindai Chengshi Fazhan yu Shehui Zhuanxing – Shanghai Dangan Shiliao Yanjiu, di si ji* (The Importing of Early Modern Western Municipal System and the Transformation of the Municipal System in Early Modern China, Early Modern Development and Social Transformation – Historical Research Based on the Shanghai Archive, Issue 4), compiled by Shanghai Dangan Guan (Shanghai Archive Museum) (Shanghai: Shanghai Sanlian Shudian, 2008), 3–17.
9 Pi Mingxiu, *Wuhan Tongshi: Wan Qing Juan (xia)* (General History of Wuhan: Volume on Late Qing dynasty, part II) (Wuhan: Wuhan Chubanshe, 2005), 17; see also Jianghan Daxue Chengshi Yanjiusuo and Wuhanshi Bowuguan, *Tushuo Wuhan Chengshi Shi* (an illustrated history of Wuhan) (Wuhan: Wuhan Chubanshe, 2010), 256–265.
10 Shao Xianchong, *Jindai Zhongguo de Xinshi Jiaotong* (New Urban Transportation Systems in Early Modern China) (Beijing: Renmin Wenxue Chubanshe, 2006), 64.
11 Li Baihao and Guo Jian, *Zhongguo Jindai Chengshi Guihua yu Wenhua* (Planning and Culture of Cities in Early Modern China) (Wuhan: Hubei Jiaoyu Chubanshe, 2008), 19–21.
12 Wu Zhilin, Hu Yidong and Wang Xie, *Wuhan Bainian Guihua Tuji* (An Illustrated History of Urban Planning for Wuhan Over a Century) (Beijing: Zhongguo Jianzhu Gongye Chubanshe, 2009), 41–42.
13 Li Baihao, Xue Chunying and Wang Xibo, "Tuxi Wuhan Jindai Chengshi Guihua, 1861–1949 (Graphic Analysis on the Early Modern Planning Schemes of Wuhan, 1861–1949)," *Chengshi Guihua Huikan* (Urban Planning Papers), no. 6 (2002): 23–28.
14 Su Yunfeng, *Zhongguo Xiandaihua de Quyu Yanjiu 1860–1916: Hubei Sheng* (Regional Studies in China's Modernization 1860–1916: Hubei Province) (Taipei: Zhongyang Yanjiu Yuan Jindaishi Yanjiusuo, 1987), 524.
15 Xu Yusu and Li Baihao, *Wuhan Jindai Lifen Jianzhu* (The *Lifen* Architecture in Early Modern Wuhan) (Wuhan: Wuhan Ligong Daxue Chubanshe, 2017).
16 Li Baihao, Xu Yusu and Wu Ling, "Wuhan Jindai Lifen Zhuzhai Fazhan, Leixing jiqi Tezheng Yanjiu (Development, Typology and Characteristics of the *Lifen* Housing Architecture of Early Modern

Wuhan: An Inquiry)," *Huazhong Jianzhu* (Huazhong Architecture), no. 3 (2000): 116–117 and no. 4 (2000): 103–105.

17 Li Baihao and Guo Ming, "Zhu Jieping yu Zhongguo Jindai Shouci Quyu Guihua Shijian (Zhu Jieping and the First Regional Planning in Early Modern China)," *Chengshi Guihua Xuekan* (Journal of Urban Planning), no. 3 (2010): 105–111.

18 Li and Guo, "Zhu Jieping," 105–111.

19 Li and Guo, "Zhu Jieping," 105–111; and Wu, Hu and Wang, *Wuhan Bainian Guihua Tuji*, 60–65.

Bibliography

Editorial Committee. *Wuhan Lishi Dituji* (Historical Maps of Wuhan). Beijing: Zhongguo Ditu Chubanshe, 1998.

Jianghan Daxue Chengshi Yanjiusuo and Wuhanshi Bowuguan. *Tushuo Wuhan Chengshi Shi* (An Illustrated History of Wuhan). Wuhan: Wuhan Chubanshe, 2010.

Li Baihao, Xue Chunying and Wang Xibo. "Tuxi Wuhan Jindai Chengshi Guihua, 1861–1949 (Graphic Analysis on the Early Modern Planning Schemes of Wuhan, 1861–1949)." *Chengshi Guihua Huikan* (Urban Planning Papers), no. 6 (2002): 23–28.

Li Baihao and Guo Jian. *Zhongguo Jindai Chengshi Guihua yu Wenhua* (Planning and Culture of Cities in Early Modern China). Wuhan: Hubei Jiaoyu Chubanshe, 2008.

Li Baihao and Guo Ming. "Zhu Jieping yu Zhongguo Jindai Shouci Quyu Guihua Shijian (Zhu Jieping and the First Regional Planning in Early Modern China)." *Chengshi Guihua Xuekan* (Journal of Urban Planning), no. 3 (2010): 105–111.

Li Baihao, Xu Yusu and Wu Ling. "Wuhan Jindai Lifen Zhuzhai Fazhan, Leixing jiqi Tezheng Yanjiu (Development, Typology and Characteristics of the *Lifen* Housing Architecture of Early Modern Wuhan: An Inquiry)." *Huazhong Jianzhu* (Huazhong Architecture), no. 3 (2000): 116–117 and no. 4 (2000): 103–105.

Liu Xianting. *Guangyang Zaji* (Notes by Guangyang). Commented and checked by Wang Beiping and Xia Zhihe. Beijing: Zhonghua Shuju Chubanshe, 1957.

Luo Weilian (William T. Rowe). *Hankou: Yige Zhongguo Chengshi de Chongtu he Shequ (1796–1895)* (Hankou: Conflict and Community in a Chinese City, 1796–1895). Translated by Lu Xiqi and Luo Dufang, proofed by Ma Zhao and Xiao Zhizhi. Beijing: Zhongguo Renmin Daxue Chubanshe, 2008.

Pi Mingxiu. *Jindai Wuhan Chengshi Shi* (An Urban History of Early Modern Wuhan). Beijing: Zhongguo Shehui Kexue Chubanshe, 1993.

———. *Wuhan Tongshi: Wan Qing Juan (xia)* (General History of Wuhan: Volume on Late Qing Dynasty, Part II). Wuhan: Wuhan Chubanshe, 2005.

Qiu Zhizhong. "Jianguo bi xian jianshi lun (On Developing the Nation by Developing the Cities)." *Shizheng pinglun* (Municipality Review), no. 8 (1948): 13–40.

Rowe, William T. *Hankow, Conflict and Community in a Chinese City, 1796–1895*. Stanford: Stanford University Press, 1989.

Shao Xianchong. *Jindai Zhongguo de Xinshi Jiaotong* (New Urban Transportation Systems in Early Modern China). Beijing: Renmin Wenxue Chubanshe, 2006.

Su Yunfeng. *Zhongguo Xiandaihua de Quyu Yanjiu 1860–1916: Hubei Sheng* (Regional Studies in China's Modernization 1860–1916: Hubei Province). Taipei: Zhongyang Yanjiu Yuan Jindaishi Yanjiusuo, 1987.

Tu Wenxue. *Wenhua Hankou* (The Culture of Hankou). Wuhan: Wuhan Chubanshe, 2006.

———. "'Hubei Xin Zheng' yu jindai Wuhan de jueqi (The New Policy of Hubei and the Rise of Early Modern Wuhan)." *Jianghan Daxue Xeubao (shehuikexue ban)* (Journal of Jianghan University, Social Science ed.) 27, no. 1 (2010): 71–77.

Wang Gang. "Jiedao de xingcheng: 1861 nian yiqian Hankou jiedao lishi xing kaocha (Formation of Streets: A Historical Study on Street Patterns of Pre-1861 Hankou)." *Xin Jianzhu* (New Architecture), no. 4 (2010): 122–128.

Weng Youwei and Zhang Xuewu. *Jindai Xifang Shizhi de Yinru yu Jindai Zhongguo Chengshi Zhidu de Zhuanxing, Jindai Chengshi Fazhan yu Shehui Zhuanxing – Shanghai Dangan Shiliao Yanjiu, di si ji* (The Importing of Early Modern Western Municipal System and the Transformation of the Municipal System in Early Modern China, Early Modern Development and Social Transformation – Historical

Research Based on the Shanghai Archive, Issue 4). Compiled by Shanghai Dangan Guan (Shanghai Archive Museum). Shanghai: Shanghai Sanlian Shudian, 2008.

Wu Zhilin, Hu Yidong and Wang Xie. *Wuhan Bainian Guihua Tuji* (An Illustrated History of Urban Planning for Wuhan Over a Century). Beijing: Zhongguo Jianzhu Gongye Chubanshe, 2009.

Xu Yusu and Li Baihao. *Wuhan Jindai Lifen Jianzhu* (The *Lifen* Architecture in Early Modern Wuhan). Wuhan: Wuhan Ligong Daxue Chubanshe, 2017.

Glossary

Bao Ding	鲍鼎
Beijing	北京
beiyang zhengfu	北洋政府
cheng zhen xiang difang zizhi	城镇乡地方自治
cheng	城
Chongqing	重庆
dayitong jianguo	大一统建国
difang zizhi	地方自治
ducheng	都城
Echeng	鄂城
Foshan	佛山
fucheng	府城
Guangyang Zaji	广阳杂记
Guangzhou	广州
guojia	国家
guomin zhengfu	国民政府
haishang shuangcheng	海上双城
Hangzhou	杭州
Hankou	汉口
Hanyang	汉阳
Huanggang	黄冈
Huangpi	黄陂
Hubei	湖北
huguang zongdu	湖广总督
Hunan	湖南
Jiangsu (Province)	江苏（省）
Jiangsu Sheng Shi Xiang Zhi	江苏省市乡制
jie	街
jiuzhou	九州
Liang Qichao	梁启超
lifen	里分
lilong	里弄
Liu Wendao	刘文岛
Liu Xianting	刘献廷
liyuan	里院
malu	马路
Ming (dynasty)	明（朝）
Nanjing	南京
Qin (dynasty)	秦 （朝）

Qing (dynasty)	清（朝）
Qingdao	青岛
Shanghai	上海
shengcheng	省城
shizhi	市制
shi	市
Song (dynasty)	宋（朝）
Suzhou	苏州
tianxia	天下
wai jiekuo nei jiexiang	外街廓内街巷
Wu Shilin	吴时霖
Wuchang	武昌
xiancheng	县城
xiang	乡
xiang	巷
xingshi yi da xingguo	兴市以达兴国
xingzheng yuan	行政院
yuzhou	宇宙
Zhang Zhidong	张之洞
zhen	镇
zhoucheng	州城
Zhu Jieping	朱皆平

19

MODERN EDUTAINMENT SPACE

Public Parks in Early Twentieth-Century China

Zhang Tianjie

In the increasing encounter between Chinese and Western civilizations since the nineteenth century, public parks emerged in modern Chinese cities as a new kind of public space. For China, the concept of public park (*gongyuan*), where common people can go for relaxation and recreation, is Western and modern.[1] Linguistically, although the Chinese characters *gongyuan* had existed in the classical Chinese lexicon, they actually referred to official gardens or land owned by the emperor, something quite different from the Western notion of the park as a public space. The term *gongyuan* was a "return graphic loan word," which refers to classical Chinese-character compounds that were used by the Japanese to translate modern European words and were reintroduced into modern Chinese.[2] A *gongyuan* with the Western concept of a public park, then, became very different from *yuanlin* (garden groves), a term used in both classical and modern Chinese. Historically, especially in Ming and Qing China, gardens groves were private or imperial ventures for the enjoyment of the owners and their invited guests and represented a highly Confucian version of conspicuous consumption among the literati.[3] While *yuanlin* meant imperial or private preserves, *gongyuan* implied public ownership and public access.

Background: Park Movement Worldwide Since the Nineteenth Century

Public parks were first promoted in industrializing Europe during the mid-nineteenth century. The construction of a public park, useful landscape within the town for the use and enjoyment of the larger public, was essentially a Victorian idea, as a response to problems of sanitation and urban growth in Britain, the forefront of the Industrial Revolution.[4] The benefits of parks were identified in physical, moral, spiritual, and political terms: parks would be the lungs for the city to refresh the air; they would improve people's health and provide places for exercises; they would be an alternative form of recreation to the tavern; and they would provide beneficial contact with nature, so elevating the spirit.[5] Besides Britain, around 1853 Napoleon III and Baron Haussmann undertook the transformation of the Bois de Boulogne and further proposed a Paris municipal park system, an unprecedented network of vast woodland reserves, large urban parks, and planted squares.[6] For French parks and gardens, the influence of mid-nineteenth-century English parks was discernable and the results of this influence in turn became influential in England.[7] And America followed suit. Inspired by Birkenhead Park in Manchester, Britain,

DOI: 10.4324/9781315851112-28

Frederick Law Olmsted and Calvert Vaux began laying out New York's Central Park in 1858. Moreover, they advanced a public park movement and further innovations of urban planning sweeping the whole of America.

The idea of building public parks also spread to Asia. After the Meiji Restoration, Japan gradually incorporated the Western concept of the public park in Meiji town and city planning and promoted public parks as a kind of place for displaying modern civilization and civility. In Tokyo, for instance, Ueno Park was established in 1873, and four more public parks were opened in the coming years, offering both recreational and educational facilities for people's enjoyment.[8] At the western edge of Asia, Turkish cities also acquired similar public spaces and urban infrastructures in the 1930s, such as Youth Park in Ankara, Kültür Park in Izmir, etc. With their pools, landscaping, casinos, tea gardens, and zoos, these parks became truly popular spaces for people from all ages, classes, and genders.[9] In general, public parks were created as an antidote to the intrinsic drawbacks of urban life.[10] Ideals of solace, escape, freedom, gregarious and relaxed pleasure, health, wholesome exercise, aesthetic culture, moral uplift, social democracy, and communion with nature all commingled in their vision.

Emergence of Public Parks in Chinese Cities

In China, precursors of public parks were built in the foreign concessions since late nineteenth century. For instance, Public Garden was opened in 1868 along the Bund in Shanghai's International settlement. It was considered the first Western-style public park in China. Covering an area of nearly 2 hm², this picturesque park embraced broad lawns and woods, long fence planting, regular beddings and pools, and a steel bandstand imported from Britain. With the development of the foreign concessions in Shanghai, Tianjin, Hankou, and other treaty ports, considerable exotic parks were laid out in various styles, such as British picturesque, French formal, Italian classic, etc. Besides the horticulture parts, in these parks there were also athletic fields for lawn tennis, green bowl, football, and other Western exercises. Open for recreation, relaxation, and fun, however, these parks usually excluded the Chinese from the beginning. These public parks, green, open, and civilized, provided challenges and in the meantime paradigms for China's own park construction.

Since the late decades of nineteenth century, some private Chinese gardens started to open for public entertainment. For example, some traditional literati gardens in Shanghai, like Shen Yuan, Xi Yuan, Zhang Yuan, and Xu Yuan, were changed to commercial open spaces blending Western and Chinese landscape components. Constructed by retired gentry-officials or modern compradors, they became popular scenic retreats and gathering sites from urban bustles.[11] These mixed-style gardens featured a couple of multistoried buildings, imported several electrical leisure facilities, and primarily catered to commercial recreation activities. Physically, they resembled traditional Chinese gardens with pavilions and lily ponds, without much of the open space characteristic of Western parks. They without exception charged a considerable admission fee, thus rejecting a large amount of the urban poor.

In the early decades of the twentieth century, after China's 1911 Revolution, public parks were promoted by the governmental authorities as a part of the reformist efforts to remake Chinese cities. In Beijing (Peking), the sacred Altar of Earth and Grain (*Shejitan*) was transformed into Central Park by the Municipal Council in 1914. A sequence of imperial altars and gardens was also opened successively to the public, for example, the Altar of Agriculture (*Xiannongtan*) in 1917, the Altar of Heaven (*Tiantan*) in 1918, and the North Sea (*Beihai*) and the Earth Altar (*Ditan*) in 1925. The traditional imperial hierarchy of space was broken down.[12] Guangzhou (Canton), the early Nationalist base, was also the seedbed of the city administration movement in the early 1920s, thanks to the support of Sun Ke (Sun Fo), Sun Yat-sen's son. During his mayorship, a series of public parks was established, and elements of "scientific" planning were introduced, emphasizing not only technological change but also social and cultural changes.[13] With the completion of Sun Yat-sen Mausoleum in Nanjing, the whole Purple Mountain was turned into the Sun Yat-sen Memorial Park in 1929. It was configured as a cultural center for the national capital, closely intertwined with Sun and Guomindang ideology.[14] In the provincial capital of Sichuan, Chengdu, Yang Sen (1884–1977), a military leader who fought his way into procession of the city in 1923, expanded Shaocheng Park with public athletic grounds and a Popular Education Institute (*Tongsu jiaoyuguan*), and devoted funds to the construction of Central Park.[15] In Wuhan, Shouyi Park was opened without an entrance fee at the foot of Snake Hill in 1924, commemorating the 1911 Revolution, and Zhongshan Park started in 1929 in honor of Sun Yat-sen as the founding father of the Chinese Republic.[16] There were more public parks in other cities: for instance, Xishan Park in Wanxian (Sichuan), Central Park in Chongqing, Zhongshan Park in Xiamen, and so on.[17] These public parks emerged mostly in treaty ports or cities with foreign enclaves, where the alien autonomy, together with the order and progress presented in the concessions, provided a challenge and a model for Chinese reformers' modernizing agenda.[18]

The newly built public parks in China began to depart from traditional Chinese gardens, although some of them were restructured from former imperial or private gardens and certain previous components remained. Usually, a traditional Chinese garden is considered as a landscape painting in three dimensions, or an artistic recreation of nature. It is composed of trees, rockeries, a pond or lake, zigzagging footpaths, winding corridors, bridges, and other garden structures for habitation, quiet viewing, and merrymaking. The elements are arranged in such a way that they are often more artistically designed than nature itself.[19] In comparison, the newly established parks used Western counterparts as a primary reference, employing the formal, symmetrical arrangement of the plan (both in its major outlines and in the patterned details of garden bedding and parterres), the artificial manipulation of water in fountains, the extensive use of grass in lawns, the sound disposal of various sports fields, and other exogenous skills. In essence, novel, civilian, open, and available for public use, these public parks stood in sharp contrast to the complex symbolism, literary elegance, and poetic meaning of private gardens, or the grandiose splendor of their imperial counterparts.

Along with the rise of Chinese public parks, local gazettes and magazines in some cities began to publish articles introducing public parks in New York, London, Paris, Tokyo, and other foreign cities. As early as 1914, *Beijing shizheng tongbao* carried an editorial that advocated public parks as one good way to help reform an unhealthy society.[20] In *Dongfang zazhi* (Eastern Miscellany), parks were juxtaposed as typical public architecture, along with municipal offices, lecture halls, schools, and churches.[21] And *Xin Hankou* in 1931 issued a timely translation of Clarence L. Brock's commentary, namely, "Developments and Values of Urban Park System in America – from 1909 to 1930."[22] These essays aimed at promoting the public's awareness of and desires for public parks.

In addition, a certain number of monographs on modern urban parks came out to offer professional knowledge. *Park* (gongyuan), a booklet written by Tong Yuming (1897–?), was published by Commercial Press in 1928 as Universal Library (wanyou wenku), No. 165.[23] Based on a French book *Promendes Parcs et jardins Publics*, Gu Zaiyan and Lu Danlin published *Zuixin gongyuan jianzhu fa* (Building Methods of Recent Public Parks) in 1928, inducting the site locating and construction of public parks in urban areas.[24] Referring to a great deal of material in Chinese, Japanese and English, Chen Zhi (1899–1989), a key figure in Chinese gardening, accomplished *Dushi gongyuan lun* (Cities and Parks) as Municipal Series (*shizheng congshu*) in 1930 and *Zaoyuanxue gailun* (Introduction to Gardening) as University Series (*Daxue congshu*) in 1935. Meanwhile, led by Chen Zhi, Zhang Shouyu (1897–1985), and Cheng Shifu (1907–1988) in the 1920s, modern gardening entered the curriculums of National Central University, University of Nanking, and National Zhejiang University. The year of 1928 saw the foundation of the Chinese Gardening Academy (*Zhongguo zaoyuan xuehui*).[25] These works enriched the knowledge of modern gardening and reinforced the momentum for Chinese park development.

Case Studies: Public Open Space for Education and Entertainment

In early twentieth-century China, vigorous park construction was deeply rooted in the profound challenge of China's nationhood from an empire to a republic. From the perspective of the republican government, public parks were generally regarded as an outward symbol for republican egalitarianism. Indeed, before the twentieth century, imperial urban planning usually offered abundant recreational space for the ruling class, but the needs of ordinary city residents were generally neglected. Folk-fairs held in Buddhist or Taoist temples or other places of worship were popular, combining cultural, commercial, social, and recreational functions. But they occurred only unfrequently and lacked natural settings. A few scenic places in suburbs were either inconvenient or lacked the necessary facilities. Without decent places for recreation and entertainment, many men were driven to seek pleasure in alcohol, gambling, and prostitution.[26] In a sharp contrast, the new public parks were promoted for not just the privileged few but for everyone; they belonged to a sort of public property, so that everyone had a right to perceive and enjoy. Through creating parks for the ordinary public, the republican government could demonstrate its resolve to break with China's imperial past and show its concern for people's welfare. Moreover, these parks were suitable public spaces to house educational facilities, athletic fields, and memorial structures, and to perform new rituals. They introduced new civility and urbanity and in the meantime inculcated the republican ideology.

Among these newly established public parks, some had been transformed from former imperial or private gardens. The physical plans and components of previous grounds were partly reshaped and partly preserved. Central Park in Capital Beijing was one of the earliest and most important cases. On National Day, October 10, 1914, the sacred Altar of Earth and Grain in Beijing was opened as Central Park, illustrating the care for the ordinary public as part of the new republican political culture. This unprecedented project was led by Zhu Qiqian (1872–1964),[27] a key political figure in the late Qing and early Republican era. He was also a pioneer incorporating the revival of Chinese building culture into his political and cultural practice between the 1900s and 1930s. He initiated a range of urban projects in order to modernize Beijing as a model city embodying republican ideologies and representing a national image. The transformation of the Altar of Earth and Grain to Central Park was regarded as one of his most successful. He once said, the objective of Central Park was "to work for the public's health, promote respectable entertainment, and maintain upstanding social customs."[28]

Zhu intentionally secularized the space, occasion, and event and changed the old ritual function and meaning. The original Altar (Figure 19.1) was made up of an inner altar and an outer altar. At the very center of the inner altar was a square, two-story, open platform for ritual performances. The configuration of the altar complex was closely related to the ceremonial procession route. When reopened as Central Park (Figure 19.2), the complex's gates, boundaries, routes, and landscape were consciously modified to meet the new functions. A new gate was opened to the south of the outer altar, so that people could easily access the Park via the newly paved Chang'an Avenue. A second gate was added later in the northwest corner, offering

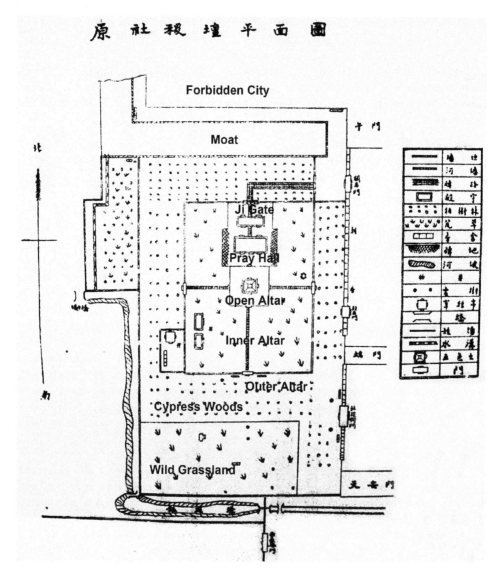

Figure 19.1 Plan of the Altar of Earth and Grain in Beijing of late Qing dynasty.

Source: Zhongyang Gongyuan Weiyuanhui, ed. *Zhongyang Gongyuan Ershiwu Zhounian Jiniance* (Commemorative album of Central Park for its 25th anniversary) (Peking: Zhongyang Gongyuan Shiwusuo, 1939), 9.

a shortcut to the museum inside the Forbidden City. The imperial relics, which were previously exclusive, were opened for everyone. The magnificent altar and palaces were preserved to inspire emotions and sensitivities of new citizens.[29] Major buildings in the inner altar were devoted to practical needs. The great hall, which once kept musical instruments for palace ceremonies, now held funeral services for the Nationalist Party leader Sun Yat-sen and other modern patriots. The smaller hall, previously the emperor's robing room, became a public library. Seven new buildings were constructed alongside the library to host exhibitions on modern themes like public hygiene, model prison, etc.[30]

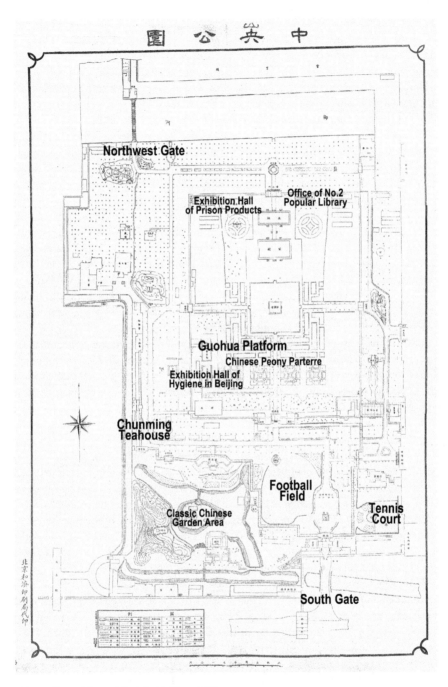

Figure 19.2   Plan of Central Park in Beijing, 1928.

Source: Beijing Municipal Government, 1928.

During the renovation, the Altar's previous imperial landscape was firstly considered as an example of cultural heritage. Nationalist sensitivity was created through its cultural implications and composition. Twenty-six planter boxes of flower beds, named the Guohua Platform, were installed in the inner altar in 1915. In an abstract geometrical form, the flowers in blossom were intentionally used to naturalize the previous rigid imperial space. Peonies, once a traditional symbol of royal power and now the national flower, were predominantly planted. They were placed along the central axis, emphasizing the centrality of the open altar. The patterns, derived from traditional decorative motifs, were employed to increase the enjoyment of the park-goers. In addition, a classic Chinese garden with artificial hill and pond was introduced at the left corner of the outer altar, so as to showcase national essence (*guocui*). Around the historical cypress woods, pavilions and buildings were reused or added for resting, entertaining, dining, and, in the meantime, appreciating the natural and cultural value of the ancient trees. In general, through recycling the traditional space and landscape, Central Park created a cultural connection between the traditional and the modern.[31]

In addition to sustaining the tradition, some other parks started to follow Western-inspired geometric planning or to combine formal and traditional Chinese garden design. For instance, Zhongshan Park in Hankou[32] started commemorating Sun Yat-sen from 1928 as the founding father of the Chinese Republic. It was an exemplary project of top priority in Hankou's urban reconstruction and the largest urban park along the Yangtze valley at that time. Based on the previous 1.3 ha of Xi Yuan, a private garden of Li Huatang, Zhongshan Park was enlarged to 12.5 ha in 1934 (Figure 19.3) and consisted of an artificial lake, old Xi Yuan, a formal garden, and various sports fields that held a number of athletic meetings.

Although it was restructured from a former private garden Xi Yuan and some previous components remained, such as rockeries, Hankou's Zhongshan Park took Western public parks as its primary design reference. Considerable exogenous skills were employed, such as the sound disposal of various sports fields, the formal, symmetrical arrangement of the plan (in its formal garden part), the artificial manipulation of water in fountains, and so on. It was also furnished with modern facilities like a meteorological observatory, nursery, library, museum, and public lavatories.[33] The park was free of charge to all visitors and fostered active recreation for young and old, men and women from all sections of society. The duo emphasis of "public" and "sports" clearly visible in public parks in Europe and America was unmistakably manifested here.[34] It was an embodiment of the concept of a new life.[35] After its opening, Zhongshan Park became a favorite site of local residents and tourists. It had to enlarge its gate due to overcrowded visitors.[36] When inspecting Hankou in 1930, Jiang Zuobin, the Secretary of the Interior of Nanjing Government, was deeply impressed. He said: "I have been to European countries and Japan, but have never visited parks as wonderful as Hankou's Zhongshan Park. As soon as I return to Nanjing, I will order all other cities to learn from Hankou to build parks . . ."[37]

Hankou's Zhongshan Park was mainly designed by Wu Guobing (1898–1989), a competent Western-trained engineer in Hankou's Public Works Bureau. With professional training on civil and mechanical engineering, and also ideas of contemporary Western modernity, Wu proposed creating a public park as a first step toward that modernity, in order to transform the listless residents. When designing Hankou's Zhongshan Park, he relied heavily on the Western public parks he had experienced firsthand. The overall layout juxtaposed the ornamental gardens with playing fields, showing a similar division of grounds as in London's parks in the early twentieth century. The horticultural parts in Zhongshan Park, especially the Lake Area and the Formal Garden, borrowed the same picturesque style as the contemporary British parks. In Hankou's Zhongshan Park, some familiar elements in British parks appeared, such as the grand fountain, the bandstand, Sigu Xuan, and Zhanggong Pavilion, while some favorite activities in Britain,

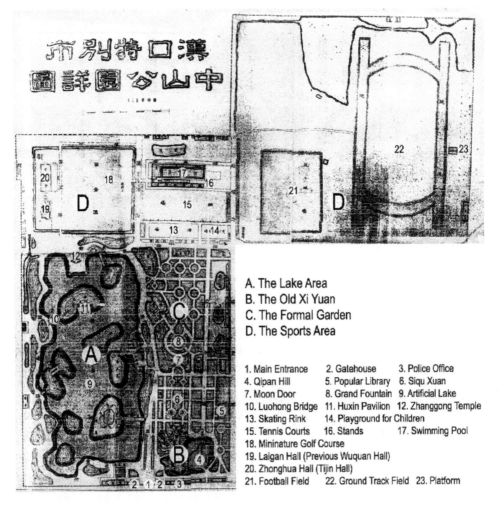

A. The Lake Area
B. The Old Xi Yuan
C. The Formal Garden
D. The Sports Area

1. Main Entrance   2. Gatehouse   3. Police Office
4. Qipan Hill   5. Popular Library   6. Siqu Xuan
7. Moon Door   8. Grand Fountain   9. Artificial Lake
10. Luohong Bridge   11. Huxin Pavilion   12. Zhanggong Temple
13. Skating Rink   14. Playground for Children
15. Tennis Courts   16. Stands   17. Swimming Pool
18. Mininature Golf Course
19. Laigan Hall (Previous Wuquan Hall)
20. Zhonghua Hall (Tijin Hall)
21. Football Field   22. Ground Track Field   23. Platform

Figure 19.3   Plan of Hankou's Zhongshan Park, 1934.

Source: Hankou Municipal Government, 1934.

such as tennis, golf, and swimming, could also be found. In Wu's own words, "I transplant what I saw in Europe to Wuhan."[38]

Besides the Zhongshan Park in Hankou, another large-scale Zhongshan Park was configured in Xiamen, a major treaty port along southeast coast. The park was a product of Xiamen's massive cityscape reconstruction in the 1920s, jointly initiated by navy bureaucrats, local gentry, merchants, and overseas Chinese.[39] In an irregularly rectangular shape, Zhongshan Park (Figure 19.4) covered an area of 16 hm², with athletic fields in the south, geometric beddings and fountain in the central area, and He'an River, pavilion, and hut in the north. The original hill and pond were preserved in the southwest corner. Integrating Western and Chinese elements, Zhongshan Park was designed by a Japan-educated architect, Zhu Shigui (1893–1981). Notably, Zhu was kind of inspired by the park design in early twentieth-century Tokyo, where he received architectural training at Tokyo Institute of Technology. The overall layout of Xiamen's Zhongshan Park showed some similarities to Hibiya Park in Tokyo, which was opened

Figure 19.4 Overview of Xiamen's Zhongshan Park, 1928.

Source: Zhou Xingnan, ed. *Xiamen Zhongshan Gongyuan Jihuashu* (The Project Plan of Xiamen's Zhongshan Park) (Xiamen: The Navy Police Headquarter of Zhangzhou and Xiamen, 1929), unpaged.

in 1903 as one of the earliest Western-style parks in Japan. Certain components, like the axis design, arrangement of museum groups, Western-style bell tower, and statues, also could be found in Ueno Park, the first public park in Tokyo. It was established following the Western example as part of the borrowing and assimilation of international practices that characterized the early Meiji period. Within Ueno Park, the Tokyo Imperial Museum was designed by celebrated British architect Josiah Conder, searching for Japanese features. Impressively, a majority of the buildings in Xiamen's Zhongshan Park, including modern facilities like the library, museum, and exhibition hall, were designed in a Chinese adaptive style pursuing both national identity and modernization.

The two Zhongshan Parks in Hankou and Xiamen were specifically laid out in Sun's honor. Worthy of note, public parks in the name of "Zhongshan" emerged all over Nationalist China under the cult of Sun Yat-sen. Among the broad efforts to deify Sun Yat-sen since the late 1920s, one of the most ambitious spatial representations was the construction of Zhongshan Park, a symbolic space for the departed Party Leader. From 1925 to 1949, there opened more than 260 Zhongshan Parks in China, not only in great metropolises but also at small counties.[40] These Zhongshan Parks were opened to all sections of the public and usually furnished with memorial halls, pavilions, steles, statues, or monuments in remembrance of Sun Yat-sen. Sun's ideals were also used to name a sequence of park components. Through a variety of means, both physically and literally, Zhongshan Parks familiarized the common people with the image and ideology of Sun Yat-sen.

What's more, ceremonies were routinely held on the dates of Sun's birthday or demise in these Zhongshan Parks. The ritual of planting trees was performed in order to keep green the memory of the Father of the Republic, to stimulate citizens' efforts to fulfill his ideals of national reconstruction and people's livelihood. Other major events such as weekly commemorative services (*jinian zhou*), which occurred from 1929 to 1937, were punctuated with a report to Sun's "undying spirit." Zhongshan Parks, holding the sequence of ceremonies, became a calendar space of collective remembering, keeping Sun Yat-sen's charisma alive and inspiring his followers to finish what he started.

Conclusion

In general, public parks in early twentieth-century Chinese cities were products of the urban reconstruction and social reform campaign, as a crucial part of the nationalist project of a strong Chinese state. They were mostly created by new gentry-officials or Western-educated technocrats who pursued both nationalism and modernization. These urban reformers recognized that behind the modern façade of concessions standing on their dignity, Chinese cities were usually dirty, disorderly, dark, unhealthy, and inefficient, an environment that encouraged drug use and gambling with few alternatives of urban life. Based on their understandings about Europe, America, and Japan, they launched public works programs and built public parks as demonstration projects, so as to create a material base from which their social reforms could be articulated.

These parks were consciously designed as a new kind of public space for education and entertainment, catering to the needs of the community's mental and physical well-being. They blended Western formal planning and traditional Chinese garden designs. Geometric parterres, artificial mountains, and water were set up, while bandstands, sundials, and drinking fountains were introduced. These didactic aspects, together with the regulations, helped mold people's character, train the unruly, and cultivate civic morality. Some of the parks were supplied with libraries, museums, exhibition halls, and other facilities, inculcating visitors with modern knowledge. A wide range of sports fields and facilities were configured and a series of athletic meetings held, encouraging men and women, young and old to do active exercises and build up their bodies. Impressive monuments were established, and memorial rituals were performed, articulating the all-encompassing cult of the party nation-state to the masses.

The public parks attracted a large number of visitors and contained a great diversity of social activities. Many residents who used to indulge themselves in smoking and gambling came out to the parks, walking, swimming, boating, or reading. Parks also became a favorite site for blind dates and other gatherings. They promoted social encounters and served the conduct of public affairs. What's more, the park-goers sometimes claimed their own rights, presenting a different emphasis from the park promoters. Although these parks were largely initiated by the government, emphasizing people's responsibility to further the development of the nation, the government's push to establish a new urban landscape and social order had to be mitigated, to a considerable degree, by residents' own interests. In essence, these new public parks entered the political, economic, and social life of the city people and contributed to the emergence of a modern urban culture.

Notes

1 Jermyn Chi-Hung Lynn, *Social Life of the Chinese in Peking* (Peking-Tientsin: China Booksellers, 1928), 59–60.
2 Lydia He Liu, *Translingual Practice: Literature, National Culture, and Translated Modernity–China, 1900–1937* (Stanford, CA: Stanford University Press, 1995), 302–329; Huang Yiren, "Gongyuan kao," *Dongfang Zazhi* (Eastern Miscellany) 9, no. 2 (1912): 1–3.
3 Literary gatherings were often held in such gardens, and their names became synonymous with poetry and intellectual discussions. See Craig Clunas, *Fruitful Sites: Garden Culture in Ming Dynasty China* (Durham: Duke University Press, 1996).
4 Alessandra Ponte, "Public Parks in Great Britain and the United States: From a 'Spirit of the Place' to a 'Spirit of Civilization'," in *The Architecture of Western Gardens: A Design History from the Renaissance to the Present Day*, ed. Monique Mosser and Georges Teyssot (Cambridge, MA: MIT Press, 1991), 373.
5 George F Chadwick, *The Park and the Town: Public Landscape in the 19th and Twentieth Centuries* (New York: F. A. Praeger, 1966), 19.

6   Florence Mary Baker, *Parisians and Their Parks: The Creation and Development of the Paris Municipal Park System, 1853–1900* (PhD Dissertation, University of California, Los Angeles, 1994), 1–2.
7   Chadwick, *Park and the Town*, 159.
8   Edward Seidensticker, *Low City, High City: Tokyo from Edo to the Earthquake* (New York: Knopf, 1983), 122–123.
9   Sibel Bozdogan, *Modernism and Nation Building: Turkish Architectural Culture in the Early Republic* (Seattle: University of Washington Press, 2001), 77–79.
10 Chadwick, *Park and the Town*, 218.
11 Cheng Xuke, Wang Tao, ed. *Shanghai Yuanlin Zhi* (Shanghai gazetteer of gardens, groves and parks) (Shanghai: Shanghai kexueyuan chubanshe, 2000).
12 Mingzheng Shi, "From Imperial Gardens to Public Parks: The Transformation of Urban Space in Early Twentieth-Century Beijing," in *Modern China* 24, no. 3 (1998): 219–254.
13 Jeffrey W. Cody, "American Planning in Republican China," *Planning Perspective* 11, no. 4 (1996): 342–346; Edward Bing-shuey Lee, *Modern Canton* (Shanghai: The Mercury Press, 1936), 132–146.
14 Charles David Musgrove, *The Nation's Concrete Heart: Architecture, Planning, and Ritual in Nanjing, 1927–1937* (PhD Dissertation, University of California, San Diego, 2002), 256–270.
15 Kristin Eileen Stapleton, *Civilizing Chengdu: Chinese Urban Reform, 1895–1937* (Cambridge, MA: Harvard University Press, 2000), 220–225.
16 Wang Changfan, ed., *Wuhan yuanlin: 1840–1985* (Wuhan Gardens, Groves and Parks: 1840–1985) (Wuhan: Wuhan shi yuanlinju, 1987), 85, 128.
17 Xishan Park was created in Wanxian (Sichuan) in 1924, Chongqing Central Park around 1926, and Xiamen Zhongshan Park from 1926. See *Zhongguo Dabaike Quanshu: Jianzhu, Yuanlin, Chengshiguihua* (Chinese encyclopedia: Architecture, landscape and urban planning) (Beijing: Zhongguo dabaike quanshu chubanshe, 1988), 568–569.
18 Joseph Esherick, "Modernity and Nation in the Chinese City," in *Remaking the Chinese City: Modernity and National Identity, 1900–1950*, ed. Esherick (Honolulu: University of Hawaii Press, 2000), 2–4.
19 Joseph Cho Wang, *The Chinese Garden* (Oxford; New York: Oxford University Press, 1998), 17.
20 *Shizheng Tongbao* (Municipal Gazette, Beijing) 1, no. 2 (1914): 9–10.
21 Gu Yaqiu, "Jianzhu Sheji yu Dushimei zhi Guanxi (The Relationship Between Architectural Design and Urban Aesthetics)," *Dongfang Zazhi* 28, no. 5 (1931): 50.
22 *Xin Hankou* (New Hankou) 2, no. 8 (1931): 9–12. *Xin Hankou* was an official periodical of the Hankou municipal government from 1928.
23 Tong Yuming, *Gongyuan* (Park) (Shanghai: The Commercial Press, 1928). The series of Universal Library, which included both Chinese classics and translations of foreign works, was composed of 1,010 titles bound in 2,000 volumes. In modern China, it was this program of Universal Library initiated by Wang Yunwu (1888–1979) that first enabled the establishment of thousands of village and town libraries, popularizing modern knowledge.
24 Gu Zaiyan and Lu Danlin, *Zuixin Gongyuan Jianzhu Fa* (Building methods of recent public parks) (Shanghai: Daolu yuekanshe, 1928); Gu Zaiyan, *Shiyong Gongyuan Jianzhu Fa* (Practical Building Methods of Public Parks) (Shanghai: The Commercial Press, 1949).
25 *Zhongguo Dabaike*, 568.
26 Mingzheng Shi, "From Imperial Gardens to Public Parks," 231–234.
27 Zhongshan Gongyuan Guanlichu, ed. *Zhongshan Gongyuan Zhi* (The Gazetteer of Zhongshan Park) (Beijing: Zhongguo Linye Chubanshe, 2002): 1–2.
28 Zhu Qiqian, "Xu (Preface)," in *Zhongyang Gongyuan Ershiwu Zhounian Jiniance* (Commemorative Album of Central Park for its 25th Anniversary), ed. Zhongyang weiyuanhui (Committee of Central Park) (Peking: Zhongyang Gongyuan Shiwusuo, 1939), 1.
29 Zhongyang Gongyuan Weiyuanhui, ed. *Zhongyang Gongyuan Ershiwu Zhounian Jiniance* (Commemorative Album of Central Park for its 25th Anniversary) (Peking: Zhongyang Gongyuan Shiwusuo, 1939), 8–9.
30 Jullie Bredon, *Peking: A Historical and Intimate Description of Its Chief Places of Interest* (Shanghai: Kelly & Walsh, 1931), 118–130.
31 Yang Tian, *Defining Building Traditions in Modern China: Zhu Qiqian, 1905–1930* (Master Thesis, University of Virginia, Charlottesville, 2007), 24–45.
32 Hankou is located at the confluence of the Yangtze River and its largest tributary, the Han River, in Central China. It was the single largest port for the collection and sale of commodities in the entire Qing empire and ranked the first among "Four Great Trading Towns in China" in the early nineteenth

century. In 1861, it was declared open as a treaty port. It became a special municipality in the Nationalist Era. From the Qing dynasty, "Wuhan" was a customary acronym of Wuchang, Hankou (Hankow),
and Hanyang tri-cities. It is also the name given to the single municipality that they today comprise.

33 Hankou shi zhengfu (Hankou's Municipal Government), ed. *Hankou shi zhengfu jianshe gaikuang* (Intro-
    duction of Hankou Municipal Development), vol. 1 (Hankou: Hankou's Municipal Government,
    1930), 37–38.

34 *Xin Hankou* 1, no. 3 (1929): 94.

35 Wu Guobing, "Jiangshan Wanli Xing (9) – Youxue Guiguo hou de Gongzuo he Shenghuo (Traveling
    Around the Country, part 9 – My Work and Life After Studying Abroad)." *Zhongwai Zazhi* 26, no. 4
    (1979): 125.

36 Wu Guobing, "Wo yu Hankou Zhongshan Gongyuan ji Shizheng Jianshe (Hankou Zhongshan Park,
    Urban Reconstruction and Me)," in *Wuhan Wenshi Zhiliao Wenku*, ed. Zhengxie Wuhanshi Wenyuan-
    hui Wenshi Xuexi Weiyuanhui, vol. 3 (Wuhan: Wuhan Chubanshe, 1999); 478.

37 Ibid., 482.

38 Wu Guobing, "Jiangshan Wanli Xing (9)," 120–127.

39 Zhou Xingnan, ed. *Xiamen Zhongshan Gongyuan Jihuashu* (The Project Plan of Xiamen's Zhongshan
    Park). Xiamen: Zhangxia haijun jingbei silingbu (The Navy Police Headquarter of Zhangzhou and
    Xiamen), 1929.

40 The statistic includes the recovered Taiwan during 1945–1949. Some were based on previous parks
    or private gardens, for example, Guangzhou's Xiushan Park, Beijing's Central Park, Tianjin Park, Tai-
    yuan's Yinghu Park, Jessfield Park in Shanghai, etc. Others were specifically laid out in Sun's honor, in
    cities such as Xiangshan (now Zhongshan), Nanjing, Hankou, Xiamen, Shantou, Ningbo and so on.
    See Chen Yunqian, "Kongjian chongzu yu Sun Zhongshan chongbai: Yi minguo shiqi Zhongshan
    gongyuan wei zhongxin de kaocha (Reconstruction of space and the worship towards Sun Yat-sen: An
    investigation with Yat-sen Park as its center in the Republic of China)," *Shilin*, no. 1 (2006): 5–7.

Bibliography

Baker, Florence Mary. *Parisians and Their Parks: The Creation and Development of the Paris Municipal Park
    System, 1853–1900.* PhD Dissertation. University of California, Los Angeles, 1994.

Bozdogan, Sibel. *Modernism and Nation Building: Turkish Architectural Culture in the Early Republic.* Seattle:
    University of Washington Press, 2001.

Bredon, Jullie. *Peking: A Historical and Intimate Description of Its Chief Places of Interest.* Shanghai: Kelly &
    Walsh, 1931.

Chadwick, George F. *The Park and the Town: Public Landscape in the 19th and Twentieth Centuries.* New York:
    F. A. Praeger, 1966.

Chen, Yunqian. "Kongjian Chongzu yu Sun Zhongshan Chongbai: Yi Minguo Shiqi Zhongshan Gongy-
    uan wei Zhongxin de Kaocha (Reconstruction of Space and the Worship Towards Sun Yat-sen: An
    Investigation with Yat-sen Park as Its Center in the Republic of China)." *Shilin*, no. 1 (2006): 1–8.

Cheng, Xuke and Wang Tao, eds. *Shanghai Yuanlin Zhi* (Shanghai Gazetteer of Gardens, Groves and Parks).
    Shanghai: Shanghai Kexueyuan Chubanshe, 2000.

Clunas, Craig. *Fruitful Sites: Garden Culture in Ming Dynasty China.* Durham: Duke University Press, 1996.

Cody, Jeffrey W. "American Planning in Republican China." *Planning Perspective* 11, no. 4 (1996): 339–377.

Esherick, Joseph. "Modernity and Nation in the Chinese City." In *Remaking the Chinese City: Modernity
    and National Identity, 1900–1950*, edited by Joseph Esherick, 1–18. Honolulu: University of Hawaii
    Press, 2000.

Gu, Yaqiu. "Jianzhu Sheji yu Dushimei zhi Guanxi (The Relationship Between Architectural Design and
    Urban Aesthetics)." *Dongfang zazhi* 28, no. 5 (1931): 49–51.

Gu, Zaiyan. *Shiyong Gongyuan Jianzhu Fa* (Practical Building Methods of Public Parks). Shanghai: The
    Commercial Press, 1949.

Gu, Zaiyan and Lu Danlin. *Zuixin Gongyuan Jianzhu Fa* (Building Methods of Recent Public Parks).
    Shanghai: Daolu yuekanshe, 1928.

Hankou Shi Zhengfu (Hankou's Municipal Government), ed. *Hankou Shi Zhengfu Jianshe Gaikuang* (Intro-
    duction of Hankou Municipal Development), vol. 1. Hankou: Hankou's Municipal Government, 1930.

Huang, Yiren. "Gongyuan Kao." *Dongfang Zazhi* (Eastern Miscellany) 9, no. 2 (1912): 1–3.

Lee, Edward Bing-shuey. *Modern Canton.* Shanghai: The Mercury Press, 1936.

Liu, Lydia He. *Translingual Practice: Literature, National Culture, and Translated Modernity – China, 1900–1937*. Stanford, CA: Stanford University Press, 1995.

Lynn, Jermyn Chi-Hung. *Social Life of the Chinese in Peking*. Peking-Tientsin: China Booksellers, 1928.

Musgrove, Charles David. *The Nation's Concrete Heart: Architecture, Planning, and Ritual in Nanjing, 1927–1937*. PhD Dissertation. University of California, San Diego, 2002.

Ponte, Alessandra. "Public Parks in Great Britain and the United States: From a 'Spirit of the Place' to a 'Spirit of Civilization'." In *The Architecture of Western Gardens: A Design History from the Renaissance to the Present Day*, edited by Monique Mosser and Georges Teyssot, 373–386. Cambridge, MA: MIT Press, 1991.

Seidensticker, Edward. *Low City, High City: Tokyo from Edo to the Earthquake*. New York: Knopf, 1983.

Shi, Mingzheng. "From Imperial Gardens to Public Parks: The Transformation of Urban Space in Early Twentieth-Century Beijing." *Modern China* 24, no. 3 (1998): 219–254.

Shizheng Tongbao (Municipal Gazette, Beijing) 1, no. 2 (1914).

Stapleton, Kristin Eileen. *Civilizing Chengdu: Chinese Urban Reform, 1895–1937*. Cambridge, MA: Harvard University Press, 2000.

Tian, Yang. *Defining Building Traditions in Modern China: Zhu Qiqian, 1905–1930*. Master Thesis. University of Virginia, Charlottesville, 2007.

Tong, Yuming. *Gongyuan* (Park). Shanghai: The Commercial Press, 1928.

Wang, Changfan, ed. *Wuhan Yuanlin: 1840–1985* (Wuhan Gardens, Groves and Parks: 1840–1985). Wuhan: Wuhan Shi Yuanlinju, 1987.

Wang, Joseph Cho. *The Chinese Garden*. Oxford and New York: Oxford University Press, 1998.

Wu, Guobing. "Jiangshan Wanli Xing (9) – Youxue Guiguo hou de Gongzuo he Shenghuo (Traveling Around the Country, Part 9 – My Work and Life After Studying Abroad)." *Zhongwai Zazhi* 26, no. 4 (1979): 120–127.

———. "Wo yu Hankou Zhongshan Gongyuan ji Shizheng Jianshe (Hankou Zhongshan Park, Urban Reconstruction and Me)." In *Wuhan wenshi zhiliao wenku*, edited by Zhengxie wuhan shi wenyuanhui wenshi xuexi weiyuanhui, vol. 3, 450–484. Wuhan: Wuhan Chubanshe, 1999.

Xin Hankou (New Hankou), 1, no. 3 (1929).

Xin Hankou (New Hankou) 2, no. 8 (1931).

Zhongguo Dabaike Quanshu. *Zhongguo Dabaike Quanshu: Jianzhu, Yuanlin, Chengshiguihua* (Chinese Encyclopedia: Architecture, Landscape and Urban Planning). Beijing: Zhongguo Dabaike Quanshu Chubanshe, 1988.

Zhongshan Gongyuan Guanlichu, ed. *Zhongshan Gongyuan Zhi* (The Gazetteer of Zhongshan Park). Beijing: Zhongguo Linye Chubanshe, 2002.

Zhongyang Gongyuan Weiyuanhui, ed. *Zhongyang Gongyuan Ershiwu Zhounian Jiniance* (Commemorative Album of Central Park for Its 25th Anniversary). Peking: Zhongyang Gongyuan Shiwusuo, 1939.

Zhou, Xingnan, ed. *Xiamen Zhongshan Gongyuan Jihuashu* (The Project Plan of Xiamen's Zhongshan Park). Xiamen: Zhangxia Haijun Jingbei Silingbu (The Navy Police Headquarter of Zhangzhou and Xiamen), 1929.

Zhu, Qiqian. "Xu (Preface)." In *Zhongyang Gongyuan Ershiwu Zhounian Jiniance* (Commemorative Album of Central Park for Its 25th Anniversary), ed. Zhongyang weiyuanhui (Committee of Central Park), 1–2. Peking: Zhongyang Gongyuan Shiwusuo, 1939.

Glossary

Beihai	北海
Beijing	北京
Beijing Shizheng Tongbao	北京市政通报
Chen Zhi	陈植
Cheng Shifu	程世抚
Chengdu	成都
Chongqing	重庆
Daxue congshu	大学丛书
Ditan	地坛

Dongfang zazhi	东方杂志
Dushi Gongyuan Lun	都市公园论
gongyuan	公园
Gu Zaiyan	顾在延
Guangzhou	广州
guocui	国粹
Guohua	国花
Guomindang	国民党
Hankou	汉口
Jiang Zuobin	蒋作宾
Jinian zhou	纪念周
Li Huatang	李华堂
Lu Danlin	陆丹林
Nanjing	南京
Nanking	南京
Shaocheng Park	少城公园
Shejitan	社稷坛
Shen Yuan	沈园
Shizheng congshu	市政丛书
Sichuan (province)	四川（省）
Sigu Xuan	四顾轩
Sun Ke	孙科
Sun Yat-sen	孙中山
Tiantan	天坛
Tongsu jiaoyuguan	通俗教育馆
Wanxian (county)	万县
wanyou wenku	万有文库
Wu Guobing	吴国柄
Wuhan	武汉
Xi Yuan	西园
Xiamen	厦门
Xiannongtan	先农坛
Xin Hankou	新汉口
Xishan Park	西山公园
Xu Yuan	徐园
Yang Sen	杨森
yuanlin	园林
Zaoyuanxue Gailun	造园学概论
Zhang Shouyu	章守玉
Zhang Yuan	张园
Zhanggong Pavilion	张公亭
Zhejiang (university)	浙江大学
Zhongguo zaoyuan xuehui	中国造园学会
Zhongshan (park or road)	中山（公园/大道/路）
Zhu Qiqian	朱启钤
Zhu Shigui	朱士圭
Zuixin Gongyuan Jianzhu Fa	最新公园建筑法

PART III

SOCIALIST–MAOIST MODERNIZATION

Spatial Construction and City Planning Under Socialist Ideology

20

SOCIALIST URBAN PLANNING IN MAO'S CHINA (1949–1976)

Li Baihao

Since 1368, when Zhu Yuanzhang established himself as the Emperor in Nanjing, there were four eras in China, namely, Ming dynasty, Qing dynasty, Republic of China, and People's Republic of China, lasting over 600 years. However, the center of authority, that is, the capital city, was always located in either Beijing or Nanjing. It is not surprising that the planning and building of these two cities as a capital have remained a focus for ongoing studies and discussions.

While Japan moved towards a centralized state system after the Meiji Restoration of 1868, China shifted after establishing the Republic in 1911 from a traditional centralized monarchy towards a loosely assembled republic of autonomous provinces, facilitating a reform in urban administration from central to local authority, initiating a modernization of urban governance. In 1921, the first modern municipality was established in Guangzhou. In 1926, to materialize Sun Yat-sen's (1866–1925) vision of a centralized state system, the Nationalist Party (Kuomintang or KMT), under Chiang Kai-shek (1887–1975), launched Northern Expedition from Guangzhou. With its success, a modern municipality system was established in Hankou, Shanghai, Hangzhou, and Ningbo; in April 1927, under Chiang and KMT, Nanjing became China's capital again, for the Republican Government (*nanjing guomin zhengfu*).

From Nanjing to Beijing: Two Ideologies for Capital City Planning

To choose Nanjing as China's capital was Sun Yat-sen's wish; so, in early 1928, Chiang Kai-shek quickly moved on in planning the capital; established a Board for Capital Development (*shoudu jianshe weiyuanhui*) and a Committee of Design, Technology, and Science for Constructing the National Capital (*guodu sheji jishu weiyuanhui*); and invited architect and engineer Henry K. Murphy (1877–1954), from the United States, and Ernest P. Goodrich (1874–1955), respectively, to be the chief advisors for the project. Chiang hoped for a quick planning and building of the capital, to demonstrate and consolidate the new government under his leadership. In late 1929, Capital Plan, or Shoudu Jihua, was completed. As the first comprehensive city plan in early modern China, Capital Plan adopted not only the scientific and rationalist ideas of urban planning from Europe and America, including functional zoning and systematic road planning, but also the Chinese tradition of planning practice and the symbolic and architectural form, to achieve an east–west synthesis. The synthesis was found not just in formal design and discourse but also in power negotiation: American advisors hoped that the ancient city wall of Nanjing, a

DOI: 10.4324/9781315851112-31

relic from the "cold-weapon era," would be preserved as modern ring-walkways or a ring-park, an idea that was at odds with Chinese leaders' vision of "breaking-down the walls and extending the avenues" (*chaiqiang zhulu*) for modernity; in a political–professional negotiation, the leaders prevailed, assuring their authority. Because of war, Capital Plan had not been fully material-ized, yet it had established a modern spatial layout for Nanjing with an east–west synthesis, or a combination of "Chinese essence with Western technology;" and ancient structures such as the Ming-dynasty city walls, or at least long parts of it, survived the modern transformations as a result (Figure 20.1).[1]

In 1949, 20 years after the release of Capital Plan, Mao Zedong (1893–1976) replaced Chi-ang Kai-shek and established the People's Republic of China, with Beijing as its capital, now center of a new state authority and new politics. However, Beijing then, despite its grand layout as an ancient capital, barely had basic facilities and the infrastructures of a modern city, and its urban conditions were very backward. To quickly change this, and to make Beijing suitable for a national capital, large-scale construction was launched. In this, nothing was more important than the making of the "Urban Planning of Beijing as a New Socialist Capital."

In May 1949, a Capital Planning Committee (*shoudu jihua weiyuanhui*) was established in Beijing, and Liang Sicheng (1901–1972) and Chen Zhanxiang (1916–2001), who studied in USA and the UK respectively, were appointed as important members of the committee, to

Figure 20.1   Preservation of the City Wall of Nanjing and its environment, as proposed in the Capital Plan (1929).

Source: Guodu Sheji Jishu Zhuangyuan Banshichu (Technical office for capital plan), *Shoudu Jihua* (Capital plan) (Nanjing: 1929).

work with other Chinese professionals on planning the capital. This was the first time comprehensive planning for the whole city of Beijing was attempted in early modern China. However, this planning project was different from any others in China in two aspects: firstly, Beijing was the capital of the previous two empires, the Ming (1420–1644) and the Qing (1644–1911), and had thus preserved the complete spatial morphology of an ancient Chinese capital with its classical planning philosophy, and secondly, the planning must demonstrate new visions of a socialist political idea and state system. For this purpose, Mao Zedong invited experts from the world's first socialist state, the Soviet Union, to participate in the planning for Beijing. The Chinese and Russian professionals proposed many different projects for the future of Beijing, which had both commonalities and differences.[2]

They shared many common positions. In terms of the nature of the city, it should be a national center, for not only politics but also culture, art, and scientific research, as well as production – it should be a large industrial city; in terms of demographic scale, Chinese planners aimed at 4 million as the limit of growth, and the Russian anticipated a growth from 1.3 million (in 1949) to 2.6 million in 15 to 20 years; in terms of spatial structure, both agreed to adopt a radial pattern for the organization of major roads; and in terms of functional distribution, an industrial production zone should be placed in the east, a landscape and leisure zone in the Western Mountain area, a zone of higher education institutions in the northwest next to the landscape area, and, wherever a work unit was placed, its living and working areas were to be placed next to each other.[3]

However, regarding the use of the old imperial center and the location of the new political center, there were radical disagreements, with a group of "outsiders" and a group of "insiders" pitted against each other.

The "outsiders," mainly represented by some Chinese professionals, proposed moving the new center outside, to be located between Yuetan (altar of the moon) and Gongzhufen (graveyard of princesses) in the west, a place due west of the old Palace City at center. The argument was that, firstly, the old Palace and the Imperial and Capital City of the Ming–Qing empire was together a complete and ideal manifestation of the classical urban planning tradition from the past, which should be protected in entirety and not broken and ruined by a new and large government complex; secondly, the old city was already densely built and there was no room for new projects; and, thirdly, by placing the new center in the west, they could maintain two centers each in their own completeness, displaying both the ancient glory of the Chinese tradition and the posture of a new age and new spirit. This proposal was best represented by the well-known Liang–Chen Plan, a joint scheme prepared by Liang Sicheng and Chen Zhanxiang (Figure 20.2).[4]

The "insiders" group, represented mostly by the Russian advisors, however, proposed that the new political center should be located in the old city center. The justification was threefold: economically, the urban buildings and facilities of the old city could be utilized; aesthetically, the cultural and architectural values of the old buildings could be fully employed; and, in terms of efficiency, when other zones were arranged around the new political core at the center, access would be most efficient in connection with the center.[5]

Because of the opposing views, no planning scheme for the capital was formally resolved and proposed as late as the end of 1953, and yet, in the real construction that was unfolding, as hindsight has made evident, development was following the ideas of the "insiders." In the late 1950s, a space before the Tiananmen (southern gate at the center leading to the Palace and Imperial City in the north) was transformed, from a closed T-shaped palace courtyard into a vast open square some five times larger than Moscow's Red Square; in the process, some ancient buildings and walls were demolished, a moat around the city wall was covered for making a

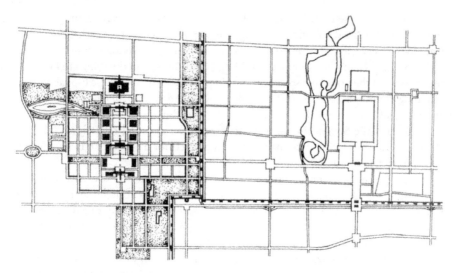

Figure 20.2 The Liang-Chen Plan (1950): New Political Center and Old City Center as separate and parallel to each other.

Source: Pan Guxi, ed. *Zhongguo Jianzhushi*, di wu ban (A history of Chinese architecture, fifth edition) (Beijing: Zhongguo Jianzhu Chubanshe, 2004), 415, Figures 16–10. By permission of Lin Zhu.

subway later on, and even the Palace City (Forbidden City) was threatened with modification. Here, the Russian advisors' proposal shared a vision with Chinese government's intentions, and the underlying political, symbolic, and cultural significance was surely more important than any technical considerations.[6]

Mao's Vision: Industrial City and People's Commune

The founding of the People's Republic was a turning point in the modern urban planning history of China, as it initiated a project of designing and building the industrial city as part of a state-led industrialization of the nation.

Although still in rural bases, the Communist Party devised a Framework of Work in the City in June 1948 and developed agendas for the new government soon to be established under their leadership: to shift from the countryside to the city and to construct a productive city.[7] In the early 1950s, China needed to recover from war, wanted technical know-how for urban construction, and hoped to industrialize quickly, and yet there was a US-led embargo against China. Because of these, Mao decided to join the Socialist Bloc and take the Soviet Union as a model. In hindsight, the government had achieved in less than 30 years what advanced capitalist countries had accomplished over a longer time and had materialized, by focusing on heavy industry first and foremost, a swift transformation from an agricultural to an industrial economy, in a mode of socialist industrialization and urbanization.

The breaking-out of the Korean War in 1950 strengthened a foundation of Mao's thought regarding prioritizing heavy industry for developing China's defense industry. In the first Five-Year Plan (1953–1957), there were 694 large and medium-sized industrial projects, of which 156 were the key works with Russian support, in the area of defense, energy, raw material, and mechanical processing.[8] To ensure that these projects had rational planning, siting, construction, and the associated designs and organizations, China adopted advice and examples from Russia in urban planning and construction and thus shaped many industrial cities, opening a new chapter in China's planning history.

Planning practice then adopted "socialism" and "industrialization" as key themes for study and exploration and developed over time in China a system of general planning suitable to a highly planned economy. In addition, in actual practice, Chinese traditional ideas and western modern planning concepts were implicitly absorbed at times, so the socialist planning in China, though originating in Russia, was not quite a copy because of Chinese interpretation involved in the process.

In 1954, Mao proposed that the aim of development was to build "Socialist Industrialization and Agricultural Socialization" (*shehuizhuyi gongyehua, nonye shehuizhuyihua*).[9] By 1956, full-scale nationalization for building a socialist economy and industry was completed, which excited Mao and encouraged him to push forward with socialist dreams. In August 1958, for speeding up the realization of communist ideals, the Central Committee of the Communist Party released a Decree on Establishing the People's Commune in the Countryside. In two months, rural China was fully communized. While historically a commune may be found around the world, as in political movements such as the Paris Commune of 1871, the "People's Commune" was Mao's design. Mao said, in 1919, that "by assembling a few new families, a new society can be created," and, in the early 1950s, noted that "it is better after all to establish People's Communes."[10] Mao's expressions soon turned into a social movement, and the Communes were built everywhere, first in the countryside, then in urban places such as factories, barracks, and schools.[11]

Architects and planners were required to contribute to the design of the Communes. A Commune was conceived, then, for a unification of politics and social life, collectivity and the person, and the urban and the rural. It asked for a closer association between different social groups (workers, farmers, students, and soldiers), militarization of organizations, a combative spirit in action, a collectivization of daily life, and an emphasis on scale and public-ness (*yida ergong*); it requested that 2000 to 6000 households be assembled into a thoroughly new "Ideal Urban–Rural Spatial Unit," and that the Communes be transformed into a communist society.[12]

For example, the Planning for People's Commune New Village of Ningbo (1959) (Figure 20.3) was composed of a living zone, a production zone, a public facility zone, an administrative zone,

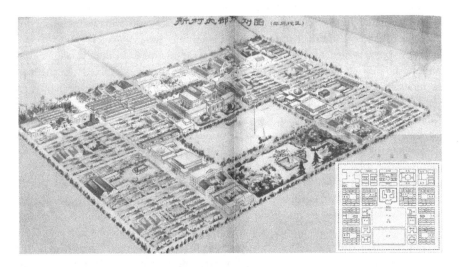

Figure 20.3 Plan for a community titled as the People's Commune New Village of Ningbo (1959).

Source: Anonymous author, Ningbo Archives.

and a square-and-park zone, with a basic principle of the living-residential areas in front and the industrial-productive areas at the back. In the whole planning scheme here, the administrative center, the square, and the park formed a central axis; on the two sides were public facilities, including an exhibition building, a cultural palace, a department store, a cinema, a theater, a library, an old-folks home, a bank, and a post-office; further outside were housing clusters each with a primary school and a kindergarten at the center, and every housing cluster in turn had four smaller housing groups, each with a collective canteen and a small park at the center. In the north, that is, at the back, were factories, a fire brigade, an agriculture research institution, a meteorological station, a Night University (open to the working population), a middle school, a hospital, and a sanatorium; the Commune was designed as a comprehensive micro-society. At the same time, the central square was large enough for a major public gathering, where the mast of the red flag and the statue of Mao, standing high at the center, expressed in spatial terms the will and the spirit of socialism.[13]

The People's Commune movement, which embodied Mao's Communist dream, lasted for 26 years, from 1958 to 1984; it was a continuation of the rural collectivization movement of the 1950s and closely associated with the campaigns of the Great Leap Forward (1958–62) and the Cultural Revolution (1966–76). It also provided, in reality, motivation and a starting point for the Rural Reform of the 1980s. To this day, we can still see elements of the People's Commune in the power structure, institutional organization, daily life, and social space of urban and rural China.

Third-Front Construction: Planning for National Defense

In the 1960s, China simultaneously faced two opponents: the United States (and the US-led western countries) and the Soviet Union (even though it shared a socialist bloc with China). Mao observed that China had to be prepared for a war against a major invading force and thought that, given the industries were focused in a few places, the population concentrated in large cities, and the transportation lines focused around the major cities, mostly on the east coast, it would be devastating if a war broke out. Because of this, large-scale projects for national defense and heavy industry were relocated to the hinterland, far away from border regions and coastal areas. Locating the industrial bases on the "third line" from the frontier was called the Third-Front or Third-Line Construction (*sanxian jianshe*), a nation-wide initiative involving a large number of schemes of urban and settlement planning, from 1964 to 1978.[14]

The Third-Line construction had clear objectives and methods. In the overall geographical distribution, the projects should be "broadly dispersed, and locally assembled"; in the layout of defense industries, the locations should be "mountainous, dispersed, and covered-up"; for the building of military and machine industries, the projects should aim for a "unification of use for peace and war, and a unification of military and civilian organizations"; for urban planning and development, it should aim for "industry–agriculture unity and urban–rural synthesis," as well as "convenience for production and livelihood"; and, in the planning and building of plants and mining bases, the rules were "production first, livelihood second; factories first, dormitories second," and the advice was to "insert a pin wherever there was a gap" (that is, to take advantage of whatever was available and possible).[15]

In the 1964–1978 period, Third-Line construction occurred to some 13 provinces and autonomous regions, each in its entirety or partially, in a total of 3.18 million km² – one-third of the overall national territory and 37% of national arable land, affecting some 40% of the overall population. These places included Sichuan, Yunnan, and Guizhou in the southwest; Gansu, Shaanxi, Ningxia, and Qinghai in the northwest; Yuxi, Exi, Xiangxi, Yuebei, and Guixibei in the middle; and Shanxi in the north (Figure 20.4).[16]

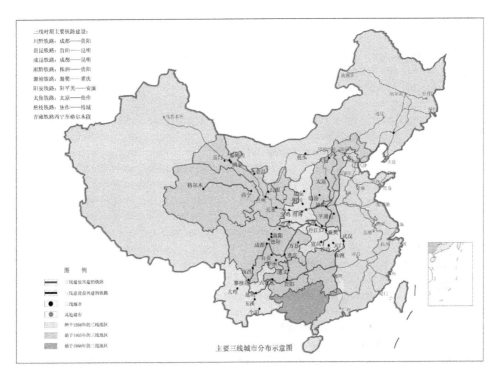

Figure 20.4   Distribution of the main cities of the Third Front (Third Line) across China.
Source: © Li Baihao.

Design for "dispersal" and "air-defense" had been the key notions of wartime urban planning, and the Third-Line construction demonstrated clearly ideas and methods of planning
against war. In preparing a war against outside aggression, the core industries and research
institutes were dispersed into remote and western regions, in deep mountainous areas, to consolidate a broad strategic rear. At the same time, the building of industries and military facilities
in these remote regions also laid down an industrial base for local development.

In the urban planning practice of Third-Front construction, settlement sites were selected
based on major industrial projects, and the layout and the design followed the principle of matching livelihood with production. For these industrial projects, some were relocated from the eastern developed areas, whereas others were newly constructed. There were three types of location
and spatial design of these industries and their associated settlements: freshly built in entirety on
a new site; partially built based on an existing city; built and dispersed into deep mountains.[17]

Constructions of the first type occurred in places less accessible but rich with material or
resources for defense and production. In this case, a city emerged very quickly from an inhab-
itable site or a small town, simply because industrial projects were now located there by the
state. With the industrial works taking absolute priority, it was the sites of these works and
the location of the natural resources that determined the shape of the settlement. Top-down
policy and planning directly affected the structure and morphology of these new cities; in other
words, these cities were not naturally developed but were made to appear and grow into a sizable settlement because of the external force of planning from the state; a primary example is
Panzhihua City.[18]

For the second type, development of industry and settlement was based on an existing city and its earlier industrial facilities, in a process of reforming and extending the existing conditions. To build industries and to promote output, the production lines took priority and the needs of the industrial zones were the guiding force in the reshaping of the old city. As a result, both the internal urban structure and the external morphology of these cities went through an important transformation, as we can find in Taiyuan.[19]

Developments of the third type took place in the inaccessible and mountainous regions. Here, military–industry bases were either resettled from elsewhere or were newly built; the bases might have a rural settlement nearby, yet they did not really form anything like a city, though the new industries, in hindsight, greatly pushed the urbanization of the place. Since the purpose was to utilize natural topography and to hide the industries in defensive locations in preparation of a coming war, the new settlements were often linear in shape, with roads meandering with natural ravines and structures built along these roads. These industrial productions were not based on an urban system and were self-sufficient and autonomous; they effectively acted as an "anti-urbanization" force for the existing cities around them but were constructive to the local place for swift development, bringing it in a few years to a level of modernity that would otherwise take decades to achieve, as in the case for Danjiangkou City.[20]

In the Third-Line period, and under the socialist and centralist system, urban planning and construction were a government business, and state politics determined the use of technical expertise and the shape of urban form. In preparation for a coming war, Third-Line planning practice utilized the strategy of dispersion and flexibly coordinated political necessity with construction possibility, thus achieving integration between politics and technology.

Prelude to a New-Modern Urban Planning: Tangshan Earthquake

In China's modern history, 1976 was a special year. On 9 September that year, Mao died, and this marked the end of the decade-long Cultural Revolution.

On 28 July that year, Tangshan, a city near Beijing, experienced an earthquake measuring 7.8 on the Richter scale, which shook the industrial city and its population of 800,000 people to complete ruins. One month after, under extreme difficulties, the Ministry of Construction assembled some 3,000 planners and other professionals from Beijing, Shanghai, and other cities to study and work on general planning of reconstruction for a new Tangshan. Based on investigations into the geological conditions prone to earthquake, the coal mine distribution, and the situation after the earthquake, the planning scheme proposed to adopt a cluster approach, to use major roads and railway lines to link three areas – the Old City zone, the Eastern Mining zone, and the Fengrun Xinqu New District zone – into one entity as a city (Figure 20.5).[21]

Based on careful analysis, the plan established principles for reconstruction: "conducive for production, convenient for living, rational in layout planning, and protective to the environment." In terms of zoning, the city should have the Old City zone, the New City zone, and the Eastern Mining zone. In the Old City zone, the Douhe River defined an industrial area to the east for steel and ceramics production, a machine production area to the north, and a residential area to the west; in the New City zone, development should go eastward, starting from an existing Fengrun town; and in the Eastern Mining zone, the plan was to reconstruct what had been destroyed, to maintain and develop the five mines of Kailuan Coal Mine, and to organize housing clusters around these. The three zones, 25 km apart from each other, established a dynamic balance with three pillars. In addition, the plan proposed to maintain seven earthquake sites for observation and research.[22]

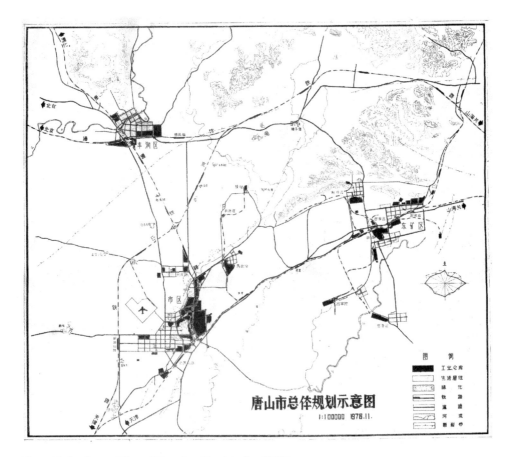

Figure 20.5   General Plan of Tangshan Municipality (1976).

Source: Taskforce for Tangshan Post-quake Reconstruction Plan, 1976; published in Wang Gang, Zhao Zhenzhong and Jiang Yongqing, "Tangshan Zhenhou Guihua Guocheng Jianshu (Brief account of the process of post-quake reconstruction of Tangshan)," *Xibu Renju Huanjing Xuekan* (Journal of human settlements in western regions), no. 4 (2014): 87; state document in public domain.

It is well known that, in the 1960s when China was in extreme economic difficulty, urban planning practice arrived at a turning point: on 18 November 1960, the state government announced that there would be "no urban planning exercise in the next three years." Since 1961, the government started to reduce the scale of construction, terminate training in urban planning, reduce the staff of planners, and disband urban planning offices – a situation that ensured a breakdown of the practice for most cities in China for more than a decade, except for special planning for the Three-Line construction.

In this context, the Tangshan reconstruction planning was not only the first urban planning exercise with national input in the Cultural Revolution period but also an event that contributed to the recovery of research and practice of urban planning, affirming that planning exercise is essential for urban building and development. In a sense, the Tangshan reconstruction planning was the prelude to a new modernization of planning practice to come in the history of modern China.

By now, China's political, economic, and social history had entered a new era of reform and opening-up. With the opening of the Third National Workshop on the City in 1978, urban planning practice entered a new era of fast and active development in the 1980s and after.

Notes

1 Guodu Sheji Jishu Zhuanyuan Banshichu, comp., *Shoudu Jihua* (Capital Plan) (Nanjing: Nanjing Chubanshe, 2006), 1–4. See also, Wang Jun, *Lishi de Xiakou* (Turning Points in History) (Beijing: Zhongxin Chuban Jituan, 2015), 65–120.

2 Zou Deci, *Xin Zhongguo Chengshi Guihua Fazhangshi Yanjiu – Zong Baogao ji Dashiji* (Investigating the Developmental History of Urban Planning of New China – General Report and Major Timeline) (Beijing: Zhongguo Jianzhu Gongye Chubanshe, 2014), 21–29.

3 Pan Guxi, ed., *Zhongguo Jianzhu Shi, di wu ban* (A History of Chinese Architecture), 5th ed. (Beijing: Zhongguo Jianzhu Chubanshe, 2004), 414.

4 Dong Guanqi, ed., *Gudu Beijing Wushinian Yanbianlu* (Fifty-year Evolution of the Ancient Capital Beijing) (Nanjing: Dongnan Daxue Chubanshe, 2006), 1–22.

5 Dong, *Gudu*, 1–22.

6 Dong, *Gudu*, 131–173; Mao Zedong, *Mao Zedong Xuanji, di wu juan* (Selected Works of Mao Zedong), vol. 5 (Beijing: Renmin Chubanshe, 1977), 95–96. See also https://en.wikipedia.org/wiki/List_of_city_squares_by_size. Accessed 1 June 2017.

7 Wang Jiaxiang, "Chengshi Gongzuo Dagang (General Notes on Leading and Managing the City)," in *Wang Jiaxiang Xuanji* (Selected Works of Wang Jiaxiang), by Wang Jiaxiang (Beijing: Renmin Chubanshe, 1989), 367–368.

8 Li Baihao and Peng Xiutao, "Zhongguo Xiandai Xinxing Gongye Chengshi Guihua de Lishi Yanjiu – yi Sulian Yuanzhu de 156 xiang Zhongdian Gongcheng wei Zhongxin (Historical Study on the Planning of Modern and Newly Emerging Industrial Cities in China – as Centered on the 156 Major Soviet-Aid Projects)," *Chengshi Guihua Xuekan* (Journal of Urban Planning), no. 4 (2006): 84–92.

9 Mao, *Mao Zedong*, 133.

10 Zhonggong Zhongyang Wenxian Yanjiushi, ed., *Mao Zedong Zaoqi Wengao* (Early Manuscripts of Mao Zedong) (Changsha: Hunan Chubanshe, 1995), 454.

11 Li Rui, *"Da Yuejin" Qingliji, xia juan* (Personal Experience of the Great Leap Forward, part II) (Haikou: Nanfang Chubanshe, 1999), 27. See also: Luo Pinghan, *Nongcun Renmin Gongshe Shi* (A History of the People's Commune in Rural China) (Fuzhou: Fujian Renmin Chubanshe, 2003), 28; and Li Duanxiang, "Guanyu Mao Zedong Chengshi Renmin Gongshe Sixiang de Lishi Kaocha ji Sikao (Mao Zedong's Thought on the Urban People's Commune: A Historical Study and Reflection)," *Dangdai Shijie yu Shehui Zhuyi* (Contemporary World and the Socialist System), no. 3 (2011): 162–166.

12 Zhonggong Zhongyang Wenxian Yanjiushi, ed., *Jianguo yilai Zhongyao Wenxian Xuanbian, di shiyi ce* (Collection of Important Documents After the Founding of the People's Republic), vol. 11 (Beijing: Zhongyang Wenxian Chubanshe, 1995), 447. See also, Wu Luoshan, "Guanyu Renmin Gongshe Guihua zhong jige Wenti de Tantao (Inquiry into a Few Issues Concerning the Planning of the People's Communes)," *Jianzhu Xuebao* (Architectural Journal), no. 1 (1959): 1–3.

13 Li Baihao, *Ningbo Chengshi Guihuashi Yanjiu Baogao* (Research Report on Urban Planning History of Ningbo) (Ningbo: Ningboshi Chengxiang Guihua Zhongxin, 2016), 128–130.

14 Li Caihua, *Sanxian Jianshe Yanjiu* (Studies in Third-Front Construction) (Changchun: Jilin Daxue Chubanshe, 2004), 14–26.

15 Zhou Yanlai, *Ershi Shiji Liuqishi Niandai Zhongguo "Sanxian" Jianshe Xulun* (The Third-Front Construction in China in the 1960s-70s) (Master's Thesis, Northwestern University, Evanston, 2003), 22.

16 Zhou, *Ershi Shiji*, 24–30.

17 Huang Li, Li Baihao and Sun Yingdan, "Fanshi Zhuanbian Lingjiedian xia de 'Sanxian Chengshi' Jianshe Guihua Shijian (The Planning Practice of the 'Third-Front' Cities at the Threshold of a Paradigmatic Transformation)," *Chengshi Guihua Xuekan* (Journal of Urban Planning), no. 1 (2013): 97–103.

18 Xiang Dong, *Ershi Shiji Liuqishi Niandai Panzhihua Diqu Sanxian Jianshe Xulun* (Third-Front Construction in the Panzhihua Area in the 1960s-70s) (Master's Thesis, Sichuan Normal University, Sichuan, 2010), 38–56.

19 Wang Ziyun, "Shanxi Sanxian Jianshe de Yanjiu (Research on the Third-Front Construction of Shanxi Province)," *Shanxi Qingnian Guanli Gangbu Xueyuan Xuebao* (Journal of the Shanxi College of Youth Cadres), no. 4 (2004): 54–58.

20 Xu Kaixi, "Hubei Sanxian Jianshe de Huigu yu Qishi (Review and Study of the Third-Front Construction of Hubei Province)," *Hubei Shehui Kexue* (Hubei Social Sciences), no. 10 (2003): 23–24.
21 Tangshan Chengshi Jianshe Zhi Bianji Weiyuanhui, ed., *Tangshan Chengshi Jianshe Zhi* (Annals of Urban Construction of Tangshan) (Tianjin: Tianjin Renmin Chubanshe, 1992), 10.
22 Shen Qingji and Ma Jiwu, "Tangshan Dizhen Zaihou Chongjian Guihua: Huigu, Fenxi ji Sikao (Planning for Post-Quake Reconstruction of Tangshan: Review, Analysis and Reflection)," *Chengshi Guihua Xuekan* (Journal of Urban Planning), no. 4 (2008): 17–28.

Bibliography

Dong Guanqi, ed. *Gudu Beijing Wushinian Yanbianlu* (Fifty-Year Evolution of the Ancient Capital Beijing). Nanjing: Dongnan Daxue Chubanshe, 2006.

Guodu Sheji Jishu Zhuanyuan Banshichu, comp. *Shoudu Jihua* (Capital Plan). Nanjing: Nanjing Chubanshe, 2006.

Huang Li, Li Baihao and Sun Yingdan. "Fanshi Zhuanbian Lingjiedian xia de 'Sanxian Chengshi' Jianshe Guihua Shijian (The Planning Practice of the 'Third-Front' Cities at the Threshold of a Paradigmatic Transformation)." *Chengshi Guihua Xuekan* (Journal of Urban Planning), no. 1 (2013): 97–103.

Li Baihao. *Ningbo Chengshi Guihuashi Yanjiu Baogao* (Research Report on Urban Planning History of Ningbo). Ningbo: Ningboshi Chengxiang Guihua Zhongxin, 2016.

Li Baihao and Peng Xiutao. "Zhongguo Xiandai Xinxing Gongye Chengshi Guihua de Lishi Yanjiu – yi Sulian Yuanzhu de 156 xiang Zhongdian Gongcheng wei Zhongxin (Historical Study on the Planning of Modern and Newly Emerging Industrial Cities in China – as Centered on the 156 Major Soviet-Aid Projects)." *Chengshi Guihua Xuekan* (Journal of Urban Planning), no. 4 (2006): 84–92.

Li Caihua. *Sanxian Jianshe Yanjiu* (Studies in Third-Front Construction). Changchun: Jilin Daxue Chubanshe, 2004.

Li Duanxiang. "Guanyu Mao Zedong Chengshi Renmin Gongshe Sixiang de Lishi Kaocha ji Sikao (Mao Zedong's Thought on the Urban People's Commune: A Historical Study and Reflection)." *Dangdai Shijie yu Shehui Zhuyi* (Contemporary World and the Socialist System), no. 3 (2011): 162–166.

Li Rui. *"Da Yuejin" Qingliji, xia juan* (Personal Experience of the Great Leap Forward, Part II). Haikou: Nanfang Chubanshe, 1999.

List of City Squares by Size. Wikipedia. https://en.wikipedia.org/wiki/List_of_city_squares_by_size. Accessed 1 June 2017.

Luo Pinghan. *Nongcun Renmin Gongshe Shi* (A History of the People's Commune in Rural China). Fuzhou: Fujian Renmin Chubanshe, 2003.

Mao Zedong. *Mao Zedong Xuanji, di wu juan* (Selected Works of Mao Zedong), vol. 5. Beijing: Renmin Chubanshe, 1977.

Pan Guxi, ed. *Zhongguo Jianzhu Shi, di wu ban* (A History of Chinese Architecture), 5th ed. Beijing: Zhongguo Jianzhu Chubanshe, 2004.

Shen Qingji and Ma Jiwu. "Tangshan Dizhen Zaihou Chongjian Guihua: Huigu, Fenxi ji Sikao (Planning for Post-Quake Reconstruction of Tangshan: Review, Analysis and Reflection)." *Chengshi Guihua Xuekan* (Journal of Urban Planning), no. 4 (2008): 17–28.

Tangshan Chengshi Jianshe Zhi Bianji Weiyuanhui, ed. *Tangshan Chengshi Jianshe Zhi* (Annals of Urban Construction of Tangshan). Tianjin: Tianjin Renmin Chubanshe, 1992.

Wang Gang, Zhao Zhenzhong and Jiang Yongqing. "Tangshan Zhenhou Guihua Guocheng Jianshu (Brief Account of the Process of Post-Quake Reconstruction of Tangshan)." *Xibu Renju Huanjing Xuekan* (Journal of Human Settlements in Western Regions) 4 (2014): 84–91.

Wang Jiaxiang. "Chengshi Gongzuo Dagang (General Notes on Leading and Managing the City)." In *Wang Jiaxiang Xuanji* (Selected Works of Wang Jiaxiang), edited by Wang Jiaxiang, 367–368. Beijing: Renmin Chubanshe, 1989.

———. *Wang Jiaxiang Xuanji* (Selected Works of Wang Jiaxiang). Beijing: Renmin Chubanshe, 1989.

Wang Jun. *Lishi de Xiakou* (Turning Points in History). Beijing: Zhongxin Chuban Jituan, 2015.

Wang Ziyun. "Shanxi Sanxian Jianshe de Yanjiu (Research on the Third-Front Construction of Shanxi)." *Shanxi Qingnian Guanli Gangbu Xueyuan Xuebao* (Journal of the Shanxi College of Youth Cadres), no. 4 (2004): 54–58.

Wu Luoshan. "Guanyu Renmin Gongshe Guihua zhong jige Wenti de Tantao (Inquiry into a Few Issues Concerning the Planning of the People's Communes)." *Jianzhu Xuebao* (Architectural Journal), no. 1 (1959): 1–3.

Xiang Dong. *Ershi Shiji Liuqishi Niandai Panzhihua Diqu Sanxian Jianshe Xulun* (Third-Front Construction in the Panzhihua Area in the 1960s–70s). Master's Thesis. Sichuan Normal University, Sichuan, 2010.

Xu Kaixi. "Hubei Sanxian Jianshe de Huigu yu Qishi (Review and Study of the Third-Front Construction of Hubei Province)." *Hubei Shehui Kexue* (Hubei Social Sciences), no. 10 (2003): 23–24.

Zhonggong Zhongyang Wenxian Yanjiushi, ed. *Jianguo yilai Zhongyao Wenxian Xuanbian, di shiyi ce* (Collection of Important Documents After the Founding of the People's Republic), vol. 11. Beijing: Zhongyang Wenxian Chubanshe, 1995.

———, ed. *Mao Zedong Zaoqi Wengao* (Early Manuscripts of Mao Zedong). Changsha: Hunan Chubanshe, 1995.

Zhou Yanlai. *Ershi Shiji Liuqishi Niandai Zhongguo "Sanxian" Jianshe Xulun* (The Third-Front Construction in China in the 1960s-70s). Master's Thesis. Northwestern University, Evanston, 2003.

Zou Deci. *Xin Zhongguo Chengshi Guihua Fazhangshi Yanjiu – Zong Baogao ji Dashiji* (Investigating the Developmental History of Urban Planning of New China – General Report and Major Timeline). Beijing: Zhongguo Jianzhu Gongye Chubanshe, 2014.

Glossary

Beijing	北京
chaiqiang zhulu	拆墙筑路
Chen Zhanxiang	陈占祥
Chiang Kai-shek	蒋介石
Danjiangkou (city)	丹江口（市）
Douhe (River)	陡河
Exi	鄂西
Fengrun (town)	丰润（县）
Fengrun Xinqu	丰润新区
Gansu	甘肃
Gongzhufen	公主坟
Guangzhou	广州
Guixibei	桂西北
Guizhou	贵州
guodu sheji jishu weiyuanhui	国都设计技术委员会
Hangzhou	杭州
Hankou	汉口
Kailuan (Coal Mine)	开滦（煤矿）
Kuomintang	国民党
Liang Sicheng	梁思成
Mao Zedong	毛泽东
Ming (dynasty)	明（朝）
Nanjing	南京
nanjing guomin zhengfu	南京国民政府
Ningbo	宁波
Ningxia	宁夏
nonye shehuizhuyihua	农业社会主义化
Panzhihua (city)	攀枝花（市）
Qing (dynasty)	清（朝）
Qinghai	青海
sanxian jianshe	三线建设
Shaanxi	陕西
Shanghai	上海

Shanxi	山西
shehuizhuyi gongyehua	社会主义工业化
shoudu jianshe weiyuanhui	首都建设委员会
Shoudu Jihua (project)	首都计划
Shoudu Jihua (book)	首都计划
shoudu jihua weiyuanhui	首都计划委员会
Sichuan	四川
Sun Yat-sen	孙逸仙（孙中山）
Taiyuan	太原
Tangshan	唐山
Xiangxi	湘西
yida ergong	一大二公
Yuebei	粤北
Yuetan	月坛
Yunnan	云南
Yuxi	豫西
Zhu Yuanzhang	朱元璋

21

DANWEI AND SOCIALIST URBANISM

Duanfang Lu

After the founding of the People's Republic in 1949, most factories, schools, and government offices were organized into a state administrative system; the work unit (*danwei*) was the basic unit of this system.[1] Since then, the work unit has functioned not only as workplace but also the principal social institution in which the lives of most urban residents are organized.[2] By 1978, around 95 per cent of urban workers belonged to a work unit of one kind or another.[3]

The fundamental importance of the work unit in Chinese society lies in its unique combination of economic, political, and social functions.[4] The work unit offers its employees lifetime employment and attendant welfare such as public housing and medical care.[5] Each work unit has its own Communist Party branch in charge of transmitting party policy, implementing social campaigns, providing political education, awarding moral merit, and making notes on employees' performance in personnel dossiers (*dang'an*). The work unit runs a variety of social services, including shops, canteens, clinics, nurseries, and libraries. It administrates many facets of everyday life: orchestrating group leisure activities, organizing local sanitation, and mediating civic disputes, to name just a few.[6]

The work unit is a territorial unit that possesses a distinctive spatial form.[7] A typical work unit integrates production, residence, and social facilities in close proximity within one or several walled compound(s). Residents may conduct most daily affairs without leaving their unit. The characteristic form of the work unit had a profound effect on urbanism under Mao. Economic reforms since 1978 have brought enormous change to the work unit, especially with the acceleration in urban restructuring since 1992.[8] Despite the changes, the influence of the work unit still persists in many aspects.[9]

As the basic building block of urban China, the work unit has been studied by scholars in disciplines ranging from sociology to political science. Important monographs include Andrew Walder's analysis of the "organized dependence" that flourished in the work unit,[10] David Bray's study of work-unit–based urban governance,[11] Yang Xiaoming and Zhou Yuhu's *Zhongguo danwei zhidu* on the institutional features of the Chinese work unit system,[12] Gail Henderson and Myron Cohen's account of daily life in a Chinese hospital,[13] and Marc Blecher and Gordon White's investigation into power and politics within the work unit during and after the Cultural Revolution,[14] among others. A volume examining the work unit as a social institution from historical and comparative perspectives was put together by Xiaopo Lü and Elizabeth Perry.[15] The number of journal articles is also growing rapidly.[16]

DOI: 10.4324/9781315851112-32

Apart from a handful of studies, most existing literature focuses on socio-political aspects of the work unit. Although the characteristic spatiality of the *danwei* has profound effects on contemporary Chinese society, disciplinary limitations have made many social researchers reluctant to include the spatial dimension in their interpretations of Chinese society. This chapter provides an examination of the work unit as an urban form and its spatial implications for the Chinese city during the socialist period. Following an introduction to the physical form of the work unit, it provides a discussion of its socio-spatial effects and the resulting urbanism. The chapter closes with a discussion of change and continuity in the work unit during the reform era.

The Work Unit as an Urban Form[17]

The site planning of a new work unit was carried out by professionals, but the subsequent development was often planned by the work unit's own Department of Basic Construction. Beginning with essential production structures and dormitories for single workers, the work unit grew naturally, expanding as the enterprise matured. During the early years, a few basic living facilities were built: apartment buildings, canteens, boiler rooms, public bathhouses, and nurseries.[18] Depending on the availability of construction funds and land, the work unit gradually built more apartments and other supporting structures such as social halls, guesthouses, and primary schools.[19] Rather than being built in a separate area, housing and facilities often occupied space adjacent to the workplace.

There is wide variation in spatial layout, resources, and size of individual work units. Units in Shanghai, for instance, are more likely to have their employees living in separate residential areas than those in Beijing. Work units in far suburban and rural areas are generally well equipped, while units near downtown areas and in small towns are less so. Depending on their rank in the bureaucratic system, the resources available to the work units vary considerably. Central units generally fare better than local units, and those in privileged fields, such as universities and major factories, are likely to receive more funding and land for construction than others. Work units also differ greatly from one another in area and population size, from those with a few hundred square metres and dozens of members, to those with thousands of square metres and hundreds to thousands of residents (Figure 21.1).

Despite the seemingly haphazard construction of individual units, some spatial characteristics are widely shared (except very small work units), be they administrative units, educational institutes, or industrial works. The common physical features can be summarized as: (1) a walled and gated enclosure; (2) a well-integrated internal circulation system; (3) close association of work and residence; (4) a high level of provision of social facilities; and (5) rationalist architectural layout and style. As mentioned earlier, economic restructuring since 1978 has brought fundamental changes to the work unit; some of the above features are no longer universal. In this and next sections, however, I treat the work unit as an archetype, leaving discussion of changes in the reform era until the last section.

Every work unit is a walled enclosure, or, if large enough, a cluster of several walled enclosures. The wall, in most cases made of brick, sets the work unit physically apart from its surroundings. There are usually several entrances through the wall from city boulevards. The main entrances are staffed by security personnel and fortified with heavy wrought-iron gates. A small janitor's room is set on one side of the main gate, which provides working and living space for the gatekeeper, on duty around the clock. There is sometimes a mailroom beside the janitor's room; unit residents come to collect mail on a daily basis.

The level of security at entrances varies from unit to unit. Some institutions, such as major administrative offices and military-related units, may subject all persons to identification

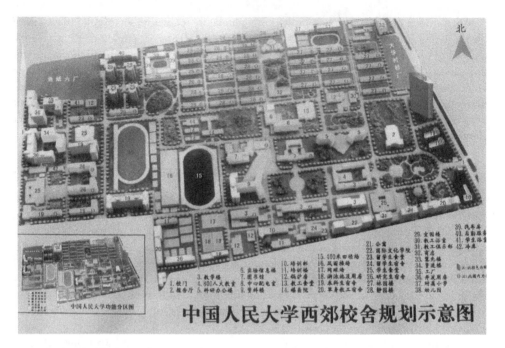

Figure 21.1 Model photo of Renmin University, Beijing (photo taken by the author in 2000). Key: 1. Main entrance; 2. Conference hall; 3. Classrooms; 4.400-student classroom; 5. Office and research building; 6. Information centre; 7. Library; 8. Central power distribution room; 9. Archive; 10. Training centre; 11. Training building; 12. Boiler room; 13. Faculty canteen; 14. Hospital; 15.400-metre track and field; 16. Sports field; 17. Tennis field; 18. Swimming pool; 19. Undergraduate dormitory; 20. Staff dormitory; 21. Apartment building; 22. International Cultural College; 23. International student canteen; 24. International student dormitory; 25. Student canteen; 26. Graduate student dormitory; 27. Lin-Yuan Building; 28. Jin-Yuan Building; 29. Yi-Yuan Building; 30. Faculty bathhouse; 31. Faculty club; 32. Shop; 33. Hui-Guan Building; 34. Xian-Jin Building; 35. Factory; 36. Development building; 37. Primary school; 38. Kindergarten; 39. Garage; 40. Services; 41. Public bathhouse; 42. Storage.

Source: © Duanfang Lu.

procedures. Others are relatively easy to enter; only those obviously not belonging to the work unit would be stopped for an identity check by the gatekeeper. The gate is closed at midnight and opened in the early morning. Once closed, coming and going for both residents and outsiders becomes difficult. Passage can only be obtained by waking the understandably displeased gatekeeper, who would only open the door for unit members he (rarely she) recognized. The working and living quarters are usually circled by separate walls. The gates between them may remain closed during work hours to prevent employees from slipping back home.

From the entrance there are roadways that form the means of circulation for pedestrians and vehicles. Far from being part of a larger urban highway system, the roadways of the work unit form a system of their own. Bounded by long boulevards for the rapid movement of city traffic, the work unit's internal circulation system is broken into short streets which give easy circulation within the unit but do not allow outside vehicles to run uninterruptedly through the unit compound. Many work units have a monumental main administration building, which serves as the centre of the work unit space. It may not necessarily be located at the actual geographical centre of the compound; instead, its symbolic importance is achieved via the arrangement of architectural elements. When the main building is located near the main entrance, the gate opens onto a spacious square with the main building on the other end of the square, facing the gate. When the square is not immediately in front of the gate, it is often approached by a broad boulevard with the main building, set at the other end of the square, facing the boulevard. In either case, great emphasis is placed on axiality and the symmetrical design of buildings and landscape.

The work unit provides public housing for its employees and their families. Usually, the living quarters (*shenhuo qu*) are close to the workplace. The only exceptions are factories that pollute the environment and work units located in highly developed urban areas where land is scarce and housing space is limited. In these cases, employees may live in separate housing areas, or spill over into downtown neighbourhoods or residential tracts managed by the municipal government. Some work units provide bus links between residence and work. Small work units may have workplace and residence within a compact area, while larger ones tend to separate them into distinct areas with walls or roadways. Residences include dormitories for single workers and apartments for families, both housed in modern-style buildings in orderly rows (Figure 21.2). The oldest ones are two to six storeys high with stairwell systems; some newest ones are high-rise buildings equipped with elevators. The design of both dormitories and apartments presents a realistic trade-off between social, utility, and housing spaces by externalizing social activities and utilities from housing units. As a number of functions are removed from

Figure 21.2 Most apartment buildings are five- to six-story walk-ups, housed in orthogonal brick and cement structures (photo taken by author in 1999).

Source: © Duanfang Lu.

351

the private domain and accommodated instead in unit social facilities, the size of residence is reduced significantly.

Both the working and living quarters of the work unit are provided with a modern infrastructure, including electricity, running water, and a sewage system. This is connected to that of the city, forming an integrated urban infrastructure system. In the case of work units in rural areas, the infrastructure is constructed from scratch at a new site and thus often forms a system of its own rather than joining with neighbouring villages. Local residents wishing to take advantage of the facilities are not allowed to do so, sometimes resulting in violent conflicts between peasants and the work unit.

The work unit provides various community facilities. Small work units have canteens, social halls, clinics, and public bathhouses. Medium-sized units may add nurseries, kindergartens, parks, libraries, sports fields, guesthouses, and shops. Large work units, especially universities and work units in remote suburban or rural areas, have such elaborate social service systems that they resemble a miniature city. In addition to the facilities listed above, they have food markets, hospitals, post offices, banks, movie theatres, workers' clubs, barbershops, and primary and high schools. While facilities in small work units are scattered in buildings throughout the unit compound, large units may have a district set aside for social services, which forms an area similar to a city's downtown. Children's playgrounds, bicycle sheds, sports fields, parks, and other recreation spaces are provided in the open areas between buildings. All these facilities are designed for the exclusive use of unit members, but enforcing such exclusivity depends on the strength of individual work units. In some cases, neighbouring units cooperate to support the joint use of such facilities as schools and hospitals.

The close proximity of work, housing, and social facilities results in a peculiar pattern of local comings and goings. Many unit residents can carry out their daily business within the unit compound, although some do daily travel beyond the unit walls. Children of small work units go to schools outside the compound. Adults living with their spouses or parents in work units other than their own have to commute by bus or bicycle. Weekends are a time when many make trips of good distances away from their work units: shopping downtown, playing in parks, or visiting relatives and friends who live in other parts of the city. Yet, the daily routine of many unit members is nonetheless confined by the unit compound. In some cases, the routines of everyday life are regulated by the use of a public address system, which provides news, announcements, information of upcoming events, music, and exercise instructions, at certain times during the day. Frequent travel along mutual pathways and shared activities at common meeting places create plenty of opportunities for people to form neighbourly bonds.

In the field of residential planning, the idea of the neighbourhood unit was introduced to China in the 1930s. It was employed by Japanese colonial planners in the planning of cities such as Changchun and Datong and used by Chinese planners in planning proposals for several major cities immediately after World War II. Socialist planners experimented with several competing residential planning ideas during the 1950s. The microdistrict (*xiaoqu* in Chinese and *mikrorayon* in Russian), an idea transmitted from the Soviet Union and essentially similar to the neighbourhood unit schema, gradually gained favour. Except a few built examples of the microdistrict, however, planners failed to actualize the model to any great extent under Mao (1949–1976). Instead, the work unit gradually became the de facto dominant form to organize the Chinese city.

Chinese urban form, as it exists today, bears little resemblance to what Chinese socialist planners had in mind. Yet by looking into the production process of space, urban form and function under Mao were nonetheless "socialist" in nature, as they were produced as part of socialist production and accumulation strategies. My study shows that the integral spatial form of the work unit was the unique outcome generated by the conflicts between the needs of capital accumulation and the necessity of labour reproduction within a peculiar socialist/Third World context.[20] Industrial expansion caused a dramatic growth in urban population in the 1950s. Under the national austerity policy, little state investment was allocated to non-productive construction. Rapid urban growth and biased investment policies together created immense scarcity of crucial consumption facilities; there was a constant shortage of housing and facilities. Much conflict was generated between the needs of accumulation and the necessity of labour reproduction.

My archival research reveals that the building of living facilities within work units was often accomplished through construction outside the state-approved plan, resource hoarding, and exchanges via informal channels. This, certainly, did not happen automatically. Instead, it was a result of the conflicted relationship between the state, work units, and planners in the construction of essential consumption facilities. Although the Chinese state was depicted as a totalitarian regime in Cold War-era research, the control of the socialist state over enterprises and labour was structurally weak. Under socialism, enterprises operate within soft budget constraints – that is, if a production unit suffers financial losses, the state will cover it sooner or later. Hence, a socialist economic system does not possess the kind of disciplinary mechanisms over enterprises characteristic of capitalism. Meanwhile, due to the lack of labour markets, layoffs, bankruptcies, and so on, the means for disciplining labour under socialism are less efficient than those under capitalism. The strong bargaining power of the work unit over the local government and the planning department, and workers over their work unit, played a key role in redirecting capital from production to consumption construction.

With the immense scarcity of consumption facilities causing severe political tension and strife during the 1950s, the state responded by imposing the responsibility of urban provision upon the work unit. Faced with political pressure from employees below and administrators above, unit leaders strived to meet the needs of their workers. The ideal model for residential development for planners was a combination of the principle of functional zoning and unitary neighbourhood planning. Due to limited resources and weak planning power, however, planners failed to actualize the model to a larger extent before 1978. In theory, public ownership and the centrally planned system should provide favourable conditions for the realization of planning ideas. In practice, construction investment was channelled through all-powerful vertical sectoral lines, over which the planning department had little control. In theory, all construction projects should be put under the supervision of planners. In practice, planners operated in the lower echelon of the power system and did not possess adequate means for regulation. The Chinese state was sufficiently pragmatic not to follow planning orthodoxies blindly, but to adapt to the changing urban reality.

Many socio-spatial effects achieved through the peculiar arrangement of the work unit are indeed similar to those of the model company town found in the capitalist society and the Soviet Union. Both are characterized by the domination of a single enterprise, the close association of workplace and residence, and the paternalistic policies that extend well beyond the requirements of production.[21] Historically, the emergence of most company towns in the West coincided with the second phase of capitalism, which was characterized by centralized industrial production.[22] What may partly explain the similarities between the work unit and the company town is that socialist society shares a number of fundamental characteristics with capitalism of this phase, including the development of heavy industries, the concentration of production, and corporate organization of production. As Lenin once pointed out, the concentration of production in capitalist societies created the economic basis for the development of socialism.[23] Although the work unit and the company town belong to two different societies often seen as oppositional, a similar economic basis – centralized industrial production (in contrast to flexible production under late capitalism) – may account for their similar characteristics. Certainly, unlike the company town, which is often located in an isolated rural location, most work units are situated in urban or suburban areas. As such, they have important implications for the city, to which I now turn.

Alternative Urbanism

The characteristic spatiality of the work unit has profound effects on contemporary Chinese society. While some commentators describe the work unit mainly as a repressive institution of state control, I contend that the work unit creates comprehensive urban effects related to community, security, equality, women's rights, employees' rights, welfare, and environmental sustainability. The work unit provides a safety net through which industrial labour is reproduced, a spatial environment that fosters social exchange, moral bonds, and equality, and a social community from which urban residents derive their social identity and sense of belonging. Certainly, the work unit has its limits on each of these facets, and its enclosed character has some negative effects upon the city as a whole. The work-unit–based city under Mao displayed an urbanism quite distinct from other societies. I shall use the past tense in this section.

Community. The work unit as the focus of urban life resulted in a small community atmosphere lacking in anonymity, a peculiar urban experience not found in other modern cities.[24] A person in the Western modern city, as typified in Edgar Allan Poe's 1840 tale "The Man of the Crowd," remains a nameless face in a crowd made up of strangers.[25] In contrast, an urbanite in Maoist China was constantly among people who knew him or her well. One experienced warm neighbourliness but was constantly subject to watchful eyes of the crowd.[26] On one hand, when difficulties arose, members of the community pitched in to help. On the other hand, gossip spread quickly when one did anything outside existing norms.[27] As a unit member remarked,

> [I]f there's a newcomer in any unit, before long everybody knows his background, history, wage grade, political behavior, whether there are any black marks on his record, what sports he's good at and with whom he does or doesn't get along. . . . A whole range of matters must go through public evaluation, such as wages, bonuses, designation as a progressive worker, being sent out to study, promotions and punishments and allocation of housing and other benefits. . . . Rumors, gossip and nasty remarks are common [too,] and this leads to pointless quarrels, making the relationships between people complicated and tense.[28]

The dense network of human relationships and the lack of anonymity inclined many to refer to the work unit as the "urban village."[29] Although the strong sense of community reduced deviance, it inevitably also had side effects such as suffocating interpersonal relations and lack of innovation.

Security and exclusivity. With clear boundaries, security gates and an internal circulation system that controls the movement of through traffic past its territory, the work unit provided a safe environment for the residents. Watchful eyes prevented outsiders from coming or going unobserved, children played without constant adult attendance, and people could walk or bike on streets safely.

With the high percentage of time spent within their own work unit, people's experiences and contacts outside were relatively few. They often spoke of events happening "out in society" (*shehui shang*), as if their work unit were entirely separated from the wider world.[30] The limited contact across work units helped to prevent large scale organized opposition beyond the unit boundary. The numerous protests during the Cultural Revolution, for instance, largely remained "cellular protests."

"Less urbanism." The city under Mao, like other socialist cities, appeared "less of an urban place," to quote Ivan Szelenzi,[31] than a typical capitalist city. Szelenzi observes that there was less urban diversity, lower density in inner urban public places, and less urban marginality in East European socialist cities.[32] The best test case of this was East Berlin, which greatly differed from West Berlin in the aforementioned aspects.

The enclosed character of the work unit resulted in less choice, social interaction, and heterogeneity at the urban level. Georg Simmel, in his analysis of the modern city, contrasts urban space, where density and diversity constantly put the individual in touch with myriad possibilities, to rural space, where individual movement and opportunities are restricted.[33] Simmel characterizes an individual living in a modern city as a mobile subject, moving across the city's social circles and choosing his or her associations to create a particular, individualized social world.[34] In the Maoist city, one's social life was largely confined within one's own work unit, which was separated from other parts of the city physically and socially.[35] As there was little provision to facilitate interactions in society at large, the urbanite in the Maoist city was restricted to the concentric social pattern centred on the work unit, with few resources available outside this circle.

As strict limits were imposed upon private commercial establishments under Mao, urban residents bought most of their daily essentials from cooperative shops run by the work unit. The streets had fewer shops, restaurants, ads, recreational centres, and other urban facilities. The social environment of the work unit encouraged socialist collectivism while discouraging social heterogeneity, which is central to Wirth's notion of "urbanism as a way of life."[36] As the greater "openness" of private life suppressed behaviour that did not conform to local norms, there was a high level of homogeneity in terms of life styles.

Equality, residential segregation, and urban marginality. A high level of social and spatial equality was maintained within the work unit. The salary difference between managers and workers was not significant enough to create major socio-economic ramifications, and they worked and lived in more or less similar buildings. To be sure, despite largely homogeneous exteriors, the internal spaces of both office and apartment buildings were differentiated. In office buildings, larger rooms or corner offices were allocated to higher ranking officials. In the case of apartment buildings, the main difference lay in the size and number of rooms of the apartment unit; other subtle differences included the orientation of the apartment unit, the floor on which it was located, and the quality of the building that housed it. Each work unit had a complicated ranking system to assign housing fairly, based on criteria such as rank, job seniority, marital status, family size, ethnic origin (minorities are given priority), and so on. Based on this system, senior workers might be ranked the same as less senior managers. Hence, despite the existence of a hierarchical system, the degree of differentiation in terms of living standards remained relatively low within the work unit.

The mechanism of residential segregation in the Maoist city bore little similarity to that found in capitalist cities. Compared with intra-unit differentiation, larger social stratification existed between units in terms of income, welfare, and environmental quality. Residential segregation in the Chinese city was most commonly expressed through the separation of different work units, instead of segregating rich, poor, and ethnic minorities into distinctive urban areas.

Like other socialist cities, the work-unit–based Maoist city displayed fewer signs of marginality.[37] The work unit system provided the majority of urban residents with lifetime employment and access to welfare benefits. Supplementary to this system, Residents' Committees created means of subsistence for those not formally employed by work units.[38] In addition to this dual safety network, there was strict control of rural immigration.[39] Peasants were kept in their respective villages through a careful coordination of the issue of residential permits (*hukou*) and work permits.[40] Migrants without correct documents could not survive in the city, as basic commodities (e.g., rice, flour, plain cloth, and oil) were rationed in urban areas. Consequently, although the city as a whole showed sign of scarcity, less extreme expressions of poverty and deviance such as homelessness and crime were found. The orderly Maoist city, devoid of urban ills such as shanty towns and prostitution, was presented as a shining counterexample to the Third World by scholars during the 1970s.[41]

Women's rights. The design of the work unit created an institutionally non-sexist environment that supported the activities of employed women and their families. In contemporary China, urban women were expected to have paid employment, while homebound women were the exception. The work unit's integration of production, residence, and social services on a manageable scale greatly facilitated the functioning of two-worker families. Public kitchens and canteens offered alternatives to cooking at home, nurseries within the unit compound reduced the time spent in commuting, and nursing rooms near workshops helped mothers to get back to work.

The Maoist city therefore contrasts sharply to the Western capitalist city in this regard, which is recognized as fundamentally dependent on the subordination of women by a vigorous feminist critique since 1970s.[42] As a result of the gender-based planning, social childcare is rarely available near office centres; the transportation pattern assumes the woman as an available full-time driver; and the whole idea of suburb is indeed based on the assumption of the self-reliant home with full-time operator – the woman.[43]

Nevertheless, residual patriarchal authority survived in Chinese domestic space; women were almost invariably expected to spend more time on housework and childcare than men. Women's double burden of work and domestic responsibilities sometimes results in household crisis.[44] In response to women's particular needs, every work unit has a women's committee that deals with a broad range of women's concerns and family disputes.

Discipline vs. employees' rights. While the modern capitalist city is based on contractual relationships between individual subjects mediated by the market, the Maoist urban society was founded on a collective labour's "organized dependence" on the work unit. Walder's famous study reveals that as the paternalism of the work unit penetrated various aspects of workers' lives, the latter were subject to the patronage of unit leaders.[45] Many commentators point out that discipline within the work unit relied not only on the presence of unit Party leaders and workshop managers but also upon mutual surveillance among workers.[46] Watchful eyes put pressure upon colleagues so that there was less chance of malingering or lateness.[47]

Yet, the managing powers and disciplinary effects of the work unit were nonetheless limited. In fact, there was widespread acknowledgment among the Chinese urban reformers that the work unit system promoted inefficiency and lack of discipline among workers. The reasons for this were multiple. First and most importantly, the guarantee of permanent employment granted employees much power to resist efficient management. Hence, when the Western ways of industrial discipline were introduced in the late 1970s, advocates of enterprise reform vigorously called for removing lifetime job security.[48]

Second, the operational logic following the ideals of the Maoist "mass line" created unique labour relations within the work unit.[49] Unit cadres were required to remain close to the employees, while workers were encouraged to participate in management. As a consequence, the power of managers was significantly weakened. Third, as David Bray rightfully points out, the spatial arrangement of the work unit was "ill suited to the creation of disciplined and individuated worker subject."[50] The close link between living and working space bred socialist collectivism rather than the logic of individual-oriented labour. The lack of clear boundary between productive activity and everyday life served to increase employees' powers to resist the discipline of workplace management.

Welfare. As mentioned earlier, lack of a society-wide welfare system meant a wide range of welfare programmes were organized via the work unit. The unit trade union was and still is the key agent to perform various welfare functions. Following the Soviet model, the trade union in China plays a different role from the trade union in capitalist society.[51] Based on the assumption that under socialism there was no need for the trade union to protect workers against the interests of the capitalist, the trade union was reconceptualized as the link between the party and the working class.[52] Although the trade union was initially designed as an extension of the party leadership in China,[53] in practice the party leadership was taken over by the unit party branch, while the trade union was mainly in charge of managing workers' welfare.[54]

Following the 1951 national policy "Labour insurance regulations," the Labour Insurance Fund was raised (3 per cent of monthly salary) to provide the payment of medical expenses, disability pensions, funeral costs and financial support for the families of workers killed in the workplace, retirement pensions, and maternity leave.[55] The work unit offered additional funding for other benefits, such as medical expenses for injuries and illness and maternity pay. The unit trade union managed 70 per cent of the Labour Insurance Fund and other resources provided by the work unit for welfare programmes. Through its role in managing many facets of everyday life meticulously on a daily basis (such as providing assistance to workers in need and organizing group leisure activities), urban workers were effectively enmeshed within a comprehensive safety net.

Environmental sustainability. The distinctive mixed land-use pattern of the work unit had important environmental significance. The close association of workplace, residence, and social facilities greatly reduced the need for urban residents to travel beyond their unit compound. Such an urban form depended little on the provision of an extensive and expensive public transport system. As Clifton Pannell observed in the late 1970s, major Chinese cities such as Shanghai and Beijing had a very small number of buses and other public transport vehicles: the number for both cities was around 2,200 in 1977, much less than other Western cities of similar sizes.[56] Without any private cars, the principal modes of circulation at the time were bicycling and walking. Energy consumption was also reduced through shared facilities such as canteens and public bathhouses. It is indeed an incredible environmental achievement to have an urban system based on minimum energy costs without generating serious dysfunctions in economic and social organization.

Despite a certain similarity the Maoist city bore with the Soviet city in terms of collectivism, "less urbanism," enterprise-based welfare systems, and so on,[57] it differed from the latter in several aspects. First, despite the desire to reduce the distance between work and home, Soviet planning tended to separate production and residence. Second, although housing in the Soviet Union was often built by industrial ministries as part of the construction of a new factory, unlike China, the housing was usually turned over to Soviet municipal authorities within six months after the construction was completed.[58] Third, the Soviet residential district was usually larger than a Chinese work unit and comprised residents from different enterprises.[59] As such, although it was held that residential design should foster a sense of neighbourliness in early Soviet planning thought (as represented in the 1920s communal housing experiments and the subsequent adoption of the microdistrict), the objective was not achieved. A 1970 study found that inhabitants in a Soviet residential district knew "only 5 to 10 of their neighbours by sight, 3 to 5 by name, and almost nothing about where they work or about their character."[60] Fourth, due to the separation between work and residence and because of weather conditions, the

Soviet urban system relied more on the provision of extensive public transport systems than the Chinese system.[61] From these perspectives, work-unit–based urbanism was indeed an alternative to both capitalist and Soviet urbanism.

Change and Continuity in the Reform Era

Changes brought by economic reforms since 1978 have been accompanied by enormous transformations of urban China. The work unit has gradually declined as the fundamental sociospatial unit of the Chinese city. This section provides a brief account of some of the most salient developments in the social and physical environment of the work unit.

The effects of reforms until the mid-1990s strengthened the role of work units in some respects.[62] Fiscal decentralization, for example, has given work units increased economic autonomy with regard to decisions on investment and resource allocation. More and better consumption facilities such as high-rise apartment buildings, convenience shops, and children's playgrounds within work units were built after the reforms. The urban reforms aiming to increase efficiency and re-commodify labour have given more managerial autonomy to unit managers to hire, dismiss, and discipline staff.[63] Certainly, the industrial restructuring since 1992 has weakened the role of state units in national economy; some, especially those in heavy industry, lose their competitiveness and become insolvent.[64] Their workers are laid off and become new urban poor after the reforms.[65]

The shift from state ownership of land and its free administrative allocation to paid transfer of land-use rights while state ownership is retained has important implications for the work unit.[66] The land value of some urban districts, especially those close to the inner city, has increased dramatically. Work units located in these districts convert part or all of their land to commercial or other uses. A most common practice is to build stores and office buildings in areas near streets and rent or sell them to private firms.[67] As residential development became increasingly profitable, some work units transferred their land-use rights to real estate companies to generate additional income. In some cases, the work units, often the ones that generate severe pollution, are relocated as a whole to remote suburban areas.[68] The land price difference between the old and new locations allows them to upgrade their workshops and other facilities. Some work units that perform poorly under a market economy but are situated in favourable locations convert themselves into real estate companies. Workshops are torn down to make way for new commercial or residential buildings. Some former unit members are included as part of the new companies while the rest are laid off or retire early.[69]

Housing reforms have brought mixed effects to the work unit. On the one hand, as the urban housing market provides other housing options, some better-off households move out of their unit apartments to private residential estates. On the other hand, the work unit plays an ongoing role in housing development and management. Although the key objective of housing reforms is to encourage urban residents to purchase their housing, the low cash salary that most unit members receive would not allow them to do so. In response to the problem, the work unit continues to provide subsidized housing for those who cannot afford to pay for "commodity housing" (*shangpin fang*) at market prices.[70] Different from the past, existing or new housing units of the work unit are sold to members at prices lower than market prices. Such purchases only provide the buyers part ownership rights while the work unit holds the rest, so the housing units cannot be sold freely. The work unit also manages the "housing accumulation fund" (*zhufang gongjijin*), which requires each employee to contribute 5 per cent of his or her salary for housing development.[71] The fund is often used to finance housing construction organized by the work unit.

Social ramifications have intensified after the reforms. The proof is the new residential land-scape: people are sorted according to their income into commodity housing ranging from affordable housing to luxury villas, housing in unit compounds and old neighbourhoods, to migrant enclaves on the edge of the city.[72] The economic performance of individual work units more than ever influences their capacity in housing and other social provisions. Profitable units are able to invest in new housing and social facilities, and sometimes buy housing units from the market and then sell them to their employees. Less successful units have limited capacity to offer housing and other benefits for their members, which places them at a disadvantaged position with regard to competing for human resources. The reforms also generate a sharp differentia-tion within the same work unit. Within the same work unit, some sub-units may perform much better than others. Some members may receive a lucrative income from their highly successful sub-unit, while others may still live on modest salary.

Accelerating marketization has resulted in an increasing mobility of capital and labour across the borders of the work unit. Some work units transform themselves into commercial compa-nies listed on the stock market, some collaborate with other private companies to develop new projects, and still others lease part of their offices or laboratories to foreign firms. The flows of capital are accompanied by flows of people. Some members leave their unit to work in the rapidly expanding private sector. Many live comfortably outside of the work unit system, while others adopt the "one family, two systems" strategy.[73] That is, one joins the private sector to seek better economic opportunities, while one's spouse remains in the state unit so that the family can enjoy various welfare programmes provided by the unit. Meanwhile, rural migrants flood into the previously exclusive work unit and take over most low paying service jobs.[74]

The central government has sought to divest the work unit from their social responsibili-ties and encourage them to open up their community facilities for outsiders' use. As a result, social services within the work unit have become increasingly market oriented. Canteens are subcontracted to individuals or private companies, the management of unit housing is taken over by newly established estate management companies (*wuye guanli gongsi*), and guesthouses and bathhouses are open to the general public. Meanwhile, unit residents no longer depend solely on their work units for social needs.[75] Society-wide health insurance and pension systems have been established. A variety of consumption options are now made available by the city: shopping malls, billiard parlours, beauty shops, video theatres, disco bars, and all kinds of clubs. Diverse urban places provide new opportunities for social interactions. As a result, the work unit no longer serves as the focus of everyday life for many; heterogeneous lifestyles mushroom both within and outside the unit compounds.

While the work unit is adapting to the new opportunities brought by the reforms, some of its features are reproduced in private companies. Corinna-Barbara Francis's study of Beijing's high-tech sector reveals that paternalistic approaches to management similar to those employed by the work unit are adopted by private firms in Haidian District.[76] Notably, similar characteris-tics in management practices and spatial arrangements can be drawn between the work unit and the various factories of Foxconn Technology Group, a Taiwanese multinational electronics con-tract manufacturing company (Figure 21.3).[77] Foxconn's largest factory worldwide in Longhua, Shenzhen, for example, has worker dormitories, a grocery store, bank, restaurants, bookstore, hospital, and its own television network within a walled complex. Like work unit employees in the previous era, workers can conduct most of their daily affairs without leaving the complex. With cheap dormitory and dining at the public canteens, Foxconn manages to deliver scale and quality at rock-bottom prices, which enables it to remain highly competitive in the global manufacturing arena. It has grown to be the world's largest electronics contractor manufacturer. Yet, with rising worker expectation, outside scrutiny, and a tighter labour market, the model is

Figure 21.3 The living quarter of Foxconn Kunshan, Wusongjiang.

Source: photo taken by author in 2015. © Duanfang Lu.

currently facing multiple challenges. It remains to be seen how the variations of the work unit may continue to unfold amid radical changes in market practices.

Notes

1 This chapter is a revised version of Chapter 3 in my book *Remaking Chinese Urban Form: Modernity, Scarcity and Space, 1949–2005* (London: Routledge, 2011), 19–46. Permission and courtesy of Routledge.

2 Franz Schurmann, *Ideology and Organization in Communist China* (Berkeley, CA: University of California Press, 1968); Xiaobo Lü and Elizabeth J. Perry, "Introduction: The Changing Chinese Workplace in Historical and Comparative Perspective," in *Danwei: The Changing Chinese Workplace in Historical and Comparative Perspective*, ed. Xiaobo Lü and Elizabeth J. Perry (Armonk, NY: M.E. Sharpe, 1997), 3–20.

3 Guojia Tongjiju Shehui Tongjisi, ed., *Zhongguo Shehui Tongji Ziliao* (Statistical Material on Chinese Society) (Beijing: Zhongguo tongji chubanshe, 1994).

4 Martin King Whyte and William L. Parish, *Urban Life in Contemporary China* (Chicago, IL: University of Chicago Press, 1984), 25.

5 During the pre-reform era, government allocated 95 per cent first jobs in urban areas; once one was assigned to a specific work unit, job changes were difficult. See Barry Naughton, "Danwei: The Economic Foundations of a Unique Institution," in *Danwei: The Changing Chinese Workplace in Historical and Comparative Perspective*, ed. Xiaobo Lü and Elizabeth J. Perry (Armonk: M.E. Sharpe, 1997), 169–194.

6 Michael Dutton, *Streetlife China* (Cambridge: Cambridge University Press, 1998).

7 E. M. Bjorklund, "The Danwei: Social-spatial Characteristics of Work Units in China's Urban Society," *Economic Geography* vol. 62, no. 1 (1986): 19–29.

8 Laurence J. C. Ma and Fulong Wu, "Introduction," in *Restructuring the Chinese City: Changing Society, Economy and Space*, ed. Laurence J. C. Ma and Fulong Wu (London: Routledge, 2005), 1–20.

9 David Bray, *Social Space and Governance in Urban China* (Stanford: Stanford University Press, 2005), chapter 7.

10 Andrew G. Walder, *Communist Neo-Traditionalism: Work and Authority in Chinese Industry* (Berkeley, CA: University of California Press, 1986).

11 Bray, *Social Space*.

12 Yang Xiaomin and Zhou Yihu, *Zhongguo Danwei Zhidu* (The Chinese Work Unit System) (Beijing: Zhongguo Jingji Chubanshe, 1999).

13 Gail E. Henderson and Myron S. Cohen, *The Chinese Hospital: A Socialist Work Unit* (New Haven, CT: Yale University Press, 1984).

14 Marc J. Blecher and Gordon White, *Micropolitics in Contemporary China: A Technical Unit During and After the Cultural Revolution* (Armonk, NY: M.E. Sharpe, 1979).

15 Xiaobo Lü and Elizabeth J. Perry, eds, *Danwei: The Changing Chinese Workplace in Historical and Comparative Perspective* (Armonk, NY: M.E. Sharpe, 1997).

16 For example, Mayfair Mei-hui Yang, "Between State and Society: The Construction of Corporateness in a Chinese Socialist Factory," *Australian Journal of Chinese Affairs* 22 (1989): 31–60; Lowell Dittmer and Xiaobo Lü, "Personal Politics in the Chinese Danwei Under Reform," *Asian Survey* 36, no. 3 (1996): 46–67.

17 The writing of this section is based on my fieldwork in Beijing, Wuhan, Guangzhou, Shanghai, Xiamen, and Gaobei in 2000, a survey of work units conducted in Beijing in 2000–2001, and my own experience with several work units and related publications.

18 To be sure, when new work units were created in remote rural areas, such as the "Third Front" enterprises, more social facilities were provided from the very beginning because of the lack of existing urban infrastructure. See for example, Barry Naughton, "The Third Front: Defence Industrialization in the Chinese Interior," *China Quarterly* 115 (1988): 351–386.

19 For a detailed account of the development of a single work unit, see You Zhenglin, *Neibu Fenhua yu Liudong: Yijia Guoyou Qiye de Ershinian* (International Differentiation and Mobility: Twenty Years of a State Enterprise) (Beijing: Shehui Kexue Wenxian Chubanshe, 2000).

20 Duanfang Lu, *Remaking Chinese Urban Form: Modernity, Scarcity and Space, 1949–2005* (London: Routledge, 2011[2006]), Chapter 4.

21 Margaret Crawford, *Building the Workingman's Paradise: The Design of American Company Towns* (London: Verso, 1995).

22 Crawford, *Building the Workingman's Paradise*.

23 Arif Dirlik, *After the Revolution: Walking to Global Capitalism* (Hanover, NH: Wesleyan University Press, 1994), 41.

24 He X., "People in the Work Unit," in *People and Prose (Sanwen yu Ren)*, ed. Shao Yanxiang and Lin Xianzhi (Guangzhou: Huacheng Chubanshe, 1993), 157–166.

25 Edgar Allan Poe, "The Man of the Crowd," in *The Fall of the House of Usher and Other Writings*, ed. David Galloway (Harmondsworth: Penguin, 1986), 179–188.

26 Gail E. Henderson and Myron S. Cohen, *The Chinese Hospital: A Socialist Work Unit* (New Haven, CT: Yale University Press, 1984).

27 Henderson and Cohen, *The Chinese Hospital*.

28 Barry Naughton, "Danwei: The Economic Foundations of a Unique Institution," in *Danwei: The Changing Chinese Workplace in Historical and Comparative Perspectives*, eds X Lu and E. J. Perry (Armonk, NY: M. E. Sharpe, 1997), 169–194, esp. 181.

29 Bin Li, "Danwei Culture as Urban Culture in Modern China: The Case of Beijing from 1949 to 1979," in *Urban Anthropology in China*, ed. Gregory Eliyu Guldin and Aidan William Southall (Leiden: E. J. Brill, 1993), 345–354.

30 Lü and Perry, *Danwei*, 8.

31 Ivan Szelenyi, "East European Socialist Cities: How Different are They?" in *Urban Anthropology in China*, ed. Guldin and Southall, 41–64. The quotation is from p. 53.

32 Szelenyi, "East," in *Urban*, ed. Guldin and Southall, 53.

33 Georg Simmel, "The Metropolis and Mental Life," in *The Sociology of Georg Simmel*, ed. Kurt H. Wolff (New York: Free Press, 1964), 409–424.

34 Peter Langer, "Sociology – Four Images of Organized Diversity: Bazaar, Jungle, Organism, and Machine," in *Cities of the Mind: Images and Themes of the City in the Social Sciences*, ed. Lloyd Rodwin and Robert M. Hollister (New York: Plenum Press, 1984), 97–117.

35 Lü and Perry, *Danwei*, 11–12.

36 Louis Wirth, "Urbanism as a Way of Life," *American Journal of Sociology* 44 (1938): 1–24.

37 Robert Park considers the existence of marginality as one of the most central features of urbanism in both "positive" and "negative" sense. On one hand, the fact that urbanites are more likely to be marginal leads to greater creativity. On the other hand, urban marginality results in more deviance such as crime and prostitution. See Robert Park, "Human Migration and the Marginal Man," *The American Journal of Sociology* 6 (1928): 881–893; and Janice Perlman, *The Myth of Marginality* (Berkeley, CA: University of California Press, 1976), 98–99.

38 Whyte and Parish, *Urban Life*, 107–228 (chapter 2).

39 Kam Wing Chan, *Cities with Invisible Walls: Reinterpreting Urbanization in Post-1949 China* (Hong Kong: Oxford University Press, 1994).

40 Tiejun Cheng and Mark Selden, "The Origins and Social Consequences of China's *Hukou* System," *The China Quarterly* 139 (September 1994): 644–648.

41 Michel Oksenberg, ed., *China's Developmental Experience* (New York: Praeger, 1973).

42 Leonie Sandercock and Ann Forsyth, "A Gender Agenda: New Directions for Planning Theory," *Journal of the American Planning Association* 58 (1992): 49–59.

43 I owe this account to Manuel Castells's lecture series on "Comparative Urban Policies," 1997, University of California, Berkeley.

44 Margery Wolf, *Revolution Postponed: Women in Contemporary China* (Stanford, CA: Stanford University Press, 1985).

45 Walder, *Communist Neo-Traditionalism*.

46 Bray, *Social Space*, 166.

47 Henderson and Cohen, *The Chinese Hospital*.

48 Dorothy J. Solinger, "Labour Market Reform and the Plight of the Laid-off Proletariat," *China Quarterly* 170 (2002): 304–326.

49 Hong Yung Lee, *From Revolutionary Cadres to Party Technocrats in Socialist China* (Berkeley, CA: University of California Press, 1991).

50 Bray, *Social Space*, 166.

51 Alex Pravda and Blair A. Ruble, eds *Trade Unions in Communist States* (Boston, MA: Allen and Unwin, 1986).

52 Emily Clark Brown, *Soviet Trade Unions and Labor Relations* (Cambridge, MA: Harvard University Press, 1966).

53 Editorial, "Shijiazhuang Gonghui Gongzuo shi ruhe Zoushang Mianxiang Shengchang de? (How has the Work of Shijiazhuang Trade Union Oriented to Production?)," *Renmin Ribao* (People's Daily) (12 May 1950): B2.

54 Lai To Lee, *Trade Unions in China, 1949 to the Present: The Organization and Leadership of the All-China Federation of Trade Unions* (Singapore: Singapore University Press, 1989).

55 Bray, *Social Space*, 104–105.

56 Clifton W. Pannell, "Past and Present City Structure in China," *Town and Planning Review* vol. 48, no. 2 (1977): 157–172.

57 James H. Bater, *The Soviet City* (London: Edward Arnold, 1980), 109–111; Ivan Szelenyi, "East," in *Urban*, ed. Guldin and Southall, 41–64; van Szelenyi, "Cities Under Socialism – and After," in *Cities After Socialism: Urban and Regional Change and Conflict in Post-socialist Societies,* ed. Gregory Andrusz, Michael Harloe, and Ivan Szelenyi (Oxford: Blackwell, 1996), 286–317; Rudra Sil, "The Russian 'Village in the City' and the Stalinist System of Enterprise Management: The Origins of Worker Alienation in Soviet State Socialism," in *Danwei,* eds Lü and Perry, 114–141.

58 Larry Sawers, "Cities and Countryside in the Soviet Union and China," in *Marxism and the Metropolis: New Perspectives in Urban Political Economy*, ed. William K. Tabb and Larry Sawers (New York: Oxford University Press, 1978), 338–364.

59 Tony French, *Plans, Pragmatism and People: The Legacy of Soviet Planning for Today's Cities* (Pittsburgh, PA: University of Pittsburgh Press, 1995).

60 Sawers, "Cities," in *Marxism,* ed. Tabb and Sawers, 351–352.

61 Poor transportation negatively affected urban functions during the early period of Soviet building. Workers at Novogireevo, for example, had to walk in the dark "through the woods in groups of ten for protection against hooligans" up until 1935. See Kenneth M. Straus, "The Soviet Factory as Community Organizer," in *Danwei,* eds Lü and Perry, 142–168.

62 Naughton, "Danwei," in *Danwei,* eds Lü and Perry, 169–194.

63 Walder, *Communist Neo-Traditionalism*.

64 The national survey in 1996 showed that the share of state units in total industrial output was 28.5 per cent, the share of collective units (including rural enterprises) 39.4 per cent, and the share of other types of enterprises 32.1 per cent. See Li Lulu and Li Hanlin, *Zhongguo de Danwei Zuzhi: Ziyuan, Quanli yu Jiaohuan* (China's work unit organization: Resources, power and exchange) (Hangzhou: Zhejiang Renmin Chubanshe, 2000), 22.

65 Solinger, "Labour," 304–326.

66 Fulong Wu and Anthony Gar-On Yeh, "Changing Spatial Distribution and Determinants of Land Development in China's Transition to a Market Economy: The Case of Guangzhou," *Urban Studies* 34 (1997): 1851–1879.

67 Bray, *Social Space*, 170.

68 Yin Huaiting, Shen Xiaoping and Zhao Zhe, "Industrial restructuring and urban spatial transformation in Xi'an," in *Restructuring the Chinese City: Changing Society, Economy and Space,* eds Laurence J. C. Ma and Fulong Wu (Abingdon: Routledge, 2005), 155–174.

69 Yin, Shen and Zhao, "Industrial," 155–174.

70 Yaping Wang and Alan Murie, "The Process of Commercialization of Urban Housing in China," *Urban Studies* vol. 33, no. 6 (1996): 971–989.

71 Wang and Murie, "The Process," 971–989.

72 Huang Youqin, "From Work-unit Compounds to Gated Communities: Housing Inequality and Residential Segregation in Transitional Beijing," in *Restructuring,* eds Ma and Wu, 192–221.

73 M. Leng, "Beijing Shimin 'Yijia Liangzhi' (Beijing residents practicing 'one family, two systems')," *Renmin Ribao, Haiwai Ban* (*People's daily,* overseas edition) (6 August 1992).

74 Dorothy J. Solinger, "The Impact of the Floating Population on the *Danwei*: Shifts in the Pattern of Labour Mobility Control and Entitlement Provision," in *Danwei,* eds Lü and Perry, 195–222.

75 Wenfang Tang and William L. Parish, *Chinese Urban Life under Reform: The Changing Social Contract* (Cambridge: Cambridge University Press, 2000).

76 Corinna-Barbara Francis, "Reproduction of *Danwei* Institutional Features in the Context of China's Market Economy: The Case of Haidian District's High-tech Sector," *China Quarterly* 147 (1996): 839–859.

77 Pun Ngai and Jenny Chan, "Global Capital, the State, and Chinese Workers: The Foxconn Experience Modern China," *Modern China* vol. 38, no. 4 (2012): 383–410.

Bibliography

Bater, James H. *The Soviet City.* London: Edward Arnold, 1980.

Bjorklund, E.M. "The *Danwei*: Social-Spatial Characteristics of Work Units in China's Urban Society." *Economic Geography* 62, no. 1 (1986): 19–29.

Bray, David. *Social Space and Governance in Urban China.* Stanford: Stanford University Press, 2005.

Brown, Emily Clark. *Soviet Trade Unions and Labor Relations.* Cambridge: Harvard University Press, 1966.

Chan, Kam Wing. *Cities with Invisible Walls: Reinterpreting Urbanization in Post-1949 China.* Hong Kong: Oxford University Press, 1994.

Cheng, Tiejun and Mark Selden. "The Origins and Social Consequences of China's *Hukou* System." *The China Quarterly* 139 (September 1994): 644–668.

Crawford, Margaret. *Building the Workingman's Paradise: The Design of American Company Towns.* London: Verso, 1995.

Dirlik, Arif. *After the Revolution: Walking to Global Capitalism.* Hanover, NH: Wesleyan University Press, 1994.

Dittmer, Lowell and Xiaobo Lu. "Personal Politics in the Chinese *Danwei* Under Reform." *Asian Survey* 36, no. 3 (1996): 46–67.

Dutton, Michael. *Streetlife China.* Cambridge: Cambridge University Press, 1998.

Editorial. "Shijiazhuang Gonghui Gongzuo shi Ruhe Zoushang Mianxiang Shengchang de? (How Has the Work of Shijiazhuang Trade Union Oriented to Production?)." In *Remmin Ribao* (People's Daily) (12 May 1950): B2.

Francis, Corinna-Barbara. "Reproduction of *Danwei* Institutional Features in the Context of China's Market Economy: The Case of Haidian District's High-tech Sector." *China Quarterly* 147 (1996): 839–859.

French, Antony R. *Plans, Pragmatism and People: The Legacy of Soviet Planning for Today's Cities.* Pittsburgh, PA: University of Pittsburgh Press, 1995.

Guojia Tongjiju Shehui Tongjisi, ed. *Zhongguo Shehui Tongji Ziliao* (Statistical Material on Chinese Society). Beijing: Zhongguo Tongji Chubanshe, 1994.

He, X. "People in the Work Unit." In *People and Prose (Sanwen yu Ren)*, edited by Shao Yanxiang and Lin Xianzhi, 157–166. Guangzhou: Huacheng Chubanshe, 1993.

Henderson, Gail E. and Myron S. Cohen. *The Chinese Hospital: A Socialist Work Unit*. New Haven, CT: Yale University Press, 1984.

Huang, Youqin. "From Work-unit Compounds to Gated Communities: Housing Inequality and Residential Segregation in Transitional Beijing." In *Restructuring the Chinese City: Changing Society, Economy and Space*, edited by Laurence J.C. Ma and Fulong Wu, 192–221. Abingdon: Routledge, 2005.

Langer, Peter. "Sociology – Four Images of Organized Diversity: Bazaar, Jungle, Organism, and Machine." In *Cities of the Mind: Images and Themes of the City in the Social Sciences*, edited by Lloyd Rodwin and Robert M Hollister, 97–117. New York: Plenum Press, 1984.

Lee, Hong Yung. *From Revolutionary Cadres to Party Technocrats in Socialist China*. Berkeley, CA: University of California Press, 1991.

Lee, Lai To. *Trade Unions in China, 1949 to the Present: The Organization and Leadership of the All-China Federation of Trade Unions*. Singapore: Singapore University Press, 1989.

Leng, M. "Beijing Shimin 'Yijia Liangzhi' (Beijing Residents Practicing 'One Family, Two Systems')." *Renmin Ribao*, Haiwai Ban (*People's Daily*, overseas ed.), 6 August 1992.

Li, Bin. "Danwei Culture as Urban Culture in Modern China: The Case of Beijing from 1949 to 1979." In *Urban Anthropology in China*, edited by Gregory Eliyu Guldin and Aidan William Southall, 345–354. Leiden: E. J. Brill, 1993.

Li Lulu and Li Hanlin. *Zhongguo de Danwei Zuzhi: Ziyuan, Quanli yu Jiaohuan* (China's Work Unit Organization: Resources, Power and Exchange). Hangzhou: Zhejiang Renmin Chubanshe, 2000.

Lu, Duanfang. *Remaking Chinese Urban Form: Modernity, Scarcity and Space, 1949–2005*. London: Routledge, 2011/2006.

Lü, Xiaobo and Elizabeth J. Perry, eds. *Danwei: The Changing Chinese Workplace in Historical and Comparative Perspective*. Armonk, NY: M.E. Sharpe, 1997.

———. "Introduction: The Changing Chinese Workplace in Historical and Comparative Perspective." In *Danwei: The Changing Chinese Workplace in Historical and Comparative Perspective*, edited by Xiaobo Lü and Elizabeth J Perry, 3–20. Armonk, NY: M.E. Sharpe, 1997.

Ma, Laurence J.C. and Fulong Wu. "Introduction." In *Restructuring the Chinese City: Changing Society, Economy and Space*, edited by Laurence J.C. Ma and Fulong Wu, 1–20. Abingdon: Routledge, 2005.

Naughton, Barry. "The Third Front: Defence Industrialization in the Chinese Interior." *China Quarterly* 115 (1988): 351–386.

———. "Danwei: The Economic Foundations of a Unique Institution." In *Danwei: The Changing Chinese Workplace in Historical and Comparative Perspectives*, edited by Xiaobo Lü and Elizabeth J Perry, 169–194. Armonk, NY: M.E. Sharpe, 1997.

Ngai, Pun and Jenny Chan. "Global Capital, the State, and Chinese Workers: The Foxconn Experience Modern China." *Modern China* 38, no. 4 (2012): 383–410.

Oksenberg, Michel, ed. *China's Developmental Experience*. New York: Praeger, 1973.

Pannell, Clifton W. "Past and Present City Structure in China." *Town and Planning Review* 48, no. 2 (1977): 157–172.

Park, Robert. "Human Migration and the Marginal Man." *The American Journal of Sociology* 6 (1928): 881–893.

Perlman, Janice. *The Myth of Marginality*. Berkeley, CA: University of California Press, 1976.

Poe, Edgar Allan. "The Man of the Crowd." In *The Fall of the House of Usher and Other Writings*, edited by David Galloway, 179–188. Harmondsworth: Penguin, 1986.

Pravda, Alex and Blair A. Ruble, eds. *Trade Unions in Communist States*. Boston, MA: Allen and Unwin, 1986.

Sandercock, Leonie and Ann Forsyth. "A Gender Agenda: New Directions for Planning Theory." *Journal of the American Planning Association* 58 (1992): 49–59.

Sawers, Larry. "Cities and Countryside in the Soviet Union and China." In *Marxism and the Metropolis: New Perspectives in Urban Political Economy*, edited by William K. Tabb and Larry Sawers, 338–364. New York: Oxford University Press, 1978.

Schurmann, Franz. *Ideology and Organization in Communist China*. Berkeley, CA: University of California Press, 1968.

Sil, Rudra. "The Russian 'Village in the City' and the Stalinist System of Enterprise Management: The Origins of Worker Alienation in Soviet State Socialism." In *Danwei: The Changing Chinese Workplace in Historical and Comparative Perspective*, edited by Xiaobo Lü and Elizabeth J. Perry, 114–141. Armonk, NY: M.E. Sharpe, 1997.

Simmel, Georg. "The Metropolis and Mental Life." In *The Sociology of Georg Simmel*, edited by Kurt H. Wolff, 409–424. New York: Free Press, 1964.

Solinger, Dorothy J. "The Impact of the Floating Population on the *Danwei*: Shifts in the Pattern of Labor Mobility Control and Entitlement Provision." In *Danwei: The Changing Chinese Workplace in Historical and Comparative Perspective*, edited by Xiaobo Lü and Elizabeth J. Perry, 195–222. Armonk, NY: M.E. Sharpe, 1997.

———. "Labour Market Reform and the Plight of the Laid-off Proletariat." *China Quarterly* 170 (2002): 304–326.

Straus, Kenneth M. "The Soviet Factory as Community Organizer." In *Danwei: The Changing Chinese Workplace in Historical and Comparative Perspective*, edited by Xiaobo Lü and Elizabeth J. Perry, 142–168. Armonk, NY: M.E. Sharpe, 1997.

Szelenyi, Ivan. "East European Socialist Cities: How Different are They?" In *Urban Anthropology in China*, edited by Greg Guldin and Aidan Southall, 41–64. Leiden: E. J. Brill, 1993.

———. "Cities Under Socialism – and After." In *Cities After Socialism: Urban and Regional Change and Conflict in Post-Socialist Societies*, edited by Andrusz Gregory, Harloe Michael and Szelenyi Ivan, 286–317. Oxford: Blackwell, 1996.

Tang, Wenfang and William L. Parish. *Chinese Urban Life Under Reform: The Changing Social Contract*. Cambridge: Cambridge University Press, 2000.

Walder, Andrew G. *Communist Neo-Traditionalism: Work and Authority in Chinese Industry*. Berkeley, CA: University of California Press, 1986.

Wang, Yaping and Alan Murie. "The Process of Commercialization of Urban Housing in China." *Urban Studies* 33, no. 6 (1996): 971–989.

Whyte, Martin King and William L. Parish. *Urban Life in Contemporary China*. Chicago, IL: University of Chicago Press, 1984.

Wirth, Louis. "Urbanism as a Way of Life." *American Journal of Sociology* 44 (1938): 1–24.

Wolf, Margery. *Revolution Postponed: Women in Contemporary China*. Stanford, CA: Stanford University Press, 1985.

Wu, Fulong and Anthony Gar-On Yeh. "Changing Spatial Distribution and Determinants of Land Development in China's Transition to a Market Economy: The Case of Guangzhou." *Urban Studies* 34 (1997): 1851–1879.

Yang, Mayfair Mei-hui. "Between State and Society: The Construction of Corporateness in a Chinese Socialist Factory." *Australian Journal of Chinese Affairs* 22 (1989): 31–60.

Yang Xiaomin and Zhou Yihu. *Zhongguo danwei zhidu* (The Chinese Work Unit System). Beijing: Zhongguo jingji chubanshe, 1999.

Yin Huaiting, Shen Xiaoping and Zhao Zhe. "Industrial Restructuring and Urban Spatial Transformation in Xi'an." In *Restructuring the Chinese City: Changing Society, Economy and Space*, edited by Laurence J.C. Ma and Fulong Wu, 155–174. Abingdon: Routledge, 2005.

You Zhenglin. *Neibu Fenhua yu Liudong: Yijia Guoyou Qiye de Ershinian* (International Differentiation and Mobility: Twenty Years of a State Enterprise). Beijing: Shehui Kexue Wenxian Chubanshe, 2000.

Glossary

Beijing	北京
danwei	单位
dang'an	档案
hukou	户口
Shanghai	上海
shenhuo qu	生活区
shehui shang	社会上

shangpin fang	商品房
wuye guanli gongsi	物业管理公司
xiaoqu	小区
Yang Xiaoming	杨晓民
zhidu	制度
Zhou Yuhu	周翼虎
Zhongguo	中国
zhufang gongjijin	住房公积金

Practice, Education, and
Knowledge Production

22

THE DESIGN INSTITUTE IN MAO'S CHINA (1950s–70s)

Ke Song

Upon the founding of the People's Republic in 1949, the new government of the Chinese Communist Party began to construct various institutional systems needed in a socialist state based on the Soviet model. The core measure was to establish socialist *danwei* (work unit) systems, to control and reorganize the whole state and society. *The danwei* work units had three types: *xingzheng*, *shiye*, and *qiye*, or administrative, institutional, and productive respectively.[1]

All units of *danwei*, under the unified leadership of the Party, functioned in the framework of a planned economy. From 1949 to the completion of "socialist transformation" in 1956, China underwent tremendous changes, which could be summarized in several aspects: 1) in terms of economic ownership, after the "Three and Five Antis" campaign (1949–52) and by the completion of the socialist transformation, private economy was replaced by a public system. 2) Politically, the Party's organizations were established in each *danwei* unit at all levels, a vertical management system that ensured a rapid conveyance of instructions from the Central Committee of the Chinese Communist Party (CCCCP) down to the grassroots level. 3) As to ideology, the entire population was led to accept socialism as the correct form of political thinking. 4) Following that, a system of socialist values and moral discussions was established.

The design institute was a specific form of *danwei* in the field of architectural design under such a state system. As an "institutional unit" (*shiye danwei*), the design institutes were directly attached to central government ministries as well as to provincial and local authorities. With this, the institutes worked on projects assigned or arranged to them by public authorities or other large work units.

Establishing the Governing Bodies and the Design Institutes

Before 1949, the construction industry in China's big cities was dominated by a large number of private design firms and builders, a situation that had no essential difference from the Western capitalist countries. In 1949, when the People's Central Government was established, there was no formal department supervising the construction sector yet. The construction of infrastructure, housing, and factories – known as "capital construction" – was managed by a "Capital Construction Office" under the Planning Bureau of the Central Financial and Economic Committee (CFEC).

DOI: 10.4324/9781315851112-34

Between 1949 and 1952, when private practice was ongoing, state government and the Party began to establish their own public design offices or firms attached to a particular public office at a certain level. These firms and offices, a year later, became well-known design institutes. For example, the Chinese Communist Party (CCP) established the Yongmao Construction Firm in 1949, and its design department was later on reorganized, many times, to become today's BIAD (Beijing Institute of Architectural Design). The CCCCP established its "construction office" then; after years of change, destruction, regroup, and renaming, this is now the well-known CAG (China Architecture Design and Research Group) of Beijing. In these earliest years, state design offices and private companies co-existed.[2]

On 11–21 June 1951, following the instructions of the CCCCP, the All-China Federation of Trade Unions held a national conference in Beijing for the unions in the building industry. The conference proposed 11 reforms, one of which was the establishment of state-owned design institutes and the separation of design from construction. The CCCCP approved the idea and required the Party to strengthen its leadership in the realms of design and construction.[3]

The years 1952–53 witnessed the establishment of many design institutes and governing bodies in the construction sector at all levels of government. One important aim was to prepare manpower and institutional forms for the forthcoming high tide of capital construction designated in the first Five-Year Plan (1953–57) – and one of the major tasks in the Plan was to ensure that the 156 Soviet-aid industrial projects were carried out successfully.

On 4 April 1952, Premier Zhou Enlai endorsed establishing a government department of construction and state construction enterprises, leading to the founding of the Ministry of Construction (*jianzhu gongcheng bu*) on 1 September. On 2–16 July of the same year, the CFEC convened the first national conference on construction affairs and requested several nationwide transformations: establishing construction-governing departments in the governments of "regions" (above and including several provinces) immediately, setting up comparable departments at provincial and municipal levels gradually, and converting all old building companies into state-owned enterprises.[4]

From October 1952 onwards, the central government held several meetings, requiring local authorities to quickly establish and enrich the institutions in capital construction sectors, including design institutes and construction enterprises, to prepare for upcoming large-scale construction in 1953. The official newspaper, *Renmin Ribao* (People's Daily), published an editorial, "The Capital Construction Should Be of the Highest Priority," advocating that the most capable cadres, technicians, and skilled workers be transferred to capital construction sectors. In August 1953, the Ministry of Construction submitted a report stating that the construction industry of the whole country had been basically transformed into state-owned, and the governing bodies in provincial and municipal levels had basically been set up. According to a document of the Central Committee, "The Decisions of the CCCCP Concerning the Ministry of Construction," the fundamental responsibilities of the Ministry were to lead the construction of industrial structures and facilities with a focus on heavy industries, and to promote mechanization in construction industry. The Central Committee also decided to move military projects to the Ministry of Defence and general civil projects to local governments and local enterprises.[5]

In this context, along with the establishment of governing bodies at all levels, the first group of state-owned design institutes was established, including Beijing Design Institute, Shanghai Civil Design Institute, Guangzhou Design Institute, Design Institute of Guangdong Province, and the design institutes in Tianjin, Gansu province, and Hunan province, among others. Some design institutes experienced name changes and restructuring in later years. In particular, the Design Institute of the Ministry of Construction (*jianzhu gongchengbu shejiyuan*) was founded by merging the Construction Office of the CCCCP and more than ten other central construction enterprises in Beijing in 1952. Later in 1954, it was renamed "Beijing Industrial and Urban Design Institute" (*Beijing gongye yu chengshi jianzhu shejiyuan*), focusing on industrial building and urban planning. In 1955, the urban planning part was taken out and it was renamed "Beijing Industrial Design Institute" (*Beijing gongye shejiyuan*). After a series of adjustments – including a "sending-down" in 1969 and a regrouping or restructuring in 1973 – it became CAG today, arguably the most renowned design institute in China.[6]

The establishment of design institutes was a major restructuring of architectural design industry in China. How to recruit design talent, especially prominent architects, and conduct "socialist thought reform" were the biggest challenges when design institutes were founded in the early 1950s. Before the founding of the People's Republic, renowned architects – mostly educated in the West, such as Yang Tingbao, Tong Jun, and Chen Zhi, among others – worked in private companies under a market economy. They concentrated in Shanghai, Tianjin, and other cities that had better economic foundations. After 1949, the Communist Party suppressed capitalist economy and provided a promising picture of socialism. At this turning point, many architects were inspired by the socialist agenda and chose to cooperate with the Party. For example, Liang Sicheng stayed at Tsinghua University as the head of the Department of Architecture and served as Deputy Director for the Architectural Society of China (ASC) in 1954. Liang's student, Zhang Bo, gave up an opportunity to work in Hong Kong and joined Beijing Design Institute; he later participated in the design of several important buildings, including the Great Hall of the People. The French-born architect Hua Lanhong (Léon Hoa) closed his design practice in France and managed to come back to China; he was appointed as a director at the Beijing Design Institute. However, other architects chose not to cooperate and left Mainland China. For example, a considerable number of prominent architects of the Republican time under the KMT or Kuomintang Party, including Guan Songsheng (Kuan Sung-sheng) and Zhu Bin, among others, moved their business to Hong Kong, Taiwan, and the United States. There were also some architects who stayed on the mainland but kept a distance from the political centre of Beijing. For example, Tong Jun, refusing to go to Beijing, chose to focus on teaching and research in Nanjing, without much involvement in design practice from the 1950s onwards.

So, why was the system of the design institutes established? First of all, the system of design institutes was an inevitable choice under the socialist planned economy, and it was also part of the Soviet model. The same institutional system made it possible for Chinese architects to directly cooperate with and learn from Soviet experts who worked in the design institutes in the Soviet Union. Secondly, in the economically difficult early years, design institutes could effectively integrate and strengthen design forces at every level of society, train young architects with solid professional foundation and loyalty to the Party, and accumulate design knowledge and expertise through collective effort. Thirdly, as institutions affiliated to the government, design institutes could efficiently implement the Party's policies, completing construction projects quickly and economically. Finally, the system of design institute ensured the Party's ideological control over design practice across the country.

It should be noted that the Chinese design institutes had made great achievements in the first Five-Year Plan, which proved the effectiveness of this system: more than half of the industrial projects were completed by Chinese design institutes (the rest were assisted by the Soviet Union), and civil projects such as railways, transportation, telecommunications, and water were mostly designed by the Chinese themselves. We should also acknowledge the great assistance provided by the Soviet Union: the industrial/civil ratio in the overall distribution of construction was 90:10, for which, as stated, a significant percentage was delivered by the Soviet Union.[7] It can be concluded that the successful completion of the Five-Year Plan was premised on both the Chinese design institutes and the aid from the Soviet Union.

Typology, Structure, and Working Methods of the Design Institute

Many features of the design institute system formulated during the Mao period are still at work today, including the typology of the institutes, divisions of labour within them, the organizational structure, and working methods.

Generally, the design institutes in China can be categorized into three types: the survey and planning design institute, the industrial design institute, and the civil design institute. The survey and planning institute is responsible for surveying, planning, and civil infrastructure. The industrial design institute is responsible for the design and planning of industrial buildings, including plants, mills, and factories. The civil design institute is responsible for the design of "civil architecture," including public buildings and housing. Due to the comprehensive nature of each institute, this classification of types is not strict. Many design institutes cover both residential and industrial buildings.

The industrial or civil design institutes can be broadly divided into three levels according to administrative relationship: those directly under central ministries, those under provincial governments, and those under municipal governments.[8] A design institute directly serves a certain level of government. In terms of the scope of the service, the higher the level, the greater the scope of services it provides. But a design institute's size, workload, and staff salary and benefits are not necessarily related to its level.

In terms of organizational structure, a design institute normally consists of several components: a Party organization and several administrative departments are responsible for the implementation of central policies and assigned tasks; a few logistics departments are responsible for financial, archives and other daily management; and the design workforce are generally organized into a number of design studios that can work independently. The Party organization overlaps with the professional organizations – a certain person can be both a Party member and professional staff. The Party, especially in Mao's China, leads all spheres of operation from daily management to design production, to ensure an ideological control in the design field. In the Mao era, to be "Red and Expert" (both socialist-minded and professionally competent) was much emphasized as a standard to judge the performance of a staff in the design institutes.

Design institutes are generally large and comprehensive. Different types of design institutes have different kinds of design studios or offices. Generally, a civil design institute has offices on structural design, HVAC design, electrical design, and drainage, among others. Some may include more specialist offices, such as those on design standardization, heritage conservation, historical research, and policy studies.

A design institute operates by forming a design team for each project, which may consist of architects and professional technicians selected from many studios and offices. In special cases, professionals from different design institutes can form a team on a nationally important project. For example, architects and professors from many institutes and university departments across China were called upon to design collectively for the Ten Great Buildings of Beijing in the late 1950s. Also, the municipal government of Guangzhou in the 1970s organized special teams to work on Guangzhou Foreign Trade Projects,[9] which consisted of architects from Guangzhou Urban Planning Bureau and Guangzhou Design Institute. The composition of a design team can vary in the process of a project, with its size ranging from several people in the conceptual design phase to a few hundred in the documentation phase.

The design institutes followed closely the policies of state authority and the Central Committee. After 1952, a design guideline – "Suitability, Economy, and Beauty When Conditions Permit" – was formulated for all design practices in Mao's China.[10] Under this formula, building standards and standard drawings were established and approved by the authorities for all construction sectors, including housing, transportation, offices, and industrial works. In addition, political movements also had direct impacts on the workings of the design institutes, especially during the Great Leap Forward (1958–65) and the Great Proletarian Cultural Revolution (1966–76).

Upon the setting-up of the system of design institutes in the early 1950s, design and construction were separated as belonging to two different types of *danwei* – design institute (*shiye danwei*, institutional) and construction enterprise (*qiye danwei*, productive), respectively. While private construction firms were transformed into state enterprises, adopting an accounting system,[11] private design companies were merged into state design institutes, to be attached to government offices and fully funded by the state – and state authority charged design fees on behalf of the design institutes.[12] In the Mao era, construction relied on state funding based on an economic plan, and market competition between the design institutes was limited, though it did exist.[13] There were organized competitions for national projects under the supervision of state authority; there were also some coordinated measuring for the performance of the different institutes – the counting of workload and the economic values created – for assessing the leadership team (of carders) and the staff of one institute against another. In addition, there were competitions between the Chinese and the Soviet design institutes in China. For example, Liu Xiufeng in a report to the Central Committee in 1957 admitted that the six industrial design institutes of the Ministry of Construction didn't have enough design tasks, showing a "slowing down"; and he recommended these design institutes to compete more actively with the Soviet design institutes for more projects in China.[14]

A History of Design and Design Thinking

In the 1950s, design institutes saw a series of nationwide debates on ideas, design, and style. This was closely related to the conditions of the time: a rising national pride after unification (of the mainland), intense global and local confrontations on ideological lines, poverty and destruction after the war, backwardness in technology and economy – all of these led to urgent actions and conflicting ideas on nation building and physical design. In 1954, in the context of learning from the Soviet Union, articles in *Jianzhu Xuebao* (architectural journal) promoted a "National Style" and associated the National Style with the ideology of socialism. Modernism was considered as the architectural form of capitalism, and several modernist buildings – along with the architects – were publicly criticized. But when National Style buildings, represented by those with the Chinese "big roofs," were completed, excessive cost became a problem and serious debates erupted, attracting the attention of the Central Committee. The criticism of Joseph Stalin and his classical architecture in the Soviet Union at the time was another reason for questioning the approach. In this context, the year of 1955 saw the launch of an anti-waste movement, in which the National Style was criticized as "revivalist" and wasteful. Architects were then more confused as to which way to go – modernist or classicist. But the Ten Great Buildings, for the tenth anniversary of the People's Republic in 1959, stimulated another tide of debate on design. Zhou Enlai and Liu Xiufeng called on architects to develop a "Socialist New Style" architecture in which all styles, "ancient or modern, Chinese or foreign," as long as it was good, could be used – and the "big roof" style was also included. So, effectively, an eclectic design approach prevailed.

In the 1960s, design institutes were more strictly controlled along with the Party's ideology shifting to the far left. The Great Leap Forward, launched in 1958, caused a serious decline in productivity in heavy industry and agriculture from 1959 to 1961, and, later on, serious famines hit the country. From 1961 onwards, in order to restore the national economy, the

Central Committee reduced the investment in new projects. Starting from 1964, along with the "Third Front Construction,"[15] Mao launched a "Design Revolution," in which various forms of "three-in-one combinations" were required to reform the established practice, increase speed, and reduce cost in construction – the combination of design, construction, and material supply, and that of cadres, professionals, and labour forces. Under this "revolution," some buildings adopted bold and new structures, eliminated decoration completely, and embraced an extreme functionalism. In the entire 1960s, ideological radicalness was repeatedly emphasized, culminating in the High Cultural Revolution (1966–1969), when the political campaigns brought everything to a standstill, plunging the country into turmoil. Apart from a few key projects, there were few design tasks in this period. Moreover, during the Cultural Revolution (1966–1967), all architectural discourses were excessively politicized, and political slogans superseded professional discussions.

Starting from the 1960s, in association with the Third Front Construction, the "send-down" policy caused a large-scale geographical re-distribution of architects in China. The direction was from the coastal area to the hinterland, and from cities to the countryside. Some of the sent-down architects were placed at provincial or municipal institutes, allowing them to engage in local design works, while others were simply arranged to do labour works unrelated to design. Design institutes at different levels experienced varying impacts. The design institutes of state ministries were most affected. For example, Beijing Industrial Design Institute under the Ministry of Construction was almost totally disbanded in 1970, and the professionals were sent down to Henan, Hunan, and other provinces. They were later recalled and the institute re-established in the following years.

From the early 1970s, Mao began to reflect on his policy mistakes of the Cultural Revolution, especially after the Lin Biao Incident of 1971.[16] Premier Zhou Enlai, representing a pragmatist faction, was appreciated and put forward again, but the radical faction, represented by Jiang Qing, Mao's wife, was also active. In confrontation with each other, they were responsible for economy and ideology respectively – while Mao was supporting both at the same time. "Grasp Revolution and Promote Production" a standard slogan of the time, became a consensus of the nation for such a balance in the mid- and late Cultural Revolution.

Meanwhile, China's diplomatic relations with the United States and other Western countries were improving dramatically. In the early 1970s, the construction of a number of important buildings for foreign affairs was the first to be proposed on the agenda, including a group of buildings in Beijing, such as the Diplomatic Residential Compounds (DRC), Beijing International Club, the Friendship Store, and a group of buildings in Guangzhou, including a new Exhibition Hall of Canton Fair, Dongfang Hotel, and Baiyun Hotel. In the mid-1970s, Zhou Enlai formally proposed plans for China's "modernization." A "43 Plan" – to spend 4.3 billion US dollars – was launched to import a large amount of technologies and equipment systems from Western countries and Japan, including those for producing chemical fibre and chemical fertilizer, which significantly eased the scarcity of food and clothes.[17] Meanwhile, a group of buildings closely related to people's everyday life, including railway stations, airports, hotels, galleries, sports venues, and telecommunication buildings, among others, were constructed in many cities. Design institutes, especially those in large cities, began to receive more tasks, so the sent-down architects were recalled to serve at their original positions. In the radical political environment of the 1960s, older architects were sidelined, so younger designers who were trained after 1949 became the main force in the 1970s. They mostly had excellent design skills but knew little about Western architectural trends, let alone Western architectural theories. In such a state of "collective unconsciousness," a highly consistent style appeared and became predominant in the 1970s, contrasting with the pluralism in the 1980s when China opened to a flooding of ideas from outside.

In addition, we should note that the Chinese design institutes had undertaken a large number of foreign aid projects in the Mao era since the mid-1950s. China's aid projects were mainly located in Mongolia, Sri Lanka, Zambia, Algeria, and other Asian and African countries. Due to China's emphasis on aid projects, many innovative architectural works appeared outside China; these include Choibalsan International Hotel (1960) in Mongolia, designed by Gong Deshun, and the Bandaranaike International Conference Hall (1973) in Sri Lanka, designed by Dai Nianci.

Summary

The system of design institute was an inevitable choice in the early days of the People's Republic as part of the Soviet model. It was a specific form of socialist *danwei* system in the field of architectural design. The system was a top-down, highly centralized management system. The institutes served the Party and the government as state apparatuses, under direct influences of official ideology. As a production unit of architectural design, the design institute maintains a preference for speed and efficiency. It adopted a design methodology privileging "practicality and economy" and Maoist socialist values, including serving the people and building for the collective and for equality. In the Mao era, all achievements in the construction industry were inseparable from the contribution of design institutes. The historical evolution of the design institutes, as they were closely related to the politics and the fate of the country, reflects neatly a shifting trajectory in state ideology, national orientation, internal economy, and policies, as well as international diplomacy; its history was also intertwined with changing aesthetics, ways of life, and consciousness of the masses. In contemporary China, the design institutes after waves of reforms in the 1990s–2000s still play a central role in design practice and the construction industry, asserting a Maoist legacy one way or another.[18]

Notes

1 In the Mao era, workers were bound to their *danwei* for life. Each *danwei* created its own housing, childcare, schools, clinics, shops, and other social services. More research can be found in Lü, Xiaobo, and Perry Elizabeth J., ed., *Danwei: The Changing Chinese Workplace in Historical and Comparative Perspective* (Armonk, NY: M. E. Sharpe, 1997).

2 Zou Denong, *Zhongguo Xiandai Jianzhu Shi* (A History of Modern Chinese Architecture) (Beijing: Jixie Gongye Chubanshe, 2003), 94–95.

3 Editorial Committee, *Zhufang he Chengxiang Jianshebu Lishi Yange ji Dashiji* (Historical Evolution and Memorabilia of Ministry of Housing and Urban-Rural Development) (Beijing: Zhongguo Chengshi Chubanshe, 2012), 105–106.

4 These regions were called *da xingzhengqu* (or *daqu*), which existed in the early years of the People's Republic from 1949 to 1954. Their governments were regarded as branches of the central government, above governments of provinces and cities.

5 Editorial Committee, *Zhufang*, 110.

6 Zou, *Zhongguo*, 95–96.

7 Liu Xiufeng (report on 25 February 1957), "Sannianlai de Huigu he Jinhou de Gongzuo (Review on the Past Three Years and Future Plan)," in *Zhonghua Renmin Gongheguo Jingji Dang'an Ziliao Xuanbian, 1953–1957. Guding Zichan Touzi yu Jianzhuye Juan* (Selected Archive Materials on the Economy of the People's Republic of China, 1953–1957: Fixed-Assets Investment and the Construction Industry), ed. Chinese Academy of Social Sciences and China Central Archive (Beijing: Zhongguo Wujia Chubanshe, 1998), 499–504.

8 According to the division of responsibility in the early years, central design institutes focused on industrial construction, while the provincial and municipal design institutes focused on civil construction. See Liu, "Sannianlai."

9 Guangzhou Foreign Trade Projects were proposed in the early 1970s for the enlarged Canton Fair (China Export Commodities Fair), which used to be the largest and the most important channel to do business with foreigners in the Mao era.

10 This formula was officially proposed as early as in the first National Conference of Construction in July 1952: "Architectural design should emphasize the principle of 'suitability, safety, and economy' – when economic conditions permit, pay a certain attention to the beauty of the building." Later in February 1955, at the Conference of Design and Construction held by the Ministry of Construction, it was simplified as "suitability, economy, and beauty when conditions permitted." See Zou, *Zhongguo*, 208–210.

11 Editorial Committee, *Zhufang*, 107–108. An economic accounting system is a system used in socialist countries under a planned economy. It is to conduct independent accounting calculations for each enterprise entity. See Ludwig von Mises, "Economic Calculation in the Socialist Commonwealth," in *Classics in Austrian Economics: A Sampling in the History of a Tradition. Volume 3. The Age of Mises and Hayek*, ed. Israel M. Kirzner (London: Pickering and Chatto, 1994/1920).

12 Chinese Academy, eds. *Zhonghua Renmin*, 349.

13 But after the reform and opening up, construction funds predominantly relied on loans, and construction enterprises operated by self-financing, while design institutes had also been restructured from *shiye danwei* into *qiye danwei*, charging design fees directly and participating in market competition. Many design institutes are currently still being restructured.

14 Liu, "Sannianlai."

15 The Third Front Construction was launched in 1964 based on concerns of national defence. Since the late 1950s and for the entire 1960s, China's relations with the Soviet Union and the United States had both deteriorated. Under such threat, Mao launched the Third Front Construction and mobilized the masses to "Prepare for the War, Prepare for the Famine." The Third Front Construction in effect industrialized part of China's most interior and agricultural regions, in national defence, technology, manufacturing, mining, metal, and electricity.

16 Lin Biao, the vice chairman of China then and the designated successor of the Chinese revolution, died in a plane crash on 13 September 1971, allegedly after attempting to assassinate Mao.

17 This was another climax of introducing industrial projects from foreign countries since the Soviet-aid projects in 1950s. Compared with the introduction of the Soviet aids in the 1950s, this time, the projects were mostly light industries imported from Western countries and Japan – China in the 1970s, after building a foundation of heavy industries, began to concentrate on improving the livelihood of the masses.

18 Zhu Jianfei. "Shejiyuan Xuanyan (The Chinese design institute: A manifesto)." In *Xi'an 2013 Jianzhu yu Dangdai Yishu Shuangnianzhan, Jianzhu Fence: West Bund 2013: A Biennale of Architecture and Contemporary Art, Volume 1: Architecture*, ed. Qin Lei and Meng Xuyan (Shanghai: Tongji Daxue Chubanshe, 2013), 112–113.

Bibliography

Chinese Academy of Social Sciences, and China Central Archive, eds. *Zhonghua Renmin Gongheguo Jingji Dang'an Ziliao Xuanbian, 1953–1957. Guding Zichan Touzi yu Jianzhuye Juan, 1953–1957* (Selected Archive Materials on the Economy of the People's Republic of China, 1953–1957: Fixed-Assets Investment and the Construction Industry). Beijing: Zhongguo Wujia Chubanshe, 1998.

Editor. "Shiyong Jingji Meiguan Jianzhu Fangzhen shi Yichan yeshi Guobao: 'Jianzhu Fangzhen 60 Nian de Dangdai Yiyi' Yantaohui Ceji (The Policy 'Suitability, Economy and Beauty' Is a Legacy and a Treasure: Notes on a Seminar Titled 'Contemporary Significance of the 60 Years of Practicing the Architectural Policy')." *Jilin Kancha Sheji* (Jilin Survey and Design), no. 2 (2013): 35–36.

Editorial Committee, ed. *Zhongguo Jianzhu Shejiyuan Chengli Wushi Zhounian Jinian Congshu: Licheng Pian* (The 50th Anniversary of the Founding of CAG/China Architecture Design and Research Group: Volume on History). Beijing: China Architecture Design & Research Group, 2002.

———, ed. *Beijing Shi Jianzhu Sheji Yanjiu Yuan 60 Zhounian Congshu, Jinian Ji* (The 50th Anniversary of the Foundation of BIAD/Beijing Institute of Architectural Design: A Commemorating Volume). Tianjin: Tianjin Daxue Chubanshe, 2009.

————, ed. *Zhufang he Chengxiang Jianshebu Lishi Yange ji Dashiji* (A History and a Historical Line of the Ministry of Housing and Urban-Rural Construction). Beijing: Zhongguo Chengshi Chubanshe, 2012.

Liang Sicheng. "Zhongguo Jianzhu de Tezheng (The Characteristics of Chinese Architecture)." *Jianzhu Xuebao* (Architectural Journal), no. 1 (1954): 36–39.

Lü, Xiaobo and Elizabeth J. Perry, eds. *Danwei: The Changing Chinese Workplace in Historical and Comparative Perspective*. Armonk, NY: M. E. Sharpe, 1997.

MacFarquhar, Roderick and John King Fairbank, eds. *The Cambridge History of China, vol. 14, the People's Republic. Part 1, the Emergence of Revolutionary China, 1949–1965*. Cambridge: Cambridge University Press, 1987.

————, eds. *The Cambridge History of China, vol. 15, the People's Republic. Part 2, Revolutions Within the Chinese Revolution, 1966–1982*. Cambridge: Cambridge University Press, 1987.

Rowe, Peter G. and Seng Kuan. *Architectural Encounters with Essence and Form in Modern China*. Cambridge, MA: MIT Press, 2002.

Shi Anhai, ed. *Lingnan Jinxiandai Youxiu Jianzhu, 1949–1990 Juan* (Excellent Architectural Works in the Modern Lingnan Region: 1949–1990). Beijing: Zhongguo Jianzhu Gongye Chubanshe, 2010.

Von Mises, Ludwig. "Economic Calculation in the Socialist Commonwealth." In *Classics in Austrian Economics: A Sampling in the History of a Tradition, vol. 3: The Age of Mises and Hayek*, edited by Israel M. Kirzner, 2–30. London: Pickering and Chatto, 1994/1920.

Wu, Xingyuan. "Cuowu de Jianzhu Lilun Bixu Pipan (A Wrong Architectural Theory Must Be Criticized)." *Jianzhu Xuebao* (Architectural Journal), no. 3 (1966): 30–32.

Yuan, Jingshen. "Guanyu Chuangzuo Xinde Jianzhu Fengge de Jige Wenti (Several Issues on Creating a New Architectural Style)." *Jianzhu Xuebao* (Architectural Journal), no. 1 (1959): 38–40.

Zhu, Jianfei. *Architecture of Modern China: A Historical Critique*. London: Routledge, 2009.

————. "Shejiyuan Xuanyan (The Chinese Design Institute: A Manifesto)." In *Xi'an 2013 Jianzhu yu Dangdai Yishu Shuangnianzhan, Jianzhu Fence: West Bund 2013: A Biennale of Architecture and Contemporary Art, vol. 1: Architecture*, edited by Qin Lei and Meng Xuyan, 112–113. Shanghai: Tongji Daxue Chubanshe, 2013.

Zou Deci, ed. *Xin Zhongguo Chengshi Guihua Fazhanshi Yanjiu: Zong Baogao ji Dashij* (Research on the Developmental History of the Urban Planning Practice of the People's Republic of China: Overview and a Historical Line). Beijing: Jianzhu Gongye Chubanshe, 2014.

Zou Denong. *Zhongguo Xiandai Jianzhu Shi* (A History of Modern Chinese Architecture). Beijing: Jixie Gongye Chubanshe, 2003.

Glossary

Beijing	北京
Chen Zhi	陈植
Dai Nianci	戴念慈
danwei	单位
Gansu	甘肃
Gong Deshun	龚德顺
Guangdong	广东
Guangzhou	广州
Hua Lanhong (Léon Hoa)	华揽洪
Hunan	湖南
Jiang Qing	江青
Kuan Sung-sheng (Guan Songsheng)	关颂声
Kuomintang (Guomindang)	国民党
Liang Sicheng	梁思成
Lin Biao	林彪
Liu Xiufeng	刘秀峰
qiye danwei	企业单位
Renmin Ribao	人民日报

Shanghai	上海
shiye danwei	事业单位
Tianjin	天津
Tong Jun	童寯
xingzheng danwei	行政单位
Yang Tingbao	杨廷宝
Yongmao (firm)	永茂（建筑公司）
Zhou Enlai	周恩来
Zhu Bin	朱彬

23

ARCHITECTURAL EDUCATION IN CHINA (1950s–1980s)

Constructing and Deconstructing

Qian Feng

After the founding of the People's Republic in 1949, China spent a three-year period undergoing "transformation and adaptation." From 1952 on, with the launch of the first Five-Year Plan, China entered full-scale construction of a socialist nation. Correspondingly, the national education system went through a large-scale reform and reconstruction to serve the effort and its socio-economic development.

The early stage of the process witnessed an adoption of Soviet ideas and corresponding institutional reform, in architectural education as in almost every field of national development. Since then, with waves of radical leftist ideology and anti-institutional efforts, the construction and deconstruction of the system of architectural education went side by side, in successive alternation. This chapter outlines this process and examines the underlying transformations.[1]

1952–1957: First Institutionalization of Architectural Education in the People's Republic

Between 1952 and 1957, under the influence of the Soviets, the first wave of institutionalization and reform of China's higher education of various disciplines, including architecture, took place. Prior to 1949, higher education in China took diverse organizational forms, including public universities, private colleges, and missionary institutions. After 1949, state government took over these schools and began to coordinate them centrally. In the early 1950s, working on these diverse and scattered universities, state authority started to reorganize the overall distribution, rearrange academic staff, build new and necessary organizations, and establish systematic plans for educating talent, academics, and professionals.

During that time, as China adopted the Soviet model, state officials heavily privileged industry. Like the Russians, they favored engineering and technological schools. In a conference of deans of engineering schools in November 1951, problems were identified: regional distribution was unreasonable; staff and facilities were scattered; bodies of knowledge to be covered in teaching were messy; teaching and practice did not match; education of the professionals was not focused enough; and the number of graduates was far less than what was needed for the industrial development of the country.[2] The policy developed to deal with the situation was

DOI: 10.4324/9781315851112-35

"focusing on the education of staff and professionals for industry-related disciplines; developing specialist colleges; reforming and strengthening comprehensive universities."[3]

This conference initiated a nation-wide reorganization of higher education institutions. By the end of 1952, three-fourths of tertiary institutions in China had been impacted. The country was divided into several regions. In each, university departments that were similar to each other were integrated into one. In the process, the emphasis was on specialized colleges and universities, whereas many old comprehensive universities were dismembered, and specialized universities strong in science, technology, and engineering emerged and developed. In this context, architectural departments scattered at different universities in a region were merged into one. The new departments of architecture, along with civil engineering sections and departments, were assembled into universities of science and technology or institutes of technology in the regions across China.

The reorganization of higher education institutions lasted from 1952 through to 1959 and resulted in the creation of eight architectural departments. They came to be known as the Old Eight (*lao ba xiao*). They included the architectural department at Tsinghua University, Tianjin University, Nanjing Institute of Technology (Southeast University today), Tongji University, South China Institute of Technology, Chongqing Institute of Architectural Engineering, Xi'an Institute of Architectural Engineering, and Harbin Institute of Architectural Engineering. These eight departments were the leading forces in architectural education in China post-1949 and have played significant roles in that historical development.

From then on, the old situation was eradicated – the numerous small schools, each with its own character and each competing with others freely, were no more, replaced by a few large and reassembled departments. These departments were centrally supervised by state authority. From this moment on, a new chapter in higher education in architecture in China began.

As China was learning from the Soviet model, the organization of the departments of architecture, both inside and outside, was altered. Before 1949, these departments belonged to the various colleges (art or engineering) within a university. Now, they were departments in an independent college or institute of technology, or a university for science, engineering, and technology. Within the department, "teaching-research groups" (*jiao yan zu*) were established for staff in the same teaching and specialist areas; there were, for example, an Architectural Design Group, a Fine Art Group, and a Building Technology Group. Some groups had subgroups, e.g. a History Sub-Group and a Basic Design Sub-Group. Staff were organized into these groups and sub-groups. State authority also requested staff to formulate standard syllabuses, to compile national textbooks, and to teach using these texts and guidelines.

Teaching ideology in China then followed the Russian model in the early 1950s, when the Soviet Union was under Stalin, who advocated ideas of "Socialist Content and National Form." Russian classicism and Baroque Style were considered as the great representatives of Russian national architecture.[4] Consequently, their teaching method turned to the model developed from the French Beaux-Arts system. Architecture was considered as a form of art, comparable to sculpture, fine art, and music.

With this influence, the classical architecture of ancient China witnessed a revival. Many National-Style buildings, often with a big Chinese roof emerged, mostly in the north around political centers. In a parallel development, architectural teaching also turned to the Beaux-Art model. Water-color rendering and pencil sketch were considered as foundational training; in design, classical compositions, monumentality, and ornamentation were considered essential for fine architecture. These ideas were basically the same as those of the American Beaux-Arts influence in China's architectural education before 1949. The new influence then took root quickly and joined the legacies of the first influence in modern China's architectural education system, making what was already mainstream into a stronger force from then on. Certain modernist ideas, such as those teaching experiments at St. John's University and Liang Sicheng's teaching of "form and environment" at Tsinghua University, were all criticized and sidelined in the major rush in the classical direction.[5]

Following the Soviet model, students were assigned to fixed classes on a definite disciplinary pathway, and cannot migrate to other disciplines and departments. National standard syllabuses were established; teaching content was detailed and regulated; students studied a set of subjects yearly as planned for the whole class; there were hardly any electives nor any freedom to choose a set of subjects by students themselves in a credit system as we find in the Anglo-American approach. Completing a fixed set of courses over a program of a few years, students were centrally distributed across the nation to where skills and workforce were needed, without much freedom given to the students to choose or seek employment themselves.

Curriculum design and planning were the core of the practice in the new system. Initially, architectural departments were asked to develop their own plans based on the Soviet model. Soon, the departments were requested to implement a universal teaching plan devised by the Soviet advisors or "Soviet Experts." In 1954, the Ministry of Education organized a conference where Soviet advisors took part, announced afterwards a unified teaching guideline for all departments of architecture across the nation, and requested the schools follow and implement. The Soviet-influenced curriculum required long teaching hours and deep learning; there were difficulties in implementation at various universities, and adjustments were made accordingly. The relevant universities also extended the initial four-year program into a five- or six-year program.

The newly established approach gradually assumed a clear system. The main pathway included three stages: foundational training, a series of design exercises, and, finally, a synthesized graduation design. Foundational training included drafting and water-color rendering; the design exercises included a sequence of studios on building types, with theory-oriented lectures delivered along the path. The typological range included residential designs, public buildings, industrial works, and urban planning. In the teaching of these first and second phases, three types of subjects were included along the learning process: painting, drawing, and fine art; building technology; and the history of art and architecture. The third or final stage was the synthesized graduation design project, where one was to test and employ all knowledge learned before.

The newly established system shared a lot with the old Anglo-American one incorporated into China before 1949, such as the interrelation between design, technology, fine art, and history in the overall arrangement, the privileging of water-color rendering in foundational training, the emphasis on fine art, and skills of drawing. There were, however, differences:

1   The Soviet or Soviet-inspired system set a greater emphasis on technology and industry-related knowledge. This was reflected in heavy teaching in these areas and in the privileging of "industrial architecture" as a special typology to be established and included in studio design teaching – a marked difference from the Anglo-American approach. This was surely to do with the policy of privileging heavy industry for the Soviet Union's national economic development – as reflected in the slogan "production first, livelihood second."

2   There was a lot of history – History of World Art, History of Western Architecture (including Russian and Soviet architecture), and History of Chinese Architecture. This was surely a common emphasis of the Beaux-Art system, but the history teaching in the Soviet-inspired system now had a new dimension: a leftist ideology with ideas of class struggle and class analysis being incorporated in history teaching. Architectural history was

then presented as the "footnote of a social history" and the reflection "a history of class struggles"; this attempt eroded the cultural depth and the humanistic educational effect of history teaching.

3   The new system paid more attention to relations with practice in reality. Inspired by the Soviet model, the new system included fixed and institutionalized periods of practice of various kinds. In every summer vacation, students needed to do practice correlated to their level of study – such as "observation practice" and "production practice." In addition, the Ministry of Education directed that design teaching should oriented towards normal or common types of buildings used in everyday life, so teaching in this period was pragmatic and closely associated with situations of real practice.

Since 1952, China's architectural education system migrated from the Anglo-American to the Soviet model. The new system had certain achievements, such as the unification of teaching and the correction of differences or gaps between different schools of architecture; but it also had several problems. For example, the system was not flexible enough and was unable to deliver teaching according to the particular character, development, and understanding of individual students; the realm for the bodies of knowledge to be learned by the students was also narrow and unitary; humanist concerns and the related subjects were largely ignored.

The purpose of the new system was to serve and to be consistent with the planned economy and the planned production of products that China was adopting, so that the system could deliver mass production of urgently needed materials and standardized professionals efficiently. But a system that had emphasized specialist knowledge and technological rationality had also suffered the loss of a synthesis of humanities and sciences found in the old system – in the old comprehensive universities in China before 1949. As a discipline for creating the human environment, it suffered a biased approach, with greater focus on pragmatics and technology and not enough on humanities and social sciences. Students generally lacked concerns for social ideals and humanistic concerns.

1958–1960: The Great Leap Forward and the First Education Revolution

From 1952 to 1957, China's architectural education followed the Soviet model, with some modifications; its main characteristics were institutionalization and normalization. However, from 1958 onwards, due to many factors, Chinese leaders began to shift away from the Soviet Union, in search for China's own path of socialist modernization. Soon, Mao started the Great Leap Forward movement and Education Revolution movement, which unfolded in ways subversive to the formalistic institution of the education system.

The Soviet-inspired system established in 1952–57 was not quite consistent with the educational ideals of the Chinese leaders. As the universities intended to uphold a high standard, the benchmarks for the entrance examination scores were quite high, and students from workers and farmers' families couldn't often reach the line and would be unable to come to the universities to study. The education system aiming at producing experts and professionals was thus at odds with the ideals of the Communist Party, which, upon entering the cities and seizing state power, wanted an open system that would serve workers, farmers, and the masses well.

Unlike some party leaders who wanted to focus on economic development, party Chairman Mao Zedong, who came from a rural background, focused more on social and moral ideals and hoped to establish an egalitarian socialist society for the whole population. He regarded the Soviet model as too departmental, hierarchical, specialist, and technocratic. He also considered it too centralized and too urban-based – a system that had ignored rural China and its peasant population. For him, the system was also too restrictive, with too much burden on the students; in other words, Mao was not pleased with the practice. In 1957, he said, education system needed reform and that the curriculum should be lessened and made more accessible, in order to allow workers and peasants' children to come and study.[6]

The political turmoil in Poland and Hungry also made the Chinese leaders more determined to steer away from the Soviet Union, to find a path of socialist development on their own. In this context, the Second Session of the Eighth NPC (National People's Congress) in 1958 passed a General Principle proposed by Mao – to "go all out, aim high, and achieve greater, faster, better, and more economically, in building socialism." He requested the population to further technological revolutions and cultural revolutions; he set up high targets for industry and agricultural production. A Great Leap Forward movement soon swept across whole China; in the field of education, the reflection of this was an "Education Revolution."

In the Education Revolution, policies went through a rapid change. As early as 1949, Mao had already established an education policy of New Democracy in his *Gongtong Gangling* (common framework) – we aim to achieve a national, scientific and people's cultural practice and education system. In February 1952, Mao said that our policy was to "allow a moral education, intellectual education and physical education to develop in full, and to cultivate a working people that is cultured and is with a socialist consciousness." Now, in 1958, Mao refined his position further: "education should serve for the politics of the proletarian class, and education should combine with work and production."[7] Shifting from "culture" to "politics," and to "work and production," a new education guideline emerged.

From this moment on, enrolment into the universities involved a review of the political background the students' families. In 1957, enrolment began to shift in favor of students with family backgrounds of workers and peasant; in 1958, there were even special groups or classes exclusively reserved for workers' and farmers' children, called *gong nong ban* (workers and peasants' classrooms), to demonstrate that education was open to the proletarian classes.

At the same time, the separation of manual labor and intellectual labor was considered the split and opposition of classes of the old society – to be eradicated in the new education system, where education was to combine work and production, so as to develop a new, communist human being. The formal and institutionalized education system established in the previous years was challenged and subverted, at times totally replaced, by on-site teaching that combined practice and real projects. With radicalization, classroom teaching came to a stop; and teachers and students formed teams to work on real projects, conducting teaching in the process.

In these project-oriented practices, architectural teachers and students produced many planning and design schemes for the People's Communes in the villages. As one of the "Three Red Flags,"[8] the building of the People's Commune was regarded as a crucial process for developing into a communist society. The Communes should work as a basic social unit in a communist society where life was highly socialized and collectivist; the members live and work there, as peasants, workers, and soldiers simultaneously, so as to eradicate class difference and urban–rural difference.

One of the greatest projects the teachers and students worked on together at the time was the design for the "Ten Grand Projects" of Beijing in 1958, for the celebration of the tenth anniversary of the People's Republic in October 1959. Teams from different universities submitted many schemes; some of them were adopted in the process of design development.

The Education Revolution of 1958 developed ideas and methods that witnessed reuse and further development in the Cultural Revolution of the 1960s and 1970s – the 1958 movement was only a prelude for an education storm to come.

1961–1966: Restoring the Education System Amid Economic Recovery

The Great Leap Forward resulted in economic slowdown and disarray. The withdrawal of Russian support and technological aid due to worsening Sino–Soviet relations made things worse – China entered serious economic hardship. To solve the problem, state authority adopted adjustment plans and restored the previous normal practice in higher education.

In early 1960, the Ministry of Education directed that "Teaching should be mainly based at classrooms; we should now plan for a comprehensive teaching practice, and gradually restore teaching at the colleges and universities."[9] Teaching at these institutions shifted in the direction of theorization, systemization, and institutionalization. In this period, the compilation of textbooks for different courses and disciplines gradually began, and the gaps in teaching due to the involvement of real practice in the previous years were now "filled up" in special classes to ensure that students did not miss anything upon graduation.

In the architectural departments, teaching followed the system installed before the Education Revolution, but with a difference. Teaching now absorbed an emphasis on practice – labor work, building practice, and work in factories or production lines were incorporated as a consequence of the Education Revolution. However, labor or practice now were no longer ad-hoc and movement-like, but formally institutionalized as part of the teaching program. This was largely due to the effort of President Liu Shaoqi (third most powerful man in China after Mao Zedong and Zhou Enlai); Liu had been trying to implement Mao's educational ideals of "work-study in factories or farms" into a formal institutionalized practice, rather than treating the Education Revolution as a social movement.

Apart from an emphasis on practice, this period also saw a new interest in technology and specialist research, due to the influence of great technological progress internationally in the field. Students in the architecture discipline were organized into teams to translate articles from overseas on the latest research and technological breakthroughs; this process, and the reading involved, informed the students about the situation of the discipline of architecture outside China.

In the teaching of design and architecture, the practice of the early 1960s mostly restored the previous academy approach before the Great Leap Forward. Design was taught in a progressive pathway, from foundational training where water-color rendering was the key component, to a series of studio exercises on projects ranging from simple to complex. Exposure to overseas architectural magazines, and the recent phases of modern architecture and technological developments included in these media, also pushed the schools in a modernist direction in architecture. The search for a national style had also shifted from the focus on palatial big roofs of the 1950s to an interest in learning from the vernacular and regional building traditions. These changes are reflected in the works of the staff and the studio exercises of the students of the time.

1966–1976: Cultural Revolution and the Second Education Revolution

When economic hardship was resolved in 1966, Mao began to push again his ideals of egalitarian socialism for the people, and his thoughts in the Great Leap Forward returned. This time, Mao launched a political movement more radical than before – the Great Proletarian Cultural Revolution; he mobilized students and the masses to criticize, attack, and topple the government offices and ruling organizations that were – according to Mao – overtly conservative, bureaucratic, and hierarchical.

In the area of education, Mao always opposed hierarchical and institutional practices; he thought that the educational practice in China at the time was overburdened by a heavy curriculum, bourgeoisie, and "few, slow, bad, and wasteful" in education production. He was also dissatisfied with Liu Shaoqi's half-work/half-study or work–study model, seeing it as a making of two-tiers with "two legs," with the children of the working classes still kept at a lower level with limited access – it was, after all, a bourgeois practice in disguise, according to Mao. What Mao wanted was "one system" – to turn all schools, even the entire society, into a "May-Seventh Commune," where one was a worker and a farmer, where one studies as a student but also exercises as a soldier.[10]

Soon, "May-Seventh Farms" and "May-Seventh Schools" appeared all over China; university professors and many intellectuals were sent down to the schools in the countryside, to receive labor reform. Mao wanted every member of society to be trained to be comprehensively and competently, able to work for industry and agriculture, and capable of being a student and a disciplined soldier as well. Mao hoped to break down the division of labor between army, industry, academy, and rural farms, in order to eradicate professional and class difference.

If the period from 1966 to 1969 was chaotic and destructive, the period since 1969 was constructive of the new. The new system emphasized "class struggle" and "revolution and criticism" in content, focused on science and technology in the arrangement of courses and departments, and emphasized the political background of the student body in university enrolment – the "worker–farmer–soldier students" (*gong-nong-bing xueyuan*) were the target of enrolment for the universities in these years. Through this second Education Revolution, the formalized and systemized higher-education system was once again deconstructed and replaced with lowly and pragmatic education practice.

Classroom teaching was once again terminated, replaced by on-site work and practice-oriented study, which was effectively a continuation of the practice in the Great Leap Forward movement. Teachers and students left the schools behind and studied and worked side by side on building sites. The organization also changed: the vertical differentiation between basic subjects and professional subjects were broken; teachers of different subjects and specializations were mixed into hybrid teams and then mixed with factory workers and "worker–farmer–soldier students" to form special task forces, to conduct teaching, studying, and working together in relation to real projects.

These reforms eroded the importance of basic and theory subjects and promoted a pragmatic education. Although the initial intention was not unreasonable in its attempt to solve problems such as the theory–practice split, the real result of the Cultural Revolution was an awful and lowly pragmatism. The practice had carried the idea to its extremes and ruined the thorough comprehensiveness of the bodies of knowledge and systems of skills. The destructive forces inflicted upon the systems and the university staff were much worse than the previous round, and the destruction was severe; teaching and learning were thoroughly derailed – they plunged into a disastrous standstill, in a political climate that was intense and highly charged.

1977–1980s: Restoring Architectural Education in the Reform Era

With the end of the Cultural Revolution and the adoption of Reform, China re-opened its doors to the world, and architectural education at universities moved back to the practice of institutionalization and normalization.

In the early days of recovery, due to urgent need, the old academy model (of the Beaux-Arts system) was directly adopted or rather just returned to. The use of ink and water-color rendering and the emphasis on the skills of graphic representations – taught in foundational studios as an entry into the learning of the design of architecture – remained the same and was much emphasized. Although modernist design exercises were gradually incorporated in the foundational studios, the basic approach remained formal and representation-oriented, emphasizing a "painterly architecture" or an "architecture of fine art" of the academy model.

Despite this, staff in many architectural departments began to search ideas and concepts of a modernist architecture in design and teaching. In thinking, the search in a modernist language was on the rise and that was combined with a new interest in the vernacular, which resulted in the testing and the production of many regional modernist works. In teaching, many schools introduced cubist and constructivist or *goucheng* ideas in the foundational studios, which promoted the creative potential in the students, to break away from the rigid and uniform system of the past.

For example, at Tsinghua University, the foundational studios introduced "the basic formal and compositional exercises" where 2-D and 3-D abstract forms were involved to develop in the students a comprehension of space and volume. At Tongji University, the foundational studio teaching introduced the Bauhaus model, which required a hands-on making process – students were asked to manually construct stationaries, to design book covers, and to design and make LP covers.[11]

At Nanjing Institute of Technology (NIT, now Southeast University) of the 1980s, a group of young staff responsible for teaching foundational studios began to explore possible ways of education reform. After an initial interest in the cubist and constructivist exercises, they shifted their focus to the latest developments in design teaching overseas and gradually developed a system of teaching centered on the ideas of "tectonics" (*jiangou*).

Conclusion: Towards a System and Further Mutations

In the first three decades of the People's Republic, China's architectural education system and its institutional framework took shape gradually. Due to radical ideologies and political movements, the process went through periods of interruption and re-orientation; the attempts at normalization and systemization were constantly counteracted by practice- and production-oriented campaigns and social movements.

Despite these interruptions, the architectural departments developed a wholesome system and method in teaching. In general, the Beaux-Arts based academy model dominated the overall approach; this was both an extension of the American model China adopted before 1949 and a result of the import of the Soviet-Russian practice in the 1950s. After several rounds of political movements and the interruptions in the educational realm, the teaching in most of the architectural departments in the 1980s – when China was recovering and reopening – maintained this system.

After three decades of development, the system in China in the 1980s had these features: a five- or six-year program in most cases; the curriculum in each of the years was mostly fixed and rigid; the subjects were mostly compulsory, with very few electives; upon entering the university department, students were constrained to a definite study and disciplinary pathway; they went through a clear and definite program over the years; and they were "assigned by the state centrally" to job "posts" where there were need across the nation. This education system reflected the planned national economy China was then adopting.

For teaching content, the first year included the practice of ink-line constructed drawings and water-color renderings in the foundational studios, emphasizing skills in pictorial representation. In the following years, a series of studios were arranged to cover different building types; and the teaching of design, history and theory, and technology were placed side by side each year along the pathway. Design philosophy followed that of the academy model in essence: symmetry, axis, proportion, balance, and the various other compositional rules in classical formal aesthetics were emphasized, at certain levels. At the same time, modern architectural principles were also adopted in reality – austerity and purity were effectively in use; ideas of *goucheng* (cubist and constructivist compositions), of space, and of tectonics were also explored and studied.

After the 1980s, the system and institution of architectural education in China continued to evolve; curriculum structure became more open and flexible, with increasingly more electives on offer; the foundational studio gradually moved out of the rendering system in favor of cultivating and promoting creativity in the students. The overall institution and the teaching system shifted increasingly to converge with the international practice of the time.

Notes

1 This research is supported by National Natural Science Foundation of China (project no.: 51778425).
2 Yang Dongping, ed. *Jiannande Richu: Zhongguo Xiandai Jiaoyude 20 Shiji (A difficult sunrise: The modern education of China in the 20th century)* (Shanghai: Wenhui Chubanshe, 2003), 120.
3 Yang, *Jiannande*, 126.
4 Zou Denong. *Zhongguo Xiandai Jianzhushi (A history of modern Chinese architecture)* (Tianjin: Tianjin Kexue Jishu Chubanshe, 2001).
5 Wu Liangyong said that the new system adopted after the Soviet-Russian model interrupted the practice Liang Sicheng and Lin Huiyin had already started previously – to introduce a teaching reform that carried modernist ideas. This interruption saddened Liang and Lin considerably, according to Wu. For this, see: Wu Liangyong. *Lin Huiyin Zuihou Shinian (The last ten years of Lin Huiyin)* (Beijing: Zhishi Chanquan Chubanshe/Zhongguo Shuili Shuidian Chubanshe, 2003).
6 Yang, *Jiannande*, 160.
7 Yang, *Jiannande*, 134.
8 The so-called Three Red Flags referred to the practice of the General Principles of Socialist Construction, the Great Leap Forward, and the People's Commune.
9 This was specified in a document titled "Interim Rules of Practice for the Higher Education Institutions Belonging to the Ministry of Education," issued by the government on 15 September 1961 – which was referred as "Sixty Points of Higher Education."
10 "May Seventh" refers to 7 May 1966, when Mao Zedong sent his directive on the idea to Lin Biao.
11 Based on my interview with Professor Zhao Xiuheng in August 2004.

Bibliography

Qian Feng and Wu Jiang. *Zhongguo Xiandai Jianzhu Jiaoyushi* (Education of Modern Architecture in China). Beijing: zhongguo jianzhu gongye Chubanshe, 1994.
Wu Liangyong. *Lin Huiyin Zuihou Shinian* (The Last Ten Years of Lin Huiyin). Beijing: Zhishi Chanquan Chubanshe/Zhongguo Shuili Shuidian Chubanshe, 2003.
Yang Dongping, ed. *Jiannande Richu: Zhongguo Xiandai Jiaoyude 20 Shiji* (A Difficult Sunrise: The Modern Education of China in the 20th Century). Shanghai: Wenhui Chubanshe, 2003.
Yu Li. *Zhongguo Gaodeng Jiaoyushi* (A History of Higher Education in China). Shanghai: Huadong Shifan Daxue Chubanshe, 1994.
Zou Denong. *Zhongguo Xiandai Jianzhushi* (A History of Modern Chinese Architecture). Tianjin: Tianjin Kexue Jishu Chubanshe, 2001.

Glossary

Chongqing Institute of Architectural Engineering　重庆建筑工程学院
gong nong ban　工农班
gong-nong-bing xueyuan　工农兵学员
Gongtong Gangling　共同纲领

goucheng	构成
Harbin Institute of Architectural Engineering	哈尔滨建筑工程学院
jiangou	建构
jiao yan zu	教研组
lao ba xiao	老八校
Liang Sicheng	梁思成
Liu Shaoqi	刘少奇
Mao Zedong	毛泽东
Nanjing Institute of Technology	南京工学院
Tianjin University	天津大学
Tongji University	同济大学
Tsinghua University	清华大学
Xi'an Institute of Architectural Engineering	西安建筑工程学院
Zhou Enlai	周恩来

24

THEORIES OF SPATIAL COMPOSITION

Design Knowledge in China up to the 1980s

Li Hua

From the late 1970s to the mid-1980s, China witnessed an unprecedented boom in publication of textbooks or reference books for teaching in architecture. These books, often compiled and published under the name of an institute or a collaboration between architectural schools and institutes, covered almost every branch for a comprehensive body of architecture knowledge, including history, design, technology, and construction. The timing is crucial. In fact, most of the first drafts or plans of these books were shaped in the 1950s and 1960s. There were very few textbooks for teaching architecture written in Chinese before – and where they did exist, they were not systematic.[1] After about a decade's stagnation in teaching and publishing in architecture during the Cultural Revolution (1966–76), a profusion of publications came into being in the 1980s, delivering a crystallization of experiences, methods, and thoughts developed in the 1950s and 1960s, and a transfer of these into a systemized body of knowledge for use at governed schools of architecture – that is, into an institutionalized form of knowledge, in the 1980s, with a long-term impact that can still be felt today. In this context, one of the most widely circulated books published at the time is *Jianzhu Kongjian Zuhelun* – a theory of spatial composition in architecture (hereafter *Spatial Composition*), written by an individual scholar (rather than a group or an institute), Professor Peng Yigang.

Spatial Composition is a book about the principles of architectural design. Completed in 1980, its first edition was publicised in 1983. After expanding twice, its third edition was issued in 2007. By 2019, it had been reprinted 50 times, and today, it is still on sale. For many architectural teachers and students in China, it has been a good introduction to the discipline of architectural design.

Composition was regarded as an essential technique of architectural design in China at least till the 1990s. In fact, when *Spatial Composition* first came out, there were three other books on the same topic – all were translations. Two of them, *Goutu Yuanli* (principles of composition, 1979)[2] and *Jianzhu Xingshimei de Yuanze* (principles of architectural aesthetics, 1982),[3] were respectively translated from the first ten and first eleven chapters of the second volume of *Forms and Functions of Twentieth Century Architecture* (hereafter *Forms and Functions*),[4] published in the United States in 1952. Another, *Jianzhu Goutu Gailun* (outline of a theory in architectural composition, 1983), was translated from a Russian book compiled and published in 1960.[5] The principles stated in *Spatial Composition* shared a lot of commonalities with not only the English and Russian books but also those published in Chinese around the same time on design principles of different building types by other scholars or institutions, such as *Gonggong Jianzhu Sheji*

DOI: 10.4324/9781315851112-36

Jichu (the foundation of design for public buildings), written and published by NIT (Nanjing Institute of Technology, now SEU or Southeast University) in 1986.[6] Common ideas can even be found in 1962's *Minyong Jianzhu Sheji Yuanli* (principles of design for civic architecture) by Tsinghua University of Beijing.[7] In other words, Peng's *Spatial Composition* is not only a work of his own but also represents shared observations and understandings of the profession in China since the 1950s. A close reading of this book is therefore important to reveal how the profession understood design and how they conceived this exercise in a broader frame of ideas and concepts. But, before that, a brief review is needed of how "spatial composition" as terminology was introduced into China in the architectural discipline.

The Notion of "Spatial Composition" in China in the 1950s–60s

To some, "space (*kongjian*) composition (*goutu, zuhe*)" may sound unusual, as the two words of the phrase come from two different or even opposite schools – modernism and the Beaux-Arts system. However, from the mid-1950s to the 1980s, it was a common phrase frequently used in professional or studio conversations; it was also an important issue that concerned architects, teachers, and scholars in China at the time. While some studies have revealed that a key characteristic in design thinking in modern China had been a hybridizing synthesis rather than conceptual opposition of the Beaux-Arts and the modernist, this chapter is more concerned with the way the hybrid developed its own life in the condition and context of China at this historical juncture.

Spatial composition, as an architectural term, first appeared in Chinese translations of Soviet architectural texts in the first half of the 1950s.[8] For example, in a 1954 Chinese translation of the initial article of 1953 in Russian, appearing in the inaugural issue of *Jianzhu Xuebao* (architectural journal), A. Kuznetsov described two aspects of designing a central square – "the first is a vertical (longitudinal) space composition" (where a highest main tower forms a centre of composition for a group of seven- to eight-storey high buildings) and "the second . . . a colonnade composition of lower buildings," whose "layout of the main buildings are arranged in a horizontal composition."[9] The most comprehensive discussion on this concept, according to Chinese architects and academics, was a 1960 book in Russian, the *Jianzhu Goutu Gailun* cited above, which contained a chapter on "Jianzhuwu goutu yu yongtu: jianzhuwu he jianzhuqun de tiliang kongjian zuhe" (the use and composition of buildings: organizing spaces and volumes of buildings and building groups); it specified that coordinating spaces and volumes, referring to treatment of vertical volumes of buildings especially, belonged to the category of "architectural composition (*jianzhu goutu*)." Though it was formally published in Chinese in 1983, its influence can be found in China over the 1960s and 1970s.[10]

While the concept of "spatial composition" in China at the time came from the Soviet Union, the impact of English publications on the meaning of the phrase and the idea at this historical juncture cannot be underestimated. Besides those on architectural composition published in the early twentieth century, the four-volume *Forms and Functions* of 1952, edited by Talbot Hamlin and supported by Leopold Arnaud (dean of architecture at Columbia University), played a crucial role. Some chapters of it were translated and published around 1980, as mentioned earlier, but photocopies of the whole book were already circulating in the 1950s. Qi Kang, professor at Southeast University and a leading figure in architecture in mid- and late twentieth-century China, recalled that,

> in the early 1960s I had opportunity to read systematically books on architectural composition, such as Pickering, Robertson, Curtis, Hamlin, and Harbeson; I later read more related books, including *Jianzhu Goutu Yuanli* (principles of composition in architecture) edited by Tsinghua University's architectural department, a valuable book for teaching then.[11]

Peng Yigang, author of *Spatial Composition*, also acknowledged that his framework drew mainly from Hamlin's *Forms and Functions* and Nathaniel C. Curtis' *Architectural Composition*.[12]

Qi and Peng's recollection suggested that the use of "spatial composition" in China then was not a replacement of the established idea of composition in the Beaux-Arts tradition, but instead a development into a new context of discussion.

The first half of the 1960s saw a period of focused systematic theorization on composition and spatial composition in China in the profession, a time that also delivered a localized Chinese interpretation. In 1962, Tsinghua University published *Jianzhu Goutu Yuanli (Chugao)* (draft for principles of composition in architecture) as shared lecture notes among universities; and in 1963, *Jianzhu Xuebao* (architectural journal), the only professional periodical in China at the time, established a column, "*Goutu* Yuanli Jiangzuo" (lectures on principles of composition), and published many articles on this matter. There were two discussions that had a long-term impact: those on the general rules of composition, and those on the layout of Chinese gardens from the viewpoint of composition. The latter focused specifically on the organization of "scenery" (*jing*) and that of "a composition of spaces in a fluid continuity as people move around" (Figure 24.1).[13] Similar observations on groups of spaces and buildings were also found then, such as "Jianzhuqun de Guanshang" (visual appreciation of building groups) by Qi Kang and

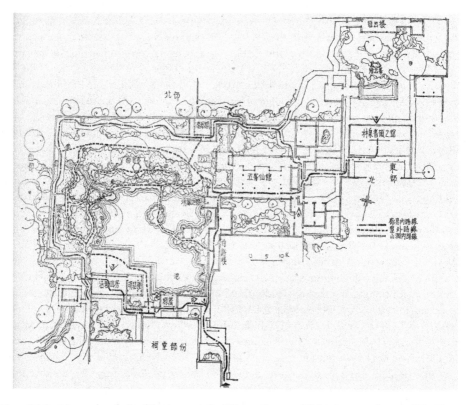

Figure 24.1 Map and analysis of "main prescribed lines of approach" for the central area of Liu Yuan or the Lingering Garden of Suzhou, made in 1963.

Source: Pan Guxi, "Suzhou Yuanlin de Guanshangdian yu Guanshang Luxian" (Viewing stations and prescribed lines of approach in the Soochow gardens), *Jianzhu Xuebao* 6 (1963), fig 4. Permission and courtesy of Pan Guxi.

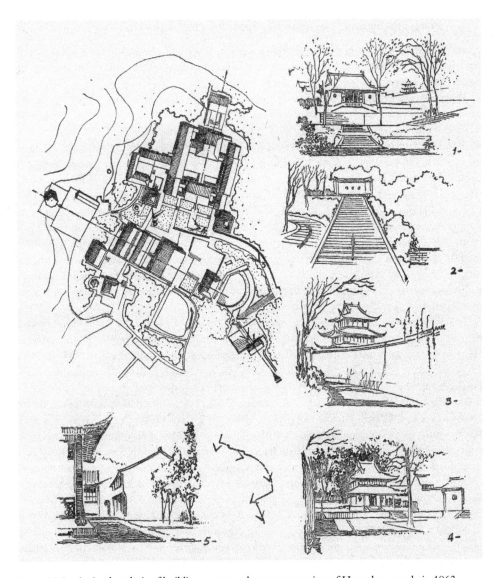

Figure 24.2 A visual analysis of building groups at hupaoquan spring of Hangzhou, made in 1963.

Source: Qi Kang and Huang Weikang, "Jianzhuqun de Guangshang" (Visual appreciation of building groups), *Jianzhu Xuebao* 6 (1963), fig 6. Permission and courtesy of Qi Kang.

Huang Weikang (Figure 24.2).[14] Their studies on the "static" and "dynamic" visual experiences among spaces and building groups in a traditional Chinese garden revealed not only a synthesis of Russian compositional theories, American ideas from *Forms and Functions*, and generic modernistic notions of space, but also a translation into modern terms of traditional Chinese painterly and poetic aesthetics – such as "shifting views with moving footsteps" and "layering of space."[15] In other words, the discussion on spatial composition in China of the 1950s and 1960s involved a self-driven Chinese construction that integrated a variety of different sources.

Peng Yigang and His *Theory of Spatial Composition in Architecture*

Spatial Composition is a theorization but also a guidebook. This is related to the author's professional position and his special approach, as well as the organization and presentation of the content in the book.

Peng, born in 1932, is a professor at the School of Architecture of Tianjin University and has been a leading figure in the "third-generation" of architects in China (the first and the second referring to those educated abroad and in China before 1940 respectively). Graduating in 1953 from the Department of Civil Engineering and Architecture at Tianjin University, Peng stayed on to teach and practice, making himself a prolific author at the same time. Peng's interest in composition had a historical reason; Peng studied under Xu Zhong, the founding head of the Tianjin University architectural department. Xu graduated in 1935 from National Central University in Nanjing, the base of Chinese architectural education in the Beaux-Arts tradition. Xu then graduated from the University of Illinois with a master's degree in 1937; though the spread of modernist teaching in the United States started in the late 1930s, Xu was already exposed to modernism there at that time. If an absorption of modernism with a Beaux-Arts base characterised Xu's overall approach,[16] then this was surely the case for Peng. In fact, Peng considered his *Spatial Composition* a modern development from Hamlin and Curtis,[17] who were both based in the Beaux-Arts tradition.[18]

Peng's focus and study on spatial composition was representative of the concern in China at the time. Pen had intended since the early 1960s to write a book on the topic, but due to political reasons, had no chance to start until 1977. Its first edition was published in 1983. In 1998, 15 years later, a chapter on post-modern architecture was added; in 2007, requested by the publisher, another chapter on "appreciating contemporary western architecture" was added.[19] It is worth noting that, from the late 1970s to late 1980s, Peng published three books – *Jianzhu Huitu Jichu Zhishi* (1978), *Jianzhu Kongjian Zuhelun* (1983), and *Zhongguo Gudian Yuanlin Fenxi* (1986) (guide to architectural drawing, spatial composition, and analysis of classical Chinese gardens, respectively). If the first focused on basic skills and the second on design principles, then the third moved on using basic skills and compositional analysis to work on a special research project – studying and extracting design methods from the design of traditional Chinese gardens. These three texts formed a progressing and internally related system of skill and knowledge. If that is the case, the middle book, *Spatial Composition*, captures some of its essential ideas.

Spatial Composition focuses on a core issue of how a form is created and developed in architectural design. Its first edition contains seven chapters. Chapter one, as introduction, describes generic regulations in the creation and development of architectural forms. Chapters two to four further explain the effect of function and structure on the generation of form; the various ways of composing a room and joining spaces of difference sizes and shapes together; and aesthetic principles for organizing forms. Chapters five to seven, finally, explain the use of compositional rules on the organization of interior spaces, external profiles, and building groups. The book contains both abstract statement of rules and practical demonstration of applications; it is accessible for reading and useful for design practice (Figure 24.3).

Another aspect that makes the book accessible and popular is its format and ample use of illustrations. *Spatial Composition* is made up of two parts – part one contains text only, occupying about one-fourth of the pages of the book, whereas part two, occupying three-fourths, is all illustrations with some concise words in the captions. The pen-and-ink drawings, depicting the design of real buildings, illustrate the rules vividly – they are visually rich and accessible and can be read on their own, forming a relatively autonomous part of the book (Figure 24.4). Drawing

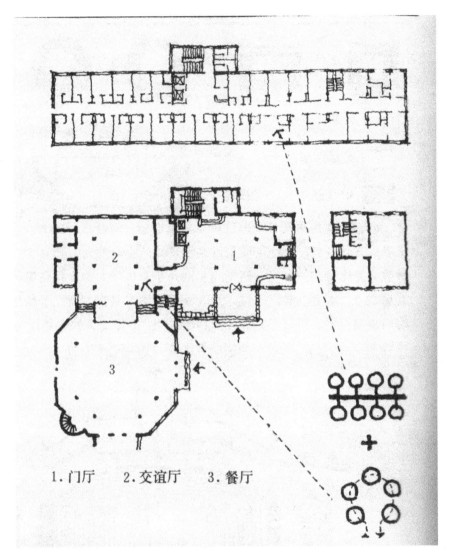

1.门厅　　2.交谊厅　　3.餐厅

Figure 24.3　Peng Yigang's analysis showing two ways of composing space in the case of Peace Hotel Beijing designed by Yang Tingbao in 1951, made in 1983. Key: 1, Reception Hall; 2, Function Hall; 3, Dining Hall.

Source: Peng Yigang, *Jianzhu Kongjian Zuhelun* (A theory of spatial composition in architecture) (Beijing: Zhongguo Jianzhu Gongye Chubanshe, 1983), 111. Permission and courtesy of Peng Yigang.

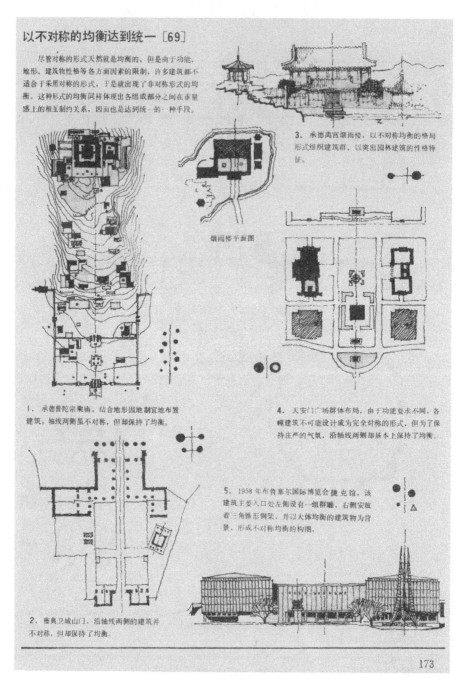

Figure 24.4 Peng Yigang's illustrations of "unity based on asymmetrical balance" each with a concise note of explanation, made in 1983.

Source: Peng Yigang, *Jianzhu Kongjian Zuhelun* (A theory of spatial composition in architecture) (Beijing: Zhongguo Jianzhu Gongye Chubanshe, 1983), 173. Permission and courtesy of Peng Yigang.

394

well with freehand sketches was a common feature of Peng's generation in architecture in China (following their teachers), although Peng's drawings in pen-and-ink displayed further his own style and strength. For sure, Peng is representative of his generation and his time not only in visual representation but also, and perhaps more importantly, in design thinking. For this reason, we need to study the book further, in its three aspects – relations between "form and content," the object of "space," and the technique of "composition."

The Issue of "Form and Content"

The relationship between "form and content" was a focus of discussion in architectural theory in China of the 1950s–60s. This theoretical discourse came from the Soviet Union in many fields of art such as literature, theatre, and fine art. In China in the architectural field, there was briefly a time of debate in the early 1950s on form, content, and their relations. From the mid-1950s on, however, with a few political campaigns waged by the government, all views were compressed into a uniform position or answer. This position was that, following a state-sanctioned materialism, economic base and social development precondition architectural form, which in turn manifests the spirit of society and its historical time. With this main perspective established, minor differences concerned the scope of content and rationalization of a form or formal system.

Chapter one of *Spatial Composition*, on "dialectics of form and content," aims to resolve the issue of "determination (*guiding xing*) of architectural form." According to Peng, this "determination" comes from "two demands and one means" – the functional and the spiritual demands, and structural techniques for materialization of form to serve the two demands. Based on the two demands, Peng divides architecture into three types – those predominantly spiritual such as a monument, those predominantly functional such as a warehouse, and those with both qualities as found in most cases. Peng further says that even for major public buildings with a high artistic expectation, functional demand still remains predominant. Peng then makes a distinction between "artistic qualities" (*yishu xing*) versus "formal aesthetics" (*xingshi mei*) in architecture: "the two are different; those with artistic qualities must have already followed rules of formal aesthetics, whereas those with these rules may not attain artistic qualities."[20] Peng is saying that an aesthetic form follows generic rules of aesthetics, whereas an artistic quality must express a certain idea; formal aesthetics is basic and generic that all designs must follow, whereas artistic qualities, for expressing ideas, are the pursuit of a higher level.

The differentiations made between these concepts are characteristic of the time, from the 1950s to the 1980s. Behind these special terms and a way of talking of that time, an underlying agenda seems to be a protection of the autonomy of design. In the early 1950s, state government issued two guidelines for architectural design, one after another: architecture must adopt "socialist content and national form," and that design must be "functional, economic and when condition permitting good-looking." The first acknowledged a spiritual quality of architecture but tended to over-politicize design; the second, on the other hand, tended to reduce architectural design into the technical operation of an engineer. Both were politically correct but were also criticized by state voices later on – the first as revivalist and formalist in a campaign against costly construction found in "national-style" architecture with ornaments, and the second as "structuralist" (a word for modernism then) for its plain and uniform look.[21] How to address the political demands of the state and to rationalize architectural design remained a practical concern and an intellectual or theoretical question – necessitating discussions on form and function, functionality, art and aesthetics, and style and character. In 1959, a symposium was organized by the Ministry of Construction and Architectural Society of China, "Housing Standard and the

Art of Architecture," which spent 13 days on the issue of "architectural art."[22] In such a climate, Peng's identification of formal aesthetics as different from art or artistic qualities of architecture was a pragmatic strategy and a way of protecting the autonomy of architectural design; it effectively claimed that design is a creative exercise that is neither ideological nor engineering-like.

The Object of "Space"

Though titled *Spatial Composition*, the book's central concern is about "architectural form and its treatment."[23] Despite this, "space" (*kongjian*) is indeed frequently used; the book also uses phrases with the word space (*kongjian*), such as *kongjian xingshi* (spatial form), *kongjian tiliang* (spatial volume), and *kongjian zuhe xingshi* (form of spatial organization). Yet, this doesn't mean that "space" commands a supreme position – for Peng and other Chinese architects of his generation, "space" is a pragmatic term subordinate to the category of form. Peng in the book says, "The so-called 'architectural form', strictly speaking, is a composite idea that is made of an assemblage of various elements including space, volume, outline, solid-and-void, convexity-and-concavity, colour, texture and ornament, among others."[24] In this frame of thinking, space is closely associated with "the main purpose of architecture" – function. According to Peng,

> architecture is to be used; and what is used is nothing other than space; for this purpose, people even consider architecture as a container – a container that contains people; when we say content determines form, we mean in architecture that function demands a form of space that is fitting and suitable.[25]

To consider form as the shape of a building and space as the volume defined by a physical enclosure was a common understanding among architects in China at the time. Talking about how function delivers a determination of quantity, form, and quality of a space, Peng says, "to achieve functional rationality, the design, for example a room, must have a suitable size, suitable shape, suitable placing of doors and windows, as well as suitable orientation of the windows; in a word, a suitable spatial form."[26] Further, Peng says, "Volume reflects space, and space is largely expressed through the plan; to secure a fine composition of volumes, one must ensure firstly a good sense of order and clarity on the play."[27] Conceiving space as a three-dimensional volume seems to be a common understanding of architects in the Beaux-Arts tradition. For example, Nathaniel Curtis from the United States wrote in his *Secrets of Architectural Composition* (1924) that "the plan of a building establishes immediately two of the three dimensions in space and implies the third; it therefore lends itself to thinking in three dimensions."[28] Translating a Russian text of 1960 into Chinese publication *Jianzhu Goutu Gailun* (outline of a theory in architectural composition) in 1983, Gu Mengchao used "volume" (*tiliang*) directly, such as "composition of spatial volumes" (*kongjian tiliang zuhe*).[29]

Although "spatial composition" as an architectural terminology came from the Soviet Union in the 1950s, "space" was already used in China in the 1930s when modernist architecture was introduced. In 1951, before the Russian discourse arrived, a textbook *Jianzhu Sheji* (architectural design) by Chen Yiqin contained a chapter, "Kongjian Zuzhifa" (methods for organizing space).[30] Though we cannot ensure Chen referred to a modernist sense of spatial flow and movement, and indeed Chinese intended to consider space as a void determined by a container in a physical sense, the arrival of "spatial composition" in China had indeed delivered ideas of space as relational, as a relation between spaces, especially in the case of an organization of interior spaces or an aesthetic appreciation of spatial layers. In Peng's *Spatial Composition*, there is a chapter on the organization of interior spaces where he claims "external form is a reflection of internal space"; he also develops a consistency whereby function determines internal space, external form, and architectural character in an orderly manner. However, like others of his generation, Peng was not a determinist, either: "the task of architectural design is to unify the contradictory demands of internal space and external form, so as to achieve a coherence between inside and outside, allowing both to perform well."[31] In other words, Peng's emphasis on the interior is more like a rational justification or internal dynamic for the genesis of form and profile in architecture.

The Technique of "Composition"

Zuhe (combining, assembling) or *goutu* (composing a visual entity), translated here as "composition," a basic skill in the Beaux-Arts system, had a long development in China. For Peng and architects of his generation in China, composition is the foundation for architectural design. Peng says,

> In my understanding, students' design capacity then was very much based on their ability of "composition." When we were correcting their designs, we always came across this issue, and couldn't explain it clearly and systematically. For sure architecture is not just about composition, it has to deal with function and other issues, yet we need composition to embody these demands so as to develop a concrete scheme; otherwise it will remain only as an idea. When we were teaching then, we used "diagram" to coordinate various functions; students understood this easily. But from this point on, we needed a specific composition to develop a complete scheme with its plans, elevations and sections. But when we reached this point, on composition, it was hard to explain well. Some teachers said you had to understand it yourself – to be felt in heart but not to be articulated in words. I thought it shouldn't be like that.[32]

It is interesting to note that the "first-generation" Chinese architects trained in the Beaux-Arts framework (primarily in the USA in the 1910s–30s) never systematically discussed this issue, but instead simply employed the idea in teaching and practice.[33] Those who actively discussed the issue in the 1950s–60s were their students. Then, the Chinese faced the problem of inheriting and renovating design knowledge handed down from the past. Peng once said, "to understand new architecture we cannot use old frameworks, but nor should we throw away eternal principles either."[34] This climate explains why there was a profusion of textbooks in Chinese for teaching architectural design from the late 1970s to the early 1980s.

According to Peng, composition has a set of universal principles. "Diversity with unity" (*duoyang tongyi*) is the first principle among these universal rules for controlling form. Chinese or international, ancient or modern, all great works, for Peng, "have followed this universal rule – diversity with unity; it is therefore the rule in formal aesthetics."[35] Similar to the writings of the topic at the time, Peng also illustrated how this universal principle was manifested, and could be used, in the specific case of securing, for example, unity via simple geometry, the main with the minor, balance and stability, contrast and subtle differentiation, rhythm and tempo, ratio and scale, among others. For the issue of different aesthetic judgement across time and between cultures, Peng claimed that

> formal aesthetic (*xingshi mei*) principles and specific aesthetic conceptions (*shenmei guannian*) belong to different categories; the former are generic, necessary and eternal laws, whereas the latter concrete standards and measurements unique to a particular

people, region and time; . . . formal aesthetic rules should manifest in all concrete art forms, despite the diversity of these forms each enriched by their specific aesthetic conceptions.[36]

In other words, formal aesthetic rules in architecture transcend historical time and local culture. This echoes Alan Colquhoun, who, when commenting on design composition in the Beaux-Arts tradition, observed that it is "a means by which rules of design common to all styles can be established."[37]

Concluding Remarks

In 1998, some 15 years after the initial publication of *Spatial Composition*, responding to the new ideas then, Peng added another chapter to the book, "Aesthetic shift and deviation in western architecture," "shift and deviation" being *bian* and *yi* in Chinese, literally "change" and "deviating, alienating." Peng claimed that there were two major changes in western architectural aesthetics – the first manifesting in the arrival of modernist technological aesthetics, and the second in post-modern and deconstructive deviating aesthetics. To Peng, the first adopted a rationalism, established a new method of design, and abandoned the classical form entirely; "nevertheless the universal formal aesthetic principles were retained and were not substantially challenged."[38] The second change, however, "has abandoned traditional aesthetic principle of unity and harmony, and has embraced instead contradiction, complexity and ambiguity, even ideas of brokenness, discontinuity, distortion, and de-construction, categories that traditional aesthetics couldn't accommodate."[39] Peng's view was much shared by many among architects of China at the time: in terms of formal aesthetics, modernism was a continuation of classical architecture, whereas post-modernism was not, belonging instead to an entirely different type of ideas.

For Peng, evidence to affirm the continuity between modernism and classical architecture was offered by Hamlin's *Forms and Functions* (1952). He found that Hamlin's ideas here in 1952, the heyday of modernism, were nearly the same as those in Howard Robertson's 1924 book, *Principles of Architectural Composition*, which didn't touch on the modern movement in architecture.[40] Hamlin's *Forms and Functions*, however, was not a work for modernism; it was, in Reyner Banham's words, "a new Guadet under the influence of the 'Beaux-Arts' system at the time of penetration of 'Modernism'."[41] The other frame of reference Peng used in his *Spatial Composition* was Curtis' *Architectural Composition* (1923), which was another salute to Guadet's *Éléments et Théorie de l'Architecture*. Colin Rowe, commenting on Hamlin's *Forms and Functions*, insightfully pointed out the author's misunderstanding of modernism – a Guadet-based composition is fundamentally different from those modernist ones found in Mondrian, Cubism, Constructivism, and De Stijl. Rowe says,

> The ideal of composition as it was understood around 1900 was a concentric one, implying generally a grouping of elements about a central space or void and a downward transmission of weights according to a gravitational scheme. Against these principles De Stijl advanced what was called "peripheric" composition, developed not toward a central focus but toward the extremities of the canvas or wall plane and involving, in a building, not a gravitational but a levitational scheme.[42]

To Rowe, Guadet's principles, though seemingly rational and universal, captured neither the inner qualities of specific styles nor their historical features and conditions. Rowe's observation is revealing for a reading of architecture of modern China.

For sure, the book *Spatial Composition* requires further analysis. But the preceding discussion has revealed to us a specific perspective on design and architecture of the profession in China from the 1950s to the 1980s and, to an extent, even today. Architectural design was and has been considered, at a basic level, as a technical practice free from ideology, history, and even culture, to which a set of skills can adapt. Design is considered to have its own, relatively independent, means and criteria, which are primarily based on form-making and formal judgement. It is considered as an engineering work with some aesthetic considerations. A certain hybrid framework of design knowledge had been established, which combined an engineering rationality, a Beaux-Arts scheme of classical composition, and some elements of modernism – a framework that emerged out of a particular juncture in China of these decades of the century, a framework that, while mutating today, retains its traces and legacies.

Notes

1 Bao Jiasheng, Professor of Architectural Design, Nanjing Institute of Technology, author of *Gonggong Jianzhu Sheji Jichu* (Foundations of design for public architecture) (1961), recalled that, when preparing this book, his teacher and a prominent "first-generation" architect of China, Yang Tingbao, advised him to "complete the book that could be used as a reference for teaching and design – China is so large a country yet with so few books on architecture." See Bao Jiasheng and Du Shunbao, *Gonggong* (Foundations) (Nanjing: Nanjing Institute of Technology Press, 1986), 363. There was a great interest in compiling textbooks for design around 1960, yet political campaigns had interrupted the effort until the late 1970s.

2 Talbot Hamlin, ed. *Goutu Yuanli* (Principles of composition), trans. Xi Shuxiang, checked by Liu Guanghua (Nanjing: Nanjing Institute of Technology, Internal Circulation, 1979).

3 Talbot Hamlin, ed. *Jianzhu Xingshimei de Yuanze* (Principles of architectural aesthetics), trans. Zou Denong, checked by Shen Yulin (Beijing: Zhongguo Jianzhu Gongye Chubanshe, 1982).

4 Talbot Hamlin, ed. *Forms and Functions of Twentieth Century Architecture* (New York: Columbia University Press, 1952).

5 Academy of Construction and Architecture of USSR, eds. *Jianzhu Goutu Gailun* (Outline of a theory in architectural composition), trans. Gu Mengchao (Beijing: Zhongguo Jianzhu Gongye Chubanshe, 1983). The book in Russian was published in 1960 by Moscow's State Press of Literature on Construction, Architecture, and Building Materials.

6 Bao and Du, *Gonggong* (Foundations).

7 Tsinghua University Teaching & Research Group in Civic Architecture, eds. *Minyong Jianzhu Sheji Yuanli: Chugao* (Principles of design for civic architecture: First draft) (Beijing: Zhongguo Gongye Chubanshe, 1962).

8 Ming Jing and Lu Yongyi, "'Kongjian Goutu': Zhongguo Xiandai Jianzhu 'Kongjian' Huayu de Yige Zhongyao Gainian ('Spatial composition': An important discourse on 'space' in architecture of modern China)," *Shidai Jianzhu* 6 (2013): 118–124.

9 A. Kuznetsov, "Huifu Eluosi Suweiai Lianbang Shehuizhuyi Gongheguo Chengshi de Zongjie (A summary of restoration for Russian cities in the Union of Soviet Socialist Republics)," trans. Cheng Yingquan, *Jianzhu Xuebao* 1 (1954): 14–28. The initial article was published in the Soviet Union in June 1953 (in a journal cited in Chinese as *Sulian Jianzhu Yishu*, or Architectural Art in USSR).

10 Information on these Russian publications are based on Chinese sources.

11 Qi Kang, "Rumen de Qishi: Ping 'Jianzhu Kongjian Zuhelun' (To enlighten the beginners: A review of the book *A Theory of Spatial Composition in Architecture*)," *Jianzhushi* 21 (1984): 164–165.

12 Interview with Peng Yigang by author (February 2007).

13 Pan Guxi, "Suzhou Yuanlin de Guanshangdian yu Guanshang Luxian (Viewing Stations and Prescribed Lines of Approach in the Soochow Gardens)," *Jianzhu Xuebao* 6 (1963): 14–18. Years before, in 1956, Pan's colleague and also teacher at Nanjing Institute of Technology, one of the leading "first-generation" architectural historians of modern China, Liu Dunzhen, said that, "the design of our traditional gardens includes a spatial composition of hills, pools, woods and rocks, along with buildings." Liu further summarized eight principles for the layout of a garden, such as irregular planning, use of basic forms, and organizing circulations, among others. See Liu Dunzhen, "Suzhou de Yuanlin (Gardens of

Suzhou)," written in 1956, in *Liu Dunzhen Wenji* (Writings of Liu Dunzhen), vol. 4, by Liu Dunzhen (Beijing: Zhongguo Jianzhu Gongye Chubanshe, 1993): 79–129.

14 Qi Kang and Huang Weikang, "Jianzhuqun de Guangshang (Visual appreication of building groups)," *Jianzhu Xuebao* 6 (1963): 19–23.

15 For a modernist reading of spatial design in traditional Chinese gardens, see Chen Wei, "'Suzhou Gudian Yuanlin' de YiYi (The significance of the book *Classical Gardens of Suzhou*)," in *Quanqiu Shiyexia de Zhongguo Jianzhu Yichang: Disijie Zhongguo Jianzhu Shixue Guoji Yantaohui Lunwenji* (Architectural heritage of China in a global perspective: Proceedings of the fourth international conference on China's architectural historiography), ed. Editorial Committee (Shanghai: Tongji Daxue Chubanshe, 2007), 45–48. See also Lu Andong, "Lost in Translation: The Chinese Garden in Modernist Discourse," in *Architecture Study 01: Words, Buildings & Drawings,* eds. Mark Cousins, Chen Wei, Li Hua and Ge Ming (Beijing: Zhongguo Jianzhu Gongye Chubanshe, 2011), 47–80.

16 See Xu Zhong, "Jianzhu yu Mei (Architecture and beauty)," *Tianjin Daxue Xuebao: Journal of Tianjin University* Z1 (1957): 128–136, and "Lun Jianzhu Fengge de Jueding Yinsu (On the decisive importance of style in architecture)," *Tianjin Daxue Xuebao: Journal of Tianjin University* 2 (1981): 1–6. This can be further verified by Xu's students' memories: Peng Yigang and Huang Weijun, "Chuantong de Jichengzhe yu Pannizhe: Yi Xu Zhong jiaoshou de chuangxin jingshen (A successor and a rebel of tradition: On professor Xu Zhong's spirit of creativity)," *Xin Jianzhu* 2 (1987): 3–4; and Bu Zhengwei, "Xu Zhong de Jianzhu Meixue Yanjiu jiqi Jiazhi, Yingxiang, Qishi (Xu Zhong's architectural aesthetics and its importance, influence and message)," *Jianzhu Xuebao* 5 (2012): 108–113.

17 Interview with Peng by author (February 2007).

18 Nathaniel C. Curtis, *The Secrets of Architectural Composition* (New York: Dover Publications, 1923), "Preface" (no pagination). See also Leopold Arnaud, "Introduction," in *Forms and Functions of Twentieth-Century Architecture*, volume 1, ed. Talbot Hamlin (New York: Columbia University Press, 1952), ix–xiii.

19 This chapter focuses on the first edition of Peng's *Spatial Composition*.

20 Peng Yigang, *Jianzhu Kongjian Zuhelun* (A theory of spatial composition in architecture) (Beijing: Zhongguo Jianzhu Gongye Chubanshe, 1983), 4.

21 Liu Xiufeng, the Minister of Construction and Civil Engineering of China, addressed the dilemma architects faced at the time in his speech at "Symposium on Housing Standards and Architectural Art" in 1959. For this, see Liu Xiufeng, "Chuangzao zhongguo de shehui zhuyi de jianzhu xin fengge (Creating new styles for a Chinese socialist architecture)," *Jianzhu Xuebao* 9–10 (1959): 3–12. On the understanding of "structuralism" and modernist architecture in China at the time, see Li Hua, "Translation, 'Mistranslation' and Translatability of Architectural Concepts," in *Architecture Study 01: Words, Buildings & Drawings,* eds. Mark Cousins, Chen Wei, Li Hua and Ge Ming (Beijing: Zhongguo Jianzhu Gongye Chubanshe, 2011), 103–130.

22 Ministry of Construction and Architectural Society of China, eds., *Zhuzhai Biaozhun ji Jianzhu Yishu Zuotanhui Fayan Huibian: Neibu Ziliao* (A compilation of speeches delivered at the symposium on housing standard and architectural art: Internal circulation) (Beijing, 1959).

23 Peng, *Jianzhu* (Spatial composition), "Xiezai qianmian (preface)," no pagination.

24 Peng, *Jianzhu* (Spatial composition), 12.

25 Peng, *Jianzhu* (Spatial composition), 12.

26 Peng, *Jianzhu* (Spatial composition), 16.

27 Peng, *Jianzhu* (Spatial composition), 59.

28 Curtis, *The Secrets,* "Preface" (no pagination).

29 For a general understanding of spatial composition in the Chinese context, Gu's translation is more accurate.

30 Chen Yiqin, *Jianzhu Sheji* (Architectural design) (Shanghai: Longmen Allied Book Company, 1952), 15–21. One of Chen's references is Percy Ash's *Theory of Architectural Design* published in 1930, a book in the Beaux-Arts tradition as well.

31 Peng, *Jianzhu* (Spatial composition), 56–57.

32 Interview with Peng by author (February 2007).

33 One of the examples can be found in: Lu Yongyi, "Tan Yuan de Jianzhu Sheji Jiaoxue yiji dui 'Buza' Tixi de Zairenshi (Tan Yuan's design teaching and a rereading of the 'Beaux-Arts' system)," *Nanfang Jianzhu* 4 (2011): 23–27.

34 Peng, *Jianzhu* (Spatial composition), 60.

35 Peng, *Jianzhu* (Spatial composition), 33.

36 Peng, *Jianzhu* (Spatial composition), 33.
37 Alan Colquhoun, "Composition versus the Project," in *Collected Essays in Architectural Criticism*, Alan Colquhoun (London: Black Dog Publishing, 2009), 178–183.
38 Peng, *Jianzhu* (Spatial composition), 85.
39 Peng, *Jianzhu* (Spatial composition), 85.
40 Peng, *Jianzhu* (Spatial composition), 85.
41 Reyner Banham, *Theory and Design in the First Machine Age* (London: The Architectural Press, 1960), 17.
42 Colin Rowe, "Review: Forms and Functions of Twentieth-Century Architecture," in *As I Was Saying, Vol. 1: Texas, Pre-Texas, Cambridge,* Colin Rowe (Cambridge, MA: The MIT Press, 1999), 107–121, esp. 115.

Bibliography

Academy of Construction and Architecture of USSR, eds. *Jianzhu Goutu Gailun* (Outline of a Theory in Architectural Composition). Translated by Gu Mengchao. Beijing: Zhongguo Jianzhu Gongye Chubanshe, 1983.

Arnaud, Leopold. "Introduction." In *Forms and Functions of Twentieth-Century Architecture*, edited by Talbot Hamlin, vol. 1, ix–xiii. New York: Columbia University Press, 1952.

Banham, Reyner. *Theory and Design in the First Machine Age*. London: The Architectural Press, 1960.

Bao Jiasheng and Du Shunbao. *Gonggong Jianzhu Sheji Jichu* (Foundations of Design for Public Architecture). Nanjing: Nanjing Institute of Technology Press, 1986.

Bu Zhengwei. "Xu Zhong de Jianzhu Meixue Yanjiu jiqi Jiazhi, Yingxiang, Qishi (Xu Zhong's Architectural Aesthetics and Its Importance, Influence and Message)." *Jianzhu Xuebao* 5 (2012): 108–113.

Chen Wei. "'Suzhou Gudian Yuanlin' de YiYi (The Significance of the Book *Classical Gardens of Suzhou*)." In *Quanqiu Shiyexia de Zhongguo Jianzhu Yichang: Disijie Zhongguo Jianzhu Shixue Guoji Yantaohui Lunwenji* (Architectural Heritage of China in a Global Perspective: Proceedings of the Fourth International Conference on China's Architectural Historiography), edited by Editorial Committee, 45–48. Shanghai: Tongji Daxue Chubanshe, 2007.

Chen Yiqin. *Jianzhu Sheji* (Architectural Design). Shanghai: Longmen Allied Book Company, 1952.

Colquhoun, Alan. "Composition Versus the Project." In *Collected Essays in Architectural Criticism*, edited by Alan Colquhoun, 178–183. London: Black Dog Publishing, 2009.

———. *Collected Essays in Architectural Criticism*. London: Black Dog Publishing, 2009.

Cousins, Mark, Chen Wei, Li Hua and Ge Ming, eds. *Architecture Study 01: Words, Buildings & Drawings*. Beijing: Zhongguo Jianzhu Gongye Chubanshe, 2011.

Curtis, Nathaniel C. *The Secrets of Architectural Composition*. New York: Dover Publications, 1923.

Editorial Committee, ed. *Quanqiu Shiyexia de Zhongguo Jianzhu Yichang: Disijie Zhongguo Jianzhu Shixue Guoji Yantaohui Lunwenji* (Architectural Heritage of China in a Global Perspective: Proceedings of the Fourth International Conference on China's Architectural History). Shanghai: Tongji Daxue Chubanshe, 2007.

Hamlin, Talbot, ed. *Forms and Functions of Twentieth-Century Architecture*. New York: Columbia University Press, 1952.

———, ed. *Goutu Yuanli* (Principles of Composition). Translated by Xi Shuxiang, checked by Liu Guanghua. Nanjing: Nanjing Institute of Technology (Internal Circulation), 1979.

———, ed. *Jianzhu Xingshimei de Yuanze* (Principles of Architectural Aesthetics). Translated by Zou Denong, checked by Shen Yulin. Beijing: Zhongguo Jianzhu Gongye Chubanshe, 1982.

Kuznetsov, A. "Huifu Eluosi Suweiai Lianbang Shehuizhuyi Gongheguo Chengshi de Zongjie (A Summary of Restoration for Russian Cities in the Union of Soviet Socialist Republics)." Translated by Cheng Yingquan. *Jianzhu Xuebao* 1 (1954): 14–28.

Li Hua. "Translation, 'Mistranslation' and Translatability of Architectural Concepts." In *Architecture Study 01: Words, Buildings & Drawings*, edited by Mark Cousins, Chen Wei, Li Hua and Ge Ming, 103–130. Beijing: Zhongguo Jianzhu Gongye Chubanshe, 2011.

Liu Dunzhen. *Liu Dunzhen Wenji* (Writings of Liu Dunzhen). Beijing: Zhongguo Jianzhu Gongye Chubanshe, 1993.

———. "Suzhou de Yuanlin (Gardens of Suzhou)." In *Liu Dunzhen Wenji* (Writings of Liu Dunzhen), edited by Liu Dunzhen, vol. 4, 79–129. Beijing: China Architecture & Building Press, 1993.

Liu Xiufeng. "Chuangzao zhongguo de shehui zhuyi de jianzhu xin fengge (Creating New Styles for a Chinese Socialist Architecture)." *Jianzhu Xuebao* 9–10 (1959): 3–12.

Lu Andong. "Lost in Translation: The Chinese Garden in Modernist Discourse." In *Architecture Study 01: Words, Buildings & Drawings*, edited by Mark Cousins, Chen Wei, Li Hua and Ge Ming, 47–80. Beijing: Zhongguo Jianzhu Gongye Chubanshe, 2011.

Lu Yongyi. "Tan Yuan de Jianzhu Sheji Jiaoxue yiji dui 'Buza' Tixi de Zairenshi (Tan Yuan's Design Teaching and a Rereading of the 'Beaux-Arts' System)." *Nanfang Jianzhu* 4 (2011): 23–27.

Ming Jing and Lu Yongyi. "'Kongjian Goutu': Zhongguo Xiandai Jianzhu 'Kongjian' Huayu de Yige Zhongyao Gainian ('Spatial Composition': An Important Discourse on 'Space' in Architecture of Modern China)." *Shidai Jianzhu* 6 (2013): 118–124.

Ministry of Construction and Architectural Society of China, eds. *Zhuzhai Biaozhun ji Jianzhu Yishu Zuotanhui Fayan Huibian: Neibu Ziliao* (A Compilation of Speeches Delivered at the Symposium on Housing Standard and Architectural Art: Internal Circulation). Beijing: Ministry of Construction and Architectural Society of China, 1959.

Pan Guxi. "Suzhou Yuanlin de Guanshangdian yu Guanshang Luxian (Viewing Stations and Prescribed Lines of Approach in the Soochow Gardens)." *Jianzhu Xuebao* 6 (1963): 14–18.

Peng Yigang. *Jianzhu Kongjian Zuhelun* (A Theory of Spatial Composition in Architecture). Beijing: Zhongguo Jianzhu Gongye Chubanshe, 1983.

Peng Yigang and Huang Weijun. "Chuantong de Jichengzhe yu Pannizhe: yi Xu Zhong jiaoshou de chuangxin jingshen (A Successor and a Rebel of Tradition: On Professor Xu Zhong's Spirit of Creativity)." *Xin Jianzhu* 2 (1987): 3–4.

Qi Kang. "Rumen de Qishi: Ping 'Jianzhu Kongjian Zuhelun' (To Enlighten the Beginners: A Review of the Book *A Theory of Spatial Composition in Architecture*)." *Jianzhushi* 21 (1984): 164–165.

Qi Kang and Huang Weikang. "Jianzhuqun de Guangshang (Visual Appreciation of Building Groups)." *Jianzhu Xuebao* 6 (1963): 19–23.

Rowe, Colin. *As I Was Saying, vol. 1: Texas, Pre-Texas, Cambridge*. Cambridge, MA: The MIT Press, 1999.

———. "Review: Forms and Functions of Twentieth-Century Architecture." In *As I Was Saying, vol. 1: Texas, Pre-Texas, Cambridge*, 107–121. Cambridge, MA: The MIT Press, 1999.

Tsinghua University Teaching & Research Group in Civic Architecture, eds. *Minyong Jianzhu Sheji Yuanli: Chugao* (Principles of Design for Civic Architecture: First Draft). Beijing: Zhongguo Gongye Chubanshe, 1962.

Xu Zhong. "Jianzhu yu Mei (Architecture and Beauty)." *Tianjin Daxue Xuebao: Journal of Tianjin University* Z1 (1957): 128–136.

———. "Lun Jianzhu Fengge de Jueding Yinsu (On the Decisive Importance of Style in Architecture)." *Tianjin Daxue Xuebao: Journal of Tianjin University* 2 (1981): 1–6.

Glossary

Beijing	北京
bian	变
Chen Yiqin	陈绎勤
duoyang tongyi	多样统一
Gonggong Jianzhu Sheji Jichu	公共建筑设计基础
goutu	构图
Goutu Yuanli	构图原理
Goutu Yuanli Jiangzuo	构图原理讲座
Gu Mengchao	顾孟潮
guiding xing	规定性
Huang Weikang	黄伟康
jianzhu (jianzhu)	建筑
jianzhu goutu	建筑构图
Jianzhu Goutu Gailun	建筑构图概论
Jianzhu Goutu Yuanli (Chugao)	建筑构图原理（初稿）

Jianzhu Huitu Jichu Zhishi	建筑绘图基础知识
Jianzhu Kongjian Zuhelun	建筑空间组合论
Jianzhu Sheji	建筑设计
Jianzhu Xingshimei de Yuanze	建筑形式美的原则
Jianzhu Xuebao	建筑学报
Jianzhuqun de Guanshang	建筑群的观赏
Jianzhuwu goutu yu yongtu	建筑物构图与用途
jing	景
kongjian	空间
kongjian tiliang	空间体量
kongjian tiliang zuhe	空间体量组合
kongjian xingshi	空间形式
kongjian zuhe xingshi	空间组合形式
Kongjian Zuzhifa	空间组织法
Minyong Jianzhu Sheji Yuanli	民用建筑设计原理
Nanjing (Institute of Technology)	南京（工学院）
Peng Yigang	彭一刚
Qi Kang	齐康
shenmei guannian	审美观念
Tianjin (University)	天津（大学）
tiliang	体量
tiliang kongjian zuhe	体量空间组合
Tsinghua (University)	清华（大学）
xingshi mei	形式美
Xu Zhong	徐中
yi	异
yishu xing	艺术性
Zhongguo Gudian Yuanlin Fenxi	中国古典园林分析
zuhe	组合

25

LIANG AND LIU

Strategies for Writing an Architectural History in the 1950s

Zhuge Jing

Liang Sicheng (1901–1972) and Liu Dunzhen (1897–1968) are the most highly regarded architectural historians in China. With their pioneering work in collaboration, they had effectively established together the discipline of Chinese architectural history in the 1930s and 1940s. However, in the 1950s, with the demand and pressure upon architectural historiography as a result of the arrival of the new state and its ideology, they began to differ significantly in their work focus. In the 1950s, Liang was undoubtedly more important in the circles of architecture and city planning in China. Liang was internationally well known; he (under the Party and the state) founded the Architectural Society of China (ASC) and *Jianzhu Xuebao* (Architectural journal); he attended major international conferences as a representative of Chinese architects; based on his manuscript completed in 1944, *Zhonguo Jianzhu Shi* (A history of Chinese architecture), Liang elaborated further the content and the theme and promoted the debate for an architecture of "national form and socialist content."[1] Liu Dunzhen, on the other hand, focused on teaching from 1949 on as a professor of architecture at Nanjing Institute of Technology and investigated ancient architecture as commissioned by the East China Bureau of Culture and Nanjing government department of cultural relics and heritage protection.[2] Before 1958, Liu published mostly his fieldwork reports and studies on ancient literature; he developed his research on houses and gardens as well. From 1958 on, he began to lead the compilation of *Zhongguo Gudai Jianzhu Shi* (A history of ancient Chinese architecture).

Although scholars such as Lai Delin have studied the respective architectural views of Liang and Liu in terms of their different perspectives on culture and society, it is surely not sufficient if we discuss only their outlooks. In and since the 1950s, their different work revealed a significant widening gap in research purpose and methodology for architectural history. On the one hand, the difference can be traced back to the 1930s–40s, when they worked for the Society of Research in Chinese Architecture (Yingzao Xueshe); on the other, the difference was increasingly clearer in the 1950s, reflecting not only their respective strategies and conditions of work, but also their different impact on the development of China's architectural history, and on redefining the relations between history and design in architecture. In this sense, a closer and more detailed study of Liang and Liu in the field of architectural history in the 1950s will assist us to understand the state of architectural history as it has arrived and its position in architecture today.

DOI: 10.4324/9781315851112-37

This chapter analyses Liang and Liu's work of the 1950s, to discover strategies they used for research and writing for architectural history and to reveal their different approaches to relations between history and design, and historiography and architecture. Further, the study aims to reveal that, despite their differences, they together contributed to the loss in the 1950s–60s of a positive contribution that architectural history once had in previous years – when it assisted actively for building a national identity and state ideology.

Liang Sicheng: Writing "Chinese Architecture" and Creating a "National Style"

In an article published in 1944, "Why Are We Studying Chinese Architecture?," Liang Sicheng, adopting optimistic views on building a new society after World War II, proposed to revive the discussion on design and creation; Liang suggested that we should connect architecture of the past to that of the future and recommended that the questions of historical research in architecture be determined from this perspective.[3] In many ways, this article anticipated Liang's shift in work after the war. In the 1950s, based in the architectural department at Tsinghua University of Beijing, Liang's main work included teaching in the classroom and leading urban planning and construction in and for Beijing. At about the same time, from 1944 when he completed the lecture notes of *Zhongguo Jianzhu Shi* (A history of Chinese architecture), to 1964 when he completed an Introduction for *Zhongguo Gudai Jianzhu Shi* (A history of ancient Chinese architecture, the sixth revision), Liang had been recursively writing on Chinese architecture;[4] he constantly explored the characteristics and history of this architecture and discussed how we may build a path from the past to the future.

The 1944 manuscript of *Zhongguo Jianzhu Shi* (A history of Chinese architecture) remains the most complete and comprehensive writing on a history of Chinese architecture Liang ever delivered in Chinese. In this manuscript, Liang emphasized the uniqueness and consistency of China's architecture over a long history and developed a set of generic characteristics of "Chinese architecture" that transcended specific time and space; these included the more material characters such as the use of material, structure, form, and layout, as well as the more conceptual ones in the so-called tendencies for an environmental thought; classical literature and historical buildings were enlisted in a parade of cases to support the claim of a generic set of characteristics, although, in each chapter, unique historical features were also described. According to Liang, architectural characteristics form a standard with which an architectural historian can judge the quality of buildings; these characteristics, further, constitute an abstract form of architecture, which in turn corresponds to a nation's characteristics, which are equally abstract and internally consistent. In actual development, the 1944 manuscript was only printed for limited circulation for teaching in 1953 and was never published until 1980. In the 1950s, Liang's theory of Chinese architecture was accessible only from his articles published in the magazines and newspapers, although they were not entirely consistent with the 1944 manuscript.

Liang's writings on "Chinese architecture" in the 1950s included two types – those on traditional architecture itself and those on relations between design and tradition as heritage. The discussion of architectural characteristics and historical evolution formed the most eminent parts in these writings. In addition, since 1949, by writing and rewriting about the features of Chinese architecture, Liang developed a renowned theory of "translation" and "translatability" (*keyi lun*), a process by which – according to him – characteristics can be carried forward from traditional to modern architecture.

In the 1944 manuscript, Liang used notions of "vocabulary" and "grammar" to explain ancient architecture of China, to assist an understanding of the tradition, although the relations between old characteristics and a new architecture to be created were not covered. But, in the 1950s, based on the study of the characteristics of Chinese architecture, Liang further developed his theory of grammar. For example, in "The Great Architectural Tradition and Heritage of Our Country" (1951), Liang considered structural rules and the composition of timber bracket sets (*dougong*) as "grammar," whereas the specific members such as *dou* and *gong* of a *dougong* set (a base and an arm of a bracket set), as well as columns and beams, are all "vocabulary." In "Introduction to Ancient Architecture" (1953), Liang reorganized the findings of the 1944 manuscript into seven characteristics of architecture of China and claimed that all of them were the aspects of a grammar, whereas the various parts formed a vocabulary. In "Characteristics of Chinese Architecture" (1954), Liang refined the observation into a list of nine characteristics[5] and proposed that architecture of different nations can each be translated – all have a translatability – from its past to a modern architecture. If we compare this to his 1944 manuscript, we find a few important differences: free plan disappeared and axial plan was emphasized to reinforce a consistency of "Chinese architecture"; a non-material setting and environment disappeared, and only material forms survived to allow formal features to depart from their context to achieve an autonomy; and certain weakness such as improper use of lime for masonry disappeared, replaced by the greatness and uniqueness of "Chinese architecture." Finally, in "Architecture of Motherland" (1954), Liang put forward two sketches as an imagined new architecture – as an example of design creation based on a study of "Chinese architecture" and methods of "translation."

It is important to note that, in his active writing, Liang's views on the evolution of architecture had also changed. Before 1953, Liang insisted that though there were regional variations, the basic characteristics of the architecture of China from the Han Dynasty (202 BC–220 AD) to the present remained consistent, that is, without fundamental change.[6] For Liang, this stability over time secured a set of characteristics of Chinese architecture consistent with its national characteristics, for a nationalism in architecture to be meaningful. These ideas, in turn, rationalized his proposition that the creation of a national style of China must be based on a study of the characteristics of Chinese architecture, with its grammar and vocabulary. However, there is a logical inconsistency between stability and the creation of a new architecture – if the tradition has been stable, why the need for a new style? So, from 1953 on (with "Gujian Xulun" or "Introduction to Ancient Architecture"), Liang started to have an evolutionary perspective – architecture was seen as developmental with arrivals of new technologies and materials and new demands of social life, yet it retained certain stable characteristics over time; architecture was then considered evolutionary, with features matching specific times but also continuous with stable national characteristics. In this way, Liang can justify his suggestion that, in the new 1950s, design can adopt new materials and technologies while inheriting the grammar of traditional Chinese architecture, for a new architecture of "national form with socialist content" that may carry forward China's architectural progress.

By tracing Liang's writing history, we can see that Liang had on the one hand retained his focus on design creation for a new architecture as he initially raised in "Why Are We Studying Chinese Architecture" (1944), and on the other elaborated much further on operational and methodological issues, as well as a theoretical basis for that. In other words, since 1949, with writing and rewriting, Liang's construction of the characteristics of Chinese architecture and its historical development was no longer merely for the scholarship of architectural history; it was increasingly for the creation of a new architecture of the national style. Over the decade, this purpose was clearer: with the selection of the features of Chinese architecture, a theory of translation and translatability emerged; historical perspective became more nuanced to balance evolution and stability; and, finally, a package of methodologies with a basic theory came into being, on which a new architecture of "national style with socialist content" can be designed and constructed.[7]

In the 1950s, the creation of a new architecture of "national form with socialist content" predominated the architectural circle in China; and scholars such as Ji Guohua and Jianfei Zhu have confirmed that Liang was indeed the leading architect in this endeavour.[8] In May 1949, upon invitation, Liang became Deputy Director for Beijing Urban Planning Committee, and following this he was deeply involved and implicated in the political life of the new state as based in Beijing, capital of the new People's Public – on which Jianfei Zhu has provided a study.[9] As the son of a renowned thinker and activist, Liang Qichao (1873–1929) of the previous Qing and Republican era, the promotion of Liang Sicheng had a certain symbolic importance. In the early 1950s, participating in supervising the planning and construction of the capital of the new Republic occupied much of Liang's focus. Some of the major issues included the placing of capitol and land use planning, as well as the form and image of designs for Beijing. Here, Liang was responsible for reviewing the major design projects for all Beijing and especially their overall form and image. This compelled Liang to develop a comprehensive reading of "national form with socialist content" and an operational methodology architects can follow in their practice.

Liu Dunzhen: History and Architecture or Double Strategies

Unlike Liang Sicheng, who was residing and working at the centre of state politics, Liu Dunzhen lived in Nanjing and worked at Nanjing Institute of Technology (NIT, now Southeast University or SEU) and did not participate directly in the discussion on "national form with socialist content." Instead, Liu responded to the demand of design for a new state and ideology in different and alternative ways. From 1949 to 1958, in architectural history, Liu's main work included the founding of a Research Unit in Chinese Architecture (Zhongguo Jianzhu Yanjiushi) as a collaboration with East China Design and Construction Corporation (Huadong Jianzhu Gongsi) of Shanghai; with this, Liu was able to continue his research on ancient architecture, especially his field investigation on vernacular houses and private residential gardens. By 1958, he had published *Zhongguo Zhuzhai Gaishuo* (Introduction to housing in China)[10] and "Suzhou de Yuanlin (Gardens of Suzhou),"[11] as two landmark achievements but also as work in progress.

In a national conference on architectural history in 1958, Liu in his speech revealed that the purpose of the survey on vernacular houses by the Research Unit as established in 1953 was to serve East China Corporation (also as Institute of Architectural Design) of Shanghai in their effort to search and design for "national form" architecture. Zhao Yue was quick to note that architects and architectural historians actually had different agendas here.[12] While architects wanted research into the "vernacular," as there were already plenty on "imperial" architecture, the work plan of the Research Unit of 1953 revealed that Liu aimed for a scope of survey as wide as possible and, for current work, "houses" were to be the main target. As it turned out, Liu worked on (vernacular) houses rather than vernacular architecture in general – he transformed an ideological category (of the vernacular versus the imperial in a class-based perspective) into a functional typological category (houses versus palaces, for example) and also concretized a generic project into a focused plan for field investigation. On the way, in real field work, more was discovered – most notably the discovery and research on Baoguosi Temple of Ningbo. In other words, Liu transformed East China Architectural Design Institute's commissioning into an opening research project, to quietly subvert the initial ideological framing and to execute a wider fieldwork on real sites and buildings.[13]

In a letter sent to the colleagues who were compiling *Zhongguo Gudai Jianzhushi* (A history of ancient Chinese architecture) in 1963, Liu clearly stated his understanding of the mode and the purpose of historical writing in architecture. He said:

> I always think that there are different ways of writing architectural history – it can be concise or detailed, it can be broad and comprehensive, or specialised and focused. But a standard architectural history should be comprehensive, synthesized and with a clear division of historical periods. Of course, history is to be used for today, so it is fine to accept that architectural history is also to be employed for architectural design. But even for design as a reference, it can be broadly or narrowly understood. If a narrow one requests a direct application, a broader approach concerns a full cultivating and understanding of architectural culture in its technological and artistic aspects. More importantly, we should adopt the perspective of a historical materialism, for a narrative on the characters of the development of architecture, and for elucidating its historical and artistic values in the perspective of a national culture.[14]

This statement is important. It revealed how Liu had integrated his own views of architectural history into a Marxist perspective as demanded by the new state and its ideology of the time. Compared to Liu's view of 1932, when he stated that architectural history was for clarifying the origins and the lines of evolution, his new articulation of 1963 revealed important changes.[15] These included: 1) one the one hand, Liu expected architectural history to deliver more and to include analysis and judgement – by using "historical materialism," we should trace a development rather than an evolution, detect underlying regularities more than description, and conclude with a judgement rather than merely a list of facts;[16] 2) yet, on the other hand, Liu still wanted to retain a diachronic description of the development of architecture – to be "comprehensive, synthesized and with a clear division of historical periods" – as the basic content of historical writing in architecture; 3) at the same time, by using a "broad" versus "narrow" differentiation, Liu incorporated the idea of "using the past for the present" into a broader purpose, which effectively reduced the importance of "providing reference materials for architectural design." Further, by clarifying the purpose and the historical-materialist framework for architectural history, this statement signalled a fundamental break away from the discursive system of architectural history of the previous time – as represented by the work of Liang Sicheng in the time of the Society (Yingzao Xueshe, 1930s–40). The concrete work on houses and gardens, as the main work of the 1950s, constituted part of this transition.

In the speech at the 1958 conference on architecture history, Liu described how he developed new understanding about houses after his 1952 fieldwork on the houses of Huizhou – while he thought the houses had artistic values, he now began to appreciate their historical values.[17] In his "Preliminary Survey of Ancient Architecture of She County in the South of Anhui Province" (1953), Liu says "these timber structures were all houses and family-ancestral temples, revealing an image of social and everyday life of the people of a bygone age, displaying significant values in the cultural and architectural histories of our country."[18] Two observations can be made here. Firstly, the fieldwork of 1952 here covered not specific houses but a study on the ancient timber constructions there – much like the work of the Society of Research in Chinese Architecture of the 1930s–40s; and these structures can be dated back to as early as the Ming Dynasty (1368–1644) and can therefore testify to the cultural and architectural conditions of the time, displaying significant historical values (for cultural and architectural histories). Secondly, judged from his speech, it is clear that Liu considered the shift from an artistic to a historical perspective on these houses a significant change.

This also suggests that Liu had a clear idea and standard as to what can be included for an architectural history – for him it was if the object had a certain historical value. Though never clearly stated what a historical value was, Liu nevertheless said in his 1958 *Introduction to Housing in China* (*Zhongguo Zhuzhai Gaishuo*) – in the preface – that we had no direct materials on the houses until now (even though we had a housing history of four thousand years, if not longer) and "in recent years we discovered several complete houses from the Ming Dynasty so now we begin to see a comprehensive picture and the various interrelations."[19] If we compare this statement with Liu's 1953 paper on the south of Anhui Province (Wannan), we can tell that for him, historical values are those that can contribute to the coherent sequential narrative of a historical development of architecture over time.

Liu had indeed appreciated the importance of houses (as in his "Diary of Dazhuangshi Chamber" of 1932 and his outline of the house based on classical literature). Nevertheless, types of houses and gardens which had no surviving cases from ancient dynasties could not be the focus for field studies nor could they be included for serious historical research. This was especially the case in the 1930s–40s, when the Society was focusing on a positivist field investigation – with classical literature study – for discovering the origins of a long tradition around and behind *Yingzao Fashi* (Manuel for construction) of 1103 of the Northern Song Dynasty (960–1127).[20] Further, compared to a historical narrative with a clear division of periods, typological study was inadequate as a mode of organization of historical knowledge for earlier times; for example, in Liang Sicheng's 1944 manuscript *A History of Chinese Architecture*, typological description was used only for the later dynasties of Song, Liao, and Jin (960–1276, 916–1125, 1115–1234) when surviving cases were found, and houses as a type only appeared for the last dynasty of the Qing (1644–1911).[21] In other words, in the time of the Society (1930s–40s), houses and gardens could not become the object of investigation as they lacked "historical values," nor could typological studies be taken up seriously, as architectural historians then were busy building up a unified "Chinese architecture" of distinctive features with a coherent history and sequential narrative.

Many scholars agreed that one of Liu's most important contributions was the expansion of the scope of architectural history of China to include houses and gardens. However, what we need is to ask more questions. During his research on houses and gardens, was he examining them in terms of their historical architectural values?

In the article "Suzhou de Yuanlin (Gardens of Suzhou)," Liu was clear that as the cases of the gardens he was studying were from the last imperial dynasty of the Qing or even after, it was their artistic rather than historical values that he was appreciating in the cases.[22] So, that article focused on the design principles of the gardens, treating the garden as an object for design and aesthetic study; this departed significantly from the approach of the Society of the 1930s–40s, which emphasized studying structures and comparing to classical construction manuals; further, in this research on gardens, irregular plan layout was considered a major characteristic.

Zhongguo Zhuzhai Gaishuo (Introduction to housing in China) – which first appeared in *Jianzhu Xubao* (architectural journal) in 1956 and was published as a book in 1958 – had two components: development outline and house types of the Ming (1368–1644) and Qing (1644–1911) dynasties.[23] The section "House Types of the Ming and Qing" was the main body of the book. Here, many cases were included based on fieldwork investigations carried out by the staff of the Research Unit in Chinese Architecture; with these cases as a base, and using the different configuration of the plans, the book provided a typological description and analysis. Though Liu had tried to trace the origins for each type, it was obvious that the focus was on case analysis rather than times and periods. Similar to the analysis of gardens, formal or "plastic" art (*zaoxing yishu*) became a main topic in the conclusion; the strength or what we can learn from the houses – according to Liu – was an economic use of material and structure and a free and flexible aesthetics.

In the New Culture movement of early twentieth-century China, housing reform was considered a crucial instrument for social reform.[24] The 1921 article "Zhuzhai Gailiang (housing reform)" by Sheng Chengyan, a graduate of Tokyo Higher College of Engineering of 1919, was arguably the most representative of these ideas.[25] Liu Denzhen's interest in housing should be understood in this context, as clearly expressed in his "Diary of Dazhuangshi Chamber" (*Dazhuangshi Biji*). In the years of the Society (1930s–40s), though houses were not the focus of research, Liu recorded conditions of local cave dwellings with a "housing reform" perspective when Liu and his team were conducting surveys on the ancient buildings in the north of Henan Province.[26] In 1941, Liu also praised highly the flexible elegance of the vernacular houses along Lijiang River of Yunnan province.[27] This also explains why Liu transformed the task of studying "vernacular architecture" demanded by East China Institute to his concrete plan of investigating the houses. In a way, Liu saw in the call for "national style" and a quest of the Institute for "vernacular architecture" an opportunity not for historical study in general, but a chance to further his interest in houses and housing reform he had long ago, for a full investigation on housing as the most basic architectural typology – even though the social ideal of improving the national character by housing reform was then replaced by a formalistic movement of creating a socialist new architecture.

Therefore, on the whole, Liu studied houses and gardens in the 1950s not for constructing a narrative in architectural history but for an analysis of the precedents for design and formal ideas as useful knowledge. So, it was for architects rather than architectural historians; and though Liu was not providing a set of formal rules, he nevertheless had provided a prospect for the architects to search and to follow certain potential rules.

On the other hand, though the "Development Outline" section of the book *Zhongguo Zhuzhai Gaishuo* (Introduction to housing in China) was brief, it was nevertheless the earliest published writing of Liu on a comprehensive history – providing thus an important case of Liu's historical writing of the time. Here, Liu attempted to specify characters of housing unique to each period using limited historical materials; he situated housing in an overall social setting and against a background of social relations; combining housing development with a division of social historical periods, he aimed for explaining the progress of architecture and housing with the factors of residential life needs and material technological possibilities, to construct a Marxist and historical-materialist framework for explaining the evolution in architectural history. As a result, this *Introduction to Housing in China*, of 1958, revealed a duality in Liu's approach for history and design, and a historical materialism for framing the discussion – together they constituted early evidence of Liu's approach to historical research and writing strategy during that time.

A History of No Use

In China, after the founding of the People's Republic in 1949, architectural history – and historical research and writing in general – confronted two challenges. Firstly, Marxist historical materialism became the only guideline to follow in historical writing; it meant that, in historical writing, one could not merely describe a list of facts, but must instead adopt historical materialism to describe a historical progress and to discover underlying forces and regulations.[28] Secondly, class perspective and realist rationality became a standard to judge the relevance of art and culture; and, to assess the importance of a cultural heritage, one must explain if it can serve the people and be used for socialist construction.[29] These two demands were written into what was considered the temporary constitution of the People's Republic, namely, the Common Program of the Chinese People's Political Consultative Conference (1949).[30] Obviously, we must assess Liang and Liu's work of the 1950s against this context. Indeed, the two adopted different strategies, with different outcomes.

Due to his social standing and the titles he assumed in Beijing in the 1950s, Liang Sicheng had no choice but to promote the ideas of "national form," to find operational design methods for the architects. As a result, he did establish a theoretical foundation and a set of methods for "national form"; these recursive writings were based on his work about Chinese architecture in the time of the Society (1930s–40s); and, by adopting Mao's theory of New Democracy (*xin minzhu zhuyi lun*) requesting that a new art should be "national, scientific and people's," Liang transformed historical writing into a tool for the political project of the government. However, to search for potential forms, Liang was effectively giving up the duty of an architectural historian; on the way, he also failed to fully appreciate state ideology and its changing position – the new Constitution of 1954 (developed from the Common Program of 1949) clarified that the general task of China of the "transitional" time was to materialize "socialist industrialization" and to achieve "socialist transformation" of agriculture, the handicraft industry, and capitalist economy (industry and commerce) – implying a shift towards industrialization beyond stylistic debate in architecture. Liang's ideas of "national form," nicknamed "big roof," was much criticized from this time on.[31] Further, in both the Common Program of 1949 and the Constitution of 1954, the official narrative was that China was a unified state of multiple nations, and Liang's singular "Chinese architecture" didn't fit that well. Finally, after the 1950s, Liang was much side-lined and criticized – a tragic figure as a result of his entanglement with state politics; he was able neither to move beyond the Society of the 1930s–40s to further the project of historical research, nor to find a new form and image successfully for the new People's Republic.

Liu, on the other hand, employed Design Institutes' need of "national form" for his further survey and study and developed a two-tier strategy for architectural and historical research, with corresponding two forms of writing – for architects and architectural historians respectively. His research on houses and gardens – as a study on types – was more an analysis than a mere linear narrative, developing thus a typological history; Liu was also clear that this typological history can serve teaching in design studios well.[32] At the same time, Liu's research also matched state demand and its ideology. After 1958, vernacular houses achieved importance that can rival the monumental architecture of palaces and temples.[33] Research on vernacular housing was much promoted by the Ministry of Construction – along with the People's Commune movement – to cover all ethnic regions of China. Vernacular housing, with its rich regional variety, was also a better type to reflect the narrative of the new republic as a "unified and multi-national country."

Research on gardens, on the other hand, could also contribute to the building of People's Parks in the cities all around. The newly formed historical research, using a temporal division of periods based on historical materialism and class struggle theory, had turned a Hegelian system into a Marxist narrative, ensuring this history of Chinese architecture as part of a history of Chinese revolution. The progressive dynamics of architectural change were now considered to have originated from the forces of productivity and the relations of production, as well as the contradiction between the working people and the ruling class. The division of periods in architectural history was also made to be the same as that in social history.

We can say that Liu had carefully ensured that his research and writing fit with state ideology well and had thus secured a room for the academic research of architectural history. Further, for Liu, architectural research and historical research were not fully separated – analyses on design and formal features can provide new ideas for the search of the origins and sequential developments in historical research, thus suggesting an important reference for determining historical values of a specific historical case.

The impact of these two kinds of writing – from Liang and Liu – was not clear until after the end of Cultural Revolution in 1976. In a long historical perspective, the full-scale expansion of the survey on vernacular houses in the late 1950s was accidental, but once houses and gardens emerged and were differentiated from "ancient architecture," the division remained significant for a long time – with the former for creative design and landscape design and the latter architectural history – until about the mid-1980s.[34] Studies on houses and gardens continued and, in our contemporary age, entered significantly into the discourse of current Chinese architects in their new effort of constructing a "Chinese tradition."[35] The typological approach adopted for the university textbook *Zhongguo Jianzhu Shi* (A history of Chinese architecture, not to be confused with Liang's manuscript of the same title of 1944) of 1982 assisted many architects well, with a function-based typological framework for reading traditional architecture.[36] On the other hand, *Zhongguo Gudai Jianzhu Shi* (A history of ancient Chinese architecture) of 1980, compiled by a team under Liu Dunzhen and adopting what Liu in 1963 had conceived as the correct format of history – comprehensive and synthesized with a chronological division of periods – received high acclaims among scholars, but was less popular and more for specialist architectural historians.[37] The mode of historical writing established in this book reached a leadership position for historical research and writing after the 1980s in two aspects. Firstly, it established a materialist history in perspective and the idea of employing the past for the present in value judgement; secondly, in analysis of architecture, though the timber structure remained the most basic, emphasis had greatly moved on to cover groups and settlement forms where courtyards and axial organizations featured prominently.[38] This latter aspect had surely contributed to the debate on national architectural traditions in the 1980s, although its overall impact for architecture of China in general is to be studied further.[39]

Returning to the 1950s–60s, whether for Liang or Liu, whatever the strategy they adopted respectively to face the crisis of historical writing, "the use of architectural history" remained a problem unresolved. In the 1930s–40s, the "nationalist" historical research in architecture under Liang was much appreciated broadly; and if the 1944 manuscript *A History of Chinese Architecture* was its most prominent achievement, then the theory of "translatability" can be understood as a concrete connection between architecture and nationalism, and between historical knowledge and design practice. Yet, after the 1950s, "function" and "technology" came forward – in a strange way – to redefine architecture's relation to state and society, and building production became more important than forms and images in the new formulations of state ideology. In a concluding speech at the closing of a 1958 conference on architectural history, Director of the Research Academy of Architectural Science, Wang Zhili (1913–2010), proposed that socialist architecture was to have seven features, none of which was to do with form.[40] Comparing to the ideas of "national form" and the practice of national style or "big-roof" architecture for a few public buildings, the large-scale industrial works and massive commoners' housing construction constituted a real landscape of architecture in China. A prevailing guideline went like this: to design we must be "pragmatic, economic, and try to achieve beauty when condition permits"; clearly, pragmatism and economic rationalism – instead of the ideas of form and image – predominated as both a limiting condition and an indication of the virtue of the new government. When Liang was criticized in 1955, it was wastefulness rather than the class issue of form or style that was the main concern in the critique; whereas in Liu's research, he had also tried to appreciate the economic wisdom in the object of study. If Liang had fallen out of favour and was criticized when his insisted nationalism was no longer relevant in the changing state ideology, then Liu had instead adopted a pragmatic approach, to further his research with the actual demand of design institutes in practice, but with the purpose of his research and writing also altered on the way. However, whether it was Liang's "translatability," Liu's design principles, or an architectural history becoming part of a revolutionary history, they had all – in making historical research useful to pragmatic construction – dissolved effectively a constructive and critical efficacy of historical research on reality, and had even deconstructed the writing of architectural history itself.

What is most ironic is that it was in the decision of writing "three histories" (of the past, early modern time, and the new republic) at the 1958 conference on architectural history that architectural history was declared to be of no use by the Ministry of Construction in the form of a state resolution.[41] In this official statement, the practice of privileging the past – of scholarship detached from politics, of research for research's sake, of research from the viewpoints of design and art, and of traditional and complex verification process in research – was targeted and criticized. The resolution says, "research must deliver a combative function for the construction of the People's Communes." It says,

> Researchers must . . . correctly understand the principles of architectural development, so as to guide practice from now on . . . (they must) correctly summarize working people's rich skills and knowledge accumulated in the historical process, so as to serve for socialist construction.[42]

In the concluding speech of the conference delivered by the Director of the Academy of Architectural Science, Wang Zhili (a revolutionary who joined the Party in 1936) directly criticized Liu Dunzhen's research on classical architecture, vernacular housing, and gardens and declared that for now architectural history was useless until it could provide service for the building of the People's Communes.[43]

Concluding Note

Despite all of this, Liang and Liu had developed two strategies for writing in architectural history in the 1950s – a contribution that cannot be ignored. The different trajectories are important to note. On the one hand, they originated from long-standing, different views on history, architecture, and the purpose of research in architectural history. On the other hand, both asserted important influence since the 1980s when debate on national form and interest in architectural history and research returned. In other words, if we do not understand Liang and Liu's work of the 1950s, we will then lose a very important perspective through which to read and examine the issues and developments in the architecture of China post-1980s.

Notes

1 For Liang's trajectory after 1949, see: Lin Zhu, *Liang Sicheng, Lin Huiyin yu Wo* (Liang Sicheng, Lin Huiyin and me) (Beijing: Zhongguo Qingnian Chubanshe, 2011), 449–452 ("Liang Sicheng Nianpu" or timeline of Liang Sicheng).

2 For Liu Dunzhen's life and profile after 1949, see: Liu Dunzhen, *Liu Dunzhen Quanji* (Complete works of Liu Dunzhen), vol. 10 (Beijing: China Architecture and Building Press, 2007), 211–215 ("Liu Dunzhen Xiansheng Shengping Jishi Nianbiao 1897–1968" or Liu Denzhen's biographic timeline 1897–1968).

3 Liang Sicheng, "Weishenme Yanjiu Zhongguo Jianzhu (Why are we studying Chinese architecture)," *Zhongguo Yingzao Xueshe Huikan* (Journal of the Society for Research in Chinese Architecture), vol. 7, no. 1 (1944): 5–12.

4 Liang's essays addressed different audiences. These included, for example, "Woguo Weidade Jianzhu Chuantong yu Yichan (The great architectural tradition and heritage of our nation)" in *The People's Daily*, 19 & 20 February (1951): 3 (both), for popular readership; "China's Art and Architecture" in *The Encyclopaedia Americana,* vol. 6 (New York: Americana Corp., 1953), 552–559, for international readers; "Gujian Xulun (Introduction to ancient architecture)" in *Wenwu Cankao Ziliao* 3 (1953): 9–30, for specialists in archaeology; and articles for architects and architectural professors such as "Zhongguo Jianzhu de Tezhen (Characteristics of Chinese Architecture)," *Jianzhu Xuebao* 1 (1954): 36–39.

5 These nine characteristics are: 1) a single building composed of three parts; 2) a plan that surrounds the core of a courtyard (compared with the 1944 manuscript, free plan disappeared while axial plan was emphasized); 3) timber frame as the main structure (emphasizing its flexibility and similarity to modern steel-and-concrete framework); 4) the use of timber bracket sets (*dougong*); 5) a unique method of raising the roof profile (*jujia, juzhe*); 6) the roof as distinctive; 7) the use of colours; 8) a unification of structure and decoration at the joineries throughout the building; and 9) colourful tiles and carved stonework.

6 Liang Sicheng, "Zuguo de Jianzhu Chuantong yu Dangqian de Jianshe Wenti (The architectural tradition of motherland and our current task of construction)," *Xin Guancha* 16 (1952): 8–11.

7 Zhu Jianfei argued that Liang's theoretical framework achieved a full completion in 1954 when Liang had reached a pick of publications in terms of quantity and clarity when three key aspects were covered in Liang's articulation – theory or ideology, historical research, and design methodology. For this see: Zhu Jianfei, "Guojia, Kongjian, Gemin: Beijing 1949–1959 (State, space, revolution: Beijing 1949–1959)," in *Zhongguo Jianzhu Liushinian (1949–2009): Lishi Lilun Yanjiu* (Sixty years of Chinese architecture 1949–2009: History, theory and criticism), ed. Zhu Jianfei (Beijing: China Architecture and Building Press, 2009), 46–71.

8 See Ji Guohua, "20 Shiji 50 Niandai Sulian Shehuizhuyi Xianshizhuyi Jianzhu Lilun de Shuru he Dui Zhongguo Jianzhu de Yingxiang (The importation of Socialist Realism from Soviet Union and its impact on the architecture of China in the 1950s)," and also Zhu, "Guojia (State)," both published in *Zhongguo* (Sixty years), ed. Zhu, 99–111 and 46–71.

9 Zhu, "Guojia (State)," *Zhongguo* (Sixty years), ed. Zhu, 46–71. See also, Jianfei Zhu, *Architecture of Modern China: A Historical Critique* (London: Routledge, 2009), 75–104.

10 Liu Dunzhen, *Zhongguo Zhuzhai Gaishuo* (Introduction to housing in China) (Beijing: Jianzhu Gongcheng Chubanshe, 1957).

11 Liu Dunzhen, "Suzhou de Yuanlin (Gardens of Suzhou)," in *Liu Dunzhen Quanji* (Complete works of Liu Dunzhen), vol. 4, Liu Denzhen (Beijing: China Architecture & Building Press, 2007), 146–199.

12 Zhao Yue, *Zouxiang Minjian Jianzhu, Tansuo Lingyizhong Chuantong: Dui Zhongguo Jianzhu Yanjiushi (1953–1965) zhi Zhuzhai Yanjiu de Yanjiu* (Towards a Vernacular Architecture, for a Different Tradition: Examining the Research on Houses by the Research Unit in Chinese Architecture (1953–1965) (Unpublished Master's Thesis, Southeast University, Nanjing, 2014), 7–26.

13 Indeed, "vernacular" and "houses" are at two different levels or planes. The point is that, when Liu changed from a commissioning task on the first to a real plan on the second, he not only materialized an abstract idea into a workable project but also subverted a class ideology or categorization into an architectural or typological one. On the way, he also liberated himself into a wider field of real sites and cases for a fruitful harvest in research.

14 Liu Dunzhen, "Zhi Yu Weiguo he Zhang Yaqing Han (zhi yi): Guanyu Minju Diaocha ji Jianzhushi Xiezuo (Letter to Yu Weiguo and Zhang Yaqing (1): On the survey of vernacular houses and the issue of writings for architectural history)," in *Liu Dunzhen Quanji: Di shi juan* (Complete works of Liu Dunzhen), vol. 10, Liu Dunzhen (Beijing: China Architecture and Building Press, 2007), 205.

15 Liu Dunzhen, "Beiping Zhihuasi Rulaidian Diaochaji (Fieldwork report on Rulai Hall of Zhihuasi Tempe in Beiping)," *Zhongguo Yingzao Xueshe Huikan*, vol. 3, no. 3 (1932): 1–17. In this paper, Liu said that "Some of the major questions we architectural historians must confront include the difference between architecture of the Ming and Qing as opposed to the earlier Tang and Song dynasties, the degree of difference and variation, the time of the departure when it took place, the intermediate phases the evolution went through, and if and where can we detect foreign influence"; therefore, our major task for research in architectural history should include "collecting the cases, determining the time they were built, identifying their similarities and differences, clarifying the characters of the time as embodied, and then seeking for a mutual verification between field investigating and the reading of classical literature." This perspective on the basic task of architectural history remained largely unchanged in and after the 1950s for Liu.

16 In Liang and Liu's self-critical writings, this kind of description with a simple listing of basic facts was described as running a pharmacy with the Chinese medicinal tradition – all herbal drugs were stored in a monotonous rows and columns of numerous cabinets.

17 Liu Dunzhen says, "In my fieldwork to the Sichuan and Yunan provinces in 1938, I began to notice vernacular houses, but only from an artistic viewpoint and just for personal curiosity; but when I was doing field survey of Ming-dynasty houses in Huizhou region of Anhui province in 1952 as commissioned by East China Ministry of Culture, I found their great achievement in layout and art, and had since changed my view acknowledging their historical values." See Liu Dunzhen, "Liu Dunzhen fayan (the speeches of Liu Dunzhen)," in *Jianzhu Lishi Taolunhui Wenjian (diyi ce)* (Documents for the conference on architectural history, vol. 1), School of Architecture Library Archive, (Nanjing: Southeast University, 1958), 9–10.

18 Liu Dunzhen, "Wannan Shexian Faxian de Gujianzhu Chubu Diaocha (Preliminary survey of ancient architecture of She County in the south of Anhui Province)," *Wenwu Cankao Ziliao* 3 (1953): 31–34. An editor's note accompanying this paper says it is rare to discover historical relics of vernacular houses when the majority discovered have been imperial and official architecture. It reveals a basically temporal or historical way of referencing ancient architecture at that time.

19 Liu, *Zhongguo Zhuzhai* (Introduction to housing), 9.

20 Liu Dunzhen, "Dazhuangshi Biji (Diary of Dazhuangshi Chamber)," *Zhongguo Yingzao Xueshe Huikan*, vol 3, no 3 (1932): 129–172. See also, Liu Dunzhen, "Beiping," *Zhongguo*, 2.

21 Liang Sicheng, *Zhongguo Jianzhu Shi* (A history of Chinese architecture) (Tianjin: Baihua Wenyi Chubanshe, 1998).

22 Liu, "Suzhou (Gardens)," 146–199.

23 Liu Dunzhen, "Zhongguo Zhuzhai Gaishuo (Introduction to housing in China)," *Jianzhu Xuebao* 4 (1956): 1–53.

24 Zhuge Jing, "Gexing, Zizhi, Pingdeng yu Guanyu Fangjian de Xiangxiang: 20 Shiji Chu Zhongguo Chengshi Zhong Dengji Juzhu Guannian zhong de Lixiang Zhuzhai – Juzhu: Cong Zhongguo Chuantong Chengshi Zhuzhai dao Xiangguan Wenti Xilie Yanjiu zhiliu (Individuality, autonomy, equality and the imagination of the room: Ideal housing for the urban middle class in China of the early twentieth century; Housing – the sixth study in Chinese traditional urban housing and the associated issues)," *Jianzhushi* 6 (2017): 61–68.

25 Sheng Chengyan, "Zhuzhai Gailiang, Zhuzhai Gailiang (xu), Zhuzhai Gailiang (zaixu), (Housing Reform, Housing Reform 2, Housing Reform 3)," *Xueyi* 3, no. 3, 4 and 5 (1921): 92–98, 112–119, 115–123.

26 Liu Dunzhen, "Henan Sheng Beibu Gujianzhu Diaochaji (Notes from the fieldwork study on ancient architecture in the north of Hebei Province)," *Zhongguo Yingzao Xueshe Huikan*, vol. 6, no. 4 (1937): 30–129.

27 Liu Dunzhen, "Xinan Gujianzhu Diaochao Gaikuang (A survey on the ancient buildings in the southwest)," in *Liu Dunzhen Quanji* (Complete works of Liu Dunzhen), vol. 4, Liu Dunzhen (Beijing: China Architecture and Building Press, 2007), 1–23.

28 The first general history of China written in this perspective is *Zhonguo Tongshi Jianbian* (Concise compilation for a general history of China) by Fan Wenlan (1893–1969) in 1941 in Yan'an of Shaanxi Province, the headquarters for the Chinese Communist Party and its Red Army from 1935 to 1948.

29 Mao Zedong, "Zai Yan'an Wenyi Zuotanhui Shangde Jianghua (Speech at Yan'an Symposium on Literature and Art)," in *Mao Zedong Xuanji* (Selected works of Mao Zedong), vol. 3, Mao Zedong (Beijing: Renmin Chubanshe, 1991), 847–879.

30 *See: Zhonguo Renmin Zhengzhi Xieshang Huiyi Gongtong Gangling (Common Program from the Chinese People's Political Consultative Conference), (Beijing: Renmin Chubanshe, 1954), 29 (Chapter Five: Policy on Culture and Education, Rule 44 and 45).*

31 Although it is commonly agreed that Liang was criticized because of the changing situation of Soviet Russia, the reality – according to a scholar, Gao Hua (1954–2011) – wasn't quite like this; Mao Zedong never really followed Soviet Union. Liang would not have been criticized so severely for costliness of his architectural vision, if it weren't because of some domestic political movement and national economic hardship China was going through at the time.

32 Liu Dunzhen says, "In the past when I lectured on Chinese architectural history I used a chronological method with a division of dynasties; but in recent years I find it inadequate. Firstly, ... Secondly, a historical study on Chinese architecture must be equipped with a patriotic spirit, and should be combined with design teaching, so that it may ground for the development of national forms. In the

periodic-chronological approach, information is organized in terms of the dynasties; if one needs to understand the forms and structures of a project or type, one has to go back and forth across the dynasties to collect various materials for a full understanding. Comparatively, a sectional approach is better; it allows direct cuts into history, for an easier teaching and communication." See: Liu Dunzhen, "Zhongguo Jianzhushi Cankao Tu Qianyan (Preface to Visual Catalogue of a History of Chinese Architecture) (1953)," in Liu Dunzhen Quanji (Complete works of Liu Dunzhen), vol. 7, Liu Dunzhen (Beijing: China Architecture and Building Press, 2007), 91.

33 Wang Zhili, "Wang Zhili Yuanzhang zai Jianzhu Lishi Xueshu Taolunhui shang de Zongjie Fayan (Concluding speech at the conference on architectural history by Director of Academy Wang Zhili)," *Jianzhu Xuebao* 11 (1958): 4–6.

34 After the Cultural Revolution (1966–76), the most established and "official" architectural journals in China, *Jianzhu Xuebao* (Architectural journal) and *Jianzhushi* (The architect), have kept a division of papers into the clusters of *gujianzhu* (ancient architecture), *minju* (vernacular houses), and *yuanlin* (gardens).

35 In recent times, the most renowned case is surely Wang Shu, a Pritzker Prize Laurette – the first Chinese national receiving the honour. In his theorization, the Chinese garden tradition is not just a heritage but a means of resistance to the rampant urbanization that has been spreading all over China in recent decades.

36 Editorial Group, ed. *Zhongguo Jianzhu Shi (diyi ban)* (A history of Chinese architecture, first edition), Beijing: China Architecture and Building Press, 1982.

37 Liu Dunzhen, ed. *Zhongguo Gudai Jianzhu Shi (diyi ban)* (A history of ancient Chinese architecture, first edition), Beijing: China Architecture and Building Press, 1980.

38 Liu, ed. *Zhongguo* (A history), 1–21.

39 Zhuge Jing, "Duanlie huo Yanxu: Lishi, Sheji, Lilun: 1980 nian qianhou Jianzhu Xuebao zhong "Minzu Xingshi" Taolun de Huigu yu Fansi (Continuity or breaking apart: History, design and theory: A review and reflection on the "national form" debate in the *Jianzhu Xuebao* journal around 1980)," *Jianzhu Xuebao* 9 (2014): 53–57.

40 The seven features are: 1) the entire social structure and its characteristics are fundamentally different from that of capitalism; 2) adopting a large-scale approach to construction . . . , with a feature of high-speed and magnitude; 3) constructing with planning and organization . . . ; 4) adopting a gradual approach with a co-use of advanced and rudimentary levels for technological progress in mechanization and industrialization; 5) on economic matters, austerity and efficient use are the basic socialist principles; 6) the approach to history, tradition, and art are essentially different to that in capitalism; 7) to take full consideration of local conditions and the specific task at hand – be local and flexible.

41 The "three histories" include: *Jianmin Zhongguo Jianzhu Tongshi* (A concise general history of Chinese architecture), *Zhongguo Jindai Jianzhushi* (A history of architecture of early modern China), and *Jianguo Shinianlai de Jianzhu Chengjiu* (Architectural achievements in the decade after the founding of the nation).

42 "Jianzhu Lishi Xueshu Taolun Huiyi Jueyi (Resolution at the academic conference on architectural history)," *Jianzhu Xuebao* 11 (1958): 6.

43 Wang Zhili, "Wang Zhili Yuanzhang zai Jianzhu Lishi Xueshu Taolunhui shang de Zongjie Fayan (Concluding speech at the conference on architectural history by Director of Academy Wang Zhili)," *Jianzhu Xuebao* 11 (1958): 4–6.

Bibliography

Editorial Group, ed. *Zhongguo Jianzhu Shi (diyi ban)* (A History of Chinese Architecture), 1st ed. Beijing: China Architecture and Building Press, 1982.

Fan Wenlan. *Zhonguo Tongshi Jianbian* (Concise Compilation for a General History of China). Beijing: Renmin Chubanshe, 1956 (First published in Yan'an, 1941).

Ji Guohua. "20 Shiji 50 Niandai Sulian Shehuizhuyi Xianshizhuyi Jianzhu Lilun de Shuru he Dui Zhongguo Jianzhu de Yingxiang (The Importation of Socialist Realism from Soviet Union and Its Impact on the Architecture of China in the 1950s)." In *Zhongguo Jianzhu Liushinian (1949–2009): Lishi Lilun Yanjiu* (Sixty Years of Chinese Architecture 1949–2009: History, Theory and Criticism), edited by Zhu Jianfei, 99–111. Beijing: China Architecture and Building Press, 2009.

Jianzhu Lishi. "Jianzhu Lishi Xueshu Taolun Huiyi Jueyi (Resolution at the Academic Conference on Architectural History)." *Jianzhu Xuebao* 11 (1958): 6.

Lai Delin. "Wenhua guan zaoyu shehui guan: Liang Liu Shixue Fengqi yu 20 Shiji Zhongqi Zhongguo Liangzhong Jianzhuguan de Chongtu (When a Cultural Perspective Encounters a Social Outlook: Difference Between Liang and Liu's Historiography and the Conflict of Two Frameworks on Architecture in China in the Mid-20th Century)." In *Zoujin jianzhu, zoujin jianzhushi: Lai Delin Zixuanji* (Into Architecture, into Architectural History: Self-Selected Works of Lai Delin), edited by Lai Delin, 139–158. Shanghai: Renmin Chubanshe, 2012.

———. *Zoujin jianzhu, zoujin jianzhushi: Lai Delin Zixuanji* (Into Architecture, into Architectural History: Self-Selected Works of Lai Delin). Shanghai: Renmin Chubanshe, 2012.

Liang Sicheng. "Weishenme Yanjiu Zhongguo Jianzhu (Why Are We Studying Chinese Architecture)." *Yingzao Xueshe Huikan* (Journal of the Society for Research in Chinese Architecture) 7, no. 1 (1944): 5–12.

———. "Woguo Weidade Jianzhu Chuantong yu Yichan (The Great Architectural Tradition and Heritage of Our Nation)." *The People's Daily* (19–20 February 1951): 3 (both).

———. "Zuguo de Jianzhu Chuantong yu Dangqian de Jianshe Wenti (The Architectural Tradition of Motherland and Our Current Task of Construction)." *Xin Guancha* 16 (1952): 8–11.

———. "China's Art and Architecture." In *The Encyclopedia Americana*, vol. 6, 552–559. New York: Americana Corp., 1953.

———. "Gujian Xulun (Introduction to Ancient Architecture)." *Wenwu Cankao Ziliao* 3 (1953): 9–30.

———. "Zhongguo Jianzhu de Tezhen (Characteristics of Chinese Architecture)." *Jianzhu Xuebao* 1 (1954): 36–39.

———. *Zhongguo Jianzhu Shi* (A History of Chinese Architecture). Tianjin: Baihua Wenyi Chubanshe, 1998.

———. *Liang Sicheng Quanji* (Complete Works of Liang Sicheng), vol. 1–9. Beijing: China Architecture and Building Press, 2001.

Lin Zhu. *Liang Sicheng, Liu Huiyin yu Wo* (Liang Sicheng, Lin Huiyin and Me). Beijing: Zhongguo Qingnian Chubanshe, 2011.

Liu Dunzhen. "Beiping Zhihuasi Rulaidian Diaochaji (Fieldwork Report on Rulai Hall of Zhihuasi Tempe in Beiping)." *Zhongguo Yingzao Xueshe Huikan* 3, no. 3 (1932): 1–70.

———. "Henan Sheng Beibu Gujianzhu Diaochaji (Notes from the Fieldwork Study on Ancient Architecture in the North of Hebei Province)." *Zhongguo Yingzao Xueshe Huikan* 6, no. 4 (1937): 30–129.

———. "Wannan Shexian Faxian de Gujianzhu Chubu Diaocha (Preliminary Survey of Ancient Architecture of She County in the South of Anhui Province)." *Wenwu Cankao Ziliao* 3 (1953): 31–34.

———. "Zhongguo Zhuzhai Gaishuo (Introduction to Housing in China)." *Jianzhu Xuebao* 4 (1956): 1–53.

———. *Zhongguo Zhuzhai Gaishuo* (Introduction to Housing in China). Beijing: Jianzhu Gongcheng Chubanshe, 1957.

———. "Liu Dunzhen fayan (The Speeches of Liu Dunzhen)." In *Jianzhu Lishi Taolunhui Wenjian (diyi ce)* (Documents for the Conference on Architectural History), vol. 1, 9–10. School of Architecture Library Archive. Nanjing: Southeast University, 1958.

———, ed. *Zhongguo Gudai Jianzhu Shi (diyi ban)* (A History of Ancient Chinese Architecture), 1st ed. Beijing: China Architecture and Building Press, 1980.

———. "Suzhou de Yuanlin (Gardens of Suzhou)." In *Liu Dunzhen Quanji* (Complete Works of Liu Dunzhen), edited by Liu Dunzhen, vol. 4, 146–199. Beijing: China Architecture & Building Press, 2007.

———. "Xinan Gujianzhu Diaochao Gaikuang (A Survey on the Ancient Buildings in the Southwest)." In *Liu Dunzhen Quanji* (Complete Works of Liu Dunzhen), edited by Liu Dunzhen, vol. 4, 1–23. Beijing: China Architecture and Building Press, 2007.

———. "Zhi Yu Weiguo he Zhang Yaqing Han (zhi yi): Guanyu Minju Diaocha ji Jianzhushi Xiezuo (Letter to Yu Weiguo and Zhang Yaqing (1): On the Survey of Vernacular Houses and the Issue of Writings for Architectural History)." In *Liu Dunzhen Quanji* (Complete Works of Liu Dunzhen), edited by Liu Dunzhen, vol. 10, 205. Beijing: China Architecture and Building Press, 2007.

———. "Zhongguo Jianzhushi Cankao Tu Qianan (Preface to Visual Catalogue of a History of Chinese Architecture) (1953)." In *Liu Dunzhen Quanji* (Complete Works of Liu Dunzhen), edited by Liu Dunzhen, vol. 7, 91. Beijing: China Architecture and Building Press, 2007.

———. *Liu Dunzhen Quanji* (Complete Works of Liu Dunzhen), vol. 1–10. Beijing: China Architecture and Building Press, 2007.

Mao Zedong. "Zai Yan'an Wenyi Zuotanhui Shangde Jianghua (Speech at Yan'an Symposium on Literature and Art)." In *Mao Zedong Xuanji* (Selected Works of Mao Zedong), edited by Mao Zedong, vol. 3, 847–879. Beijing: Renmin Chubanshe, 1991.

———. *Mao Zedong Xuanji* (Selected Works of Mao Zedong), vol. 3. Beijing: Renmin Chubanshe, 1991.

Renmin Chubanshe. *Zhonguo Renmin Zhengzhi Xieshang Huiyi Gongtong Gangling* (Common Program from the Chinese People's Political Consultative Conference). Beijing: Renmin Chubanshe, 1954.

Sheng Chengyan. "Zhuzhai Gailiang, Zhuzhai Gailiang (xu), Zhuzhai Gailiang (zaixu) (Housing reform, Housing reform 2, Housing reform 3)." *Xueyi* 3, no. 3–5 (1921): 92–98, 112–119, 115–123.

Wang Zhili. "Wang Zhili Yuanzhang zai Jianzhu Lishi Xueshu Taolunhui shang de Zongjie Fayan (Concluding Speech at the Conference on Architectural History by Director of Academy Wang Zhili)." *Jianzhu Xuebao* 11 (1958): 4–6.

Zhao Yue. *Zouxiang Minjian Jianzhu, Tansuo Lingyizhong Chuantong: Dui Zhongguo Jianzhu Yanjiushi (1953–1965) zhi Zhuzhai Yanjiu de Yanjiu* (Towards a Vernacular Architecture, for a Different Tradition: Examining the Research on Houses by the Research Unit in Chinese Architecture (1953–1965). Unpublished Master's Thesis. Southeast University, Nanjing, 2014.

Zhongguo Yingzao Xueshe. *Zhongguo Yingzao Xueshe Huikan* (Journal of the Society of Research in Chinese Architecture), vol. 1–7. Beijing: Zhishi Chanquan Chubanshe, 1930–1945.

Zhu Jianfei. "Guojia, Kongjian, Gemin: Beijing 1949–1959 (State, Space, Revolution: Beijing 1949–1959)." In *Zhongguo Jianzhu Liushinian (1949–2009): Lishi Lilun Yanjiu* (Sixty Years of Chinese Architecture 1949–2009: History, Theory and Criticism), edited by Zhu Jianfei, 46–71. Beijing: China Architecture and Building Press, 2009.

———, ed. *Zhongguo Jianzhu Liushinian (1949–2009): Lishi Lilun Yanjiu* (Sixty Years of Chinese Architecture 1949–2009: History, Theory and Criticism). Beijing: China Architecture and Building Press, 2009.

———. *Architecture of Modern China: A Historical Critique*. London: Routledge, 2009.

Zhuge Jing. "Duanlie huo Yanxu: Lishi, Sheji, Lilun: 1980 nian qianhou Jianzhu Xuebao zhong "Minzu Xingshi" Taolun de Huigu yu Fansi (Continuity or Breaking Apart: History, Design and Theory: A Review and Reflection on the "National Form" Debate in the *Jianzhu Xuebao* Journal Around 1980)." *Jianzhu Xuebao* 9 (2014): 53–57.

———. "Gexing, Zizhi, Pingdeng yu Guanyu Fangjian de Xiangxiang: 20 Shiji Chu Zhongguo Chengshi Zhong Dengji Juzhu Guannian zhong de Lixiang Zhuzhai – Juzhu: Cong Zhongguo Chuantong Chengshi Zhuzhai dao Xiangguan Wenti Xilie Yanjiu zhiliu (Individuality, Autonomy, Equality and the Imagination of the Room: Ideal Housing for the Urban Middle Class in China of the Early Twentieth Century; Housing – the Sixth Study in Chinese Traditional Urban Housing and the Associated Issues)." *Jianzhushi* 6 (2017): 61–68.

Glossary

Anhui (Province)	安徽省
Baoguosi (Temple)	保国寺
Beijing	北京
Dazhuangshi (Chamber)	大壮室
Dazhuangshi Biji	大壮室笔记
dou	斗
dougong	斗拱
gong	栱
Gujian Xulun	古建序论
Han (Dynasty)	汉朝
Henan (Province)	河南省
Huadong Jianzhu Gongsi	华东建筑公司
Huizhou	徽州
Ji Guohua	吉国华
Jianfei Zhu	朱剑飞

Jianzhu Xuebao	建筑学报
Jin (Dynasty)	金朝
keyi lun	可译论
Lai Delin	赖德霖
Liang	梁
Liang Qichao	梁启超
Liang Sicheng	梁思成
Liao (Dynasty)	辽代
Lijiang (River)	丽江
Liu	刘
Liu Dunzhen	刘敦桢
Ming (Dynasty)	明朝
Nanjing	南京
Nanjing (Institute of Technology)	南京工学院
Ningbo	宁波
Qing (Dynasty)	清朝
She (County)	歙县
Song (Dynasty)	宋朝
Suzhou de Yuanlin	苏州的园林
Tsinghua (University)	清华大学
Wang Zhili	汪之力
Wannan	皖南
xin minzhu zhuyi lun	新民主主义论
Yingzao Fashi	营造法式
Yingzao Xueshe	营造学社
Yunnan (Province)	云南省
zaoxing yishu	造型艺术
Zhao Yue	赵越
Zhongguo Gudai Jianzhu Shi	中国古代建筑史
Zhongguo Jianzhu Shi	中国建筑史
Zhongguo Jianzhu Yanjiushi	中国建筑研究室
Zhongguo Zhuzhai Gaishuo	中国住宅概说

Architecture in Socialist China:
Nationalism and Modernism

26

NATIONAL STYLE

Thinking and Building for a New Republic in Beijing (1949–1959)

Jianfei Zhu

The 1950s appears to be a critical time in the history of modern China. It is the first decade of the People's Republic. It is a decade when design institutes, university departments, and key aspects of historical knowledge, all still in use today, were first established. It is a decade when "Chinese architecture," based on earlier research, was *precisely* comprehended as a system and a "national" tradition, one that can be employed immediately to design new forms for the new republic. From a political, institutional, and disciplinary viewpoint, the 1950s seems *foundational*, not only for the Mao era (1949–78) but, more importantly, for post-Mao and contemporary China in hidden and subtle ways. It is therefore important, if we are to understand this decade in this perspective, to read the events and discussions concerning the "national" tradition and the use of it for design, in relation to the founding of the republic with its political aspirations.

This chapter aims to trace a few events and debates, occurring as they did around key individuals, publications, and design projects in Beijing of this decade.[1] It is not a historical survey, but rather an analytical study, on the "national" discourse in historical research *and* design creation, in the political context of the Chinese capital of the 1950s. It aims to address three questions. Firstly, how was "Chinese architecture" as a body of historical knowledge systemized and objectified, and how was that knowledge employed in the creation of a National-Style architecture? Secondly, how were the party and state authority involved with a Maoist ideology and Soviet influence, and how was the authority related to the architectural profession, in a power-knowledge nexus, that turned out to be productive, despite subsequent criticisms? Thirdly, what was the underlying formal, visual, and epistemological basis of the National Style, and how was that related to the earlier historical research, and through that, western traditions in Renaissance and early modern Europe, where methods of visualization played a key role? Knowledge, politics, and form are the three focuses in this study of a key decade of modern China.

In this investigation, some individuals such as Liang Sicheng and Liu Xiufeng will be studied. But a romantic narrative on persons, especially Liang, idolized as a tragic hero in China today, is consciously avoided. The study here concerns a *social* production of ideas and projects, not the success or failure of individuals whose presence are here considered as a joint or a current, though critical, of a social history. Foucault's research is exemplary.[2] He traces a formation of modern systems of knowledge as developed at specific institutional sites across a historical development; at these sites and moments, a cast of "scientific" gaze upon bodies and objects, as in a

DOI: 10.4324/9781315851112-39

panopticon prison devised by Jeremy Bentham, constitutes a key point at which power, knowledge, and visualization are found to be mutually productive. Bentham is important in this study not as a person, but rather as a critical joint in a social history of ideas and institutions. Benedict Anderson's thesis that a "nation" is an imagined community, with creations and inventions, is also a useful guide for a study on twentieth-century efforts of nation building.[3] Nevertheless, his privileging of the European Enlightenment as *the* beginning of modern nationhood is avoided, as China of tenth to thirteenth century (Song dynasty), if not earlier, already had features of modern nationhood, based on various recent studies.[4]

Social and Institutional Change

The People's Republic of China was founded on 1 October 1949. Soon architects were "collectivized" into state-owned design institutes and university departments. They were to follow the leadership of the part and state government in constructing a new nation. They were required to study socialist ideas and to develop a new architecture for the new China. As led by the CCP (Chinese Communist Party), China had just achieved unity and independence (on the mainland) and was engaged in industrialization and socialist transformation. The nation was to become "socialist" and was ideologically opposed to local feudalism and western imperialism, capitalism, and the associated bourgeois culture.

The party waged a few social campaigns. This includes "Land Reform" (1950), "Suppression of Counter-Revolutionaries" (1951–2), various "anti-" movements on corruption and subversive forces (1951–2) in different walks of life, and "Thought Reform" (1951–2) for intellectuals and professionals. In 1953, a "Socialist Transformation" for eradicating private economy was initiated and was completed in 1956. The first Five-Year Plan was announced in 1953, which included the building of 694 industrial projects, hitherto the most ambitious in China. In 1954, State Council was established, together with the National People's Congress and state Ministries. For the architects, they were absorbed into state-owned "design institutes" or national universities around 1952. An "Architectural Society of China" (ASC) was established in 1953, and Zhou Rongxin, a CCP member, was appointed as Director, while Liang Sicheng and Yang Tingbao, the two most respected in the profession in China, were appointed the first and second Associate Directors. In 1954, the Ministry of Construction was established, and the Minister was Liu Xiufeng, while the Deputy Ministers were Wan Li, Zhou Rongxin, and Song Yuhe. Liu, Wan, Zhou, and Song were all CCP members. A vertical relation between the party and the profession was found here, as in other organizations; the professionals, who had studied before 1949, many overseas in capitalist countries and especially the United States, were now expected to study Mao's writings and the ideas of CCP, and to follow the party in a social transformation theorized as progressive.

Among all in the profession, Liang Sicheng is arguably the first person we need to observe closely, as he was in such a prominent position nation-wide in interactions between the party and the profession, as Liang was based in Beijing (while Yang Tingbao and Liu Dunzhen were in Nanjing). Liang studied at the University of Pennsylvania in 1924–7; upon returning to China, he established a department of architecture at the Northeastern University in Shenyang, one of the earliest in China. From 1931 on, he joined Yingzao Xueshe (Society for Research in Chinese Architecture); with Liu Dunzhen and Liang's wife Lin Huiyin, and others, the Society conducted the first "scientific" survey and documentation of ancient Chinese buildings from 1931 to 1944. Upon the conclusion of World War II, Liang became the head of the architectural department at Tsinghua University in 1946; he went to the United States in 1946–7 to lecture at Yale and Princeton and for a joint design of the UN Headquarters in

New York, representing the then Republic of China under KMT (Kuomintang or National-ist Party). In 1949, with the CCP's People's Republic established, Liang, as the head of the department and a member of CPPCC (Chinese People's Political Consultative Conference), was soon heavily involved in a torrential wave of debates on a new architecture for the ris-ing republic. What happened from this point on in Liang's trajectory in the 1950s is what we need to observe. In important ways, Liang is a critical lead for us to understand a *social* production of a tradition of "Chinese architecture" in relation to the task of designing for a new nation.

There are three moments in the 1950s when we can identify intensities in design and design discourse: the early, the middle and the end of the decade (1949–50, 1953–4 and 1958–9 respectively). While the second and third are "peaks" of intensities in theorizing, design, and construction, the first includes iconic projects for the republic just established. At all these moments, historical sources were employed to produce new designs, which requires a closer observation.

First Moment, 1949–50: The Iconic

Given Liang's position, he was involved in projects of the highest national importance, such as the National Emblem and the Monument to the People's Heroes, and the planning of Beijing. For the Emblem, after an invited competition, the design by Liang and his wife Lin, as based at Tsinghua University, won the endorsement of Mao and Premier Zhou Enlai. After refinement the design was finalized and announced in 1950.[5] The design revealed three features required in the brief: representing China, representing a state government, and being formally solemn and splendid. The prominent "Chinese" feature was the use of colors – gold stars in a sky of red – to render a warm and festive splendor.

For the Monument, to be placed at the center of Beijing, Liang was responsible for archi-tectural design (whereas others were responsible for sculptural work and historical narrative). Zhou Enlai, besides other CCP leaders, was heavily involved in the process concerning the height, the site, and the orientation of the monument. The design was finalized in 1952, and the monument was built in 1958. During the design, key issues debated were the typology and the scale. It was argued that a Chinese typology of *bei* was better that the Roman col-umn and Egyptian obelisk, as it had to have Mao's epigraph "Long Live the People's Heroes" inscribed on its surface, and such an epigraph was referred in Chinese as *beiwen* or "inscription upon a *bei*." Yet the Chinese *bei* or memorial tablet was characteristically small, about two to three meters high – "gloomy" and "lacked a heroic spirit" and must be "radically transformed."[6] When completed, the monument stood 37.94 meters in height, at the center of a vast open space, the Tiananmen Square just cleared upon eradication of old walls and laneways. The leap from a *bei* of two to three meters to the new monument at 38 meters was a radical transforma-tion, a spatial revolution in the most literal sense. But it was part of a larger transformation of Beijing in 1959, something we will explore soon.

For the planning of the Chinese capital, Liang was involved and then sidelined, as his proposal of locating the new center outside the imperial hub was not favored. By 1953, a definite plan, known as Changguanlou Plan, was adopted by the central government.[7] It was in fact a plan developed by CCP members acting as planners with Russian Soviet advice. The plan was bold and assertive, not only in locating the new complex at the old center but also in various projections of growth and industrialization, and the spatial dimensions speci-fied as needed for such a projective development (which still turned out to be conservative decades later).

Second Moment, 1954: Theorizing a National Style

At the opening of ASC (Architectural Society of China) in 1953, Liang as the first Deputy Director delivered a speech. In 1954, the official journal of ASC, *Jianzhu Xuebao* (architectural journal, *Xuebao* thereafter) was published under Liang as the editor for its first and second issue, in June and December respectively. As an active participant in the debate on a new architecture for the nation, Liang was a prolific writer on "national styles" and "socialist realism." Yet his writing was unclear, until 1953, after a visit to Moscow early in the year, when he witnessed buildings of classical styles considered as "national" and "socialist-realist" in the Soviet Union. In 1954, we can identify a *culmination* of Liang's writing on National Style and socialist realism in terms of clarity of ideas, quantity of publications, and the scope of issues covered. This intensity of Liang's writing in 1954 also coincided with a peak of construction in the National Style around 1954 and 1955. Among Liang's publications and the two issues of *Xuebao* he edited, all in 1954, we can identify a *tripartite* framework that had clearly emerged.[8] It included three areas: an ideological theory, a historical study of ancient Chinese architecture, and a design methodology. The first argued for a socialist-realist architecture that needed a national tradition for a national style; the second provided scholarly studies to objectify a national tradition; and the third provided a method of employing that national tradition to design a socialist-realist national architecture.

This tripartite framework can be found in the contents of the two issues of *Xuebao*. In the first, for example, there were articles translated from Russian on socialist realism; there was one article by Liang on the indigenous building tradition titled "Characteristics of Chinese Architecture"; there was also an article by Zhang Bo featuring a real project then under construction in Beijing, the Xijiao Guesthouse (known today as Friendship Hotel), which adopted features of Chinese architecture, such as the prominent curved roofs. In the second issue, this three-part structure was repeated.

In Liang's own writings published in 1954, such a tripartite structure is directly manifested. Here we can identify three of his writings published that year, as best representations of his ideas developed then, each covering one of the three areas of this framework. The first was his speech in 1953, published in 1954 in *Xin Jianshe* (new construction), titled "On Socialist Realism in Architectural Art and the Issues of Study and Use of National Heritage."[9] The second was his "Characteristics of Chinese Architecture" in the first issue of *Xuebao* as mentioned earlier.[10] Liang's book printed in 1954 for a small circulation, *A History of Chinese Architecture*, his manuscript of 1944, can also be included as a key text for this second area on history.[11] The third writing, covering the third issue on how to design, was a pamphlet titled *Architecture of Motherland*, which included specific design methods, and two famous sketches of imagined new buildings in the National Style.[12]

It is important to note that the manuscript competed in 1944 was based on the work of Yingzao Xueshe (Society of Research in Chinese Architecture) in the 1930s and early 1940s. Further, the article "Characteristics of Chinese Architecture" was a revised and shortened version of the introduction chapter of the book. This article has identified nine features of the Chinese building tradition and has claimed that this tradition had a "grammar" and a "vocabulary" that can be "translated" into modern buildings. In the pamphlet published in 1954, Liang further articulated that, in this translation, grammar and vocabulary can migrate onto new designs regardless of scale and height; and specific principles and sketches were provided to demonstrate how this may work.

The issues of *Xuebao* in 1954 reveal two other dimensions of practice in China at the time: a geo-political alliance with Russia and the socialist bloc, and an intense "constructivism" – buildings of the National Style were designed and constructed instantly, with many completed around 1955. Apart from a rush to construct and industrialize, a practical reason for instant,

almost simultaneous materialization was a parallel testing of ideas in practice *and* theorization –
theory doesn't predate practice. Many buildings in the National Style were designed before or
during Liang's writing in 1953–4. In fact, the rise of nationalism in design occurred in the early
1950s amid a surge of national pride after 1949. In other words, Liang was not a pioneer or a
pioneering leader of this movement. He was, instead, given his position nation-wide, a leading
theorist, in that he had provided a most comprehensive framework for the National Style.

Third Moment, 1958–9: New Urban Typology

Liang's theorization of the National Style – nicknamed the "big roof" – was criticized in 1955
as wasteful in cost and idealistic in thinking, when Khrushchev criticized Stalin's classical architecture. Later on, there was a gradual distancing of architectural thinking in China from that in
Soviet Russia, and Liang's ideas of the big roof or national forms were re-appreciated, in a larger
framework tolerant of more "styles" in the late 1950s. In September 1958, a project for celebrating the tenth anniversary of the People's Republic was announced. It included the construction
of ten Grand Buildings in Beijing. A nation-wide collaboration soon started, and ten designs
were finalized in a few weeks, followed by instant construction on the ten sites. Two were on
the eastern and western sides of Tiananmen Square, so the grand projects in fact included the
newly expanded square at the center of the Chinese capital. The ten buildings, together with
the square, were all completed in ten months, in late September 1959, ready for the National
Day celebration on 1 October 1959 (Figures 26.1 and 26.2).

Figure 26.1   Cultural Palace of Nationalities, Beijing, 1959. Architect: Zhang Bo.

Source: Photo taken in 2009. © Jianfei Zhu.

Figure 26.2   Tiananmen Square viewed from the southeast, with two of the ten Grand Buildings – Great Hall of the People to the west (left) and Museum of Revolution and History to the east (right), Beijing, 1959. Architect: Zhao Dongri, Zhang Bo, and Zhang Kaiji.

Source: Photo taken after 1977 when Mao's Mausoleum was added to the south. Source: Lu Bingjie, *Tian An Men* (Shanghai: Tongji Daxue Chubanshe, 1999), Fig. 1, p. 16.

Thinking and theorizing in architecture in 1958–9 were closely related to the Grand Buildings. This time, like the planning of Beijing, the party was directly involved. Relevant CCP leaders, eminently Zhou Enlai, Wan Li, and Liu Xiufeng, had all talked about these projects. For the profession, Liang was sidelined as a leading theorist after a few rounds of organized criticism on his ideas of the National Style. Although he joined the CCP in 1959, this didn't change the situation. For theorizing on design, a more collective discussion occurred, under the leadership of the party. This was best represented in an invited symposium. When the designs were settled and the construction was on the way in Beijing, some 30 noted architects across China with relevant CCP leaders attended a conference in Shanghai titled "Housing Standards and the Art of Architecture," from May to June 1959. The speeches of the ten prominent architects were published in the June, July, and August issues of *Xuebao*, starting with that of Liang – a sign of respect.[13] And, finally, the concluding speech by Liu Xiufeng, Minister of Construction, was published in the September–October joint issue of *Xuebao* in 1959, where the newly completed ten buildings and the square were fully featured.

Liu's speech, titled "Creating New Styles for a Chinese Socialist Architecture," was a theoretical treatise on architecture and design, ever written by a state leader in modern China, acting both as an official guide and an academic argument.[14] It was cautious, specific, and carefully balanced with Marxist dialectics. It included well-known ideas expressed by Zhou Enlai and articulated by Wen Li for the grand projects, as well as hidden notions accepted then.

Two such ideas are important. The first was that the big roof was fine and can be employed sometimes, and the national heritage should be critically inherited.[15] The second was that we need to explore more forms and styles, and that, "all excellent ideas, past or present, Chinese or overseas, should be adopted and synthesized, for our use here" (*gujin zhongwai, yiqie jinghua, jianbao bingxu, jiewei woyong*).[16] This is a very Chinese approach that has a great message that should be discussed elsewhere. For the current study, this explained an eclectic collection of formal approaches in the ten buildings: four in the National Style with Chinese roofs, two in western classicism (on the east and west side of the Square), one with a Russian spire, and three in a modern or art-deco style. As pointed out by Zhang Bo, a student of Liang who had designed two of the ten buildings, the underlying ideas of the 1959 theory was still under the sway of Liang's "translation" theory, which treated forms as "styles" to be applied on a modern structure.[17]

The real breakthrough of the 1958–9 moment was an extension of the large scale of single buildings of the mid-1950s to a greater urban dimension in 1959: the breakthrough was the new urban dimension and, with that, the emergence of an urban typology, of straight avenues and a vast square, with monumental buildings around it.[18] The best manifestation was the east–west Chang'an Avenue and Tiananmen Square, with the Monument at the center and the large monumental buildings to the east and west (Figure 26.2). The emergence of the Square, measuring 500 meters east–west and 880 meters north–south, along with the grand objects around it, was a key breakthrough – the moment of a great spatial revolution. The leap from a small *bei* to the Monument, 38 meters high, at the center of the square, was only part of this larger spatial revolution of 1959. The next important breakthrough, to counter-balance the modernity of the heroic objects, was the horizontality of the overall profile in central Beijing, an impact asserted from the vast imperial palace at the north overlooking the new urban typology of the square and the avenue. As noted by Zhao Dongri and Zhang Bo, who designed the Great Hall of the People and the square together, the horizontal stretch of the square, and of the Hall and the Museum to the west and the east, each 40 meters high, as reflected in a height–width ratio of the square in an east–west section at 1/12.5 or 40m/500m, corresponded with the horizontal profile of the imperial palace at the north, where the sky and the horizontal lines predominate.[19] In this way, as noted by Zhao, the square had absorbed a grand "aura" from the vast palace built five centuries earlier.[20]

Back to 1954: Ideology, History, and Design

However, as mentioned, apart from these urban dimensions and a tolerance of more styles, the 1959 theory remained within a frame of the 1954 conceptualization. The National Style still dominated the scene; the various forms were still considered as styles to be translated across; and the ideological framework remained "Chinese," "socialist," and "realist." In addition, Liu's writing was general, whereas Liang's was both diverse and concrete, with clear reference to historical research and modern design. For these reasons, we need to go back to Liang of 1954 for a clearer understanding of the 1950s as a whole.

The key messages of the three areas in the tripartite theory of Liang can be further excavated and distilled (Figure 26.3). In the first area of ideological theorization, Liang followed Mao's idea that art should serve politics and be "realist" (rather than abstract) for a "socialist" construction.[21] The ideological agenda this architecture should serve, following CCP's theory, is two-fold: national independence against imperialism and socialism against capitalism. The formal language of this architecture should be realist in expressing a national tradition, against abstract

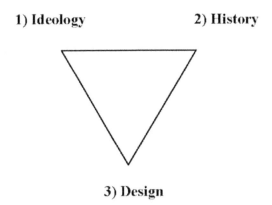

1) Ideology   **2) History**

3) Design

1) 'On Socialist Realism…' (speech 1953, article in *Xin Jianshe*, 2, 1954) + 7 articles (1950-3)

2) 'Characteristics of Chinese Architecture' (*Jianzhu Xuebao*, 1, 1954) + *A History of Chinese Architecture* (book, 1954) + 1 article (*Jianzhu Xuebao*, 2, 1954)

3) *Architecture of Motherland* (with 2 sketches) (pamphlet, 1954)

Figure 26.3   A tripartite framework in Liang's theorization of the National Style in 1954.

Source: Conceived and drawn by author. © Jianfei Zhu.

modernism from the imperialist and capitalist countries. So, architecture in China should adopt "national forms" and be "socialist-realist." Regardless of our ideological views today, there was a critical or progressive agenda in that this architecture supported national liberation and socialist strive for social justice.

In the second area, a historical study of building tradition of China, the article "Characteristics of Chinese Architecture" enlisted nine features, three of which were to do with the curved roofs: the curved profile, the *juzhe* structure within, and the *dougong* bracket sets projecting the roof into space – tectonic aspects of palatial and religious structures, *not* vernacular buildings.[22] This list of nine features was a simplified version of a complex listing of features in the introduction chapter of the manuscript completed in 1944, which in turn was based on massive research of pre-modern buildings across China in the 1930s–40s by the research society (Yingzao Xueshe) headed by Liang and Liu Dunzhen.[23] In other words, a rich and complex body of knowledge was now, in 1954, under the pressure of the time, compressed into a succinct list of nine prominent features, so that the so-called Chinese national tradition could be identified, objectified, and employed. At this moment, a system was constructed, and a tradition was *invented*. The process was selective and had privileged temples and palaces of northern China, including that in Ming–Qing Beijing (1420–1911).

In the third area of design, Liang followed Mao's idea that tradition should be critically inherited and that we should "discard feudalist garbage and absorb democratic essences," democratic being people's.[24] So, the imperial palace had a class content that must be discarded, but it also had beautiful formal features loved by the people – profile, structure, proportion, color – which should be inherited. In this Maoist critical transformation, as understood in Liang, the *imperial* became the *national* that belonged to *the people*. For design, the question is how to inherit the Chinese tradition critically and selectively. At this point, Liang provided two principles. Firstly, traditional forms can be translated onto modern buildings regardless of size and height; secondly, in this translation, overall silhouettes are most important and proportion is important as well, whereas decorative details are less important. Liang then supplied two sketches of imagined new buildings, to illustrate what a new Chinese architecture might look like following his principles. One depicts a horizontal block three- to five-stories high, the other a tower of 35 stories. They were pencil sketches with light watercolor rendering, set in a perspective, with shades and shadows or chiaroscuro, which rendered the buildings solid, massive, and monumental, as objects in open space.

Liang himself may not be aware that there was such a neat triangular framework, yet all ideas and relations between and across this triangle were there by 1954. This is arguably the most important framework for understanding design thinking in China of the 1950s. With this triangle, many events, ideas, and interrelations, within or around this structure and the year it appeared, can be identified and their importance appreciated. For example, Liang's visit to Moscow in 1953 was critical in clarifying for Liang the actual meaning of national style and socialist realism (historical relations from 1953 to 1954). Mao's writings (1940s), and the associated ideas from Stalin and the Soviet Union (1930s–40s), as cited in Liang in 1953–4, were important, concerning the relation between art and politics, and critical inheritance of tradition (internal issues of the first area). The relation between historiography and creative design, the second and third area in the structure, was critical as well in supplying historical knowledge for creative design. Further, the design of the National Style of the 1950s seems to have a relation to not only historical research of the 1930s–40s but also formal design of the 1930s in Nanjing when architecture of "Native Chinese Form" was called upon and experimented with, with which Liang was also involved (relations from 1930s to 1954).

With this triangle of 1954, we can speculate that the source of ideas for the National Style of the 1950s was three-fold. Firstly, Mao's ideas that art must serve society and politics, and tradition must be critically inherited, as explained in his "Talks at the Yan'an Forum on Literature and Art" (1942) and "On New Democracy" (1940).[25] Secondly, Stalinist classicism in concrete examples and theoretical discourse of socialist realism (up to 1954, before Khrushchev criticized Stalin in late 1954). And, finally, American-European influences in design and historical research that can be traced back to the 1930s when a new Chinese architecture was explored in design and when historical research was conducted, by Chinese graduates trained mostly in the United States in the 1920s in a Beaux-Arts program. This program in turn, can be traced back to classical France (before and after 1789) and further back to Renaissance Italy. All these sources of influence – Mao, Stalin, the 1930s design in Nanjing, the Beaux-Arts classicism imported from the States – are already known in the academic circles in China today. The exception, and arguably a deeper line of influence, is the connection from creative design back to historical research of the 1930s, and further back to classical France and Italian Renaissance, where a way of seeing was imported, reaching fruition in China in 1944 and then 1954, before leaping onto a creative surface for imagining new buildings in Beijing. This deserves a closer look.

Vision and Form: Importing Objects and Modernity

The research on ancient buildings, carried out by the Yingzao Xueshe society, and academically led by Liang and Liu Dunzhen from 1931 to 1944, included a systematic visual documentation of these buildings surveyed, studied, and compared in a "scientific" manner.[26] The documentation adopted graphic techniques originating in post-Renaissance and early modern Europe. Various sources suggest that Liang's work in 1944 followed Banister Fletcher's *History of Architecture* of 1901,[27] and that in turn followed J-N-L Durand's work on "world architecture" of 1801–9.[28] As collected in the 1944 manuscript, the visualizing techniques included chiaroscuro, perspective, orthogonal projection, and universal comparison (of plans and formal types across sites and times). The actual representations included *single* buildings in photos, watercolors, and line drawings (plans, sections, and elevations), and sets of *many* buildings in line drawings at one scale for cross-comparison. From describing single buildings to re-grouping them on abstract platforms for universal comparisons, the Chinese buildings were increasingly isolated, purified, and objectified. The shades and shadows, the precise line drawings, the Chinese and English notations written on the plates, and the four-line borders framing these plates have all contributed to the making of a new perspective and a new space of knowledge (Figure 26.4). These 70 visual representations completed by 1944 had constructed a new gaze and a pure and abstract space of modern knowledge of ancient Chinese structures, now considered as isolated and purified objects.[29]

Erwin Panofsky has made it clear in his *Perspective as Symbolic Form* (1997) that linear perspective, or for that matter a whole set of visual techniques developed with the perspective after the Renaissance, carries with it not just a scientific way of seeing, but also a culturally specific or a "symbolic form" of seeing and knowing.[30] This "symbolic" way of seeing assumed a cone of visual rays casting, from a fixed eye, through a window, upon the world – a monocular capturing of things standing still at a disembodied distance. It enacted a Cartesian split or disembodiment, separating the realms of subject and object, turning bodies into objects. In other words, the historical research of Liang and others in the research society of the 1930s was not just "scientific," but was in fact culturally and epistemologically specific, with a new perspective and its "bias": a dualistic Cartesianism that disembodies things into pure objects. It is a re-reading and re-representation to the modern mind of a tradition known and practiced for centuries in another paradigm.

In other words, the scientific historical research (1931–44) was also a *creative* cultural practice, in the sense that a new perspective was projected upon a field of things, and with this, a new way of seeing and understanding this field was achieved, in which these things turned out to be something else – pure objects in a universal open space. When this was achieved in 1944, and made to reappear in 1954, the next leap onto a creative surface of imagination, for a new architecture as monumental objects in 1954, can be followed (Figure 26.5). The process from the 1930s to the 1950s, from historical research to creative design, was closely related: it all involved a gaze, an act of seeing to search for things as objects, an act of seeing that also desires new buildings as objects.

The rise of modern buildings in Beijing as monumental objects was surely to do with other practical factors (the scales of function, structure, production). But this frame of seeing offered a visual and symbolic methodology that facilitated and justified the arrival of heroic objects. In addition, this new way of seeing things as objects in architecture should also be considered as part of a generic importation of western modernity in China in art, science, and industrialization, where, for example, realism in fine art, as led by Xu Beihong and others, had also played a central role in forming a visual culture of modern China.[31]

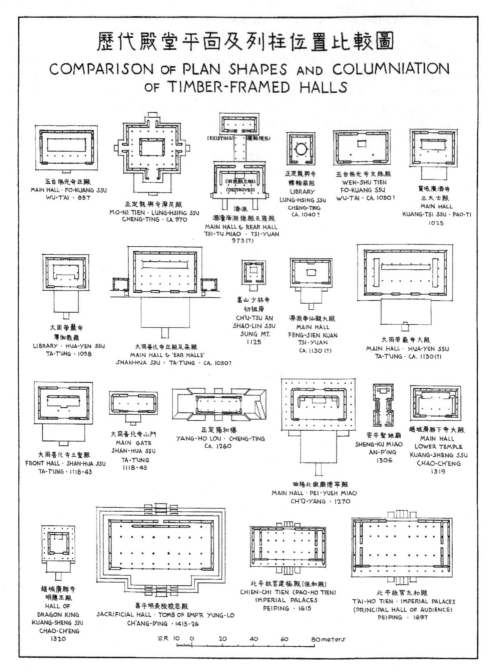

图21 历代殿堂平面及列柱位置比较图

21 Comparison of plan and columniation of timber-frame halls

Figure 26.4 Documentation of ancient Chinese buildings by Liang and others of the Yingzao Xueshe research society completed by 1944.

Source: Liang Sicheng, *Liang Sicheng Quanji*, vol. 4 (Beijing: Zhongguo Jianzhu Gongye Chubanshe, 2001), p. 219. By permission of Lin Zhu.

Figure 26.5 Imagining a new Chinese architecture: one of the two sketches by Liang in 1954.

Source: Liang Sicheng, *Liang Sicheng Quanji*, vol. 5 (Beijing: Zhongguo Jianzhu Gongye Chubanshe, 2001), p. 233. By permission of Lin Zhu.

Conclusion: The 1950s as Foundational

In the 1950s, there was a party–profession interaction as well as a history–design relationship. In the first, a vertical relation was established where state authority with its ideology directed the work of the profession, in a power–knowledge dynamic that was "productive" of each other, as Foucault has theorized elsewhere. The professional discourse on tradition and design would not be so produced without the pressure from the party and state government; the party-led state, on the other hand, would not be visually, formally, and spatially manifested and materialized without the design service and academic discourse provided by the profession. This power–knowledge relation had in fact traversed several realms here: authority, ideology, historical knowledge, design creativity, form, visualization, and epistemology.

Within the work of the profession is the second, a "horizontal" relationship, between history and design. Here a body of historical knowledge was compressed into a concise system, under political pressure and a practical need to identify a unified tradition and to create a new national architecture. In the process, a tradition of "Chinese architecture" was created. This in turn facilitated the creation of a new Chinese architecture, much larger in scale and more as an object in the urban context, but nevertheless having retained some Chinese features, such as the roof and an urban horizontality.

In this process, there was a *selective* reading of the tradition in which northern and socially superior ancient architecture (palaces and temples) were privileged to represent a diverse field of practices. In this process, there was also a *political* transformation of the meaning of this major tradition: imperial architecture was re-appreciated as a national tradition now belonging to the people in socialist China, through a Maoist "critical inheritance" of the past. In this context, this new architecture was also *progressive* as it supported national and social liberation.

Further, in studying, summarizing, and employing the tradition, from the 1930s to the 1950s, there was an act of *objectification*, aided by the lens adopted from the west; this new way of seeing was then transferred onto a creative surface and facilitated the design of modern Chinese buildings as objects and monuments, as manifested in Liang's sketches, the massive buildings of the mid-1950s, and the greater urban typology of the Grand Buildings with the Avenue and the Square.

The mode of design practice was also very special, in three ways. Firstly, the profession followed the ideological and moral leadership of the party and state government; secondly, all in the profession worked in a collectivist way, in state-owned design institutes, and a few at university departments, with collaborations within and across; thirdly, there was often an urgent need to design and construct immediately with a "constructivist" dynamic. Though they appear communist or Maoist, as found in the 1950s, 1960s, and 1970s, when we include pre- and post-Mao periods, that is, the 1930s and 1990s and after 2000, these patterns, to a varying degree, still survive. In the 1930s, architects worked in private offices, but they also followed the moral and ideological call of the state for a Chinese architecture; in current China after 1990 or 2000, moral leadership of the state, collaborative ethics in design across it, and a "constructivism," remain characteristic. So, the design practice of the 1950s, although more political, is representative, and foundational for China thereafter.

To summarize, the decade laid down a base for the discipline and the profession of architecture of modern China. A body of knowledge on the national tradition was established with a selective and political reading and a process of objectification, which had shaped later understandings leading also to criticism and modifications. A mode of design practice was also established, which remains characteristic today: a history–design connection, a search for national and cultural expressions in design, a leadership of the state, a relational and collaborative ethics, and a "constructivism" for instant materialization.

Notes

1 This chapter is a revised and developed version of Chapter 4 published in my *Architecture of Modern China: A Historical Critique* (London: Routledge, 2009), 75–104. Permission and courtesy of Routledge.
2 Michel Foucault, *Discipline and Punish: The Birth of the Prison*, trans. Alan Sheridan (London: Penguin, 1977), 195–228.
3 Benedict Anderson, *Imagined Communities* (London: Verso, 1983), 1–7.
4 Francis Fukuyama, *The Origins of Political Order: From Prehuman Times to the French Revolution* (London: Profile, 2012), 19–21, 128–138, 147–150, 291–295.
5 Qin Youguo, "Liang Sicheng, Lin Huiyin yu guohui sheji (Liang Sicheng, Lin Huiyin and the design for the national emblem)," in *Liang Sicheng Xiansheng Baisui Danchen Wenji* (A collection of essays at the 100th birthday of Liang Sicheng), ed. Editorial Committee (Beijing: Qinghua Daxue Chubanshe, 2001), 111–119.
6 Liang Sicheng, "Renmin yingxiong jinianbei sheji jingguo (An account of how the Monument to the People's Heroes was designed)," in *Liang Sicheng Quanji* (Complete works of Liang Sicheng), vol. 5, Liang Sicheng (Beijing: Zhongguo Jianzhu Gongye Chubanshe, 2001), 462–464.
7 Dong Guangqi, *Beijing Guihua Zhanlue Sikao* (Reflective studies on Beijing's planning strategies), (Beijing: Zhongguo Jianzhu Gongye Chubanshe, 1998), 313–323.
8 This was first identified in Zhu, *Architecture*, 84–86.

9 Liang Sicheng, "Jianzhu yishuzhong shehuizhuyi xianshizhuyi he minzu yichan de xuexi yu yuanyong de wenti (On socialist realism in architectural art and the study and use of national heritage)," in *Liang*, vol. 5, Liang, 185–196.

10 Liang Sicheng, "Zhongguo jianzhu de tezheng (Characteristics of Chinese architecture)," *Jianzhu Xuebao* 1 (1954): 36–39.

11 Liang Sicheng, "Zhongguo jianzhu shi (A history of Chinese architecture)," in *Liang Sicheng Quanji* (Complete works of Liang Sicheng), vol. 4, Liang Sicheng (Beijing: Zhongguo Jianzhu Gongye Chubanshe, 2001), 1–222.

12 Liang Sicheng, "Zuguo de jianzhu (Architecture of motherland)," in *Liang*, vol. 5, Liang, 197–234.

13 The ten architects were, in the order of appearance, Liang Sicheng, Liu Dunzhen, Ha xiongwen, Chen Zhi, Zhao Shen, Wu Liangyong, Wan Tan, Dai Fudong, Jin Oufu, and Chen Boqi.

14 Liu Xiufeng, "Chuangzao zhongguo de shehui zhuyi de jianzhu xin fengge (Creating new styles for a Chinese socialist architecture)," *Jianzhu Xuebao* 9–10 (1959): 3–12.

15 Liu, "Chuangzao," 9.

16 Liu, "Chuangzao," 10; and Zhang Bo, *Wode Jianzhu Chuangzuo Daolu* (My life-long journey in architectural design) (Beijing: Zhongguo Jianzhu Gongye Chubanshe, 1994), 157.

17 Zhang, *Wode*, 150–151, 156–157.

18 Zhu, *Architecture*, 96–99.

19 Zhang, *Wode*, 154, 177, 179; and Zhao Dongri, "Tiananmen Guanchang (The Tiananmen Square)," *Jianzhu Xuebao* 9–10 (1959): 18–22.

20 Zhao, "Tiananmen," 21.

21 Liang, "Jianzhu yishuzhong shehuizhuyi xianshizhuyi (On Socialist Realism)," 185–196.

22 Liang, "Zhongguo jianzhe de tezheng (Characteristics)," 36–39.

23 Liang, "Zhongguo jianzhu shi (A History)," 1–222.

24 Liang, "Zuguo de jianzhu (Architecture of Motherland)," 228–229, 233–234.

25 Mao Zedong, "Zai Yanan wenyi zuotanhui shang de jianghua (Talks at the Yan'an Forum on literature and art)," "Xin minzhu zhuyi lun (On new democracy)," in *Mao Zedong Xuanji* (Selected works of Mao Zedong), vol. 3, vol. 2, Mao Zedong (Beijing: Renmin Chubanshe, 1970), 804–835, 623–670.

26 Liang, "Zhongguo jianzhu shi (A history)," 1–222.

27 Liang Sicheng, "Liang Sicheng de fayan (Liang Sicheng's talk)," *Jianzhu Xuebao* 11 (1958): 6–7; and Lin Zhu, *Koukai Luban de damen: Zhongguo yingzao xueshe shilue* (Opening a door to the world of Lu Ban: A brief history of the Society for Research in Chinese Architecture) (Beijing: Zhongguo Jianzhu Gongye Chubanshe, 1995), 32–33.

28 David Watkin, *The Rise of Architectural History* (London: The Architectural Press, 1980), 23–24, 85–86.

29 These included 70 renderings and line drawings, and a larger collection of photos, completed by 1944, making their appearance in the 1955 book in Chinese and, as a simplified version, in 1984 in English: *A Pictorial History of Chinese Architecture* by the MIT Press.

30 Erwin Panofsky, *Perspective as Symbolic Form*, trans. Christopher S. Wood (New York: Zone Books, 1997); see also Martin Jay, "Scopic Regimes of Modernity," in *Vision and Visuality*, ed. Hal Foster (Seattle: Bay Press, 1988), 3–23.

31 Zhu, *Architecture*, 34–40; also Zou Yuejin, *Xin Zhongguo Meishu Shi: A History of Chinese Fine Arts, 1949–2000* (Changsha: Hunan Meishu Chubanshe, 2002), 1–15, 35–67.

Bibliography

Anderson, Benedict. *Imagined Communities*. London: Verso, 1983.

Dong Guangqi. *Beijing Guihua Zhanlue Sikao* (Reflective Studies on Beijing's Planning Strategies). Beijing: Zhongguo Jianzhu Gongye Chubanshe, 1998.

Editorial Committee, ed. *Liang Sicheng Xiansheng Baisui Danchen Wenji* (A Collection of Essays at the 100th Birthday of Liang Sicheng). Beijing: Qinghua Daxue Chubanshe, 2001.

Foster, Hal, ed. *Vision and Visuality*. Seattle: Bay Press, 1988.

Foucault, Michel. *Discipline and Punish: The Birth of the Prison*. Translated by Alan Sheridan. London: Penguin, 1977.

Fukuyama, Francis. *The Origins of Political Order: From Prehuman Times to the French Revolution*. London: Profile, 2012.

Jay, Martin. "Scopic Regimes of Modernity." In *Vision and Visuality*, edited by Hal Foster, 3–23. Seattle: Bay Press, 1988.

Liang Sicheng. "Zhongguo jianzhu de tezheng (Characteristics of Chinese Architecture)." *Jianzhu Xuebao* 1 (1954): 36–39.

———. "Liang Sicheng de fayan (Liang Sicheng's Talk)." *Jianzhu Xuebao* 11 (1958): 6–7.

———. "Jianzhu yishuzhong shehuizhuyi xianshizhuyi he minzu yichan de xuexi yu yuanyong de wenti (On Socialist Realism in Architectural Art and the Study and Use of National Heritage)." In *Liang Sicheng Quanji* (Complete Works of Liang Sicheng), edited by Liang Sicheng, vol. 5, 185–196. Beijing: Zhongguo Jianzhu Gongye Chubanshe, 2001.

———. "Renmin yingxiong jinianbei sheji jingguo (An Account of How the Monument to the People's Heroes Was Designed)." In *Liang Sicheng Quanji* (Complete Works of Liang Sicheng), edited by Liang Sicheng, vol. 5, 462–464. Beijing: Zhongguo Jianzhu Gongye Chubanshe, 2001.

———. "Zhongguo jianzhu shi (A History of Chinese Architecture)." In *Liang Sicheng Quanji* (Complete Works of Liang Sicheng), edited by Liang Sicheng, vol. 4, 1–222. Beijing: Zhongguo Jianzhu Gongye Chubanshe, 2001.

———. "Zuguo de jianzhu (Architecture of Motherland)." In *Liang Sicheng Quanji* (Complete Works of Liang Sicheng), edited by Liang Sicheng, vol. 5, 197–234. Beijing: Zhongguo Jianzhu Gongye Chubanshe, 2001.

———. *Liang Sicheng Quanji* (Complete Works of Liang Sicheng), vol. 4–5. Beijing: Zhongguo Jianzhu Gongye Chubanshe, 2001.

Liang, Ssu-Ch'eng. *A Pictorial History of Chinese Architecture*. Cambridge, MA: MIT Press, 1984.

Lin Zhu. *Koukai Luban de damen: zhongguo yingzao xueshe shilue* (Opening a Door to the World of Lu Ban: A Brief History of the Society for Research in Chinese Architecture). Beijing: Zhongguo Jianzhu Gongye Chubanshe, 1995.

Liu Xiufeng. "Chuangzao zhongguo de shehui zhuyi de jianzhu xin fengge (Creating New Styles for a Chinese Socialist Architecture)." *Jianzhu Xuebao* 9–10 (1959): 3–12.

Mao Zedong. *Mao Zedong Xuanji* (Selected Works of Mao Zedong), vol. 2–3. Beijing: Renmin Chubanshe, 1970.

———. "Xin minzhu zhuyi lun (On New Democracy)." In *Mao Zedong Xuanji* (Selected Works of Mao Zedong), edited by Mao Zedong, vol. 2, 623–670. Beijing: Renmin Chubanshe, 1970.

———. "Zai Yanan wenyi zuotanhui shang de jianghua (Talks at the Yan'an Forum on Literature and Art)." In *Mao Zedong Xuanji* (Selected Works of Mao Zedong), edited by Mao Zedong, vol. 3, 804–835. Beijing: Renmin Chubanshe, 1970.

Panofsky, Erwin. *Perspective as Symbolic Form*. Translated by Christopher S. Wood. New York: Zone Books, 1997.

Qin Youguo. "Liang Sicheng, Lin Huiyin yu guohui sheji (Liang Sicheng, Lin Huiyin and the Design for the National Emblem)." In *Liang Sicheng Xiansheng Baisui Danchen Wenji* (A collection of Essays at the 100th Birthday of Liang Sicheng), edited by Editorial Committee, 111–119. Beijing: Qinghua Daxue Chubanshe, 2001.

Watkin, David. *The Rise of Architectural History*. London: The Architectural Press, 1980.

Zhang Bo. *Wode Jianzhu Chuangzuo Daolu* (My Life-Long Journey in Architectural Design). Beijing: Zhongguo Jianzhu Gongye Chubanshe, 1994.

Zhao Dongri. "Tiananmen Guanchang (The Tiananmen Square)." *Jianzhu Xuebao* 9–10 (1959): 18–22.

Zhu, Jianfei. *Architecture of Modern China: A Historical Critique*. London: Routledge, 2009.

Zou Yuejin. *Xin Zhongguo Meishu Shi: A History of Chinese Fine Arts, 1949–2000*. Changsha: Hunan Meishu Chubanshe, 2002.

Glossary

bei	碑
Beijing	北京
beiwen	碑文
Chang'an (avenue)	长安（街）
Changguanlou	畅观楼
dougong	斗拱

gujin zhongwai	古今中外
jianbao bingxu	含包并蓄
Jianzhu Xuebao	建筑学报
jiewei woyong	皆为我用
juzhe	举折
Kuomintang (Guomindang)	国民党
Liang Sicheng	梁思成
Lin Huiyin	林徽因
Liu Dunzhen	刘敦桢
Liu Xiufeng	刘秀峰
Mao (Zedong)	毛（泽东）
Shanghai	上海
Shenyang	沈阳
Song Yuhe	宋裕和
Tiananmen (square)	天安门（广场）
Tsinghua (university)	清华（大学）
Wan Li	万里
Xijiao (guesthouse)	西郊（宾馆）
Xin Jianshe	新建设
Xu Beihong	徐悲鸿
Xuebao	学报
Yan'an (forum)	延安（文艺座谈会）
Yang Tingbao	杨廷宝
Yingzao Xueshe	营造学社
yiqie jinghua	一切精华
Zhang Bo	张镈
Zhang Kaiji	张开济
Zhao Dongri	赵冬日
Zhou Enlai	周恩来
Zhou Rongxin	周荣鑫

27

TOWARDS A REGIONAL MODERNISM IN CHINESE ARCHITECTURE (1930s–70s)

Eduard Kögel

This chapter examines different approaches to regional modernism in China. I will use the case of the architects Xi Fuquan (1902–1983), Hsia Changshi (1903–1996),[1] Feng Jizhong (1915–2009), and Shang Kuo (1927), who searched for an architecture based in function, climate, and, last but not least, structural features of regional building traditions. The timeframe for the study covers roughly 50 years from the 1930s to the 1980s. In this period, the named architects consciously searched for a regional logic in architectural heritage with the hope that they could continue a building tradition without mimicry of styles. Despite some similarities in the architectural concepts and in their dealings with formal problems, they did not form a group or movement but rather searched individually for new forms of expression.

The proclamation of the People's Republic of China on 1 October 1949 by Mao Zedong in Beijing had a tremendous effect on the practice of architects and planners. However, the changes came slowly, and it took several years to streamline the architectural vocabulary in the various regions of the huge country. Whereas the Soviet advisers became strongest in the then new capital Beijing, the architects in Shanghai and in Guangzhou continued with their conceptions as before. In Beijing, architecture and urban planning came under the strict surveillance of the Communist Party, and the architects created a socialist model with "Soviet" characteristics. I examine here the above-named architects who searched for unique solutions far beyond the political demands. Their legacy is an important contribution to the establishment of a sustainable architecture, long before this term was used in such a context. The examples discussed here testify that these architects used their knowledge, learned in European institutions but embedded it in the local culture, basing it on the analyses of regional factors, economic possibilities, and societal demand. The analyses of function in traditional architecture without pictorial reference led to unique expressions, which can even today serve as references for an adaptive architecture. But the named architects and their production also illustrate that Chinese architects worked throughout the last century – against great odds – on a renewal of architectural tradition based on adaptive technology, spatial continuation, and narrative expressions.

Xi Fuquan: First Challenge

The development of a locally motivated modern architecture in China has its roots in the 1930s, when the first architects returned from their education in Europe. In contrast to the

DOI: 10.4324/9781315851112-40

first generation of architects educated in the USA and exposed to the American version of a Beaux-Arts curriculum,[2] some of the returnees from Europe brought with them fresh ideas picked up from the discourse stimulated by the Modern Movement or such institutions as the Bauhaus in Germany. One of them was Xi Fuquan (until 1949 he used the name Fozhien Godfrey Ede), who studied architecture at the Technische Hochschule Darmstadt in Germany, where he graduated as Diplom-Ingenieur in 1926, before he continued his studies in Chinese architectural history under the supervision of the Berlin-based architectural researcher Ernst Boerschmann, with a doctoral thesis about the design of the Qing Dynasty tombs in Beijing in 1929.[3] Boerschmann was an expert in the history of Chinese architecture and taught at the Technische Hochschule Berlin. As Boerschmann's doctoral student, Xi learned about the importance of Chinese architectural history, but as an architect he understood the discourse around the Modern Movement in Germany during his stay between 1922 and 1930. These were the formative years for the avant-garde with the Bauhaus as a leading institution. Examples like the Weissenhof Estate in Stuttgart or the new social housing estates in Berlin by architects such as Mies van der Rohe, Walter Gropius, or Bruno Taut were discussed in public and expert circles. The discourse in Germany left a deep impression on the thinking of Xi Fuquan, which is proved not only by his architectural projects in Shanghai but also in his written statement about the need for modernization in Chinese architecture. The paper was published in the late 1920s and gives a clear understanding of his mission. Xi argues for a radical modern approach in order to catch up with the development in Western countries.

> My ancestors owned junks, donkey carts and oil lamps. Why do I give up the junk for the steamboat, why do I leave the cart and use the automobile, why do I take electric light instead of the miserable oil lamp – though all of those achievements come from Europe? I do not use them because they come from Europe, but because they are better than the things handed down by the ancestors. Cars, motorboats and electric bulbs are obviously a change for the better and also a progress; and also the house I will live in, in the future, is it not better and more progressive?[4]

He argues that although many buildings in China had recently been erected in the Western style,

> only the exterior style was copied, the real meaning was ignored: sometimes half Chinese, half Western, sometimes neither Chinese nor Western. It is the same as if one would install a motor into a donkey cart or use sails on the steamboat. It is not perfect in form or function, it will even lag behind the old solution.[5]

It is a clear argument for a focus on a functional and contemporary solution that should be based in the Chinese culture but furnished with all possibilities of technical progress. Since China did not yet have any university courses for architects, Xi was sure that "the success will not come over-night, but in a few decades, we will see it in retrospect."[6]

His own work reflects the attitude discussed in the article published before he returned home and opened an office in Shanghai.[7] In one of his first works, the Hongqiao Sanatorium or Convalescent Hospital (1934), Xi Fuquan adapted principles learned from the German architect Richard Döcker, to accomplish an adaptive architecture that reacts to the function, climate, and economy. The function of a modern tuberculosis hospital had to reflect the need of the patients for fresh air and sun. Between 1926 and 1928, Stuttgart-based architect Richard Döcker had built a terraced hospital in Waiblingen. Two years later he published a book on the topic of terraced building typologies, in which about half of the examples focused especially on hospitals.[8] The healing potential of the sun and the UV radiation were precisely described and Döcker published schematic sectional drawings to illustrate the terraced building typology and how it should function in the course of the year. He analyzed the sun exposure, the terraces, the shading devices, and the glazed opening of the façade (Figure 27.1).

When Xi Fuquan designed the Hongqiao Sanatorium, he did it in great awareness of Döcker's work. The only wing of the four-story building with about 100 beds was terraced; the glazed windows and doors to the terraces were covered with horizontal shading devices placed on the wall panels, which separated the terraces for hygienic reasons. Above the shading device a small window allowed the sun to enter the patients' rooms and provided ventilation. The radical functional design resisted the use of aesthetic elements from Chinese tradition. The sub-division of the big floor-to-ceiling window in the lobby followed an irregular pattern as found in traditional Chinese shelves or in the radical geometric compositions of the Dutch artist Piet Mondrian. The double layers of reference and the functional requirement led to a building that was truly based in modern principles but integrated local climatic and cultural requirements into the detail of the final design.[9] In the field of functional requirement for hospitals, no reference to traditional Chinese examples was possible, since new knowledge and medical insights

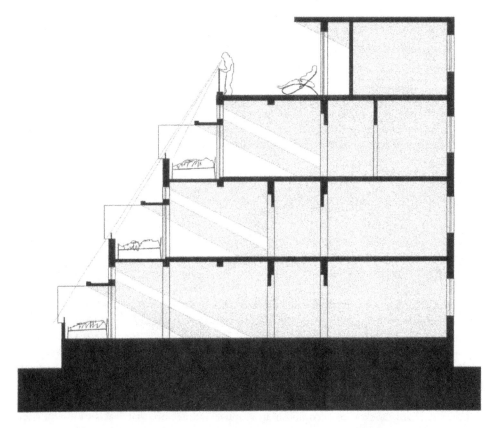

Figure 27.1 Sectional drawing of the Hongqiao Sanatorium designed by Xi Fuquan in 1933 with stepped terraces and shading device across the separating walls.

Source: © Eduard Kögel.

called for new design ideas. Xi Fuquan used his experience from Germany and searched for solutions that fitted in the local environment. As expressed in his statement, he opposed integrating a "motor" into a Chinese pavilion and he opposed a stylistically European architecture, which was en vogue in Shanghai in those years.[10]

Hsia Changshi: Response to the Climate

With the end of the Second Sino-Japanese War in 1945, Hsia Changshi returned from the war capital Chongqing to his hometown Guangzhou in Southern China, where he served as professor at Zhongshan University.[11] He had studied in the German cities of Karlsruhe and Tübingen. In Karlsruhe he got a degree as Diplom-Ingenieur in architecture in 1928 and in Tübingen he received a doctoral degree in art history with a focus on architectural history.[12] After his return to China, in 1934 he accompanied German architectural historian Ernst Boerschmann on a trip through the central provinces, visiting and documenting ancient temples.[13] Like Xi Fuquan, he had a profound knowledge of Chinese architectural history and the role it could play in the renewal of architectural concepts. During the war-years he worked in Shanghai, Kunming, and Chongqing. Back in his hometown Guangzhou after the war, Hsia investigated local building tradition and garden culture.[14]

The traditional Lingnan architectural style refers to the region of Guangzhou. It consists of stones, bricks, and tiles wrapped around the outside of a wooden framework. Lingnan style impresses with its dignity and heaviness. In the 1950s and 1960s architects like Hsia Changshi, Mo Bozhi, and Chen Boqi adapted technology and design to the local climate and developed new methods for sun-shading, insulation, and ventilation. Hsia Changshi analyzed the spirit of Chinese landscape architecture and created his own architectural language with a strong focus on climate-responsive issues.[15]

Before Hsia returned to China in 1932, he worked briefly in the office of Le Corbusier in Paris and learned about the development of the brise-soleil for buildings in tropical zones.[16] It took until the 1950s for Hsia to receive commissions in Guangzhou for institutional buildings at the university, where he applied a façade-system in tune with the ideas of Le Corbusier.[17] He experimented with shading devices and double roof structures in the search for a contemporary regional architecture that responded to the local climate and economy. But his first major building in 1951, the Pavilion for Aquatic Products from Lingnan Region in Guangzhou, had such an independent poetic narrative that party members soon criticized it as "boxes and columbaries of American or Hong Kong style" and "streamlines of notorious capitalism characters."[18] The circular floor plan with complex circulation was complemented by an abstracted concrete boat topped by a mast and placed at the corner of the pond in front of the pavilion. Despite the pictorial expression, the pavilion represents rational principles and adapted the climatic condition of the subtropics.

In the following years, Hsia further investigated the possibilities of climate-adaptive responses in contemporary architecture. The façade for the 1953 Biochemical Institute at Zhongshan University in Guangzhou shows best the discourse and first solutions. The institute is organized on a simple floor plan with the main staircase at the west and a secondary staircase at the east end of the rectangular volume. The main entrance at the west was located at ground floor level, whereas the entrance for the secondary staircase was one story below at the level of the basement. The whole ground floor was occupied by one open-plan laboratory. On the upper levels, a middle corridor gave access to a row of offices towards north and south. The façade on the ground floor was fully glazed with only the load-bearing columns between the windows. The floors above had a different, much smaller window format. The openings were designed

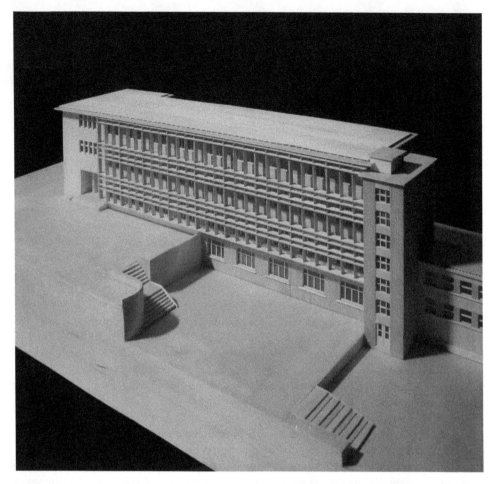

Figure 27.2 Model of the Biochemical Institute in Guangzhou designed by Hsia Changshi in 1953. The concrete brise-soleil builds an independent system in front of the façade.

Source: © Eduard Kögel.

according to function and need. However, on the south side an almost independent concrete brise-soleil system overlaid the façade and served in a functional way the shading of the skin of the building. The composition of horizontal and vertical plates worked independently from the façade and gave the institute a radical modern expression (Figure 27.2). With the concrete structural overlay, the conventional skin of the building was given a rational rhythm, which rewrote all acceptable standards of the state-controlled aesthetics. A second element introduced in Hsia's designs is the vault-construction for a double roof with cross-ventilation. It consists of brick vaults with repetitive character, which are responsible for the appearance of the roof. With these measurements, Hsia tried to reduce the climatic impact on the buildings and hoped for a new expression of regional characteristics in architecture. He interpreted the big roof with large overhangs in traditional architecture as a device against the impact of direct sun penetration. With his double roof structure with cross-ventilation and the concrete brise-soleil on the south façade, Hsia Changshi tried to renew the form and optimize the function for multistory buildings created with new materials.

Shang Kuo: Poetry With Local Flavor

In contrast to the other architects discussed here, Shang Kuo was not educated abroad but graduated in 1957 from Tianjin University. Afterwards he worked for several years at the Research Institute of Building Science at the Ministry of Construction (1957–1965) in Beijing, before he continued as an architect at the Design Institute in Guilin.[19]

During the period when Shang Kuo worked at the Ministry of Construction, he investigated native dwellings in Zhejiang province. With great care and many detailed drawings, Shang not only documented the traditional heritage, but also searched for elements to solve contemporary problems. The result of the study was presented at an international conference in 1964 in Beijing. In the published paper one reads:

> It is a task of significance for us, architects, to investigate and study seriously our traditional vernacular dwellings, and to assimilate the positive factors therein which are of any service for today's living requirements, so that we can create houses which are more suitable to our living customs, more fit to be built with local material and more in tune with the taste of the general public.[20]

However, the more important part of Shang's professional life came with the design of tourist infrastructure in the 1970s in Guilin. The monsoon-influenced subtropical climate of the region, with its unique scenery of karst topography and conical mountains, rapidly turned the city into one of China's most popular tourist destinations. In the characteristic environment of picturesque mountains with age-old caves and historic cultural references, Shang Kuo developed a unique style by using aspects of traditional design in a new way.

The Reed Flute Cave in the northeast of the city near the Peach Blossom River needed facilities such as a restaurant, pavilion, entrance building, teahouse, bridge, covered walkways, and a parking lot for the tourist coaches. In front of the cave was a small lake, which Shang Kuo used in the orchestration of the different buildings in the scenic landscape around a circular pathway for the visitors: from the parking lot via the entrance building on an upward path to the two-story entrance pavilion at the Reed Flute Cave. The visitors entered at the upper level and returned on the lower level of the open pavilion. From there a footbridge led the people across a valley towards a neighboring conic karst mountain with a teahouse on its slope. Then the path again descended towards the lake and passed a pavilion floating on the water. A zigzag bridge led across the lake to a peninsula with a further pavilion in front of the parking lot. The loop road for the visitors emphasized the particularities of the scenic area in a very organic way by using the rich landscape as a backdrop for the sensitive design of the small, individual buildings. All pavilions have reference to features of traditional archetypes, but none of them copies or tries to hide the nature of their design and materiality. All of them are made of concrete, and the pitched roof, sometimes geometrically folded, refers to vernacular prototypes. The asymmetric composition of open platforms with integrated rock formations, the shifted composition of volumes, the translucent walls, and the outreaching walkways integrate each building into the landscape. In addition, the material used for the buildings bound them to the place. Natural stone, concrete, and plastered walls formed a strong image of a regional modern approach that was backed by covered platforms in the subtropical climate (Figure 27.3).

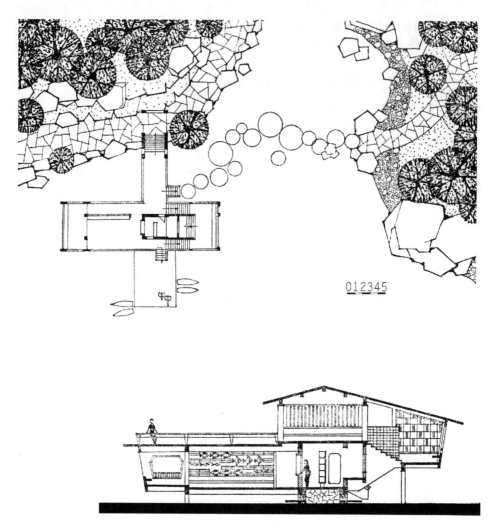

Figure 27.3   The leisure pavilion designed by Shang Kuo floating on the water of the lake in the 1970s.
Source: © Eduard Kögel.

To highlight Shang Kuo's architectural approach, I will focus on the boat-pavilion in the lake. Pillars support the concrete building, which appears to float above the water. The floor plan is shaped like an asymmetrical cross with a bridge connecting to the path along the shore of the lake. The platform continues on the waterside of the pavilion, providing access to the rowing boats. From the other side, circular steppingstones in the water allow alternative access. The pavilion consists of two levels; the lower above the water is used as lounge, with the open terrace on the second floor as its roof. The pavilion is open to the surrounding environment and allows visitors to relax in the sun or in the shade of the building on the water. An asymmetrically sloped roof covers the connecting staircase. In the original design by Shang Kuo, the roof was painted with red and white stripes to resemble a textile, tent-like cover. But the local party commissioner vehemently opposed such a flirtation with the design of the United States flag, as he called it. This small episode simply illustrates the pressure on architects in the 1970s to find a way through all the political pitfalls at the end of the Cultural Revolution.[21] The individual departure from the given model – but not clearly defined idea of socialist realism – challenged the watchdogs of Communist Party aesthetics. However, with the reference to his studies of asymmetrical vernacular buildings in Zhejiang in the early 1960s, Shang Kuo could prove his ingenious interpretation of age-old principles of vernacular design.

Like the small boat-pavilion, all other buildings are designed with an asymmetrical layout, with pitched concrete roofs in a rational but adaptive style. The integration of natural rocks on the platforms as part of the composition shows his idea to combine nature with the new buildings and make it part of the visitors' experience. Not only the overall design of the location of the different facilities but also the unique design approach combines environment and culture. With the found qualities of the site, Shang Kuo transformed the area around the Reed Flute Cave into a contemporary park by using traditional principles and modern instruments. In an article, he declared the general aims of his design for the scenic spot:

> In considering the formal treatment of the buildings, it aims at assimilation of vernacular building idioms and architectural elements of the traditional garden, such as covered ways, bridges, pavilions and so on. At the same time, modern technical possibilities should be fully utilized for creating a new-type of landscape representative of our era.[22]

By the time of implementation in the mid of 1970s, the buildings at Reed Flute Cave stood as a unique approach in the modern history of Chinese architecture. They illustrate a vernacular modernism based on traditional models and in consideration of regional climatic conditions. The scenic arrangement within the landscape turned the area into a landscape park with reference to the art of historic garden design. The individual buildings, however, were designed and built with contemporary materials, which provides a perfect example of how the adaptive approach could continue local qualities without resorting to vernacular timber architecture.

Feng Jizhong: Pavilion in a Garden

In 1946, Feng Jizhong returned from his studies in Vienna and worked in Nanjing and Shanghai. His first major commissions after the establishment of the People's Republic of China included in 1952 the East Lake Guesthouse and the Tongji Hospital in Wuhan.[23] The hospital building is a strict, rational four-story complex with a functional layout based on the need for efficient daily use. In his design, there is no reference to Soviet classicist styles or to the then so-called National Style with the big roof or other decorative applications of Chinese traditional architecture. This was in huge contrast to the architectural production in Beijing under the surveillance of the party.

However, the conceptual independence of Feng is represented by the floor plan for the East Lake Guesthouse in Wuhan, which is the opposite to the rational layout of the hospital. The complex is split into two parts, each with a complicated geometry adapted to the topographic condition at the shore of the lake. During his first visit to the site, Feng closely observed the environment near the water and integrated the program with two building groups just a few meters apart. Each complex was again split into several elements and positioned at different heights on the gentle slope with views across the water. The view towards the lake and the given topography became the guiding principles for the layout. Because each part of the building was set on a different level, the composite four-sided pitched roofs formed a landscape of their own above each building part, reflecting the given topography. The use of simple materials like local natural stones, vertical steel-framed windows, and smooth, matte, yellowish plaster augmented the design strategy, placing the guesthouses in the environment and making them part of it.

The general political development, as well as Feng's assignment as dean of the architectural department at Tongji University and the bad treatment he underwent during the Cultural Revolution, prevented further projects in this direction. It took until the late 1970s for another significant opportunity for architectural experimentation to appear with the reconstruction of the Square Pagoda Garden in Songjiang near Shanghai. Feng Jizhong designed several smaller, new elements in the garden, like a hut, an entrance gate, and a trench across a hill, clad on three sides with stone and covered only by the leaves of the trees. Such a poetic interpretation of spatial enclosure made some officials furious, and they demanded that his interventions be demolished during the Anti-Spiritual-Pollution-Campaign in 1983.[24] However, the most important pavilion built in the Square Pagoda Garden survived and is located at the furthest-flung corner of the premises on a small island: the Helouxuan Teahouse. The simple bamboo construction supports a huge thatched, grass-clad roof. The bamboo poles are painted white, while the knots that bind them together are painted black. This irritating black-and-white puzzle in space creates an almost surreal framework, since the white parts of the construction tend to disappear in the bright light outside the open pavilion. The construction stands on

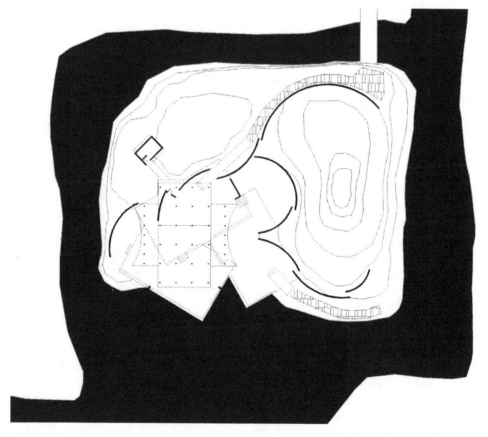

Figure 27.4   Plan of Helouxuan Teahouse, Songjiang, Shanghai, 1982. Architect: Feng Jizhong.
Source: © Eduard Kögel.

Figure 27.5 The interior of the bamboo construction at Helouxuan Teahouse.
Source: © Eduard Kögel.

platforms, which rotate on three overlapping rectangular levels and overlap the water of the lake and the garden. The hill on the island is marked off by freestanding, semi-circular screen wall elements made of red bricks. With these elements, the architectonic space is marked far beyond the cover of the roof or the reach of the platforms. The deconstruction of the architectonic elements, like wall, platform, and roof, are composed in an organic way and mediate the spatial relation between inside and outside. The ambiguity between space, ground, and cover makes the small teahouse a statement for a radical modern approach by using simple traditional means. The use of cheap and locally available material like bamboo for the construction, grass for the roof, and bricks for the walls brings the building very close to vernacular patterns. However, the conscious use of humble material and the creative composition of spatial relations locate the teahouse in both the traditional heritage and the field of creative search for a contemporary spatial concept in Chinese architecture. The Singaporean architect and critic William Lim once wrote about the teahouse: "There is a wonderful ambience of reflective repose, making the place an ideal environment suited for contemplation, just like a traditional teahouse." (Figures 27.4 and 27.5)[25]

The official criticism from party members in 1983 led to a meeting, in which the architect was unfairly blamed for all sorts of aspects. The critics did not follow the invitation of Feng to visit the site and to look at the buildings personally. Most probably they were indignant because he departed from the then usually applied model solution with an individualized strategy in which every part had its own form and function. The obvious cultural meaning of Feng's interventions frightened the officials, who were still trying to avoid any alternative to the streamlined aesthetics of the party.

Conclusion

The discussed examples demonstrate that up to the 1980s quite a few architects actively searched for a modern vernacular building strategy in tune with the economic possibilities and cultural traditions. The strong will for individual answers beyond the then party-sanctioned model solutions created difficulties for all of the architects discussed here. The political narrow-mindedness prevented any movement or broad discourse. In contrast, the simplified official aesthetic program was used to denounce every single person who attempted to establish alternative positions. The given diffusive aesthetic ideals of the party were used as a political tool in the class struggle and prevented suitable expressions based on a rational thought pattern.

In the early 1950s, Xi Fuquan's office was nationalized and he "disappeared" into the new design field for the light industry.[26] In Guangzhou, Hsia Changshi and his colleagues established against all odds an idea of Lingnan Architecture, based on principles of climate responsive strategies and applications. This is probably the strongest outcome of the discussed approaches, which generated such fine examples as the Baiyunshan Village[27] or the Kuangquan Guesthouse, both designed by Mo Bozhi and his colleagues in the 1970s. During the Cultural Revolution, the revolutionary committees "reeducated" Hsia Changshi in the countryside, and between 1968 and 1972 he was imprisoned. Afterwards, with failing health, he emigrated to Germany.[28]

Full of hope, Feng Jizhong commented on the new architectural development after the Cultural Revolution in 1981:

> The creation of a contemporary Chinese vernacular architecture still requires tremendous effort. Nevertheless in new buildings recently constructed in southern China, . . ., favorable attempts have been made to inter-relate the landscape organically with architecture and to create architectural space within a Chinese tradition.[29]

He did not say it, but it is clear that he was referring to the examples from Guangzhou and Guilin, where the abovementioned experiments of Hsia Changshi (and his followers, like Mo Bozhi and others) and Shang Kuo in Guilin gave hope for the renewal of architectural culture after the political extremes of the Cultural Revolution. Feng's own contribution, to an architecture with Chinese characteristics but without the use of striking references to formal expressions of tradition, is clearly documented in his approach to the redesign of the Square Pagoda Garden in Songjiang as well as in the earlier guesthouses in Wuhan. His contribution with small interventions in a period of great change in early 1980s makes Feng Jizhong, despite his small oeuvre, an important architect in twentieth-century China.

Shang Kuo's small pavilions in Guilin also represent an outstanding contribution to the discourse about the continuation of regional architecture with modern materials and translated spatial concepts. While the historic pavilions often served private pleasures with only exclusive users, the demands of a mass society called for public utilities in the service of the young leisure industry with a focus on foreign as well as domestic guests. The radical integration between landscape and architectonic space made the buildings an exceptional contribution to the search for a local approach to modernization. However, the political climate during 1970s also challenged his poetic interpretation – as the example of the red and white stripes on the roof of the pavilion earlier illustrates – and gave the architect a hard time to explain the socialist content of the buildings.

From the 1980s onward, the large-scale urban development and the commercial attitude of the market-driven architectural production often ignored any reference to local know-how. Due to the closure of the universities during the Cultural Revolution, a generation of architects was missing. The isolation from the international discourse did the rest. The old generation, educated in foreign systems, searched for a renewal of traditions in the hope of establishing a discourse with rational arguments and the logic found on site. After the construction of millions of square meters of buildings without any cultural meaning, some small signs of hope can be seen in the last 15 years. Maybe now the dream of Xi Fuquan from the late 1920s is coming true, and finally a Chinese architecture is evolving that refers to function and regional logic without stylistic mimicry. The work of some architects of the younger generation, like Wang Shu, Liu Jiakun, or standardarchitecture, negotiates a world of standard solutions and globally available materials with individualized and tailor-made architecture that critically responds in one way or another to regional issues. The work of Xi Fuquan, Hsia Changshi, Feng Jizhong, and Shang Kuo can be seen as a thin line of headstrong individuality in tune with the need for difference. Their work must be called – in the true meaning of the word – avant-garde, fought, as it was, in "trench warfare" against the massive force of the dominant ideological architecture.

Notes

1 The family name Hsia in modern transcription is Xia. However, he used all his life the transcription Hsia and all related documents in the archives in Germany can be found under this name. Therefore, I decided to use Hsia in this paper.

2 For this aspect, see Jefferey W. Cody, Nancy S. Steinhardt and Tony Atkin, eds, *Chinese Architecture and the Beaux-Arts*. (Honolulu: University of Hawai'i Press, 2011).

3 Fozhien Godfrey Ede (Xi Fuquan), *Die Kaisergräber der Tsing Dynastie in China, Ihr Tumulusbau* (The Imperial Tombs of the Qing Dynasty in China) (PhD Dissertation, Josef Rother Buchdruckerei, Berlin and Neukölln, 1930).

4 Xi Fuquan, "Woguo zhi Jianzhu Tan (Architecture and construction in our country)," *Zhong De Nian-jian* (Chinese students year book in Germany) (c 1927), 89–90.

5 Xi, "Woguo," 89–90.

6 Xi, "Woguo," 89–90.

7 For his work before 1949, see: Kan Liu, Lun Li and Tammy Sau Lyn Chau, "The Transculturation in Architecture between Berlin and Shanghai: The Case of Architect Xi Fuquan (1902–1983)," in *Bridging Urbanities, Reflections on Urban Design in Shanghai and Berlin*, eds Bettina Bauerfeind and Josefine Fokdal, (Münster: LIT-Verlag, 2011), 43–54.

8 Richard Döcker, *Terrassentyp, Krankenhaus, Erholungsheim, Hotel, Bürohaus, Einfamilienhaus, Siedlungshaus, Miethaus und die Stadt* (Terrace type, hospital, recreation home, hotel, office building, family house, settlement house, tenement house and the city) (Stuttgart: Julius Hoffmann Verlag, 1930).

9 Xi Fuquan, "Shanghai Hongiao Liaoyang Yuan (Hongqiao sanatorium in Shanghai)," *Zhongguo Jianzhu: The Chinese Architect*, no. 1 (1933): 3–8.

10 The building has been demolished today.

11 In the 2009 Shenzhen & Hong Kong Bi-City Biennale of Urbanism/Architecture, Hsia's life-time work was showcased in an exhibition, "Under the Sun: Hsia Changshi, A Retrospective," curated by Feng Jiang, Xiao Yiqiang and Song Gang, staff of the Department of Architecture, South China University of Technology, Guangzhou.

12 For his education, see Eduard Kögel, "Between Reform and Modernism: Hsia Changshi and Germany," *Nanfang Jianzhu* (South architecture), no. 2 (2010): 16–29.

13 Eduard Kögel, "Networking for Monument Preservation in China: Ernst Boerschmann and the National Government in 1934," *Journal of Chinese Architectural History*, no. 10 (2013): 339–372.

14 Xia Changshi and Mo Bozhi, "Mantan Lingnan Tingyuan (On the gardens of the Lingnan region)," *Jianzhu Xuebao* (Architecture journal), no. 3 (1963): 11–14. His lifetime investigation led to a book on garden art in 1995.

15 Xia Changshi, "Yaredai Jianzhu de Jiangwen Wenti (Problems of cooling for buildings in the subtropical region)," *Jianzhu Xuebao* (Architecture journal), no. 10 (1958): 36–39.

16 From 1930 on, Le Corbusier worked on projects in North Africa, where he developed his idea of the sun-shading system.

17 The layout and the aesthetic appearance have relations to the Ministry of Education and Health Build-
ing in Rio de Janeiro in Brazil. This building was designed and built between 1935 and 1943 by Lucio
Costa, Affonso Eduardo Reidy, and others. Le Corbusier was invited for advice. It is obvious that Hsia
Changshi closely watched the architectural development in other tropical regions.

18 He Jingtang and Liu Ye, "Jinian Yidai Jianzhu Zongshi Xia Changshi (Commemorating master architect Xia Changshi)," *Xin Jianzhu* (New architecture), no. 5 (2002): 51.

19 Yang Yongsheng, ed., *Zhongguo Jianzhushi: Noted Architects in China* (Beijing: Dangdai Shijie Chubanshe, 1999), 125.

20 Wang, Chi-ming. *Dwelling Houses of Chekiang Province,* ed. Ministry of Building Construction (Beijing, 1964), 471. Besides the written account, the paper has more than 30 pages with line drawings
of vernacular houses in Zhejiang. Shang Kuo told the author in a conversation in 2006 that the paper
was entirely prepared by him, but due to the political circumstances it was presented and published by
Wang Chi-ming.

21 Information from Shang Kuo given to the author in a conversation in Beijing, 2006.

22 Shang Kuo, "Guilin Ludiyan Fengjing Jianzhu de Chuangzuo Fenxi (Analysis on the creative design of
landscape architecture in the Reed Flute Cave of Guilin)," *Jianzhu Xuebao* (Architectural journal), no.
3 (1978): 11–15.

23 Tongji University College of Architecture and Urban Planning, ed., *Jianzhu Rensheng: Feng Jizhong
Fangtanlu* (A life for architecture: Interviews with Feng Jizhong) (Shanghai: Kexue Jishu Chubanshe,
2003), 27–31.

24 Tongji, ed., *Jianzhu,* 60.

25 William Lim and Hock Beng Tan, *The New Asian Architecture: Vernacular Traditions and Contemporary
Style* (Hong Kong: Periplus Editions, 1998), 43.

26 I do not know of a study about his work after 1949.

27 See Charlie Q. L. Xue, *Building a Revolution: Chinese Architecture Since 1980* (Hong Kong: Hong Kong
University Press, 2006), 119–123.

28 For a detailed story of his return to Germany, see Kögel, "Between Reform and Modernism," 16–29.

29 Chi-chung Feng (Feng Jizhong), "People's Republic of China," in *International Handbook of Contemporary
Developments in Architecture,* ed. Warren Sanderson (Westport & London: Greenwood Press, 1981), 232.

Bibliography

Bauerfeind, Bettina and Josefine Fokdal, eds. *Bridging Urbanities: Reflections on Urban Design in Shanghai and
Berlin.* Münster: LIT-Verlag, 2011.

Cody, Jefferey W., Nancy S. Steinhardt and Tony Atkin, eds. *Chinese Architecture and the Beaux-Arts.* Honolulu: University of Hawai'i Press, 2011.

Döcker, Richard. *Terrassentyp, Krankenhaus, Erholungsheim, Hotel, Bürohaus, Einfamilienhaus, Siedlungshaus,
Miethaus und die Stadt* (Terrace Type, Hospital, Recreation Home, Hotel, Office Building, Family
House, Settlement House, Tenement House and the City). Stuttgart: Julius Hoffmann Verlag, 1930.

Ede, Fozhien Godfrey (Xi Fuquan). *Die Kaisergräber der Tsing Dynastie in China. Ihr Tumulusbau. Ihr Tumu-
lusba* (Imperial Tombs of the Qing Dynasty in China). PhD Dissertation. Josef Rother Buchdruckerei,
Berlin and Neukölln, 1930.

Feng, Chi-chung (Feng Jizhong). "People's Republic of China." In *International Handbook of Contemporary
Developments in Architecture,* edited by Warren Sanderson, 232. Westport and London: Greenwood
Press, 1981.

He, Jingtang and Liu Ye. "Jinian Yidai Jianzhu Zongshi Xia Changshi (Commemorating the Great Master
Architect Xia Changshi)." *Xin Jianzhu* (New Architecture), no. 5 (2002): 50–51.

Kögel, Eduard. "Between Reform and Modernism: Hsia Changshi and Germany." *Nanfang Jianzhu* (South
Architecture), no. 2 (2010): 16–29.

———. "Networking for Monument Preservation in China: Ernst Boerschmann and the National Government in 1934." *Journal of Chinese Architectural History,* no. 10 (2013) 339–372.

Lim, William, and Tan Hock Beng. *The New Asian Architecture: Vernacular Traditions and Contemporary Style.*
Hong Kong: Periplus Editions, 1998.

Liu, Kan, Lun Li and Tammy Sau Lyn Chau. "The Transculturation in Architecture Between Berlin and
Shanghai: The Case of Architect Xi Fuquan (1902–1983)." In *Bridging Urbanities: Reflections on Urban*

Design in Shanghai and Berlin, edited by Bettina Bauerfeind and Josefine Fokdal, 43–54. Münster: LIT-Verlag, 2011.

Sanderson, Warren, ed. *International Handbook of Contemporary Developments in Architecture*. Westport and London: Greenwood Press, 1981.

Shang, Kuo. "Guilin Ludiyan Fengjing Jianzhu de Chuangzuo Fenxi (Analysis on the Creative Design of Landscape Architecture in the Reed Flute Cave of Guilin)." *Jianzhu Xuebao* (Architectural Journal), no. 3 (1978): 11–15.

Tongji University College of Architecture and Urban Planning, ed. *Jianzhu Rensheng: Feng Jizhong Fangtanlu* (A Life for Architecture: Interviews with Feng Jizhong). Shanghai: Kexue Jishu Chubanshe, 2003.

Wang, Chi-ming. *Dwelling Houses of Chekiang Province*. Beijing: Ministry of Building Construction, 1964.

Xi, Fuquan. "Woguo zhi Jianzhu Tan (Architecture and Construction in Our Country)." *Zhong De Nianjian* (Chinese Students Year Book in Germany) (1927): 89–90.

———. "Shanghai Hongiao Liaoyang Yuan (Hongqiao Sanatorium in Shanghai)." *Zhongguo Jianzhu: The Chinese Architect*, no. 1 (1933): 3–8.

———. "Yaredai Jianzhu de Jiangwen Wenti (Problems of Cooling for Buildings in the Sub-Tropical Region)." *Jianzhu Xuebao* (Architectural Journal), no. 10 (1958): 36–39.

Xia, Changshi (Hsia, Changshi) and Mo Bozhi. "Mantan Lingnan Tingyuan (On the Gardens of the Lingnan Region)." *Jianzhu Xuebao* (Architectural Journal) 3 (1963): 11–14.

Xue, Charlie Q.L. *Building a Revolution: Chinese Architecture Since 1980*. Hong Kong: Hong Kong University Press, 2006.

Yang, Yongsheng, ed. *Zhongguo Jianzhushi: Noted Architects in China*. Beijing: Dangdai Shijie Chubanshe, 1999.

Glossary

Baiyunshan (resort)	白云山庄
Chen Boqi	陈伯齐
Feng Jizhong	冯纪忠
Guangzhou	广州
Helouxuan (teahouse)	何陋轩（茶舍）
Hongqiao (sanatorium)	虹桥（疗养院）
Hsia (Xia) Changshi	夏昌世
Kuangquan (guesthouse)	矿泉（别墅）
Lingnan	岭南
Liu Jiakun	刘家琨
Mo Bozhi	莫伯治
Shang Kuo	尚廓
Songjiang	松江
Tongji (hospital)	同济（医院）
Tongji (university)	同济（大学）
Wang Shu	王澍
Wuhan	武汉
Xi Fuquan	奚福泉
Zhongshan (university)	中山（大学）

28

FOR A MODERNISM

Huang and Feng at Shanghai's Tongji Architectural Programme

Lu Yongyi

How to define the beginning of China's modern architecture and delineate its development is a complex question.[1] By now, most historians use the end of the 1920s as a key starting point for Western modernism to arrive in China. It is also commonly understood that when the Modern Movement thrived and when modernism gained influence internationally, they had a hard time in China.

Rich explanation has been given to this situation. Firstly, the first generation of Chinese architects had received mostly a Beaux-Arts education in western countries, for which the University of Pennsylvania had made its significant contribution. Secondly, when they finished education and returned to China, they faced a twofold mission: to catch up with international trends for modernization, on the one hand, and to search for a formal language to represent a Chinese national identity, on the other. As a result, an eclectic style combining western Beaux-Arts methods and features of Chinese palatial architecture was widely adopted. Named "Chinese Native Style" by state authority, it could accommodate both modern functions and new technologies, while simultaneously retaining the visual grandeur found in China's traditional architecture. Some explained this as follows: "the compatibility of this system with traditional Chinese Architecture was perhaps more seamless than that in any other part of the world to which the Beaux-Arts architecture was exported."[2] But in reality, it was more complex, since modernism was also introduced as a "progressive" architecture in the early 1930s. With passion for this "new architecture" among young Chinese professionals, intense debate occurred with the emergence of an "International Style" – and all the discussions concerned issues of cultural identity.

In Shanghai, for example, we saw not only the practice of western predecessors such as Rudolf Albert Hamburger (1903–80), Ladislaus Edward Hudec (1893–1958), and Richard Paulick (1903–78), but also the works by pioneering Chinese architects, such as Hongqiao Sanitorium with its distinct modernist features, designed by Xi Fuquan (Fohjien Godfrey Ede, 1902–83). But what that means and why modernism did not really evolve in China continue to be heated topics to this day among critics and scholars. Some argued that architects in China did not really have a commitment to a new culture or a social progressive program – they were not concerned about creating social housing on a rational and economic ground but instead acting as servants for the market, so that it was hard to say if they were not adopting merely another

DOI: 10.4324/9781315851112-41

style replacing Art Deco.[3] Others attribute the failure of modernism in China to the primitive levels of China at the time in industrialization, standardization, and construction management.[4]

This chapter focuses on two predecessors who contributed to the dissemination and development of modernism in architecture in China in the 1940s and 1950s – Henry Jorsen Huang (1915–75) and Feng Jizhong (1915–2009). They joined Tongji University in 1952, along with other colleagues determined to develop modernism in architecture; they turned Tongji into an epicentre for disseminating the philosophy, education system, and design methodology of architectural modernism in China. However, their quests and historical contributions have not yet attracted enough attention.

From St John's to Tongji: Huang's Education Philosophy for Modernism

Henry Jorsen Huang (Huang Zuoshen) is one of the earliest Chinese students who received education in architectural modernism in Europe and North America. Huang first studied at the AA School in London in 1933–37, when the school was moving away from the Beaux-Arts system and the English began to accept and develop modernism.[5] Figures in modernism such as Le Corbusier, Erich Mendelsohn, and Russian Constructivists were becoming familiar to the students. Particularly, Walter Gropius' visit to London and his lecture there left a strong impression on this young Chinese student.[6] Upon graduating from the AA, Huang went to GSD at Harvard in 1939 for the next two years to study. GSD then was also at a turning point, when Gropius from the Bauhaus of Germany and Joseph Hudnut, who was committed to reforming the education system, began to promote modernist education system in architecture there. Although the reform itself was controversial, Huang's encounter there and then had certainly secured him a deeper and wider understanding of architectural modernism than many other Chinese students. On this, Gropius' idea of "Total Architecture" and Marcel Breuer's design teaching in the studios had clearly inspired him to reform architectural education in China later on.[7]

In late 1941, amid the Sino-Japanese War, Huang graduated and returned to Shanghai, China. The next year, he joined the renowned St John's University, a Baptist university founded by American missionaries, and established the Department of Architecture with the support of Yang Kuanlin, Dean for the School of Engineering.[8] With modernism in mind, Huang aimed to establish a system totally different from the Beaux-Arts approach (already well adopted locally) at the very beginning of the program development. Despite the limiting condition, St John's gained impressive success in just ten years: it established an education system with modernist ideas; it recruited architects, planners, and educators – working in a modernist perspective – from China and abroad; and together they fostered a generation of young architects.

In particular, German architect Richard Paulick, who had worked with Gropius on the buildings of Bauhaus in Dessau, joined St John's University in 1943.[9] Huang's friends and classmates from his overseas years were also invited to join and teach.[10] Later, the first batch of graduates from St John's also joined the university, turning the university into the most active centre for teaching and promoting modernism in architecture.

It may be difficult to fully appreciate how architectural education was delivered there.[11] But a careful reading of Huang's two speeches from the 1940s – "The Training of an Architect" and "On Chinese Architecture," which are the only two essays from him that we have now – may reveal key features of his basic approach to the teaching of architecture there.[12] For him, the first thing was to provide a totally new definition of the architectural discipline to respond to the needs of the time and society.

> So today, the most significant change has been the reorientation of architect's relationship with society. Instead of thinking of himself as an artist associating only with privileged classes; the architect of today thinks himself as a reformer whose job is to provide the background for society to live in. . . . So it (architecture) should combine many purposes; purposes of use and function, structure, tools and material, also drawing inspiration from human and social sources. There are many sides of the architect's relationship with his society, namely, the technical, aesthetic, social and political. Hence we see that the cliché "art for art's sake" is no longer adequate.[13]

Huang believed that architects should have the responsibility of establishing a new order for society. For this sake, he compared three "present means of studying architecture" – "the university school of architecture, the technical building school, and an apprentice to an architect's office." He thought that architectural education within these three approaches had all failed to meet the requirements of modern society.[14] For him, new education institutions should emphasize both "the technical and the intellectual."

> The technical program includes drawing, mathematics, strength of materials, acoustics, heating and ventilation, building methods, sanitation, and so on, and the intellectual program includes politics, philosophy, history, sociology, psychology, literature and art, in order to provide a background for the understanding of present civilization and its relation to that of the past.

Huang also promoted the openness of architectural discipline, by firstly emphasizing that "the role of architecture and town-planning as arts of civilization in general . . . because one influences another," and secondly extending architecture into landscape, interior design, and other design areas.[15] Despite the limited size of staff, Huang tried his best to implement ideas of "Total Architecture" into design studios that ranged from hospital to villa design, and from stage setting to student suits – even the master planning of Shanghai in 1946.

Huang advocated that architectural education should incorporate scientific and rational thinking, social practice, and creativity. He indicated that "instruction in architecture today tries to find the solution of a problem in the nature of a problem itself, contrary to the old form of architectural education which approached its problems from without, with preconceived ideas and proscriptions."[16] He implemented this idea in every aspect in the education. For example, in the studio of hospital design, students were required to respond to the location, site conditions, and the needs of doctors and patients. For this reason, he advocated that students must "go from their drawings boards to their technical realities," move on directly to investigate the hospitals, and, after using, experiencing, and communicating, work on and establish the brief and then move on to finish the design. For Huang, it was a necessary process through which students could develop abilities to analyse and organize comprehensive problems in areas from function to material, and even to social aspects such as modern management and state governance.

Huang strongly opposed to the notion of modern architecture as "simply a rigid style," and he believed a true architectural education was not to pursue a rigid "architecture of a period" but to develop a "contemporary architecture."[17] So, for him, the first task was to go back to construction itself and to understand and master new technologies. Huang arranged a particular theoretical subject, "Time and Life: On Mechanics," in which he introduced new technological inventions of power machines and industrial products. For the use of materials, he introduced subjects including "pattern and texture," "pottery exercise," "bricklaying exercise," and "techniques workshops." He said,

> The students must understand that architecture depends on the nature and the character of materials and construction. For the organic quality of a building it does not matter if either wood, brick, stone, concrete, or steel was used for construction. All materials used in constructions are considered equal, provided the material used is adequate for certain purposes, not in any way enhancing the very character of such a material being used. All prejudices for or against certain materials should be made clear as being unreasonable.[18]

Clearly, Huang put more emphasis on searching for materiality and its presence in construction, which approximates the ethos of modernism in architecture. Huang always propagated the words of theorist Sir Thomas Jackson: "architecture does not consist in beautifying buildings; on the contrary, it should consist in building beautifully."[19]

At St John's, if there was a central idea that totally opposed the Beaux-Arts system, that must be the notion of space since, according to Huang, "Space is the core of modern architecture." Huang implemented this principle in the design process taught there, emphasizing that "the conception of the building is so designed in terms of volume – of space enclosed of planes and surfaces – as opposed to mass and solidity." For sure, his notion of space came from various sources, including Bauhaus, Mies, and Giedion. On the last, Giedion's *Space, Time and Architecture: The Growth of a New Tradition* was used as an important reference for teaching design theory at St John's.[20] Further, Huang added his own reading to the ideas of space and "spatial design" – firstly, space was a thinking tool for organizing functions, and then, secondly, space also involved an artistic language to inspire one's physical and psychological experience. Explaining Mies' German Pavilion in Barcelona's EXPO, Huang guided students to appreciate a "spacious flowing space" and related it to *qiyun shengdong* (rhythmic vitality), a Chinese phrase describing dynamic movement of land profiles in the mountain-water (*shanshui*) landscape painting – something he appreciated a lot himself.[21]

Finally, based on and apart from the scientific rationality emphasized, Huang's program strongly advocated "originality" and "heuristic education," in which students were guided to "find and develop students' infinite potential," rather than being spoon-fed and dictated to.[22] For him, "experimental exercises can be carried out to its fullest extent, and careful consideration given to individual inclination." According to the memoirs of his students, in their studio learning, a dream, a drama, or an abstract painting, among others, could be a source of inspiration for design, "for he may find the limitations encountered in this field a new challenge to his ingenuity and imagination."[23]

Design: From Stage Set of "Rossum's Universal Robots" to Tongji Faculty Club

Unfortunately, very few documents have been left with us from St John's architectural department. Photos of a stage set, designed by Huang and his students, were among these few surviving images (Figure 28.1). This was a set for "Rossum's Universal Robots,"[24] a drama composed by his brother, the famous dramatist Huang Zuolin's Kugan Jutuan (hard-working theatre).[25] The set adopted abstract forms, with segments forming a whole by scattering, layering, and hanging, in a manner that departed from the ideas of centrality and stability and of a representation

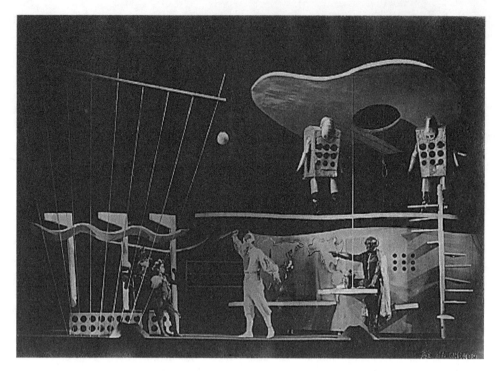

Figure 28.1 Stage scene of "Rossum's Universal Robots," Shanghai, mid-1940s; stage set designed by Henry J. Huang and his students.

Source: Photo taken in the mid-1940s. From and by permission of Henry Huang's family (Huang Zhi).

of a scene used in traditional stage design. With juxtaposition, non-hierarchical composition, abstract forms, and the infinite depth of the backdrop, the stage deconstructed traditional perspective space, creating a flowing and extensive space and bringing the audience to an unfamiliar world full of metaphors.

Like many intellectuals of his time in China, Huang retained a strong national concern and sentiment. In his speech in the 1940s, he publicly advocated that education in architecture should follow the principle of Constitution (of China then), and "be consistently nationalist, scientific and popular."[26] Commenting on international influence, Huang confessed that "we took them (buildings of foreign styles) quite rightly as signs of progress perhaps not knowing in what way," and "I do regret that we should discard so much of our own heritage."[27] At the same time, he opposed the practice of "Chinese Native Style" (which typically used traditional Chinese roofs atop a modern structure) and openly advocated a contemporary approach, saying that "a contemporary Chinese architecture capable of coping with modern requirements and yet remaining still true to our cultural tradition cannot come about so easily by adopting a Chinese exterior and a western interior."[28]

Concerning cross-cultural thinking, Huang had his own observations. According to him, ideas like "a building could be raised to architecture by the poetry in construction" were western, whereas on the Chinese side, Li Jie's *Yingzao Fashi*, the monumental treatise on the building construction (printed in 1103), was not enough for a comprehensive understanding of Chinese architecture. For Huang, the Chinese tradition had "two forces going to the making of Chinese architecture independently of each other": "on one hand, the master builders supplying the physical needs, and on the other hand, the scholars unconsciously applied the intellectual efforts." And although the intellectuals' consideration of architecture is unconscious, unlike Leon Battista Alberti's *Treatise on Architecture*, China still had great creators in architectural art such as Confucius, whose thinking on ritual system resulted in the Forbidden City as a masterpiece, and intellectuals including Li Yu, Cheng Yuwen, and Cao Xueqin, among others, whose construction and residence turned traditional Chinese gardens into poetic places.[29]

Huang connected notions of space in modernist architecture to spatial experience found in traditional Chinese architecture. For him, the character of the Forbidden City cannot be presented in any single building, because it was built as a ritual space with a long axial "approach" in the "Chinese manner." He asked students to experience walking on the axis in the Temple of Heaven compound, and likened it to "walking on the rising road, while cypresses sinking down and people going above to the sky."[30] But he appreciated the Ming-dynasty imperial tomb in Nanjing more, thinking that this architectural complex was a spatial sequence both majestic and harmonious with the mountains around it. In contrast, he criticized the Sun Yat-sen Mausoleum, built in 1925, arguing that the wide monumental steps were an invasion to nature. However, what he appreciated most were freedom and seclusion of space in the garden house of Chinese ancient literati. He cited *Qingxian Gong* (On idleness) by Cheng Yuwen of Ming dynasty, to imagine his ideal house:

> Inside the gate is a footpath and the footpath must be winding. At the turning of the footpath there is an outdoor screen and the screen must be small. Behind the screen there is a terrace and the terrace must be level. On the banks of the terrace there are flowers and the flowers must be fresh. Beyond the flowers is a wall and the wall must be low. By the side of the wall there is a pine and the pine tree must be old. At the foot of the pine tree there are rocks and the rocks must be quaint. On the rocks there is a pavilion and the pavilion must be simple. Behind the pavilion there are bamboos and the bamboos must be thin and sparse. At the end of the bamboos there is a house and the house must be secluded . . .[31]

Huang "discovered" features of Chinese houses and gardens – such as respecting the site, free layout, interconnection between man-made and nature – and found a compatibility with the architecture of modern masters such as Wright, Mies, and Aalto. He did not have enough of a chance to test out this kind of design, but Tongji Faculty Club, completed in 1956 and designed by his students, Li Dehua and Wang Jizhong, is an excellent test and practice of this "compatibility."

The faculty club was a building less than 2,000 sq. meters in floor area and was located on campus in an area called Tongji New Village (Figures 28.2 and 28.3). It was arranged according to site conditions and composed of functional spaces; it adopted a "picturesque composition"; and it had no "front" façade nor a monumental entry, either. Architects here had paid more attention to spatial organization and spatial interconnectedness. The interior had no corridors; the entry and the staircase were found in the centre, a space that connected a ballroom, a reading room, a cafeteria, and other functional rooms in various directions. The spaces and rooms had no hierarchy among them; most of them had no doors – allowing free entry and exit in a flowing space. On the outside, there were platforms, extended walls, and semi-enclosed courtyards. When the floor-to-ceiling doors were open, the space of the ballroom could then extend outward, turning the courtyard into part of the

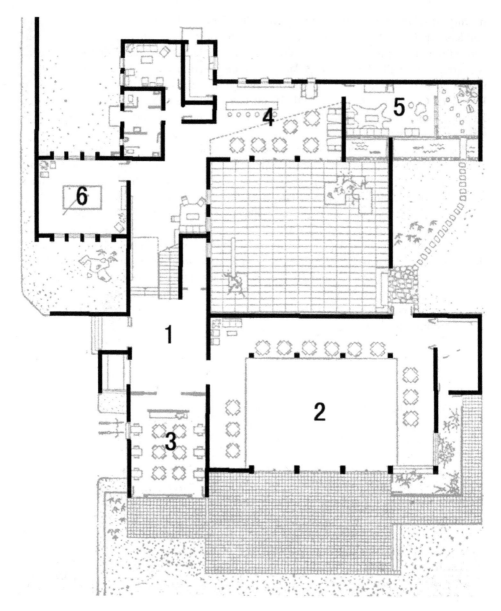

Figure 28.2 Plan of Tongji Faculty Club (1. entrance, 2. dancing hall, 3. chess room, 4. bar, 5. lounge, 6. billiard room), Shanghai, 1956. Architect: Wang Jizhong and Li Dehua.

Source: *Tongjidaxue Xuebao* (Journal of Tongji University), no. 4 (1958), 7; with permission and courtesy of Journal of Tongji University Editorial Office.

café. In this way, the idea of a flowing space from Mies, the free layout found in the Chinese houses, and the rich design from the Chinese garden – such as shifting and zigzagging spaces, solid–void interpenetrations, and inside–outside interflows – were fully incorporated into this design; it provided a welcoming home for busy teachers to come to, relax in, and enjoy at any time.[32]

Figure 28.3   Courtyard of Tongji Faculty Club. Photo taken in 1956.

Source: Jianzhu Xuebao, no. 6 (1958), 18; with permission and courtesy of *Jianzhu Xuebao* Editorial Office.

Design Methodology: Feng and His "Compositional Principles in Spatial Design"

Another important founder of the Tongji University architecture department was Feng Jizhong (1915–2009). A body of ideas titled *Kongjian Sheji Zuhe Yuanli* (compositional principles in spatial design, hereafter *Principles*), conceived and developed by Feng, is the earliest exploration of a methodological framework for design teaching in China with the principles of architectural modernism. Feng's ideas and approach to design, appealing to both rational and poetic considerations, has won him a high standing in the history of architecture of the twentieth century in China.

Feng graduated from the Department of Civil Engineering, St John's University, and then started architectural study in Vienna's Technische Hochschule in 1936. Recent study on the history of Technische Hochschule Vienna offers better understanding on what shaped or constructed Feng's belief on modern architecture in these early years.[33] Carl König was considered as the core figure at the Hochschule, leading "the König" school. Many of his students and assistants later were Feng's teachers, such as Karl Holey, Erwin Johannes Ilz, and Siegfried Theiss. According to Feng's idea, the Hochschule was differentiated from art school and the Bauhaus as well by emphasizing engineering subjects and advocating that "the first thing is the foundation of technology and the foundation of history, then finally comes to the idea of design."[34] So, the understanding of architecture based on technological rationality was the core approach in design teaching, which emphasized the use of new technology; but teaching there also emphasized intensive reading in architectural and building history. According to the studies available, "the König" – inherited from Emmanuel Viollet-le-Duc and Gottfried Semper – advocated a comprehensive and scientific study of history of building as a foundation for creation of the new and as a secure way of preventing oneself from going for mere superficial forms or images – considered a dead end in such as teaching philosophy.[35]

The writings of *Principles* began as a draft textbook written by Feng for guiding design teaching in the early 1960s. Scholars have considered the text as developing an alternative to the Beaux-Arts systems much adopted elsewhere in China: it advocated notions of space developed in architectural modernism to replace ideas of typologies and formalist organization, and the idea of design principles to replace the classical approach of pupils learning from the masters.[36] Feng's *Principles* aimed at establishing design principles and design methods in line with modern architecture. Feng noted that within the Beaux-Arts system there was a methodology that made it work in its framework, and that, for students working for "free creation" in a modernist perspective, they also needed a methodology. He criticized the idea that "architectural education has only the results of architectural design, but no experience accumulated in the process,"[37] and suggested that if modern architecture could not establish a design methodology, it would not reach the rationality it wanted to achieve and would end up in a superficial pursuit of styles.

As to the core of this methodology, Feng's concept of space in his *Principles* was apparently much inspired by Giedion, as he mentioned. However, the technological rationality in Technische Hochschule Vienna contributed to another foundation for Feng's methodology. For Feng, the handbook that everyone had a copy of at the Hochschule – Ernst Neufert's *Architects' Data* – gave him a direct inspiration.[38] Neufert's book provided a body of knowledge ranging from conceptual design to design principles of all types of functional spaces. What was "greatly appealing" to Feng was a common knowledge that lay under the specific functionalities,[39] so that the core skills of the architect were to organize spaces according to needs and conditions.[40]

We can now enlist some contributions made by Feng's *Principles*:

1   It established a teachable design method in studio education. Assuming that a common notion in architectural design is about spatial organization, *Principles* here classifies four types of spatial design – in his own words – "spatial formation (for large space), spatial sequence, spatial ordering, and combination of many spaces." It provides a perspective to go beyond a function-based typological thinking and a concrete and operational design method on buildings that departs from the grand discourse of architecture of the historians.

2   It translates functionalism in modern architecture into concrete spatial design. *Principles* specifies that "functional requirement must be placed in a dominant position" and design be conceived as a process of "concrete shaping of functions"; functions here include people's activity and the placing and movement of things, as well as ventilation, lighting, visual design, and acoustics. A "main space" forms a core, surrounded by auxiliary spaces; and the ways of connecting spaces – sequencing, ordering, and combining – can be arranged according to human needs and functional circulations.

3   It translates structural rationality in modern architecture into concrete spatial design. *Principles* emphasizes that "architectural space is composed of a structural system and its construction," that it presents a "relation between force and structure," and that it "must be outside functional space" to reveal a dominance of function. If the two (architectural and functional space) are in conflict, economy can secure balance and control for a unification of the two. Every step of design for some spatial composition is a spatial communication with structural situations such as column distances, structural units, a grid of columns, and some units inserted from elsewhere.

As we can see, *Principles* has put forward a shaping or composing method that is made of three aspects, namely "functional space, architectural space, and solid form." It reminds us of Hugo

Häring's organic functionalism.[41] But it also establishes a "constructing" method with another three aspects – "structural space, architectural form, perceptive processing" – revealing a strong influence from the principles of structural rationality taught at Hochschule. Feng recalled a moment as a student there: commenting on the Doric order of Greek architecture, a teacher explained that the fillets of the capital was there for grooving the flute on the shaft, so everywhere there was "a correlation between engineering and form."[42]

From Huagang Teahouse to Square Pagoda Garden

Feng was committed to reforming the traditional Beaux-Arts system, but never became so radical as to abandon history. He wanted to learn from all valuable resources, especially Chinese traditional culture. While his designs of the 1950s revealed more interest in functionalism and structural rationalism,[43] his projects of the 1960s, namely East Lake Guesthouse of Wuhan and Huagang Teahouse of Hangzhou, represented a rich collection of inspirations from Mies, Aalto, and Chinese traditional house-gardens. The Teahouse, attracting the most attention in architectural circle at the time, adopted the look of a vernacular house (Figure 28.4). Compared with Tongji Faulty Club, the generous site here allowed a more open and flexible design; and the functional units were not only combined but also penetrate and interrelate together in a manner that was more dynamic. The most distinctive was the asymmetrical roof covering the flowing spaces below, acting like a wedding curtain (in the local tradition) that represented "an affinity with the soil."[44]

Unfortunately, the roof of the teahouse was criticized as similar to a "Taoist priest's hat," a symbol of "feudalism and capitalism" (whatever the logic behind this accusation); and was therefore removed during construction. The text of *Principles* was also criticized; and Feng had no room to practice and experiment in the early 1960s, let alone during the Cultural Revolution (1966–76). After the Cultural Revolution, when China started to reform and open up, more scholars began to use and explore notions of spatial compositions or compositions in spatial design, as a methodological project.[45] Ideas and notions around "compositions" were adopted gradually in architectural schools. But the trend moved on in historical studies for summarizing spatial typologies of the past, while Feng's initial rationalist emphasis was somewhat ignored. Around that time, post-modernism was introduced into China, encouraging criticism of architectural modernism as overlooking and ignoring urban context and accumulated tradition. Architectural discourse in China once again fell into a debate on styles in design exercises – do we want it Chinese or western, modern or traditional, etc.

Upon this debate, Feng had clear and independent thinking. On the one hand, he remained committed to rationalism and modernism in architecture, but on the other, he began to look for ways to enrich human dimensions of architecture. He was more concerned about urban renewal and urban historical context. In addition, he aimed to go beyond the limitations of his *Principles* by absorbing new western theories such as architectural phenomenology and environmental psychology, by re-interpreting the ideas behind Chinese gardens and the philosophy of relations between "nature and humans," and by enriching his notions of "space" to a new level for creating harmonies between people and place.

Fangtayuan Park, or Square Pagoda Garden, completed in the early 1980s, represented a new height in Feng's understanding and practicing around ideas of space. This is a modern park combining historical structures, including a Song-dynasty pagoda, a Ming-dynasty screen wall, and a Qing-dynasty temple hall, as well as other landscape features such as stone bridges, ancient trees, farmland, rivers, and low-lying lands. Following the natural condition of the site, Feng skilfully integrated natural and artificial, ancient and modern, into a rich whole. Here,

Figure 28.4 Design model for Huagang Teahouse, Hangzhou, early 1960s. Architect: Feng Jizhong.

Source: Photo taken in the early 1960s. From and by permission of College of Architecture and Urban Planning, Tongji University.

space remained the guiding concept in planning and design, but it was no longer understood as merely a sequencing connection of functions and landscapes; it was, rather a more complex reading of spatial ideas and experiences rooted in the Chinese literati tradition concerning nature and natural landscape. In this manner, Feng worked round the key notions of *kuang*

Figure 28.5 Helouxuan Pavilion in Square Pagoda Garden, Songjiang, Shanghai, 1982. Architect: Feng Jizhong.

Source: Photo taken in 2019. Permission and courtesy of © Li Yanbo (2019).

(open expensiveness) and *ao* (deep and mysterious), *dong* (dynamic, active) and *jing* (silent, static, peaceful), and integrated historical fragments, and developed a unique spatial narrative and spatial-temporal experience.[46]

The highlight of the project is a teahouse called Helouxuan (rustic pavilion), a bamboo-structured pavilion with a thatched roof – inspired by local traditional houses but with new and dynamic ideas (Figure 28.5). It included several ideas. Firstly, a space of *yi dong*, ideas on the move, or a flow of ideas and consciousness, was employed; by using a roof, curving walls, and three rotating platforms, and by organizing baroque-like movements and shifting of orientations, a rich space was created that interrelated people and built structures with the natural surroundings in a rich and subtle manner. Secondly, a space of *shikong zhuanhuan* (spatial-temporal shifting) was employed – one moves in and through the pavilion, with views shifting at every turn as one meanders around the place; one lingers and realizes the presence and the flowing of time in space through the movement along the curving walls, the glittering lights and shadows on the ground, and the changing juxtaposition of old and new everywhere when one turns back, looks aside, or glances around.[47]

Conclusion

Huang and Feng had taken significant steps towards the development of a modern architecture in China. While most Chinese professionals in the field considered modernism as an "International Style," Huang and Feng explored deeper principles at a more basic level. Sharing beliefs in functionalism and structural rationalism and emphasizing space as a key concept and design as a problem-solving process, they both attempted to reconstruct an epistemology and methodology to go beyond Beaux-Arts thinking and the stylistic understanding of modernism.

Many have stressed that the backwardness in building technology and industry was one of the key reasons behind the difficult development of architectural modernism in China. Huang and Feng's studies and designs, nevertheless, seem to have suggested an alternative answer. Instead of making a "new architecture" with new materials and structures, they searched for a "de-familiarization" of traditional spaces and constructional forms, so that new possibilities can be found with a new use of historical elements and a hybrid of modernity and tradition. The Faculty Club, the Teahouse, and Helouxuan Pavilion (of Square Pagoda Garden) all attracted great appreciation when "critical regionalism" became a hot topic in China in recent times.

Huang and Feng were not alone in being interested in revitalizing Chinese culture and tradition. What made them exceptional was their approach to this. They both were critical of the practice of "Chinese Native Style" (where imperial or palatial roofs were used on modern structures); considering it a projection of the image of the nation-state, they regarded it as a superficial imitation of China's architectural tradition for a symbolic image of political authority. Leaving aside ideological discussions concerning (if we should adopt) "Chinese learning as core and western learning as instrument (*zhongxue weiti, xixue weiyong*)," they preferred to explore a deeper understanding of spatial organizations of traditional architecture and landscape design, and a method of transferring spatial cultures from antiquity to modern architecture. Specifically, Huang's observation on the poetics of Chinese gardens centred on a combination of artisans' garden-making and intellectuals' meditative life, saturated with or reflected on paintings and poetry. Feng, on the other hand, had a more theoretical interpretation of the poetics of gardens in his later years; he claimed that the garden was about "describing an overall world of ideas and images comprehensively and intuitively, about searching for the vivid, the incomplete, the ambivalent, the dramatic, the unsure; about letting the human subject wonder and drift . . . with a free mind."[48] Going beyond stylistic concerns, and moving beyond the duality of China and the west and tradition and modernity, Huang and Feng had aimed for a new synthesis – "joining the ancient and becoming the new," as advocated by Feng.

Like many others, Huang and Feng's exploration of architectural modernism encountered tough times. Due to the wars of the 1940s, the experiment in architectural education for Huang and his colleagues at St John's was much limited. After 1949, when the People's Republic of China was established, universities nationwide were reorganized; when the staff from St John's joined Feng and others at Tongji University in 1952, it was widely expected that the group would be a forerunner in the development of modern architecture in China. However, state authority called for "socialist realism" and "socialist content with national form" in art and architecture in the early and mid-1950s, which prolonged the use of Chinese forms and roof features – a reuse or an imitation of palatial or imperial roofs upon modern structures using Beaux-Arts design thinking. In this context, Tongji Faculty Club and Huagang Teahouse were criticized as being not socialist but "bourgeois." Feng moved away to focus on design methodology for teaching, to avoid frontline debates on ideological issues, yet his *Principles* was also criticized as "western and bourgeois." Ironically, Liang Sicheng's (1901–72) framing of "national form" – using ideas of vocabulary, grammar, and translation – was for socialist architecture in

China in the 1950s also criticized as wasteful and improper. For a long while, architects didn't know what was correct in architecture, and the important contributions by these pioneers such as Huang and Feng were ignored for decades – until recent times. Of the two, while Feng had the opportunities to continue his exploration with China opening up in the 1980s, culminating in the work of Square Pagoda Garden, Huang ended his life of less at 60 years in 1975, at the end of the Cultural Revolution. The historical episode outlined here, revealing intellectual and personal trajectories alike, may serve as an academic study and a humanistic reflection as well.

Notes

1 Special thanks to Associate Professor Qian Feng (Tongji University), Mr Huang Zhi (son of Huang Zuoshen, residing in USA), Professor Li Hua (Southeast University), Associate Professor Zhao Dongmei (Shanghai Jiaotong University), and Mr Edward Bottoms (Architectural Association of School of Architecture, London) for their support with this chapter.
2 Nancy S. Steinhardt, "Chinese Architecture on the Eve of the Beaux-Arts," in *Chinese Architecture and the Beaux-Arts*, eds. Jeffrey W. Cody, Nancy S. Steinhardt and Tony Atkin (Honolulu: University of Hawaii Press; Hong Kong University Press, 2011), 5.
3 Jia Beisi and Jia Yunyan, "'New Architecture' or 'Revolution'–the choice of Chinese pioneer architects," in *Zhongguo Jindai Jianzhu Xueshu Sixiang Yanjiu*: Research on China's Modern Architectural Academia, eds. Zhao Chen and Wu Jiang (Beijing: Zhongguo Jianzhu Gongye Chubanshe, 2003), 26–30.
4 Li Haiqing, "Lixiang zhuyi yu shehui xianshi (Between ideality and reality)," in *Zhongguo Jindai Jianzhu Xueshu Sixiang Yanjiu* (Research on China's modern architectural academia), eds. Zhao Chen and Wu Jiang (Beijing: Zhongguo Jianzhu Gongye Chubanshe, 2003), 44–47.
5 Based on emails from Mr Edward Bottoms (18 February 2012), head of archives at the AA School of Architecture London.
6 Based on Henry Huang's memoirs from the archives at Tongji University, as provided by Qian Feng.
7 See Anthony Alofsin, *The Struggle for Modernism: Architecture, Landscape Architecture, and City Planning at Harvard* (New York: Norton & Co. 2002).
8 Yang Kuanlin studied in the Department of Civil Engineering at the University of Michigan from 1911 to 1916 and started his practice in China in the 1920s. Known as one of the masters of China's first generation of building structure design, Yang completed many influential buildings from the 1930s to the 1950s. In the 1940s–50s, he worked as Dean of the School of Civil Engineering at St John's University in Shanghai.
9 Richard Paulick (1903–1979) had worked with Walter Gropius in the 1920s before coming to Shanghai and opening a design office there in 1933 – first with his brother, called "Paulick and Paulick, Architects and Engineers," and later to as "Modern Homes, Interior Designers." Introduced by Gropius, he became a professor at St John's University in 1943, teaching interior design and urban planning in the architecture department. He was involved with the Greater Shanghai Plan in the late 1940s. He went back to GDR (German Democratic Republic) in 1950 and became a "National Architect" there.
10 Huang's friends and classmates who taught at St John's University included A. J. Brandt, Nelson Sun, Chester Moy, Wang Dahong, Zheng Guanxuan, Eric Cumine, Lu Qianshou, Chen Zhanxiang, and Zhong Yaohua.
11 For the Department of Architecture of St John's University, see Qian Feng and Wu Jiang, *Zhongguo Xiandai Jianzhu Jiaoyushi, 1920–1980* (Education of modern architecture in China, 1920–1980) (Beijing: Zhongguo Jianzhu Gongye Chubanshe, 2008), 101–118.
12 Henry J. Huang, "The Training of an Architect" and "On Chinese Architecture," in *Huang Zuoshen Jinian Wenji: Commemorative Accounts of Huang Zuoshen*, ed. College of Architecture and Urban Planning, Tongji University (Beijing: Zhongguo Jianzhu Gongye Chubanshe, 2012), 8–14, 22–30.
13 Huang, "The Training," 8.
14 Huang primarily criticized the pedagogy of some leading architectural schools then in China – based on Beaux-Arts systems – such as National Central University of Nanjing and Hangchow University of Hangzhou.
15 Huang, "The Training," 10.
16 Huang, "The Training," 11.

17 Luo Xiaowei and Li Dehua, "Shengyuhan daxue zuinianqing de yige xi, jianzhu gongchengxi (The youngest department at St John's University, the department of architecture and engineering)," in *Huang Zuoshen Jinian Wenji,* ed. College of Architecture and Urban Planning, Tongji University (Beijing: Zhongguo Jianzhu Gongye Chubanshe, 2012), 131.

18 Huang, "The Training," 13.

19 Huang, "The Training," 8.

20 We have no further information on Huang meeting S. Giedion when the latter was giving lectures at Harvard. But the publication of Giedion's book two years later certainly captivated Huang; and the book became a key reference in Huang's teaching on architectural theory at St John's.

21 Liu Zhong, "Liu Zhong Xiansheng Shuxin (a letter to Mr. Liu Zhong)," in *Huang Zuoshen Jinian Wenji,* ed. College of Architecture and Urban Planning, 160.

22 Luo and Li, "Shengyuhan daxue zuinianqing de yige xi, jianzhu gongchengxi," 131.

23 Huang, "The Training of an Architect," 12.

24 Formerly known as "Rossum's Universal Robots, R.U.R.," a satiric play written by Czech novelist and playwright Karel Èapek in Czech in 1920, which described the coexistence and the conflict between humans and factory-produced robots.

25 Kugan Jutuan (hard-working theatre) was founded by the famous drama and film artist and playwright Huang Zuolin (the elder brother of Huang Zuoshen), with Huang Zongjiang and Shi Hui in 1942. With the faith in "work hard and work together," the theatre became one of the earliest and most influential professional theatres with a strong character of innovation in China at the time.

26 Constitution here refers to that of the Republic of China, passed by the National Assembly with the KMT government in Nanjing in 1946, claiming to establish a democratic republic with the features "of the people, by the people and for the people."

27 Huang, "On Chinese architecture," 24.

28 Huang, "On Chinese architecture," 25.

29 Huang, "On Chinese architecture," 130.

30 Qian and Wu, *Zhongguo,* 118.

31 Huang, "On Chinese Architecture," 132.

32 Li Dehua, Wang Jizhong, "Tongjidaxue jiaogong julebu (The Tongji University Faculty Club)," *Tongji Daxue Xuebao: Journal of Tongji University,* 1 (1958): 5–16.

33 Christopher Long, "An alternative path to modernism: Carl König and architectural education at the Vienna Technische Hochschule, 1890–1913," *Journal of Architectural Education* 55, no. 1 (Sep 2011): 21–30.

34 Feng Jizhong, *Jianzhu Rensheng: Feng Jizhong Zishu* (Architecture and Life: Feng Jizhong's Self-description) (Beijing: Dongfang Chubanshe, 2010), 54.

35 Feng, *Jianzhu Rensheng,* 54.

36 Gu Daqing, "Kongjian yuanli de xueshu ji lishi yiyi (Academic and historical significance for the studies on the principles of spatial composition)," in *Feng Jizhong he Fangta Yuan* (Feng Jizhong and the Square Pagoda Garden), ed. Zhao Bing (Beijing: Zhongguo Jianzhu Gongye Chubanshe, 2008), 94–95.

37 Feng Jizhong, "Tantan jianzhu sheji yuanli wenti (Conversation on the issues concerning the principles of architectural design)," Feng Jizhong, *Jianzhu Xianzhu: Feng Jizhong Lungao* (Chords of architecture: A collection of Feng Jizhong's essays), (Shanghai: Shanghai Kexue Jishu Chubanshe, 2003), 12–17.

38 Feng, *Jianzhu Rensheng,* 55–56.

39 Ernst Neufert, a Bauhaus member in the early 1920s, once closely worked with Gropius for some Bauhaus buildings. His book *Architects' Data,* published in 1936, promoted a rationalized and standardized process of modern architectural design and was widely read in Europe and the United States in the architectural field.

40 Feng, "Tantan," 12–17.

41 Feng was a good friend of German-Chinese architect Chen-kuen Lee. There should be further research into how Lee, Hans Scharoun, and the historian Ernst Boerschmann influenced Feng. See Feng, "Liuxue Aodili (My studies in Austria)," *Jianzhu Xianzhu,* 48–51.

42 Feng, *Jianzhu Rensheng,* 55.

43 For example, Feng designed a project for the Shanghai No. 1 Bus Terminal (1951). Its sawtooth-shaped roof of large-span reinforced concrete shell structure was the first in China adopting this structural type. Feng, *Jianzhu Rensheng,* 114.

44 Feng, *Jianzhu Rensheng,* 168.

45 Peng Yigang's *Jianzhu Kongjian Zuhelun* (On compositions in architectural space) (Beijing: Zhongguo Jianzhu Chubanshe, 1983) is a representative case here.
46 *Kuang* (wide) and *ao* (profound) are Feng's concepts derived from the literary interpretations of spatial qualities of natural landscape by the renowned Tang-dynasty poet and writer Liu Zongyuan (773–819). See Feng Jizhong, *Yugu Weixin: Fangtayuan Guihua* (Join the past, become the new: Planning the Square Pagoda Garden) (Beijing: Oriental Press, 2010), 69.
47 Feng, *Yugu Weixin*, 69, 80, 142.
48 Feng, *Jianzhu Rensheng*, 230.

Bibliography

Alofsin, Anthony. *The Struggle for Modernism: Architecture, Landscape Architecture, and City Planning at Harvard*. New York: Norton & Co., 2002.

Cody, Jeffrey W., Nancy S. Steinhardt and Tony Atkin, eds. *Chinese Architecture and the Beaux-Arts*. Honolulu: University of Hawaii Press, Hong Kong University Press, 2011.

College of Architecture and Urban Planning at Tongji University, ed. *Huang Zuoshen Jinian Wenji: Commemorative Accounts of Huang Zuoshen*. Beijing: Zhongguo Jianzhu Gongye Chubanshe, 2012.

Feng Jizhong. "Liuxue Aodili (My Studies in Austria)." In *Jianzhu Xianzhu: Feng Jizhong Lungao* (Chords of Architecture: A Collection of Feng Jizhong's Essays), edited by Feng Jizhong, 48–51. Shanghai: Shanghai Kexue Jishu Chubanshe, 2003.

———. *Jianzhu Xianzhu: Feng Jizhong Lungao* (Chords of Architecture: A Collection of Feng Jizhong's Essays). Shanghai: Shanghai Kexue Jishu Chubanshe, 2003.

———. "Tantan jianzhu sheji yuanli wenti (Conversation on the Issues Concerning the Principles of Architectural Design)." In *Jianzhu Xianzhu: Feng Jizhong Lungao* (Chords of Architecture: A Collection of Feng Jizhong's essays), edited by Feng Jizhong, 12–17. Shanghai: Shanghai Kexue Jishu Chubanshe, 2003.

———. *Jianzhu Rensheng: Feng Jizhong Zishu* (Architecture and Life: Feng Jizhong's Autobiographic Account). Beijing: Dongfang Chubanshe, 2010.

———. "Zai Weiyena (In Vienna)." In *Jianzhu Rensheng: Feng Jizhong Zishu* (Architecture and Life: Feng Jizhong's Autobiographic Account), edited by Feng Jizhong, 16–21. Beijing: Dongfang Chubanshe, 2010.

———. *Yijing yu Kongjian* (Space and Poetic Prospect). Beijing: Dongfang Chubanshe, 2010.

———. *Yugu Weixin: Fangtayuan Guihua* (Join the Past, Become the New: Planning the Square Pagoda Garden). Beijing: Oriental Press, 2010.

Gu Daqing. "Kongjian yuanli de xueshu ji lishi yiyi (Academic and Historical Significance for the Studies on the Principles of Spatial Composition)." In *Feng Jizhong he Fangta Yuan* (Feng Jizhong and the Square Pagoda Garden), edited by Zhao Bing, 94–95. Beijing: Zhongguo Jianzhu Gongye Chubanshe, 2008.

Harbeson, John F. *The Study of Architectural Design, with Special Reference to the Program of the Beaux-Arts Institute of Design*. New York: The Pencil Points Press, 1926 (Reprinted in 2008).

Huang, Henry J. "On Chinese Architecture." In *Huang Zuoshen Jinian Wenji: Commemorative Accounts of Huang Zuoshen*, edited by College of Architecture and Urban Planning at Tongji University, 22–30. Beijing: Zhongguo Jianzhu Gongye Chubanshe, 2012.

———. "The Training of an Architect." In *Huang Zuoshen Jinian Wenji: Commemorative Accounts of Huang Zuoshen*, edited by College of Architecture and Urban Planning at Tongji University, 8–14. Beijing: Zhongguo Jianzhu Gongye Chubanshe, 2012.

Jia Beisi and Jia Yunyan. "'New Architecture' or 'Revolution' – the Choice of Chinese Pioneer Architects." In *Zhongguo Jindai Jianzhu Xueshu Sixiang Yanjiu: Research on China's Modern Architectural Academia*, edited by Zhao Chen and Wu Jiang, 26–30. Beijing: Zhongguo Jianzhu Gongye Chubanshe, 2003.

Lai Delin. "Liang Sicheng, Lin Huiyin Zhongguo jianzhushi xiezuo biaowei (Liang Sicheng and Lin Huiyin's Writings on the History of Chinese Architecture)." In *Zhongguo Jindai Jianzhushi Yanjiu: Study on the History of China's Modern Architecture*, edited by Lai Delin, 313–330. Beijing: Qinghua Daxue Chubanshe, 2007.

———. *Zhongguo Jindai Jianzhushi Yanjiu: Study on the History of China's Modern Architecture*. Beijing: Qinghua Daxue Chubanshe, 2007.

Le Corbusier. *Zouxiang Xin Jianzhu* (Vers Une Architecture). Translated by Wu Jingxiang. Beijing: Zhongguo Jianzhu Gongye Chubanshe, 1981.

Li Dehua and Wang Jizhong, "Tongjidaxue jiaogong julebu (The Tongji University Faculty Club)." *Tongji Daxue Xuebao: Journal of Tongji University* 1 (1958): 5–16.

Li Haiqing. "Lixiang zhuyi yu shehui xianshi (Between Ideality and Reality)." In *Zhongguo Jindai Jianzhu Xueshu Sixiang Yanjiu: Research on China's Modern Architectural Academia*, edited by Zhao Chen and Wu Jiang, 44–47. Beijing: Zhongguo Jianzhu Gongye Chubanshe, 2003.

Liu Zhong. "Liu Zhong Xiansheng Shuxin (A Letter to Mr. Liu Zhong)." In *Huang Zuoshen Jinian Wenji: Commemorative Accounts of Huang Zuoshen*, edited by College of Architecture and Urban Planning at Tongji University, 223–224. Beijing: Zhongguo Jianzhu Gongye Chubanshe, 2012.

Long, Christopher. "An Alternative Path to Modernism: Carl König and Architectural Education at the Vienna Technische Hochschule, 1890–1913." *Journal of Architectural Education* 55, no. 1 (September 2011): 21–30.

Luo Weidong. "Mishi Wendelu (Mies Van der Rohe)." *Jianzhu Xuebao* (Architectural Journal), no. 5 (1957): 52–60.

Luo Xiaowei and Li Dehua. "Shengyuhan daxue zuinianqing de yige xi, jianzhu gongchengxi (The Youngest Department at St John's University, the Department of Architecture and Engineering)." In *Huang Zuoshen Jinian Wenji*, edited by College of Architecture and Urban Planning at Tongji University, 127–133. Beijing: Zhongguo Jianzhu Gongye Chubanshe, 2012.

Peng Changxin. "Diyu zhuyi yu xianshi zhuyi: Xia Changshi de xiandai jianzhu gouxiang (Regionalism and Realism: Xia Changshi's Ideas on Modern Architecture)." *Nanfang Jianzhu* (Southern Architecture), no. 2 (2010): 36–41.

Peng Yigang. *Jianzhu Kongjian Zuhelun* (On Compositions in Architectural Space). Beijing: Zhongguo Jianzhu Chubanshe, 1983.

Qian Feng and Wu Jiang. *Zhongguo Xiandai Jianzhu Jiaoyushi, 1920–1980* (Education of Modern Architecture in China, 1920–1980). Beijing: Zhongguo Jianzhu Gongye Chubanshe, 2008.

Steinhardt, Nancy S. "Chinese Architecture on the Eve of Beaux-Arts." In *Chinese Architecture and the Beaux-Arts*, edited by Jeffrey W. Cody, Nancy S. Steinhardt and Tony Atkin, 3–22. Honolulu: University of Hawaii Press; Hong Kong: Hong Kong University Press, 2011.

Zhao Bing, ed. *Feng Jizhong he Fangta Yuan* (Feng Jizhong and the Square Pagoda Garden). Beijing: Zhongguo Jianzhu Gongye Chubanshe, 2008.

Zhao Chen and Wu Jiang, eds. *Zhongguo Jindai Jianzhu Xueshu Sixiang Yanjiu: Research on China's Modern Architectural Academia*. Beijing: Zhongguo Jianzhu Gongye Chubanshe, 2003.

Glossary

ao	奥
Cao Xueqin	曹雪芹
Chen Zhanxiang	陈占祥
Cheng Yuwen	程羽文
dong	动
Fangtayuan (park)	方塔园
Feng Jizhong	冯纪忠
Hangzhou	杭州
Helouxuan (pavilion)	何陋轩
Hongqiao	虹桥
Huagang (Teahouse)	花港（茶室）
Huang Zuolin	黄佐临
Huang Zuoshen	黄作燊
jing	静
Kongjian Sheji	空间设计
kuang	旷
Kugan Jutuan	苦干剧团
Li Dehua	李德华
Li Jie	李诚

Li Yu	李渔
Liang Sicheng	梁思成
Lu Qianshou	陆谦受
Luo Xiaowei	罗小未
Qingxian Gong	《清闲供》
qiyun shengdong	气韵生动
Shanghai	上海
shanshui	山水
shikong zhuanhuan	时空转换
Sun Yat-sen	孙逸仙（中山）
Tongji	同济
Wang Dahong	王大闳
Wang Jizhong	王吉螽
Wuhan	武汉
Xi Fuquan	奚福泉
xixue weiyong	西学为用
Yang Kuanlin	杨宽麟
yi dong	意动
Yingzao Fashi	《营造法式》
Zheng Guanxuan	郑观宣
Zhong Yaohua	钟耀华
zhongxue weiti	中学为体
Zuhe Yuanli	组合原理

29

BUILDING CANTON FAIR

Towards a Regional Modernism in Southern China (1950s–1980s)

Jiang Feng

Twice every year, during the weeks of the Canton Fair, it is almost impossible to book flights to and from Guangzhou.[1] Hotels raise their room prices significantly but remain full. One might assume this is the result of the historically recent manufacturing boom in the Pearl River Delta – and China in general – but surprisingly, the popularity of the Canton Fair preceded China's "open door policy." The Canton Fair went through the challenging times of the People's Republic of China; and designers of the various buildings of the fair had to address, with architecture, paradigm shifts in national policies (Figure 29.1). Due to its special economic and political relevance, the buildings of the Canton Fair implicitly represent the diverse manner of China's urban development and architectural movements.

Prologue

The Canton Fair, also known as the Biannual China Export Commodities Fair, was founded in 1957. It was the most important international trade event in People's Republic of China, and it has never been interrupted, even during the Cultural Revolution. China was in great need of many critical supplies from overseas, and the Canton Fair was established in order to earn foreign exchange.[2] To some extent, the Canton Fair was outside of ideological struggles. Mao Zedong once pragmatically summarized the relations between China and other countries: "No matter how reactionary they are, as long as they want to do business with us, want to establish diplomatic relations with us, we should win them over."[3]

Guangzhou, the city known in Western countries as Canton, has been developing international trade continuously for about 2000 years and was one of China's most important treaty ports in history. For many decades, Guangzhou was the only port in China that was open to international shipping. Guangzhou was far away from the political center in the north, and close to Macau – a city with international communities managed by the Portuguese since the sixteenth century – and Hong Kong, a British enclave since the mid-nineteenth century. Moreover, Guangdong Province, of which Guangzhou is the capital, is the major hometown of overseas Chinese. Therefore, Canton has geopolitical and social capital advantages in connecting to the outside world.

The Canton Fair creates great opportunities for architects, as exhibition halls, hotels, and transportation facilities need to be developed. One of the first questions when establishing the

DOI: 10.4324/9781315851112-42

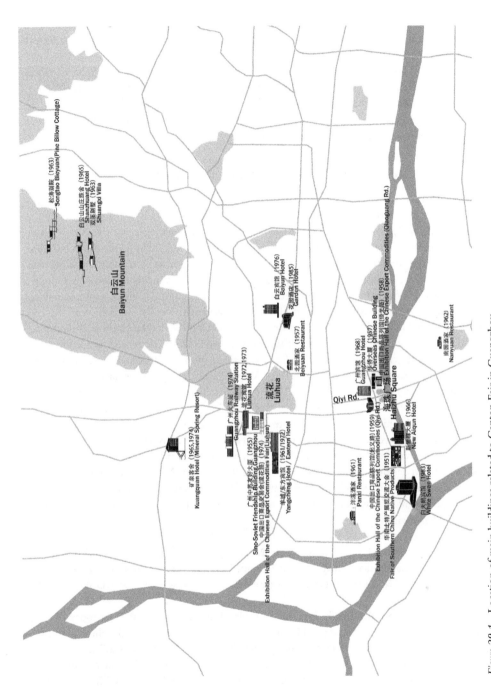

Figure 29.1 Location of main buildings related to Canton Fair in Guangzhou.

Source: Conceived and drawn by author. © Jiang Feng.

Canton Fair was: What is the proper place to hold the fair? Canton's historical trade center, "Thirteen Hongs,"[4] had been reduced to smoke and ashes in the fire of 1856, during the second Opium War. Other relevant questions were: What kind of architecture should the Canton Fair utilize? What messages did the People's Republic want to send its people and the outer world through the architecture of the Canton Fair? Would the event trigger significant progress towards a new architecture for a new China?

Soon after the foundation of the Canton Fair, China experienced the "Three Years of Great Famine," the Cultural Revolution, and other historical events such as the breakdown of Sino–Soviet relations, the establishment of Sino–US diplomatic ties, and the diplomatic normalization of the Sino–Japan relations. The architecture of the Canton Fair had to respond to the evolving ideologies as the political condition was evolving.

Act One (1957–1959): Location and Relocation

Over the first three years, the Canton Fair was held in three different main exhibition halls. Locations and scale varied from year to year.

The opening of Canton Fair was on April 15, 1957, in a rental space of the Sino–Soviet Friendship Building. The winter before that, another fair had been held in the same building to gain experience for organizing the Canton Fair. The Sino–Soviet Friendship Building was built in 1955, for the Exhibition of Economic and Cultural Achievements of USSR in Guangzhou. The 19,700 m² building, accompanied by several plazas and green fields, was erected on an 11.4-hectare site to the west of Yuexiu Hill. Total investment was 2.8 million Yuan, or 130 Yuan/m² (not including equipment). Compared to the Sino–Soviet Friendship Building in Shanghai, which cost over 300 Yuan/m², it was very cost efficient. The project was completed in only five months, including design and construction, with construction even continuing through the rainy season known as Dragon Boat Water.[5] Finally, the project realized the target of "greater, faster, better and more economical." The chief architect of the Sino–Soviet Friendship Building was Lin Keming (1900–1999). Mai Yuxi, She Junnan (1916–1998), and Jin Zeguang from Guangzhou Municipal Design Institute were also on the design team. Lin treated the exhibition hall as a showcase in itself and emphasized artistry and ideology. The figuration of the main façade followed the Zhdanov Style. The premier principle of Lin's design was to achieve a good layout and aesthetic appearance. Soviet Union architect Andreyev suggested reducing floor area and volume and simplifying decorations. The final result, according to Lin himself, met the requirement of use, but "as for the artistic level, is far below the exhibition halls in Beijing and Shanghai."[6]

The first session of Canton Fair was attended by 1,223 merchants. They came from 19 countries and regions, including Hong Kong, Macau, Japan, Singapore, Malaysia, Indonesia, Thailand, Burma, Cambodia, Canada, Great Britain, Belgium, France, and others.[7] The gross export turnover was 17.54 million US dollars (the exchange rate was fixed at 1 USD = 2.4618 CNY at the time).

In the spring of 1958, the Exhibition Hall of China Export Commodities (at today's No. 2 Qiaoguang Road) located southeast of Haizhu Square was completed, and the third session of Canton Fair was moved there while the Sino–Soviet Friendship Building was still rented by the fair (Figure 29.2). Designed by Mai Yuxi, the hall was composed of several distinct volumes and the total floor area was 14,500 m². Adjacent to the north was the Overseas Chinese Building built in 1957, designed by Mai Yuxi and Zhu Shizhuang. Compared with the Oversea Chinese Building "with a little flavor of national decorations,"[8] the new Exhibition Hall is quite modern. The total cost of construction is 2.8 million Yuan, averagely 96 Yuan/m².[9]

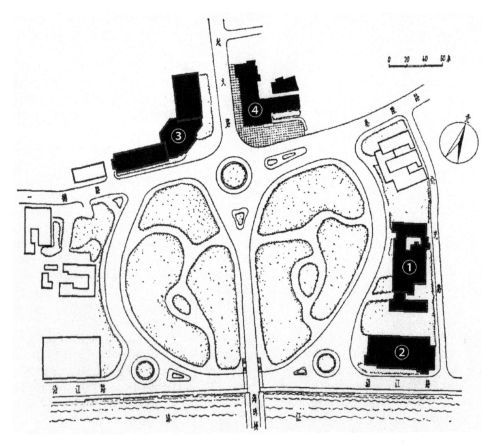

Figure 29.2　Master Plan of Haizhu Square, Guangzhou. 1) Oversea Chinese Building, 1957; 2) Hall on Qiaoguang Rd, 1958; 3) Hall on Qiyi Rd, 1959; 4) Guangzhou Hotel, 1968.

Source: Guangzhou Chengshi Guihuachu Shejizu, "Guangzhou Binguan (Guangzhou Hotel)," *Jianzhu Xuebao*, no. 2 (1973): 18; with permission and courtesy of *Jianzhu Xuebao* Editorial Office.

The sixth session of Canton Fair was held in the autumn of 1959, and the main venue moved to the new China Export Commodities Exhibition Hall at No. 1, Qiyi Road, located at the northwest side of Haizhu Square. To celebrate the ten-year anniversary of the liberation of Guangzhou, Haizhu Square was redesigned. A statue of a People's Liberation Army soldier was put on the axis of the square. The eight-story new hall was 33,893 m^2 in size, with a total cost of 3 million Yuan. The hall was in a simplified neo-classical style, symmetrical in plan and figuration. It exposed a Beaux-Arts origin through the proportion and detail treatments. There are roof gardens on top of both wings. Lin Keming was the main architect, while Mai Yuxi and Zhu Shizhuang were on the design team as well. Lin carried out the Beaux-Arts tradition while adopting the simplified socialist classical style in his design, to follow the changing ideology of the time. Haizhu Square became the first stable location of the Canton Fair. It was close to the Tianzi Dock, Haizhu Bridge, and Dashatou Railway Station, the terminal of Canton-Kowloon Railway, and was therefore conveniently located for transportation. Haizhu Square is also an important node on the city axis. The axis, as suggested by Henry Murphy, was set up in the 1920s and used by the municipal government of the Republic of China to express the city's spirit.[10] Through the urban design and the new arrangement of Haizhu Square and the Canton Fair, the new government led by the Communist Party of China was trying to endow the axis with new content and new meaning.

A certain proportion (varying between 1% and 0.1%) of the gross turnover of Canton Fair was kept as handling fees for running the Fair, including maintenance and expansion of the buildings. From the 1956 trial fair to 1966, the 11 years' gross turnover of Canton Fair was 3,826.1 million US dollars. The total handling fee was 23.06 million Yuan, within which 7.1 million Yuan was put into construction works.[11]

Lin Keming played a key role in the design of the early Canton Fair buildings. He was an architect as well as an official of the Construction Bureau of Guangzhou City at that time. Lin graduated from the Lyon campus of École des Beaux-Arts[12] and was taught by Tony Garnier, a pioneer of concrete construction and the proponent of the Industrial City. During the Republic of China period, Lin worked as a consultant for the Sun Yat-sen Memorial Hall in Guangzhou and designed a series of National Style buildings, such as the Sun Yat-sen Library and several buildings on the Shipai campus of National Sun Yat-sen University. Lin was skilled at various styles, not only neo-classical and traditional Chinese, but also modern. His design also addressed the need to adapt to the humid and hot climate of "South China" (Guangdong Province) – his contemporaries, architects Hsia Tchang-sie (Xia Changshi, 1905–1996) and Chen Boqi (1903–1973), developed climate-adaptive design in South China (Guangdong) through the research and practice of ventilation, shading, thermal insulation, and damp proof.

Lin Keming had designed several modern buildings before, including the Dade Road Theater, Campus of Xiangqin University in Shiliugang, and his own house on Yuexiubei Road. Lin designed the master plan and two exhibition pavilions for the Fair of Southern China Local and Special Products in 1951, which happened at the original site of Thirteen Hongs. That fair was the first time that International Style buildings were presented collectively in the People's Republic. More than ten architects from different institutions were invited to design the 12 pavilions of the Fair. All the pavilions were designed as semi-permanent buildings, and they reshaped the new character of architecture of South China (Guangdong) as transparent, light, and lucid. However, the International Style buildings soon encountered strong ideological critique. *Jianzhu Xuebao* (Architectural journal), second issue of 1954, published a reader's letter forwarded from *The People's Daily*, in which the author Lin Fan criticized these buildings as "Old Peony of capitalist countries," "cubic boxes, pigeonhole, streamline in American style and Hong-Kong style," and stated that "people require architects to carry out criticism and self-criticism."[13] Maybe because of the strong critique and his identity as a technical official, Lin Keming consciously stayed close to the requirement of mainstream ideology and ceased designing modern-style buildings for a long time after. Whether in the Sino–Soviet Friendship Building finished in 1955, Exhibition Hall on Qiyi Road in 1959, or the Yangcheng Hotel in 1961, he generally obeyed the principle of "Socialist content, national forms."

Act Two (1963): Modern Garden Buildings and a Lin Xi Task Force

Since 1963, several garden villas have been built on Baiyun Mountain for the leaders of the country, who often visited Guangzhou because of the Canton Fair. Architect Mo Bozhi (1914–2003) was in charge of Shanzhuang Hotel and the Shuangxi Villa (Twin-streams villa). These resort buildings didn't need to convey ideological meaning; instead, they expressed both the spirit of modernism and elaborations on the theme of the traditional garden.

After the "Three Years of Great Famine" from 1959 to 1961, China started to import rice, and it was necessary to gain more foreign currency. Therefore, the Canton Fair became even more important to China. Many leaders of the country, such as Liu Shaoqi, Zhou Enlai, Chen Yi, Dong Biwu, and He Long came to Guangzhou more frequently than before to inspect the fair. Where to properly accommodate such high-level leaders? The answer was Baiyun Mountain. Through the province's leader Tao Zhu's effort of planting pine trees all over the mountain in the 1950s, Baiyun Mountain was transformed from a tomb hill to a resort with a beautiful landscape. Shuangxi Villa was built in 1963 and Shanzhuang Hotel in 1965. The Kuangquan Hotel, also known as the Mineral Spring Resort, resulted from the renovation of old warehouses in 1964 and was expanded in 1974. About the same time, gardens like the Orchid Garden and Songtao Bieyuan (literally, "Pine Billow Cottage") designed by Zheng Zuliang (1914–1994) and Li Muxiang, among others, were also completed. Kuangquan Hotel was described as – in China – "the first complex to develop planning traditions by combining landscape with buildings to create elegant effects of organic interpenetration of interior with exterior space."[14] However, Shanzhuang Hotel, which adopted the same approach, was built earlier, and the garden-based innovation of Kuangquan Hotel was not completed until 1974.

Mo Bozhi (1914–2003), born in a contractor's family in Dongguan, was familiar with traditional buildings, gardens, and construction techniques from a very young age. After graduating from the Civil Engineering Department of National Sun Yat-sen University in 1936, he started to do some construction work. Mo met architect Dr. Hsia Tchang-sie when both of them were working on the construction of the Burma Railway in Yunnan Province. Hsia defended his PhD thesis at Tubingen University in 1932, then guided Ernst Boerschmann on a nine-month investigation of ancient Chinese buildings.[15] Hsia became a proofreader for Zhongguo Yingzao Xueshe (Society for Research in Chinese Architecture) in 1934 and took part in the investigation of Suzhou gardens and historic buildings in 1935. Hsia Tchang-sie started to investigate and study Lingnan (South China) traditional gardens in the late 1950s. Hsia was a mentor and friend of Mo and they studied *tingyuan* (courtyard-gardens) together. Mo designed three garden restaurants in Guangzhou: North Garden in 1957, Panxi Restaurant in 1961, and South Garden in 1962. In history, a garden was a special place for rich families and refined scholars. Common people were not able to enjoy gardens. Garden restaurants allowed them to experience the interest and charm of traditional gardens. These practices also built the foundation for Mo Bozhi's future effort to combine modern architecture with traditional gardens.

Mo Bozhi concentrated on architectural design after that. Because he was not educated as an architect, he didn't draft much and instead focused on thinking and construction issues. Although some architects underestimated Mo because he only made quick sketches, he has come to be seen by many as a leader of his time in architectural thinking. He led a team to design Shanzhuang Hotel,[16] whose members included Chen Weilian (1935–1985), Wu Weiliang, Cai Dedao, and Lin Zhaozhang. All of them graduated from the Architecture Department of South China Institute of Technology or its predecessor, the Architectural Engineering Department of National Sun Yat-sen University. Because the team was called on by Lin Xi, the vice mayor of Guangzhou, it was also dubbed the "Lin Xi Task Force." Later, the team worked on other important projects. It was organized temporarily, so there was no fixed name. Different researchers refer to it by different names, including Foreign Trade Projects Design Group, or Tourism Design Group.

Spring is the key element in Mo Bozhi's modern garden buildings. Two streams cross the Shuangxi Villa. Three stacked springs run through the Shanzhuang Hotel. These remind us of Frank Lloyd Wright's Falling Water House. There are other similar characters, such as the use of stone walls and flag stone paving, and the sense of a stretched horizon, among others. Mo Bozhi was successful in creating picturesque images and dynamic space through the treatment of topography and the use of the courtyard garden, independent galleries, and chromatographic glass. Mo chose poetic images and artistic conceptions of traditional gardens instead of Wright's prairie. Some vernacular forms and construction techniques were also used in these buildings, such as the tiger-skin stonewall, which appeared in villa buildings in Wuhan and Guilin as well. The local tradition in Guangzhou, however, only used rectangular stones – so Mo's approach was a generic or non-local vernacular. When relations between domestic architects and the outside were cut off, the influence of world architecture ceased at theories and works of masters such as Wright and Le Corbusier whom they knew prior. For many Chinese architects, Mo Bozhi's works recalled of Frank Lloyd Wright, and they put him in the place where Wright occupied in their minds. Mo became an idol in China.

These modern garden buildings on Baiyun Mountain were related to the Canton Fair very closely although they were not a direct part of it. The experiments of combining modern architecture with traditional gardens proved to be successful. Later, many hotels built for the Canton Fair adopted the approach. Gardens became a fixed part of Lingnan modern architecture from then on. Accordingly, it has become a favorite among architects since then to create picturesque views and spaces.

Act Three (1965–1968): New Aiqun Hotel and Guangzhou Hotel – A Sudden Swerve

Sino–Soviet relations deteriorated in 1960 and broke off in 1965. What would be the ideological direction of Canton Fair architecture? To continue in the Socialist Style, turn to the International Style, or find a third way?

Two special cases emerged, the New Aiqun Hotel and the Guangzhou Hotel, both designed by Mo Bozhi with other members of the Lin Xi Task Force: Mo Junying, Wu Weiliang, Cai Dedao, and Lin Zhaozhang, among others. During the autumn Canton Fair of 1964, there were far more guests than expected and they came in a concentrated period. With additional impacts from the 15th anniversary of the People's Republic on the National Day as well as a typhoon that delayed the merchants returning home, accommodation was seriously insufficient. As a result, the New Aiqun Hotel and the Guangzhou Hotel were built to accommodate more foreign guests in the future.

The original Aiqun Mansion was a famous high-rise building completed in 1937, designed by Chen Rongzhi (1902–1979) and Li Bingyuan. The steel structure building, in a Gothic Revival style, was an imitation of the Woolworth Building in New York. Aiqun Mansion had served Canton Fair since the very beginning. The municipal government decided to build an 18-story hotel as an extension of the Mansion, and it was named the New Aiqun Hotel. Unlike the vertical line emphasized on the old Mansion, the elevation of the new hotel built in 1965 adopted horizontal lines. This might be the first time a high-rise building used horizontal strip windows in Guangzhou, and perhaps even in mainland China. At that time, a façade dominated by horizontal lines was considered capitalist i.e. a symbol of capitalism.

Another interesting case is the Guangzhou Hotel. The 4,300 m² site is again near Haizhu Square, opposite the old Exhibition Hall at Qiyi Road. Should the building itself be symmetrical and also symmetrical to the Exhibition Hall? What is the right style? The design had to answer these questions. The site was once considered for a commercial building. She Junnan proposed a draft for it, a composition with several cubic volumes in different heights with the main building facing the Pearl River. She Junnan's friends advised him not to adopt a design considered as *feng-zi-xiu* (feudalist, capitalist, and revisionist).[17] Later, it was decided to build Guangzhou Hotel at the site. Mo Bozhi picked up and finished the design with the Lin Xi Task Force based on She's thinking. When an article about the building was published in *Jianzhu*

Xuebao, the author – representing the architects – was "Design Group of Guangzhou Municipal Planning Bureau."[18] The 27-story hotel used parallel horizontal strip windows on the main façade as well. It was the tallest building in China at the time. Construction began in early 1966, but it took longer than expected to complete because the Cultural Revolution broke out. The project was on and off until it was finally completed in April 1968. During the Spring Fair of that year, Guangzhou Hotel accommodated Japanese merchants.

Later, Liuhua Hotel, Eastern Hotel, and Baiyun Hotel adopted strip windows to dominate the elevation without exception. It was appropriate for a hotel and easily constructed at a lower cost and in a shorter timeframe. Several years later, Mo Bozhi and the Task Force designed the 34-story Baiyun Hotel, the tallest building in mainland China upon completion, on which the influence of the Guangzhou Hotel is very clear.

Act Four (1974): Another Move and a Corbusian Interpretation in Guangzhou

After diplomatic relations were established between China and many western countries in 1972, as well as normalization of Sino–Japanese relations in the same year, more and more guests from capitalist countries were invited to attend the Canton Fair. This required the construction of larger exhibition buildings and more hotels. The Central Government granted financial support to develop foreign trade projects. In 1974, Canton Fair moved to Liuhua Road, where the Sino–Soviet Friendship Hall was located. The railway station, a bus terminal, and the telecommunications building were also moved there to support the Fair. Several hotels were built to accommodate international guests, including Liuhua Hotel, Eastern Hotel, and Baiyun Hotel. Teams from different institutions in Guangzhou were organized to design these projects. The collective design was signed in the name of the team. She Junnan, Mo Bozhi, and Lin Keming each led their respective teams. She Junnan, leading his colleagues from Guangzhou Municipal Design Institute, designed the Exhibition Hall of the Chinese Export Commodities Fair (Figure 29.3), Liuhua Hotel, and Eastern Hotel (Figure 29.4). Mo Bozhi led another team and

Figure 29.3 Exhibition Hall of China Export Commodities Fair, Liuhua Rd, Guangzhou, completed in 1974.

Source: © Lin Zhaozhang and Shi Anhai. With permission and courtesy of Lin Zhaozhang.

Figure 29.4   Eastern Hotel, Liuhua Rd, Guangzhou, completed in 1974.

Source: Zeng Zhaofen, ed., *She Junnan Xuan Ji* (Selection works of She Junnan) (Beijing: Zhongguo Jianzhu Gongye Chubanshe, 1997), 227.

finished the design of Baiyun Hotel (Figure 29.5). Lin Keming stayed active and was the chief architect of Guangzhou Railway Station.

Because the friendship was gone, the Zhdanov-Style façade of the Sino–Soviet Friendship Hall was blocked from view by the new Exhibition Hall acting as an extension of the old. She Junnan was in charge of the design of the project. The total investment was 20.75 million Yuan, and the total floor area was 110,500 m² after the extension.[19] She Junnan and his team used a brise-soleil shading system and openwork rosettes for the front elevation. She Junnan (1916–1998) was born in Vietnam and graduated from Tangshan Institute of Technology at Communication University in 1941. In 1948, he founded an office with his former teacher, Lin Bingxian (1900–1986, bachelor's degree, Ohio University), in Hong Kong, then moved back to mainland China in 1951. He thought architecture was for human values, not for the creation of things, and emphasized the importance of organizing space.

When She Junnan was commissioned to design Eastern Hotel, he had to face the existing old wing (former Yangcheng Hotel) designed by Lin Keming in 1961. The old wing has a symmetrical façade with some traditional decoration elements, enclosing a courtyard on three sides. She Junnan designed a modern building connecting the existing one, together forming a large garden. After finishing the design, She Junnan wrote an article on his thinking for the design. He was quite satisfied with offering more public open space for the guests, with a "roof garden at the top and a transparent stilt or *piloti* floor on the ground."[20] This reminds us of Le Corbusier's five points for a new architecture. The new wing has a free plan with a garden on the ground, an asymmetrical free façade, and very long strip windows. The Eastern Hotel can be seen as an interpretation of Le Corbusier's ideas. Maybe because of this, many Chinese architects of the time voiced high appreciation for She Junnan. It was a time when China didn't know the

Figure 29.5   Baiyun Hotel, Huanshi East Rd, Guangzhou, completed in 1976.

Source: Lin Rujian and Lu Yuanding, eds, *Zhongguo Zhuming Jianzhushi Lin Keming* (Renowned Chinese architect Lin Keming) (Beijing: Kexue Puji Chubanshe, 1991), 171; with permission and courtesy of Lu Yuanding.

new works of Le Corbusier, and most Chinese architects had no chance to design during the Cultural Revolution; She Junnan's works were read as a continuation of Le Corbusier's architecture and were thus highly regarded as a pillar for professionals.

At this time, the Canton Fair buildings generally turned towards the International Style. This was also influenced by the idea of making the Canton Fair more open and showing another face of socialist China. Most of the buildings had a strong feeling of modernism while also adaptive to the climate and cultural tradition of southern China. Later they came to be known as part of the Lingnan School – *lingnan* referred to the region and was vaguely referred to as South China. Mo Bozhi and She Junnan were the two leading figures. Both were educated in China, but both were considered aware of international standards and trends. Mo was good at traditional techniques and garden architecture. She Junnan was good at modern technology and space composition. Both Mo Bozhi and She Junnan were regarded as great masters who could catch the pulse of world architecture.

Act Five (1983): Garden in the Cage

White Swan Hotel, a new hotel with investment by Hong Kong entrepreneur Fok Ying-Tung, opened on February 6, 1983. Soon it became one of the most famous hotels in China. The hotel is located at the riverside on Shameen (Shamian) Island, the foreign concession area in Guangzhou. Mo Bozhi and She Junnan were the co-chief architects of the hotel. This was the first time the two famous architects had been in charge of a project together, and it was also the last project finished by the Lin Xi Task Force.

The site is a piece of reclaimed land, facing the broad water of the Pearl River. In history, the famous landscape here was E'tan Yeyue (night moon of swan pond). The site is 350 meters long east–west, and 60~80 meters wide north–south, with a total area of 36,000 m². Following the shape of the site, the 28-story main building is shaped in plan like a Chinese waist drum, and a lower podium extends to the south, to obtain the best view of the Pearl River. A modern garden was put on the west side. In the interior atrium, under a glass roof, there is a small traditional garden. A Tibetan-style pavilion stands atop an artificial rock hill of about ten meters high. Beside the pavilion, a waterfall falls into a pool below. On the rock above, three Chinese characters are chiseled: *gu xiang shui*, meaning literally "water of hometown," as a title for the scenery. The scene, especially the chiseled words, has evoked strong resonance from visitors, especially overseas Chinese who have left their hometown for decades or longer.

Because of the limited width of the site, the garden was inside the building.[21] Mo Bozhi considered this an interior atrium designed with garden features, rather than a proper garden that was covered to make it an interior space.[22] The atrium was in a centrally air-conditioning environment. Although sunlight could still come through the glass roof, in an interior space, the sense of a garden was primarily for a visual experience. The garden lost its outdoor environment and failed to provide the feeling of subtle changes of time, seasons, and weather. When none of these could be experienced, what the visitors encountered was not actual nature. Guangzhou was stepping into an active technology era. To the decision makers, climate adaptive design widely used in the prior passive technology era was not necessary anymore. Instead of a stilt floor, a ground floor enclosed by large glass walls became popular. And the garden was put into the interior, or would even disappear entirely. The interior garden here only acts as a symbol of traditional culture. When the significant sense of the subtle change of time, environment, and plants is ignored, the garden becomes a decoration and loses its essence as a representation of nature. In fact, it is also a closure of modernism in essence. White Swan Hotel is effectively a turning point for the Lingnan School to go downhill.

Garden Hotel, another famous hotel with investment by another Hong Kong entrepreneur, Richard Charles Lee, opened up in 1985. Hong Kong architect Szeto Wai finished the design based on the sketch drawn by I. M. Pei. A fascinating outdoor garden with a high rock mountain, waterfall, and fishponds was designed to reference the origin of the hotel's name. It is the last call of traditional gardens in Lingnan modern architecture.

Epilogue

Canton Fair was a platform for Lingnan, or South China, architecture. In those tough years, it was a central stage for exploring a Chinese modern architecture. At the beginning, architectural form swung between Soviet Union style and economic rationalism, while finally a simplified socialist classicism was dominant. When Sino–Soviet relations deteriorated, regional consciousness awakened. Architects started to explore climate-adaptive design and merge aspects of traditional gardens into modern architecture. On Baiyun Mountain, picturesque modern garden buildings created an impression similar to Frank Lloyd Wright's Prairie Houses. New Aiqun Hotel and Guangzhou Hotel were two special experiments to design something in a "capitalist" style – with horizontal lines. After diplomatic relations between China and many western countries thawed, Canton Fair architecture turned to a version of the International Style that combined with gardens when the main exhibition site moved to Liuhua Road. She Junnan epitomized the thought, skill, and technology of the Lingnan School. He designed with climate, garden tradition, horizontal lines, and distinct volumes all together.

Through a retrospective of the Canton Fair, we can find the core resources of the "new" of the Lingnan School: modernism, traditional gardens, and vernacular techniques. Canton Fair pushed forward the development of a modern architecture as situated in and reflective of the southern local tradition in the Lingnan region of China – broadly referred as South or southern China; in the process, Canton Fair marked the summit of this southern regionalist modern architecture or the Lingnan School. For sure, climate-adaptive design, garden tradition, and the simultaneous use of vernacular and modernism were adopted. We may recognize it as regionalist modern architecture.

Architecture also shaped the Canton Fair and established an open and modern image of the Fair for the world. Canton Fair was a very special event; and that is why its architecture could explore an approach quite different from the mainstream National Style. Also, because of the specificity, Canton Fair buildings were located in very special places and mainly built for a privileged minority. In some cases, the buildings didn't show true respect to the sensibility and rationality of the site but paid more attention to the visual effect and comfort, and the creation of cultural symbols. For an example, White Swan Hotel built a ramp bridge in the Pearl River to guide the guests directly to the lobby, but at the same time the bridge cut the visual relationship between Shameen (Shamian) Island and the broad river.

Tracing the distinct solutions provided across decades, the locations of the Canton Fair are also an indicator of the direction of urban development in Guangzhou. In 2003, Canton Fair was relocated once again. This time, it was moved southward to Pazhou Island. The area and volume are much bigger than before. The plan is to construct 700,000 m² of buildings, 395,000 m² of which were built during the first stage. This time, a hi-tech mega-structure design was selected. The proposal was from AXS, Japan. The new exhibition center is close to Hai'ao Pagoda, which was built in Ming dynasty and acted as one of the three lighthouses for entering Canton, is also very close to Whampoa Harbor, the historic anchorage point for foreign merchant marines.

The past of Canton Fair not only is carved into the memory of the city but also still influences the life of Guangzhou today. During the fair, international visitors and the Chinese chat everywhere, on the street, at mobile phone markets, in clothes shops, restaurants, and teahouses. In the teahouses, only those who get up very early can enjoy a leisurely morning as usual, not influenced by the tides of familiar strangers.

Notes

1   The author wishes to thank Yang Wenjun and Li Jun for collecting data and preparing for illustrations for the research that is resulted in this paper. Thanks should also go to Liyan Yang, David Gregory, and Francesca Frassoldati for sharing generously their observations and suggestions. This paper is dedicated to the memory of Liyan Yang.

2   Because the trade settlement between socialist countries was by book-entry, it could not create foreign currency. Canton Fair soon played the most important role in international trade in China. According to the record, in the 1970s, the gross export turnover of Canton Fair contributed to 41.7% of China's total export.

3   Mao Zedong, *Mao Zedong Xuanji* (Collected works of Mao Zedong), vol. 7 (Beijing: People's Press, 1999), 63.

4   The "hongs" were major business houses in Canton. The Thirteen Hongs were the original Qing-dynasty merchants of China responsible for foreign trade. "Thirteen Hongs" was an area for the "foreigners' quarters" or "barbarian houses." It became very prosperous when Emperor Qianlong limited westerners to the port of Canton in 1757, and faded from the scene after the First Opium War (1839–1942).

5   Lin Keming, "Zhongsu Youhao Dasha De Sheji Yu Shigong (The design and construction of the Sino-Soviet Friendship Building)," *Jianzhu Xuebao*, no. 3 (1956): 58–67.

6   Lin, "Zhongsu," 62.

7   Ouyang Xiang, "Guangjiao Hui Kefu Yaoqing de Guobie (Diquebie) Zhengce yu Zhongguo Jingji Waijiao de Zhengce Quxiang – yi 1972 nian Zhongmei Guanxi Zhengchanghua qian wei Zhongxin de Lishi Kaocha (Policy on countries or places to be invited for Canton Fair and its relations to the policy orientation of China's economy-related diplomacy – a historical study based on the situations before the 1972 Sino-US normalization)," *Dangdai Zhongguo Shi Yanjiu* (Historical studies of contemporary China), vol. 19, no. 3 (May 2012): 49–56.

8   Mo Bozhi et al., "Guangzhou Haizhu Guangchang Guihua (Planning of Haizhu Square in Guangzhou)," *Jianzhu Xuebao*, no. 8 (1959): 18.

9   Mai Yuxi, "Guangzhou Zhongguo Chukou Shangpin Chenglieguan (The exhibition hall of Canton Fair)," *Jianzhu Xuebao*, no. 12 (1958): 23–25.

10 Feng Jiang, "Guangzhou Bianxing Ji: Cong Wanqing Shengcheng dao Minguo Diyizuo Xiandai Chengshi (Transformation of Guangzhou: From a provisional capital city of the Late Qing to the first modern city of the Republican era), *Chengshi yu Quyu Guihua Yanjiu: Journal of Urban and Regional Planning*, no. 3 (2013): 107–128.

11 Guangzhoushi Difangzhi Bianzuan Weiyuanhui, *Guangzhoushi Zhi* (Guangzhou local chronicles), vol. 7 (Guangzhou: Guangzhou Chubanshe, 2000), 365–367.

12 Different articles use different names for this school, such as "Leon School of Architecture," "Leon Polytechnic Institute." In Hou Youbin's study on Yu Binglie, when Yu and Lin Keming studied there, it was a branch of École des Beaux-Arts. See Hou Youbin and Li Wanzhen, *Yu Binglie* (Architect Yu Binglie) (Beijing: Zhongguo Jianzhu Gongye Chubanshe, 2012).

13 Lin Fan, "Renmin Yaoqiu Jianzhushi Zhankai Piping He Ziwo Piping (People Require Architects to Carry out Criticism and Self-criticism)," *Jianzhu Xuebao*, no. 2 (1954): 122–124.

14 Dan Cruickshank, ed., *Sir Banister Fletcher's A History of Architecture*, Twentieth Edition (Oxford: Architectural Press, 1996), 1563.

15 Eduard Kögel, "Between Reform and Modernism: Hsia Changshi and Germany," *Nanfang Jianzhu* (Southern architecture), no. 2 (2010): 16–29.

16 According to Lin Zhaozhang'e lecture, Hsia Tschang-sie (Xia Changshi) designed the serpentine veranda between the canteen and the lobby of the hotel.

17 Zeng Zhaofen, ed., *She Junnan Xuan Ji* (Selected works of She Junnan), (Beijing: Zhongguo Jianzhu Gongye Chubanshe, 1997), 174–176.

18 Guangzhou Chengshi Guihuachu Shejizu, "Guangzhou Binguan (Guangzhou hotel)," *Jianzhu Xuebao*, no. 2 (1973): 18–22.

19 Guangzhoushi, *Guangzhoushi Zhi*, 357.

20 Zeng, *She Junnan Selected Works*, 102.

21 Cai Dedao, "Bai Tian'e Binguan (White Swan Hotel)," *Jianzhu Zhishi* (Architecture knowledge), no. 5 (1984): 16–18.

22 Mo Bozhi, *Mo Bozhi Wen Ji* (Collected essays of Mo Bozhi), (Beijing: Zhonggup Jianzhu Gongye Chubanshe, 2012), 154–155.

Bibliography

Cai Dedao. "Bai Tian'e Binguan (White Swan Hotel)." *Jianzhu Zhishi* (Architecture Knowledge), no. 5 (1984): 16–18.

Cruickshank, Dan, ed. *Sir Banister Fletcher's A History of Architecture*, 20th ed. Oxford: Architectural Press, 1996.

Feng Jiang. "Guangzhou Bianxing Ji: Cong Wanqing Shengcheng dao Minguo Diyizuo Xiandai Chengshi (Transformation of Guangzhou: From a Provisional Capital City of the Late Qing to the First Modern City of the Republican Era). *Chengshi yu Quyu Guihua Yanjiu: Journal of Urban and Regional Planning*, no. 3 (2013): 107–128.

Feng Jianming. *Guangzhou "Luyou Sheji Zu" (1964–1983) de Jianzhu Chuangzuo Yanjiu* (A Research on the Design Practice of the "Tourist Architecture Design Group" of 1964–1983 in Guangzhou). Master's Research Thesis. South China University of Technology, Guangzhou, 2007.

Garrett, Valery M. *Heaven Is High, the Emperor Far Away: Merchants and Mandarins in Old Canton*. Hong Kong: Oxford University Press, 2002.

Guangzhou Chengshi Guihuachu Shejizu. "Guangzhou Binguan (Guangzhou Hotel)." *Jianzhu Xuebao*, no. 2 (1973): 18–22.

Guangzhoushi Difangzhi Bianzuan Weiyuanhui. *Guangzhou Shi Zhi* (Local Chronicles of Guangzhou), vol. 7. Guangzhou: Guangzhou Chubanshe, 2000.

Hou Youbin and Li Wanzhen. *Yu Binglie* (Architect Yu Binglie). Beijing: Zhongguo Jianzhu Gongye Chubanshe, 2012.

Kögel, Eduard. "Between Reform and Modernism: Hsia Changshi and Germany." *Nanfang Jianzhu* (Southern Architecture), no. 2 (2010): 16–29.

Lin Fan. "Renmin Yaoqiu Jianzhushi Zhankai Piping He Ziwo Piping (People Require Architects to Carry Out Criticism and Self-criticism)." *Jianzhu Xuebao*, no. 2 (1954): 122–124.

Lin Keming. "Zhongsu Youhao Dasha De Sheji Yu Shigong (The Design and Construction of Sino-Soviet Friendship Building)." *Jianzhu Xuebao*, no. 3 (1956): 58–67.

Mai Yuxi. "Guangzhou Zhongguo Chukou Shangpin Chenglieguan (The Exhibition Hall of Canton Fair)." *Jianzhu Xuebao*, no. 12 (1958): 23–25.

Mao Zedong. *Mao Zedong Xuanji* (Collected Works of Mao Zedong), vol. 7. Beijing: People's Press, 1999.

Mo Bozhi. *Mo Bozhi Wen Ji* (Collected Essays of Mo Bozhi). Beijing: Zhongguo Jianzhu Gongye Chubanse, 2012.

Mo Bozhi et al. "Guangzhou Haizhu Guangchang Guihua (Planning of Haizhu Square in Guangzhou)." *Jianzhu Xuebao*, no. 8 (1959): 18–19.

Ouyang Xiang. "Guangjiao Hui Kefu Yaoqing de Guobie (Diquebie) Zhengce yu Zhongguo Jingji Waijiao de Zhengce Quxiang – yi 1972 nian Zhongmei Guanxi Zhengchanghua qian wei Zhongxin de Lishi Kaocha (Policy on Countries or Places to Be Invited for Canton Fair and Its Relations to the Policy Orientation of China's Economy-Related Diplomacy – a Historical Study Based on the Situations Before the 1972 Sino-US Normalization)." *Dangdai Zhongguo Shi Yanjiu* (Historical Studies of Contemporary China) 19, no. 3 (May 2012): 49–56.

Shi Anhai, ed. *Jinxiandai Youxiu Lingnan Jianzhu: 1949–1990 Juan* (Outstanding Architecture of the Lingnan Region of the Modern and Early Modern Eras: The 1949–1990 Volume). Beijing: Zhongguo Jianzhu Gongye Chubanshe, 2010.

Zeng Zhaofen, ed. *She Junnan Xuan Ji* (Selection Works of She Junnan). Beijing: Zhongguo Jianzhu Gongye Chubanshe, 1997.

———, ed. *Mo Bozhi Wen Ji* (Collected Writings of Mo Bozhi). Guangzhou: Guangdong Keji Chubanshe, 2003.

Glossary

Aiqun Hotel & Mansion	爱群大厦
Baiyun Hotel	白云宾馆
Baiyun Mountain	白云山
Cai Dedao	蔡德道
Chen Boqi	陈伯齐

Chen Rongzhi	陈荣枝
Chen Weilian	陈伟廉
Chen Yi	陈毅
Dade Road	大德路
Dashatou Railway Station	大沙头火车站
Dong Biwu	董必武
Dongguan	东莞
E'tan Yeyue	鹅潭夜月
feng-zi-xiu	封资修
gu xiang shui	故乡水
Guangdong	广东（省）
Guangzhou	广州（市）
Hai'ao Pagoda	海鳌塔
Haizhu Bridge	海珠桥
Haizhu Square	海珠广场
He Long	贺龙
Hsia Tchang-sie (Xia Changshi)	夏昌世
I. M. Pei	贝聿铭
Jianzhu Xuebao	建筑学报
Jin Zeguang	金泽光
Kuangquan Hotel	矿泉客舍
Li Bingyuan	李炳垣
Li Muxiang	利慕湘
Lin Bingxian	林炳贤
Lin Keming	林克明
Lin Xi	林西
Lin Zhaozhang	林兆璋
Lingnan	岭南
Liu Shaoqi	刘少奇
Liuhua Hotel	流花宾馆
Liuhua Road	流花路
Mai Yuxi	麦禹喜
Mo Bozhi	莫伯治
Mo Junying	莫俊英
Panxi Restaurant	泮溪酒家
Pazhou Island	琶洲岛
Qiaoguang Road	侨光路
Qiyi Road	起义路
Shameen (Shamian) Island	沙面（岛）
Shanzhuang Hotel	山庄旅舍
She Junnan	佘畯南
Shiliugang	石榴岗
Shipai campus	石牌校区
Shuangxi Villa	双溪别墅
Songtao Bieyuan	松涛别院
Sun Yat-sen	中山／孙中山
Szeto Wai	司徒惠

Tangshan Institute of Technology	唐山工学院
Tao Zhu	陶铸
Thirteen Hong	十三行
Tianzi Dock	天字码头
tingyuan	庭院
Whampoa Harbor	黄埔古港
Wu Weiliang	吴威亮
Xiangqin University	勷勤大学
Yangcheng Hotel	羊城宾馆
Yuan	元
Yuexiu Hill	越秀山
Yuexiubei Road	越秀北路
Zheng Zuliang	郑祖良
Zhongguo Yingzao Xueshe	中国营造学社
Zhou Enlai	周恩来
Zhu Shizhuang	朱石庄

PART IV

CONTEMPORARY HISTORIES
CHINA IN THE WORLD

Architects and the Issue of Autonomy

30

CRITICAL PRAGMATISM

Architects as Reflexive Individuals in Contemporary China

Li Xiangning

In March 2010, an exhibition themed "Projects Across China: Architecture Stories of Three Studios From 1999 to 2010" and a symposium were held in Beijing. It is a joint exhibition on the works of Atelier Liu Jiakun, Mada Spam, and Urbanus, the three very active and representative architectural firms in contemporary Chinese architecture. All three firms were established in 1999, the same year that the UIA World Congress of Architecture was held in Beijing. The decade witnessed growth and expansion of Chinese privately operated architectural firms and their competition with state-owned design institutes. This exhibition may symbolize the particular voice gradually heard from this unique group in contemporary Chinese architectural practice. Encountering similar dilemmas of contemporary artists,[1] private architectural firms are nearly excluded from all official design awards (including the National Survey and Design Awards and the Architectural Society of China's Design Awards) because they are outside of the state-owned institute system. However, they dominate the international and domestic exhibitions and media reports and become idols of the mass media and architecture students.

According to research about Chinese leading architectural journals,[2] among the top 40 architects whose works have been reported and commented on the most since 2000, the individual architectural practices account for 60%; the architects who teach in architecture schools and own relatively independent studios in medium and large design institutes account for 27.5%, while full-time architects from the state-owned medium and large design institutes account for only 12.5%.

Since the establishment of New China in 1949, the key player in Chinese architectural practices has always been the state-owned medium and large design institutes. Privately operated architectural firms began to emerge in the 1980s, and, arguably, they started to draw public attention as practices independent of state ownership since Yungho Chang founded Atelier FCJZ (*fei chang jian zhu*) in 1993, after he returned to China from the States. The discussion about experimental architecture among architectural journals like *The Architect, World Architecture Review*, and other magazines is in effect attention paid to the practice of then budding individual architects like Yungho Chang, Liu Jiakun, Wang Shu, Zhao Bing, and Tang Hua, among others. And an experimental paradigm, different from that of the mainstream, state-owned architecture institutes, emerged from the practices of these rising star architects. Their "experiments," in some way, have thrown a challenge to the mainstream model and gained momentum for the architecture culture with the latest Western architecture theories and practice as

DOI: 10.4324/9781315851112-45

reference. A new movement finally took place, and architecture, as a new contemporary culture public, attracted more and more public attention and enthusiasm.

Encouraged by the success of preceding individual architects, more and more graduated architecture students decide to found their own architectural firms to conduct independent architectural practice. Many of the current individual architects studied overseas, and some even worked for several years in Western architectural firms. Most of them are based in China's major cities. By the virtue of the urbanism and culture there, they are frequently seen at architectural exhibitions and reported on by mass media. In Shanghai's 2013 Westbund Biennale of Architecture and Contemporary Art, which served as a comprehensive and complete review of China's contemporary architecture since the year 2000, nearly 70 Chinese architects were selected and participated in the exhibition, mainly individual architects. Among them, about 35% were from Beijing, 30% from Shanghai, and the remaining 35% from all other regions of China.

Different from the experimental architectural practices in the 1990s, today there are a larger number of younger individual architects with more diversified patterns of practice. Without evident common guiding principles or revolutionary commitment, they work for the government, private developers, small private owners, and other different sorts of clients, and more flexible and adaptive strategies have evolved. "Critical pragmatism" may be an appropriate term to describe the collective practices of contemporary Chinese individual architects of the new millennium.

This chapter tries to sort out the practices of individual architects in China from 1990s' "experimental architecture" to a contemporary approach of "critical pragmatism." A shift of practical strategies, in response to changing social reality and spatial production systems, will be discussed. Current opportunities and challenges brought on by the latest new technology and social transformations will also be examined.

Experimental Architecture as Resistance

No matter whether the term "experimental architecture" is agreed upon or not, it is indisputable that in the 1990s a kind of "new" architectural practice "different" from the past practice appeared in the Chinese architecture. Such "new" and "different" aspects are reflected in not only architecture image but also a more independent way of thinking and manner of working. Many scholars in China described this "new" architectural practice as "experimental architecture," and accordingly the designers were tagged as "experimental architects," most of whom are emerging individual architects. Over the course of ten years, these "experimental architects" have turned into a group of star architects with vigorous creativity and outstanding works executed now and then in contemporary China.

As a matter of fact, the so-called experimental architecture and experimental architects are closely bound up in the specific social economy and cultural backdrop of China in the late 1980s and early 1990s. At the time, a new trend was surging, in contemporary art or architecture, with the desire of breaking through tradition and communicating with the world. Development of contemporary art (the "85 New Tide" art movement as an important node) and introduction and translation of foreign architectural theories set the stage for Chinese "experimental architecture." If the ten years between the mid-1980s and mid-1990s can be thought as the "preparation period"[3] of Chinese "experimental architecture," Chinese "experimental architecture" boomed in the following decade starting in the mid-1990s, witnessing a number of emerging architects, buildings, and architecture events and recording the development trajectory of Chinese experimental architecture – the phenomenon coming into being as a response to the social transition period of China.

Yungho Chang, Ma Qingyun, Wang Shu, Liu Jiakun, and Tang Hua were definitely the leading figures of the Chinese "experimental architects." Yungho Chang and Ma Qingyun were educated abroad and established their own architectural firms successively. In 1993, Yungho Chang established Atelier FCJZ, and two years later, Ma Qingyun founded his Mada Spam. In 1996, Yungho Chang completed the reconstruction project for Xishu Bookstore in Beijing, which is arguably known as the first and most famous example in Chinese experimental architecture. Chang's Split House of the commune by the Great Wall put forth efforts in addressing issues of material and structure. Chang also discussed the relation between Chinese tradition and modern urbanism through installation works such as "Bamboo City." Tianyi Square of Ningbo and reconstruction of the entrance of the Garden of Winding Water (Qu Shui Yuan) in Shanghai Qingpu district, designed by Ma Qingyun, both illustrate his reflection of China's current urbanism. The irony and banter often found in his works have fully replied to the rapidly growing new urban fabric and the decline, death, and renewal of the old urban quarters. He borrowed this idea and used it as the theme of the 2005 Shenzhen Biennale, of which he was the chief curator.

Different from Yungho Chang and Ma Qingyun, Wang Shu and Liu Jiakun were home-grown architects. Wang Shu's thorough comprehension of and strong interest in Chinese traditional culture had made him a traditional cultural man, persistent in references to traditional cultural artistic conceptions in his architectural design. His early work, Wenzheng Library of Suzhou University, was designed as pure white with simple modern volumes, which implied the special reference to Chinese traditional gardens. Although he read Western authors like Roland Barthes and Jacques Derrida, Wang Shu insisted on using in his buildings traditional Chinese materials as dark blue brick, wood, ceramic tile, and rammed earth and applying traditional construction technology in his buildings and art installations. Such exploration in "Chinese-ness" was perfectly demonstrated in the Xiangshan Campus of China Academy of Art and Ningbo History Museum. Liu Jiakun used to work for a state-owned design institute. He showed his interest in literature from an early stage of his career and even published his own novel. He established his office in the city of Chengdu in Sichuan Province, and self-consciously defined himself as an architect "working in the west (of China)" – meaning a less-developed inland part of the country. His designing works, Mrgadava Museum of Stone Sculpture and the faculty building of the sculpture department in Sichuan Academy of Fine Arts, applied regional materials and construction, revealing his unique understanding of China's architecture in the western region and local cultural characteristics.

Public attention to Tang Hua resulted from his proficient command of modernistic form, which was very rare in the Chinese architects of the time. He was the first among all Chinese architects to have his solo exhibition in Shanghai Art Museum. On the list of "experimental architects," we can also find younger architects like Dong Yugan, Zhu Jingxiang, Zhang Lei, Urbanus, Wang Yun, Zhu Pei, Atelier Deshaus, Standard Architecture, and so on.

Apart from architects and their works, there are a series of architecture events (exhibitions, forums, etc.) that evolved around Chinese "experimental architecture." In the "experiment and dialogue" (*shiyan yu duihua*), a symposium on Chinese young architects and artists held in Guangzhou in May 1996, the term "experimental architecture" (*shiyan jianzhu*) was put forward. In 1998, two Chinese scholars, Wang Mingxian and Shi Jian, published an article in *Literature & Art Studies*, "China's Experimental Architecture in the 1990s." In 1999, Wang Mingxian curated an exhibition entitled "Chinese Young Architects' Experimental Architecture," during the 20th UIA World Congress of Architecture; Yungho Chang, Zhao Bing, Tang Hua, Wang Shu, Liu Jiakun, Zhu Wenyi, Xu Weiguo, and Dong Yugan participated in the exhibition. In 2000, a documentary exhibition of five architects (namely, Yungho Chang, Wang Shu, Ma Qingyun, Dong Yugan, and Zhu Jingxiang) was held in Shanghai's "top-art" gallery – known as Room with a View – designed by Wang Shu. In 2001, the "Tu Mu – Young Architecture of China" exhibition was held in Berlin Aedes East Gallery with the participation of Ai Weiwei, Yungho

Chang, Liu Jiakun, Ma Qingyun, Wang Shu, and a Nanda Jianzhu group (including Zhang Lei and Zhu Jingxiang). This exhibition marked the first appearance of Chinese architects as a group on the international stage. In 2002, *Time + Architecture* magazine published a special issue on *Zhongguo Shiyan Jianzhu*, an experimental architecture journal from China, and reviewed the works of the architects under the umbrella of "experimental architecture" (*shiyan jianzhu*). One year later, an exhibition in Beijing titled "Ten Years of FCJZ" (*feichang jianzhu shinian*), curated by Atelier FCJZ, was taken as another landmark in Chinese experimental architecture. This exhibition highlighted the practice of Yungho Chang as an individual architect, and it inspired more young architects and students to explore thoughtful and independent architectural practice beyond the mainstream official architecture design institute system.

Although it might be difficult to clearly define "experimental architecture" in China, a rough list of related key words will help with understanding of this concept: young architects, individual practice, privately operated architectural firms, avant-garde, marginality, contemporariness, Chinese-ness, etc. Some of these words indicate the age of architects; some, as Rao Xiaojun pointed out in his article, "express a strong questioning attitude and challenge gesture towards orthodox or mainstream architecture trends and ideas from the very beginning."[4] As Wang Mingxian put it in his article,

> since the 1980s, the Chinese architects have broken the limitation set by the pure architecture tradition, and attempted to draw and extract the internal essence of the Eastern architecture from classical art. The experimental architecture of 1990s has proved the young architects' efforts in mastering traditional spirit more broadly and thoroughly. They are not content with extraction of traditional cultural details any more, but try to establish a new evaluation system under the condition of cultural exchange at present times, to seek and interpret an Eastern culture that can counterweigh the Western culture.[5]

Another critic, Jianfei Zhu, points out more clearly that the new architects (mainly referring to Wang Shu, Liu Jiakun, and Yungho Chang) are apt to be "right-leaning, conservative, personal, narrowly-narrative, emphasizing autonomous issues of architecture itself, tectonics, light and personal aesthetic experience; but the architecture before 1976 are almost completely opposite: left-leaning, (politically) radical, collective, broadly-narrative, irrespective of architecture itself."[6] I myself would rather use the term "resistance" or "refusal" to describe the attitudes of the independent individual architects, to use architecture as vehicle to challenge the Western and Chinese mainstream architectural discourse and ideology, with or without consciousness in their pursuit of avant-gardism.[7]

Diversified Architectural Practice and Critical Pragmatism

Back to the ten-year exhibition "Projects Across China: Architecture Stories of Three Studios From 1999 to 2010" by Liu Jiakun, Mada Spam, and Urbanus. The exhibition title geographically summarizes the cities (Beijing, Shanghai, Shenzhen, Xi'an, and Chengdu) where the three firms and their branches are located, but we can also find such information delivered: compared with the 1990s' experimental architecture movement with only several representative architects, today's China has witnessed individual architects establishing their own tribes and clusters in several important cities. Most of them are the main force, between their forties and fifties, such as: Yungho Chang, Ma Yansong, Wang Hui, Zhu Pei, Zhang Ke, Hua Li, Li Hu, Dong Gong, Li Xinggang, Li Xiaodong, Wang Yun, Wu Gang, Dong Yugan, and Xu Tiantian in Beijing; Ma Qingyun, Liu Yichun, Chen Yifeng, Zhuang Shen, Yuan Feng, Zhang Ming, Zhang Bin,

Rossana Hu, Liu Yuyang, Zhu Xiaofeng, Tong Ming, Li Li, Li Linxue, Yu Ting, Zhang Jia-jing, and Bu Bing in Shanghai; Zhang Lei, Ge Ming, Fu Xiao, and Zhou Ling in Nanjing; Liu Xiaodu, Meng Yan, and Liu Heng in Shenzhen; Liu Kecheng in Xi'an; Wei Chunyu in Chang-sha; Liu Jiakun in Chengdu; Wang Shu in Hangzhou; Wang Weiren, Zhu Jingxiang, and John Lin in Hong Kong; and Huang Shengyuan and Xie Yingjun in Taiwan. There are also some young architects in their thirties emerging with demonstrated talent, such as Han Tao, Tao Lei, Wang Shuo, Feng Guochuan, Fan Ling, and Wang Yan, among others.

These individual architects meet and communicate in various publications, exhibitions, col-lective design activities, and seminars, revealing different the subpopulation characteristics of dif-ferent cities. In addition, they participate in the architectural education of well-known Chinese architectural schools in small groups. Recently, Tongji University of Shanghai and Tsinghua University of Beijing have successively invited more than ten individual architects to teach as guest studio professors. With a focus on architectural practice, these architects also develop their career in multiple dimensions, including exhibitions, writing, teaching, academic research, and cultural communication. Such a state is quite different from that of their predecessors in Chinese architecture, even those in the contemporary state-owned design institutes. Confronting the complex social and cultural environment and featuring different living conditions and practice strategies, they are seeking their personal positions in a network of intricate tensions between the forces of autonomy and social reality, globalization and localization, and politics and form.

Firstly, they are confronted with the relation between architectural autonomy and social real-ity. The "post-critical" architectural theory in America developed in the previous decade advo-cates a kind of "reflective" architectural practice, which can reflect reality. Rather than a mere avant-garde resistance or simple refusal, it identifies an approach that incorporates the forces of capital and social reality. Two representatives of such a theory, Sarah Whiting and Robert Somol, have participated more than once in the debate in the symposiums and in journals such as *Time + Architecture* in China, adding an impact to the discussion. For Chinese architects, the chance to build their designs gives them the greatest benefit for living in the world's biggest building factory and also wins them more attention and more say on the international stage. Architecture has always struggled between autonomy and reliance on capital and politics. The contemporary architecture discipline is unable to ignore social economy and political culture to realize its pure autonomy. Therefore, the majority of these architects, facing reality, are trying to achieve a critical position through cooperating with reality with an aim to make the most of it.[8] Diversity in client types, such as government, real estate developers, cultural institutes, and individual proprietors, and constant variability in project nature and scale, may explain why few architects are maintaining a complete and persistent architecture language and are instead constantly changing strategies. After all, there are few architects who enjoy the right of picking up clients as one wishes, as Wang Shu does. The approach is also reflected in a critical realism – to survive and develop in the market, some individual architectural firms must resort to some short-term, expedited commercial designs and mass residential projects with quick returns to support the production of more interesting public or cultural buildings that consume time and energy. They are clearly aware of the difference between the two types of design, so those "cash dispenser projects" would not be shown in publications or exhibitions. The survivalist approach reflects a touch with reality a contemporary architect cannot avoid.

Secondly, they are confronted with the tension of the processes of globalization and that of localization. Thanks to an international perspective brought by their overseas education, many young architects in today's China are sensitive enough to take the initiative to think over the position of architectural practice in relation to globalization and localization and aim to make an interpretation of "Chinese-ness" in a contemporary manner. They have adopted a global modern form to deal with local issues and conditions – this may be a temporary and make-shift strategy for a while, but it has nevertheless developed or presented a reasonable balance between a design ideal and complex social reality. Among these individual architects in China, we can find those who preside over international architectural education as deans and heads of architecture schools with their overseas education background and architectural practice at home, such as Yungho Chang and Ma Qingyun;[9] those who win international building projects through constant participation in international competitions, like Ma Yansong; and those who are educated in China but internationally accredited through persistent exploration of "Chinese contemporary" architectural identity, like Wang Shu. The dual practice formulated by real construction in China and exposure in international architectural exhibitions and professional media enables each individual architect to find his or her own position in between the poles of globalization and localization. Another figure worth mentioning is Ma Yansong and his design firm, MAD. His few built-up works have maintained consistent formal identity and design quality. His recent work, Ordos Museum, is a perfect combination of cutting-edge concepts and nonlinear forms (Figure 30.1). His Absolute World Towers, accomplished in 2012 in Canada,

Figure 30.1 Ordos Museum, Ordos; completed in 2011. Architect: Ma Yansong (MAD Architects).

Source: Permission and courtesy of © Ma Yansong; photographer: Shu He.

Figure 30.1 (Continued)

and the Lucas Museum of Narrative Art in Chicago, which he recently won through competition with Zaha Hadid, UN Studio, and several other European firms, have made him the
first contemporary Chinese architect who has built important public architecture in the West.
His recent practice tries to combine the architecture of nonlinear forms with Shan Shui City
(mountain–water–city) originating from ancient Chinese ideas.

Finally, they have to achieve a balance between politics and form. Form, as a matter of fact,
is an important part of the core of architecture discipline. No matter how an architect claims
his/her works are divorced from formalism, form has taken root in architecture in any case.
Architectural competitions and tendering in China – affecting a general trend as a whole – have
been adopting a formal judgment one way or another. Whatever the approach an evaluation
takes, what to be resolved in the end is a proposition of form. The trajectory of contemporary
Chinese politics has inevitable influence on architectural form. City policy makers with obscure
political desires and aesthetic taste may eventually decide the formal criteria of architecture
and urban design. However, politics can also have positive influence on architecture and urban
design if given a proper guidance. The "Qingpu-Jiading" effect is an exemplary case. Dr. Sun
Jiwei, the leading figure in the district government, meticulously selected from a list of best

Figure 30.2 Long Museum, Shanghai; completed in 2012. Architect: Liu Yichun.

Source: Permission and courtesy of © Xia Zhi & Liu Yichun.

contemporary individual architects to design projects in the district. Some young and talented individual architects seized the opportunity and started their career here. These two suburban districts of Shanghai have served as an experimental laboratory for young architects, for them to become known and to step onto the contemporary architectural stage of China; these include Liu Yichun, Zhuang Shen, and Zhu Xiaofeng, among others. Most of their early architectural works were executed here. At the same time, these works take on certain special features because of the provincial characteristics of the two districts as elegant, traditional water-towns. As Dr. Sun is taking up his new posts in Xuhui district and then in Pudong new district, a group of high-quality buildings will be erected there soon – works designed by leading contemporary individual architects, invited by Sun. The recently built Long Museum, a work designed by Liu Yichun, is an exemplary building with high overall construction quality and a sensational design deliberation (Figure 30.2).

Current Opportunities and Challenges

For more than two decades, and continuing today, China has embraced rapid social, economic, and cultural change. Discussion of contemporary Chinese architecture typically involves complaints about limits and restriction, while much of the construction activity in China is described negatively as shortsighted operations impelled by expedient value judgments. In contrast, positive expositions identify individual Chinese architects whose works stand as manifestos of resistance to the existing attitudes of society and also of mainstream professional architects, both Chinese and international. A gap becomes apparent between the good taste and neat architectural articulation of the buildings selected and exhibited worldwide, and the mass construction that permeates all of China. What chances will there be for Chinese architecture in the near future? Is there an opportunity for a better Chinese architecture as a whole, rather than just a matter of exemplary but dispersed works? Will there be an approach to Chinese architecture that positively represents an urban transformation that could not be fitted into any of the social-urban paradigms that the West has experienced?

It is true that, these days, most new Chinese architecture may be considered as some kind of makeshift, temporary solution. But confronting a society marked by uncertainty, and currently inhabiting an instant urban environment that could be thoroughly reconfigured within a few years, what is the point of imagining monuments? The pursuit of quantity, speed, efficiency, and ephemerality has been for many years seen to be lacking in quality, deliberation, eternity, etc. However, might we not take those characteristics of the contemporary Chinese ethos as stimulating challenges? Instead of retreating to Chinese cultural tradition and finding nostalgic motifs for design, we might seek architectural positions responsive to massive change at the urban scale. If we could develop a Chinese model of urban development that is a new proposition – an alternative to the models pursued and propagated by the West – could we not develop a new value system in making judgments about contemporary Chinese architecture?

Interaction between the traditional core of architecture discipline and the new technological innovation has provided new chances to review the practice of contemporary Chinese individual architects and therefore look for the way for future development and the possibility of making special contributions to architecture. What we now observe from contemporary Chinese architecture is mostly variations of typical Western modernism architecture, regarding space, dimension, structure, material, function, or, if going a little further, light, poetics, and tectonics. From the practice of these individual architects, it is hard to find an independent and insistent architectural language (which Wang Shu's works may have), or mature strategies that are responsive to the rapid transformation taking place in contemporary Chinese cities, as well as continued attempts in architecture innovation and industrialization. But still, some trends can be noticed in the practice of individual architects, and these may become driving factors for the future architectural evolution in China.

Digital building technologies (including 3D printing, kinetic architecture, and BIM system) and international waves of parametric architecture brought by today's digital innovation have greatly influenced the practice of Chinese individual architects. Xu Weiguo, Yuan Feng, Song Gang, and Wang Zhenfei are China's representational pioneers in this direction. They have organized a series of international digital architecture workshops between 2012 and 2014. Apart from inviting leading architects and theorists in international digital architecture for discussion on Chinese architecture practice, they also developed a new direction for digital design and construction through their own built works. Xu Weiguo, from Tsinghua University, was the first to introduce digital approaches into architecture teaching and practice at the beginning of the twenty-first century. And the completion of some parametric buildings by those architects in recent years, such as the "silk wall" and teahouse project built by Yuan Feng in Shanghai for his workshop, and Yujiabao Engineering Command Center by Wang Zhenfei, has demonstrated the possibility that digital building technology has taken root and is developing in China. Such an innovation means not only creative changes in fancy forms, but also changes in the architectural culture and way of space production. If we take Lanxi Court in Chengdu, designed by Yuan Feng (Figure 30.3), as example, the architect adopted digital construction technology and combined Chinese traditional material (brick in this case) and way of construction. Recent development in 3D-printed concrete houses in China also reveals a chance of industrialization and mass production in the near future. At the same time, the digital architecture practice by

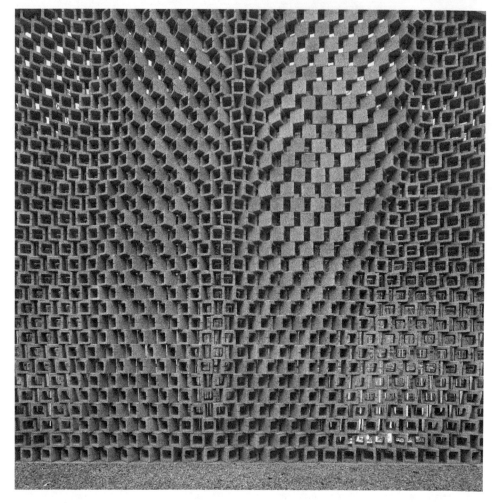

Figure 30.3 "Silk Wall," Shanghai; completed in 2011. Architect: Yuan Feng.

Source: Permission and courtesy of © Archi-Union Architects & Yuan Feng.

individual architects has also begun to influence the architects of state-owned institutes. The practice combining parametric and BIM construction technologies may change the production model of future Chinese architecture. A recent example is the headquarters of Phoenix Publishing & Media Group designed by Shao Weiping, chief architect of BIAD, the biggest state-owned design institute.

Another trend developing simultaneously with digital architecture is the increasing concern about social justice and building ethics in the practice of individual architects. One symbolic event has been the appraisal of the China Architecture Media Awards since 2006, which exerts an influence on the public and professional fields. Advocating "civil architecture," this award places the architectures' common and social character and contribution to society in a more important position than architecture aesthetics and designs itself. Award-winning projects such as the Gehua Youth and Cultural Center by Li Hu's Open Architecture studio; Maosi Ecological Experimental Primary School by Wu Enrong and Cultural Center by Fu Xiao; and the Xinya Primary Schools by Zhu Jingxiang have all pushed forward a kind of public culture value. The award, forum, and related media report greatly improved the social impact of a group of young and middle-aged individual architects. Due to the recent occurrence of several natural disasters, public participation and social ethic values are highlighted during public spontaneous relief. The design and construction activities for public welfare with architects and artists involved, like post-earthquake reconstruction, bring to the contemporary young architects more concern about people's livelihoods, social equity, and justice. More projects are appearing with a higher sense of social responsibility, like the "Tulou Commune" – affordable apartments for low-income groups in cities designed by Urbanus adopt the form of traditional southern Hakka dwellings – ring-shaped earthen buildings (Figures 30.4 and 30.5). Inspiration from regional architectural style and user-friendly design approach have both been mobilized to create a nice form.

A new trend correlative to increasing social responsibility and equity in architecture is that more individual architects turn their eyes to the countryside, design and construct country buildings, and even take part in its social reconstruction. Until nearly ten years ago, architects had concentrated on architecture design and construction in cities, ignoring the countryside because of its unfavorable economy and culture condition. However, in recent years, the crowded streets and industrial pollution in cities have lost attraction for architects, who then turn to the countryside where idyllic pastoral dreams still can be realized. In addition, the Chinese government has begun to pay attention to countryside development during the new urbanization progress, beginning with the design and construction of a number of Hope Primary Schools. The School Bridge project in Fujian province designed by Li Xiaodong won the 2012 Aga Khan Award for Architecture, and serial rural construction designed by Hong Kong architect John Lin, including House for All Seasons, made him win the 2013 Ralph Erskine Award from the Swedish Association of Architects. As some artists, designers, and social workers are stationed in the countryside and participate in community reconstruction there, some individual architects also persevere in building the countryside and even move out of their cities to become a member of the local community, such as Huang Shengyuan's Field-Office Architects in Taiwan Yilan, and Wang Hao, Zhao Yang, Huang Yingwu, and Chen Haoru, who have attracted a lot attention for their architecture activities in mainland China's countryside.

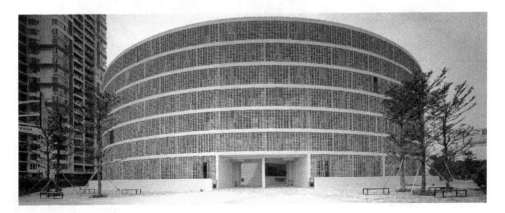

Figure 30.4 Tulou Commune, low-income apartment block (external view), near Guangzhou; completed in 2008. Architect: Urbanus.

Source: Permission and courtesy of © URBANUS; photographer: Yang Chaoying.

Figure 30.5 Tulou Commune, low-income apartment block (internal view), near Guangzhou; complete in 2008. Architect: Urbanus.

Source: Permission and courtesy of © URBANUS; photographer: Yang Chaoying.

Among the rural architectural practices, one individual architect deserves special attention: Xie Yingjun from Taiwan. He conducts low-cost residence projects simultaneously in Taiwan and on the mainland. The combined application of a lightweight steel frame system and local building materials techniques greatly reduce the construction cost. Unlike most architects, who are building neat projects pursuing design quality as first priority, Xie Yingjun pays more attention to the possibility of a low-cost industrial system. He himself has invested in a factory to research and develop new structural and building systems that can be mass produced and industrialized. With local villagers taking part in his construction practice, he has created a chance for social mobilization. He is clearly aware of the contrast between China's abundant mass production of buildings and the lack of an industrial system. Subconsciously, we are drifting away from the ideas of the Deutscher Werkbund and of Le Corbusier's own dream of housing industrialization. Often, Xie's contribution to mass construction and the industrial system is taken merely as a social or socially oriented practice, whereas in reality his system of designing and construction is an essential core that cannot be ignored.

Conclusion

Nowadays, the external environment for Chinese architects has greatly improved compared to the situation ten years ago. Young architects are even able to complete large-scale buildings with high construction quality. At the same time, the main challenge confronting these architects is how to choose among an ocean of styles, to hold their own positions, and to maintain a continuity of formal identity and design strategy in an ever-changing social and political world. We cannot deny that the flooding of Western architecture images makes a total or partial copy of form and concept from Switzerland, the Netherlands, Spain, or Japan a shortcut that saves time and money. This pragmatic approach, lacking self-consciousness, introspection, and critique, will eventually result in failure. Pragmatic or expedited operation erodes or at least poses a threat to social consciousness and self-criticality.

Although contemporary Chinese architectural practices have drawn international attention and Chinese architects have entered the spotlight on the international stage, the lack of theorization and design criticism about Chinese architecture is indeed a great concern for many. We see either superficial architectural criticism published by Western journalists and researchers, or Chinese scholars' research following popular Western theories and discourses. What we truly lack is a specific critical discourse that not only recognizes the complicated cultural contexts and social realities of China but also communicates and shares frameworks with the audience in the West. However, if we look at the discourses and theories that have greatly influenced contemporary architects in China in the last two decades, it is quite disappointing that we end up using only Western theories and methodologies, with rare exceptions.

Although the individual architects have contributed a large number of good-quality works over decades, they have not responded forcefully to the distinctive characteristics of contemporary Chinese urbanism, such as bigness, swiftness, cheapness, uncertainty, and so on. As a result, subconsciously, people see the Chinese architects as not proficient enough to counterweigh Western architects, in the eyes of both the general public and professionals. In my own experience, I often ask my architectural students about their favorite contemporary architects. Among various answers they gave, I. M. Pei is the only Chinese. Wang Shu has started to enter the list, but only after he received the Pritzker Architecture Prize. Even so, voices questioning the impartiality of the award are often heard among architects in China. Lack of self-confidence is another reason why most landmarks in China's big cities are designed by international architectural firms.

Therefore, as we rejoice in the fine and interesting buildings springing up under the Chinese individual architects' efforts, we have to be aware that a future improvement of design and building quality also relies on independent critical consciousness. Reflecting the ethos of our society and manifesting it in built forms, paying more attention to social connotation of architecture, and exploring the latent influence of new technological innovations – these might be the impetus for the architects of China to move forward in the future, where greater works may be expected.

Notes

1 Today, China's official system of art academies and state-sanctioned associations of artists and painters are totally different from the "independent contemporary artists" that have emerged in the recent decades.

2 The study and report conducted for 2013 Westbund Biennale of Architecture and Contemporary Art, by Wang Kai, Zeng Qiaoqiao and Li Xiangning. It was based on publications of China's five leading architecture magazines. They are: *Jianzhu Xuebao* (Architectural journal), *Time + Architecture*, *Shijie Jianzhu* (World architecture), *Jianzhu Shi* (The architect), and *Xin Jianzhu* (New architecture).

3 Shi Jian, "Shiyanxing Jianzhu de Zhuanxing: Houshiyangxing Jianzhu Shidai de Zhongguo Dangdai Jianzhu (Transformations of Experimental Architecture: The Contemporary Chinese Architecture in Post-experimental Age)," in *Zhongguo Jianzhu 60 Nian (1949–2009): Lishi, Lilun he Piping: Sixty Years of Chinese Architecture (1949–2009): History, Theory and Criticism*, ed. Zhu Jianfei (Beijing: China Architecture & Building Press, 2012), 296.

4 Rao Xiaojun, "Shiyan Jianzhu: Yizhong Guannianxing de Tansuo (Experimental architecture: A conceptual exploration)," *Time + Architecture,* no. 2 (2002): 13.

5 Wang Mingxian and Shi Jian, "Jiushi Niandai Zhongguo Shiyanxing Jianzhu (Experimental architecture of China in the 1990s)," *Wenyi Yanjiu: Literature and Art Studies*, no. 1 (1998): 121.

6 Jianfei Zhu's talk at the opening of the exhibition "Tumu @ Home" in 2002, as quoted in Li Wuying, "Shi fan chuangtong er bushi qianwei: Tumu huijia zhangji (It is anti-traditional rather than avant-garde: Notes on the exhibition of Tumu @ Home)," *Jianzhu Shibao: Construction Times* (20 August 2002).

7 See Li Xiangning, "Zuowei Dikang de Jianzhuxue: Wang Shu he ta de Jianzhu (Architecture as resistance: Wang Shu and his architectural works)," *Shijie Jianzhu* (World architecture), no. 5 (2012): 30–33.

8 See Li Xiangning, " 'Make-the-most-of-it' architecture and Chinese young architects," *City*, 12, no, 2 (13 Aug 2008): 226–236.

9 Yungho Chang was the head of MIT Department of Architecture, and Ma Qingyun is the current dean of USC School of Architecture and Planning.

Bibliography

Chang, Yung Ho. *Pingchang Jianzhu*. Beijing: Zhongguo Jianzhu Gongye Chubanshe (China Architecture & Building Press), 2002.

Li Wuying. "Shi fan chuangtong er bushi qianwei: Tumu huijia zhangji (It is Anti-Traditional Rather Than Avant-Garde: Notes on the Exhibition of Tumu @ Home)." *Jianzhu Shibao: Construction Times*, 20 August 2002.

Li Xiangning. " 'Make-the-Most-of-It' Architecture, Young Architects and Chinese Tactics." *City* 12, no. 2 (July 2008): 226–236.

———. "Zuowei Dikang de Jianzhuxue: Wang Shu he ta de Jianzhu (Architecture as Resistance: Wang Shu and His Architectural Works)." *Shijie Jianzhu* (World Architecture), no. 5 (2012): 30–33.

———, ed. *Dangdai Zhongguo Jianzhu Duben* (Contemporary Chinese Architecture Reader). Beijing: Zhongguo Jianzhu Gongye Chubanshe (China Architecture & Building Press), 2016.

———. *Mapping China: Construction and Deliberation in Chinese Metropolis*. Barcelona: Actar, Forthcoming.

Liu Jiakun. *Cishi Cidi* (Here and Now). Beijing: Zhongguo Jianzhu Gongye Chubanshe (China Architecture & Building Press), 2002.

Qin Lei. "Zhongguo Dangdai Jianzhu Zai Haiwai de Zhanlan (Overseas Exhibitions of Contemporary China's Architecture)." *Time + Architecture*, no. 1 (2010): 41–47.

Rao Xiaojun. "Shiyan Jianzhu: Yizhong Guannianxing de Tansuo (Experimental Architecture: A Conceptual Exploration)." *Time + Architecture*, no. 2 (2000): 12–15.

Shi Jian. "Shiyanxing Jianzhu de Zhuanxing: Houshiyangxing Jianzhu Shidai de Zhongguo Dangdai Jianzhu (Transformations of Experimental Architecture: The Contemporary Chinese Architecture in Post-experimental Age)." In *Zhongguo Jianzhu 60 nian (1949–2009): Lishi, Lilun he Piping: Sixty Years of Chinese Architecture (1949–2009): History, Theory and Criticism*, edited by Zhu Jianfei, 296–313. Beijing: China Architecture & Building Press, 2012.

Wang Mingxian and Shi Jian. "Jiushi Niandai Zhongguo Shiyanxing Jianzhu (Experimental Architecture of China in the 1990s)." *Wenyi Yanjiu: Literature and Art Studies*, no. 1 (1998): 117–126.

Wang Shu. *Sheji de Kaishi* (The Beginning of a Design). Beijing: Zhongguo Jianzhu Gongye Chubanshe (China Architecture & Building Press), 2002.

Wang Ying and Wang Kai. "Zitai, Shijiao yu Lichang: Dangdai Zhongguo Jianzhu yu Chengshi de Jingwai Baodao yu Yanjiu de Shinian (Gestures, Perspectives and Positions, Notes on Overseas Reportage and Studies on Contemporary Chinese Architecture and Urbanism in Recent 10 Years)." *Time + Architecture*, no. 4 (2010): 102–109.

Xu Weiguo. "Shuzi Xinrui: Zhengzai Yongxian de Zhongguo Xinyidai Jianzhushi (Digital Avant-Garde: Emerging Architects in China)." *Time + Architecture*, no. 1 (2011): 40–45.

Xue, Charlie Q.L. *Building a Revolution: Chinese Architecture Since 1980*. Hong Kong: Hong Kong University Press, 2005.

Zhu, Jianfei. *Architecture of Modern China: A Historical Critique*. London and New York: Routledge, 2009.

———, ed. *Zhongguo Jianzhu 60 Nian (1949–2009): Lishi, Lilun he Piping* (Sixty Years of Chinese Architecture 1949–2009: History, Theory and Criticism). Beijing: Zhongguo Jianzhu Gongye Chubanshe (China Architecture & Building Press), 2012.

Zhu Tao and Zhao lei. "Zhege Zhichi Nage: Jianzhu, Meiti yu Gongmin Shehui Jianshe (One Supports Another: Architecture, Media and the Building of a Civil Society)." *Xin Jianzhu* (New Architecture), no. 3 (2009): 16–19.

Glossary

Ai Weiwei	艾未未
Beijing	北京
Bu Bing	卜冰
Changsha	长沙
Chen Haoru	陈浩如
Chen Yifeng	陈屹峰
Chengdu	成都
Dong Gong	董功
Dong Yugan	董豫赣
Fan Ling	范凌
fei chang jian zhu (**FCJZ**)	非常建筑
Feng Guochuan	冯果川
Fu Xiao	傅筱
Ge Ming	葛明
Gehua Center	歌华（营地体验）中心
Han Tao	韩涛
Hangzhou	杭州
Hua Li	华黎
Huang Shengyuan	黄声远
Huang Yingwu	黄英武
Jiading	嘉定
John Lin	林君翰
Lanxi Court	兰溪庭
Li Hu	李虎
Li Li	李立
Li Linxue	李麟学
Li Xiaodong	李晓东
Li Xinggang	李兴钢
Liu Heng	刘珩
Liu Jiakun	刘家琨
Liu Kecheng	刘克成
Liu Xiaodu	刘晓都

Liu Yichun	柳亦春
Liu Yuyang	刘宇扬
Long Museum	龙美术馆
Ma Qingyun	马清运
Ma Yansong	马岩松
Maosi	毛寺
Meng Yan	孟岩
Nanjing	南京
Ningbo	宁波
Pudong	浦东
Qingpu	青浦
Qu Shui Yuan	曲水园
Rao Xiaojun	饶小军
Rossana Hu	胡如姗
Shan Shui	山水
Shan Shui City	山水城市
Shanghai	上海
Shao Weiping	邵韦平
Shenzhen	深圳
Shi Jian	史建
shinian	十年
shiyan jianzhu	实验建筑
shiyan yu duihua	实验与对话
Song Gang	宋刚
Sun Jiwei	孙继伟
Suzhou	苏州
Taiwan	台湾
Tang Hua	汤桦
Tao Lei	陶磊
Tianyi Square	天一广场
Tong Ming	童明
Tongji University	同济大学
Tsinghua University	清华大学
Tu Mu	土木
Tulou	土楼
Wang Hao	王灏
Wang Hui	王辉
Wang Mingxian	王明贤
Wang Shu	王澍
Wang Shuo	王硕
Wang Weiren	王维仁
Wang Yan	王彦
Wang Yun	王昀
Wang Zhenfei	王振飞
Wei Chunyu	魏春雨
Wenzheng Library	文正图书馆
Wu Enrong	吴恩融

31

ARCHITECTS AS AUTHORING INDIVIDUALS

Y. H. Chang, Liu Jiakun, and Wang Shu

Hing-Wah Chau

A new generation of Chinese architects has emerged since the mid-1990s.[1] This can be considered a significant breakthrough in the development of Chinese architecture from a historical perspective as independent architectural profession was in abeyance for four decades (1950s–1980s). After the establishment of the People's Republic of China in 1949, private architectural firms were gradually absorbed by state-owned design institutes, in which architects were employed as "engineers" for implementing official instructions and enforcing government policies. Unlike the anonymous collective production in the past, Chinese architects nowadays enjoy more freedom of individual expression.

The emergence of Chinese architects as authoring individuals was closely associated with the cultural liberalisation in China under the Open Door Policy of Deng Xiaoping in the post-Mao era. The import of western ideas through extensive translation of foreign publications and the intense intellectual discussion among Chinese artistic circles led to the '85 Movement (*'85 Meishu Yundong*), which was labelled "The Enlightenment of Chinese Avant-Garde" by Gao Minglu.[2] Compared with the vibrant and radical contemporary art in China, the development of Chinese architecture apparently lagged behind its artistic counterpart in the 1980s.[3] Chinese architectural practitioners were generally bewildered by the arrival of various western theories, including the historicist Post-Modernism and were unprepared to digest the imported discourse, struggling to reconcile the Beaux-Arts tradition with the Post-Modern eclectic fashion. Within this situation, young Chinese architects were inspired by the experimental art in China.[4] The Chinese Contemporary Architectural Salon (*Zhongguo Dangdai Jianzhu Wenhua Shalong*) was founded in 1986, launching a series of academic activities for exploring the relationship between architecture and culture.[5] The exploratory nature of experimental art and the possibility of the development of experimental architecture in China were discussed in a symposium among young Chinese artists and architects in Guangzhou on 18 May 1996, titled "Dialogue Between South and North: 5.18 Symposium Among Young Chinese Architects and Artists" (*Nanbei Duihua: 5.18 Zhongguo Qingnian Jianzhushi, Yishujia Xueshu Taolunhui*).[6] According to Wang Mingxian, a co-founder of the Chinese Contemporary Architectural Salon, this was the first symposium to discuss experimental architecture in China and the idea of experimental architecture in China was initiated by him and Rao Xiaojun in the mid-1990s.[7] Although the term, "experimental architecture" (*shiyan jianzhu*) has not been clearly defined in the Chinese context and has been criticised for being too ambiguous, it was a label that could highlight

DOI: 10.4324/9781315851112-46

the works of some emerging Chinese architects.[8] Deviating from mainstream conventions, the young "experimental" architects demonstrated their efforts to explore boundaries and to protest against the mainstream architectural practice.[9]

After the Southern Tour of Deng Xiaoping in 1992, the economic growth in China was strengthened under the so-called socialist market economy with Chinese characteristics. In response to the expansion of entrepreneurs, design-oriented developers and the middle class in society, significant reforms of state-owned design institutes have been carried out to enhance their competitiveness.[10] Along with the re-structuring of official design institutes, the re-institutionalisation of the architect registration system in China in 1994–95 initiated a fundamental change in architectural practice, enabling architects to work independently and to define their individual positions outside the official system.[11]

During the initial stages of their private practices in the 1990s, independent architects were marginal and peripheral. The first public occasion for having a dialogue between marginal and mainstream architects in contemporary China was the exhibitions held in Beijing during the twentieth International Union of Architects (UIA) Congress in 1999. In parallel with a retrospective exhibition displaying 55 architectural works by stated-owned design institutes from 1959 to 1999, young architects made their debuts in the "Experimental Architecture by Young Chinese Architects" exhibition (*Zhongguo Qingnian Jianzhushi Shiyan Zuopinzhan*) curated by Wang Mingxian.[12] Such an experimental architecture exhibition was considered to be inappropriate and was requested to be cancelled three days before its opening under hierarchical censorship. Despite the discrimination and hardship during the curatorial process, after a series of intense negotiation and discussion, this exhibition was finally held at the Beijing International Convention Centre, the main exhibition venue of UIA Congress, and successfully generated discourse and attracted media coverage.[13]

Marginal practices of young Chinese architects have gradually attracted the attention of their western counterparts. Some of the practitioners were invited to display their works in the "TU MU: Young Architects in China" exhibition, curated by Eduard Kögel and Ulf Meyer, in Berlin in 2001.[14] Since it was the first time for contemporary Chinese architects to show their works overseas, when their works were re-exhibited in the subsequent "TU MU @ Home" exhibition, accompanied with a public seminar in Shanghai in 2002, it initiated another round of discussion among Chinese architectural circles.[15]

Chang, Liu, and Wang

Some Chinese architects involved in these three significant exhibitions have demonstrated persistent self-conscious practice and reflective thinking, which deserve close observation. Among them, Yung Ho Chang (b. 1956), Liu Jiakun (b. 1956), and Wang Shu (b. 1963) are selected for analysis here. This does not imply that other architects participating in these exhibitions are unimportant. The reasons for selecting Chang, Liu, and Wang are not only because they were the only three architects who participated in all three exhibitions, but also their influence and outstanding performance in terms of their works and discourse production.

After ten years of Cultural Revolution (1966–76), universities in China were re-opened and the entrance examination system for higher education was resumed in 1977. Chang and Liu were within the first cohort of students receiving tertiary education, followed by Wang, who started his studies in 1981.[16] Chang and Wang studied architecture at the same school, the Nanjing Institute of Technology (NIT), which was renamed as Southeast University in 1988 and was regarded as "the most important base camp for the Beaux-Arts education" in China.[17] After the transplantation of the Beaux-Arts architectural pedagogy to China in the 1920s, it became a nationwide educational model.[18] Although the Bauhaus teaching approach was adopted by several architectural schools, it was only implemented for a short period of time due to social upheavals in the 1930s–40s, the unification of the national architectural education under the Beaux-Arts tradition in the early 1950s, and the interruption by the Cultural Revolution in the 1960s–70s.[19] Having studied three years at NIT, Chang went to the US in 1981 for further study at Ball State University (1981–83) and the University of California, Berkeley (1983–84). The technical training at NIT laid a good foundation for him, while the liberal American curriculum provided him more freedom for reflective thinking and exploration.[20] Although Liu and Wang did not study abroad, they were inspired by western theories and overseas examples as Chinese versions of foreign books and articles became available in China under Deng Xiaoping's Open Door Policy.[21]

Chang, Liu, and Wang are self-conscious in expressing their thinking through writing. They have published their writing since they were university students. When Chang was an architectural student in the US in the early 1980s, he was aware of the differences between the American liberal teaching pedagogy and the rigorous architectural training in China at that time. He published his articles in the Chinese architectural journal, *New Architecture*, in the 1980s to share his learning experience and, subsequently, his teaching methods in the US to his Chinese counterparts.[22] Through studio teaching, he emphasised the importance of paying attention to everyday life and making sensitive observation of surroundings. Similar views were also raised by Wang in his article published in the Chinese journal, *Architect* in 1984.[23] Compared with Chang and Wang, Liu was more interested in novel writing. His first published novel, *Mucking Around* (*Youhun*, 1980), expresses his personal reflection about the meaning of life.[24]

The publication of monographs has facilitated these architects in defining their critical positions in contemporary Chinese architecture. Among them, Chang was a pioneer in publishing his first monograph, *Feichang Jianzhu* (1997), which compiles the conceptual exploration of his early practice.[25] His subsequent books, *For a Basic Architecture* (2002) and *Architectural Verb* (2006), show the transformation from his early conceptual narratives to tectonic concern, involving materiality and construction.[26] By comparison, Liu and Wang, both locally trained architects who did not study abroad, show their substantial sensitivities to the use of regional resources and local craftsmanship in their *Now and Here* (2002) and *The Beginning of Design* (2002) respectively.[27] Liu accentuates his regional response, whereas Wang reiterates the importance of learning from artisans and everyday life as the beginning of design.

These three architects have close connections with educational institutions. Chang taught at four universities in the US for a decade: Ball State (1985–88), Michigan (1988–90), Berkeley (1990–92), and Rice (1993–96). His study and teaching experience in the US enabled him to be immersed in western ideas and concepts. Chang established the Graduate Centre of Architecture (GCA) at Peking University in 1999, while Wang launched an architectural programme at the China Academy of Art in Hangzhou after his doctoral research at Tongji University (1995–2000). Chang introduced tectonic studios at GCA to equip students with hands-on experience of dealing with materials, construction, and structure. The series of publications by GCA was an effective strategy to distinguish the school from the traditional Beaux-Arts curriculum, highlighting Chang's tectonic pursuit.[28] Similarly, Wang encourages students to gain hands-on construction knowledge, but with a particular focus on folk building techniques with an aim to continue and transform regional culture and traditions. The academic environment enabled these architects to enjoy more freedom of expression and to develop their individual architectural approaches. Although Liu has not taught as a faculty member in a university, he has maintained a working relationship with the Sichuan Fine Arts Institute in Chongqing, which commissioned him to design for the Sculpture Department building (2004) and the new campus for the Design Department (2006) in Chongqing.

Among the selected architects, Chang was a forerunner to set up his own atelier in China, namely *Feichang Jianzhu* (FCJZ), in 1993.[29] Regardless of the staggering economic growth in China in the 1990s, most of his early design commissions were either unrealised or small in scale, yet his architectural practice was inspiring to many architectural students and architects, including Liu and Wang.[30] Wang's Amateur Architecture Studio was established in 1998 during his doctoral research. Liu worked at the Chengdu Architectural Design Institute (CADI) after his graduation in 1982, but, aiming for a greater degree of independence, he finally decided to resign in 1997 despite the ample training opportunities and good promotion prospects at CADI.[31] After passing the professional architect registration examination, he opened Jiakun Architects Studio in 1999. The establishment of independent practice enabled these architects to assert their design authorship in the pursuit of their own trajectories of design thinking.

The Trajectory of Chang's Design Thinking

Chang's design practice may be divided into three phases: the Conceptual Phase, the Tectonic Phase, and the Urban Intervention Phase. The first phase (1981–98) covers his conceptual experimentation in the US, ranging from his studio assignment "Bike Story" (1982–83), the "Bachelor Apartment" for the Shinkenchiku Residential Design Competition (1986), smoking pipe models (1989), and the "Head House" installation (1990), to his early projects in China, including the Luoyang Kindergarten (1992), the Book-Bike Store (1996), the Upside-Down Office (1997) and the "Sliding Folding Swing Door" installation (1998) (Figure 31.1).

In 1998, Chang published the article "Basic Architecture," arguing for the importance of the tectonic quality of architecture and highlighting the relationship between materiality, construction, form, and space, in opposition to external ideologies and superficial ornamentation.[32] During the Tectonic Phase (1998–2002), his awareness of tectonic relations was enhanced by

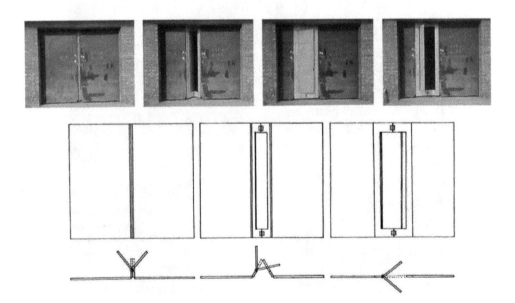

Figure 31.1   Sliding Folding Swing Door Installation, Beijing, 1998. Architect: Yung Ho Chang.

Source: Laurent Gutierrez and Valérie Portefaix, eds., *Yung Ho Chang/Atelier Feichang Jianzhu: A Chinese Practice* (Hong Kong: Map Book Publishing, 2003), 24, 37. Permission and courtesy of © Yung Ho Chang.

the realisation of his early architectural works, such as the Morningside Centre of Mathematics (1998), the Mountain Dialogue Space (1998), and the Split House (2002). The emphasis on materiality and construction has been further elaborated in his article "Learning from Industrial Architecture" (2000) and his second monograph, *For a Basic Architecture* (2002).[33]

Chang's competition entry for the Central China Television (CCTV) Headquarters, Beijing (2002), in collaboration with Toyo Ito, and his article "On Urban Research" (2003), express

Figure 31.2 Top Floor Art Gallery, Shanghai, 2000. Architect: Wang Shu

Source: Wang Shu, *Sheji de Kaishi* (The Beginning of Design) (Beijing: Zhongguo Jianzhu Gongye Chubanshe, 2002), 97. Permission and courtesy of © Wang Shu.

his concern for the relationship between architecture and the city.[34] In the Urban Intervention Phase from 2002 onwards, he has been involved in a series of planning-related works, such as the Jianchuan Museum Town (2003), the Qianmen revitalisation (2008), and the Jiading Advertisement Base (2013).

The division of Chang's design practice into three phases does not imply that his particular concern is limited within a single phase. The second and third phases signify his awareness of tectonic quality and urban intervention, but his conceptual experimentation and tectonic exploration have been continued from the first and second phases to nowadays, as exemplified by the inventive use of Chinese roof tiles of the Tea Pavilion installation for the Seoul Design Fair (2010), the seeing and framing of the Audi Haus car display stand (2011), and the use of light-weight materials for the FRP House in Nanjing.[35]

Figure 31.3 Teaching Building no. 14, Xiangshan Campus, China Academy of Art, Hangzhou, 2007. Architect: Wang Shu.

Source: © Jianfei Zhu.

The Trajectory of Liu's Design Thinking

Liu worked for CADI for more than ten years after graduation, so the first phase of his design practice may be considered as the State Design Institute Phase (1982–97). In 1997, Liu published the seminal article "A Narrative Discourse and A Low-tech Strategy," signifying the Regional Phase (1997–2006).[36] Significant works in this phase include the Xiyuan Leisure Camp (1996); the artists' studio series in rural areas near Chengdu: the Luo Zhongli Studio (1996), the Dan Hong Studio (1997), the He Douling Studio (1997), and the Wang Hai Studio (1997); his installation "Follow the Wind" (2002); the Luyeyuan Stone Sculpture Museum, Chengdu (2002); and the Design Department, Sichuan Fine Arts Institute, Chongqing (2006).

From 2006 onwards, the social dimension of Liu's design practice has become more explicit, starting from his proposed public access within the private residential development, the Time Rose Garden Phase III, Guangzhou (2006), and his engagement with recent traditions in the series of exhibition halls of the Cultural Revolution Clock Museum, Anren (2007) (Figure 31.4). The climax of the Social Critique Phase (2006–present) was his response to the devastating Sichuan earthquake in 2008, including the erection of the Hu Huishan Memorial House (2009) to commemorate the death of an ordinary school girl and the production of Rebirth Bricks by utilising the debris of the ruined areas (Figure 31.5).

The Trajectory of Wang's Design Thinking

Similarly, Wang's design practice may also be classified into three phases. The Early Phase (1988–97) covers his early formal experimentation, especially his deconstructivist experimentation

Figure 31.4 Exhibition Hall of Seals, Cultural Revolution Clock Museum, Anren, 2007. Architect: Liu Jiakun.

Source: © Hing-Wah Chau.

Figure 31.5 Hu Huishan Memorial House, Anren, 2009. Architect: Liu Jiakun.

Source: Permission and courtesy of © Liu Jiakun; photographer: Mao Weixi.

for the Community Complex for Youth, Haining in Zhejiang Province (1989), and the Fengleqiao Subway Entrance, Hangzhou (1991). During this period of time, he also participated in some planning projects, such as the Campus Improvement Planning of the China Academy of Arts (1993) and the Zen-Heart Tea Centre, Hangzhou (1994). Both projects expressed his interest in geometric superimposition and formal manipulation.

After working for several years as a freelance designer and a worker on construction sites, Wang spent five years (1995–2000) at Tongji University, Shanghai, to complete his doctoral research in history and theory with a focus on the city. In 1998, Wang established his atelier, Amateur Architecture Studio. He considers his architectural design as an amateur activity rather than a professional practice and emphasises the importance of continuous self-improvement and transformation through learning from daily life.[37] To him, a sensitive observation of the praxis of life is required in order to generate an appropriate design to suit actual needs.[38] He criticises the conventional approach of architectural professionals who only focus on architecture itself and consider it to be more important than other issues.

In 1997, Wang completed the interior design of his own residence, Hangzhou, with a strong emphasis on craftsmanship and detailing. This demarcates the Handcraft Phase (1997–2002), which is distinguishable from his early deconstructivism and planning projects. Another key example of this phase is the Top Floor Art Gallery in Shanghai (2000), in which he closely collaborated with artisans on site for handling different materials and construction details (Figure 31.2). In the West Lake International Sculpture Exhibition, Hangzhou (2000), he even directly participated in the whole construction process of his exhibit, "Earth Tamping," to gain hands-on experience in handling the traditional building material of rammed earth. All these works, together with the Wenzheng College Library, Suzhou (2001), are collected in his first monograph, *The Beginning of Design* (2002).[39] The book title reiterates his advocacy of learning from the beginning through everyday life and the collaboration with artisans outside the ambit of professional architectural knowledge.

After the completion of his doctoral research, Wang started to teach at the China Academy of Arts, Hangzhou. Since the early 2000s, he has carried out a series of research projects near Ningbo. Folk construction techniques, traditional building forms, and materials have been incorporated in his new architecture, as exemplified by the Xiangshan Campus, Hangzhou (2004, 2007) (Figure 31.3), and the Five Scattered Houses, Ningbo (2006). Having a keen interest in Chinese literati traditions of calligraphy, landscape painting, and garden design, his series of works in the Literati Phase (2002–present) reflect his design inspiration coming from cultural resources, with an aim to strive for the continuity and transformation of traditional culture to cope with contemporary needs.

Although Wang's design practice can be briefly analysed in three phases, his formal experimentation and artisan attitude continue to subsequent phases, while his interest in Chinese literati traditions can be traced back to his entrenched practice of Chinese calligraphy.[40] On the whole, the trajectory from early deconstructivist experimentation to the revitalisation of Chinese literati traditions can be easily observed in Wang's design practice.

Despite different trajectories of design thinking of these three Chinese architects, their individual practices can be analysed and compared in terms of conceptual studies, tectonic expression, use of tradition, and social awareness.

Conceptual Studies

Chang's conceptual experimentation is closely related to his architectural education in the US. He has explicitly expressed his gratitude for meeting "excellent teachers" there, especially Rodney Place of Ball State University, who "completely changed" his understanding of architecture.[41] Since Place studied under Robin Evans and taught at the Architectural Association (AA) in the 1970s, so the AA's teaching approach, as well as Evans's methods of observation, influenced Chang via Rodney Place.[42] One of Place's design studios in which Chang participated was titled "Use, Overuse, Misuse," requiring students to observe an everyday object that could fulfil all three aspects.[43] Chang selected the bicycle as his research focus under the theme of the "Bike Story" (1982–83). He interacted with teenagers on the street and used a camera to record how they used their bicycles to jump over kerbs, steps, and ramps. Through the "misuse" and "overuse" of different elements on the streets, these bicycle riders creatively converted an urban space into an exciting playground.[44] This recalls Henri Lefebvre's emphasis on everyday life concerning sensory experience of space (1974), Ian Borden's analysis of the skateboarder's spatial production in ordinary places (2001), and Quentin Stevens's analysis on transgressive, playful uses of urban spaces (2007).[45]

Through teaching, installations and competitions, Chang concentrated on conceptual studies in his early days. In 1987, he attended an academic conference in Beijing and shared his conceptual ideas there. In response to the theme of the conference relating to the evaluation and prospect of Chinese architecture, he queried the validity of old methods in the pursuit of new architecture and called for the courage to question established norms critically. By using René Magritte's *The Treachery of Images* (1929) and Michel Foucault's *This is not a Pipe* (1973) as illustrations, Chang emphasised the crucial role of the thinking process and critical mentality for obtaining a new perspective on familiar contexts.[46] Inspired by Magritte's *The Treachery of Images*, Chang created a series of full-scale "smoking pipe" models. Despite their close resemblance to the appearance of actual pipes, they can be divided into halves, exposing various internal arrangements and negating their apparent function as a pipe.[47] Through a series of images of smoking pipe models, the thinking process of his experimentation is illustrated, transforming and suspending the everyday object of the smoking pipe.

Influenced by Magritte's thought-provoking statement, "This is not a pipe," Chang not only developed his full-sized smoking pipe models but also applied such reflective practice to architectural elements. In the "Sliding Folding Swing Door" installation (1998), he added a new swing door and a folded door frame between a pair of abandoned garage sliding doors. During the door opening process, the three actions of sliding, folding and swinging could be carried out sequentially.[48] This is an insightful installation challenging the conventional notion of the door.

Similar to Chang's challenge to conventional norms, Wang's design practice expresses his conscious subversion of mainstream conventions. After graduation, he deliberately kept a distance from official design institutes or private developers, which was in striking contrast to his peers, who were busy immersing themselves in numerous projects due to the building boom in the 1990s. During his doctoral research at Tongji University, Wang was involved in the design of his own residence in Hangzhou in 1997. He sought the possibility of creating a "private garden" within a 50-square-metre residential unit, which was much smaller than the smallest private garden in Suzhou, the Garden of Residual Grains (*Canliyuan*).[49] The Garden of Residual Grains has only one traditional Chinese pavilion on the highest level, serving as the primary visual attraction within the overall layout. Likewise, Wang designed a "pavilion" in his residence as a visual focus, which was in an oblique disposition within the overall orthogonal arrangement. Instead of keeping the standard partitioning of the residential unit, he removed the doors and non-structural walls there. In addition, two wall openings were provided for a bedroom to facilitate the dynamic flow of space, which became a desirable place for his 2-year-old son to play hide-and-seek. According to his observation, his son could perceive the spatial quality intuitively through personal interaction with the space at play.[50] To Wang, a private garden is a living world full of stimulating experience, no matter how small it is.[51] Within his small residence in Hangzhou, Wang even designed eight timber light fittings instead of installing proprietary lighting products. The light fittings had comparable forms with the cubic pavilion near the window and were scattered around the residential unit. Sharing a family resemblance, the light fittings were named "Eight Uninhabitable Houses."[52] The relationship between various "architectural objects" within an interior was expressed, involving the conceptual studies of scale conversion.

Comparatively, Liu's design experimentation is more contextually based. He accentuates the importance of using regional resources and appreciating existing conditions during the design process. Against the temptation of moving to the developed east coast of China, such as the globalised metropolis of Shanghai, for more opportunities to practise, Liu prefers to stay in Chengdu, the western part of China, where he is more familiar with its locality. In response to the less developed situation, he used the term "low-tech strategies" to introduce his early works, which can appropriately highlight his design approach with due consideration of limited resources, aiming to strike a balance between architectural quality, low-technical skills and budget.[53] He explicitly distinguishes "low-tech strategies" from "low-tech style," which is merely a superficial expression.[54] To Liu, developing a design strategy that can deal with realistic constraints is far more important than maintaining a consistent appearance across his works.

In the early installation, "Follow the Wind" (2002), Liu used cheap local materials of balloons, agricultural membranes and Chinese fans to create a temporary covered gathering space at low cost. Agricultural membranes, being lifted up by balloons, could provide effective shading against strong sunlight in summer. During the hot season, people could use the hanging Chinese fans to achieve the cooling effect, while during windy days, the movement of the membranes could vividly express the flow of the wind.[55] The mobile shelter was easily erected and dismantled at different locations, fulfilling functional needs and expressing the sense of lightness. "Follow the Wind" was a conceptual manifestation of Liu's "low-tech strategies."

Tectonic Expression

Besides conceptual studies, another salient feature of these architects is their tectonic pursuit against external ideologies and superficial ornamentation dominant in Beaux-Arts tradition and eclectic Post-Modernism. Chang's awareness of tectonic relations can be illustrated in his architectural works, such as the Morningside Centre of Mathematics, Beijing (1998), having a minimalist treatment of materials. His article "Learning from Industrial Architecture" (2000) also draws a distinction between ontological aspects of architecture and "fine arts" decorative tradition in the past.[56] His tectonic approach can be traced back to his earlier work, the Book-Bike Store, Beijing (1996), which was both a conceptual exploration and a tectonic manifestation.

In the now-defunct Book-Bike Store, Chang continued to develop the recurrent theme of bicycle-wheel, such a ubiquitous everyday object in China. He was inspired by conceptual art, especially the exposure to Marcel Duchamp's work in the US, which was "an incredible experience" to him.[57] In comparison with the mounting of a wheel to a kitchen stool in Duchamp's work, Chang installed bicycle wheels under bookshelves. As the location of the bookstore was originally planned as a passage for bicycles to pass through, the bicycle wheels of the bookshelves responded to the specificity of the site. The use of translucent glass panels and steel frames without any extravagant ornamentation expressed his interest in the exposure of materials and the interplay between translucency and transparency.

After becoming the founding head of the GCA in Peking University in 1999, Chang extended his tectonic concern to architectural teaching. He criticised the adverse impact of the Beaux-Arts teaching approach as merely concerning the two-dimensional graphic representation and external appearance of buildings rather than four-dimensional architectural experience and spatial quality.[58] Against typical architectural programmes in China producing "renderers" or "architectural artists" in his view, Chang emphasised the importance of hands-on experience with materials, structure, and construction.[59] In the compulsory first-year tectonic studio at GCA, postgraduate students were required to design and build a small functional facility, such as a wood workshop, within budget and schedule.[60] Through material testing, product procurement, structural calculation, detailed design and direct participation in the whole construction process, Chang cultivated in his students first-hand knowledge of materiality and construction.[61]

Chang's influence is not limited to China.[62] He not only commented on Chinese architectural education but also opposed a theory-based teaching approach in the US. As the Head of the Department of Architecture, Massachusetts Institute of Technology (MIT, 2005–2010), Chang carried out a series of curriculum reforms there. One of the key reform elements was to strengthen students' first-hand exposure to materials and their direct participation in construction.[63] He appreciates the technical teaching approach in Europe and Japan and criticises the significant reduction of practical components in architectural curricula in the US, leading to "a narrow intellectualisation" within the ivory tower.[64]

Similar to Chang, Liu's early works express his design focus with purist treatment of materials. In response to the native context, the title of his first monograph, *Now and Here* (2002), reinforces this line of thinking by emphasising the full use of regional resources and geographical circumstances. Locally available materials were used in his early works, such as pebbles obtained from adjacent rivers for wall construction in the Xiyuan Leisure Camp, Chengdu (1996), and the Luo Zhongli Studio, Chengdu (1997).

One of Liu's salient works is the Design Department, Sichuan Fine Arts Institute, Chongqing (2006). The teaching buildings have distinguishing materials on the facades. Holes of perforated concrete blocks are exposed instead of being concealed to enhance the texture of the elevations. Cementitious corrugated panels are stacked on top of each other to show their dynamic undulating edges. The protrusion and recess of corrugated panels further enhance both visual and tactile qualities. Galvanised metal sheets with folded edges facing outside form a compatible pattern with the fenestration. Other inexpensive building materials, such as quarry tiles and external plastering, are also used on the facades to meet the tight construction budget. Liu's concern for materiality and construction is closely related to buildability, utilisation of local resources and economic feasibility. Existing limitations and inherent problems stimulate him to develop appropriate strategies to circumvent inadequate local construction skills, resulting in a tactful solution to address practical issues and respond to existing conditions.

Likewise, Wang has a keen interest in materiality and handcraft. He was influenced by his father and grandfather who made timber furniture and toys in his childhood.[65] During the design of his own residence in Hangzhou, Wang taught timber artisans how to produce the light fittings for creating the dramatic lighting effect in the interior. The extensive use of timber and the eight handcrafted "uninhabitable houses" exemplify his concern for the tectonic quality of the work.

The visibility of handcraft on material surfaces was clearly shown in Wang's now-defunct Top Floor Art Gallery, Shanghai (2000), in which marks and scratches on steel panels were purposely exposed (Figure 31.2). Different materials were juxtaposed without any transition or concealment, expressing the inherent qualities of materials. Rather than using proprietary products, catches and latches were made by local ironsmiths for the continuity of folk craftsmanship.

Use of Tradition

Chang, Liu, and Wang, as Chinese architects, are explicit in engaging with cultural traditions through their works. One common theme of Chang's early works is his engagement with Chinese characters. An early example was the Zhengzhou Kindergarten project (1993), in which the layout was based on the transformation of the Chinese character, *yuan*. He emphasised the enclosing structure of the character for developing the courtyard arrangement of the kindergarten.

Apart from the use of Chinese characters, Chang engages with material traditions. For the Seoul Design Fair in 2010, he designed the Tea Pavilions for exploring the potential of traditional Chinese roof tiles. Rather than following the usual wet-fixing method, the roof tiles were dry-fixed and tied together by steel cables to form an arch profile. The lightness of materiality was clearly expressed. The use of contemporary assembly method to connect traditional roof tiles demonstrates his engagement with material traditions in an inventive manner.

Wang is regarded as "the most humanistic and literary architect" in contemporary China.[66] Referring to the rich legacy of Chinese traditions, Wang is obsessed with Chinese literati traditions, ranging from Chinese garden design and landscape painting to calligraphy.[67] One significant work by Wang is the Xiangshan Campus of the China Academy of Art in Hangzhou (Phase I, 2004; Phase II, 2007). When the Academy planned for its new expansion, a site to the east of the Hangzhou mountains was selected rather than conventional government-zoned higher education districts. During the site selection, natural landscape was considered far more important for campus setting even though there was a temporary lack of infrastructural provision there. This is in line with the traditional practice of locating Chinese academies in secluded mountains away from cities as scenic landscape, delicate gardenand teaching pedagogy can be mutually enlightening.[68] Engagement with the landscape and daily encounters with nature have been considered as a crucial way for nurturing students' aesthetic value and cultivating reflective thinking.[69] By referring to Chinese landscape painting, Wang points out that architecture itself only plays a small part in the overall composition, while the major concern is its relationship with nature. Based on this understanding, rigorous grids with architectural axiality and clear demarcation of zoning were not adopted for the campus design. Instead, teaching buildings in the Xiangshan Campus are located around the central small hill, following the undulating profile of the natural landscape sensitively.[70] Existing farmlands and streams have been protected for preserving the pastoral scenes of the original site.

Teaching buildings of the Xiangshan Campus Phase I are mainly in courtyard typology, being fully enclosed or bounded on three sides. It was common for traditional Chinese academics to adopt an orderly layout to arrange teaching areas around a series of courtyards along a dominant main axis. Comparatively, Phase I courtyard buildings are organised in a more responsive manner for engaging with the topography of the hill. In contrast to the relatively static and formal arrangement in Phase I, the Phase II campus design shows Wang's more elaborate formal manipulation, creating tension between buildings in a playful manner. Regardless of the contrasting design between these two phases, family resemblance among buildings is achieved by the use of dominating colours of white plastered walls, grey roof tiles, and natural woodwork.

Teaching buildings in Phase I are connected by bridges to enable users to walk from one building to another in all weathers. Similar to stroll as a bodily movement for exploring a garden setting, the provision of bridge connection in the campus facilitates sensory experience, allowing users to access to courtyards with varying atmosphere. Spatial movement is further reinforced in Phase II through the sinuous building form with external ramps and steps on the facades. Such a three-dimensional walkway system connects different buildings, courtyards and activity spaces together, encouraging outdoor learning programmes, informal gathering and discussion. Meandering experience is comparable to the dynamics of viewing traditional Chinese horizontal scrolls. Chinese landscape paintings do not "depict the visual image statically," but instead "convey a perception of the experience of travelling amidst real landscapes of natural beauty."[71] Similar to horizontal scrolls, the elaborate external walkway system in Phase II invites visitors to participate in meandering movement for unfolding a continuity of dynamic spatial sequence of the campus layout.

As exemplified in the Xiangshan Campus, Wang has not confined himself to a mere imitation of the past nor an exercise in nostalgia. Instead, he demonstrates a conscious transfer of ideas from the Chinese cultural tradition to architectural and campus design. Some of the wall openings are designed in resemblance to exquisite tracery and window latticework of traditional Chinese architecture, yet the scale has been enlarged to cover entire facades for achieving the visual impact. In addition, Wang has developed curvilinear roofs for some teaching buildings, such as Teaching Building no. 14 in Phase II, which has a water body in front (Figure 31.3). The striking curvilinear roof and the water reflection on the pond serve as a visual focus in the campus environment. Cultural inheritance is taken as a source of inspiration, resulting in new articulation with reference to the past.

Compared with Chang and Wang, Liu prefers to make a reference to recent traditions in his work. Before studying architecture at the Chongqing Institute of Architecture and Engineering, he lived in the Wenzhou rural area for three years (1975–78).[72] The experience of village living during the late Cultural Revolution provided inspiration for his novel writing. His last novel, *The Conceptual Planning of the Mingyue New City* (*Mingyue Gouxiang*, 1996), illustrates a utopian blueprint of a collective way of living under socialism, which is a mockery of the irrational social phenomena he encountered in the Mao era.[73]

The Cultural Revolution, as a significant event to Liu, has been integrated into his architectural design. Red bricks were widely used during the period of planned economy in China in relation to the working class, so for the Cultural Revolution Clock Museum, Anren (2007) in Sichuan Province, he used red bricks to correlate with the theme of the museum (Figure 31.4).[74] The popular political slogan in the Mao era − "rebellion is not a crime, there are reasons in rebellion" (*Geming Wuzui, Zaofan Youli*) − is shown on the boundary wall by using red bricks, whereas the arrangement of having a religious church setting with a statue of Mao Zedong at the altar is an embodiment of power relationships, arousing visitors to have a reflection of Mao's dominant role in the ten-year long massive upheavals (1966–76) in society.

Social Awareness

Chang, Liu, and Wang have not confined themselves to a narrow concern with architectural forms but have expressed their social awareness to a certain degree. Chang's Qingxi Hillside Housing project (1995) was an attempt to respond to the ineffective use of valuable land resources in China.[75] In contrast to the common phenomenon of extensive villa development, the residential units of the Qingxi Hillside Housing were proposed to be attached together to achieve higher density, yet they were equipped with introverted courtyards for residents to enjoy outdoor activity spaces. His further response to the housing issue was exemplified by the "1K House Project" at MIT in 2009. Students were required to design affordable houses at a unit cost of barely one thousand US dollars. Apart from catering for victims of natural disasters, this is a proactive way under a concerted effort of an interdisciplinary team to address world poverty by empowering impoverished people to participate in regional revitalisation through the construction of affordable housing.[76] Under the three fundamental principles of affordability, liveability and sustainability, the first "1K House," namely the Pinwheel House, was erected in Sichuan Province in 2011.[77] The design studio was a practical response to tackle the fundamental issue of housing need in society.

Both Chang and Wang criticise the planning policies in China of creating wide streets and grand public squares. From Chang's perspective, the "unconditional acceptance of existing planning guidelines" can lead to a confrontational and isolated urban environment.[78] In the Jiading Advertisement Base in Shanghai, Chang deliberatively controls the width of streets and provides a variety of programme and public spaces for enhancing the liveability and walkability of the environment. Similarly, Wang considers that the conventional approach of providing roads as wide as 40 to 60 metres is "impossible for the formation of city life."[79] In the Zhongshan Road Revitalisation, Wang insisted on reducing the width of the road to 12 metres for maintaining the proportion of urban space. Against the common *tabula rasa* approach, Wang successfully convinced the local government to revitalise the old Hangzhou city centre along Zhongshan Road without any massive destruction or relocation of residents. This is not merely a single urban project for the old Hangzhou city centre, but also an exemplar of an alternative way of urban revitalisation in China.

Liu's social response was explicitly expressed after the devastating Sichuan earthquake in 2008. Being compassionate for the profound sorrow of a couple who had lost their daughter in the earthquake, Liu designed and constructed the Hu Huishan Memorial House at his own cost (Figure 31.5). Taking a common refugee tent as its prototype, the simple building form without exaggeration can arouse people's memory of the earthquake. Although this house is small in scale to commemorate an ordinary secondary school girl, to Liu, this is the most meaningful work of his professional career because "the concern for every single ordinary life is the foundation of revival of a nation."[80] Owning to its sensitive correlation with the controversial collapse of school buildings in the earthquake, this memorial house is not allowed to be opened by the government; yet, it can still offer a critique provoking widespread public concern and discussion in society.

Conclusion

Based on the preceding analysis and comparison, the three selected Chinese architects, in varying degrees, share a family resemblance of salient features in terms of their conceptual studies, tectonic expression, use of tradition and social awareness. Through experimentation, they are courageous to challenge existing norms and mainstream conventions. They aim to return to ontological tectonic quality of architecture against extravagant decoration and superficial appearance. Facing the phenomenon of globalisation and homogenisation, they strategically position themselves within local contexts and cultural traditions. They are proactive in expressing their social awareness and reflective thinking in the pursuit of self-conscious practices and design authorship. They are the representative figures signifying the emergence of architects as authoring individuals under the socio-economic transformations in contemporary China.

The salient features identified are not unique to Chang, Liu, and Wang, but can also be found in the works of other independent Chinese architects. Examples include the conceptual experimentation of the "Shanshui City" by Ma Yansong, proposing the harmonious co-existence between urban life and nature; the clear formal logic and material expression of the Concrete Slit House in Nanjing (2007) by Zhang Lei; the incorporation of traditional craftsmanship and local construction methods in the Museum of Handcraft Paper in Yunnan (2010) by Hua Li; as well as the social response of the Tulou collective housing in Guangzhou (2008) by Urbanus (the partnership of Liu Xiaodu, Meng Yan, and Wang Hui) for low-income migrant workers. Of course, the development of contemporary Chinese architecture will continue to unfold. More young architects, especially those born in the 1970s, 1980s, and even later, will emerge, awaiting further research.

Notes

1 This article derives from my PhD research at the University of Melbourne (2010–2014). I would like to express my special gratitude to Professor Jianfei Zhu, Associate Professor Gregory Missingham, and Associate Professor Peter Raisbeck for their valuable advice and comments.
2 Gao Minglu et al., *'85 Meishu Yundong: 80 Niandai de Renwen Qianwei (The '85 Movement: The Enlightenment of Chinese Avant-Garde)* (Guilin: Guangxi Shifan Daxue Chubanshe, 2008).
3 Gao Minglu, *Total Modernity and the Avant-Garde in Twentieth-Century Chinese Art* (Cambridge MA: The MIT Press, 2011).
4 Wang Mingxian, "80 Niandai de Jianzhu Sichao (Architectural Thinking in the 1980s)," in *'85 Meishu Yundong: 80 Niandai de Renwen Qianwei (The '85 Movement: The Enlightenment of Chinese Avant-Garde)*, eds. Gao Minglu et al., 412–441 (Guilin: Guangxi Shifan Daxue Chubanshe, 2008).
5 Gu Mengchao, Wang Mingxian and Li Xiongfei, eds., *Dangdai Jianzhu Wenhua yu Meixue (Contemporary Architectural Culture and Aesthetics)* (Tianjin: Tianjin Kexue Jishu Chubanshe, 1989).
6 Rao Xiaojun and Yao Xiaoling, "Shiyan yu Duihua: Ji 5.18 Zhongguo Qingnian Jianzhushi, Yishujia Xueshu Taolunhui (Experiment and Dialogue: A Record of 5.18 Symposium among Young Chinese Architects and Artists)," *Jianzhushi (Architect)* 72 (October 1996): 80–83. Some young emerging Chinese architects attended this symposium, including Yung Ho Chang, Wang Shu, and Ma Qingyun.
7 Wang Mingxian, "Jintian, Zuotian (Today, Yesterday)," in *Xin Guancha (New Perspective)* 5: 2–3, ed. Shi Jian, *Chengshi Kongjian Shiji (City Space Design)* 3 (2010).
8 Zhu Tao, "Fansi xuyao Yujing (Reflection needs Context)," in *Xin Guancha (New Perspective)* 5: 4–13, ed. Shi Jian, *Chengshi Kongjian Shiji (City Space Design)* 3 (2010). Roan Ching-yueh, "Xianzhi, zhuding

sizai Taxiang? (Is Deserting the Fate for Prophets?)," in *Xin Guancha* (*New Perspective*) 5: 20–23, ed. Shi Jian, *Chengshi Kongjian Shiji* (*City Space Design*) 3 (2010).

9   Chau Hing-wah, "'Shiyan Jianzhu'? 'Dangdai Jianzhu'?: Sikao Dangdai Zhongguo Shiyanxing Jianzhu ('Experimental Architecture'? 'Contemporary Architecture'?: Thinking on Contemporary Chinese Experimental Architecture)," in *Xin Guancha*. (*New Perspective*) 6: 2–8, ed. Shi Jian, *Chengshi Kongjian Shiji* (*City Space Design*) 4 (2010). Guanghui Ding, *Constructing a Place of Critical Architecture in China: Intermediate Criticality in the Journal Time + Architecture* (Farnham, Surrey, England; Burlington, VT: Ashgate, 2015), 100.

10 Jianfei Zhu, "The Chinese DI: A Manifesto," Text for an exhibition at West Bund 2013 Biennale of Architecture and Contemporary Art, Shanghai, 19 Oct 2013.

11 A tentative registration examination was held in Liaoning in late 1994 and the first national registration examination was held in the end of 1995. The National Management Committee of Registered Architects promulgated a list of Class 1 architects in July 1996. Charlie Q. L. Xue, *Building Practice in China* (Hong Kong: PACE, 1998), 125 & 131.

12 Yung Ho Chang, Liu Jiakun, Wang Shu, Tang Hua, Dong Yugan, Zhao Bing, Xu Weiguo, and Zhu Wenyi participated in the "Experimental Architecture by Young Chinese Architects" exhibition in 1999.

13 Wang Mingxian, "Kongjian Lishi de Pianduan: Zhongguo Qingnian Jianzhushi Shiyanxing Zuopinzhan Shimo (Fragments of Spatial History: Beginning of Experimental Works by Chinese Young Architects)," *Jinri Xianfeng* (*Avant-garde Today*) 8 (2000): 1–8.

14 "TU MU" denote "earth" and "timber" respectively. They were commonly used building materials in ancient China. "TU MU: Young Architects in China" exhibition involved nine Chinese architects: Yung Ho Chang, Liu Jiakun, Wang Shu, Zhang Lei, Ma Qingyun, Ai Weiwei, Ding Wowo, Wang Junyang, and Zhu Jingxiang. Eduard Kögel and Ulf Meyer, *TU MU: Young Architecture of China*. (Berlin: Aedes, 2001).

15 Jianfei Zhu made a concluding speech at the seminar of the "TU MU @ Home" exhibition, highlighting the micro narratives of independent Chinese architects against the grand narratives of the nation-state. Li, Wuying. "Shi Fanchuantong er bushi Qianwei: 'Tu Mu Hui Jia' Zhan Ji (Against Tradition not Avant-Garde: 'TU MU@Home' Exhibition Record)," *Jianzhu Shibao* (*Architecture Times*), 30 August 2002, www.abbs.com.cn/jzsb/read.php?cate=5&recid=3129. Accessed 16 June 2012.

16 Yung Ho Chang entered the Nanjing Institute of Technology in 1977, while Liu Jiakun entered the Chongqing Institute of Architecture and Engineering in 1978.

17 Gu Daqing, "An Outline of Beaux-Arts Education in China: Transplantation, Localisation, and Entrenchment," in *Chinese Architecture and the Beaux-Arts*, eds. Jeffrey W. Cody, Nancy S. Steinhardt, and Tony Atkin, 73 (Honolulu: University of Hawai'i Press; Hong Kong: Hong Kong University Press, 2011).

18 Gu, "An Outline of Beaux-Arts Education in China: Transplantation, Localisation, and Entrenchment," 73–90.

19 Some architectural teachers promoted modern architectural education in China, including Lin Keming of Xiangqin University (1932–37), Xia Changshi (Hsia Changshi) and Chen Boqi of Chongqing University (1940–43), Huang Zuoshen (Henry Jorson Huang) of St. John's University (1942–52), and Feng Jizhong (Feng Chi-Chung) of Tongji University in the early 1960s. Qian Feng and Wu Jiang, *Zhongguo Xiandai Jianzhu Jiaoyushi 1920–1980* (*Education of Modern Architecture in China 1920–1980*) (Beijing: Zhongguo Jianzhu Gongye Chubanshe, 2008), 41–70, 91–118, 206–208.

20 Liu Jiakun and Yung Ho Chang, "Zhuanzhedian de Jingli: Liu Jiakun/ Zhang Yonghe Duitan (Experiencing the Turning Point: A Dialogue between Liu Jiakun and Yung Ho Chang)," *Shidai Jianzhu* (*Time + Architecture*) 4 (2012): 45.

21 Hing-wah Chau, "Wushi Taidu, Huiying Chujing: Liu Jiakun Jianzhushi Fangtan (Pragmatic Attitude to respond to the Context: An Interview with the Architect, Liu Jiakun)," *HKIA Journal* 64 (2012): 82–83. Hing-wah Chau. "Dangdai Zhongguo Jianzhu de Taolun: Wang Shu Jiaoshou Fangtan (Discussion of Contemporary Chinese Architecture: An Interview with Prof. Wang Shu)." *HKIA Journal* 56 (2009): 100.

22 Yung Ho Chang, "Zixingche de Gushi: Yige Zhongguo Liuxuesheng de Jiaxin Zhailu (Bike Story: Summary of Family Letters from a Chinese Overseas Student)," *Xin Jianzhu* (*New Architecture*) 1 (1983): 83–84. Yung Ho Chang, "Taipingyang Bian de Laixin ('Letters from the other side of the Pacific Ocean,")" (1985) trans. Wang Shijun, *Xin Jianzhu* (*New Architecture*) 3 (1988): 75–79.

23 Wang Shu, "Jiuchengzhen Shangye Jiefang yu Juzhu Linong de Shenghuo Huanjing (Commercial Districts of Old Towns and the Living Environment of Laneways)," *Jianzhushi* (*Architect*) 18 (Mar 1984): 104–112.

24 Liu Jiakun, "Youhun (Mucking Around)," *Sichuan Wenxue* (*Sichuan Literature*) 10 (1980): 22–28.

25 Yung Ho Chang, *Feichang Jianzhu* (Haerbin: Heilongjiang Kexue Jishu Chubanshe, 1997).

26 Yung Ho Chang, *Pingchang Jianzhu* (*For a Basic Architecture*) (Beijing: Zhongguo Jianzhu Gongye Chubanshe, 2002). Yung Ho Chang/ Feichang Jianzhu, eds., *Jianzhu Dongci: Chang Yonghe/ Feichang Jianzhu Zuopinji* (*Architectural Verb: Collection of Yung Ho Chang/ FCJZ*) (Taibei: Tianyuan Chengshi, 2006).

27 Liu Jiakun, *Cishi Cidi* (*Now and Here*) (Beijing: Zhongguo Jianzhu Gongye Chubanshe, 2002). Wang Shu, *The Beginning of Design* (Beijing: Zhongguo Jianzhu Gongye Chubanshe, 2002).

28 Yung Ho Chang, *[Wu] Shangxia Zhuzhai*. (*[Without] Upside-down* House) (Beijing: Zhongguo Jianzhu Gongye Chubanshe, 2001). Lu Xiang, Huang Yuan et al., *Beida Jianzhu 2: 79 Hao Jia +*. (*Peking University Architecture 2: No. 79A+*) (Beijing: Zhongguo Jianzhu Gongye Chubanshe, 2002).

29 The name *Feichang Jianzhu* (FCJZ) expresses Chang's interest in Chinese texts having multiple meanings based on different ways of interpretation. As a noun phrase, it means "unusual architecture" or "special architecture," while as a gerund, it denotes "unusual construction." If it is interpreted as an adjective phrase, it can convey the meaning of "very architectural." Chang, *Feichang Jianzhu*, 1.

30 Chau, "Pragmatic Attitude to respond to the Context: An Interview with the Architect, Liu Jiakun," 82. Zhao Xing, " 'Feichang Jianzhu Feichang Shinian' Yantaohui Jishi (Record of the Seminar on the Unusual Ten Years of Feichang Jianzhu)," *Jianzhushi* (*Architect*) 108 (Apr 2004): 52.

31 Chau, "Pragmatic Attitude to respond to the Context: An Interview with the Architect, Liu Jiakun," 82.

32 Yung Ho Chang, "Pingchang Jianzhu (Basic Architecture)," *Jianzhushi* (*Architect*) 84 (Oct 1998): 27–37.

33 Yung Ho Chang and Zhang Lufeng, "Xiang Gongye Jianzhu Xuexi (Learning from Industrial Architecture)," *Shijie Jianzhu* (*World Architecture*) 7 (2000): 22–23. Yung Ho Chang, *Pingchang Jianzhu* (*For a Basic Architecture*) (Beijing: Zhongguo Jianzhu Gongye Chubanshe, 2002).

34 In the CCTV design competition, Yung Ho Chang and Toyo Ito received the second prize. Hironori Matsubara, "Low-rise as New Symbol," trans. Deng Yi, *Times + Architecture* 2 (2003): 42–44. Yung Ho Chang, "Kuanyu Chengshi Yanjiu (On Urban Research)," *Shidai Jianzhu* (*Time + Architecture*) 2 (2003): 96.

35 Hing-wah Chau, "Discourse Production: Yung Ho Chang's Cross-cultural Practice, Narratives and Projects," *Architecture and Culture* 2, no. 2 (2014): 205–212.

36 Liu Jiakun, "Xushi Huayu yu Diji Celue (A Narrative Discourse and A Low-tech Strategy)," *Jianzhushi* (*Architect*) 78 (Oct 1997): 46–53.

37 "I even oppose the so-called architects of architecture; otherwise, I will not name my office as Amateur Architecture Studio. This involves a basic attitude, that is, to work in actual living conditions aiming for self-improvement and transformation." Li Dong and Wang Juzheng, eds., "Fan Xueyuan de Jianzhushi (Architects against Institution,")" *Jianzhushi* (*Architect*) 122 (Aug 2006): 28.

38 "architecture should not only rely on rational spatial logic as basis, it should also depend on direct observation of daily lives." Wang Shu, "Kongjian Shihua: Liangze Jianzhu Sheji Xizuo de Chuangzuo Shouji (Space Poetry: Creation Manuscripts of Two Architectural Designs)," *Jianzhushi* (*Architect*) 61 (Dec 1994): 85.

39 Wang Shu, *The Beginning of Design* (Beijing: Zhongguo Jianzhu Gongye Chubanshe, 2002).

40 Wang Shu. *Imaging the House*. Zurich: Lars Müller, 2012.

41 MIT 150 Infinite History Project Team, *Interview with Prof. Yung Ho Chang*, http://mit150.mit.edu/infinite-history. Accessed 30 June 2012.

42 Jianfei Zhu, "Criticality in between China and the West," *The Journal of Architecture* 10, no. 5 (2005): 487. Jianfei Zhu, "Robin Evans in 1978: Between Social Space and Visual Projection," *The Journal of Architecture* 16, no. 2 (2011): 267–290.

43 Chang, "Bike Story: Summary of Family Letters from a Chinese Overseas Student," 83.

44 Yung Ho Chang, "Zixingche de Gushi (Bike Story)," (1982–83) *Feichang Jianzhu* (Haerbin: Heilongjiang Kexue Jishu Chubanshe, 1997), 4.

45 Henri Lefebvre, *The Production of Space* (1974), Eng. trans. David Nicholson-Smith (Oxford: Blackwell, 1991). Iain Borden, *Skateboarding, Space and the City: Architecture and the Body* (Oxford; New York: Berg, 2001). Quentin Stevens, *The Ludic City: Exploring the Potential of Public Spaces* (London; New York: Routledge, 2007).

46 Yung Ho Chang, "Sixiang de Guocheng yu Guocheng de Sixiang: Xunzhao Xinjianzhu (The Process in Thinking and the Thinking in Process: In the Search of New Architecture)," (1988) in *Zhongguo Jianzhu Pingxi yu Zhanwang* (*Review and Prospect of Chinese Architecture*), eds. Gu Mengchao and Zhang Zaiyuan (Tianjin: Tianjin Kexue Jishu Chubanshe, 1989), 42–44.

47 Yung Ho Chang, "Yandou: Gainianxing Wuti (Smoking Pipe: Conceptual Object)," (1989) *Feichang Jianzhu*, 68–71.

48 Chang, *For a Basic Architecture*, 61.

49 The Garden of Residual Grains has an area of only 140 square metres and was built in Qing Dynasty. It is not open to the public and is located at 34 Zhuangjia Bridge Lane, Suzhou. Liu Dun-zhen, *Chinese Classical Gardens of Suzhou*, trans. Chen Lixian (New York: McGraw-Hill, 1993), 139.

50 Wang Shu, "Zao Yuan Ji (Record of Making Garden)," *Jianzhushi (Architect)* 86 (Feb 1999): 80–81.

51 Wang, "Record of Making Garden," 81.

52 Wang Shu, "Bage Buneng Zhude Fangzi (Eight Uninhabitable Houses)," *Jianzhushi (Architect)* 87 (Apr 1999): 76–83.

53 Liu, "A Narrative Discourse and A Low-tech Strategy," 46–53.

54 Liu Jiakun, "Wo zai Xibu zuo Jianzhu (My Architectural Practice in Western China)," *Shidai Jianzhu (Time + Architecture)* 4 (2006): 46.

55 Liu, *Now and Here*, 140–145.

56 Chang and Zhang, "Learning from Industrial Architecture," 22–23.

57 "You know, I came from kind of an isolated society at that time. To be exposed to Marcel Duchamp, and French new wave movies, all of that, was an incredible experience." MIT, *Interview with Chang*, http://mit150.mit.edu/infinite-history. Accessed 30 June 2012.

58 Yung Ho Chang, "Kuanyu Jianzhu Jiaoyu (About Architectural Education)," *Jianzhushi (Architect)* 98 (Apr 2001): 14–15.

59 Stanley Collyer, "Interview: Yung Ho Chang with Stanley Collyer." *Competitions* 10 no. 4 (2000–2001 Winter): 39.

60 Yung Ho Chang, "Back to School: Architectural Education – the Information and the Argument," *Architectural Design* 74 no. 5 (Sep/ Oct 2004): 89.

61 Lu Xiang, Huang Yuan et al. *Beida Jianzhu 2: 79 Hao Jia + (Peking University Architecture 2: No. 79A+)* (Beijing: Zhongguo Jianzhu Gongye Chubanshe, 2002).

62 Jianfei Zhu, "Criticality in between China and the West," 479–498.

63 Yu Bing, ed. "Interview with Yung Ho Chang," *Domus+78: Chinese Architects & Designers* (Beijing: Zhongguo Jianzhu Gongye Chubanshe, 2006), 22.

64 Wang Fei and Ding Junfeng, eds., "Interview with Yung Ho Chang," (2008) in *Inter-views: Trends of the Top Architecture and Urbanism Programs in Europe and North America* (Beijing: Zhongguo Jianzhu Gongye Chubanshe, 2010), 10–23.

65 Huang Yuanshao, *20 Zhongguo Dangdai Qingnian Jianzhushi (20 Chinese Architects)* (Beijing: Zhongguo Jianzhu Gongye Chubanshe, 2011), 180.

66 Yu, *Domus + 78: Chinese Architects & Designers*, 298.

67 Wang Shu, "Introduction," *Imaging the House* (Zurich: Lars Müller, 2012), n.p.

68 Wu Xin, "Yuelu Academy: Landscape and Gardens of Neo-Confucian Pedagogy," *Studies in the History of Gardens & Designed Landscapes: An International Quarterly* 25, no. 3 (2005): 156–157.

69 Wu Xin, "History, Neo-Confucian Identity, and Landscape at the Yuelu Academy," in *Interlacing Words and Things: Bridging the Nature-Culture Opposition in Gardens and Landscape*, ed. Stephen Bann, 65, 67, 76 (Washington: Dumbarton Oaks, 2012).

70 Yu, *Domus + 78: Chinese Architects & Designers*, 300.

71 Wang, *Imaging the House*, n.p.

72 Peng Nu, "Benzhi shang bu jinjin shi Jianzhu (Not merely architecture in nature)," in *Now and Here*, eds. Wang Mingxian and Du Jian, 164 (Beijing: Zhongguo Jianzhu Gongye Chubanshe, 2002).

73 Liu Jiakun, "Mingyue Gouxiang I (The Conceptual Planning of the Mingyue New City I)," *Jintian Wenxue Zazhe (Today Literary Magazine)* 1 (1996 Spring): 189–225. Liu Jiakun, "Mingyue Gouxiang II (The Conceptual Planning of the Mingyue New City II)," *Jintian Wenxue Zazhe (Today Literary Magazine)* 2 (1996 Summer): 111–158.

74 Chau, "Pragmatic Attitude to respond to the Context: Interview with the Architect, Liu Jiakun," 84.

75 Yung Ho Chang, "Qingxi Podi Zhuzhaiqun: Huo Meiguo Di 43 Jie 'Jinbu Jianzhu' Jiang Zuopin (Qingxi Hillside Housing: Receiving the 43rd Progressive Architecture Citation Award)," *Shiji Jianzhu (World Architecture)* 2 (1996): 57–59.

76 Peter Dizikes, "A True Bargain House: First Prototype built from MIT's Effort to construct Houses for $1,000 each," *MIT News*, 15 September 2011, http://web.mit.edu/newsoffice/2011/1k-house-prototype-0915.html. Accessed 30 June 2012.

77 The "Pinwheel House" was designed by the student, Ying Chee Chui, in the "1K House" design studio led by Yung Ho Chang, Tong Ciochetti, and Dennis Shelden in 2009 at MIT. "Housing the

Victims of Natural Disaster: A Prototype of the 1K House recently built in China," *Plan: Review of the MIT School of Architecture and Planning* 80 (Dec 2011).

78 Yung Ho Chang, "Phenomena and Relationships: A Hypothetical Reorganisation of the First Shenzhen Biennale of Urbanism/ Architecture, a Message passed to the Next Curator," in *Chengshi, Kaimen!: 2005 Shoujie Shenzhen Chengshi/ Jianzhu Shuangnianzhan* (*City, Open Door!: The First Shenzhen Biennale of Urbanism/ Architecture*) ed. Yung Ho Chang, 21–22 (Shanghai: Shanghai Renmin Chubanshe, 2007).

79 Wang Shu, "Zhongshan Road," *Lotus International* 141 (2010): 109.

80 Liu, "Am I practising Architecture in the Western China?" 91.

Bibliography

Auyang, Jianghe. "Jianzhu zuowei Bendi Shiwu de Chouxiang: Jianzhushi Liu Jiakun Fangtan (Architecture as an Abstract of Local Things)." *Jintian Wenxue Zazhe* (Today Literary Magazine) 85 (Summer 2009): 65–92.

Bertin, Vito. *Leverworks: One Principle, Many Forms*. Beijing: China Architecture & Building Press, 2012.

Borden, Iain. *Skateboarding, Space and the City: Architecture and the Body*. Oxford and New York: Berg, 2001.

Cen, Wei. "'Hongse Niandai': Liu Jiakun de 'Dushi Xiezuo' (Red Age: Liu Jiakun's Writing for Urban)." *Shidai Jianzhu* (Time + Architecture) 5 (2002): 48–51.

Chang, Yung Ho. "Zixingche de Gushi: Yige Zhongguo Liuxuesheng de Jiaxin Zhailu (Bike Story: Summary of Family Letters from a Chinese Overseas Student)." *Xin Jianzhu* (New Architecture) 1 (1983): 83–84.

———. "Taipingyang Bian de Laixin (Letters from the Other Side of the Pacific Ocean, 1985)." Translated by Wang Shijun. *Xin Jianzhu* (New Architecture) 3 (1988): 75–79.

———. "Sixiang de Guocheng yu Guocheng de Sixiang: Xunzhao Xinjianzhu (The Process in Thinking and the Thinking in Process: In the Search of New Architecture, 1988)." In *Zhongguo Jianzhu Pingxi yu Zhanwang* (Review and Prospect of Chinese Architecture), edited by Gu Mengchao and Zhang Zaiyuan, 42–44. Tianjin: Tianjin Kexue Jishu Chubanshe, 1989.

———. "Cong 'Hou Chuang' dao 'Kan de Youxi' (From 'Rear Window' to 'Visual Game')." *Shidai Jianzhu* (Time + Architecture) 2 (1994): 34–37.

———. "Qingxi Podi Zhuzhaiqun: Huo Meiguo Di 43 Jie 'Jinbu Jianzhu' Jiang Zuopin (Qingxi Hillside Housing: Receiving the 43rd Progressive Architecture Citation Award)." *Shiji Jianzhu* (World Architecture) 2 (1996): 57–59.

———. *Feichang Jianzhu*. Haebin: Heilongjiang Kexue Jishu Chubanshe, 1997.

———. "Pingchang Jianzhu (Basic Architecture)." *Jianzhushi* (Architect) 84 (October 1998): 27–37.

———. "Kuanyu Jianzhu Jiaoyu (About Architectural Education)." *Jianzhushi* (Architect) 98 (April 2001): 14–19.

———. "Vertical DenCity: 'Upside Down Office' Cummins Asia Headquarters, Beijing, 1997." In *Asian Architects 2*, edited by Tan Kok Meng, 200–201. Singapore: Select Publishing, 2001.

———. *[Wu] Shangxia Zhuzhai* ([Without] Upside-Down House). Beijing: Zhongguo Jianzhu Gongye Chubanshe, 2001.

———. "Jianzhu = (n.) Architecture & (v.) to Build." *Dialogue: Architecture+Design+Culture* 62 (September 2002): 43–46.

———. *Pingchang Jianzhu* (For a Basic Architecture). Beijing: Zhongguo Jianzhu Gongye Chubanshe, 2002.

———. "Kuanyu Chengshi Yanjiu (On Urban Research)." *Shidai Jianzhu* (Time + Architecture) 2 (2003): 96.

———. "Back to School: Architectural Education – the Information and the Argument." *Architectural Design* 74, no. 5 (September–October 2004): 87–90.

———. "Di San Zhong Tai Du (The Third Attitude)." *Jianzhushi* (Architect) 108 (April 2004): 24–26.

———. *Zuo Wen Ben* (Yung Ho Chang Writes). Beijing: Sanlian Shudian, 2005.

———. "City of Object a.k.a. City of Desire." In *Totalstadt: Beijing Case*, edited by Gregor Jansen, 370–371. Köln: Walther König, 2006.

———. "Phenomena and Relationships: A Hypothetical Reorganisation of the First Shenzhen Biennale of Urbanism/ Architecture, a Message passed to the Next Curator." In *Chengshi, Kaimen!: 2005 Shoujie Shenzhen Chengshi/ Jianzhu Shuangnianzhan* (City, Open Door!: The First Shenzhen Biennale of Urbanism/ Architecture), edited by Yung Ho Chang, 21–22. Shanghai: Shanghai Renmin Chubanshe, 2007.

————. "My Father and I." *Abitare* 32 (October–December 2012): 11.

————. "Phenomena and Relationships: A Hypothetical Reorganisation of the First Shenzhen Biennale of Urbanism/ Architecture, a Message passed to the Next Curator." In *Chengshi, Kaimen!: 2005 Shoujie Shenzhen Chengshi/ Jianzhu Shuangnianzhan* (City, Open Door!: The First Shenzhen Biennale of Urbanism/ Architecture), edited by Yung Ho Chang, 20–31. Shanghai: Shanghai Renmin Chubanshe, 2007.

Chang, Yung Ho and Feichang Jianzhu, eds. *Jianzhu Dongci: Chang Yonghe/ Feichang Jianzhu Zuopinji* (Architectural Verb: Collection of Yung Ho Chang/ FCJZ). Taibei: Tianyuan Chengshi, 2006.

Chang, Yung Ho and Zhang Lufeng. "Xiang Gongye Jianzhu Xuexi (Learning from Industrial Architecture)." *Shijie Jianzhu* (World Architecture) 7 (2000): 22–23.

Chang, Yung Ho and Zhou Rong. "Duihua: Xiayige Shinian (Conversation: The Next Decade)." *Jianzhushi* (Architect) 108 (April 2004): 56–58.

Chau, Hing-wah. "Dangdai Zhongguo Jianzhu de Taolun: Wang Shu Jiaoshou Fangtan (Discussion of Contemporary Chinese Architecture: An Interview with Prof. Wang Shu)." *HKIA Journal* 56 (2009): 100–103.

————. " 'Shiyan Jianzhu'? 'Dangdai Jianzhu'?: Sikao Dangdai Zhongguo Shiyanxing Jianzhu ('Experimental Architecture'? 'Contemporary Architecture'?: Thinking on Contemporary Chinese Experimental Architecture)." In *Xin Guancha* (New Perspective) 6: 2–8, edited by Shi Jian. *Chengshi Kongjian Shiji* (City Space Design) 4 (2010).

————. "Wushi Taidu, Huiying Chujing: Liu Jiakun Jianzhushi Fangtan (Pragmatic Attitude to Respond to the Context: An Interview with the Architect, Liu Jiakun)." *HKIA Journal* 64 (2012): 82–87.

————. "Zhongguo Shichang Jingji zhong de Feichang Jianzhu (FCJZ in the Chinese Market Economy)." *Shidai Jianzhu* (Time + Architecture) 6 (2012): 148–152.

————. "Duili Tongyi: Zhang Lei Jiaoshou Fangtan (Unity of Opposites: An Interview with Prof. Zhang Lei)." *Shidai Jianzhu* (Time + Architecture) 1 (2013): 68–71.

————. "Chengshi Sheji, Cailiaoxing yu Lishigan: Zhang Yonghe Jiaoshou Fangtan (Urban Planning, Materiality, and Historicity: An Interview with Prof. Yung Ho Chang)." *HKIA Journal* 67 (2013): 68–71.

————. "Discourse Production: Yung Ho Chang's Cross-Cultural Practice, Narratives and Projects." *Architecture and Culture* 2, no. 2 (2014): 205–212.

————. "*Xianfeng? Houfeng? Youfeng?*: An Analysis of Selected Contemporary Chinese Architects, Yung Ho Chang, Liu Jiakun and Wang Shu (1990s–2000s)." *Frontiers of Architectural Research* 4, no. 2 (2015): 146–158.

————. "Consumerism, Urbanisation and Wang Shu's Architecture: The Use of *Spolia* and Vernacular Traditions." In *Reuse in an Accelerated World*, edited by Robert Crocker and Keri Chiveralls. London and New York: Routledge, 2018 [To be published].

Collyer, Stanley. "Interview: Yung Ho Chang with Stanley Collyer." *Competitions* 10, no. 4 (Winter 2000–2001): 38–45.

Deng, Jing and Zhong Wen-kai. "Dui Liu Jiakun Sichuan Meiyuan Xin Xiaoqu Sheji Yishuguan de Liangzhong Yuedu (Two Interpretations of Liu Jiakun's Work: The Art and Design Building in the New Campus of Sichuan Academy of Fine Arts, Chongqing)." *Shidai Jianzhu* (Time + Architecture) 1 (2008): 94–103.

Ding, Guanghui. " 'Experimental Architecture' in China." *Journal of the Society of Architectural Historians* 73, no. 1 (March 2014): 28–37.

————. *Constructing a Place of Critical Architecture in China: Intermediate Criticality in the Journal Time + Architecture* (Farnham, Surrey and Burlington, VT: Ashgate, 2015).

Ding, Guanghui, Jonathan Hale and Steve Parnell. "Constructing a Place for Critical Practice in China: The History and Outlook of the Journal *Time + Architecture*." *Architectural Research Quarterly* 17, no. 3–4 (2013): 237–252.

Ding, Wowo, Zhang Lei and Feng Jinlong. *Ouzhou Xiandai Jianzhu Jiexi: Xingshi de Luoji* (The Analysis of Modern Architecture in Europe: The Logic of Form). Nanjing: Jiangsu Kexue Jishu Chubanshe, 1998.

Ding, Wowo, Feng Jinlong and Zhang Lei. *Ouzhou Xiandai Jianzhu Jiexi: Xingshi de Yiyi* (The Analysis of Modern Architecture in Europe: The Meaning of Form). Nanjing: Jiangsu Kexue Jishu Chubanshe, 1999.

Dirlik, Arif. "Markets, Culture, Power: The Making of a 'Second Cultural Revolution' in China." *Asian Studies Review* 25, no. 1 (2001): 1–33.

Dizikes, Peter. "A True Bargain House: First Prototype Built from MIT's Effort to Construct Houses for $1,000 Each." *MIT News*, 15 September 2011, http://web.mit.edu/newsoffice/2011/1k-house-prototype-0915.html. Accessed 30 June 2012.

Edelmann, Frédéric and Jérémie Descamps. *Positions: Portrait of a New Generation of Chinese Architects*. Paris: Cité de l'architecture, 2008.

Feng, Jinlong, Zhang Lei and Wowo Ding. *Ouzhou Xiandai Jianzhu Jiexi: Xingshi de Jiangou* (The Analysis of Modern Architecture in Europe: The Tectonic of Form). Nanjing: Jiangsu Kexue Jishu Chubanshe, 1999.

Feng, Lu. "'Cishi Cidi' de Xianshi (Reality of 'Here and Now')." *Jianzhushi* (Architect) 129 (October 2007): 47–48.

Frampton, Kenneth. "Foreword: From Where I'm Standing – A Virtual View." In *Asian Architects 2*, edited by Tan Kok Meng, 16–18. Singapore: Select Publishing, 2001.

Fu, Rong. "Zhang Lei: Ronghe Qinggan de Cailiao yu Jianzao (Zhang Lei: The Materials and Construction with Emotion)." *Chengshi Huanjing Sheji* (Urban Environment Design) 7 (2010): 138.

Gao, Minglu et al. *85 Meishu Yundong: 80 Niandai de Renwen Qianwei* (The 85 Movement: The Enlightenment of Chinese Avant-Garde). Guilin: Guangxi Shifan Daxue Chubanshe, 2008.

Gao, Minglu. *Total Modernity and the Avant-Garde in Twentieth-Century Chinese Art*. Cambridge, MA: The MIT Press, 2011.

Gao, Minglu et al. *85 Meishu Yundong: 80 Niandai de Renwen Qianwei* (The 85 Movement: The Enlightenment of Chinese Avant-Garde). Guilin: Guangxi Shifan Daxue Chubanshe, 2008.

Ge, Ming. "Shenglue de Shijie: Zhongguo Meishu Xueyuan Xiangshan Xiaoyuan Jishu (An Elliptical World: An Interpretation of Xiangshan Campus of Chinee Academy of Art)." *Shijie Jianzhu* (World Architecture) 8 (2005): 96–102.

Gu, Daqing. "An Outline of Beaux-Arts Education in China: Transplantation, Localisation, and Entrenchment." In *Chinese Architecture and the Beaux-Arts*, edited by Jeffrey W. Cody, Nancy S. Steinhardt and Tony Atkin, 73–90. Honolulu: University of Hawai'i Press; Hong Kong: Hong Kong University Press, 2011.

Gu, Mengchao, Wang Mingxian and Li Xiongfei, eds. *Dangdai Jianzhu Wenhua yu Meixue* (Contemporary Architectural Culture and Aesthetics). Tianjin: Tianjin Kexue Jishu Chubanshe, 1989.

Gu, Mengchao and Zhang Zaiyuan, eds. *Zhongguo Jianzhu Pingxi yu Zhanwang* (Review and Prospect of Chinese Architecture). Tianjin: Tianjin Kexue Jishu Chubanshe, 1989.

Gutierrez, Laurent and Valérie Portefaix, eds. *Yung, Ho Chang: A Chinese Practice*. Hong Kong: Map Book Publishers, 2003.

Hao, Shuguang. *Dangdai Zhongguo Jianzhu Sichao Yanjiu* (Research on Architectural Thoughts in Contemporary China). Beijing: Zhongguo Jianzhu Gongye Chubanshe, 2006.

Ho, Jiang. "Dangdai Zhongguo Shiyan Jianzhu de Xianfengxing (The Avant-garde Sense of China's Contemporary Experimental Architecture)." *Xin Jianzhu* (New Architecture) 2 (2006): 93–95.

Hu, Heng. "Qingsong, huo Zuidi Xiandu de Lixing: Kuanyu 'Dongguan Ligong Xueyuan Jiaogong Shenghuoqu (Sprezzatura, or the Minimal Rationality: A Review on the Staff Residence in Dongguan Institute of Science and Technology)." *Shijie Jianzhu* (World Architecture) 2 (2007): 69–71.

———. "Lishi ji Quaigan: Zhang Lei Shiji de Jiangsu Liyang Xinsijun Jiangnan Zhihuibu Jinianguan (History as a Delight: New 4th Army Jiangnan Headquarters Memorial Designed by Zhang Lei, Liyang, Jiangsu)." *Shidai Jianzhu* (Time+Architecture) 2 (2008): 82–87.

———. "Yuwang Luoji zhong de Cailiao Weizhi (Material and Desire)." *Shijie Jianzhu* (World Architecture) 4 (2011): 24–26.

Hu, Qiguang. "'Shiyan Jianzhu' Xianxiang de Paoxi yu Shenshi (Analysis and Examination of the Phenomenon of Experimental Architecture)." *Jianzhushi* (Architect) 112 (December 2004): 72–79.

Huang, Yuanshao. *20 Zhongguo Dangdai Qingnian Jianzhushi* (20 Chinese Architects). Beijing: Zhongguo Jianzhu Gongye Chubanshe, 2011.

———. *Liuxiang: Zhongguo Dangdai Jianzhu 20nian Guancha yu Jiexi (1991–2011)* (Flow and Tendency: Observation and Analysis of Two Decades of Chinese Contemporary Architecture (1991–2011)), vol. I–II. Nanjing: Jiangsu Renmin Chubanshe, 2012.

Huang Xiao and Wu Lili, eds. *Zhongjie Kaishi: Zhongguo Dangdai Yishujia Fangtanlu*, 34–37. Changsha: Hunan Meishu Chubanshe, 2002.

Köegel, Eduard. "From Simplicity to Sophistication: The Work of Zhang Lei." *World Architecture* 4 (2011): 16–23.

Kögel, Eduard and Ulf Meyer. *TU MU: Young Architecture of China*. Berlin: Aedes, 2001.

———. "Deguoren Kan Jinri Zhongguo Jianzhu: Qunti de Bianyuan (German View on Chinese Contemporary Architecture)." Translated by Chen Yifeng. *Architecture & Design* 1 (2002): 100–101.

Lai, Delin. "Zhongguo Wenren Jianzhu Chuantong Xiandai Fuxing yu Fazhan zhi lu shang de Wang Shu (Wang Shu and the Revival and Development of Chinese Literati Architectural Tradition)." *Jianzhu Xuebao* (Architectural Journal) 5 (2012): 1–5.

Lefebvre, Henri. *The Production of Space (1974)*. Translated by David Nicholson-Smith. Oxford: Blackwell, 1991.

Li, Dong and Wang Juzheng, eds. "Fan Xueyuan de Jianzhushi (Architects Against Institution)." *Jianzhushi* (Architect) 122 (August 2006): 26–36.

Li, Wuying. "Shi Fanchuantong er bushi Qianwei: 'Tu Mu Hui Jia' Zhan Ji (Against Tradition not Avant-Gade: 'TU MU@Home' Exhibition Record)." *Jianzhu Shibao* (Architecture Times), 30 August 2002, www.abbs.com.cn/jzsb/read.php?cate=5&recid=3129. Accessed 16 June 2012.

Li, Xiangning. "Chuanyue Qujing Miyuan: Wang Shu Zuopin Jiedu (Wandering Through a Meandering Garden: Dissecting the Works of Wang Shu)." *Shidai Jianzhu* (Time + Architecture) 5 (2002): 44–47.

———. "'Make-the-Most-of-It' Architecture: Young Architects and Chinese Tactics." *City* 12, no. 2 (2008): 226–236.

———. "Architecture as Resistance: Shu Wang and His Architecture." *Architecture and Urbanism: Chinese Edition* 4 (2009): 145–149.

Li, Zheng. "Chenjing yu Xuanhua: Zhongguo Meishu Xueyuan Xiangshan Xiaoqu Kongjian Yuedu (Stillness and Blatancy: Xiangshan New Campus of the China Academy of Fine Arts)." *Jianzhu Jishu yu Sheji* (Architecture Technology and Design) 7 (2008): 118–127.

Ling, Jie and Li Baotong. "Chidu, Manbu: Zhongguo Meishu Xueyuan Xiangshan Yierqi Gongcheng Bijiao (Scale, Wander: Comparisons Between Phases 1 and 2 of Xiangshan Campus)." *Shinei Sheji yu Zhuangxiu* (Interior Design Construction) 3 (2008): 50–58.

Liu, Dun-zhen. *Chinese Classical Gardens of Suzhou*. Translated by Chen Lixian. New York: McGraw-Hill, 1993.

Liu, Jiakun. "Youhun (Mucking Around)." *Sichuan Wenxue* (Sichuan Literature) 10 (1980): 22–28.

———. "Yuzhong Xiaolu Hualiuliu (Slippery Footpath in the Rain)." *Huacheng* (Flower City) 1 (1981): 64–76.

———. "Yingxiong (Hero)." *Qingnian Zuojia* (Young Writers) 6 (1983): 64–66.

———. "Gaodi (High Land)." *Wenxueyuan Congshu* (Art Academy Book Series), vol. 2. Sichuan: Sichuan Wenyi Chubanshe, 1993, 2–13. Originally published in *Qingnian Zuojia* (Young Writers) 5 (1984): 54–58.

———. "Huisemiao he you Kuishu de Tingyuan (A Grey Cat and a Courtyard with a Chinese Pagoda Tree)." In *Wenxueyuan Congshu* (Art Academy Book Series), vol. 2. Sichuan: Sichuan Wenyi Chubanshe, 1993. Originally published in *Qingnian Zuojia* (Young Writers) 9 (1987): 87–93.

———. "Mingyue Gouxiang I (The Conceptual Planning of the Mingyue New City I)." *Jintian Wenxue Zazhe* (Today Literary Magazine) 1 (Spring 1996): 189–225.

———. "Mingyue Gouxiang II (The Conceptual Planning of the Mingyue New City II)." *Jintian Wenxue Zazhe* (Today Literary Magazine) 2 (Summer 1996): 111–158.

———. "Xushi Huayu yu Diji Celue (A Narrative Discourse and a Low-tech Strategy)." *Jianzhushi* (Architect) 78 (October 1997): 46–53.

———. *Cishi Cidi* (Now and Here). Beijing: Zhongguo Jianzhu Gongye Chubanshe, 2002.

———. "Kuanyu Wo de Gongzuo (About My Work)." *Shinei Sheji yu Zhuangxiu* (Interior Design Construction) 11 (2002): 68.

———. "Wo zai Xibu zuo Jianzhu (My Architectural Practice in Western China)." *Shidai Jianzhu* (Time + Architecture) 4 (2006): 45–47.

———. "Gei Zhu Jianfei de Huixin (A Letter to Jianfei Zhu)." Translated by Shi Chee Chia. *Shidai Jianzhu* (Time + Architecture) 5 (2006): 67–68.

———. "Kuanyu Wo de Gongzuo (About the Work)." *Jianzhu yu Wenhua* (Architecture & Culture) 5 (2007): 74–75.

———. "Wo zai Xibu zuo Jianzhu Ma? (Am I Practising Architecture in the Western China?)." *Jintian Wenxue Zazhe* (Today Literary Magazine) 85 (Summer 2009): 65–92.

———. *Blog for Wenchuan Earthquake*, http://wenchuan512.blogbus.com/. Accessed 17 January 2012.

Liu Jiakun and Yung Ho Chang. "Zhuanzhedian de Jingli: Liu Jiakun/ Zhang Yonghe Duitan (Experiencing the Turning Point: A Dialogue Between Liu Jiakun and Yung Ho Chang)." *Shidai Jianzhu* (Time + Architecture) 4 (2012): 44–49.

Liu Jiakun, Stanislaus Fung and Zhao Yang. "Liu Jiakun Fangtan (Interview with Liu Jiakun)." *Shijie Jianzhu* (World Architecture) 1 (2013): 94–99.

Liu, Qing. "Zhang Lei: Sheji Xuyao Yizhen Jianxue (Zhang Lei: Design Must Be Spot on)." *Chengshi Huanjing Sheji* (Urban Environment Design) 6 (2009): 130–131.

Liu, Xianjue. *Zhongguo Jinxiandai Jianzhu Yishu* (Early Modern and Modern Chinese Architecture). Wuhan: Hubei Jiaoyu Chubanshe, 2004.

Liu Yichun. "Chuang fei Chuang, Qiang fei Qiang: Zhang Yonghe de Jianzao yu Sibian (Window, Wall or Not: Construction and Dialectical Thinking in the Works of Yung Ho Chang)." *Shidai Jianzhu* (Time + Architecture) 5 (2002): 41.

Lu, Duanfang, ed. *Third World Modernism: Architecture, Development and Identity*. London and New York: Routledge, 2011.

Lu, Erming and Yi Feng, eds. *Zhongguo Dangdai Qingnian Jianzhushi Zuopinxuan* (Memories and Solutions of Young Architects: Chinese Architecture Since 1980). Beijing: Encyclopedia of China Publishing House, 1997.

Lu, Xiang, Huang Yuan et al. *Beida Jianzhu 2: 79 Hao Jia +* (Peking University Architecture 2: No. 79A+). Beijing: Zhongguo Jianzhu Gongye Chubanshe, 2002.

Luna, Ian, ed. *On the Edge: Ten Architects from China*. New York: Rizzoli, 2006.

Matsubara, Hironori. "Low-Rise as New Symbol." Translated by Deng Yi. *Shidai Jianzhu* (Times + Architecture) 2 (2003): 42–44.

Meng, Tan Kok, ed. *Asian Architects 2*. Singapore: Select Publishing, 2001.

MIT School of Architecture + Planning. "Housing the Victims of Natural Disaster: A Prototype of the 1K House Recently Built in China." *Plan: Review of the MIT School of Architecture and Planning* 80 (December 2011), http://sap.mit.edu/resources/portfolio/1khouse/. Accessed 30 June 2012.

Muynck, Bert de. "Local Hero." *Mark* 19 (April–May 2009): 73–85.

Nederlands Architectuurinstituut, ed. *China Contemporary: Architecture, Art, Visual Culture*. Rotterdam: NAi, 2006.

Peng, Nu. "Benzhi shang bu jinjin shi Jianzhu (Not Merely Architecture in Nature)." In *Cishi Cidi* (Now and Here), edited by Wang Mingxian and Du Jian, 163–195. Beijing: Zhongguo Jianzhu Gongye Chubanshe, 2002.

Peng, Nu and Zhi Wenjun. "Zhongguo Dangdai Shiyanxing Jianzhu de Pingtu (A Mosaic of Contemporary Experimental Architecture in China: Theoretic Discourses and Practicing Strategies)." *Shidai Jianzhu* (Time + Architecture) 5 (2002): 20–25.

Peng, Nu, Zhi Wenjun and Dai Chun, eds. *Xianxiangxue yu Jianzhu de Duihua* (Dialogue Between Phenomenology and Architecture) Shanghai: Tongji University Press, 2009.

Qian, Feng and Wu Jiang. *Zhongguo Xiandai Jianzhu Jiaoyushi 1920–1980* (Education of Modern Architecture in China 1920–1980). Beijing: Zhongguo Jianzhu Gongye Chubanshe, 2008.

Qin, Lei. "Dangdai Zhongguo Shiyanxing Jianzhuzhan Shilu (Documents of Contemporary Experimental Architecture Exhibitions)." *Shidai Jianzhu* (Time + Architecture) 5 (2003): 44–47.

———, ed. "Liu Jiakun: Zaishengzhuan (Liu Jiakun: Rebirth Brick)." *Domus China* 26 (October 2008): 44.

Qin, Lei and Yang Fan. "Zhongguo Dangdai Jianzhu zai Haiwai de Zhanlan (Overseas Exhibitions of Chinese Contemporary Architecture)." *Shidai Jianzhu* (Time + Architecture) 1 (2010): 41–47.

Qing, Feng. "Yulinnanlu 3 Hao 11 Dong 2 Danyuan 7 Lou (Yulinnanlu no. 3 Block 11 Unit 2 7/F)." *Jianzhushi* (Architect) 125 (February 2007): 82–89.

Rao, Xiaojun. "Bianyuan Shiyan yu Jianzhuxue de Biange (Edge Experiment and the Change of Architecture)." *Xin Jianzhu* (New Architecture) 3 (1997): 19–22.

———. "Shiyan Jianzhu: Yi Zhong Guangnianxing de Tansuo (Experimental Architecture: A Conceptual Exploration)." *Shidai Jianzhu* (Time + Architecture) 2 (2000): 12–15.

Rao, Xiaojun and Yao Xiaoling. "Shiyan yu Duihua: Ji 5.18 Zhongguo Qingnian Jianzhushi, Yishujia Xueshu Taolunhui (Experiment and Dialogue: A Record of 5.18 Symposium Among Young Chinese Architects and Artists)." *Jianzhushi* (Architect) 72 (October 1996): 80–83.

Roan, Ching-yueh. "Dialogue: Ching-Yue Roan vs. Wang Shu." *Architectural Keywords: 30 Ways to Read East Asian Architects*, 228–235. Taipei: Garden City, 2008.

———. "Xianzhi, zhuding sizai Taixiang? (Is Deserting the Fate for Prophets?)." In *Xin Guancha* (New Perspective) 5: 20–23, edited by Shi Jian. *Chengshi Kongjian Shiji* (City Space Design) 3 (2010).

Rowe, Peter G. and Seng Kuan. *Architectural Encounters with Essence and Form in Modern China*. Cambridge, MA: MIT Press, 2002.

Ruan, Xing, ed. *New China Architecture*. Singapore: Periplus, 2006.

Shi, Jian. "Shiyanxing Jianzhu de Zhuangxing: Hao Shiyanxing Jianzhu Shidai de Zhongguo Dangdai Jianzhu (Transformation of an Experimental Architecture: A Post-Avant-Garde Era in Contemporary China)." In *Zhongguo Jianzhu Liushinian (1949–2009): Lishi Lilun Yanjiu* (Sixty Years of Chinese

Architecture (1949–2009): History, Theory and Criticism), edited by Jianfei Zhu, 296–313. Beijing: Zhongguo Jianzhu Gongye Chubanshe, 2009.

Shi, Jian and Feng Keru. "Zhang Yonghe Fangtan (Interview: Yung Ho Chang)." *Domus China* 1 (July 2006): 1–14.

Stevens, Quentin. *The Ludic City: Exploring the Potential of Public Spaces.* London and New York: Routledge, 2007.

Tang, Hua. "Jiakun." *Jianzhushi* (Architect) 129 (October 2007): 31–32.

Wang, Fei and Ding Junfeng, eds. "Interview with Yung Ho Chang (2008)." In *Inter-views: Trends of the Top Architecture and Urbanism Programs in Europe and North America*, 10–23. Beijing: Zhongguo Jianzhu Gongye Chubanshe, 2010.

Wang, Lu, ed. "World Architecture." *Zhang Lei Material Volition* 4 (2011).

Wang, Mingxian. "Kongjian Lishi de Pianduan: Zhongguo Qingnian Jianzhushi Shiyanxing Zuopinzhan Shimo (Fragments of Spatial History: Beginning of Experimental Works by Chinese Young Architects)." *Jinri Xianfeng* (Avant-garde Today) 8 (2000): 1–8.

———. "80 Niandai de Jianzhu Sichao (Architectural Thinking in the 1980s)." In *85 Meishu Yundong: 80 Niandai de Renwen Qianwei* (The 85 Movement: The Enlightenment of Chinese Avant-Garde), edited by Gao Minglu et al., 412–441. Guilin: Guangxi Shifan Daxue Chubanshe, 2008.

———. "Jintian, Zuotian (Today, Yesterday)." In *Xin Guancha* (New Perspective) 5: 2–3, edited by Shi Jian. *Chengshi Kongjian Shiji* (City Space Design) 3 (2010).

Wang, Mingxian and Shi Jian. "90 Niandai Zhongguo Shiyanxing Jianzhu (90s Chinese Experimental Architecture)." *Wenyi Yanjiu* (Literature & Art Studies) 1 (1998): 118–127.

Wang, Shu. "Jiuchengzhen Shangye Jiefang yu Juzhu Linong de Shenghuo Huanjing (Commercial Districts of Old Towns and the Living Environment of Laneways)." *Jianzhushi* (Architect) 18 (March 1984): 104–112.

———. "Wannan Cunzhen Xiangdao de Neijiegou Jiexi (Analysis of the Inner Structure of the Laneways in the Wannan Vernacular Architecture)." *Jianzhushi* (Architect) 28 (October 1987): 62–66.

———. "Siwu Shouji: Kongjian Shiyu Jiegou (The Manuscript of the House of the Dead: The Poetic Structure of Space)." M. Arch. Southeast University, Dhaka, 1988.

———. "Kongjian Shihua: Liangze Jianzhu Sheji Xizuo de Chuangzuo Shouji (Space Poetry: Creation Manuscripts of Two Architectural Design)." *Jianzhushi* (Architect) 61 (December 1994): 85–92.

———. "Sheji de Kaishi (The Beginning of Design)." *Jianzhushi* (Architect) 85 (December 1998): 82–85.

———. "Zao Yuan Ji (Record of Making Garden)." *Jianzhushi* (Architect) 86 (February 1999): 79–85.

———. "Bage Buneng Zhude Fangzi (Eight Uninhabitable Houses)." *Jianzhushi* (Architect) 87 (April 1999): 76–83.

———. "Shijian Tingzhi de Chengshi (Stagnating City)." *Jianzhushi* (*Architect*) 96 (October 2000): 39–60.

———. "Sheji de Kaishi/ 3 (The Beginning of Design/ 3)." *Jianzhushi* (*Architect*) 97 (December 2000): 82–85.

———. *Xugou Chengshi (Fictionalising City).* PhD. Tongji University, Shanghai, 2000.

———. *Sheji de Kaishi* (The Beginning of Design). Beijing: Zhongguo Jianzhu Gongye Chubanshe, 2002.

———. "Na Yi Tian (One Day)." *Shidai Jianzhu* (Time + Architecture) 4 (2005): 97–106.

———. "Hengfang yu Chuifang de Guanyunfeng (Horizontal and Vertical Guanyun Stone)." *Shidai Jianzhu* (Time + Architecture) 1 (2006): 125.

———. "'Zhongguoshi Zhuzhai' de Kenengxing: Wang Shu he Ta de Yanjiushengmen de Duihua (Possibilities of 'Chinese-Style Housing': A Dialogue Between Wang Shu and His Students)." *Shidai Jianzhu* (*Time + Architecture*) 3 (2006): 36–41.

———. "'Thinking by Hands' an Experiment on the Reconstruction of Living Places in Collapsing Traditional Cities." In *Refabricating City: Hong Kong & Shenzhen Bi-city Biennale of Urbanism/ Architecture*, edited by The Hong Kong Institute of Architects, 45. Hong Kong: The Hong Kong Institute of Architects, 2007.

———. "Yingzao Suoji (Record on Construction)." *Jianzhu Xuebao* (Architectural Journal) 7 (2008): 58–61.

———. "Ziran Xingtai de Xushi yu Jihe: Ningbo Bumuguan Chuangzuo Biji (The Narration and Geometry of Natural Appearance: Notes on the Design of Ningbo Historical Museum)." *Shidai Jianzhu* (*Time + Architecture*) 3 (2009): 66–79.

———. "Poumian de Shiye (The Field of Vision on Section)." *Shidai Jianzhu* (Time + Architecture) 2 (2010): 81–88.

———. "Zhongshan Road." *Lotus International* 141 (2010): 106–111.

———. *Imaging the House.* Zurich: Lars Müller, 2012.

Wang, Shu, Xu Jiang et al. *Tiles Garden: A Dialogue Between City, Between an Architect and an Artist* (China Pavilion – 10th International Architecture Exhibition, La Biennale di Venezia, 2006). Hangzhou: China Academy of Art, 2006.

Wang, Shu and Lu Wenyu. "Jianzhu Rushan (Architecture as a Mountain)." *Chengshi Huanjing Sheji* (Urban Environment Design) 12 (2009): 100–105.

———. "Xunhuan Jianzao de Shiyi: Jianzao Yige yu Ziran Xiangsi de Shijie (Poetics of Construction with Recycled Materials: A World Resembling the Nature). *Shidai Jianzhu (Time + Architecture)* 2 (2012): 66–69.

Wang, Shu and Hsieh Ying-Chun. *Illegal Architecture*. Taipei: Gardencity, 2012.

Webb, Michael. "Campus Calligraphy: China Art Academy, Hangzhou." *The Architectural Review* 1337 (July 2008): 54–57.

Wöhler, Till. "Ningbo Museum." *The Architectural Review* 1357 (March 2010): 56–63.

Wu, Xin. "Yuelu Academy: Landscape and Gardens of Neo-Confucian Pedagogy." *Studies in the History of Gardens & Designed Landscapes: An International Quarterly* 25, no. 3 (2005): 156–190.

———. "History, Neo-Confucian Identity, and Landscape at the Yuelu Academy." In *Interlacing Words and Things: Bridging the Nature-Culture Opposition in Gardens and Landscape*, edited by Stephen Bann, 65–80. Washington: Dumbarton Oaks, 2012.

Xu, Jie and Zheng Jing. "Zai Xianshi Zhong Fasheng: Dui Liu Jiakun Jinqi Zuopin Zhong 'Chuli Xianshi' Celue de Gaixi (Occurrence in Reality: Brief Interpretation of the Strategy of 'Dealing with Reality' in Liu Jiakun's Recent Works)." *Jianzhushi (Architect)* 129 (October 2007): 49–51.

Xue, Charlie Q.L. *Building Practice in China*. Hong Kong: Pace, 1998.

———. *Building a Revolution: Chinese Architecture Since 1980*. Hong Kong: Hong Kong University Press, 2006.

Yi, Na and Li Dong. "Jieyu Lilun Sibian he Jishu Zhijian de Yingzao (Construction Between Theoretical Thinking and Technology)." *Jianzhushi (Architect)* 120 (April 2006): 16–25.

Yu, Bing, ed. *Domus+78: Chinese Architects & Designers*. Beijing: Zhongguo Jianzhu Gongye Chubanshe, 2006.

Zhang, Wenwu. "Dui Zhongguo Dalu Shiyan Jianzhu de Renshi (Experimental Architecture in Mainland China)." *Shidai Jianzhu (Time + Architecture)* 2 (2000): 16–19.

Zhao Xing. "'Feichang Jianzhu Feichang Shinian' Yantaohui Jishi (Record of the Seminar on the Unusual Ten Years of Feichang Jianzhu)." *Jianzhushi (Architect)* 108 (April 2004): 52–55.

Zhi, Wenjun, Dai Chun and Xu Jie, eds. *Contemporary Architecture in China: 2008–2012*. Shanghai: Tongji Daxue Chubanshe, 2013.

Zhi, Wenjun and Xu Jie, eds. *Contemporary Architecture in China: 2004–2008*. Shenyang: Liaoning Kexue Jishu Chubanshe, 2008.

Zhong, Wenkai. "A Sense of Reality in Building Practice in China: A Review of Jiakun Liu's Recent Works." *Architecture and Urbanism* 22 (August 2008): 164–169.

Zhou Rong. "Jianzhushi de Liangzhong Yanshuo: Beijing Shizilin Huisuo de Jianzhu yu Chaojianzhu Yuedu Biji (Two Types of Discourse From Architects: Decoding the Micro and Macro Architectural Discourse of Shizilin Private Club)." *Shidai Jianzhu (Time + Architecture)* 1 (2005): 90–97.

Zhu, Jianfei. "Beyond Revolution: Notes on Contemporary Chinese Architecture." *AA Files* 35 (Spring 1998): 3–14.

———. "An Archaeology of Contemporary Chinese Architecture." *2G: International Architectural Review* 10 (1999) (Special issue: Instant China: Notes on an Urban Transformation): 90–97.

———. "Criticality in Between China and the West." *The Journal of Architecture* 10, no. 5 (2005): 479–498.

———. "China as a Global Site: In a Critical Geography of Design." *Critical Architecture*, edited by Jane Rendell et al., 301–308. London: Routledge, 2007.

———. *Architecture of Modern China: A Historical Critique*. London: Routledge, 2009.

———, ed. *Zhongguo Jianzhu Liushinian (1949–2009): Lishi Lilun Yanjiu* (Sixty Years of Chinese Architecture (1949–2009): History, Theory and Criticism). Beijing: Zhongguo Jianzhu Gongye Chubanshe, 2009.

———. "Robin Evans in 1978: Between Social Space and Visual Projection." *The Journal of Architecture* 16, no. 2 (2011): 267–290.

———. "The Chinese DI: A Manifesto." Text for an exhibition at West Bund 2013 Biennale of Architecture and Contemporary Art, Shanghai, 19 October 2013.

Zhu, Jianfei and Hing-wah Chau. "Yung Ho Chang: Thirty Years of Exploring a 'Design Discourse'." *Abitare* 32 (October–December 2012): 32–39.

Zhu, Tao. "'Jiangou' de Xunuo yu Xushe: Lun Dangdai Zhongguo Jianzhuxue Fazhan zhong de 'Jiangou' Guannian (Promises and Assumptions of Tectonics: On the Emerging Notions of Tectonics in Contemporary Chinese Architecture)." *Shidai Jianzhu* (*Time + Architecture*) 5 (2002): 30–33.

———. "Babu zouxiang Feichang Jianzhu (Eight Steps Towards Feichang Jianzhu)." *Jianzhushi* (Architect) 108 (April 2004): 32–43.

———. "An Architect Who Has Changed His 'Peaceful Heart' in the Great Quake." *Architecture and Urbanism* 22 (August 2008): 158–161.

———. "Fansi xuyao Yujing (Reflection Needs Context)." In *Xin Guancha* (New Perspective), edited by Shi Jian, 5: 4–13; *Chengshi Kongjian Shiji* (City Space Design) 3 (2010).

Zou, Denong. *Zhongguo Jianzhushi* (A History of Modern Chinese Architecture). Tianjin: Tianjin Kexue Jishu Chubanshe, 2001.

———. *Zhongguo Xiandai Jianzhu Yishu Lunti* (Issues on Chinese Modern Architecture). Jinan: Shantung Kexue Jishu Chubanshe, 2006.

Zou, Denong, Wang Mingxian and Zhang Xiangwei, eds. *Zhongguo Jianzhu Liushinian (1949–2009): Lishi Lilun Zonglan (Sixty Years of Chinese Architecture (1949–2009): A General Survey of Its History)*. Beijing: Zhongguo Jianzhu Gongye Chubanshe, 2009.

Glossary

'85 Meishu Yundong	'85 美术运动
Anren	安仁
Canliyuan	残粒园
Chen Boqi	陈伯齐
Dan Hong Studio	丹鸿工作室
Deng Xiaoping	邓小平
Dong Yugan	董豫赣
Feichang Jianzhu	非常建筑
Fengleqiao Subway Entrance	丰乐桥人防地道口
Feng Jizhong	冯纪忠
Gao Minglu	高名潞
Geming Wuzui, Zaofan Youli	革命无罪，造反有理
Haining	海宁
He Douling Studio	何多苓工作室
Hua Li	华黎
Huang Zuoshen	黄作燊
Huishan Memorial House	胡慧姗纪念馆
Jiading Advertisement Base	嘉定国际广告创意产业基地
Jianchuan Museum Town	建川博物馆聚落
Jianzhushi, Yishujia Xueshu Taolunhui	建筑师，艺术家学术讨论会
Jinhua Architecture Park	金华建筑艺术公园
Liu Jiakun	刘家琨
Liu Xiaodu	刘晓都
Lin Keming	林克明
Luoyang Kindergarten	洛阳幼儿园
Luo Zhongli Studio	罗中立工作室
Luyeyuan Stone Sculpture Museum	鹿野苑石刻博物馆
Ma Yansong	马岩松
Meng Yan	孟岩
Mingyue Gouxiang	明月构想
Nanbei Duihua: 5.18 Zhongguo Qingnian	南北对话：5.18中国青年建筑师，艺术家学术讨论会

Ningbo	宁波
Ningbo Tengtou Pavilion	宁波滕头案例馆
Qianmen revitalisation	前门重建
Qingxi Hillside Housing	清溪坡地住宅群
Rao Xiaojun	饶小军
Sanhe House	三合宅
Shanshui City	山水城市
shiyan jianzhu	实验建筑
Tulou	土楼公舍
Wang Hai Studio	王亥工作室
Wang Hui	王辉
Wang Mingxian	王明贤
Wang Shu	王澍
Wenzheng College Library	文政学院图书馆
Wenzhou	温州
Xia Changshi	夏昌世
Xiangqin University	勤勤大学
Xiangshan Campus	象山校园
Xiyuan Leisure Camp	犀苑休闲营地
Youhun	游魂
yuan	园
Yung Ho Chang	张永和
Yunnan	云南
Zhang Lei	张雷
Zhengzhou	郑州
Zhongguo Dangdai Jianzhu Wenhua Shalong	中国当代建筑文化沙龙
Zhongguo Qingnian Jianzhushi Shiyan Zuopinzhan	中国青年建筑师实验作品展
Zhongshan Road	中山路

State Design Institutes
in the Reform Era

32

FROM MAO TO MARKET

Evolution of the State Design Institutes in China

Charlie Q. L. Xue and Guanghui Ding

Initially following the Soviet Union's practice but much transformed in China's own political evolution, the state-owned architectural design institutes, born in the early 1950s, have been a major force of design production in the People's Republic.[1] As a public institution under the party and the state, design institutes were the predominant agent for delivering civil and industrial building designs in Mao's China and for providing a wider variety of design services for the state and private sector in post-Mao China.[2] Growing with the People's Republic, the institutes have made substantial contributions – they have redefined the built environment, modernized the physical fabric of society, culture, and daily life, and supported the modernization of the nation.[3]

This chapter examines the changing relationship of China's design institutes with state, society, and market. It looks into how economic force influenced politics and design institutes, and how design institutes responded to the changing context of the country. It is argued that design institutes were employed as a means by the party-state to implement the task of construction and reconstruction of urban architecture, with an aim, among others, to maintain a legitimacy that is politically, economically, and culturally crucial to Chinese people and society. Over the past six decades, the primary task of China's design institutes has been transformed from service provision into profit-making where the state – relative to society – remains a leading beneficiary when market economy is introduced, whereas the architects, who worked in the institutes in the recent decades of reform and opening-up, are increasingly assuming a mediating role, where possible, to negotiate a constructive position between state, society, and market.

The Emergence of State-Owned Design Offices in China

A state-owned design institute by definition is a concrete system through which the state carries out the production, distribution, and consumption of architectural resources. Although the birth of state-owned design institutes in China was the result of a centrally planned economy established in the early 1950s, the history of a government office supervising building construction can be traced back to the Zhou dynasty (ca. 1046–221 BC), when the position of *dongguan* was created to lead and supervise the official and public construction activities. The existence of such a state institution over a long history, although under different rubrics in

DOI: 10.4324/9781315851112-48

different dynasties, contributed to the coordination and accomplishment of significant architectural projects.[4] However, the architectural profession in the modern sense, in modern China, did not appear until the 1920s, when the first of several generations of Western-trained Chinese architects returned and started various activities in commercial practice, scholarly research, and academic teaching, with offices, societies, and university departments being established.[5] Following what they had learned overseas, some pioneering architects opened their own private design firms and were active in the building industry in many key cities in China.

When the People's Republic was established under the Chinese Communist Party (CCP) in 1949, some practicing architects moved to Taiwan and Hong Kong while the majority stayed, assuming that the CCP's success in the civil war would deliver hope and give them a renewed faith in their future. As the economy was in ruins after the war, one of the most important tasks for the country was to recover and reconstruct, which was important for the newly established authority. As stipulated by the "Common Program of the CPPCC (Chinese People's Political Consultative Conference)" of 1949, private economy was described as necessary and acceptable for China then, in a period described as "New Democracy." One year later, the "Provisional Regulations for Private Enterprises" set out the condition under which the private sector was to be protected.[6] At the same time, apart from private design firms operating as allowed, the government also established a few public design offices, including, among others, a "Design Office" directly belonging to the state government of Beijing and an "East China Architectural Design Firm" in Shanghai.

However, the co-existence of private, official, and co-operative sectors did not last for long. In January 1952, the government initiated a campaign against the owners of private firms.[7] In April of the same year, "Decisions for Establishing an Official Architectural Department and State-own Architectural Firms" was promulgated, which aimed to strengthen the government's control over design and construction. Radical political campaigns through mass mobilization were launched, to discredit private businessmen and to facilitate their subsequent absorption into state organizations. This seriously interrupted any growth of private economy.[8] Soon, a considerable number of private firms were dismantled and incorporated into state offices or public–private joint operations.

Five-Year Plans and Organization of Design Institutes

The year of 1953 saw the launch of the first Five-Year Plan, a Stalinist practice in planning and managing economy and development. The Plan called for large-scale construction and the forming of organizations of specialists, technicians, and managers. To meet this demand, the state-owned design firms, following the Soviet system, were restructured into design institutes; and these institutes were each divided into offices covering some of these specializations – civil architecture, industrial buildings, structure design, electro-mechanical facilities, and master planning. A design institute, as a socialist *danwei* (work unit), included administrative offices overseeing professional service, finance, and staff's livelihood that covered catering, accommodation, healthcare, childcare, and the education of staff's children.[9]

Such a comprehensive organization, putting many functions together, was conceived as such to serve more efficiently the building of a socialist industrialization across the nation. Within such an institute, it typically consisted of design sections each with architects and civil engineers, as well as service engineering sections with other professionals. The institute also consisted of a Chief Architect's Office, a Chief Engineer's Office, a technical office for compiling standard detail drawings, a library, and a managing office – a chief architect or engineer here was the equivalent of design director in a private design firm. A design institute in Beijing and Shanghai typically had a staff of several hundred, approaching one thousand. In the 1950s and 1960s, there were ten in Beijing and several in Shanghai for the institutes of this scale.

The establishment of state-owned design institutes was part of the party's endeavor to legitimize its leadership and to materialize its vision of making a socialist modern nation through the construction of buildings, factories, infrastructure, and cities. From 1953 to 1966, the Beijing Institute of Architectural Design completed a total floor area of 26.5 million square meters covering various types such as hotel, housing, hospital, educational and commercial office, and industrial and military building.[10] In 1956 in particular, the built-up area by the Beijing institute was 1.86 million square meters.[11] According to Zhou Rongxin, the then Deputy Minister of Architecture and Civil Engineering, this significant achievement proved convincingly the party's determination to improve the built environment of the people and that the socialist design production was far more efficient than the private practice of the previous Republican time before 1949.[12]

The proliferation of design institutes at many administrative levels, including state, province, and municipality and, later on, large organizations such as universities, reflected a strong will and power of the central state in rationally distributing design talent and other architectural resources across the nation with a centrally planned vision and design.[13] In particular, at state level, the setting up of design institutes to be attached to a range of state ministries – the list was increasing over decades – such as "machinery," "aerospace," "metallurgical," "coal," "petroleum," "chemical," "electronics," "textile," and "nuclear industry," among others, testified to the government's ongoing determination for industrialization. Geographically, apart from those attached to a province and a capital and other cities, there were also those attached to a "region" (across several provinces), such as Central China, Northeast China, Northwest China.

In the initial stage of the 1950s, Soviet architects and engineers provided important support, designing the main industrial structures and facilities for the 156 heavy industrial projects, for which the Chinese professionals assisted on minor facilities and residential accommodations. For instance, an automobile plant built in the city of Changchun was one of the aid projects designed by Soviet professionals, whereas the Chinese, led by Wang Huabin and his colleagues from East China Design Institute for Industrial Architecture from Shanghai, delivered designs for workers' dormitories and other facilities.

Like many other Soviet-style organizations, the design institutes were based on bureaucratic rather than professional principles. It is interesting to note that these institutes didn't charge fees, as the whole nation was considered as one unified community. Titles, ranking, and pay levels of the professionals were centrally determined in accordance with a mixture of criteria, which included but were not limited to the levels of skill and expertise.[14] The administrative authorities at various levels made decisions on the recruitment and career path of a professional, where architects, as professionals, delivered only technical drawings and did not assume the right of site supervision.[15]

Despite the domination of the design institutes, private design firms did not disappear until 1957, when "Socialist Transformation" was fully accomplished. Despite the official statement, which described that the professionals happily joined the state institutes, many in fact were reluctant. But the ongoing teaching and campaigning from the government cultivated gradually a collective spirit and a sense of pride and responsibility in designing for the nation.

The Interplay of Ideology and Design

The swift completion of "Socialist Transformation" (1953–57), erasing all "capitalists" in just a few years, gave party leaders an illusion that communism could be achieved shortly. The intent in launching the Great Leap Forward was to transform China from backward agriculture into an advanced industrialized and communist power, yet in reality it resulted in a number of disasters.[16] A large meeting of the Politburo of the Central Committee of the Chinese Communist Party held in Beidaihe in August 1958 declared the building of "People's Communes" across rural China and the constructing of several major landmark buildings in Beijing. The former was an institutional exploration of collectivization, while the latter was an architectural manifesto with a political message. Both shared a radicalized idea to encourage and accelerate socialist construction.

The erection of Ten Great Buildings in 1959, to celebrate the 10th anniversary of the People's Republic, was part of the effort to transform the landscape of the historic center of Beijing (Figure 32.1).[17] Representing China's great socialist achievement to the nation and the world,

Figure 32.1   Premier Zhou Enlai visiting the building site of Beijing Railway Station and listening to the architect Chen Deng'ao's presentation, 1959.

Source: Editorial Committee, ed., *Zhongguo Jianzhu Sheji Yanjiuyuan Chengli Wushi Zhounian Jinian Congshu: Licheng Pian* (Beijing: Qinghua Daxue Chubanshe, 2002), 37, 62. Permission and courtesy of CADG (China Architecture Design & Research Group).

it assumed enormous political and cultural importance. Shortly after the decision, authorities mobilized design professionals of design institutes and senior professors at prestigious architecture schools across China to submit design schemes or advice. And, for sure, a large number of design proposals were received.

One of the ten, the Great Hall of the People, was no doubt the most important and representative, as it assumed such an important location and function (to the east of the Tiananmen Square facing east, a great hall for the Chinese People's Political Consultative Conference or CPPCC).[18] Just one month after the call, 34 design institutes in Beijing and a number of design professionals and architectural students nation-wide submitted 84 plans and 189 elevations for the competition. The project's initial function was quite ambiguous, consisting of an auditorium for 10,000 people, a banquet hall for 5,000 people, and some office rooms, leaving designers a large space for imagination and speculation. After studying these requirements and observing the site personally, Liu Ren, Deputy Secretary of the Party of Beijing, felt that the previous area requirement of 70,000 square meters could not accommodate these programs, nor could it respond to the scale of the site, let alone embody the vision Mao had. Later, he instructed the design office of the Beijing Planning Authority, which provided schemes, to expand the scale, without telling other shortlists.[19]

During the next stage of competition, Zhao Dongri, Shen Qi, and Tao Zongzhen, architects from the Beijing Planning Authority, presented a revised proposal with a classical colonnade. Compared with other proposals, this scheme, now at 170,000 square meters, assumed a distinctive feature – a scheme that was selected. Many rounds of fierce debate occurred, concerning the Western style, the over-sized scale, and the various practical concerns regarding the capacity and time needed to complete. Party leaders such as Wan Li, Deputy Mayor of Beijing and the director of the Ten Great Projects, and, more importantly, Premier Zhou Enlai, intervened and made decisions regarding scale and formal style. While the scale had to be maintained, the eclectic formal approach was also supported – "all good ideas in design, ancient or modern, Chinese or overseas, can be absorbed here for us," according to Zhou. For construction, to ensure speedy progress, more than ten construction companies and some tens of thousands of skilled builders selected from across China were working together, 24/7, for the Great Hall alone, and a comparable scale of efforts was put on the other of the ten projects as well across Beijing. In a great socialist cooperation, the forces worked efficiently and finally delivered the ten buildings, in 11 months – a miracle in world comparison.

The construction of the Ten Great Buildings revealed a perspective and a capacity of the central authority to distribute intelligence and resource across the nation according to need. This highly uneven allocation of resources in a period of scarcity was often praised as an embodiment of the advantage of socialism – concentrating forces on major projects. Whereas the erection of these state monuments represented the institutes' active response to the call of the party, the design of some civic projects under limited circumstances by a few architects demonstrated a strong commitment to other public and social needs. Two creative projects may well illustrate this contribution.

When monumental design was prevailing in the mid- and late 1950s, Xia Changshi, a professor and architect of a design office affiliated with South China Institute of Technology, finished a hostel near the Dinghu Mountain in Zhaoqing, a city in a southern province of Guangdong.[20] This moderate building adopted local, accessible, and recyclable materials such as wood, bamboo, and stone under the limit of both budget and construction time allowed. The project exhibited an integrated approach by embedding itself carefully in between a few existing buildings and maintaining the topographic character of the site. A comparable example in resisting both standardized and wasteful design in the same period was Hua Lanhong's project of the Xingfucun (happy village) Neighborhood in Beijing. Hua, one of the principal architects in the Design Institute of Beijing Planning Authority, experimented with an alternative layout of veranda style dwellings.[21] By using inexpensive materials, including bricks and timber, the architect created a wide range of housing units with landscaped gardens and courtyards, which responded well to the diverse requirements of the residences (Figure 32.2).

The Great Leap Forward gave rise to a bold increase in capital construction investment and a proliferation of backyard iron and steel factories, at the expense of agricultural production and the natural environment. The subsequent famine and economic recession forced the authorities to formulate new economic strategies. In the design field, the size of the profession declined drastically.[22]

In 1964, Mao and the central government launched a campaign titled "Design Revolution" to deal with existing design problems, including a tendency of "detaching design from politics, reality, and people." After years of practice, the Chinese professionals gradually grasped the complex techniques by learning from the Soviet Union, yet knowledge transfer did not always engage and match well with local reality. In a period of recovery from famine and recession, from the early to the mid-1960s, architects and engineers of the institutes concentrated their effort on two main areas: housing design in urban and rural areas, and industrial projects.[23] In order to resist the so-called bourgeois inclination to be big, foreign, and all-embracing, state authorities advocated a dramatic reduction of cost of non-productive buildings.[24] Architectural production was much constrained by the reality of scarcity and the policy of austerity.

When political turmoil started to spread across Chinese society after the eruption of the Cultural Revolution in 1966, professional practice of the design institutes suffered gravely from the campaigns of "class struggles." Later, many design professionals were criticized as "feudal-ist," "capitalist," and "revisionist" and were sent to reform camps. With the design institutes

Figure 32.2 Xingfucun (happy village) Neighborhood, Beijing, 1957. Architect: Hua Lanhong.
Source: © Guanghui Ding.

disbanded and their staff sent down, the functioning was fully interrupted – until the early 1970s, when they were recalled gradually into the institutions in the city.

The Reform of the Design Institute

With the Cultural Revolution coming to an end in 1976 when Mao died, the party began to shift its policy from "revolution" to "economic development," which was basically engendered by Deng Xiaoping, who resumed power in the late 1970s (Figure 32.3). In 1978, Deng launched reform and opening-up, and steered China towards socialist market economy and active engagement with the outside. Like many state-owned institutions, the design institutes began a process of reforming its organization and management structure. The first action was the "Implementation of Fee Charge for Design Service" at pilot institutes in 1979. By doing this, authorities encouraged some institutes to charge design fees and to remove gradually central funding. After that a series of reform policies were issued – all aimed to promote and support market practice of the institutes with more managerial autonomy granted.

Although there was a construction boom and an expansion of some design institutes (establishing branch offices in Shenzhen, Zhuhai, Haikou, and other cities in the south) in the 1980s, design practice was actually very much constrained by the old bureaucratic rules and a competitive mechanism was much needed. Dai Nianci, a senior chief architect in Beijing and the former Deputy Minister of the Ministry of Urban–Rural Construction and Environmental Protection, contemplated deeply the problem and searched for ways of moving forward. For this, he opened a small design studio, *Jianxue*, under the protection of the Ministry, and tested various ideas with a few selected projects – included an affordable housing project, the Fahuasi Residential Community of Beijing, before he passed away in 1991.[25]

Figure 32.3   Professionals from Design Institute of the Ministry of Construction discussing on city planning after the 1976 earthquake, Tangshan 1976.

Source: Editorial Committee, ed., *Zhongguo Jianzhu Sheji Yanjiuyuan Chengli Wushi Zhounian Jinian Congshu: Licheng Pian* (Beijing: Qinghua Daxue Chubanshe, 2002), 37, 62. Permission and courtesy of CADG (China Architecture Design & Research Group).

Individual experiments such as this paralleled official moves for the reform of the professional system of architecture. And open-minded officials with a professional background, such as Dai mentioned earlier, and Gong Deshun and Zhang Qinnan, played critical roles in pushing the reform. With increasing exchange and cooperation since the early 1980s between the Architectural Society of China (ASC), the American Institute of Architects (AIA), the Royal Institute of British Architects (RIBA), and the Hong Kong Institute of Architects (HKIA), new educational and professional frameworks of architecture were established in China, including the National Supervision Commission for Higher Education in Architecture in 1992 and the National Registration Architect Management Committee in 1995, both of which were modelled after the American system.[26] After years of endeavor, the architect's legal status was formally recognized through the promulgation of the "Regulations of Registered Architect" in 1995.[27] Zhang even envisaged the establishment of a new interconnected framework he called AIR (Accreditation–Institute–Registration), an integrated system headed by the ASC, the Institute in the middle, for improving architects' status and expanding their rights in design and construction.[28]

In many ways, the reinstating of the professional system in the mid-1990s laid down a solid basis for the subsequent reforms of the structure of the state design institutes – a process that was part and parcel of a larger nation-wide reform of the state-owned enterprises (SOEs). The strategy to improve the performance and competitiveness of the SOEs was to introduce a modern enterprise system, which had been a central agenda for the economic reform of China since 1994. In 1995, for the reform of state design institutes, the central state authority decided that large-scale state institutes were to remain as state-owned, whereas medium and small-sized institutes were to be privatized, so as to make the former nationally and internationally competitive while reducing the financial burden for the latter.

The role of state authority was also changing: whereas it had been a plan maker, it was now a capital holder, for the SOEs, allowing it to enjoy the statutory rights and interests of a major shareholder.[29] In this sense, the bifurcation of the "large" and "small" institutes also reflected a political distribution of holding: large-size institutes were restructured into incorporated companies where the state owned a dominant proportion of the company's shares, while medium- and small-sized institutes were transformed into private firms by diversifying ownership. Most of these privately run companies still keep the name of "design institute." Through merging and joint venture, some "flagship" SOE design institutes become groups of 3–4,000 staff each, such as CADG (China Architecture Design and Research Group), BIAD (Beijing Institute of Architectural Design), and the Shanghai Modern Group. Their fee-earning ability is close to the firms in Hong Kong, Europe, and North America.[30] In the 1950s, around 10,000 people were working in the state design institutes; after 60 years of evolution, there were around 1.7 million professionals working in the building design industry, including the public and private sectors (Figure 32.4).[31] The civil and industrial buildings in the cities, especially the ubiquitous residential projects, were the primary works of design institutes at various levels.

A remarkable phenomenon in China is that universities with an architecture school usually have a design institute attached (Figure 32.5). The practice started in 1958, when the first such institute was established at Tongji University of Shanghai. Some half a century later, the Tongji University Architectural Design and Research Institute now has grown into a group consisting of 30 companies and 3,000 staff.[32] Other universities run their design companies as well, to integrate teaching, research, and design practice and to financially support the parent organizations. According to our estimation, there are around 300 such university-owned design institutes in China today.

Due partly to reputation and strength and partly to multiple links with local authorities (who were often investors or clients), the design institutes, compared with private design

Figure 32.4 Interior of the Design Institute of Shenzhen University, Shenzhen, 2004.
Source: © Charlie Q. L. Xue.

firms, enjoyed a special privilege in China and gained numerous commissions from public and private sectors. This connection had an impact on the work of institutes, as interesting and radical designs often had to give way to authority's interest in a centralized image, and to pragmatic rationality or practical pressures such as efficiency and quantity. On the other hand, the proximity with state authority also required a social contribution – the institutes' active work in post-earthquake reconstruction in Sichuan Province after 2008 and Qinghai Province after 2010 illustrated how they were mobilized to deliver intensive design services for people in need.

Despite the long-established proximity with state authority, the design institute cannot easily compete with internationally renowned design firms. The provision of creative designs, strong technology, and effective management secured a superior position of these international offices in many high-profile public projects. And, for this, the domestic design institutes often played the role of a local design collaborator or a producer of construction documents. The rising profile of small and private design firms in China since 2000 has also challenged the old institutes, as the former tended to offer innovative design solutions to specific contexts for a client.

To improve competitiveness, design institutes have made structural reforms toward specialization within an institute, in several directions. It could be specialization in terms of types (housing, hospital, education, sport, office, and hotel), disciplinary areas (architecture, urban planning, landscape, structure, and building services engineering), or design phases (conceptual

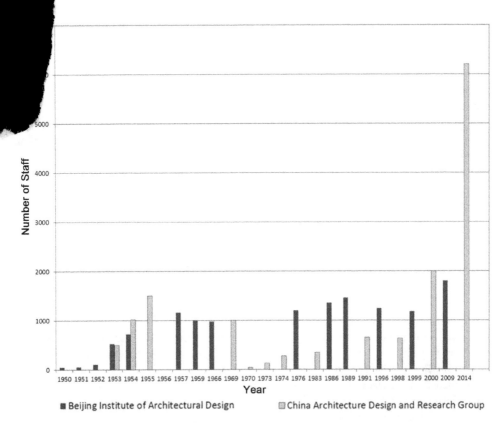

Figure 32.5 Staff size of two state-owned design institutes from the 1950s to the 2010s. Note: In 2000, four state-owned design institutes, including the Design Institute of Ministry of Construction were amalgamated into CADG (China Architecture Design and Research Group). The figure of CADG before 2000 reflects the employee number of the Design Institute of Ministry of Construction.

Source: © Charlie Q. L. Xue.

design, preliminary design, technical drawing, and service).[33] The spreading and decentralizing framework also gave rise to the emergence of a number of financially and administratively "independent" units within one institute, to provide both freedom to experiment and protection when needed.

Within a framework of the institute, efforts were made to encourage a relative autonomy so that creative individuals may be found, supported, and allowed to grow and prosper. For this, individual studios were established within. A well-known example is Cui Kai Architecture Studio, established within CADG (China Architecture Design and Research Group) – one of the earliest such offices in China – in 2003. Led by Cui Kai, himself a creative architect and Deputy Director of CADG, the studio has a staff of 30, has been successful in winning competitions and commissioning, and has been active in delivering high profile – and much acclaimed – cultural and public projects.

For a studio like this, the security of the large institute and the freedom of the small office provided a good mixture; the established reputation of the institute and the more creative flair of the studio also formed a positive inter-relationship. The product of Cui Kai Studio is often

much appreciated – designs in which tradition and modernity, buildings and the city, fo
landscape are mediated with interesting ideas. Well-known cases include his Desheng U
a cluster of five-story buildings forming a street with a vista towards an ancient city gate,
engmen, in the northwest corner of the old city of Beijing, and Yinxu Museum of 2006,
the entire facility was buried into the landscape with narrative corridors surrounding a (
courtyard facing the sky.[34]

The emergence of celebrity studios within a design institute is an active response to
changing architectural market, particularly the increasing requirement to express "culture" by
the profession and the population. A number of well-known projects produced recently by
those studios led by Cui Kai, Cheng Taining, He Jingtang, and Xing Tonghe, to name just a
few, demonstrate their commitment to the expression of culture in an architecture of quality
under the pressure of the market. Yet, a few masterpieces do not represent the whole situation
of design production by the design institutes. It would be fair to say that the majority produced by the institutes was first and foremost the product of the market. In today's situation,
a judicious balance between commercial requirement and cultural pursuit remains a major
challenge.

Conclusion

The evolution of the design institutes revealed a changing relationship of individual architects
with state, society, and market. As part of a Soviet-style planned economy, the centralization
of private firms into national design enterprises enabled the state to focus on strategic parts of
the industrial and military sector, and on reconstruction of the cities. Central authority had
maintained a strong leadership in design practice through ideological means by formulating
principles – that a building should be "practical, economic and, where possible, beautiful" – and
also practical means by controlling the distribution of all resources.

Since the 1980s, reform in the context of opening-up and economic liberalization effectively promoted the autonomy of the architects. Following the policies of the state, the design
institutes began to accumulate capital by providing their professional service to the public and
private clients in the lucrative market. The direct link established between an individual's performance and his/her compensation encouraged the initiatives of the professionals, in a process
that was dismantling the old management system – the so-called "iron rice bowl," the life-long
job security. Such a straightforward market-driven strategy, though effective in promoting productivity and income, had not always being supportive of critical experimentations nor conducive necessarily to the production of works of cultural values.

Since the 1990s, to produce works of cultural values was increasingly expected among
the profession as well as by state authority, largely because China was more exposed and
image building became more of a concern on a global stage. With a convergence of the
desires of the architects, the design institutes, and state authority, the emergence of the
"studios" within the large institutes was a natural result – an attempt to balance between
collective practice and individual creativity, commercial productivity and experimental exercise, within the framework of the institute. The works produced by these studios, generally
speaking, have displayed the capacity of the individual architects to mediate the aspirations of
diverse concerns – personal, social, economic, cultural, and political. With social and cultural
responsibilities, they were able to work towards a synthetic mediation between the forces of
state, society, and market in their design practice. One would hope that, with further development, the state design institutes, as a public office, would deliver more for the collective
society as a whole.

Notes

1 This chapter is part of a study supported by the National Natural Science Foundation of China, Project No. 51878584. We are grateful for the valuable advice provided by Professor Jianfei Zhu and Dr. Jing Xiao.

2 Steven N.S. Cheung, *Zhongguo de Qiantu* (China's Future) (Hong Kong: Arcadia Press Ltd., 2002), 156.

3 For useful reference, see Li Feng, *"Critical" Practice in State-owned Design Institutes in Post-Mao China (1976–2000s): A Case Study of CAG* (China Architecture Design and Research Group) (Master's Thesis, The University of Melbourne, Sydney, 2010).

4 Cui Maoxin, Jin Lei and Li Chen, eds., *Jianzhu Zhongguo Liushinian: Jigou Juan 1949–2009* (Sixty years of Chinese architecture: Institutions 1949–2009) (Tianjin: Tianjin University Press, 2009), 11.

5 See Thomas Kvan, Bingkun Liu and Yunyan Jia, "The Emergence of a Profession: Development of the Profession of Architecture in China," *Journal of Architectural and Planning Research* 25, no. 3 (2008): 203–220; Peter G. Rowe and Bing Wang, "Formation and Re-formation of the Architecture Profession in China: Episodes, Underlying Aspects, and Present Needs," in *Prospects for the Professions in China*, eds William P Alford, William Kirby, and Kenneth Winston (Oxford: Routledge, 2011), 257–282.

6 *Zhongguo Renmin Zhengzhi Xieshang Huiyi Gongtong Gangling* (The common program of the Chinese People's Political Consultative Conference) (Beijing: People's Press, 1952), 3.

7 See Sun Ruiyuan, *Sanfan Wufan Yundong* (The three-anti and five-anti campaigns) (Beijing: Xinhua Press, 1991).

8 T. J. Hughes and D. E. T. Luard, *The Economic Development of Communist China 1948–1958* (London, New York and Toronto: Oxford University Press, 1959), 84.

9 See David Bray, *Social Space and Governance in Urban China: The Danwei System from Origins to Reform* (Stanford: Stanford University Press, 2005).

10 See Wu Desheng, et al. eds., *Beijingshi Jianzhu Sheji Yanjiuyuan Chengli Wushi Zhounian Jinianji, 1949–1999* (Album for the fiftieth anniversary of Beijing Institute of Architectural Design, 1949–1999) (Beijing: China Architecture and Building Press, 1999), 42.

11 Zhou Rongxin, "Shenru Kaizhan Jianzhujie de Fanyoupai Douzheng (Carrying out deeply the Anti-rightist struggle in the architectural community)," *Jianzhu Xuebao* (Architectural Journal), no. 9 (1957): 1–4.

12 Zhou, "Shenru," 1–4.

13 Before the Three-anti and Five-anti campaigns, architectural educators were permitted to engage with practice either privately or publicly. After that, many educators collaborated with their own universities or other public sectors to design projects. See Charlie Q. L. Xue, "Zhongguo Tese de Jianzhu Shejiyuan (Design institutes with China's characteristics)," *Time + Architecture*, no. 1 (2004): 27–31; Xiao Yiqiang and Chen Zhi, "Huanan Ligong Daxue Jianzhu Shejiyuan Fazhan Licheng Pingxi (A review of the growth and development of the Architecture Design and Research Institute of SCUT)," *Nanfang Jianzhu* (South architecture), no. 5 (2009): 10–14.

14 The titles of design professionals, for example, included "assistant engineer," "engineer," "senior engineer," and "engineer at professor level." Since the mid-1950s, titles of "architect" were abolished, while those of "engineer" were kept.

15 As everything belonged to the state, it was not necessary to supervise each other. See Zhang Qinnan, "Wushinian Cangsang: Huigu Guojia Jianzhu Shejiyuan de Lishi (Fifty years' vicissitudes: A retrospect of the history of sate-owned institute of architectural design)," in *Jianzhu Baijia Huiyilu Xubian* (Sequel of One Hundred Architecture Memoirs), Yang Yongsheng (Beijing: Intellectual Property Publishing House Co. Ltd/China Water & Power Press, 2003), 100–106, 100.

16 For useful reference, see Frank Dikötter, *Mao's Great Famine: The History of China's Most Devastating Catastrophe, 1958–62* (London: Bloomsbury, 2011).

17 See Qu Wanlin, "1949–1959 Nian Guoqing Gongcheng ji Jingyan Qishi (The project of the Ten Great Buildings and its experience)," in *Dangdai Zhongguo Chenggong Fazhan de Lishi Jingyan: Diwujie Guoshi Xueshu Nianhui Lunwenji* (The historical experience of contemporary China's successful development: Proceedings of the fifth national history conference), ed. Zhang Xingxing (Beijing: Contemporary China Publishing House, 2007), 280–289.

18 See Hung Chang-tai, *Mao's New World: Political Culture in the Early People's Republic* (Ithaca, N.Y.: Cornell University Press, 2011).

19 Zhao Dongri, technical director of the Design Institute of Beijing Planning Authority, knew Liu Ren well since the 1940s. Given this personal connection, it would not be surprising if Liu had given a special support to Zhao.

20 Xia Changshi, "Dinghushan Jiaogong Xiuyangsuo Xiujian Jiyao (Notes on the design of Dinghushan Hostel)," *Jianzhu Xuebao* (Architectural journal), no. 9 (1956): 45–50.

21 Hua Lanhong, "Beijing Xingfucun Jiefang Sheji (The design of the Xingfu village neighborhood)," *Jianzhu Xuebao* (Architectural Journal), no. 3 (1957): 16–35.

22 *Zhonggong Zhangyang Jingjian Jianzao Duiwu Renyuan de Jueding* (Decisions of the Central Committee of the Chinese Communist Party on the reduction of construction personal) (Beijing: Beijing Municipal Archives, 1961).

23 During this period, the published buildings on the pages of *Jianzhu Xuebao* (Architectural journal) were primarily housing and industrial projects.

24 The *Jianzhu Xuebao* (Architectural journal) published an issue introducing the experience of reducing the cost of non-productive buildings in the third issue of 1966.

25 The full name of the office he established was "Jianxue & Jianzhu Design Office" or "Jianxue yu Jianzhu Gongchen Shiwusuo." For his experiments, see Dai Nianci, "Ruhe Jiada Zhufang Midu: Zhufang Jianshe de Yige Juyou Zhanluexing de Wenti (How to increase housing density: A strategic problem of housing construction)," *Jianzhu Xuebao* (Architectural journal), no. 7 (1989): 2–5.

26 See Charlie Q. L. Xue, *Building Practice in China* (Beijing: China Architecture and Building Press, 2009).

27 The establishment of the journal *Jianzhushi* (The architect) in 1979 by Yang Yongsheng and his associates can be regarded as an endeavor to restore the title of "architect," which had been replaced by the titles of "design technician" or "engineer" (*shejishi* or *gongchengshi*). For discussion of the titles, see Lin Leyi, "Tantan Women Jianzhushi Zheyihang (Discussion on the profession of our architects)," *Jianzhushi* (The architect), no. 1 (1979): 7–9; Chen Zhanxiang, "Jianzhushi Lishi Diwei de Yanbian (The evolution of architect's position in history)," *Jianzhu Xuebao* (Architectural journal), no. 8 (1981): 28–31.

28 Zhang, "Wushinian Cangsang," 104.

29 Shen Hong and Zhao Nong, *China's State-owned Enterprises: Nature, Performance and Reform* (Singapore; London; Hackensack, NJ: World Scientific, 2013), 215.

30 This can be found from the annual ranking of *World Architecture*, London, since 2000.

31 *Zhongguo Jianzhuye Nianjian* (China building industry yearbook) (Beijing: China Architecture and Building Press, 2012).

32 Figures were obtained through the authors' investigation.

33 Cui Maoxin, Jin Lei, and Li Chen, eds, *Jianzhu Zhongguo Liushinian: Jigou Juan 1949–2009* (Sixty years of Chinese architecture: Institutions 1949–2009) (Tianjin: Tianjin Daxue Chubanshe, 2009), 54.

34 Zhang Nan and Cui Kai, "Yinxu Museum," *Jianzhu Xuebao* (Architectural journal), no. 1, (2007): 34–39.

Bibliography

Bray, David. *Social Space and Governance in Urban China: The Danwei System from Origins to Reform*. Stanford: Stanford University Press, 2005.

Chen Zhanxiang. "Jianzhushi Lishi Diwei de Yanbian (The Evolution of Architect's Position in History)." *Architectural Journal*, no. 8 (1981): 28–31.

Cheung, Steven N.S. *Zhongguo de Qiantu* (China's Future). Hong Kong: Arcadia Press Ltd., 2002.

Cui Maoxin, Jin Lei and Li Chen, eds. *Jianzhu Zhongguo Liushinian: Jigou Juan 1949–2009* (Sixty Years of Chinese Architecture: Institutions 1949–2009). Tianjin: Tianjin Daxue Chubanshe, 2009.

Dai Nianci. "Ruhe Jiada Zhufang Midu: Zhufang Jianshe de Yige Juyou Zhanluexing de Wenti (How to Increase Housing Density: A Strategic Problem of Housing Construction)." *Jianzhu Xuebao* (Architectural Journal), no. 7 (1989): 2–5.

Dikötter, Frank. *Mao's Great Famine: The History of China's Most Devastating Catastrophe, 1958–62*. London: Bloomsbury, 2011.

Dong Zhikai and Wu Jiang. *Xin Zhongguo Gongye de Dianjishi: 156 Xiang Jianshe Yanjiu, 1950–2000* (The Industrial Cornerstone of New China). Guangzhou: Guangdong Economic Press, 2004.

Eckstein, Alexander. *China's Economic Development: The Interplay of Scarcity and Ideology*. Ann Arbor: The University of Michigan Press, 1976.

Editorial. "Zhengque de Sheji Cong Shijian Zhong Lai (Correct Design Comes from Social Praxis)." *People's Daily*, 22 April 1965.

Hua Lanhong. "Beijing Xingfucun Jiefang Sheji (The Design of the Xingfu Village Neighborhood)." *Jianzhu Xuebao* (Architectural Journal), no. 3 (1957): 16–35.

Hughes, T.J. and D.E.T. Luard. *The Economic Development of Communist China 1948–1958*. London, New York and Toronto: Oxford University Press, 1959.

Hung, Chang-tai. *Mao's New World: Political Culture in the Early People's Republic*. Ithaca, NY: Cornell University Press, 2011.

Jin Oubu. "Quanguo Diyijia Guoying Jianzhu Shejiyuan Chengli Qingkuang: Qinghe Huadong Jianzhu Sheji Yanjiuyuan Chengli Wushi Nian (The Establishment of China's First State-Owned Architectural Design Institute: Celebrating Fiftieth Anniversary of East China Architectural Design and Research Institute)." In *Jianzhu Baijia Huiyilu Xubian* (One Hundred Architecture Memoirs, Sequel), edited by Yang Yongsheng, 107–110. Beijing: Intellectual Property Publishing House Co. Ltd., China Water & Power Press, 2003.

Kvan, Thomas, Liu Bingkun and Jia Yunyan. "The Emergence of a Profession: Development of the Profession of Architecture in China." *Journal of Architectural and Planning Research* 25, no. 3 (2008): 203–220.

Li Feng. *"Critical" Practice in State-Owned Design Institutes in Post-Mao China (1976–2000s): A Case Study of CAG (China Architecture Design and Research Group)*. Master's Thesis, The University of Melbourne, Melbourne, 2010.

Lin Leyi. "Tantan Women Jianzhushi Zheyihang (Discussion on the Profession of Our Architects)." *Jianzhushi* (The Architect), no. 1 (1979): 7–9.

Liu Jingliang, Liu Jun, Zhang Yongchen, Wang Li and Wang Houhe. "Tianjinshi Jianzhu Shejiyuan (Tianjin Institute of Architectural Design)." In *Jianzhu Zhongguo Liushinian: Jigou Juan 1949–2009* (Sixty Years of Chinese Architecture: Institutions 1949–2009), edited by Cui Maoxin, Jin Lei and Li Chen, 88–99. Tianjin: Tianjin University Press, 2009.

Lou Chenghao and Tao Weijun. *Chen Zhi: Shiji Rensheng* (Chen Zhi: A Century's Life). Shanghai: Tongji University Press, 2013.

Ma Licheng. *Datupo: Xin Zhongguo Siying Jingji Fengyunlu* (Big Breakthrough: The Record of Private Economy in New China). Beijing: Zhonghua Gongshang Lianhe Chubanshe, 2006.

Qu Wanlin. "1949–1959 Nian Guoqing Gongcheng ji Jingyan Qishi (The Project of the Ten Great Buildings and Its Experience)." In *Dangdai Zhongguo Chenggong Fazhan de Lishi Jingyan: Diwujie Guoshi Xueshu Nianhui Lunwenji* (The Historical Experience of Contemporary China's Successful Development: Proceedings of the Fifth National History Conference), edited by Zhang Xingxing, 280–289. Beijing: Contemporary China Publishing House, 2007.

Rowe, Peter G. and Bing Wang. "Formation and Re-formation of the Architecture Profession in China: Episodes, Underlying Aspects, and Present Needs." In *Prospects for the Professions in China*, edited by William P. Alford, William Kirby and Kenneth Winston, 257–282. Oxford: Routledge, 2011.

Shen Hong and Zhao Nong. *China's State-Owned Enterprises: Nature, Performance and Reform*. Singapore, London and Hackensack, NJ: World Scientific, 2013.

Sun Ruiyuan. *Sanfan Wufan Yungdong* (The Three-Anti and Five-Anti Campaigns). Beijing: Xinhua Chubanshe, 1991.

Wu Desheng et al., eds. *Beijingshi Jianzhu Sheji Yanjiuyuan Chengli Wushi Zhounian Jinianji, 1949–1999* (Album for the Fiftieth Anniversary of Beijing Institute of Architectural Design, 1949–1959). Beijing: China Architecture and Building Press, 1999.

Xia Changshi. "Dinghushan Jiaogong Xiuyangsuo Xiujian Jiyao (Notes on the Design of Dinghushan Hostel)." *Jianzhu Xuebao* (Architectural Journal), no. 9 (1956): 45–50.

Xiao Yiqiang and Chen Zhi. "Huanan Ligong Daxue Jianzhu Shejiyuan Fazhan Licheng Pingxi (A Review of the Growth and Development of the Architecture Design and Research Institute of SCUT)." *Nanfang Jianzhu* (South Architecture), no. 5 (2009): 10–14.

Xu, Yi-chong. "The Political Economy of SOEs in China and India." In *The Political Economy of SOEs in China and India*, edited by Xu Yi-chong, 1–18. Houndmills, Basingstoke, Hampshire and New York: Palgrave Macmillan, 2012.

Xue, Charlie Q.L. *Building a Revolution: Chinese Architecture Since 1980*. Hong Kong: Hong Kong University Press, 2006.

———. *Building Practice in China*. Beijing: China Architecture and Building Press, 2009.

———. *World Architecture in China*. Hong Kong: Joint Publication Ltd., 2010.

Zhang Nan and Cui Kai. "Yinxu Museum." *Jianzhu Xuebao* (Architectural Journal), no. 1 (2007): 34–39.

Zhang Qinnan. "Wushinian Cangsang: Huigu Guojia Jianzhu Shejiyuan de Lishi (Fifty Years' Vicissitudes: The Retrospect of the History of State-Owned Institute of Architectural Design)." In *Jianzhu Baijia*

Huiyilu Xubian (One Hundred Architecture Memoirs, Sequel), edited by Yang Yongsheng, 100–106. Beijing: Intellectual Property Publishing House Co. Ltd., China Water & Power Press, 2003.

Zhongguo Jianzhuye Nianjian (China Building Industry Yearbook). Beijing: China Architecture and Building Press, 2012.

Zhongguo Renmin Zhengzhi Xieshang Huiyi Gongtong Gangling (The Common Program of the Chinese People's Political Consultative Conference). Beijing: People's Press, 1952.

Zhou Rongxin. "Shenru Kaizhan Jianzhujie de Fanyoupai Douzheng (Carrying Out Deeply the Anti-Rightist Struggle in the Architectural Community)." *Jianzhu Xuebao* (Architectural Journal), no. 9 (1957): 1–4.

Zhu, Jianfei. *Architecture of Modern China: A Historical Critique*. London and New York: Routledge, 2009.

Glossary

Beidaihe	北戴河
Beijing	北京
Cheng Taining	程泰宁
Cui Kai	崔恺
danwei	单位
Deng Xiaoping	邓小平
Deshenmen	德胜门
Dinghu	鼎湖
dongguan	冬官
Fahuasi (housing)	法华寺（居住区）
Gong Deshun	龚德顺
Haikou	海口
He Jingtang	何镜堂
Hua Lanhong	华揽洪
Jianxue	建学
Liu Ren	刘仁
Shanghai	上海
Shen Qi	沈其
Shenzhen	深圳
Tao Zongzhen	陶宗震
Tongji (university)	同济（大学）
Wan Li	万里
Wang Huabin	王华彬
Xia Changshi	夏昌世
Xing Tonghe	邢同和
Xingfucun	幸福村
Yinxu	殷墟
Zhang Qinnan	张钦楠
Zhao Dongri	赵冬日
Zhaoqing	肇庆
Zhou Enlai	周恩来
Zhou Rongxin	周荣鑫
Zhuhai	珠海

33

THE CHINESE DESIGN INSTITUTE

A Critique of "Critical Thinking"

Jianfei Zhu

Established in Mao's China in the 1950s with Soviet influence and the Chinese Communist Party's directives, the architectural design institute, state-owned and collectivist, was the main institutional form of design practice in China for decades. In the reform era since the 1980s, with the introduction of market economy, the design institutes began to go through transformations, to make themselves more competitive as commercial firms. Today, some of the biggest design institutes are providing important contributions in China and are active overseas as well. Interestingly, they remain state-owned in a socialist country while competing as a "capitalist" force in the market. This phenomenon and the Chinese design institute in general have not been studied in a critical perspective yet – in the sense of dealing with political, ethical, and formal issues of design practice in a social context.

This chapter aims to investigate the design institute in contemporary China and explore its significance in a comparative perspective.[1] Scholarship in the west is useful here. While studies on professional practice explore immediate issues (visualization, documentation, digital technology, global service, community participation, to name a few),[2] the debate on "critical architecture" in relation to a philosophical tradition deals with the ethical and political aspects of practice in relation to state, market, and society. The second body of discussions, for sure, is more relevant to the present study. These discussions will form an important counterpoint here. For this purpose, a review of the debate is needed – albeit very briefly and at a huge cultural distance, before we turn to the Chinese case.

"Critical Architecture" and a Critical Tradition in Europe and North America

There can be as many "critical architectures" as there are moments when the word "critical" is used in any studio discussion. The recent and formulated positions of a critical architecture are probably those arguing for a "critical regionalism" in the 1980s by Kenneth Frampton, Alexander Tzonis, Liane Lefaivre, and others.[3] Yet, the confronting debate, with several polemic positions, on what should be the critical in architecture emerged only recently, when Michael Hays' 1984 essay was re-discovered and Rem Koolhaas was found to be paradigmatic and forward-looking by a younger generation (labeled as "post-critical" around 2000), and in serious

DOI: 10.4324/9781315851112-49

conferences such as the one on "critical architecture" at University College London in 2004.[4] In hindsight, this debate involved at least three positions. The first may be termed as "critical" or "formal-critical"; it was self-consciously claimed in the writings of Peter Eisenman and academically articulated in K. Michael Hays, and in both cases the formally pure and resistant works of Mies van der Rohe were cited as pioneering. The ideas here argued for the use of austere and autonomous forms, to oppose a status quo around the project, such as an established tradition or a commercial behavior.[5] The second has been termed "post-critical," and its arguments were found in the writings of Michael Speaks, Robert Somol, and Sarah Whiting, who aimed at challenging the first. They all cited Rem Koolhaas as a pioneering figure who, according them, had actively engaged with the world around them; they called for a break from the positions of Eisenman and Mies, an engagement with realities, and the use of "intelligence," instead of ideology, to learn rather than to critique the real and the other.[6] The third, however, may be termed as "social-critical."[7] It was promoted by scholars of a Marxian tradition as represented more recently by Hilde Heynen. This position advocated critical engagement with realities, in order to address social issues and to help build a better and fairer society, as many had attempted in central Europe with socialist municipal governments (such as Hannes Meyer). In the eyes of the third position, the first two were all "formal" and not really critical, whereas a really "critical" position should address social ills and injustices and aim for building for a better society to come.

These positions, especially the first and the third, were related in various ways to a critical tradition developed since the eighteenth century in Europe. It started with Immanuel Kant, developed from Friedrich Hegel to Karl Marx, and arrived in modern forms in the Frankfurt School.[8] While Kant (*Critique of Pure Reason*, 1781) criticized "pure reason," so as to limit its scope and to protect realms of ethics and aesthetics, Marx — with reformed Hegelian notions of history — criticized the products of "pure reason" when it reached a capitalist age, namely the instrumental reason of industrial capitalism (labor as commodity, alienation, surplus value) and the associated ideologies (that of capital, market, and the state). The Frankfurt School theorists expanded further the scope of critique to cover social, cultural, artistic, symbolic, and psychological areas; of industrial modernity, to critique reason, modernity, and modern systems; and to call for transformations for a better and fairer society to come.

This lineage of ideas captures a central current of thinking of the critical tradition developed in modern Europe. This critical thinking was historically associated with bourgeois revolutions against the "ancien régime." It included and still includes a progressive politics of protecting a natural state or civil society of free individuals, against oppressive regimes ancient or modern. In this framing, the oppressive regimes were initially the feudal kingship, and later on the list includes state bureaucracy, market forces, and capital or capitalist greed. In this critical tradition, state government is a problem, if not an enemy, of a "natural" civil society of free individuals. John Locke's *Two Treaties of Government* (1689) is a primary articulation about the state that needs to be limited with checks and balances.[9] Contemporary theorization, such as Habermas' writing, also considers state authority as one of the main adversary forces to be resisted.[10]

A few features of this tradition must be noted now: 1) state authority is looked upon as a basic problem, if not obstacle, for a desirable or progressive agenda; 2) there is a dualist thinking with a clear opposition at work; 3) there is an "outside" that permits autonomy to exist and critical forces to perform – an outside that accommodates all these opposing entities. In the Chinese tradition, on the other hand, all these assumptions are absent in its moral philosophy, which generates cases for alternative thinking.

Progressive Architecture and State Authority in Modern China

If we review the various currents and developments in the architecture of modern China, we can identify a few strands of "progressive" architecture – progressive in a local and histori-cal sense, covering either a political or a design agenda.[11] For example, the building of the People's Commune in the Cultural Revolution of the 1960s–70s for idealist social equality, and the awakening of a sense of "form" in the 1990s for an "architectural" advancement, are both considered progressive in their specific context. In modern China, six groups of such designs can be identified. They may be briefly enlisted here: 1) the Chinese Native-Style architecture of the 1930s, under the Republican Government based in Nanjing (an architec-ture that served for national independence against western imperialism and colonialism); 2) the National-Style architecture of the 1950s based mostly in Beijing (an architecture that served or served to represent national independence and socialist construction); 3) architecture of the People's Commune in the late 1960s and early 1970s (to experiment with a political utopia of communism); 4) functionalist and modernist architecture of socialist China of the 1960s–70s (welfare facilities and public buildings, including those for trade and foreign affairs); 5) designs with socialist agendas in the reform era of market economy (aid or disaster-relief projects, low-cost housing, buildings for a "socialist countryside"); 6) a pure and formal architecture emerging in the late 1990s, to express personal experience (light, space, texture), autonomous formal language (material, tectonics, form), and abstract interpretations of local traditions (gar-den design, literati aesthetics, vernacular traditions), to transcend earlier modern traditions in China, as found in Yung Ho Chang, Liu Jiakun, and Wang Shu. Of these six cases, only in the last one do we find a relative independence or autonomy of state authority, in that architects can explore their own positions. But even in this case, the autonomy is in fact partial: all these architects are still related to government through state-owned universities and many other state institutions of all levels.

In all these cases, state authority is the force behind, and often leading, the progressive agendas in architecture of modern China, in the Republican, socialist (Maoist), and reform periods. It is important to note that, in pre-modern China, in the Chinese tradition, state authority typically assumed a moral and comprehensive leadership over many spheres of society, including building and construction. This, in turn, is rooted in the Confucian moral-political tradition in which state authority is considered or expected to be a "sage ruler," a disciplined and cultured figure who leads by moral example. Persons, families, states, the world of nations, and nature (heaven) are considered to be interrelated moral entities; within this totality, state leaders play a central role in securing a good functioning of all under heaven.[12] In the western tradition, as in the critical thinking outlined earlier, however, state or government is conceived as a problem, often as an obstacle to a civil soci-ety of free individuals. In this framework, a civil society of individuals is naturally right and inherently progressive (or its search for autonomy and freedom is considered natural and right), whereas state authority is structurally an obstacle to the naturally right and the pro-gressive, even though state government is also theorized as necessary.[13] In its recent mani-festation, in the writing of Habermas, a late member of the Frankfurt School, it is argued that to protect a life-world of the civil society, it is necessary to build a "dam" to block the "flooding" of the invading forces of state authority and market economy.[14] This contrast in the basic conception of statehood between Europe and China is profound and may prove significant in a new moral-political debate in the world, at least in our discussion about the design institute.

The Chinese Design Institute

After the founding of the People's Republic in 1949, the design institutes were the only form of design practice in mainland China; in the reform era after 1978, despite the transformation of their structures and the arrival of other forms of practice, the design institutes remained as a major and pervasive force. Some of the most noted ones, and also the largest, include CAG (China Architecture Design and Research Group, headquartered in Beijing), BIAD (Beijing Institute of Architectural Design), ECADI (East China Architectural Design and Research Institute, Shanghai), and SIADR (Shanghai Institute of Architectural Design and Research), the last two being parts of a conglomerate, the Modern Group (Shanghai), also known as "Shanghai Xian Dai."

CAG was and still is a body belonging to the Ministry of Construction of the People's Republic. CAG, large in staffing (1000 in the 1950s and 4000 in the 2010s), is especially comprehensive in the range of expertise it covers, which includes technological research, establishment of design codes, historical research, and heritage conservation, in addition to planning, design, and project management. Their design works are influential as well. Well-known works include: Beijing Central Telegraph Building (Figure 33.1) and China Art Gallery of the 1950s, National Library of the 1980s, Ministry of Foreign Affairs of the 1990s, railway stations in Lhasa and Suzhou of the 2000s (Figure 33.2), and the National Olympic Stadium of 2008 (with Herzog and de Meuron). Renowned architects include Lin Leyi, Chen Deng'ao, Dai Nianci, Gong Deshun, Cui Kai, and Li Xinggang.[15]

Figure 33.1   Central Telegraph Building, Beijing, 1957. Architect: Lin Leyi at CAG.

Source: Photo taken in 2009. © Jianfei Zhu.

Figure 33.2   Railway Station, Suzhou, 2006. Architect: Cui Kai at CAG.

Source: Photo taken in 2014. © Jianfei Zhu.

Another major institute in Beijing, BIAD, is renowned for designing large-scale public buildings in the Chinese capital. Most government and public buildings in Beijing come from this office. Noted ones include: Beijing Children's Hospital, Friendship Hotel, Great Hall of the People (Figure 33.3), Museum of History and Revolution, and Tiananmen Square itself, all of the 1950s; the list also includes Apartment Blocks for Foreign Diplomats and Chairman Mao's Mausoleum of the 1970s, Beijing Western Railway Station of the 1990s, and Terminal 3 of Capital Airport (with Norman Foster) and Grand National Theatre (with Paul Andreu) of

Figure 33.3   Great Hall of the People (left) and Grand National Theatre (right), Beijing, 1959 and 2007 respectively. Architect: Zhao Dongri and Zhang Bo of BIAD (left); a joint design between Paul Andreu and BIAD (right).

Source: Photo taken in 2008. © Jianfei Zhu.

the 2000s (Figure 33.3). Renowned architects include Hua Lanhong (Leon Hoa), Zhang Bo, Zhao Dongri, Zhang Kaiji, Ma Guoxin, Zhu Xiaodi, Zhu Jialu, Li Chengde, Shao Weiping, Jin Weijun, and Wang Ge.[16]

In Shanghai, in Modern Group, ECADI is particularly strong in technology, especially in super high-rise, foundation structure, and geotechnical engineering. Their well-known works include Sino–Soviet Friendship Mansion of the 1950s; Shanghai Center, Shanghai Grand Theatre, and Shanghai Planning Exhibition Hall of the 1990s; Pudong Airport Terminal 2 of the 2000s; and Shanghai World Expo Axis and Complex, Expo Cultural Center, Zhengda Himalayas Center (Figure 33.4), and China Central Television (CCTV) Headquarters of the 2010s (Figure 33.5). Many of these are collaborations with overseas architects, including Rem Koolhaas, Arata Isozaki, and Paul Andreu, for CCTV, Zhengda, and the Pudong Airport respectively. Well-known ECADI architects include Wang Huabin, Zhao Shen, Wu Jingxiang, Fang Jianquan, Cai Zhenyu, and Wang Xiao'an.[17]

Historical Development

Partially influenced from the collective practice of the Soviet Union, but more directly framed by socialist transformations the government was implementing under the Chinese Communist

Figure 33.4   Zhengda Himalayas Center, Shanghai, 2011. Architect: a joint design by Arata Isozaki, Jiang
Huangcheng and ECADI (Shanghai Modern).

Source: Photo taken in 2014. © Jianfei Zhu.

Figure 33.5   CCTV, Beijing, 2008. Architect: a joint design by OMA, ARUP and ECADI (Shanghai Modern).

Source: Photo taken in 2009. © Jianfei Zhu.

Party, practicing architects and the related professionals, hitherto working in private offices, were organized to work in state-owned design institutes after 1949.[18] These design institutes, as a public office, were attached to administrative organs of various levels, such as municipal, provincial, and "regional" governments (for example, Shanghai Municipal ADI, Jiangsu Province ADI, East China ADI, Southwest China ADI), as well as certain government ministries (such as those attached to Ministry of Construction, Ministry of Railways, Ministry of Mechanical Engineering). In the high Cultural Revolution (1968–71), some of the biggest institutes were criticized and banished but restored soon after; for the most part in the Mao period (1949–76), however, they functioned well as instruments of state and state-led society.

In the post-Mao era (since 1978), under Deng Xiaoping, economic reform started and market economy was introduced from the early 1980s on. During 1979–83, design institutes began to charge fees and introduced performance-based incentive salaries and responsibility systems, which transformed the nature of the organization from "administrative" to "commercial."[19] In the following years (1984–86), the state government issued various directives to regulate an emerging design market: a tendering system, private practice protocol, and a hierarchical classification of design offices in four classes in terms of capacity. In 1992–95, with the market expanding, national registration systems were established to regulate the qualification of architects and the related professions. At the same time, as marketization developed, the reform of the design institute reached a point of bifurcation: under the directive of "keep the large, let go the small," local design institutes now began to be fully privatized and assumed forms of shared ownership with many private holders, whereas the largest design institutes remained state-owned, to become "national" and "central" companies controlled by state government, through SASAC (State-owned Assets Supervision and Administrative Commission). In the late 1990s, these largest design institutes moved in this direction further, turning themselves into large design and engineering firms of international standards while being state-owned. China's joining the World Trade Organization in 2001 facilitated the opening of the Chinese market further. In the 2000s, a pluralistic design market was established in China where different types of design practice competed side by side – state design institutes, local private design institutes, commercial firms, semi-academic offices (ateliers and studios), cross-border joint ventures, international design firms, and many hybrid bodies inside and in between these entities can all be found in contemporary China.

In Mao China, belonging to the central government, the design institutes received central funding and did not charge a design fee in principle. With a large staff (at 1000 often), a design institute tended to be comprehensive in its technical service. There were some specializations among them. In general, however, they covered a broad range of work (design, planning, research, conservation, among other tasks) and, in the case of design, a variety of types, including civil, industrial, and infrastructural. Against this background, the reform of the design institute in the post-Mao framework of the past three decades is significant. In hindsight, three main changes have occurred: 1) the charge of fees and the instituting of a performance-based incentive systems, shifting "administrative" offices into "commercial-industrial" firms; 2) a bifurcation of the small and the large – small local offices became private while the largest remained state-owned; 3) a national governance of the market with measures including tendering systems, a classification of design practices, and a licensing regime to examine and register qualified architects and other professions. All these shares one central theme: *the introduction of the market*. And the most striking phenomenon in terms of the result of this market reform is not a retreat but an *advancement* of state authority – a spreading control over the market and a growth of the state-owned design institutes in capacity and magnitude.

Working with "Creative Individuals"

Since the late 1990s, there have been a growing number of "creative" or "star" architects from abroad designing landmark buildings in China. All of these works are the product of a joint effort between these architects and a local design institute, often a large state-owned entity. Playing the role of an unsung hero, they provide local knowledge and practical solutions, so that the master's design can be approved, documented, constructed, and completed. For example, the new headquarters of China Central Television (CCTV), designed by OMA and Arup, was a joint project with ECADI, who provided practical expertise so that it can be built at all, in China, with local methods, materials, and labor force (Figure 33.5). For the National Olympic Stadium (the Bird's Nest), Herzog and de Meuron worked with CAG for a comprehensive pragmatic assistance, so that it could be constructed. For the Grand National Theatre (Fig 33.3) and Terminal 3 of Capital Airport, as designed by Paul Andreu and Norman Foster respectively, the local collaborator is BIAD. For the "creative" architects within China, the pattern remains. Whether it is Yung Ho Chang (who has assumed many roles in China and the United States) or Wang Shu (who won the Pritzker Architecture Prize in 2012), there is always a design institute working with them to materialize their projects with pragmatic skills provided. A preliminary survey discovers a persistent pairing of creative architects with a local technical support, a design institute: Arata Isozaki – BIAD; Kengo Kuma – Modern Group (SIADR); Steven Holl – Shenzhen General ADI; Yung Ho Chang – Baiyun ADI, IADR (of China Academy of Science); Wang Shu – Suzhou Construction, Hangzhou ADRI, DI of Landscape Architecture (China Academy of Art); Liu Jiakun – Chengdu ADI; Zhang Lei – ADI in Yangzhou and at Nanjing University and Hunan University; Ma Qingyun (MADA spam) – ADI in Shanghai (Zhongjian) and at Shenzhen University, among others.

The design institutes cultivate their own talents as well. One of the most tangible ways of achieving this is the establishment of semi-autonomous ateliers or "workshops," often known as a "studio" titled under the name of a leading architect, such as "Cui Kai Studio." The purpose is manifold, according to rationalizations from one of the institutes: to promote the branding and reputation of the institute, to improve the quality of design proposals, to promote the value of creative individuals, to assist and guide early-career staff, and to help develop overall skills with a heightened academic environment in the institute.[20] So far, the most well-known studios are found in Beijing. In CAG, Cui Kai Studio, Li Xinggang Studio, and Chen Yifeng Studio are the most influential. In BIAD, Ma Guoxin Office, UFo (unforbidden office, led by Shao Weiping), Hu Yue Studio, and Wang Ge Studio are among the most noted.

It is obvious that the design institute supports creative efforts in architecture both without and within. It supports those edgy or creative architects in materializing formally innovative works. It also develops its own creative edge, for formally (sometimes culturally and socially) interesting works, to improve the institute as more than a mere practical and technical force. However, on the whole, judging from the internal composition of the institutes and their positions in the design market, it must be acknowledged that the Chinese design institutes remain a practical, technical, and state force: a competent and comprehensive design agent of the state serving society and the nation as a whole.

Synthesis, Not Opposition

Given that the design institutes are supporting and cultivating formal creativity, and yet remain in their basic character a technical, pragmatic, and state agent in design service, the design institutes, such as CAG, BIAD, and the Modern Group, are now attaining a duality and a synthesis of apparently opposing types of ideas and operations: pragmatism and creativity, technology and form, state institution and market practice, comprehensive character and focused specialization, collectivist ethos and a flair of individualism. To be accurate, there are three main types of syntheses in the workings of the institute: 1) technical pragmatism with formal creativity in design approach, 2) state governance with market practice in politico-economic operation, and 3) collective spirit with a degree of liberal individualism in the mode of practice.

The reason the institutes are now becoming synthetic or accommodative of different types of operations is, arguably, its state-owned background in Mao's socialist system that today aims to be market-oriented as well, without abandoning its state nature. The basic or fundamental duality synthesized here is that of state and market and, with this, comes the other dualities, such as collectivism and individualism, as well as pragmatic functionalism and formal creative innovation. In a broader perspective, the design institute in fact is a form of SOE or state-owned enterprises formed in the reform era, which are the leading sector in China's economy today. The institutes, and the SOEs in general, reflect a synthetic character of China today as a whole, a state-led market economy, described in China as "socialist market economy" and in the west, perhaps incorrectly, as "state capitalism."

State leadership of design market and especially of design institute can also be read as the continuation of a long tradition formed, at the latest, in the Song dynasty (906–1279), where state authority supervised design and construction of major projects nation-wide in a *gongguan* system. It produced, among others, a state guide on building construction, *Yingzao Fashi* (1103), one of the oldest in the world. The state-owned design institute and a broader state leadership over construction, land use, and urban growth reflect a generic Chinese or Confucian tradition where the state assumes a moral and comprehensive leadership over many spheres of human society, including culture, economy, and technology. In this ethical-political tradition, the state is considered a moral agent first and foremost, in a large ecological whole that involves persons, families, state-society, a world of nations, and the all-encompassing nature.

There are arguments put forward today on a China-led political economy of a global scale (or one centered on China and East Asia). One of these is Giovanni Arighi's *Adam Smith in Beijing* (2007).[21] It argues that China's (and East Asia's) pre-modern economy, and what China is arriving at now, is a state-led market economy, a path Adam Smith actually argued for – one that privileges governance over market, seeing market as a tool of governance, not the other way around (a situation that defines "capitalism" according to the author). Characteristic to this path is a labor-intensive, resource-saving, and energy-saving model that requires human relational ethics and strong governance, whereas the capitalist path developed in Europe is labor-saving, energy-consuming, and technology-intensive, which has generated modern capitalism with high per capita income and consumption. Combining the two models, but with the western moving towards the eastern path, China, and East Asia as a whole, is more likely to lead the development of the world, with a population much larger than what the European model was catering for. Considering the scarcity of land and resource, and the size of world populations, the state-led market economy, rather than intensive capitalism, is more likely a path of modernization for the world. The Chinese design institute, in our current study, may serve as a case for the larger argument, a case in which synthesis, collaboration, and a relational-collective ethics, rather than opposition and autonomy, are some of the primary modes of thinking.

Theorization: Towards a Different Ethics

The design institute manifests the tradition of a comprehensive state leadership of society, economy, and technology. It leads to a major issue we need to ponder, namely the ethical foundation of state government and how it was formed in China vis-à-vis Europe. While state government is considered a problem to be opposed and limited in one tradition, it is considered as a moral agent in the other, in an ecological totality from persons to nature. If a comprehensive, synthetic, and relational ethics is considered rational, then the oppositional, analytical, and "critical" logic, and the critical oppositions it produces, may be reviewed in a new light, perhaps to be not abandoned altogether but rather reemployed in a new perspective.

A study of the design institute should encourage us to imagine a new ethics of design in which collaboration, networking, and hybrid synthesis are the key characteristics – a new perspective that sees no "enemy." This new ethics should challenge ideas of autonomy, opposition, resistance, and dualist binary, at a basic or fundamental level.

This study should also encourage us to revise the mode of thinking and writing on modern architecture, of the world or a region. So far, a history of modern architecture has been written with a focus on the individual, rather than a collective and a relational dynamic conditioning any creative design. And if the Chinese case is to be accommodated, then the writing of modern architecture may have to be revised in basic conception.

China and East Asia have been combining western and indigenous traditions for about a century by now. Combining the two, but leaning to the native tradition as a basic outlook more recently when "westernization" has reached a point, China and the region are likely to assert a new ethics, while still absorbing synthetically western and outside influences. While state governance, relational ethics, ecological culture, labor-intensive practice, and collective wealth rather than high per capita consumption, are likely to be its main aspects, a western critical outlook, with a healthy assumption of an "outside" and a distance, to counter a negative tendency of relational ethics (sliding into corruption) should also be its important component. Although this sounds contradictory, or difficult to implement, a synthetic and difficult combination is possible, as evidenced in history, especially the history of modern Asia where westernization has been a persistent practice. This new ethics, which includes moral statehood, relational ethics, and externalized criticality, may not be easy, but is likely to be part of a new horizon of the twenty-first century.

Notes

1 This chapter is developed from my lecture notes of recent years, an exhibition staged in Shanghai, and a paper published in Chinese: Zhu Jianfei, "The Chinese DI; a Manifesto," exhibition installation, West Bund Biennale of Architecture, Shanghai, 2013; and Zhu Jianfei, "Shejiyuan: Yizhong Sheji Shijian Xingshi de Duter Yiyi" (Design institutes in China: The political philosophy of a special form of design practice), *H+A Architecture*, no 1 (2015): 134–137.

2 For studies on professional practice, see the four papers by Dana Cuff, Paolo Tombesi, Christopher Hight, and David Salomon, in "Section 5, Design/Production/Practice," *The Sage Handbook of Architectural Theory*, eds C. Greig Crysler, Stephen Cairns and Hilde Heynen (London: SAGE, 2012), 383–443.

3 Kenneth Frampton, "Towards a Critical Regionalism: Six Points for an Architecture of Resistance," in *The Anti-Aesthetic: Essays on Postmodern Culture*, ed. Hal Foster (Seattle: Bay Press, 1983), 16–30.

4 George Baird, "'Criticality' and its Discontents," *Harvard Design Magazine*, no. 21 (2004), www.gsd. harvard.edu/hdm. Accessed 5 November 2004; Jianfei Zhu, "Criticality in between China and the West," *The Journal of Architecture* 10, no. 5 (November 2005): 479–498; Jane Rendell, Jonathan Hill, Murray Fraser and Mark Dorrian, eds. *Critical Architecture* (London: Routledge, 2007).

5 Peter Eisenman, "Critical Architecture in a Geopolitical World," in *Architecture beyond Architecture*, eds Cynthia C. Davidson & Ismail Serageldin (London: Academy Editions, 1995), 78–81. See also K. Michael Hays, "Critical Architecture: Between Culture and Form," *Perspecta 21, The Yale Architectural Journal* (1984): 15–29.

6 Michael Speaks, "Design Intelligence: Part 1: Introduction," *A+U* 12, no. 387 (2002): 10–18. See also Robert Somol and Sarah Whiting, "Notes around the Doppler Effect and Other Moods of Modernism," *Perspecta 33: Mining Autonomy* (2002): 72–77.

7 Hilde Heynen, "A Critical Position for Architecture," in *Critical Architecture*, eds Jane Rendell, Jonathan Hill, Murray Fraser and Mark Dorrian (London: Routledge, 2007), 48–56.

8 Stephen Eric Bronner, *Of Critical Theory and Its Theorists* (London: Routledge, 2002), 11–38. See also Jianfei Zhu, "Opening the Concept of Critical Architecture," in *Non West Modernist Past: On Architecture and Modernities*, eds William S. W. Lim and Jiat-Hwee Chang (Singapore: World Scientific Publishing, 2012), 105–116.

9 Bertrand Russell, *A History of Western Philosophy* (London: Unwin Paperbacks, 1984), 601–610.

10 Jürgen Habermas, "Further Reflections on the Public Sphere," in *Habermas and the Public Sphere*, ed. Craig Calhoun (Cambridge, MA.: MIT Press, 1992), 421–461.

11 Zhu, "Opening," 107–110, 113–114; see also Jianfei Zhu, *Architecture of Modern China: A Historical Critique* (London: Routledge 2009).

12 Jianfei Zhu, "Ten Thousand Things: Notes on a Construct of Largeness, Multiplicity, and Moral Statehood," in *Common Frameworks*, ed. Christopher C. M. Lee (Cambridge, MA: GSD, 2013), 27–41; Jianfei Zhu, "Political and Epistemological Scales in Chinese Urbanism," *Harvard Design Magazine* 37 (2014): 74–79.

13 Russell, *Philosophy*, 601–610.

14 Habermas, "Further Reflections," 421–461.

15 www.cadreg.com. Accessed 10 May 2013.

16 www.biad.com.cn and www.biad-ufo.cn. Accessed 18 September 2013; Editorial Committee, ed., *BIAD: Beijing Institute of Architecture Design and Research: A Collection of Works 1949–2009* (Tianjin: Tianjin University Press, 2009).

17 www.xd-ad.com.cn/cn/cn.html. Accessed 19 September 2013; see also: Zhang Hua, "Shanghai Xiandai Jianzhu Sheji Jituan (Shanghai Modern Group for Architecture Design)," in *Jianzhu Zhongguo Liushi Nian (1949–2009): Jigou Juan* (Constructing China for sixty years 1949–2009: Volume on Institutionalization), ed. Editorial Committee (Tianjin: Tianjin University Press, 2009), 72–78; Editorial Committee, ed., *Liushi Nian (1952–2012) Jinian Ce: Shanghai Xiandai Jianzhu Sheji Jituan Chengli 60 Zhounian Jinian* (Commemorating the Sixty Years 1952–2012: For the 60th anniversary of the founding of Shanghai Modern Group), (Beijing: Beijing Chengshi Chubanshe, 2012); Editorial Committee, ed., *Liushi Nian (1952–2012) Sheji Zuoping Ji: Shanghai Xiandai Jianzhu Sheji Jituan Chengli 60 Zhounian* (Works of the Sixty Years 1952–2012: For the 60th anniversary of the founding of Shanghai Modern Group) (Beijing: Beijing Chengshi Chubanshe, 2012).

18 Editorial Committee, ed., *Jianzhu Zhonguo*. See also Xue Qiuli, *Zhongguo Jianzhu Shijian: Building Practice in China* (Beijing: China Architecture & Building Press, 2009). I would like to thank Xue Qiuli for generously sharing his data for my exhibition (The Chinese DI, 2013).

19 Information on the structure and the reform of the design institutes was obtained from my field trips in 2011 to CAG (China Architecture Design and Research Group), TADI (Tianjin Architectural Design Institute), BIAD (Beijing Institute of Architectural Design), Shanghai Modern Group, Nanjing University Architectural Design Institute, SADI (Shenzhen General Institute of Architectural Design and Research), CADI (Chongqing Architectural Design Institute), SPADI (Sichuan Province Architectural Design and Research Institute), CSWADI (China Southwest Architectural Design and Research Institute); and my interviews with Ouyang Dong (June 28), Li Keqiang (June 28), Wen Bing (June 30), Liu Jun (July 1), Zhang Zheng (July 2), Li Xinggang (July 2), Zhu Xiaodi (July 2), Jin Weijun (July 2), Liu Enfang (July 4), Li Ding (July 4), Zhang Lei (July 6), Meng Jianming (Sept 11), Li Bingqi (Sept 29), Li Chun (Sept 30), and Li Xiongwei (Oct 1), and above all Cui Kai over many years. I thank them all for sharing insights, information, and experience.

20 Based on emails and conversations with Cui Kai, Vice Director and Chief Architect of CAG in 2012–14.

21 Giovanni Arrighi, *Adam Smith in Beijing: Lineages of the Twenty-First Century* (London: Verso, 2007), 13–96.

Bibliography

Arrighi, Giovanni. *Adam Smith in Beijing: Lineages of the Twenty-First* Century. London: Verso, 2007.

Baird, George. "'Criticality' and its Discontents." *Harvard Design Magazine*, no. 21 (2004), www.gsd.harvard.edu/hdm. Accessed 5 November 2004.

www.biad.com.cn. Accessed 28 December 2021.

Bronner, Stephen Eric. *Of Critical Theory and Its Theorists*. London: Routledge, 2002.

www.cadg.com.cn. Accessed 28 December 2021.

Calhoun, Craig, ed. *Habermas and the Public Sphere*. Cambridge, MA: MIT Press, 1992.

Crysler, C. Greig, Stephen Cairns and Hilde Heynen, eds. *The Sage Handbook of Architectural Theory*. London: Sage, 2012.

Editorial Committee, ed. *BIAD: Beijing Institute of Architecture Design and Research: A Collection of Works 1949–2009*. Tianjin: Tianjin University Press, 2009.

———, ed. *Jianzhu Zhongguo Liushi Nian (1949–2009): Jigou Juan* (Constructing China for Sixty Years 1949–2009: Volume on Institutionalization). Tianjin: Tianjin University Press, 2009).

———, ed. *Liushi Nian (1952–2012) Jinian Ce: Shanghai Xiandai Jianzhu Sheji Jituan Chengli 60 Zhounian Jinian* (Commemorating the Sixty Years 1952–2012: For the 60th Anniversary of the Founding of Shanghai Modern Group). Beijing: Beijing Chengshi Chubanshe, 2012.

———, ed. *Liushi Nian (1952–2012) Sheji Zuoping Ji: Shanghai Xiandai Jianzhu Sheji Jituan Chengli 60 Zhounian* (Works of the Sixty Years 1952–2012: For the 60th Anniversary of the Founding of Shanghai Modern Group). Beijing: Beijing Chengshi Chubanshe, 2012.

Eisenman, Peter. "Critical Architecture in a Geopolitical World." In *Architecture Beyond Architecture*, edited by Cynthia C. Davidson and Ismail Serageldin, 78–81. London: Academy Editions, 1995.

Foster, Hal. *The Anti-Aesthetic: Essays on Postmodern Culture*. Seattle: Bay Press, 1983.

Frampton, Kenneth. "Towards a Critical Regionalism: Six Points for an Architecture of Resistance." In *The Anti-Aesthetic: Essays on Postmodern Culture*, edited by Hal Foster, 16–30. Seattle: Bay Press, 1983.

Habermas, Jürgen. "Further Reflections on the Public Sphere." In *Habermas and the Public Sphere*, edited by Craig Calhoun, 421–61. Cambridge, MA: MIT Press, 1992.

Hays, K. Michael. "Critical Architecture: Between Culture and Form." *Perspecta 21, the Yale Architectural Journal* (1984): 15–29.

Heynen, Hilde. "A Critical Position for Architecture." In *Critical Architecture*, edited by Jane Rendell, Jonathan Hill, Murray Fraser and Mark Dorrian, 48–56. London: Routledge, 2007.

Lee, Christopher C.M., ed. *Common Frameworks*. Cambridge, MA: GSD, 2013.

Lim, William S.W. and Jiat-Hwee Chang, eds. *Non West Modernist Past: On Architecture and Modernities*. Singapore: World Scientific Publishing, 2012.

Rendell, Jane, Jonathan Hill, Murray Fraser and Mark Dorrian, eds. *Critical Architecture*. London: Routledge, 2007.

Russell, Bertrand. *A History of Western Philosophy*. London: Unwin Paperbacks, 1984.

Somol, Robert and Sarah Whiting. "Notes Around the Doppler Effect and Other Moods of Modernism." *Perspecta 33: Mining Autonomy* (2002): 72–77.

Speaks, Michael. "Design Intelligence: Part 1: Introduction." *A+U* 12, no. 387 (2002): 10–18.

www.xd-ad.com.cn/zh/. Accessed 28 December 2021.

Xue Qiuli. *Zhongguo Jianzhu Shijian: Building Practice in China*. Beijing: China Architecture & Building Press, 2009.

Zhang Hua. "Shanghai Xiandai Jianzhu Sheji Jituan (Shanghai Modern Group for Architecture Design)." In *Jianzhu Zhongguo Liushi Nian (1949–2009): Jigou Juan* (Constructing China for Sixty Years 1949–2009: Volume on Institutionalization), edited by Editorial Committee, 72–78. Tianjin: Tianjin University Press, 2009.

Zhu, Jianfei. "Criticality in Between China and the West." *The Journal of* Architecture 10, no. 5 (November 2005): 479–498.

———. *Architecture of Modern China: A Historical Critique*. London: Routledge 2009.

———. "Opening the Concept of Critical Architecture." In *Non West Modernist Past: On Architecture and Modernities*, edited by William S.W. Lim and Jiat-Hwee Chang, 105–116. Singapore: World Scientific Publishing, 2012.

———. *The Chinese DI; a Manifesto*. Exhibition Installation. Shanghai: West Bund Biennale of Architecture, 2013.

———. "Ten Thousand Things: Notes on a Construct of Largeness, Multiplicity, and Moral Statehood." In *Common Frameworks*, edited by Christopher C.M. Lee, 27–41. Cambridge, MA: GSD, 2013.

———. "Political and Epistemological Scales in Chinese Urbanism." *Harvard Design Magazine* 37 (2014): 74–79.

———. "Shejiyuan: Yizhong Sheji Shijian Xingshi de Duter Yiyi (Design Institutes in China: The Political Philosophy of a Special Form of Design Practice)." *H+A Architecture*, no. 1 (2015): 134–137.

Glossary

Baiyun (design institute)	白云（设计院）
Beijing	北京
Cai Zhenyu	蔡镇钰
Chen Deng'ao	陈登鳌
Chen Yifeng	陈一峰
Cui Kai	崔恺
Dai Nianci	戴念慈
Deng Xiaoping	邓小平
Fang Jianquan	方鉴泉
Gong Deshun	龚德顺
gongguan	工官（制度）
Hangzhou	杭州
Hu Yue	胡越
Hua Lanhong	华揽洪
Hunan	湖南
Jiangsu	江苏
Jin Weijun	金卫钧
Li Chengde	李承德
Li Xinggang	李兴钢
Lin Leyi	林乐义
Liu Jiakun	刘家琨
Ma Guoxin	马国馨
Ma Qingyun	马清运
Mao (era)	毛泽东（时代）
Nanjing	南京
Pudong	浦东
Shanghai	上海
Shao Weiping	邵韦平
Shenzhen	深圳
Suzhou	苏州
Tiananmen (square)	天安门（广场）
Wang Ge	王戈
Wang Huabin	王华彬
Wang Shu	王澍
Wang Xiao'an	汪孝安
Wu Jingxiang	吴景祥
Xian Dai	现代（集团）
Yingzao Fashi	营造法式
Yung Ho Chang (Zhang Yonghe)	张永和

Zhang Bo	张镈
Zhang Kaiji	张开济
Zhang Lei	张雷
Zhao Dongri	赵冬日
Zhao Shen	赵深
Zhengda (center)	正大（中心）
Zhongjian (group)	中建（集团）
Zhu Jialu	朱嘉禄
Zhu Xiaodi	朱小地

CBDs: Global Spectacles

34

OBJECTS IN TERRITORIES ALONG AVENUES

Spatial Planning in Beijing and Shanghai

Peter G. Rowe and Har Ye Kan

Axiality and symmetry are fundamental principles of Chinese architecture and spatial design that have endured since the imperial times. While the importance of four-sided enclosures or attaining spatial magnitude through horizontal aggregation has diminished as features in modern urban planning, axes have continued to be defining elements in the organization and creation of distinct urban-architectural territories in Chinese cities today. As China shapes its own standing on the international stage, these axes and their accompanying circumscribed spheres of action for architectural production engage both global movements and local specificities. Unlike the central north–south axis that was the overarching feature in traditional city planning, the prominent axes and territories that were codified since the People's Republic of China traverse the cities largely in an east–west manner, providing a counterpoint to the conventional north–south spines. Much as the associated spatial transformations have been considerable, these operations in fact adhere to underlying situational logics of the past. Two notable cases are Chang'an Avenue in Beijing and the Yan'an Elevated Road-Century Avenue in Shanghai, both of which are intrinsically bound to the making of the respective metropolises as global cities in the twenty-first century.

Axes served as the basis of spatial organization in imperial Chinese city planning. Deployed to attain balanced orders in the arrangement of major buildings, gates, and the subdivision of cities into smaller districts, the central north–south axes of traditional Chinese cities are inherently conceptual. This is contrary to the western notion of axes as conduits facilitating visual connection and movement through space as experiential sequence, as in the case of Rome, where Pope Sixtus V developed a plan in which circulation routes would relate key architectural monuments located at the ends of the axes to each other. Moreover, the imaginary north–south line along which a series of landmarks and territories were composed in the Chinese context is highly symbolic, representing the social order emanating out beyond both ends of the axes and on either side, and the harmonious coexistence of man and nature. The east–west axes in modern Chinese urban planning, however, depart from the time-honored notions associated with the static, inaccessible central north–south axes. Instead, these east–west axes are dynamic, entailing movement and progression along major rights-of-way while stringing together urban-architectural territories of civic importance. To be sure, this concept of "articulation of experience along an axis of movement through space" that is akin to armatures in the western context[1] is not entirely foreign to China, given the Beaux-Arts influenced plans of broad boulevards and

DOI: 10.4324/9781315851112-51

grand vistas proposed during the Republican period.[2] What is novel, though, is the determination of an additional primary east–west axis in each city, establishing a different socio-spatial order that re-interprets tradition while accommodating the re-making of the city for the future.

Beijing's East–West Axis: Chang'an Avenue

In 2004, the municipality of Beijing approved the 2004–2020 Master Plan for the city, which proposed a spatial structure comprising "Two Axes – Two Corridors – Multiple Centers," where the "two axes" refer to the north–south central axis that had been a legacy of imperial Beijing, and an east–west axis constituted by Chang'an Avenue (Figure 34.1). The plan marked the first time the east–west axis was officially codified and referred to alongside the predominant north–south axis. The existence of this axis, however, dates further back in time as an artifact of the communist regime. Spanning a total length of more than 20 kilometers, Beijing's east–west axis emanates from Chang'an Avenue, flanked by the Forbidden City and Tiananmen Square, where it meets the historic north–south axis. From there, it extends out from East and West Chang'an Avenues to Jianguomen Outer Street and Fuxingmen Outer Street, before terminating at the East and West Fifth Ring Roads. At the core of this east–west axis is an administrative district anchored by Tiananmen Square, with important office buildings located immediately on the southern edge of Chang'an Avenue. This configuration was proposed by the Soviet expert Barannikov in his plan for Beijing in the early 1950s, and further elaborated by Zhu Zhaoxue and Zhao Dongri. According to Zhu and Zhao, "work should be done to develop one more axis for the city which . . . will be as remarkable as the existing north–south axis."[3] It must be said that the east–west axis in the Zhu–Zhao scheme was not Chang'an Avenue, but the ladder block of administrative buildings to the south, resulting in a conceptual axis much akin to the north–south alignment of imperial offices and landmarks.

By the end of the Cultural Revolution, the Zhu–Zhao plan had barely materialized. In fact, these developments along Chang'an Avenue were closer to a scheme proposed by Chen Gan in 1959, who had argued for the thoroughfare to be the east–west axis of the city, symbolizing innovation in contrast to tradition as embodied by the north–south axis.[4] Monumental additions constructed during the Tenth Anniversary of the People's Republic included the People's Heroes Monument, the People's Great Hall, the Revolutionary History Museum, and the Minzu Cultural Palace. Towards the end of the Cultural Revolution hiatus, only two other well-known buildings were completed along Chang'an Avenue: the Beijing Long-Distance Telephone Exchange and the east tower of the Beijing Hotel. Together, these landmarks effectively shifted Zhu–Zhao's conceptual east–west axis from the ladder block to Chang'an Avenue itself, as was advocated for by Chen Gan, thereby elevating the significance of this major right-of-way. A key report entitled "Information on the Existing Conditions of Chang'an Avenue," published in June 1978, lent further impetus to the avenue, identifying it as an "arterial road of paramount significance in the capital."[5] This formed the basis for a plan of Chang'an Avenue where the varying road widths of the avenue, which then ranged from 35 to 47 meters, were to be widened to a boulevard of uniform width of 120 meters.[6] Although Chang'an Avenue never quite attained the intended width, it was later transformed into a uniform ten-lane route for motor vehicles traveling in both directions, flanked by generous bicycle lanes and setbacks on either side, making it one of the world's widest urban thoroughfares.

The turning point for Chang'an Avenue came about in the 1990s when the capital sought to redefine its role through the 1991–2010 Master Plan. In this document, the city was to become an "international city operating in all respects with additional functionality and structure,"

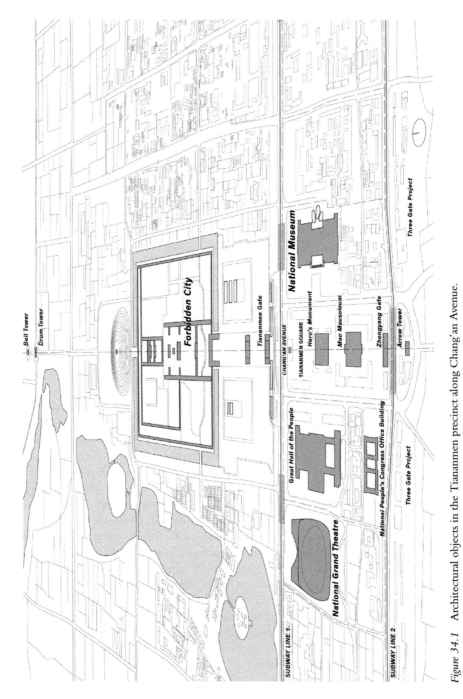

Figure 34.1 Architectural objects in the Tiananmen precinct along Chang'an Avenue.

Source: Drawn by Michael Sypkens, a graduate of the Harvard Graduate School of Design.

including encouragement of a further shift to the tertiary sector.[7] More specifically, with regard to Chang'an Avenue, the plan called for the

> continued completion of the redevelopment of Tiananmen Square and along both sides of East and West Chang'an Avenue, with a focus on locating major state administrative organizations and large-scale cultural amenities, as well as appropriate amount of commercial services amenities along the street, thereby forming a majestic, beautiful and modern central plaza and east–west axis.[8]

A central business district (CBD) with financial, commercial, cultural, and office functions was to be developed between Jianguomen at the Second Ring Road and the Third Ring Road. Counterbalancing this new CBD on the west was the designation of Financial Street along the Second Ring Road, and the Wukesong Olympic Complex further afield adjacent to the Fourth Ring Road. Closer to the center, older commercial areas such as Wangfujing and Xidan bordering the east and west of the Forbidden City received facelifts in conjunction with the development of these new urban-architectural precincts. The Chang'an armature here thus embodied the modern re-interpretation of the traditional Chinese north–south axis. It is not strictly perspectival in its manner of appreciation as in the Western notion of an axis. Rather, it entails an unfolding of spatial events or episodes that are more dispersed, engendering a sense of an almost infinite extension and open-endedness that reflect the underlying temporal framework of continual growth and progress aspired for the city. At the same time, the past continues to assert itself, with inner areas like Tiananmen Square, Wangfujing, and Xidan maintaining their overall figural integrity. This integrity is not limited to these historic areas alone but also shapes the compositional quality of emergent architectural territories, including the city's center, the CBD, and Financial Street.

Two outstanding, if not provocative, architectural projects proclaiming Beijing's contemporary place in the world can be found in two of these territories. The first, located within the vicinity of Tiananmen Square adjacent to the Great Hall of the People on Chang'an Avenue, is the National Grand Theater, by Paul Andreu and ADP (Figure 34.1). The China Central Television (CCTV) Headquarters complex, by Rem Koolhaas and Ole Scheeren of the Office of Metropolitan architecture (OMA) constitutes the second project, located in the city's new CBD (Figure 34.2). Apart from their similar expressive forms embodying a hyper-modernism that has become synonymous with "New China" in the twenty-first century, both projects are also comparable in their responses to the situational logics and underlying principles of Beijing's persistence of place. Each of these projects, if taken alone, inadvertently comes across more as architectural objects. While they might at first glance seem out of place, this is quickly proven otherwise, as each project fits into and in fact reifies the distinctive nature of the territories for which they were designed. In fact, closer inspection suggests their continuities with the horizontality and monumentality of the city's large block configurations and, more importantly, their correspondence with their respective contexts.

The National Grand Theater of China, also known as the National Center for the Performing Arts, opened in 2007 to much fanfare as well as controversy. Located along West Chang'an Avenue right next to the Great Hall of the People, the 5,500-seat theater assumed the form of a super ellipsoidal shell engineered by Setec. Spanning 212.4 meters in the east–west direction parallel to Chang'an, and 143.8 meters in the north–south direction, this cultural superstructure seemingly floats in a lake created by the shallow-plinth demarcating the 11.8-hectare site boundaries. The complex is accessed by a 60-meter-long transparent passage under the lake from the north, transporting the public through this theatrical gesture to a world of drama

Figure 34.2 CCTV Headquarters complex in the Beijing CBD.

Source: Drawn by Michael Sypkens, a graduate of the Harvard Graduate School of Design.

and imagination beyond. The axiality and symmetry of the composition is continued on the southern segment, landscaped with two passages aligned diagonally with the outside corners of the site. Inside the shell, the east–west axis of the ellipsoid becomes the organizational element, with the larger opera house at the center flanked by the concert hall to the east and the theater to the west. Clad in titanium and a refined tracery of glazing, arching up across the front of the building and illuminating the lobby within, the project features a constant interplay among conditions of transparency, partial transparency, void space, and volumetric modulation, as well as somberness and light.[9] Territorially speaking, this resplendent, futuristic theater is located beyond the conservation domain of the Forbidden City and lies within the ladder block structure of Chang'an Avenue – a precinct that inherently permits and in fact encourages a degree of unconventional approaches to the urban form. This potential to accommodate the avant-garde was certainly the case here, with Andreu's design emerging out of an international competition that saw the client group, comprising officials from the Beijing Municipal Government, the then Ministry of Construction, and the Ministry of Culture, playing a growing role in the eventual architectural expression of the building. Much as the project was variously criticized by influential architects, engineers, and scholars as being "irrational" and "alien in the historic city of Beijing,"[10] it also received affirmations, for "symbolizing the hopes of the time" and being "forward looking into the twenty-first century."[11] The interests of the client group for a hyper-modern outcome, and an unabashed iconicity as evinced from the evolving design schemes,[12] certainly speaks of their conceptions of China's present and her future, and Beijing's emergence as a global city in this millennium.

The second object in a territory along Chang'an is the CCTV complex, located in the CBD precinct and is, more precisely speaking, the first phase of this new urban undertaking (Figure 34.2). While the entire territory will eventually occupy a tract of land some 7 square kilometers, this initial phase is smaller in area at around 4 square kilometers and is generally defined by Chaoyang Road to the north and the Tonghui River to the south, straddling the Third Ring Road. The master plan was prepared by Johnson Fain Partners in 2001, and subsequent urban design and landscape guidelines were drawn up by the Tsinghua University Urban Planning and Design Institute in 2003. Intended to create a "live–work" environment, the plan was composed of office, residential, and retail functions. It sought to transform the original hodgepodge of lower-rise buildings and former "work unit" or *danwei* complexes into a dense assemblage of tall towers, high- and mid-rise infill projects, as well as mixed-used projects of similar rise. Embracing the large block configuration of the CBD, the CCTV project encompasses a considerable site of 10 hectares comprising three buildings, each with its own functional logic. Opened finally in 2012 after a fire destroyed part of the complex, the most conspicuous feature of this ensemble is the vast CCTV Headquarters with its square loop structure. Situated on the southwestern corner of the subdivided urban block, two towers rise to a height of 234 meters from a ground plinth before they are enjoined at the top by an L-shaped cantilevering bridge. Together, these various sections house a combination of administrative, news broadcasting, production, and auxiliary service functions, integrating programs and activities that were dispersed in different parts of the city, allowing for an inherent and much anticipated connectedness and collaborative potential. This sense of unity is expressed in not only the innovative interlocking structure but also the irregular glazed grid of soft grey glass that lends a tone of quiet monumentalism to the overall project.

Conceived of as an "anti-skyscraper," the CCTV Headquarters also seeks to defy the singular image conventionally projected by architectural objects.[13] Instead, it assumes a myriad of facets, appearing, in the words of the architects, "sometimes as big and sometimes as small, and from some angles it is strong and from others weak."[14] Accompanying this 473,000 square meter building is the Television Cultural Center to the north, assuming a more informal disposition with its playful angular form. Here, the architects drew upon the quality of the surrounding urban fabric to recreate an urban microcosm, with most of the public programs, such as a theater, digital cinemas, and recording studios accommodated in the first four floors. Rising above this folded podium is a 100-meter tower for a five-star hotel, complete with ballrooms, restaurants, bars, shops, and recreational amenities, as well a conference and exhibition center. In addition to these components in OMA's winning design are a two-story, ring-shaped service building on the northeastern parcel and a large media park comprising several structures for outdoor broadcasting and entertainment. Knitting the four sub-blocks into a coherent whole is a soft, pixelated landscape design of circulation paths, gardens, and plazas by Inside Outside from Amsterdam, endowing the formerly gated *danwei* site of the Beijing Automobiles and Motorcycles Manufacturing Company with an open, park-like setting. Setting aside the monikers the project has earned with the public, what OMA achieved here is, quite objectively speaking, a well-qualified and inventive approach in terms of the architectural expression and the urban design strategy in tackling the physical rigidities and scale of China's typical superblock configuration. The striking, hyper-modern form echoes the state discourse on "national form" of the times, befitting again not just the nature of CCTV as the media organ of the state, but also heralding the "New China" and, by extension, the "New Beijing."

Shanghai's East–West Axis: Yan'an Elevated Road-Century Avenue

Shanghai's east–west axis transpired at around the same period as the turning point for Chang'an Avenue in Beijing during the country's opening up and the onset of Deng Xiaoping's reforms (Figure 34.3). In 1984, the Scheme of the Urban Master Plan for Shanghai Municipality was submitted to the central authorities and approved by the State Council in 1986. Based on preliminary sketches in the early 1980s by the Shanghai Urban Planning and Design Institute (SUPDI) led by Huang Fuxiang, the Scheme proposed development in the eastward direction of Pudong.[15] In line with the overarching state policy issued during the Third Plenary of the Eleventh Party Committee in 1984, where the country was to shift to a "planned commodity economy" and then to a "socialist market economy" by 1992, Shanghai was identified as a "key-point city" and slated to be the "head of the dragon" for the Yangtze-River Delta Region. Before the 1986 plan was revised in 1995, Zhu Rongji, the mayor of Shanghai from 1987 to 1991, sought technical assistance from the Institut d'Aménagement et d'Urbanisme de la Région Île-de-France (IAURIF), or the Development and Town Planning Institute of the Paris Region, and l'Établissement Public pour l'Aménagement de La Défense (EPAD). This gave rise to the formation of the Group Français d'Appui au Développement de Shanghai-Pudong, or the French Back-up Group for the Development of Shanghai-Pudong. Among the key findings from this Chinese–French joint committee of experts was the development of Shanghai's east–west axis, along and adjacent to the Yan'an roadway in Puxi, and into Pudong through Lujiazui along Century Avenue, already sketched out earlier by Huang Fuxiang and his colleagues at SUPDI.[16]

The east–west armature of Shanghai thus ostensibly emerged as the outcome of major planning and investment movements that converged in the 1980s and 1990s. On the western half of the axis, Yan'an Road was reinforced as the primary right-of-way through Puxi with the construction of the Yan'an Elevated Road in 1995 above the existing route. This 16-kilometer new artery essentially linked Hongqiao International Airport to prominent civic spaces such as Yan'an Expressway Park and the Renmin precinct, subsequently rejoining the East Yan'an Road

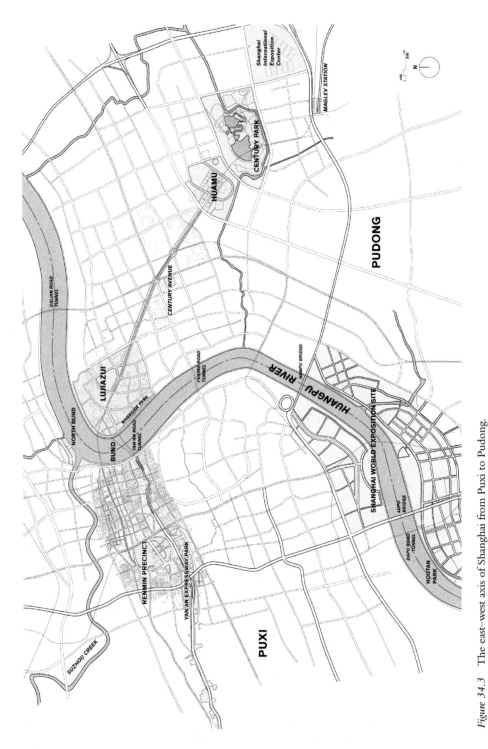

Figure 34.3 The east–west axis of Shanghai from Puxi to Pudong.

Source: Drawn by Michael Sypkens, a graduate of the Harvard Graduate School of Design.

Tunnel to Pudong. The eastern half of the axis continues in Pudong above grade with Lujiazui West Road, which leads up to the new financial center at Lujiazui, continuing eastwards along the Century Avenue boulevard that terminates in the Huamu Administrative precinct, Century Park, and the Shanghai International Exposition Center. Beyond Century Avenue, the armature traverses a series of municipal expressways before culminating in the Pudong International Airport, covering a total distance of some 37 kilometers. By the 2006–2010 Land Use Plan, this axis was graphically apparent with the east–west corridor of commercial and civic functions designated along the Yan'an Elevated Road and Century Avenue, and reinforced by the "Sketch Map of Comprehensive Planning of Shanghai Cultural Facility" that further articulated an east–west connection of major civic territories.[17]

Like Chang'an Avenue, Shanghai's east–west axis is associated with territories of contemporary urban-architectural production that have since become part and parcel of the city's identity, bridging its past with its future. Puxi came into prominence with the establishment of Shanghai as a treaty port in 1842 and, over much of the twentieth century, anchored the city's growth. Back then, Yan'an Road was already a major thoroughfare. Named Edward VII Avenue or Zhongzheng Road during the treaty port era, the road was in fact the Yangjing-bang creek before it was covered over and was of great significance as it demarcated the border between the International Settlement and the French Concession. The 6.4-kilometer road ran almost perpendicular to the Bund, and at the height of Shanghai's golden age in the 1920s and 1930s, it had developed into an east–west axis stringing together various districts of importance. Starting on the east at the Bund was the financial and commercial district. This evolved into a major entertainment district with the race course and a cluster of popular dance halls and theaters. Finally, on the western edge of the road was a mixture of automobile companies and landmarks, including the famous Aili Garden and the Bubbling Well Cemetery.[18] After the communists came into power, the road was renamed Yan'an Road and remained as a major right-of-way, stringing together some renowned civic spaces. The race course just north of Yan'an Road was redeveloped into the city's administrative core, known as Renmin Square, and further to the west, Aili Garden, which fell into disrepair during the War of Resistance against the Japanese, was taken over by the new government and rebuilt as the monumental Sino–Soviet Friendship Mansion in 1955; the Bubbling Well Cemetery close by was similarly redeveloped into Jing'an Park.

If Puxi represented Shanghai's past, Pudong was a vision of the city's future. The definitive Pudong New Area Master Plan of 1992 prescribed the institutional and spatial parameters for this vast undertaking of some 522 square kilometers in area. Prior to the 1992 plan, several international consultations and local planning efforts helped to lay the groundwork, including a partnership entered into by Shanghai city officials and the IAURIF in 1985. This French inclination revealed not only an admiration of Francois Mitterrand's ambitious revitalization of Paris through his so-called *Grand Projets* and the statist form of urban development, but also a sustained acknowledgement of the quality of planning and urban form in the city's historic French concession. The development of Pudong saw the participation of foreign architects, and a major force in this regard was Arte Charpentier, who was commissioned to envision a unifying element that would connect the various parts of the Pudong plan while projecting a strong image of this ascendant metropolis. This gave rise to the design for Century Avenue, a 5-kilometer long boulevard measuring 100 meters in width, modeled after the Champs-Elysées.[19] Extending from Puxi on the west, Century Avenue linked the three distinct urban-architectural precincts, providing continuity through its uniform width as well as its landscaping, composed of a sequence of gardens that enhance the urban amenity, inviting pedestrians to stroll, pause, and engage with the unfolding spatial episodes in the same vein as Chang'an Avenue (Figure 34.4).

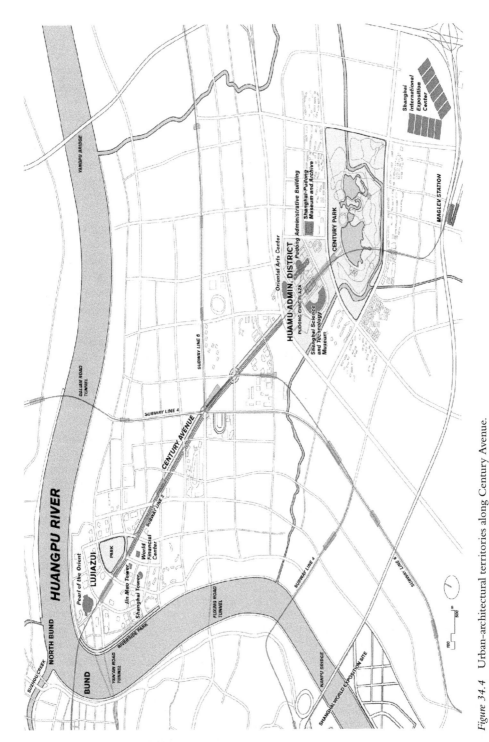

Figure 34.4 Urban-architectural territories along Century Avenue.

Source: Drawn by Michael Sypkens, a graduate of the Harvard Graduate School of Design.

The past and the future of the city were therefore integrated by this axial gesture, and in the words of the framers of the plan, at once "respect[ing] history but build[ing] for the future."[20]

While contemporary projects such as the Hongqiao Intermodal Hub, the Shanghai Grand Theater, the Shanghai Museum, and the 28-hectare Yan'an Expressway Park have served as architectural and landscape highlights for precincts along the western armature of Shanghai's east–west axis, the focus of this article is on several notable pieces along Pudong's Century Avenue, including a trio of skyscrapers in Lujiazui and the Shanghai Oriental Arts Center, again by Paul Andreu and ADP, in collaboration with the East China Architectural Design Institute (ECADI). Plans for Lujiazui's 1.9 square kilometer tract of land to be a constellation of towers and the symbol of the "New Shanghai" were drafted as early as the 1990s. Allusions to this high-rise aspiration were materialized with the 468-meter-tall Oriental Pearl Tower by ECADI, which broke ground in 1991. The following year, a group of international architects and planners were invited to participate in the Chinese–French consultancy and provide urban design ideas for the new financial and commercial district, alongside a team from the SUPDI. The final scheme for this center of "New Shanghai" was derived from the SUPDI proposal, which had a distinctive east–west axis, although it also incorporated aspects of other proposals, like the central green spaces in Dominique Perrault's and Richard Rogers' proposals. More importantly, driven by a concern for image and the creation of a memorable skyline, the final reference design also designated the trio of skyscrapers near the core of Lujiazui of around 400 meters and above in height, with rings of buildings diminishing in height from this central core at 300 meters and then 200 meters.[21]

Across the street from the 421-meter-tall Jin Mao Tower by Skidmore, Owings, and Merrill is the Shanghai World Financial Center by Kohn Pedersen Fox, the second in the trinity of super-tall towers. Soaring to a height of nearly 500 meters, this elegant project houses a mix of offices and retail uses in the lower floors, the 300-suite Park Hyatt Shanghai in the floors above, and a sky arena on the top affording visitors a panoramic view of the city. Unlike the design of Jin Mao, which references the tiered structure of a traditional Chinese pagoda, the World Financial Center is characterized by "heightened simplicity" with its chisel-like monolithic form.[22] From a square base, the 382,000 square meter tower ascends towards the sky, tapering towards the top along two "cosmic arcs" where the building culminates in a trapezoidal "sky portal."[23] Where the Jin Mao was a figural re-interpretation of local building traditions, here the World Financial Center draws upon cultural symbols like the square representing the earth, weaving these into an architectural allegory that in fact stems as much from engineering and efficiency considerations as they do from cultural ones. Politically sensitive references in the design, regardless of whether they were unintentional, were likewise addressed. For instance, the original circular cut-out at the top of the building after the traditional moon gate, which caused considerable public dissatisfaction for its resemblance to the rising sun, a symbol of Japan and a reminder of the Sino–Japanese War of 1937 to 1945, was replaced expediently by the trapezoidal shape. Clad in a diaphanous glass skin, the steel and aluminum structure exudes an exceptional lightness, enlivening the Lujiazui precinct with its distinguished yet unimposing presence.

Rounding out the trinity is the 632-meter-high mixed-use Shanghai Tower by Gensler which was completed in 2015. Situated south of the Jin Mao, the project is the tallest of the trio, symbolizing "the emergence of modern China as a global financial power."[24] Spatially configured like its two counterparts to be a "city within a city," the tower seeks to create a vertical community, stacking programs one above another, beginning from a retail zone and a light-filled garden atrium or "sky lobby" at the base, to several vertical sections of office space, followed by a hotel and boutique office, and capped with observation and cultural facilities.

In contrast to the strict geometry of the Jin Mao and the streamlined form of the World Financial Center, the asymmetrical Shanghai Tower rises from the ground in a dynamic, spiraling manner. Sculpted intentionally to ensure that the building would be able to withstand typhoon-force winds common in Shanghai, the tower also has a transparent second skin that wraps around the building under the curtain wall, creating atriums that double up as public spaces as well as insulation pockets to reduce energy consumption. Other sustainable design strategies include wind turbines on top of the tower to generate power for the building's exterior lighting, and a rainwater collection system incorporated into the tower's spiraling parapet. Taken together, the three projects have certainly responded to the nature of Lujiazui as China's premier financial district, providing a visual anchor in the cacophony of skyscrapers articulating Shanghai's ascension as a global city.

At the eastern terminus of Century Avenue is the Shanghai Oriental Arts Center, one of several noteworthy projects in the Huamu administrative and cultural district. Symbolically centered on the expansive Century Square Plaza flanked by a *parterre* garden landscape, the programmatic scope of this precinct was to accommodate governmental functions, including the Shanghai Pudong People's Government Building, as well as venues for a variety of civic uses like the Science and Technology Museum and the Shanghai-Pudong Museum and Archive. Here, the axial alignment connecting with Century Avenue is sustained through the square plaza around which other prominent buildings are located within a park-like setting. The Oriental Arts Center, situated adjacent to the Pudong People's Government Building, is smaller in scale at 40,000 square meters compared to the National Grand Theater in Beijing, and houses a concert hall, a drama theater, and a modest music performance hall, as well as an exhibition area and a multi-media center. Unifying the performance venues is an upward-curving, continuous glass and steel skin tracing the outline of the building while carving out interior circulation space between the façade and the internal volumes. At dusk, the glistening pearl grey façade gradually regains its transparency, revealing the rich enamel tiled volumes and the playful tubular struts supporting the external frame. Relieved of the weight of history, monumentality, and symbolism evinced in Beijing, this new administrative center of Pudong, like the Lujiazui precinct, is afforded a freedom and contemporaneity in architectural expression that was certainly well tapped by Andreu and his team in the Oriental Arts Center.

Lines of Order, Spheres of Action

Since the late 1980s, Chinese cities have undertaken massive capital investments in promoting urban development. In Beijing and Shanghai, these investments and planning efforts have been tied to a conscious re-fashioning of the two leading metropolises into global cities, prefiguring the arrival of "New China." As discussed, a prominent feature of planning in these two cities during this period is the formal articulation and codification of axes, and in particular, the east–west axis. In both cases, the contemporary east–west axes were grounded in situational logics of the place, whether it was their importance as thoroughfares through major urban districts in the past or their modern invention and extension by planners in response to existing practices and future developments. More importantly, the east–west axes of Chang'an Avenue and Yan'an Elevated Road-Century Avenue were deployed purposefully for the establishment of a new socio-spatial order, resulting in the creation of associated territories and spheres of urban-architectural action that effectively re-activated the two cities for the roles they were to assume in the country's ascension. Even in the recent Master Plan updates, the east-west axes continue to be emphasized as a key part of the urban framework to support new spheres of urban-architectural action.

The 2016–2035 Beijing Municipality Master Plan, for instance, called for the east-west axis to extend out to the 5th Ring Road, terminating around the Shougang-Yongding River-Xishan Mountain Range to the west and near the Grand Canal-Chaobai River Systems to the east. Similarly, the 2017–2035 Shanghai Municipality Master Plan reiterated the role of the north-south Huangpu River and the east-west Yan-an Road-Century Ave as the "two development axes guiding the compact, functional clustering around the urban core".[25]

For Beijing and Shanghai, the rich architectural outcomes are befitting of the time and place. Like many other practices and policies in China, though, the definition of axes and indeed, the east–west axis, has been widely adopted as far north as Harbin and south as Shenzhen. Outside of Beijing and Shanghai, the extent to which these urban axes have been thoughtfully adopted to organize the form and programs in their respective cities, however, is open to question. More often than not, the planning and design significance of these axes need to transcend mere diagrammatic lines and arrows and consider how the actual elements of urban design can be woven together to lend coherence to the place without being blinded solely by the desire for image-making and over-building. At the architectural scale, the projects or objects described here responded to and worked within their prescribed territories, bringing across what is prescient in the past and present into the future. Context, clearly, is key. And here, it is about context that takes into account the where and the when, acknowledging the mutability of both as China's cities poise themselves for further growth but also renewal.

Notes

1 Edmund Bacon, *Design of Cities* (London: Penguin Books, 1967), 123.
2 These included the Capital Plan for Nanjing (1928) and the Plan for Greater Shanghai (1929). See Peter Rowe and Seng Kuan, *Architectural Encounters with Essence and Form* (Cambridge, MA: MIT Press, 2002), 24–55.
3 "Opinions of Zhu Zhaoxue and Zhao Dongri on Planning for the Capital's Reconstruction," in *Records of Beijing's Urban Construction Since the Founding of New China* (Vol. 1, City Planning), compiled by the Editorial Board of the Editorial Committee for the Book Series on the History of Beijing's Construction, 2nd edition, November 1995, cited by Wang Jun, *Beijing Record: A Physical and Political History of Planning Modern Beijing* (Singapore: World Scientific, 2011), 129.
4 Chen Gan, *Jinghua Daisi Lu – Chen Gan Wenji* (*Records and Reflections on the Chinese Capital: A Collection of Essays by Chen Gan*) (Beijing: Beijingshi Chengshi Guihua Sheji Yanjiuyuan, 1996), 23–33, 72, cited by Yu Shuishan, "Redefining the Axis of Beijing: Revolution and Nostalgia in the Planning of the PRC Capital," *Journal of Urban History* 34 (2008): 597.
5 Editorial Committee, *Chang'an Jie Xianzhuang Ziliao* (*Information on the Existing Conditions of Chang'an Avenue*) (Beijing: 1978), foreword.
6 This proposal was not unprecedented, as Chen Gan had suggested the widening of Chang'an Avenue to 120 meters as early as the 1950s.
7 Beijing Municipal Government, *Beijing Municipality Master Plan 1991 to 2010* (1996).
8 Beijing Municipal Government, *Beijing Municipality Master Plan 1991 to 2010* (1996).
9 Paul Andreu, "Grand National Theater, Beijing," *AV Monografías*, 109–110 (2004): 34–39; Paul Andreu, "National Grand Theatre," *A+U*, 399 (2003): 54–59.
10 Charlie Xue, *Building a Revolution: Chinese Architecture Since 1980* (Hong Kong: Hong Kong University Press), 41.
11 Yu Jun, "Wo Lai Wei Andelu Bianjian Yu Peng Peigen Xiansheng Shangque (Defense for Andreu and Discussion with Mr Peng Pei-gen)," *Jianzhu Xuebao (Architectural Journal)*, 3 (2001): 31–33.
12 Clearly shown by proposals at various stages of the competition. See Editorial Committee, *Zhongguo Guojia Dajuyuan Jianzhu Sheji Guoji jingsai Fang'an Ji* (*A Collection of Design Schemes for the International Architectural Competition of the National Grand Theater P. R. China*) (Beijing: China Architecture & Building Press, 2000).
13 Rem Koolhaas, Lecture on Monumentality (Cambridge, 2003), Harvard University Graduate School of Design.

14 Paul Goldberger, "Forbidden Cities," *New Yorker*, 30 June 2008, www.newyorker.com/arts/critics/skyline/2008/06/30/080630crsk_skyline_goldberger. Accessed 13 March 2014.

15 Interview with Huang Fuxiang, 8 January 1994.

16 Interview with Huang Fuxiang, 8 January 1994.

17 Shanghaishi Chengshi Guihua Guanliju, *Shanghai Chengshi Guihua* (*Shanghai Urban Planning*) (Shanghai: Shanghai Urban Planning and Administration Bureau, 2006).

18 Cheng Zai and Wu Jianxi, *Lao Shanghai Baiye Zhinan: Daolu Jigou Changshang Zhuzhai Fenbutu* (*Commercial Directory of Old Shanghai: Maps Showing the Distribution of Roadways, Institutions, Factories, and Residences*) (Shanghai: Shanghai Shehui Kexue Chubanshe, 2008).

19 Pierre Clement, "Shanghai: Squares and Public Spaces" in *Shanghai: Architecture & Urbanism for Modern China,* ed. Seng Kuan and Peter G. Rowe (Prestel: Munich, 2004), 148–154.

20 Kerrie L. MacPherson, "The Shanghai Model in Historical Perspective," in *Shanghai: Transformation and Modernization Under China's Open Policy*, eds. Y. M. Yeung and Y. W. Sung (Hong Kong: The Chinese University Press), 517–518.

21 Seng Kuan, "Image of the Metropolis" in *Shanghai: Architecture & Urbanism for Modern China,* ed. Seng Kuan and Peter G. Rowe (Prestel: Munich, 2004), 90.

22 William Pedersen, "Strategie e pianificazionè," *l'Arca*, 109 (1996): 10.

23 KPF, "Shanghai World Financial Center," *KPF*, www.kpf.com/projects/shanghai-world-financial-center. Accessed 29 December 2021.

24 Gensler, *Shanghai Rising: A Symbol of China's Ascension*, http://du.gensler.com/vol5/shanghai-tower/#/shanghai-rising. Accessed 13 March 2014.

25 Beijing Municipal Commission of Planning and Natural Resources, "Beijing Chengshi Zongti Guihua (2016-2035)" (Beijing Municipality Master Plan (2016–2035)), http://ghzrzyw.beijing.gov.cn/zhengwuxinxi/zxzt/bjcsztgh20162035/202001/t20200102_1554600.html . Accessed July 9, 2022. The State Council Information Office of the People's Republic of China, "Shanghaishi Chengshi Zongti Guihua (2017-2035 Nian) Xinwen Fabuhui" ("Shanghai Municipality Master Plan (2017-2035) Press Conference"), http://www.scio.gov.cn/xwfbh/gssxwfbh/xwfbh/shanghai/Document/1615545/1615545.htm. Accessed July 9, 2022.

Bibliography

Andreu, Paul. "National Grand Theatre." *A+U* 399 (2003): 54–59.

———. "Grand National Theater, Beijing." *AV Monografías* 109–110 (2004): 34–39.

Bacon, Edmund. *Design of Cities*. London: Penguin Books, 1967.

Beijing Municipal Government. *Beijing Municipality Master Plan 1991 to 2010*. Beijing: Beijing Municipal Government, 1996.

Cheng Zai and Wu Jianxi. *Lao Shanghai Baiye Zhinan: Daolu Jigou Changshang Zhuzhai Fenbutu* (Commercial Directory of Old Shanghai: Maps Showing the Distribution of Roadways, Institutions, Factories, and Residences). Shanghai: Shanghai Shehui Kexue Chubanshe, 2008.

Clement, Pierre. "Shanghai: Squares and Public Spaces." In *Shanghai: Architecture & Urbanism for Modern China*, edited by Seng Kuan and Peter G. Rowe, 148–154. Munich: Prestel, 2004.

Editorial Committee. *Chang'an Jie Xianzhuang Ziliao* (Information on the Existing Conditions of Chang'an Avenue). Beijing: China Architecture & Building Press, 1978.

———. *Zhongguo Guojia Dajuyuan Jianzhu Sheji Guoji Jingsai Fang'an Ji* (A Collection of Design Schemes for the International Architectural Competition of the National Grand Theater P.R. China). Beijing: China Architecture & Building Press, 2000.

Gensler. "Shanghai Rising: A Symbol of China's Ascension." http://du.gensler.com/vol5/shanghai-tower/#/shanghai-rising. Accessed 13 March 2014.

Goldberger, Paul. "Forbidden Cities." *New Yorker*, 30 June 2008, www.newyorker.com/arts/critics/skyline/2008/06/30/080630crsk_skyline_goldberger. Accessed 13 March 2014.

KPF. "Shanghai World Financial Center." *KPF*, www.kpf.com/projects/shanghai-world-financial-center. Accessed 29 December 2021.

Kuan, Seng. "Image of the Metropolis." In *Shanghai: Architecture & Urbanism for Modern China*, edited by Seng Kuan and Peter G. Rowe, 84–95. Munich: Prestel, 2004.

MacPherson, Kerrie L. "The Shanghai Model in Historical Perspective." In *Shanghai: Transformation and Modernization Under China's Open Policy*, edited by Y.M. Yeung and Y.W. Sung, 493–528. Hong Kong: The Chinese University Press.

Pedersen, William. "Strategie e pianificazionè." *l'Arca* 109 (1996): 2–13.

Rowe, Peter G. and Seng Kuan. *Architectural Encounters with Essence and Form*. Cambridge, MA: MIT Press, 2002.

Shanghaishi Chengshi Guihua Guanliju. *Shanghai Chengshi Guihua* (Shanghai Urban Planning). Shanghai: Shanghai Urban Planning and Administration Bureau, 2006.

Wang, Jun. *Beijing Record: A Physical and Political History of Planning Modern Beijing*. Singapore: World Scientific, 2011.

Xue, Charlie. *Building a Revolution: Chinese Architecture Since 1980*. Hong Kong: Hong Kong University Press, 2005.

Yu, Jun. "Wo Lai Wei Andelu Bianjian Yu Peng Peigen Xiansheng Shangque (Defense for Andreu and Discussion with Mr Peng Pei-gen)." *Jianzhu Xuebao* (Architectural Journal) 3 (2001): 31–33.

Yu, Shuishan. "Redefining the Axis of Beijing: Revolution and Nostalgia in the Planning of the PRC Capital." *Journal of Urban History* 34 (2008): 571–608.

Glossary

Beijing	北京
Chang'an (Avenue)	长安（街）
Chaobai (River)	潮白河
Chaoyang (Road)	朝阳（路）
Chen Gan	陈干
danwei	单位
Deng Xiaoping	邓小平
Fuxingmen	复兴门
Hongqiao	虹桥
Huamu (district)	花木（区）
Huang Fuxiang	黄富厢
Jianguomen	建国门
Jin Mao (Tower)	金茂（大厦）
Jing'an (Park)	静安（公园）
Lujiazui	陆家嘴
Minzu (Cultural Palace)	民族（文化宫）
Pudong	浦东
Puxi	浦西
Renmin (Square)	人民（广场）
Shanghai	上海
Shougang	首钢
Tiananmen (Square)	天安门（广场）
Tonghui (River)	通惠（河）
Wangfujing	王府井
Wukesong	五棵松
Xidan	西单
Xishan	西山
Yan'an (Elevated Road)	延安（高架桥）
Yangjingbang (Creek)	洋泾浜
Yongding (River)	永定河
Zhao Dongri	赵冬日
Zhongzheng (Road)	中正（路）
Zhu Rongji	朱镕基
Zhu Zhaoxue	朱兆雪

35

ICONIC ARCHITECTURE IN CHINA (2000s)

Historical Reading versus Marxist Critique

Ming Wu

As a result of China's rapid economic development and urbanization during the past three decades, a new Chinese cityscape across the country, and its global cities in the making, has been created. This fundamental change of landscape was an integral component of a profound socio-economic and political transformation induced by Deng Xiaoping's post-Mao reform beginning in 1978. Under a new state leadership, the reform liberated China from the Maoist planning economy and ideological conflicts and opened the country to the rest of the world. With an active market economy and opening up, China also became a magnet for foreign capital. As a counterpart of neoliberalism that originated in the UK and America of the late 1970s, the state in post-Mao China is considered as having embraced a pro-development mode of political-economic practice, especially since the early 1990s.[1] China's pro-market reform and opening up responded closely to "the progress of neoliberalization on the world stage" and "the increasing geographical mobility of capital" that have put pressures on different geographic localities, including countries, regions, and cities.[2] However, it needs to be emphasized that it was also driven by China's aspiration to national self-strengthening and modernization under the new conditions of contemporary globalization.

Architectural Spectacle as a Problem

Taking the world by surprise for the speed and scale of construction, China's new cityscape is marked by its blossoming contemporary iconic buildings, characterized by bold architectural statements and bearing names of renowned international architects. After Gehry's Guggenheim with its "Bilbao effect," communicating positive images to promote cities has become the most sought-after strategy among various others to attract capital investment in an increasingly competitive global economy. China's most important cities, such as Beijing and Shanghai, quickly picked up this strategy. They constructed their own flagship architectural projects and iconic buildings, often involving participations of renowned international architects to brand and market themselves. The resultant spectacle of iconic buildings not only becomes an expression of audacity backed by China's recent economic achievement but also asserts its new aspiration in the age of globalization.

Guy Debord argues that "the spectacle is not a collection of images; rather, it is a social relationship between people that is mediated by images."[3] For Debord, it consolidates and

DOI: 10.4324/9781315851112-52

reproduces the hegemony of social and power structures through a synthesis of consumption, commodity fetishism, and mass media. When inducing passive identification with the spectacle, it can become political power on its own. Examining the representation of the social world following a more analytical approach, Pierre Bourdieu contributes to the understanding of spectacle by offering insights into the economics of symbolic capital in the form of "distinction" that is produced and circulates in fields of cultural production and consumption.[4] It is argued that symbolic struggles over distinction are one significant aspect of the field of social and power struggles, and they determine partially the reality of objective classification within the social world.[5] The spectacle can be accordingly considered as "symbolic capital" and "marks of distinction" that are ready to be transformed into more tangible economic capital and political capital. Not constrained to the social world, David Harvey relates Bourdieu's idea of symbolic capital to the contemporary process of globalization where traditional "monopoly privileges" derived from natural geographical distances and institutional barriers to trade have been significantly diminished.[6] Harvey argues that distinctive and non-replicable cultural claims have been increasingly sought by different localities across the globe as collective symbolic capital that has a significant drawing power upon the flow of capital in the recent bout of uneven geographic development.[7] In addition to its effect in social stratification and oppression, the spectacle of iconic buildings often associated with the place-bound identity has thus become one of the most powerful constitutive elements in the competition for global capital flows and local economic growth between cities, regions, and countries.

Existing literature on the topic of high-profile architectural projects in the age of globalization is rich. So far geographers and social critics, for instance David Harvey and Sharon Zukin, have dominated the discourse on the phenomenon of new flagship architectural projects across the globe. Inclining to Marxism in approach and examining the new physical and social landscape represented by the spectacle of iconic buildings, they tend to emphasize its association with the interests of capital accumulation as considered socially destructive and prone to further stratification of society. When significant attention has recently been drawn to China's rapid urbanization and "transnational architectural production,"[8] some scholars who are interested in how the phenomenon unfolds in China are apt to align themselves with a similar Marxist stand. Adopting the social theory of spectacle and symbolic capital, Anne-Marie Broudehoux and Xuefei Ren investigate China's highest-profile architectural projects through a lens of market logic and power relation in both geopolitical and social terms.[9] Critical of its affiliation to state power and oppressive potential, their writings observe the production of architectural spectacle as a means of social control and contributary factor in severe polarization of the Chinese society. They consider it as a self-assertion of China's rise as a geopolitical power and facilitating restructuring of territorial social elites.

In the meantime, there is attentive work dedicated to the design and contextual aspects of China's new flagship architectural projects. Not concerned with social theory and its critical perspective, in his study of Beijing's emergent territories of urban production, Peter G. Rowe reveals certain situational logics that the architectural projects responded to and were defined by in their place, time, and design.[10] Viewing them as being conservative with regard to Beijing's earlier urban compositional principles and persistent features in a more abstract manner, Rowe argues that its new architectural geographies, with a further emphasis on technical prowess and display, offer forward-looking design opportunities that further enhance the already distinctive character of Beijing.[11]

Distanced from the abovementioned, Jianfei Zhu adopts both a long historical view and the idea of a "capitalist world-system" from Immanuel Wallerstein when examining China's new landscape.[12] Aware of its nature as "a spectacle with great symbolic capital," Zhu relates it to "a moment in China's own history in modernization and integration with the global community."[13] He affirms an enrichment of formal languages and disciplinary knowledge of modern Chinese architecture, which is attributable to the recent significant participation of overseas architects in China who introduced radical modernism into the country through its new iconic buildings. For Zhu, those new iconic buildings, with their radical architectural ideas, serve as "a representation of a new nation, its aspiration and a new state leadership," when China is in search of continuing national self-strengthening and modernization at the present time.[14]

In short, a significant body of research on the production of iconic buildings in China has been made. However, when adopting critical social theories, it tends to examine the question from a Marxist standpoint, emphasizing power struggles between classes or society and state authority within China. When pointed to its architecture and disciplinary implication, it often overlooks a geopolitical and social perspective. When adding historical and world-system dimensions to the social and formal analysis, it does not single out the phenomenon as a primary problem but investigates it as an episode integrated into the country's long national and formal development. In response, this chapter aims to focus on the collaboration between China and international architects in producing new global architectural icons. Also adopting the concept of spectacle and symbolic capital, it is nevertheless intended to question the conventional Marxist approach and comprehend the spectacle in relation to China's present national development and geopolitical positioning in the world. For this purpose, three of the most significant new architectural icons of contemporary China designed by overseas star architects are selected for close observation. They are the Grand National Theatre (GNT), the CCTV headquarters (CCTV), and the National Olympic Stadium (NOS).

A Contrasting Metaphor in Historical Context

The Grand National Theatre in Beijing is arguably the most important public building in China at the advent of the new millennium, not only for its role as the most prestigious performing arts centre of the country and its ultra-modern architecture design, but also because of its significant location in the centre of the capital city of China (Figure 35.1). Towards the southwest of the intersection of the two central axes of Beijing, on the southern side of Chang'an Avenue opposite to the Forbidden City, and on the western side of the Great Hall of the People that flanks Tiananmen Square, the GNT occupies a site of 118,900 square metres.[15] Designed by Paul Andreu of ADPi in association with BIAD (Beijing Institute of Architectural Design), the main body of the building is a giant oval shell with a span of 212 metres from east to west, 143 metres from north to south, and a height of 46.68 metres.[16] With a spatial structure made up of 148 arch-shaped steel trusses, it is covered with about 30,800 square metres of Japanese-made titanium plate, and about 6,700 square metres of French-made ultra-transparent glass that imitates a curtain opening gradually from top to bottom on the northern side of the shell facing Chang'an Avenue.[17] The ellipsoid shell as an object is then completely surrounded by an artificial lake that makes it look like it is floating on water. The route leading to the theatre lobby starts with a sunken square along Chang'an Avenue that is followed by a glass-roofed passageway of some 60 metres long underneath the lake connecting to an underground entrance hall. Entering the oval-shaped shell from the underground, there is a huge public space accommodating three independent enclosures, namely an opera house (2416 seats), a concert hall (2017 seats), and a theatre (1040 seats).[18]

The NGT was the first of a number of large public buildings in Beijing that started to be commissioned to globally renowned architects through international competitions with state investments at the turn of the century. In comparison with other projects, the NGT had long

Figure 35.1 Grand National Theatre, Beijing, completed in 2007. Architect: Paul Andreu with BIAD.
Source: Photo taken in 2007. © Jianfei Zhu.

been conceived on the same site since the 1950s when the government decided to reconstruct Tiananmen Square and build the Ten Buildings to commemorate the tenth anniversary of the People's Republic. While the project was postponed at the time, design schemes produced then were in conformity with a National Style.[19] They were invariably similar to the formal language of the Great Hall of the People and the Museum of Revolution and History, on the two sides of Tiananmen Square nearby. A dramatic change was, however, heralded by a two-round process of international competition organized by the city government for the NGT between April 1998 and August 1999. No selected entry was considered to have satisfied the expectation during the first round, as the government was keen on having a first-class international performing arts venue and a creative architectural statement to display its ambition in the eyes of the world. Thereafter, in contrast with his original idea of a rectilinear box, Andreu's renewed design, embracing a completely new form of a giant ellipsoid dome, was picked as the winning scheme in the second round.[20]

The giant oval shell, which seemed to radically violate convention and the context of Tiananmen Square, trigged an intense debate. Supporters from a young generation of architects and intellectuals considered the design progressive, forward-looking, capable of providing Beijing and China a new iconic building in the twenty-first century. However, resentment and criticism towards the futuristic blob were overwhelming. A group of outraged "academicians" from the China Academy of Science and Engineering and senior architects took their protests to media and the central government, and accused the Andreu scheme of unnecessary high cost, being unreasonable and impractical, and, probably most importantly, of ignoring the context of Tiananmen Square. Local Beijingers were also sceptical about the giant glass-and-titanium dome. They joked about it by "claiming it resembles a colossal turtle egg or, worse, a floating silver turd from outer space."[21] Driven by the urge to present a new image of Beijing and China to the world, determined to show its power and confidence through a daring architectural statement, the government sided with those supporting Andreu's design. Despite the prevalent challenge and criticism, the construction of the project started in April 2000. Upon its completion in July 2007, the GNT became one of the most important landmarks and iconic buildings of modern China, generating worldwide media exposure and visibility.

As the very source of the controversy, it is the outrageous design of the NGT in relation to its sensitive site and context of Tiananmen Square that underlies its overpowering iconic effect. According to Andreu, rather than respecting the context through imitation and assimilation, his scheme aimed at producing a resonance by putting different architectures together. Testifying to this claim, while its symmetrical and primitive form in association with a modest height indicates an implicit consistency with the characters of majesty and horizontality of Tiananmen Square and Beijing, the NGT deviates significantly in formal language from the existing monumental buildings and the urban fabric. It presents a sharp contrast to the centuries-old Forbidden City through a glittering futuristic dome in combination with the latest modern materials. Embarking on a more neutral abstraction and minimalist approach in overall building form, it also distinguishes itself from the Great Hall of the People and the Museum of Revolution, which adopted classical proportions in combination with socialist realism. It is this upsetting of decency and deference that has not only provoked resentment but also contributed to the iconicity of the NGT.[22] The contrasting futuristic ultra-modern design made the building a distinctive metaphor for departure from the past of ideological conflicts towards a promising future. It served as a bold new image of Beijing and modern China. It is clearly what the state was after from the NGT, in search of a symbol of national development and economic modernization in the age of globalization.

A Typological Alternative to the Skyscraper

Beijing in 2001 won its bid to be the hosting city for the 2008 Olympic Games, a mega-event that could generate local urban economic growth and promote Beijing and China through extensive global media coverage. To build a new image of Beijing to impress the world audience was imperative. International design competitions were promptly organized by the government to select the best architects worldwide to design ground-breaking landmark venues for Olympic Beijing. The headquarters of China Central Television, designed by the 2000 Pritzker Prize winner Rem Koolhaas and his partners from OMA, in association with ECADI (East China Architectural Design & Research Institute), became a prominent representative of those new landmarks. Located in Beijing's new Central Business District around the intersection of Chang'an Avenue and the city's Third Ring Road, the CCTV headquarters in combination with another building, the Television Cultural Centre, and some affiliated facilities composed a complex with a total area of 558,000 square metres.[23] Aimed at integrating the entire process of TV-making into a collective of interconnected activities, the CCTV building is made of a three-dimensional loop with two slightly oblique towers rising from a common platform and joined by a giant 75-metre cantilevering L-shaped overhang on top.[24] The building is then wrapped by an exoskeleton structure of triangulated grids immediately underneath its tempered glass surface. The triangulated grids not only serve as the building's primary support, but also stretch and contract in density according to the actual stress and load distribution.

Bending six angled tubes into the loop equivalent to a 180-storey building, the CCTV building also claims to substitute an interdependent, reciprocal, and "truly" three-dimensional experience for the banal typology of one-dimensional skyscraper that is hierarchical and only thrusts relentlessly upwards.[25] Competing against other renowned international architects, including SOM, KPF, Philip Johnson, Toyo Ito, and Dominic Perrault, Koolhaas's win of the commission in 2002 was attributable not only to its radical design but also to his cunning response to the government's call for a distinctive architectural icon.[26] When condemning that the skyscraper has been widely adopted by Asia to the exclusion of almost all others, and yet exhausted and not keeping pace with contemporary business and urban life, Koolhaas states that he put himself against all the 300 skyscrapers that have been planned for Beijing's Central Business District.[27] Arguing that "the 301st would certainly be a feint echo, not the desired landmark," Koolhaas designed an exceptional mutant, which is a big, bulky, looped-tube shape with a 70-storey height and, most importantly, is not a skyscraper.[28]

For Koolhaas, the CCTV building is a desirable architectural manifestation for his prolonged yet idiosyncratic formal and programmatic investigation to date. It started from promoting a "culture of congestion" that was driven by technology and economics and was exemplified by the skyscraper in Manhattan. It evolved to argue for a "theory of Bigness" that "can sustain a promiscuous proliferation of events in a single container." It denounced lately the skyscraper as an obsolescent symbol of business that "can deny instead of promote interaction and communication," and thus urged on "new configurations of the contemporary metropolis."[29] Materialising Koolhaas's latest campaign to "kill the skyscraper," the CCTV headquarters received great support from the Chinese government that mobilized substantial economic capital, political power, and other resources for its realization. What underpinned the overwhelming generosity was clearly an attempt to secure a status of active patronage of cutting-edge architects and pioneering contemporary architectural ideas that were globally "accredited."

As another intended new architectural icon for Beijing and China, the CCTV headquarters shares some common features with the GNT. They were both designed by renowned overseas architects. Both buildings presented on a massive scale distinctive abstract forms that could emanate a sense of modernization and progress. When materializing these distinctive and even terrifying forms demanded great local building capabilities and would generate astronomical construction and maintaining costs, both buildings became the source of controversy and triggered intense debates about their formal extravagance and engineering outrage. Yet, they were both favoured by the Chinese government. Differences between them in generating values of distinction are also conspicuous. The GNT was engaging a contrasting resonance with its immediate and significant historic urban context, whereas the CCTV building gained its vantage-point more through patronizing Koolhaas, arguably one of the most iconic contemporary architects who had been considered as persistently pushing the frontier of architectural thinking.

Tectonic Formation as a Symbol for the Beijing Olympics

The National Stadium was the very protagonist among the 31 stadiums prepared for Olympic Beijing, as it was the centre stage and the highest-profile architectural project for the Olympic spectacle.[30] Its design was attributed to another two laureates of the Pritzker Prize, Jacques Herzog and Pierre de Meuron, in collaboration with CAG (China Architectural Design & Research Group) and Chinese artist Ai Weiwei. Joined by another two major sports facilities, the National Gymnasium and the National Aquatics Centre, the NOS was seated in the Olympic Park on the northern extension of the central axis of Beijing. Conceived by the designers as a gigantic collective vessel seen from both a distance and close up, the NOS was however nicknamed the Bird's Nest for its interwoven steel structures resembling a bird's nest. Embracing a dramatic spatial grid-like formation, it achieved a pure and minimalist bowl shape, integrating seamlessly its structure, façade, and roof.[31] When enjoying a saturated media exposure through the 2008 Olympics, the Bird's Nest, with the other iconic sports facility the National Aquatics Centre, nicknamed the Water Cube, became the much-celebrated symbol of Olympic Beijing and modern China (Figures 35.2 and 35.3).

The symbolic significance of the NOS has been emphatically illustrated not only through its strategic location, aligning it with some of the most important landmarks of Beijing, but also by its role as the central stage of the Beijing Olympics, including housing the spectacular opening ceremony, directed by the renounced film director Zhang Yimou. This significance could only

Figure 35.2 Cover of *Architectural Record*, Issue 07 ("Beijing Transformed"), 2008, featuring the National Olympic Stadium, Beijing, 2008. Architect: Herzog & de Meuron with CAG.

Source: Permission and courtesy of *Architectural Record* Editorial Office.

Figure 35.3 National Olympic Stadium under construction, Beijing, completed in 2008. Architect: Herzog & de Meuron with CAG.

Source: Photo taken in 2007. © Jianfei Zhu.

be explained by what it meant to the country and the nation that Beijing, the capital city of China, would host the Olympics. The Olympics as a potentially highly profitable mega-event could generate local economic growth and urban regeneration, and provide the opportunity for image building in global interurban competitions. Yet, the 2008 Olympics involved much higher stakes for Beijing and China; namely, "they represented to the world China's rise as a new global power, backed by the dynamic Chinese economy and consolidated under the rule of the Communist party."[32] In association with such extraordinary national symbolism, the project of the NOS surely aspired to a great new architectural icon to promote the Beijing Olympics. It was similar rather than different to the projects of GNT and CCTV headquarters in searching for reputable overseas architects and outstanding designs through international design competitions. In October 2002, the government organized a competition with an "overwhelming number of international design teams and jury member" to make Beijing "gather the best architectural designs from the world for Olympic stadium."[33] Among 13 invited entries, including eight from established international firms and three from joint ventures, Herzog and de Meuron's design was again challenged by local cultural conservatives for a similar reason. Yet, it was picked as the winning scheme by the 13-member jury, whose six architectural experts were all international architects, including prominent figures such as Rem Koolhaas, Kisho Kurosawa, Jean Nouvel, and Dominique Perrault.[34]

Winning the Pritzker Prize one year later than Koolhaas in 2001, Herzog and de Meuron's work has been considered among contemporaries as a primary counterpoint to Koolhaas's pursuance of a programmatic synthesis, and has become itself an icon of "territorial value" in architecture.[35] Since their early presence in the field of architecture in the late 1980s, Herzog and de Meuron have been identified as "an anomaly within the contemporary architectural avant-garde." Rejecting the external influence of function and programme as well as denouncing stylistic expression, they assumed a basic adequacy of architecture's inner materiality and tectonics.[36] In contrast to their contemporaries, often interested in "radical geometries and cross-disciplinary forays," Herzog and de Meuron deliberately confined themselves within the conventional architectural discipline. Somewhat suppressing image and iconography, they decided to focus on normative materials, technique, and constructions in search of their fundamental nature and unexpected formal potential.[37] Frequently presenting overly simple and even austere forms, their work was often intent on impressing people with certain radicalism and novelty in architectonics that were yet an outcome of creative handlings of the most typical materials and structures. In recent years, their highly exposed, distinguishable work has made them two of the most sought-after international architects. Meanwhile, Herzog and de Meuron were widely recognized for their consistency in giving attendant importance to potentially new sensibilities based on architecture's inherent materiality and tectonics. On par with Koolhaas, they are iconic figures in the global architectural production who have arguably shaped another distinctive paradigm for the development of the discipline of architecture in the world.

Like the CCTV building to Koolhaas, the NOS offered Herzog and de Meuron a great opportunity, willingly supported by the Chinese government in various senses, to expand their exploration of the new sensibility and formal potential of architecture's inner materiality and tectonics. As a result, again bearing the name of the world celebrity architects, it presented on an unprecedented scale a simple and primordial architectural form that surprised the global audience with its imaginative, spatial grid-like formation. At the cost of enormous economic, political, and human resources. which were again difficult to justify in any normal sense, the NOS staged a gigantic "tactile" material form whose images circulated around the world due to the saturated Olympic-related reporting. In conjunction with the mega-event of the Olympics, with "great marks of distinction" attached to its overwhelming tectonic form as well as the name of the star architects, the NOS served as another predominant architectural icon that represented new Beijing and modern China in the global media.

A New Symbolic Form

These three architectural projects of national significance have all demonstrated a decisive attempt of the Chinese state to engage with the production of architectural spectacle in the age of contemporary globalization. Prestigious international architects and their designs were sought after by the government, almost in ignorance of the criticism and opposition from the local academicians and architects as well as the public. The resultant bold architectural statements supported by the state both economically and politically served as an overpowering exhibition of symbolic capital.

Underpinning the spectacle of iconic buildings, the more fundamental economy of symbolic capital and market logic were at work. The marketing of architecture in search of symbolic capital and instant fame in the world marketplace was foremost reflected by the Chinese state's eager patronage of the prominent overseas architects and their speculative architectural experiments. Being associated with these iconic architects and their cutting-edge designs, China could claim the status of being a sophisticated and open-minded patron of contemporary global architectural culture. Nevertheless, the struggle for symbolic capital driven by the recent bout of capitalist globalization was most conspicuously manifested by the signature buildings themselves. With their pervasive images circulated instantaneously in the global media, in the form of a daring integration of radical aesthetics and creative structure solutions at an unprecedented massive scale, the bold architectural statements, facilitated by advanced building technology, displayed great marks of distinction. Aspiring to the elaboration of distinctive contemporary identities and place branding, having mobilized enormous economic, political, and human resources, these iconic buildings served to offer Beijing and China monopoly privileges in the global competition for tourists and foreign capital investments.

The synthesis of formal inquiries in architecture and the economic and political power of the state generated great symbolic capital that responded to the pressures put on all geographic localities by the global progress of neoliberalization. Yet, the Chinese state has often been accused of adopting a ruthless neoliberal approach to political-economic practice where "considerations of economic growth and development have trumped every other concern, particularly those of democracy and social justice," as found in the works of David Harvey and Wang Hui.[38] In accordance with a similar critical stand, the production of iconic buildings in China was frequently criticized for its affiliation to the hegemonic power of the state and elite classes, as well as its association with capitalist acquisition at significant social costs. As found in Anne-Marie Broudehoux's work, it was condemned for not only enforcing a cruel coalition between the state power and global capitalism in securing capital accumulation, but also serving as instruments to govern and regulate Chinese society.[39] While aligned with Broudehoux in social critique, Xuefei Ren nevertheless states that the phenomenon "has to be understood within a broader conception of power, one that goes beyond pure market logic."[40] For Ren, the spectacle of these state-sponsored megaprojects also demonstrated China's rise as a geopolitical power and a new nation.

Often read as a service to hegemonic power and rampant capitalist acquisition, the spectacle needs a close scrutiny. While the criticism of the production of iconic buildings in China found in Broudehoux's and Ren's work is not incorrect, their ideas are not enough. The emergent iconic buildings in China have specificities that could only be comprehended in conjunction with the country's concrete historical conditions, that is, conditions of its national development. Through his critique of the critical theory in the West, Jianfei Zhu questions a confrontational dualism in the Marxist and the Frankfurt School tradition that emphasizes "class" and "class struggle," and views the market and state authority in opposition to society.[41] Critical of the conventional framework focusing on class or state-society confrontation within a society and the use of the idea in a global expansion with a flat universalism, Zhu rather favours the recent notion of geopolitical critique in the West. He further elaborates a concept of relational logic rooted in Chinese tradition and demonstrated in the country's history in modernization where state authority assumed the leadership. As an alternative to the critical theory conventionally used, Zhu puts forward a relational logic that supports the idea of the state as a leader working with market and society in search of a balanced development.[42]

If this is correct, a new and supplementary reading of the new architectural icons under investigation can be proposed. Understood from a historical perspective, China's recent socio-economic and political transformation was the latest phase of the country's prolonged pursuance of national self-strengthening and modernization since the late Qing dynasty. In the past, there was the "Self-Strengthening Movement" during the late Qing dynasty, after its humiliating defeats in confrontation with the industrialized Western powers. It was a period of institutional reforms intended to strengthen China through economic and military modernization. Later, the national project of the Republic and the socialist project of the People's Republic in the Mao period accomplished national unification and independence in the age of imperialism. In the present, the post-Mao project led by the new state and embracing market economy is striving for economic growth and further national development under the new conditions of globalization. From a geopolitical point of view, the historical transformation led by the post-Mao state also manifested China's new standing in integration with the global community. Engaging in dialogue with its core powers, China is striving to shift from a periphery towards the centre of the global stage.

Existing literature has provided rich observations of how, across the globe, high-profile architectural projects could be affiliated to the state power and/or elite classes, as well as associated with capitalist acquisition at significant social costs. It is also evident that the state in post-Mao China did prioritize economic growth and development over many other concerns in competition with other geographic locations in the process of global neoliberalization. Therefore, a critical attitude towards China's emerging new landmark buildings with a focus on class and society-state relations is much needed. Nevertheless, despite a recent achievement of China's dual historical and geopolitical project, it is still at large a developing country falling behind the developed countries and core nation-states in the West. This moment in the history of China's self-strengthening, modernization, and integration with the global community arguably necessitated the spectacle of iconic buildings in Beijing. With cutting-edge designs facilitated by advanced construction innovation, these buildings of national significance were offering China great collective symbolic capital. Readily convertible to more tangible economic capital and political power according to Debord and Bourdieu, it provided real supports for the country's continuing struggles for economic success in the increasingly competitive world marketplace.

When the concrete historical conditions are understood, the meaning of this emergent landscape can be revealed. As an outcome of active collaborations between China and prominent overseas architects, with great marks of distinction, these spectacular buildings brand and market Beijing and China favourably in the increasingly competitive global economy. Willingly sought after and promoted by the post-Mao state, with radical formal and tectonic expressions, they symbolize on the world stage a new nation, its aspiration, and a new Chinese state. Representing this historical moment of China's dynamic engagement with the world market and the global community, the spectacle of iconic buildings in Beijing is essentially a new symbolic form for China's national development in the age of contemporary globalization.

Notes

1 David Harvey, *A Brief History of Neoliberalism* (New York: Oxford University Press, 2005); see also Wang Hui. Theodore Huters, ed. *China's new order: Society, politics, and economy in transition* (Cambridge, MA: Harvard University Press, 2003).

2 Harvey, *Neoliberalism*, 1–2, 87, 92.

3 Guy Debord, *The Society of the Spectacle*, Translated by Donald Nicholson-Smith. (New York: Zone Books, 1994), 12.

4 Pierre Bourdieu, *Distinction: A Social Critique of the Judgement of Taste*, Translated by Richard Nice (Cambridge, MA: Harvard University Press, 1984).

5 Bourdieu, *Distinction,* 253.

6 David Harvey, *Spaces of capital: Towards a critical geography* (New York: Routledge 2001), 394–395.

7 Harvey, *Spaces*, 398–399, 405.

8 Harvey, *Spaces*; David Harvey, *The condition of Postmodernity: An Enquiry into the Origins of Cultural Change* (Oxford and Cambridge, MA: Blackwell, 1990); David Harvey, "From Space to Place and Back Again, in *Mapping the Futures: Local Cultures, Global Change*, ed. Jon Bird et al., 3–29 (London and New York: Routledge, 1993); and see also Sharon Zukin, *Landscapes of Power: From Detroit to Disney World* (Berkeley: University of California Press, c1991).

9 Anne-Marie Broudehoux, *The Making and Selling of Post-Mao Beijing* (London and New York: Rout-ledge, 2004); and see also Xuefei Ren, *Building Globalization: Transnational Architecture Production in Urban China* (Chicago, IL; London: University of Chicago Press, 2011).
10 Peter G. Rowe, *Emergent Architectural Territories in East Asian Cities* (Basel: Birkhauser, 2011).
11 Rowe, *Emergent*, 40.
12 Jianfei Zhu, *Architecture of Modern China: A Historical Critique* (London: Routledge, c2009), 169–170, 194–195.
13 Zhu, *Architecture*, 206.
14 Zhu, *Architecture*, 196.
15 Charlie Q. L. Xue, Zhigang Wang, and Brian Mitchenere, "In search of identity: The develop-ment process of the National Grand Theatre in Beijing, China," *The Journal of Architecture* 15, no. 4 (August 2010): 517.
16 Paul Andreu, *National Grand Theatre of China, Beijing*, www.paul-andreu.com/pages/projets_recents_operapek_g.html. Accessed 15 July 2014; and see also Xue et al., "In search of identity," 517.
17 Xue et al., "Identity," 517.
18 Andreu, *Theatre*.
19 Xue et al., "Identity," 519–521.
20 Xue et al., "Identity," 526.
21 Thomas J. Campanella, *The Concrete Dragon: China's Urban Revolution and What it Means for the World* (New York: Princeton Architectural Press, c2008), 140–143.
22 See Charles Jencks, *The Iconic Building* (New York, NY: Rizzoli International Publications, Inc., 2005), 7–8, for his definition of the iconic building.
23 William B. Millard, "Dissecting the Iconic Exosymbiont: The CCTV Headquarters, Beijing, as Built Organism," In *Content*, by AMOMA, Rem Koolhaas, and et al. (Köln: Taschen, 2004), 486.
24 OMA, *CCTV – Headquarters, China, Beijing 2002: New Headquarters of China Central Television*, www.oma.eu/projects/2002/cctv-%E2%80%93-headquarters/. Accessed 15 July 2014.
25 Jencks, *Building*, 111.
26 Jencks, *Building*, 107.
27 AMOMA, Rem Koolhaas, and et al., *Content* (Köln: Taschen, 2004), 473.
28 Jencks, *Building*, 107.
29 Rem Koolhaas, *Delirious New York: A Retroactive Manifesto for Manhattan* (London: Thames and Hud-son, 1978), and see also Rem Koolhaas, "Bigness, or the problem of large." In *S, M, L, XL.*, by Rem Koolhaas and Bruce Mau (New York: Monacelli Press, 1995), 511; and see also AMOMA et al., *Content*, 474–477.
30 Xuefei Ren, *Building Globalization: Transnational Architecture Production in Urban China* (Chicago, Ill.; London: University of Chicago Press, 2011), 140.
31 Herzog & de Meuron, *226 National Stadium*, www.herzogdemeuron.com/index/projects/complete-works/226-250/226-national-stadium.html. Accessed 15 July 2014.
32 Ren, *Globalization*, 145.
33 Ren, *Globalization*, 148.
34 Ren, *Globalization*, 149.
35 Rafael Moneo, *Theoretical Anxiety and Design Strategies in the Work of Eight Contemporary Architects*, Translated by Gina Cariño. (Cambridge, MA; London: MIT Press, c2004), 4.
36 A. Krista Sykes, ed., *Constructing a New Agenda: Architectural Theory 1993–2009* (New York: Princeton Architectural Press, c2010), 152–153.
37 Moneo, *Anxiety*, 262–266.
38 Harvey, *Neoliberalism*; and see also Wang, *Order*.
39 Broudehoux, *Beijing*; and see also Anne-Marie Broudehoux, "Images of Power: Architectures of the Integrated Spectacle at the Beijing Olympics." *Journal of Architectural Education* 63, no. 2 (March 2010): 52–62; Anne-Marie Broudehoux, "Spectacular Beijing: The Conspicuous Construction of an Olym-pic Metropolis." *Journal of Urban Affairs* 29, no. 4 (2007): 383–399.
40 Ren, *Globalization*, 4.
41 Jianfei Zhu, "Opening the Concept of Critical Architecture: The Case of Modern China and the Issues of the State," in *Non West Modernist Past: On Architecture & Modernities*, eds. William S. W. Lim and Jiat-Hwee Chang (Singapore: World Scientific, 2012), 113.
42 Zhu, "Critical," 111–116.

Bibliography

AMOMA, Rem Koolhaas et al. *Content*. Köln: Taschen, 2004.

Andreu, Paul. *National Grand Theatre of China, Beijing*, www.paul-andreu.com/pages/projets_recents_operapek_g.html. Accessed 15 July 2014.

Bourdieu, Pierre. *Distinction: A Social Critique of the Judgement of Taste*. Translated by Richard Nice. Cambridge, MA: Harvard University Press, 1984.

Broudehoux, Anne-Marie. *The Making and Selling of Post-Mao Beijing*. London and New York: Routledge, 2004.

———. "Spectacular Beijing: The Conspicuous Construction of an Olympic Metropolis." *Journal of Urban Affairs* 29, no. 4 (2007): 383–399.

———. "Images of Power: Architectures of the Integrated Spectacle at the Beijing Olympics." *Journal of Architectural Education* 63, no. 2 (March 2010): 52–62.

Campanella, Thomas J. *The Concrete Dragon: China's Urban Revolution and What It Means for the World*. New York: Princeton Architectural Press, 2008.

Debord, Guy. *The Society of the Spectacle*. Translated by Donald Nicholson-Smith. New York: Zone Books, 1994.

Hall, Tim and Phil Hubbard, eds. *The Entrepreneurial City: Geographies of Politics, Regime, and Representation*. Chichester and New York: Wiley, 1998.

Harvey, David. *The Condition of Postmodernity: An Enquiry into the Origins of Cultural Change*. Oxford and Cambridge, MA: Blackwell, 1990.

———. "From Space to Place and Back Again." In *Mapping the Futures: Local Cultures, Global Change*, edited by Jon Bird et al., 3–29. London and New York: Routledge, 1993.

———. *Spaces of Capital: Towards a Critical Geography*. New York: Routledge, 2001.

———. *A Brief History of Neoliberalism*. New York: Oxford University Press, 2005.

Herzog & de Meuron. *226 National Stadium*, www.herzogdemeuron.com/index/projects/complete-works/226-250/226-national-stadium.html. Accessed 15 July 2014.

Jencks, Charles. *The Iconic Building*. New York, NY: Rizzoli International Publications, Inc., 2005.

Kipnis, Jeffrey. "The Cunning of Cosmetics (A Personal Reflection on the Architecture of Herzog & de Meuron)." In *Constructing a New Agenda: Architectural Theory 1993–2009*, edited by A. Krista Sykes, 154–164. New York: Princeton Architectural Press, 2010.

Koolhaas, Rem. *Delirious New York: A Retroactive Manifesto for Manhattan*. London: Thames and Hudson, 1978.

———. "Bigness, or the Problem of Large." In *SMLXL*, edited by Rem Koolhaas and Bruce Mau, 494–517. New York: Monacelli Press, 1995.

Koolhaas, Rem and Bruce Mau. *SMLXL*. New York: Monacelli Press, 1995.

Millard, William B. "Dissecting the Iconic Exosymbiont: The CCTV Headquarters, Beijing, as Built Organism." In *Content*, edited by AMOMA, Rem Koolhaas et al., 490–491. Köln: Taschen, 2004.

Moneo, Rafael. *Theoretical Anxiety and Design Strategies in the Work of Eight Contemporary Architects*. Translated by Gina Cariño. Cambridge, MA and London: MIT Press, 2004.

Olds, Kris. *Globalization and Urban Change: Capital, Culture, and Pacific Rim Mega-Projects*. Oxford: Oxford University Press, 2001.

OMA. *CCTV – Headquarters, China, Beijing 2002: New Headquarters of China Central Television*, www.oma.eu/projects/2002/cctv-%E2%80%93-headquarters/. Accessed 15 July 2014.

Ren, Xuefei. "Architecture and Nation Building in the Age of Globalization: Construction of the National Stadium of Beijing for the 2008 Olympics." *Journal of Urban Affairs* 30, no. 2 (2008): 175–190.

———. *Building Globalization: Transnational Architecture Production in Urban China*. Chicago, IL and London: University of Chicago Press, 2011.

Rowe, Peter G. *Emergent Architectural Territories in East Asian Cities*. Basel: Birkhauser, 2011.

Sklair, Leslie. "Iconic Architecture and Capitalist Globalization." *City* 10, no. 1 (April 2006): 21–47.

———. "Iconic Architecture and the Culture-Ideology of Consumerism." *Theory Culture & Society* 27, no. 5 (September 2010): 135–159.

———. "The Transnational Capitalist Class and Contemporary Architecture in Globalizing Cities." *International Journal of Urban and Regional Research* 29, no. 3 (September 2005): 485–500.

Sykes, A. Krista, ed. *Constructing a New Agenda: Architectural Theory 1993–2009*. New York: Princeton Architectural Press, 2010.

Wang Hui and Theodore Huters, eds. *China's New Order: Society, Politics, and Economy in Transition.* Cambridge, MA: Harvard University Press, 2003.

Xue, Charlie Q.L., Hailin Zhai and Brian Mitchenere. "Shaping Lujiazui: The Formation and Building of the CBD in Pudong, Shanghai." *Journal of Urban Design* 16, no. 2 (May 2011): 209–232.

Xue, Charlie Q.L., Zhigang Wang and Brian Mitchenere. "In Search of Identity: The Development Process of the National Grand Theatre in Beijing, China." *The Journal of Architecture* 15, no. 4 (August 2010): 517–535.

Zhu, Jianfei. *Architecture of Modern China: A Historical Critique.* London: Routledge, 2009.

———, ed. *Zhongguo Jianzhu 60 Nian (1949–2009): Lishi Lilun Yanjiu = Sixty Years of Chinese Architecture (1949–2009): History, Theory and Criticism.* Beijing: Zhongguo Jianzhu Gongye Chubanshe, 2009.

———. "Opening the Concept of Critical Architecture: The Case of Modern China and the Issues of the State." In *Non West Modernist Past: On Architecture & Modernities*, edited by William S.W. Lim and Jiat-Hwee Chang, 105–116. Singapore: World Scientific, 2012.

Zukin, Sharon. *Landscapes of Power: From Detroit to Disney World.* Berkeley: University of California Press, 1991.

Glossary

Ai Weiwei	艾未未
Beijing	北京
Chang'an	长安
Deng Xiaoping	邓小平
Ren, Xuefei	任雪飞
Shanghai	上海
Wang Hui	汪晖
Zhang Yimou	张艺谋
Zhu, Jianfei	朱剑飞

Urban-Rural Reintegration

36

URBAN–RURAL
DEVELOPMENT IN CHINA
AND A WAY FORWARD WITH
"NEW URBANIZATION"

Wang Jianguo

To put it concisely, the path of urbanization of China after 1949 – when the People's Republic was founded – has followed a zigzag trajectory of "opening, closing, and opening again." It has deeply embodied the political agenda and economy policy of state government; it was also closely associated with land policies adopted in the late 1950s.

From 1949 to 1957, Land Reform policies distributed land to farmers extensively, which stimulated greatly agricultural production. During this time, with Soviet aid, China launched its first Five-Year Plan in 1953; some 156 large-scale construction projects were implemented across the nation's major urban centers during these years. The gap of prices for agricultural and industrial goods and the differentiated policies for city vis-à-vis country began to emerge and were widening; a certain discrimination against agriculture was already evident.

The Great Leap Forward movement, initiated in 1958, saw the establishment of Cooperatives and People's Communes in the countryside, which reclaimed land from farmers. These collectivist rural organizations also adopted a Household Registration System. This registration system was increasingly strict, acting effectively as a barrier to keep farmers from coming into the cities – to lessen the burden on the cities for public service and social security. In hindsight today, this system directly caused the "urban–rural split or duality" that is now widely criticized – a structure whereby the urban and rural populations lived with totally different systems in the provision of education, welfare, and social security.

In the 1960s, China launched the Great Proletarian Cultural Revolution. While in the realm of state ideology "politics predominates" (*zhengzhi guashuai*), in economic development everything was slowing down; a movement called "up to mountains and down to countryside" (*shangshan xiaxiang*) was waged, which saw many urban residents, intellectuals, and students being sent to rural China. The directed flow of urban population to rural hinterland was in fact to divert surplus manpower – that which cannot be absorbed in the existing urban industry – from urban centers. In this period, it was openly stated that "large cities must be restricted for their development"; in fact, for medium and small-sized cities, the growth was also very slow or weak. Urbanization in China then basically came to a standstill.

Since 1978, the Reform and Opening-up have seen a lease of land back to farmers by the state government – for farmers to rent them for production. The policies made the peasants rich and living standards were much improved when land became "pots of gold"; the policies also

DOI: 10.4324/9781315851112-54

resolved problems in employment and social security, offering a senior population with more to live by. Unfortunately, this favorable approach did not last long; in the fast and accelerated pace of urbanization in China, the rural land adjacent to cities and towns was quickly monopolized and acquired in the primary market. The land was bought at a low price and sold to the highest bidding in so-called land finance, a practice that harmed the interests of the rural population once again.

Problems in China's Urbanization: An Analysis

On the whole, from 1949 to 1978, urbanization was initially slow for a long and then proceeded to go up and down by the end of the 1980s. In this period, urban development evolved within the model of a "planned economy" with a biased approach – privileging for industrial, especially heavy industry; cities were regarded as centers of production. The campaigns of "up to the mountains and down to the countryside" and "building for the third front" (China's strategic rear) had led to an anti-urbanization development that was against natural historical trends. Urbanization in this period was below 20%, at 10.6% in 1949, and going up to 17.9% in 1978 – an increase of 7.3% over only three decades. But from 1978 on, urbanization accelerated – the rate escalated to 26.44%, 45.68%, and 51.27% in 1990, 2008, and 2011 respectively; the speed of urbanization was three times the world's average during the same period. In 2013, urbanization in China reached 53%, meaning that the city had outstripped the country in the demographic balance, and from then on China had fundamentally altered its long-held condition of "nation-building upon agriculture." However, upon a closer look, things were more complex: the spatial accommodation of people in the city didn't lead to a social and administrative absorption of them into the city in state systems. There were some 260 million rural-to-urban migrant workers who were not accepted into the city system due to the strict rules of the Household Registration System – they were still treated as rural population (and urban services were not open to them). In this sense, the rate of urbanization in China was around 35% (Figure 36.1).

What appeared to be glorious rates of urbanization of China on the surface covered up in reality serious problems in terms of effectivity and substance of real social development.

Firstly, there were a few key factors pushing for excessive urbanization; these included "demographic bonus" because of low labor cost, "land bonus" from cheap land collected from

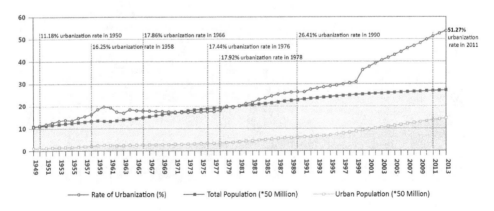

Figure 36.1 China's urbanization rate, 1949–2013.

Source: © Wang Jianguo Research Team.

farmers, and incentive-oriented performance review of government officials during their terms. These factors pushed and accelerated urbanization, resulting in over-exhaustion of land, resources, and environment, with low efficiency and endless greed. At the same time, with an aggressive approach of "cities above countryside," farmers were losing land, their ways of life, and their skills of production in a new and alien setting; they were also arranged into compact and rigid residential blocks in the cities. This "forced urbanization" was a nightmare to most farmers, deprived of their homeland and their rural culture and ecology robbed from them – while their bodies and minds were also caged into rigid grids of control.

Secondly, demographic moves into the cities and social welfare provision for them lagged far behind the expansion of urban space and urban land of some large cities. With special privileges in state policy, location, and resources, a few large cities grew into mega-scale giants at an astonishing speed unmatched in the history of global urban development. In comparison, however, many medium and small-scale cities fell behind and backward, with large areas of rural China even more so, being neglected and almost forgotten. Because of a serious unevenness in resource distribution and an unbalanced approach to development, there has been a grave polarization that has resulted in breaking up any reasonable continuity between cities, townships, and villages.

In this case, the phenomenon of "no-where" – places that were "neither city nor country" – was widespread; because of fast development, rural areas that were not demolished and urbanized fast enough were soon enclosed into enclaves, to become the now well-known *Cheng Zhong Cun*, urban-villages or villages-inside-the city. Many cities have these urban-villages, or "one city, two administrations," with hundreds of thousands of villagers enclosed. These are some of the hardest problems in urban renewal projects in China today (Figure 36.2). Solutions

Figure 36.2 An urban village in Guangzhou.

Source: Photo taken in 2013. © Wang Jianguo.

to these issues have now been included in a scheme of the current New Urbanization plan titled "Three Sets of One Hundred Million People."[1]

The problems of fast urbanization, in the realm of architecture and urban design, have led to fragmentation and heterogeneity in the form, texture, and scale of urban structures at various levels, as the consequence of a bankruptcy of value systems and frames of judgment. Song Chunhua, former chairman of the Architectural Society of China, once said that, amid fast urbanization, rough and poor-quality designs and construction were tolerated; Song further claimed that cities were congested, depressing, unhealthy, and no longer habitable – indeed, that cities were increasingly "unlike us." Further, cities were increasingly similar; old places with memory were disappearing, whereas new sites of meaning or intensity were rare. Political arrogance of officials, commercial gestures by developers, and the absence of architects' voices had also led to disastrous outcomes in architecture and urban design.[2]

Today, people observe that your "hometown is where you can no longer return to"; this confirms that we now have serious problems in the countryside. Today, traditional and effective building methods handed down over generations, and regionally based ways of life and cultural-aesthetic values – rich and varied like the bio-diversity of the natural world – are fast disappearing. In research projects on architectural cultures of the regions of Jiangsu Province, we discovered that government offices at various levels had been developing the countryside as if developing cities; they adopted industrial models for developing villages and rural communities. As a result, villages became micro urban districts, farmland became housing estates, and streams and rivers became underground sewage systems – an entire agricultural civilization and its ecological basis were being quickly ruined, in a manner that was out of control.

More basically, the balance between development and environment for a sustainable growth and the inherent contradiction between economy and resource are now the most serious problems facing us. Because of low efficiency in land use, poor capacity for reuse of water and energy, and weak protection for the ecological environment, China's urbanization of the past three decades has caused, for every 1% development, an additional 1,004 square kilometers of urban land, new energy consumption of 60 million tons of coal, and an additional use of 1.7 billion cubic meters of urban water – and a fall of 0.0073 on the environmental quality index. The result is serious dysfunction and weakening of the ecological systems, with serious harm to the healthy growth of cities and townships.[3]

Nanjing: Urban Planning and Morphological Growth From 1978 to 2008

Nanjing, known as the "capital of six dynasties," is one of the ancient capital cities of China. By now, it has an urban history of 2470 years. Sun Yat-sen, that father of modern Chinese revolution, said in 1917 in his *Nation-Building Strategy* that Nanjing had tall mountains, deep waters, and broad plains; combining these three natural gifts into one, it was a city of exceptional conditions rarely found among the great cities of the world.

In its modern development, Nanjing's periods of growth have been closely related to the making of urban planning schemes at key points over time. During the 80 years from 1919 to 1998, Nanjing has gone through some 14 schemes of urban planning at different scales and with different emphases. Among them, the Capital Plan of 1929 for the Republic of China, and the General City Plan for Nanjing – state council approved – of 1980 and 1992 after the founding of the People's Republic of China (1949), are among the most significant and consequential.

During the 60 years from 1949 to 2008, Nanjing's development has had three major turning points – 1978, 1995, and 2003. If we include other background factors, the urban development of Nanjing can be described as having four periods.

Period One (1949–1978). Because of socio-political turbulence and the anti-urban Cultural Revolution, the growth of Nanjing was slow; urban construction was concentrated in the old city and moved northward, with many industrial bases built along the southern bank of the Yangtze River. The time from 1956 to 1960 saw a small peak in urban construction, with 70% of total investment into industrial production, and less than 30% on non-productive sectors; urban growth was weak and sluggish.

Period Two (1979–1994). With some 200,000 carders and urban youth – who had been sent down to the countryside – returning to Nanjing, and with newly established work-units (*danwei*) moving in as well, the city experienced a great shortage of accommodation, in the so-called famine in housing. These demographic and land pressures thus pushed the urban space of Nanjing out of the old city walls at a significant scale, especially for housing space and land. One of the typical examples is the Nanhu Housing District, which was specifically built for the youth returning from the countryside.

With the growth of the economy and upgrading of industrial production, industrial bases gradually moved out into sub-urban and rural areas, while urban centers began to acquire more commercial functions. The Jinling Hotel, built at a central location, stood 37 stories and 110 meters high; completed in 1983, it was at the time the tallest building in China. This hotel broke and altered the horizontal profile of Nanjing and marked the arrival of a high-rise era in Nanjing in which traditional street fabric and a mountain–water urban landscape (a city among hills, lakes, and rivers) were increasingly threatened.

Period Three (1995–2001). The city entered a period of stable development. From 1998 on, Nanjing maintained a growth of 7 million square meters of construction per year; urban development adopted a program of "infrastructural growth led by road construction." After several years, the three basic difficulties of Nanjing at the time – water supply, power provision, and road networks – were largely resolved. After a reorganization of administrative zones of the city, Nanjing's urban growth witnessed a gradual expansion in a concentric manner, with an emerging pattern of several large development zones, a new town, with three new urban districts, all placed around the main city. The diversification of investment facilitated high-rise development for commercial and office use in the old city in the central area. By 2002, high-rise buildings inside the old city walls – of the Ming dynasty (1368–1644) – counted for over 70% of all highrises in Nanjing (Figures 36.3 and 36.4).

Period Four (2001–2008). Apart from a few urban villages whose demolition would be too costly, the entire core city of Nanjing had been basically fully occupied and built-up. In this stage of development, the government announced an adjustment strategy for urban layout – "One Dispersion and Three Concentrations" – to disperse population and function away from the core of the old city, and to concentrate building projects into new districts, factories into industrial zones, and colleges into university towns. In this period, the old city core and newly developed outskirts of Nanjing became more closely interrelated in land use patterns and functional distribution; peripheries were increasingly internalized as part of the city. However, dispersion of population and function from the old city was not so successful; population density there had in fact increased, reaching 30,400 per square kilometer. The old city was more congested, and the pressure for conservation of historical architecture and urban fabric became more severe, with more debates and conflicting arguments on the issue.

Figure 36.3   Beiji Ge Hill of Nanjing in 2002.

Source: Photo taken in 2002. © Wang Jianguo.

Figure 36.4   Beiji Ge Hill of Nanjing, surrounded by high-rises, in 2011.

Source: Photo taken in 2011. © Wang Jianguo.

If we translate the urban maps of Nanjing at the turning-point years (1940, 1978, 1995, 2003, and 2008) into vector graphs with Arc map software, we can observe, monitor, and analyze the morphological growth of the built areas of Nanjing over its modern history (Figure 36.5).

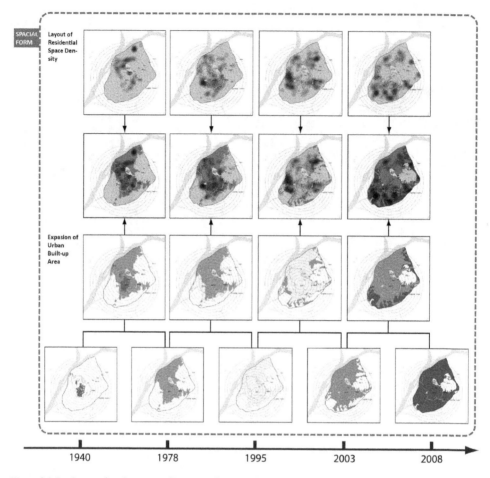

Figure 36.5 An overlapping map of Nanjing showing the expansion of urban built-up areas and the building density of residential spaces.

Source: © Wang Jianguo Research Team.

The case study of Nanjing reveals that the radical expansion of urban territory and increasing formal heterogeneity characterized a solid and objective transformation in China's urban development that was beyond our subjective standing or intention. Although the growth had been plan-guided and was orderly – as much as possible – in Nanjing, the dynamics of economic expansion, the policies of "development is the truth," and the "invisible hand" of the market had been ceaselessly escaping and breaking away from the top-down planning guidance for orderly construction. This led to many notorious problems with Chinese urbanization, such as the imbalance of urban and rural development, issues of villages-inside-city (or urban-villages), the erosion of historical culture and regional tradition, and the various symptoms of urban pathologies, among others.

Urban–Rural Development for New Urbanization: Recommendation

Based on the situation of and problems with China's urbanization today, we propose the following recommendations for optimizing the process of development.

Urban-Rural Coordination with Compact Development

1   *Integrated Development Strategy for City and Country.* First of all, we must adopt a coherent and comprehensive approach for city and countryside as one and on equal footing, for socio-economic planning and problem management. At the same time, we must also consider and manage well the relations between the ecological space, social space, and economic space of cities and their surroundings.[4] We should comprehensively manage land use practice in both city and countryside – to strictly control industrial land use, to reconstruct existing sites and plots, to reshuffle the use and space for many key program areas, and to gradually resolve the splitting urban–rural duality within government policies. At the moment, the "Five Golden Flowers" in the urban–rural coordinated development of the Jinjiang District of Chengdu[5] and the "Seven Villages" for the urban development of Lintong of Xi'an are providing us with useful ideas and experiences.[6]

2   *Moderating Scale, Quantity, and Intensity for a Gradual Development.* We must tailor the design for the specific site or plot. We must resolutely avoid rough and wasteful practices, the provision of land free of charge or with low price, and chaotic competitions – all those that characterized so much the fast urbanization of China in the recent past. The distribution of land use patterns and the scale of these developments must be considered with limits and boundaries; the ideas and practices of "garden city," "greater London plan," and "organic dispersion of functions," as tested before and elsewhere, were based on similar reflections.

3   *Towards a Compact City.* The specific conditions of China suggest that we must adopt a pathway of densification and compact development. Although China has broad territory, land useful for cities and large-scale settlements is in fact quite limited. As early as 30 years ago, scholars suggested that we must "build cities within cities." The model of the compact city is based on the principle of sustainable development, with three basic pieces of advice – densification, mixed use, transport-oriented. This advice is particularly useful for China's new urbanization today; it can prevent new "villages-in-cities" from appearing again.

Utilizing Local Resources for a Consolidated Development

A key piece of advice in today's new urbanization is – for new plots of development – no or minimal destruction of trees, filling of lakes, and demolition of buildings; its spirit is to develop with a wise use of specific local conditions. In fact, using local materials, taking full advantage of local conditions, and sustaining local cultures and expressions are the common principles of all civilizations across times for building a settlement.

In today's new urbanization, we must consider the capacity of the site and respect its specific natural and environmental characteristics. We must study and compile systematically regional wisdom and local building methods of all places where architecture and natural ecology work together in harmony; we should inherit and develop further the holistic thinking found in historical urban and rural settlements where the dynamics of built form, micro climate, material provision, and energy supply were coordinated. In addition, we must especially respect folk customs and traditions and improve rural living conditions with maximum protection of existing form and layout of the villages and the living customs of the villagers; we must develop urban or rural renewal schemes that are flexible and variegated.

Building the Right Institutions for Sustainable Development

To secure rational and orderly urbanization, institutional establishment and institutional functioning are the key. Firstly, we must establish a correct relationship between government and market – we must free the invisible hand of the market but also manage properly the visible hand of the state. Based on the demands of new urbanization, we must fully revise or even newly establish various legal, policy, and development systems, such as those for Household Registration, Land Profit Distribution, Rural Land Transfer, Tendering for Land Development, Medical Service, Housing Provision, and Social Pension, among others. We must gradually eradicate the polarizing and discriminative urban–rural dual system and abolish through reforms of the Household Registration System the terms and institutional differentiations associated with or described as "migrant workers," "external population," and "drifting people." We must implement non-discriminative policies for all nationals of China.

The central government has clearly proposed that "we must thoroughly integrate the ideas and rules of ecological civilization into the whole process of urbanization, and adopt a new urbanization path that is compact, intelligent, green and low-carbon." We therefore need to maintain a priority for ecological development in top-level designs by state systems and institutions, push forward programs for sustainable building and green architecture, and thoroughly implement government standards and procedures for energy saving. We must ensure that any development is based on assessments of environment capacity and fully secure a coherent "Unity of Four Planning" – developmental planning, ecological planning, land use planning, and spatial planning – and aim for multiple wins on several fronts with development.

The essence of new urbanization we are proposing is urban–rural unity in a coordinated approach. For this purpose, it is also urgent today that we provide systematic training to professionals who specialize in rural design and planning. Because production mode, land right, lifestyle, and cultural tradition in rural China are different from that in the city, planning and design for villages and rural communities have their own aims, contents, methods, technology, and ways of presentation – we cannot simply follow those urban models. Although China's National People's Congress has changed its "Urban Planning Law" to "Urban and Rural Planning Law," professional interest in research and implementation in planning remains on the cities; in planning education at universities and colleges, the focus also remains urban – village and rural settlement planning and design are much ignored with no important standing in the curriculum. Because of this, the central government should advise, and university departments and local planning institutes implement, various education programs to train village designers and planners – free of charge if at all possible. In staffing for local government offices, we must also ensure that there are specialized personnel at levels of towns and townships in the making and administrating of planning; an attractive package must also be in place to channel professionals into these positions for rural design and planning. In addition, encouraging and supporting local technicians and craftsmen, and developing local building techniques and methods, are critical as well to ensure sustainable development for rural and urban China as a whole.

Notes

1 The Government Working Report of 2014 has specified that, in the near future, we need to resolve the problems of "three sets of one hundred million people" – to assist one hundred million rural-to-urban migrants to settle down into cities and townships, to improve the living conditions of one hundred million people residing in slums and urban-villages, and to guide one hundred million people to settle and be urbanized in their nearby areas in the hinterland in western and central China.

2 Wang Jianguo, "Cong fansi pingxi dao lujing jueze: 2013 zhongguo dangdai jianzhu sheji fazhan guoji gaoduan luntan zongshu (From reflexive analysis to strategic choice: A review of the advanced international forum of 2013 on contemporary architecture of China)," *Jianzhu Xuebao* 1 (2014): 2.

3 Science and Technology Development Center at Ministry of Housing and Urban-Rural Development of China, ed., *Zhongguo Jianzhu Jieneng Fazhan Baogao: Jiyou Jianzhu Jieneng Gaizao 2014,* (Report on building energy efficiency in China: Energy-saving renovation for old buildings 2014), (Beijing: Zhongguo Jianzhu Gongye Chubanshe, 2014), 4.

4 Zhu Dajian, "Ruhe zouxiang genghao de chengzhenhua (How to move on for a better urbanization)," *Chengshi Zhongguo* 6 (2013): 30–33.

5 The municipal government of Chengdu has built in the urban–rural integrated area of Jinjiang District, for about 12 square kilometers in all, five tourism-cum-agriculture zones, each branded respectively as "Fragrant Farm Houses," "Happy Forest of Plum Blossom," "Vegetable Farms of the Jiang's," "Chrysanthemum Gardens with Eastern Fences," and "Moonlight over Lotus Ponds" – together called "Five Golden Flowers." The project was awarded with National Four Stars for developing landscape and tourism.

6 In the Lintong area of Xi'an, on the northern slopes of Lishan Mountains, attempts were made to fully utilize the resources of hills, valleys, streams, rivers, springs, forests, heritages, and housing dwellings. Following the given ecological conditions, the project has developed village-based tourism and leisure products and has successfully combined into one diverse program for agricultural exhibition, village tourism, leisure holiday, sports, and health and wellness.

Bibliography

Liu Kung, Wang Jianguo, Tang Peng. "The Development of Residential Space in the Old Town of Nanjing Since 1978." *Frontiers of Architectural Research* 1 (2012): 280–286.

Luo Sidong. "Xinxing chengzhenhua daolu weishenme shi zhongguo de biranxuanze: Zhongmei chengshihua lishijincheng de bijiaoyanjiu (Why New Urbanization Is an Inevitable Choice for China: A Comparative Study of Historical Processes of Urbanization in China and the United States)." *Renmin luntan: Xueshu qianyan* 21 (2013), http://theory.people.com.cn/BIG5/n/2013/1231/c40531-23993192-3.html. Accessed 3 July 2014.

Science and Technology Development Center at Ministry of Housing and Urban-Rural Development of China, ed. *Zhongguo Jianzhu Jieneng Fazhan Baogao: Jiyou Jianzhu Jieneng Gaizao 2014* (Report on Building Energy Efficiency in China: Energy-Saving Renovation for Old Buildings 2014). Beijing: Zhongguo Jianzhu Gongye Chubanshe, 2014.

Wang Jianguo. "Xiangcun jianzhu de zaidixing tese jiqi pinzhi tisheng (Rural Architecture: Local Characteristics and Ways of Promoting Its Qualities)." *Jiangsu Jianzhu* 1 (2012): 28–33.

Wang Jianguo, Gu Xiaoping, Gong Kai and Zhang Tong. "Jiangsu jianzhu wenhua tezhi jiqi tisheng celue (Characteristics of Architectural Culture in Jiangsu Province and Our Strategies for Their Promotion)." *Jianzhu Xuebao* 1 (2012): 103–106.

Wu Qi. "Lintong Kaifa: Ruhe pojie rongzi nanti (Lintong Development: How to Crack the Financing Problems)." *Sanlian Shenghuo Zhoukan* 49 (2013), www.lifeweek.com.cn/2013/1210/43525.shtml. Accessed 3 July 2014.

Zhu Dajian. "Ruhe zouxiang genghao de chengzhenhua (How to Move on for a Better Urbanization)." *Chengshi Zhongguo* 6 (2013): 30–33.

Zhu Tiezhen. "Zhongguo chengshihua de lishi Jincheng (The Historical Process of China Urbanization)." *Zhongguo Chengshi Fazhan Wang: Chinacity.org.cn,* 29 March 2010, www.chinacity.org.cn/cstj/zjwz/53974.html. Accessed 3 July 2014.

Glossary

Cheng Zhong Cun	城中村
Chengdu	成都
Jiangsu (province)	江苏（省）
Jinjiang (district)	锦江（区）
Jinling (hotel)	金陵（饭店）
Lintong (area)	临潼（区）
Nanjing	南京
shangshan xiaxiang	上山下乡

Song Chunhua	宋春华
Sun Yat-sen	孙逸仙（孙中山）
Xi'an	西安
Yangtze (river)	扬子江（长江）
zhengzhi guashuai	政治挂帅

Geopolitical Differentiations

37

"CHINESE CULTURAL RENAISSANCE" AND A CHINESE NEOCLASSICISM

Taiwan (1960s–80s)

Chao-ching Fu

The Cultural Revolution began on the Chinese mainland in 1966. It called for the destruction of the "four olds," namely, ideas, cultures, customs, and habits of old times. In response, the Nationalist Government decided to celebrate the 101st anniversary of the birthday of the national father, Sun Yat-sen; President Chiang Kai-shek delivered a speech entitled "The Commemoration Speech of the Dedication of the Chinese Cultural Hall at Zhongshan Lou (Sun Yat-sen Tower)." The participants in the celebration suggested that the national father's birthday should be declared "Chinese Cultural Renaissance Day." This recommendation was recognized by the Nationalist Government. Under the chairmanship of President Chiang Kai-shek, the Chinese Cultural Renaissance Promotion Committee was established in 1967. Branch committees were established throughout Taiwan to mobilize efforts to promote this movement; this was the Nationalist Government's first structured plan for Taiwanese cultural development. The policy for duplicating ancient objects, including buildings, had a great influence on the emergence of Chinese classical-style architecture in Taiwan.[1] Guided by the so-called Policy of Cultural Renaissance Principle, new stadiums, theaters, music halls, and galleries were required to "merge the characteristics of Eastern and Western architecture, and to enhance our architectural style."[2]

Emergence of the Chinese Cultural Renaissance Movement and Zhongshan Lou

With its mixture of Eastern and Western architectural characteristics, Zhongshan Lou in Yangmingshan National Park provides a strong example of following these guidelines. In fact, the beginning of the Chinese Cultural Renaissance Movement coincided with the completion of Zhongshan Lou, demonstrating the combination of architecture and political ideology. The plan to construct the building began in 1965 when the Nationalist Government prepared to commemorate Sun Yat-sen's centennial birthday and revive traditional Chinese culture. Xiu Ze-lan, the most famous female architect at that time, was appointed to design the building.[3]

Zhongshan Lou occupies a site larger than 130,000 square meters. Thirty-four meters high, it is a multifunctional complex with a floor area of over 18,000 square meters. The complex has a grand auditorium, the Zhonghwa Wenhua Tang (Chinese Culture Hall), which can seat

DOI: 10.4324/9781315851112-56

1800 people, a large restaurant, and various small- to medium-sized meeting rooms. To address the difficulty of including so many halls and rooms in the same building under a giant roof, the architect integrated various Chinese classical-style roofs. A *luding* (casket-shaped roof) was used for both the primary and secondary entrances. A double-eaved *yuancuanjian* (circular conical roof) is positioned over the entrance lobby, which is flanked by a *juanpeng* (curved gable roof) structure on both sides. The grand auditorium is crowned by a double-eaved *xieshan* (gable-and-hip roof). However, the inside of the building reveals several awkward manipulations, since the room spaces do not necessarily match their roofs. All of the roof tiles are green, in contrast with the red raffles under the roofs. All doors, windows, furniture, and lighting fixtures are decorated in Chinese classical styles. Certain ornaments are in the style of the Shang dynasty. Although the proportions of the façade cannot be compared with its classical prototype, and its composition is rather eclectic, the rich classical decorations and numerous *dougong* (bracket sets) yield a strong sense of classicism (Figure 37.1).

The building previously served as an exclusive convention site for the National Assembly of the Nationalist Government. It was the eminent location for the head of state to receive distinguished foreign guests or host state banquets. Despite criticism from academics for its inaccurate classical proportions, governmental officials praised the building for its political implications. For example, Sun Yat-sen's grandson Sun Ke declared the building the optimal model of the Chinese Cultural Renaissance Movement. Even though reinforced concrete was used as the building material, its essence and ornaments embodied Chinese culture. Sun Ke's praise was reflected in President Chiang Kai-shek's opening ceremony speech, entitled "The Memorial Remarks for the Chinese Culture Hall at Zhongshan Lou." Chiang praised the building as "a landmark for the reconstruction of national culture in the anti-Communist revival base Taiwan."[4]

Figure 37.1   Exterior of Zhongshan Lou, Yangmingshan, Taipei, 1966. Architect: Xiu Ze-lan.

Source: Photo taken in 2013. © Chao-ching Fu.

National Palace Museum in Taipei

As a country with a long history, China has built several museums since the 1920s. The Central Museum in Nanjing and the Jiangwan Museum in Shanghai, two of the most important examples, were both designed in the Chinese classical style. Taiwan's National Palace Museum houses the largest and finest Chinese art collection in the world. The museum was originally located in the Forbidden City in Beijing before being relocated to Taiwan in 1948, where it was officially inaugurated on October 25 of that year. The museum was intended to preserve the imperial collections and palatial treasures of the Chinese dynasties and allow present and future generations to admire their cultural heritage. During the wartime period of 1931 to 1948, the museum's collections were moved several times from one place to another before finally arriving in Taichung County, Taiwan. To house these national treasures, a new museum project was initiated. The construction of this new museum was intentionally to duplicate the image of the Palace Museum in Beijing. The fact that some of the architectural vocabularies were derived from those in Wumen supports this idea.[5]

In 1965, a new National Palace Museum was built in the Taipei suburb of Waishuanxi, and the "Regulations for the Provisional Board of Directors of the National Palace Museum" were enacted by the Executive Yuan. The new museum was christened "Zhongshan Museum" in honor of the nation's founding father, Dr. Sun Yat-sen, and was first opened to the public on the centenary of his birthday in 1966. The design of the new National Palace Museum highlights the association between Chinese classical-style architecture and the Beaux-Arts tradition. As the architect Huang Bao-yu noted, the museum is "a neo-renaissance Chinese architecture which satisfies the Chinese people in general and foreign tourists in particular."[6] The final design is extremely sophisticated and can be regarded as a great victory of Beaux-Arts practice in Taiwan. The dual-character of Chinese classicism and Beaux-Arts is evident in the design.

While most of building's ornaments are in the Chinese classical style, the spatial design of the site plan and the interior organization of the rooms carefully follow the Beaux-Arts tradition. If we compare the site plan and the perspective drawings of the National Palace Museum with other Beaux-Arts projects, the similarities are easily detected. A *luding* (casket-shaped roof) dominates the central structure of the museum. Continuous pre-cast *dougong* (bracket sets), especially *renzigong* (inverted V sets) and *yidousansheng* (brackets of one cap-block supporting three arms and three small blocks), are the main features on the wall. The museum stands on a hill with a spacious foreground. A six-pillar, five-bay classical-style archway forms a symbolic entrance. An axial road leads from the base of the hill to the archway, and several sets of steps lead to the upper level where the museum sits. The original spatial arrangement of the museum is simple and straightforward (Figure 37.2).

The main square structure is composed of a grand exhibition hall and four surrounding galleries. Four smaller square rooms interlock at the corners of the main square to form additional exhibition halls. The overall space resembles a *mintang*, the grand worship hall in the Qin palace. However, this conformity to the shape of the *mintang* at the expense of adequate circulation and lighting has been criticized by both the public and architectural professionals. Although the Palace Museum in Taipei was designed and constructed before the beginning of the Chinese Cultural Renaissance Movement, it became a strong base for the promotion of the movement. The Nationalist Government used it to support the claim that it was the legitimate government of China, which was based on the notion that it remained the sole preserver of traditional Chinese culture when the Cultural Revolution erupted in mainland China. The National Palace Museum thus served as a major political symbol for the Nationalist Government during the 1960s and 1970s to counter political movements in mainland China. Using the

Figure 37.2   Panoramic view of the National Palace Museum, Taipei, 1966. Architect: Huang Bao-yu.
Source: Photo taken in 2012. © Chao-ching Fu.

museum's collection as a political tool, the Nationalist Government launched the Chinese Cultural Renaissance Movement, promoting the idea that while the Communists sought to change, perhaps destroy, traditional Chinese culture in the name of Communism, Taiwan's Nationalist Government sought to preserve it. The museum became a symbol for Chinese mainlanders that represented the atmosphere of their original homeland.[7]

New Confucius Temples Across Taiwan

In the 1970s, new Confucius temples were built in response to the destruction of such temples in China during the Cultural Revolution. The Confucius temples of Taichung (1975, Taiwan Provincial Public Works Bureau) and Kaohsiung (1976, Chen Bi-tan, Lu Yu-feng) are the most representative examples. There is a prototype for the spatial organization in Confucius temples. *Dacheng men* (the gate of great achievement) is the main entrance to the primary architectural complex. *Dacheng dian* (the hall of great achievement) is the main hall of a Confucius temple. The tablet of Holy sage Confucius is located at the central niche inside the *dacheng dian*; while the tablets of his 12 disciples are worshipped at four separate tables. The *dongfu* (eastern wing) and *xifu* (western wing), containing the worship tablets for notable Confucian scholars, are followed by the rooms for sacrificial implements and musical instruments, respectively. *Chongsheng ci* (the shrine for the sage) is located behind the main hall. A school is typically located beside the temple complex; the school gate is called the *zute chihmen* (the gate to virtue), and *minlun tang* (the hall of edification) is the main hall of the school. Founded during the Ming dynasty, the Tainan Confucius Temple is the best example of a traditional Confucius temple in Taiwan.

The new Confucius temples built to counter the Cultural Revolution in China typically follow traditional paradigms of spatial organization using Chinese classical styles. The Taichung Confucius Temple follows the prototype of the Qufu Confucius Temple in China; its design was supervised by Kung Te-cheng, a high-ranking officer and descendent of Confucius. Designed in the Chinese classical style, it contains all the gates, halls, and other facilities required for a typical Confucius temple. The golden-yellow glazed tiles in various halls are visually powerful in the surrounding area, and the image of the temple differs from traditional Taiwanese Confucius temples. After its construction, the Nationalist Government premier, Chiang Ching-kuo,

Figure 37.3 Front view of *Dacheng dian* of the Taichung Confucius Temple, 1975. Architect: Taiwan Provincial Public Works Bureau.

Source: Photo taken in 2011. © Chao-ching Fu.

praised the Taichung Confucius Temple as a model for new Confucius temples in other cities and counties (Figure 37.3).[8]

The architect's Kaohsiung Confucius Temple originally attempted to surpass the restricted model of the Taichung Confucius Temple by applying a distinct site plan. The two axes are arranged perpendicular to each other, as opposed to the traditional parallel model. The main axis contains the major spaces of a Confucius temple, passing from a half-moon pond to a square to the *chongsheng ci*. The secondary axis begins at the same square of the main axis and passes a *hongmen* (the school entrance) to the courtyard compound of the school, *wenchang tzu* (wenchang worship shrine) and *minlun tang*. Golden-yellow tiles are used on all the buildings along the main axis. The *linghsin men* is a five-bay pailou and the *dacheng men* is a five-bay structure with a *xieshan*-style roof. The *dacheng dian* is crowned with a double-eaved *fudian*-style roof and colonnades surround the hall. The *chongsheng ci* is topped by a single-eaved *fudian*-style roof. Green tiles are used on the buildings along the secondary axis. The *wenchang tzu* is a single-eave *xieshan*-style roof building and the *minlun tang* exhibits the *juanpeng*-style roof. Regarding the structural considerations, the architect did not believe in following a particular system, whether a Qing model or a Sung model; he acknowledged that the slope of the roof resulted from continuous revisions and intuition-based modifications.[9]

Fo Guang Shan in Kaohsiung

Religious facilities, including Buddhist temples, were forced to close in China during the Cultural Revolution. Consequently, promoting and supporting various religions became a policy of the Chinese Cultural Renaissance Movement in Taiwan. The year 1967 simultaneously witnessed the establishment of Fo Guang Shan (Buddha's Light Mountain) and the beginning of the Chinese Renaissance Movement. Founded by Venerable Master Hsing Yun, Fo Guang Shan is an international Chinese Mahayana Buddhist monastic order based in Taiwan. The construction of Fo Guang Shan began in 1967. After nearly half a century of development, Fo Guang Shan is now a Buddhist park with several facilities, including worship halls, schools, exhibition halls, and a cemetery. Most of the buildings were designed in the Chinese classical style. Among them, *Dabei dian* (1971), *Buer men* (1973), *Daxiong baodian* (1981), and *Puxian dian* (1985) are famous for their architectural uniqueness. In 1975, a 36-meter-high statue of Amitabha Buddha, surrounded by hundreds of small statues, was consecrated and became a symbol of Fo Guang Shan.[10]

Buer men (the non-duality gate), the formal gateway along the main axis, was designed in the traditional pailou style. Behind the gate, there are 500 white jade arhat statues. Each sculpture appears lifelike with different features and expressions. *Dabei dian* (the hall of great compassion) was the first important building completed. Construction on the hall began in December 1968 and was completed in 1971. In the hall, there stands a 6-meter-high image of Guanyin (Avalokitesvara Bodhisattva) in white, gazing upon all living beings with love and compassion. The four walls of the *Dabei dian*, which was Fo Guang Shan's first Chinese classical-style building, are replete with many smaller images of Avalokitesvara in the style of the Dunhuang Caves.

Daxiong baodian (the great hero jeweled hall, 1981), the main hall of Fo Guang Shan, was personally designed by the founder, Venerable Master Hsing Yun. The four Chinese characters of *daxiong baodian* are inscribed on a wooden tablet above the entrance. The hall is a 13-bay building, making it the largest Buddhist structure in China and Taiwan at the time it was built. The attempt to surpass the magnificence of the *Taihe dian* (hall of supreme harmony) in the Forbidden City is evident. *Daxiong baodian* has a double-eaved *fudian*-style roof, the highest-ranked roof in Chinese classical architecture. On either side of *Daxiong baodian* are the *dongchan* and *xijin*, one for people gatherings and the other for administration. The roofs of these two adjacent buildings are in the single-eaved *fudian* style. All three buildings are decorated with colorful *dougong* under the eaves. The roof tiles are golden-yellow, similar to those of Chinese palaces.

Daxiong baodian occupies an area of about 3,570 square meters and is 30 meters high. Three 7.8-meter Buddha images with different hand gestures sit in meditation in the decorated shrine, where they are worshipped. In the center is the Sakyamuni Buddha of the saha world; to the left is the Bhaisajaguru Buddha (Medicine Buddha) of the Eastern lapis lazuli world; and to the right is the Amitabha Buddha (Buddha of Infinite Light) from the Western Pure Land of Ultimate Bliss. To the left and right of the images are the largest Buddhist bell and drum in Taiwan. The bell is made of pure beaten copper and weighs 3.8 metric tons. It took two years and two castings to complete. The four interior walls are filled with Dunhuang-style stone niches enshrining 14,800 smaller images of the Sakyamuni Buddha. Since there are no columns in the shrine to obstruct the view, it can accommodate 1,000 people for morning and evening chants or Buddhist religious services. Since Fo Guang Shan played a leading role in Taiwan's Buddhist circles, its new buildings became prototypes for other Buddhist temples. Beginning in 1970, demolishing old buildings and constructing new ones became a common practice for many historical Buddhist temples in Taiwan.

Addition to Grand Hotel in Taipei

The Taipei Grand Hotel was financed by the Nationalist Government and began operating in 1952. The architect Yang Zhuo-cheng was asked to design the hotel in the Chinese classical style. In the 1960s, the hotel became world famous because of its Chinese classicism and hospitality. A need for additional space was identified at the end of the 1960s, and the Taipei Grand Hotel Addition (1971, Homu Architects, Yang Zhuo-cheng) continued to function as a tourist attraction (Figure 37.4).

Figure 37.4   Front view of the Grand Hotel Addition, Taipei, 1971. Architect: Yang Zhou-cheng.
Source: Photo taken in 2013. © Chao-ching Fu.

This construction also raised crucial questions regarding new Chinese classical-style buildings. Can Chinese classical styles be used, and how should they be expressed in high-rise buildings? In the history of Chinese architecture, numerous pagodas provided high-rise images in ancient times. However, the pagoda as a prototype is outdated in modern society. Therefore, architects had to find new solutions to build tall buildings in the Chinese classical style. The Grand Hotel is located on the former site of a Japanese Shinto shrine and has been a Taipei landmark since its completion. Considering cultural and urban identity, some scholars and architects have responded positively to using the Chinese classical style in a high-rise hotel. Others, however, have suggested that implementing the classical style hampers the creativity of designers. Wang Da-hong paradoxically suggested that

> understanding traditional culture is necessary. However, one should not trap oneself in copying. The Grand Hotel is merely a kind of scenery that lacks the simple and solemn characteristics of the Chinese style; however, it is a Chinese-style object that exhibits regional features. Such result is superior to those pirated foreign examples.[11]

Visual effect is a key point of the Chinese classical high-rise building. Aside from pagodas, Chinese classical architecture is mostly comprised of low-rise buildings. Thus, adjusting the visual alignment in a high-rise Chinese classical building is crucial for ensuring that the proportions are correct. Accordingly, the structural system of the roof of the Grand Hotel Addition adopted a method that contradicted the principle of a traditional *xieshan* roof. This demonstrated the contradiction between an authentic Chinese classical structure and a high-rise building decorated with classical Chinese.[12] However, the classical style exterior of the Grand Hotel Addition was welcomed by government officials and the public because of the political atmosphere of that time. Today, the Grand Hotel remains one of Taipei's most famous landmarks and is used for state banquets. It is also a tourist attraction because of the ideal views of the Taipei cityscape from almost every room.

Chiang Kai-shek Cultural Center in Taipei

President Chiang Kai-shek passed away on April 4, 1975. In July of that year, the Nationalist Government established a committee to discuss a possible Chiang Kai-shek memorial and park. Though the project was reminiscent of the Zhongshanling (Sun Yat-sen Mausoleum) in Nanjing in the 1920s, the Chiang Kai-shek Memorial surpassed the scale of its predecessor. After two phases of competition, the committee selected two proposals by Yang Zhuo-cheng. The committee asked the architect to integrate the buildings from his two proposals into a single project. The large memorial was completed in 1980, and the accompanying National Theatre and Concert Hall were finished in 1987. The site was named Chiang Kai-shek Memorial Park and later renamed Chiang Kai-shek Cultural Center. The Nationalist Government considered Chiang Kai-shek a "national liberator," and thus, the construction of his memorial warranted the utmost attention and reverence from the entire nation.

In retrospect, the construction of the Chiang Kai-shek Cultural Center was the penultimate work of public architecture promoted by Taiwan's Chinese Cultural Renaissance Movement. The role of the memorial in this movement is not limited to its physical features. The complex revealed the differing perceptions of the term "modern architecture" among Taiwanese administrators and architects. For most architects, "modern architecture" suggested that designs should not be based on or burdened by the restrictions of Chinese classical decorations or built forms. Examining the other submissions to the design contest reveals that all architects except the winner chose to exclude the features of the Chinese classical style; these architects did not think officials would define modern architecture in terms of a "decorated exterior with a modern interior design." However, the Chinese classical design style revived in twentieth-century national architecture was the ideal form cherished by members of the Nationalist Government.

Yang's design places the memorial at the east end of Chiang Kai-shek Memorial Park, which covers more than 240,000 square meters. The primary axis of the memorial complex runs east to west: the five-bay, blue-tiled pailou archway in the southwest functions as the main entrance. A horizontal tablet placed across the top of the pailou reads *dazhung chihzheng* (great centrality and perfect uprightness), and every part of the pailou is decorated in the Chinese classic style. The *Dachung men* (the gate of great loyalty) stands to the north of the park and the *Daxiao men* (the gate of great piety) stands to the south. After passing through the main entrance and walking several hundred meters to the end of the complex, one arrives at the main memorial building. The building has a square floor plan and is crowned with a double-eaved *pachiao zhanchiendien* (octagonal conical roof). The blue-glazed roof tiles used in this building contrast with the white walls; it sits atop a three-layered platform foundation and rises 76 meters above the ground (Figure 37.5).

The memorial's main entrance features a set of double doors that open into the main hall, each standing 16 meters high and weighing 75 tons. When asked about the design concept of the complex, architect Yang Zhuo-cheng explained that it combined elements of the Lincoln Memorial in Washington, D.C., the Taj Mahal in India, Tiantan in Beijing, and the Sun Yat-sen Mausoleum in Nanjing; this explains the small pond on the primary axis and a pair of memorial columns in front of the main hall in the original designs.[13] The design of the memorial contains strong political symbolism. The blue and white building and the red flowerbeds echo the colors

Figure 37.5 Bird's-eye view of the Chiang Kai-shek Cultural Center, Taipei. Architect: Yang Zhou-cheng.
Source: Photo taken in 2010. © Chao-ching Fu.

of Taiwan's national flag. The octagonal shape represents the number eight, which is tradition-ally associated with abundance and good fortune in Asia. The two sets of white stairs leading to the main entrance have 89 steps, each representing Chiang's age at death. The architect explained that the three layers of the foundation represent *san min chu yi* (the three principles of the people) and the four-sided square and eight-sided roof represent the followers of Chiang Kai-shek from *sumen pafeng* (four directions and eight orientations). As such, political ideology is very clearly embedded in the design of the complex.[14]

A large statue of Chiang Kai-shek dominates the main hall, facing the viewers who enter the hall at the end of the staircase. The center of the main hall ceiling is emblazoned with an elaborate and symbolic caisson that illustrates a *chingtein baizu* (the white sun in the blue sky), which is the insignia emblem of the Nationalist Party. To match the design of the memorial, the National Theatre and Concert Hall required a classical style; however, the functions of pro-fessional theatres and concert halls appeared less critical as compared with their classical shells. The Concert Hall was the final building constructed in the project. It has a three-part *xieshan* roof above the main structure and a *luding* roof portico in front of both the north and south entrances. Instead of applying a *xieshan* roof to the entire National Theatre, this building was crowned with a large *fudian* roof.

Both the National Theatre and the Concert Hall have yellow-golden glazed roof tiles. The forms of the two buildings, including their corresponding colonnades, are almost identical; both buildings feature red columns lined with white balustrades and painted *dougong* under the eaves. The floor plans differ slightly but are quite similar. While these buildings serve as the favored arts-oriented facilities of the Nationalist Government, the construction process forced officials to address concerns regarding classical models applied to new architecture.

Conclusion

From Zhongshan Lou to the Chiang Kai-shek Cultural Center, the Nationalist Government continued to favor colorful glazed-tile roofs and ornaments, regarding the classical revival as the appropriate national style. When government officials requested designs for public projects, such as national martyrs' shrines, Confucius temples, and memorial complexes, the architects awarded contracts consistently utilized orthodox classical styles. In the early 1980s, however, Taiwanese regionalist architecture arose, and its adherents were among the first to challenge the classical Chinese form for recognition as the national architecture of Taiwan. By 1990, much of the Nationalist Party's power was replaced by the Democratic Progressive Party. Although the Nationalist Party lost its power to undertake large-scale construction projects, the projects constructed during its rule were already completed. As of the 1990s, the Chinese classical form only appeared in occasional commercials.

Notes

1 The Cultural Revolution, which began in May 1966 and ended in October 1976, was a political movement led the Communist Party that resulted in severe setback and heavy loss in economy, society, and culture on the Chinese mainland. Customs, values, and ideas from the past, including religious practice and cultural relics, were among the primary targets criticized and attacked.

2 Chao-ching Fu, *Zhongguo Gudian Shiyang Xin Jianzhu: Ershi Shiji Zhongguo Xin Jianzhu Guanzhihua de Lishi Yanjiu* (New architecture in classical Chinese styles: Historical studies in the institutionalization of new Chinese architecture of the twentieth century) (Taipei: Nantian Shuju, 1993), 273–274.

3 Fu, *Zhongguo*, 273–274.

4 Fu, *Zhongguo*, 273–274.

5 Li-fu Wang, Chien-lang Lee, and Chao-lee Kuo. *Taipei Jianzhu* (Architecture in Taipei) (Taipei: Architects' Association of Taipei, 1985), 130.

6 Bao-yu Huang (Boyle Huang), *Jianzhu Zaojing Jihua – Huang Baoyu Lunwenji* (Architecture, landscape and urban planning – selected works of Boyle Huang) (Taipei: Dalu Shudian, 1975), 754.

7 The purpose of preserving and venerating the National Palace Museum and its collection in this way was to help legitimize the Nationalist Government as the sole government of China, by and with an appeal to Chinese conservatism and nationalism in the 1960s and 1970s. However, in recent times, with the rising of opposition party and the waning of the Nationalist Government's influence in Taiwan, and due to the introduction of democracy, the National Palace Museum has changed its focus and has been showing more on the history of indigenous culture and the pieces on loan from museums from abroad.

8 Fu, *Zhongguo*, 276–278.

9 Fu, *Zhongguo*, 276–278.

10 Chao-ching Fu, *A History of Modern Architecture in Taiwan* (Taipei: Architecture Institute of Taiwan, 2013), 206.

11 Da-hong Wang, quoted in Chun-jen Lee, "Fang Wang Da-hong (Interview with Wang Da-hong)." *Chinese Architect*, (January–February 1979): 74.

12 Wang, Lee, and Kuo, *Taipei Jianzhu*, 137.

13 Li-mei Liu, "Fang Yang Zhou-cheng Jianzhushi tan Taipeishi Zhongzheng Jiniantang zhi sheji (Interview with architect Yang Zhou-cheng on the design of Chiang Kai-shek Memorial Hall)." *Chinese Architect*, (August 1976), 5.

14 Fu, *A History*, 201.

Bibliography

Alumni Association of Department of Architecture and Urban Design at Chinese Culture University, ed. *Lu Yujun Jiaoshou Lunwen Ji* (Collection of Works of Professor Lu Yu-chun), vol. 2. Taipei: Alumni Association of Department of Architecture and Urban Design at Chinese Culture University, 1988.

Chang, Chiao-hao. "In Search of Style." *Free China Review* (June 1987): 2–13.

Chao, Chia-chi, ed. *Taiwan Jianzhu* (Architecture in Taiwan). Taichung: Taiwan Sheng Jianzhushi Gonghui, 1995.

Chen, Kai-shao. *Taiwan Jianzhu de Xiandai Yuyan* (A Modern Language of Architecture in Taiwan). Master Thesis, National Cheng Kung University, Tainan, 1933.

Cody, Jeffrey W., Nancy S. Steinhardt and Tony Atkin, eds. *Chinese Architecture and the Beaux-Arts*. Honolulu: University of Hawaii Press, 2011.

Fu, Chao-ching. *Zhongguo Gudian Shiyang Xin Jianzhu: Ershi Shiji Zhongguo Xin Jianzhu Guanzhihua de Lishi Yanjiu* (New Architecture in Classical Chinese Styles: Historical Studies in the Institutionalization of New Chinese Architecture of the Twentieth Century). Taipei: Nantian Shuju, 1993.

———. "The Story of Glazed Tiles atop the Memorials of KMT Heroes." *Dialogue*, (November 2002): 45–51.

———. *Taiwan Jianzhu Modenghua de Gushi* (The Story of Modernization of Architecture in Taiwan). Taipei: Council for Cultural Affairs, 2006.

———. *Taiwan Jianzhu de Shiyang Mailuo* (The Stylistic Context of Architecture in Taiwan). Taipei: Wunan Tushu Chuban Gufeng Youxian Gongsi, 2013.

———. *A History of Modern Architecture in Taiwan*. Taipei: Architecture Institute of Taiwan, 2013.

Huang, Bao-yu (Boyle Huang). *Jianzhu Zaojing Jihua – Huang Baoyu Lunwenji* (Architecture, Landscape and Urban Planning – Selected Works of Boyle Huang). Taipei: Dalu Shudian, 1975.

Lee, Chien-lang. *Taiwan Jianzhu Bainian* (One Hundred Years of Architecture in Taiwan). Taipei: Meizhao Wenhua, 1995.

Lee, Chun-jen. "Fang Wang Da-hong (Interview with Wang Da-hong)." *Chinese Architect*, (January–February 1979): 72–74.

Liu, Li-mei. "Fang Yang Zhou-cheng Jianzhushi tan Taipeishi Zhongzheng Jiniantang zhi sheji (Interview with Architect Yang Zhou-cheng on the Design of Chiang Kai-shek Memorial Hall)." *Chinese Architect* (August 1976): 4–9.

Wang, Da-hong. "Chinese Architecture, Can It Survive?" *Peiyehchuan Journal* 4, no. 1 (1962): 1–2.

Wang, Li-fu, Chien-lang Lee and Chao-lee Kuo. *Taipei Jianzhu* (Architecture in Taipei). Taipei: Architects' Association of Taipei, 1985.

Glossary

Beijing	北京
Buer men	不二门
Chen Bi-tan	陈碧潭
Chiang Ching-kuo	蒋经国
Chiang Kai-shek	蒋介石
chingtein baizu	青天白日
Chongsheng ci	崇圣祠
Dabei dian	大悲殿
Dacheng dian	大成殿
Dacheng men	大成门
Dachung men	大中门
Daxiao men	大孝门
Daxiong baodian	大雄宝殿
dazhung chihzheng	大中至正
dongchan	东禅
Dongfu	东庑
dougong	斗栱
Dunhuang	敦煌
Fo Guang Shan	佛光山
Fudian	庑殿

Guanyin	观音
Hsing Yun	星云
Huang Bao-yu	黄宝瑜
Jiangwan	江湾
juanpeng	捲棚
Kaohsiung	高雄
Kung Te-cheng	孔德成
linghsin men	棂星门
Lu Yu-feng	吕裕丰
luding	盝顶
Ming dynasty	明朝
Minlun tang	明伦堂
Mintang	明堂
Nanjing	南京
pachiao zhanchiendien	八角攒尖顶
pailou	牌楼
Puxian dian	普贤殿
Qin (dynasty)	秦（朝）
Qing (dynasty)	清（朝）
Qufu	曲阜
renzigong	人字栱
san min chu yi	三民主义
Shang dynasty	商朝
Shanghai	上海
sumen pafeng	四面八方
Sun Ke	孙科
Sun Yat-sen	孙中山
Sung (dynasty)	宋（朝）
Taichung	台中
Taihe dian	太和殿
Tainan	台南
Taipei	台北
Tiantan	天坛
Waishuanxi	外双溪
Wang Da-hong	王大闳
wenchang tzu	文昌祠
Wumen	午门
xieshan	歇山
Xifu	西庑
xijin	西净
Xiu Ze-lan	修泽兰
Yang Zhuo-cheng	杨卓成
Yangmingshan	阳明山
yidousansheng	一斗三升
Yuan	院
yuancuanjian	圆攒尖
Zhonghwa Wenhua Tang	中华文化堂

Zhongshan	中山
Zhongshan Lou	中山楼
Zhongshanling	中山陵
zute chihmen	入德之门

38

ARCHITECTS AS REFLEXIVE INDIVIDUALS

Taiwan and Hong Kong Since the 1950s

Ke Song

In the post-World War II decades, Taiwan and Hong Kong had drastically different socio-political backgrounds. As a result, their trajectories of architectural development also differed. Many scholars have done substantial works on the architectural histories of Taiwan and Hong Kong,[1] but few have studied them together. This chapter attempts to do so in order to contribute to a more comprehensive history regarding a larger Chinese region, including mainland China, Taiwan, and Hong Kong, and to reveal the hidden connections in and across this region.

The chapter also proposes to focus on three individual architects, including Wang Da-hong (1917–2018), Chen Chi-kuan (1921–2007), and Rocco Yim (1952–). These three architects have responded to their times critically. Their works constitute a continuous line of quest for the adaptation of Western modernism in a Chinese context, by demonstrating different possibilities to synthesize modernist spatial principles and Chinese cultural and architectural traditions.

Post-War Architectural Development in Taiwan and Hong Kong

Taiwan was under Japanese colonization from 1895 until 1945, when Japan was defeated in World War II. Prior to 1945, only Japanese have the privilege to practice architectural design. In the process of modernization, Japanese architects brought Western architecture to Taiwan. During the colonial period, Taiwanese were only allowed to study architecture in one single university, Waseda University in Tokyo.[2] Among those few of them, we know Chen Jen-ho as a rare case.[3] At the end of the World War II, following the withdrawal of the Japanese, there was an extreme shortage of architects in Taiwan. After being defeated by the Chinese Communist Party (CCP), the KMT government retreated to Taiwan in 1949. Many architects came here from mainland China with the KMT, including Kwan Sung-sing (b. 1892), Lu Yu-jun (b. 1904), Yang Cho-cheng (b.1914), and Wang Da-hong. These architects were mostly educated in the Western countries before World War II. They could be categorized as first-generation architects in Taiwan. Foreign architects also exerted important influence on the development of Taiwan architecture. Many of them were invited by Christian groups in Taiwan, including Justurs Dahinden,[4] Kenzo Tange, Anthony Stoner, Gottfried Böhm, and I. M. Pei.[5] Among them, I. M. Pei played a special role. Because of his Chinese background and significant international influence, he received important commissions from both the KMT government and Christian groups in Taiwan, including Tunghai University (1954–1964) and the Republic of China Pavilion at the

DOI: 10.4324/9781315851112-57

1970 Expo in Osaka. On the Tunghai project, he worked with Chen Chi-kuan and Chang Chao-kang (b. 1922). Chen and Chang both studied in the US and finally came back to Taiwan and Hong Kong after the Tunghai project. In the Expo project, Pei supervised a group of younger generation architects, including Cheng Mei (b. 1930)[6] and C. Y. Lee (b. 1938).[7] Cheng and Lee had a similar trajectory to Chen and Chang, studying in the US and returning to Taiwan after working with Pei.

From the 1980s, Taiwan architecture was deeply affected by the global wave of postmodernism. C. Y. Lee adopted a historicist manner to express Chinese culture and identity in architecture, as represented by the Hung Kuo Building in Taipei (1989). Han Pao-teh (b. 1934),[8] as an educator, was also motivated by the postmodern ethos, and he promoted an architecture culture that could be appreciated by both academics and the general populace.[9] In recent years, architects including Kris Yao (b. 1951), Hsieh Ying-chun (b. 1954),[10] and Huang Sheng-Yuan (b. 1963) distanced themselves from postmodernism by rejecting historicist iconography and populist decoration. Yao used simple forms to create dynamic space. Hsieh and Huang engaged with wider social issues.

As to the development of Hong Kong architecture after World War II, Charlie Q. L. Xue has provided a comprehensive introduction.[11] Around the late 1940s, after the KMT government retreated to Taiwan, the CCP began to take over major cities, including Shanghai, the economic and financial centre of the Far East in the 1930s and 1940s. Many people of the upper class in Shanghai fled to British Hong Kong to escape communism. Many renowned architects of the first generation came to Hong Kong around 1949, including Robert Fan (b. 1893), Luke Him Sau (b. 1904), Eric Cumine (b. 1905), and Sü Gin Djih (b. 1906).[12] These Chinese architects and those Western architects working in the Public Works Department and other companies, such as the P&T, together dominated the architectural design market in post-war Hong Kong. In 1950, the first architectural department of Hong Kong was established in the University of Hong Kong (HKU) under the leadership of Gordon Brown (1912–1962). The first batch of HKU graduates, including Jackson Wong and Andrew King-fun Lee started their own firms in the late 1950s and early 1960s. However, compared to the architects in post-war Taiwan, Hong Kong architects in the 1950s and 1960s, including those from Shanghai, were mostly commercial. They absorbed modernism, especially the International Style, in the context of the fast economic development but lacked a critical reflection on either Chinese culture or local identity. Chang Chao-kang[13] was an exception in this regard. With close connections with Pei, Wang Da-hong, and Chen Chi-kuan, he retained an intellectual and scholarly attention to architecture as a culture. But, probably for the same reason, he didn't build much in Hong Kong.

Since the 1970s, Hong Kong architects, including Chung Wah-nan (b. 1931) and Tao Ho (b. 1936), have been striving for local architectural culture and an identity for Hong Kong. Chung and Ho were both trained in Western universities, the Bartlett School of Architecture at University College London and Harvard University, respectively. They returned to Hong Kong in the 1960s and designed important public buildings, including Peak Tower (1972) by Chung and the Hong Kong Arts Centre (1977) by Ho. The architectural language of their works emphasized geometry and mass composition, showing the influence of "late modernism" as manifest in the works of Louis I. Kahn and I. M. Pei. Rocco Yim was trained locally in Hong Kong in the 1970s, but soon demonstrated a rare design talent in a series of small projects and by winning an international competition in 1983. Compared with the late modernism of Chung and Ho or the postmodernism of C. Y. Lee in Taiwan, Yim's works were lighter in visual appearance, more dynamic in composition, and less decorated in detailing, and therefore closer to the works of Kris Yao. In the 1980s, following the opening up of mainland China, many Hong Kong architects became increasingly engaged in the projects in mainland China, where they faced the same issues about the expression of Chinese culture that mainland and Taiwan colleagues had been grappling with in the past few decades. In recent years, many younger architects of Hong Kong working in the mode of partnerships, such as Oval Partnership, AD+RG, CL3, Gravity, and individual architects like Wei-jen Wang and Gary Chang, began to attain international fame thanks to the rising economy of both mainland China and Hong Kong as well as accelerating globalization.

Among the above-mentioned architects in Taiwan and Hong Kong after the 1950s, I focus on three names, Wang Da-hong, Chen Chi-kuan, and Rocco Yim. Wang Da-hong and Chen Chi-kuan are among the first generation of Taiwan, but Rocco Yim is much younger and still active now. The three architects' life trajectories overlapped, together offering us an overall understanding of the history of Taiwan and Hong Kong architecture from the 1950s to now.

These three stand out against pure commercial architects because they insisted on individual thinking and especially displayed a self-consciousness about their own relations with both political authority and market. Also, as a result, they not only rejected the conventional and old architectural approaches of the time, but also opened up new possibilities of design approaches or attitudes. Therefore, they could be considered as "critical" in two aspects: 1) they were critical thinkers of the political and cultural condition of their times, and 2) they were important nodes in the history of architectural innovation.

We can identify distinctive architectural approaches from the representative works of the three architects. Wang Da-hong designed a series of houses for himself, in which he made reference to traditional Chinese courtyards. At the same time, he also designed the monumental Sun Yat-sen Memorial Hall with a unique roof structure reminiscent of Chinese traditional roofs. Chen Chi-kuan's works concentrated on the campus of Tunghai University, including the iconic Luce Memorial Chapel, and other buildings with introverted courtyards. Similar to Wang, he attempted to restore a Chinese spatial tradition by referencing Chinese courtyards. Rocco Yim's early works concentrated in Hong Kong; the dynamic composition reflected the vitality of this high-density contemporary Asian metropolis. His later works, especially those in mainland China, were exemplary in creating innovative forms by taking inspiration from Chinese cultural symbols. The three architects actually shared commonalities, especially in the intention of synthesizing modernism and Chinese cultural identity, but differed in attitudes and specific architectural approaches. Wang Da-hong and Chen Chi-kuan both have a deep sympathy for Chinese traditional literati, and both attempted to achieve an elitist taste and a high culture in architecture. Rocco Yim had less echo with the tradition, but more interest in the possibilities of interpreting cultural tradition and identity in an innovative and contemporary way. His architecture aimed to have a more inclusive audience, satisfying both connoisseurs and the general public.

Wang Da-hong

Wang Da-hong was born in Beijing in 1917, during World War I. His family came from Dong-guan, Guangdong. His father, Wang Chung-hui, was an important politician in the Republic of China and the first Minister of Foreign Affairs, later Minster of Justice and the judge representing China in the International Court of Justice in The Hague, Netherland. Wang Da-hong in his childhood lived with his father, moving from one place to another in China and Europe. Wang finished primary school in Suzhou and later attended middle school in Nanjing. One year later, he moved to Paris with his father, then attended a boarding school in Switzerland after 1930.[14] He studied architecture at Cambridge University (1936–1939) for his bachelor's. From 1941 to 1942, he studied under Water Gropius at the Graduate School of Design of Harvard, with classmates including I. M. Pei and Philip Johnson. After graduation, from 1945 to 1947, he temporarily worked as a translator for the Chinese embassy in the US. In this period, he designed three works as "paper architecture," which became the prototypes for his own houses later. In 1948, Wang Da-hong returned to Shanghai and formed the practice called Five United with Luke Him Sau, Huang Zuoshen, Chen Zhanxiang, and Zheng Guanxuan. From 1949 to 1952, following KMT's retreat from mainland, Wang Da-hong temporarily stayed in Hong Kong and finally opened his own practice in Taipei after 1952.

Wang's works spanned a wide range, from individual houses to national monuments. Several lines were entangled together throughout Wang's career. The first line comprised the three houses for his own family, including the house on Jianguo South Road (1953), Hong-Lu Apartment (1964), and Hong-Ying Apartment (1979). The three houses shared similarities, all reflecting an intention to synthesize the Chinese cultural and architectural tradition more closely with the spatial principles of modernism. Wang's own house on Jianguo South Road was his first project in Taiwan. It was a simple box enclosed by a rectangular courtyard. According to Shyu Ming-song's research, Wang's plan shared similarities with Mies' 1934 Court House project.[15] But subtle and critical differences were identifiable. The entry of Wang's house did not face south to the front door of the courtyard, but rather faced the west wall. In this way, the front yard could be undisturbed by the footpath towards the entry, and the footpath was prolonged to provide a transitional experience from the outside to the inside. One could not see the entry of the house directly, but needed to turn around before entering the house. This subtle treatment about the entry and footpath actually reflected a conscious intention to pay tribute to Chinese cultural and architectural tradition, which was different from Mies' composition (Figure 38.1).

Figure 38.1 Wang Da-hong's house on Jianguo South Road, Taipei, 1953 (reconstructed in 2014). Architect: Wang Da-hong.

Source: Photo taken in 2018. © Jianfei Zhu.

At the level of architectural detail, Wang's intention to synthesize modernist aesthetics and Chinese traditional forms was more evident. Simple and elegant furniture of modernist aesthetics also conveyed a distinct Chinese sense. The gourd-like pendent sculpture was not only a modern artwork, but also a traditional Chinese symbol of fortune. The moon window became a signature of Wang's own houses and a trope that reoccurred in his later two houses.

The second line was about the expression of monumentality, represented by the competition for the National Palace Museum (1961) and Sun Yat-sen Memorial Hall (1972). In these two projects, he used an innovative structure system to create new monumental images. In the design of the National Palace Museum, he adopted the inverted umbrella roof. This kind of structure represented the advancement of structural technology in the post-war period, but Wang also saw its potential to symbolize Chinese traditional roofs. The same approach was carried out in the design of the Sun Yat-sen Memorial Hall, featuring a distorted Chinese big roof (Figure 38.2). His approach formed a contrast with the prevailing revivalist approach exemplified by the Grand Hotel (1973) and the Chiang Kai-shek Memorial Hall (1980) designed by Yang Cho-cheng.

The third line was paper architecture and architectural fictions. As a lover of literature and poems, Wang was imaginative and internally passionate. He designed the Monument to the Moon Conquest (1969), which was published on *Progressive Architecture*. The monument was intended to be a gift of Taiwan people to the US similar to the Statue of Liberty as a gift of French people, but was abolished due to the deterioration of the diplomatic relationship between the US and Taiwan. From 1966 to 1977, during the design process of the Sun Yat-sen

Figure 38.2 Sun Yat-sen Memorial Hall, Taipei, 1972. Architect: Wang Da-hong.
Source: Photo taken in 2018. © Jianfei Zhu.

Memorial Hall, Wang also translated the novel *The Picture of Dorian Gray* by Oscar Wilde into Chinese as *Du Lian Kui*, in which the setting of the story was changed to Taipei. He was often more productive in the internal spiritual world when there were more setbacks in the real world. The struggle between internal ideals and external reality endured throughout his life. Wang was close to the traditional Chinese intellectual who strove to not only externally serve the nation and society, but also internally achieve heights in the cultural and spiritual realm.

Chen Chi-kuan

Chen Chi-kuan was born in Beijing in 1921 and attended middle schools in Nanjing. He graduated from the Central University in Chongqing in 1944. After graduation, he worked as an English translator for the Chinese expeditionary army in India and Burma, who were fighting against Japan. In 1946, he came back to Nanjing to work as an architectural designer in Kwan, Chu, and Yang Architects, the most well-known architectural firm in China at the time. From 1948 to 1951, he studied at the Graduate School of Design of Harvard under Gropius. After graduation, he worked in Gropius' office and then taught at MIT for years. In 1954, I. M. Pei invited Chen Chi-kuan and Chang Chao-kang to work on the project of Tunghai University founded by the United Board for Christian Colleges in China. Chen began to travel frequently between Taiwan and the US.

From 1954 to 1956, the first phase of the university was supervised by I. M. Pei, Chang Chao-kang, and Chen Chi-kuan. Chang and Chen were believed to assume different roles in the first phase. Chang paid much attention to the tectonic details of the buildings, while Chen's interest concentrated in the overall master plan and the disposition of architectural spaces.[16] The planning of Wenli Boulevard was the central focus in this period (Figure 38.3). The boulevard

Figure 38.3   Wenli Boulevard, Tunghai University, Taichung, 1957.

Source: Photo taken in 2018. © Jianfei Zhu.

pointed to the mountains far away, forming an axis that anchored the whole campus in a vast landscape. The buildings on the two sides of Wenli Boulevard were carefully planned according to the compositional principles of traditional Chinese painting. Much attention was paid to the open space in between buildings, where topography, distance, and atmosphere could be sensed in a way similar to the disposition of the empty space in a Chinese painting.[17]

After 1957, Chang went to the US, and Chen became the major designer for the second phase from 1958 to 1964.[18] The iconic Luce Memorial Chapel was completed in 1963. More importantly, Chen conducted a series of architectural experiments in this period, featuring a consistent use of white walls, including Condon House (1959), the Architectural Department (1961), the Dormitory for Female Staff (1962), and the Art Centre (1963). Compared with the buildings of the first phase, tectonic details were less emphasized, largely due to the absence of Chang in this phase. The white wall became an ideal architectural vocabulary for Chen Chi-kuan, because with the disposition of white walls, he could focus on the poetics of space itself instead of the tectonics. The pervasive use of white walls led to a more radical experiment with the spatial typology of courtyard in this period. Compared with the regular courtyards of the first phase buildings, the types of courtyards of the "white wall" buildings were diverse and innovative (Figure 38.4).

Condon House had an H-shaped floor plan. The perforated walls formed two semi-enclosed courtyards at both the front and the back. The Architectural Department was in a rectangular shape, reminiscent of Mies' Crown Hall at Illinois Institute of Technology. The

Figure 38.4 Female Staff Dormitory, Tunghai University, Taichung, 1962.

Source: Photo taken in 2018. © Jianfei Zhu.

internal space could be flexibly divided according to the actual needs. The Art Centre was a semi-underground courtyard, with an entrance leading downwards to the courtyard at the centre. It didn't conform to the traditional Chinese courtyard, rather reflecting a pragmatic response to the topography. The Architectural Department and the Art Centre featured the inverted umbrella structure as a basic module to organize the floor plans. This approach was probably inspired by the roof structure of Wang Da-hong's competition entry for the National Palace Museum and shared a similar intention to express a sense of Chinese-ness through this modern structural component. In the design of the Dormitory for Female Staff, Chen further suppressed the expression of tectonic details, but focused on the spatial flow, displaying a rhythm of light and shadow, a contrast between openness and enclosure, and a spatial continuity from inside to outside. This building was modest but was highly praised by later architects and scholars, including Zhu Xiaofeng, who commented that the feature and atmosphere of this building reflected Chen's humanistic and artistic care as a traditional intellectual.[19]

Chen was appointed as the Dean of Architecture of Tunghai University in 1960, a position he held until 1965. After 1965, Chen established his own office in Taipei, but completed few works as remarkable as the projects for Tunghai University. Probably, the rising market economy diluted the cultural and intellectual interests as well as socio-political concerns in architecture. In his later life, Chen shifted his interest towards fine art and demonstrated a rare talent in Chinese painting.

Rocco S. K. Yim

Rocco S. K. Yim was raised and educated in Hong Kong. He finished his architectural education at the University of Hong Kong (HKU) in 1976 and opened his office, Rocco Design Associates, in 1979. He was internationally recognized as early as in 1983 by winning the first prize for the L'Opéra de la Bastille international competition. Yim's entry displayed clear geometric relations and a sensibility about the urban context, featuring a curved external area for the public, echoing the shape of the Colone de Juillet at the centre of the roundabout.

Around the 1980s, he completed a series of small hostel projects such as Moon Tung Wan Youth Hostel (1983), Pak Sha O Youth Hostel Extension (1985), and Tai Mo Shan Youth Hostel (1988) (Figure 38.5). Being located in the rural areas of Hong Kong, these projects demonstrated Yim's adept skills to deal with topography, space, formal language, and materials. He used various courtyards to resolve the difficulties of topography and the issues of connectivity between the new extensions and the existing buildings. The vernacular building materials and modernist formal language were combined to create a modern architecture that had traditional sense. His design approach was close to the proposition of "critical regionalism" – the emerging discourse of that time probably influenced Yim.

Since the 1990s, Yim has designed numerous iconic and significant public buildings in Hong Kong, mainland China, and overseas, including Lok Fu Shopping Mall (1991), Citibank Plaza (1992), Graduate Hall, the University of Hong Kong (1998), Hong Kong Station Development (1998, 2004), iSQUARE (2009), Guangdong Museum (2010), HKSAR Government Headquarters (2011), W Hotel in Guangzhou (2013), and Yunnan Museum (2013). By now, he has published several monographs, including *The City in Architecture* (2003), *Being Chinese in Architecture* (2004), *Presence* (2012), and *Reconnecting Cultures* (2013).[20] As a "star architect," he is not just skilful in design practice but also very articulate in theoretical thinking.

Figure 38.5   Pak Sha O Youth Hostel Extension, Hong Kong, 1985. Architect: Rocco Yim.

Source: Permission and courtesy of © Rocco Design Architects Limited.

Among his designs and writings, two lines of architectural innovation could be identified. The first was the continual experiments for an architectural language to reflect the dynamics and excitement of the dense, vertical, and dynamic urban context of Hong Kong. When Yim had just begun his career in Hong Kong, postmodernism was arising as an international trend. He actively absorbed this new theory, but at the same time kept a distance from it. He expressed a discontent about the over-emphasis on culture and past tradition. In particular, he disagreed with the extravagant forms and the literal transposition of traditional elements or symbols from the past, which were common in postmodernist designs.[21] Yim had an alternative understanding about the prevailing postmodernism. He said,

> Architecturally, I embrace this new postmodernism, an authentic position which takes as its point of departure, not preoccupation with nostalgia but an emphasis on constructive engagement with divergent actualities within globalization, informed by the presence of the city and tempered by a renewed urban sensibility.[22]

He deliberately freed architecture from traditional values in order to create an "authentic" and "relevant" architecture for the contemporary cities. Therefore, he pointed to the need to capture an ongoing tradition embodied in the current urban condition. He believed this condition could offer a regional otherness within globalization and provide the necessary energy to reinvigorate architecture.[23]

Despite the generic modernist formal language reminiscent of the Miesian International Style, his architecture was an authentic architecture rooted in his deep understanding of the spatial typologies of Hong Kong. As the densest urban area and one of the most rapidly growing cities in the past few decades, Hong Kong has characteristic urban and architectural forms. The small plots of buildable land and the high land values force buildings upward. The irregular urban fabrics and the loaded programs require complicated plan forms. The sloping topography naturally organizes the city at several levels. Escalators, bridges, and steps knit together to form a three-dimensional interconnected infrastructure that links many parts of the urban fabric. In the design of the high-rise tower as a typical building type for Hong Kong, for example, the Citibank Plaza, Yim fully exploited the potential of this building type. For him, a tower has panoramic views at the top, stacked floors in the middle portion, and, most importantly, the three-dimensional interconnected and permeable public spaces for pedestrians at the lower levels.[24] Yim also paid considerable attention to the circulation and movement of both people and vehicles in all types of construction, no matter the podium of a vertical tower or a horizontal complex. Architecture for him was actually an integrated part of the urban fabric and a city in microcosm.

Despite his contempt for the postmodernist use of traditional symbols, the second line of his architectural innovation was about the architectural expression of Chinese cultural identity and tradition. Since 1983, Rocco Design had been building in mainland China, taking advantage of the opening up and fast development of China's economy. Instead of the physical urban context he had focused on in previous works in Hong Kong, the cultural context became more significant in defining forms of buildings in mainland China. The expression of Chinese-ness became a foremost question confronting him when dealing with government clients in mainland China. His critical attitude towards postmodernism continued to inspire him to adopt a rational and inclusive perspective to rethink the notions of culture and tradition. For him, culture was not just nostalgia for the past, but also a sensibility and consciousness about the contemporary reality. He said,

> Architecture is the embodiment of culture. Culture stems from the past, but it goes beyond just tradition or heritage. Culture actually deals with the present. It is about contemporary living and current attitudes, tempered by the past, towards space, material, the perception of beauty and balance of values.[25]

In design practice, Yim often took inspiration from traditional forms both man-made and natural, by looking at the spatial strategies and formal configuration. But after a rigorous process of formal operation, the final outcome was actually tailored to contemporary use and needs.[26] This approach was marked by the publication of *Being Chinese in Architecture* in 2004 and a series of iconic museums in mainland China.

For example, Guangdong Museum in Guangzhou, facing the Opera House by Zaha Hadid, brought Yim into the international spotlight at the highest level. The box volume was lifted up above a man-made terrain extending into the building. Although it escaped the high-density character of Hong Kong, the repertoire of ramps and bridges still conveyed the same idea of three-dimensional inter-connectivity as in Hong Kong. The facade was carved deeply with a series of L-shaped incisions – this formal manoeuvre gave the building an iconic image and demonstrated a unique expression of Chinese culture. The building was therefore extolled as a "hollowed-out treasure box," and the facade was said to resemble the traditional ivory carving technique in Guangdong province. All of these metaphors and cultural connotations were important for a successful project in mainland China, but we cannot ignore that these incisions also enriched the interface between the inside and the outside, providing spaces for people to actually enjoy natural light, fresh air, and city views. The synthesis of the two different approaches regarding spatial dynamics and cultural symbolism respectively was achieved in Yim's works. In this regard, Yim surpassed Rem Koolhaas' more limited notion of "culture of congestion," which only captured contemporary metropolitan conditions, and dove into the realm of cultural expression.[27] As a result, Yim's architecture was both contemporary and Chinese-specific, rooted in both urban and cultural contexts.

Conclusion

As discussed earlier, the architectural histories of mainland China, Taiwan, and Hong Kong were actually highly comparable, despite the distinct trajectories of each region. If studied together, we may find interesting connections. For example, Wang Da-hong and Chen Chi-kuan were forerunners in synthesizing Chinese spatial conception and modernism not just in Taiwan but also in the entire Chinese region. Their early experiments echoed with the parallel quests in mainland China, for example Mo Bozhi's works in the late 1960s and the 1970s in Guangzhou and Feng Jizhong's work in the 1980s in Shanghai. These architects together demonstrated the compatibility between modernist spatial principles (flowing space and the penetration between inside and outside) and Chinese traditional conception of space (especially the artfully choreographed and labyrinth-like spatial experience manifest in the southern gardens). Despite the limited communication between mainland China and Taiwan, Wang Da-hong and Chen Chi-kuan might be still known by architects in mainland China. The historical connections between these architects deserve further investigation.

The three architects analysed here, Wang Da-hong, Chen Chi-kuan, and Rocco Yim, constitute a continuous history about critical architects and critical architecture. They together presented the best works in the two opposing dimensions respectively regarding space and culture. To put it simply, Wang and Chen put Chinese traditional culture at the centre of their architectural design – architecture was regarded as a symbolic spatial system to achieve a cultural ideal or imagination. But Yim focused on architectural space itself in relation to the reality of contemporary cities, especially the density, topography, and dynamism of Hong Kong. He also actively responded to the cultural discourse regarding Chinese-ness, but considered culture as external reference and connotation added onto architecture.

From Wang Da-hong and Chen Chi-kuan to Rocco Yim, we see a continuous line about the evolution of spatial typology. They developed different spatial typologies as reference systems for different purposes. Wang Da-hong imitated Chinese gardens for the design of his own houses, in both detached house and apartments. Despite being detached from both mainland

China and the immediate urban context of Taiwan, his gardens maintained a spiritual continuity from mainland China to Taiwan and from ancient times to his time. In the case of Chen Chi-kuan, the series of courtyards on the campus of Tunghai University were to nurture young students with a Chinese cultural identity. This purpose was not just conforming to Chen's own will, but was also supported by the Christian group behind the university, who hoped to root Christianity into Chinese culture. This Chinese expression also coincided with the revival movement of Chinese culture advocated by the KMT government. Lastly, Rocco Yim jumped out of the reference to typical architectural typologies of garden and courtyard and began to explore more possibilities to engage with both Chinese tradition and contemporary urban environments. His aim and approach to find an authentic architecture for contemporary China provided a fresh inspiration for today's practice.

Notes

1 Important works include: Charlie Q. L. Xue, *Hong Kong Architecture, 1945–2015: From Colonial to Global* (Singapore: Springer, 2016); Shyu Ming-song, "Cuguang yu Shiyi: Taiwan Zhanhou Diyidai Jianzhu de Duoyuan yu Youxian (Roughness and Poetry: The Diversity and Limitation of the First Generation Architecture in Postwar Taiwan)," *Shidai Jianzhu: Time + Architecture*, no. 5 (2016): 110–119.

2 Ulf Meyer, *Architectural Guide Taiwan* (DOM Publishers, 2012), 11.

3 Chen Jen-ho was born in Taiwan and graduated from Waseda University (1941–1945). He opened his office in 1951 in Kaohsiung and designed high-quality modernist buildings, but his name was not well known even in Taiwan. Xu, "Cuguang Yu Shiyi," 114–116.

4 Justurs Dahinden, born in 1925, was a Swiss architect and scholar.

5 Meyer, *Architectural Guide*, 12.

6 Cheng Mei was born in Shanghai and moved to Taiwan in 1949. He studied architecture at National Cheng Kung University, ETH, and MIT. Cheng established Fei & Cheng Associates in 1974 with his classmate in MIT, Philip T. C. Fei. This firm is now one of the largest architectural firms in Taiwan.

7 C. Y. Lee designed Taipei 101, the world's tallest skyscraper from 2004 to 2010.

8 Han Pao-teh was an important architectural educator, writer, and museum director in Taiwan. He served as Dean of the Faculty of Architecture at Tunghai University from 1967 to 1977, bringing together professors educated overseas and nurturing talented architects. He published numerous books and articles, and edited and founded influential architectural magazines, including *Jianzhu Shuangyue Kan* (Architecture Bi-monthly), *Jianzhu yu Jihua* (Architecture and Planning) and *Jing yu Xiang* (Sphere and Image). Since the late 1960s, his office Han Kwang Architects has won several commissions and has been known for first undertaking historical preservation projects in Taiwan.

9 Shyu Ming-song, "Han Baode de Dacheng Jianzhu yu Nayidai (Han Po-Teh's Mahayana Architecture and That Generation)," *Shidai Jianzhu: Time + Architecture*, no. 2 (2017): 114–123.

10 Hsieh has been helping people rebuild their homes since the devastating earthquake in Taiwan in 1999. Hsieh represented Taiwan in Venice Architecture Biennale 2006 and Venice Biennale of Contemporary Art 2009.

11 Xue, *Hong Kong Architecture*.

12 Wang Haoyu, and Yang Guodong, "1949 Nian hou Yiju Xianggang de Huaren Jianzhushi (Architects from Mainland China to Hong Kong after 1949)," *Shidai Jianzhu: Time + Architecture*, no. 01 (2010): 52–59.

13 Chang graduated from St John's University in Shanghai in 1946 and pursued further education at Illinois Institute of Technology, MIT, and Harvard in the US. He worked in New York in the 1950s until he was invited by Pei to work on the Tunghai project. In the 1960s and 1970s, he worked in both Hong Kong and Taiwan and travelled frequently between the two places. After the opening up of mainland China in 1978, he travelled to various parts of China over 70 times, to investigate Chinese architectural traditions. These works were published in Chao-Kang Chang and Werner Blaser, *China: Tao in Architecture* (Basel; Boston: Birkhäuser Verlag, 1987).

14 Shyu Ming-song, *Jianzhushi Wang Dahong: 1942–1995* (Architect Wang Da-Hong: 1942–1995) (Tongji Daxue Chubanshe, 2015), 34.

15 Shyu, *Jianzhushi*, 73.

16 Shyu Ming-song, "Liangge Shijian Zhier: Zaonian Donghai Daxuexiaoyuan de Wutuobang (Two of the Two 'Events': Utopia of the Early Tunghai University Campus)," *Shidai Jianzhu: Time + Architecture*, no. 3 (2016): 140.

17 Shyu, "Liangge," 15.

18 Zhu Xiaofeng, "Xingzhi de Xinsheng: Chen Qikuan zai Donghai Daxue de Jianzhu Tansuo (Formal Evolution: Chen Qikuan's Architectural Exploration in Tunghai University)," *Jianzhu Xuebao* (Architectural Journal), no. 1 (2015): 74.

19 Zhu, "Xingzhi," 80.

20 Eliza Hope, and Kate Ryan, eds., *The City in Architecture* (Melbourne: Images, 2002); Rocco Design, *Being Chinese in Architecture: Recent Works in China by Rocco Design* (Hong Kong: MCCM Creations, 2004); Jessica Niles DeHoff, and Maki Fumihiko, eds., *Reconnecting Cultures: The Architecture of Rocco Design* (London: Artifice, 2013).

21 Gary Hack, "Introduction," in *The City*, ed. Hope and Ryan, 6.

22 Rocco Yim, "A Contemporary Urban Sensibility," [First Published in 1998] in *The City*, ed. Hope and Ryan, 23.

23 Yim, "A Contemporary," 19.

24 Hack, "Introduction," 8.

25 Rocco Yim, "Introduction," in *Reconnecting Cultures*, ed. DeHoff and Fumihiko, 6.

26 Yim, "Introduction," 6.

27 Kenneth Frampton, "Beneath the Radar: Rocco Yim and the New Chinese Architecture," in *Reconnecting Cultures*, ed. DeHoff and Fumihiko, 10–13.

Bibliography

Chang, Chao-kang and Werner Blaser. *China: Tao in Architecture*. Basel: Birkhäuser Verlag, 1987.

Chung Wah Nan. *Contemporary Architecture in Hong Kong*. Hong Kong: Joint Publishing, 1989.

DeHoff, Jessica Niles and Maki Fumihiko, eds. *Reconnecting Cultures: The Architecture of Rocco Design*. London: Artifice, 2013.

Design, Rocco. *Being Chinese in Architecture: Recent Works in China by Rocco Design*. Hong Kong: MCCM Creations, 2004.

Hope, Eliza and Kate Ryan, eds. *The City in Architecture*. Melbourne: Images, 2002.

Meyer, Ulf. *Architectural Guide Taiwan*. Berlin: DOM Publishers, 2012.

———. *Architectural Guide Hong Kong*. Berlin: DOM Publishers, 2013.

OCAT Shanghai, ed. *Jiuwei de Xiandai: Feng Jizhong/Wang Dahong Jianzhu Wenxianji* (Modernism Revisited: Feng Jizhong/Wang Dahong Archives). Shanghai: Tongji Daxue Chubanshe, 2017.

Shyu Ming-song. *Jianzhushi Wang Dahong: 1942–1995* (Architect Wang Da-Hong: 1942–1995). Shanghai: Tongji Daxue Chubanshe, 2015.

———. "Cuguang yu Shiyi: Taiwan Zhanhou Diyidai Jianzhu de Duoyuan yu Youxian (Roughness and Poetry: The Diversity and Limitation of the First Generation Architecture in Postwar Taiwan)." *Shidai Jianzhu: Time + Architecture*, no. 5 (2016): 110–119.

———. "Han Baode de Dacheng Jianzhu yu Nayidai (Han Po-Teh's Mahayana Architecture and That Generation)." *Shidai Jianzhu: Time + Architecture*, no. 2 (2017): 114–123.

———. "Liangge Shijian Zhier: Zaonian Donghai Daxuexiaoyuan de Wutuobang (Two of the Two 'Events': Utopia of the Early Tunghai University Campus)." *Shidai Jianzhu: Time + Architecture*, no. 3 (2016): 135–143.

Wang Haoyu and Yang Guodong. "1949 Nian hou Yiju Xianggang de Huaren Jianzhushi (Architects from Mainland China to Hong Kong after 1949)." *Shidai Jianzhu: Time + Architecture*, no. 1 (2010): 52–59.

Xue, Charlie Q.L. *Hong Kong Architecture, 1945–2015: From Colonial to Global*. Singapore: Springer, 2016.

Zhu Xiaofeng. "Xingzhi de Xinsheng: Chen Qikuan zai Donghai Daxue de Jianzhu Tansuo (Formal Evolution: Chen Qikuan's Architectural Exploration in Tunghai University)." *Jianzhu Xuebao* (Architectural Journal), no. 1 (2015): 74–81.

Glossary

C. Y. Lee	李祖原
Chang Chao-kang	张肇康
Chen Chi-kuan	陈其宽
Chen Jen-ho	陈仁和
Chen Zhanxiang	陈占祥
Cheng Mei	陈迈
Du Lian Kui	《杜连魁》
Fei & Cheng (Associates)	宗迈(事务所)
Feng Jizhong	冯纪忠
Han Pao-teh	汉宝德
Hsieh Ying-chun	谢英俊
Huang Sheng-yuan	黄声远
Huang Zuoshen	黄作燊
Hung Kuo (Building)	宏国(大楼)
Jianzhu Shuangyue Kan	《建筑双月刊》
Jianzhu yu Jihua	《建筑与计划》
Jing yu Xiang	《境与象》
Kris Yao	姚仁喜
Kwan Sung-sing	关颂声
Kwan, Chu, and Yang (Architects)	基泰(工程司)
Lu Yu-jun	卢毓骏
Luke Him Sau	陆谦受
Mo Bozhi	莫泊治
Rocco S. K. Yim	严迅奇
Sü Gin Djih	徐敬直
Sun Yat-sen	孙逸仙
Tunghai (University)	东海(大学)
Wang Chung-hui	王宠惠
Wang Da-hong	王大闳
Wenli (Boulevard)	文理(大道)
Yang Cho-cheng	杨卓成
Zheng Guanxuan	郑观萱

PART V

THEORIZATION

Culture and Epistemology

39

TEN LAMPS OF ARCHITECTURE IN CHINESE CULTURE

Wang Guixiang

In the two thousand-year-old discourse *De Architectura Libri Decem* (*Ten Books on Architecture*), the ancient Roman architect Vitruvius formulates the oldest known requirements of mankind for architecture. His three best-known principles that integrate arts into technology are the qualities of "*firmitas, utilitas, venustas*" (strength, utility, beauty).[1]

The *Shang Shu* (Book of documents), one of the five Confucian Classics, records a concept of similar content by the legendary Chinese ruler Yu the Great, or Dayu. Dayu says,

> Oh! Think of these things, O Emperor. Virtue is seen in the goodness of the government, and government is tested by its nourishing of the people. There is water, fire, metal, wood, the earth, and grain – these must be duly regulated; there are the rectification of *virtue*, the means for the *conveniences*, and the securing abundant means of *welfare* – these must be attended to in and with *harmony*.[2]

In Dayu's view, to govern the state is to nourish the people, which, in turn, is closely related to various branches of production and industry such as water conservation (water), metal fabrication (fire and metal), palace construction (wood and earth), and farming (grain). All these branches shall follow the three basic principles of *virtue, convenience,* and *welfare* (*zhengde, liyong, housheng*), and build upon the core concept of *harmony* (*he*).

The Warring States philosopher Confucius highly praises the government activities of Dayu, which include building:

> I can find no flaw in the character of Dayu. He used himself coarse food and drink but displayed the utmost filial piety towards the spirits. His ordinary garments were poor, but he displayed the utmost elegance in his sacrificial cap and apron. He lived in a humbled palace but expended all his strength on peoples' welfare. I can find nothing like a flaw in Dayu.[3]

The words of Confucius here essentially follow Dayu's idea of virtue, convenience, and welfare in balanced harmony. What he calls "humbled palace but expended all his strength on peoples' welfare" is his interpretation of Dayu's view on virtue.

DOI: 10.4324/9781315851112-60

Three Principles of Traditional Chinese Architecture

On the basis of the three Vitruvian qualities just mentioned, the nineteenth-century English theorist John Ruskin defines seven moral concepts that should be embodied in all architecture. They are recorded in his seminal work *Seven Lamps of Architecture* – the lamps of sacrifice, truth, power, beauty, life, memory, and obedience.[4]

So, in line with Ruskin, why should we not be able to discover these lamps of wisdom in the several thousand-year-long history of China? Supposing there are such universal practical laws, then, how did the Chinese incorporate their own folk culture and wisdom into their construction of cities, palaces, and gardens? Now, I shall express my thoughts and say a few words to answer the questions posed.

On the Highest Excellence

Ancient Chinese people believed that the proper government of a state lay in nourishing the people. Only the rectification of virtue (*zhengde*) could achieve this goal, which refers to upholding the noble moral as expressed in the following famous line: "What the Great Learning teaches, is to illustrate illustrious virtue; to renovate the people; and to rest in the highest excellence."[5]

What is meant by "the highest excellence" (*zhishan*) is the benevolence of the kind and the high style of the cultivated. For palace construction, this denotes "frugality" (*jiejian*) and for the spatial design of a palace complex, this denotes "balanced harmony" (*zhonghe*).

The Lamp of Frugality (Jiejian)

One should be frugal and not extravagant when building palaces, so as not to waste limited manpower. To advocate thriftiness in palace construction and curtail building activity runs like a leitmotif through the several thousand-year-long history of Chinese thought. For example, the Warring States philosopher Mozi explains:

> The guiding principles for these buildings were these: the house shall be built high enough to avoid the damp and moisture; the walls thick enough to keep out the wind and cold; the roof strong enough to stand snow, frost, rain, and dew; and the walls in the palace high enough to observe the propriety of the sexes. These are sufficient, and any expenditure of money and energy that does not bring additional utility shall not be permitted.[6]

The emperor has always gained reputation by being moral, which, largely if not fully, depended upon his thriftiness, especially regarding construction projects:

> I heard the virtue of the Han is outstanding. Emperor Xiao Wendi set an example and was frugal himself. When he was outside the capital, he saved on labor imposed on his subjects. . . . Xiao Wendi wished to build a platform and estimated that he might need a hundred *jin* (gold or a unit weight of gold). But after assessing the financial situation of the people, he abandoned the plan and did not build it. The heaped-up soil of the earthen foundation has survived to this day in its original form. He also issued an imperial edict not to build a large burial mound for him upon his death. Therefore, at

that time, all under heaven was in great harmony. The common people could make a living, and virtue prevailed amongst their descendants.[7]

In the eyes of Confucians, the supreme virtue of the emperor was to follow the economic thought of the ancient sage-kings. We know about the palace of Tang Yao that "the thatch of his roof was left untrimmed, and the raw timber of his beams was left unplaned,"[8] and about Dayu that "he used himself coarse food and drink" and "lived in a humbled palace but expended all his strength on peoples' welfare." The Western Han Emperor Xiaowen wished to build a summer resort with an open terrace to enjoy the cool, but he abandoned the plan. The estimated costs would have been roughly equal to the property of ten families. The Tang Emperor Taizong built Yuhua Palace where "the Main Hall was tiled, but the other (buildings) were thatched. This was to allow for some relief from the heat (in summer) and to be frugal."[9] Such examples became paradigms of how the emperor should behave and were advocated by Confucian scholars of succeeding generations.

Confucius himself specifically mentions the concept of "frugality." In his discussion of ancient ritual culture, he defines it as the ultimate source of the ceremonial system:

> Lin Fang asked what the first thing was to be attended to in ceremonies. The Master said: "A great question indeed! In festive ceremonies, it is better to be sparing than extravagant. In the ceremonies of mourning, it is better that there be deep sorrow than a minute attention to observances."[10] Thus, we can see that being economical has fundamental significance for traditional Chinese culture.

The Lamp of Harmony (zhonghe)

The three principles of virtue, convenience, and welfare must be in harmony. If so, then all things are in a state of equilibrium and follow the "middle path" (*zhongdao*) without leaning towards either side. This concept reflects the attitude that ancient Chinese adopted towards everything:

> While there are no stirrings of pleasure, anger, sorrow, or joy, the mind may be said to be in the state of equilibrium. When those feelings have been stirred, and they act in their due degree, there ensues what may be called the state of harmony. This equilibrium is the great root from which grow all the human acting in the world, and this harmony is the universal path, which they all should pursue. Let the states of equilibrium and harmony exist in perfection, and a happy order will prevail throughout heaven and earth, and all things will be nourished and flourish.[11]

Without the middle path, everything becomes either unrestrained (*kuang*) or impetuous (*juan*). The arrogant man becomes frivolous. The aloof man stays reserved and does not act. The middle path lies somewhere in between. As the Warring States philosopher Mencius argues:

> A great artificer does not, for the sake of a stupid workman, alter or do away with the marking line. Yi did not, for the sake of a stupid archer, change his rule for drawing the bow. The superior man draws the bow but does not discharge the arrow. The whole thing seems to leap before the learner. Such is his standing exactly in the middle of the right path. Those who are able follow him.[12]

All things should follow this right path. The superior man should position himself in the middle of the right path, and "superior architecture" should follow the right path by way of balanced design.

In ancient Chinese thought, the concept of balanced harmony first appears with respect to music (*yue*) in particular with the modulations of the voice (*yinyue*):

> When music and dance are in balance it may be called the state of complete harmony. Let this state exist in perfection, and a happy order will prevail throughout heaven and earth, and all things will be nourished and flourish. The audience will be affected, their benevolence be inspired, their idleness be punished, and therefore, people will become good-natured and honest in character.[13]

Music is associated with ritual (*li*) which, in this combination, considerably influenced Chinese critical thinking and writing: "Ritual is reverence and refinement, music is balance and harmony."[14]

Music and architecture are fraternized art forms. Music needs harmony, and palace architecture needs balance. If the ruler succeeds in balancing the living space (*dazhong zhiju*),[15] people will enjoy what they should enjoy, things will be put where they should be put, and the state of complete harmony will be achieved. Then, he is considered to be a true superior man. For the common people, to dwell in a well-balanced house, to nourish well-balanced energy (*qi*), and to live a well-balanced life is what constitutes the superior man.

A well-known line by the philosopher Laozi reads: "All things leave behind them the Obscurity out of which they have come; and go forward to embrace the Brightness into which they have emerged, while they are harmonized by the Breath of Vacancy."[16]

A palace inhabited by people is a spatial environment with negative *yin* holding the *yang* (*fuyin baoyang*) that must be flushed with energy to be in harmony:

> Thus, a door shut may be pronounced *kun* (a feminine principle), and the opening of the door *qian* (a male principle). The opening succeeding the being shut may be pronounced a change; and the passing from one of these states to the other may be called the constant course. The appearance of anything is what we call a semblance; when it has received its complete form, we call it a definite thing. The divining-plant having been produced, the sages set it apart and laid down the method of its employment – what we call the laws of divination. The advantage arising from it in external and internal matters, so that the people all use it, stamps it with a character which we call spirit-like.[17]

Through provision of a proper amount of space and a spatial layout with negative *yin* holding the *yang*, houses can achieve the *yin–yang* harmony – if frequently opening and closing the door to increase circulation – and thus, the effect of the balanced living space can unfold in full.

On Rituals and Music

Chinese buildings follow the Confucian system of rites and music. The Western-Jin poet Ruan Ji reflects:

> The covers of a vehicle, banners and flags, palaces, food and drink – these are the utensil necessary for ritual. Bells, drums, lutes, singing and dancing – these are the

tools for music. When ritual exceed the proper amount, the hierarchical order is dis-harmonious. When music is out of tune, the relationship between human and nature is disturbed. Ritual provides order, music calms people's heart. Ritual governs from outside; music educates from inside. Only if ritual and music are properly adjusted, all things under heaven will be in peace.[18]

Palace architecture, hence, is an instrument for the implementation of ritual. Ruan Ji further explains: "To determine the correct order by distinguishing between high and low ranks and high and low grades, this is called rituals."[19]

In the past, residential architecture has been strictly divided into grades and, officially, there was no transgression. This embodies the idea of *dazhuang* (great, correct, and firm, or more broadly "greatness") and highlights the ceremonial aspect of palace architecture. However, Ruan Ji also argues: "To settle down, to experience affection but not sorrow, this is called joy."[20] A suitable and stable dwelling symbolizes the delight and joy that it brings – which fits with the concept of *shixing* (suitable form, or more broadly "properness") in Chinese architecture.

The Lamp of Greatness (dazhuang)

The *dazhuang* hexagram is one of the divinatory symbols (*gua*) in the *Zhou Yi* (Book of changes). It is often discussed in combination with palace architecture when explaining how the ancient sages created things by viewing them (literally, observing images and creating implements):

> In the highest antiquity they made their homes in winter in caves, and in summer dwelt in the open country. In subsequent ages, for these the sages substituted houses, with the ridge-beam above and the projecting roof below, as a provision against wind and rain. The idea of this was taken, probably, from *dazhuang* – the thirty-fourth hexagram.[21]

The *Xiang Zhuan* (Treatise on the symbolism of the hexagrams) in the *Zhou Yi* explains the virtue of this divinatory symbol:

> The trigram representing heaven and above it that for thunder form *dazhuang*. . . . The hexagram is the symbol of strength that serves to put things in motion. . . . Thunder and lightning rolling above in the sky and making all things shake and move are emblems of great power. *Qian* is represented by heaven and indicates strength. Thunder belongs to heaven, so it is the symbol of "strength that serves to put things in motion," and hence it expresses "*dazhuang*." . . . The superior man, in accordance with this, does not take a step which is not according to propriety.[22]

The *dazhuang* hexagram embraces the ancient ritual system that finds expression in hierarchical order. This hierarchy was almost omnipresent with examples embracing every aspect of Chinese life. In architecture, for example, the number of bays in memorial shrines and temples formed the mark of distinction:

> In the ancient times, the temple of the Son of Heaven was seven bays wide, that of princes five bays, that of high officials three bays, and that of low officials two bays. The common people offered sacrifices in their homes.[23]

Likewise, the height of the hall podium formed the mark: "The hall podium of the Son of Heaven was nine *chi* tall, that of princes seven *chi*, that of high officials five *chi*, and that of low officials three *chi*."[24]

Also, the decorative pattern of clothes and hats formed the mark:

> In ritual, ornament formed the mark of distinction. The Son of Heaven wore his upper robe with the dragons figured on it, princes, the lower robe with the axes embroidered on it, Great officers, their lower robe with the symbol of distinction, and other officers, the dark-colored upper robe, and the lower one red. The cap of the Son of Heaven had twelve pendants of jade beads set on strings hanging-down of red and green silk, that of princes, nine, that of Great officers of the highest grade, seven, and if they were of the lowest grade, five; and that of other officers, three.[25]

Last but not least, the use of colors for the columns in a palace formed the mark:

> In autumn, the columns of Huan Palace were painted red. According to ritual laws, red is the color for the Son of Heaven, that for princes is black and white, that for officials is grey, and that for common people is yellow. The red columns are a violation of ritual laws.[26]

From this passage, we can know that there was a hierarchical system for palace architecture. The imperial palace was considered most important and ranked highest. It was the residence of the emperor and built for the supreme ruler in feudal society. As it was the residence of the Son of Heaven, it had to fulfill certain requirements: "How is a capital city? Large. How is a military camp? Crowded. The residence of the Son of Heaven must be large and filled with people."[27]

Only if the imperial palace in the capital was strongly fortified and marvelously decorated was it able to demonstrate the Mandate of Heaven and the power bestowed upon its son – which was the fundamental idea of the statesman Xiao He and also the reason for the analogy between *dazhuang* hexagram and palace.

In other words, the imperial palace reflects the respect and awe for the emperor. Government buildings (*yashu*) reflect the power and authority of local officials. Monasteries and temples reflect the veneration and worship for a Buddhist or Daoist deity. Main halls (*zhengting*) in the houses of the common people reflect the obedience and respect for the older generation. These phenomena are likewise rooted in the meaning of *dazhuang*. They provide a key to the understanding of traditional Chinese architectural culture – even if their underlying concept of strict class division may appear outdated to us in the light of the changed conditions in our modern society.

The Lamp of Properness (shixing)

How is it that we associate architecture with music? Music lies in properness (*shi*), or to put it differently, in the appropriate arrangement of tones and their harmonic concordance. Properness and harmony are hereby the defining qualities, as Confucius once put it: "I could follow what my heart desired, without transgressing what was right."[28]

Music is what the heart desires, but properness is what holds us back and lets us avoid extremes. The Daoist philosopher Zhuangzi pointedly addresses the problem of "properness":

> A shoe fits when you forget about your foot; a belt fits when you forget about your waist; the mind fits when you forget about right and wrong; opportunity fits when

there is no internal transformation or external imitation. One who begins with what fits and never experiences what doesn't fit has the fitness that forgets about what fits.[29]

People of the Warring States period also raise the issue with regard to space and elaborate the need for an appropriate scale in architecture:

> Once Duke Ai of the state of Lu was about to have a huge palace building erected. Gong Xuanzi remonstrated with him, "if the palace is too huge and you share it with many other people, it will become very noisy; and if you stay with few people, it simply makes you melancholy. We wish you build a palace building of the right size." . . . Then Duke Ai of Lu ordered the construction work to stop and remove structural planks and dismissed the workers.[30]

The encyclopedic compendium *Lüshi Chunqiu* (Spring and autumn annals of Master Lü) connects the idea of appropriate scale in palace architecture with the traditional *yin–yang* theory:

> If the house is large, there is an excess of *yin*; if the tower is high, there is an excess of *yang*. Excess of *yin* causes lameness; excess of *yang* causes paralysis. These are the harmful results of not restraining the *yin* and *yang*. This was why the early kings did not reside in large houses nor build lofty platforms. . . . They made palaces and pavilions sufficient to protect themselves from dampness and heat, but no more.[31]

In the Western Han dynasty, the Confucian scholar Dong Zhongshu summed up the basic idea behind it, calling it *shizhong* (moderation): "High platforms result in excessive *yang*, huge houses result in excessive *yin*. This destroys the harmony of the world. Thus, the sage would not act in this way. He would prefer moderation."[32]

Evidently, a building should not be too tall and the interior space not too large in order to maintain the harmony between the *yin* and *yang*. In a grand palace, the buildings of the outer-court are often over-pronounced, and the open space of the outer-court is over-sized in comparison to the whole complex. A good example is the Ming-Qing Forbidden City in Beijing, where the open space of the three great front halls accounts for two-thirds of the total depth of the entire complex, but the living space in the rear only for about one-third. The three rear ceremonial halls are also large and massive structures. However, 12 small-sized courtyard clusters surround them. They are similar in scale to those of the common people, because this is the place where the daily life of the emperor and his imperial concubines took place.

Even the main hall for administration of daily affairs of the Qing emperor – the Hall for Mental Cultivation (Yangxindian) – is located in the western rear corner of the Forbidden City. The scale of the building and courtyard is not much different from ordinary Beijing courtyard houses (*siheyuan*). Only the important ceremonies on the occasions of enthronement or inauguration of the first day of each year (*gushuo*) were held at the Hall of Supreme Harmony (Taihedian) to demonstrate the *dazhuang* of imperial architecture. The daily life of the emperor lacked such a space momentum and ceremonial extravagance. Ordinary palace architecture was scaled down to a suitable form much closer to normal living space.

On Beauty

Ancient Chinese people also thought that one of the essential factors of building was "beauty" (*mei*). The *Lunyu* (The analects), quoting Zigong, says:

> Let me use the comparison of a house and its encompassing wall. My wall only reaches to the shoulders. One may peep over it and see whatever is valuable in the apartments. The wall of my Master is several fathoms high. If one does not find the door and enter by it, he cannot see the ancestral temple with its beauties, nor all the officers in their rich array. But I may assume that they are few who find the door.[33]

It is the expression of "ancestral temple with its beauties" that denotes the beauty of the building. The text then mentions three stages of house building:

> The Master said of Jing, a scion of the ducal family of Wei, that he knew the economy of a family well. When he began to have means, he said: "Ha! Here is a *collection*!" When they were a little increased, he said: "Ha! This is *complete*!" When he had become rich, he said: "Ha! This is *beautiful*!"[34]

Although this is about vernacular rather than imperial architecture, we can discern three aesthetic concepts that correspond to different levels of wealth on an ascending order: *he* (collected), *wan* (completed), and *mei* (beautiful). It is noteworthy that Confucius placed most emphasis on "beauty" as the supreme requirement. Beauty in architecture, therefore, was considered a luxury based on worldly possessions; but even if so, it was a goal pursued by the people of ancient China.

The Lamp of Simplicity (zhipu)

Beauty possesses the different qualities of *wen* (culture) and *zhi* (substance). The Master said:

> Where substance is in excess of culture, we have crudeness; where culture is in excess of substance, we have the manners of a court scholar. When the culture and substance are equally blended, we then have the man of virtue.[35]

Both qualities are essential. Neither elaborate culture nor material substance can be omitted. But substance is more important: "Do people know that if something is beautiful in the outward appearance, color and sound, it must have inner beauty that derives from its substance."[36] Confucius points to the imbalance between *wen* and *zhi* that has become accentuated over time:

> The men of former times in the matters of ceremonies and music were rustics, it is said, while the men of these latter times, in ceremonies and music, are accomplished gentlemen. If I have occasion to choose, I follow the men of former times.[37]

The Neo-Confucian scholar of the Song dynasty Zhu Xi explains this well. Quoting Master Cheng, he says:

> The men of former times handled ornamentation and substance in matters of ceremonies and music properly, but at the time of Confucius, this was commonly

referred to as simple and artless and these men as rustics. The men of latter times overemphasized ornamentation in ceremonies and music at the expense of substance, but at that time this was commonly referred to as sophisticated and polished and these men as accomplished gentlemen. At the end of the Zhou dynasty, ornamentation had become predominant which is why the people back then called it in that way – without knowing that elaborate ornamentation had taken the upper hand.[38]

The proper handling of the two qualities of beauty brings us back to the essentials. Then, beauty lies in simplicity, and such kind of beauty can be described as "simple and plain" (*zhipu*). The superior man is balanced in outward grace and solid worth (*wenzhi binbin*), and he will dislike ornaments if there is one too many. Confucius praises the people of the past for their self-refinement (*wen* and *zhi* in balance) but admonishes the people of his time for their focus on ornamentation.

The *Huainanzi* (Collected essays of prince Lu An, lord of Huainan) describes how and why "substance" creates true beauty that does not depend on external things:

> Xi Shi and Yang Wen are bestowed with a pretty countenance, white teeth, and nice figures and therefore appear beautiful to other without making up or wearing any fragrant ornaments; Mo Mu and Pi Sui were born with ugly cheek, askew mouth, chicken breast, and crookback and therefore do not look beautiful even after being beatified with make ups.[39]

The same is true for architecture. Building material, structure, space, and the shapes and proportions of the building are the essential qualities of architectural beauty. But the ornamentation that adorns the outside is a superfluous thing added afterward rather than a decisive factor for true beauty.

Therefore, beauty with focus on substance results in an architectural beauty without superfluous decoration, a "simple and plain" beauty as described by Zhu Xi, who emphasizes Confucius' view on simplicity:

> The Master said: "To be resolute and firm, simple and slow in speech is to approach true goodness." Master Cheng said: "*Mu* (simple) is to be simple; *ne* (slow in speech) is to be slow in speech. These four are characteristics that approach true goodness."[40]

Having said all this, then, it is quite understandable that Confucian scholars of succeeding generations became more inclined to simple beauty. Many intellectuals enjoyed a subdued lifestyle and simple and natural living space. The Eastern Jin scholar Tao Yuanming described this in one of his poems: "ten acres of land and house, a thatched cottage of eight or nine rooms, elms and willows shading my back court, peach and plum trees extending my front hall."[41] And the Tang poet Bai Juyi (courtesy name Letian) recalls approvingly, "a house with the size of ten *mu*, a garden of five *mu* with a pond and thousands of bamboos."[42]

Simplicity and plainness are particularly important factors in architecture that represent traditional Chinese aesthetics. For example, the grey walls of Beijing courtyards and the quiet elegance of their roofs, the whitewashed walls and black roof tiles of dwellings of the Jiangnan region (the southeast, around the Yangtze River delta) – there are no words to describe their simple and plain beauty.

The Lamp of Ingenuity (qili)

The term *qili* (enchanting, beautiful, with intricacy or elaboration) often describes the enchanting atmosphere and beautiful scenery where the platform of a multi-storied building is embellished with a balustrade, such as in the following two passages: "a secluded house, a private room – a balustrade around the spacious platform, a balcony suspended from the building high up in the sky. The lofty pavilion and the stone platform are interwoven and complement each other."[43] And,

> inside the building, small rooms in a confined space – outside the building, a surrounding corridor spacious and generous. The height of the floor rises by three steps, walking through the building one passes through seven doors. This is an archive known as Dongguan, a vast collection of documents.[44]

What the two passages refer to is architectural space. Chinese people like to view open space from a certain position to achieve a twisted, winding, scattered, or drifting effect. The individual buildings within this landscape setting are likewise enchanting and, moreover, ingeniously constructed, as evidenced in this description:

> What skillful craftsmanship! The delicate latticework gives the observer an open and spacious impression of the room. Amidst the clouds and mist, the building is slender and tall. Spiritual beings rise and suddenly appear on the horizon. Timbers are densely piled up in successive layers. Columns rest on top of columns atop beams. Brackets are placed in-between to support and stabilize the structure.[45]

Here we learn about the remarkable beauty of a high-platform building. And it is exactly in this passage that the two terms – skillful (*gongqiao*) and delicate (*qishu*) – are put together. They then become associated with each other and combined into a compound (*qiqiao*) that denotes "ingeniously built, ingenuity." A good example to demonstrate this are bracket sets (*dougong*), which have always attracted attention through their skillful mounting and magnificent carving. The beauty of their shape and construction is repeatedly recorded in historical literature:

> A thousand posts, a hundred brackets, they overlap and mutually support each other. Short columns atop beams covered with embroidery, jade-cladded rafter heads – they compete with each other in their reflections . . . so exquisitely and ingeniously constructed that without wind, the wooden structure makes no sound; so perfectly glazed that without wiping the tiles are clean without dust.[46]

Or, in another description:

> Curved beams stretching across buildings, strong and big like *dazhuang*. The local forest officers are called upon to contribute logs, and large numbers of carpenters are recruited. Thousands of cap blocks enchantingly uphold the upturning eaves floating in the air; hundreds of brackets form the structural frames shaped like rainbows.[47]

The bracket sets with interlocking timbers, the crossbeams atop that look like rainbows floating in the air, and the upturning flying roof eaves – they all evoke the elegant beauty that locks the spectator into a reverie. However, innumerable steps need to be taken to achieve this effect, and historical texts often touch upon requirements for craftsmanship, for example: "that which is artistically made is called craftsmanship."[48]

But the main purpose of craftsmanship lies in practical use: "Even the most skilled artist meticulous in his work cannot create something more beautiful than this. Its enchantment lies in its use, and the grace of its mechanical design never ends."[49]

What is described here are artifacts that are stunning in technical construction and physical appearance, and this includes palace architecture. The workflow and production process must show a certain degree of order regardless of how skillfully built or visually appealing such art and architecture is – not least because wisdom lies in organized things. Or, to put it differently, how shall we discuss artfulness when things are messy and disorderly? Mencius explains this: "Commencing to achieve harmony is the work of wisdom. Terminating it is the work of sage-ness. For wisdom, we may liken it to skill, and for sage-ness, we may liken it to strength."[50]

Therefore, simple but ingeniously built are two characteristics of Chinese traditional architecture that are seemingly in contradiction. In practice, they represent two sides of the same coin that are equally important. A building can be plain like a cold moon reflected in water or dazzling like flowers in full bloom. It can be a rough hut on an earthen podium with a crooked threshold leading into a secluded room – the grace of a modest and self-disciplined gentleman. Or, it can be a striking palace on a tall stone platform with beautiful roofs and ingeniously built halls and pavilions – the pride and glory of a nation. Chinese traditional architectural beauty can be found in both cases.

On Taste

The aesthetic taste of a nation or a society is not only a construct of the past but also a product of one's time. But this taste has many facets, and between noble and vulgar aesthetic taste are often worlds apart. The ancient Chinese advocated elegant refinement (*ruya*) and carefree unrestraint (*fanglang*) – an apparent contradiction that created the unique artistic taste of China.

The Lamp of Refinement (ruya)

Refinement in Chinese art – the elegant style of a learned and refined scholar – is somewhat close to "noble" and "solemn" art in the West. The Xiao-Liang recluse He Yin observes:

> With the manners and morals of the time declining, dispute and deception commonly occur changing the atmosphere of a place, and indeed, everything has changed. Since people nowadays are devoid of noble spirit and neither refined not well-educated, no one can forecast the future direction that the society will take.[51]

Such refinement mainly stems from knowledge and accumulated experience. In ancient China, a refined scholar was described as follows (here, exemplified by Xie Yiwu):

> He was versed in all the four subjects taught by Confucius and had all the nine virtues of a sage. He was benevolent to the people of his time and possessed the wisdom of the universe. At a young age, he had become learned and refined in the six arts. He was able to practice astrology, to collate classical canons, to explore the mysteries of the universe, to observe the law inside the changes of the world, and to predict the future through the study of celestial phenomena. He was in harmony with the virtue of heaven. Therefore, on the basis of all these, he was thus of great help to the emperor.[52]

This slightly differs from the ancient Roman approach in Vitruvius' *Ten Books on Architecture*, which also emphasizes manual skills and practical knowledge – "the architect's expertise is enhanced by many disciplines and various sorts of specialized knowledge . . . [but] born both of practice and of reasoning" – but achieves the same result.[53]

The refined Chinese style was first promoted by men of letters and refined scholars (*wenren yashi*) and thus became known as the "way of gentlemen." Confucius praises Yan Hui, one of his disciples, for his plain, simple, and noble sentiments typical of this style:

> Admirable indeed was the virtue of Hui! With a single bamboo dish of rice, a single gourd dish of drink, and living in his mean narrow lane, while others could not have endured the distress, he did not allow his joy to be affected by it. Admirable indeed was the virtue of Hui![54]

In comparison with the expression *qinghua* (fresh and natural), the meaning of refined becomes even more obvious. A learned and refined person is of noble and elegant character. A fresh and natural person is beautiful and pure. The two exist side by side and complement each other. The Northern Wei emperor once praised the Great Officer Gao Lu: "He was refined in manner, dressed in plain clothes, and possessed a fresh and not artificial spirit, and thus, was respected as an outstanding man of the state in his old age."[55]

In other words, only if noble and refined is it a man of good taste; and only if pure and indifferent to fame or gain will his personality truly shine. The same applies to landscapes and dwellings. The living environment praised by Chinese intellectuals also embodies the two concepts of noble and elegantly refined but also fresh and resplendent. The following passage describes such a scene:

> A garden in the front, a cultivated field in the back, I live in my house as if it was located in a mountain valley. A zither on my left, a book on my right, not bound by society I am in high spirits. Sima Xiangru declined the emperor's invitation, but he was able to compose a text like *Fengchan*. Upon resignation, Tao Yuanming lived in seclusion in Pengze, but he left us the excellent work *Guilai* (returning). Nothing is more delightful than being a carefree refined scholar![56]

The sentiment of residing in the mountains, the pleasure of playing with zither, chess, calligraphy, and painting, the atmosphere of a relaxed view of the mist and clouds in the twilight: this is life refined and gentle at its extreme – and a mood noble and pure at its best.

Refined is also understood as *qingzheng* (clear and upright), for example, in the following passage about Wang Xie, Northern Wei Minister of the Masses (*situ*) of Pengcheng: "Although living alone, he never lost his spirits. He wholeheartedly admired those who were refined and treated them with respect. He was honest, simple and frugal, and free of corruption."[57]

Finally, refined can be paired with the term *qingsu* (clear and honest), for example, in the following description about a Southern dynasty's official: "The secretary's given name was Mi, his courtesy name was Sixuan, another name was Mu. He became famous in his early age for his refinement, purity of character and literary skills."[58]

In essence, *qingsu* as well as *qingzheng* and *qinghua* build upon the idea of *qing* (clear). In the Chinese context, "clear" and "noble" are similar in meaning, which is why in succeeding dynasties, exemplary people were described as *qinggao* (morally lofty). The term as well as other expressions like refined, honest, tranquil, noble, thrifty, simple, and straightforward then became synonyms in art and architecture. By way of analogy, it was used as a specialized term to describe a particular building style and nature setting.

The Lamp of Unrestraint (fanglang)

The people of the past described spring as follows: "In the first period of spring, the peach blossom begin to bloom, the trees sprout vigorously – free and open (*fanglang*) – thanks to the *yang* energy."[59] The image of plants in full bloom is an analogy for this season, when everything is full of vigor and vitality. The myriad things grow and thrive. This denotes the concept of unrestraint.

The Eastern Jin calligrapher Wang Xizhi takes the term *fanglang* out of context and uses it to describe artistic taste:

> others identify themselves with what they like and abandon themselves to unrestrained joy. Though people may differ in their choices or temperaments, they invariably find temporary contentment, when they come upon something that delights them. They are so happy that they even forget they will be old soon.[60]

Freed from material and physical constraints, untrammeled and joyful – this probably denotes the kind of pleasure that is intrinsically good and stimulates artistic spontaneity. Chinese intellectuals of succeeding generations pursued this pleasure and enjoyed the wilderness of mountains and rivers, and the private garden scenery with a pond.

In the Qin dynasty, Xiao Shi "roamed unbound through the landscape."[61]

The Song-dynasty poet An Changqi says: "resigned over a certain matter and never took up his career as an official anymore. With an attendant, he wandered around Guangdong and soaked up the landscape."[62]

The Tang Buddhist monk Yaoshan, "with unbridled ambition, rambled freely around the landscape to meet future disciples."[63]

In the Song dynasty, Abbot Fayin of Juehai'an temple "lived with unrestrained freedom and self-assurance in his later years; and called himself the Undisciplined Man of Wusong."[64]

The Eastern Jin scholar Xie Lingyun resigned office and found refuge in the mountains where he compiled his masterpiece, *Shanju Fu* (A Rhapsody on Mountain Dwelling). One passage reads as follows:

> My thatched hut lies amidst the rocky forest; water is guarding the stone steps. When I open the window, I see mountains, stretching my head I see distant peaks and below a stream clear as a mirror. Halfway between the ridges, there is another building that allows my gaze to wander all around, not too far away, I can turn around to see the window of my own hut *xiguang*. Descending along the ridge, the path is densely covered by bamboo, from the north all the way to the south, this place is known as bamboo grove.[65]

The Ming official Jiang Xiao is described as "brilliantly talented, he was a kind and chivalrous man. Dismissed from office in his early years, he enjoyed his life building rockeries and ponds in his garden. Always delighted, he forgot everything around him, finding it hard to leave."[66]

The Eastern Jin recluse Tao Yuanming recalls home in his poems, *Guiyuan Tianju* (Return to my garden and fields):

> The tame bird longs for his old forest, the fish in the house-pond thinks of his ancient pool. I will break the soul at the edge of the Southern moor. I will guard simplicity

and return to my fields and garden. My land and house, a little more than ten acres. In the thatched cottage, only eight or nine rooms. Elms and willows shade the back verandah, peach and plum trees in rows before the hall.[67]

His garden and fields, his thatched cottage, and his trees – these are the places that he yearns for. His unrestrained lifestyle was praised and celebrated in succeeding generations.

The Tang poet Du Fu has a line that reveals his admiration for Tao Yuanming's leisurely and carefree life: "Xie Lingyun led his life in carefree leisure, while Tao Yuanming enjoyed his easeful pleasure."[68]

The Song poet Su Shi remembers:

I do not regret that I spent ten years to look after this garden of five *mu*. The once sparse orange and paulownia trees have flourished. The clear pond reaches the foot of Tiger Hill, strange stones like turtles in the lake. Whoever knocks on the door is a welcome guest – rich or poor – enjoy yourself playing flute and drinking wine. I am an unrestrained man, living in the southwest of the country. My cottage still exists, but no one takes care of my small garden.[69]

The owner of the garden here creates his own living space with orange and paulownia trees, a pool with rockery, and a shabby cottage (*bilu*). His garden – about five-*mu* large – provides the perfect setting for his unrestrained lifestyle and longing for the wilderness of nature. It is the ideal place to stroll around but also to find some rest.

On Space

Chinese people paid full regard to Confucian rites and emphasized "squareness" (*fangzheng*) and "orthogonality" (*duanzhi*) in palace and house construction. These ideas stand in sharp contrast to the spatial design of twists and turns that was likewise popular. This thus forms another apparent contradiction in the history of Chinese traditional architecture, although – in practice – the regular and irregular design concepts complement each other. They constitute the last two lamps of architecture in Chinese theory.

The Lamp of Squareness (fangzheng)

Chinese have always paid special attention to the "square" concept. The *Book of Changes* describes the second line of the *kun* hexagram: "The second line, divided, shows the attribute of being straight, square, and great. Its operation, without repeated efforts, will be in every respect advantageous."[70] The commentary explains: "A dwelling is centered correctly if it responds to the character of the land."[71]

The two expressions "straight, square, great" and "centered correctly" illustrate not only how the people of the past understood the *kun* hexagram but also how the spatial idea of "squareness" gradually took shape in ancient Chinese thought. City planning, for example, has always built upon the square. The most-known passage in the *Zhouli Kaogong Ji* (Craftsmen's records of the Zhou rituals) reads:

When artisans designed a capital, they made the city nine-*li* long and three gates on each side of the city walls; in the city, nine roads from north to south and nine roads from west to east, and each road was as wide as nine wagons abreast; the ancestral shrine was in the left while the altars to the gods of soils and grain on the right; audience chambers were in the front while the market was at back; the market and the audience chambers comprised an area of one hundred-step square.[72]

The Western-Han scholar Chao Cuo further articulates this: "When artisans designed a city, they built the walls, set up neighborhoods and divided them into house units."[73] The design described here includes three kinds of "square" spaces: first, cities (*chengyi*) that were laid out in a square; second, neighborhoods known as wards or blocks (*lifang*) with each neighborhood block being one *li* square in area and square or rectangular in shape; third, individual houses with each neighborhood block being divided into several rectangular, local house units (*fangzhai*).

The "square" design concept relies upon the ideas of *zheng* (rectified, right, or correct in positioning) and *zhi* (upright, straight, a straight line). The Tang compilation *Yiwen Leiju* (Collection of Literature Arranged by Categories) records Dong Zhongshu's thoughts on palace design: "If the land is high, it is filled with *yang*; if the house is wide, it is filled with *yin*. Therefore, houses should have a suitable form and be placed *correctly* (*zheng*)."[74]

Here especially noteworthy are the expressions "suitable form" and "placed correctly," which demonstrate the need for properness and rectification. This perception of space became typical for Chinese traditional architecture and, moreover, drew attention in neighboring regions. Bak Jiwon a famous Korean scholar of the Joseon dynasty, analyzes the differences in spatial design between the two countries:

> Chinese houses must have an area of several hundred paces (*bu*) equal in length and width. The ground of the building site is cleaned and planed; then the compass is used to determine the directions. Next is the construction of the platform. . . . The main gates to enter and exit are located in the central bays; the front and back doors must be aligned with each other. In case of three buildings, there are six doors, and in case of four buildings, there are eight doors. With all doors opened, one can see from the door of the innermost room to the outermost gate – as straight as an arrow. This is what is called "my heart is as straight as the open doors", which is a metaphor for being fair (*zheng*) and honest (*zhi*).[75]

What Bak Jiwon refers to are the houses of ordinary people, but the same spatial design principles are ingrained in various other Chinese building types ranging from palaces and government buildings to religious architecture such as monasteries, temples, shrines, and altars. That is to say, the typical Chinese layout is square and follows the cardinal directions. It is highly symbolic and ideological. It is the visual expression of a certain divinatory constellation – the *kun* hexagram – that denotes "straight, square, and great," and in the figurative sense, being fair, honest, at ease, and confident. It thus embodies the concept of rectification of the people's virtue that is recorded in the *Zhou Yi*.

The Lamp of Irregularity (yuqu)

Chinese never took the art of designing lightly and never, for example, simply drew lines on a drawing board with a foot-long wooden strip (*chidu*). Even if the people of the past strived for square and orthogonal design, they alternatively took a contradictory approach with twists and turns (*yuqu*). Therefore, the regular city plan based on a grid coexists side by side with an organic layout, as the philosopher Guanzi observes:

> Always situate the capital and urban centers either at the foot of a great mountain or above the bank of a broad river. To ensure sufficient water, avoid placing them so high as to approach the drought level. To conserve on the need for canals and embankments, avoid placing them so low as to approach the flood level. Take advantage of the resources of Heaven and adapt yourself to the strategic features of the Earth. Hence city and suburban walls need not rigidly accord with the compass and square, nor roads with the level and marking line.[76]

What is called "not accord with the compass and square . . . nor . . . the level and marking line" contrasts the typical square and orthogonal plan. In building practice, city planners were often confronted with special topographic conditions that led to adaptations, as we are told in the *Shishuo Xinyu* (A new account of the tales of the world) in case of the Southern dynasties' city of Jiankang.[77] The Eastern Jin prime minister Wang Dao explains that the city plan cannot be as direct and straight as in the north because Jiangnan (southeast China or Yangtze River Delta area) is crisscrossed by many rivers and lakes and the land is narrow and insufficient. Rather, it should take twists and turns and adapt to local conditions. Looking at late-imperial cities in Jiangnan, we can indeed see free forms with irregular and winding streets when the city layout harmonizes with nearby mountains.

Irregularity and versatility are also common artistic techniques in palace and garden design. The people of the Qing dynasty perceived the Western Park of the Forbidden City in Beijing as a garden-like palace complex because of its winding paths and variegated scenic areas:

> In the courtyard, water is collected in a pool with connecting corridors on the sides. Behind the building grows slender bamboo, and to the west lies the Chun'ouzhai (a hut or house). Turning west from Dechangmen (a doorway), there is a gate facing east, passing through it and heading southward along the winding mountain path, one arrives at the Chun'ouzhai.[78]

Today, the Chinese art of making gardens can still be seen at the imperial park ensembles of the Qing dynasty, for example the Yiheyuan and the Chengde Summer Resort. In the south, the private gardens in Jiangnan artfully imitate organic natural forms, and this borrowed scenery (*qiaomiao yinjie*) meshes perfectly together with real landscape. Not surprisingly, the specialized language of classical garden art is devoid of terms like "squareness" and "orthogonality" but full of expressions for natural elegance. However, it is difficult to identify a single pattern for the making of traditional Chinese gardens. The diversity and variety in design can be summarized under the term "irregularity," which is exactly what is meant by this lamp.

Conclusion

Past Chinese scholars often discussed traditional city planning, architecture, and garden art. Their thoughts built upon the three basic principles of virtue, convenience, and welfare in balanced harmony. In the spirit of John Ruskin's *Seven Lamps of Architecture*, we can re-arrange their ideas under five thematic topics and identify ten lamps of architectural wisdom in Chinese theory:

The first theme – on moral values – includes the Lamp of Frugality and the Lamp of Harmony.

The second theme – concerning rituals and music – comprises the Lamp of Greatness and the Lamp of Properness.

The third theme – on beauty and aesthetics – is manifested in the Lamp of Simplicity and the Lamp of Ingenuity.

The fourth theme – for scholarly taste and the way of gentlemen – includes the Lamp of Refinement and the Lamp of Unrestraint.

The fifth theme – on spatial design for convenience and social welfare – manifests itself in the Lamp of Squareness and the Lamp of Irregularity.

Notes

1 Ingrid D. Rowland and Thomas Noble Howe, eds. and trans., *Vitruvius: Ten Books on Architecture* (Cambridge: Cambridge University Press, 1999).

2 *Shang Shu* (Book of documents), *Yu Shu* 3: 6. English translation follows James Legge, *The Shoo King or the Book of Historical Documents, Vol. 3.1 of The Chinese Classics* (Taipei: SMC Publishing, 1992), 55–56. Here and thereafter, the phonetic transcriptions of Chinese names in Legge's translations have been changed to *pinyin*.

3 Confucius, *Lunyu* (The analects) 8:21. Legge, "The Confucian Analects," in *Hanying Si Shu* (The Chinese English four books), ed. Liu Zhongde and Luo Zhiye (Changsha: Hunan Chubanshe, 1992), 133.

4 John Ruskin, *Seven Lamps of Architecture*, ed. Liu Rongyue, trans. Zhang Lin (Jinan: Shandong Huabao Chubanshe, 2006).

5 *Liji* (Record of rites) 42:1. Legge, *Hanying Si Shu*, 3.

6 Mo Di, *Mozi* (Works of Mozi), *juan* 1, 6:1. Ian Johnston, ed. and trans., *The Mozi: A Complete Translation* (New York: Columbia University Press, 2010), 39.

7 Ban Gu, *Han Shu* (Book of the Former Han), *juan* 75, Sui Liang Xia Hou Jing Ji Li Zhuan 45, Ji Feng Zhuan.

8 Hang Fei, *Hanfeizi* (Works of master Han Fei) 49: 3. Theodore de Bary and Irene Bloom, eds., *Sources of Chinese Tradition, Vol. 1: From Earliest Times to 1600* (New York: Columbia University Press, 1999), 199.

9 Wang Pu, *Tang Huiyao* (Important Documents of the Tang), *juan* 30, Yuhuagong.

10 Confucius, *Lunyu* 3: 4. Legge, *Hanying Si Shu*, 79.

11 *Liji* 31: 1. Legge, *Hanying Si Shu*, 25–27.

12 Mencius, *Mengzi* (Works of Mengzi) 13:41. Legge, *Hanying Si Shu*, 531–533.

13 Zhu Zaiyu, *Lülü Jingyi* (A clear explanation of that which concerns the equal temperament), outer chapters, 9: 8.

14 Xun Kuang, *Xunzi* (Works of Xunzi) 1: 12.

15 For further information see Yan Kejun, "Quan Houhan Wen (Complete prose of the Later Han)," *juan* 89, Zhong Changtong 3, in *Quan Shanggu Sandai Qin Han Sanguo Liuchao Wen* (Complete prose from high antiquity, the Thee Dynasties, Qin, Han, Three Kingdoms, and Six Dynasties).

16 Laozi, *Daode Jing* (The classic of the dao and of virtue), 42. The English translation basically follows Legge but some architectural terms are modified: James Legge, *Tao Te Ching or The Tao and Its Characteristics by Lao-Tse* (Rockville: Arc Manor, 2008), 66.

17 *Zhou Yi* (Book of changes), *Xici shang* 11. Translation follows Legge but some architectural terms are modified: James Legge, *The Yi King (The I Ching)*, (New York: Dover, 1993), 372.

18 Ji Yun (Ji Xiaolan) and Lu Xixiong, eds, *Qinding Siku Quanshu* (Complete library of the four treasuries), Jibu, Zongjilei, Han Wei Liuchao Sanbaijia Ji, *juan* 34, Wei Ruan Jiji Tici, Lun, Lelun.

19 Ji and Lu, eds, *Qingding, juan* 34, Wei Ruan Jiji Tici, Lun, Lelun.

20 Ji and Lu, eds, *Qingding, juan* 34, Wei Ruan Jiji Tici, Lun, Lelun.

21 *Zhou Yi*, Xici xia 2. Legge, *The I Ching*, 385.

22 *Zhou Yi, Yijing* 34:1. See also: Wang Bi and Kong Yingda, ed. & annotated, *Zhou Yi Zhengyi* (Rectified connotation of the Zhou Yi), *juan* 4, Xiajing, Xian Zhuan. The translation of the main text follows Legge, *The I Ching*, 309.

23 Ji and Lu, eds, *Qinding Siku Quanshu*, Jibu, Zongjilei, (Yuan) Su Tianjue Bian, *juan* 35, Yuanwen Lei, Yuji, Luoshizu Puxu.

24 *Yili Zhushu* (Ceremonies and rites with commentaries), annot. by Zheng Xuan and Jia Gongyan, *juan* 15, Yan Li 6, sub-commentary. Chi is a unit of length used in ancient China and in East Asia, although its actual length varied over time and place. In Han-dynasty China (206 BC – 220 AD), 1 chi = 23.09 cm. See https://zh.wikipedia.org/wiki/ and https://en.wikipedia.org/wiki/Chi_(unit). Accessed 4 April 2018.

25 Zheng Xuan and Kong Yingda, eds & annotated, *Liji Zhengyi* (Rectified connotation of the Liji), *juan* 23, Liqi 10. Legge, "*Liji*," in *Sacred Books of the East, Vol. 27* (Oxford: Clarendon Press, 1885), 400.

26 Gu Liangchi, *Chunqiu Guliang Zhuan* (Guliang commentary on the *Spring and Autumns Annals*), Zhuang Gong, 23rd year of Duke Zhuang: 3.

27 He Xiu and Xu Can, ed. & annotated, *Chunqiu Gongyang Zhuang Zhushu* (Gongyang commentary on the *Spring and Autumns Annals*), Huan Gong, 9th year of Duke Huan: 1.

28 Confucius, *Lunyu* 2: 4. Legge, *Hanying Si Shu*, 71.

29 Zhuang Zhou, *Zhuangzi* (Works of Zhuangzi), outer chapters, 19: 13. Victor Mair, ed. and trans., *Wandering on the Way, Early Taoist Tales and Parables of Chuang Tzu* (New York: Bantam Books, 1994), 184.

30 Liu An, *Huainanzi*, 18: 32. Zhai Jiangyue and Mou Aiping, trans., *The Huainanzi: A Guide to the Theory and Practice of Government in Early Han* (Guilin: Guangxi Normal Press, 2010), 1384–1385.

31 Lü Buwei, *Lüshi Chunqiu* (The annals of Lü Buwei), *juan* 1, 3: 3. English translation modified after John Knoblock and Jeffrey K. Riegel, trans., *The Annals of Lu Buwei* (Stanford: Stanford University Press, 2000), 69.

32 Dong Zhongshu, *Chunqiu Fanlu* (Abundant dew of Spring and Autumn Annals) 77: 1.

33 Confucius, *Lunyu* 19: 23. Legge, *Hanying Si Shu*, 251.

34 Confucius, *Lunyu* 13: 8. Legge, *Hanying Si Shu*, 179.

35 Confucius, *Lunyu* 6: 18. Legge, *Hanying Si Shu*, 111. Modification in the English translation is made to render the discussion more consistent.

36 Dai De, *Dadai Liji Buzhi* (The book of rites of the elder Dai) 69: 26.

37 Confucius, *Lunyu* 11: 1. Legge, *Hanying Si Shu*, 155.

38 Zhu Xi, *Sishu Zhangju Jizhu* (Collected commentaries on the Confucian four books), Lunyu Jizhu 11: 1.

39 Liu An, *Huainanzi* 19: 6. Zhai Jiangyue et al., *Huainanzi*, 1413.

40 Zhu Xi, Sishu Zhangju Jizhu, Lunyu Jizhu 13: 27. Daniel Gardner, ed., Learning to be A Sage: Selections from the Conversations of Master Chu Topically Arranged (Berkeley: University of California Press, 1993), 75.

41 Lu Qinli, *Xianqin Han Wei Jin Nanbeichao Shi* (Poetry of the former Qin, Han, Wei, and the Northern and Southern dynasties), Jin Shi *juan* 17, Tao Yuanming, "Guiyuan Tianju Shi Wu Shou (Five poems on returning to dwell in the country)" (Beijing: Zhonghua Shuju, 1983), 989.

42 Cao Yindeng et al, *Quan Tang Shi* (A complete collection of Tang poetry), *juan* 461, Bai Juyi, Chishangpian.

43 Yan Kejun, *Quan Shanggu Sandai Qin Han Sanguo Liuchao Wen*, *juan* 45, Cui Qi, Qi Juan.

44 Yan, *Quan*, *juan* 50, Li You, Dongguan Ming.

45 Yan, *Quan*, *juan* 52, Zhang Heng 1, Xijing Fu.

46 Yan Kejun, "Quan Liang Wen (Complete prose of the Liang)," *juan* 52, Wang Sengru 2, Zhongsi Bei, in *Quan Shanggu Sandai Qin Han Sanguo Liuchao Wen*.

47 Guo Maoqian, *Lefu Shiji* (Music bureau collection), *juan* 15, Yanshe Geci 3, Gongtiaoqu Wu Shou.

48 Zheng and Jia, *Yili Zhushu*, *juan* 15, Yanli 6, sub-commentary.

49 Yan Kejun, "Quan Jin Wen (Complete Prose of the Jin)," *juan* 81, Yin Ju, Jingyudeng Fu, in *Quan Shanggu Sandai Qin Han Sanguo Liuchao Wen*.

50 Mencius, *Mengzi* 10:1. Legge, *Hanying Si Shu*, 453.

51 Yao Silian, comp., *Liang Shu* (Book of the Liang), *juan* 51, Liezhuan 45, Chushi Zhuan, He Yin.

52 Fan Ye, comp., *Houhan Shu* (Book of the later Han), *juan* 82.1, Fanshu Liezhuan 72.1.

53 Rowland and Howe, *Vitruvius*, 21.

54 Confucius, *Lunyu* 6: 11. Legge, *Hanying Si Shu*, 109.

55 Wei Shou, comp., *Wei Shu* (Book of Wei), *juan* 54, Liezhuan 42, Gaolu Zhuan.

56 Wei Wei, et. al., comp., *Sui Shu* (Book of Sui), *juan* 76, Liezhuan 41, Wenxue, Wang Zhen Zhuan.

57 Sima Guang, *Zizhi tongjian* (Comprehensive mirror for aid in government), *juan* 143, Qiji 9, Dong Shihou 2.

58 Tao Hongjing, *Zhengao* (Declarations of the Perfected), *juan* 20, Jizhenjian 2.

59 Zhang Zongfa, *Sannong Ji* (Records of the three departments of agriculture), Zhongchun.

60 Zhang Yanyuan, *Fashu Yaolu* (Critical survey of calligraphy), *juan* 10, Youjun Shuji. See also Luo Jingguo, ed. and trans., *Guwen Guanzhi Jingxuan* (A selection of classical Chinese essays from *Guwen Guanzhi*) (Beijing: Waiyu Jiaoxue yu Yanjiu Chubanshe, 2005), 16.

61 Zhao Daoyi, *Lishi Zhenxian Tidao Tongjian* (Comprehensive mirror of perfected immortals and those who embodied the dao through the ages), *juan* 3, Xiao Shi.

62 Zhao, *Lishi*, *juan* 49, An Changqi.

63 Shi Decheng, *Chuanzi Heshang Bodiao Ge* (Songs of rowing a boat by the buddhist monk Chuanzi). Lingyin Shan Qing Xu.

64 Pu Ji, *Wu Deng Huiyuan* (Compendium of five lamps), *juan* 18, Linji Zong, Nanyue 2 Shisan Shi 2, Yun Juyou Chanshi Fasi, Juehai Fayin Anzhu.

65 Yan Kejun, "Quan Song Wen (Complete prose of the Song)," *juan* 31, Xie Lingyun 2, *Shanju Fu*, in *Quan Shanggu Sandai Qin Han Sanguo Liuchao Wen*.

66 Chen Tian, *Mingshi Jishi* (Chronicle of Ming poetry), Yiqian, *juan* 8, Jiang Xiao, Poem 1.

67 Ji and Lu, *Qinding Siku Quanshu*, Jibu, Biejilei, Han-Wudai, (Jin) Tao Yuanming, Tao Yuanming Ji, *juan* 2, Guiyuan Tianju Si Wu Shou, Poem 1. See also: Acker, "Five Poems on Returning to Dwell in the Country," in: *Classical Chinese Literature*, 499.

68 Cao Yindeng et al., *Quan Tang Shi* (A complete collection of Tang poetry), *juan* 218, Du Fu, Shijuge. See also: Wu Juntao, trans., *Du Fu Shi Yingyi Yibaiwushi Shou* (Tu Fu: One hundred and fifty poems) (Xi'an: Shaanxi Renmin Chubanshe, 1985), 152.

69 Su Shi, *Su Shi Ji* (Collected works of Su Shi), *juan* 18, Poem 118, "Jiti Meixuan Yiyuanting." Mu is a unit of area used in ancient China; in the Song dynasty (960–1279), 1 mu = 573 sq meters; see https://sizes.com/units/mu.htm (Accessed 4 May 2018).

70 Legge, *The I Ching*, 60.

71 Wang and Kong, *Zhou Yi Zhengyi*, *juan* 1, Shangjing, Qian Zhuan.

72 *Zhouli Kaogong Ji* (Craftsmen' records of the Zhou rituals), in *Zhouli*, Dongguan Kaogong Ji. See also: Feng Jiren, *Architecture and Metaphor: Song Culture in the* Yingzao Fashi *Building Manual* (Honolulu: University of Hawaii Press, 2012), 31.

73 Ban, *Han Shu*, *juan* 49, Yuan Ang and Chao Cuo Zhuan.

74 Ouyang Xun, *Yiwen Leiju* (Collection of literature arranged by categories), *juan* 61, Juchubu 1, Zongzai Juchu.

75 Bak Jiwon, "Yeolha-ilgi (Dairy on the travel to Jehol), 58," in *Mingchao yu Chaoxian Wangchao Difang Chengshi ji Jianzhu Guizhi Bijiao Yanjiu* (A Comparative Study of Local Urban Planning and Architecture Regulations Between the Ming and Joseon Dynasties), ed. Baek Sohun (PhD Thesis, Tsinghua University, Beijing, 2013), 88.

76 Guangzi, *Guanzi* (Writings of Guanzi) 5: 1. See also: W. Allyn Rickett, trans., *Guanzi* (Princeton: Princeton University Press, 1998), 116.

77 For further information see Liu Yiqing, *Shishuo Xinyu* (A new account of the tales of the world), Yuyan 2.

78 E'Ertai et al., *Guochao Gongshi* (A history of the dynastic palace), *juan* 15, Gongdian 5, Xiyuan Zhong.

Bibliography

Baek Sohun. *Mingchao yu Chaoxian Wangchao Difang Chengshi ji Jianzhu Guizhi Bijiao Yanjiu* (A Comparative Study of Local Urban Planning and Architecture Regulations Between the Ming and Joseon Dynasties). PhD Thesis. Tsinghua University, Beijing, 2013.

Bak Jiwon. *Yeolha-ilgi* (Dairy on the Travel to Jehol), vol. 4. Seoul: Munyewon, 2012.

Ban Gu, comp. *Han Shu* (Book of the Former Han). Annotated by Yan Shigu. Beijing: Zhonghua Shuju, 1962.

Cao Yindeng et al. *Quan Tang Shi* (A Complete Collection of Tang Poetry). Beijing: Zhonghua Shuju, 1960.

Chen Tian. *Mingshi Jishi* (Chronicle of Ming Poetry). Shanghai: Shanghai Guji Chubanshe, 1993.

Confucius. *Lunyu* (The Analects), Si Shu Wu Jing ed. Beijing: Yanshan Chubanshe, 2011.

Dai De. *Dadai Liji Buzhi* (Book of Rites of the Elder Dai). Compiled by Kong Guangsen. Beijing: Zhonghua Shuju, 2013.

De Bary, Theodore and Irene Bloom, eds. *Sources of Chinese Tradition, vol. 1: From Earliest Times to 1600.* New York: Columbia University Press, 1999.

Dong Zhongshu. *Chunqiu Fanlu* (Abundant Dew of Spring and Autumn Annals). Zhengzhou: Zhongzhou Guji Chubanshe, 2010.

E' Ertai et al. *Guochao Gongshi* (A History of the Dynastic Palace). Beijing: Beijing Guji Chubanshe, 1994.

Fan Ye, comp. *Houhan Shu* (Book of the Later Han). Hangzhou: Zhejiang Guji Chubanshe, 2000.

Feng Jiren. *Architecture and Metaphor: Song Culture in the "Yingzao Fashi" Building Manual.* Honolulu: University of Hawaii Press, 2012.

Gardner, Daniel, ed. *Learning to Be a Sage: Selections from the Conversations of Master Chu Topically Arranged.* Berkeley: University of California Press, 1993.

Gu Liangchi. *Chunqiu Guliang Zhuan* (Guliang Commentary on the Spring and Autumns Annals). Shenyang: Liaoning Chubanshe, 2000.

Guangzi. *Guanzi* (Writings of Guanzi). Beijing: Zhonghua Shuju, 2009.

Guo Maoqian. *Lefu Shiji* (Music Bureau Collection). Beijing: Zhonghua Shuju, 1979.

Han Fei. *Hanfeizi* (Works of Master Han Fei). Beijing: Zhonghua Shuju, 2013.

He Xiu and Xu Can, eds. and annotated. *Chunqiu Gongyang Zhuang Zhushu* (Gongyang Commentary on the Spring and Autumns Annals). Shanghai: Shanghai Guji Chubanshe, 1990.

Ivanhoe, Philip J. and Bryan W. Van Norden, eds. *Readings in Classical Chinese Philosophy.* New York: Seven Bridges Press, 2001.

Ji Yun (Ji Xiaolan) and Lu Xixiong, eds. *Qinding Siku Quanshu* (Complete Library of the Four Treasuries), Tsinghua Digital (Wenyuange) ed. Shanghai: Shanghai Renmin Chubanshe, 1999.

Johnston, Ian, ed. and trans. *The Mozi: A Complete Translation.* New York: Columbia University Press, 2010.

Knoblock, John and Jeffrey K. Riegel, trans. *The Annals of Lu Buwei.* Stanford: Stanford University Press, 2000.

Laozi. *Daode Jing* (The Classic of the Do and of Virtue). Hangzhou: Zhejiang Guji Chubanshe, 2001.

Legge, James, trans. *The Shoo King or the Book of Historical Documents, vol. 3.1 of the Chinese Classics.* Taipei: SMC Publishing, 1992.

———. "The Great Learning," "The Confucian Analects," "The Works of Mencius." In *Hanying Si Shu* (The Chinese English Four Books), edited by Liu Zhongde and Luo Zhiye, 2–23, 65–556. Changsha: Hunan Chubanshe, 1992.

———. *The Yi King.* Rpt. *The I Ching.* New York: Dover, 1993.

———. *Tao Te Ching or the Tao and Its Characteristics by Lao-Tse.* Rockville: Arc Manor, 2008.

Liji (Record of Rites), Si Shu Wu Jing ed. Beijing: Yanshan Chubanshe, 2011.

Liu An. *Huainanzi* (Collected Essays of Prince Liu An, Lord of Huainan). Shanghai: Shanghai Guji Chubanshe, 1989.

Liu Yiqing. *Shishuo Xinyu* (A New Account of the Tales of the World). Xi'an: Shanxi Chubanshe, 2004.

Liu Zhongde and Luo Zhiye, eds. *Hanying Si Shu* (The Chinese English Four Books). Changsha: Hunan Chubanshe, 1992.

Lü Buwei. *Lüshi Chunqiu* (The Annals of Lü Buwei). Chinese Text Project Online, https://ctext.org. Accessed 9 January 2013.

Lu Qinli. *Xianqin Han Wei Jin Nanbeichao Shi* (Poetry of the former Qin, Han, Wei, and the Northern and Southern Dynasties). Beijing: Zhonghua Shuju, 1983.

Luo Jingguo, ed. and trans. *Guwen guanzhi jingxuan* (A Selection of Classical Chinese Essays from *Guwen Guanzhi*). Beijing: Waiyu Jiaoxue yu Yanjiu Chubanshe, 2005.

Mair, Victor H., ed. and trans. *Wandering on the Way, Early Taoist Tales and Parables of Chuang Tzu.* New York: Bantam Books, 1994.

———. *The Columbia History of Chinese Literature.* New York: Columbia University Press, 2002.

Mencius. *Mengzi* (Works of Mencius), Si Shu Wu Jing ed. Beijing: Yanshan Chubanshe, 2011.

Minford, John and Joseph S.M. Lau, eds. *Classical Chinese Literature: An Anthology of Translations, vol. I, from Antiquity to the Tang Dynasty.* New York: Columbia University Press, 2000.

Mo Di. *Mozi* (Works of Mozi). Beijing: Zhonghua Shuju, 2007.

Ouyang Xun. *Yiwen Leiju* (Collection of Literature Arranged by Categories). Shanghai: Shanghai Guji Chubanshe, 1985.

Pu Ji. *Wu Deng Huiyuan* (Compendium of Five Lamps). Beijing: Zhonghua Shuju, 1994.

Qin Chuan, ed. *Si Shu Wu Jing* (Four Books and Five Classics). Beijing: Yanshan Chubanshe, 2011.

Rickett, W. Allyn, trans. *Guanzi*. Princeton: Princeton University Press, 1998.

Rowland, Ingrid D. and Thomas Noble Howe, eds. and trans. *Vitruvius: Ten Books on Architecture*. Cambridge: Cambridge University Press, 1999.

Ruskin, John. *Seven Lamps of Architecture*. Edited by Liu Rongyue and translated by Zhang Lin. Shandong: Huabao Chubanshe, 2006.

Shang Shu (Book of Documents). *Si Shu Wu Jing*. Beijing: Yanshan Chubanshe, 2011.

Shi Decheng. *Chuanzi Heshang Bodiao Ge* (Songs of Rowing a Boat by the Buddhist Monk Chuanzi). Shanghai: Huadong Shifan Daxue Chubanshe, 1987.

Sima Guang. *Zizhi Tongjian* (Comprehensive Mirror for Aid in Government). Beijing: Zhonghua Shuju, 2007.

Su Shi. *Su Shi Ji* (Collected Works of Su Shi). Xi'an: Shanxi Guji Chubanshe, 2006.

Tao Hongjing. *Zhengao* (Declarations of the Perfected). Beijing: Zhonghua Shuju, 2011.

Wang Bi and Kong Yingda et al., eds. and annotated. *Zhou Yi Zhengyi* (Rectified Connotation of the Zhou Yi), Shisan Jing Zhushu Congshu ed. Shanghai: Shanghai Guji Chubanshe, 2008.

Wang Pu, comp. *Tang Huiyao* (Important Documents of the Tang). Beijing: Zhonghua Shuju, 1955.

Wei Shou, comp. *Wei Shu* (Book of the Wei). Beijing: Zhonghua Shuju, 1974.

Wei Wei et al., comp. *Sui Shu* (Book of the Sui). Beijing: Zhonghua Shuju, 1973.

Wu Juntao, trans. *Du Fu Shi Yingze Yibaiwushi Shou* (Tu Fu: One Hundred Fifty Poems). Xi'an: Shaanxi Renmin Chubanshe, 1985.

Xun Kuang. *Xunzi* (Works of Xunzi). Xi'an: Shanxi Guji Chubanshe, 2003.

Yan Kejun. *Quan Shanggu Sandai Qin Han Sanguo Liuchao Wen* (Complete Collection of Prose from High Antiquity, the Thee Dynasties, Qin, Han, Three Kingdoms, and Six Dynasties). Beijing: Zhonghua Shuju, 1965.

Yao Silian, comp. *Liang Shu* (Book of the Liang). Beijing: Zhonghua Shuju, 1973.

Zhai Jiangyue and Mou Aiping, trans. *The Huainanzi: A Guide to the Theory and Practice of Government in Early Han*. Guilin: Guangxi Normal Press, 2010.

Zhang Yanyuan. *Fashu Yaolu* (Critical Survey of Calligraphy). Shanghai: Shanghai Chubanshe, 2013.

Zhang Zongfa. *Sannong Ji* (Records of the Three Departments of Agriculture). Shanghai: Shanghai Guji Chubanshe, 1995.

Zhao Daoyi. *Lishi Zhenxian Tidao Tongjian* (Comprehensive Mirror of Perfected Immortals and Those Who Embodied the Dao Through the Ages). Yangzhou: Jiangsu Guangling Guji Keyinshe, 1997.

Zheng Xuan and Jia Gongyan, eds. and annotated. *Yili Zhushu* (Ceremonies and Rites with Commentaries), Shisan Jing Zhushu Congshu ed. Shanghai: Shanghai Guji Chubanshe, 2008.

Zheng Xuan and Kong Yingda, eds. and annotated. *Liji Zhengyi* (Rectified Connotation of the Liji), Shisan Jing Zhushu Congshu ed. Shanghai: Shanghai Guji Chubanshe, 2008.

Zheng Xuan and Kong Yingda et al., eds. *Shisan Jing Zhushu Congshu* (Thirteen Classics with Annotations and Sub-Commentaries). Shanghai: Shanghai Guji Chubanshe, 2008.

Zhou Yi (Book of Changes). *Si Shu Wu Jing*. Beijing: Yanshan Chubanshe, 2011.

Zhouli Kaogong Ji (Craftsmen' Records of the Zhou Rituals). Chinese Text Project Online, https://ctext.org. Accessed 9 January 2013.

Zhu Xi. *Si Shu Zhangju Jizhu* (Collected Commentaries on the Confucian Four Books). Beijing: Zhonghua Shuju, 2011.

Zhu Zaiyu. *Lülü Jingyi* (A Clear Explanation of That Which Concerns the Equal Temperament). Beijing: Renmin Yinyue Chubanshe, 1996.

Zhuang Zhou. *Zhuangzi* (Works of Zhuangzi). Shanghai: Shanghai Guji Chubanshe, 2013.

Glossary

An Changqi	安昌期
Bai Juyi (Letian)	白居易（乐天）
Bak Jiwon	朴趾源
Beijing	北京
bilu	敝庐

bu	步
Chao Cuo	晁错
Chengde	承德
chengyi	城邑
chi	尺
chidu	尺牍
Chun'ouzhai	春耦斋
Confucius	孔子
Dayu	大禹
dazhong zhiju	大中之居
dazhuang	大壮
Dechangmen	德昌门
Dong Zhongshu	董仲舒
Dongguan	东观
dougong	斗栱
Du Fu	杜甫
duanzhi	端直
Duke of Ai of Lu State	鲁哀公
Eastern Jin (dynasty)	东晋（朝）
Emperor Xiaowen	孝文帝
fanglang	放浪
fangzhai	方宅
fangzheng	方正
Fayin	法因
Fengchan	封禅
fuyin baoyang	负阴抱阳
Gao Lu	高闾
Gong Xuanzi	公宣子
gongqiao	工巧
gua	卦
Guanzi	管子
Guilai	归来
Guiyuan Tianju	归园田居
gushuo	告朔
he	合
he	和
He Yin	何胤
housheng	厚生
Huainanzi	淮南子
Huan Palace	桓宫
jian	俭
Jiang Xiao	蒋孝
Jiangnan	江南
Jiankang (city)	建康（城）
jiejian	节俭
jin	金
Joseon (dynasty)	朝鲜王朝

juan	狷
Juehai'an	觉海庵
kuang	狂
kun	坤
Laozi	老子
li	礼
lifang	里坊
liyong	利用
Lunyu	论语
Lüshi Chunqiu	吕氏春秋
mei	美
Mencius	孟子
Mi Sixuan (Mi Mu)	谧思玄（谧穆）
Ming (dynasty)	明（朝）
Ming-Qing	明清
Mo Mu	嫫母
Mozi	墨子
mu	亩
Northern Wei (dynasty)	北魏
Pengcheng	彭城
Pengze	彭泽
Pi Sui	仳傕
qi	气
qian	乾
qiaomiao yinjie	巧妙因借
qili	绮丽
Qin (dynasty)	秦（朝）
Qing (dynasty)	清（朝）
qinggao	清高
qinghua	清华
qingsu	清素
qingzheng	清正
qiqiao	绮巧
qishu	绮疏
Ruan Ji	阮籍
ruya	儒雅
Shang Shu	尚书
Shanju Fu	山居赋
Shishuo Xinyu	世说新语
shixing	适形
shizhong	适中
Siheyuan	四合院
Sima Xiangru	司马相如
situ	司徒
Su Shi	苏轼
Taihedian	太和殿
Tang (dynasty)	唐（朝）

Tang Emperor Taizong	唐太宗
Tang Yao	唐尧
Tao Yuanming	陶渊明
wan	完
Wang Dao	王导
Wang Xie	王飔
Wang Xizhi	王羲之
wen	文
wenren yashi	文人雅士
wenzhi binbin	文质彬彬
Western Han (dynasty)	西汉（朝／时期）
Wusong	五松
Xi Shi	西施
Xiang Zhuan	象传
Xiao He	萧何
Xiao Shi	萧史
Xiao-Liang	萧梁（国）
Xie Lingyun	谢灵ff
Xie Yiwu	谢夷吾
Yan Hui	颜回
Yang Wen	阳文
Yangxindian	养心殿
Yaoshan (monk)	药山和尚
yashu	衙署
Yiheyuan	颐和园
yin–yang	阴阳
yinyue	音乐
Yiwen Leiju	艺文类聚
yue	乐
Yuhua Palace	玉华宫
yuqu	纡曲
zheng	正
zhengde	正德
zhengting	正厅
zhi	直
zhi	质
zhipu	质朴
zhishan	至善
zhongdao	中道
zhonghe	中和
Zhou Yi	周易
Zhouli Kaogong Ji	周礼·考工记
Zhu Xi	朱熹
Zhuangzi	庄子
Zigong	子贡

40

DERIVING ARCHITECTURAL THEORY FROM CHINESE PHILOSOPHY

Thinking With Xunzi

David Wang

In the Greco-European lineage of ideas, there exists a continuous line of writing about the visual attributes of buildings. This is true from at least Vitruvius (first century BCE) to our own day.[1] Furthermore, a fair amount of this writing explains why the visual attributes of buildings of one cultural period must be different from those of another cultural period. Adolf Loos: *Ornament is Crime!* Or Mies van der Rohe: *Less is More!* Or Robert Venturi: *Less is a Bore!* These are just a few recent examples.

In contrast, in the profound output of Chinese ideas over the centuries – let us say from the beginning of the Zhou period (1046 BCE) to the end of the Qing dynasty (1911 CE); that's almost three millennia – there is no continuous line of contemplation over the visual attributes of buildings; certainly not over why these attributes should change from era to era. The relatively few documents typically quoted today in the architectural literature – for instance, the *Kaogong Ji* from Zhou period, the *Yingzao Fashi* from the Song dynasty, or the *Lu Bang Jing* from Ming times – these all focus on matters of trade or carpentry methods rather than on philosophical outlooks that energize architectural theory, as is the case in Western treatises.

Why this difference? In the Greco-European tradition, buildings bear the responsibility of empirically reflecting a culture's highest philosophical aspirations. In this regard, Western architecture has always been about metaphysics in physical form. When the human body was the emblem of cosmic ratios, buildings reflected the proportions of the human body.[2] When the machine became the new cultural "epiphore,"[3] architects had to "open their eyes!" to see the beauty of steamships and airplanes as the bases for design.[4] But in my recent book, *A Philosophy of Chinese Architecture Past, Present, Future*, I explain why Chinese buildings over the centuries did not have this self-conscious burden to embody ever-changing philosophical ideals in physical forms. It is not in the nature of Chinese philosophy to be teleological, in the sense of constantly pushing forward in search of new truths. If Chinese buildings did reflect philosophy, they reflected *unchanging* Confucian social relations, as exemplified in the *siheyuan* (courtyard) typology.[5] All of this changed after 1840, the year that marks the First Opium War. After 1840, and with increasing momentum as China entered into her tumultuous twentieth century, not only did the term *architect* first emerge on the Chinese horizon of ideas; not only did *architecture* first emerge as a "profession"; there also began all sorts of attempts to *theorize* what exactly is "Chinese architecture" – resulting in a smorgasbord of hybrid styles.

DOI: 10.4324/9781315851112-61

All of the above sets the stage for this present chapter: I derive some ways to theorize Chinese architecture from the pre-Qin dynasty philosopher Xunzi (d. 238 BCE). What possible relevance can Xunzi have for today's building boom in China? As just noted, *the very awareness for architecture as a theoretical object of concern was itself a product of Western intervention into Chinese culture.* Architecture as a self-conscious idea, hence architectural theory as self-conscious formulations about the visual attributes of buildings, came into China with the steamship, with the railroad, with guns and cannons and with the opium trade. These foreign interventions enabled and enforced a new-found necessity to theorize, of all things, the looks of buildings. This is because even as China tried to reject the Western "foreign devils," she embraced their technology and ultimately their scientific outlook. In the midst of this love –hate relationship, rationalizations for retaining Chinese *ti* (essence) while taking advantage of European *yung* (utilitarian function) generally resulted in the realization that not much *ti* remains after embracing *yung*. It is precisely because of this vacancy of *ti* that current Chinese architectural theory does not have historic anchorage in China's own ideological traditions. In this regard, theorizing Chinese architecture these days is emblematic of the larger inclination of post-1840 Chinese culture *to continue to look to the West*, with the default assumption that China's own philosophical traditions, moored in Confucian ritual, Daoist indeterminacy, and Buddhist idealism, cannot possibly have relevance for "scientific modernity." This default presupposition imposes limitations for theorizing architecture in China as we move forward into the twenty-first century.

We can put this in a slightly different way. Critical theory is a recent trend in architectural theory in China.[6] Yet, the deployment of this term may be another nod to Western trends.[7] Critical theory grew out of the Frankfurt School in Germany, active in the 1920s and 1930s. It sought to explain why Marxism, which looked so promising in the aftermath of the Russian Revolution of 1917, was unable to account for the horrors of WWI (1914–18), followed by Stalin and Hitler. James Bohman has pointed out that the *disposition* of critical theory is now so pervasive it is necessary to distinguish between the capitalized Critical Theory denoting the original Frankfurt School, and many other "critical theories." What is the common denominator? "In both the broad and the narrow senses . . . a critical theory provides the descriptive and normative bases for social inquiry aimed at decreasing domination and increasing freedom in all . . . forms."[8] In other words, critical theory renders the theorist a social activist, an agent of change to free people from various forms of social oppression real or imagined. And, true to its Marxist roots, an anti-capitalist posture is ingrained in criticalist thinking. To cut to the chase, the whole Marxist *oeuvre* has roots outside of China. Yes, China herself embraced Marxism in the twentieth century. But this simply exemplifies China's propensity to embrace ideologies external to her own culture, and then is left to sort out the aftermath with the tired caveat: "with Chinese characteristics." Architecturally, we see this often, for example, in the little "Chinese hats" that grace the tops of modernist skyscrapers all over China. In contrast, looking to Xunzi as an *indigenous* source for deriving architectural theory assures that the "Chinese characteristics" of the resulting system would truly touch upon the *ti* of historic Chinese ways of being.

In what follows, I first summarize Xunzi's place in Chinese philosophy, explaining why his thought is particularly fit for deriving an indigenous Chinese architectural theory. I then expand on three specific points: Xunzi's thought in relation to architectural tectonics; Xunzi and cultivation of craft as a basis for excellent praxis; Xunzi and architectural education.

The Unfortunate Unpopularity of Xunzi, Architecturally Considered

Any introduction to Chinese philosophy lists three names for early Confucianism: of course Confucius (b. 551 BCE), then Mencius (b. 372 BCE), then Xunzi. The first two draw enormous accolades; Xunzi not so much. Why? Xunzi discerned that human nature is *e*, or bad.[9] To the Chinese cultural mind, this denigration of human nature is quite inconvenient. In his anthology of Chinese thought, Wing-Tsit Chan notes that two thousand years of philosophical tradition from the Han period to the nineteenth century largely neglected Xunzi, perhaps because he was too "tough-minded" compared to the "tender-minded" Mencius.[10] After all, it is often said that Xunzi's ideas informed the brutal practices of the short-lived Qin dynasty (221–207 BCE), because one of his students, Han Fei, was the leading Qin theorist. But it is precisely Xunzi's doctrine of the badness of human nature that provides entrée towards an indigenous Chinese architectural theory. This is because permeating Xunzi's philosophy are prescriptions for culti-vating *e*-bad human nature through ritual protocols (*li*) to render it, if not good, at least ordered.

> I say that human nature is the original beginning and the raw material, and deliberate effort is what makes it patterned, ordered, and exalted.[11]

The reference to raw material is germane because Xunzi consistently uses images from craft and construction to illustrate cultivation of moral character. Put another way, for Xunzi, *crafting wayward human nature into social excellence is akin to crafting raw material into tectonic excellence*. This is why it is unfortunate that Xunzi's thought was neglected throughout the long centuries of China's history. When the onslaught of Western ideas in the nineteenth century overwhelmed the Qing dynasty – and again, architectural awareness in China emerged as a fruit of this West-ern imposition – the possibility of Xunzi's thought for developing an indigenous architectural tectonic sensibility was not there.

Why did Xunzi sideline himself with his view that human nature is *e*-bad? Being third in line in early Confucianism, by Xunzi's day the "warring states" of China had been warring for over two centuries. Imagine the history of the United States filled with *continuous* bloodshed; the sons and daughters of one state killing the sons and daughters of neighboring states, and vice versa – nonstop for two hundred and fifty years – and one gets a sense of the despondency of those times. Why all the bloodshed? For Confucius three centuries before Xunzi, this question was not on the table. Even though the Zhou polity had frayed into multiple fiefdoms by his day, the actual Warring States Period (475–221 BCE) commenced only after Confucius passed from the scene. Confucius was thus less concerned about bloodshed; his gaze was towards an idealized Zhou culture some five hundred years earlier. The technical terms he championed linked this idealized society to natural patterns, the totality of which is *tian* (heaven). Within this social-cosmic system, prescribed ritual protocols (*li*), enacted by social roles, resulted not only in har-monious community; even cattle prices remained low.[12] This is because humane benevolence (*ren*) finds expression in *li*-ritual between all social roles. When enacted properly, a moral power called *de* (virtue) emanates from the ruler down, holding together a social–ethical–cosmic unity. Thus: "The one who rules through the power of virtue is analogous to the pole star: it simply remains in its place and receives the homage of the lesser myriad stars."[13] All of this is high on ideals; the sparseness of words in the Confucian *Analects* suggests it is low on details.

Mencius continued the idealism of Confucius; but by now, the bloodshed of war had been ongoing for at least a century. Even though Mencius was still some 150 years before Xunzi, something more was needed to explain the ongoing violence. Mencius is famous for saying that human nature is *originally* good; but like a mountain whose trees are axed and its grass consumed by cattle so that the mountain loses its original pristine nature, so human nature loses its original heart of humanity (*ren*).[14] The destruction of the mountain is a parable of the devastation of war in Mencius's day. Human nature is good, but circumstances compromise this goodness. Thus in Mencius we see a bifurcation between the interior life – that is, we see the emergence of a

Confucian psychology of the goodness of human nature – versus external circumstances. The key is to cultivate elements of the original good residing within: "If you let people follow the feelings (of their original nature), they will be able to do good . . ."[15]

But Mencius's formulations did nothing to end the warfare. It is therefore not difficult to see that, by Xunzi's day over a century after Mencius, idealized notions of human goodness simply did not have the evidence to back them up. Xunzi: "Mencius says: people's nature is good, but they all wind up losing their nature and original state. I say: if it is like this, then he is simply mistaken."[16] Two traits stand out in Xunzi. First, among early Chinese thinkers, he comes closest to what Western parlance calls an empiricist. Xunzi does not idealize; he looks to empirical evidence for his formulations. "One performs the rain sacrifice and it rains. Why? I say: there is no special reason why. It is the same as when one does not perform the rain sacrifice and it rains anyway."[17] This sounds quite accessible to contemporary ears. The second trait is that Xunzi gives explanatory details for why or how things are. The key example is his view of social rituals (*li*). Xunzi was a Confucianist, so he promoted *li*. But whereas for Confucius *li* simply emanated from the cultivated person without effort, for Xunzi *li* were utilitarian means to keep *e*-bad human inclinations in check. "Ritual cuts off what is too long and extends what is too short. It subtracts from what is excessive and adds to what is insufficient. It achieves proper form for love and respect."[18] Ritual protocols, then, were tools of social training for Xunzi. And then:

> the ink-line is the ultimate in straightness, the scale is the ultimate in balance, the compass and carpenter's square are the ultimate in circular and rectangular, and ritual is the ultimate in the human way.[19]

Note again images of building construction to illustrate the powers of moral cultivation via *li*-ritual. Xunzi's discernment that human nature is *e*-bad required detailed explanations of social cultivation; what better than construction processes to show how to straighten out recalcitrant material? What is the result of analogizing moral cultivation to construction detailing? The answer is an entire material culture – which is to say, *architecture*, writ large:

> Meats and grains, the five flavors . . . Fragrances and perfumes . . . carving and inlay, insignias and patterns . . . bells and drums, pipes and chimes, lutes and zithers . . . Homes and palaces, cushions and beds, tables and mats . . . Thus, ritual is a means of nurture.[20]

Carvings and inlay; cushions and beds; *homes and palaces*. The rigors of moral cultivation via *li*-ritual, as a means of nurture, go hand-in-hand with achieving the assemblages of material environments, as expressions of culture. I now develop the aforementioned applications of Xunzi's thinking for formulating an indigenous Chinese architectural theory.

Deriving a Tectonic Rationale via Xunzi

By tectonics, I mean *a philosophy of jointure, in which micro-scale details of assemblage result in macro-scale expressions of moral orderliness not only in buildings, but also in society.*

Consider a detail from a contemporary building (Figure 40.1). This project is well published, cited in anthologies of current cutting-edge architecture in China. But note the detailing at the base of the mullions; also the uneven grouting in the glass block units. Anyone familiar with construction in China can attest that this level of shoddiness is common. Recently I asked a Chinese colleague regarding this pervasive problem. His response was that there is so much

Figure 40.1 Detail of a new building in a city of southeastern China.

Source: © David Wang.

construction these days there is not enough labor to go around; untrained workers do much of the work. But this answer is not satisfying. For this kind of shoddiness to pass muster, many levels of management must accept it, not to mention the client; not to mention the general public.

The condition shown here (in Figure 40.1) is not simply a matter of unskilled labor; it touches on a philosophical weltanschauung. At the root of our issue is a non-unitary, but rather a fluid, basis for conceiving the material fabric of the cosmos. In the Greco-European tradition as early as Democritus (b. 460 BCE), the atomic structure of materiality was a point of philosophical speculation; the early Greeks saw the cosmos as comprised of *units* somehow held together. In Plato's *Timaeus*, enormously influential in the Christian Middle Ages, the primal elements of matter are geometric shapes: fire a pyramid, earth a cube, so on.[21] Fire, earth, water, and air are then joined "with little pegs too small to be visible . . . fastening the courses of the immortal soul in a body which was in a state of perpetual influx and efflux."[22] And then:

> the ratios of their numbers, motions, and other properties, everywhere God . . . has exactly perfected and harmonized in due proportion.[23]

This proportional view of the cosmos has obvious moral overtones embedded right into how "little pegs too small to be visible" connect one material to the next. There is indeed flux, but overcoming flux is the constancy of harmonious proportions, all traceable to God, which both Plato and Aristotle held to be the prime mover.[24] Thus, embedded in the

Greco-European outlook is a presumption that excellent jointure of materials – because such jointure reflects moral values – comes out of this unitary way of imagining the elemental fabric of the cosmos.

In the Chinese case, matter (including humans) is not comprised of discreet units. All is *qi*, produced by the oscillation of *yin* and *yang*.[25] The *yin-yang*, in turn, comprises the 64 hexagrams of the *Yi Jing* (or "I Ching" as popularly known), a long-standing shamanistic text used to prognosticate future conduct for health and social benefit. When the hexagram that applies to a particular problem is determined by random processes (such as tossing yarrow sticks), the recipient knows that even this hexagram is morphing to the next. The point is that empirical form is not comprised of fixed units held together with tiny pegs and distributed according to a logic of moral-geometric proportions. Everything moves, and keeps moving; and keeping in step with this constant flux is something like keeping in step with *de*-virtue. Thus, Laozi taught that the sage accomplishes everything "without action" (*wuwei*),[26] which is to say, without departing from how the natural flux of things unfolds spontaneously. For his part, Confucius held that by the time he was 70 he "could follow my heart's desire without transgressing moral principles."[27] This was Confucius's way of keeping in step with the flux of spontaneous nature. But these are idealizations. At the pedestrian level, keeping in step with nature is an endlessly busy affair. For instance, in his work on the Ming carpentry manual *Lu Ban Jing*, Klaas Ruitenbeek has shown that, when building a house, one never knows how to locate "the center" without complicated geomantic rituals – only to have the center shift the following year.[28] Note how this activity does not inform the jointure of material assemblies themselves, but rather their *placement* in a fluid and amorphous cosmos. In this outlook, fixed compositions of tectonic jointure have less responsibility to represent moral excellence.

It is different with Xunzi. He rejects the assumption that human nature, being good, can simply express itself effortlessly "without transgressing moral principles." For Xunzi, because human nature is *e*-bad, one has to *work* at it. Again, construction imagery:

> Through steaming and bending, you can make wood as straight as an ink-line into a wheel. And after its curve conforms to the compass, even when parched under the sun it will not become straight again. . . . The gentleman learns broadly and examines himself thrice daily.[29]

A trait of Xunzi's thought is going from small scale to large as one continuous logic. It is none other than Xunzi who gives us the image of traveling a thousand miles by taking single steps (his image is the plodding turtle).[30] The large, the empirically visible, depends on details at small or unseen levels. "Even if one's outer form is good, it will pose no impediment to becoming a petty man if one's heart and chosen course are bad."[31] This is a small-to-large, invisible-to-visible logic. We can use this lens to view the problem shown in Figure 40.1. If the detailing is shoddy, even if the building's "outer form" receives accolades, it would not pass muster on a Xunzian accounting of excellence.

Architectural theory based on Xunzi, then, begins at details of jointure. Cultivating (crafting) materiality excellently presumes an initially unformed, perhaps recalcitrant – perhaps *e*-bad – raw material requiring intervention of standards of excellence. Xunzi speaks of "making clear what is the *yi*" for a given context.[32] Usually translated "righteousness," in Xunzi *yi* can also refer to "a certain set of ethical standards that were created by the ancient sage kings to bring order to the people."[33] On Xunzi's view, a given task has an accompanying correct standard. One must make clear what the appropriate standard is if the external "ornament" (his term) is to be *yi*-right, which is to say, excellent. I now develop on this.

Xunzi and the Moral Elevation of Craft: Integrating *Li*-ritual With *Li*-principle

In China, *moral refinement, and hence cultural excellence, has historically not required embodiment in material objects*, at least not to the level found in Greco-European ideas. For Aristotle, virtue accrues through practices that focus human activities into material productions reflecting moral excellence. Therefore, the excellence of an object of art participates in moral virtue, e.g., "men will be good or bad builders as a result of building well or badly."[34] Or again, "the virtue of man also will be the state or character which makes a man good and which make him do his own work well."[35] In contrast, Wan Juren, in describing the Confucian idea of a moral person (*cheng ren*), writes this:

> The aim of such a person's life does not lay in pursuing the sort of specialized craft or skill that would result in material achievement. . . . The possession of skills such as . . . craftsmanship is thus not a necessary prerequisite to becoming a perfected person . . . the first and primary task for a person hoping to possess virtue is to forge his or her moral character and cultivate a personal, internal virtuous nature, rather than to externally pursue any kind of technical perfection or realization of material end.[36]

And so historically, while Confucianism is very detailed in defining moral relations between persons, moral relations between persons and things are less clear; even less clear are moral connections between things and things (read: excellence in tectonic jointure). This may be due to the lack of imperative to reflect virtue in objects of craft. It is true that, by the time of the Ming dynasty thinker Wang Yangming (1472–1529), the influence of Buddhism led this Confucian philosopher to say that even *tiles and stones* can form one benevolent (*ren*) "body" with human beings.[37] But this again is idealist speculation short on details. During the Qing period, promoters of "evidential learning" (*kaozheng*) rejected Wang's idealism in their search for more empirical grounding. Again, it is unfortunate they were not predisposed to look to Xunzi, whose formulations were rich with reliance on empirical evidence.

Another thinker the Qing evidentialists dismissed was Zhu Xi (1130–1200) of the Song dynasty. But Zhu and his Neo-Confucian predecessors promoted a concept that, had Qing thinkers embraced Xunzi, might have served as an entrée into architectural thinking along Chinese lines during the European ideological onslaught. I am referring to *li*-principle. Pronounced the same as *li*-ritual, *li*-principle is a different character, and quite a different basis for philosophizing a worldview. This is not the place to trace the pedigree of this term from early Chinese philosophy. For our purposes vis-à-vis Xunzi, we only need to note that Zhu Xi elevated *li*-principle to perhaps *the* key Confucian technical term in his day.

What is *li*-principle? Neo-Confucianism held that *li*-principle is in all things. To illustrate, Zhu uses the moon and its reflections on water.[38] It is not that *li*-principle is the moon, and reflections of moonlight are somehow less substantive. The moon and its reflections are both *li*; and in this way Zhu gives materiality a metaphysical weight it did not have in earlier Confucianism. The way to becoming a sage is to penetrate to the *li*-principle in things, and one does this by another term Zhu retrieves from the past: the "investigation of things" (*gewu*).[39] Zhu Xi was short on detail on how exactly to *gewu*. He would deny this, but the influence of Buddhism in his day suggested that, if one investigated things sincerely and seriously, enlightenment will simply come. This is one reason Zhu's idealism did not appeal to Qing evidentialists.

But if the evidentialists were more open to Xunzi, *li*-principle could have indeed provided a philosophical basis to "investigate" materiality, and material jointure, from *within* a Confucian framework. *Li*-principle just may be an alternative reading to the Platonic "little pegs" holding the cosmos together; an alternative reading that can train a *Confucian* eye towards the detailed jointure of things to things without abandoning Confucian moral values – in fact, it brings moral rectitude to bear on cultivations of tectonic jointure.

It is at this point that, for instance, the Qing evidentialist Dai Zhen (1724–1777) sought to redefine principle purely through empirical terms:

> *Li* is a name given to the examination of the minutest details with which to make necessary distinctions. This is why it is called the principle of differentiation. In the case of the substance of things, we call it "fiber in muscle," "fiber in flesh," and "pattern and order." When the distinctions obtain, there will be order without confusion.[40]

Dai Zhen's evidentialist bearing led him to excise anything metaphysical from Zhu Xi's earlier outlook. The focus is now on the details of things – perhaps the "little pegs" that stitch all things together. Unfortunately for our purposes, Dai Zhen looked to Confucius and Mencius but, alas, not to Xunzi. The irony is that, while he stressed "evidentialism," Da harked back to idealistic Confucianism, with a view of the goodness of human nature that was insufficient to motivate study of evidence-based details at small scales. But couldn't we consider these details – fiber in muscle, for instance – to be the *li*-principle(s) Zhu Xi held was in all things, now evidentially considered? On this view, the jointure of materials excellently at the level of details, then, becomes a practice of moral cultivation.

A contemporary practitioner who follows through from small-scale details to larger forms is Wang Shu, the 2102 Pritzker Prize winner. The way he conducts his practice may itself be a commentary. Wang Shu practices out of his Amateur Studio in Hangzhou while teaching at the China Academy of Art. The name of his studio signals resistance against the spirit of market-driven mass production so typical of Chinese architectural practice today. Wang often begins his day with tea and calligraphy. His accounts of the creative process indicate he waits for the site to tell him what it wants to be (I adapt this wording from Lou Kahn; there are curious resonances between Wang's approach and Kahn's). What emerges are forms connected to the regional land-scape, somehow birthed out of the timeless site, from details to "outward form." Wang's Ningbo Museum is an exemplar of this approach (Figure 40.2).

> There used to be thirty beautiful traditional villages here. When I started the design, only half were left, and the others were ruined. I decided to collect the materials from the ruins and use them to build this new museum so that the vanished memory, the haptic felling, and the time past would be collected and preserved.[41]

We can say Wang's approach might resemble critical regionalism, à la Kenneth Frampton.[42] But to limit this approach to Frampton is a missed opportunity. The tectonic care, resulting in the form of the building evoking a timeless sense of place, exemplifies a Xunzian integration of *li*-principle with *li*-ritual. I now conclude with some thoughts for architectural education, centered around the educator–practitioner as an echo of the Confucian *shi*, who embodies *li*-ritual in how he or she investigates *li*-principle towards excellent tectonic practice. In this regard, Wang Shu might be one exemplar.

Figure 40.2   Ningbo Museum, Ningbo, completed in 2008. Architect: Wang Shu.

Source: Inset shows recycled tiles, bricks, and stones in the walls. © David Wang.

Xunzi and Architectural Education

For Xunzi and Confucianism in general, the gentleman (*shi*, or *junzi*) is the crux to a successful moral society. "The gentleman is crucial for the Way and the proper models, and one cannot lack him for even a moment."[43] At the outset, I noted that the very notion of "architect" came from the European influx in the late Qing. The ensuing history of architectural practice in China witnesses attempts either to make it a profession along Western lines, or, during the heyday of the Mao regime, to harness architectural practice as an extension of state ideology.[44] Post-Deng Xiaoping, the explosion of architectural practice as part of "capitalism with Chinese characteristics" resulted in great varieties of norms, from government supported design institutes employing thousands, to smaller private practices, to university-based design institutes associated with schools of architecture.

These university-based design institutes offer a particular opportunity for return to a *shi* model, this time with the architect–scholar–practitioner, as *shi*, articulating a path for communal well-being through excellent praxis. Currently in most university design institutes, the same rush towards monetary gain is prevalent. Some students feel like draftspersons in a firm, with little time to actually learn a coherent architectural curriculum – and then they graduate. But there are those who navigate against this tide. One is Liu Jiaping, of the Green Architecture Research Center at the Xi'an University of Architecture and Technology; his can be a type of *shi*-based practice (Figure 40.3). Liu is now well known in China for bringing his interdisciplinary team to participatory design events among China's rural populations. I have witnessed first-hand his work in designing and building "green" cave dwellings in northern Shaanxi Province; also solar-powered farm housing outside of Lhasa in Tibet. In each case,

Figure 40.3 Liu Jiaping with colleagues and students at Xi'an University of Architecture and Technology.
Source: Permission and courtesy of © Liu Jiaping.

Liu's team proposes iterative designs, with local residents having the prerogative of rejecting and/or modifying the proposals. Liu's work over the last 20 years has produced a generation of young architects and drawn wide national attention. Indeed, the Chinese Academy of Engineering now recognizes Liu as a *yuanshi*, one of only a few architects in China to receive this national honor.

Another example is Li Baofeng (Figure 40.4), former dean of the architecture program at the Huazhong University of Science and Technology, who limits his projects to ones that give his students experience in studying how a building relates to its site. Li does indeed use local labor; but he devises methods such that limitations of local materials and local labor are strategically harnessed for the aesthetics of the overall design. An example is his recent Dinosaur Museum in Hubei Province, where local concrete, combined with recycled materials from demolished buildings (à la Wang Shu), were tectonically integrated into a serpentine form that appears to grow out of the land (Figure 40.5).

Neither Liu Jiaping nor Li Baofeng premise their practice on a Xunzian integration of *li*-ritual with *li*-principle. This is my overlay on their work, as examples of how current praxis can be "read" through a lens from China's own philosophical lineage. Xunzi's philosophy accommodates the notion that raw materials, as raw, can be cultivated towards tectonic excellence in the process of producing excellent architecture. The architectural scholar–practitioner stands at the nexus between raw materiality, on the one hand, and the health, welfare, and safety of the public, on the other. This Confucian platform gives a profound basis to recognize just how deeply meaningful "health, welfare, and safety" can be. All of this requires the emergence of the architect understood as the cultivated person, the teacher, the enlightened administrator, the *shi*, who brings beautiful architectural expressions into being by following his or her heart's desire, "without transgressing moral principles." My point is that, in Xunzi, we can formulate

Figure 40.4   Li Baofeng with his students in his studio at Huazhong University of Science and Technology.

Source: Permission and courtesy of © Li Baofeng.

Figure 40.5   Dinosaur Museum, Shiyan, Hubei Province, completed 2012. Architect: Li Baofeng.

Source: Permission and courtesy of © Li Baofeng.

a Chinese philosophical basis for theorizing the visual attributes, and the formal bearing, of buildings. The result would be an indigenous expression of Chinese architecture, truly with Chinese characteristics.

Notes

1 I say "at least since Vitruvius" because Vitruvius himself refers to earlier works on buildings. For example: "It was a wise and useful provision of the ancients to transmit their thoughts to posterity by recording them in treatises, so that they should not be lost, but, being developed in succeeding generations through publication in books." Vitruvius, Book VII, Introduction in *The Ten Books on Architecture*, translated by Morris Hicky Morgan (Dover Publications, 1960), 195.

2 Vitruvius, Book III, Chapter 1, "On Symmetry: In Temples and in the Human Body" in *The Ten Books on Architecture.*, 72–75.

3 This is a term from Tzonis and Lefaivre in their "The Mechanical Body versus the Divine Body: The Rise of Modern Design Theory" in *Journal of Architectural Education* 29, no. 1 (1975): 4–6.

4 Le Corbusier, "Eyes Which Do Not See," in *Towards a New Architecture* (New York: Dover, 1986), 85–148.

5 David Wang, "Homes for Plato and Confucius" in *A Philosophy of Chinese Architecture Past, Present, Future* (Routledge, 2017), 37–58.

6 For example, see Guanghui Ding, "'Experimental Architecture' in China" in *Journal of the Society of Architectural Historians*, Vol. 73, No. 1 (March 2014): 28–37: "in which editors and contributors collectively formulated a critical ideology of experimental architecture." Also Jianfei Zhu, "Criticality in between China and the West, 1996–2004" in *Architecture of Modern China: A Historical Critique* (London and New York: Routledge, 2009), 129–167.

7 See George Baird, "Criticality" and its Discontents" in *Harvard Design Magazine*, Fall/Winter 2004. www.harvarddesignmagazine.org/issues/21/criticality-and-its-discontents. Accessed 26 October 2017. Also Robert Somol and Sarah Whiting, "Notes around the Doppler Effect and Other Moods of Modernism" in *Perspecta 33: Mining Autonomy* (MIT Press, 2002), 75.

8 James Bohman, "Critical Theory," Stanford Encyclopedia of Philosophy, https://plato.stanford.edu/entries/critical-theory/. Accessed 26 October 2017.

9 "Human nature is bad. Their goodness is a matter of deliberate effort." *Xunzi*, Chapter 23, 1–5. Translated by Eric L. Hutton (Princeton University Press, 2014), 248.

10 Wing-Tsit Chan, "Naturalistic Confucianism: Hsun Tzu" in *A Source Book in Chinese Philosophy* (Princeton University Press, 1963), 115.

11 *Xunzi*, Chapter 19, 360, in Hutton, 210.

12 "After three months of his administration vendors of lamb and pork stopped raising their prices." Sima Qian (Ssu-ma Chien), "Confucius" in *Records of the Historian*. Translated by Yang Hsien-yi and Gladys Yang. (Beijing: Foreign Language Press, 1979), 8.

13 Confucius, *Analects* 2.1, translated by Edward Slingerland (Indianapolis: Hackett, 2003), 8.

14 *Mencius* 6A:8 in Chan, *A Source Book*, 56.

15 This statement continues: "The feeling of commiseration is what we call humanity (*ren*); the feeling of shame and dislike is what we call righteousness (*yi*); the feeling of respect and reverence is what we call propriety (*li*); and the feeling of right and wrong is what we call wisdom (*zhi1*)." *Mencius* 6A:6, in Chan, *A Source Book*, 54.

16 *Xunzi*, Chapter 23, 60, in Hutton, 249.

17 *Xunzi*, Chapter 17, 175–180, in Hutton, 179.

18 *Xunzi*, 19, 300–305, in Hutton, 209.

19 *Xunzi*, 19, in Hutton, 205.

20 *Xunzi*, 19, 10–20, in Hutton, 201.

21 Plato, *Timaeus*, 55d – 56b, translated by Benjamin Jowett, in Edith Hamilton and Huntington Cairns, *The Collected Dialogues of Plato* (Princeton University Press, 1961), 1181.

22 Plato, *Timaeus*, 42e – 43a, 1171.

23 Plato, *Timaeus*, 56c, 1182.

24 Plato, *Timaeus*, 57e, 68d, 1183, 1192. Also Aristotle, *Metaphysics* 7, 1072a, 20–25; 1072b, 25–30, in Richard McKeon, *Introduction to Aristotle* (New York: Modern Library, 1947).

25 "The two produced the three. And the three produced the ten thousand things. The ten thousand things carry the *yin* and embrace the *yang*, and through the blending of the qi they achieve harmony." Wing-Tsit Chan, *Tao-te Ching* 42, in Chan, *A Source Book,* 160.

26 *Daodejing (Tao-te-Ching)* 2, in Chan, *A Source Book,* 140.

27 *Analects* 2.4, in Chan, *A Source Book,* 22.

28 Klaas Ruitenbeek, *Carpentry and Building in Late Imperial China: A Study of the Fifteenth-Century Carpenter's Manual* Lu Ban Jing. (Leiden: E.J. Brill, 1993), 55–61.

29 *Xunzi*, Chapter 1, 1–5, in Hutton, 1.

30 *Xunzi*, Chapter 2, 150–155, in Hutton, 13.

31 *Xunzi*, Chapter 5, 10–15, in Hutton, 32.

32 Xunzi, Chapter 19, 430–435, in Hutton, 212.

33 Eric Hutton, "Appendix I" in Hutton, 346.

34 Aristotle, *Nicomachean Ethics,* Book II.1, 1103b, 5–10, in McKeon 332.

35 Aristotle, Book II.6, 1106a, 20–25, in McKeon, 338.

36 Wan Junren, "Contrasting Confucian Virtue Ethics and Macintyre's Aristotelian Virtue Theory," translated by Edward Slingerland, in Robin R. Wang, ed., *Chinese Philosophy in an Era of Globalization* (Albany, N.Y.: State University of New York Press, 2004), 146.

37 Wang Yangming, "Inquiry on the Great Learning" in Chan, *A Source Book,* 659–660.

38 Zhu Xi (Chu Hsi), "The Complete Works of Chu Hsi" in Chan, *A Source Book,* 638.

39 This term is from *The Great Learning*, an early Zhou document Zhu Xi elevated to be one of "The Four Books" of Confucianism. The other three are *Doctrine of the Mean, Analects*, and *Mencius*. (No mention of *Xunzi*!).

40 Tai Chen (Dai Zhen), "Commentary of the Meanings of Terms in the Book of Mencius" in in Chan, *A Source Book*, 711.

41 Wang Shu, *Imagining the House*, section 3 (Zurich, Switzerland: Lars Muller Publishers), 2012–2013.

42 Kenneth Frampton, "Towards a Critical Regionalism: Six Points for an Architecture of Resistance," In *Postmodern Culture*, ed. Hal Foster (London and Sydney: Routledge, 1987), 16–30.

43 *Xunzi*, Chapter 14, 45–55, in Hutton, 142.

44 I learned the most about this topic in Xiao Hu, *Reorienting the Profession: Chinese Architectural Transformation Between 1949–1959* (Doctoral Dissertation, University of Nebraska, Lincoln), 2009.

Bibliography

Aristotle. *Nicomachean Ethics*. Edited by Richard MaKeon. New York: Modern Library, 2001.

Baird, George. "Criticality and Its Discontents." *Harvard Design Magazine*, Fall–Winter 2004, www.harvarddesignmagazine.org/issues/21/criticality-and-its-discontents. Accessed 26 October 2017.

Bohman, James. "Critical Theory." *Stanford Encyclopedia of Philosophy*, https://plato.stanford.edu/entries/critical-theory/. Accessed 26 October 2017.

Chan, Wing-Tsit. *A Source Book in Chinese Philosophy*. Princeton: Princeton University Press, 1963.

Chu Hsi. "The Complete Works of Chu Hsi." In *A Source Book in Chinese Philosophy*, edited and translated by Wing Tsit-Chan, 638. Princeton: Princeton University Press, 1963.

Confucius. *Analects*. Translated by Edward Slingerland. Indianapolis: Hackett, 2003.

Ding, Guanghui. "'Experimental Architecture' in China." *Journal of the Society of Architectural Historians* 73, no. 1 (2014): 28–37.

Frampton, Kenneth. "Towards a Critical Regionalism: Six Points for an Architecture of Resistance." In *Postmodern Culture*, edited by Hal Foster. London and Sydney: Pluto Press, 1987.

Hsun Tzu. "Naturalistic Confucianism: Hsun Tzu." In *A Source Book in Chinese Philosophy*, edited and translated by Wing Tsit-Chan, 115–135. Princeton: Princeton University Press, 1963.

Hu, Xiao. *Reorienting the Profession: Chinese Architectural Transformation Between 1949–1959*. Doctoral Dissertation. University of Nebraska, Lincoln, 2009.

Lao Tzu. "The Natural Way of Lao Tzu." In *A Source Book in Chinese Philosophy*, edited and translated by Wing Tsit-Chan, 136–176. Princeton: Princeton University Press, 1963.

Le Corbusier. *Towards a New Architecture*. Translated by Frederick Etchells. New York: Dover Publications, 1986.

Mencius. "Mencius." In *A Source Book in Chinese Philosophy*, edited and translated by Wing Tsit-Chan, 54–56. Princeton: Princeton University Press, 1963.

Plato. *Timaeus*. Translated by Benjamin Jowett. Edited by Edith Hamilton and Huntington Cairns. *The Collected Dialogues of Plato*. Princeton: Princeton University Press, 1961.

Ruitenbeek, Klass. *Carpentry and Building in Late Imperial China: A Study of the Fifteenth-Century Carpenter's Manual Lu Ban Jing*. Leiden: E.J. Brill, 1993.

Sima Qian (Ssu-ma Chien). *Records of the Historian*. Translated by Yang Hsien-yi and Gladys Yang. Beijing: Foreign Language Press, 1979.

Somol, Robert and Sarah Whiting. "Notes around the Doppler Effect and Other Moods of Modernism." *Perspecta 33* (2002): 75.

Tai Chen (Dai Zhen). "Commentary of the Meanings of Terms in the Book of Mencius." In *A Source Book in Chinese Philosophy*, edited and translated by Wing Tsit-Chan, 711. Princeton: Princeton University Press, 1963.

Tzonis, Alexander and Liane Lefaivre. "The Mechanical Body Versus the Divine Body: The Rise of Modern Design Theory." *Journal of Architectural Education* 29, no. 1 (1975): 4–6.

Vitruvius. *The Ten Books on Architecture*. Translated by Morris Hicky Morgan. New York: Dover Publications, 1960.

Wan Junren. "Contrasting Confucian Virtue Ethics and Macintyre's Aristotelian Virtue Theory." In *Chinese Philosophy in an Era of Globalization*, translated by Edward Slingerland and edited by Robin R. Wang, 146. Albany, NY: State University of New York Press, 2004.

Wang, David. *A Philosophy of Chinese Architecture Past, Present, Future*. London and New York: Routledge, 2017.

Wang Shu. *Imagining the House*. Zurich, Switzerland: Lars Muller Publishers, 2012–2013.

Wang Yangming, "Inquiry on the Great Learning." In *A Source Book in Chinese Philosophy*, edited and translated by Wing Tsit-Chan, 659–660. Princeton: Princeton University Press, 1963.

Xunzi. *Xunzi*. Translated by Eric L. Hutton. Princeton: Princeton University Press, 2014.

Zhu, Jianfei. *Architecture of Modern China: A Historical Critique*. London and New York: Routledge, 2009.

Glossary

Dai Zhen	戴震
de	德
Deng Xiaoping	邓小平
e	恶
gewu	格物
Han Fei	韩非
Huazhong	华中
Hubei	湖北
junzi	君子
Kaogong Ji	考工记
kaozheng	考证
Lhasa	拉萨
Li Baofeng	李保峰
li-ritual	礼
li-principle	理
Lu Ban Jing	鲁班经
Liu Jiaping	刘加平
Ningbo	宁波
Ming (dynasty)	明朝
qi	气
Qin (dynasty)	秦朝
Qing (dynasty)	清朝
ren	仁
shi	士

siheyuan	四合院
Song (dynasty)	宋朝
tian	天
ti	体
Wang Shu	王澍
Wang Yangming	王阳明
wuwei	无为
Xi'an	西安
Xunzi	荀子
yi	义
Yi Jing (I Ching)	易经
yin and *yang*	阴阳
Yingzao Fashi	营造法式
yuanshi	院士
yung	用
Zhu Xi	朱熹
Zhou (dynasty)	周朝

41

FIGURATION

Writing, Memory, and Cities
in Chinese Culture

Shiqiao Li

If we think along the line of "linguistic relativity" with Edward Sapir and Benjamin Whorf, can we consider the intense interest in the "syntax of architecture" – among them Wittkower's Palladian diagrams, Rowe's mathematics of villa design, Alexander's pattern language, Stiny's shape grammar, Hillier's and Hansen's space syntax, Lynch's good city form, and Eisenman's critical diagrams – a function of the alphabetic language? The alphabet is modular; it strategizes on modular relationships between parts and whole, and it creates complexity through large amounts of relatively small sets as building blocks. This has been a highly productive principle for design and theory in the western cultural context: both as a design act of piecing together larger and more complex building systems with smaller and simpler sets of components, and as a theoretical act of understanding by breaking down complex environmental conditions into smaller and repeatable units. Mathematics provides an inalienable abstract model, and genetics offers biological confirmation for this way of thinking; architecture, in this sense, is intensely engaged with ways of putting components together. It is a common and no doubt correct instinct to assume that there are deep connections between the way language works and the way the human mind thinks; structuralism thrives on this assumption and traces the connections between the structure and function of language and all aspects of cultural life as consequences of linguistic structure and function.

How does the Chinese language – the use of large number of figures rather than small number of letters in alphabets, the conception of immanent figures rather than that of transcendental symbols – influence architectural thinking and production in China? Could it be possible that the syntax-inspired tectonics has never been the poetic center of Chinese architecture, and attempts to retrofit "architecture" in Chinese historiography and design excluded a vast potential rooted in its linguistic strategy? The Chinese language, I argue, formulates distinct memory and production strategies that give rise to how Chinese cities accumulate their heritage in the built environment and how they produce aesthetic orders in materials and space.

Writing Before Speech

One of the most basic assumptions of structuralism, as was already apparent in the works of Ferdinand de Saussure, is to see language as a "speech act": a system of phonetic differentiations supplemented by notational methods in alphabetic letters. "In setting up the science of

DOI: 10.4324/9781315851112-62

language within the overall study of speech, I have also outlined the whole of linguistics," Saussure writes at the start of *Course in General Linguistics*.[1] Continuing this way of understanding language, Walter Ong declares that "Thoughts are nested in speech, not in texts, all of which have their meanings through reference of the visible symbol to the world of sound" in his defense of the oral culture.[2] The phonetic notations are relatively abstract and not invested heavily in meaningful graphic forms. Sinologists, such as Marcel Granet, Herrlee Glessner Creel, John DeFrancis, and William Hannas, have long stressed that in the Chinese cultural context, the Chinese language is not primarily a speech act; it is instead a "writing act." For DeFrancis and Hannas, the Chinese language should be described more appropriately as the Chinese writing system. The difference between speech and writing has extensive consequences. Granet suggests that the Chinese "emblem" is immanent; it is both a sign and a thing in its own right. There are perhaps two ways of understanding this condition. First, things are not reduced to categories of types, and then to systems of types that characterize knowledge; instead, things all have their own reasons, despite typological similarities. This is almost like the Borges's notion of a map of an empire that is the size of the empire itself, a condition that troubles the western imagination, but seems to have less difficulty in the Chinese imagination of all things, framed as "ten thousand things" (*wanwu*). Second, there is a parallel system of figures (*xiang*) that captures the specificity of things, also in very large numbers, in the linguistic strategy. This is the set of the figure-based characters. The authoritative eighteenth-century imperial dictionary of Chinese characters, the *Kangxi zidian* (1716), contains about 49,000 characters; about 6,000 characters are generally in use today. A literate Chinese uses between 4,000 and 5,000 characters, while the Japanese and the Koreans use about half of this number. These large quantities of characters are made from 214 semantic components known as radicals, and 800 semi-phonetic indicators; but there are no consistent rules for making a character with these components.[3]

Lothar Ledderose argues that the Chinese writing system is also modular,[4] but this is perhaps confusing gridded amalgamation of components with module. This difference is significant enough for Freud to use the Chinese writing system to stand in for the irreducibility of the psychic contents to reason and abstraction (features of the alphabet and the module): they "have more than one of even several meanings, and, as with Chinese script, the correct interpretation can only be arrived at on each occasion from the context."[5] John DeFrancis and William Hannas suggest that, compared with alphabetic languages, the Chinese writing system exhibits a "high degree of graphic redundancy" and "high incidence of homophony";[6] it seems to be a flawed modular system and an obstacle to attain certain levels of intellectualization.[7] Modularity is made of purified, abstracted, standardized, and independent units. In the Chinese writing system, one cannot be quite certain if this is the case; Ledderose's own example of the 24 versions of the pair of characters *shijie* (world) that appear in the *Lotus Hand Sutra* (1055–1093) demonstrates 24 different ways of writing/carving them.[8] One is not quite sure if the stroke, or the character, or something in between, should be considered as the "module"; if the character is the module, then the set is simply too large to be convincing as a modular system. This is perhaps why the movable type printing, developed in China since the eleventh century, should be seen more like a technique to assemble large numbers of characters quickly, rather than being an example of a modular system. The Chinese literati never seem to have valued movable type highly; it only became sensationalized in writings in the west. In the world of the Chinese writing system, there is no doubt that the order of value begins with calligraphy (where each character is written with a propensity emanating from calligraphic situatedness), then woodblock printing (where each character is carved with a consideration of fixed context), and movable type printing (where characters are formed prior to the surrounding distribution and meanings of other characters). Movable type printing was perhaps seen to be a compromise of the aesthetic experience, often used for low-cost production;[9] prestigious textual projects remained to be produced with carved woodblock printing. The low cultural status of movable type seems to provide an explanation for the curious fate of the project to print an imperial book collection with copper movable type under Yongzheng (reigned 1722–1735) – an emperor who is known for his fascination with western culture – which, despite the massive quantity of types used, only produced 64 copies; nothing else was printed with the copper types and they were melted down to make coins in 1744.[10] This hierarchy of prestige seems to have remained the case well into the early twentieth century; when Zhu Qiqian and Tao Xiang published a high-quality reconstituted version of the eleventh-century building manual the *Yingzao Fashi* in 1925, they used carved woodblock instead of movable type or twentieth-century printing techniques such as lithography.[11] If anything, there seems to be a strong force in China to move away from modularity despite the enormous promise of efficiency and structure inherent in the idea of the module.

DeFrancis and Hannas claim that the Chinese characters are basically under-developed phonetic systems; in this, they perhaps under-estimated the central importance of the Chinese language as a writing system, and their "structuralist" importance to much of the cultural life in China. Writing in the 1980s, Walter Ong pronounced that there "can be no doubt that the characters will be replaced by the roman alphabet," despite the fact that the "loss to literature will be enormous."[12] There were two kinds of attempts in China in response to this perception in the twentieth century. First, there has been a construction of an oral culture in China – gathered from elements of rural and popular manifestations – to serve a new cultural and political agenda since the May Fourth era. Second, there were several attempts to convert the Chinese writing system to a system of phonetic symbols in the twentieth century, which give us the system of *pinyin* as the main method of Romanizing Chinese characters used today. Lu Xun, one of the most radical intellectuals in early twentieth-century China, claimed that China would perish if it did not abandon the square words, which echoed a common sentiment shared by other influential reformers and revolutionaries such Cai Yuanpei, Qu Qiubai, Qian Xuantong, and Mao Zedong. From the late twentieth century, the Chinese writing system has been profoundly challenged by the use of digital technologies, which have had a visible impact on the ability of the young population in China to write Chinese characters. In response to this trend, in January 2013, the Ministry of Education re-introduced calligraphy in primary education, stressing that calligraphy is "the beginning of systematic education of pupils, and the foundation for life-long learning."[13] The Chinese culture, despite the fears of Lu Xun and the proclamations of Ong, DeFrancis, and Hannas, did not vanish, and the Chinese writing system seems to have defended successfully against all kinds of attempts to undermine its use; the fact that it has secured its position despite various attempts of reform inspired by the alphabetic languages indicates its deep and extensive cultural significance in China. In the Chinese writing system, the figurative does not return in the form of dreams resulting from syntactical repression;[14] here, it finds its home.

As if to defend its status of written text, the Chinese writing system, for most of its life and before modernization inspired by alphabet-based languages, resisted punctuation marks, which, of course, are a function of speech and the breathing patterns associated with speech. Formal speech in Chinese is slow and deliberate; this may be related to the need to avoid misunderstanding because of the large number of homophones, but aesthetically it seems to present a phonetic representation of the visual presence of characters. Here, speech seems to pay homage to writing. One of the most consistent pieces of advice on writing in the context of alphabetic languages is to see if the text "sounds right." As Walter Ong tells us, to "think of readers as a united group, we have to fall back on calling them an 'audience', as though they were in fact listeners."[15] In the Chinese linguistic context, there is not such a clear sense of speaking text; how the characters are pronounced differ considerably from region to region, and from time to time in any case. In Chinese, writings have to "look right"; all important texts aspire to calligraphy. Christopher Connery, in his study of Chinese scholar/officials (*shi*) in the Han dynasty, proposed the notion of "textualized life"; it is a life in which writing of texts is inseparable from authority and imperial officeholding, which became "codified in the Han, and continued, in a general way, throughout Chinese history."[16] The literarily accomplished emperor Cao Pi (187–226) wrote, in his *Authoritative Discourses: On Writing*, that writing survives eternally while life and body (the conditions of speech) are limited by time.

The way in which the Chinese writing system influenced the examination systems in Europe is another interesting case to understand the speech and writing divide. The history of examinations in the west had been primarily one of oral examinations; it had been, before the eighteenth century, conducted almost exclusively in the forms of question and answer, disputation, determination, defense of a thesis, and delivery of a public lecture. The much longer history of examinations in China, in contrast, had conducted exclusively in writing. "Writing is the only Test by which a Man of Sense desires to be try'd," the popular *Gentleman's Magazine* touted in 1755 the virtues of the Chinese written examination system.[17] There is a strong case to be made that the writing-centered Chinese examinations system – much admired by western scholars in the eighteenth century – had influenced the substitution of written for oral examinations in the introduction of civil service systems in France and Britain.[18] In the Chinese cultural context, there is a great deal of discomfort in seeing disputation and dialogue as the defining acts of decision making, and there is a deep-rooted reliance on reading and the recitation of texts as the center of meaning and authority.

Picasso's instinct was perhaps right: "If I were born Chinese, I would not be a painter, but a writer. I'd write my pictures."[19] When this sentence is translated into Chinese, it becomes invariably a sentence about Picasso wanting to be a calligrapher. Picasso's statement is perhaps more than a wish to become a calligrapher; if becoming a calligrapher is about writing *well*, Picasso seems to be intrigued by the amazing thought to "write pictures" prior to writing well. The Chinese artist Xu Bing was struck by Picasso's comment on writing pictures; to him, it touched the core of Chinese civilization. The Chinese terms for civilization, *wenhua* and *wenming*, refer to "textualization" and "understanding text"; neither is connected with the meaning of *civitas* that implies public speech. Describing his *Landscript* series, in which the brush strokes in the traditional Chinese landscape paintings do not paint the landscape but write it with square words; "I learned that *cun fa* is a kind of writing."[20] *Cunfa*, or brush methods, is one of the central techniques in traditional Chinese painting, forming an important part of any instructional manuals of painting. The most well-known and widely used manual is called *Manual of the Mustard Seed Garden* (*Jieziyuan huazhuan*, 1679), a step-by-step guide to brush stroke types and techniques highly popular since the late seventeenth century. For example, the method of painting stone is here broken down as having five steps: outline (*gou*), texture (*cun*), rub (*ca*), dot (*dian*), and render (*ran*). The methods of painting stone textures, *cunfa*, are based on brush stroke techniques analogically termed as lotus leaf *cunfa* or folded ribbon *cunfa*. Here, the Chinese landscape painting becomes a function of the brush, and the brush is the primary instrument in the materialization of the Chinese square words. If Monet's landscape dissolves objects into the indistinct continuum of light, Xu Bing's *Landscript* crystalizes them into the Chinese square words. It is perhaps not a coincidence that the act of "painting" is often described in Chinese as an act of writing (*xie*); life painting is "writing the raw" (*xiesheng*) and poetic painting is "writing the mental state" (*xieyi*).

Memory Without Location

Reflecting on his reform ideas at the start of the twentieth century, Liang Qichao thought that although there were a massive number of records from the past, China never had history. As Max Weber and Karl Jasper contemplated and formulated the idea of defining characteristics of intellectual traditions already set in place by 200 CE (the Axial Age), they observed that the Confucian civilization was unique in sustaining an order of the past; all other independently developed civilizations – Greek, Zoroastrian, Buddhist, Hindu, Judaic – began with a deity or an impersonal principle, therefore allowing a possibility to break from the past. This seemingly paradoxical condition – the Chinese culture that lives among an order of the past but does not seem to have an intellectual project of history – may not be so strange when we consider the culture as deeply rooted in its writing system. In the western cultural context in which the break with the past became developed as intellectual history, memory of the past has come to be symbolized by the status of the relic. The relic essentially no longer functions as it was intended; it takes on the new function of marking a temporal break. Is it feasible to link the spatial *loci* of memory in the relic in the west to the deep-rooted distrust of the written text, such as the Platonic proposition that writing creates the appearances of knowledge, and not the substance of knowledge, rehearsed in *Phaedrus*. From Piranesi to Soane, ruins of buildings have a unique place in the western imagination, in a way that still has not been quite understood in China, where every ruin awaits reconstitution. In China, the order of the past, I would like to argue, is primarily preserved through the integrity of the characters and texts; this is memory without location. Of course, we are presenting slightly idealized conditions here, and the twentieth century brought the western conception of the intellectual project of history to China and produced amazing achievements. However, despite these achievements, the "order of the past" that Weber and Jasper articulated continues to serve an important role in the Chinese cultural life; I would like to see this manifestation in two ways, the preservation of texts and the reconstitution of ancient buildings. In the context of fast and extensive urbanization in China today, the reconstitution of ancient buildings has a uniquely powerful impact on the Chinese city as it is experienced politically, culturally, and aesthetically.

The key to this seeming paradox is that the Chinese culture thrives on canonical texts rather than canonical relics; the Chinese canonical texts are perpetually reconstituted. The process of reconstitution, perhaps unique to texts as the central enterprise of a civilization, is general known as "evidential research" (*kaozheng* or *kaoju*), a tradition of scholarship that reached its height in the eighteenth century (Qing dynasty). Traditional philologists were scrupulous and thorough; they scoured vast literary fields and examined diverse physical facts to detect internal inconsistencies and factual errors of the texts, as well as errors attributable to scribes and printers, in an attempt to revise and to create a better version of the text. Evidential research was central to the Chinese scholarly tradition for many centuries and carried high cultural prestige;[21] it was regarded by Chinese reformers such as Kang Youwei and Liang Qichao as evidence of a traditional respect for historical facts. Kang Youwei, founder of the so-called New Text School, was able to use this method to pronounce Confucius a "reformer" to justify his reform ideas. Liang Qichao, in his "Outline of Qing Scholarship," saw in this tradition a development comparable to that of philology and textual criticism centered on the Greek and Roman antiquity in Renaissance Europe.[22] Even cultural iconoclasts of early twentieth-century China such as Hu Shi and Lu Xun had enormous respect for evidential research as one of the essential achievements of the Chinese civilization.[23] In all its ambition to establish correctness, evidential research, it is crucially important to recognize, is a tradition of "correcting texts" instead of one of "correcting facts." In putting a canonical text right (*zheng*), evidential research provided an extraordinary care to the principal surrogate of the empire of figures, the Chinese writing system. What sets apart the Chinese philological tradition from that in the west is the deeply and widely held belief that the canonical texts themselves were sufficient as "originals" when they become the "right texts" in the right form (*shanben*). Instead of "text as relic" in the western city, we encounter "relic as text" in the Chinese city. The concept of the "original copy" of canonical texts seems to be an ambiguous one. Here, writing becomes both the medium of meaning and the medium of memory.

It is interesting to note that the production of corrected texts (*shanben*) came, in some cases, with the destruction of a historical document; often printers would use pages of an existing book to be pasted on woodblocks to be carved for printing, destroying the original in the process. The central conception embedded in the printing of texts – a reconstitution rather than a combination of preservation and reproduction – does not rely on the authenticity of the location of text. This perpetual reconstitution of text, it would seem, provides a compelling archetype for the production of many other aspects of the material culture in China of which buildings constitute an important part. If we take a moment to think with Picasso and Xu Bing that the Chinese cultural landscape is written rather than designed, and that buildings in such cultural landscape appear to be texts rather than relics, we can perhaps understand that ancient buildings in China are in permanent need to be reconstituted in order to have a role in the "current order of the past." In many ways, both the relic and the reconstituted entity can serve the purpose of the text-like status of ancient buildings. Like his father Liang Qichao, Liang Sicheng also lamented the lack of an intellectual project of the architectural history; in "Architecture and the Restoration Plan for the Temple of Confucius," Liang Sicheng remarked in 1935 that

> the only objective of past repairs was to replace the old building with a glorious and sturdy new building; if this meant the demolition of the old building, it would be all the more praise-worthy as virtuous achievements of a high order.[24]

The state heritage conservation legislation in China today – its Venice Charter–inspired heritage conservation law established in 1982 – demands authentic locations to be preserved without alteration and relocation. This heritage conservation law in China is clearly in conflict with the ancient sensibility of reconstituting antiquity; it has been a very difficult law to reinforce in China. It is very common to visit ancient sites in China, only to be told that many, if not all, parts of the ancient sites had been built in various later ages. Out of the "three famous towers of the Jiangnan Region" that claim heritage of many centuries – Yellow Crane Tower (Huanghelou), Pavilion of Prince Teng (Tengwangge), Yue Yang Tower (Yueyanglou) – one was constructed in the nineteenth century; the other two were built in the late twentieth century with reinforced concrete and air-conditioning. Similar situations are very common in China; this is of course not to suggest that the relic has no cultural value in China, but to argue that cultural heritage in China is not exclusively grounded in location-authenticated information.

Colonies of Beauty and Violence

I would like to characterize the power of the writing system as figuration, a plastic power of forming figures rather than symbols in its linguistic strategy to formulate meanings. Figuration is principally surrogated by the writing system; it is also more than the writing system. It is a way to understand, order, and shape the world. The writing system begins with singular units of graphic forms and one-syllable sounds. This method of creating a language cannot be more different from the alphabetic one; it sets off an entirely different cultural path that shapes almost all things in life differently. As our review of sinological and structuralist insights suggests, this initial linguistic step put writing before speech; it creates a distinctive force that impact on the built environment. The first site of this plastic force is the body; memorizing and reproducing, in good writing form, the large set of characters produce a visible impact on the body that artists such as Xu Bing (*The Book from Sky*, 1987–1991) and Qiu Zhijie (*One-thousand-time Copy of Lantingxu*, 1990–1997) tried to come to terms with. The vigor of the writing system comes with a strong corporeal and intellectual force.

Figuration lays out a gridded system of signs and things, it projects a figure-based classification system that does not rely on typological differentiations or artificial modularity, it imposes an "empire of figures" that extends its influence into the production of things to force function to follow form, and it produces and reproduces a sense of completeness through its standardization, gridded amalgamation, and completeness of each component to demand seemingly a similar completeness in political, social, and knowledge production. The formative power of figuration should not be under-estimated, even in today's cultural context of global exchange of ideas; the figure insists on its own form of adaptation to external influences.[25]

In the built environment, the plastic power of figuration produces a focus on the figurative potentials of what I would like to call "objects of value." These objects, unlike objects of epistemological value and objects of historical value in the western cultural context, are about the figure and its essentialization. This condition is perhaps traditionally most observable close to the scene of writing: the scholar's desk and the scholar's garden. Here, the elements of the environment – its water, vegetation, and earth – become figured into ponds and streams, miniature plants in basins, and rockery. The aesthetic order here is perhaps best highlighted by contrasting the Chinese garden to the lawn in the western cultural context. Thorstein Veblen commented that "the aesthetic purpose of the lawn is a cow pasture";[26] the aesthetic purpose of the Chinese garden is to be like painting (*ruhua*), which is, in turn, to be like writing. Chinese paintings are amazingly writing-like, in the shared use of brush stroke techniques, in the interplay between texts and images, and in the temporal unfolding of painted scrolls as an archetypal reading act. The progression from writing to painting takes many further steps to project writing onto more remote environments; this is where one finds extensive stone carvings of texts, as well as scenic narrations to read landscape as writing. In the Greco-Roman tradition, writing on buildings does not demand its own separate materiality, and writing on landscape is seen to be graffiti;[27] in the Chinese tradition, writing on landscape is essential to any form of understanding of landscape.[28]

Moving further away from the scene of writing, it is important to understand that traditional Chinese buildings, like paintings, are dominated by texts; texts announce and accompany every artificially constructed threshold such as a gate, a door, a notable scene, an important office. Most often, they are present through scrolls and tablets, distinctly separate from the buildings themselves. Like the iconic seals on paintings, these scrolls and tablets bearing writing seem to have a different status; they are sites of extraordinary levels of creativity and poetic evocation, in ways that are very unlike the relatively conventional building forms. Moving through a Chinese garden or a grand courtyard is an experience of these prominent and delightful texts; their ability to invoke past stories, literary and poetic sensibilities, and levels of creativity are often excluded from scholarship of Chinese architecture. It is a misfortune for traditional Chinese architecture to be represented purely as physical objects, and not as forms of writing as they were first conceived and constructed. To attain a level of literary awareness to be able to appreciate the achievement of Chinese architecture has not been part of the education of architects in China today; much of western scholarship on Chinese architecture focus on retrofitting formal analyses, which misplaces the poetic center of Chinese architecture.

It is perhaps from this understanding that one gains insights into the numerous transformations of the built environment, in terms of the relationship between textual signs and architecture, and in terms of the creation of "cultural parks" in China. Texts have a bewildering range of appearances in Chinese cities; all spatial thresholds are framed with texts in red background at the time of the Chinese New Year, and text scrolls on government buildings certainly tap into the valence of this traditional architectural feature for status of authority. Commercial buildings use texts to excess; often commercial buildings in Chinese cities are fully covered with textual signage, announcing the prime importance of text and the subservient status of architecture. If this is disturbing to many architectural critics, it is perhaps grounded not in the use of text but in the overuse of texts in commercial context. If the highly cultivated traditional literati gardens result from the cultivation of sophisticated sense of *poesis* arising from writing, then the absence of this cultivation could be seen to be responsible for the production of "illiterate gardens" in China. The twentieth century has been a particularly difficult time for Chinese culture; the loss of confidence in its writing-based civilization undermined the quality and sophistication of traditional cultivation, while the aspirations to modernize were often materialized in poorly hybridized forms. Perhaps the hybrid modernity – which seems to be successful economically – is still finding its cultural voice. In the meantime, vast stretches of land in China have been transformed, resulting from "bad writing." The rush to build development areas in Chinese cities – a trend that produced 38,600 square kilometers of "development zones" in 2005, which are one and half times of the entire existing urban area of China[29] – tremendously accelerated the development of illiterate gardens in China.

Having separated literature from architecture in education and practice in twentieth-century China, it is perhaps propitious to re-examine their well-established inter-dependency in China. To insist on orality and spatiality in China disengages its cultural character and tradition; but to return to the calligraphy and literacy in traditional China would also mean a return to the same set of intellectual predicaments that prompted radical reforms and revolutions in the early twentieth century. This is a complex process of restoration and innovation; it is a future in which Chinese architecture can find levels of comfort and flourishing comparable to its past achievements. Can literary cultivation take place next, rather than in opposition, to syntactical orders? Can writing re-organize spatiality? What are the dangers of "over-writing"? Erwin Panofsky defended the literary in the syntactically dominated western art by developing the frameworks of "iconography" and "iconology";[30] the fact that this "semantic distribution" in western arts has to be defended is perhaps a reflection of its relatively low intellectual status in art. If we were to formulate a defense of art in the Chinese writing system, they would probably have to be one of "visuality" and a "visualogy." This may indeed be one of the readings of the argument for a "visual culture" in the Ming dynasty – an unviable enterprise at first glance – in Craig Clunas's *Empire of Great Brightness*; rescuing Chinese art from its literary dependency would be a counterpoint to the literacy-dominated Chinese art and architecture. Understanding the writing-based cultural heritage will certainly formulate a different set of theoretical questions for a radically different set of outcomes in the built environment in which Chinese architecture may be able to find its form.

Notes

1 Ferdinand de Saussure, *Course in General Linguistics* (New York: Philosophical Library, 1959), 17.
2 Walter Ong, *Orality and Literacy: The Technologizing of the Word* (Abingdon: Routledge, 2002), 74.
3 William Hannas, *The Writing on the Wall: How Asian Orthography Curbs Creativity* (Philadelphia: University of Pennsylvania Press, 2003), 246.

4 Lothar Ledderose, *Ten Thousand Things: Module and Mass Production in Chinese Art* (Princeton: Princeton University Press, 2000).

5 Quoted in Jacques Derrida, "Freud and the Scene of Writing," in *Writing and Difference*, by Jacques Derrida (Chicago: The University fo Chicago Press, 1978), 209.

6 William Hannas, *Asia's Orthographic Dilemma* (Honolulu: University of Hawai'i Press, 1997), 172.

7 John DeFrancis, *The Chinese Language: Fact and Fantasy* (Honolulu: University of Hawai'i Press, 1984).

8 Ledderose, *Ten Thousand Things*, 12–13.

9 Ledderose, *Ten Thousand Things*, 139–140.

10 Ledderose, *Ten Thousand Things*, 141–142.

11 Li Shiqiao, "Reconstituting Chinese Building Tradition: The *Yingzao fashi* in the Early Twentieth Century," *Journal of Society of Architectural Historians* 62, no. 4 (2003): 470–489.

12 Ong, *Orality and Literacy*, 86.

13 www.moe.gov.cn/srcsite/A26/s8001/201301/t20130125_147389.html. Accessed 29 December 2021.

14 Derrida, "Freud and the Scene of Writing," 209.

15 Ong, *Orality and Literacy*, 73.

16 Christopher Leigh Connery, *The Empire of the Text: Writing and Authority in Early Imperial China* (Oxford: Rowman & Littlefield, 1998), 81.

17 Quoted in Teng, Ssu-Yü. "Chinese Influence on the Western Examination System," *Harvard Journal of Asiatic Studies*, no. 7 (1943): 267–312.

18 Teng, "Chinese," 267–312; also in Ledderose, *Ten Thousand Things*, 101.

19 Dore Ashton, ed., *Picasso on Art, A Selection of Views* (New York: Da Capo Press, 1972), 131.

20 Xu Bing, "An Artist's View," in *Persistence – Transformation: Text as Image in the Art of Xu Bing*, eds Jerome Silbergeld and Dora C. Y. Ching (Princeton: Princeton University Press, 2006), 109.

21 Benjamin Elman, *From Philosophy to Philology, Intellectual and Social Aspects of Change in Late Imperial China* (Los Angeles: UCLA Asian Pacific Monograph Series, 2001).

22 Liang Qichao, *Qindai Xueshu Gailun* (Outline of Qing scholarship) (Beijing, 1920).

23 Wen-hsin Yeh, *The Alienated Academy: Culture and Politics in Republican China, 1919–1937* (Cambridge MA: Harvard University Press, 1990), Chapter One, Language and Learning, pp. 7–48.

24 Lin Zhu, *Jianzhushi Liang Sicheng* (Architect Liang Sicheng) (Tianjin: Tianjin Kexue Jishu Chubanshe, 1997), 64.

25 For more details on these propositions, see Li Shiqiao, *Understanding the Chinese City* (London: Sage Publications, 2014).

26 Thorstein Veblen, *The Theory of the Leisure Class*, ed. Martha Banta (Oxford: Oxford University Press, 2007; first published in 1899), 90.

27 Lawrence Keppie, *Understanding Roman Inscriptions* (Baltimore: Johns Hopkins University Press, 1991).

28 This practice is described in Robert E. Harrist, Jr., "Reading Chinese Mountains: Landscape and Calligraphy in China," *Orientations*, no. 31 (December 2000): 64–69; *The Landscape of Words, Stone Inscriptions from Early and Medieval China* (Seattle and London: University of Washington Press, 2008). Craig Clunas, *Empire of Great Brightness: Visual and Material Cultures of Ming China, 1368–1644* (Honolulu: University of Hawai'i Press, 2007), 109.

29 Qiu Baoxing, *Duiying Jiyu yu Tiaozhan* (Response, opportunity and challenge) (Beijing: Zhongguo jiangong chubanshe, 2009), 54.

30 Erwin Panofsky, *Meaning in the Visual Arts* (London: Peregrine Books, 1970).

Bibliography

Ashton, Dore, ed. *Picasso on Art: A Selection of Views*. New York: Da Capo Press, 1972.

Clunas, Craig. *Empire of Great Brightness: Visual and Material Cultures of Ming China, 1368–1644*. Honolulu: University of Hawai'i Press, 2007.

Connery, Christopher Leigh. *The Empire of the Text: Writing and Authority in Early Imperial China*. Oxford: Rowman & Littlefield, 1998.

De Saussure. Ferdinand. *Course in General Linguistics*. New York: Philosophical Library, 1959.

DeFrancis, John. *The Chinese Language: Fact and Fantasy*. Honolulu: University of Hawai'i Press, 1984.

Derrida, Jacques. *Writing and Difference*. Chicago: The University of Chicago Press, 1978.

Elman, Benjamin. *From Philosophy to Philology: Intellectual and Social Aspects of Change in Late Imperial China*. Los Angeles: UCLA Asian Pacific Monograph Series, 2001.

Hannas, William. *Asia's Orthographic Dilemma*. Honolulu: University of Hawai'i Press, 1997.

———. *The Writing on the Wall: How Asian Orthography Curbs Creativity*. Philadelphia: University of Pennsylvania Press, 2003.

Harrist, Robert E. Jr. "Reading Chinese Mountains: Landscape and Calligraphy in China." *Orientations* 31 (December 2000): 64–69.

———. *The Landscape of Words: Stone Inscriptions from Early and Medieval China*. Seattle and London: University of Washington Press, 2008.

Keppie, Lawrence. *Understanding Roman Inscriptions*. Baltimore: Johns Hopkins University Press, 1991.

Ledderose, Lothar. *Ten Thousand Things: Module and Mass Production in Chinese Art*. Princeton: Princeton University Press, 2000.

Li Shiqiao. "Reconstituting Chinese Building Tradition: The *Yingzao fashi* in the Early Twentieth Century." *Journal of Society of Architectural Historians* 62, no. 4 (2003): 470–489.

———. *Understanding the Chinese City*. London: Sage Publications, 2014.

Liang Qichao. *Qindai xueshu gailun* (Outline of Qing Scholarship). Beijing: Beijing chubanshe, 1920.

Lin Zhu. *Jianzhushi Liang Sicheng* (Architect Liang Sicheng). Tianjin: Tianjin Kexue Jishu Chubanshe, 1997.

www.moe.gov.cn/publicfiles/business/htmlfiles/moe/moe_714/201301/147389.html. Accessed 21 September 2017.

Ong, Walter. *Orality and Literacy, the Technologizing of the Word*. Abingdon: Routledge, 2002.

Panofsky, Erwin. *Meaning in the Visual Arts*. London: Peregrine Books, 1970.

Qiu Baoxing. *Duiying Jiyu yu Tiaozhan* (Response, Opportunity and Challenge). Beijing: Zhongguo jiangong chubanshe, 2009.

Teng, Ssu-Yü. "Chinese Influence on the Western Examination System." *Harvard Journal of Asiatic Studies*, no. 7 (1943): 267–312.

Veblen, Thorstein. *The Theory of the Leisure Class*. Edited by Martha Banta. Oxford: Oxford University Press, 2007 (first published in 1899).

Xu Bing. "An Artist's View." In *Persistence – Transformation: Text as Image in the Art of Xu Bing*, edited by Jerome Silbergeld and Dora C.Y. Ching, 109. Princeton: Princeton University Press, 2006.

Yeh, Wen-hsin. *The Alienated Academy, Culture and Politics in Republican China, 1919–1937*. Cambridge, MA: Harvard University Press, 1990.

Glossary

ca	擦
Cai Yuanpei	蔡元培
Cao Pi	曹丕
cun	皴
cunfa	皴法
dian	点
gou	勾
Huanghelou	黄鹤楼
Jieziyuan Huazhuan	芥子园画传
Kang Youwei	康有为
Kangxi Zidian	康熙字典
kaoju	考据
kaozheng	考证
Lantingxu	兰亭序
Liang Qichao	梁启超
Liang Sicheng	梁思成
Lu Xun	鲁迅
Mao Zedong	毛泽东
Qian Xuantong	钱玄同
Qiu Zhijie	邱志杰
Qu Qiubai	瞿秋白

ruhua	如画
shanben	善本
shi	士
shijie	世界
Tao Xiang	陶湘
Tengwangge	藤王阁
wanwu	万物
wenhua	文化
wenming	文明
xiang	象
xie	写
xiesheng	写生
xieyi	写意
Xu Bing	徐冰
Yingzao Fashi	营造法式
Yongzheng (emperor)	雍正（皇帝）
Yueyanglou	岳阳楼
zheng	正
Zhu Qiqian	朱启钤

42

SIGNS OF EMPIRE

Scale and Statehood in Chinese Culture

Jianfei Zhu

Roland Barthes' 1970 reading of Japan, *Empire of Signs*, offers a distant perspective. His unfamiliarity with local language and customs generated subtle and visually intense observations – musings on symbolism ranging from the use of chopsticks to calligraphic brush strokes – of a world so different from his own.[1] In this realm of images, the oriental ideogram, *kanji* (Chinese characters used in Japan), featured prominently. In his notes on symbolism in Japanese culture, Barthes uncovered a world of scripts that are inescapable in cities of Japan and East Asia at large. Though he wrote of an "emptiness" of meaning, what remains most impressive of Barthes' work is the titular "empire," a *dispersion of visual* signs and scripts, an image that has captured so well some key features of the *kanji* characters. Two comments should be made here: since the characters have shared roots in China, Japan, and other countries in East Asia, along with a whole realm of similar practices, Barthes' work has a broader relevance when thinking of the differences between East Asia and the West. Further, Barthes focused on culture, not politics, let alone relations between them. He did not explore an underlying relationship between an empire of signs and signs of empire – that is, the role a system of signs plays in the construction of the state. Such a relationship is important in understanding East Asia, where the use of the characters is related to a holistic worldview and a comprehensive statehood. This chapter aims to explicate this relationship in the case of China.[2]

For this purpose, an outline of Chinese thought is useful – particularly in comparison with European thought. As a working hypothesis, we may say that a critical difference between Chinese and European thought lies in the assumption of an *inside* and an *outside*. If European thinking has conceived a transcendental outside to the world, an outside in which God, an unmoved mover can create the world by delivering the first cause (like a sculptor, standing outside a sculpture, creating the work of art, to follow Aristotle's analogy), Chinese thinking has conceived the universe as self-generated, developed from within.[3]

European thinking has evolved with the logic of the outside – externalizing, excluding, and opposing – in the use of ideas of autonomy, where entities can be separated from each other. This externalization is exemplified in modern analytical science, the practice of critique, the idea of universal law, the "separation of powers," and the various oppositions between political parties, and between categories such as nature and culture, modern and tradition, and state regime and civil liberty. The Chinese thinking, on the other hand, has evolved along the logic of the inside: the universe is *zi-ran* or self-evolved; the world is here and inherent (immanent);

DOI: 10.4324/9781315851112-63

all entities are always already related to each other, with a natural or universal ethics governing the flow of all things.

Such Chinese thinking is useful, even radical in a postmodern critique of transcendence, autonomy, and dualist opposition in the West. But this approach is not about a blurred relatedness; rather, it has a structure and an ethics. That is, it offers a remedy to a lost relativism and cynicism in postmodern thinking as well. Further, as a practiced tradition, it is more complex and balanced than some contemporary polemics that are radical but not comprehensive. For example, in the West, ideas of multiplicity have been celebrated recently, at the cost of oneness and relatedness. This is epitomized in Gilles Deleuze and Felix Guattari's privileging of difference and rhizomatic logic, over the oneness of a "tree" structure.[4] However, according to Chinese thinking, multiplicity and oneness, difference and relatedness, are two sides of a same condition.

Through a complex web of ideas in Confucianism, Daoism, and other schools of East Asian thought, the Chinese have produced a framework of worldviews and political ethics that include six related propositions: (1) a relatedness in thinking that prevents the possibility of autonomy, opposition, and opposing dualism (yin and yang are not oppositional, but interrelated and mutually transformative); (2) a simultaneous understanding of oneness and multiplicity – the universe is a large oneness that contains ten thousand multiplicities – a harmony of differences; (3) the universe is all-inclusive and inherently "good"; there is a holistic bio-ethical order that connects the body, the person, the family, the state, the world, and nature, in that their moral functions are interrelated; (4) state government is part of this natural-ethical order; (5) the emperor or the head of the state should be a moral leader who ensures manifestations of the inner good of all humans; (6) state government should comprehensively lead many spheres of social lifeworlds.

These propositions can be summarized into two essential propositions: there is a construct of a large oneness with diverse multiplicities in natural reality,[5] and there should be a moral statehood that leads all realms of social life. The central hinge in Chinese culture is a connection between the two – epistemology and political ethics, between a holistic view of the world as a web of connections and a political proposal that a comprehensive state should and can ensure the moral functioning of all humans. Historically, a state-society hybrid was developed in which state government had extensive moral influence over the population, and, in turn, the population looked up to the state as a moral leader. One practical mechanism by which to achieve this condition was the civil-service examination system established in the seventh century, which recruited the best students from the population to become state officials. A meritocracy was established in which officialdom, following the emperor as Sage Ruler, was expected to be competent, disciplined, highly educated, and morally superior to society at large.

This cultural construct manifests itself in concrete spheres of practice. Let us examine three such spheres: *systems of signs* (game sets and the Chinese script), *signifying surfaces* (books and paintings), and *constructed things* (buildings and cities). While the first is epistemological, as it involves signs for seeing and knowing, the second and the third relate to a political empire: they incorporate signs into bodies of knowledge, aesthetic compositions, and construction technologies employed for state governance.

Systems of Signs: For Seeing and Knowing

Chinese script is arguably the most important system of signs in China, and East Asia at large (Figure 42.1). But other systems of signs, for example Chinese games such as weiqi (go) and mahjong, shed light on Chinese modes of seeing and knowing. If we compare weiqi with chess, which has a similar grid structure, it is clear that weiqi comprises a more expensive spatial system. In chess, there are 64 (8 × 8) positions with 16 pieces for each player; in weiqi, there are

361 (19 × 19) positions on the board. In the latter, one player has 180 pieces and the other has 181 pieces. With so many positions and pieces to oversee, the weiqi player must take a more strategic, top-down approach. Weiqi requires dynamic observation – players must be able to shift their views from global to local, between "here" and "there," across a larger space and more actively than in the case of chess. Weiqi encompasses a dispersed multiplicity of options that is unified by a strategic oneness of the board

Mahjong's systemic logic is more complex than either chess or weiqi. The mahjong set consists of 144 tiles with a messy system in numerical and semantic order. It includes four sets of five series (which contains 9, 9, 9, 4, and 3 pieces respectively) and a set of one series (with two groups of four pieces each). The semantic ordering of these pieces is messy as well, with different coexisting systems: the first three sets of nine pieces are named "pancakes," "strings," and "ten-thousands" respectively; the following sets are named "orientations," "primary cards," "flowers," and "seasons." A mahjong set is an order of disorder, a system that contains unsystematic chaos. It is a system accommodating a broad coexistence of radical multiplicities.

Chinese script has fifty thousand characters. Each character is a square word composed of a few radicals, each of which is composed of several strokes (Figure 42.1). There are a few hundred radicals (214 according to one account). Radicals are not alphabets; they provide some semantic suggestions and at times indefinite phonetic specifications. Additionally, radicals cannot be composed linearly as in an alphabetic language. Rather, they are combined in a few directions in the square. There is no logical progression from radicals to characters. Rules of forming a character remain implicit and vague, so one has to memorize each character as an

Figure 42.1 Flags and two Chinese characters *wan sui* ("ten thousand years"), Tiananmen Gate, Beijing, 2007.
Source: © Jianfei Zhu.

absolute given, as an absolute "singular," in the process of mastering this language. The written language cultivates a cultural mindset: to learn it, one must have humility, be open to outliers, and be more likely to accept than to reject or to challenge.

Chinese characters are visual signs rather than phonetic scripts. Defined by a graphic figure, each is a sketch of a view that refers to a thing or an idea. To comprehend a Chinese text is an experience of viewing rather than reading. Half abstract and half figurative, each character encapsulates a window upon the world. A character precipitates a direct opening to things and ideas. It restores a primary connection from seeing to knowing, from signs to ideas, a connection that is removed in the abstraction of alphabets.

The visuality of Chinese characters lends an experiential quality to the script and has elevated the practice of calligraphy to an art form. The malleability of the characters' form has produced a visual and textual culture in which a text can run in different directions (vertically or horizontally) and in which calligraphy, poetry, and painting are interconnected media. Often a short poem, phrase, or a single character is written on a wall scroll; a poem describing a sentiment may be written down inside a landscape painting. As a whole, Chinese script is a world of singular sketches or windows – "centers," "vanishing points," and "ideologies" – a large construct of diverse, local, and specific worldviews.

Signifying Surfaces: For Governing

In China, the largest books and the largest artworks (such as landscape paintings) were produced at the imperial court. Two of the most prominent books in Chinese historiography are Sima Qian's *Shi Ji* (91 BCE) and Sima Guang's *Zizhi Tongjian* (1084). The former contains 520,000 words in 130 volumes and spans a history of 3000 years, and the latter is 3 million words in 294 volumes that cover more than 1,500 years.[6] Scrolls (of paper or silk) have been made since the seventh century, and bound books have been produced since the tenth century. With printing, papermaking, and publication technologies always developing, book production became ever more impressive. The largest paper encyclopedia made in human history is *Yongle Dadian* (*Yongle Encyclopedia*), completed in 1408, with 370 million Chinese characters in 22,937 volumes. Later, in 1782, the first copy of the largest collection of published works in China, *Siku Quanshu* (*Complete Library of the Four Treasures*) was completed; it contained 800 million written Chinese characters.[7]

As productions of the imperial court, the scale of the projects reflected the power of the centralized state, which was related to the scale of land and population that the state was able to coordinate. As the largest collections of bodies of knowledge covering history, ethics, political discourse, and other areas such as language, economy, and technology, they secured a moral and intellectual superiority of the authority of the state – a meritocracy rooted in the Confucian theory of moral statehood.

Another signifying surface that reflects scale and statehood is painting. The royal Chinese court has always had an academy of painting, which was developed extensively in the Northern Song Dynasty (960–1127). Chinese painting takes on various formats: small paintings collected in albums or mounted on fans for detailed scenes (such as birds and flowers); medium-sized and larger wall scrolls for human figures or, more commonly, natural landscapes; and long horizontal scrolls to depict social gatherings, urban scenes, and especially natural landscapes with multiple perspectives. The last format, the horizontal landscape scroll, represents one of the most distinctive Chinese approaches to painterly composition.

In the Northern Song Dynasty, a growing interest in the horizontal landscape scroll and the development of the imperial academy of painting coincided and conjoined fostering a profusion of masterpieces in the early twelfth century.[8] Two of the most prominent landscape scrolls are Wang Ximeng's *Qianli Jiangshan Tu* (*A Thousand Li of Rivers and Mountains*) (1113, 51.5 ×

Figure 42.2 Wang Ximeng, *A Thousand Li of Rivers and Mountains* (color on silk, 51.3 x 1191.5 cm), 1113, Palace Museum, Beijing. A Section.

From: wikimedia commons (public domain).

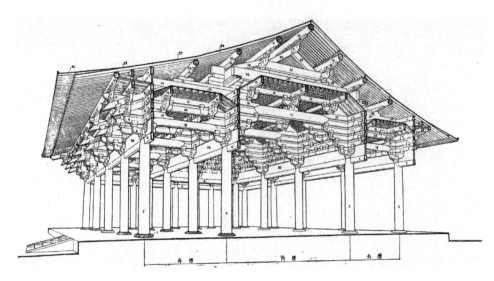

Figure 42.3   Timber structure of Foguangsi Temple, built in 857.

From: Liu Dunzhen, *Zhongguo Gudai Jianzhu Shi* (Beijing: Zhongguo Jianzhu Gongye Chubanshe, 1980), fig 86–6, 129. Permission and courtesy of Liu Dunzhen's family.

1191.5 cm) and Zhang Zeduan's *Qingming Shanghe Tu* (*Along the River During the Qingming Festival*) (1085–1145, 25.5 × 525 cm). Both were made under Emperor Huizong (r. 1100–1126), who himself was an accomplished calligrapher and painter. While the later work represented the capital of Northern Song China and its surrounding rural landscape, the earlier one depicted an imaginary landscape, combining features from northern and southern China. In the urban–rural landscape of *Along the River During the Qingming Festival*, hundreds of human figures, along with other details (bridges, boats, donkeys, horses, interiors, courtyards, and storefronts), are meticulously painted. In *A Thousand Li of Rivers and Mountains*, human figures with other details (boats, bridges, birds, trees, huts, and villages) were rendered across a larger and longer scroll surface, to be viewed over time, as the scroll is being unrolled (Figure 42.2).

These empires of signs contain signs of empire in specific ways. Embodying a holistic view of all-inclusiveness, they also reveal a political gaze of the court – the emperor's concern with social prosperity and a land of majestic rivers and mountains, to be protected against decline and invasion respectively – which were also interrelated. Additionally, these awe-inspiring artworks, still stored in state museums, reflect aspects of Chinese meritocracy in which the state acts as a "humanistic" leader in art, culture, and intellectual discourse.

Constructed Things: For Governing

In China, the construction of buildings, building groups, cities, and infrastructures is typically state-supervised. The earliest surviving book in China on the design and construction of a building is *Yingzao Fashi* (*State Building Standards*), published in 1103 by the imperial court of the Northern Song Dynasty.[9] Written by Li Jie, an official in charge of construction, its aim was to control the use of revenue and to standardize building practice. It specified the use of labor and material, and described methods of assembling precut timber parts into a building in a few structural typologies. For each type, there were eight sizes to correspond to a social hierarchy of the inhabitant of the building – a higher standing was matched with a larger size permitted

Figure 42.4 The Imperial Palace, Beijing, 1930s.

From: Wulf-Diether Graf zu Castell-Rüdenhausen, *Chinaflug: Als Pionier der Lufthansa im Reich der Mitte 1933–1936* (Berlin: Atlantis-Verlag, 1938), 64. Permission and courtesy of Wulf-Diether Graf zu Castell-Rüdenhausen's family.

by the state. The structural elements were to be precut into precise shapes and dimensions before being assembled into a temple or a palace hall – up to several thousand precut parts could be needed for the construction of a large temple or a pagoda. This system, or the completed building itself, is an *empire of parts*, a construct of large oneness with a multiplicity of details and specifications (Figure 42.3). Again, as supervised by the state, they contained signs of a centralized empire, whose government acted as a leader in many spheres, including construction.

Because of the use of timber, the size of a single building in China is limited, and expansion occurs horizontally via courtyards arranged along central axes. The construction of the largest building groups was supervised by the state. The best examples are the palace and imperial tombs from the Ming and Qing Dynasties, found in Beijing and its vicinity. In the case of the Imperial Palace of Beijing (1420), a set of formal rules for design based on feng-shui teaching and the associated literature specified simultaneous control of a smaller and a larger composition (about 30 meters and 300 meters away from a point of observation), which were considered as static "forms" and dynamic "currents" respectively.[10] The majestic Forbidden City (753 × 961 meters) inside Beijing, an empire of courtyards with a sea of golden roofs, is one such result of this literature (Figure 42.4). In each of the imperial tombs of the Qing Dynasty (located northeast and southwest of Beijing), the group of arches, gateways, pavilions, shrines, side buildings, a memorial hall, and hilltop burial ground is arranged with the same set of rules, but at larger scales extending to the surrounding hills and mountains. The sublime layout displays a compositional design at small, medium, large, and extra-large scales, with static forms and dynamic currents stretching to the mountains, whose dancing ranges are considered as "dragons" that breathe vitality into the landscape.

A significant number of cities in China were administrative centers. Among the large ones, such as provincial or imperial capital, the master-plan performed an ordering at both large and small scales. Beijing, the capital of Ming and Qing China from 1420 to 1911, for example, had a grand order for state authority (with the palace and altars on the main axes) and an extensive field of networked local centers (chiefly temples dotted across the city and further afield outside the city walls).[11] The city was conceived of as a large, unifying oneness with an extensive field of multiplicities.

Cities in China must be understood in the larger context of a national geography. Due to early unification of many warring states into one empire in the Qin and Han Dynasties (221 BCE–220 CE), a network of cities as administrative centers across the continent was established.[12] A system of postal routes was built connecting these cities in the direction of the imperial capital. This geopolitical composition dictated that cities be state-cities, not city-states. Unlike the European city-states, where autonomy has led to conflict between cities and institutions, Chinese state–cities belong to the state, which umbrellas all cultural, political, and religious institutions, creating a unification across the continent. This situation manifests a different construct of statehood in China, one that is large in scale and comprehensive in its sphere and scope of coordination.

If a single temple is a micro empire of parts, then the ensembles of these structures, the cities and the networked geography of the state, are larger, scalable empires of parts and sites. Each is a construct of oneness with extensive multiplicities. Here, the art and technology of constructions of different scales are employed for and by the comprehensive state.

Towards an Ethics of Inclusion

We have observed systems of signs, signifying surfaces, and constructed things – three spheres of practice in which a construct of largeness and multiplicity is found, and in which an inclusive epistemology correlates with an inclusive statehood.

This Chinese framework, at least its surface structures, entered a deep crisis in the nineteenth century, and a long process of westernization followed. Today, as China is industrialized and, as it is integrating but also moving beyond "communism" and "capitalism," there is a renewed interest in China's own culture and its core Confucian political ethics. There is ground to argue that China may develop a different modernity in the following decades in which the native framework facilitates a departure from the established Western model and its underlying framing of options or terminologies.

In a global dialogue, this new modernity, or the Chinese tradition within it, may serve as a new critical voice concerning Western constructs, both classical and current. For the notions of oppositions and autonomy, Chinese thinking can provide systems of relatedness. For an exhausted relativism in postmodern thinking, it can provide new "certainties" of bio-ethics and of pragmatic empiricism. For the polemics of multiplicity and difference (leading to identity politics and violent conflicts), it can provide a balanced insight that multiplicities can and should coexist peacefully in a larger oneness. For the practice of excessive individualism, it may reveal the efficacy and wellbeing of a dense, co-present, and governed social life. Finally, for the logic of the alphabet, it can supply an empire of signs – visual, experiential, multidimensional – with which a primary engagement with matter and immanence may be restored.

Notes

1 This chapter is a revised version of my essay "Empire of Signs of Empire" first published in *Harvard Design Magazine*, no. 38 (2014): 132–141. Permission and courtesy of Harvard Graduate School of Design.

2 An initial version of this chapter was published: Jianfei Zhu, "Empire of Signs of Empire: Scale and Statehood in Chinese Culture," *"Do You Read Me?" Harvard Design Magazine*, no. 38 (2014): 132–141. Revisions are made to clarify several points in the current publication.

3 For a full explanation, see Jianfei Zhu, "Ten Thousand Things: Notes on a Construct of Largeness, Multiplicity, and Moral Statehood," in *Common Frameworks: Rethinking the Developmental City in China*, ed. Christopher C.M. Lee (Cambridge, MA: Harvard Graduate School of Design, 2013), 27–41.

4 Gilles Deleuze and Félix Guattari, *A Thousand Plateaus: Capitalism and Schizophrenia*, trans. Brian Massumi (Minneapolis: University of Minnesota Press, 1987), 3–25.

5 This construct is fully explained in Zhu, "Ten Thousand Things," 27–41.

6 Editorial Committee, ed., *Zhongguo Da Baike Quanshu: Zhongguo Lishi*, vol. 2 (Encyclopedia of China: History of China) (Beijing: Zhongguo Da Baike Quanshu Chubanshe, 1992), 936–937; vol. 3, 1618–1619.

7 Editorial, *Zhongguo Da Baike Quanshu*, vol. 2, 966; vol. 3, 1412–1413.

8 Cai Han, "Beisong Hanlin Tuhuayuan Ruogan Wenti Kaoshu (Exposition of a few issues concerning the imperial academy of painting and calligraphy in the Northern Song Dynasty)," *Zhejiang Daxue Xuebao* 36, no. 50 (2006): 176–180.

9 See Liang Sicheng, *Liang Sicheng Quanji* (Complete works of Liang Sicheng) (Beijing: Zhongguo Jianzhu Chubanshe, 2001) 7: 5–27; and Pan Guxi and He Jianzhong, *Yingzao Fashi Jiedu* (Reading *Yingzao Fashi*) (Nanjing: Dongnan Daxue Chubanshe, 2005), 1–19.

10 Wang Qiheng, ed., *Fengshui Lilun Yanjiu* (Studies in Feng Shui theory) (Tianjin: Tianjin Daxue Chubanshe, 1992), 117–137.

11 See Jianfei Zhu, *Chinese Spatial Strategies: Imperial Beijing 1420–1911* (London: RoutledgeCurzon, 2004), 61–90, 222–234.

12 Editorial, *Zhongguo Da Baike Quanshu*, vol. 1, 155, 510–511; vol. 3, 1401–1406. See also Dong Jianhong, *Zhongguo Chengshi Jianshe Shi* (A history of urban construction in China) (Beijing: Zhongguo Jianzhu Gongye Chubanshe, 1989), 158–188.

Bibliography

Cai Han. "Beisong Hanlin Tuhuayuan Ruogan Wenti Kaoshu (Exposition of a Few Issues Concerning the Imperial Academy of Painting and Calligraphy in the Northern Song Dynasty)." *Zhejiang Daxue Xuebao* 36, no. 50 (2006): 176–180.

Deleuze, Gilles and Félix Guattari. *A Thousand Plateaus: Capitalism and Schizophrenia*. Translated by Brian Massumi. Minneapolis: University of Minnesota Press, 1987.

Dong Jianhong. *Zhongguo Chengshi Jianshe Shi* (A History of Urban Construction in China). Beijing: Zhongguo Jianzhu Gongye Chubanshe, 1989.

Editorial Committee, ed. *Zhongguo Da Baike Quanshu: Zhongguo Lishi*, vol. 2–3 (Encyclopedia of China: History of China). Beijing: Zhongguo Da Baike Quanshu Chubanshe, 1992.

Liang Sicheng. *Liang Sicheng Quanji* (Complete Works of Liang Sicheng). Beijing: Zhongguo Jianzhu Chubanshe, 2001.

Pan Guxi and He Jianzhong. *Yingzao Fashi Jiedu* (Reading Yingzao Fashi). Nanjing: Dongnan Daxue Chubanshe, 2005.

Wang Qiheng, ed. *Fengshui Lilun Yanjiu* (Studies in Feng Shui Theory). Tianjin: Tianjin Daxue Chubanshe, 1992.

Zhu, Jianfei. *Chinese Spatial Strategies: Imperial Beijing 1420–1911.* London: Routledge Curzon, 2004.

———. "Ten Thousand Things: Notes on a Construct of Largeness, Multiplicity, and Moral Statehood." In *Common Frameworks: Rethinking the Developmental City in China*, edited by Christopher C.M. Lee, 27–41. Cambridge, MA: Harvard Graduate School of Design, 2013.

———. "Empire of Signs of Empire: Scale and Statehood in Chinese Culture." *Harvard Design Magazine*, no. 38 (2014): 132–141.

Glossary

feng-shui (fengshui)	风水
Han (dynasty)	汉（朝）
Huizong (emperor)	徽宗（皇帝）
Li Jie	李诫
Ming (dynasty)	明（朝）
Qianli Jiangshan Tu	千里江山图
Qin (dynasty)	秦（朝）
Qing (dynasty)	清（朝）
Qingming Shanghe Tu	清明上河图
Shi ji	史记
Siku Quanshu	四库全书
Sima Guang	司马光
Sima Qian	司马迁
Song (dynasty)	宋（朝）
Wang Ximeng	王希孟
weiqi	围棋
Yingzao Fashi	营造法式
Yongle Dadian	永乐大典
Zhang Zeduan	张择端
zi-ran (ziran)	自然
Zizhi Tongjian	资治通鉴

Political Ethics

43

THE STATE FUNCTION OF ARCHITECTURE

Shiqiao Li

The role of architecture in the exercise of governance of place is significantly influenced by the nature of political power. In the Chinese cultural context, political power can be understood as distinctly more "immanent" than "transcendental"; it is invested heavily in the material classifications and distributions of things to the extent that it can perhaps no longer be seen as a system of signifiers serving the function of symbolizing power. These classifications and distributions of things are the operational substances of political power: the sizes and quantities of materials, colors of fabrics and material surfaces, schemes of decorations, and numbers of intercolumniations do not just symbolize status and privilege. They are status and privilege. This state of political affairs depends on a conception of power that is object-based rather than abstract; this object-based conception of power is an integral part of a much larger framework of cultural life that is, I argue, grounded in the Chinese writing system and *poiesis* inherent in the writing system. If the nature of investing in signifiers of political power in the western cultural context calls for political institutions to actualize the operative specificities – the contractual details in constitutions, laws, parliamentary procedures, and policing – that produce efficacy of power, then the nature of Chinese investment in the classifications and distributions of things are already a form of "political institutions" of some sort, giving political power in the Chinese cultural context a distinct character. Chinese architecture, in this sense, can be understood to primarily serve what may be described as a "state function" and only secondarily generate its own "professional" and "aesthetic" domains that we are very accustomed to discussing.

The Immanence of Power

It is perhaps important to understand that this immanent nature of political power in China has not changed in a fundamental way, just as Confucianism and the Chinese writing system have retained their integrity, despite changes in interpretations and forms, for over two millennia. Architecture in China today possesses, at least in some important aspects, the state function as it once did in imperial China. It is of course a fact that China has incorporated and internalized many influences from the west – both directly and through Japan – since the early twentieth century. These influences repositioned the relationship between political power and architecture in many ways: the Republican Revolution in 1911 strived to remove the association between political power and the imperial system of dress codes and palaces that framed it. Sun Yat-sen's

DOI: 10.4324/9781315851112-65

vision for China was decisively influenced by his western education in medicine, and in culture in general. His Chinese suit for himself as the head of new Chinese republic, a relatively minor detail among his revolutionary introduction of western style political institutions to China, paralleled the western suit; in moving away from the strict hierarchical codifications of colors and materials in the Chinese imperial system of dress codes, the new Chinese suit, in its simplicity, manifested his aspiration to bring to China a notion of equality of persons that was increasingly attained in western countries, and that became one of the key inspirations for his revolution in China. It is from the times of the Republican Revolution when "architecture," understood primarily as a distinct discipline and aesthetic domain, was first introduced to China. Other momentous events in the twentieth century following the Republican Revolution, such as the May Fourth Movement, the Communist Revolution, the Cultural Revolution, and the Open Door Policy, all seem to indicate abrupt and chaotic moving away from Chinese tradition. However, abrupt and chaotic changes should not eclipse the reality that both Confucianism and the Chinese writing system remain perhaps the most powerful underlying forces that newer forms of political and social practices can be conducted. In other words, continuity recasts new influences in defining ways.

In the western cultural context, even at moments of intense union between power and materials exemplified by the French monarchy and its courtly material lives, power can probably still be understood as being transcendental; the trappings of power, so to speak, are symbolic and not inherent in the symbols themselves. During the centuries between the Renaissance and Industrial Revolution, European royal palaces, king's bed chambers, his or her art collections, thrones, and crowns served as signifiers of political power rather than as systems of material classifications and distributions that contain power. The country houses and art collections of the courtiers, larger and more magnificent than those of the English monarchy in the seventeenth century, could exist precisely because of the notion of the transcendentality of power; this would have been an impossible condition in the context of imperial China. It is of course apparent that power is always connected with materials; Aristotle explicitly linked the level and scale of judicious expenditure with the magnificence of persons,[1] and Christopher Wrens realized that architecture has its "political use" after spending a good portion of his life attempting to establish the English Crown and the Anglican Church through the materiality of architecture.[2] However, there is an important difference between the power that is believed to reside in materials and that seen to be symbolized by materials.

The history of power in the western cultural context can also be understood in one way as a history of the decoupling of power from materials; it can be seen as a process of power being gradually abstracted from materials. The transcendentality of power, at least in the secular context, gives us a way to understand this removal of display of valuable material possessions around powerful persons since the twentieth century; today's secular political leaders appear to be in an ordinary state of dressing and decoration. This ordinariness of politically powerful persons is, it would seem, highly orchestrated; it is of course an illusion – the perfect equality of appearances belies the stark contrast of power status measured in many other ways – resulting from the western political ideal of equality and universality of rights. The transcendentality of power allowed the "modern constitution," in Latour's terms, to purify political power of its material and corporeal associations; power emanates from a contract and an elected office, rather than from material and corporeal substances. The efficacy of western political power becomes increasingly produced through the institutions of power. A key moment of this purification took place in the debate between Robert Filmer's political power inherent in the body of the king and John Locke's monarchical power instituted in the contract between the king and his subjects. In *Patriarcha, or, The Natural Power of Kings* (1680), Filmer argued for the notion of divine right, which was inherited through a long blood line tracing back to Adam; in *Two Treatises of Government* (1689), Locke advocated the idea of the ruler and the ruled entering into an agreement based on the notion of natural rights of human beings. The 1689 English Bill of Rights emerged precisely as a prototype of an institution of power that relocated power from the body of James II to the fictive body of the Parliament. The decoupling of power from materials, it may be argued, released architecture into a territory where it had to formulate an ontological framework. Architecture became possible when political power was separated from its materiality. The intense intellectual interest in treatises of architecture in late seventeenth century – in the form of translations of Vitruvius and Palladio, and in the form of new definitions of the grounds of architecture by Wren and Ware – can be seen as part of that effort. By removing it from the monopolization of power, architecture emerged to articulate its professionalization and aestheticization; a body of knowledge and a disinterested academic discipline became established. The incorporation of architectural education into the university system was one important stage in the professionalization and aestheticization of architecture. Under these conditions, architecture has a different kind of role to play in contemporary politics; instead of becoming sites of immanent political power, architecture is used as instruments of power. From the Urban Areas Act in South Africa, to the Israeli settlements based on fortification design in Palestinian territories, to the construction of the Berlin Wall, architecture provides a material and spatial strategy of violent policing of communities divided by ideology and privilege.

Neither the symbolic, nor the professional, nor the instrumental functions of architecture can describe adequately the realities of the built environment in China. The immanence of power, as a deeply rooted cultural condition in China, places a pervasive importance in the legitimacy of things (*wu*) as having some form of ontological status; this is deeply intertwined with its linguistic strategy of meaning in figures (*xiang*) as inherent locations of meanings. Perhaps paralleling the alphabetic linguistic strategy, knowing and understanding in the western cultural context often meant the ability to reduce a larger set of things to a smaller set of things – seeking instruments of abstraction and transcendentality – with mathematics and alphabetic systems as their archetypes. The moment of knowing becomes the moment of reduction; hence induction, despite its apparent logical flaws, is used commonly as a path to knowledge. This is the scheme of knowledge laid out in Francis Bacon's *The Advancement of Learning* (1605), which served as one the foundational texts for western modernity. In the Chinese cultural context, mathematics was not an archetype; instead, it was numerology. Mathematics reduces and numerology does not. The strategy of meaning of the Chinese writing system makes use of a very large set of figures; similarly, knowing and understanding demands an intellectual engagement with a much larger set of things – normatively indicated as ten thousand things (*wanwu*) as well as ten thousand figures (*wanxiang*). Each thing, instead of being considered as an iteration of a type, is seen to have its own reason; "ten thousand things all have their own principles, and it is easy to follow them but difficult to go against them," claimed the influential eleventh-century Confucian scholar Cheng Hao.[3] Furthermore, "outside *Dao* there are no things and outside things there is no Dao."[4] Contemporary scholars of the Song and the Ming dynasties (tenth to seventeenth centuries, when book publishing was at its height) are often astonished by the penchant habit of Chinese authors to describe objects, not through best representatives of types but through evenly spread lists and rankings; the Ming novel *Jin Ping Mei* displays a "mania for objects" that can be seen to suggest an entirely different realm of significance for materiality,[5] and the myriad Ming-dynasty books on almost all subjects relished the opportunities to endlessly document lists and rankings of things and people.[6] This "lists mania" conveys a very different conception of groupings of things – immanent rather than abstract – which can indeed be seen as a provocation to the western mind; Foucault's use of Borges's fictitious "Chinese encyclopedia" as his springboard to launch a deep critique of western modernity demonstrates the far-reaching implications of two different kinds of thoughts. Foucault's work poses questions on Chinese thought (how can order be possible?) as well as on western thought (how can we have freedom if difference is not legitimate?). In the Chinese context, it is not abstract order – and the documentation of abstract order – that dictates knowledge; it is the activities embedded in the propensities of situations that lead to efficacy. One of the most striking manifestations of the immanence of power in things in today's China appears in the realm of economic life – the exchange of goods as being always already embedded in all exchanges in life – where efficacy is not tied to theoretical modeling only, but also to embedded economic activities constituting the propensity of situations.[7] Like in the late Ming dynasty (sixteenth century) when China's economic activities were by far the largest in the world,[8] the current increase of economic activities in China, against the incessant advice and pressure emanating from tenants of neo-liberal economic modeling, is testament to the strength of a form of economic life grounded in the notion of immanence. This is no small distinction; it can be seen to be the heart of the "great divergence" between Europe and China since the seventeenth century as presented by Kenneth Pomeranz,[9] and at the center of the current rise of East Asia again as a prominent place for world economic activities. It certainly makes a big difference in terms of how the state functions through architecture.

The Politics of *Cai* and *Jian*

A consistent feature in construction in imperial China, for many centuries, was that buildings were distinguished and classified by numbers and sizes of building components, and not by typological distinctions. In the history of western architecture, particularly since the Renaissance, buildings and their functions find increasingly tight fit with one another; spiritual buildings and popular entertainment venues have very different appearances. We can perhaps describe this feature as the tectonic quality of buildings. Their looks correspond to their functions. In the Chinese imperial building examples such as those of the Forbidden City in Beijing, there is only one type: made of roof, columns and windows, and ground floor. All functions seem to have to be forced into this type. The building type is then stretched to form corridors, enlarged to give it higher imperial significance, and reduced to become pavilions; out of these manipulations, there is a formal system that is organized around the sizes and numbers of building components. *Cai* (timber size) and *jian* (intercolumniation) are two defining measures, as they are used in manuals of construction related to the construction of official buildings in imperial China. In the twentieth century, Chinese architects and historians of Chinese architecture have viewed these two measures as a form of modularity similar to that of the diameter of the classical order in the western architectural tradition.[10] But this is misleading. *Cai* and *jian* are not modular. The eight grades of timber size and the numbers of intercolumniations contained in the Song-dynasty manual of construction *Yingzao Fashi* (1103) convey the imperial practice of buildings as material grades. The Qing dynasty construction manual, *Gongcheng zuofa zeli* (1734), adopted a system of 11 grades.[11] The 8 and 11 grades of *cai* do not give us 8 or 11 kinds of buildings or styles; they are the same building in 8 and 11 sizes. They reflect material hierarchy in the most material ways. The *Yingzao Fashi*, unlike western architecture treatises, is a demonstration of the state occupation of architecture in imperial China. The official records in China were filled with descriptions of the graded distributions of buildings; very little attention was paid to the function and structure of these buildings.[12]

In the eighteenth-century imperial collection *Siku quanshu*, the *Yingzao Fashi* as well as other building-related books were classified under the "governance" (*zhengshulei*) section of the branch of "histories" (*shibu*).[13] This classification perhaps indicates the importance of imperial orders from the past, as they were embedded in the materiality of buildings. The imperial administrative structure in China saw the construction of buildings as part of the establishment of rituals, to be formulated by ritual offices, among them the Court of Imperial Sacrifices (Taichang Si) and the Ministry of Rites (Li Bu), in ways that were far removed from any conception of "architecture" in the western cultural context. Ministry of Rites was charged with devising ritual ceremonial details – exceedingly material in all their operational aspects – in relation to those of auspicious (*ji*, concerning temples of heaven, earth, ancestry), funeral (*xiong*, concerning funeral rituals, tombs and burial sites), military (*jun*, concerning rituals associated with military hierarchies), reception (*bin*, concerning settings for the reception of foreign embassies), and celebration (*jia*, concerning celebratory occasions such as accessions and weddings). Each courtly event would concern ritual planning of one or several of these types of rituals, involving not only exact and detailed specifications of clothes, music and dance, food and drinks, but also those of spatial settings and building forms. Nothing was left out of this tightly controlled materialization of imperial privilege and power.[14] Among the six ministries of the imperial administration – those of Personnel, Revenue, Rites, Works, Punishment, War – the Ministry of Works responsible for construction and cities ranked perhaps the lowest. It was the Ministry of Rites that masterminded the core moral and aesthetic values through its defining role in the formulation of Confucian rituals and the examination system. Rites have been central to Confucianism; and rites are material. The Song dynasty assertion of Confucian rites through building was part of a much larger attempt to expel the mixing of Chinese culture with those of the steppe tribes; the love of riding-based games such as polo and hunting in the Tang era (618–907) gave way to that for sedentary and contemplative learning.[15] The political project of the Song dynasty (960–1279) to restore imperial Confucianism through extensive re-establishment of ancient rites placed a high demand on the regularity of buildings. The *Yingzao Fashi* compiled by Li Jie in 1103 can be seen as a culmination of the materiality of rites; the eight ranks of structural timber usage determined material and spatial ritual orders in close parallel to the hierarchical ritual orders determined at the Ministry of Rites.[16] From the founding era of the Chinese culture during the Han dynasty (206 BCE–220 CE), Confucian rites have been central to Chinese governance; this "imperial Confucianism"[17] relied heavily on the ontological status of materials in its monopolization of the aesthetic realm in Chinese life, making it the physical manifestations of rites.

In the eagerness to equate documents such as the *Yingzao Fashi* and *Gongcheng zuofa zeli* to those by Vitruvius and Palladio, we have neglected to point out that these documents were documents of governance, which was distributed to a great degree through material grades. The endeavors of the pioneering scholars of Chinese architecture in the twentieth century, to a large extent, were focused on retrofitting a realm of "architecture" in this rites-based Chinese building tradition to match that of the western conception of architecture. This seems to be the primary goals of the works of Osvald Sirén (1879–1966), Ito Chuta (1867–1954), and Ernst Boerschmann (1873–1949), as well as those of the first generation of architects and scholars trained in the western architectural tradition, such as Liang Sicheng (1901–1972), Lin Huiyin (1904–1955), and Liu Dunzhen (1897–1968). The resulting "history of Chinese architecture" gained tremendous momentum as a project of intellectual reform in twentieth-century China;[18] it also presents Chinese architecture in the light of western historiography. The rise of architectural history in China obscures many fundamental features of its building tradition; our understanding of Chinese architecture in the twentieth and twenty-first centuries, it seems, began with a flawed perspective. The immanence of power, and its history through the materiality of buildings in imperial China, gives us a different starting point to examine many important features of contemporary Chinese architecture.

The Immanent State in Buildings and Cities

If we pause to examine long-term continuities rather than short-term adaptations, this imperial tradition of material grades can be seen to have had a range of important manifestations in contemporary Chinese cities; it certainly gives us insight into why, despite features taken from western or international norms of architectural practice, Chinese cities appear to have distinct formal characters. Today, the state function of Chinese architecture is a complex system of status and privileges that is interwoven with normative state functions from central to local. Compared with western cities such as London and Paris, the Chinese city, both ancient and contemporary, never achieved similar levels of political independence; they have always been part of the state function. Without this municipal independence, it is difficult for Chinese cities to attain some degree of architectural and urban distinction outside the well-established material orders. In the context of the immanence of power, Chinese cities tend to converge towards similar urban ideals and forms, whether it is through courtyards and gardens, or through municipal centers, planning museums, and prestigious architectural projects. Many factors contribute to the making of the Chinese city, from the way its design and construction capacity are organized, to the grading system of cities that, like the past material-based grading systems in the imperial hierarchies, gives each city a certain material limit.

An understanding of the state function of architecture in China must begin with an understanding of the numerous and powerful "institutes of architectural design" as work units (*danwei*). This is a key aspect of the state function of architecture that has tremendous impact on the Chinese city. Work unit is a general term used to describe a wide variety of places to live and work established since the 1950s, ranging from government ministries to large industrial complexes, universities, and institutes of architectural designs. In line with the ancient sensibility, work units are hierarchical and not typological; their ranks are determined by their sizes and centrality to the government rather than by the types of work: they are either central (*zhongyang*), local (*difang*), or grass-root (*jiceng*). Being part of a work unit does not just mean having a job; its membership means a combined "provision of housing, free medical care, child care centers, kindergartens, dining halls, bath houses, service companies, and collective enterprises to employ the children of staff, the *danwei* provides its members with a complete social guarantee and welfare services."[19] The work unit is both a unit of production, a system of care, and a method of human management; for many decades since the establishment of the work unit in the mid-twentieth century, a person always belonged to a work unit and abided by the rules and regulations of that unit. All inter–work unit matters, official and personal, required "introduction letters" from one's work unit. The work unit is an extraordinary crystallization of a wide range of demands in the Chinese city: cultural heritage, social welfare, ideological control, labor management, and economic viability.[20] All these demands were carried out through material grades of the work units, as well as similar grading systems within the work units.

Danwei remains a powerful institutional form for the production of architecture in China today, although many *danwei* operations have adopted features from business corporations and large architectural firms around the world. There is an emerging hybrid that is highly effective. Both as a *danwei* and as a production unit of architectural design, the state-owned Design Institute (*shejiyuan*) plays a uniquely important role in Chinese architecture. Established in the 1950s to take up the task of designing the reconstruction of China after decades of wars, these design institutes reinvented themselves to become some of the most productive and influential architectural design institutions in China. They combine state legitimacy with cost effectiveness as well as professional and technical competence, becoming increasingly competitive in the context of international competitions. Among the design giants in today's China, Shanghai Xiandai Architectural Design (SXDA), China Architecture Design & Research Group (CAG), Beijing Institute of Architectural Design (BIAD), Shenzhen General Institute of Architectural Design and Research (SADI), and Architectural Design and Research Institute of Tongji University (TJAD) all came from this background, and all are outstanding as effective design institutions; they overshadow private design firms. From the Tiananmen Square (1950s) to the Olympic Games (2008) and Shanghai Expo (2010), these design institutes combined their state legitimacy with an ancient tradition and contemporary demand. The BIAD, for instance, employed about 1,500 professionals in 2009; it has 29 "ateliers," each led by a talented and recognized architect or engineer. From its establishment to today, BIAD has designed an astonishing 15 billion square meters of floor space all over China.

Architectural design firms and architects are graded in contemporary Chinese cities: grade one (*jiaji*), grade two (*yiji*), or grade three (*bingji*) for design firms, and class one (*yiji*) or class two (*erji*) for registered architects. These parallel the grading system of the vast array of bureaucratic positions standardized throughout China. Perhaps unique in the world, Chinese cities also have a strict system of grades, which is accompanied by distinct levels of resource distribution. In orders of importance, Chinese cities belong to one of five categories: capital, provincial capital, provincial city, prefecture city, and towns. In order of administrative differentiations, at the top of the ranking order of cities are Special Administrative Regions (Hong Kong, Macau), Special Economic Zones (Shenzhen, Zhuhai), followed by Direct Administrative Cities (Beijing, Tianjin, Shanghai, Chongqing), Provincial Capitals, Sub-Provincial Cities, Prefecture Cities, County Cities, and a bottom layer of large number of towns.[21] None of these are typological differentiations; they are state functional categories. The state determination of the grades of cities in China has an immense impact on the ways in which these cities develop in the context of emulations and competitions for prestige, status, and resources. This impact is particularly strong in the design of new administrative centers. In the late 1990s, when the city of Shenzhen planned its new administrative center to materialize its status of Special Economic Zone (for which there was no precedent), it followed Beijing's axial plan – a combined spatial arrangement of the Imperial Palace and Tiananmen Square – against the backdrop of a hill. Although designed by the New York–based architectural firm Lee/Timchula Architects, this new administrative center revisits an ancient diagram of order in Beijing that had been reconstituted in the 1950s. The Shenzhen administrative center is dominated by the roof of the City Hall; its gigantic size and disconnection with the function of the roof highlight the nature of this roof as a figure, perhaps a contemporary reconstitution of the imperial rooflines of Beijing. Kisho Kurokawa's landscape master plan for the Shenzhen city center in 1997 adds a layer of richly narrated artificial landscape called "urban score"; certainly more literary than musical, the urban score invents a narrative for Shenzhen that works together with the ordered administrative center. Arata Isozaki's Cultural Centre – made of a concert hall and a library – stands as a figurative object; while typologically different, the concert hall and the library have almost identical exterior forms, perhaps recalling the absence of typological differentiation in the Chinese architectural tradition.

Between Tiananmen Square and the new administrative center of Shenzhen – two temporal and geographical ends of the state function of architecture – there lies a vast landscape of similar looking administrative centers in Chinese cities. In the complex rankings of cities, the city of Dongyang in Zhejiang Province is a lowly Prefecture City with a population of

820,000. Traditionally known for its woodcarving and talent (as seen in the number of successful candidates in the imperial examinations), today it is known for its production of modern building materials and its provision of filming sites (the film studio city of Hengdian falls within its administration). The new city center is built across the Dongyang River from the traditional city center, laid out as a grand diagram, dominated by the massive Administrative Centre, which is larger than those in many larger cities; spread along a grid next to the main building are a series of buildings indicating other government functions, such as the procuratorate, the public security bureau, the trade and commerce building, and a court house. While the Administrative Centre is designed in a contemporary style, the Dongyang People's Court House and Administrative Building are modeled loosely on western classical designs with Corinthian porticoes and a dome. Constructed by local construction firm Guanghong Construction in 2004 and winning several provincial construction awards, the Administrative Centre and the People's Court House are rather generic in designs; they are certainly far removed from the high-profile public building projects in Beijing and Shenzhen. However, their unremarkable designs are more than compensated for by their bulk; the expansive square in front of the Administrative Centre shares the same diagrammatic quality as those of Beijing and Shenzhen, and the contrived western classicism sits uncomfortably in the context of a traditional Zhejiang prefecture. The large administrative center of Dongyang gives us another view of the state function of architecture: the oversized administrative center can be seen as an expression of a political aspiration grounded in its extraordinary economic success. Beyond the overwhelming visual and spatial experience of the architecture, the central ambition here appears to have little to do with architecture; it is the political ambition to advance the municipal status of Dongyang in the strict system of grading cities that perhaps motivated the gigantic endeavor of the city.

It is entirely possible to assemble, from the enormously complex and fast-moving productions of architecture in China today, stories of Chinese architecture and the Chinese city that resemble accounts of architecture in the western tradition: perhaps forms of critical regionalism, perhaps works of cultural specificity nevertheless addressing similar universal architectural concerns. The increasing presence of western architects in China makes this form of story-telling compelling and important; the market place has a levelling effect that provides a common platform for architecture to formulate practicality and iconicity that seem to be fundamental to today's world financial operations. However, beyond all these possible narratives of Chinese architecture, the state function of Chinese architecture, its cultural tradition of the immanence of power, and the architectural and urban strategies from those in power constantly seeking status and influence through the materiality of architecture in Chinese cities should be considered to be one of the key narratives. Architecture has never played the same role in China as in the west; it is important that they should be considered in this way when we attempt to understand Chinese cities. The end of China's long-lasting imperial administration at the beginning of the twentieth century did not lead to the abandonment of the association of power with materials; it merely put it through a profound process of transformation. Emerging from this transformation is perhaps a complex picture of municipal dependence on the state, systems of classification of cities, design institutes and architects, and newer forms of architectural practices that are inspired by western traditions of architecture. All these exist in China as layered conditions; while it is important to acknowledge the emerging new profession and discipline of architecture in China with their tremendous advancements and achievements, it is also crucial to emphasize that all these accomplishments are framed within a much larger and more deeply rooted tradition of the state function of architecture.

Notes

1 Aristotle, *Nicomachean Ethics*, 1122b, 10–15, in Richard McKeon ed., *The Basic Works of Aristotle* (New York: The Modern Library, 2001), pp. 935–1112.
2 Lydia M. Soo, *Wren's "Tracts" on Architecture and Other Writings* (Cambridge: Cambridge University Press, 1998), 153.
3 Cheng Hao and Cheng Yi, *Er Cheng Ji* (Collected Works of the Two Chengs) (Beijing: Zhonghua Shuju, 1981), "Yishu," (Chapter 11), 123.
4 Cheng, *Er Cheng Ji*, 73.
5 Naifei Ding, *Obscene Things: Sexual Politics in Jin Ping Mei* (Durham, NC and London: Duke University Press, 2002), 188–189.
6 Craig Clunas, *Empire of Great Brightness, Visual and Material Cultures of Ming China, 1368–1644* (Honolulu: University of Hawai'i Press, 2007), 131–136.
7 Michael Keith, Scott Lash, Jakob Arnoldi, and Tyler Rooker, *China Constructing Capitalism, Economic Life and Urban Change* (Abingdon: Routledge, 2013).
8 Andre Gunder Frank, *ReOrient: Global Economy in the Asian Age* (Berkeley and Los Angeles: University of California Press, 1998).
9 Kenneth Pomeranz, *The Great Divergence, China, Europe, and the Making of the Modern World Economy* (Princeton and Oxford: Princeton University Press, 2000).
10 Li Shiqiao, "Reconstituting Chinese Building Tradition: The *Yingzao fashi* in the Early Twentieth Century," *Journal of Society of Architectural Historians* 62, no. 4 (2003): 470–489.
11 Liang Sicheng, *Qingshi Yingzao Zeli* (Construction methods of Qing dynasty) (Beijing: Society for Research in Chinese Architecture, 1934).
12 Liang Sicheng, *Zhongguo Jianzhushi* (History of Chinese architecture) (Hong Kong: Joint Publishing, 2000; first completed 1943), 10.
13 Xu Subin, *Jindai Zhongguo Jinazhuxue de Dansheng* (The beginning of Chinese modern architecture) (Tianjin: Tianjin daxue chubanshe, 2010), 15.
14 Zhao Zhongnan et al., *Mingdai Gongting Dianzhishi* (History of Imperial Rituals of the Ming Dynasty) (Beijing: Zijincheng Chubanshe, 2010).
15 Jacque Gernet, *A History of Chinese Civilization*, trans. J.R. Foster (Cambridge: Cambridge University Press, 1982), 331.
16 Song dynasty documents, such as *Sanlitu* by Nie Chongyi in 962 and the chapters in the Song encyclopedia *Taiping yulan* compiled in 983, convey an overarching concern for the restoration of rites. See Jiren Feng, *Chinese Architecture and Metaphor: Song Culture in the Yingzao Fashi Building Manual* (Honolulu and Hong Kong: University of Hawai'i Press, 2012).
17 John King Fairbank and Merle Goldman, *China: A New History* (Cambridge, MA: Harvard University Press, 1998), 62.
18 Li Shiqiao, "Writing a Modern Chinese Architectural History: Liang Sicheng and Liang Qichao," *Journal of Architectural Education*, no. 56 (2002): 35–45.
19 Li Hanlin, "China's Danwei Phenomenon and the Mechanisms of Conformity in Urban Communities," *Sociology Research* 5 (1993): 23–32, translated and quoted in David Bray, *Social Space and Governance in Urban China: The* Danwei *System from Origins to Reform* (Stanford: Stanford University Press, 2005), 3–4.
20 Bray, *Social Space and Governance in Urban China*; Lu Duanfang, *Remaking Chinese Urban Form, Modernity, Scarcity and Space, 1949–2005* (London and New York: Routledge, 2006).
21 Gu Chaolin, *Zhongguo Chengshi Tixi: Lishi, Xianzhuang, Zhanwang* (The system of Chinese cities and towns, history, current conditions and prospects) (Beijing: Shangwu yinshuguan, 1992).

Bibliography

Aristotle. *Nicomachean Ethics*, 1122b, 10–15, in Richard McKeon, ed., *The Basic Works of Aristotle*, 935–1112. New York: The Modern Library, 2001.
Bray, David. *Social Space and Governance in Urban China: The Danwei System from Origins to Reform*. Stanford: Stanford University Press, 2005.
Cheng Hao and Cheng Yi. *Er Cheng Ji* (Collected Works of the Two Chengs). Beijing: Zhonghua Shuju, 1981.

Clunas, Craig. *Empire of Great Brightness: Visual and Material Cultures of Ming China, 1368–1644.* Honolulu: University of Hawai'i Press, 2007.

Ding, Naifei. *Obscene Things: Sexual Politics in Jin Ping Mei.* Durham, NC and London: Duke University Press, 2002.

Fairbank, John King and Merle Goldman. *China: A New History.* Cambridge, MA: Harvard University Press, 1998.

Feng, Jiren. *Chinese Architecture and Metaphor: Song Culture in the Yingzao Fashi Building Manual.* Honolulu and Hong Kong: University of Hawai'i Press, 2012.

Frank, Andre Gunder. *ReOrient: Global Economy in the Asian Age.* Berkeley and Los Angeles: University of California Press, 1998.

Gernet, Jacque. *A History of Chinese Civilization.* Translated by J.R. Foster. Cambridge: Cambridge University Press, 1982.

Gu Chaolin. *Zhongguo Chengshi Tixi: Lishi, Xianzhuang, Zhanwang* (The System of Chinese Cities and Towns: History, Current Conditions and Prospects). Beijing: Shangwu Yinshuguan, 1992.

Keith, Michael, Scott Lash, Jakob Arnoldi and Tyler Rooker. *China Constructing Capitalism: Economic Life and Urban Change.* Abingdon: Routledge, 2013.

Li Shiqiao. "Writing a Modern Chinese Architectural History: Liang Sicheng and Liang Qichao." *Journal of Architectural Education,* no. 56 (2002): 35–45.

———. "Reconstituting Chinese Building Tradition: The *Yingzao fashi* in the Early Twentieth Century." *Journal of Society of Architectural Historians* 62, no. 4 (2003): 470–489.

Liang Sicheng. *Qingshi Yingzao Zeli* (Construction Methods of Qing Dynasty). Beijing: Society for Research in Chinese Architecture, 1934.

———. *Zhongguo Jianzhushi* (History of Chinese Architecture). Hong Kong: Joint Publishing, 2000 (completed 1943).

Lu, Duanfang. *Remaking Chinese Urban Form, Modernity, Scarcity and Space, 1949–2005.* London and New York: Routledge, 2006.

Pomeranz, Kenneth. *The Great Divergence: China, Europe, and the Making of the Modern World Economy.* Princeton and Oxford: Princeton University Press, 2000.

Soo, Lydia M. *Wren's "Tracts" on Architecture and Other Writings.* Cambridge: Cambridge University Press, 1998.

Xu Subin. *Jindai Zhongguo Jianzhuxue de Dansheng* (The Beginning of Chinese Modern Architecture). Tianjin: Tianjin Daxue Chubanshe, 2010.

Zhao Zhongnan et al. *Mingdai Gongting Dianzhishi* (History of Imperial Rituals of the Ming Dynasty). Beijing: Zijincheng Chubanshe, 2010.

Glossary

Beijing	北京
bingji	丙级
cai	材
Chongqing	重庆
danwei	单位
Dao	道
defang	地方
Dongyang	东阳
erji	二级
Gongcheng Zuofa Zeli	工程做法则例
Guanghong (Company)	广宏（建筑公司）
Hengdian	横店
ji	吉
jia	嘉
jiaji	甲级
jian	间

jiceng	基层
Jin Ping Mei	金瓶梅
Liang Sicheng	梁思成
Lin Huiyin	林徽音
Liu Dunzhen	刘敦桢
Shanghai	上海
shejiyuan	设计院
Shenzhen	深圳
shibu	史部
Siku Quanshu	四库全书
Sun Yat-sen	孙逸仙
Tai Chang Si	太常寺
Tianjin	天津
Tongji (university)	同济（大学）
wanwu	万物
wanxiang	万象
wu	物
Xiandai (group)	现代（集团）
xiang	象
xiong	凶
yiji	一级
yiji	乙级
Yingzao Fashi	营造法式
Zhejiang	浙江
zhengshulei	政书类
zhongyang	中央
Zhuhai	珠海

44

POLITICAL SPACE AND MORAL STATEHOOD

Jianfei Zhu

This chapter explores a conceptual dialogue between Han Fei (c. 283–233 BC) and Jeremy Bentham (1748–1832), between a Chinese theory of centralized authority and a European approach to centralization of institutional and state power. On the China side, Beijing, capital of Ming and Qing dynasty (1420–1911) will be studied as a case in which the Chinese tradition was embodied and, in that city, a spatial machine of control will be identified and analyzed. On the European side, we will read the development as identified by Michel Foucault concerning the rise of a disciplinary control at local and state level. Between these two lines, following François Jullien, we will explore comparability of a political space of dynastic China with a disciplinary space of early modern Europe. Differences between them and overall diversions of the two political traditions will be discussed as well.

Bentham, Foucault, and Jullien

It is well known that Michel Foucault had studied institutions formed in early modern Europe, such as clinics, hospitals, asylums, and especially prisons. Foucault examined them as disciplinary grounds on which problems of knowledge, power, the body, space, and surveillance became intertwined. Rational knowledge was accumulated from a space of defined power relations in these settings in which human bodies, as objects of the gaze of an enquiring mind, were detained, placed, observed, studied, and normalized for a moral or productive purpose. In the case of the prison, in its formation in the eighteenth and nineteenth century, Foucault identified a precise and "analytical" space of a disciplinary power relationship, a pattern that was generalized into a modern disciplinary society ruled by state apparatuses above and managed with surveillance devices at institutional nodes on ground. Jeremy Bentham's design of an ideal penitentiary, the Panopticon, was regarded as a critical breakthrough in this process (Figure 44.1).[1]

François Jullien, furthermore, indicated similarities between Bentham's panoptic principles and the Legalist ideas Han Fei advised to the emperors in China. Articulated in *The Propensity of Things* (1995), Jullien proposes to read diverse areas of practice in traditional China, such as waging a war, forming a state authority, composing a poem, organizing a landscape painting, as well as theorizing on dynastic history, from the point of view of a single Chinese word, *shi*, meaning propensity and powerful tendency in a situation.[2] Reading these areas one after another, Jullien discusses comparability between Chinese and European cases. Sun Zi's *The Art*

DOI: 10.4324/9781315851112-66

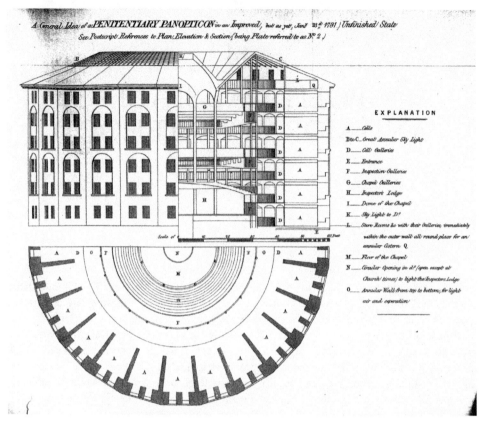

Figure 44.1   Plan, elevation, and section of a Panopticon designed by Jeremy Bentham.

From: John Bowring, ed., *The Works of Jeremy Bentham*, Vol. 4 (Edinburgh: William Tait, 1843).

of War (fourth century BC) is compared with Carl von Clausewitz's *On War* (1832), in that both are the first treatises on realities of war that can be analyzed in a rational manner in the two cultures.[3] Principles of the Panopticon are then related to Han Fei's Legalism in that, for Jullien, Bentham's ideas were already explored and practiced in China at a larger scale.[4]

Bentham's Panopticon is a prison in a circular shape with a watchtower at the center.[5] While the prison guard at the center is dimly lit, the prison inmates are in the cells placed around the periphery, well lit by the windows on the peripheral wall behind and the directed skylights above. While the guard can see all the inmates with ease, the inmates, mutually separated by cell walls but visually open to the center, cannot actually see the guard clearly, because of the distribution of light and spatial location. With this, an asymmetry of visibility is established, the controlling *effect* of the watching eye can thus be prolonged all the time, and the effect can then be self-internalized by the inmates themselves, on the body but more so upon the soul (Figure 44.2). The precise design, the analytical space, the rational and functional architecture, now *works* as a machine of power, 24/7 and on its own. The actual presence or absence of the guard is no longer important – the machine works "automatically," with a central mechanism of the set-up, the asymmetrical eye-power radiating, effectively, from center to periphery.

Figure 44.2 A prisoner, in his cell, kneeling at prayer before the central inspection tower.

From: N. Harou-Romain, *Plan for a Penitentiary* (1840).

Han Fei, Legalism, and Dynastic Beijing

It is often said that after the Han dynasty (206 BC–AD 220), Chinese imperial rule was based on a synthesis of Confucianism and Legalism, that is, a combination of moral idealism and political realism, of a cosmological ethics of the emperor as Son of Heaven and a realist functionalism of the throne as the center of complete control. However, when we examine research literature on Chinese capital cities such as Beijing, we encounter descriptions of the city's formal

715

and symbolic layout representing the Son of Heaven, rather than a real space of state authority and its effective operation.[6] On the one hand, operative practice and a space that sustains it, a field of spatial practice, are ignored. On the other, the realist tradition of Legalism is not taken up seriously in the established scholarship. A convention that privileges a semantic reading of classical texts such as *Kaogongji* (notes on construction) has contributed to this bias in research. The classic describes an ideal plan for a capital city: it should be symmetrical, centralized, and square in shape, with a careful placement of the temple and the shrine, and the palace and the market. The idea of the emperor as a central figure between heaven and earth, who follows ways of heaven and leads all humans on earth, is clearly expressed in the layout prescribed in the text. These features can be found to a certain extent in real capital cities such as Beijing. The grand axis, the concentric layout, and the symbolic posture representing the authority of the Son of Heaven are thus repeatedly described in almost all academic literature on the city of dynastic Beijing. But, if there was indeed an ancient and long-standing synthesis of Confucianism and Legalism in the approach to imperial rule in China, where was the Legalist tradition in Beijing? Han Fei's Legalism emphasized principles of *shi*, *fa* and *shu*, namely, the use of powerful positioning, the setting-up of rules and regulations, and the employment of techniques of investigation.[7] How were these ideas applied and their corresponding practices constituted in the space of Beijing (Figure 44.3)?

Beijing of the Ming and Qing dynasty (1420–1911) involved layers of spatial practices that together constituted a pragmatic and functioning domain of power relations. Beijing was excessively deep. Walls and distances separated the inner center from the outside, creating an excessive inequality between inside and outside, center and periphery. Along the central axis, standing at Daqingmen (the southern front gate of the Imperial City), one had to walk 1,750 meters and pass seven gates to reach Qianqingmen (the southern gate to the inner court of the Palace City), and 2,000 meters and 14 gates to reach an inner courtyard beyond. There was a division of Inner Court and Outer Court, spatially and in organization. While eunuchs and palace ladies served the emperor in the former in internal spaces, ministers and officials assisted the emperor in governing the empire in the latter, in spaces mostly outside the Palace and Imperial City. Serving the body and the mind of the emperor respectively, the inner and the outer courts, that is, people who worked in the two areas, often competed, opposed, and even confronted each other at times. There was therefore a triangular structure of the throne as an organization: the emperor at the top interacted with the eunuchs and ladies on the one hand, and the ministers and officials on the other, while the two parties also interacted (officially or informally) in competition for imperial attention. Each of the three lines of this triangle involved a set of power relations: to delegate and to limit power in the first, to remain close yet be kept afar in the second, and to collaborate but also to compete and even oppose in the third. These three sets of power relations constituted a spatial politics and a political space of the inner structure of imperial authority.[8]

For the emperor's management of the empire, the emperor–minister/official connection was most important. There was always a tension between them: while the emperor needed the ministers and formal departments of the government, he also wanted to limit their power. In historical evolution, there had been a gradual diminishing of the power of the minsters and the formal offices, with an outward move of their locations and, at the same time, an inward move of a small and secretarial office to be closer to the inner palace. In the Ming and Qing dynasties, Emperor Zhu Yuanzhang abolished *zaixiangzi* (the prime-minister system) in 1380, thus restricting the power of the government and assuming for himself hitherto the most authoritarian position in China's imperial history.[9] In the 1420s, Neige (inner cabinet), often translated as Grand Secretariat, was established *inside* the Palace City, at its southeast corner next to the eastern gate (Donghuamen). In the 1730s, Junjichu (military affairs office), translated as Grand

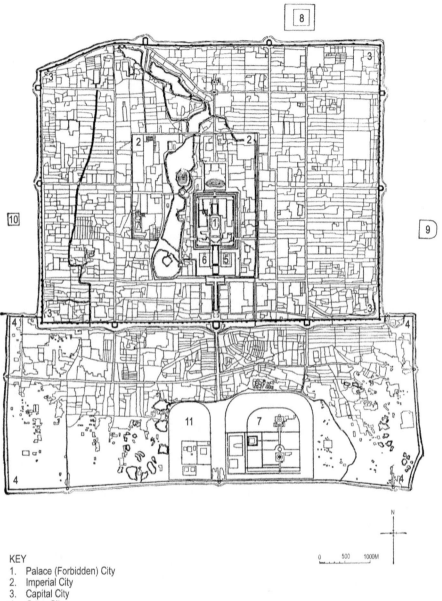

KEY
1. Palace (Forbidden) City
2. Imperial City
3. Capital City
4. Outer City
5. Temple of Ancestors
6. Altar of Land and Grain
7. Altar of Heaven
8. Altar of the Earth
9. Altar of the Sun
10. Altar of the Moon
11. Altar of Agriculture

Figure 44.3 Plan of Beijing in early Qing dynasty (1553–1750).

Source: Adapted from Liu Dunzhen, *Zhongguo Gudai Jianzhushi* (Beijing: Zhongguo Jianzhu Gongye Chubanshe, 1980), fig 153–2, 280.

Council, was established at a location *further inside*, which was much closer to the emperor's residence (in the northwest corner of the courtyard to the south of the residence Yangxindian). These developments marked an outward move of formal departments and an inward move of smaller offices to be closer to the emperor. In daily practice, officials and ministers walked to the front gate of the inner palace (Qianqingmen) from the eastern gates of the Palace and Imperial City, in a southeast-to-northwest diagonal direction. They had to walk 1,260 meters and pass four gates to reach the gate or, when necessary, 1,600 meters and 11 gates to reach an inner chamber in the deepest region behind the gate (Figure 44.4).[10]

The overall triangular structure of imperial authority assumed a pyramid of power relations centered on the throne at the apex. Higher political positions were placed at more internal locations. The inside–outside spacing corresponded with and supported the high–low differentiation of political positions. Based on this, the efforts of extending depth, by the use of walls and distances, and by externalizing formal government offices, contributed to the rise of the height of the throne at the center. In this pyramid of many relations, as said, the emperor–minister connection was most critical. On this lifeline of imperial governance, together with the ministers' visits in person, "memorials" (reports) flowed in and "directives" (emperor's decrees and replies) flowed out.[11] Based on the previous hierarchical system, a new vertical differentiation was established in the mid-Qing (1720s–30s): ordinary memorials were sent to Neige (Grand Secretariat) before reaching the emperor, whereas "palace memorials," secret reports on critical matters, should reach Junjichu (Grand Council) directly, to be read and offered a reply by the emperor quickly and, after that, to be sent via Junjichu to a specific official or general anywhere in the Chinese empire, *bypassing* Neige and any formal government offices. The speed of sending the imperial directives across the country was set at 300 to 600 *li* (150–300 km) a day.[12] In abstract terms, the vertically layered and strictly asymmetrical communication, the inward flows of reports and outward flows of decrees, created a one-way assertion of the gaze *and* control of the emperor, that is, the imperial eye-power, from inside to outside, center to periphery, that is, from the throne down to the whole empire.

Han Fei's theories of *shi*, *fa*, and *shu* were manifested in this spatial practice. Han Fei, discounting Confucian theory on the importance of human qualities of the ruler, argued for the importance of *shi*, a powerful tendency in a situation or a set-up:

> it is authority and position that should be relied upon, whereas talent and wisdom are not respected. . . .. Talent and wisdom are not sufficient to subdue the masses, but authority and position are able to subject even men of talent.[13]

In imperial Beijing, the pyramid supported a powerful position of the throne. The excessive extension of depth in spatial terms and in institutional positioning of the offices (in 1380, 1420s, and 1730s) promoted significantly the great and powerful height of the throne. Han Fei's second key idea, *fa* (rules and regulations that should work, so that "the emperor needs to do nothing"), corresponded to the strict institutional structuring, as well as a complex spatial division and relative distancing, for the system of the one-way assertion of the eye-power of the throne to work like an operating machine. Han Fei's third idea, *shu* (technique of seeing and investigating on staff and outside while remaining invisible), can be found, in terms of spatial and institutional design, in the asymmetrical visibility established whereby the emperor can "see" the outside and assert decrees while remaining invisible to the outside: the forming and the exercising of imperial eye-power. These three ideas of Legalism were related; they were aspects of one tectonic of an operating authority, on the principles of the pyramid, and of deep centralization and institutionalization.

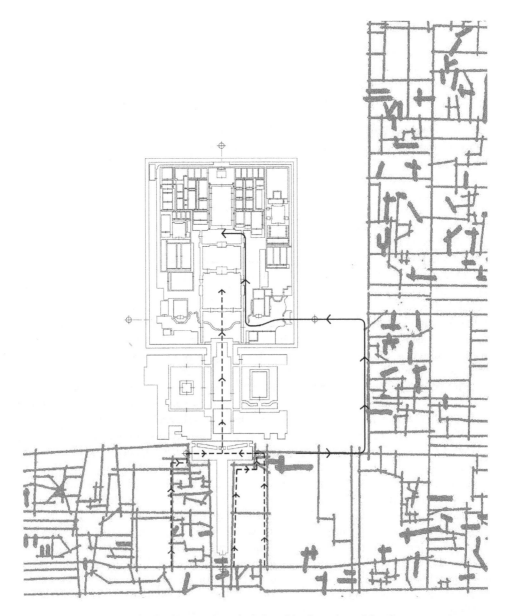

Figure 44.4 Ministers and officials' routes into the Palace City for an imperial audience.

From: Jianfei Zhu, *Chinese Spatial Strategies: Imperial Beijing 1420–1911* (London: Routledge Curzon, 2004), fig 5.10, 141. Permission and courtesy of Routledge.

This research doesn't repudiate the conventional idea that there was a Confucian, moralist, and symbolic tradition, and a corresponding formal, aesthetic, and ceremonial architecture of the city in Beijing. Rather, this study leads to an acknowledgment of a duality in the capital. The political culture and space of Beijing involved a synthesis of Confucianism and Legalism, a combination of a symbolic layout representing the Son of Heaven, with an invisible, pragmatic, and instrumentalist space facilitating the emperor's control over the government and the empire.

Europe and China, Comparability and Difference

Jullien has indicated comparability between Han Fei's Legalism and Bentham's panoptic design. What is really comparable, it seems, is a historical process of rationalization in the use of state power in China and Europe. Scholars such as Jacques Gernet and Francis Fukuyama have indicated that rationalization or modern state formation occurred earlier in China, since the Qin and Han dynasties (221–206 BC, 206 BC–AD 220).[14] A thoroughly rationalized state bureaucracy was established in the Song (960–1279), and by the time of early Ming (1368–1420s), state government had become ponderous and over-institutionalized. In Europe, according to Jullien, the process took off in the Renaissance. Niccolo Machiavelli's *The Prince* (1513) began to consider "effective truth" and "clash of interests" in the politics of governing. A theory of total centralization of state power emerged in Thomas Hobbes' *Leviathan* (1651). John Locke's *Treatises on Government* (1689) further proposed ideas of government as a contract and argued for the need to separate state powers (executive and legislative), to counterbalance the centralized state suggested in Hobbes; a system was established in Locke for a liberal philosophy of modern statehood in Western Europe and North America where separation of three powers (the third being judicial), protection of individual's property and liberty, and legitimacy of state government to be approved with a contract with the people were enshrined as sacred principles.[15] In the meantime, rational centralization of state power continued at operative levels nevertheless. In this, Jeremy Bentham's Panopticon in the 1790s brought about a new rigor in asserting and reproducing state power at local institutions, in the design of walls and windows of a building, to be populated across a governed country. The design was, in his words, "a great and new instrument of government," "a new mode of obtaining power of mind over mind in a quantity hitherto without example."[16] According to Foucault, the panoptic idea was generalized later on at many levels in the nineteenth century, into state apparatuses and into a social and institutional fabric of a "carceral archipelago," producing together a disciplinary society and state.[17]

If Beijing was an imperial capital practicing Legalism handed down from antiquity and was perfecting it in late imperial China (1368, 1420s, 1730s), the Panopticon was then a breakthrough in producing centralized state power at local institutions leading to a generalized nation-state of a disciplinary society in the nineteenth and twentieth century in the west. While the first was a capital ruling an empire, the second was a design of a local institution that was generalized onto a national political geography. Despite the differences, the two can be compared for their internal logic and design. Both were instrumentalist; both were institutionalized spatial machines of power; both discounted the importance of humans in the mechanization of control; both assumed an abstract pyramid in which spatial depth correlated with political height; and both involved a central mechanism – the asymmetrical visibility, the one-way assertion of eye-power, from center to periphery.[18]

What happened beyond this point, that is, how the two traditions departed from here, is worth contemplating.[19] There seem to be two important differences. The first is time and scale – China had established this "modern" and "instrumental" state much earlier and at a continental scale comparable to, if not larger than, the whole of Europe, which suggests more differences, qualitative ones revealing an alternative political culture, which leads to the second difference. Here, Europe and China depart substantially. While the west has adopted an instrumentalist statehood counterbalanced with ideas of openness, opposition, and "checks and balances," the Chinese imperial system, formulated over a long time, counterbalanced the instrumentalist practice with a moralistic Confucianism, functionalist rationalism with a human relatedness, and the "modern" civil government with an absolute monarchy, as Sage Ruler, with moral leadership. The first is based on conceptions of openness, autonomy, opposition, and a "natural state" of competition; the second is based on ideas of relatedness, "moral statehood," and a universal ethics for all beings, human and nonhuman. This neat symmetry of east and west, of Europe and China, came into an end in the late nineteenth century. What happened after was China's "modernization" on the model of the west in many aspects, but selectively in the realm of state politics. The problem in this struggling process, still ongoing today, is to find an open and representative government that is also a continuation of China's tradition of relatedness and moral leadership. It can be argued that, when the process of absorbing western ideas reaches a point, an alternative philosophy of relatedness may arise.

Notes

1 Michel Foucault, *Discipline and Power: The Birth of the Prison*, trans. Alan Sheridan (London: Penguin Books, 1977), 195–228.
2 François Jullien, *The Propensity of Things: Towards a History of Efficacy in China*, trans. Janet Lloyd (New York: Zone Books, 1995).
3 Jullien, *Propensity*, 25–38.
4 Jullien, *Propensity*, 39–57.
5 Jeremy Bentham, *The Panopticon Writings*, ed. Miran Bozovic (London: Verso, 1995), 31–34. See also Foucault, *Discipline and Punish*, 200–204.
6 Discussions and analyses in this section on dynastic Beijing are based on Jianfei Zhu, *Chinese Spatial Strategies: Imperial Beijing 1420–1911* (London: Routledge Curzon, 2004).
7 Editorial Group, *Hanfeizhi Jiaozhu* (Annotated and studied translation of Han Fei's writings) (Nanjing: Jiangsu Renmin Chubanshe, 1982).
8 Zhu, *Chinese Spatial*, 143–148.
9 Zhu, *Chinese Spatial*, 133–148.
10 Zhu, *Chinese Spatial*, 108–122.
11 Zhu, *Chinese Spatial*, 149–155.
12 Zhu, *Chinese Spatial*, 153–154.
13 Editorial Group, *Hanfeizhi*, 38, 297–298, 570–571, 589; see also Zhu, *Chinese Spatial*, 170–176.
14 Jacques Gernet, "Introduction," in *Foundations and Limits of State Power in China*, ed. S. R. Schram (London: School of Oriental and African Studies, 1982), xv–xxvii. See also Francis Fukuyama, *The Origins of Political Order: From Prehuman Times to the French Revolution* (London: Profile Books, 2012), 19–22, 90–92, 110–150.
15 Bertrand Russell, *A History of Western Philosophy* (London: Unwin, 1984), 596–616.
16 Bentham, *Panopticon Writings*, 39.
17 Foucault, *Discipline and Punish*, 205–216, 293–308.
18 Zhu, *Chinese Spatial*, 179–193.
19 Ideas expressed in this paragraph are explained further elsewhere: Jianfei Zhu, "Ten Thousand Things: Notes on a Construct of Largeness, Multiplicity, and Moral Statehood," in *Rethinking the Developmental City in China*, ed. Christopher C. M. Lee (Cambridge, MA: Harvard University Graduate School of Design, 2016), 34–45.

Bibliography

Bentham, Jeremy. *The Panopticon Writings*. Edited by Miran Bozovic. London: Verso, 1995.
Editorial Group. *Hanfeizhi Jiaozhu*. Annotated and Studied Translation of Han Fei's Writings. Nanjing: Jiangsu Renmin Chubanshe, 1982.
Foucault, Michel. *Discipline and Power: The Birth of the Prison*. Translated by Alan Sheridan. London: Penguin Books, 1977.
Fukuyama, Francis. *The Origins of Political Order: From Prehuman Times to the French Revolution*. London: Profile Books, 2012.
Jacques, Gernet. "Introduction." In *Foundations and Limits of State Power in China*, edited by S.R. Schram, xv–xxvii. London: School of Oriental and African Studies, 1982.
Jullien, François. *The Propensity of Things: Towards a History of Efficacy in China*. Translated by Janet Lloyd. New York: Zone Books, 1995.

Lee, C.M., ed. *Rethinking the Developmental City in China*. Cambridge, MA: Harvard University Graduate School of Design, 2016.

Russell, Bertrand. *A History of Western Philosophy*. London: Unwin, 1984.

Schram, S.R., ed. *Foundations and Limits of State Power in China*. London: School of Oriental and African Studies, 1982.

Zhu, Jianfei. *Chinese Spatial Strategies: Imperial Beijing 1420–1911*. London: Routledge Curzon, 2004.

———. "Ten Thousand Things: Notes on a Construct of Largeness, Multiplicity, and Moral Statehood." In *Rethinking the Developmental City in China*, edited by Christopher C.M. Lee, 34–45. Cambridge, MA: Harvard University Graduate School of Design, 2016.

Glossary

Beijing	北京
Daqingmen	大清门
Donghuamen	东华门
fa	法
Han (dynasty)	汉（朝）
Han Fei	韩非
Junjichu	军机处
Kaogongji	考工纪
li	里
Ming (dynasty)	明（朝）
Neige	内阁
Qianqingmen	乾清门
Qing (dynasty)	清（朝）
shi	势
shu	术
Sun Zi	孙子
Yangxindian	养心殿
zaixiangzi	宰相制
Zhu Yuanzhang	朱元璋

Methodology

45

STUDIES ON ARCHITECTURE OF ANCIENT CHINA

As in Part I

Chen Wei, Li Hua, and Jianfei Zhu

Research on ancient Chinese architecture, starting from the 1920s with domestic and international scholars, and especially those from the Society of Research in Chinese Architecture – the so-called first-generation scholars of modern China in the field, including Liang Sicheng (1901–1972) and Liu Dunzhen (1897–1968) – has by now covered a journey of nearly a hundred years. In the process, the work of many scholars over five generations has, like rivers converging into the sea and rocks rising up to form a mountain, grown into a majestic collection of vast scholarship. The massive work on historical texts and actual buildings, and the fieldwork with their research results of the first-generation scholars, established a basic system of references, providing a solid foundation for deepening and widening studies of subsequent generations. The 12 chapters collected here are really a very small sample; they cannot represent the vast scholarship accumulated by now. Thankfully, with the approval of many from the second to the fifth generations, the selected chapters have displayed interesting manifestations on approach and methodology. Together they have also formed a perspective on architecture of ancient China in this book. Though limited in coverage, they highlight interesting features that can be briefly outlined here.

Nancy S. Steinhardt's chapter, "The Chinese City in the Service of the State," provides a panoramic review of cities of heads, kings and emperors from prehistory to late dynasties, including both early settlements and the primary and secondary capitals of imperial dynasties; the chapter employs archaeological discoveries – on city walls, city moats, burial grounds, palace sites, and temple traces – for a description of state cities and imperial capitals. It delivers a historical survey on these cities in China. However, because it has introduced a perspective – the "service of the state," it allows itself to go beyond a mere description of the cities. For example, for Longshan Culture (3000–1900 BC), it focuses on urbanization for a study on urban centres; for Six Dynasties (222–589), it explores a relationship with north Korea; and for the Song dynasty (960–1279), it exams the economic policy of Wang Anshi (1021–1086) for the rise of coastal cities. In other words, the chapter adopts a "chronology-with-cases" approach; it has a major chronological line but, under the idea of "serving the state," it also embeds a series of cases on certain themes with varying scope and content. This is very different from the approach often adopted in China, where such a history would be a chronology of the major cities, such as Chang'an, Luoyang, Kaifeng, Beijing, Lin'an, and Nanjing. The chapter does not discuss much about Lin'an of Southern Song (1127–1279) and Nanjing of

DOI: 10.4324/9781315851112-68

early Ming (1368–1420); in fact, it hardly mentions Nanjing. Is this because it hadn't served the state long enough, or the two were marginal in location and political status? In any case, focusing on "servicing the state," describing a 6000-year history of cities with focused cases with a rhythm of "relaxation-and-intensity," and not being confined to the boundary and character of the capital cities themselves seem to constitute some key features and methods of this chapter.

Another chapter that offers an important survey is Ho Puay Peng's "Vernacular Architecture: Themes and Variations Over a Large Country." What makes it different from Steinhardt's is its adoption of a geographic platform on which climatic environment and local culture provide main factors for the shaping of vernacular form. Here, siting based on fengshui, rationalizing layout, structural systems, building material, and ornamental aesthetics are some of the methodological focuses. We note that the research narrative unfolds with dynamic shifts between cases, such as that of village and house, shrine and residence, Han Chinese and other ethnicities, south and north, and Han and European (or southern European) traditions. We may describe the approach as a "structural assemblage." Instead of a strict description of house types according to different regions, or a classification of village settlements versus individual buildings, this chapter follows a certain structural relationship to discuss individual cases and types, or uses certain types such as ancestral shrines or houses for a locally substantiated condition, thus allowing us to see both "trees" and "forests."

In Part I, there are four chapters that have adopted a "sectional observation." They are Heng Chye Kiang's "Imperial Cities: Critical Changes in Urban Paradigm from Sui-Tang to Song," Gu Kai's "*Literati* Gardens of the Jiangnan Region," Xu Jia's "Landscape Urbanism: Urban–Rural Relations in Hangzhou of Southern Song China," and Shen Yang's "Confucian Authority: Analysis of School-Temples at Imperial Academy of Beijing." All four of these chapters focus on a special case or set of cases, as a sectional cut into a historical development. How have they determined the point for such a section? From what angle and with what questions have these sectional cuts been made? The answer seems to lie in the relation between cases and questions. An important issue here is which takes primacy. The first two chapters emphasize primacy on historical cases, which then leaves theorization as an open process; whereas the second two seem to have emphasized theorized themes, which may preclude richness and complexity in the process of research.

Another three chapters that can be grouped together methodologically are Cheng Jianjun's "Yang Yunsong and the Jiangxi School of Fengshui Practice in Southern China," Dong Wei's "Fengshui Practice and Urban Development in Ancient China," and Chang Yu-yu's "Carpentry in Vernacular Building Practice." All three are about vernacular practice in design and construction, covering fengshui methodology, operational techniques, historical figures, and productional practice. It is important to note that these chapters, while analysing vernacular design and building practice as embedded in the obscure past, also establish a relationship between ancient narratives and modern knowledge on siting, designing, and constructing. These chapters have delivered a mature and deep study at multiple levels, even though there is yet to be an agreement between them on the origin of the ancient theories. But from these chapters we can already learn a lot on, for example, inheriting relations between ancient manuscripts and practicing masters, and the wide application of these teachings on a variety of areas of practice – such as topographic siting, city planning, designing and building, vernacular house organization, palace architecture construction, and the building of imperial tombs, as well as a special concern for coordination between time and environment. This system is comparable to ancient Chinese medicine – the teaching is both a toolkit for solving problems of human life and an interpretative framework for anticipating future problems of human life – as we find in Master Yang's

"Three Harmonies," which concerns regulations of birth, growth, and death. We have not quite understood this teaching yet, but these chapters have opened a window for us. The "interpretative" approach is not about explaining only; it is a search for reasoning. Chang Yu-yu has also studied the topic deeply, decoding operational secrets and secretive teaching in the hierarchy of masters and craftsmen in a local *chuandou* timber-building tradition of Fujian Province. In other words, the knowledge and production system of vernacular construction handed down from the past has its own narrative theories and social organizations of masters, like that in Chinese medicine; the scale and scope of teaching and popular use are vast. These chapters have only revealed the tip of the iceberg.

If we are looking for a study that uses numerical and geometric relations to examine classical Chinese architecture, especially its developed group design, then the excellent example has to be Fu Xinian's "Typical Design Features of Ming Palaces and Altars in Beijing." The study examines how, on a plan of axes and grids, the east–west and north–south lengths of many systems of different scales built since the early Ming dynasty – the city, the palace complex, and the palatial courtyards large and small – display regular ratios; the areas of the courtyards and the palace cities also display a regularity of integer multiplications. The chapter then explores cultural and design meanings in these regular ratios. One of the key issues here is the measuring units used. The paper uses *bu*, *zhang*, metre and area; and since Ming-dynasty Beijing was built on the Yuan-dynasty capital Dadu, we need to inquire further about the relationship between a standard unit of length in the Yuan and the Ming. Further, we need to examine the relations between early and middle Ming in terms of continuity. This requires onsite historical studies at the buildings and in the city; and then overlapping that information onto the numerical study of the formal layout, which requires highly refined and strict *kaozheng* (evidential) and quantified data analysis. Clearly, the current work is convincing: as based on the modular grids, there are integer multiplications or formal ratios, so that we can detect how the complex layouts of the groups and courtyards were organized and determined. Of course, if readers know more about the distribution of zones and functions – the outer and inner courts in the south and north respectively – and other differentiations such as front and rear for temples, they will be able to appreciate more about the ratios and multiplication.

Compared to Fu Xinian, who studies by tracing from the end product backwards, Pan Guxi, in his "*Yingzao Fashi*: The Book and Methodical Issues for Studying It," starts from the beginning of a design production, this time in the Northern Song dynasty, studying an architectural manuscript of 1103, *Yingzao Fashi* (*Building Standard*). Pan examines the context and the process in which the book came into being as well as the identity and standing of the author; Pan then reads into the book's preface closely. From these, Pan states clearly that the manuscript was not just for building design but was also, more importantly, for strengthening the control and management of construction and for reducing wasteful capital spending – and therefore it also had a certain legal standing. By examining the origins or initial contexts of the manuscript, Pan's approach thus departs from the previous reading, which focused on architecture and design. By reading into the three steps discussed in the book, Pan further ascertains that the control had a formula of three stages – a determination of magnitude, a fixing of budget, and an adjustment on labour and material use depending on a shifting scale. According to Pan, by shifting the scale and scope in a regular framework within or under a controlling system, the level of flexibility and adaptability had reached remarkable sophistication by then. Aside from the study on the book itself, Pan has also cross-compared the relevant content of *Mengxi Bitan* (*Dream Pool Essays*) of the same time, as well as architecture of the Song dynasty. On the whole, Pan's work is strong and well grounded in its argument and evidence and thus provides important breakthroughs.

Although equally focusing on a specific case, Chen Wei's "Chan Lang Pavilion of Suzhou" looks into it over a long time. The chapter examines the phrase "chan lang" (a river name or a reference to clear water and symbolic associations) in terms of its meaning and use over the course of 2000 years, as well as the evolution of garden design based on the phrase over 1000 years. The chapter aims to cover the richness and complexity, as well as literary culture and grounded materiality, that has been accumulating on the scholar gardens in China as found in this case. It seeks to discern the change and contribution made in specific times across history, and to appreciate the formation of the scholar-garden culture of China. This temporal and semantic approach is in fact a dynamic search for origin and evolution; the theoretical narrative thus established may provide a contribution to the sustaining of the tradition.

As outlined earlier, the chapters collected for ancient China (Part I) have adopted various methods: "chronology-with-cases," "structural assemblage," "sectional observation," "interpretation," "reasoning on design," "studying the initial text," and "temporal semantic study." The descriptions may not be exact, but they characterize a certain pathway between the object and the purpose in research. Historical research, especially on ancient architectural history, tends to be obscure since the subject is far in the past and is covered with thick layers of clothing and dust. We may adopt a variety of methods, but three principles seem to be important: to approach historical authenticity; to discover historical complexity; and to open historical eyes to appreciating some rationality of the past. For these principles, especially the third, working towards an "understanding" becomes a lighthouse of guidance.

The third principle, or the practice that follows it, sets us apart from first-generation scholars on ancient Chinese architecture. The work of the first-generation, as eminent historian Fu Sinian (1896–1950) said, is "to search up and down, in heave and on earth, using our hands and feet, to look for things and artifacts." For the first generation, it was important to discover the sites and buildings, so as to detect their function and type, to ascertain time of construction, to describe the character, and to establish a system of historical knowledge. But, in this collection, our purpose is mainly to understand, to adopt a mindset of knowing for a closer appreciation of the past. Here, adopting a broad or a middle perspective, focusing on topics or cases, these chapters have sketched some outlines and revealed some parts of a rich heritage of ancient Chinese architecture at three levels – the imperial, the scholar-gentry, and the vernacular.

For the imperial and official, on imperial capitals and state cities, our knowledge is still being updated as archaeological discoveries are constantly being made. For scholar culture or gentry society, for research on garden design, current scholarship has covered many more aspects – delivering an understanding far more enriched than before; yet, more refined work is needed on how to understand changes over time; and if we expand the scope to include landscape gardening and design, then there is so much more to cover on regions and regional difference. For folk society and vernacular culture, there remain a vast amount of work to do, requiring us to use our "hands and feet," and our "mouths," to do field work and to conduct interviews, to discover and to decode; given the scale of China and her rich range of ethnicities, tough effort is needed to move in this direction. Having said that, the current collection has already made a step forward; these chapters have revealed an alternative in reading ancient Chinese architecture, a richness in the methods adopted for a variety of topics and cases, and a perspective one can expect in the development of historical research in the future. We look forward to more guidance, participation, and contribution from the readers soon.

Glossary

Beijing	北京
bu	步
chan lang	沧浪
Chang Yu-yu	张玉瑜
Chang'an	长安
Chen Wei	陈薇
Cheng Jianjun	程建军
chuandou	穿斗（架）
Dadu	大都
Dong Wei	董卫
fengshui	风水
Fu Sinian	傅斯年
Fu Xinian	傅熹年
Fujian (province)	福建（省）
Gu Kai	顾凯
Han (people, culture)	汉（人、文化）
Hangzhou	杭州
Heng Chye Kiang	王才强
Ho Puay Peng	何培斌
Jiangnan (region)	江南（地区）
Kaifeng	开封
kaozheng	考证
Liang Sicheng	梁思成
Lin'an	临安
Liu Dunzhen	刘敦桢
Longshan (culture)	龙山（文化）
Luoyang	洛阳
Mengxi Bitan	梦溪笔谈
Ming (dynasty)	明（朝）
Nanjing	南京
Pan Guxi	潘谷西
Shen Yang	沈旸
Song (dynasty)	宋（朝）
Sui-Tang	隋唐（时期）
Wang Anshi	王安石
Xu Jia	徐佳
Yang Yunsong	杨筠松
Yingzao Fashi	营造法式
Yuan	元（朝）
zhang	丈

46

PERSPECTIVES ON ARCHITECTURE OF (MODERN) CHINA

As in Parts II–V and Part I

Jianfei Zhu, Li Hua, and Chen Wei

If we review all chapters collected from Part II to Part V, we discover that there are six themes covered, as studies of the 2010s covering mostly the architecture of modern China. These six themes can be briefly summarized.

Knowledge. As a system of knowledge to be passed on in education and as a system of professional practice to be governed, "architecture," as we use the term today, is a *western* idea introduced to China in the late nineteenth century. Its subsequent development in China, in terms of knowledge production, is captured in this book in three aspects – education, design thinking, and historical writing. On education, Xu Subin's "Emergence of 'Architecture'," Qian Feng's "Architectural Education in China (1950s–1980s)" and, to an extent, Lu Yongyi's study on "For a Modernism: Huang and Feng at Shanghai's Tongji Architectural Programme" have all examined modern teaching programmes on architecture in China from the earliest time on, a process in which a state ministry on education or construction played a leadership role. On design thinking, Li Hua's "Theories of Spatial Composition: Design Knowledge in China up to the 1980s," and Lu Yongyi's study on the Tongji programme, both in the 1980s, exposed a special time in China, one that accumulated the work of the previous decades at the dawn of Reform and Opening-Up. On historical writing, Zhuge Jing's comparison of Liang Sicheng and Liu Dunzhen exposed a complex situation for the historians of architecture in modern China, in the 1950s–70s especially, caught in a conflict between ideology and research, historiography and design research, formalism and (Marxist) materialism, imperial architecture and vernacular culture, among others.

Design and Design (or Stylistic) Positioning. On the topic of design language, there are chapters on nationalism, modernism, and "autonomous" design. Zhou Qi and Ji Qiu's "Chinese Classical Revival" in the 1930s, Jianfei Zhu's "National Style" in the 1950s, and Chao-ching Fu's "Chinese Neoclassicism" of Taiwan in the 1960s–80 have picked up some of the major phases of a nationalist architecture of modern China. On the other hand, Eduard Kögel's "Towards a Regional Modernism in Chinese Architecture (1930s–70s)", Lu Yongyi's "Huang and Feng at Shanghai's Tongji Architectural Programme," and Jiang Feng's " Building Canton Fair: Towards a Regional Modernism in Southern China (1950s–1980s)" have examined the rise of modernism with a southern vernacular connection. If the nationalist design discourse was promoted by state government, regional modernism here was also subtly tolerated by the

DOI: 10.4324/9781315851112-69

state and left to happen in the "remote" (therefore critical) south. For critical and experimental designs by the "autonomous" architects in a more liberal situation – when permitted by the state – Li Xiangning's "Critical Pragmatism" and Hing-Wah Chau's "Architects as Authoring Individuals" examine the development in mainland China since the 1990s, while Ke Song's "Architects as Reflexive Individuals" explores this in Taiwan and Hong Kong since the 1950s.

Practice, Professionalism, and Autonomy. On the issue of the mode of design practice, the focus here centres on three conditions, each as a problem: the rise of the modern profession and state administration of the trade in the 1930s, the instituting of a socialist design production in the form of the "design institute" in Mao's China and after, and an antithesis to that in mainland China after the Mao era or outside in Hong Kong and Taiwan since earlier times. Here Wang Xiaoqian's "The Architect as a Profession in Republican China" of the 1930s examines the first, whereas Ke Song's "The Design Institute in Mao's China (1950s–70s)," Charlie Q. L. Xue and Guanghui Ding's "From Mao to Market," and Jianfei Zhu's "A Critique of 'Critical Thinking'" are working on the design institute in Mao and post-Mao times. Further, the three chapters by Li, Chau, and Song, which consider issues of autonomy as noted earlier, can also be included in this cluster, concerning a critical case that has institutionally opposed the state. Again, the state government plays a central role as either a positive agent or an invisible force that produces its opposite, in a logical and historical sense.

Society and Social Space: Institutions, Cities, and Countryside. In this cluster, four issues are addressed by the chapters: making the modern city; socialist planning and the work unit; city-country (dis)integration; and the building of CBDs (central business districts) in a neoliberal economy – the first and second covering republican and socialist times in a sequential manner, while the third and fourth consider contemporary conditions at two ends of a spectrum. For the making of the modern city in China in the republican time (1910s–40s), Li Baihao's "From Hankou Town to Greater Wuhan" and Zhang Tianjie's "Modern Edutainment Space: Public Parks in Early Twentieth-Century China" reveal two facets of urban and social modernization then. Into the 1950s and thereafter, in socialist China, Li Baihao's "Socialist Urban Planning in Mao's China (1949–1976)" and Duanfang Lu's "*Danwei* and Socialist Urbanism" provide a multi-scalar observation at regional, urban, institutional, and neighbourhood levels on a socialist production of space in Mao China. Further, Wang Jianguo's "Urban–Rural Development in China" address a more recent situation of massive urbanization, at an unprecedented speed and scale in world history, resulting in a mega-urban or an urban–rural condition of extreme heterogeneity; Wang moves forward to provide advice for a "new urbanism." In the opposite direction, while the city is expanding outward, it is also refocusing on its urban cores; here the building of radian objects in China's city centres, as in Beijing and Shanghai, is the topic in Peter G. Rowe and Har Ye Kan's "Objects in Territories Along Avenues: Spatial Planning in Beijing and Shanghai" and Ming Wu's "Iconic Architecture in China (2000s)." In all these cases, state government again plays a leading role, in republican, socialist, and contemporary times.

Technology and Its Challenge. Although various papers have touched on the use of technology, one paper addresses it and its challenge in early modern China. Li Haiqing's "Building Technology in Republican China and Its Historical Legacies" explores the introduction of modern building technologies, its achievements, and its difficulties in the context of war, turbulence, national disunity, and industrial backwardness. In terms of backwardness, it actually explains a generic situation of modern China. Li's paper can also be connected up to premodern China, to the practice of timber construction for imperial architecture and vernacular practice, as covered in Part I by Pan Guxi's "*Yingzao Fashi*" and Chang Yu-yu's "Carpentry in Vernacular Building Practice" respectively.

Theorization or the Use of Broader Perspectives. Although many chapters have a level of theorization, those collected in Part IV aim specifically for theorization with a broader spectrum and deeper examination. Here, the work has three approaches: those on or with a history of philosophical and aesthetic ideas *in* the Chinese tradition; those using modern categories of cultural practice (writing, memory, and epistemology); and those using modern categories but centring on socio-political issues (state and political ethics). For the first, Wang Guixiang's "Ten Lamps of Architecture in Chinese Culture" and David Wang's "Thinking With Xunzi" provide a reading into the foundation of the culture of building in ancient China, using China's own words and categories. For the second, Shiqiao Li's "Figuration: Writing, Memory, and Cities in Chinese Culture" and Jianfei Zhu's "Signs of Empire" explore the strategy of writing in the Chinese tradition by using modern and analytical categories, bringing as it were an alien insight into the ancient system for debate on an international platform. For the third, Li's "State Function of Architecture" and Zhu's "Political Space and Moral Statehood," adopting these alien or external perspectives but on a socio-political field, shift to a more difficult problem of the Chinese approach to statehood.

State as a Methodological Centre

Reviewing the studies in these six clusters, it becomes apparent that "the state," or the ideas, forces, conditions, and agencies covered by this category, constitutes one of the most important methodological focuses in all these Parts (II–V, that is, modern China since 1911) just outlined. Here the state has appeared at least in two forms. Firstly, it has appeared as an active agent, as state authority or central government. This is manifested in the role of leadership over spatial production, including city planning, architectural design, and building construction. It is manifested in other realms of social practice as well, with a comprehensive impact on spatial production and formation, such as work-unit and neighbourhood organization (of the Mao era) and urban modernization (before and after Mao's time), as well as other specific campaigns such as inward relocation for war preparation of the 1960s–70s and outward engagement with global economy to the coast (since the 1980s). Active state leadership is also manifested in other fields, such as professionalism and university education (in republican, socialist, and reform times). As an active agent, state authority has also promoted nationalist discourse, to be manifested in the national-style (or Chinese neoclassical) architecture found at different moments of modern China – chiefly the 1930s, 1950s, and 1970s–80s in Nanjing, Beijing, and Taipei respectively. The state had also produced briefly, in limited cases, versions of modernism for state architecture, as found in Beijing and Guangzhou of the 1970s.

Secondly, the state has appeared as a producer or generator through social dynamics – willingly or otherwise – of alternative or opposite agents, forces, and conditions. The chief manifestation of this is the rise of private and independent architects as an "individual," who opposed – structurally at least – the ideas and forces of the state and its design institutes, or their architects as a "collective," in late Reform time in mainland China (since the 1990s). In design language, the alternative to the state and its nationalist discourse has been the various strands of regional modernism found in the south (which in turn were associated with state-sponsored modernism) of the 1970s; since the 1990s, the alternative or sometimes critical thrusts (but with the state's tolerance) was then found in the new generation of "independent" architects with their contemporary ideas and experimentations.

Connecting to Part I (Ancient China): Continuity and Discontinuity

If we are connecting times before and after 1911, i.e. from premodern to modern China, we then have to acknowledge a huge break or discontinuity in between, as occurring not just around 1911 (the end of China's last dynasty) but in fact over a much longer time, at least a century, from the mid-nineteenth to mid-twentieth century. For the production of the built environment in China, the focus of this collection, we may observe this major break, and any discontinuities and underlying continuities, in three aspects – architecture as a physical condition, social and intellectual practice for the making of that condition, and the role of the state for and in the production of the condition.

For the first, the physical condition, the break is extreme or radical; in modern China, the whole building technology and industry, the social programs or institutions as "functions," the scale of the structure and the form, and the associated urban scale, space, and form were radically different from that in the past, resulting in excessive heterogeneity when new and old fabric coexist (a common condition in modern East Asia, in contrast to modern Europe where such a radical difference is harder to find). For the second, the social and intellectual practice for architecture, the modern approach was also radically different, as chiefly manifested in professional practice, university education, and research and writing, that is, in the modes of design practice and in the systems of creating and transferring architectural knowledge.

Three Roles of the State

If in these two aspects we are witnessing extreme difference or radical change, then in the third, for the role of the state, we are observing a complex situation in which a persistence of the central role of the state survived. The specific systems in modern China (at least in the republican and socialist time on the mainland) were surely different from the imperial or dynastic systems, yet a rather powerful presence of state authority remained, securing a certain persistent role of the state and its methodological importance for research on architecture of China. Matching our observation on the state in modern China, the situation in ancient China, as covered in Part I, also leads us to see the state appearing in two roles or capacities – as an active agent and as a generator of different (if not opposite) forces. As an active agent, the imperial court and government ministries led the planning of major (administrative) cities and the construction of monumental structures (palaces, offices, major temples, city walls, and drum and bell towers, among other key infrastructures). As a producer of other and alternative forces, it had also supported associated strata of social worlds (gardens, temples, academies, schools) and tolerated and structurally secured a folk or vernacular lifeworld at the base of the social hierarchy – vernacular discourse and practice for building shrines, houses, villages, and settlements (in the use of fengshui and vernacular carpentry). The differentiation between the imperial and the vernacular in the past was arguably more organic and interrelated than in modern times, revealing a third role of the state that is more prominent in the past – state as a cultural force.

In ancient China, with a comprehensive approach of ethics and an assumption of the state as a moral leader, state governance tended to be wide-ranging, with a broad influence over and into society and culture, in religion, education, art practice, and intellectual pursuit. If architecture and the built environment can be viewed as an aesthetic, cultural, and anthropological realm, then indeed the whole settlement, in technology, discourse, and form, was shaped by a culture in which the state played a leadership role. The so-called vernacular discourse-practice of fengshui and timber carpentry, for example, were in fact interrelated to an imperial industry of designing and planning, such as that for the building of imperial Beijing in the fifteenth century (when folk masters from Jiangxi and Suzhou were involved; see Cheng Jianjun and Chang Yu-yu's chapters). A symbolic universe permeating all aspects of Chinese life, saturated with words, stories, and mythologies, and the associated writing and visualization, and acting and performing, had bathed the construction practice in a culture in which the imperial court acted as a Sage Ruler. Modern China was supposed to have stripped off all these feudal and imperial practices, but the state (republican or socialist) in fact still played these cultural roles. Both the dominant national style and the less noted state modernism in mainland China were promoted by state authority; the liberal or critical practice of vernacular modernism of the 1970s and the internationally exposed contemporary design of the "autonomous" architects since the 1990s were in fact also supported or tolerated by the central government. In Taiwan, this observation remains, although the condition was not quite the same – but the Confucian culture secured the pattern in any case.

Emerging Trends: An Incomplete Observation

Based on the chapters from this collection, and based on our reading, a few tendencies can be found. Firstly, even though "modern China" has not quite arrived or settled, and mutations are expected, the historical condition of modern China, as a break away from the dynastic and imperial past through wars and revolutions, is now fully established. As we move further away from 1911 or that turbulent time, modern history is now unavoidable and modern architecture of China is increasingly important for research. By extension, contemporary architecture in China is also increasingly significant for scholarly investigation. The time when "Chinese architecture" means "ancient Chinese architecture" is over. When this is the case, scholarship on any episode of "Chinese architecture" contains inevitably a long perspective where ancient and modern (and contemporary) histories are *connected*, no matter how turbulent it was in the transition from ancient to modern China. Scholarly research that interconnects the ancient and the modern, and even that using a modern perspective to view the past, are expected to be on the rise. Scholarship on modern and current architecture of China is also expected to grow substantially.

Secondly, when ancient and modern conditions are studied together, or at least when modern and contemporary architecture of China are increasingly important, a methodological tolerance is needed, so that, on top of history and historical methods, sociology and cultural studies (and other disciplines in social science and humanities) will be increasingly employed for their theories, concepts, and methodologies. For this purpose, some key concepts or categories, as experimentally used here in this collection, may be employed more often in the future. These categories are in fact clusters of ideas and issues. They include: state (authority, ideology, nationalist discourse, governance over spatial production in design and planning, geopolitics, international relations, aid projects); agent (state authority, the profession, design institutes, architects as a "collective," architects as "individuals," architects from "outside," other agents and forces in the use and production of the built environment); space (work-units, institutions, public space, places, city and country, gardens and the landscape, villages and settlements, geopolitical space of borders and transactions, world space of connections and tensions); knowledge (education, historical writing, design criticism, institutional control of the use of skills or professionalism, architectural research and writing); and design or design as intervention (agenda, positioning, criticality, service, public realm, public interest, statement, vision, and desire). These clusters of ideas are also interconnected, as a network of networks, with other networks to be joined where necessary.

Thirdly, with the increasing use of sociology and cultural studies for their ideas and concepts, efforts of theorization are likely to be on the rise, in a more radical exploration of new knowledge. For this, as tested in this collection, two approaches may be adopted. One is an attempt to theorize by using internal categories in auto-narratives in China, such as the ideas in Confucianism or Daoism, for example "ritual," "benevolence," "Sage Ruler," "Dao," "yin and yang," and a universe of ancient words, texts, and classics behind these. The other is theorization by using external categories, often modern and analytical terms such as "script," "memory," "signs," "visibility," or "power relations" for a reading or deconstruction, with alien light casting onto the cases, offering an opening into some international or cross-cultural communication. The two are not mutually exclusive, and both are often used together. The logic, however, is different. Both have pitfalls – the first a close-door relativism, and the second an ahistorical universalization. When the two are used together, a productive tension may be secured, when internal terms and ideas are met with modern and analytical perspectives as rays of light illuminating a mysterious condition within a case.

If the current collection reflects a landscape of contemporary scholarship on the architecture of China, then it seems to suggest a certain methodological liberation, where social and cultural methods are being increasingly introduced, to work with historical and architectural perspectives, for a revelation of something called "Chinese architecture." This is still changing and evolving, with a long history stretching back over a few millennia in which the state has played a major role, but where the tradition also retains vast potential, allowing new transformations to come in the future.

Glossary

Beijing	北京
Chang Yu-yu	张玉瑜
Chang'an (avenue)	长安（街）
Chao-ching Fu	傅朝卿
Charlie Q. L. Xue	薛求理
Cheng Jianjun	程建军
danwei	单位
Dao	道
David Wang	王元生
Duanfang Lu	卢端芳
Feng Jiang	冯江
fengshui	风水
Guanghui Ding	丁光辉
Guangzhou	广州
Har Ye Kan	简夏仪
Hing-Wah Chau	周庆华
Ji Qiu	季秋
Jianfei Zhu	朱剑飞
Jiangxi	江西
Ke Song	宋科
Li Baihao	李百浩
Li Haiqing	李海清
Li Hua	李华
Li Xiangning	李翔宁

Liang Sicheng	梁思成
Liu Dunzhen	刘敦桢
Lu Yongyi	卢永毅
Mao (era)	毛泽东（时期）
Ming Wu	吴名
Nanjing	南京
Pan Guxi	潘谷西
Qian Feng	钱锋
Shanghai	上海
Shiqiao Li	李世桥
Suzhou	苏州
Taipei	台北
Taiwan	台湾
Tongji (university)	同济（大学）
Wang Guixiang	王贵祥
Wang Jianguo	王建国
Wang Xiaoqian	汪晓茜
Xu Subin	徐苏斌
Xunzi	荀子
yin (and) yang	阴阳
Zhang Tianjie	张天洁
Zhou Qi	周琦
Zhuge Jing	诸葛净

Appendix
TIMELINE: CHINESE HISTORY

Xia	2070–1600 BCE
Shang	1600–1046 BCE
Western Zhou	1046–771 BCE
Eastern Zhou	770–476 (Chunqiu), 475–221 (Zhanguo) BCE
Qin	221–207 BCE
Han	202 BCE– 8 CE (Western), 25–220 (Eastern)
Three kingdoms	220–280
Jin	266–420
Northern–Southern dynasties	420–589
Sui	581–619
Tang	618–907
Five dynasties	907–979
Song	960–1127 (Northern), 1127–1279 (Southern)
Liao	937–1125
Jin	1115–1234
Yuan	1271–1368
Ming	1368–1644
Qing	1644–1912

Hong Kong	1842–1997	British colony
	1997–	returning to PRC
Macau	1887–1999	Portuguese colony
	1999–	returning to PRC
Republic of China (ROC)	1912–1949	under Sun Yat-sen & Chiang Kai-shek
	1949–	relocated to Taiwan
People's Republic of China (PRC)	1949–1976	under Mao Zedong
		(1966–76: Cultural Revolution)
	1976–	post-Mao or contemporary
		(since 1978: Open and Reform)

INDEX

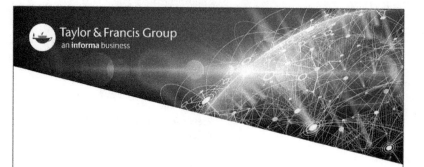

9 780415 729222